# The Fitzgeralds and the Kennedys

# THE FITZGERALDS

### AND

# THE KENNEDYS

## DORIS KEARNS GOODWIN

St. Martin's Press
New York

Library of Congress Cataloging-in-Publication Data
Goodwin, Doris Kearns.
    The Fitzgeralds and the Kennedys : an American saga / Doris Kearns
Goodwin.
        p.    cm.
    Includes index.
    Reprint. Originally published: New York : Simon & Schuster, 1987.
    ISBN 0-312-06354-7
    1. Fitzgerald family.   2. Kennedy family.   3. United States—
Biography.   I. Title.
CT274.F58G66   1991
929'.2'0973—dc20                                                   91-21711
                                                                      CIP


First published in the United States of America by Simon and Schuster, Inc.

10 9 8 7 6 5 4

*For my husband, Richard*

# THE
# FITZGERALD
# FAMILY

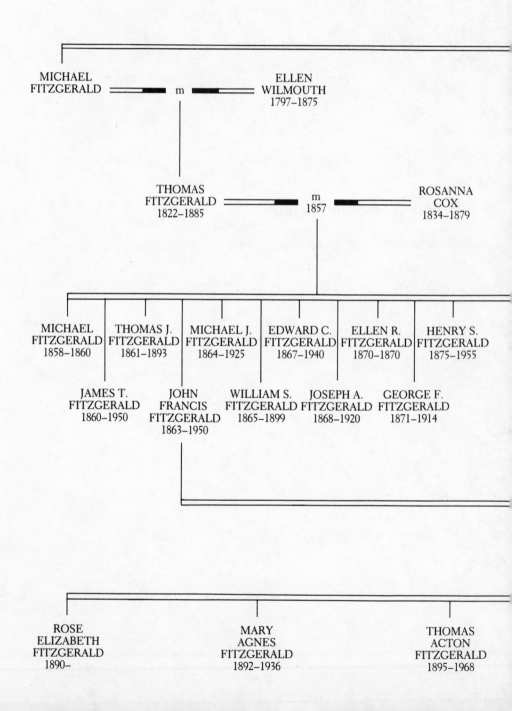

JAMES
FITZGERALD

MICHAEL
FITZGERALD —— m —— ELLEN
WILMOUTH
1797–1875

THOMAS
FITZGERALD —— m —— ROSANNA
1822–1885      1857      COX
1834–1879

MICHAEL
FITZGERALD
1858–1860

THOMAS J.
FITZGERALD
1861–1893

MICHAEL J.
FITZGERALD
1864–1925

EDWARD C.
FITZGERALD
1867–1940

ELLEN R.
FITZGERALD
1870–1870

HENRY S.
FITZGERALD
1875–1955

JAMES T.
FITZGERALD
1860–1950

JOHN
FRANCIS
FITZGERALD
1863–1950

WILLIAM S.
FITZGERALD
1865–1899

JOSEPH A.
FITZGERALD
1868–1920

GEORGE F.
FITZGERALD
1871–1914

ROSE
ELIZABETH
FITZGERALD
1890–

MARY
AGNES
FITZGERALD
1892–1936

THOMAS
ACTON
FITZGERALD
1895–1968

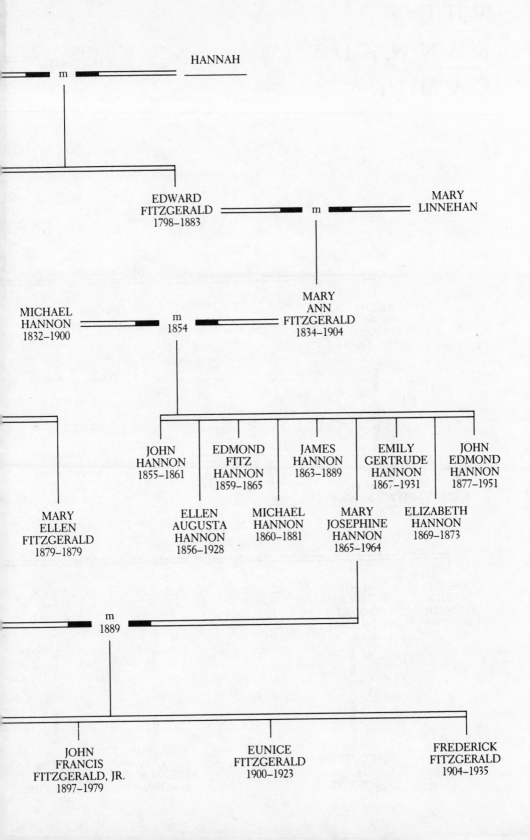

HANNAH
m

EDWARD
FITZGERALD
1798–1883
m
MARY
LINNEHAN

MARY
ANN
FITZGERALD
1834–1904

MICHAEL
HANNON
1832–1900
m
1854

JOHN
HANNON
1855–1861

EDMOND
FITZ
HANNON
1859–1865

JAMES
HANNON
1863–1889

EMILY
GERTRUDE
HANNON
1867–1931

JOHN
EDMOND
HANNON
1877–1951

MARY
ELLEN
FITZGERALD
1879–1879

ELLEN
AUGUSTA
HANNON
1856–1928

MICHAEL
HANNON
1860–1881

MARY
JOSEPHINE
HANNON
1865–1964

ELIZABETH
HANNON
1869–1873

m
1889

JOHN
FRANCIS
FITZGERALD, JR.
1897–1979

EUNICE
FITZGERALD
1900–1923

FREDERICK
FITZGERALD
1904–1935

# THE
# KENNEDY
# FAMILY

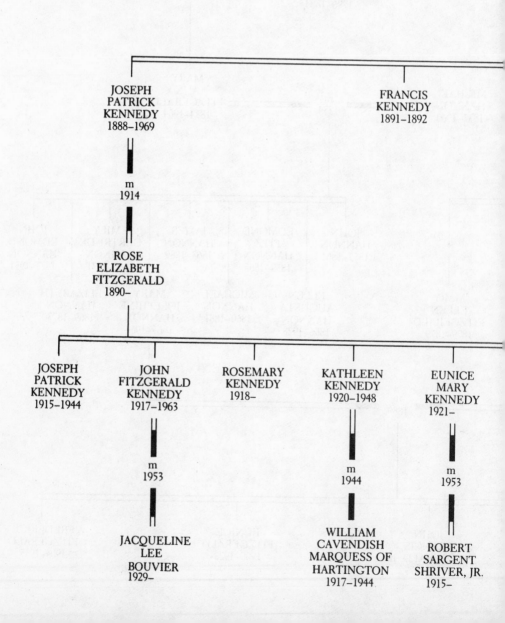

PATRICK
KENNEDY

JOSEPH
PATRICK
KENNEDY
1888–1969

FRANCIS
KENNEDY
1891–1892

m
1914

ROSE
ELIZABETH
FITZGERALD
1890–

JOSEPH
PATRICK
KENNEDY
1915–1944

JOHN
FITZGERALD
KENNEDY
1917–1963

ROSEMARY
KENNEDY
1918–

KATHLEEN
KENNEDY
1920–1948

EUNICE
MARY
KENNEDY
1921–

m
1953

m
1944

m
1953

JACQUELINE
LEE
BOUVIER
1929–

WILLIAM
CAVENDISH
MARQUESS OF
HARTINGTON
1917–1944

ROBERT
SARGENT
SHRIVER, JR.
1915–

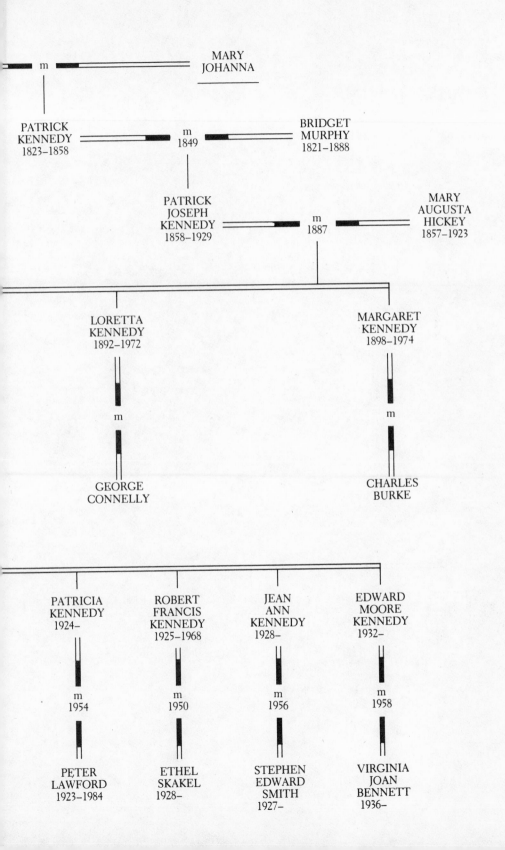

m

MARY
JOHANNA
_____

PATRICK
KENNEDY
1823–1858

m
1849

BRIDGET
MURPHY
1821–1888

PATRICK
JOSEPH
KENNEDY
1858–1929

m
1887

MARY
AUGUSTA
HICKEY
1857–1923

LORETTA
KENNEDY
1892–1972

MARGARET
KENNEDY
1898–1974

m

m

GEORGE
CONNELLY

CHARLES
BURKE

PATRICIA
KENNEDY
1924–

ROBERT
FRANCIS
KENNEDY
1925–1968

JEAN
ANN
KENNEDY
1928–

EDWARD
MOORE
KENNEDY
1932–

m
1954

m
1950

m
1956

m
1958

PETER
LAWFORD
1923–1984

ETHEL
SKAKEL
1928–

STEPHEN
EDWARD
SMITH
1927–

VIRGINIA
JOAN
BENNETT
1936–

# CONTENTS

Preface                                                                    xiii


### BOOK ONE: THE FITZGERALDS
### (1863–1915)

| | |
|---|---:|
| 1. The Immigrant World | 3 |
| 2. Pageants and Processions | 21 |
| 3. "The Other Boston" | 40 |
| 4. Great Expectations | 58 |
| 5. Apprentice to the Boss | 69 |
| 6. A Long Courtship | 77 |
| 7. The Boy Politician | 92 |
| 8. A Most Energetic Mayor | 110 |
| 9. "Eyes Full of Laughter" | 130 |
| 10. "Guilty as Charged" | 151 |
| 11. A Child of Mary | 174 |
| 12. The Mayor's Daughter | 190 |
| 13. Harvard College '12 | 208 |
| 14. "Banking . . . could lead a man anywhere." | 234 |
| 15. The Balance Shifts | 242 |


### BOOK TWO: THE KENNEDYS
### (1915–1940)

| | |
|---|---:|
| 16. A Stranger Among Friends | 267 |
| 17. Learning the Tricks of the Trade | 289 |
| 18. Separation and Resolve | 301 |

19. "The Wall Street Racket"                    322
20. "This is . . . a gold mine."                339
21. Growing Up Kennedy                          349
22. The Young Mogul                             369
23. "Gloria needs handling . . ."               381
24. The *Queen Kelly* Curse                     398
25. Riding the *Roosevelt Special*              419
26. Policing Wall Street                        436
27. The Model Son and the Pied Piper            456
28. Children of Privilege                       475
29. Tempting the Gods                           494
30. Arrival in London                           512
31. At the Court of St. James's                 531
32. "Peace for Our Time"                        548
33. The Long Weekend                            574
34. "Hostages to Fortune"                       590

## BOOK THREE: THE GOLDEN TRIO
### (1941–1961)

35. The Circle Is Broken                        621
36. "Hero in the Pacific"                        645
37. Forbidden Romance                           661
38. "Now it's all over."                         683
39. Shadowboxing                                698
40. The Young Congressman                       722
41. The Lone Survivor                           742
42. "Shooting for a Star"                        750
43. Triumphant Defeat                           769
44. Burying the Religious Issue                 787
45. A Tip of the Hat                            809
    Notes                                       819
    Bibliography                                891
    Index                                       905

# PREFACE

I was first attracted to this family history almost a decade ago, out of my lifelong absorption in American history, and my special interest in the presidency. There were also other, more intimate reasons. My father was the son of Irish immigrants. His accounts of his heritage, and his family's struggle to establish a place for themselves in a strange, harsh and promising land, had illuminated my childhood musings and fueled my young ambition. My own journey from our family's roots in Brooklyn does not compare with the rise of the Fitzgeralds and the Kennedys from the slums of Boston's North End to the White House, which is the subject of this book. But there was a resonance, a sense of identity.

Indeed, as I progressed, it became apparent that the story of the Fitzgeralds and the Kennedys—despite its unique magnitude—was both symbol and substance of one of the most important themes of the second century of American life: the progress of the great wave of nineteenth-century immigration, the struggle of newcomers to force open the doors of American life so zealously guarded by those who had first settled the land.

That story—in an undefinable sense, both real and metaphorical—culminated with the inauguration of John Fitzgerald Kennedy, which is where I end my book. The rest of the Kennedy story—his Administration and his death, the rise and assassination of one brother, the political career of another—is a part of American political history, copiously chronicled in hundreds of volumes to which little can be added, at least until the passage of time has given us a different historical perspective.

The sources of this history are detailed in the notes to this volume. But the source that most profoundly influenced the texture of this work does not fit readily into any standard academic category: the city of Boston itself. Living here allowed me a journey through time, past streets and buildings once populated by the subjects of my work. Thus, I stood at the altar of St. Stephen's Church where John Francis Fitzgerald was baptized more than a century ago, walked to the corner where the young Irish newsboy had his first glimpse of wealthy, cultured Beacon Hill whose influential Yankee residents were to be both adversary and model for his own ambition.

Boston is a city that has preserved much of its past. And that past came alive again as I went through the pages of old newspapers, read descriptions in antique deed books, studied the journals of priests who had chronicled the births, the uncertain, often fragile lives and the deaths of their immigrant parishioners. The examinations and report cards of a century had been carefully filed away at the Boston Latin School, the Eliot Grammar School and Harvard Medical School.

My research took me far beyond the Boston area: to England, the site of Joe Kennedy's most luminous public achievement and his greatest tragedies and defeats; to New York and Hollywood; to Washington, Palm Beach and Hyannis Port. For the history of this family traversed boundaries and continents. But at its heart—in the end as in the beginning—it was a Boston story.

After nearly three years of research, I discovered that over one hundred and fifty cartons of papers belonging to Joe and Rose Kennedy had been shipped for safekeeping from the attic of their house at Hyannis Port and from the Kennedy office in New York to the Kennedy Library. Those cartons had never been catalogued or processed. They were crammed with thousands of manila folders, a multitude of envelopes stuffed with the memorabilia of a couple who kept almost every scrap of paper—old diaries, old report cards, letters, tax returns, bills, notes, memos, family pictures, canceled checks, travel vouchers, and dance cards.

Once I was granted access to these papers they proved a biographer's treasure: the hitherto unexamined records of almost fifty years. It required over two years of work simply to read and categorize these documents, but they were to give both detail and dimension which would not otherwise have been possible.

These same records greatly increased the yield of my interviews with friends, associates and members of the Kennedy family. I had, for example, talked with Rose Kennedy without being able to elicit any more than the anecdotes continually repeated in other volumes and in her own memoirs. Now, however, I could show to her, during our interviews, her letters dating from the early 1900s and handwritten notes from all her various trips, and read to her entries from the diary she kept while her husband was ambassador to Great Britain. This material resurrected long-buried memories which she generously, often excitedly, shared with me.

Perhaps no American family—with the possible exception of the Adams family—has had a more vivid and powerful impact on the life of their times. But the Kennedy tale—the spiral compound of glory, achievement, degradation and almost mythical tragedy—exerts a fascination upon us that goes beyond their public achievements. For it is in the end the tale of a family that has managed to retain its bonds despite all the disintegrating forces of twentieth-century life.

Nor are the ambitions and achievements of individual family members only accidentally related. Through this generational history, the reader will, I hope, be able to see more clearly the inescapable impact of family relationships over time, the repeated patterns of behavior, both enviable and dubious, the same strengths and the same weaknesses that crop up again and again. It is a tale, repeated in three generations, of great achievement followed by decline and failure—self-inflicted or at the hands of a merciless fate.

And even though the story might be the stuff of legend—if we lived in a time for legends—it is not timeless. Each person and each generation reflected the changing circumstances of the world they lived in: the small world of neighborhood, mounting personal affluence, family ties; and the larger world of depressions and reckless booms, diplomacy, wars, and, above all, politics, which was the arena whose mastery transformed the Kennedys from successful Americans, fortunate inheritors of the American dream, to subjects of the interest and passions of an entire world. I have tried to relate those aspects of the historical setting essential to informed understanding of the actions, ambitions, beliefs and moral code of each generation; hoping thereby to avoid the error of imposing the values, ideology and prejudices of the present on a very different past.

Through this blending of public and private history, I have tried to tell the story of the Fitzgeralds and the Kennedys—the world that made them, and which, in part, they made.

I wish to acknowledge first the indispensable assistance of my research associate and friend, Linda Vandegrift, whose devotion to this book over the nine-year period was equal to my own. She brought to the task an inexhaustible curiosity, an instinct for what was significant and what was not, and, above all, the imagination to identify with each of the figures and periods we were studying. Indeed, without her, *The Fitzgeralds and the Kennedys* would never have come into being.

I am grateful to Senator Edward M. Kennedy and the Kennedy family, who permitted me to examine the papers of Joseph P. Kennedy and Rose F. Kennedy without ever asking to see a page of what I had written.

I am also grateful to the scores of people I interviewed over the years who gave so generously of their time and their memories without asking anything in return. They include Helen Barron, Lem Billings, Dinah Bridge, Charles Burke, Marjorie Mills Burns, Thomas Cabot, Mary

Keane Campbell, Al Chandler, Mary Jo Gargan Clasby, George Cukor, Francis Curley, John Henry Cutler, Marnie Devine, Bill deLong, Luella Hennessey Donovan, Morton Downey, Mary Duffy, Rose Keane Ellis, Phil Fine, Edward Fitzgerald, Father John Fitzgerald, Polly Fitzgerald, Sally Fitzgerald, Thomas Fitzgerald, Sister Jean Ford, Allen Fox, Judge John Fox, John Kenneth Galbraith, Edward Gallagher, John Galvin, Joseph Gargan, Frederick Goode, Jr., Oscar Handlin, Edward Hanify, Geraldine Hannon, Linda Hart, Pamela Churchill Harriman, Mary Heffernan, Julia Fitzgerald Hill, Cy Howard, Sisters Alice and Gabriella Husson, Sumner Kaplan, Edward M. Kennedy, Joan Bennett Kennedy, Rose Fitzgerald Kennedy, Helen Keyes, Ann Gargan King, Henry Cabot Lodge, Alice Lynch, Kerry McCarthy, Mary Lou McCarthy, John McCormick, Marguerite Curry Monahan, Frank Morrissey, Marion Fitzgerald Mullen, Regis Fitzgerald Murphy, Deborah Greene Muse, Clem Norton, Dave Powers, George Pumphret, Francis Russell, Eunice Kennedy Shriver, Robert Sargent Shriver, Jr., William Sutton, Barbara Fitzgerald Value, Samuel Wakeman, Jr., Frank Waldrop, Thomas Wangler, John B. White, Eunice Ford Williams, Page Huidekoper Wilson, Howard Wishnee, Judge Charles Wyzanski.

There are others who sustained me in different ways during the long course of this writing. I owe a special thanks to Bill Bott and Barbara Loughlin for their trust in me and my project. I am also grateful to Bruce Haas, Arnold Hiatt, Jeff Rosenhouse and Arthur Snyder. I am indebted to Cynthia Stocking for the skill and patience that enabled her to complete the task of typing and retyping a manuscript that stretched to nearly two thousand pages. I thank Brad Simon for his research and Barbara Anderson for her checking of the facts.

To Bill Goldstein I give my thanks for his careful reading of the manuscript and for his wise suggestions. I owe thanks as well to Jean Stein and to my sister, Jeanne Kearns. And from the bottom of my heart, I thank my friend Janna Malamud Smith, who read and edited the entire manuscript at every stage.

I wish to express a special thanks to the staffs of the various libraries where I worked over the last nine years. It is hard to imagine a warmer working situation than the Kennedy Library. From the earliest days when the papers were still stored in the Federal Records Center in Waltham to the creation of the new library in Dorchester, William Johnson and Deborah Greene Muse provided more help, encouragement and companionship than I ever expected to find in the archives of any institution. And when the time came for choosing the photographs, no one could have been more helpful than Alan Goodrich. I am also grateful to the wonderful staff at the Boston Public Library, where so much of the material for my book was found, to Rodney Armstrong at the Boston Athenaeum and to Jim O'Toole at the Boston Archdiocese Archives.

And to the entire staff of the Concord Public Library I feel a special gratitude for giving me a second home over all these years as I sat, day after day, writing this book in longhand, in the warmth and beauty of the wood-paneled reading room.

At Simon and Schuster I owe a special thanks to Vera Schneider for the skillful job she did in copyediting and indexing, to Ann Godoff for her insightful suggestions on every chapter and to Henry Ferris for his consistent warmth and good cheer. And to my editor, Alice Mayhew, who encouraged me from the first day to the last without ever once losing faith in the project despite the inordinate time it took to be completed, I am more grateful than she will ever know.

On this book, as on everything connected with my writing life, I owe a special debt to my agent, Sterling Lord. He has always been there when I needed him and I shall never forget it.

And, finally, I reserve my deepest thanks to my husband, Richard Goodwin, who conceived the idea for this book a decade ago and who helped me through every single day of labor.

DORIS KEARNS GOODWIN

*Concord, Massachusetts*
*November 1986*

# BOOK ONE

# THE
# FITZGERALDS
## (1863-1915)

# CHAPTER 1
# THE
# IMMIGRANT
# WORLD

On the twelfth of February, 1863, on a morning described in the Boston newspapers as "below freezing" and "cloudy" with a cold wind blowing hard from the north, a tiny boy, John Francis Fitzgerald, not yet one day old, was carried by his father to St. Stephen's Church for baptism.

For the father, Thomas Fitzgerald, the rushed baptism spoke to the extreme fragility of life in the North End, the immigrant quarter of Boston, where three infants out of ten died before the age of one. Believing that an unbaptized child would be forever prevented from entering the kingdom of heaven, condemning his parents to haunting visions of a little soul howling in the night, searching for water that would never be found, Thomas had arranged for the baptism within twelve hours of the baby's birth.

The journey to the church from the wooden tenement house on Ferry Street in which the baby had been born took the father and son through a maze of narrow alleys and dark lanes, dignified by the name of streets, as Ferry emptied into North, North wound into Richmond and Richmond opened onto Hanover Street, the bustling, congested center of commerce in the North End.

Turning north on Hanover Street, the child and his father passed by dozens of narrow storefronts, crowded one beside the other, housing apothecaries, grocers, saloon keepers, watchmakers, tailors and dressmakers, all just beginning a long day of work, until they finally came to a large majestic structure that stood in commanding contrast to its congested surroundings, a breakwater of order and elegance against the chaotic tide of life in the slum.

St. Stephen's Church, considered then by many observers the most beautiful of all the Catholic churches in Boston, had originally been commissioned in 1802 as a Congregational church by the old Boston families of learning and wealth. Designed by the city's most famous architect, Charles Bulfinch, to echo the beauty of Italian Renaissance churches, this stately red brick structure boasted a splendid classical interior: it was symmetrically proportioned as a perfect square, its dimensions all determined by the height of its Doric columns, its every detail related in perfect harmony to every other based upon the ideal proportions of the human body.

But its life as a church of Boston's elite had not lasted for long. For within fifty years, with the onrush of the Irish immigrants into the narrow cobblestone streets surrounding the wharves, the North End had become Boston's most densely populated slum. The old Protestant families had fled to Beacon Hill and the Back Bay, abandoning their homes and their churches. With their worshipers gone, the Protestants sold their Bulfinch church to the Catholics, whose ever-expanding population provided an instant membership of over five thousand people.

Having been through the baptismal ceremony three times before with the birth of his first three sons, Thomas Fitzgerald understood that when he arrived at the church he was to knock on the door to announce his presence and then wait outside with the baby and the baby's sponsors while the parish priest, the Reverend Charles Rainoni, prepared the holy compound of oil and balm, the blessed salt and the natural water to be used in the sacrament.

Once his own preparations were completed, Father Rainoni, carefully attired in a flowing white surplice and a long purple stole of embroidered silk that was to be worn only for baptisms, advanced to the threshold, where he asked the name of the child to be baptized.

By Catholic custom at the time, the selection of a name was a serious task, for the people believed then that a child would develop the characteristics of whomever he was named after. Even the poorest of Catholic parents owned Butler's *Lives of the Saints* so that they could choose a saint by whose example the child might be excited to a holy life and by whose prayers he might be protected. Other considerations also prevailed in the naming of an Irish child, such as the desire to honor a grandparent or another close relative. And, at a time when the death of a child was a common event, a new baby would often be named for a dead one, emphasizing its role as a substitute. Thus, the Fitzgeralds' first son, born in 1858, was named Michael after both Michael the Archangel and his paternal grandfather, Michael Fitzgerald, and later, after the first baby Michael died of hydrocephalus before he was two, another Michael was christened in 1864. Their next son, James, born in 1860, was named for both Saint James the Apostle, and for Thomas' younger brother James, while Thomas Junior, born in 1861, obviously carried on his father's own name as well.

As for the name John, it was said at the time that if parents wanted their son to be either a great writer or a great orator he should be named John, after Saint John the Apostle, the author of the mysterious Book of the Apocalypse, or after the golden-mouthed Saint John Chrysostom.

History does not record which ancestors, if any, Tom Fitzgerald and Rosanna Cox had in mind in choosing the name John. We know only that once the name was chosen by that generation, it would be passed on for generations to come.

When the chosen name had been announced, Father Rainoni put a grain of blessed salt into the mouth of the infant. By this ancient ceremony, reflecting the Biblical saying "the salt of the earth," the child was admonished "to procure and maintain in his soul true wisdom and prudence, for which salt is an emblem inasmuch as it seasons and gives a relish to all things." Then the priest proceeded to the solemn prayers used to cast from the soul the Devil under whose power all humans were born by original sin. "I exorcise thee . . . in the name of the Father and of the Son and of the Holy Ghost."

All these initial ceremonies the priest performed in the entry of the church, to signify that the infant was not worthy to enter into God's place of worship until the Devil had been cast out of him. But after the prayer for exorcism, the priest placed the end of his purple stole on the child and brought him into the church, saying, "John Francis, come unto the temple of God, that thou mayest have part with Christ unto life everlasting. Amen."

At the baptismal font, the priest anointed the child upon the breast and between the shoulders with holy oil, which outward unction was to represent the inward anointing of the soul by divine grace, fortifying him against his passions and his sexual desires. Then, with both godparents holding their godchild, the priest poured the water upon the infant's head three times in the form of a cross, saying at the same time these exact words: "John Francis Fitzgerald, I baptize thee in the name of the Father and of the Son and of the Holy Ghost."

The ceremony over, the priest recorded the event for history in the large black baptismal book which has been kept for more than a century, its leather bindings now torn and frayed, among the records of St. Stephen's, so that even today we can read Rainoni's original entry penned in black ink on a blue page: "Feb 12 Bap John Francis born 11 inft of Thomas Fitzgerald and wife Rosa Cox."

From what we know of the texture of the daily life of the Fitzgerald family, it is easy to understand the magic of the Catholic Church at this time and in this place. For the sheer beauty of the church building alone opened up to them, as to all their neighbors in the North End, an inner world of sounds, smells and sights in stark contrast to the world outside.

Against the clamor of the teeming life in the streets—where Thomas Fitzgerald worked from dawn to dusk as a peddler—the church provided a hushed and solemn refuge. In the soft, gray silence, broken only by whispered talk and the rustle of footsteps, one could find that rarest of possessions in the city slum—privacy. In the din of the cramped tenement house, as Irving Howe has observed in World of Our Fathers, "space was the stuff of dreams; a room to oneself, a luxury beyond reach." Yet here, in the dark, vaulted silence of the church, amid the gleam of the soft brasses of the candlesticks on the large elaborate altar, each worshiper could feel utterly alone.

And there was a rich, musty smell inside—not the unbearable odor rising from the one water closet which the Fitzgerald family shared with all their neighbors in the tenement house (twenty-four adults and thirteen children) along with the customers of the saloon which occupied the first floor, nor the stench of rotting food and waste only intermittently carted away by a neglectful Sanitation Department, but the fine smell of aging wood and the clinging fragrance of burnt incense.

A contemporary observer, writing in The Atlantic Monthly in 1868, explained the pull of the Catholic Church on the immigrant community in these terms:

If there is any such thing as realized, working Christianity, it may be seen in one of [the] poor, densely peopled Catholic parishes, where all is dreary, dismal desolation, excepting alone in the sacred enclosure around the church, where a bright interior cheers the leisure hours; where pictures, music and stately ceremonial exalt the poor above their lot; and where a friend and father can ever be found. . . . All in their lot, all in their surroundings, is mean, nasty, inefficient, forbidding—except their church.

Amid the rich surroundings of his church, an immigrant's mind could soar high into the realm of hopes, away from the world of facts, hunger, dirt and despair, away from the tyranny of the here and now to a mysterious romantic regime dominated by the promise of life eternal in a celestial community, governed by its own rites and images, filled with its own possibilities.

Poor and unfortunate though these immigrants might be, they were admonished to find compensation for their miserable lot in this world in the knowledge that a far loftier role awaited them in the next. In the standard nineteenth-century spiritual book Catholics were told:

You may be a poor man—striving by wearying, ceaseless toil for a poor living, you may have had little schooling, you may lack comforts of this life and feel envious sometimes to see your Protestant friends so much better off in this world's way . . . but there is something you possess which our poor friends with all their wealth cannot purchase—the true religion of Jesus Christ.

Acceptance of one's position was the central message pervading Catholic readers, daily catechism and Sunday sermons in the nineteenth century. This religious dictum reinforced the self-denying and pessimistic view of the world which the Irish peasants carried with them across the Atlantic, their mental baggage from the Old World. In the New World, this gospel of acceptance was to bear bitter fruit, for "no slum was as fearful as the Irish slum." Of all the immigrant nationalities in Boston, the Irish fared the least well, beginning at a lower rung and rising more slowly on the economic and social ladder than any other group. The degradation endured for generations by the poor peasant in the Old World combined with a Catholic value system in which the preparations for one's death and rebirth eclipsed the affairs of the immediate present to produce an acceptance of conditions in the New World which few other people would have tolerated.

Yet the story of the Fitzgerald family is the story of the slow escape from the grind of mere subsistence. It is a tale not of acceptance but of gradual progress and achievement; of mobility, not resignation, and of ever-expanding horizons. In the immigrant slums, Oscar Handlin has argued in *Boston's Immigrants*, one in a hundred lived and prospered and stood to be looked at as a living monument of the American dream, but ninety-nine in a hundred were lost, never to be heard of. What do we know about the early experience of Thomas Fitzgerald in Boston that numbered him among that "one in a hundred" who lived and prospered and distinguished the story of his family from that of the overwhelming majority of Irish immigrants?

The home at 30 Ferry Street to which the Fitzgerald party returned after the christening consisted of two doorless rooms no larger than closets, which were used to house the pilings of straw that served as beds, and a kitchen twelve by ten feet. Six short steps from the outer wall to the hall measured the full extent of the family's living quarters. Behind a makeshift wall lived the family of the tailor Owen McLaughlin, his wife, Bridget, and their two children, and next to them the family of a laborer, Michael Sullivan, his wife, Nancy, and their three children. On each of three floors, the same pattern prevailed: the lives of nine families separated only by the thinnest of walls and a dark, open well of stairs.

If there was no escape from the crowded conditions of tenement life, the Fitzgeralds' quarters were on the top floor and their kitchen fronted onto the street, providing them with sunlight, a considerable advantage in their struggle for survival. Of all the ills associated with tenement housing, an investigator in Boston singled out insufficient light and air —occasioned by the haphazard partition of apartments and the building of one tenement house right up against another—as the primary cause of death and disease. In the typical tenement building, the investigator reported, "all the lower rooms are very dark . . . in some rooms on the ground floor the ceiling is only 6¼' high . . . in the rear houses the only windows . . . look on 3 and 5 storied walls only 4.4 inches away." From such buildings—with the exception of some of the rooms on the uppermost floors—sunlight was almost completely excluded.

A vivid testimony to the value that tenement dwellers placed on the golden sun is provided by Jacob Riis in his classic work on tenement life, where he describes a conversation with a twelve-year-old girl, the daughter of a Polish capmaker, whose fondest dream was to move to a front room where "sunlight comes right into your face." In her rear rooms, she knew the exact month—June—and the exact hour of the day when the sun's rays shone into their home, providing a momentary respite from the gloom of the gray walls.

John Francis Fitzgerald, too, long remembered his own family's description of the warmth and the pleasure of their Ferry Street kitchen on a sunny day. And it was there in that kitchen on the twelfth of February, 1863, that the Fitzgeralds held the customary christening dinner, to which the parish priest, the baby's sponsors and the family's relatives were invited.

Since the thirty-two-year-old mother Rosanna had given birth only the day before, the duties of preparation most likely fell upon the baby's paternal grandmother, Ellen Wilmouth Fitzgerald, who was living right around the corner on North Street. Evidently lack of space did not prevent the assembling of the whole Fitzgerald clan, which included Thomas' three younger sisters, Bridget, thirty-five, and Hannah, thirty-four, both married with children, and Ellen, twenty-four, who was about to be married. Also present at the christening dinner, and central to the story of the Fitzgeralds' rise from poverty, was Thomas' youngest brother, James, a forceful young man of twenty-five with dark-blue eyes and a deep, gruff voice, who, in the tangled course of events following the family's immigration to America, had become the person upon whom the rest of the family pinned its hopes.

The invisible loyalties which brought the Fitzgerald sisters and brothers together, on this as on so many other occasions, particularly those surrounding birth, marriage and death, had been born across the ocean in the boggy countryside of western Ireland where the small farm and the ancestral graves they had left behind provided a common stock of memories, myths and values that would stay with them all the rest of their lives. In the little farming community of Bruff where the Fitzgeralds had grown up, the christening of a baby was considered one of the central events in a person's life, occasioning a large, joyous celebration at the crossroads, to which all the members of the village were traditionally invited. Here, however, in the cramped world of the city, the christening celebration was typically a much smaller, less important affair.

But this particular christening held an importance that went beyond its appearance; for at the gathering of the clan an agreement was reached which changed the direction of Thomas Fitzgerald's life. After years of dreaming that he would eventually settle on a farm in the Midwest, Fitzgerald decided on this day to go into business with his brother James and to build his family's future in the old North End.

A broad-chested, powerfully made man with a handsome face and a ruddy complexion, Thomas Fitzgerald, or Cocky Tom as he was commonly called for his having one cocked eye, had lived in America for more than ten of his forty years, and seven of these years had been spent right where he now was, in the heart of Boston's Irish slum. Yet, all these years the city had remained for him an alien and forbidding place

—a place he had never intended as his home but only as a way station until he could save enough money to move his family away from the port of landing, through the interior cities of transit to the farms of the Midwest, where the open lands reached away in plenty and where once again he could be in a position to till the soil, the only livelihood he had ever wanted, the only labor he considered worthy of a man.

In the Old Country where Thomas was born, nearly every boy was brought up to be a potato farmer. At the age of seven, under the direction of his father, Michael Fitzgerald, Thomas had learned to dig the trenches for the potatoes, and by the time he was ten he was involved in the sowing of the fields. While he worked beside his father, his sisters were thrown in with their mother, learning to feed the pigs and the chickens, to rake the ashes in the hearth and to prepare the big meal at lunchtime when the men and the boys came back from the fields. For every member of the family at every age, there were a special set of tasks, allowing them all to share in the common enterprise of cultivating the soil, creating among them all, as Thomas later explained to his sons, an unbreakable bond with each other and—he thought—with the land.

John Fitzgerald later said that when he listened to his father talk about his childhood in Ireland, he thought there must be no more wonderful place in all the world to grow up in. For though the family slept on a mud floor in a one-room thatched cabin on a tiny plot of rented land, and though, like all Catholics in Ireland, they were prevented by British law from voting, holding office, owning land or even attending school, they had all the food, warmth and companionship they needed to feel spirited and gay.

But, as anybody who knows the history of Ireland knows, the potato failed. It is now understood that the blight of the potato in 1845—which caused the failure of four successive crops, sentenced one out of every six peasants to death by starvation and forced more than a quarter of the Irish population to emigrate—was caused by the invasion of a fungus which can be treated by spraying with a copper compound. But when this microscopic organism made its first appearance on the potato plant, in the fall of 1845, as a whitish fringe, there was no comprehension of the nature of the blight nor any understanding of how to stop its spread. Under ordinary weather conditions, the fungus might have died of its own accord over the cold winter months, but the unusual warmth of January and February and the extraordinary wetness of the spring of 1846 favored the spread of the blight to an extent which had not been recorded before or since. First, the endless weeks of rain allowed the diseased shoots left in the ground from the year before to form millions of new spores, and then the continuously moist earth provided an underground system of canals allowing the destructive spores to swim from plant to plant and field to field, working their way into every leaf and tuber, reducing green and healthy plants to decay, turning entire fields into blackened, stinking masses of decomposing rot.

So completely did the conditions of life and the existence of the people in this least industrialized of all Western nations depend upon the soil, and in particular upon the potato, that the partial failure of one year's crop and the total failure of the next produced a national famine. Helpless before the fate overtaking them, the starving peasants turned to the British government for help, but the relief measures which the British adopted proved indescribably inadequate to the scope of the disaster.

Before the Great Famine, as it came to be called, the Irish had regarded the idea of leaving their country as the most appalling of fates. But now, terrified and desperate in the wake of starvation and fever, they made their way out of Ireland by the tens of thousands. The first major exodus took place during the winter and spring of 1846 and 1847, when hordes of panic-stricken peasants simply fled, borrowing or burrowing their way onto the great "coffin ships," so named because of the great numbers who died on board, their precise destination mattering less than the desire to escape a land they now believed to be cursed. As would be expected, the poorest class of farmers went first; all those who retained even the slightest resources for survival stayed behind in the hope that the next year's crop would see them through. But when the two succeeding crops also failed, hope turned to terror, and by 1848 even the better and more energetic farmers readied themselves to leave.

It was in this second wave of emigration, which lasted roughly from 1848 to 1855 and presumably encompassed the better class of farmers, that the Fitzgeralds came to America. In what order and by what means they came we are not sure, though family tradition suggests that James, the youngest boy, came first, followed by the three girls and their mother, Ellen, who is listed upon her arrival as a widow (evidence that her husband, Michael, had died before they left), and still later by the oldest brother, Thomas, who, legend suggests, clung to the family's land until there was absolutely no hope of survival.

"As I heard it told," second cousin Mary Hannon Heffernan recalled, "James came over as a little boy in 1848 or 1849 with his uncle Edmond Fitzgerald and his first cousin, Mary Ann Fitzgerald, Edmond's daughter. He was only ten or eleven at the time and he got desperately sick on board the ship. Everyone in the family was terrified that if the captain saw how sick the boy was, he would think it was typhus and simply throw him overboard. But there was a wonderful woman on the ship, a

Mrs. Williams, who took care of him. Day and night she kept him covered up with a blanket, insisting that it was only a bad cold. Then, near the end of the voyage, they ran into a terrible storm with winds so high that the ship turned itself completely around, and they were sure they were headed back to Ireland until the moment they landed in Boston."

That after a raging storm and six weeks at sea their sense of direction could have deceived them is not at all surprising. But the sensation of turning around suggests the possibility that before the storm the ship was headed somewhere else, perhaps to New York. In other words, had it not been for the high winds blowing them north, the first Fitzgeralds might have ended up in Brooklyn or the Bronx and a different tale would now be told. For, once the first members of the family settled in the North End, all the others came, drawn as by a magnet to the same congested spot.

It is a fragmentary memory, yet powerful in its suggestion of the severe emotional dislocation experienced by millions of immigrants at this time who were forced to separate themselves forever from the whole circle of people and places on which they had depended, sailing across an unknown ocean to an unknown land. What internal terror there must have been for so many people to take such a spectacular risk, and how the terror must have persisted long after their arrival in America! For many of the Irish, the Church was the only salve for their anxiety, but others, the Fitzgeralds among them, found a powerful substitute for loss in the prevailing American ideology, the ideology of opportunity and success.

Family tradition holds that when Thomas Fitzgerald first arrived in Boston, he accompanied his cousin Mary Ann and her new husband, Michael Hannon, to the little farming community of Acton, twenty-five miles west of Boston, where he worked as a farm laborer for three years in the hope of saving up enough money to buy and cultivate his own plot of land.

But his meager wages as a laborer apparently kept him living so close to the margin that he was unable to accumulate the surplus he needed to alter his position, and by 1857 he had moved back to Boston, occupied as a peddler. Although his original intention was to stay in the city only as long as it took to save up the money to travel to the Midwest, he, like so many thousands of his fellow immigrants who harbored similar dreams, was somehow trapped, destined to live the rest of his days separated from the world of nature, fenced off from the realm of birds and beasts and growing things that had once given meaning and structure to his entire being.

What thwarted his escape from the city? That he started out as a peddler seemed at first a fortunate choice, for in the nineteenth century, in the days before retail stores or supermarkets, there was money to be made in peddling, though success usually called for the peddler, his bag of stock upon his back, to move widely and freely about the country, traveling for hundreds of miles to far distant points where his supply of tools, clothes, books and candlesticks was needed and his news from the city eagerly awaited. For those with ingenuity, ambition and an entreprenurial spirit, there were, already, some inspirational examples of thriving enterprises and large fortunes built upon the peddler's trade: by such men as Daniel Drew, Jim Fisk, Collis P. Huntington and Cyrus H. McCormick.*

But unlike the classic peddler, fueled with the thirst for adventure, Thomas Fitzgerald never took to the open road; he became, instead, a street peddler with a narrow route of trade circumscribed by the wharves and the docks of the immigrant district. Up each morning before dawn, carrying a large wicker basket under his arm, he would meet the returning fishing boats at Lewis Wharf and spend the morning tramping up and down the crowded cobblestone streets until he had sold all the codfish and haddock his basket could carry. Then, back to the wharf for the afternoon's catch and another strenuous route. It was, in the words of Irving Howe, "backbreaking and soul destroying work."

That Thomas never developed a wider route of travel is not to be wondered at when we consider that his five years in peddling coincided with marriage and the rapid growth of his family. On the fifteenth of November, 1857, only one month after he had obtained his peddling license, he was married to Rosanna Cox, daughter of Irish immigrants Philip and Mary Cox. Rosanna was twenty-three when they married at St. Stephen's Church; Thomas was already thirty-five. But like so many of the Irish, who tended to marry later in life than the native Americans, he soon made up for lost time: in the first five years of his marriage, four sons were born.

Nor should we wonder at the difficulties Thomas faced in trying to save up his meager profits for his distant dream. Though the dollars he earned, measured in terms of potatoes, compared favorably with what he had earned in Ireland, here for the first time he was faced with the

* The best story of a peddler's progress was yet to be written: In the latter half of the nineteenth century, young Dick Sears, a telegrapher in a little train station in North Redwood, Minnesota, would decide one day to buy up an unclaimed shipment of watches for a small sum which he then peddled for a fine profit. His success persuaded him to leave his telegrapher's job for the peddler's road. As his watch business grew, he found himself in need of someone to keep his watches in repair, and in answer to an ad a young man named Alvah Roebuck was hired—a fortuitous choice leading, in time, to the gigantic enterprise of Sears, Roebuck and Company

necessity of purchasing his own food and clothing and at costs high beyond anything he could possibly have imagined at home.

Yet before six years had passed Thomas had saved up the money he figured he needed to pick up his family, move to the Midwest and purchase a farm. Then, just before he planned to leave, came the christening dinner for John Francis where, according to the story he later told, he received an offer from his younger brother James to stay in the city and go into business with him. The year before, James had purchased a small grocery store at 310 North Street, which he now wanted to expand; if Thomas joined him in the business and contributed his savings, they could add a supply of "bottled goods" to the stock of food already there and operate the store together as grocer and clerk. Though the idea of becoming a clerk in a store failed to correspond to any vision of happiness Thomas had hitherto entertained, he accepted his brother's proposition. From that moment on, the city became his permanent home, the locale in which the life experience of all his children would be played out.

When asked later by his son John why, against his deepest wishes, he had given up his vision of a life in the country and accepted his brother's offer, Thomas listed three reasons: his wife, his relatives and his church. That at the moment of decision he should have been held to the city by these associations is not at all surprising: millions of immigrants were.

All during the middle years of the nineteenth century, the Irish were implored by politicians, by newspapers and by social agencies to leave the cities and go west. Typical of such entreaties is the following passage in an article in the leading Catholic newspaper, *The Pilot*, in 1864:

> If we could sit by the side of every emigrant at home, this is what we would say . . . America . . . has room and work and wages for every soul of the starving poor of Europe . . . The emigrant who comes with a spirit of active industry and enterprise may soon gain an independence for himself and for his children. But it is not by lingering in the crowded haunts of men that he will do this. The cities are overrun, thronged with candidates for labor . . . But there is a resource which is always open, always inviting, which is never glutted, which always has room for more and that is the land—employment upon the land.

Despite these oft-repeated words of advice and the splendid image of green meadows and open fields, only the exceptional few, estimated at less than ten percent, became farmers, among them Henry Ford's grandfather John Ford, who cleared what was then primeval forest near Dearborn, Michigan, and made a farm; the vast majority remained huddled together in the grassless cities. Possibly if when they first landed they had had enough resources to push their way into the country, this concentration would not have occurred, but the Irish had always been a highly social people, and once they had tasted of the close life in the city, where they could meet their friends and relatives on every corner, they were unwilling to give it up. It is said that the women, especially, were afraid to cut loose from the streets and the stores and all the objects of daily life that had now grown familiar; they had already experienced the harrowing process of leavetaking when they said goodbye to the land of their birth, and one such grief was enough.

Contributing to the immigrants' fear of moving, if the choice actually arose, were the bleak tales told of the isolation of life on the American farm, where, in contrast to Ireland, the ample space was too ample, creating an emptiness that seemed more troubling than the overcrowding of the slum. Then, too, there was the fear of losing their church and finding themselves in a faraway place without a priest close by, a loss the Fitzgeralds no doubt contemplated more carefully than most, having experienced the special aesthetic pleasures of belonging to a church as magnificent as St. Stephen's.

Though the explanations Thomas gave for remaining in the city centered mainly on the fear of leaving the familiar for the unknown, it is reasonable to suppose that he also felt drawn in a positive way to the opportunity of going into business with his brother James. John Fitzgerald later remembered his father saying that he had always felt there was something special in his younger brother's character, that from the very first months when he had watched his brother working in the grocery store, he had sensed in his bones that James possessed an uncanny instinct for business which would lead him someday to achieve considerable success. And Thomas' instincts were right, for eventually James became one of the wealthiest men in the North End.

The story that comes down to us suggests that James, of all the Fitzgerald children, adapted the most readily to the challenge of life in the New World. Whereas his sisters and brothers retained all their lives many characteristics of western Ireland, James, with his ready will and raw intelligence, made himself thoroughly comfortable in the city.

The first job young James found turned out to be that of an assistant in the very grocery store he would eventually own and operate for fifty years. Apparently, the boss was pleased with the way the boy handled himself and he made sure that James acquired a thorough understanding of the store, its goods, its prices and its customers. Shrewd and clever, with a faculty for judging people, James learned to recognize which customers could be given credit and which could not. Always alive to necessity, he educated himself in the arts of weighing, measuring and reckoning, of bargaining, selling and even purchasing, and by the time he was sixteen he had risen to the responsible position of clerk.

In his twentieth year James made the acquaintance of his future wife, Julia Adeline Brophy. Julia, possessed of an educated mind and refined temperament, was the granddaughter of Thomas Cass, a sharp-witted, successful trader who had accumulated a substantial amount of property in the North End. How it came to pass that she, who no doubt had other more suitable prospects, could have chosen a barely educated clerk remains an interesting question of history and most likely a revelatory comment on James's special character.

Through his marriage, James developed a business relationship with his wife's uncle Cornelius Doherty, one of the most successful grocers in the North End, which enabled him, when he was only twenty-four, to get his start as an independent proprietor. Though the exact nature of the business relationship is unclear, it is recorded in the city records that in 1862 James Fitzgerald received a sum of over $1,000 from the merchant Doherty. It is also recorded that in that same year James became "the grocer" at 310 North, and, considering that the average salary of a clerk at that time was two dollars a day, it is reasonable to assume that Doherty's loan provided the cash Fitzgerald needed, beyond his own savings, to purchase the store.

Upon becoming a grocer, James had entered one of the few spheres of business in which immigrants had an advantage over their native competitors. "Where they relied on the patronage of their compatriots, they prospered," Handlin observed. "Food dealers—butchers, fruiterers, and above all, grocers—dealt directly and intimately with immigrant women who preferred to purchase from those who spoke their own language, carried familiar food stuffs and served them as a friend, confidant and advisor."

But the best money in the grocery business came when the grocery doubled as a saloon, ministering to the needs of the women by day and the men by night. Such expansion was the rationale behind the partnership James offered to his brother Tom; for with Tom's savings he could stock his store with supplies of beer, gin, whiskey and wine, while at the same time keeping his barrels filled with the conventional supplies of sugar, flour, potatoes, crackers, tea, soap, candles and kindling wood.

As a combination grocery-groggery, the store at 310 North came to serve as an informal social center for all manner of neighborhood folk, and it was, as well, the locale for some of young John's earliest memories. Shopkeeping in those days was a family business; whenever she could—that is, whenever her state of pregnancy allowed her to be up and around—Rosanna Fitzgerald worked with her husband in the store.

All his life John would remember the room in the back where he and his brothers were left to play amid the wooden casks and the barrels filled with flour while their mother handled the customers out front. For some children, the confinement of the small, cluttered room would have been torture, but not for John, who, as he recalled, "loved the sense of being right in the middle of everyone, where everything was happening." Later he could remember his mother telling him that when he was an infant all she ever had to do to keep him from crying was place him on a blanket in full view of the store, where he would sit contentedly for hours totally absorbed in the passing scene.

The traffic would begin soon after dawn, when the neighborhood women streamed in to fill their cans and their jugs with flour and milk for the morning meal. Then, in the afternoons, they were back again for more flour and their daily supply of meat—there being neither money to buy nor room to store articles bought in bulk. For the typical immigrant family, depending as they did upon the credit of the store-keepers, the cost of food was very large—nearly half of their income—while the quality received, in a business noted for its sharp practices, was generally very low.

Yet the combination of meager wages and irregular employment which forced the typical immigrant into a relationship of credit with the storekeeper, and trapped him into buying inferior food in small quantities at high prices, assured a good profit for the grocer, and gradually the store at 310 North began to prosper. With a growing margin of profit behind them, Tom and Rosanna were able to provide their own family with a steady supply of decent food, affording them a measure of control over their daily life which few of their neighbors were able to enjoy. In contrast to the dominant experience of the slum, where food was a constant source of worry and concern, John Fitzgerald long relished the memory of good food and pleasant mealtimes at his home; he spoke of eating fish as well as meat and of having fresh vegetables every day, and he particularly remembered Sunday nights when his mother made flapjacks which he loved to drown in butter and syrup or molasses.

If the store did well by day, it thrived by night as the neighborhood men, home from a long day of hard work, began to drop in for drinks. The saloon at that time was not simply a bar as we know it today. In the twelve-block area of the North End, over 540 different establishments—ranging from groceries like the Fitzgeralds' to billiard parlors and bowling alleys—served liquor; and in none of these places, according to a study by a Committee of 50 in the 1880s, was drinking the sole function. The typical "saloon" in the immigrant quarters, as committee chairman John Koren described it, supplied many legitimate wants besides the craving for intoxication. [It] is here the workingman's club, in which many of his leisure hours are spent, and in which he finds more of the things that approximate luxury than in his home . . . In winter [it] is warm, in summer cool, at night it is brightly lighted, and it is almost always clean . . . it is not enough to say that [the] sense of discomfort pervading the dark tenement house, with its tired, unkempt wife and restless children, leads to its use. No, at bottom, it must be a craving for fellowship underlying the unrest of the workingman's hours that draws him into the saloon.

It has often been said, only partly in jest, that among the Irish there are only two types of drinkers: alcoholics and teetotalers, those who give in completely to liquor's seductive appeal and those who guard themselves completely against it. In this context, it is curious to note that of the nine sons eventually born to Thomas and Rosanna Fitzgerald, three followed their father's path to success by entering into some aspect of the liquor trade at some point in their lives, while three ended up as heavy drinkers and died young. It seemed as if the blessings that accrued to some members of the family as a result of the liquor trade had brought a curse upon the others, as if the profits built upon the backs of stumbling men had exacted a price in the ledger of family accountability. "Whenever anything bad happened in the family," a Fitzgerald relative remembered, "my mother would sigh deeply and then with fear and bitterness in her voice she would say, 'It's the curse of the liquor money, I know it.'"

By the fall of 1866, when Johnny was three and a half years old, his father, Thomas, had accumulated enough money to move his family into larger quarters in a three-story brick building at 435 Hanover Street. By this time, Johnny and his two older brothers, Jimmy, six, and Thomas, five, had been joined by two younger brothers, Michael, two, and William, one, and Rosanna was pregnant with Edward, who would be born the following March. But the move was more than simply a move of necessity compelled by the growing size of the family. For with the assistance of his brother, who had invested in real estate himself the year before, Thomas was able to buy the entire three-story building from Micah Dyer for $6,550, thereby shifting his status from tenant to landlord and solving another major concern of all immigrant families—the disproportionate share of income that had to go for rent.

Though nothing, at first glance, could seem less similar than the experience of owning and operating a tenement in a packed city slum and the situation Thomas had originally hoped to create for himself of owning a farm in the country, the signing of the papers, which marked him for the first time in his life as an owner of property, provided him with a great feeling of accomplishment. Many years later, John Fitzgerald remembered his father saying near the end of his life that "beyond his family, nothing he had done before and nothing he accomplished since meant as much to him as the possession of that small white document that testified to the fact that Thomas Fitzgerald at the age of forty-four was finally the owner of his own home."

In the long view, the change from tenant to landlord brought a substantial increase in the degree of control Thomas was able to exert over the physical conditions of his family's daily life: windows that were patched up, a workable fire escape, a lighted hallway, stairs that were kept in repair, a clean toilet. "Only people who have never known the absence of these rudimentary amenities," observed Irving Howe, "would be inclined to minimize their values."

In their new quarters, behind a storefront which Thomas would eventually convert into his own grocery store, allowing him to go into business completely on his own, the Fitzgerald family boasted a parlor with two windows and a kitchen heated by a coal stove, and, for the first time in their married life, Tom and Rosanna enjoyed the privacy of their own bedroom, separated by a flight of stairs from a big room in which all the children slept together, with their beds "lined up like a dorm." Though the physical conditions were still a long way from the next generation's vision that in a comfortable home each member of the family should have a separate room, the fact that the children were separated from their parents had a significant impact on their growing up. In most of the tenements at that time, the children slept in the same room if not in the same bed as their parents, a circumstance which inevitably led to their sexual precocity and made it difficult to put them to sleep before the parents themselves were ready for bed. In their new home, however, as John Fitzgerald later recalled, there was a clear distinction between the boys' room upstairs and their parents' room downstairs. Only when his younger brothers were infants did they have to sleep in their parents' room; once they were able to crawl, they were allowed upstairs with the rest of their brothers.

Many years later, John Fitzgerald told a friend that sometimes, when he watched one of his little brothers being carried to bed in his parents' room, he wished he were smaller so that he too could be allowed to sleep there. The wish itself is testimony to the progress the Fitzgeralds had made: only a boy who did not consciously remember the terribly cramped conditions of his earlier house at 30 Ferry Street would have wished away his separate bedroom.

In the course of his long life Fitzgerald spoke only in the most positive terms of the "warm and wonderful house" in which he had grown up; but every now and then, for a political speech on his "rise to success," he liked to use as his starting point a description of "the dingy tenement on Ferry Street," where he was born, "that had no bathroom or electric lights or any other conveniences—not even a humble accordion, let alone a harmonica or piano"; and then, having roused his audience to sympathy and not wanting to break the rhythm of their emotions, he conveniently forgot to mention that the brick home on Hanover Street where he actually grew up represented a marked improvement over the ratty wooden tenement in which he was born.

Another interesting sign of the gradual betterment of conditions at 435 Hanover Street emerges in the body of statistics gathered for the census, the city directories and the reports of the tax assessors which suggest that from 1868 on, at any one time, at least twelve people, on the average, occupied the uppermost floor as boarders. As cramped and limiting as life had once been for the Fitzgeralds, so it now was for the families of Cornelius Mahoney, a stevedore; Michael Conlan, a fisherman; Thomas Cochran, a laborer; and Thomas Acorn, a painter. While the Fitzgerald family spread out on two floors, these four families had to live huddled together behind a jumble of thin walls on a single floor.

There is no way of knowing how Thomas treated his renters at 435 Hanover, but stories abound that, once secure in the possession of property, the Irish landlord, "like an apt pupil . . . merely showing forth the result of the schooling he had received, reenacting in his own way the scheme of the tenements, collected rents with the same avidity as the Yankee owners had from him." And we do know that, with the money he earned from his rentals in just three years, Thomas was able to buy two additional tenements, at 4 Webster Place and 379 Hanover.

With time, as these properties added up, Tom Fitzgerald grew more worldly, learning from the experience of his brother. Though he himself never became in any sense a wealthy man, as his brother eventually did, Thomas was able, through his business, to get a grip on his life and to achieve a mastery of sorts over the struggle for existence. If he accumulated little more through his long years of toil as a peddler on the streets and a clerk in a groggery, this in itself was a substantial achievement, for, with food and shelter guaranteed by the store and the tenement, his children experienced the small pleasures of life—a bed with a mattress, a vacation at the seashore, a bath at the public bathhouse, the chance for an education—that broadened their horizons and transmitted to them a feeling of power at odds with the dominant fatalism so characteristic of the slums.

# CHAPTER 2
# PAGEANTS
# AND
# PROCESSIONS

Among the growing boys, eventually numbering nine with the birth of Joseph in 1868, George in 1871 and Henry in 1875, Johnny was the smallest. Always in motion, always struggling to reach a position of vantage, he battled with his puny body as with a reluctant animal that had to be mastered.

Every night, when all his brothers had gone to sleep he would complete one hundred sit-ups on the narrow strip of the wooden floor that ran in front of the lined-up beds. Then, in the early morning, before the sun came up, he would venture outside to the alleyway behind his tenement house, where he would drag his body through an ordeal of exercises designed to strengthen his torso, his arms and his legs. Under cover of darkness he intended to tauten his muscles and build his stamina so that, despite his size, he could become an athlete and compete with his oldest and tallest brother, Jimmy.

This self-imposed regimen went on for months until one night, his teeth clenched in a grimace as he strained to pull himself up off the floor, he noticed his brother Jimmy sitting up and staring at him. At first, so it seemed, Jimmy didn't understand what was going on, but as soon as he did he started to laugh, and his laughter grew louder and louder until Johnny finally dived into bed and hid his face under the blanket. All that night Johnny stared at the ceiling, the echoes of his brother's laughter worse, he remembered, than the roar of lions, but when morning came he had decided upon a course of action which carried him irresistibly forward. As he saw it, he had a choice to make now that his secret had been shamefully exposed: either he could give in to Jimmy's superiority or he could turn his shame around by competing against him in the full light of day. He decided to become a runner and to work at it with all the energy he possessed. In so doing, Johnny manifested what would become his characteristic approach to life, in which all difficulties represented no more than way stations to be conquered on the road to success. In choosing to overcome his physical inadequacy, he exhibited a familial trait that would show itself again and again in succeeding generations.

From that moment on, he devoted his whole mind to the task of propelling his body forward as swiftly and smoothly as an animal in pursuit of prey. Wherever he went, he ran: to school in the morning; home in the evening; on errands; to see friends. When he had nothing to do for a moment, he would practice his breathing and his starting release, fidgeting with the overflow of energy that was in him. He soon became a familiar figure in the North End, his skinny chest expanded to a newfound strength, as he regularly padded through the crowded streets, past the rows of shabby houses, past the shops and saloons, along the dingy waterfront, his racing legs reaching toward a goal that wasn't mere victory in a race but a claim to supremacy.

So complete was his concentration on the task in hand and so resolute his will that it was only a matter of time until he began winning some races against his brother Jimmy and then against increasing numbers of the neighborhood boys as well. Soon it became "the neighborhood sport to beat little Johnny." Week after week he found himself pitted against boys who were taller, stronger and more coordinated than he, but they ran without his urgency or his sense of purpose. And, as a result, he was always the first to cross the finish line.

More than fifty years later, Fitzgerald still felt proud of his accomplishment: "We used to run on the sidewalks and cobblestones of Hanover Street and I could always beat any of the boys. I could also sprint around the loop of old Fort Hill in a shorter time than any competitors. As a sprinter my distance was from 120 to 150 yards. I won the half mile distance cup in Boston in one year. I was a champ."

Through this experience as a champion sprinter, Johnny developed a confidence in the mastery of his will over his body which would follow him from swimming to football to baseball and allow him to achieve a success in the world of athletics which he later claimed had affected the course of his entire life: "I attribute my good physical condition, my mental alertness and the consequent capacity for work to an athletic youth." It was not the individual victories that mattered, it was the sense of his potentiality being fulfilled and completed, the knowledge of what could be accomplished when his whole mind and body were directed toward a task—a knowledge he would put to good use in his first job of political organization.

In the North End of Johnny's youth, there was not a single playground, nor a gymnasium, nor even, as Fitzgerald later put it, "a single blade of grass" on which the children could play. For most of the immigrant children, caught as they were in a daily struggle for sheer survival, the lack of playing facilities was simply taken as a matter of course. As long as there were streets and roofs and cemeteries available, as long as there was space to move their limbs about, they did not wish for something they had never known and they organized their games to fit the terrain.

What with this lack of facilities, the games of the children necessarily took on a makeshift quality. Johnny later remembered all manner of contests: contests to see who could climb up the lamppost at the corner of Hanover and North in the shortest time, who could jump from curb to curb across Harris Street in the fewest number of steps; who could kick a can up the hill at the cemetery in the fewest kicks; who could jump from the highest point off the Warren Avenue bridge.

Without a playing field, the only places for playing ball were the narrow cobblestone streets, but the level of congestion was so high from the peddlers, the storekeepers and the soapboxers who trafficked on these streets that even stickball, played with a rubber ball and with a broomstick for a bat, was forbidden, and policemen, brandishing clubs, patrolled the area to enforce the decree.

Undeterred, Johnny organized a system whereby two boys would take turns standing at each end of the street to tip off the rest when the police were coming. Then, as the boys on his teams got better, he moved the games to "larger facilities" at Union Wharf, where a wide-open space of wooden planks provided a more spacious field of play. This time, he took a different approach to the police: he made friends with the cop whose daily beat included Commercial Street, and together they worked out a system where the boys were allowed to play undisturbed for nearly an hour each day.

Not all of Fitzgerald's early memories of the North End were so positive. Many years later he would point to his broken middle finger and use it as an indictment of the conditions which forced him to slide into first on the rough cobblestone streets. "See that finger?" he would say. "I have a baseball finger caused by playing ball in the North End." And, until the end of his life, he would still remember the unbearable dreariness of the North End in the long winter months when the friendly streets had vanished between banks of dirty snow and when, in the absence of a recreation center, the children had no escape from their stuffy rooms, which, with their windows all boarded up and nailed down against the cold, were as dark as prisons.

Beyond his recollections of athletic mastery, most of Fitzgerald's memories of childhood revolved about the wide array of traditional festivities and ceremonies where children regularly took part in the games, amusements, rituals, pageantry and merriment of the adults. Organized mainly by the Church, these great seasonal festivals were the dominant means by which the Irish community strengthened its collective bonds. It is hard for us, living as we do in our more isolated world of the twentieth century, to understand the meaning which community fairs, parish processions and holiday pageants used to hold in the everyday life of the immigrant families. So powerful was the emotional impact of these seasonal festivities on Fitzgerald as a child that he would spend much of his adult political life searching for their modern-day equivalents.

As the rhythmic world of nature faded in the New World, the immigrants directed the whole weight of their longings into the festivals and liturgical celebrations of the one familiar body they still had left—the Catholic Church. Down through the ages, these religious festivals and celebrations had provided men and women, faced with the bitterness and uncertainty of life, with the chance to gather together and express ceremonially their feelings about the inevitability of nights and days, the changing seasons and the certainty of birth and death. And now, for the Irish immigrants in the North End, these same festivals served an additional purpose as well: they kept alive the memories of the life and the land they had left behind and helped to fit those memories into urban Boston.

In Fitzgerald's youth, the celebrations of the Catholic Church formed an organic unit which consisted of three festivals or seasons: Christmas, preceded by Advent and followed by Epiphany; Easter, preceded by Lent; and Pentecost, followed by the rest of the year. Through the rich and varied celebrations associated with each of these cycles, where "times of waiting alternate with times of fulfillment, the lean weeks of Lent with the feasts of Easter and Pentecost, times of mourning with seasons of rejoicing," the first-generation immigrants kept their city-born children in touch with the emotions of the changing seasons and the rhythms of nature.

It was a regular custom with the Fitzgerald family, as with most Catholic families in the North End in those days, to mark the first Sunday of Advent, four weeks before Christmas, with the hanging of the Advent wreath and a reading from the Scriptures. The season of Advent was a period of preparation, a little Lent, during which good Catholics were not allowed to have weddings or attend public dances.

After the abstinence of Advent came the fulfillment of Christmas, symbolized forever in Johnny's mind by the mystery and wonder of midnight Mass. Years later, Fitzgerald told his daughter Rose that in his early childhood, before he was allowed to go to midnight Mass, he would lie awake in his bed, awaiting the sound of the church bells that were rung at vespers to announce the coming of the Savior. Then, on the stroke of midnight, he could hear the thunderous chords of the organ as it opened the processional march, and still later the voices of the choir as they sang "It Came Upon a Midnight Clear."

But not even this experience prepared him, he later said, for "the glory and the beauty" of the midnight Mass when he was finally allowed to attend. The church on Christmas Eve was decorated with garlands of green and beautiful flowers. The shiny white altars were dotted with red flames from dozens of small white candles which surrounded a great central one that symbolized Christ, the Light of the World. "It was so beautiful I thought I would faint," Fitzgerald recalled.

By ancient custom, the six weeks after Christmas were meant to be a time filled with merrymaking and dancing. During these "carnival weeks"—as they were sometimes called—the Fitzgeralds visited back and forth among themselves, sharing food, talk and fellowship late into the night. It was also a time for church suppers and for dances.

When the last day of the carnival season arrived, the families gathered together for the Shrovetide feast, a celebration traditionally associated with games and boisterous fun before the forty days of the Lenten fast. For young Fitzgerald, the Shrovetide feast held a special pleasure, for at supper that night it was customary to eat pancakes—reflecting an old English custom of using up all the eggs, butter and milk originally prohibited during Lent—and pancakes were his favorite food. Though the rules of the Lenten fast had relaxed by the mid–nineteenth century so that dairy products were no longer forbidden, the old traditions persisted, rooted in the depths of common memory.

The beginning of Lent was Ash Wednesday, when all the faithful were exhorted to kneel before the priest and receive on their forehead a sign of the cross with ashes. Once, Fitzgerald remembered, he was given the responsibility of bringing his younger brothers to church to receive their ashes. Always fascinated by the decorum of the church, Johnny took care to prepare his brothers ahead of time for the special etiquette involved.

All went well until his youngest charge, Joseph, reached the altar and knelt before the priest. The priest dipped his thumb into the ashes and moved toward the kneeling boy, his lips just beginning to form the words of the solemn declaration which accompanied the mark of the cross: "Remember that thou art dust and unto dust shalt thou return." Then, just as his thumb touched Joseph's forehead, the boy let out a frantic scream and raced up the aisle toward the door. The priest simply moved on to the next person, and it was up to Johnny to lead his little brother back to the altar amid the stares of a thousand eyes. That moment lingered in Fitzgerald's memory, tinged with humiliation, so that years later he could never go through the ceremony of Ash Wednesday without a tug of fear in his heart.

During the Lenten fast that followed, Fitzgerald took great pains to help his little brothers with their fasting, their resolutions and their daily prayers. It seems that whenever Rosanna needed help with the boys, she turned to Johnny. And Fitzgerald later admitted that there was something nice about having this responsibility. It made him feel older than his years. Each night during Lent, he would gather his younger brothers round his bed and inquire whether they had faithfully kept their Lenten resolutions. The reward for their constancy was a round of bedtime stories, which ranged from hoary tales of monsters and ghosts to biographies of patron saints. From his earliest days, Johnny was known as the best storyteller in the family. His capacious memory seemed to soak up everything he read or heard, and he was able to retell these tales with such enthusiasm, laughter and dramatic gestures that he kept his audience spellbound, oblivious of time and begging for more.

The Lenten fast led up to Holy Week, a time Fitzgerald associated with the coming of spring, with open windows, crowded doorways and throngs of people gathered on the streets. More somberly, Fitzgerald remembered sitting through his first Tenebrae service on Holy Thursday, his hand reaching for his mother's as, one by one, the candles on the altar were extinguished, plunging the church into total darkness to symbolize the desertion of Christ by his disciples. The solemn mood continued through Good Friday, when, as Johnny later remembered it, "the church stood desolate and bare, its altar draped in black, its statues all covered in purple."

As Easter was preceded by forty days of sorrow, it was followed by fifty days of rejoicing leading up to Whitsunday, the Feast of Pentecost, commemorating the day the Apostles received the Holy Spirit. Once again the narrow streets of the North End became resplendent with the pageantry of a colorful procession, equal to any at Rome, as children crowned with wreaths and wearing colored sashes marched in line, carrying flowers, banners, mottoes and little images.

Tying together the past and the present, the old order and the new, these great religious festivals were so deeply woven into the fabric of young Johnny's life that long after he had become thoroughly acclimatized to the hurried style of city life he still responded deeply to all manner of traditional pageantry, and he still viewed the changing seasons through the calendar of the Christian year. Indeed, when he reached the height of his political career he would spend substantial time and money in an attempt to recreate these festivals for the children of the modern world. "Personally," he would later write, "I believe about the best use to which public money is appropriated, outside of money to care for the unfortunates, is for holiday celebrations."

Through all of Johnny's memories of the great festivals of his childhood days runs the theme of helping out his mother: taking his little brothers to church on Ash Wednesday, reminding them of their Lenten resolutions and telling them stories at bedtime. We hear of him also at the age of seven and eight accompanying his mother to Jordan Marsh's department store to help pick out clothes for his brothers, and, a little later, helping her bundle up and march the boys to the public baths. And still later, when his younger brothers were too old to be taken to the women's bath, Johnny was said to be the one who dragged them through the clouds of steam in the men's bathing room, scrubbed them clean and returned them, red-skinned and shivering, to their mother on the other side. "For some reason," Fitzgerald later wrote, "it was my trust to boss the family."

That it was Johnny and not his two older brothers, Jimmy and Tommy, who took on this protective role is suggested by the accounts of his relatives who universally remember him with a rush of warmth as "the one who taught the others how to swim, how to play ball and how to whistle through their fingers," "the mainstay of the family," "the one who kept the whole family together." The picture that emerges is of Johnny marching off into the streets with two or three adoring brothers tagging along behind. "I've always wondered," niece Regis Fitzgerald Murphy later mused, "when was John Francis young? Whenever catastrophe or illness came he was the one they all turned to."

When he was five years old, still too young for the first grade and a decade too early for Boston's experimental kindergarten, Johnny was curious to know about this institution called school that kept his older brothers, Jimmy and Tommy, away from home most of the day. One morning he decided to follow his brothers as they threaded their way through the milling crowds of people and peddlers' carts up Hanover Street and down North Bennett, where the small one-story primary school stood on the east side of the street.

Keeping his distance, Johnny stayed across the street until the last of the pupils scrambled up the short stairs and in the door, and then he ran around to the side of the building and stationed himself beneath a small open window. (Each of the four classrooms in the Ware primary school boasted one rectangular window which was supposed to be kept open all year round.) There, crouched on his knees, he listened to the morning's routine.

The first voice he heard was that of a teacher reading a passage from the Bible. This was followed by some singing and then a recitation period in which each child was called upon to come to the front of the room, where he was to read aloud from his reader, his body erect, his knees and feet together, and the tips of his shoes touching the edge of a board in the floor. While these recitations were taking place, Johnny saw a small boy, not much bigger than he, running down the street, late for school. Through the open window, he traced the sound of the latecomer's footsteps as he raced into class. There was a moment of stillness and then a strange clapping sound followed by a succession of screams so loud and so horrible that they stayed in Johnny's memory for the rest of his life. Frozen in his crouched position, he closed his eyes until the screams finally stopped and a different sound, the echoes of marching footsteps, filled the air. (In the primary schools, the children marched around the room every morning for at least ten minutes.) Lulled by the marching, Johnny was just beginning to relax when it happened again: the sound of a whip or a cane, he couldn't tell which, striking an object, followed by a piercing cry.

That Johnny was not exaggerating his experience is confirmed by the testimony of Boston School Superintendent Samuel Eliot. In his first year of office in 1879, Eliot issued some scathing observations on the use of corporal punishment in the primary and grammar schools: "There is no question about the disorder it now excites, the sounds more like those of a menagerie than those of a school, the sullen looks, the disturbed feelings, the outward and inward effects." And the school reports for 1880 recorded 157 blows in one school in a period of a month and 130 in another in the space of twenty-one days.

Slowly, Superintendent Eliot began to see that the frequent resort to physical violence was only a symptom of a deeper malady in an educational system that defined its tasks in terms of instilling order, punctuality, regularity and attention in its students. In each of his semiannual reports, the reformist Eliot dissected a different aspect of this problem, focusing particularly on the poor methods of teaching.

"English grammar might be like a window but it is apt to be a wall, through which there is no seeing," Eliot wrote. "Its technicalities, long since vanished from common speech and writing, are conjured up in books & exercises only to perplex the minds of young people . . ." "History stands like a skeleton . . . far from recalling the past, it frightens it away to return no more . . ." "That the love of reading should survive is proof how deep and inexhaustible its sources are." Little wonder, Eliot concluded, that in a system of such little inspiration, discipline becomes the only way teachers can keep control of the class.

That the educational problems Eliot observed characterized the system as a whole, from its schools in the Back Bay and on Beacon Hill to its schools in the North and South Ends, is clear from a sampling of the memoirs of any number of distinguished Bostonians ranging from Henry Adams to Henry Cabot Lodge, all of whom regarded their early educational experiences with hostility and disdain.

Yet the failures of the primary-school system affected the child of the slum far more deeply than the child of means, who had many other outlets for learning. And for the Irish Catholic child there was the additional problem of a system that was Protestant in orientation and openly prejudiced against Catholicism. William O'Connell, who later became Boston's third cardinal, described his early years in the Lowell, Massachusetts, schools in the 1860s as "a perfect torture."

We lived actually in an atmosphere of fear [O'Connell wrote]. We sensed the bitter antipathy, scarcely concealed, which nearly all these good women in charge of the schools felt toward those of us who had Catholic faith and Irish names. For any slight pretext we were severely punished. We were made to feel the slur against our Faith and race . . . to understand our inferiority to the other children, blessed with the prop of Protestant inheritance and English or Puritan blood.

The greatest trial to the Catholic students . . . was the use of a bigoted history of England. Even the glorious case of Saint Thomas à Becket was distorted in such a way as to make Henry II, a tyrant, the hero of the tragedy, and Saint Thomas an arrogant, unreasonable subject . . . When later we arrived at the Reformation in England, we were told that all the leaders . . . even Cromwell were great saints, and that Wolsey and Catherine were traitors . . . Even the glorious name of Thomas More was slurred over and belittled, Mary Tudor was a target for endless vilification and scorn; and Elizabeth, the bastard of Anne Boleyn, was exalted upon a pedestal of glory . . . In fact, nothing that was Catholic was right, as nothing that was Protestant could possibly be wrong.

An even more virulent form of prejudice against Catholic pupils had flared up in the North End in the decade before John Fitzgerald was born. On March 14, 1859, a young Catholic boy, Thomas Wall, was severely beaten by his teacher for refusing to participate in the morning reading of the Protestant Bible. As the story was told and retold, the boy had been instructed by his priest at St. Mary's that to read the Protestant Bible was to commit a sin. With the fear of hell on his mind, he chose to disregard his teacher's order, which subjected him to a whipping which lasted more than half an hour, left his hands cut and bleeding and caused him to faint. The beating became a cause célèbre in the Catholic community. That night large crowds of Catholic parents came together, and the next day over three hundred Catholic pupils joined together in refusing to read the required scriptural passage. The boys were immediately suspended from school and their parents notified that the indispensable condition of reinstatement was conformity to the objectionable rules. In the meantime, they were warned, they would be liable to arrest and imprisonment for truancy.

In response, Wall's father filed a suit against the headmaster alleging assault and battery on his son, but the Yankee-dominated court dropped all the charges and ordered the rebellious students back to school, arguing that foreign priests were attempting to take from the schoolroom the Bible that had been its household god from the infancy of our country. At this juncture, the Catholics gave in, though the incident sparked the development of the parochial-school system that would eventually—but not in time for John Fitzgerald—take nearly half of the Catholic students in the city away from the public schools.

So it was that the fear Johnny experienced as he stood outside the window on that cold and windy morning had a strong basis in reality. But the determined boy refused to be dominated by his initial feeling. After kneeling in terror for more than an hour, he peeked through the window and then he saw the villainous woman—Miss Kate Sawyer. With her black hair pulled tightly back from her long, thin face, with her long black dress and her black shoes, she looked to him like a wicked witch, and he quickly dropped down out of sight. But, moments later, as he told his own story, he summoned his courage back, and when school was dismissed for lunch he followed her as she walked up Salem Street and turned into a local grocery store. From the doorway he heard her voice as she talked with the owner, and he was surprised to hear how soft it sounded. Then, still more surprisingly, he saw her lean down and pat the head of a little girl who darted out from behind the counter. When the teacher herself turned to come out, Johnny turned and ran all the way home. But the next week he followed her every day into the store until she finally smiled at him and asked him his name. From that moment on he knew he was safe, and all summer long he looked forward to school.

We can see here in the young boy's ability to charm a potential enemy the threads of a pattern that would characterize his behavior all his life. He seemed to possess the unusual gift of responding to things that troubled him by moving toward them rather than backing away. Even at this early age, his positive approach to school set in motion a positive cycle, distinguishing his educational experience from that of all his brothers. His enthusiasm was contagious, and his teachers responded in kind as he showed a natural ability for reading, spelling and writing and developed a set of sharp arithmetical skills. At the end of three years, he was promoted to the Eliot Grammar School, a significant attainment which less than 10 percent of the students who lived in the North End at that time achieved.

On the late afternoon of January 27, 1870, the Fitzgerald household was filled with a general rejoicing. After eight sons, Rosanna Fitzgerald had given birth to a fair-skinned, blue-eyed little girl. Though Johnny was only in his sixth year, he remembered the occasion so clearly that seventy years later he described it to a friend: "I can still remember my grandmother coming out into the kitchen to tell my father that the new baby was a girl. I had just come home from school, and he lifted me up in his arms and brought me into the bedroom, where I saw the baby lying next to my mother. My father bent down and kissed the baby's forehead and then took my mother's hand, and I'll never forget what he said: 'Well, Rosie, we've finally got our little girl and she's as beautiful as an Irish morning.' "

They named her Ellen Rosanna after her mother and her grandmother, and as Johnny remembered it they watched over her with special care. "Every time she got a fever, my mother was sure she was going to die," Fitzgerald recalled. "I don't know why, but she seemed to worry about little Ellen all the time. Later, I wondered if it had been a premonition."

Rosanna's high anxiety at the first sign of her child's sickness was not uncommon in the Irish community at that time. Since so many mothers had actually seen one or more of their children wake up healthy in the morning and die before nightfall of smallpox, typhus or cholera, and since so little was understood about the causes and nature of disease, it is not surprising that they interpreted the early symptoms of any illness as a prelude to death. The diary of the Reverend Hilary Tucker, a Catholic priest in the South End in the 1860s, is filled with stories of being called to administer last rites to feverish children whose parents mistakenly assumed they were dying. "The poor people, God bless them," Tucker wrote in 1862, "the moment a croup or a big flea bit[e]s them, send for the priest. This shows the strength of their faith, but it so often verges on superstition, and especially [tries] the patience of the poor priest."

Yet, if they tended to multiply the situations in which death seemed to be looming, the Irish parents had good reason to be anxious about steering their children through their first five years in life. For though the mortality rates for young children born in Boston in the 1870s were not as severe as in the Puritan days, when Cotton Mather, seeing eight of his fifteen children die before the age of two, wrote that "a dead child was a sight no more surprising than a broken pitcher or a blasted flower," they were still alarmingly high. The annual reports of the City Registrar for the early 1870s showed that out of every one hundred children born in Boston, nearly twenty would die before their first birthday and another fifteen would be dead before the age of five. Beyond the age of five, Boston's mortality rates compared favorably with other cities', but the shocking percentage of deaths in Boston in the early years was higher than in any other city in the United States, matched only by the most unhealthy of English towns—Liverpool and Newcastle.

Alarmed by these annual statistics, Boston's Board of Health appointed a committee of five physicians to conduct a thorough investigation of the mortality rates of Boston. The committee's report, issued in 1875, attributed Boston's high rate of death to the large proportion of foreign immigrants, whether foreign born or children of foreign parentage, who suffered much higher death rates than those which prevailed among the purely native population.

The report also found that of the total foreign-born population of the city, over two-thirds consisted of the Irish, giving Boston the largest proportion of Irish inhabitants of all the great cities in the United States. And, compared with all the different foreign races domiciled in the U.S. —Germans, English, Welsh, Swedes, French, Italians, etc.—the Irish exhibited the greatest mortality rate. The source of Boston's problem, as the committee saw it, was therefore abundantly clear—it was the Irish, whose "inborn predisposition to certain constitutional diseases (consumption and cancer) together with various unwholesome habits and traditions in matters of hygiene" accounted for the disproportionate rates of death in the city as a whole.

Against this interpretation, which essentially blamed the Irish as a nationality for their excessive susceptibility to death and diseases, there was a different interpretation which stressed the poverty of the Irish immigrants rather than their nationality and placed the blame on the squalid conditions under which the Irish lived in their crowded, unventilated, unsanitary tenements. Analyzing the cholera epidemic in the North End in 1849, a medical committee observed: "This whole district is a perfect hive of human beings, without comforts and mostly without common necessaries; in many cases, huddled together like brutes without regard to sex, or age . . . , grown men and women sleeping together in the same apartment, and sometimes wife and husband, brothers and sisters in the same bed."

So it was that despite the comparative means her parents possessed, young Ellen Fitzgerald was subjected from birth to the same unwholesome conditions of tenement life that threatened the existence of every child of the slum. Yet, as the winter months gave way to the balmy days of April and May, the baby was, as Fitzgerald was later told, "in the bloom of health." And the grocery store at 310 North Street was also prospering. R. G. Dun & Co. (later Dun & Bradstreet) reported in 1870 that "James Fitzgerald is making money in business, assisted by his brother (Thomas), both working attentively."

Then came the sweltering months of summer, marked in 1870 by an unprecedented heat wave and an almost total absence of rain, and in the first weeks of August the dreaded disease of cholera came once again to the North End, killing more than eighty children in twelve days.

In the nineteenth century, cholera was considered "the most fatal disease known to the annals of medicine." Though its cause would not be known until 1883, when the German bacteriologist Robert Koch isolated the *Vibrio cholerae* bacillus, which is transmitted by feces-contaminated drinking water and food, experience had taught that it attacked the poor, living in crowded, unsanitary conditions, in a much larger proportion than the rich, and that its transmission was favored by the high temperatures found in the summer months.

The explosive character of the 1870 scourge suggested a simultaneous infection probably caused by water contaminated with sewage. Just three months earlier, a group of physicians had warned the city about the sanitary problems in the district of the North End. And a later commission report, "The Sewage of Boston," found that in the poorer areas of the city there were several hundred "open mouthed" cesspools.

. . . the water occasionally evaporates from these traps during the summer, exposing the contents to the air and leaving direct communication between the sewers and the outer air. . . . No dispensary physician who has [the Haymarket] district can have failed to notice the deleterious influence of such conditions upon the health of people who are absolutely powerless to help themselves.

As Rosanna Fitzgerald watched the disease spread down Hanover Street, its fatal progress marked by the appearance of a black ribbon on the door of each stricken house, she redoubled her efforts to protect her family. In a later conversation, Thomas Fitzgerald told his son John that she would not allow anyone in the family to eat any fruit or meat that summer until it was personally inspected by her, that every morning she disinfected the privy with dry earth and lime and that she hung newspapers over the screenless windows in an attempt to keep out the flies which were thought to carry the disease. Yet, despite her precautions, on the cloudy morning of August 16, 1870, cholera struck the Fitzgerald household, and the person it struck was the one who was the least able to fight back: little Ellen Rosanna, six months old.

Fitzgerald was told later that his sister had been put to bed the night before in perfect health but that when she awakened in the morning, the disease had already set in.

"Indeed, it is folly to talk of curing cholera," Dr. Thomas Hawkes Tanner wrote in 1872, "when the principles which should guide us are undecided. Until we know whether recovery depends on a persistence of the intestinal evacuations or suppression of them, how can we prescribe?" In the absence of scientific prescription, the people relied on a variety of folk remedies: mustard poultices and hot turpentine frictions over the abdomen; frequent doses of Dr. Strickland's anticholera mixture (opium, cayenne pepper, camphor and calomel); and hot-water bottles to the soles of the feet and the calves of the legs.

Which of these remedies Rosanna Fitzgerald tried we do not know; we know only that nothing she did was successful in arresting the deadly progress of the disease, in which diarrhea and vomiting produce a cumulative dehydration followed by agonizing muscle cramps and extreme thirst. The disease then advances rapidly into a second stage characterized by extreme collapse: the skin becomes cold, dry and wrinkled, the features become pinched, the cheeks hollow, the eyes sunken, and the voice is reduced to a hoarse whisper. This condition can result in death within one day. Such was the case of Ellen Rosanna, who was dead before the first day of her illness had passed.

There is no record of where or when she was buried—her body does not lie with the rest of the Fitzgerald family at Holy Cross Cemetery, Malden. We do know, however, that, to prevent the spread of the disease, the body was supposed to be removed from the house immediately, placed in a hermetically closed casket and buried privately. There were other measures to be taken as well; we can assume Rosanna Fitzgerald took some of them, since not one of her seven boys came down with the disease. "The sickroom is to be emptied of furniture, curtains, and carpets," the authorities advised, "while sawdust wetted with diluted carbolic acid is as an excellent disinfectant to sprinkle over the floor. All the excreta are to be received in pans containing disinfectant fluid and then at once buried in the ground. Soiled bed and body linen are to be soaked in a solution of chloride of lime."

That the Fitzgerald family was deeply affected by the loss of this little girl is clear from the length of time John Fitzgerald held on to his memory of her short life and his understanding of her painful death. Yet they had a consolation for their loss in the idea of heaven, in the belief that Ellen's death in this world was just the beginning of her eternal life in a far better world, a world where she would meet her brother Michael—who had died ten years before almost to the day— and where, in peace, happiness and comfort, the two of them could anticipate the time when the whole family would be together once again.

Yet, if the idea of heaven lessened the personal pain for the parents of the dead child, it did not lessen the injustice of a society in which the child of poverty was three times more likely to die before the age of five than the child of means. Boston's renowned minister Edward Everett Hale spoke to this point in an essay on an earlier cholera epidemic. "In the epidemic among children in the summer of 1864," he wrote,

> 1,000 children of less than five years of age died in Boston in 100 days. I suppose that of the Boston people who read these pages not one in ten knows that there was any such epidemic. If the deaths had been proportional among all classes of society, at least ten of these deaths would have taken away infants from the parish of which I am minister, which embraces 1% of the population of the city. But that is a body of people in comfortable circles, living in comfortable houses. And, in fact, in that epidemic, not one of our children died.

Unlike his parents, who found their solace in the Church, young Johnny responded to his sister's death with frantic activity, a pattern of response that would characterize his family for generations to come. On the day after Ellen's burial, he entered a swimming contest at Lewis Wharf, and, with all the neighborhood children watching, he came in first. "I felt it was important to do something great to take away the sadness," Fitzgerald later recalled, "and winning the swimming meet was the only thing I could think of to do."

When he walked through the iron gates of the Eliot Grammar School, Johnny was entering one of Boston's oldest schools, established in the early eighteenth century. Entering with Johnny in the sixth and lowest grade (the numbering system ran backward from six to one) were 180 boys from three different primary schools. Each year, however, marked a gradual attrition in the numbers as the necessity for work in the Irish slum ate away at educational opportunity. By the fourth grade, when the children reached eleven and twelve, the total had dropped almost by half, to 108. The number remained constant until a huge exodus took place between the second and first grades. Of the 110 children who left the second-highest grade in June 1876, only thirty-five, John Fitzgerald among them, reappeared after the long summer vacation to enter the first or final grade. The explanation is simple: during that period, a large majority of the students reached fourteen, the magic age when they were legally allowed to quit school and go to work—a choice fully understood and even expected in a community which depended upon the labor of its children in order to survive.

For those who remained, the curriculum and the teaching were on a much higher level than what we think of today as grammar school. John Fitzgerald later looked back with justifiable pride on the quality of the education. To teach at the grammar-school level, the aspiring teacher had to pass a wide-ranging examination that tested his or her knowledge in psychology, music, Latin, history, geography, English history, American history, civil government and the principles of education. In contrast to the all-female primary-school staffs, male teachers, known as "masters," were now mixed in almost equal numbers with females, who were called assistants and typically were paid only half of the male teachers' annual salary of $2,700. Though the material was still largely taught through textbooks—Swinton's *Language Lessons*, Warren's *Common School Geography*, Worcester's *History* and Cooley's *Natural Philosophy* —and though learning was still largely through recitation, it was not as mechanical as in the earlier grades, since the teachers were better equipped to move beyond the books in order to create curiosity and interest in the child.

We have no official record showing John Fitzgerald's ranking among the thirty-five graduates, but the family tradition has it that he graduated near the top of his class and that during his six years at the Eliot School he emerged as a natural leader among his peers. And whatever his ranking, we know that in the immigrant community at that time the sheer attainment of a grammar-school diploma was considered a substantial achievement, which ranked in popular regard with graduation from high school in another district or the obtaining of a college degree in yet more favored circles.

For each of the thirty-five graduates and for their families, the June graduation ceremony was an occasion for wearing their best clothing, despite a warning issued by the School Department the year before on the need to guard against forcing "a needless indulgence" on families suffering from an actual need of food and clothing. As Mary Antin, author of *The Promised Land*, explained: "A mother who had scrubbed floors for years to keep her girl in school was not going to have her shamed in the end for want of a pretty dress . . . There was not a girl who came to school in rags all the year round that did not burst forth in sudden glory on Graduation Day. Fine muslin frocks, lace-trimmed petticoats, patent leather shoes, perishable hats, gloves, parasols, fans— every girl had them." And a similar level of pride marked the appearance of the boys.

Though he would go on to higher education, to John Fitzgerald the Eliot School remained the most tangible object of his childhood affections and loyalties. As soon as he could afford the entrance fee, he became an active member in the old graduates' association, and more than thirty years later he played a prominent role in organizing a public commemoration of the school's two hundredth birthday. Such loyalty to the neighborhood school was typical in the immigrant community at that time, for the graduate of a grammar school carried with him not only the dignity of his initial achievement but a store of sentiments, traditions, memories and friendships which deepened as the years went by.

At the age of fourteen, Johnny was full of the most unshakeable self-confidence. He was a sturdy youth, courageous and defiant, a bright boy with a bright face, a ruddy complexion and clear blue eyes. He had a curious, receptive mind and was forever asking questions with an intense desire for an intelligent reply. The world seemed an exciting place where something interesting was always happening to him.

In September of 1877, Johnny obtained a license to hawk newspapers on the streets of Boston—an enterprise which engaged him for nearly two years until he returned full time to school. In that town, in those days, newspaper selling was a lucrative business: the 1,100 minors licensed as newsboys cleared an average of $2.50 a week, which was more than the average weekly salary of an experienced clerk. On these earnings, the newsboy (fittingly described by one former hawker as half child and half man, with the worldliness of a man and the sensitivity of a child) not only supported himself but often provided a large share of his family's income. And for those who were willing to stick to their work through the bitter cold of winter mornings and the steamy summer afternoons, the job was uncommonly secure.

With the passing years, the immigrant newsboy of the nineteenth century has acquired a picturesque image. "The unwritten story of their rise," Frank Mott writes,

> would be a romantic chapter in the history of American journalism. They appeared on the streets of the large cities as soon as the penny papers became established—a heterogeneous, loud-voiced, shrewd lot . . . The ragged, shouting, insistent . . . newsboy . . . was something new to the world. Often he was a thorough street gamin . . . but again, he was the sole support of a widowed mother and selling papers was for him a stepping stone to independence and fortune: such as he were the heroes of many edifying novels and plays.

Even in the haze of memory, the impulse to romanticize the newsboy's lot must be resisted. Year after year, educators, reformers and philanthropists alike despaired at the harmful features of this most visible form of child labor, arguing that "the late hours, the indiscriminate handling of money and the contagion of the street often undermines the character and health of these boys," placing them "constantly in the way of temptation" and "leading them directly into crime." Moreover, the necessity of getting up at half past three or four in the morning in order to buy their papers and be at their corners by six or seven "brings them to school tired out and altogether unfitted to do the classroom work, or so completely exhausted they go to sleep at their desks."

Having finished grammar school, Johnny was in a different position from most of his fellow workers. Amid a large fleet of boys frustrated by conflicting aspirations and divided desires between school and work, his talents and his capacities moved in one direction. The goal of making money united all elements of his vibrant personality, assuring his success. Moreover, at fourteen, Johnny was already a sophisticated student of human nature, ready to respond to the fascinating range of characters he encountered each day in the process of selling his papers. From childhood, he had loved the sport and the gossip of political life; he had listened for hours to the men talking politics in his father's store; now, as he stood on the street, his bundle of papers under his arm, his voice calling out the headlines of the day, he experienced himself as a participant in that larger world.

During his first weeks on the job, he would get up at three o'clock in the morning to be first in line to pick up his papers and thus first on the street. In those days, a carrier visited each newspaper office in order to collect his assortment of papers for the day. For Johnny it was a ten-minute walk up Hanover Street and across Congress to the corner of State Street where the old *Traveler* stood. From there he turned right to reach the *Advertiser* on Court Street and then right again on Washington, where the *Journal* and the *Herald* stood on opposite sides of the street. To the left it was half a block to the *Post* on Water Street and then another half block to the *Transcript* at the corner of Milk. Then he would walk up Milk to State, where the *Globe*'s original building was situated.

Even at this early hour, the newspaper offices were filled with dozens of people—editors, reporters, office boys and apprentices—milling around the tall black rotary press that stood in the center of the printing room like an organ in a church. When the machine was working, the room was filled with the smell of damp newspapers and of fresh printing ink, and everybody's eyes followed the roll of paper as it fed into the press with four feeders and four takers off, permitting ten thousand copies of a four-page newspaper to be printed in an hour.

Fitzgerald later said that from the moment he set foot in his first newspaper office he knew he was going to like the work. Naturally gregarious, brimming over with curiosity and a love of adventure, he must have responded at once to the hum of life in the newsroom, the quickened pace, the noisy atmosphere and the continuous talk. But, as much as he might have enjoyed staying around for hours, making himself useful in a dozen different ways, he understood that a newcomer's only hope of turning a profit was to arrive on the streets before the workingmen began their day's work. For in contrast to the experienced newsboys, who all had regular corners, the newcomers were obliged to sell their papers by roaming up and down the streets, a far more difficult task, since most people habitually bought their papers at the same corner every day.

Johnny evidently went about his relationship to the city streets in the right spirit. He walked everywhere, this day up Tremont and down Charles, that day up Washington and down Beacon. His wanderings took him into strange and new parts of the city where he had never been before and introduced him to new types of people. A shrewd judge of character, he took pleasure in guessing from outward demeanor which paper each passerby wanted and would take it from his bundle before he was even asked. He made it a practice to scan all the papers before he began—a substantial achievement, given the crowded pages and the tiny nonpareil type which confronted readers at that time—and, with his knowledge of the leading stories, he could choose which headlines to call out.

Johnny's diligence and enthusiasm met their reward. According to his own account, he was always the first of the newsboys at large to sell out his entire bundle of papers, and at times he even completed his work before any of the regulars were done. At the same time, with his uncanny faculty for making friends, he developed a network of new relationships all over the city. The job was all that he had expected it to be and more.

# CHAPTER 3

# "THE
OTHER
BOSTON"

Johnny's years as a newsboy witnessed a series of dramatic developments in journalism which, in turn, reflected the sweeping changes that were taking place in American economic and social life. A consequence of the great industrial expansion of the time, with its mushrooming urban centers, its multiplication of factories, smokestacks and mills, and its spread of literacy, was the rise of the newspaper to a new position in American life. Writing in the late 1870s, Justin Winsor observed that "the newspaper press of the U.S. has attained an importance . . . unparalleled in any other country. Nowhere does the number of newspapers bear so large a proportion to the population, nowhere else are newspapers so universally read."

These years also witnessed the birth of a much livelier and more dramatic concept of news—a pronounced shift away from editorial comment and party politics toward human-interest features, fictionalized serials, sports and amusement. Reflecting the changed conditions of city life—the hurried pace, the rise of organized spectator sports, the development of mass entertainment and the desire for an escape from the daily struggle for survival—this new journalism, as it was called at the time, produced an immense growth in the numbers of people who read newspapers.

The stimulus of the Civil War had enlarged the scope of newspapers as well. Wartime necessity had taught readers to value a paper's rapid and accurate reporting of the news. Before the war, most of the leading dailies were morning papers, distinguished mainly by their editorial columns and their party identification. But the war had whetted the public appetite for up-to-the-minute news on the results of battles, and, as a result, "extra" editions—which eventually evolved into evening papers—were commonly issued in the afternoons.

Coming into the newspaper field in this era of dramatic change, Johnny witnessed the rise and fall of a number of Boston dailies. He developed a keen interest in understanding why some of the older papers remained vigorous, changing with the changing times, while others, unable or unwilling to depart from tradition, began to languish. Years later, when he became the publisher of a weekly paper, *The Republic*, he was fond of maintaining that his boyhood experiences as a newsboy had taught him "more about the business of publishing than any of those fancy colleges across the river." He was probably right.

An even deeper seal was set on Johnny's young consciousness through his acquisition of the choicest hawking corner in the city of Boston—the corner of Park and Beacon Streets, facing the trees, the benches and the grassy space of the Common in one direction and the front of the State House, with its long sweep of broad stone steps, its terraced lawn and its familiar gilded dome, in the other. When Johnny first began selling papers, the corner belonged to a neighbor, a tall, spare boy named Fred, several years older than he and very serious.

To Johnny, Fred appeared as a heroic figure. In three years he had established a reputation as the most energetic and enterprising of all the newsboys; from the earnings of his profitable stand, he supported his widowed mother and grandmother and his five younger sisters and brothers.

Johnny made it a practice each morning to fall in line with Fred as he gathered up his bundle of papers on Newspaper Row, and at night he would deliberately schedule his own route to end up by Fred's corner so that they could walk home together. He soon discovered that Fred shared his love of history and fascination with politics, and they became friends. In the free hours during the afternoons, they would often go together to the Boston Public Library to read in the cavernous reading room. Johnny later said that he felt in Fred a kindness, a maturity and a conscience he had never encountered before. At length they began to spend their Saturdays together as well, and Johnny introduced the bookish boy to baseball, swimming, football and coasting.

Wrapped about with Johnny's goodwill, Fred slowly lost his reluctance and began to talk about himself. He told Johnny that his family had enjoyed a steady income with his father working as a lamplighter, until a dreadful accident occurred. One night, when his father was standing with his back to the street, his hands directing the long pole toward a jet of gas, he was struck from behind by a heavy wagon pulled by runaway horses. Positioned only inches away, Fred watched helplessly as his father's skull was shattered against the lamppost. The terror of that night took a terrible toll on the thirteen-year-old boy. He dropped out of school, never to return, and for weeks he was barely able to speak. When he finally recovered enough to function in the world, he threw himself so completely into his responsibilities as the new head of the family that he had little time or energy for anything else.

All this Fred shared with Johnny, and as the months went by their friendship continued to strengthen. Every day of their crowded lives they managed to spend some time together—talking, laughing, reading or playing ball.

Then, in the middle of January 1878, Fred fell sick with bronchitis, which developed into tuberculosis—or consumption, as it was commonly called. His body wasted away to a skeleton, but he refused to stay in bed, understanding only too well the governing structure of the newsboy's world in those days. As another former newsboy later described it, once a boy had worked up a corner by coming regularly for a period of time and establishing it into a profitable stand, it became his property and all the other newsboys recognized it as his. No matter how small he was and no matter how big and tough his competitor, this right was respected. But the moment a boy stopped coming regularly, his stand was up for grabs.

Johnny responded to the situation with an urgent and obstinate force. Recognizing that Fred would never get well unless his work load was lightened, Johnny conceived of a plan whereby he would take responsibility for both his own and Fred's bundles of papers. All that Fred had to do was drag himself to the corner at the start of the day so that his presence could be noted and recorded; then he could go home and stay in bed while Johnny took care of the rest, his abundant energy allowing him to work double time. This went on for several weeks, until one particularly cold morning when Fred, pale and shivering, his eyes glowing with fever, collapsed. Johnny propped him up and pulled him home, where he was put to bed, and though he tried every morning until the February morning when he died, he never could get up again.

All the while his friend was dying, Johnny reported each day as usual to the Beacon Street corner, but as the news of Fred's illness spread, first one and then another of the older newsboys began to drop around, eying the corner with suspicion. Johnny knew it was only a matter of time until one of them took over, for it was, after all, the best stand in the city. To let it go to a newcomer was unthinkable. He also knew, however, that he had a short period of grace while the potential rivals argued among themselves, and in this period he laid out his course of action.

Johnny figured that Fred's successor was most likely to emerge from the ranks of "the hawks," as the toughest group of newsboys liked to call themselves. Were he to defend himself against these waiting foes, he would need allies, and he knew at once where those allies could be found. There was a scattered group of young newsboys who stood in terror of the older bullies. Walking home alone at night, most of them had been roughed up and robbed a number of times by one or more of the hawks and then told that they'd be left alone so long as they agreed to split a portion of their weekly profits with the gang. Fearful of losing even more if they failed to comply, most of them had given in and kept their silence. But with each passing week their hatred of the bullies grew stronger; they were ripe for some kind of revolt.

Johnny based his plan on the psychology of numbers: he organized the younger boys in patrols of six to walk home together each night. In return for the protection this gave them at night, the younger boys stood by Johnny at the start of each day to help him establish his position on the corner of Beacon and Park. Johnny's offensive took the hawks by surprise. At length, fearing they might lose their licenses if one of the younger boys tipped off the police about the extortion scheme, they decided to let both the corner and the racket go, lying in wait for a break in Johnny's ranks. Then, with the passage of time, a new element came into play: the corner was becoming Johnny's. And once it was so recognized, no one could take it away.

·  ·  ·

It was through his experience of selling papers at the corner of Beacon and Park that Fitzgerald saw "the other Boston" for the first time—not the teeming city of immigrant poverty but the clean, cultured world of Beacon Hill, a world aloof and untouched by the vices of time, a world inhabited by an impeccable Yankee elite later referred to as the Boston Brahmins. From his central location on Beacon Street—aptly described by Oliver Wendell Holmes as "the sunny street that holds the sifted few" —Johnny stood right in the middle of the most aristocratic quarter of the city, in sight of some of the finest and most elegant residences in all of New England. Within a few minutes' walk, under the spreading elms of stately Mount Vernon Street, along gracious Chestnut Street, down the quaint slope of Pinckney with its houses standing endwise to the sidewalk, or in Louisburg Square, Johnny observed entire neighborhoods filled with splendid, spacious mansions of quiet dignity such as he had never dreamed existed. He was astonished at the beauty of their terraced lawns, their elaborate arched entrances and large bay windows.

For the first time in his life, Johnny saw a profusion of silk-hatted liveried coachmen sitting erect in open victorias, carrying couples, elegantly attired, on their way to parties—the gentlemen resplendent in frock coats, fancy waistcoats and high hats, the ladies in lace shawls and billowing dresses, holding delicate parasols above their heads. In the winter, the hacks were replaced by covered sleighs with coachlike bodies cozily lined with red plush or silk, and Johnny watched as men in fur caps and ladies snugly tucked in beside them in fur robes, their hot-water bottles held in tiny muffs to keep their hands warm, glided over the hard-packed snow, sleigh bells jingling in the frosty air. For the child of the slum, this was a glimpse of happy privilege at the highest pitch— a glimpse which remained printed on John Fitzgerald's memory in such a way that forty years later he was able to recreate for his daughter Rose both the sights and the sounds of Boston society as he first encountered it on Beacon Hill.

In truth, Johnny had confronted these Bostonians before, though never in the full context of their world. From earliest childhood, he had participated in the legendary snowball fights between the North Enders and the Beacon Hillers of which so many Brahmins later boasted in their memoirs. Restricted by their parents from playing near the marshes or on the back of Beacon Hill where the foreigners had built their humble settlements, the Brahmin boys took great delight in waging what they described as "Homeric" and "savage" combats against the children of the immigrants on the only playing ground available to both groups—the Boston Common.

To a visitor watching the spectacle at midcentury, it must have seemed an odd affair. The two groups were strangers to each other; neither had anything to say in which the other might have displayed the slightest interest; there was not between them even the beginnings of friendliness or even of sportsmanship. On the one side, a homogeneous group of carefully manicured young gentlemen in woolen suits, knee pants, cotton stockings, Eton collars and caps; on the other, a motley assortment of Irish youths, looking bigger and tougher in their worn and shabby pants, baggy coats and ill-fitting caps, their sheer presence inspiring fear in the hearts of many of the upper-class boys. Looking back later, Charles W. Eliot, who became the president of Harvard University, vividly remembered the pains and griefs of these boyhood encounters on the Common, which became linked forever in his mind with all sorts of dark and childish fears. "It was no small deliverance," he recalled, "to outgrow the fear of bigger boys, particularly of Mason-Streeters and of North-Enders, and of dogs and ferules, and of the imaginary imps and robbers that haunted dark rooms, and lurked under beds and in closets, and hid behind trees in the dim woods, and among the rocks upon the lonely shore."

Yet, for most of the Brahmin boys, these ritualistic challenges were later remembered as the high point of their childhood days; for the contest was not as one-sided as it seemed at first glance. Living so close to the Common, the Beacon Hillers had a great advantage: they could prepare their snowballs the day before, leave them to freeze overnight and carry them in large baskets to the field of battle. Then, in the midst of combat, if they scored a direct hit on the cheeks or the chin, they could draw the "mucker's" blood. ("Muckers" was the name the Brahmin boys used for the Irish youths.) But in the end the Beacon Hillers were generally defeated by the North Enders.

For most of the children in the North End, such fleeting images of the well-to-do remained their only contact with the insular world of the Boston Brahmins. But to Johnny, standing day after day at the center of Beacon Hill, the ways of the Brahmins became familiar, and this familiarity would color his ambitions and his hopes just as surely as his daily experience in the North End. Those days and nights on the Hill opened up for him a different world—a world whose pleasures and privileges he would crave as long as he lived.

Johnny's years on the corner of Beacon and Park witnessed the waning days of an extraordinary period in the history of Boston's elite. From the beginning of the century through the Civil War, Boston had enjoyed a position as the trading capital of America, a dominance made possible in large part through the great speed of her native clipper ships, with their long, slender lines, their tall raking masts and their overhanging bows, which outbid any competitor for the Far Eastern trade. Prosperity in shipping had fostered prosperity in manufacturing as well; the first factories in America were developed in Massachusetts. With the wealth gathered from the sea, a score of old Boston families, the Lowells, the Cabots, the Lees, the Higginsons, the Tracys and the Jacksons, had turned to manufacturing, and in this turn a revolutionary new system of factory organization was born. For the first time, all the processes of manufacturing a complex commodity were carried on in the same place under a single management; raw cotton went in at one end and came out finished cloth at the other.

With both its merchants and its manufacturers moving forward, Boston had enjoyed its most prosperous era. In the first half of the nineteenth century, Boston's available capital was greater even than New York's; cotton, railroads, textile mills and mining operations were all financed from Boston, and Boston's banking system stood at the center of the entire region. It was, in short, a dazzling time, a time, as *Fortune* magazine later described it, "when Boston was a great port and Boston ships were great ships and Boston banks were great banks and the name of Boston carried the Union Pacific over the Continental Divide."

Moreover, in its moment of economic triumph, Boston, affectionately dubbed "the hub of the universe" by Oliver Wendell Holmes, possessed unchallenged authority in the cultural world as well. As commerce, that great civilizing agency, began to rouse the New England imagination with the tales of travelers, and as the Industrial Revolution and the textile mills on the Merrimack began to weave a new pattern of life, New England produced a cultural renaissance, a phenomenal burst of literary activity. More than a century and a half later, historians would still marvel at the extraordinary concentration of intellectuals, writers and poets who flowered together in the same time and in the same place.

The wondrous parade began in the field of history, with the coming of age of an exceptional group of scholars—George Ticknor, William Prescott, Francis Parkman, George Bancroft, John Motley and John Palfrey—whose large, splendid works on Spain, Mexico, Peru, the Netherlands and the United States would blaze a new trail in the narrative writing of history. These same years also witnessed an explosion of literary activity in the writing of stories, novels, poems and essays which, taken together, proclaimed the birth of a new American literature. In the two decades before the Civil War an array of books was produced in New England—including the works of Ralph Waldo Emerson, Nathaniel Hawthorne, Henry David Thoreau, Henry Wadsworth Longfellow, John Greenleaf Whittier and Louisa May Alcott—which, in the critic Perry Miller's words, "still staggers our realization."

The unusual coherence and community which marked Boston's literary life in these golden years can be traced in part to the remarkable pattern of living which had been established in Boston and existed nowhere else in the United States. As in Florence in the Renaissance or England in the sixteenth century, early-nineteenth-century Boston had a leading core of citizens who lived in town, saw each other regularly and married into one another's families; who patronized the arts and letters and interested themselves in local institutions. In an age of increasing privatism, Boston's men of wealth still believed in public responsibility and in familial values.

By the nineteenth century, the "city set on a hill" had, by Puritan standards, become a secular city and religion had yielded its centrality to commerce and politics, but the nonmaterialist ideal of living remained formidable enough to produce in Boston, more than in any other city in the United States, a culture in which the life of the mind was accorded a dignified and important place. It was this tradition that led New England's men of commerce to consecrate large portions of their money to learning, to the building of libraries, the endowment of universities, the support of free lectures and the publication of books.

And still there was something more. When a Brahmin family had accumulated a certain wealth, instead of trying to build it up still further it would, often enough to take notice, step out of business altogether and try to accomplish something in politics, public service, education, medical research, literature or the arts. Surely there were families like this in other cities, but in Boston, as Samuel Eliot Morison observed, "there were so many of them as to constitute a recognized way of life." One has only to think of the Quincys, who produced three generations of Boston mayors plus a president of Harvard (indeed, Brahmin leadership in the mayor's office was typical down to the Civil War); the Lodges (two senators, a poet, a museum director); the Lowells (a jurist, an educator, an author, a judge, a historian, an astronomer, a president of Harvard and two poets); the Phillipses (a philanthropist, an educator and an abolitionist); the Shattucks (four generations of medical reformers); the Holmeses (a clergyman, an M.D. author, a Supreme Court justice); the Eliots (a mayor, a superintendent of schools, a president of Harvard); the Peabodys (an educator, two professors, an architect, a headmaster and a poet) and what they collectively accomplished in public service, education and the arts to see what was meant by the uniqueness of Boston.

And then, of course, there was the incomparable Adams family, which produced a patriot-governor, two Presidents, a diplomat, a historian and a writer, with each succeeding generation spurred on by the achievements of the past. "I must study politics and war," John Adams had said at the start of the family dynasty, "that my sons may have the liberty to study math and philosophy. My sons ought to study math and philosophy, geology, natural history and naval architecture, navigation, commerce and agriculture, in order to give their children a right to study painting, poetry, music, architecture, statuary, tapestry and porcelain."

These curiously blended families produced a vigorous leadership caste whose houses were alive with the hurry and bustle of politics, reform, combat and crisis. Always in touch with the central currents of contemporary life, they took on the task of directing the destiny of their city and their nation with the same self-confident vigor with which they had sailed the seven seas and built the first factories. In the middle decades of the nineteenth century, Boston was animated by the conviction that commerce and politics, word and deed, thought and action, interact. The politicians and the merchants, the poets and the storytellers, the essayists and the philosophers shared the sense of belonging to a community which believed in the disciplined use of words in writing and speaking to provide moral guidance and political leadership to society, a community full of idealism and humanitarianism, experimental theories and radical thoughts.

It was the time in the life of the mind of New England when Channing was preaching the optimistic doctrines of unitarianism, when Emerson was inventing the idea of inner perfectibility, and when Margaret Fuller was speaking out for women's rights. It was the time of *The Dial* and Brook Farm; it was the time when Hawthorne's brother-in-law, Horace Mann, later known as the father of the common school, was revolutionizing America's ideas about public education, when Dorothea Dix was leading her crusade to reform prisons, almshouses and insane asylums, and when Samuel Gridley Howe was pioneering in social reforms for the handicapped.

Of all the cities Charles Dickens visited in America, he reserved his highest praise for Boston, "where the tone of society [was one] of perfect politeness, courtesy, and good breeding," and where he found "the air so clear, the houses were so bright and gay; . . . the bricks were so very red, the stone was so very white . . . the knobs so marvellously bright and twinkling . . . that every thoroughfare in the city looked exactly like a scene in a pantomine." "I sincerely believe," Dickens concluded, "the public institutions and charities of the capital of Massachusetts are as nearly perfect as the most considerable wisdom, benevolence and humanity can make them."

Through his readings in school, Johnny developed a heroic image of Boston's "merchant princes" who had built their fortunes out of their own enterprise and then turned their energies back to the benefit of their city. In his fertile imagination, he could see himself standing in their place, accumulating a fortune and then using it to improve the welfare of his city. Even as a young boy he felt a special tie to Boston, a feeling that his history and the history of Boston were magically intertwined. Though that other Boston was as far removed from his own life in the North End as Ireland was from America, he felt curiously connected to all the old parts of Boston, convinced that the heritage of the patriots and the abolitionists, the clipper ships and the counting houses, belonged to him as much as it did to anyone else. Required to read Dickens' glowing description of Boston in school, Johnny took it so to heart that years later he could still recite large portions of it to his daughter Rose.

But even as Charles Dickens proclaimed the glory of Boston, the city's days of dominance were coming to an end. Ironically, it was the Civil War, which tinged the Bostonians with their culminating glory, that served as the agency of their dissolution. While the best energies of the city's leading citizens were absorbed in the tasks of preserving the Union and freeing the slaves, the nation and the city were changing in such far-reaching ways that the old Bostonians returning from the battlefields of war barely recognized the world they had left behind. The stimulus of the Civil War had enormously quickened the tempo of the age, hastening the spread of the Industrial Revolution, the expansion of the railroads and the development of the factory system. "The headlong growth of business," observed historian John Higham, "made the city, the machine, and the capitalist the controlling forces in American culture." The dawn of a new spirit was rising in the land, but for Boston it was sunset; her building days were over.

With the ending of the Civil War, the interior of the continent rapidly sprang into civilized life. A wholly new America was shaping itself—a vastly expanded America in which the balance of power, in numbers of population, in wealth, in productivity and in speculation, was rapidly shifting to the West, opening up vast natural resources and creating a national market capable of absorbing them, an America with which Boston had as yet little relationship. It was a time of recklessness and rapid change calling on men of a practical and opportunistic turn of mind; those who could not adapt to the new conditions were left behind, stranded. Such was Boston's fate. In the postwar era, her enterprise and vitality were gone. Refusing to follow the way the other parts of the country were hastening, Boston turned its mind backward and clung to the past.

As compared with all the other great cities of the East which did manage to move in harmony with the buccaneering spirit of the new order, Boston alone failed to create a substantial route of trade connecting it with the vitality of the ever expanding West. Undertaken with vigor in the 1850s, the construction of railroads came to a premature close at the end of the war. To be sure, it would have taken a great deal of Yankee ingenuity to enable Boston's railroads to compete with the Erie Canal, which had established a link between New York and the fertile plains of the trans-Allegheny West, but the point is that Boston's capitalists never really tried.

And without a direct link to the Midwestern markets, Boston's foreign commerce languished: line by line the ships from Canton, from Calcutta, from Russia and from the western coasts of Africa began to change their routes, sending Boston's trade into a permanent decline. By 1880 Boston's export trade had declined to 30 percent of the prewar decade, and the harbor stood relatively empty. The waterside streets no longer thronged with sailors, the welcoming wharves became sorely dilapidated, and, as Charles Francis Adams observed, grass began to grow in front of the once bustling warehouses, from the counting-room windows of which the old merchant princes had looked down on the decks of their vessels. In the prewar era, prosperity in shipping had fostered prosperity in manufacturing; so now the steady decline in commerce went hand in hand with a marked decline in Boston's manufacturing position. Throughout Boston's manufacturing community, the spirit of aggressive enterprise was gone. By the mid-1880s, Boston had even lost its edge in the manufacture of readymade clothing.

Why this decline occurred is a complex question, although many old Bostonians liked to point to the massive influx of immigrants in the mid–nineteenth century as *the* reason for Boston's decline. For years, these old Bostonians argued, Boston had retained a remarkably homogeneous population. Geographically unsuited to receive large numbers of immigrants—its small area surrounded on all sides by water—it had increased its population slowly during the half century following the American Revolution. Before 1830, the number of immigrants from abroad landing in Boston annually had never exceeded 2,000; before 1840 it reached 4,000 only once (1837) and most of these were transients, westward bound. Compared to other great port cities these numbers were exceptionally small, and of those who remained the overwhelming majority were drawn from a narrow range of mostly English-speaking countries. As a result, Boston was allowed to preserve its original air of homogeneity longer than the other large cities. A visitor from New York in the 1840s, observing the crowd in the streets, exclaimed, "Why, all these people are of one race. They behave like members of one family, whereas with us a crowd is an assembly of all the nations upon the earth."

In this closely knit community in which the leading families spent most of their time together, went to the same schools and shared the same religion, in which most things were within easy walking distance of one another, an aristocratic way of life had been sharply defined which, it can fairly be said, contributed to Boston's great accomplishments and achievements in the prewar era. In the aftermath of the Civil War, however, as industrialism and immigration pressed forward with a speed which seemed to leave all the old landmarks behind, this comfortable way of life was threatened with disruption. For all Americans in all parts of the country, the Industrial Revolution introduced massive elements of confusion and recklessness into everyday patterns of life. Yet, while others were able to overlook this confusion in the heady atmosphere of optimism and cheer produced by the humming mills and the smoking factories, the Bostonians, precisely because their culture had been the most coherent, despaired and withdrew into themselves. The familiar world they knew was slipping from its moorings and they were fearful of the crude open seas into which they were plunging. To them, the postwar world represented the triumph of materialism and unabashed vulgarity, the loss of traditional standards and distinction in manners and dress, the end of dignity and repose. They saw change going on and they interpreted it as decay.

The most dramatic change, the influx of immigrants, can be traced, ironically, to the central position which Boston originally held in the shipping trade, a position which induced the famous British steamship company the Cunard Line to establish its terminus in Boston in 1841, and before long others followed its route, adding considerably to Boston's importance as a port. But Cunard's decision had other consequences in the years ahead as the necessity of the poor became the opportunity of the wealthy. In the wake of the massive exodus from Ireland following the potato famine, Sam Cunard recognized the profits to be made in filling his ships bound for America with immigrants and then returning with cargo for Europe. By 1850, the Cunard Line was making more than a dozen such trips a year, bringing throngs of destitute Irish from the port of Cork to Boston. So it happened that a startled and scarcely prepared Boston, whose population was already too large for the confines of the original peninsula, was suddenly flooded by the unanticipated arrival of thousands of immigrants. In the nine years up to 1845, only 33,346 immigrants had landed in Boston. In 1847, in a single year, somewhere over 37,000 arrived in a city of 114,366.

Moreover, in contrast to the earlier immigrants who chose to move on rather than settle under the unfavorable conditions dictated by Boston's physical, economic and social structure, the penniless Irish newcomers had no choice but to remain in a city which had no space in which to lodge them, trying to eke out a miserable existence in an atmosphere of cultural homogeneity that was rigidly forbidding to aliens. As a result, Boston's population swelled from 85,475 in 1840 to 136,881 in 1850. In 1855 there were 55,000 Irish in Boston—more than 34 percent of the total population of the city. The numbers alone make it easy to understand the shock Boston received from its Irish "invaders." In contrast, New York, though receiving a far larger absolute number of famine immigrants, was three times Boston's size in population—371,223 in 1845 compared with Boston's 114,366—and its area was six times as large. Moreover, New York in the 1840s was more fluid and diverse in its makeup, a boisterous and open city, far readier than Boston to tolerate the new arrivals.

In the long view, the influx of the Irish immigrants spoke of a richer and more varied culture for Boston, but at the time it must have been a wrenching experience for the old Bostonians to witness the transformation of their cherished, well-ordered city into a slum-ridden metropolis. For even with the land that was added by cutting down the hills and filling in the Back Bay, Boston's space was still wholly inadequate for housing the newcomers, and overcrowding occurred on a fantastic scale. By the second half of the nineteenth century, large areas of Boston had lapsed into slum regions of tenements and lodging houses, spreading too rapidly to control. Obliged to find shelter wherever and however they could, the Irish were easy prey for speculative landlords who utilized every yard, garden and court, every cellar and every attic, to yield the maximum number of hovels that might pass as homes. By 1873 more than sixty thousand Irish, one fifth of the population, dwelt in tenements.

The once fashionable North End was the first section to give way; by the 1870s the West and South Ends had been destroyed as well. The narrow and crooked streets where Sam Adams and John Quincy had dwelt among their fellow patriots, merchants and artisans lost their familiar character, rotten now and choked wth dust, straightened out and widened to make room for the mushrooming tenements. In the process, many of the Revolutionary landmarks disappeared. New buildings arose upon sites that had once been shaded by great trees, in gardens where birds had sung; gone from the city was the atmosphere of quiet repose for which Boston had been so widely acclaimed. Almost everywhere one looked, life had become abrasive and clamorous.

Despite the best ideals of the Brahmins, a proletariat was in the making, rapidly shattering the sentimental hope of a shared community life. For with the slums and the poverty came all the attendant problems of pauperism, disease, vice and crime which Boston had heretofore largely escaped. And at the other end of the scale, "power and arrogance accumulated no less swiftly," defying all the initial hopes for moderation. Many individual Yankees benefited greatly in this new industrial era, but typically their excess profits came, not from their pitting themselves against the risks of the open seas as in the old days, but from the impoverishment, brutality and debasement of their fellow citizens. As a consequence, the contrast between the poor and the rich grew sharper and eventually the sodden wretchedness of the slums cast a pall over the entire city.

Feeling that their way of life was vanishing beneath their feet, the old Bostonians recoiled in despair. Overwhelmed, they retreated, withdrawing from their active, robust lives in the once spirited neighborhoods of the North and South Ends to the higher and more rarified ground of Beacon Hill and the Back Bay. There, in the seclusion and safety of their cultivated gardens, surrounded by leather chairs and rare books in their elegant town houses, they were able to forget the slums, the immigrants and the vulgar industrialism engulfing their city. The recoil of fashionable Boston took the form of Anglophilism, in which the ideas, customs and social standards of the British aristocracy assumed an enormous sway. The British influence affected everything about Boston society in the late nineteenth century—from its literary taste to its taste in clothing, from its custom of afternoon tea to its cotillion, from its hunt balls to the names chosen for the new Back Bay streets—Berkeley, Clarendon, Dartmouth, Exeter, Gloucester and Hereford. "The more the center of gravity of the nation shifted to the West," Van Wyck Brooks argued, "the more the Boston mind, thrown back upon itself, resumed its old Colonial allegiance."

Anglophilism served as a bulwark against the immigrant invasion; by stressing tradition, lineage and decorum, it sanctioned the Brahmins' position by right of birth, tying them by invisible bonds to one another, directing them in their tastes and associations, separating them forever from the parvenus and the foreigners. As each year went by, the mood of retreat deepened: by the 1870s, a substantial portion of Boston's elite had abandoned city living altogether to build large and gracious estates in the country, where their souls could respond once again to the romance of the rural ideal and to the pleasures of good conversation with weekend guests of their own choosing. Disentangled from the ebb and flow of the real world, the Brahmins found again the quiet and the repose they had lost. But in the shifting of their residential patterns, they gave geographic borders to the ethnic and class cleavages of their city, destroying forever the community ideals which had shaped Boston's earlier identity.

This mood of retreat had significant economic consequences too as the older families began, branch by branch, to withdraw from productive enterprises, choosing instead to salt away their capital in family trust funds which left only a small part of the inheritance fluid, just enough to bring up and educate the children. The rest of the estate was then thoroughly tied up beyond reach, with specific provisions denying the heirs the right to borrow against their inheritances. Developed as a holding action against the future, these trusts enabled the Boston elite to protect their wealth against the materialism of the postwar era. As a consequence, in contrast to the experience in other cities—where the fortunes of the old nineteenth-century families were typically squandered by the twentieth century according to the cherished American maxim of shirtsleeves to shirtsleeves in three generations—the old Boston families were able to prolong their power and position for generations. In the second quarter of the twentieth century *Fortune* magazine declared: "The great family trusts stand between the Bostonians and the activities of contemporary life like the transparent but all too solid glass which separates the angel fish of an aquarium from the grubby little boys outside." Indeed, so well did this system work that more than a century later most of Boston's first families could still trace their lives of privilege to their original family trusts.

The trustee system had a deadening impact on Boston's economy, immobilizing its capital for generations. By nature, tradition and design, the trustees chosen to manage the funds were conservative investors; their task was to multiply the family's capital in a cautious, steady manner, not to take risks. "I never invest in anything I can't see from my office window," an old Bostonian once observed. By the 1870s and 1880s, a mood of guardianship had replaced the earlier mood of enterprise.

With the ebbing of Boston's economic vitality, its mind appeared to atrophy as well. The springtime feeling, the joyous sense of awakening, that had marked its development in the decades before the war gave way to a mood of cheerlessness, of nostalgia and retrospection. The golden era of New England's literary dominance had come to an end; in its place appeared a sad sterility that masked itself in superiority, a genteel culture arrogant in its rejection of all the fresh and vital impulses arising in the West and the Midwest, in the writings of such men as Mark Twain or Bret Harte.

In politics as in literature the Enlightenment was over in Boston, and the progressive spirit passed on to New York and the West. The ardor of reform that had burned fiercely in the decades before the war subsided into a well-bred interest in temperance, Negro schools and foreign missions. Finding it easier to extend their human sympathies to the Negroes in the South than to the Irish in their own corner, the native Bostonians became more interested in admiring their past accomplishments than in moving forward.

The generation of Brahmins who matured after the Civil War—the sons and grandsons of the merchant princes and the manufacturing pioneers—were a different breed from their daring fathers, almost a caricature of the earlier ideal. By and large—there were always exceptions—they were content to be secretaries of the Somerset Club and of Harvard College rather than secretaries of state; successful members of fashionable law firms rather than judges or statesmen; genealogists and antiquarians rather than historians; doctors with lucrative practices rather than contributors to public health and the development of medicine. Whereas the fathers had championed the public-school system and the Boston Latin School, the sons were enrolled almost from birth in private schools and tapped for membership in private clubs where they could respond to people of their own class and to conversation on their own level.

By the 1880s, the archetype of a once virile and creative ruling group had become the Back Bay gentleman who lived on the income from his income, who ate his oatmeal every day even though he hated it, and who carried his umbrella under his arm even on the sunniest of days: the John Adamses had yielded to the George Apleys.

Paradoxically, while the old Brahmin world was being swept away, it was at its most fervent; while the days of the Brahmins' intellectual, industrial and political supremacy were drawing to a close, the social life of the period reached its zenith, shining down to us even now like a masterpiece of art, a portrait in pastels of polite ladies drinking tea and making conversation, of sporting gentlemen in silk top hats, set against a soft background of calling cards and gaslit chandeliers, of butlers in striped trousers and children's nurses all in white, of drawing rooms and dancing schools, of private clubs and cotillion balls. Insulated in its privileges, ideas and habits, still commanding a very large portion of the wealth, prestige, social dominance and standing in the community, the Brahmin society became more difficult to penetrate than ever before.

It was this fleeting moment, this moment of high privilege and exquisite social form, that young John Fitzgerald caught in 1879 from his special position at Beacon and Park. Standing there on his corner, looking up at the lighted windows, he pictured the people inside, sitting beside a bright fire, reading, talking and sipping wine, and he wanted more than anything else in the world to share in their company.

Indeed, the one interior glimpse he was afforded of a Beacon Street home remained with Fitzgerald throughout his life. It chanced that one particularly cold evening, when he had stayed on his corner longer than usual in order to sell out an extra late edition of the *Boston Globe*, he saw a large, kindly-faced Irish woman, laden with bundles, trying to negotiate her way up the slippery street, and he offered to carry her packages home. Her destination was 31 Beacon, a large red brick mansion which stood across from the Common only a short distance down from the golden-domed State House. In this elegant home she had worked for nearly fifteen years as the second cook, and now, since the master was away for the evening, she invited Johnny in for a warming cup of tea.

Seated in the servants' kitchen, Johnny was possessed of an enormous curiosity about the organization of the household; in particular, he was fascinated with the large number of servants required to keep such a place functioning: a butler, a house footman who waited on tables and cleaned the pantry, a valet, a cook, a second cook, a housemaid who attended to bedrooms, dressing rooms and bathrooms, a parlormaid who was responsible for the drawing room and the library, and a ladies' maid whose duties included hairdressing, packing and mending. Never shy in moments like this, Johnny asked his new acquaintance if she would take him through some of the rooms upstairs before he had to go. It was during this tour that he came upon the children's playroom, providing the vision that would remain in his memory.

"That playroom was the most extraordinary sight," Fitzgerald later recalled, "filled with the most elaborate wooden toys you could ever imagine—beautifully carved miniature soldiers and horses, hand-painted boats with movable parts, wood-burning locomotives and bright-red fire engines with tall ladders."

In coming upon the children's playroom, supervised by a governess and cordoned off from the world of adults, Johnny was also encountering an entirely different and more distinct concept of childhood from the one he had experienced in the North End, where life was much less segmented and the separation between childhood and adulthood much less clear. Yet, as he later reconstructed the scene, his thoughts on entering the room and seeing "all those toys, neatly stacked on shelves," ran in a more personal direction. "I stood in the doorway and made a promise to myself that someday, when I had children of my own, I would be in a position to give them all the toys that these children of privilege had enjoyed."

Johnny learned that the owner of the house was a distinguished gentleman named Henry Cabot Lodge, a proper Bostonian descended from Cabots and Higginsons, as well as Lodges, a Harvard graduate who was the author of a large number of scholarly articles. In the months ahead, Johnny would hear the name of Lodge more and more frequently; that summer Lodge would deliver the July Fourth oration at Faneuil Hall, and that fall he would win the Republican nomination from Nahant for a seat in the state legislature, thereby launching a long and successful political career which would eventually take him to the Senate of the United States.

As time went by, however, Johnny was to remember that evening from an even more curious point of vantage. For, surprising as it would have seemed to him as he sat in the servants' quarters flushed with excitement, there would be a train of events in which he would meet up in person with the master of 31 Beacon. Indeed, in the intricate patterning of incidents that would shape the course of Fitzgerald's life, his destiny and that of his children would intertwine over and over with the figure and the family of Henry Cabot Lodge.

# CHAPTER 4
# GREAT
# EXPECTATIONS

Fornor all his fascination with the glittering world of Beacon Hill, Fitzgerald's social life remained where it had always been, in the Irish North End. From all accounts, the Fitzgerald family, expanded now to nine boys, was extraordinarily close. It was not merely that all the brothers continued to live at home and contribute their earnings to the family even after they were old enough to leave school and live on their own; nor simply that most of their leisure-time activities—which consisted largely of visiting with relatives and participating in a wide range of religious rituals—were framed in a family context. More than that, the nine boys and their parents were deeply attached to one another; they were a tightly knit tribe.

Then, suddenly, in the spring of 1879, the family experienced a wrenching transformation with the unexpected death of their mother, Rosanna, at the age of forty-eight. That winter Rosanna had given birth to her twelfth child, a baby girl whom she named Mary for her mother, Mary Cox. Family history records the pregnancy as a difficult one, and four days after her birth the baby died, her death certificate simply listing "debility" as the cause.

Two months later, still weak and tired, Rosanna found herself pregnant again, and this time her vaunted endurance gave way. On the morning of March 10, 1879, as Rosanna's granddaughter Regis Fitzgerald Murphy heard the tale, Thomas took all the boys to a picnic, sponsored by the church, at Caledonian Grove. The weather had warmed up rapidly after an early March snowstorm, but Rosanna did not feel well enough for an outing, so she stayed at home. Later that afternoon, a man on horseback came riding through the North End bearing the false news of a dreadful accident on the train carrying the St. Stephen's picnickers to Caledonian Grove. Upon hearing the story, Rosanna collapsed on the floor, and two hours later she died. On her death certificate the cause of death is given as "cerebral apoplexy," a term used at the time to describe a sudden shock.

Whether Rosanna could have survived with medical help we do not know. We only know that by the time her family arrived home she was already dead, having died grieving for a family she thought she had lost. The following day a two-line obituary ran in the *Boston Herald*: "In this city, 10th instant, Rosa Fitzgerald. Funeral from her late residence 465 Hanover Street. March 12 at 8:30 o'clock. Relatives and friends invited."

Years later one of Fitzgerald's favorite memories was of his sitting at his mother's feet listening to the story of her girlhood days in Ireland. He loved her description of the rolling green hills and the happy life she had led on the farm before the famine came. And then the hard resolution to leave it all—relatives, neighbors and homestead—to seek whatever life she could find in an unknown and faraway land. She was scarcely a woman when she began the distressful passage across the ocean, her life in limbo until the ship reached Boston, where, in the cobblestone streets surrounding the wharves, she found a new home and a new life with Thomas Fitzgerald. To a child it was a great romance, an adventure story without equal.

Seen from a less romantic perspective, however, her life story suggests a perpetual weariness which is more than her own: she typifies a civilization and an epoch where constantly pregnant women would work themselves to exhaustion. Hers is the familiar story of countless immigrant women who defined their worldly possibilities entirely through their husbands and their children. She was indispensable in life, but only vaguely remembered in death.

Perhaps the story of Rosanna Fitzgerald would best be told if the story of the house at 465 Hanover Street could be told. In this connection, while there is an old photograph which shows us the tenement house on Hanover Street where the store and the Fitzgerald quarters once stood, there is not a single picture of Rosanna Fitzgerald, nor even one of those classic photos of husband and wife, standing side by side, stark, abstract, beyond emotion. With Thomas, at least, we have some hints that allow us to reconstruct how he looked. It was generally said in the family and repeated to the grandchildren that of all the sons Michael most resembled his father, and since we know that Michael was a big, strapping man with blue eyes and brown hair we can guess that Thomas too was large and husky. And then we have the peculiar feature of his cocked eye, which, precisely because it was peculiar, lived on in memory. With Rosanna, however, we have no clues whatsoever, since neither of her two little girls survived to an age where they might have been seen or said to resemble their mother and since she herself died before any of her sons had children of their own to keep the memory of her face and figure alive.

"The only thing I remember hearing about her," said Julia Fitzgerald Hill, "was that she was pregnant all the time." Speaking in a similar fashion, Regis Fitzgerald Murphy said she had always wondered what it must have been like for her grandmother, "bearing one baby after another, and then having to bring up all those boys in that little house with no one, not even a daughter, to help her out."

It is hard to refute the dominance of pregnancy in Rosanna Fitzgerald's life. In the twenty-one years of her marriage, she bore Thomas Fitzgerald twelve children: her first child was born when she was twenty-three, nine months to the day after her wedding; and she was pregnant with her thirteenth child when she died at the age of forty-eight. Here, then, was a woman whose body scarcely had time to recover from one pregnancy before her abdomen began once again to distend.

There is, fittingly, one lasting remnant to Rosanna's memory in a grassy plot framed by a low stone wall at Holy Cross Cemetery in Malden, Massachusetts, where a tiny stone marker bears her name, followed in large block letters by the simple epitaph MOTHER. It is curious to note that standing next to this tiny marker, casting a shadow upon it, is a large, handsome granite memorial, built in the shape of the Bunker Hill Monument, which bears the name of Thomas Fitzgerald in the center surrounded by the names of six of his nine sons. Rosanna, having died first, was buried before the family decided upon a joint memorial. So it happened that in death Rosanna Fitzgerald was finally permitted to stand alone.

In the months that followed Rosanna's death, there grew in Thomas Fitzgerald the ambition that one of his sons should become a doctor. All that summer, John Fitzgerald later remembered, his father kept dwelling on the need to fight back against the terrible illnesses which had taken his wife and little girls away from him. He had seen his first little girl die from cholera, and nearly a decade later he had watched his second daughter die after only four days of life. But this last death, the death of his wife from a totally unexpected and wholly mysterious shock to the brain, had stirred some kind of longing in his heart, the desire that someone in his family do something big in the field of medicine, discover a cure or develop a great skill. Then, perhaps, some solace could be found.

There was never any question that John was the one to fulfill his father's dream. Alone among the boys, he had the combination of brains, talent and drive to commit himself to what would amount to at least seven more years of schooling—four years of high school and three of medical school. In an age when only 4 percent of all boys and girls between fourteen and seventeen attended secondary school, it would represent a considerable achievement for the entire Fitzgerald clan if one of their number graduated from high school, to say nothing of the more distant dream of medical school.

But it would also entail a considerable sacrifice, not only in the loss of working income which John would otherwise have contributed to the family's support, but also in the cost of the textbooks and all the other school supplies the family would be required to purchase. For, in those days, even the most enlightened educators did not believe that textbooks or even blank paper should be furnished by the state free of charge. In the school superintendent's report for 1878, Sam Eliot wrote: "There are large numbers of our children who cannot buy the books or the stationery, but . . . for the city to play the benefactor is no benefaction."

In sending John to the prestigious Boston Latin School and later to Harvard Medical School, his father intended no injustice to the other boys. Indeed, as the story is told by one of Thomas Fitzgerald's grandsons, the decision was a collective one: "After Rosanna Fitzgerald's death, Thomas and all the boys got together and decided to send Johnny to school. If there was any envy on the part of the others, I never heard it said. For while they were all the most wonderful boys, Johnny had always been the cleverest and the most ambitious, the only one who had really come to love reading and learning for its own sake. As I heard it, all the others admired his intelligence, and, in an age when mutual help by family members was essential for survival, they all got behind him and gave him the shove."

A new life began for Johnny in September 1879 when he entered the alien and musty halls of the historic Boston Latin School. Until now, he had gone to school with his neighborhood friends, who were predominantly Catholic and Irish. But in entering the Latin School Johnny was entering a school which had been founded by English colonists in 1635, only five years after the founding of Boston itself. Over the years the proper Bostonians had championed the Latin School as a truly public institution where the sons of the humblest artisans could read Virgil and Demosthenes beside the sons of the most aristocratic citizens.

By the time Johnny arrived, however, the Brahmins were in full retreat from their democratic ideals as the exploding immigrant population was increasingly placing its sons in a minority position in the public system. Forced to choose between their educational idealism and the exposure of their sons to "the contact of a Paddy in the public classroom," the Brahmins concentrated their energies on the founding of an entire system of private schools where their sons could be enrolled from birth and educated with people of their own class. In the decades following the Civil War no fewer than eight preparatory schools opened their doors, including Middlesex, Groton, St. Paul's and St. Mark's.

In this same period, ironically, just as the wealthy Yankees were beginning their exodus from the public schools, the Catholic Church was inaugurating its own plans for a system of parochial education where its young could be schooled in the more secure atmosphere of its own kind. Having witnessed the humiliations which so many Irish children had suffered from the teachers of the older stock, Archbishop Williams announced in 1880 that he would withdraw Catholic children from the public schools wherever practicable. The embryonic parochial system was slow in taking root, however, as few Irishmen could afford its costs. Even so, old New England seethed at the very idea of parochial education. Even as they removed their own sons, the upper-class Yankees still believed in the public school as an Americanizing force and feared that if the Irish segregated their children from the rest of the community the next generation would be even more detached from America's traditions than their immigrant parents had been. In this context the story was told and retold of the appalling day when James Russell Lowell saw two Irishmen staring at George Washington's statue in the Boston Public Garden and heard one of them ask the other who the figure was.

So it happened that when John Fitzgerald arrived at the Latin School, he found himself surrounded by an ethnically mixed group of bright and ambitious students—Irish boys wishing to be lawyers or doctors, Jewish boys wishing to be professors, and Yankee Protestant boys whose families were unable to afford the expense of a private preparatory school. For the first time in his life, he had to work hard just to keep up with his class. And in the process, in listening to lectures on Shakespeare's plays and Milton's poems and being called upon to translate Homer's *Iliad* and Cicero's orations, his mind was deepened and stretched.

When Johnny first arrived, the Latin School was housed on Bedford Street in downtown Boston. "It seemed a vast rambling old shell of a building," the writer George Santayana recalled, "bare, shabby and forlorn to the point of squalor . . . No blackboard was black, as they were indelibly clouded with ingrained layers of old chalk . . . Every desk was stained with generations of inkspots and cut deeply with initials and scratched drawings."

Then, in 1881, the school was moved to a new three-story building on Warren Street designed after the German plan of a hollow square with corridors on all sides. On the first two floors were the library, the large lecture hall and the laboratory; the third floor contained the heart of Latin's pedagogy: twenty-four recitation rooms, where students were called upon in order of class rank to translate from Ovid, Virgil and Xenophon and to recite from memory long portions of the plays of Sophocles and Shakespeare, scenes from Hawthorne's *Tanglewood Tales* and Walter Scott's novels, and the complete orations of Burke, Pitt, Webster, Everett and Sumner. Even the study of mathematics was oral: the schoolmasters called upon the boys to solve problems aloud and to state the general method of their solution.

Afterward, Fitzgerald would say he owed a great deal to the Latin School for helping him to develop oratorical skills and for giving him dramatic practice in the art of debating. Indeed, even during his years as a student he would put these ripening skills to good use—in conducting tours for groups of visitors who came through the North End in search of America's political roots, which were everywhere to be seen, as Fitzgerald liked to say, in "these narrow old streets where history seemed to come alive." Having absorbed American history on his own for as long as he could remember, this son of Irish immigrants brought to the tours a knowledge so deep and an enthusiasm so broad that even the most fretful old Yankee, alarmed at the future of his country, could not have listened to his performance and emerged unimpressed.

During one of these tours, Fitzgerald had an experience he would long remember. On a warm Sunday afternoon in May 1882 he was guiding an English couple and their daughter, "one of the most beautiful young girls" he had ever seen, on a long tour which had taken them from Faneuil Hall, where so many spirited speeches preceding the Revolution were made, to North Square, which had been the seat of Boston's gentility before the Revolution, when it was adorned with fine trees and dignified by spacious mansions. Turning south on North Street, he had guided his little party past the low wooden house where Paul Revere had lived to the site of the old Green Dragon Tavern, headquarters of the patriot leaders, where the Boston Tea Party was organized and where the North End Caucus met at night to formulate its plans. At the end of the tour, according to his custom, he had arrived at the door of the Old North Church, in whose steeple were hung the original lanterns which Paul Revere used to warn his countrymen of the march of the British troops to Lexington and Concord.

While Fitzgerald did not think of himself as superstitious, he always managed to end his tours at the door of this same old church. Someday, he kept telling himself, he would do it differently, but for now, so long as he still carried within himself the old Catholic dread of ever setting foot inside a Protestant church, he would end his tour here, which allowed him, if his customers should ask to be taken inside, to say that while they were certainly welcome to enter, the hour was late and the time had come for him to be on his way.

On this occasion, however, just as he was about to take his leave, the English couple pleaded with him to stay just a little longer so that he could accompany them up the steeple where the historic lanterns were housed. In the presence of their beautiful daughter, he felt he could not refuse, so he drew a quick breath and opened the door. After all, he told himself, long before this he had experienced an almost overwhelming curiosity to see what would happen if he went inside the Old North Church. Could all the tales he had heard of Catholics being struck dead for entering a Protestant church be true? When he stepped across the threshold, as he later described it, a sudden terror he had never known before took possession of him, and his mind raced back to the catechism of his youth. Still, he was determined to go on, so he braced himself against the wall to shake off the trembling in his knees and led his new friends through the darkness to the site of the lanterns. Whereupon, in a mood of exultation at having conquered his fear, he burst forth with the words of Longfellow's famous poem on Paul Revere.

As the touring party emerged from the Old North Church, the news-boys had begun to hawk the evening papers, but Fitzgerald was so filled with good feelings from the flattering words of praise the English family had bestowed upon him that he failed at first to hear the startling news that was being shouted out at every corner: "Extra! Extra! Assassinated —Lord Frederick Cavendish, Britain's new Chief Secretary for Ireland, struck without warning in Phoenix Park, Dublin!"

The scorching words were not lost on the English gentleman, who bought the paper at once and began to read the story aloud to his wife and daughter. According to the early reports, the news of the killing was so monstrous that many refused to believe it. On the morning of the day that was to bring his death, Lord Frederick Cavendish had arrived in Ireland to a tumultuous welcome from the Irish people. As a member of the family of the famous Dukes of Devonshire, whose holdings were among the most magnificent in all of England and Ireland, Lord Frederick had enjoyed many summers at Lismore Castle, the family seat in Ireland, where his father had consistently showed himself an enlightened and liberal landowner. And beyond his personal attachment to the Irish countryside, Lord Frederick carried with him the conciliatory policies of the Liberal Prime Minister, William Gladstone, who was his intimate friend and his uncle by marriage. So it seemed that with the swearing-in of the new Chief Secretary "a brighter day had dawned for Ireland."

That evening, Lord Frederick went for a walk through picturesque Phoenix Park, and there, at approximately ten minutes after seven, he was suddenly attacked by four men wearing slouch hats who repeatedly plunged knives into his breast and throat and then escaped in a waiting carriage. At the time of these early reports, there was no clue to the assassins' identity or their motive. What was most bewildering was why any Irishman would want to kill Lord Frederick when he represented the best hope for any constitutional effort to ameliorate the condition of Ireland.*

In the aftermath, irreparable damage was done to the relations between England and Ireland. For, as it happened, Lord Frederick's older brother, Spencer Compton Cavendish, the Marquess of Hartington, was a leading figure in Gladstone's Liberal Party, an immensely powerful man whose support Gladstone sorely needed if ever he hoped to find a peaceful solution to the Irish question. But after the slaying Hartington became unalterably opposed to Irish Home Rule and led a dissident faction of Liberal Unionists whose votes in Parliament effectively killed its chances for over a generation.

While none of these events could have been foreseen on that warm Sunday afternoon of May 7, 1882, it was clear to the English family that a foul murder had been committed by some wicked Irishmen against one of their own. As the father finished reading the story, he beckoned to his wife and daughter to follow and abruptly turned his back upon the confused Fitzgerald, stopping only long enough to throw the paper into the lad's face. When Fitzgerald tried to follow them down the street, the girl turned around and told him, in a wrathful tone he would remember all his life, to stay back where he belonged.

It is a memorable story, made all the more memorable by the fact that Fitzgerald would one day have a granddaughter, Kathleen, who would

---

* At the trial of the murderers the following year, it was made evident that the plot was never intended against Lord Frederick but against Under-Secretary Thomas Burke, with whom he was walking.

marry Lord Frederick Cavendish's great-grandnephew, William Cavendish, the ninth Marquess of Hartington.

In June 1884, along with thirty other students from an entering class of 103, Fitzgerald passed the Latin School's demanding final examinations. A copy of one of the exams given in this period remains in the files of the Boston School Committee. It opens with Latin, calling upon the students to translate Cicero and Virgil at sight and to explain the syntax of *honore, salutis* and a dozen other words. In the section on history, the students are asked first to describe the forms of government and the classes into which the people were divided in Greece during the Heroic Age, and then to explain the causes of the Peloponnesian Wars and the terms of surrender and finally to evaluate Caesar's campaigns in Gaul. In the field of English, the students are called upon to write an account of Mark Antony in Shakespeare's Forum scene and to render Macauley's estimate of Milton as a poet. There follows a series of complex problems in algebra and geometry, and a long section on physics which calls for an illustration of the laws of attraction and repulsion between currents of electricity and for an explanation of the laws of Manotte and the lines of Fraunhofer.

So highly was the Latin School diploma regarded in Fitzgerald's day that he was admitted directly to Harvard Medical School in September 1884 without having to pass the entrance exams or to present a college diploma. Of the 102 students in his entering class, more than half held at least an A.B. degree and all the others—except those, like Fitzgerald, who were specially exempted—had successfully passed an exam given the previous June which demanded a rich training in physics, botany, geometry and algebra as well as English composition and translations from Latin, French and German.

As he walked through the halls of the medical building, which stood on the corner of Boylston and Exeter Streets, Fitzgerald found himself surrounded by a large number of Harvard graduates, young men with old Yankee names such as Edward Erastus Bancroft, Henry Francis Sears and William Sohier Bryant. But, since entry into medicine was still easier than entry into law or business at this time, there was also a substantial sprinkling of Irish students in his class, including ten graduates of Holy Cross and Boston College. Irish or Yankee, they were all males. Harvard's experiment of letting in one female in 1850 had come to an end when the medical students rioted in protest and the young woman withdrew her application. (It would be sixty years, in 1945, before women would finally be admitted into Harvard Medical School.)

When Fitzgerald entered Harvard Medical School in the fall of 1884,

*J*ohn F. Fitzgerald and Patrick J. Kennedy, the two men whose families would join together to create an American political dynasty, are shown here vacationing in Asheville, North Carolina, in 1895.

# THE FITZGERALDS

In an age when the people looked to politics for their entertainment and when campaigns resembled carnivals—with kerosene torches, spangled banners, marching parades and colorful speeches—Fitzgerald's dramatic presentation and vigorous movements touched all the proper chords. He is shown here with President William Howard Taft in Boston; at a Fourth of July celebration in Concord, Massachusetts; and with his wife Josie, in Palm Beach.

# THE KENNEDYS

Joe Kennedy's mother, Mary Augusta Hickey, shown at top with her husband, P. J. Kennedy, had been born under circumstances far more comfortable than the poverty in which her husband grew up. P.J. moved cautiously from one step to the next, however, and eventually his modest tavern prospered to the point where he was able to purchase one of the nicer homes in East Boston. At bottom, P.J., second from left, is shown playing cards with a group of his friends in 1899.

Rose Fitzgerald was her father's favorite child and chosen companion. Father and daughter, people said, were cut from the same mold. Here she is shown with her younger sister Agnes and her brother Tom; traveling abroad with her father; and in Palm Beach with her father and mother.

As the firstborn, Joe Kennedy, pictured above at age two, always held a special place in his parents' hearts. He walked through Boston Latin with an assured step and with an expectation that things would generally go his way. He was president of his class, colonel of his drill regiment, and captain of the baseball team, pictured here with Joe in the center. Joe, en route to Europe with Harvard friends Joe Merrill, left, and John Hannon, center.

*T*his newspaper photo records the first meeting of Rose Fitzgerald, age five, and Joe Kennedy, age seven, in 1895. The occasion was a joint family picnic at Old Orchard Beach, Maine. John Fitzgerald is seated on the post at left with Rose beside him. Joe Kennedy, with his finger in his mouth, is in center of the second row beside his aunt, Katherine Hickey. Behind them, in a black-and-white bonnet, is Mary Kennedy. The man in the white cap with a heavy mustache, second on Mary Kennedy's left, is P. J. Kennedy. Josie Fitzgerald stands by the post at extreme right, holding her daughter Agnes.

*J*oe and Rose met again at Old Orchard Beach, Maine, when Rose was sixteen. "I shall always remember Old Orchard as a place of magic," Rose recalled years later, "for it was the place where Joe and I fell in love." Second from the left is P. J. Kennedy, then Rose Fitzgerald and John Fitzgerald. Second from right is Joe Kennedy.

No other occupant of City Hall was so widely known, so frequently photographed, so often a figure of fascination in the papers as John Fitzgerald.

$W$ith the marriage of Joe and Rose, shown here emerging from the ceremony in October 1914, the balance of power shifted once and for all from John Fitzgerald to Joe Kennedy.

medicine was in a transitional period. In the three preceding decades, great breakthroughs had occurred in the knowledge of physiological processes—the most spectacular the conclusive demonstration that certain diseases as well as the infection of surgical wounds were caused by minute living organisms. This discovery would change the whole face of pathology and would effect a complete revolution in the practice of surgery.

It was also a time of great improvement in the curriculum of Harvard Medical School. Until the 1880s, the requirements for becoming a doctor were meager: with a high-school degree or frequently less, a candidate could take a haphazard series of "courses" and end up certified in less than two years. As of the 1870s, the exams at Harvard Medical School consisted merely of nine professors spending five minutes each questioning the candidate. To pass, it was necessary only to satisfy five of the nine professors; thus, a candidate could fail four of his nine subjects and still get a degree. Under a system as loose as this, it was not surprising that a scandal erupted when a Harvard-trained doctor mistakenly poisoned his patient.

Spurred on by the scandal, Harvard's president, Charles Eliot, introduced a series of sweeping reforms in the medical school which led the way to similar changes throughout the country. By the 1880s the curriculum had been lengthened to three years instead of two, and at the end of each year written examinations were administered in the various subjects to determine whether the candidate could continue at the next level. When President Eliot first introduced these reforms he was informed by Professor Bigelow that half the medical students could barely write and that it was ridiculous to expect them to pass written exams. He was also warned that his prerequisite of a college degree or the passing of an admissions exam would drastically reduce the number of students, which it did, almost by half. But Eliot persisted, and by the time Fitzgerald arrived the school was prepared to offer him a substantial education.

While he was pursuing his first-year courses in anatomy, physiology, chemistry and pharmacology, Fitzgerald continued to live with his father and his brothers in his family's home in the North End, where he remained an active member of his neighborhood organizations, finding time for both his studies and his social life. But there is no record of his performance at Harvard Medical School that first year, since, two weeks before the final exams, covering the entire year's work, his father died and the medical career of John Francis Fitzgerald came to an abrupt end.

· · ·

There is some evidence that the pneumonia which took the sixty-two-year-old Thomas Fitzgerald's life ran a rapid course. The last will and testament that he made out and signed in the presence of three witnesses is dated May 19, 1885, the very day of his death, and his signature on it is shaky.

It was an unusual will for an old-country Irishman, inasmuch as it rejected the right of primogeniture with the decree that all the real estate and personal property to which "I may die seized or be entitled to, be divided equally among all my children, share and share alike." Written in the presence of Matthew Keany, James O'Brien and Edward Fegan, the will also decreed that none of the real estate be sold until the youngest of his children (Henry, aged ten) reached the age of twenty-one, and then the income realized should be divided equally and devoted to the care and maintenance of all his children. In this way, the dying Thomas Fitzgerald ensured that his nine sons would have a home as long as they needed one.

Since no executor was named and no objection issued, James T. Fitzgerald, the eldest son, was named administrator of the estate, which was appraised in an inventory made on December 5, 1885, at $18,162. The real-estate holdings included the Fitzgerald home and grocery store at 465–467 Hanover, appraised at $6,000; the house and land at 378–381 Hanover, worth $9,000; and the house and land at 4 Webster Place, worth $3,000. These were the tenement buildings which Thomas and his brother James had purchased over the years. Beyond this, the grand total of Thomas Fitzgerald's personal estate was $162: $150 in cash and $12 in furniture.

Thomas Fitzgerald had not had an easy life. Forced to leave the land of his birth as a young man, he had never realized his dream of returning even once to western Ireland, which would forever hold for him the spacious memories of his early youth upon the farm. Having settled for the city, he had seen three of his children die and had lost his wife at an early age. Nor had he achieved fame or fortune. The short account of his life which the Boston papers ran the day after he died simply said: "He was a plain, frank, noble hearted man, open of speech and upright in his dealing."

# CHAPTER 5

# APPRENTICE
# TO
# THE
# BOSS

After his father's death, Fitzgerald turned to the Irish boss of the North End for help. At the funeral, the local parish priest had suggested to Fitzgerald that the only course of action, now that both his parents were dead and five of his nine brothers were still under age, would be to split the family apart, which would mean sending one or two of the younger boys to each of their three aunts. Fitzgerald was adamant in his insistence that the family stay together. However, with his older brother James, aged twenty-five, just beginning in a new business and already the father of three children under five, his brother Thomas, aged twenty-four, receiving only $2.50 a day as a clerk, and Johnny himself producing nothing but expenses at medical school, he did not see how he could make it work. In his predicament, he turned, as did the great majority of his fellow Irish in the North End, to the most respected man in the district —the neighborhood boss, Matthew Keany.

From their earliest years in America, the masses of Irish immigrants crowding into the growing cities had developed a characteristic style of politics known to history as "machine politics" or the "ward boss" system. Built upon the inability of existing governments to meet the demands of the immigrant poor, the ward boss system constituted a shadow government at the local level, a supplementary structure of power in which the newly arrived immigrants willingly gave their votes to a network of local political bosses in exchange for all manner of help in the daily challenge of survival. In time, as the local bosses gained more and more power in more and more city neighborhoods, the Irish in Boston, New York and Chicago virtually took over the Democratic Party at the local level.

Fitzgerald found the bluff and genial Keany in his usual position, behind his desk in the back room of the red brick grocery store at One Prince Street which he had owned for twenty-five years. A steady and industrious man, large and husky, with wavy dark hair, a thick walrus mustache and bushy eyebrows, Keany had started in the grocery trade at an early age and by diligent, hard work had become the proprietor of the Prince Street store, which he then built into one of the most prosperous groceries in the city, with an abundance of vegetables and fruits in crates and baskets covering half the sidewalk. Little known in public life until the outbreak of the Civil War, he became an ardent supporter of the Union cause and was elected to the Common Council, where he did much to facilitate troop recruitment. Once the war and its immediate aftermath came to an end, he retired from elective office, but in the eyes of his neighbors he had proved himself a natural leader of men, and he went on to become the undisputed boss of the North End.

Into this low-ceilinged room which served as his headquarters, thousands of men and women had entered over the years in search of assistance. By Keany's word, a man's son could be liberated from prison, a widow provided with food, an aspiring peddler issued a permit and a destitute father given a coffin to bury his infant child. Ward politics in those days was an intricate system built upon loyalty in which the boss served as a protector of his people in return for their votes on election day. In Keany's ward, the ties that bound his people to him were unusually tight, as he had become for them over the years not only a friend and a protector but an oracle whose advice was generally sought before any significant decision was made.

Fitzgerald found Keany in animated conversation with a young priest who, along with Keany, was an organizer of the Home for Destitute Catholic Children. As Fitzgerald entered, the boss was assuring the priest that he would have the help he needed in the planning for the children's picnic, which was to be held the following month. As the priest stood up to leave, Keany beckoned Fitzgerald over, introducing him as one of the most promising young men in the North End, a man who would one day make his dead father proud by becoming a famous doctor. Then, with an affectionate clap on the back, Keany ushered the priest out and turned his undivided attention to the young man.

The meeting that day would change the course of Fitzgerald's life. He began the conversation by telling the boss of his terrible fear that in the wake of his father's death he and his brothers were going to be separated. But, he added, he had a plan. He had thought it out. There was only one thing to do. He would leave Harvard immediately, take a job and, with the money he made, hire a housekeeper so that the family could stay together in the Hanover Street home. The only question was, could the boss help him find a good job?

Fitzgerald's request put Keany in a difficult position. On the one hand, he felt honor bound to his friend Thomas Fitzgerald—whose last will and testament he had witnessed only three days before—to help this boy upon whom Thomas had placed such high hopes to become a doctor. On the other hand, Keany himself had long harbored a different dream for this talented young man. Having observed John Fitzgerald closely over the years through all the organizational work he had done for the church and the local Neptunes Associates, an organization of neighborhood men, the boss had seen in him the superior faculties of command, the fascination with combinations and intrigues and the torrential energy that to him suggested the promise of a natural politician, with more potential than any other young man in his district. Indeed, there were many times, as he told Fitzgerald much later, when he thought he understood Fitzgerald's ambitions better than his father, detecting long before this crisis that the boy's most absorbing passion lay with politics rather than medicine.

Now that Cocky Tom was dead, Keany felt all the more compelled to help Fitzgerald stay his original course. To the boy's request for a job he offered instead the money for school plus an additional sum to pay a housekeeper. The boss spoke in an affectionate tone, but one of command. The boy, however, was not to be driven from his decision. Even with the money Keany offered, he would feel absurdly useless staying in school. The time had come for him to earn a living.

All the while he spoke, Fitzgerald later recounted, Keany was studying him with sharp eyes, weighing his words on the scales of his experience and considering what to do next. Once he realized that Fitzgerald could not be moved, he changed his tack and suggested that if the boy really was determined to stop school and get a job, why not start out as an apprentice to the boss? The work would not be simply a means of making money but the chance to study politics and prepare for a political career (that is, if such a career appealed to him!). Keany had barely finished making his offer when Fitzgerald leaped up from his seat, threw his arms around the older man and said he'd report for work the following morning.

So Fitzgerald began to study ward politics, which, as party historian M. Ostrogorskii once observed, was "not the Politics of Aristotle, nor even that of Columbia College," but was nonetheless "a science which demands great application and certain natural aptitudes." It consisted first of a sort of empirical psychology, a study in depth of the men in a district: the intricacies of their family relationships and their social organizations; the strengths of their various needs and their willingness to trade their votes for the satisfaction of those needs; their capacity for loyalty and their susceptibility to threats. There was no better place for Fitzgerald to continue his study of human nature than from Matthew Keany's headquarters—where he reported all summer long in order to help the boss dispense the hundred and one favors regularly awarded in the course of a day, favors which spread the boss's influence, like a huge spider web, over the entire district.

The day-by-day workings of a ward boss who bears a considerable resemblance to Matthew Keany has been richly described by Boston writer Joe Dineen in his novel *Ward Eight*. Set in the North End in about the same period, the novel centers on a young man, not unlike Fitzgerald, who starts out as the boss's apprentice and takes over the reins of power when the old man dies. More revealing than a dozen essays on ward politics is the passage which describes the boss's early-morning sessions with his young lieutenant.

"Ye'd better get yer pencil and write these things," was the first instruction.

"Mugsy Dwyer has gone to Holy Ghost Hospital for the Incurables. He'll never come back except in a pine box. See that he has all the tobacco, corncobs, and whatever he wants, and a glass of beer as often as he pleases," he paused. "Let him have whisky if he craves it," he said. "He might as well stay plastered if it makes the dying easier . . . Mickey Dunn's Aunt Liz had another heart attack . . . Here's the prescription [for nitroglycerin]. . . . Have Mulrooney fix the bulkhead down by the Merchants and Miners Wharf. One of the brats fell through it yesterday . . . And 'Fingers' Flynn will be getting out Saturday noon. Have somebody meet him at the jail and take care of him.

" . . . And about those new vestments, tell Father Duffy two hundred dollars and not a nickel more . . . I'll give that much to God, and to hell wid it. That's all I can think of now. I'm going home and take a nap."

While the complexion of Ward 6 would change in the 1890s as large numbers of Italians from the barren hillsides of southern Italy and thousands of Jews from Russia and eastern Europe would make their way into the old North End, the district was still predominantly Irish when Fitzgerald began his work with the boss. This meant that many of his daily assignments involved him with the scores of Irish associations familiar to him since his earliest days—St. Stephen's Church, the Charitable Irish Association, the Ancient Order of the Hibernians, the Neptunes Associates. As the months of summer passed, he learned which men in each organization could be counted upon to help him in the implementation of the boss's orders; in the process, he began building his own political force which would later become the foundation of his own substantial success.

Then, in the autumn months, as the elections drew near, the technical part of Fitzgerald's learning began, as he came to understand the elaborate machinery of the party organization, the wheels within wheels —the primaries, the nominating conventions, the campaigns, the elections—and all the intricate procedures involved in the filing of the nominating papers, the printing up of the party ballots and the final rounding up of all the votes on election day.

Fitzgerald long remembered the pride he felt when the boss first designated him a "heeler" for the ward, one of the chosen few whose responsibility it was to ensure that only the "right" party members attended the local meetings designed to choose the delegates for the nominating conventions. Each year, in early September, the boss drew up a checklist of the voters in the ward who were fixed on the right side; it was these men the heelers were dispatched to round up from their homes and their saloons on primary day. If the heelers did their job well, the proceedings took little time, as the hand-picked meeting invariably supported the boss's slate of delegates. But if a group of outsiders appeared at the door, the heelers were responsible either to prevent their entry or, failing that, to conduct a second roundup, this time of "the personators," the men who were willing to "vote the cemetery." This last task was the one Fitzgerald relished the most, for, as he liked to boast, time was of the essence and since he was still the fastest runner in the North End he was able "to round up more dead people in a shorter time than any other heeler."

So long as the boss's slate of delegates was kept intact, the process of choosing the nominees for office—for the city Common Council, the state legislature and the Congress—was entirely automatic. Since it was the city committee's practice to order the names of the candidates on the ballot in the same sequence in which their nominating papers were filed, it was in the interest of each ward leader—there were twenty-two at the time—to see to it that *his* candidates filed the papers first. More

than any other practice during this era, this one, the rewarding of the
first group through the door, produced the most absurd demands on the
heelers. But this was Fitzgerald's world, and he accepted each challenge
with the delight of a natural competitor whose exploits grew legendary
as time went by. It was said that on one occasion, while a large gathering
of a rival leader's forces were keeping an all-night vigil at the front door
of the city committee headquarters, Fitzgerald climbed up a tree and
came down through a skylight. And on another occasion it was reported
that he managed to persuade the night janitor of the building to exchange roles with him, so that on the morning of the filing day he was
able to present himself, the nominating papers in the pocket of his
janitor's uniform, at the office of the city committee before the doors to
the building were even opened.

As a reward for filling the post of heeler so well, Fitzgerald was advanced to the speakers' bureau, where he joined a small group of men
selected by the boss to give rousing speeches on behalf of the boss's
nominees. The boss himself was not a man who felt comfortable speaking before the public, but he was brilliant at turning the talent of others
to his own account. And from the first time he heard the young Irishman speak, despite the slight lisp that stayed with Fitzgerald all his life,
Keany took the measure of his extraordinary capacity as an orator. In
an age when the people looked to politics for their entertainment and
when campaigns resembled carnivals—with kerosene torches, spangled
banners, marching parades and colorful speeches—Fitzgerald's dramatic presentation and vigorous movements touched all the proper
chords. So effective was "little Fitzie," as he came to be called, not only
in arousing his audiences but in getting to the best street corners first
(every night there was a struggle to see which speakers could set up their
soapboxes and portable platforms in the most populous places), that the
boss rapidly advanced him to the ranks of his "shock troopers." These
were the most elite of the boss's speakers, whose job it was to infiltrate
the meetings of the enemy and then, by heckling, wit and strength of
voice, undermine the opponent and turn the audience around in favor
of the boss's man.

Through his far-ranging apprenticeship, Fitzgerald was treated to
a view of the ward system at every phase of its development—from the
days of its planting, when the boss distributed his assistance to families
in the district, through its cultivation at the primary, the convention and
the campaign, to its harvesting when the elections finally took place and
the boss reaped his rewards. It was during this final phase that Johnny
came up against the hardest test of his early political education.

On the day before the elections Keany told Fitzgerald he wanted him
to be a checker at the precinct headquarters at the Eliot School. It was

the checker's job to sit where the voters deposited their marked ballots into the ballot box and determine exactly how each voter voted. In those days—before the requirements of the Australian system of secrecy—when each party still printed its own ballots, there were several ways to determine how each voter was voting. First of all, the checker could determine which party's ticket the voter was using by noting the shade of the ballot he slipped into the box. Although Massachusetts had passed a law in the early 1870s prescribing that all ballots be printed on plain paper and without any mark to distinguish one party's ballot from another, the parties had skillfully evaded the law by using different shades of white, ranging from shiny white to cream.

In a district that was as heavily Democratic as Fitzgerald's, however, this simple question of party loyalty was less important than the more elaborate test of whether every Democrat had voted exactly the way the boss had instructed. If, as it sometimes happened, there were two men, the boss's man and a rival candidate, running for the same office, the ballots had to be closely inspected to discern which one the voter had chosen. But the checkers had their ways—beginning with the distribution of pencils so hard that all the Xs came through to the surface in a pattern which the checker could interpret as the folded ballot was slipping through the rollers.

In the days before this particular election in 1888, an undercurrent of opposition had arisen. It happened that one of the boss's nominees for the Common Council was an aggressive man who had a reputation for "unbridled arrogance and abusing power." There was talk in the street that some of the North Enders were going to defy the boss on this one and vote for a rival boss's candidate. Having heard these rumors, Keany was determined to catch the defectors early in the day so that reports of their swift and heavy punishment could be turned back on the streets as a warning to the rest of the voters.

With Keany, revenge was not taken in anger, it was simply his method of politics: these men had already bound themselves to him by accepting his favors, all he asked in return was their vote. Perhaps this blustery fellow was not the best candidate; if so, the boss would discard him the next time around. But for now, loyalty demanded that all his men rally around his candidates, including the objectionable ones.

So it was that Keany put his most trusted men on duty with instructions to identify the defectors as they slipped their ballots into the box by a raise of the arm which notified a gang of waiting heelers to retaliate. In some instances, the punishment could be administered immediately: if the defector had a city job or one supplied by the boss, he would be told on the spot that he was fired. With others, the web took longer to spin; but no one escaped the boss's wrath: a rebellious landlord would return to his tenement to find a group of investigators from the city's Health Department responding to complaints about the sanitary conditions of his buildings; a defecting saloon keeper would receive a hefty fine from the police for having stayed open after hours; an unfaithful merchant would be boycotted. And everyone would understand that all of these actions were the result of one man's word.

For himself, Fitzgerald had no trouble with the system. Harsh as the punishment seemed, it was only the corollary of the assistance Keany provided. But when the day of the balloting dawned, there arose for the faithful Fitzgerald an agonizing dilemma. It chanced that one of the men who had threatened to vote against the boss's candidate—based on a scuffle at the docks in which he lost the use of one of his eyes—was the uncle of the newsboy Fred, the friend and companion of Fitzgerald's youth. After young Fred's death, his paternal uncle had come to live with the family in the North End, where Keany had found him a steady job on the docks. A loyal man who was willing to work hard, he had done well by his dead brother's family, with whom Fitzgerald had kept in close touch. But on this occasion, when he saw the big man approach the precinct booth, Fitzgerald dropped his head; he knew the pride and independence of the family and feared the worst. As the uncle picked up his ballot, he said nothing; he merely glanced at Fitzgerald, a glance Fitzgerald would remember all his life.

Years later, Fitzgerald recalled that as he turned the rollers and discovered the uncle's X beside the rival name, he became conscious of a loud throbbing in his heart. He knew that if he turned the man in, all would be lost for Fred's family. Yet he felt that his first loyalty had to be to Matt Keany. To desert Keany was to lose everything he'd been working for since his father's death. Drawing a deep breath, he raised his arm to signal the defection and turned back to his work. But try as he might, he could never block from his mind the sight of the boss's heelers as they swarmed about the uncle to let him know that his job at the docks had vanished and that there was nothing else in the city he was qualified to do.

The reward for Fitzgerald's faithfulness came several months later when the boss secured for him a position in the Customs House which not only allowed him to work at Boston Harbor but also left him plenty of time to continue his political education. And the job had an additional benefit: since a clerkship in the Customs House provided the substantial sum of $1,500 a year plus benefits, Fitzgerald was finally able to think of marrying the beautiful Josie Hannon, the girl with whom he had been in love since the first day they met.

# CHAPTER 6
# A
# LONG
# COURTSHIP

Mary Josephine Hannon, or Josie as she was called, was just thirteen on the Sunday afternoon in the autumn of 1878 when the fifteen-year-old John Fitzgerald first saw her standing in the kitchen of her family's farmhouse in the quiet country town of Acton, twenty-five miles west of Boston. Early that morning the Fitzgerald family had boarded the Fitchburg Railroad at Causeway Street for a day's outing to the Hannon farm. Mary Ann Hannon, Josie's mother, was a first cousin of John Fitzgerald's father, Thomas, and it was with Mary Ann and her husband, Michael Hannon, that Thomas had lived when he first came to America.

The trip from Boston to Acton took just under an hour, but it brought the Fitzgeralds into a world so different from their life in the North End that it must have seemed as if they had moved backward a half century in time. As the train sped west, the jumbled sights and thunderous sounds of the city rapidly receded, giving way to long stretches of farmland. "On both sides of the Fitchburg railroad," observed a reporter who had traveled west toward Acton in this same period, "you can see as you pass along large farmhouses and barns in the distance. The farmers here furnish large quantities of milk for the Boston market, hence, they keep large herds of cows. A large amount of hay fodder and root crops are gathered for feeding stock." Through Belmont, Lexington and Concord, deeper and deeper into the country, the train made its way to the small depot at Acton, where, once the steam whistle's echo had died upon the air, nothing could be heard but the chir-chir of insects and the twitter of birds.

Fitzgerald would remember the details of this September day until the end of his long life—holding in his mind the simple beauty of the countryside, the smell of the cool, fresh air and the first sight of the young girl who would eventually be his wife for sixty-one years. The short walk from the railroad station to the house where the Hannons lived took the Fitzgeralds along a dirt path until they reached a grassy hill and, beyond it, a wooden fence enclosing the Hannon property. The house itself was rather small—smaller than the Fitzgeralds' house on Hanover Street—but to Fitzgerald the beauty of its setting more than made up for the simplicity of its structure. The front door opened onto a small hall, immediately behind which a steep flight of stairs led up to the three bedrooms on the second floor where the six Hannon children and their grandmother slept. To the right of the hall was a closed wooden door, behind which stood the "parlor," where a wall-to-wall carpet lay over the rough floor, and matching chairs stood across from a love seat. "Irish families," writer Joe Dineen explained, "entertained in the kitchen. The parlor was a showroom, to be viewed from the threshold and to be occupied only during death-wakes, courtings, piano lessons and Christmas. The head of many an Irish family got into this room only when he died." To the left of the hall was the all-purpose kitchen/dining room, which led through one door to the Hannons' bedroom and through another to the back kitchen and the outdoor toilet. It was at the black soapstone sink, beside the large wood stove that furnished heat for the entire house, that John Fitzgerald found Josie Hannon. "The first time I saw her, I knew," Fitzgerald later wrote, "I knew this was it."

Numerous accounts of Josie's beauty as a young girl provide a ready explanation for Fitzgerald's immediate attraction. She had an abundance of lustrous black hair, which was drawn up in a swirl upon her head to expose a slender neck and that clear white complexion and dusky-rose cheeks that so often mark the beauty of the Irish girl. She looked out upon the world with dark, shining eyes beneath broad level brows. And perhaps most arresting of all, she stood perfectly erect; her slender figure with its small hips gave the impression of a tall, graceful fir tree. Years later, even up to her ninetieth birthday, her grandchildren would remark on the dignity of her bearing. "What I remember most about her," said her granddaughter Mary Jo Clasby, "is that she always stood absolutely straight. She never had a bottom, so her figure went straight down. And somehow even with age she never bent over, not even a little bit."

The imagination, stimulated by Fitzgerald's reminiscences, takes delight in picturing the first meeting between this unlikely pair over a hundred years ago: first the image of John Fitzgerald at fifteen, his small stature redeemed by a large handsome head and a husky frame, his entire figure molded by action, his movements, his glance, his voice full of energy and enthusiasm as he rushed into the kitchen, nearly shouting out his warm hello. Then the image of Josie quietly turning toward him, her eyebrows lifted in polite inquiry, her manner one of composure and observation. There was a stillness about her which balanced his exuberance: one imagines her response to his eager hello as a gentle half-smile where only the corners of her lips turned up slightly. And then, as Fitzgerald remembered it, no sooner had she smiled than she withdrew from the room, scurrying upstairs with a faint rustling of her long skirts.

Fitzgerald did not see Josie again the rest of that day. He spent the afternoon picking apples with her brothers, Michael, seventeen, and Jimmy, fifteen. But he decided then and there, from that first glance, that this girl would someday be his—a decision which would meet substantial opposition and engage him in a campaign that would last eleven long years before reaching a successful conclusion.

The most immediate barrier to Fitzgerald's success was Josie's extreme shyness, a trait that stayed with her throughout her life. When any friend or relative is asked to recall Josie Hannon, the first adjective chosen is "shy," invariably followed by "withdrawn, reserved, and proper." "I can never imagine her flirting or teasing with anyone," her niece Geraldine Hannon later said. "When I try to imagine her as a young girl, the picture in my mind is already the proper woman with her hat on her head and her white gloves in her hands." "Father was an extrovert," Rose Kennedy recorded in her memoirs. "Mother was innately rather shy and reserved. He would talk with anybody about anything. When she spoke, it was usually directly and to the point. He enjoyed being with people of all kinds . . . she was happiest with friends and close members of her family." Yet, as her granddaughter Mary Jo Clasby put it, "her shyness did not make her a doormat; on the contrary, to those whom she allowed into her life, she showed herself to be a very strong-willed, even formidable person."

If Josie had been an experienced coquette, she could not, in those early days, have proceeded more winningly than by her shyness and by the sense of distance she invariably created. For in this Victorian age, the ideal woman stood upon an unreachable pedestal, blending silence and sympathy, shyness and reserve.

And beyond this generalized Victorian ideal lay the particular picture that Catholic ideology painted of young womanhood. "Politeness with proper and modest reserve should be the constant rule," girls were told by *Donahoe's*, a popular Catholic monthly, "affection and familiarity are out of the question. For a young woman to make one of the other sex her friend or familiar companion . . . is a thing which should be unheard of." As for flirting, *Donahoe's* went on, "the act is not very different from that of an abandoned woman. A girl who flirts seems to be lost to all sense of decency, almost as much so as [those] who shamelessly walk at night up and down the avenues in the hope of attracting attention."

So it was that with her shy demeanor, beautiful face and slender figure, Josie Hannon must have looked just the way John Fitzgerald had always wanted a girl to look; and, as he later told his daughter Rose, the perfection of her mother's image created the power of their romance. No matter what he later discovered in her nature, he could never undo the impact of that first impression.

In the months following their initial meeting, a relationship slowly developed between Fitzgerald and Josie. Years later, niece Geraldine Hannon was told, "After Uncle Johnny's mother died, his father brought the boys out to the Hannon farm more often. Grandmother Hannon was a wonderful cook and Thomas no doubt realized the importance of a female influence on his nine motherless boys. And Thomas had always loved the country. Remembering his own childhood in Bruff, he wanted his boys to grow up with a knowledge of country life."

Most Irish immigrants, trapped by the web of survival in the slums of the city, had neither the means, the access nor the leisure time to rediscover the joys of country life. For better or worse, the city was now their permanent and only home. When psychologist C. Stanley Hall tested a sample of Irish children in Boston in 1891, he found their ignorance of nature shocking: "Butter was said to come from buttercups, meat to be dug from the ground and potatoes picked from trees." Over half of the children entering Boston's primary schools had never seen a plow or a spade, a robin or a squirrel, the woods or the country. Six out of ten had never been bathing and nine out of ten were unable to distinguish an elm tree from an oak or a willow.

Thus Thomas' regular trips to Acton assured his sons a wider experience than that enjoyed by most of their neighbors on Hanover Street. "Compared to Boston," niece Geraldine Hannon said, "Acton then was like Tom Sawyer and Huck Finn. There was a local woman who smoked a pipe and served as a voluntary undertaker. When anyone died she would take the front door off and use it as a board to lay the dead person on and then stay with the corpse in the parlor until the funeral took place. All the local people helped each other out. There was a big rock up on the hill where Michael Hannon put his cows to pasture. That was where all the farmers met to talk and find out what was going on and who needed what."

That the community spirit of the small town was still strong enough to encompass most of its residents is reflected in the annual reports for the town of Acton, where the section "Support of the Poor" reads as if it had been written in a much earlier and simpler age, especially when it is compared to the complex, already bureaucratic reports of the "overseers for the poor" written in Boston at the same time. In 1868, for example, the entire sum paid out by town funds for support of the poor totaled only $157.49 and read as follows: "For medical expenses and supplies for Mrs. Murphy $13.50; coffin and robe for child $10.00; for assistance rendered travellers $5.75; for support and burial Asa Oliver $48.32; for George Robbins at reform school $13.00." In that same year the support of the poor in Boston totaled over $70,000 and encompassed ten different agencies.

Fitzgerald was a student at Boston Latin in the early years of their courtship; Josie, after finishing grammar school in her fifteenth year, had become a seamstress in a local dress factory. Over time, the wellsprings of her character, so different from his, must have seemed less mysterious to him, though it is doubtful whether he understood then the depth of her reserve or that he ever contemplated the possibility that beneath her shyness lay a deeper chill, a permanent shadow brought on by the troubled course of her early life.

Josie, the sixth of nine children, was born in Acton on October 31, 1865, when her mother was thirty-one and her father thirty-three. Before she was born the Hannons had seen their eldest son, John, born a year after their marriage in 1854, die at the age of six from "inflammation of the lungs." Then, while Josie was being carried in her mother's womb, at the end of the second month of pregnancy, the next oldest son, Edmond, died just before his sixth birthday of "brain fever," the term commonly used at the time for a high temperature. Still left when Josie was born were Ellen, aged nine, Michael, five, and James, two.

As we have seen, this pattern of repeated bereavements was also experienced in the Fitzgerald family in the death of their firstborn son and their two infant girls. But the Hannon family experienced death and bereavement beyond the average and through causes more individual and harder to accept than childhood disease.

When Josie was two, a third daughter, Emily, was born and two years after that a fourth daughter, Elizabeth, a pretty little girl with dark ringlets and dark eyes, who was called Lizzie and who became Josie's favorite sister. Behind the Hannon house, down the hill, was a small pond where Lizzie was told never to go unless accompanied by an adult. But.on a sunny afternoon in early December 1873, when she was nearly four, she eluded eight-year-old Josie's watch and, with her best friend, who lived nearby, walked down to the edge of the pond. In the warmth of the winter sun, the ice on the pond was breaking up and, as the family later reconstructed the scene, the large chunks of ice floating on the surface caught the attention of the two little girls. As they drew nearer the edge, their clothing got caught in the bushes that grew on the side of the pond, and when they tried to extricate themselves they pushed themselves farther and farther into the cracking ice. By the time Josie realized that Lizzie was missing and her father ran down to the pond, the two little girls were fully submerged in the water. When he pulled them out, neither one was alive.

"This was something the family never got over," said Mary Heffernan, daughter of the oldest Hannon girl, Ellen. "My mother often spoke of it. It had been so simple and so quick, she used to say. No one could believe it. My mother was still haunted years later by the image of her father, half mad with shock and grief, carrying the two little girls in his arms to the little playmate's house. Her parents were one of the three or four Catholic families in all of Acton and the two families had spent much time together. It must have been unbearable for him to face not only the loss of his own daughter but the responsibility for the death of the daughter of his closest friend as well."

Four years later, when Josie was twelve, the last child, a son, was born to her parents. He was named John Edmond after his two dead brothers and grew up fearing that his name had brought a curse upon him, a fear that was sadly realized when he had barely reached his teens. The story is told by his daughter Geraldine: "When he was thirteen he walked his mother to the train station one morning before going to school. She was going into Boston for the day. He had high laced shoes on, and his foot got caught in the track. The train was pulling in right then and he had time only to get his body out of the way, which saved his life but mangled his leg. He had two operations on his leg, both without ether. When the first one didn't work and it looked like he might die, they cut his leg below the knee." Despite his heavy artificial leg, John Edmond would live out a full life, eventually marrying and producing children, the only one of the Hannon boys to survive into manhood.

A different and more fatal curse fell upon the two older sons, Michael and Jimmy. In the autumn of 1881, three years after Fitzgerald had first met Josie and joined her brothers in picking apples from their father's orchard, Michael Hannon, Jr. died. On his death certificate the cause is given as "congestion of the lungs," but the family history records the real cause as alcoholism. "It's the curse of the Irish," Mary Heffernan said, "always has been and always will be."

The family history suggests that alcohol wreaked its vengeance on Jimmy Hannon as well, weakening his constitution to the point where the consumption he contracted in the winter of 1888 proved fatal. The issue of the local paper for the week of April 26, 1889, recorded simply: "James Hannon, who has been sick with consumption for the past winter, died on Saturday last and was buried from his late home on Monday. He was 25 years of age and was born in this village and has always lived here. He was at one time employed on the Fitchburg road."

So it happened that five out of the nine Hannon children died, leaving only three girls and a crippled boy. It is of course impossible now to know in detail the impact of these tragedies on the innermost dimensions of the Hannons' family life, but we can imagine that, particularly with the three later deaths, the family had to deal not only with the losses themselves but with a complex web of guilt and self-reproach—with the fear that they had somehow contributed to the deaths by failing to provide the proper physical care and emotional support.

Nor is it possible to trace the particular impact of the family's losses on each individual child, though later accounts suggest that over the three living girls there hung forever a pall of sorrow and withdrawal. Maurice Heffernan, an easy, outgoing man, who married Ellen, the oldest girl, when she was twenty-nine, used to tell his children, "I married your mother just in time or she'd have been like the rest of them." And Emily, the youngest surviving girl, never married. "She had a boyfriend," her niece Mary Heffernan said, "whom she loved very much. His name was Jack Connors. But he drank too much and she was too afraid, so she never married. Through her twenties and thirties, until her parents died, she stayed at home. I remember she planted a beautiful old-fashioned garden in front of the house, with sturgis, sweet pea and rose bushes all fenced in with chicken wire. And on Saturdays when her father would come back from the railroad, blackened with soot, she would bathe his face and brush his hair."

Into this home, darkened by the shadows of death, John Fitzgerald brought energy, sunshine and finally, for Josie, escape. "I can see how John F. must have impressed Josie," niece Geraldine Hannon said. "He was a great character, a diamond in the rough, a man of such incomparable force. And he was always cheerful. It is probable that Josie had never met anyone so entertaining and so confident in himself as John F. was. Even for us, years later, it was high adventure whenever he came to visit. He'd pile us all in his car—which wasn't really his, for each visit he'd have a different car on loan. Evidently he told a different dealer each time that he was interested in that car and wanted to try it for a day. Then, after making us all stuff old newspapers into our coats to keep us from getting cold, he'd tell his chauffeur to take it up to sixty miles an hour so we could feel the wind in the open car. Then he'd whisk us out into the woods to get these fuzzy, soft mullen leaves which he'd use to bring color to his cheeks. And all the while he was talking, talking to anyone and everyone."

"She could not help being intrigued by him," Josie's daughter Rose suggested. "It was a clear case of opposites attracting. His vigor, charm and sheer joy in living were contagious. I can just imagine him walking into that house and within five minutes having them all smiling and active."

For his part, Fitzgerald interpreted Josie's reserve as a personal challenge. Had she been warmer from the start it is possible he would have lost interest in her. But as it was, her temperamental coolness kept Fitzgerald coming back to her year after year even though in many ways they were not well-suited as a couple.

More than his visits to her house Josie enjoyed the time they spent together away from Acton. There was something proud in Josie, something almost haughty, which would always keep her from enjoying the simple country life in Acton because of the lowly position the Hannons occupied on the social and economic ladder.

Poverty, like riches, is always comparative. And though the Hannons owned their own home, made their own clothes and could always feed themselves from the proceeds of the farm, they were nevertheless among the poorest residents in the town. In a valuation of real and personal estate in 1872, Michael Hannon's entire property was listed as consisting of his house, valued at $150, three quarters of an acre of land worth $50 an acre, and two swine. By the next valuation, in 1889, his renovated house was worth $650, a barn $325, and his land, now four and a half acres, $550. By then his personal property had also increased to include a horse worth $50, a cow worth $20 and a yearling worth $15, but the total worth of his estate was only $1,525, lower than that of the average Acton resident and considerably lower than the $18,000 left in Thomas Fitzgerald's estate at the time of his death four years before.

Though the difficulties in being poor were less imposing in rural areas than in the city, there is some evidence that the psychological effect of being a little worse off than most of her neighbors and friends affected Josie Hannon negatively, just as John Fitzgerald drew positive strength from being a little better off than most of his circle.

"There was always a great pride and sense of grandeur in the Hannon women," Geraldine Hannon said. "Even Grandmother Hannon, with the little money they had, insisted on going to Jordan Marsh for her clothes instead of to the country store of Tuttle, Jones and Wetherbee where almost everyone else in the town bought their clothes"—along with their hemp carpets, spring beds, Alaska refrigerators, and ice chests. "Grandmother insisted on style even if it meant having only a couple of dresses, one for morning wear and one for afternoon. I was told she would never leave her room in the morning without a high lace jabot on. All the girls inherited this pride; Josie had the most of all."

Throughout her life Josie took pains to cultivate her appearance. She was fond of fine clothes and jewelry, and with her instinctive taste she enjoyed the consciousness of making an impression. "Even in her eighties and nineties," granddaughter Marian Fitzgerald Mullen recalled, "she looked when she came out of her room as if she had just stepped out of Bonwit Teller's. For years she used tape on her face to ward off the wrinkles, and until the very end she kept her hair jet black."

Visiting Fitzgerald in Boston, Josie shared in a manner of life larger and more plentiful than her own. Regis Fitzgerald Murphy, daughter of John F.'s younger brother Michael, remembers her father's accounts of Josie's visits to the Hanover Street house where eight of the boys and their father continued to live after their mother's death: "Whenever Josie was coming, the neighbors would know because there'd always be a big bustle inside—the sound of the boys cleaning up the place—and the stairs were newly carpeted. It was John F.'s doing, of course. And John F. would bring a relative down to play the piano in the parlor for Josie. She would play 'Rock-a-Bye Baby' and John F. would sit beside Josie, proud as a peacock."

And on each of these visits Fitzgerald would give Josie a present, usually an article of clothing or a piece of jewelry which he picked out himself. Priding himself on his taste and always generous with the money he had, he enjoyed nothing more than the knowledge that through him this beautiful somber young girl was beginning to bloom and flower afresh. "He was enchanted with her and so proud of her beauty and her great refinement," Rose Kennedy recalled. "She loved the theater, and he told me he enjoyed nothing better than taking her there when they were courting, so he could watch the impression she made as she walked in on his arm, her head held high and her carriage erect."

In the middle of the 1880s, Fitzgerald's future was still uncertain. His job as a customs clerk provided a regular income, but it was likely to come to an end with a change of administration, and where he would go from there was not yet known. But Josie was in a situation which gave a value to any change—so strong was her desire to leave Acton and the past behind her.

In contrast to her somewhat sad associations with Acton, the neighboring town of Concord had captivated Josie from the first time she had seen it as a little girl, so much so that whenever Johnny visited she asked him to take her there. Concord was indeed an enchanting town in the 1880s: rich in wildflowers and meadow grasses, in philosophy and literature, in art and nature. "Concord has a winsome loveliness," a visitor wrote in 1884. "The quiet saunterer finds no end of choice bits to please the eye about this delightful village. First the famous houses, then the Revolutionary houses, and, at last, the quiet glimpses of country and river scattered about the old town."

Both Josie and Fitzgerald were great walkers, and Josie long remembered the romance of breezy, springlike afternoons when they explored together the old North Bridge and the Wright Tavern, the homes of Emerson, Thoreau, Hawthorne and Alcott, the monuments at Sleepy Hollow Cemetery and the banks of the Concord and Sudbury Rivers. The rich historic associations brought forth Fitzgerald's inexhaustible stock of knowledge and anecdotes. Everywhere they went, she later recalled, he talked as knowledgeably as a trained guide, and she marveled at his buoyant energy, his immense curiosity and his vivid descriptions.

At the old North Bridge, where the first battle of the Revolution was fought on the nineteenth of April, 1775, he recited from memory—in a ritual that he would repeat for his daughter Rose and she in turn would practice on her children—the words of Ralph Waldo Emerson inscribed on the bronze statue representing a Minuteman in the act of discharging his gun across the river into the ranks of the British soldiers: "By the rude bridge that arched the flood / Their flags to April's breeze unfurled / There once the embattled farmers stood / And fired the shot heard round the world."

Then as they walked to the other side of the river, the spot where the first two British soldiers fell and were buried, he reminded Josie that it was the British who had fired the first shots, wounding three and killing two, before Major Buttrick of Concord finally gave the order, "Fire, fellow soldiers, for God's sake, fire," that began the war for American independence.

A short distance from the battleground, approached by an avenue of black ash trees, stood the "Old Manse," originally the home of Emerson's grandfather and later the honeymoon cottage for Sophia and Nathaniel Hawthorne, where Hawthorne wrote *Mosses from an Old Manse*.

Having read A *Wonder-Book* and *Tanglewood Tales* at the Latin School, Fitzgerald spoke with familiarity of Hawthorne's works, and Josie, in her quieter way, could not help but share his excitement in seeing this silvery old house, with its dormer windows and battered gambrel roof, steeped in the magic of Hawthorne's imagination.

One doubts that Josie spoke a great deal during these historical and literary discourses. For one thing, she had probably never been encouraged much, by her family or society, to express her thoughts on history or literature. "The girl who knows everything," wrote the editors of *Donahoe's* in October 1890, "makes herself obnoxious by flaunting recently acquired knowledge . . . young men dread her; old ones have the utmost contempt for her . . . she is losing her womanliness."

Nor had the Acton school system given her the high-quality education that John Fitzgerald had received at the Boston Latin School. Though she and her sisters were listed each year on the honor roll for perfect attendance at both South Acton Primary and South Acton Grammar, the town reports suggest a school system concerned more with absenteeism and with discipline than with the subject matter taught. "That there has been an evident lack of efficient discipline in some of our schools, we will not deny," concluded the school report for 1870–71. "Neither will we admit the Teachers are wholly to blame." (All the teachers were female, remembered by Josie's older sister Ellen as "all rather sour," but the school committee decided that "to make out the extra money required for employment of a male teacher . . . we would be obliged to shorten our winter terms which are now too short.") And in 1876 a separate heading was allocated for absenteeism: "This evil is becoming more and more prevalent in our schools and we have no remedy."

But Fitzgerald's knowledge had a fertilizing quality, and the stories he told Josie made a deep impression upon her. So much so that thirty years later she was able to repeat them to her daughter Rose. "When we lived in Concord," Rose recalled, "my mother took me to the beautiful Sleepy Hollow Cemetery, where, on a steep knoll overlooking the valley, the graves of Emerson, Thoreau, Hawthorne and the Alcotts lay together in a cluster, and she still remembered my father pointing out to her that in death as in life only a narrow path separated these four literary families."

Besides its historic associations and its literary heritage, Concord had a slow, lovely, winding river on which, Josie later recalled, "we spent many a romantic afternoon, canoeing up and down among the water lilies, waiting to find the most perfect picnic spot."

Slowly their intimacy ripened. They took long horseback rides together over the country hills, and Johnny discovered that on horseback

Josie proved herself—in spirit and in skill—more than his equal. "My mother loved riding and excelled at it," Rose Kennedy recorded in her memoirs. "One of my most vivid memories is of her riding sidesaddle at a gallop . . . [the horse's] mane and tail flying, and her own long thick, lustrous dark-brown, nearly black hair—fallen loose from the hairpins —streaming behind her. She was magnificent and it seemed to me perfectly beautiful . . . My father was enchanted with her and very proud of her. When both were old, and someone asked him to look back and name the happiest day of his life, he said, 'When I got the girl I wanted, Mary Josephine Hannon.' "

It is not certain when John Fitzgerald proposed to Josie, but family memories suggest it was sometime in 1887, more than two years before the marriage actually took place. The stumbling block was the opposition of Josie's parents to the idea of her marrying her second cousin. The common ancestor from whom both Josie and Johnny descended was a great-grandfather named James Fitzgerald. James Fitzgerald had two sons: Edmond, who married Mary Linnehan and produced a daughter, Mary Anne Fitzgerald, Josie's mother; and Michael, who married Ellen Wilmouth and produced a son, Thomas Fitzgerald, Fitzgerald's father.

According to the official canon law of the Catholic Church at the time, second cousins fell within the third degree of consanguinity, which meant, as Catholic couples were told in the marriage manuals, that a dispensation was required, and such dispensations were "not mere matters of form . . . they will not be given unless there are grave reasons for doing so," and "a tax for some charitable object must be given when obtaining a dispensation."

Despite this hoary rhetoric, the process of receiving a dispensation in the case of second cousins should have been fairly routine. It was a matter of taking the application—which consisted of a genealogical chart demonstrating the degree of closeness of the relationship—to the local parish priest, who would then apply for the dispensation from the chancery, in this case from Archbishop Williams in Boston. Once it was granted, a notation would be made in the archdiocese book and a copy sent to the priest of the parish where the marriage was to take place.

Why, then, in John Fitzgerald's case, did it take so long? The best guess is that the real impediment was not the Church itself, but the Hannon family, who, in trying to persuade Josie not to marry John, may have had the local priests on their side.

This conclusion is supported by a story niece Mary Hannon Heffernan remembers hearing, that "each week when John F. would visit, he would bring a letter from a different priest in his own parish suggesting that his marriage to Josie would be legitimate in the eyes of the Church, but still the family remained opposed. For more than canon law was at stake. Their real fear was that by marrying within the family Josie would produce retarded and weak children."

There was no way for Fitzgerald to allay this fear, but over time his persistence, steadiness and inexhaustible energy simply wore Josie's parents down. Once the Hannons agreed to the marriage, there still remained the need to secure an official dispensation, which was granted on the seventh of September, 1889. In an official red leather book with gold tooling which sits in the archdiocese library, there is the following entry: "Marriage impediment. Consanguinity in 3rd degree. John Fitzgerald and Mary Hannon. Rev. McCall in Concord. Donation $1.00."

After eleven years of waiting, John Fitzgerald refused to wait any longer. The wedding was set for September 18, 1889, at St. Bernard's Catholic Church in Concord. Due to the shortness of notice and to the fact that the Hannon family was still in official mourning for the death of Josie's brother Jimmy the previous April, the family decided to keep the wedding small and simple.

The only description we have of the wedding itself comes from a news item in the *Concord Enterprise*:

> The marriage of Miss Mary Hannon . . . and Mr. J. F. Fitzgerald, president of the Neptune Associates of Boston, was solemnized in Concord on Thursday last. The wedding party was confined to the relatives and intimate friends on account of a recent death in the bride's family. Elegant wedding gifts were presented by Mr. Fitzgerald's associates in the Customs House, from the Neptune society and classmates in the Boston Latin School. The bridal party left immediately after the ceremony for an extended tour of the White Mountains.

After the honeymoon, Fitzgerald took Josie back to his family's home at 465 Hanover Street, where six of his brothers still lived. It is easy to imagine the difficulties the new bride must have experienced as she settled into married life in these cramped, crowded quarters, trying to adjust not only to the habits of an energetic husband but to the comings and goings of his brothers as well. Whereas John Fitzgerald flourished in continual social contact, so that the dormitorylike conditions of Hanover Street imposed little hardship on him, it was harder for a sensitive girl like Josie who valued solitude and privacy and could not find it. At least on the farm, solitude could always be found in the hills or on the country roads.

There was another adjustment, even more difficult, that Josie would be called upon to make. In the happy days of their courtship, as she later told her daughter Rose, "she always had her Johnny to herself." In their long walks and on their picnics, she knew she was the center of his energy, and the knowledge warmed her like the sun. "John Fitzgerald always had this amazing quality to make you feel special when you were with him," Mary Jo Clasby remembered. "Each of us grandchildren felt when we were with him that he or she was *the* most special person in his life. I thought about it later and I came to understand that when he put me on a train to go back to Lowell after I had spent a wonderful, magical day with him in Boston, he probably never thought about me again until I saw him the next time, but no one could have made me realize that at the time."

"It was not easy for a woman like Josie to live with a magnetic figure like John F.," recalled his grandniece Rose Ellis. "When she saw him turn his fantastic warmth beyond her to his brothers and their families, or to his colleagues and his friends, she felt terribly jealous. If only she had realized that he had enough love and feeling to encompass all the world with his left hand while he still had her in his right hand, she could have been happy. But she wanted him all to herself—and that was the one thing he could never give her."

Two months after their honeymoon, Josie learned she was pregnant and the exultant father-to-be decided it was time for them to move into a place of their own. Three years earlier the Fitzgerald family had purchased a building at 4 Garden Court Street, and it was to this three-story red brick house standing directly across from the site of what had once been Governor Hutchinson's mansion that Fitzgerald now moved his pregnant wife.

July 22, 1890, dawned hot and steamy. By midmorning the temperature had already reached 89 degrees, and it would climb to 95 by the late afternoon when Josie began her contractions. "All along John F. kept saying it was going to be a girl," recalled Geraldine Hannon. "He was so sure of this it almost seemed as if he willed it. Unlike most men, who long for a son, he wanted a little girl so much—perhaps because his own household had been without a female since the death of his mother and little sister more than ten years before. And he probably figured his words would make it happen."

Later that night, Fitzgerald's wish came true. A little girl was born, healthy and strong, with her mother's clear white skin, dark hair and finely chiseled face. It is said that John Fitzgerald was so excited that he ran up and down the streets of the North End, knocking on his neighbors' doors to tell them the happy news.

She was named Rose Elizabeth in memory of her grandmother, Rosanna Cox Fitzgerald, and her mother's little sister, Elizabeth Hannon, but from the first time her father held her in his arms she was *his* little girl; his love for her, he later told a friend, was greater than any feeling he had ever known. For in the clear, trusting expression on her face and the bright curious way her blue eyes looked out upon the world, he could see his beautiful Josie as she too might have been had not the sorrows of her childhood taken a toll which he now realized was permanent. But with little Rosie, as he called her, he had the chance to love again, and into her he poured all his magnificent hopes and enthusiasms and all his remarkable vitality.

# CHAPTER 7
# THE
# BOY
# POLITICIAN

With the birth of his first child, Fitzgerald decided the time had come to make his first move into elective politics. Having left the Customs House to set himself up in the insurance business with his brother Henry, a business which benefited greatly from his many contacts, he was in a position to take the time to run for political office. For his initial foray, he chose to stand for the Common Council, the lowest branch of the city government, a body of seventy-five men, elected three each by twenty-five wards.

With Keany's backing, Fitzgerald's name appeared on the chosen slate of three for Ward 6 and his victory was assured. But even Keany was surprised when the mid-December returns revealed that his young apprentice had topped the list, gathering more votes than either of his fellow victors: Charles Carroll, a dealer in secondhand building materials, and Neil Doherty, a liquor dealer.

A striking portrait of the rough-and-tumble Council is provided in the diary of Beatrice Webb, the British socialist, who visited Boston in the 1890s.

The Council was the lowest depth in representative bodies that we have yet explored. Its powers are limited practically to concurring with the

Aldermen in voting the appropriations. It has no patronage, and was until lately not paid. The members then gave themselves carriage-rides and dinners, so now they get £60 a year ($300) in lieu . . . half the members were youths between 20 and 35, striplings describing themselves as law students, medical students, clerks, telegraphists, stenographers, with half a dozen bartenders and billiard markers. . . . There were two young ne- groes (law students), two Russian Jews (very sensible men, small dealers) and about thirty Irish—three different Donovans for instance. There were car-drivers, hackmen, labourers and mechanics; a few little grocers, a peddler or two—the whole forming the queerest debating society kind of legislative body I ever saw. But the council had a beauté de diable—these young men with the cleanest of collars and cuffs and nice jacket suits, had a distinctly more pleasing appearance than the flashy, overfed dissipated ward politicians of the New York and Philadelphia Councils.

Undaunted by the Council's lowly reputation, Fitzgerald used the Thursday-night sessions as a personal platform to argue for the creation of a public park in the North End. In an era when public services on behalf of the poor were not yet considered legitimate functions of gov- ernment, it was not an easy crusade, and Fitzgerald ran into substantial opposition from Council members who lived in the better parts of the city. But, powered as he was by the memories of his childhood, Fitzger- ald never gave up, and his many speeches on the subject showed the oratorical flair that would later carry him to higher office.

"The North End contains thirty-five thousand people and is congested as no other part of the city is congested," Fitzgerald argued, "yet not one dollar has ever been appropriated by the city of Boston for a breath- ing space or a park. . . . It is well enough," he continued, poking fun at a councilman from a wealthy neighborhood, "for Mr. Quinn, under the quiet influence of the Rose of Sharon on a summer afternoon, basking beneath the trees, and swinging in a hammock, as I can see him in imagination," to ask that this money not be appropriated, but the chil- dren who were dying in the North End in the summertime from all kinds of contagious diseases needed "a chance to get a breath of God's pure, fresh air."

The more he spoke, the more votes Fitzgerald gathered, and after two months, during which he never let up, the Council finally authorized $350,000 for the creation of the North End Park on Commercial Street. It was a triumphant moment, a happy blending of his past with his present that he would cherish for the rest of his life.

While Fitzgerald was making a name for himself in the Common Council, Matthew Keany was taken down with a fatal case of pneu- monia. Even as the old boss lay ill in his bed, all the political leaders in Ward 6 began making plans, jockeying to determine who would inherit the kingdom Keany was leaving behind. For young Fitzgerald, this was a difficult time. The loss of the bushy-haired Keany was the loss of a second father, a kindly mentor who, more than any other man, had guided his political career. Yet ambition compelled him, even as he spent his days at Keany's bedside, to spend his nights gathering friends and allies in a quest to take over the leadership of the ward himself. Keany died on February 27, 1892, "the saddest day of my life," Fitzgerald later described it, "next to the death of my parents."

Responding once again to his grief with energetic action, Fitzgerald took it upon himself to take charge of the funeral arrangements, naming the pallbearers and the honorary pallbearers, organizing the seating in the church and the line of procession to Calvary Cemetery. The ceremony itself, held at St. Stephen's, was a grand affair. "Never," *The Republic* observed, "was such an imposing scene known in the North End. All classes paid homage to the dead. The clergy, state officials, city dignitaries, the poor and the orphan mingled their tears at the bier of one they had known and loved."

In the confusion of the weeks following Keany's death, Fitzgerald accomplished the remarkable transition from young protégé to new boss of the North End. How this came about remained a mystery at the time. "Fitzgerald is as different from Keany as creme de menthe is from New England rum," a reporter observed. "He is in a class by himself . . . a blend of audacity, vigor, force and perseverance." Having just passed his twenty-ninth birthday, he was viewed as a boy by some of the old-timers, but, with favored access to all the index cards and secret lists that Keany had kept in his safe for decades, he knew exactly whom to approach for support and how best to make that approach in a district that was changing its complexion year by year.

Throughout the 1880s Fitzgerald had witnessed the gradual movement of his fellow North Enders to better homes and neighborhoods in the surrounding areas of Dorchester, Charlestown and South Boston. In these same years the North End was becoming home to a large contingent of Italian immigrants from southern Italy and to thousands of Russian Jews, gathered together in a triangular section along Hanover Street, Endicott Street and Prince Street. Recognizing these shifts before he died, Keany had instructed Fitzgerald both to begin forging contacts with these newer groups and to make certain that as each loyal Irishman departed he understood that his name would remain on the voting lists forever, to be activated by a simple trip to "the dear old North End" on election day.

When Keany died, Fitzgerald was arguably the only man who could hold the machine together, the only bridge between the old politics of the seventies and eighties and the new politics of the nineties. And if this was not strictly true, surely no one else in the district possessed his remarkable energy, his supreme confidence in himself and his powers of articulation. Nor, it seems, did any rival possess his instinct for the exercise of power—an instinct which, combined with his short, stocky, handsome appearance, would soon bring journalists to depict him as the Little Napoleon of Ward 6.

As the newly constituted boss of the old North End, Fitzgerald lost no time in nominating himself for higher office, boldly choosing to skip both the Board of Aldermen and the state House of Representatives to stand for a seat in the thirty-five-member state Senate. Had Keany still been alive, Fitzgerald later admitted, he would probably never have taken such a risk, for Keany was a cautious man who wanted Fitzgerald to build his power step by step. But in the absence of Keany's restraining hand Fitzgerald's audacity triumphed. Gathering together the members of his newly formed organization, which he called the Jefferson Club, Fitzgerald announced that he intended to run for the state Senate against George McGahey, who was then in power in the neighboring Ward 7. Under ordinary circumstances, his move would have brought certain defeat, for, even though he could be assured of Ward 6's support to balance McGahey's support in Ward 7, Martin Lomasney's Ward 8 was also included in the senatorial district and at this point Fitzgerald had not even met the powerful boss of the West End.

Recognizing the importance of Lomasney's support, Fitzgerald decided to visit "the Mahatma," as Lomasney was called, in the latter's headquarters on Causeway Street in the West End. Later Fitzgerald described this first meeting in vivid detail, recalling the powerful presence Lomasney projected as he sat in his chair surrounded by a half-dozen loyal aides. A thickset, well-muscled man whose most outstanding feature was a hard rocklike jaw that made him a cartoonist's friend, Lomasney was a bachelor whose entire life was given to the building of his political machine, the Hendricks Club. He lived a simple, low-key life, renting a small apartment and wearing the same old battered straw hat year round, but to the people of the West End he was a god. Arriving early each morning at his headquarters, Lomasney worked 365 days a year, caring for "his" people in all phases of their lives, relieving thousands, as he liked to put it, of "the inquisitorial terrors of organized charity."

Behind his gold-rimmed spectacles, Lomasney's piercing gray-blue eyes must have seen in young Fitzgerald the towering ambition that would eventually bring the two of them into bitter conflict, giving Lomasney, as he himself later put it, "more sleepless nights than any other individual." But at this first meeting Fitzgerald greatly impressed Lomasney as "a pink-cheeked youngster" with a remarkable personality. So much so, Fitzgerald liked to believe, that when the talk turned to the senatorial race Lomasney agreed to lend his invaluable support. But, unbeknown to Fitzgerald, his character traits were not the issue; for, as it happened, Lomasney was carrying a personal grudge against McGahey stemming from a convention in 1890 when McGahey voted against Lomasney's closest friend, Ned Donovan. Now, with this race two years later, Lomasney had found his revenge. When the election took place in the fall of 1892, Fitzgerald became one of the youngest senators on Beacon Hill.

These were turbulent years at the State House, years which saw Massachusetts take the lead in shaping progressive legislation to respond to all manner of social evils brought about by the Industrial Revolution. "The United States in the eighties and nineties was trembling between two worlds," the historian Arthur Meier Schlesinger has written, "one rural and agricultural, the other urban and industrial. In this span of years the fateful decision was made." But as the country became a nation of cities, there rose a whole new range of social problems which legislatures all across the country were just beginning to grapple with. During his years as a state senator, Fitzgerald voted with the progressives on a wide range of bills relating to the rights of the working people, including bills to provide minimum wages for manual labor ("compensation for said day's work shall be, in no case, less than two dollars"); maximum hours for women and children in manufacturing establishments; and regulation of the industrial evils classed under the title of the "sweating system," whereby clothing was manufactured in filthy and disease-infected tenements which implied the continuous oppression of the workers by the employers.

During his second term at the State House, Fitzgerald began to emerge as a major figure in the local press. Describing him as "the most called for man at the state-house," the Boston Daily Advertiser wrote a series of glowing articles about the young Senator. "Is Senator Fitzgerald here? is a question that the Senate doorkeeper has to answer all day long while his messengers jocosely suggest that he ought to wear a bell which will make his whereabouts known anywhere in the building. He possesses the reputation of looking after the personal welfare and interest of his constituents very industriously."

In 1894, the first nine wards of Boston—stretching from East Boston and Charlestown to the North and West Ends, plus parts of the South End, Winthrop and downtown Boston—formed the only solidly Democratic congressional district in the state of Massachusetts. From his position as the leader of the populous Ward 6, Fitzgerald decided in the fall of 1894 to make a run for the House seat in the Ninth Congressional District, the same district from which his grandson would launch his political career half a century later.

It would be an uphill battle all the way, for the incumbent Congressman was Joseph O'Neil, a leading light in city boss P. J. Maguire's galaxy of Irish politicians who could bridge the gap between the Irish in the slums and the Yankee reformers on Beacon Hill. For three terms, O'Neil had served his district well, proving himself both an effective errand boy for Boston businessmen and a rich source of patronage for the local bosses. Having prospered substantially over the years, the self-made O'Neil had little sympathy for the radicalism many Irish laborers had absorbed from the Knights of Labor in the eighties; from his vantage, the moderate reform programs of Yankee Democrat Mayor Nathan Matthews seemed the safer route.

The year 1894, however, was not one for moderate solutions. In the wake of the Wall Street panic of 1893, a serious economic depression had set in all across the country, marked by a series of railroad and bank failures, the closing of factories and mills, hundreds of commercial failures and a severe drop in prices. In Massachusetts, the number of jobless grew steadily, reaching the point where one out of four workers was unemployed. In city after city in the state, large numbers of destitute men were appearing at police stations, seeking some place to sleep. As winter set in, the tensions deepened, and on February 20, 1894, Beacon Hill went through, according to the *Post*, "what it had never gone through before." Five thousand unemployed men and their sympathizers invaded the State House, demanding that public bodies "allay the starvation" caused by the widespread unemployment.

With his city in turmoil, Mayor Matthews devoted a major address to the depression, but his narrow definition of reform allowed him simply to repeat the hackneyed call for the generosity and public spirit of the citizenry. Under the stress of the crisis, Maguire's coalition of cooperation, forged by self-made politicians like O'Neil from their soft perches on the ladder of success, lost its logic and appeal.

Claiming to represent the poor and downtrodden against the established leaders who had broken their ties with the slums, Fitzgerald stepped in at just the right moment. Hailed as "the boy candidate," Fitzgerald canvassed every ward, appealing to the voters to "give youth a chance." Night after night, he took his message of hope to the streets, accompanied everywhere he went by a loyal cadre of friends bearing cannon crackers and torches, roman candles and horns which turned his arrival at every corner into a triumphal parade. "If noise, fireworks, red lights, bands and banners and a huge overflow of enthusiasm . . . are any indications," the *Advertiser* predicted, "young Mr. Fitzgerald certainly has some foundation for his extremely sanguine hopes of success." In contrast, O'Neil ran a more dignified and formal campaign, without screaming supporters or pyrotechnic displays.

Yet, for all his derring-do, Fitzgerald never could have succeeded had it not been, once again, for the support of Martin Lomasney. At a time when nominations were still made by caucuses, the power of the local bosses was supreme, and, besides Maguire, O'Neil had the backing of three of the most powerful ward bosses in Boston—P. J. Kennedy of East Boston, Jim Donovan of the South End and Joseph Corbett of Charlestown. As it happened, this trio was then challenging Lomasney for control of the Democratic city machine. Lomasney viewed the congressional race as an opportunity to show his strength.

The caucuses in September of 1894 were the first ever held by Massachusetts Democrats at which the secret Australian system of balloting was used, and as a consequence there were scenes of turmoil and fighting in almost every ward. The polls opened at 4 o'clock and it was not until midnight that the boxes were closed and the work of counting began. All night large crowds filled the wardrooms as the votes were tallied on large sheets of white paper. By morning, the astonishing result was clear: John Fitzgerald had defeated Joe O'Neil to become the Democratic nominee for Congress.

Later that morning, having not slept even one hour the night before, Fitzgerald showed the mark of perseverance that would eventually carry him to his goal of becoming His Honor the Mayor. All through the campaign, he had been careful to say and do nothing that would give offense to the ward bosses who were backing O'Neil. On the contrary, he frankly confessed that, far from deprecating the support of the powerful bosses of East Boston, Charlestown and the South End, he regretted he could not have it for himself. Then, to prove his point, he set out on the morning of his victory to visit with each member of the opposing trio, P. J. Kennedy, Jim Donovan and Jim Corbett.

"Now that the fight is over, P. J., let's shake hands," Fitzgerald said during his early-morning visit to P. J. Kennedy's home in East Boston. And they did, but before Fitzgerald left he spotted P. J.'s sandy-haired blue-eyed son, who would have been six years old at the time. Responding to the child with his customary warmth, Fitzgerald lifted him up onto his lap and gave him a lollipop. If this is true, it is the first recorded meeting between John Fitzgerald and his four-year-old daughter's future husband, Joseph Patrick Kennedy.

Compared to the nomination fight, the general election was easy, but

Fitzgerald never let up. The baffling economic conditions had spawned a rash of strikes, which, in turn, had given birth to a nativist movement convinced that immigration was responsible for the industrial unrest and that the time had come for a general restriction on all new immigrants. Gathering strength in the Republican Party, the nativist movement developed a strong anti-Catholic tinge, culminating in the formation of the American Protective Association (APA), a secret organization whose members took an oath never to vote for a Catholic, never to employ one when a Protestant was available and never to go on strike with Catholics.

In the election campaign, Fitzgerald shrewdly linked the APA to the Republican Party and, by implication, to his Republican opponent, ex-Alderman Randolph Gore. In speech after speech he denounced the APA, demanding that Republicans come out of their hiding places and speak out like men to tell what they thought of the existence of "a secret society which was stabbing in the back a certain loyal class of citizens." These same men, Fitzgerald argued, might be good fellows on the street and they might go into hysterics at the tale of the indignities perpetrated in Samoa, yet "they have not uttered a single word in defense of the Roman Catholic people of the country."

Carrying the same theme into the Jewish neighborhoods of the North and West Ends, Fitzgerald implored the Jews to stand up against the APA. "I cannot see," he argued in a major address at Baldwin Hall, "how the Jewish people can remain quiet and observe the secret machinations against their fellow citizens. Unless you go forth on Tuesday and throttle this prospective monster, how do you know that the next step will not be against the Jew?"

It was an effective approach. On election day, November 6, 1894, Fitzgerald emerged as the new Congressman from the Ninth District. "Fitzgerald will carry a great responsibility on his young shoulders," the *Post* reported, "he will stand alone in the 54th Congress for the Democrats of Massachusetts."

In 1895, when Congressman Fitzgerald arrived in Washington D. C., the city was still Southern in atmosphere, with its leisurely pace, its tree-lined streets and its spacious parks and squares. "Compared with New York or Chicago," wrote an English visitor, "Washington, although it is full of commotion and energy, is a city of rest and peace. The inhabitants do not rush onward as though they were late for the train or the post. . . . It looks a sort of place where nobody has to work for his living or, at any rate, not hard."

Congress was in session only four or five months a year, with the sessions starting in December and ending in the spring before the unbearable summer heat set in. In the House of the 1890s members talked and laughed, frequently with their feet propped on desks above the ever present spittoons, in an atmosphere as relaxed as that of a hotel bar-room. Members transacted all business from their individually carved oak desks on the huge oblong floor arranged as an amphitheater, with seats and desks radiating from the Speaker's dais.

Like most of his fellow congressmen, Fitzgerald elected to live in a boardinghouse, leaving his family at home. Since Congress was in session only a few months a year, it made little sense to uproot wives and children from their homes and their schools, and as a consequence the Washington boardinghouse remained a central institution in the life of the town. For his part, Fitzgerald found a room at the Hotel Wellington, a small boardinghouse located near the Capitol at 1325 G Street, N.W. But no sooner had he arrived in Washington and selected his desk than he requested a leave of absence for ill health. As it happened, the young Congressman was suffering from tuberculosis and had been ordered by the doctors to spend the winter in the South to recover his health. During his prolonged stay in Asheville, North Carolina, Fitzgerald was joined by his new ally, P. J. Kennedy, and while the two were out horseback riding one day a picture was taken which remains in the family archives nearly a century later.

Returning to Washington in April of 1896, Fitzgerald made up for lost time with an eloquent speech on behalf of the Catholic Church in its operation of the contract school system for Indians. As one of only three Catholic congressmen in the 350-member House, Fitzgerald spoke out against what he perceived as a tide of anti-Catholicism on the part of his fellow congressmen, arguing that a conspiracy was under way to have the Indian children go uneducated and untaught just to make a stab against the Church, whose efficient operation of the schools had never been questioned.

In the months that followed, Fitzgerald spoke out on a number of local issues, including the expansion of the Boston port, the preservation of the frigate *Constitution*, and the extermination of the gypsy moth. On the national level, he supported the Democrats in their push for taxing incomes rather than levying higher duties on foreign products, and he became a leading spokesman in favor of continuing America's policy of unrestricted immigration.

In 1896, the movement to restrict immigration found its ideal spokesman in the person of Henry Cabot Lodge, the Republican Senator from Massachusetts. At the age of forty-six, Lodge was well on his way to becoming one of the most powerful figures in Washington. Having entered politics from Harvard University, where he had been a brilliant and rising young historian, Lodge personified the Yankee gentleman, the scholar-in-politics. Tall and slender, with a Vandyke beard and a serious demeanor, Lodge had served four terms in the House of Representatives before assuming the illustrious Senate seat of Webster and Sumner in 1893.

As a historian, Lodge had to admit that there once had been a time when America's policy of unrestricted immigration had exerted a positive influence upon the country. But to his mind the earlier immigrants, the British, the Irish, the Scandinavians and the Germans, represented a totally different and higher class of people from the massive hordes of Italians, Greeks, Hungarians, Poles, Bohemians and Rumanians who had been migrating to America in large numbers in the late eighties and early nineties. These "new immigrants," Lodge argued, these strange peoples from strange lands, had among them a high proportion of desperately poor and displaced persons who tended to concentrate in Eastern cities, aggravating problems of health, government and housing. Worse still, they represented a different "race," alien to the great Anglo-Saxon race which had founded and settled America.

If this immigration continued, Lodge argued in a major speech in the Senate in 1896,

> it involves, in a word, nothing less than the possibility of a great and perilous change in the very fabric of our race. . . . If a lower race mixes with a higher race in sufficient numbers history teaches us that the lower race will prevail. . . . In other words, there is a limit to the capacity of any race for assimilating and elevating an inferior race and when you begin to pour in in unlimited numbers people of alien or lower races of less social efficiency and less moral force you are running the most frightful risk that a people can run. The lowering of a great race means not only its decline, but that of civilization.

As his first move toward shutting out these undesirables, Lodge introduced a bill which required that all who sought entrance to America must know how to read or write in their own language. It was the perfect exclusionary device, aimed directly at the new immigrants from southern and eastern Europe, most of whom had never had an opportunity to learn to read or write.

Today, with the perspective of nearly a century behind us, it is obvious that the Italian, the Pole, and the Slav of the eighties and nineties were no more upsetting to the American character than the German of the eighteenth century or the Irishman of the nineteenth, or, for that matter, the Pilgrim and the Puritan of the seventeenth. On the contrary, without the influx of the new immigrants at the turn of the century, America would not have become the vital country it did. But in the nationalist nineties the danger seemed great and Lodge's bill passed the Senate by a vote of 34 to 31.

When the exclusionary bill was introduced to an even more receptive House, Fitzgerald listened with great distress to "the insidious arguments" of his fellow congressmen, arguments which would have excluded his own mother from entering the United States. Deciding to respond with a major speech, he spent weeks working on a comprehensive statement in opposition to the bill which he delivered on the floor of the House on January 27, 1897.

"Mr. Speaker," he began, "I am utterly opposed to this bill in its present form. . . . It is fashionable today to cry out against the immigration of the Hungarian, the Italian and the Jew; but I think that the man who comes to this country for the first time—to a strange land without friends and without employment—is born of the stuff that is bound to make good citizens. I have stood on the docks in East Boston and watched the newly arrived immigrant gaze for the first time on this free land of ours. I have seen the little ones huddle around the father and mother and look with amazement on their new surroundings."

From this emotional beginning, Fitzgerald went on to catalogue the many contributions the Jewish and Italian immigrants had made to America, concluding that the literacy test was a "latter-day attempt to set people against people" and preserve the very frontiers of European nationalism which America, if left alone, would slowly but inexorably obliterate.

It was a speech he would always be proud of, though there was no doubt when the vote was taken, recording 195 yeas, 37 nays and 123 not voting, that the sentiment of the House went the other way. Years later Fitzgerald liked to tell the story of his meeting Henry Cabot Lodge in the Senate chamber shortly after the speech. "You are an impudent young man," Lodge reportedly said. "Do you think the Jews or the Italians have any right in this country?"

"As much right as your father or mine," Fitzgerald responded. "It was only a difference of a few ships."

Fitzgerald later said that after the bill passed the Congress he took his case to the White House, where, sitting alone with President Cleveland on a long Saturday afternoon, he argued so persuasively against the bill that Cleveland decided to veto it. While Fitzgerald's influence was probably not as large as he liked to believe, history does record that on March 2, 1897, thirteen days before McKinley was scheduled to be sworn in, Cleveland vetoed the literacy bill as a radical departure from U.S. national policy relating to immigration, thereby keeping America's doors open for another twenty years. It was a courageous decision on Cleveland's part; its effect, as Fitzgerald correctly observed, "was to bring millions of immigrants to these shores who would otherwise have been kept out."

While Fitzgerald was dividing his time between Washington and Boston, Josie remained at home with her growing family. Two years after Rose was born, a second daughter, Agnes, arrived, and then a boy, who was named Thomas after Fitzgerald's father. These were difficult years for Josie, since Fitzgerald was seldom at home, leaving the entire responsibility for the physical maintenance of the home and the nurturing of the children in her hands. Sitting alone in the city with three small children, she longed for a home in the country that would bring her nearer to her parents and siblings. "Once Mother got it in her mind to move out to Concord, nothing could stop her," Rose later recalled. "It was a tough decision for Father, for he knew he'd be criticized for living away from his district and his people, but he saw how much it meant to Mother and he finally agreed."

So, in 1897, the Fitzgeralds moved to a large wooden house on the main street of West Concord, which was known then as Concord Junction. Set back from the road on a little hill, the house boasted a broad veranda, a glassed-in conservatory, a large barn and henhouse and a sizable tract of land. Best of all, as far as Josie was concerned, the house was only two blocks away from the street where her brother John Hannon lived and a ten-minute carriage ride from her parents' home in Acton.

"These were wonderful years," Rose recalled of the six years she spent in Concord between the ages of seven and thirteen, "full of the traditional pleasures and satisfactions of life in a small New England town: trips with horse and buggy to my grandparents' house, climbing apple trees, gathering wildflowers in the woods behind the house."

During these years in Concord, Josie gave birth to two more children: a son, John Francis Fitzgerald, Jr., and a daughter, Eunice. (A sixth child, Fred, named after Fitzgerald's newsboy friend, would be born after the family moved back to Boston.) As the oldest child, Rose enjoyed her privileged status, though she later admitted that sometimes she felt that her mother was so busy with each new baby that "she didn't have as much time for me as some of my friends whose families were smaller." However, Rose observed, "this made me more self-reliant and independent."

Since there was no Roman Catholic church in Concord Junction at the time, on Sundays the Fitzgeralds made the three-mile trip to St. Bernard's Church in Concord Center by horse and carriage. For Josie, the distance from her home to the church was the only drawback in an otherwise idyllic setting. A deeply religious woman for whom, as Rose said, "the Church was a pervading and abiding presence," Josie drilled her children regularly in their catechism lessons and talked to them about the fasts and feasts of the Church. "Every night during Lent my mother would gather us in one of the rooms of the house, turn out the lights—the better to concentrate—and lead us in reciting the Rosary. I'm sure my knees ached and that sometimes I wondered why I should be doing all the kneeling and studying and contemplating and praying. But I became understanding and grateful."

In contrast, Fitzgerald was, in Rose's words, "so deeply involved in the affairs of the world that he took religion for granted without thinking much about it. Going to Mass was simply natural and normal and gave him the opportunity (I say this with love and without sacrilege) of communicating not only with God, but with many of his friends and political constituents."

During these years, a directive was issued by the archdiocese in Boston commanding all Catholic parents to send their children to Catholic schools.

> This is the command of the Catholic Church [Donahoe's observed], and she must be obeyed to please her Divine Father. Our Holy Father . . . says that these Catholic schools are the only places for Catholic children to receive their education and that a father or mother, claiming to be a Catholic, is a poor misguided Catholic who will send a Catholic boy or girl to schools where they may be certain, if they do not lose their faith, that they will, at least, have it weakened.

In spite of this directive, Fitzgerald sent his children to the Concord public schools, believing, as he told his brother Henry, that the public schools were training grounds for success in the world. Anticipating such reasoning, Donahoe's argued that "even if it were true that there is a better education in the affairs of the world in the public schools than there is in the Catholic schools . . . the first and highest law of God is to 'seek first the Kingdom of Heaven and His Justice,' and not to seek first success in the Kingdom of the World, which is the only object and the only teaching of the present system of public schools."

For her part, Josie would have much preferred giving her children a parochial education, but the West Concord Grammar School, a small school with five teachers and 190 pupils, had the compensating advantage of being only three blocks from the house. From the start, young Rose proved herself a hard-working and intelligent student. "Some children will study less if their father is in an important position," she later observed, "thinking they can get by. I studied more because I thought I was more conspicuous on that account."

In her memoirs, Rose pointed out that her father was seldom home during these years and that, as a result, the direction and care of the children was left largely to her mother. "It is a price which members of a political family have to pay," she noted flatly, never giving voice to the sadness she must have experienced every time her father went away. For a young girl who adored her father as much as she did, his long absences from home must have seemed interminable. Yet in later life Rose refused to dwell on her feelings of loss, determined to keep intact the romantic idea of Fitzgerald as the perfect father.

Even from the distance of more than seven decades, Rose could still remember "the absolute thrill" of driving in the carriage to meet her father when he arrived from Washington at the train station in Concord. "The minute he saw me he would pick me up in his arms and twirl me around and then he would make me close my eyes while he pulled a wonderful present from his bags. To my mind, there was no one in the world like my father. Wherever he was, there was magic in the air."

In the summer of 1900, after serving three terms in Congress, Fitzgerald publicly announced that he did not want to run again. Having entered Congress with the rallying cry that "the people believe in rotation," he reluctantly agreed that the time had come when that same cry would be used against him. Yet, if he seemed to be stepping out of politics he was in fact preparing the way to reach his real goal—the mayorship of Boston. But before he could make any further plans he had to leave Concord.

All along, Martin Lomasney had warned Fitzgerald that if he wanted a future in the Democratic Party he had to move his family back to Boston. "Father knew that Lomasney was right," Rose recalled, "but Mother loved Concord so much he stayed in the country as long as he could, all the while keeping his voting registration in the North End." Then in 1903 the issue of Fitzgerald's residence became a public issue when a complaint was brought before the board of election comissioners. Although the board found, with no explanation, that he was legally a citizen of Ward 6, Fitzgerald decided that the time had come to return to Boston.

Fortunately for the peace of the family, Fitzgerald had enough money by now to afford a large mansion at 39 Welles Avenue in Dorchester, which Josie soon came to love. Perched on a hill, with a curving driveway, the gracious house boasted a mansard roof with a turret, big parlors, a solarium, a library, a billiard room and a music room.

The money had accumulated over the past two years with Fitzgerald's purchase of a small Catholic weekly, *The Republic*, originally owned by P. J. Maguire. At the time of the purchase the paper was steadily losing money in the hands of the Maguire family, and Fitzgerald managed to buy it for only $500. Initially the announcement was received with surprise by the Boston politicians, who predicted that if Fitzgerald tackled political issues aggressively in the paper he would be hurt politically, "if he does have aspirations for the future and there is no doubt he does." But *The Republic*'s new publisher Fitzgerald devised an entirely new strategy for the paper which involved absolutely no political risk.

"I knew the success of a newspaper depended on its advertising revenue," he said, "and that advertisers look to women, who spend most of their money in the big stores that did most of the advertising. I accordingly made the paper more readable to women by publishing society notes." In Fitzgerald's "Society & Clubdom notices," John Cutler observed, "he cleverly mingled the social doings of Catholic women with those of the more patrician matrons of the Back Bay in the manner of an Irish Cholly Knickerbocker, who knew that names make news."

Moreover, as a powerful city boss, Fitzgerald was in an excellent position to sell ads. "Sixty percent of the shoppers of Boston are Catholic," he told George Raymond, one of Boston's biggest advertisers, "and my paper is the only effective medium for reaching them." Besides, he added, "if you should want anything in the Massachusetts legislature or at City Hall, I can get it for you." According to Cutler, Fitzgerald's energetic promotion built a dying enterprise into a thriving business that netted him profits of $25,000 a year.

As far as Fitzgerald was concerned, however, *The Republic* was merely a way station on the road to the mayorship. Even as early as 1901, the Boston papers observed that a strong movement for Fitzgerald as mayor was beginning. Reporting on a large banquet held at Fanueil Hall to honor Fitzgerald, *Practical Politics* observed that "the entire demonstration, gold watch and all, was arranged for political effect. . . . He has learned wisdom with experience and years and now he is using the wily tactics of a diplomat, his manners and his methods are alike pacific and he relies on persuasion rather than force."

But if Fitzgerald hoped to run for mayor right away, his hopes were dashed by the decision of Patrick A. Collins to seek the nomination in 1901. Considered one of the most respected men in Boston politics, Collins had returned from his post as consul to Great Britain to seek the

Democratic nomination, and with the backing of the party's board of strategy his election was assured. Once Collins was in office, Fitzgerald dared not oppose him for reelection, and so the years went by until September of 1905, when the fifty-year-old mayor, vacationing in Hot Springs, Virginia, contracted pneumonia and died.

The sudden death of Mayor Collins precipitated a wild contest for his successor. With the Democratic primary set for November 14, 1905, eight weeks away, Fitzgerald moved first, mobilizing his machine into immediate action on the assumption that Martin Lomasney would be with him. "Fitzgerald did not have my verbal promise," Lomasney later wrote, "but he didn't need it the way we felt early in that year and of course, he had every right to think I would be with him." But as it happened, the other ward bosses, anxious to eliminate Fitzgerald's rising star, came up with the one candidate who could tear Fitzgerald and Lomasney apart—Ned Donovan, Lomasney's closest friend. "Without Lomasney," the *Boston Herald* reported, "the strategists believed Fitzgerald would fade as dew before the morning sun."

In five years as city clerk, Donovan had established himself pretty solidly in the affections of the various bosses who sat on the powerful board of strategy—the citywide alliance of Democratic leaders—and though he had no idea of running for mayor himself, he was unable to resist the pressure put upon him by such powerful figures as Jim Donovan and P. J. Kennedy. "I knew they were working on Ned," Lomasney later recalled, "but I'd hoped they would not get anywhere with it." But when Ned came to Lomasney and said, "I want it. I want the honor, Jim Donovan is with me and are you going to stand in my way," Lomasney had no choice. "It was one friend talking to another . . . 'Don't say another word, old sport . . . if it means that much to you, I'll go the limit.' "

Though Fitzgerald was temporarily stunned by Donovan's entry into the race, "he soon recovered his poise," Lomasney remembered, "and set out to answer the challenge." Fitzgerald came up with the interesting strategy of running a solo campaign against the whole system of bossism. From his headquarters he issued a statement that he would not have a strategy board to manage his campaign but would instead be his own campaign manager. "I am making my contest single-handedly," he shouted as crowds roared with delight, "against the machine, the bosses and the corporations." Linking himself to the progressive reformers all across the country, he said, "The victory of Jerome in New York, Weaver in Philadelphia and Moran in Boston* encourages me to believe

---

* William Travers Jerome was reelected district attorney in New York, John Weaver mayor of Philadelphia, and John B. Moran district attorney in Boston.

that [my] policy . . . to banish graft and jail the grafters is a policy which the people will endorse on primary day."

Yet, even as he posed as the man who could smash bossism, the real strength behind the Fitzgerald candidacy was the implied promise that "the gang in City Hall for four years would be cleaned out to make room for another gang"—in other words, the gang that was out wanted in and Fitzgerald was smart enough to gather to his banner all the disaffected politicians who had been left out by the regular organization.

On the stump, Donovan was no match for the magnetic Fitzgerald. As Donovan was not in the best of health when the campaign began, he could manage only three or four speeches a night, while Fitzgerald, aided in moving from ward to ward by the speed of a large automobile, averaged more than ten speeches a night on a schedule which "no candidate had ever attempted." For three weeks, reporters observed, Boston "throbbed with excitement" as Fitzgerald whipped the crowds into a frenzy of delight, climaxed by a whirlwind finish on primary eve in which he spoke in each of the twenty-five wards. Ending his tour in his old hometown ward at the Jefferson Club on Hanover Street, Fitzgerald, one reporter wrote, was "surrounded by a procession of cheering and yelling constituents who carried red fire that illuminated the streets and the faces of hundreds of dwellers who appeared at the window." The reporter recorded, "It was an exciting and beautiful sight and formed a fitting climax in the most remarkable speaking tour ever made by a political candidate in Boston."

On primary day, Fitzgerald won the nomination by a vote of 28,130 to 24,387 for Donovan, giving the regular Democratic machine the worst beating it had suffered in many years. Yet, ward politics being what they were, all of the Democratic leaders, save one, patched up their differences with Fitzgerald and fell in line before the regular election. Only Martin Lomasney held out, not so much because he was angry with Fitzgerald as because he felt that both he and Ned had been used by the regular machine who were now backing the victorious Fitzgerald. The time had come, Lomasney decided, to teach the machine a lesson.

In the general election Fitzgerald faced a divided Republican Party, with Louis Frothingham, Republican Speaker of the Massachusetts House of Representatives, running as the organizational candidate and Henry Dewey, former judge of the Municipal Court of Boston, running an independent campaign. As it happened, Dewey had been running for mayor for months when the death of Mayor Collins occurred. Anticipating the renomination of Collins, the Republican leaders had paid little attention to the race. But when the death of Collins opened the door to the Fitzgerald–Donovan fight, the Republicans recognized the opportunity for victory and moved at once, with the help of Henry Cabot Lodge, to recruit Frothingham, a substantial figure in Massachusetts politics. With the backing of the Republican organization, Frothingham won the primary, but Dewey was so bitter that he elected to stay in the race.

On election eve, Lomasney called all the active followers in the Hendricks Club down to headquarters. "I am not going to support Fitzgerald," he told them, suggesting that he was turning against his party and voting for Frothingham. "There is no deal on, no promises. I don't think [Fitzgerald] can be beaten, but I'm not going to lay down and be with the gang that has done such a job on us. Now I am going to put the lights out for two minutes. I haven't had time to check up to see who is here and who is not. If anybody here doesn't want to go through with me, just slide out in the dark and there'll be no hard feelings. Whoever goes out can come back the day after election and we'll be friends again. . . . I have decided what should be done to save the organization in the future and it doesn't make any difference if you all walk out. I'll fight just the same."

So Lomasney put out the lights. They sat in the dark for two minutes, and there wasn't a move. Not a chair scraped and nobody moved to the door. When he put the lights on every man was just where he'd been when he put them out—an amazing tribute to "the Mahatma."

On election day, Lomasney's ward went for Frothingham, the first time it had voted Republican in years. But even without Lomasney, Fitzgerald won, gathering 44,171 votes to 36,028 for Frothingham and 11,608 for Dewey. "Thank God for old Dewey," Fitzgerald said in private, while in public he hailed the dawn of a new era.

# CHAPTER 8

# A MOST
# ENERGETIC
# MAYOR

O n January 1, 1906, in the presence of a crowd of men, women
and children described by the
*Boston Post* as "the largest that has ever been present . . . to witness the
inaugural exercises of any mayor" of Boston, the Honorable John Francis Fitzgerald was inducted into office.

The new year had started with a midnight squall which laid a fresh
blanket of snow upon the city's streets, but inaugural morning dawned
bright and clear under a cloudless blue sky and a strong, glittering sun
which brought the temperature up to a springlike 45 degrees. Inspired
by the balmy weather and by the abounding vitality of their youthful
new mayor, the people of Boston turned out by the thousands to watch

the festivities. By midmorning, an immense crowd had formed on School Street; the air was full of conversation, expectation and anticipation.

Inside the City Hall, that "lunatic pile of a building," as Edwin O'Connor once described the great grim gray structure, the City Council chamber was crowded to overflowing. Long before ten o'clock all the seats available for spectators and all the standing room in the balconies had been appropriated. On the floor of the chamber, precedent was broken as large numbers of women were seated in small wooden chairs. (Never before on inaugural day had women been allowed on the Council floor.) In the packed balconies too, the bulk of people consisted of women—it was said that women, in particular, felt the power of Fitzgerald's charm. Indeed, Fitzgerald was known about town as something of a ladies' man.

Ten o'clock passed and the crowd on the street shuffled with impatience as the mayor-elect failed to appear; his progress to City Hall had been retarded by all the well-wishers lining his path. Finally, when the "monster automobile" containing Fitzgerald, his wife and his family turned into School Street, there was "wild applause" and "sustained cheering." As the auto stopped and the inaugural party alighted, "Fitzgerald was actually overwhelmed with ovations and demonstrations." "Never before," the *Boston Evening Transcript* reported, "was there such a demonstration on inaugural day."

From the car to the entrance of the City Hall, Fitzgerald's passage was "a continued ovation and his countenance fairly shone with pleasure at the great reception accorded to him." Similar enthusiasm was evident on the face of his "glowing" wife, Josephine, elegantly attired in gray velvet with a Continental hat of Malta lace, and his five "exuberant" children: Rose, fifteen, in a garnet velvet suit with hat to match and ermine furs; Agnes, thirteen, in blue velvet with white beaver hat and a set of white fox furs; Eunice, five, in a lace frock; Thomas and John Junior, ten and eight, in black velvet Eton suits. The youngest child, Fred, still an infant, had been left at home.

After the approach of the inaugural party into the chamber, the prayer was offered by Reverend Dennis J. O'Farrell, pastor of St. Stephen's, the North End church where John Fitzgerald and all his brothers had been baptized, had received their first communion and had heard their first midnight Mass, and then the Chief Justice administered the oath, making Fitzgerald the thirty-fifth mayor of Boston.

At last he began his inaugural address, speaking first in a low voice, which he soon raised so that every word could be easily heard. "What we need above everything else in this juncture," he suggested, "is a reawakening of civic pride," a return to the days of Boston's dominance when a common devotion inspired the whole population, a return to the days when Boston was "a beacon to the whole American nation. . . . Who said 'Boston' called up an image in which love of liberty, commercial enterprise, intellectual distinction and large, practical philanthropy were blended in almost equal proportions."

But, he told them, that glorious reputation was in danger of being lost unless the new generation, "moulding their ideals to the pattern of the splendid past," proved themselves worthy successors, in vigor and initiative, of the old merchant princes, the founding fathers of the great Brahmin families.

The applause at this point was "loud" and "enthusiastic." With these words, Fitzgerald had spoken to the increasing anxiety felt by the Yankees, reduced now to only 11 percent of the population, that their beloved old city would eventually disappear beneath the crushing force of all the new immigrants, who, they feared, knew little and cared less about the city's triumphant past. These same words registered on the predominantly Irish audience—those of Irish descent now constituted close to 40 percent of Boston's population—as a powerful call to leadership. This was not a new theme for Fitzgerald. Throughout his career, he had urged his Irish brethren to participate more fully in Boston's community life; again and again, he had advised his fellow Catholics not to be provincial in their own separate schools, but instead to "go to school with the superior men, read their words, listen to them, talk to them." ("We ought to be proud of a city as historic as ours," he would later tell the Young Men's Catholic Association. "We ought to know its history by heart, its record in war, the names of its great men, its commerce, government and institutions. It should be our ambition to advance its fame and leave it greater than we found it.")

Turning to the present in his inaugural address, Fitzgerald characterized the economic situation of Boston as one of "stagnation," "halt," and "decline." Against the vigorous form of the merchant princes, he opposed the pale existence of their sons and grandsons, whose conservative control of Boston's financial institutions and enterprises had exerted a "deadening impact" upon the entire community. Living on the reputation of their fathers, filling their days with the desire to keep hold and sit still, their wills trapped in a hapless pursuit of gentility, these men were managing the city's economic activities with a "persistent disregard" for the "interests of Boston." The time had come, Fitzgerald urged, for a new leadership caste, who would manage the city's enterprises "with imagination and risk, with the hope that profit would follow upon improvement and development."

At the heart of this call for new economic leadership stood the figure of the new mayor, with his boundless energy, his thirst for action and his fierce belief that the history of Boston was central to the history of the entire nation. With the monies of the city treasury at his disposal, and the munificence of the old entrepreneurs as his ideal, he intended to create "a bigger, better and busier Boston," its wharves alive once more with the bustle and activity of commerce, its streets humming with new factories, schools, hospitals and public buildings, its landscape dotted with new parks and playgrounds, baths and gyms.

The speech went on for fifty-seven pages, much of which Fitzgerald read, yet the audience—accustomed to detailed inaugurals in those days —remained attentive and enthusiastic through the entire reading. Finally he reached his concluding paragraph, which took note of the fact that a critical attitude toward the American city was in the air in 1906. Through the investigative journalism of Lincoln Steffens, Frank Norris, Upton Sinclair and David Graham Phillips cities had gained an unenviable reputation as natural homes of political corruption, crime, and vice. Yet, Fitzgerald argued, cities could not be wished away by a nostalgic yearning for a rural past. Given "the tendency of the American people . . . to live together in large communities," it was in the city, with all its scandals and its throbbing life, in all its dark and its glistening aspects, that "the problems of self-government" must be worked out.

At the end, amid a roar of enthusiasm, Fitzgerald smiled his great dimpled smile and, while the photographers' smoke was still clearing away, left the chamber for the mayor's office. There he inaugurated a new custom of holding a public reception for the long line of citizens stretching up and down the corridors, out the door and into the street.

Celebration filled the remaining hours of inaugural day. First there was a family luncheon at the Quincy House, followed by a large banquet for all the members of the Board of Aldermen and the Common Council. Heretofore it had been the custom for the new mayor to dine the thirteen aldermen, but Fitzgerald invited the seventy-five councilmen as well, arguing that the Council deserved equal consideration with the Board. Later in the afternoon, he took an automobile ride to the Ferncroft Inn at Danvers, where he dined with his brothers and a few intimate friends. Still later he returned to the Quincy House for another party tendered to him by a number of his old-time friends in the North End.

Long past midnight, tired and happy, Fitzgerald returned to his home on Welles Avenue and to his bed. From the moment of his rising until now, he later told a friend, the pomp and revelry of the day had exceeded his greatest anticipation. But just before he dropped off to sleep he thought of the one thing that would have made his inauguration perfect: he wished that his parents had been with him to share in his pride at becoming the first child of immigrant parents to reach the mayorship in Boston.

For the city, the mayor's inaugural ushered in a mood of resurgent hope. His energetic call for action and his forceful plea for a revitalized economy evoked a uniformly warm editorial response, typified by the conclusion in the *Boston Globe* that "no more interesting and attractive address has recently been delivered by an incoming mayor." Even the Yankee reformers who had vigorously opposed Fitzgerald's election joined in the initial applause which followed the new mayor through his early weeks. After all, Fitzgerald was speaking their language when he promised an "efficient, economical, honorable government," a government run on "a businesslike basis," with no soft jobs, no graft and no waste.

In the first weeks of his administration, Fitzgerald seemed to be every-where—filing economic-reform bills before the Council, announcing evidence of collusion between a group of milk dealers and inspectors, calling for a new boulevard along the Charles River, championing parks and athletic activities, leading the grand march at the firemen's ball, heading the cotillion at the ball of the Catholic Literary Union, ringing church bells in honor of the White House wedding of Alice Roosevelt and Nicholas Longworth, talking constantly on all manner of subjects ranging from graft to development to Irish Home Rule, and greeting visitors in a working day that began before sunrise and ended after midnight.

"As Mayor," *Practical Politics* reported on January 20, "John Francis Fitzgerald is setting a faster pace than any of his predecessors. . . . He is personally looking after details at City Hall which his predecessors ignored, he keeps his secretaries and stenographers on the jump and he shows no sign of letting go." The mayor's office, freshly painted in a pleasing shade of green, embodied the new spirit of activity. Where once formality and aloofness had reigned—Mayor Collins had rarely arrived at City Hall earlier than 10 A.M. and often left before 3 P.M.—there was now an informal, welcoming air, with lights burning until well after midnight and "a steady stream of visitors, of not one but many races, who whenever a door was left for a moment unguarded, hurried them-selves, as it were, with swift and noiseless force into the room of the chief executive."

A reporter for the *Boston Post* in 1906 observed the scene on a typical day:

The doors opened and the avalanche descended. "First come, first served," said the Mayor informally, as one by one the men slid into the great leather chairs or fell into various attitudes about the room. Number one was a little old man who almost fell into the Mayor's arms, but was saved by the Mayor's strong right hand. . . . Number two was a serious little man, quite as much of a fighter as the Mayor and he kept talking away persistently till he evidently accomplished his object. In the meantime, Tom Curley ambled in and completely filled a huge arm chair not far from the Mayor's desk, gazing on the scene with pensive complacency. . . . Numbers three and four came together and the Mayor lost no time telling them: "It was a very bad state of affairs," punctuating his sentences with rapid running of his fingers through his thick dark hair, which strangely parts in the back on the left side in a long slanting line. . . .

In thirty-two minutes, the reporter noted, Fitzgerald disposed of exactly twenty-six callers. There was "no waste of time on frivolities" and yet "no apparent turning down of a visitor by an abrupt dismissal." It was "remarkable," the reporter concluded, a tribute to the mayor's personality which seemed "to shake off all cares as a Newfoundland sheds water off his back" and the focusing powers of his mind, "ready without any notice to concentrate itself at once on the subject of the minute."

Yet even the ubiquitous Fitzgerald could not find enough hours in the regular day both to accommodate the waiting throng and to carry out his other duties. "I had been in City Hall two or three days," he later said, "and I saw that it was impossible for me to do the public business within the specified hours and see the multitude of people who used to want to see me." Not wishing to turn away his visitors, he decided to defer all matters concerning the departments—such as the signing of documents, contracts, notes or bonds—until after business hours. "It resulted in the fact," Fitzgerald claimed, "that I never went home to dinner once during my administration, except on Sundays and holidays."

The administration which Fitzgerald headed was divided into forty-four departments, ranging from the Bath Department to the Health Department, from the Lamp Department to the Library Department, from the Parks Department to the Water Department. In Fitzgerald's era as mayor, the city had much more money at its disposal than the state of Massachusetts. In 1905 the city spent $33 million, the state $9 million. So it happened that a man who up to this time had had no formal business training was all at once responsible for the work of a great organization which employed 12,000 people, spent $100,000 a day and affected the interests of nearly 600,000 people.

This meant, as Fitzgerald described the situation in an article for New

*England Magazine* written shortly after he assumed office, that the mayor must instantly "familiarize himself with an immense mass of executive details. Questions relating to transportation, street construction and paving, protection from fire, water service, sanitation, buildings, taxation, health, the care of the sick, the poor, the vicious, the homeless young—these and a hundred of other problems are presented to him as part of his daily duty." And most of this business, remember, was brought to Fitzgerald only after five o'clock.

Nor did the mayor's work come to an end when the last department head had departed. One evening's "leisure" was catalogued by a reporter who attended Fitzgerald through it: "It included six banquets, at each of which the mayor spoke, seven dances and socials, and a visit, just as dawn was breaking, at a humble house in the tenement district, where an acquaintance lay dead. At eight the next morning the Mayor was at his desk."

It was, as these flattering accounts suggest, an auspicious beginning for the new mayor. The press, intrigued by the novelty of the first colorful mayor in decades, was more interested in Fitzgerald's personality than in his messages. No other occupant of City Hall had been so widely known, so frequently photographed, so often a figure on the front pages of the paper. They wrote stories commenting on his dress, his voice and his dancing; they followed the activities of his six brothers and his six children. They portrayed him as charming and well-mannered, funny and impetuous.

The only concern the reporters expressed in these early weeks was the fear that even a man of Fitzgerald's abnormal energy had his limits; they predicted collapse unless he took things more easily. "The Mayor should go slow," *Practical Politics* urged. "His is not a strong physique. He has a strong and far reaching voice but the lungs behind that voice require intelligent and considerate treatment." Despite these and other warnings, Fitzgerald kept up his exhausting pace. He absolutely loved the job; he savored completely the hectic routine of his long, full days. Basking in the admiration of friend and foe alike, he no doubt thought that he could accomplish things no other politician could accomplish, that he alone could combine the general principles of good government with the daily demands of practical politics.

Whatever vision Fitzgerald may have held of the great "businesslike" reforms he would bring about in the interests of the people as a whole, the very nature of the political machine which had brought him into power and sustained him in office made it impossible for him to work objectively for the "public interest." Trained by the system of ward politics, his whole life pragmatically geared to satisfying the immediate needs of his special constituents, he could not suddenly change this orientation to a point of view which stressed efficiency, planning and good government. The machine was built upon rounding up votes and winning elections. For half a century it had used the public payroll to finance itself, dangling contracts, licenses, appointments and jobs as powerful lures to attract and bind together a complex web of party workers, city employees, contractors, politicians, reporters, judges, vendors, and solicitors of privileged licenses. The ideal of the machine was individual, not social; it was held together, to use Josiah Quincy's colorful phrase, by "the cohesive power of public plunder," by the strivings of thousands of individuals for personal gain.

And, in the end, despite his brave new words about ending corruption and graft and his vigorous promise "that no man will be appointed to a place unless an actual necessity for an appointment arises," John Fitzgerald was the offspring of this machine. He had lived all his life by the machine's code of ethics, which stressed patronage, personal loyalty and personal obligations above all else. However much he wanted to run an efficient and honorable government, he couldn't simply change his mode of consciousness overnight. It would be, at best, a gradual shedding and even then the old habits were likely to remain, deeply rooted in the depths of his nature.

It must not be supposed from this, however, that Fitzgerald was simply saying one thing and doing another, that he never meant to reform any part of the system in the first place. Fitzgerald was no theorist. It probably never occurred to him that there was a fundamental conflict between his inaugural goals and the practical realities of sustaining the political machine. Indeed, from his earliest days in politics Fitzgerald had been able to compartmentalize his actions so that he could hold on to an image of himself as a "good" man and a "reformist politician" even as he found himself willing to turn in the uncle of his best childhood friend in order to please the boss and work his way up the political ladder.

Not many days would pass, however, as one astute reporter had prophesied at the time of the election, before the contradictions inherent in Fitzgerald's regime would be made clear. "Fitzgerald would go into city hall," the reporter predicted, "bound by more promises, direct or implied, than any other man who ever entered the executive chamber. He is facing a condition, possibly not far away, where he must make good and where promises will not avail." From his days as Keany's apprentice, Fitzgerald had worked within the ward system, tirelessly converting his political resources—access, information and offices—into jobs for the people of Ward 6. Campaigning for mayor, however, he had run as an outsider, with no access to the city payroll or the city treasury. Promises were his only currency, and promises he had liberally given in exchange for support. In each neighborhood he had set up an employment bureau with a clerk in charge to catalogue the names, desires and qualifications of every applicant for public work. Now all these people, with no time to lose, had to be brought within the compass of the city government, and their numbers, given the wall that civil service had built around a steadily larger segment of the public service, far exceeded the positions under the new mayor's control.

For a short period, Fitzgerald's ingenuity proved equal to the task. Putting his experience as a civil-service clerk to good use, he figured out how to circumvent the system in order to bring his own men on board. For supporters whose talents did not include the ability to pass the civil-service exam, he provided "provisional" or "emergency" appointments which allowed hundreds of men to be appointed without a fuss, and then, once they were on the payroll, they were simply kept on. For those whose qualifications did not fit any particular job opening, he created a host of novel job categories which conveniently fell outside the civil-service listings; in the early weeks, dozens of tea warmers, rubber-boot repairmen, brick slingers, barn bosses and watchmen to hire other watchmen were hired. By administrative order, he increased the deputy collectors of taxes from sixty-two to eighty-three and he added eight additional deputy sealers to the Department of Weights and Measures. Next he turned his attention to the scores of private companies anxious to stand well with the new administration; surely, he told them, there must be openings for his men in construction, on the streetcar lines, in the telephone company and in the gas company.

Just as quickly as all these new jobs were created, they were filled, and still the office seekers surged around City Hall. Leaving nothing to chance, Fitzgerald exerted his efforts on behalf of a pension system for city employees too old for proper service. In his inaugural, he had called for "a properly graded pension scheme, based upon an equitable basis of financial contributions, not merely as a measure of philanthropy but of actual economy and efficiency as well." His proposal immediately attracted favorable support among reformers who saw the pension scheme as a way of reducing the swollen city payroll and lowering the city tax rate. While Fitzgerald too spoke the language of efficiency and waste, he saw the pension scheme in a very different light: if he could provide a secure retirement for all the old employees currently on the payroll, hundreds of new jobs would be opened up which he could fill with younger men.

Given the cross-purposes which motivated Fitzgerald on the one hand

and the reformers on the other, it was inevitable that their relations would one day come to an open break. And they did. When the annual list of city employees appeared, "containing almost 14,000 names of men and women who draw pay from the city and county," there were cries of outrage from the Good Government Association, the Municipal League and the various progressive papers. "It is the most remarkable collection of names ever printed under city auspices," the *Boston Journal* reported, "and the list alone shows how the payrolls are padded by the employment of scores of men who do not labor . . . it is estimated that one person in every forty-two of the city's population are drawing money from the city treasury."

For days, the *Journal* continued its attack on this "amazing exposure of payroll graft," focusing on different sections of the list each day. "Three men are still paid for duty at the abandoned Mt. Washington Avenue Bridge, which once connected South Boston with the city proper and which now is used as a storage yard by contractors: Thomas Cloney, drawtender, 1200; Samuel Edgeworth, first assistant, 1200; Daniel Ford, first assistant, 900. This bridge cannot be used except for the payment of salaries." Another "remarkable exhibit" was found in the street-watering division, where there were "8 bicycle tallymen . . . each of whom receives $2 a day. Their duties are to follow up the street sprinkling men and see that they water the streets." Taking all these cases together, the *Journal* concluded that that year was to be "a record year for the payroll grafters."

An even stronger outburst of criticism followed Fitzgerald's departmental appointments. When he first assumed office, taking note of the waste that was prevalent in all departments, Fitzgerald had promised to exercise the utmost care in selecting qualified men as his administrative chiefs, men who would "subject their departments to a thorough examination" and then reconstitute them "on a proper basis," insisting upon "an adequate return for every dollar spent." But when the time came to make these administrative appointments, Fitzgerald yielded his high ambitions and used the positions as he earlier had said he would not do— as rewards for his political supporters. Once again the imperatives of his campaign determined his later actions. Because he had launched his quest for the mayoralty as an outsider, effectively running against the recognized leaders of the city, he had gathered under his banner an army of discontented people who felt they had not been used rightly by the established powers. Fitzgerald later admitted that he was never fully satisfied with the caliber of these men, that he was anxious to rebuild his ties with his old associates, but in the course of the campaign he had made a number of commitments which he now had to honor.

The first test came with the selection of a new superintendent of streets. This appointment, the most important one he had to make, was a particularly sensitive one in light of recent investigations which had targeted the Street Department as the most unwieldy, the most extravagant and the most corrupt of all the departments. If Fitzgerald really did intend to reconstitute his departments on a businesslike basis, then "the huge leisure class employed by the street department," as Louis D. Brandeis once called the thousands of street employees, was the place to begin. For weeks, the city was filled with speculation; then, on March 2, along with several other appointments, Fitzgerald unveiled his choice for superintendent: James Doyle, a pub keeper who had been expelled from the legislature the year before for election fraud. Doyle's appointment produced widespread criticism in the press and renewed cries of outrage from the various reform groups. Still, the inner circle at City Hall stood firm; Doyle had been one of the earliest backers of Fitzgerald's campaign, and his support had given Fitzgerald hundreds of votes in a ward where he needed them. And for that support a price had to be paid. "The Mayor's appointments are out," lawyer George Nutter wrote in his diary on March 2, "and some of them pretty bad. Doyle is Superintendent of Streets—a man rejected by the people for street commissioner, expelled from the legislature for fraud and the appointee because of the Hotel Somerset agreement. It is said Fitzgerald signed a paper at that time agreeing to the appointment as the price of support."

Fitzgerald's succeeding appointments produced mixed reactions in the press. James Nolan, a popular liquor dealer in East Boston with no knowledge of building construction or repair, was made superintendent of public buildings; John Leahy, a whitewasher and furniture polisher, became superintendent of sewers, a post which called for a civil engineer; Tim Crowley of Ward 8, recently acquitted in Superior Court of trying to shoot Martin Lomasney's brother, was appointed deputy sealer of weights and measures. At the head of the Collecting Department was placed a man who had never managed any business or any office that would qualify him for the executive duties of this important office; a saloon keeper replaced a doctor on the Board of Health.

With a few notable exceptions, the evidence suggests that in making his appointments to head the city departments Fitzgerald was motivated more by the need to reward past supporters than by the desire to find the most experienced or qualified candidates. As a result, according to a subsequent report, "a steady deterioration in the technical competency and moral strength of the heads of the departments" took place, leaving the administrative business of the city, by and large, in the hands of men "without education, training, experience or technical qualifications of any sort."

. . .

Yet the mayor's popularity survived this initial flurry of criticism. While the reform organizations railed against his widespread use of patronage, on the grounds that it demoralized the entire work force, destroying the skill that comes with experience and the security that comes from basing appointments and promotions upon merit, the general public, still regarding patronage as the natural order for a democracy, rallied around their activist mayor. Within the immigrant community, despite the acceptance of civil service on principle, there remained a widespread sentiment that the civil-service exams, geared to proficiency in grammar, spelling and arithmetic, were elitist, impractical and exclusionary.

Just a year earlier, a striking display of these sentiments had been exhibited in the public's reaction to the conviction of the two Curleys, James and Tom (not related), for taking the civil-service exam for mail carriers in the place of two other men, Fahey and Hughes. The night before the jailing, hundreds of people had crowded into the streets to celebrate the Curleys for their dramatic effort to overcome "an unfair system" which, with its "unnecessary educational standards," was presenting the better-educated citizens with "an unwarranted advantage." For despite the difficulties Fahey and Hughes would have encountered in the exam, both men, most people believed, could have performed the duties of mail carrier with ease. In derogating the impersonal code of civil service in favor of the bonds of friendship and loyalty, the two Curleys had earned the undying support of their constituents, who resoundingly returned James to the Board of Aldermen and Thomas to the Massachusetts House of Representatives while they were under conviction, and greeted them as triumphant heroes upon their release from jail.

Moreover, while the evils of an administrative system built upon patronage seemed obvious to the middle-class reformers who could afford to measure municipal performance by its efficient use of funds and its low tax rate, the overwhelming needs of the immigrants led them to measure government by a different yardstick: by the results it produced —by its ability to provide jobs and parks, schools and hospitals, roads and baths. Former Mayor Josiah Quincy understood this when he pleaded with the reformers to take a broader conception of the functions of the city. The object of the city, he argued, is "to promote the welfare of its citizens, in the broadest sense"; and to that end, "spending money liberally for the common good could be exceedingly beneficial." If necessary, he said, "it is even wiser to submit . . . to a certain amount of waste or even dishonesty than to leave essential municipal duties unfulfilled."

And, in order to produce results, as one leading voice for good government recognized, a mayor *had* to acknowledge and reconcile in some way the claims of patronage and the powers of the machine politicians. Speaking of what would result, given the cumbersome structure of the bicameral system in Boston, with seventy-five Council members and thirteen aldermen, if a mayor refused to accommodate the entrenched politicians, the *Herald* allowed: "His administration would likely come to a deadlock, and hence what he avoids in the way of the evils of patronage may be more than offset by his inability to carry through positive and advantageous municipal measures."

In time, events would take a turn, and the reformers' critiques would find a more sympathetic audience, but for the first months of his administration Fitzgerald enjoyed a substantial and widespread popularity. Judging only the concrete, the broader aspect of things escaping them, the people of Boston applauded Fitzgerald's continuing display of action. Day by day he was more in the public eye than any other man, captivating audiences with his plea for a "bigger, better and busier Boston," charming reporters with his sense of the dramatic, his swift repartee and his affable manner. In meetings, in speeches, and in press conferences, his mastery of the details of his office astonished many who had long before taken his measure. And, more important, his efforts seemed to be paying off: before the end of his first month in office, the Board of Aldermen passed his order for a consumptives' hospital; by early February, the School Committee approved his plan for a high school of commerce; and by the summer his bill for taxing corporations was making its way through a special joint committee on taxation in the state legislature.

Never losing his energy or enthusiasm, he continued to thrive on activity and to find entertainment in the most routine tasks: speaking at a welcoming banquet for Archbishop William O'Connell in April 1906; traveling to Washington to sell War Secretary Taft fifty acres of land on Deer Island for a United States fortification in May; presenting a Dorchester High diploma to his fifteen-year-old daughter Rose in June—the first city magistrate privileged to preside at his own daughter's graduation; showing up at Oak Island in July, surrounded by an exuberant crowd of several hundred small boys as he personally directed the field day events at the annual summer outing of St. Stephen's Parish. The following month he lunched with Prince Wilhelm of Sweden, and a few weeks later he appeared in New York at a welcoming reception for William Jennings Bryan, where his style, his exuberance and his good humor made him stand out even in what was called "a glittering crowd." "He outdid himself," one reporter wrote, "and looked as though he would certainly make old Broadway sit up and take notice." Clad in a light-gray sack suit with a necktie of dark red and green, sporting his famous Panama upon his head, the mayor possessed, the reporter observed, "the rare faculty of wearing with perfect serenity and harmony things that would look out of place on most men." All in all, reviewing his first six months in office, one had to conclude that things were going well for John Fitzgerald.

So much did the political life of the city center upon the mayor that when he went away in August for his summer vacation the press and "half the city" traveled with him. In these days before the spread of the automobile, families usually went for their vacations to one particular place and settled there, with trunks, servants and children, for weeks or months. For Irish Catholic families in Boston at the turn of the century, the most popular place was Old Orchard Beach, Maine, a summer resort built along one of the longest beaches on the Atlantic coast.

Known as "the city of the sea," with an assemblage of hotels and cottages crowded thickly all along the seafront, its red roofs, peaked gables and gaudy turrets curving with the sandy shore, Old Orchard was described in a contemporary guidebook as "the typical watering place for those who detest the name of solitude." Packed with "shops, cafes, booths, fruit-stands, shooting galleries, bazaars without end," with "newsboys, hotel porters and bootblacks," Old Orchard gave the appearance of having sprung up in a night, "like a colony of red, white and orange toadstools after a summer shower." Yet, beyond the crowded beachfront, the craggy rocks and the crashing surf, as far as the eye could see, lay the expanse of the dark-blue sea, providing "one of the most magnificent vistas in all the world." For the sociable Irish, with their Celtic love of beauty, it was the ideal resort.

Fitzgerald first took his family to Old Orchard in the early 1890s when Rose was still an infant, and year after year they returned. Though they never owned a house there—each year they rented a different cottage or stayed in one of the bustling hotels—eventually the place would serve in memory as the summer base of the Fitzgerald family.

It was there at the age of five that Rose Fitzgerald first met a seven-year-old freckled boy named Joseph Patrick Kennedy, P. J. Kennedy's eldest son. A group photograph taken from the beach shows Rose and Joe seated together on the porch of a large white hotel, surrounded with relatives from both families. Rose, her thick curls falling out beneath her white hat, is leaning happily against her father; Joe, in plaid blouse and cap, is seated beside his Aunt Katherine and in front of his mother. Altogether there are over thirty people in the picture, a striking assemblage of toddlers and adults, of handlebar mustaches, white summer suits and large summer bonnets.

And it was there, a decade later, in the summer of 1906, that Rose's romance with Joe Kennedy began. A student at the Boston Latin School, the tall sandy-haired Joe Kennedy was as confident in his striking good looks as Rose Fitzgerald was in hers. Talkative and clever, driving and masterful, he had, Rose recalled, "the most wonderful smile that seemed to light up his entire face from within and made an instant impression on everyone he met."

They went well together, these two—they shared a vital ambition to live life to its fullest which seemed to ally them against all that was commonplace in everyday life. If ever there was a pair whose experiences in childhood matched, it was Joe and Rose: born to conquer, they had each grown up as the favored child in a favored family, secure in the love and admiration of a wide circle of friends and acquaintances, proud of the honors they were carrying away in school, with Rose consistently ending up at the top of her class while Joe was elected president of his, colonel of his drill regiment and captain of the baseball team.

"I shall always remember Old Orchard as a place of magic," Rose Kennedy said when she was nearly ninety years old, "for it was the place where Joe and I fell in love. It was a magical place for our parents as well, because so many of their friends and relatives went there. They all came up at the same time, they took cottages right near one another and they visited back and forth constantly. At Old Orchard there was something for everyone—lawn tennis, fishing and skeet shooting for the men, carriage rides and concerts for the women, and for the children a merry-go-round and boardwalk games. And, of course, there was always the beach, the beautiful white sandy beach which stretched out for miles. I can still picture my mother sitting in a large porch rocker where all the mothers sat tilting their chairs so they could see their children splashing in the water. In the evenings after dinner, the families would gather in the big dining room of the Brunswick Hotel, and afterwards, by the light of old kerosene lamps, the men would play cards and the women would talk."

In his first term as mayor, as Boston drowsed in the summer heat, Fitzgerald spent most of the month of August on the cooler shores of Old Orchard. On July 27, 1906, the *Boston Post* reported that "Mayor Fitzgerald shook the dust of the streets of Boston from his patent leathers and took the two o'clock train for Old Orchard," where he and his family would spend the rest of the summer in a $12,000 cottage known as Bleak House. As the press reported it, life at Old Orchard was informal, vigorous and athletic, a whirlwind of activity with Mayor Fitzgerald, not surprisingly, at the center of the whirlwind. Various dispatches from Old Orchard describe him bowling along the beach in his chauf-feured auto accompanied by dozens of joyous children, defying the tremendous pounding of storm waves to swim his daily swim with his daughter Rose, giving impromptu speeches at the nearby campground, scoring a 91 in candlepins and even becoming a hero at an afternoon baseball game when he "displaced a hired pitcher on a picked nine, and in the remaining seven innings, struck out 16 men on the opposite team, which in the first two innings, had been winning."

Nor was politics left behind. "Hardly a day passed," the press reported, "that Fitzgerald did not have some visitors from Boston and the mental strain was intense." As His Honor sat on the veranda of Bleak House, lawyer Timothy Coakley came by, a few days later Joe Corbett and still later P. J. Kennedy, Jim Doyle and Jim McClellan. Before the end of the summer a majority of the ward leaders had made their way to the sands of Old Orchard. Carefully noting each of Fitzgerald's visitors, reporters speculated on the possibility that a new strategy board, made up of selected ward leaders, was coming into existence.

But, reporters observed, in Old Orchard, as in Boston, Fitzgerald spent far more of his time with his six brothers than he did with any of the regular politicians. His inner circle of advisers were all Fitzgeralds. As the pattern of his administration had developed, usually four or five and sometimes all six brothers would show up at City Hall shortly after 5 P.M. and remain with the mayor for hours at a stretch, advising him, arguing with him, amusing him, relaxing him. The same closeness pre-vailed at Old Orchard; wherever the mayor went, he was accompanied by Jim, Eddie, George, Mike, Joe or Henry.

It was during this summer of 1906, observing Fitzgerald's continued reliance upon his brothers and taking stock of his first six months in office, that journalists began to refer to the Fitzgeralds as "the royal family." It was, at the time, a good-natured remark, suggesting the power, the prominence and the camaraderie of the Fitzgerald brothers. It was said that never before had the city been run by a band of brothers all of whom seemed to possess an instinctive understanding of politics and public life. Irish to the core, by turns affectionate and raging, rowdy and wise, the Fitzgerald brothers acted as extensions of the mayor's power, distributing patronage, delivering orders and bearing messages. "Henry S. and James T. and possibly two of the other brothers act as the mayor's confidential men," *Practical Politics* reported, "and no other confidential man is needed." Not all people took to the Fitzger-alds. They were considered loud and noisy by some and arrogant by others. Yet, for the most part, they confronted the city with the vitality and confidence of a genial and high-spirited clan.

Though their relationship was often tense and stormy, John Fitzgerald was probably most involved with his oldest brother, Jim. Still the best-looking and by far the most self-sufficient of all the Fitzgeralds, Jim was considered, by 1906, "an extremely wealthy man" and a most influential figure in Charlestown, where he was not only the proprietor of the Bunker Hill House, one of the largest hotels in the city, but also the owner of three barrooms, including the successful tavern at Sullivan Square which, on a Sunday or holiday, his granddaughter was told, would net him a profit of $1,000.

They were not the least alike, these two successful brothers. John Fitzgerald was the conspicuous one, the one who cherished the limelight, the loud and chatty one. Jim was invariably cool and distant, a man who preferred to exercise his power from behind the scenes. At different times he gave financial support to each of his brothers. It was said that over the years he contributed $50,000 to John's campaigns, that he helped George and Eddie set up their businesses and that he gave Henry the $16,000 he needed to buy the Elcho Cigar Company, a manufacturing plant which employed 105 cigarmakers who turned out by hand one of the most popular brands of cigars in all New England. Yet, if Jim was generous with his money, he was sparing with his emotions; affection and love were far more difficult for him to give. According to family legend, if one of the brothers did something wrong or displayed a weakness, it was John Fitzgerald rather than Jim who stood by him, providing sympathy and understanding. Similarly, if one of the children became sick, it was John, teddy bear in hand, who showed up at the bedside, not Jim.

If John Fitzgerald was deeply though uneasily attached all his life to his oldest brother, Jim, he was probably closest and most relaxed with his youngest brother, Henry. Here the bond between the two was an association of similar natures avid for work and ambitious for power. With his small frame, ruddy complexion and blue eyes, Henry so resembled John Fitzgerald that he would often be approached on the street as "Mr. Mayor." Their partnership dated back to John's first foray into the insurance business, when he invited Henry, then only fifteen, to be his clerk. Within a matter of weeks, John Fitzgerald later said, he recognized how clever and industrious Henry was and he put him in charge of all patronage activities in the North End.

When Henry turned twenty-eight, Fitzgerald deepened his brother's involvement in politics by engineering his election to the State House. The following year Henry married Margaret Herlihy of Charlestown and bought a house on Lyndhurst Drive in Dorchester, only half a block away from his brother's large white house on Welles Avenue. Living so close together, the two families grew up as one. When Fitzgerald became mayor, Henry became his alter ego, his confidant and trouble-shooter. "See Henry," was the mayor's constant refrain when someone came to him about a job. By the summer of 1906 it had become a cliché to say that Henry Fitzgerald was the second most powerful man in the city.

Of the middle four surviving brothers, Eddie was the most gregarious, the most unconventional, and in many ways the most endearing. Jovial and hearty, warm and witty, Eddie has been variously described by his descendants as "a wonderful character," "a natural politician," "the funniest of them all." It was said that children adored him, and that he couldn't go ten feet on the streets of Boston or the beach at Old Orchard without a wild assortment of people, birds and animals following after him. With John Fitzgerald's help, Eddie had obtained a liquor license and had bought a controlling interest in a tavern on Hanover Street before he was thirty. As he prospered, he bought into several other taverns and eventually became the owner of a thriving hotel, the Hotel Warren. A bachelor all his life, he lived with his brother Michael in the winter and with his brother Henry in the summer. Generous and caring by instinct, he would regularly order his hotel restaurant to feed all the hungry people in his neighborhood. A man of excess, he ate too much and drank too much, but luck and a strong constitution favored him, and, as his nephew Tom put it, "he had a good long run before the food and liquor finally got to him at the age of 73."

George was a milder edition of Eddie, slimmer, more conventional and more reserved. Like Eddie, he had started out as a clerk in Jim's store, and then with Jim's help he had gone out on his own as a brewery salesman. A shrewd and careful businessman, he was already doing well when he married Lizzy, "a dazzling beauty," and became the father of a son, Ned. In 1903 George and Lizzy moved to Dorchester, where George became the chairman of the ward committee. Some of his relatives believe that even then George was drinking more than was good for him, but if so, few spoke of it at the time. The stronger memory is the image of heads turning as George and Lizzy strolled along the beach at Old Orchard, her long black hair falling loosely behind the black velvet ribbon she always wore, his handsome face radiating happiness and pride. Yet those summers were possibly the last happy times for the couple, for the drinking would get worse, eventually leading George to a nervous breakdown and an early death in McClean Hospital at the age of forty-three.

Michael, one year younger than John, was a policeman at Station 9 when his brother became mayor. For many years, he too had been known "to hit the bottle too much," but when he finally married at the age of thirty-eight he took the pledge, and he rarely drank to excess again. His wife was Elizabeth Theresa Degnan, the youngest daughter of the kindly Irish woman, Ellen Degnan, who had watched over the Fitzgerald boys when their parents died. In rapid succession five children were born, and Michael moved his family to a house in Copps Hill Terrace in the North End. Michael was observant by nature, and his police work brought him into contact with all manner of people, contractors and prostitutes, pickpockets and crooks, debtors and drunks, who gave him a perspective on city life which his brother greatly valued. In return, the mayor secured for Michael the position of health inspector, which brought shorter hours and better pay, allowed him an occasional afternoon off to watch the Red Stockings play ball, and gave him the chance to join with his brothers in their nightly sessions at City Hall and their summer vacations at Old Orchard Beach.

Of all the brothers, Joe, five years younger than John Fitzgerald, had the hardest time making his way. Genial and good-natured, he had returned from the Spanish–American War with a severe form of malaria in which the parasites had localized in his brain and left him, in the words of relatives, "a little dippy." Old-timers still recall a hot summer day at Old Orchard when Joe, followed by dozens of adoring kids, marched up and down the beach in his full military uniform, giving orders to himself and singing songs. Unable to secure a job on his own, Joe had been supported by his brothers until 1905, when John interceded with Mayor Collins and secured him work delivering the daily traffic report from the Warren Avenue Bridge to City Hall. For this service, one performed by the mail service from all other bridges for one cent a day, Joe received an annual salary of $1,100 and the satisfaction of earning his own living. In the years ahead opposing politicians would use Joe's position against Fitzgerald, publicly ridiculing Joe as "the human postage stamp," but in the heady days of the Fitzgerald reign the family's powerful position cast a friendly light on Joe's eccentricities.

There were, to be sure, disadvantages for the mayor in having his brothers so visible in city affairs. Their errors and excesses could not be easily repudiated or ignored. Nor could their power and access be easily forgiven. Politicians disgruntled by their inability to see the mayor more often would direct their frustration and resentment against the brothers, claiming that "the Fitzgerald dynasty" had appropriated to itself a kinglike power, complaining that Fitzgerald had "syndicated" the office of the mayor, dividing it up into seven parts.

But Fitzgerald refused to credit any of this gossip. As he saw it, his brothers had always been his closest friends, his favorite companions. Becoming mayor of the city did not "diminish one whit" his affection or loyalty to them; on the contrary, he needed them more than ever. If there was any talk in the city of the extended roles his brothers were playing, Fitzgerald said he had "no apology to make." Nine boys, he explained, had grown up together and had lived together for fifteen years without a father or a mother. "Two of the boys died some years ago. Seven of us remained. There was the warmest kind of attachment always between us. In every political campaign of mine they have been of inestimable service to me. If I were to be without their assistance tomorrow I would not think of running for public office ever again."

"There was only one problem with our summers in Maine," Rose Fitzgerald Kennedy recalled; "they never lasted long enough." In this familiar vacationer's lament there was an additional meaning provided by the geography of Old Orchard, where the seasonal scales tip early. By the middle of August the days in Maine have more of early fall than of summer in them, the air grows chilly, darkness comes sooner, and along the back roads some of the leaves have already begun to turn. There comes a difference in the light, a difference in the air, an indefinable shifting, and then, slowly but surely, all the vacationing families begin to pack up and leave.

Holding out longer than most, the Fitzgeralds finally returned to Boston on September 14, 1906. "Although it was late in the day," the *Boston Evening Record* reported, "the news that the chief executive was once more in City Hall brought the usual throng of politicians and seekers after everything and he put in several strenuous hours seeing visitors before leaving for his home on Welles Avenue which had been completely renovated since the Fitzgerald family had been out of town."

As the autumn turned to winter and the mayor began his second year in office, reporters found him moving at an even faster pace, impossible as that seemed. On January 13, 1907, he appeared at the Waldorf-Astoria in New York as a dinner guest of Frederick A. Heinze, the copper king. The following month he greeted President Theodore Roosevelt, who had come to Boston on a private trip and sat with him in the center box at the Symphony Ball of the Young Men's Catholic Association. In March he returned to New York and then back to Boston to be an honored guest at the St. Stephen's Catholic Lyceum. On May 23 he received Baron Kuroki, the Japanese general in the Russo–Japanese War, and three weeks later the Duke of Abruzzi, mountain climber and explorer.

# CHAPTER 9
## "EYES FULL OF LAUGHTER"

I t is little wonder that Rose Fitzgerald at seventeen wanted time
to stand still, for at that age she
seemed to have everything a girl could have: an open, ardent nature
filled with wonder and belief; a radiant complexion and eyes full of
laughter; a fine, slim figure and plenty of new clothes; a strong, active
mind and abundant opportunity to engage it in stimulating conversation. As her father's chosen companion, she had privileged access to all

manner of political and social events, ranging from front-row theater seats to box seats at the ball park, from the head table at banquets to the reviewing stand at rallies.

"We all stood in admiration of her," recalled Margaret Curry, one of her companions from Dorchester. "As we saw it, she lived in a special world of infinite possibility, a happy world of movement, vitality and action. I can still picture her in my mind walking down the hallway at school in one of her fancy challis blouses and a woolen skirt that reached down to her ankles. The bottom part of the skirt was stitched all around with a stitch so heavy that the whole skirt swayed as she walked. There was something so enchanting in that swaying walk of hers that we all started wearing challis blouses with woolen skirts."

There is a remarkable photograph of Rose, taken at about this time, showing her seated on the edge of an air duct on the deck of a ship. In it she is wearing a good-looking striped blouse with a full skirt. Her thick black hair is caught up in a braided bun, her head tilted, her face flushed with excitement. There are the square chin, the straight nose and the fine cheekbones which with maturity would become the handsome and familiar face of the Kennedy matriarch, but there is nothing of the matriarch's expression in the dancing smile and the bright, full eyes. It is an altogether captivating image of budding womanhood, of an untamed and unbroken spirit.

All through her girlhood years, in contrast with her mother's experience, Rose had been encouraged to express herself; her remarks had been attended to; she had been expected to have intelligent opinions. Curling up in her bedroom, she had devoured books on history, politics, romance and travel, and the breadth of her reading showed. "Brimming with animation and charm and girlish spirits," one reporter wrote at the time, "she displays depth and strength of mind rarely found in so young a woman. Undoubtedly her father's influence upon her life has broadened her outlook, so that she lives much more vividly than most girls of her age."

In her element in almost any sphere, she had no idea as yet what it was she wanted to do. Her chief ambition was still of a more general nature: to be one of the best, to move in a realm of light, a world of challenge. When she thought of her future, her dreams focused on a college education, and from there she imagined possibilities as varied as a career in music or in politics.

The college Rose had chosen was Wellesley, a small private women's college situated on three hundred acres of wooded hilly land on the shores of Lake Waban, twenty miles west of Boston, and with her intelligence and her grades she was accepted for admittance in her junior year of high school. She later contended that she had had her heart set on Wellesley for a long time, from "a golden afternoon" when, as a girl of thirteen, she had first visited the school with her father. Bathed in the physical beauty and the intellectual excitement of the atmosphere, she persuaded three of her close friends, Ruth Evans, Vera Legg and Marguerite O'Callaghan, to apply to Wellesley, and when all of them were finally accepted there was great rejoicing.

It would have been difficult for Rose to choose a college more in keeping with her temperament. Since its founding in 1875 for the purpose of giving to young women opportunities for education equivalent to those provided in the best colleges for young men, Wellesley had developed an exceptional curriculum, an elite student body and a reputation as one of the finest colleges in the entire country. In 1900, its departments of English literature and psychology—steeped in talent, including medieval scholar Sophie Jewett, poet Katharine Lee Bates (author of "America the Beautiful"), and internationally known philosopher Mary Calkins—had won a gold medal at the Paris Exposition.

Moreover, a special set of circumstances had combined at the turn of the century to bring together at Wellesley an extraordinary group of committed women whose driving intellectual powers and sense of mission (as the first generation of female college graduates in America) put them in the forefront of the movement to better the conditions of workers and the poor and to right the wrongs of industrial society.

This was the period when Wellesley faculty members Katharine Coman, Emily Greene Balch and Edith Abbott were breaking new ground in the teaching of political economics, with courses offered in the industrial history of the United States and of England, the development of modern socialism, the regulation of trusts, the evolution of the factory system and the problem of child labor. A friend of Jane Addams and a moving force in the creation of Denison House, Boston's settlement house, Miss Coman was nationally recognized as a leader in the Consumers League, which carried on a continual campaign to abolish sweatshops and to better conditions in factories. Miss Balch, also a powerful force in the settlement movement, was an exuberant, inspired teacher who inaugurated the concept of fieldwork at Wellesley by taking the students to institutions for paupers and the feebleminded, to reform schools and prisons. Spare of figure, unmindful of clothes, Balch would later become the second American woman—Jane Addams was the first —to win the Nobel Peace Prize. Edith Abbott, the third teacher in this exceptional group, taught a rich assortment of courses on immigration and the labor movement; her writings on immigrant groups are still widely read today.

In those days Vida Scudder, professor of English, and Ellen Hayes, professor of mathematics, also figured largely in the Wellesley scene. Both women were nonconformists who rebelled against the inequalities they saw around them; both were members of the Socialist Party when it was not even considered respectable to be a member of a trade union; together, they inspired a generation of Wellesley students to an active regard for child welfare, settlement houses and woman suffrage. By 1907, the year Rose Fitzgerald was scheduled to start her freshman year, the excitement of the place had reached a feverish pitch; everywhere one looked there were new reform groups springing up: an Equal Suffrage League, the Somerset Y, the student branch of the Women's Christian Temperance Union, the College Settlement Association, a Single Tax League, and much more. It was, in short, a fascinating place; indeed, for a young girl like Rose Fitzgerald with a vibrant mind and an active temperament, there was probably no better school in all of America.

While the days were passing for Rose in happy anticipation of her college experience, there was a movement under way which was to have calamitous results for Fitzgerald and for all the members of his family.

At eleven o'cock Tuesday morning, July 30, 1907, the seven members of the newly created Finance Commission arrived at the small office of former Mayor Nathan Matthews in the Ames Building to hold their first organizational meeting. It began simply enough with the election of Matthews as chairman and the appointment as secretary of J. Wells Farley, a young, energetic lawyer, and as counsel Michael Sughrue, who had filled the office of district attorney and was an expert in criminal practices. But the completion of these routine matters set in motion a process which, for months and months, would occupy the very center of Fitzgerald's life.

The commission had been constituted by the state legislature in response to "the uneasy feeling in the community that waste and extravagance were flourishing" to an extent greater than ever before. It had long been common knowledge that the city treasury had become a field for exploitation by contractors and political leaders, and that thousands of dollars were wasted each year through the excess prices paid for materials and supplies to favored contractors who then returned the favor by financing the party machine from their swollen profits. But by the turn of the century, as the city government became increasingly involved in the wildly lucrative business of conferring franchises upon companies to operate streetcar lines, to deliver gas, light and coal and to provide telephone services, the scale of the corruption had become so colossal that it seemed to one observer that "the moral salvation and the very solvency of the city were at stake."

Awakened by a sense of impending doom, disillusioned by the course of Fitzgerald's administration, and stimulated by the nationwide character of reform, Boston's progressives had sharpened their demand that something be done about the city's corruption and graft. In November 1906 the *Boston Herald* had spoken for many reformers when it called for a statewide commission to investigate the financial condition of the city government. A number of large cities had already taken this route; the previous decade had witnessed major investigations of municipal affairs in New York, Chicago, San Francisco, Cleveland, St. Louis, Albany, Philadelphia and Cincinnati.

The interesting wrinkle in Boston's situation was that soon after the reformers called for action, the mayor himself—who was expected to be the prime target of the investigation—had issued his own proposal for the establishment of a finance commission with wide license to examine the business of the city. According to the mayor's plan—which was the one ultimately adopted—the commission was to be composed of seven "representative, able and impartial" citizens.

It had taken a few months for the state legislature to act on the mayor's proposal, but when it did the new commission found itself with broad investigatory powers, including the authority to summon witnesses, compel the release of documents and take testimony. In the meantime, the City Council had appropriated the substantial sum of $50,000 for expenses.

Fitzgerald's reasons for proposing the investigative committee remain an interesting puzzle, for, in spite of the rising tide of criticism from reformers, he still enjoyed widespread popularity with the public at large. Perhaps he recognized that sooner or later, with or without his approval, the Republican state legislature would take some kind of action, and that if this was inevitable it was better that he be the author of the plan. Perhaps, as George Nutter argued, in spite of the cumbersome mechanism for nominating members Fitzgerald had in mind a committee he could dominate, "a whitewashing committee" similar to the one Boss Tweed had constituted in New York with John Jacob Astor at its head; reporting at the height of Tammany Hall's corrupt power, this New York committee had certified that the affairs of the city were being administered "in a correct and faithful manner."

Or perhaps Fitzgerald simply assumed that this committee, like most bodies comprised of busy private citizens working without compensation, would merely run its course with an occasional meeting, sporadic interviews and a dull report, and in the meantime its very existence would provide a release of tension. The progressive reformer Joseph Lee recognized this possibility when he wrote: "Usually when a committee is appointed, the citizen feels that now he can turn over and go to sleep. Its creation is regarded not as a preliminary to action but as a substitute. When, after a three years doze, it reports in six volumes, the newspapers give it six lines and there an end."

It is also possible, given Fitzgerald's remarkable ability to see himself in the best light, that he fully believed that the commission would find him innocent of any wrongdoing no matter how long and hard it worked.

In any case, the proposal was made, and once made it could not be unmade, even as events took a turn very different from Fitzgerald's original expectations. The first sign of unusual life and activity on the part of the new Finance Commission came at the end of its first business meeting, when its members decided to meet again, not at the accustomed interval of two weeks or a month, but at nine o'clock the following morning; and this meeting was succeeded by another the following day and another the day after that. "As a matter of fact," Commissioner John Moors reported, "the members not only gave the greater part of their business hours to this public duty (to their serious financial loss in important instances) but they also devoted to it their Sundays, holidays, summer vacations and many of their nights." The commission's commitment to its work was indeed impressive; it was even said that one prominent member became so involved in the investigation that he forgot to take his rubbers off through an entire month of good weather.

The growth of civic passion is a peculiar thing. Every member of this commission had achieved considerable success in his private occupation: Nathan Matthews and George Ernst in law; Samuel Carr and George Crocker in finance; John Sullivan in business; John Kennedy in labor; and John Moors in banking. Four of the seven were graduates of Harvard University, and a fifth Harvard later adopted with an honorary degree. In another era, all of these men might have lived full and contented lives without any connection with public affairs. But as members of the generation which came to maturity at the turn of the century, all of them, even as they were pursuing their own ambitions, were acutely aware that, in Richard Hofstadter's words, "there was something special about the political and social life of their time which sharply marked it off from the preceding era."

An activist spirit was in the air, a new consciousness of the need for change. The long-awaited reckoning with the industrial order was now at hand; the people were determined to make a new life for themselves, to regain control of their economic destiny. It was an age fascinated with politics; its greatest heroes and its greatest villains were its politicians. In this atmosphere it is little wonder that all the members "made the work of the Commission their first interest in life."

Like impatient hounds on the scent of game, the commission decided not to wait to issue an official, polished report, but instead to run with each set of its findings, preliminary as they might be, "so long as every line was weighed and tested to be sure that it told the truth in such a way that the facts would surely support it." It was a farsighted decision, for with each sensational report the commission's prestige and reputation grew stronger. The first report, issued on August 7, 1907, only eight days after the commission's first meeting, focused public attention on the waste and inefficiency of the Department of Weights and Measures, specifically calling on the mayor to withdraw his improvident appointment of eight unnecessary deputy sealers of weights and measures. As Massachusetts Civic League member Joseph Lee wrote two years later:

> It was a report calculated to make us all sit up, and we have been taking notice ever since. It was direct, simple, specific, saying what was the matter with a certain city office and what ought to be done about it. Similar detonations followed in rapid succession for a year and a half, each one getting more space in the papers than most commissions ever get at all. There were no opinions, no epithets, no back talk; just hard, concrete, undeniable fact.

In a previous era when the newspapers were more closely identified with the political and financial power of the city, this first report and the 126 which followed in the next eighteen months would most likely have been soft-pedaled on the ground that it was not good for Boston or for local commerce to make a public row or to drag the fair name of the city through the mud. But by 1907, exposure had become the order of the day; there was excitement and romance in the business of investigation and in the spreading of information. People loved to read about corruption, and the newspapers loved to satisfy the people's desires.

Fitzgerald responded to the first batch of commission reports, issued over successive weeks in August 1907, in an uncharacteristically subdued manner. For once in his life he said very little. From the sands of Old Orchard came only the flat comment that when he returned home he would surely look into the various matters mentioned. In the meantime, he intended to take in as many salt baths as he possibly could.

September 1 found Fitzgerald back in Boston faced with a far more troubling announcement: the Finance Commission had scheduled a series of public hearings on the peculiar manner in which Fitzgerald's new Supply Department had let out contracts for coal. The head of the Supply Department was a man named Michael Mitchell, one of Fitzgerald's closest and oldest friends. A large man with broad shoulders, bushy hair, thick eyebrows and a thick black mustache, Mitchell radiated warmth and goodwill. In the first year and a half of Fitzgerald's administration, the two men had seen each other nearly every day. They had dined together at least once or twice a week; and in the evenings after work they could often be seen walking together arm in arm. If the commission had any evidence against Mitchell, it would surely implicate Fitzgerald as well.

When the Supply Department had originally been created, in February 1906, Fitzgerald hailed it as the solution to the problems of inefficiency, waste and corruption. By consolidating all of the city's purchases into one central department instead of letting each make its own purchases, the mayor's office, for the first time, would be able to search and scrutinize all the payments made from the city treasury. The centralization of purchases would also, Fitzgerald had said, "secure lower prices for our city" and "tend to prevent wasteful and unnecessary purchases." In particular, Fitzgerald had promised, the new department would overhaul the wasteful methods by which the city went about making its enormous purchases of coal.

When Fitzgerald first approached Mitchell about taking on the superintendency of the new department, Mitchell had expressed substantial reservations. While he had experience in purchasing and supplying the paraphernalia of mourning—for fifteen years he and his sister had run a successful undertaking business in Charlestown—he was not prepared, he felt, to superintend nearly one million dollars a year for the purchase of materials and supplies, ranging from coal and oil to flagstones and drainpipes, from spruce lumber to iron castings. In addition, as one newspaper account suggested, he was worried that if he took on a job as demanding as this he would be unable to carry out his responsibilities as undertaker. His preference, the *Boston Evening Record* reported, was for the post of assistant auditor, which would have allowed him to split his hours between his undertaking business and the city government.

Fitzgerald and Mitchell had met when they served together in the city government. Fitzgerald was instantly attracted to Mitchell's magnetic personality and his ready ability to win the confidence of others. Mitchell, in turn, was drawn to Fitzgerald's raw force and bounding energy, which was greater than his own. As the years passed, their friendship deepened, until by 1906 Mitchell was the one person—outside of his brothers—to whom Fitzgerald felt he could turn in absolute trust.

Over the years, Mitchell had grown almost as attached to Fitzgerald's children as he was to Fitzgerald himself. A bachelor who lived with his sister, Mitchell regularly took his vacations with the Fitzgerald family, joining them at Old Orchard in the summers and at Hot Springs, Virginia, in the winters. "We simply adored him," Rose remembered. "He was always so kind and so interested in everything; he reminded me of a big, comfortable teddy bear. I can still remember the long letters he sent us when we were away at school. They were filled with the most wonderful descriptions of people and events. And whenever he came to our house, his pockets would be stuffed with trinkets and chocolates for all of us children."

It was, in fact, by appealing to Mitchell's loyalty that Fitzgerald finally persuaded him, against his will, to accept the position of superintendent of supplies. "He took the position," *Practical Politics* reported, "not because he needed the money, for he did not, but because he felt that it would be helpful to the mayor to have a friend in that position." Indeed, so important was the new department to Fitzgerald's plans that both men assumed from the start that the mayor's office would be involved in all the major decisions.

When Fitzgerald received word of the impending public hearings, his first thoughts, he later told Eddie Gallagher, ran back to Mitchell's original hesitations about taking the job, and, without his knowing why, an ominous sense of foreboding passed over him. Yet never in his darkest moments could Fitzgerald have foreseen the grueling test to which Mitchell's friendship would be put nor the long and embarrassing chain of events that would crowd in upon his entire family as a consequence of the hearings about to begin.

The first session of what became known as the "Coal Graft Hearings" opened on a rainy Thursday morning, the third of September, in the meeting room of the Old School Committee Building on Mason Street in an atmosphere charged with excitement and anticipation.

The first witness, George P. Koch, took the stand at 10:30 A.M. Koch, chief clerk in the Supply Department, stated that in his present job he worked directly under Michael Mitchell, superintendent of supplies. For two hours Sughrue kept Koch on the stand, plying him with questions in an attempt to discover the methods by which coal was purchased by the city. Throughout his entire testimony, much of which was purely routine, the witness, a thin and pale-faced man, appeared uncommonly nervous; his hands were seen to tremble and on several occasions his voice cracked. During the intense questioning Koch admitted that he could not give a single instance where a coal contract had been advertised for bid and awarded to the lowest bidder.

At these words, there was a stir in the room. It was common knowledge that the law required public advertisement for all contracts over $3,000 unless the mayor, with good reason, expressly approved the private deal. For example, Sughrue interrupted, in May of 1906 a large contract for thirty thousand tons of coal was not advertised in the papers. Instead, it went directly to the W. C. Niver Coal Company, whose agent, Maurice Klous, received the lion's share of all the city contracts for coal. "For what reason?" Koch was asked. "I do not know," he replied. At this point, Sughrue informed the committee that a summons had been issued for Klous but that Klous had left the city and was nowhere to be found. Later in his testimony Koch admitted that from the start there were complaints about the quality of the coal supplied by Klous, but the city continued to deal with him nonetheless. Then, with the strong whiff of politics in the air, and with Koch wiping the sweat from his brow, Sughrue called the next witness.

The afternoon session resumed with Mitchell in the stand. He had not slept for several days, he later told a friend, so anxious was he about the hearing—not because he had done anything wrong, but because he feared the commission would find out the truth, the fact that he had never really taken hold of the department, that he had left all the major decisions to the mayor and the mayor's brothers while he himself had felt obliged to continue his undertaking duties.

Mitchell was artless and inexperienced at testifying, and his efforts to conceal his ignorance only made things worse for him. As the tone of Sughrue's questions grew sharper, Mitchell looked as if he had withdrawn into himself. At the end of each answer his voice trailed off, as if he feared that if he went on talking he might say something ill-advised. All afternoon long, Sughrue made the most of Mitchell's discomfiture, taking every occasion he could to expose the man's ignorance of his job. Finally, he brought Mitchell to admit that the May 14 contract was but the first of six contracts let to Klous and the Niver Coal Company in the course of his superintendency, and that all but one of these had been let without public advertisement, though just why Klous had been chosen above all others he could not clearly say.

Then, just before the session came to a close, Sughrue produced two dramatic documents which would, he suggested, far better than the halting testimony heard so far, provide the commission with a true understanding of the motivating force behind the lucrative contracts Mitchell had made with Klous. The first, a letter written by Klous to James Donovan, the former superintendent of streets, on December 9, 1905, was presented as the tip of the iceberg, illustrating the nature of the hold which certain favored contractors had upon the city government:

> We are this date in receipt of your letter asking our support for the candidacy of Daniel Flanagan, aspirant for the board of aldermen, and the writer wishes to personally assure you that he will deliver at least 300 votes for your candidate, represented by the employees of this company and as many more as our combined efforts will secure for him.
>
> Very truly yours,
> W. C. Niver Coal Co.
> Maurice H. Klous

The second document presented was a personal telegram sent to Mitchell at the Sea Shore Hotel, Old Orchard Beach, on August 9, 1907, expressing Klous's regrets at being unable to join Mitchell and "the boys." In Sughrue's mind, these two documents served to reinforce the view emerging from the testimony that with Mitchell it was friendship and politics that mattered, not which company could deliver the best coal at the least price.

When the hearings resumed on Wednesday afternoon, Mitchell was back on the stand for another grueling examination. For two hours, the hapless undertaker tried in vain to answer the barrage of technical questions about the poor quality of the coal Klous had supplied. Incapable of feigning, Mitchell was forced to acknowledge that he himself knew very little about coal.

At this startling admission, a burst of coarse laughter ran through the room and Sughrue, sensing victory, brought an immediate end to the testimony. When Mitchell left the stand, he was a beaten man. He walked out, the *Boston Evening Record* reported, "moistening his lips nervously and wiping his face."

The mayor's aides had listened in dismay to the hearing that day, and as they saw it Mitchell's showing had not been a good one. Granted, the position in which the beleaguered superintendent found himself was a difficult one, but the mayor must remember that elections were coming up in three months and, unless some way could be found to defuse the Finance Commission, Mitchell's continued presence in the administration could do great damage to Fitzgerald's hopes for reelection.

Mitchell's resignation was the only answer, but it might be difficult to achieve, the aides believed, for Mitchell had a large number of loyal friends who were telling him that he must stop being so defensive, that he must remember he had done nothing wrong and that he must stick it out in order to vindicate himself and restore his good name. Mitchell's friends were probably right; had he stayed in his office and told the commission how the Department of Supplies really worked, it would have been clear to all that he was simply a stand-in for the mayor himself. But when Fitzgerald approached Mitchell directly and asked him to resign, Mitchell promptly agreed. "Mitchell's loyalty to the mayor was simply unbelievable," a friend later recalled.

The news of Mitchell's resignation produced sprawling headlines in all the city papers, and for days the city talked of little else. But if Mitchell's action took reporters by surprise, the mayor's quick response seemed even more surprising. "Hardly had the mayor [received Mitchell's resignation]," the *Journal* reported, "when he turned to the other side and telephoned to William J. Smith, the purchasing agent of the school department, offering him the same position at Smith's own price." Then the mayor sent out copies of Mitchell's resignation letter to the press, enclosed with a flat thirty-word statement to the effect that, having failed to receive as yet a copy of the coal probe testimony, for which he had asked, he could say nothing about Mitchell's resignation. Not a word of praise for his old friend, nor even an expression of sadness that events had brought Mitchell to this difficult decision.

Even before the Finance Commission filed its formal report, which, issued in November, would describe the "lamentable picture of dishonesty and greed" resulting from the application of "the spoils system" to municipal government, it was plain that it had scored an unimagined triumph. Already, the mayor had instructed his Law Department to begin suit for recovery of excess payments made to the Niver Coal Company for delivery of inferior-grade coal in place of the best fuel, and the district attorney had announced that he would begin a grand-jury probe of the whole affair. And the commissioners knew that a high-level resignation was just the sort of publicity coup they needed at the outset to ensure continuing attention to a complicated investigation. In short, the commission's prestige had been greatly enhanced at the expense of the discredited Mitchell and the disreputable Klous.

The sudden turn of events which led to Mitchell's resignation caught his many friends by surprise, and several of them spoke aloud of their feelings, directing their wrath at Fitzgerald for having Mitchell resign and then for failing to issue a public statement of praise and support. Their angry comments apparently made the rounds on Newspaper Row. To avoid a public split between Mitchell and the mayor, Jim and Eddie Fitzgerald drafted a statement which they asked Mitchell to issue under his own name. The Fitzgerald brothers knew their man: having stuck with the mayor through the whole ordeal by never once even hinting at the mayor's role in all the coal decisions that had been made, Mitchell would not back down now. His loyalty was too intense. The statement was released to the papers Friday night, September 6, over Mitchell's signature:

> There is absolutely no truth to the statement that my friends are sore with Mayor Fitzgerald over my resignation. My resignation was my own act, and in order that no embarrassment would come to the administration. I am more loyal to Mayor Fitzgerald than ever, if that could be possible, and I find this sentiment among the people I meet.

Mitchell's enduring loyalty provides testimony to the warmth and power of Fitzgerald's personality. Fitzgerald was one of those rare men who could demand sacrifice of others without making them feel he was using them for his own ends. Indeed, it is likely, given the values of the political machine, that Fitzgerald never even experienced his actions during the hearings as a betrayal of any kind. Just as he had given loyalty to his own boss, Matthew Keany, under difficult circumstances, so Mitchell was now exhibiting that same loyalty to him. And as soon as the hearings were over, Fitzgerald told a friend, he would make sure that Mitchell had everything he needed to resume his business and his rightful place within the community.

If Fitzgerald seemed at first to escape the baleful effects of the hearings, the Finance Commission's melancholy shadow spread over Rose in a most unexpected way. Indeed, as a result of the commission's proceedings, all of Rose's plans for the future were upset.

The first indication of trouble came at a family discussion which took place, as Rose long remembered it, on a Sunday evening in early September, "right after the hearings had ended and just before I was scheduled to begin Wellesley." When she first sat down, Rose vividly recalled, she noticed her father's cheek twitching and she felt oddly apprehensive. But when Fitzgerald began talking in his usual confident tone about an upcoming political event, she felt better and settled back in her chair. Then it came. His face set hard, his voice determined, John Fitzgerald looked directly at Rose and said that he and her mother had decided she was still too young for Wellesley and had enrolled her instead at the Convent of the Sacred Heart in Boston. That was it. There was no further discussion.

Rose was startled and confused, but she never said a word in protest. In her experience, a daughter simply did not argue with her father. It did enter her mind, however, as she sat in silence, that there was a betrayal in his words, but no sooner had the shocking thought rushed into her head than she dismissed it as impossible and unworthy. Immediately, a host of images flashed into her memory—the picture of the two of them walking together with arms entwined, the picture of her father beaming with pride as he handed her high-school diploma to her . . . Surely, she told herself, her father's words meant only what they said, that she was still too young for Wellesley. Patience, that was all she needed, patience. Yet even as she tried to put the best possible face on the situation, something warned her of peril.

As it turned out, Rose's apprehensions were not misplaced; for beneath her father's words of postponement lay a permanent change of heart against sending his daughters to college. Though the situation was obscured for her at the time by her optimistic temperament and her uncanny ability to adapt herself to the wishes of her father as if the adaptation were in her own best interest, the fact was that her father's decision reflected a concern for *his* needs and not hers.

The previous day, it seems, Fitzgerald had met the Archbishop of Boston, William O'Connell, on a corner and their conversation had turned to the schooling of Rose and Agnes. Hearing that Rose was planning to go to a Protestant college, the Archbishop was very upset, fearing the impact of the decision on other Catholic girls because of Fitzgerald's position in the community. "Your talk with me settled the matter as far as I was concerned," Fitzgerald wrote to O'Connell years later, "and when I brought back your suggestions to the family there was no further discussion and both girls went to the Sacred Heart."

The future Cardinal was an imperious man of great propriety and moral rectitude who dreamed of leading the Irish Catholics of his city into a new era which would see them obtain proper dignity and genuine respect. Accustomed to the cultured manners of the cosmopolitan circle he had inhabited while he was rector of the North American College in Rome, O'Connell regarded with distaste the coarse and vulgar ways of the typical Irish politicians. From the very first, he had determined to keep his distance from the self-promoting mayor. The disgraceful hearings only reinforced O'Connell's view that with Fitzgerald the Irish were caught in an outdated mold. The word went out to every parish: from that moment on, Fitzgerald was no longer to benefit from his connections with the Church; he should no longer take part in strictly parish functions; he was, after all, just another politician.

It was in this context that the discussion about the Fitzgerald girls' schooling took place. O'Connell had set as a priority the advancement and improvement of Catholic education; in his view, all good Catholics should attend Catholic schools. Anxious to please this powerful man, Fitzgerald readily agreed to shift his daughter from Wellesley College to the Academy of the Sacred Heart.

The incident haunts the imagination. It is impossible to overestimate the importance of this event in the young girl's maturing sensibilities. When asked at the age of ninety to describe her greatest regret, she was silent for a moment and then, with a bitterness of tone which she did not often allow herself to betray, she said, "My greatest regret is not having gone to Wellesley College. It is something I have felt a little sad about all my life."

In the presence of such long-lasting emotion, one cannot help but feel that through this experience Rose suffered an injury that went deeper than the loss of a college. This was, after all, as far as we can tell, the first major defeat Rose sustained at the hands of her father. Until this moment, John Fitzgerald had been the unquestioned center of her universe. Whatever he wanted for her was right. But now he was asking her to surrender to a paternal edict which she not only profoundly disagreed with but she could not understand. For seventeen years he had offered her everything, telling her she could do or be whatever she wanted. Now he was taking it all back and telling her, in essence, that she was only an appendage to his political needs.

If Fitzgerald's ambition had become a vehicle of pain for his daughter, Fitzgerald probably did not experience it that way. So adept was he at seeing what he wanted to see that he no doubt convinced himself that the Convent of the Sacred Heart would be a much better school for Rose than Wellesley. He was not a mean man, nor was he capable of consciously hurting someone he loved. He was capable, however, of putting his own ambition first and then rationalizing that in the end his behavior would bring benefits to everyone, not just himself.

For her part, manifesting a pattern of behavior that would be revealed again and again, Rose smothered her feelings of resistance and bowed to her father's powerful will. In mid-September 1907, while her three friends were busy unpacking their trunks at Wellesley, she boarded a streetcar to begin her year as a day student at the Sacred Heart Convent on Commonwealth Avenue, and with enforced discipline she adjusted herself remarkably well.

But the repercussions of this abrupt shift in plans would be felt in her for years to come. It was as if a mask had fallen, allowing her to see her father for the first time, tainting forever the quality of his reactions with a recognition of his self-absorption. Though they would still remain the closest of friends—all their lives, indeed, they would share a special intensity—their relationship had imperceptibly slipped onto a new footing. A barrier had been raised, a measure of detachment forged which would allow Rose, when the time came, to go against her father on a matter of even greater importance—the choice of a husband. With this detachment, however, the whole tone of her life seemed to change.

Never again would she appear quite so radiant, so vigorous and so high-spirited as she had been at seventeen.

The Sacred Heart convent which Rose entered in 1907 was one link in a chain of many. Founded by Madame Sophie Barat in the chaos of the French Revolution, the Sacred Heart Society had developed an exclusive order of first-rate academies which had become the schools for the daughters of the Catholic aristocracy all over the world. From the beginning, the society had a definite plan of studies and a fixed curriculum designed to fit "the feminine mind, character and vocation," and to consider "the position these girls were to fill when they took their places in the social world." "Knowing as we do," the official philosophy stated, "that in the ordinary course of Providence, our children are destined to become wives and mothers of families, our education endeavors to prepare them to fulfill this vocation as perfectly as may be."

Following the original pattern laid down in France, a highly centralized order of Sacred Heart schools developed, the same the world over, as Mary McCarthy observed in her book *Memories of a Catholic Girlhood*:

> the same blue and green and pink moiré ribbons awarded for good conduct, the same books given as prizes on Prize Day—the same congés, or holidays, announced by the Mère Supérieure . . . the same gouter, or tea, the same retreats and sermons, the same curtsies dipped in the hall, the same early-morning chapel with processions of girls, like widowed queens, in sad black-net veils, the same prie-dieu, the same French hymns ("Oui, je le crois"), the same glorious white-net veils and flowers and gold vessels on Easter and Holy Thursday and on feasts peculiar to the order.

There was nothing ordinary about the Sacred Heart schools. The Sacred Heart girls were not ordinary Catholics; they were daughters of the best families. The Sacred Heart nuns were not ordinary nuns; they were "the Ladies of the Sacred Heart," educated women of fine families who had freely chosen the life of learning, teaching and contemplation. And the subjects taught were not ordinary subjects, like math, biology and English. Instead, as outlined in the official plan of study, they included religion ("the foundation of our whole work of education"), apologetics ("once well grounded in Faith, work to forearm them against attacks which this faith will encounter in the world"), the fine arts ("to train for the kingdom of heaven . . . is not complete without training in the love of the beautiful . . . it develops the precious power of admiration, of reverence"), literary training ("gives greater breadth and keenness to the mind, greater delicacy of feeling") and experimental science ("The object of all these branches of natural sciences is the visible creation . . . the work of God").

In addition to these academic subjects, the Sacred Heart curriculum, as Rose later characterized it in her memoirs, was "unusually concerned with the practical things of this world. It was assumed that the girls when they married would be devoting their lives to kinder, kirche and kuche (children, church and cooking) and needed to prepare for all the duties implied in that expression. It was further assumed that they would have servants to do all the actual work, but in order to instruct and supervise the servants and to run an efficient household they should be proficient in what has been called 'domestic science.' "

The philosophy behind this heavy emphasis on domestic science is clearly spelled out in the official plan of study, which prescribes instruction in cooking, needlework, first aid, packing, preparing for journeys, writing orders to shops, making beds, dusting private rooms, and the other arts of housewifery: "Linking the highest natural graces of a woman with these lowliest occupations is considered essential to prevent the woman of the household from being left to the mercy of servants' tempers or of head cooks on strikes . . . helpless dependence on servants is too great a risk to be accepted." As for learning needlework, "the fundamental handicraft of women," the program pointed out that "if fortune deals hardly with them (the Sacred Heart girls) and they are thrown on their own resources later in life . . . to make their own clothes is a form of independence for which they will be very thankful." And "if it is not needed as a means of gaining a livelihood, it is a heaven sent blessing, providing as it does an interest and joy which saves from idleness and its unfortunate results: boredom, indolence, frivolous conversation and dangerous reading."

It was not easy to enter this system from the outside, as Rose discovered when she started classes that September. "My studies did not dovetail very well with studies in the uppermost forms. I knew Latin, Roman and Greek history and grammatical French very well but knew nothing of medieval history and literature, nor could I understand spoken French. I also had no training in psychology or logic which was part of the curriculum at the convent. However, I never thought of remonstrating with Father."

There is a homeliness of detail here which camouflages the more fundamental nature of the contrast Rose encountered between her previous experience in the college preparatory courses at Dorchester High and the schooling she would receive at the convent. For the Sacred Heart system was designed above all to provide "an anchorage in faith," "the happiness of knowing that one's life is governed by convictions and not merely by custom." Never again would knowledge be presented to her objectively, for its own sake; never again would the subjects she studied be approached from various points of view, considering all sides of the matter.

In the end, the picture that emerges of the intellectual world at the convent suggests a fiery world of martyrs and villains, of truths and fallacies, of good eras and bad eras, of right ways to think and wrong ways to think. Looking back many years later to her first encounter with this curriculum, Rose observed flatly but accurately that "the world in which I found myself when I entered the Sacred Heart Convent was very different from the world I had known."

On October 8, 1907, three weeks after the humiliating hearings which resulted in Superintendent Mitchell's resignation, George Koch, the longtime clerk in the Department of Supplies, was found in his Jamaica Plain room with all the doors and windows locked and the two gas jets open. What inner torment lay behind Koch's decision to take his life cannot be known. It can only be inferred from the timing of his act and from the remarks of his landlord that the hearings had cast an even larger shadow than previously suspected.

Throughout his testimony Koch had appeared excessively nervous, answering the most routine questions as if he were dreading a terrible discovery. And when he was finally told that he could step down he was shaking so badly, one observer noticed, that his knees gave way beneath him. That he was deeply troubled about something—something that reached beyond the emerging story of the coal fraud—was obvious, but at the time Attorney Sughrue was unable to penetrate his wall of silence.

However, if Koch intended, in taking his life, to take his secrets with him to the grave, his plan misfired when his landlady detected the smell of gas, broke open a window and found Koch unconscious but still alive in his bed. An ambulance hurried him to City Hospital.

The news of his attempted suicide circulated quickly on Newspaper Row, along with the excited suspicion that the man's despondency was linked in some unexplained way to the Finance Commission probe. Questioned by reporters, the landlord confirmed that Koch had been "much worried over the investigation in his department by the Finance Commission and that he had been called before District Attorney Moran in private conference, which seemed to weigh upon his mind." In addition, the landlord said, Koch had been working very hard in recent weeks, often staying at City Hall into the evening, and he had not had a vacation for two years.

The next day, J. Wells Farley, the Finance Commission secretary, went to City Hospital to see Koch. Being of a sympathetic nature, Farley evidently established a feeling of trust in Koch which Sughrue had been unable to produce.

The story Koch told Farley, and subsequently retold before a public hearing and a grand jury, described a state of municipal affairs in which bribery had become so endemic that few public officials could escape its corroding influence. The situation he described, in the words of the report the Finance Commission later released, was "a perfected development of the spoils system as applied to Municipal Government." The first stage, the distribution of offices and contracts as a reward for party service, appeared innocent enough. If there were two men equally qualified for a particular job, why not give the job to the loyal party man? But, as Koch's story illustrated, "honest graft" of this kind shaded imperceptibly into a system of organized bribery in which the city's money was looked upon as an inexhaustible pool, the legitimate property of those best able to grease their way in with a well-timed present here or a handsome payoff there. Under this system, the prices paid for contracts were often double or even triple the going rates, with the excess profits divided between the individual contractors and the politicians or middlemen who made the lucrative deals possible.

In the course of his hospital-bed confession, Koch admitted that, as the second in command of the Supply Department, he had regularly received gifts from a number of different contractors. While he was not the official head of the department, much of the responsible work fell upon him, since the nominal head (Mitchell) was so frequently absent from his office attending to his private business. In answer to Farley's probing questions, Koch produced a list of contractors from whom he had obtained gifts—including Maurice Klous, the infamous agent for the W. C. Niver Coal Company, from whom he had received money on two or three occasions.

Continuing on, Koch admitted that he had also received money from a Mr. Patrick Bowen, an ex-alderman who had come by the office several times on behalf of Maher Brothers, a firm that was seeking a contract to furnish flagstones to the city. As the story came out in Koch's "deathbed testimony," the city had bought the flagstones for years from a reputable firm, Cuddihy Brothers, paying the market price of thirty-three and a half cents a square foot. Then, soon after Fitzgerald got in, the Cuddihy contract was canceled and a new contract was made without competition with the Maher Brothers firm. Though the new contractor charged the city double the original amount—sixty-seven cents a square foot—the city completed the transaction and went on to award five additional contracts to the same firm at the same high price. Later estimates put the loss to the city at $14,000.

Shortly after this, according to Koch, on the day the contract was signed, ex-Alderman Patrick Bowen had come into his office and told him that Maher Brothers wanted to present a suit of clothes to him. Two or three days later Koch found on his desk a $50 bill which he assumed came from Mr. Bowen, since Bowen had been in his office that morning and there was no one else he could think of who had been there that day and could have left such a sum.

With these damaging admissions, Farley drew the hospital interview to a close, but not before making one last attempt to widen the circle of guilt. Had Koch ever heard of Mitchell receiving any money from any of these contractors? Farley asked. No, Koch replied, to his knowledge the only present Mitchell ever received was a pair of cuff buttons from Maurice Klous. Nor did he know of any consideration paid to anyone higher up. "In spite of the desperate condition I was in," Koch was later quoted as saying, Farley "kept pressing me to tell him something on Fitzgerald. I can't, I answered, because I know nothing against him. But he kept on urging me. Tell me something we can use. We must get him by hook or crook."

While Farley had failed to establish a direct link to Fitzgerald, he had succeeded in extracting a sensational interview which became the basis for a new set of Finance Commission hearings—which, in turn, rocked the city even more than the coal hearings and provided the evidence for a grand-jury investigation of Michael Mitchell and Thomas Maher, senior partner in the Maher Brothers firm.

Upon hearing of Koch's testimony, Mayor Fitzgerald immediately suspended the confessed clerk and issued a statement expressing his great surprise: "In view of the record of Mr. Koch that he had received money in connection with the discharge of his duties, whether it be a legal offense or not, no man can accept either a bribe or a money gratuity under my administration and remain connected with it." Fitzgerald then went on to criticize the Finance Commission for releasing the testimony at a public hearing just a few days before the municipal election.

Fitzgerald was no doubt correct in his assessment of the political motivation behind the commission's timing; it was hardly an accident that they chose to schedule the hearings just four days before the mayoral election.

As the battle lines developed, the Republicans chose George Albee Hibbard as their candidate for mayor. Hibbard, Boston's postmaster, was the former head of the local Republican machine. A conservative Yankee, he pledged that, if elected, he would "clean up the mess" in Boston's city government. But Fitzgerald was accustomed to professional politicians like Hibbard, and while he recognized that the mood of the city had come a long way from the halcyon days of his victory in 1905, he also knew that this time, after two hard years of juggling appointments and rebuilding old ties, he would have the Democratic machine behind him—P. J. Kennedy, Joe Corbett, Joe McClellan, James Donovan and, most important, Martin Lomasney. Indeed, notwithstanding all the charges against the Fitzgerald administration, had the election been a straight two-way contest between Fitzgerald's Democratic machine and Hibbard's Republican machine, Fitzgerald would have emerged the victor.

The more troubling result of the Finance Commission's investigation was the unexpected candidacy of John A. Coulthurst, nominated as a reform candidate under the banner of William Randolph Hearst's Independent League party. Coulthurst was a relative newcomer to politics, but his fiery oratory, which held Fitzgerald's performance up to the great reformist pledges he had made upon coming into office, appealed to a large number of normally Democratic voters embarrassed by the public dishonor the hearings had stamped upon their municipal government. It was this independent vote which defeated Fitzgerald. When the voters went to the polls on December 10, 1907, Coulthurst stunned the party professionals by amassing over 15,000 votes—more than enough to give Hibbard, with 38,112, a narrow plurality over Fitzgerald, who ran a frustrated second with 35,935 votes.

For a man who had never before lost an election, Fitzgerald faced his first defeat cheerfully. There was nothing savage in his words, no rage against his enemies, only the clear determination to try again another day. He had learned from many years' experience that in politics the wheel turns round and round. "What of the future?" he was asked shortly after he had heard the final results. "We held a conference a little while ago," he said with a broad smile on his face, "and began our planning for the next election." And, "in a way," he added, "the defeat will be a good thing . . . since it will allow me more time with my family."

CHAPTER 10

# "GUILTY
# AS
# CHARGED"

The real political fight, however, had just begun, for within two weeks of Fitzgerald's defeat the district attorney, John B. Moran, had issued summonses to Fitzgerald, Mitchell, Maher, Koch and Bowen to appear before a grand jury to give testimony in regard to the flagstone contract.

It was a dull, warmish day on December 23, 1907, when the twenty-two members of the grand jury—all of them men—took their seats in the jury room of the Suffolk County Courthouse at Pemberton Square. Drawn from lists made up at City Hall in accordance with the state regulation that "women, insane persons and minors are incompetent to serve," the grand jurors were charged in this case to hear the state's evidence with regard to the flagstone fraud and then to decide by majority vote whether the evidence was sufficient to require Mitchell or Maher or anyone else to stand trial.

By far the most sensational happening of the flagstone probe came the day after Christmas when Mayor Fitzgerald made a record appearance before the grand jury, submitting himself to the examination of the district attorney for nearly four hours. "As nearly as can be learned," the *Boston Journal* reported, "it was the first time in the history of the city that a mayor has been called as a witness before the indicting body."

There was a large crowd of reporters in the corridors of the courthouse at 12:45 when the mayor showed up. Though the proceedings of the grand jury were required to be conducted secretly—it having been held contempt of court for newspapers or individuals to publish anything definitely pertaining to the investigation—experience taught that "background information" could often be obtained from the various witnesses while they paced up and down the hallway or sat on the bare wooden bench outside the jury room waiting to be called. Then, too, through the windows reporters could catch glimpses of the facial expressions of the people on the stand, even if they couldn't hear what was being said. Moreover, in this instance, given the unusual nature of his appearance, Fitzgerald had agreed to make a public statement when he finished his testimony.

To the surprise of the waiting reporters, Fitzgerald was "smiling" and appeared "not at all tired" when he emerged at six o'clock from his long ordeal. "It was quite a new experience for me," he said, "and it was interesting, so much so that I didn't notice the time slipping by, although I stood all the time." He then proceeded to state positively that the city had been "fooled" in the flagstone contract into paying double the price, though he refused to accept any responsibility for any part of the situation. As an excuse for not knowing that the city was getting fooled when the contract was made, he likened the city to a big business corporation and declared that though the head was responsible for its dealings, he had to rely implicitly on the honesty, integrity and ability of his department chiefs.

From the tone of this statement and even more from the portions of Fitzgerald's grand-jury testimony which came out in an odd and circuitous way at the subsequent trial, it is clear that, at some point, Fitzgerald decided to place the responsibility for the flagstone contract on the shoulders of Michael Mitchell. When asked by the district attorney why as mayor he had approved the contract without taking bids, he said he did so because Mitchell told him that the Maher brothers were the only ones who could supply the stone and that the prices had advanced. Fitzgerald also said that he had never met the Maher brothers, that they had never been in his office and that he knew no more of them than if they lived in China.

Fitzgerald's testimony before the grand jury was extremely damaging to Mitchell, especially when it was coupled with the refusal of the Maher brothers to say what they had done with the money they received from the contracts, on the grounds that it might incriminate them.

While no one believed that Mitchell had received a cent of the money —indeed, at the subsequent trial, testimony would be heard from Thomas Maher declaring, "I say that as true as there is a God in heaven, I never paid Mitchell any money"—and while most people believed that Mitchell's only fault was that he did not know what he ought to have known about his department, he was the one upon whom the full responsibility fell. Refusing to speak on his own behalf, never wavering in the loyalty he felt toward Fitzgerald which Fitzgerald apparently failed to return, Mitchell became the scapegoat of the whole sordid affair.

To see Fitzgerald's betrayal before the grand jury as far as possible through his own eyes, it is necessary to remember how desperately he had been driving himself through the previous month before the election and to imagine the private grief and anger he must have felt at losing the mayoralty on the heels of the sensational exposures of the Supply Department which Mitchell had headed. It is also likely, as Mitchell's attorney Daniel Coakley later argued, that Fitzgerald believed that the grand jury would never indict Mitchell and that if this was the case, since the deliberations were secret, no one on the outside would ever hear any part of the testimony he gave. After all, as Fitzgerald's biographer John Henry Cutler wrote, for years "Democratic politicians of Boston had learned to gain control of the grand jury"; in case after case, when prominent politicians were involved, despite the evidence presented, the jurors invariably returned "nol pro" bills.

In believing that the grand jury would never indict Mitchell no matter what was said in the privacy of the proceedings, Fitzgerald displayed a certain hubris which we will see again and again in his life story and in the story of his family. It seemed as though the very courage and defiance that had lifted Fitzgerald from the slums of the North End to the mayor's seat in Boston carried with it a disregard of ordinary restraints which allowed him to take wanton risks with others. Had he known that Mitchell would be indicted on the basis of his testimony before the grand jury, it is hard to believe he would have acted as he did. But even if we grant the reigning expectation that the process could be controlled by politics, the charge still holds that Fitzgerald took a terrible risk with the life and dignity of his best friend.

For, as it happened, this particular grand jury defied all expectations and came back with a batch of indictments, causing "the biggest sensation in political circles in years." Journals of the period attributed the stunning results to the work of the strangely solitary district attorney, John B. Moran. Moran, a small man with "a grim face and burning eyes," had burst unexpectedly onto Boston's political stage in the autumn of 1905 when he single-handedly conducted a "most remarkable political campaign" as an independent candidate for Boston district attorney.

A serious and austere man who lived alone in two small rooms, wore no jewelry and owned "neither horse, dog, auto, frock coat, Prince Albert nor plug hat," Moran had presented to the Boston electorate a radical platform calling for "official freedom from politicians and grafters; official action in the grand jury instantly on receipt of information from the press and private sources without waiting for the lower court; no intimacy with jurors and rigid enforcement of laws against grafters and bribers." On the basis of this platform, Moran had won the backing of Hearst's crusading newspaper the *Boston American*, whose stirring editorials helped him achieve a victory which left the regular parties "thunderstruck."

Still, few were prepared for the grand jury's stunning return of no fewer than eight indictments. (Beyond the flagstone case, Moran had submitted evidence on two other cases, which became known as the "Codman Street land deal" and the "July Fourth larceny.") "So large a number of prominent men have never been indicted at one time by a Suffolk County grand jury," the *Boston Post* reported. Among those indicted were Thomas Maher and Michael Mitchell, charged jointly with a series of larcenies aggregating $28,000.

As the indicted men arrived at police headquarters to be formally placed under arrest, the inspectors had a great deal of trouble making a way for them through the huge crowd. Finally a lane was carved through the triple row of spectators, and the squad of men—the defendants, their counsel and their bondsmen—marched through, holding their arms before their faces to defeat the efforts of the photographers.

The experience of being arrested was an agonizing one for Mitchell. For this simple man, respect counted for everything. The humiliation of the arrest stripped away his long-held reputation for honesty; a new round of embarrassments set in. On top of everything, there was the vexatious problem of what to do about his sister Catherine, who had been so deeply affected by the grand-jury proceedings, the rumors and the endless newspaper gossip that she had fallen ill and taken to her bed, and despite all of his best efforts there seemed to be nothing he or anyone else could do to bring her back to health. For a family who had once stood so high in Charlestown, the whole business was a bad blow. Nor was this the end of the matter, for events still more painful awaited.

Ironically, at the very moment Mitchell was being preyed upon by the torment of his arrest, Fitzgerald was making his way through the elaborate ceremony surrounding the inauguration of the new mayor, George

Albee Hibbard. For, as chance would have it, January 6 marked both inaugural day and the day the indictments were handed down; indeed, the general merriment in the vicinity of City Hall made a strange contrast with the solemn mood just two blocks away at Pemberton Square.

The violence of the contrast must have held a special meaning for Fitzgerald, particularly if he thought back to the tremendous pleasure of the same scene just two years before, when, on a clear and beautiful springlike day, he had enjoyed the matchless delight of the thunderous applause and the high expectations that accompanied his own inauguration as mayor. Now, on a far colder day, born of a New Year's storm which had swept over New England, leaving record low temperatures and a howling wind in its wake, Fitzgerald felt the negative force of the alternating current of political life, the harshness of its contrasts where defeat and victory, like winter and summer, mark two entirely different modes of life and thought.

All in all, the early months of 1908 must have been a time of anguish for the defeated mayor. For despite his confident declaration that he would run again, he must have known that, with the shadow Mitchell's trial was certain to cast upon his first administration, it would take all the energy, the commitment and the intelligence he had to win another term and earn a second chance. Moreover, as a defeated candidate, he would face bitter opposition within his own ranks; in April he was forced to withdraw from the field of candidates running for chairman of the Democratic State Committee, in the clear recognition that he could not win. And still he faced the relentless probe of the Finance Commission, which had twelve more months to exist before its authority ran out and was determined to find something on Fitzgerald so that he could never occupy the mayor's chair again.

It was in this context that Fitzgerald decided to send his two oldest daughters, Rose and Agnes, to boarding school in Europe, preceded by a family vacation in Ireland, England and France. Outwardly, the story of the girls' year at the Sacred Heart Convent at Blumenthal, Holland, may be summed up in terms of the progress of the Irish, with the Fitzgerald family ready to imitate the elite of their generation. "In those times," Rose Kennedy wrote in her memoirs, "it was considered a great advantage for a young person to have gone to school 'abroad' . . ."

But the real story lies elsewhere, in Fitzgerald's desire to shield his daughters from the vicious struggle that lay ahead, the nasty charges and countercharges, the likelihood that he would have to take the stand against Mitchell at a public trial, or, even worse, the chance that he himself might be brought into court on any one of a series of Finance Commission charges. Then, too, as *Practical Politics* observed, a trip to

Europe would serve Fitzgerald's political purposes as well, allowing him to escape being drawn into all the factional fights that were sure to erupt in the summer months before the fall primaries.

Having made up his mind that a trip to Europe would be good, Fitzgerald proceeded to draw up elaborate plans with boyish enthusiasm, booking passage on the steamer *Cymric* on July 18, 1908, bound for Liverpool. The timing of his departure could not have been more fortuitous. Just five days before he was set to sail, a story leaked to the papers that the Finance Commission intended to press charges against Fitzgerald as a result of a secret investigation made into his private bank accounts. The story hinted that a record of his deposits would reveal the existence of big sums of money supplied by the gas, electric, light, street-car and railway corporations just at the time their contracts were coming up for renewal.

Upon reading the story Fitzgerald immediately contacted his one friend on the Finance Commission, the labor representative John F. Kennedy, who was initially dumbfounded by the story, as he knew of no such investigation. Kennedy soon discovered, however, that without telling him, fearing he in turn would tell Fitzgerald, and without securing the full sanction of the commission, Attorney Sughrue and Commissioner Sullivan had indeed conducted a private probe of Fitzgerald's bank accounts. Moreover, they had discovered the existence of four large deposits of $10,000 each and were just on the verge of learning whether these deposits had been made in cash, as they suspected, or by check. Furious that Sughrue and particularly Sullivan would act behind the commission's back, Kennedy charged that it was an "investigation urged by personal spite, prejudice and general nastiness." Commissioner Sullivan apparently took the allusion to himself and advanced toward Kennedy with his fists raised. Kennedy accepted the challenge, but before they could come to blows Nathan Matthews intervened.

Naturally, a story of this nature produced good copy in the press, which saw the near-fight as an indication of a far deeper friction growing within the commission. Taking full advantage of the commission's embarrassment at seeing its internal rows splashed across the front pages, and apparently believing that he could make a good showing before the commission's lawyer, Fitzgerald graciously agreed to appear before that body on July 15 to answer any questions they might have regarding his bank accounts.

It was a brilliant stroke, for it allowed him to reveal in public and to the surprise of the commission that he had nothing to fear about an investigation into those four mysterious $10,000 deposits, since all had been made by check and were easily traceable. As Fitzgerald explained it, the first two deposits, made by his brother Jim, were secured on two mortgages on two pieces of property that Jim owned on Pleasant Street and La Grange Street; both were traceable through the Registry of Deeds. As for the two deposits made by himself, after the first big fight for the mayoralty he had had many bills pressing for payment, so he had $10,000 transferred from the account of his newspaper, *The Republic*, to his personal account. A similar transaction covered the second deposit. Then, with a dramatic flourish, he offered to cancel his trip to Europe if any further explanations were necessary.

Fitzgerald's performance caught the commission off guard and left it with no choice but to say in public that it was completely satisfied with Fitzgerald's explanation and had no further plans to continue the investigation. Having moved too precipitously, the commission lost its chance to pursue the matter further.

Yet, even as Fitzgerald once again evaded trouble, the recognition of his luxurious lifestyle raised unanswered questions about his personal finances. Beyond his mansion in Dorchester, there were frequent trips to the South in the winter and to the coast of Maine in the summer, as well as extensive outlays for his trips to Europe. Yet his government salaries were hardly lavish: the City Council paid $300 a year, the state Senate $750 and the Congress $5,000. Even assuming that he obtained additional money through his successful operation of *The Republic*, there remains the likely possibility that he was using his public office for private gain. Though no charge of corruption was ever substantiated, the gap between his legal income and his high level of spending would seem circumstantial evidence enough to suggest that something underhanded was going on.

In a mood of triumph, Fitzgerald invited all his friends to a "glorious send-off party" at the harbor before the *Cymric* sailed at two o'clock Saturday afternoon, July 18. Fitzgerald's brothers Henry, George and Eddie were there, as were ex-Alderman Patrick Bowen, Commissioner John F. Kennedy, City Treasurer Charles Slattery, Father O'Farrell of St. Francis de Sales, Father Roman of St. Peter's, P. J. Kennedy and Eddie Gallagher, along with scores of other prominent politicians and leading churchmen. Even Martin Lomasney sent one of his closest friends to represent him. In those days, Rose later observed, "trips to Europe were no minor affairs . . . with flags and music playing, handkerchiefs waving, we were in a sea of smiles and shouts, and the smoke of photographers' flash powder. There were confetti, balloons, and all the marvelous trappings that used to make sailing on a big liner such an exciting and glamorous experience."

Shouting cheers for the "smiling and defiant" Fitzgerald, the huge crowd stayed until the big steamer backed slowly out of the dock with the ex-mayor waving an American flag that somebody had thrust into his hands while Agnes and Rose waved huge bandana handkerchiefs.

When Fitzgerald first told Rose that she was going to a convent school abroad to study for a year, she reacted with dismay; it seemed so far away from her family, her friends and her growing romance with Joe Kennedy, whom she had been seeing steadily ever since their reencounter the previous summer at Old Orchard. But the more she thought about the trip, the more excited she became; she had not as yet divested herself of the youthful impression that every new adventure would exert a positive influence upon her life. There was, moreover, the compensation of a grand tour of Europe with her parents and her sister in the two months preceding the opening of school—a prospect Rose regarded as "the fulfillment of a girlhood dream." From her father she had inherited a fascination with faraway places; like him, she greeted the thought of travel with a childlike, unrestrained ardor. Later in their lives, indeed, Fitzgerald would fondly refer to his daughter as "my rambling Rose."

As a young girl, Rose had spent many a Saturday afternoon in Boston's Symphony Hall listening to the celebrated lecturer Burton Holmes, whose vivid travelogues had unlocked the imagination of an entire generation of young Bostonians. It is little wonder that the idea of actually seeing London and Paris for the first time conjured up in Rose a vast vision of romance.

As the S.S. *Cymric*, "as comfortable and as nice as a house," made its way slowly across the Atlantic, Fitzgerald, with characteristic openness, found something interesting to discuss with everyone he met and managed to form a number of those strange, quick ocean friendships which, as he put it, one comes to regard "with as much affection as though they had been the friends of a lifetime." Josie, for her part, enjoyed herself "immensely," while Rose and Agnes lost no time joining the other young people aboard in the daily deck games of shuffleboard and ringtoss. In a letter written on July 22, to her brother Tom from "the middle of the ocean," Rose reports that since it is her birthday "we are going to be allowed to go down and see all the steerage passengers way way down in the boat."

Fitzgerald had originally intended to stop off at Queenstown and travel through Ireland before landing on English soil, but when he discovered that this itinerary would bring him to London after the Parliament had adjourned, he changed his plans and landed in Liverpool, whose splendid dock system arrested his attention at once. From there they took the train to London and, as Rose reported in notes she jotted down during the trip, spent five hectic days taking in English architecture and history, ranging from Westminster Abbey to the Old Tower, where, Rose noted, "little princes murdered, Lord Dudley and brothers imprisoned."

On August 1 the Fitzgeralds crossed the Irish Sea to Dublin. In a long letter to the *Boston Post*, Fitzgerald described his feelings upon first seeing the land of his parents. "I hardly closed my eyes all night, so anxious was I to get the first possible glimpse of Erin's Isle. It was just breaking day as I came upon the upper deck of the vessel with Mrs. Fitzgerald and my two girls and saw the headlands of the Irish coast looming up with Fastnet Light ahead. We sat enraptured for an hour while the mist, lifted by the powerful rays of the rising sun coming up out of the ocean, disappeared in the distance."

As an old man looking back, John Fitzgerald would remember this first trip through Ireland as the high point of his travels, recalling most vividly his visit to the small farmhouse on Palantine Road in Bruff where his father, Tom, had been born. Seen through the sentimental eyes of an immigrant's son returning to the homeland, the entire area around Bruff and the neighboring village of Lough Gur where Michael Hannon was born appeared "indescribably lovely."

Not unexpectedly, when the memory of this same trip to Ireland came back to Rose Kennedy, it came in a different shape. As a child of the next generation in the New World, she had less comprehension of her ancestral background. On the day the Fitzgeralds went to the old homestead her journal entry simply noted "Bruff" with no further elaboration.

From Ireland the Fitzgeralds traveled to France and then on to Switzerland, where they took a train up the Jungfrau, heard the music of the cowbells and saw the lion at Lucerne. In late August they proceeded to Germany, where, Rose reported, her father was "impressed with the neatness and discipline, the warmth and companionability and above all the vitality and forceful energy of the people." Finally, they moved on to Brussels and then out to Blumenthal, where the adult Fitzgeralds placed Rose and Agnes in the convent school for the year and then left for home.

Upon his return, Fitzgerald found that in his absence the district attorney, John Moran, the man who held Michael Mitchell's fate in his hands, and the man who had played such a determining role in Fitzgerald's decision to go abroad, had contracted a serious case of tuberculosis. As the autumn turned to winter, Moran's condition failed, and on the evening of February 5, 1909, in a hospital room crowded with friends, the forty-nine-year-old district attorney died.

Moran's death gave Fitzgerald and Mitchell the precious gift of hope —hope that the temporary district attorney appointed by Governor Eben Draper would fail to take action on a case as potentially explosive as the flagstone case, leaving it up to the next district attorney who was to be elected in November. Then, if luck ran with the Democrats, the man might be a friend—indeed, there was already talk in Democratic circles of running a man named Pelletier for district attorney—and if he won, the case might never go to trial, for Pelletier's closest friend was Daniel Coakley, Mitchell's lawyer.

The mood of the Democrats turned even more upbeat when Governor Draper announced Arthur Hill, "one of the mildest and least aggressive looking men in the city," as his choice for the acting district attorney. Born into "a family of scholars, bookworms and bluebloods," Hill had grown up in Cambridge, where for twenty-five years his father was a professor of rhetoric at Harvard. It was said that his house had so many books in it that every room was a library and there was no place for a kitchen. As might be expected, he went to Harvard, graduated from Harvard Law School and then became attached to a prominent Boston law firm. "Innocent, green, and boyish looking," he was, in the words of one reporter, "the last man one would pick for a successful prosecuting attorney."

In the early spring, Hill put ex-Alderman George Battis on trial for larceny, charging him with having kept for himself part of the money he had drawn to purchase prizes for the 1906 Fourth of July athletics winners. Since Battis was the first to go on trial of the eight men indicted with Mitchell and Maher, the whole city watched with interest. All during the trial, Battis' lawyer, one of the best criminal lawyers in the city, treated Hill as if he were a boy, patting him on the shoulder and apologizing for what he had to do to him. When the jury came back unable to reach an agreement, the politicians chuckled and said, "What did I tell you?"

Pretty soon, however, they were astonished to find Battis put on trial again, and even more astonished to find that Hill was having the jurors watched day and night by detectives. Two inspectors from police headquarters were assigned to each juror so that there would be no chance at all for a briber to get anywhere near. It was also noticeable that Hill had learned from the weaknesses in the first trial. The criminal lawyer stopped treating him as an artless youth and no longer patted him on the shoulder. When the jury came back this time, the verdict was guilty and Battis was sentenced to three years in prison.

In the subsequent weeks, case after case came to trial. In each of them, Hill had the juries watched, and in each of them, one after another, verdicts of guilty came in. At the end of two months, the mild-mannered Hill had brought back more convictions than the wild-eyed Moran had secured in nearly two full terms. But all this was a prelude. For, as *Harper's Weekly* observed, "the climax of excitement came when Mitchell and Maher were placed on trial."

The trial of Michael J. Mitchell and Thomas F. Maher, charged with conspiracy to defraud the city, opened on a stifling Monday afternoon, the twenty-first of June, before an overflowing crowd of politicians, reporters, sketch artists, messengers and spectators. By noontime all the seats available in the high-ceilinged chamber of the Superior Court had been taken, and still the curious kept coming; they stood in the corners, sat on the windowsills and appropriated all the benches in the corridors.

With the jury in the box, District Attorney Hill rose. In his opening statement he outlined the government's case: that the defendants had conspired together so that crosswalk flagging which had been purchased from another dealer at thirty-three and a half cents a square foot had been bought for sixty-seven cents a square foot, the result being that the city was defrauded.

"Gentlemen of the jury," Hill said, turning dramatically toward Fitzgerald, who was sitting with the other waiting witnesses, "the state believes that Mayor Fitzgerald relied upon the word and recommendations of Mitchell. It will be shown that Mitchell was responsible for the city's part of the flagstone contracts. It is true that the mayor authorized the awarding of these contracts of over two thousand dollars without bids, but he did so because Mitchell made . . . . false statements to him. These statements were, in effect, that the Maher Brothers concern had control of the flagstone market in the city and also that the prices had advanced."

When Hill finished his opening statement he crossed over to where Fitzgerald was sitting and proceeded to engage him in pleasant conversation—a curious gesture, intended perhaps to underline the state's position that Fitzgerald, whom they expected to be a friendly witness on their side, was not to blame in any way for these transactions.

Six witnesses were then sworn in. The former mayor was the first to rise and walk to the bar to be placed under oath. "He seemed to take a decided interest in the proceedings," the *Journal* reported, "and bowed and smiled at the various friends he noticed that dotted the courtroom." There was, however, as reporters were quick to notice, one man toward whom Fitzgerald failed to incline his head—and that man was Daniel Coakley, the feisty Irishman who was Mitchell's lawyer. During an unusual career, Coakley had been a horsecar operator, a referee of prizefights, a reporter on the *New York Sun*, sporting editor of the *Boston*

*Herald*, and a member of the state legislature before he enrolled in law school and took up the practice of criminal law. Flamboyant and glib, he combined his law practice with an active interest in politics. In 1905 he had lined up with Fitzgerald in his first campaign for mayor and was partly instrumental in bringing about the coup by which Fitzgerald won over the heads of all the most powerful bosses. When he became mayor, Fitzgerald rewarded Coakley with a lush appointment as commissioner of parks.

But, for many months now, stemming back to Fitzgerald's damaging testimony against Mitchell before the grand jury, reporters had detected "a noticeable coolness" in the relationship between the two former friends. The year before, a story had circulated that Coakley was planning to sue Fitzgerald for legal services, and this story was followed up by the observation that when Fitzgerald sailed to Europe Coakley had failed to send flowers to the ship. What lay behind this break was Coakley's strong feeling that Fitzgerald had betrayed Mitchell, a feeling that Coakley would have to keep in harness during the course of the trial, for reasons that will be made clear; but once the trial was over, Coakley's anger would gain possession of him, turning into an obsession that would rear itself again and again with disastrous results for Fitzgerald's political career.

The second day of the trial found New England at the start of a devastating heat wave which would last for the remainder of the week, leaving over twenty dead and causing scores of people to drop in the streets each day. With the thermometers showing temperatures of more than 103 degrees, the strict rules of courtroom decorum had to be somewhat relaxed: fans were supplied to the witnesses, jugs of water were carried in by the hour, and more frequent recesses were called. As a result, the progress of the trial was considerably slowed down.

Michael Cuddihy, whose firm had held the flagstone contract before Maher Brothers, testified that when the contract was taken from him and awarded at double the original price to Maher Brothers he was still willing to sell at thirty-three and a half cents per square foot. The witness also testified that when he heard that the contract had been lost he went to see Mitchell, requesting the reason why, but Mitchell told him that he must see the mayor.

After Cuddihy concluded his testimony, the district attorney placed John Wells Farley, the former Finance Commission secretary, on the stand. Under cross-examination by Coakley, Farley was led to recall an interesting exchange with Maher back in the fall of 1907, when he had first told Maher that the case looked like one for the district attorney and pressed Maher to say whether he had given any money to Mitchell.

"Mr. Farley," Maher had replied, "I don't know what you are, but I am a Catholic and I say that as true as there is a God in heaven, I never paid Mitchell any money." At that, the hundreds who had crowded into the courtroom visibly stirred and Mitchell's taut body relaxed for the first time in days.

Mitchell's relaxation did not last long, however, for the next witness was George Koch. Presently employed as a purchasing agent for a Lynn concern and recently married for the first time, Koch displayed during his entire testimony an unimpaired composure which stood in sharp contrast to the extreme nervousness he had exhibited in all of his public appearances the year before. Koch testified that on at least three occasions he had pointed out to Mitchell that the price of the Maher contract was double the old price.

With the conclusion of Koch's testimony, the dramatic moment that everyone had long been waiting for finally arrived: the testimony of the prosecution's star witness, ex-Mayor Fitzgerald. Having built up his case for the conspiracy in slow and painstaking detail, District Attorney Hill now hoped to rest his argument with the man whose testimony before the grand jury had unquestionably been the severest and the most damaging to the defendants. But in this calculation Hill failed to consider that Fitzgerald possessed a mind shrewder and more clever than his own, combined with a temperament capable of pulling off the boldest of maneuvers.

All through his initial testimony, from his first to his last moments on the stand, Fitzgerald maintained a remarkably cool countenance; not for a single moment did he allow himself to seem out of sorts, impatient or ruffled. In answer to the preliminary questions, he listed his occupation as newspaper publisher and told of the work of the Supply Department leading up to the appointment of Mitchell as purchasing agent.

"What experience had Mitchell that fitted him for this position?" Hill asked.

"He had had business experience as an undertaker," Fitzgerald replied.

"His business as an undertaker was retail, was it not?" Hill asked.

"Well, yes," Fitzgerald said, with a broad smile on his face. "I am not sure that I ever heard of a wholesale undertaker." There was a burst of laughter in which everybody, including Judge Sanderson, joined.

From there, Hill proceeded to the core of his case.

HILL: Now, do you recall the Maher contract incident?

FITZGERALD: No.

HILL: Do you remember giving your sanction to the contract?

FITZGERALD: I do not.

Flustered and confused by Fitzgerald's unexpected response, Hill handed a copy of the first Maher contract to Fitzgerald in order to refresh the latter's memory, and then, after a few moments, he asked again, "Do you remember having sanctioned this contract?"

"I do not," answered the ex-mayor.

Once more Hill repeated his question, and this time the witness began a response.

FITZGERALD: The system of the Mayor's office—

HILL: I don't care what the custom of the Mayor's office was, Mr. Mayor, but I want an answer, yes or no. Did you sanction that contract?

COAKLEY: I object to this method of questioning, because the District Attorney is here attempting a sort of cross-examination.

HILL: I think I have a right to cross-examine, because this testimony is a great surprise to me.

Finally, Fitzgerald admitted that by law the contracts could not have been made without his signature, but as to any of the details surrounding the making of this particular contract, such as whether he had asked the department head for information on the contract, he repeated his claim that he did not recall. The mayor's repeated answer of "don't recall" exasperated Hill and he cried out, "Well, we can try this case with the testimony taken before the grand jury. Your memory was fresher then."

As the district attorney reached over to take the transcript of the grand-jury testimony from the table, attorneys Coakley and Carney, representing Mitchell and Maher, jumped up and objected, citing case after case against the admission of grand-jury minutes into a trial. The district attorney responded that he was not going to read the minutes aloud, he was simply going to use the grand-jury testimony to refresh Fitzgerald's mind.

HILL: Do you remember being asked by Moran whether you had talked to Mitchell about the prices for contracts?

FITZGERALD: I do not recall.

HILL: Your memory is pretty good, isn't it, Mr. Fitzgerald?

FITZGERALD: Yes, considering the many things that come to me for some years past.

The district attorney then read some of the questions of the late District Attorney Moran, again with the view of refreshing Fitzgerald's memory. As recorded in the minutes, Moran had asked, "What information did you have regarding those contracts?" Fitzgerald had answered, "I called Mitchell up on the telephone and asked him if it was the best he could do."

HILL: Do you recollect saying that to the grand jury, Mr. Fitzgerald?

FITZGERALD: I don't recall it, and will not answer except those things I remember.

From the grand-jury testimony, the district attorney read, " 'Question: If you had known that the stone could have been had at half as much, would you have signed the contract? Answer: I would not have made the contract.' Do you remember saying this?" Hill asked.

"No, I do not," Fitzgerald replied.

After two hours on the stand, all the mayor was able to recall was that the papers in the present case had been brought to him in Old Orchard, and he said he did not recollect telephoning to Mitchell as he had testified before the grand jury.

HILL: Do you remember telling the grand jury that you understood later that what Mr. Mitchell told you you had found not to be in accordance with the facts?

FITZGERALD: I believed at the time that Mr. Mitchell told me the truth.

And on it went until the judge finally called an adjournment with Fitzgerald still on the stand.

By seven o'clock the next morning, June 29, 1909, the city papers were on the stands with sprawling headlines which informed everyone of Fitzgerald's surprising testimony, or rather lack of testimony, and described the lively tilts between the attorneys and the witnesses in such an engaging manner that hundreds of additional spectators showed up at court in the hopes of gaining entrance to what was now turning out to be the most spectacular trial in recent history. "Necks were craned, bodies stretched upward and forward," the Globe observed, as "people filled every public seat, overflowed into the bar inclosure and occupied extra chairs brought in by obliging officers."

Fitzgerald was already in court when the court was called to order, and he appeared "somewhat flushed" when he took the stand again as the chief witness of the day. All in all, the newspaper accounts had been most unflattering toward his performance and the cartoonists had enjoyed a field day with his inability to recall, but Fitzgerald knew that he was caught in a trap of his own making and that the decision to forget was the best strategy he could follow. As *Practical Politics* observed:

> The fact remains that the whole trouble grew out of Mayor Fitzgerald's testimony before the grand jury when the case was first under consideration. He talked too much and talked unwisely. He made a speech to the grand jury and with it he threw discretion and his subordinate [Mitchell] to the wind. When the case came up for trial he had to repeat his grand jury testimony in open court or forget what he had said there. To have repeated it would have been fatal; to forget was dangerous. He chose the wiser course.

At the sound of the gavel, Hill started right in.

> HILL: Have you thought over your evidence before the grand jury since you left the courtroom last night, Mr. Mayor, and are you able to remember any more about it?
>
> FITZGERALD: I have considered it carefully and am not able to recollect any more than I told yesterday . . .
>
> HILL: Do you recollect saying that you had called up Mr. Mitchell on this particular case and that he told you the Maher Brothers were the only agents who could furnish the material?
>
> FITZGERALD: No.
>
> HILL: Do you recollect saying they had done this cleverly?
>
> FITZGERALD: I do not.

Hill was considerably exasperated at the ex-mayor's lack of memory, and several times during the day he made remarks about "this unfortunate lapse of memory," but before the session came to an end the district attorney seemed to regain his composure, finishing up his examination of Fitzgerald on a strong and compelling note.

> HILL: Did you realize the purpose of your appearance before the grand jury? Did you swear to tell the truth?
>
> FITZGERALD: Yes, sir.
>
> HILL: And did you not tell the grand jury anything but the truth?
>
> FITZGERALD: Yes, sir.
>
> HILL: So anything you definitely told the grand jury then as true was true?

FITZGERALD: Yes, sir.

HILL: Well, if you told the grand jury that you spoke to Mitchell about these flagstone prices, was it true?

FITZGERALD: If I so testified, it was true.

At this moment, unquestionably the most triumphant in his long and weary examination, the district attorney announced that he was finished with the witness.

Now it was time for the cross-examination of the witness by the lawyers for the defendants. Coakley kept Fitzgerald on the stand for nearly half an hour with a line of inquiry so subtle and so fascinating as to suggest the intriguing possibility that at some point before the trial Fitzgerald and Coakley had agreed together on the "don't recall" strategy which Fitzgerald had stuck to throughout his entire testimony. How this strategy evolved we do not know for certain. From the later remarks of Eddie Gallagher it would seem that Coakley approached Fitzgerald with both the idea and the clear threat that unless Fitzgerald agreed, Mitchell would be put on the stand to testify on his own behalf that with the flagstone contract, as with all the others, he was simply following the wishes of Fitzgerald. But all these messy revelations could be avoided if Fitzgerald agreed to "forget" his grand-jury testimony and if he managed to keep his agreement, no matter how embarrassing it became or how much damage he seemed to be doing to his political reputation. For without Fitzgerald's grand-jury testimony, Coakley believed, Mitchell would never be convicted.

Such a scenario would explain why, for most of the trial, Coakley kept his fury at Fitzgerald under wraps, and why, at times, he even seemed to be acting in concert with Fitzgerald, directing most of his courtroom interventions toward the goal of making Fitzgerald's performance more effective.

"What was the custom in the mayor's office," Coakley asked Fitzgerald during cross-examination, "in regard to looking up matters for the mayor's decision?"

In his long reply, which Coakley helped to elicit, Fitzgerald sought to show that there was such a vast mass of business during his term at City Hall and so many people who brought him papers to sign and documents to read, that he couldn't possibly remember who told him what in regard to any one particular contract; in fact, documents came to him in baskets piled five feet high and in an ordinary day he would sign his name anywhere from fifty to seventy-five times.

With this established, Coakley then took aim at Hill's final line of questioning, which had cleverly brought Fitzgerald to admit that whatever he had testified before the grand jury must have been true. As Hill had intended, these questions put Fitzgerald on the spot: to admit that he had not told the truth before the grand jury would be to admit perjury, which clearly Fitzgerald did not wish to do; yet, to end his testimony averring that what he had said at the grand jury was true was surely not the conclusion Fitzgerald had intended to leave in the jury's minds.

Attacking the problem head on, and making the fullest use of his celebrated powers of cross-examination, Coakley immediately recalled Fitzgerald's attention to the moment when Hill had led him to say that if he had testified at the grand jury that he had spoken to Mitchell about the flagstone price, then it must have been true.

COAKLEY: You are not infallible, are you, Mr. Fitzgerald?

HILL: I hardly think you should ask that. (laughter)

FITZGERALD: No, not infallible.

COAKLEY: I meant to show that many of these matters were negotiated by subordinates and at the grand jury the mayor may have testified *in good faith* that he thought he talked with heads of departments when it was really done by subordinates and he just signed papers after their investigation.

Isn't it likely that Mr. O'Connell, Mr. Dolan or some other office attaché might have given you the information instead of Mitchell?

FITZGERALD: It is likely . . . I may have made some mistakes in my testimony, of course.

This was the moment Coakley was waiting for. The point having been made, he turned to the judge, signifying that he was finished with this witness, and, after six hours of testifying, Fitzgerald was finally allowed to step down.

When the court reconvened at two o'clock, the trial moved swiftly on to its conclusion. At 2:45 Prosecutor Hill announced that his evidence was all in and that the government rested its case.

Then Coakley took most of the packed courtroom by surprise with his sudden announcement that the defense would rest, without presenting any testimony or evidence on Mitchell's behalf.

In his closing statement, Coakley addressed the jury on behalf of Michael J. Mitchell. As he stood before the jurors and began to speak, a hushed silence fell over the courtroom: Coakley's reputation as a bold and forceful orator was well known and widely respected. He began, predictably enough, given the drift of all the objections he had raised during the trial, to address the inadmissibility of the mayor's grand-jury testimony. Assuming that it was upon the ex-mayor's testimony alone that the district attorney had relied to prove a conspiracy, he said that as far as Fitzgerald's evidence was concerned "it was as if he never appeared on the stand."

Then, turning to face the crowd as well as the jury, he burst unexpectedly into a savage attack on Mayor Fitzgerald. The angry tone with which he spoke made a strong impression upon the reporters in the crowd. If seemed as if all the pent-up anger against Fitzgerald that he had been constrained for days and days to keep inside, so long as utility prescribed a temporary alliance, had been swelling so rapidly that it simply exploded.

> If Fitzgerald told the truth while on the witness stand in this trial, he gave false testimony before the grand jury. The District Attorney in his argument will talk about the "unfortunate lapse of memory" here by John Fitzgerald. In anticipation of that assumption, Michael J. Mitchell says to you here, through his counsel, myself, that there was no unfortunate lapse of memory here but, if the stenographer told the truth, Fitzgerald had an excess of memory back in the grand jury room, or, in other words, he falsified there and he has told you the truth here. What does he tell you? Simply this: I don't remember that Mitchell made any representations to me. . . .
>
> I care nothing for mayors, ex-mayors, future mayors maybe. I appear for no man but Mitchell, whose reputation in the community stands head and heels over the reputation of any witness that has appeared here. Assuming there is a case here, wherever the evidence may lead, to the ex-mayor if you will, it never points to Michael J. Mitchell.

The sting of Coakley's blazing attack was sufficient to cause a slight tremor on the part of the audience, but the strong language and irritability Coakley displayed were soft in comparison with the "scorching" attack which came next, when the district attorney stood up for his closing remarks and declared that when Fitzgerald came into court he "did not come with the purpose of telling the truth to this jury" but "to throw the government's case."

Like the counsel for the defense, the district attorney dwelt briefly on the evidence relative to the indictment and then turned his full attention to Fitzgerald. At times it seemed as if Mitchell and Maher were almost forgotten in the eagerness of both attorneys to retaliate against Fitzgerald.

Now I am coming to the testimony of Mr. Fitzgerald. I want to state that
. . . we had to put him on as a witness, but as for relying on him, that is
another story.

He failed to recollect anything about the original transactions—those
transactions which were one of worst blots on his administration when he
was mayor. . . . All of that has fled from his mind as if the whole matter
had never occurred. Again and again, he said, "I don't recollect."

. . . He failed to recollect that he testified before the grand jury that
Mitchell told him that Maher Brothers were the only ones who had this
quality of stone, that Mitchell told him that this was the same price that
had been paid by other administrations, that Mitchell misinformed him as
to the facts, that he relied on Mitchell's misinformation and that he
pointed out to the grand jury how cleverly they had worked it.

. . . I want to say . . . that Mr. Fitzgerald when he came here did not
come with the purpose of telling the truth to the jury, and did not tell the
truth to this jury, and that his object was to throw the government's case
because he probably thinks we rely upon him. Why did he want to throw
the government's case?

Is there any reason for his coming here and practically refusing to testify
except that he was afraid that if the whole truth came out it would not be
only the defendants that would be there in the dock? I tell you, gentlemen,
I don't know whether we have got all the conspirators or not, but I know
we have proved a conspiracy here and proved it up to the hilt. Whether
everybody who is in this thing was brought up or not I can't tell you, but
I promise you this: If it ever comes out that any other man or men are in
this thing, whether their names are Patrick or John or Henry or whatever
their names are, that I will put them where those two defendants are.

The jury began deliberation at three o'clock in the afternoon. At nine-
fifteen it became known that the twelve men had reached a definite
conclusion, for one by one they were seen slipping out the backdoor of
the courthouse onto Somerset Street and quietly leaving for their
homes.

The fact that an agreement had been reached so early seemed to be
regarded as a favorable sign to the friends of the defendants who had
hung around the courtroom to await any news from the jury room.
Then, as chance would have it, from a source that was apparently considered wholly reliable, a tip was circulated that the jury had rendered a
verdict of not guilty. How and when this news reached Mitchell we do
not know; we only know that he spent the night in Charlestown cele-
brating with all his loyal friends who had remained by his side throughout the ordeal.

At Nantasket Beach, where the Fitzgerald clan had gathered, everybody also took it for granted that Mitchell had been acquitted. There was much rejoicing, and a defiant Fitzgerald took the occasion to issue a reply to the district attorney's closing speech:

> Mr. Hill descended to the level of a blackguard. He even went further. Though claiming aristocratic training and surroundings, he showed the traits of a hireling. Mr. Hill's speech was meant for a campaign document against me this fall, in payment for his appointment to his present office. If he really meant what he said, he will present the evidence before a grand jury and ask for an indictment for perjury. I dare him to do so.

All that night, Mitchell later told a friend, he was unable to sleep. While he was heartened by what now seemed to be a strong prospect of acquittal, he was clearsighted enough to know that nothing was certain until he actually stood at the bar and heard the jury foreman say the words "Not guilty." In the dawning light his worries multiplied, and by the time he got out of bed he was shaking so much he could hardly button his vest.

The courtroom was packed long before the appointed time of nine-thirty. Finally, after eight long days, the moment they had all been waiting for had arrived. As the judge mounted the steps to his rostrum and the defendants took their places at the bar, the twelve members of the jury filed in.

At the words of the clerk, "Gentlemen of the jury, have you agreed upon a verdict?" the foreman, Charles Reid, spoke up: "We have."

In the strained silence, the clerk went on: "Do you find the defendants, Michael J. Mitchell and Thomas F. Maher, guilty or not guilty?"

And Reid announced, "We find the defendants Michael J. Mitchell and Thomas F. Maher guilty as charged in the indictment."

When the verdict was announced, reporters observed that "Mitchell was almost overcome." He dropped woodenly into his chair and "tears sprang to his eyes." Maher, it was said, "paled slightly" but seemed to take the announcement "in a more stoical manner." Mitchell's stunned friends immediately encircled him with sympathy and comfort, but he remained slumped in his chair, disgraced and inconsolable.

When the time for the sentencing arrived, at two o'clock on Friday afternoon, July 9, 1909, every seat in the courtroom was taken, as it had been at every stage of the trial. Turning first to the attorneys for the defense, the judge asked what they had to say on the matter of the sentence.

Maher's lawyer, Francis Carney, spoke first, telling the judge that

Maher had asked him to make a special plea for Mitchell. "The fact that Mitchell stands with him, Maher says, makes his position the more difficult. . . . Mr. Maher wants you to know that absolutely no money went to Michael J. Mitchell. . . . If it is a crime to deal with the city as with others, then my client is guilty, but Mitchell is innocent."

At that, Carney returned to his seat and Coakley rose to speak. "Maher," Coakley said, "has manfully said that Mitchell is innocent, and if you feel that Mitchell was an innocent tool of somebody else I ask that you show him clemency."

After hearing both the defense and the prosecution, Judge Sanderson delivered a remarkable speech explaining his own rationale for the sentence he was about to impose. Ordinarily, he said, a heavier sentence would be imposed upon Mitchell, who was a public official and therefore entrusted with the responsibility of protecting the public, than upon Maher, who was a private contractor, but there was an unusual situation here since the foreman of the jury had come up to him after the verdict to speak on Mitchell's behalf. Representing the entire panel, the foreman had said they thought that Mitchell "was not so deep in the matter as somebody else who was not charged, that there was more guilt attaching to others in connection with this transaction than to Mitchell and that they hoped the court would take this into consideration when sentencing Mitchell."

The judge's announcement caused a commotion in the courtroom as many of the spectators audibly hazarded guesses as to whom the foreman of the jury was referring to when he spoke of someone more to blame than Mitchell. Rapping for order, the judge went on to say that while he was willing to take the jury's plea for Mitchell into consideration, the facts were that Mitchell was the public servant in charge, that he did not attempt by anything he said to shift that responsibility to anyone else or to claim that he was an innocent victim for some other person. Moreover, the main object of a sentence is not its effect on the individual sentenced—who a good many times has suffered as much before the sentence as he will suffer after—as it is to protect the community from future crimes of the same kind and to keep others up to the proper standard. For that reason, he could not agree to a simple fine or a sentence of probation. He had decided instead to sentence both men to the House of Correction on Deer Island for one year at hard labor.

Later that day, a rumor circulated that the convicted Mitchell was planning to make a statement that would implicate others, even up to the ex-mayor himself, and would cause a sensation. This report had the effect of arousing great interest along Newspaper Row, where reporters anxiously awaited the explosive document. But when it came, it was simply another glowing tribute to Mayor Fitzgerald. "John F. Fitzgerald is the squarest of men I have ever known," the statement read. "His political enemies try to give a different opinion but everyone who knows him as I have known him has the same opinion I have." As the story was later told, this "remarkable tribute" was once again the handiwork of brother Jim, who, early that evening, had sent a finished typewritten statement into the Charles Street Jail for Mitchell to sign.

The public's interest in Mitchell and Maher did not end with their commitment to Deer Island. For days, the newspapers carried dramatic follow-up stories provided by unnamed and often conflicting sources. On Sunday, for instance, the *Boston American* reported that while Maher had maintained his usual calm as he was being booked in, Mitchell had fallen into a faint "when the grim walls of the prison loomed before him," and "it was necessary to take him to the hospital." Competing with one another for the most trivial of details, the newspapers ended up describing the daily diets of the prisoners as if they were describing the menu at a state dinner.

After this first flurry of interest, however, the newspapers turned their attention elsewhere, and then began for Mitchell what he later described to Eddie Gallagher as "a long nightmare"—long, monotonous days no longer buoyed up by the hectic tension of the trial and the crowds. "The curse of the place," Mitchell told Gallagher, "was all the hours you had to sit there all by yourself, thinking and worrying and never really understanding how it had all happened to you. One day you'd be okay and think you could make it through, the next day you'd know all too well that your life would never again be the same. You'd start saying to yourself, So this is how all those years of hard work have ended up. And then, oh God, you'd feel so bad you couldn't even get out of bed."

# CHAPTER 11
# A CHILD
# OF
# MARY

With Mitchell safely in jail, there was one piece of unfinished business Fitzgerald had to attend to: it was time to bring his daughters home from the convent. For months, Rose and Agnes had been writing home, begging their parents to let them come home in July after the school year was over. While they both agreed that Blumenthal was "an excellent place" to study at, "for we are free from all distractions and we are in contact with such cultured people," they both kept stressing that one year so far away from home was more than enough and that they were terribly lonely.

Of the two girls, Agnes was the more explicit in her longing to come home; she dreamed constantly of the day "we will be altogether again in the dear old U.S.A." And she told her parents that once she finally returned it would be some time before anyone would induce her again to leave America's shores. But Rose too, while absorbing convent life more fully than her sister, confessed that she would be "terribly disappointed" at being told she must stay over for another year.

All during the spring, however, even into the early summer, Fitzgerald had refused to listen to his girls' request. Not knowing how Mitchell's trial would turn out, he wanted to keep the option open of leaving them abroad, away from the scandal and the rumors and away from Mitchell's torment. But now that the trial was completed and the loyal Mitchell had gone willingly to jail, Rose and Agnes could finally come home. "You can't imagine our surprise," Agnes wrote on July 28, "when we received the telegram from Papa saying he was coming. We didn't receive the telegram until the day before he arrived. Oh how happy we were and when we *saw* him I can't tell you our great joy. I think he looks the same as ever so I don't suppose Rose and I could have changed a great deal."

Speaking for herself, Agnes was no doubt correct. From all accounts, the experience of boarding school had not changed the shy and warm-hearted younger sister in any noticeable way. But with Rose it was a different story. Whether she fully realized it at the time or not, the evidence suggests that, by channeling certain aspects of her character while deflecting others, the year at Blumenthal had changed her in fundamental ways. To understand the nature of this change, we must move backward to the previous September when the Fitzgeralds deposited their daughters at the convent.

When the time came for the girls to be left at Blumenthal, Rose admitted to a "sudden feeling of intense loneliness." Cut off from the protection of family and friends, parted from every familiar object, she felt that everything seemed "cold, distant, and strange." The one great solace she had was the presence of her sister Agnes, with whom she was, in her words, "extremely close."

They were different in temperament: Agnes was softer and more easygoing than Rose, not so bold or so competitive, far more her mother's child. "I was the one with lots of ideas," Rose recalled. "I would be the one to say, 'Let's have a party.' She would think that a marvelous inspiration and would plan the menu, set and arrange the table and I would invite the people. I would say, 'Let's take a trip to so and such'; again, marvelous and she would pack our bags. I liked one kind of beau. She liked another kind."

But the deeper affinity was unmistakable: heredity had infused into both girls a vital interest in people, a perceptive cast of mind and an innate desire to please. Moreover, their closeness in age had bound them together through much of their girlhood; at home they were forever in each other's company, sharing both their bedroom and their bath, their clothes and their books. And from all accounts they got on remarkably well. Whereas with her brothers Rose assumed a patronizing air which decidedly irritated them and made them in turn exhibit considerable anger and jealousy toward her, with Agnes she was always patient, loving and warm. In all the family letters there is not a hint of rivalry, of anger or even of strong irritability between the two. On the contrary, they seemed to take a genuine comfort in each other's company—a comfort which they both needed more than ever in the unaccustomed surroundings of Blumenthal.

The world in which Agnes and Rose found themselves at Blumenthal was a hundred years away in time from twentieth-century America. In all things—in architecture, in ritual and in way of life—the Blumenthal tradition was one of monastic simplicity. All members of the Blumenthal community, including the mother superior, the teaching nuns and all the boarding students, were housed in the same building—a large stone structure, three stories high, with tall arched windows on every side. For quarters, the Fitzgerald girls were assigned a small room on the second floor sparsely furnished with two beds, a washstand, a prie-dieu, a writing table and a small space for Bibles and books.

There was no central heating in the old granite building, and the cold in the bedrooms and the classrooms could be very numbing. Not long after she was settled in, Agnes described in a letter addressed to her mother a morning "so cold that they gave us all a cup of hot water and whiskey with bread and butter at ten o'clock." Later she spoke of a wind "so sharp, it goes right through you," while Rose reported that her hands had turned "a purplish bluish color" and that she had had frost on her feet for a few weeks. Yet, as the situation was described by Mary Magiore, an Irish girl in residence with Rose and Agnes who later became a writer and the wife of the Irish playwright Padraic Colum, "nobody thought of complaining much." "We snuffled with colds," Mary Colum wrote, "and our hands and feet, but especially our hands, became covered with chilblains. There was a point, I remember, when these broke or split and became very painful." But if any of the girls talked aloud about their aches, they were told "to meditate on the sufferings of our Lord on the Cross" so they would not be tempted to overestimate their own puny pains.

More difficult than the cold, however, was the rigid schedule, "with penalties for those who did not or could not keep to it," which governed every aspect of life in the convent, and the ceaseless supervision of behavior, designed "to prevent evil, detect faults and remedy them." For Rose and Agnes, as newcomers to boarding life, the first challenge was to synthesize in their minds the mass of minutiae on which convent life was based and to teach their bodies to behave accordingly. "It is hard to understand how things are at boarding school," Rose admitted in an early letter to her parents. "Everything is marked out for a certain period of time and we have hardly any free periods." It was "the same routine" day after day, week after week. No changes, not even on Saturdays.

"Not only the first days, but the first year was difficult," Mary Colum contended,

> for convents, like courts and camps, have a traditional ritual handed down through centuries, and to get into the pattern was not easy. . . . All the conventions and customs of a convent were both fascinating and difficult to get used to. Everything I did seemed to be wrong. I kept my seat when I should be standing up; I wore my house shoes when I should be wearing outdoor shoes; unwittingly I made myself audible so conspicuously during silences that for the rest of the year I hardly spoke at all.

The day at Blumenthal began at 6 A.M., in the cold gray of dawn, with bells that rang through every corridor in the older wing of the house where the students slept in their tiny rooms. From a distance came the voice of the mistress intoning the rising prayer, "Sacred Heart of Jesus and Immaculate Heart of Mary . . ." and then the sound of a hundred bodies dropping to their knees and responding in unison, "I give you my heart." No one was allowed to get up before the prescribed hour, nor was anyone allowed to stay in bed, not even for a minute's slumber, once the rising bell had rung.

There was a strict rule in the convent that there should be no conversation in the early morning; except for reciting their morning prayers, which were to be said "in a loud voice, steady and distinct," the girls had to keep silent from the rising bell at six until the end of breakfast at eight-thirty. Years later Rose Kennedy would recall "the loneliness of waking up on those raw and chilly mornings when the only sound you heard was the rustling of garments as dozens of girls in dozens of rooms stepped behind dozens of curtains to slip off their dressing gowns."

The girls were expected to be washed, dressed and ready for assembly by six-fifteen sharp, when the tolling bell announced the voice of Christ summoning the entire convent to prayer. During the recitation of the morning prayers, the girls were supposed to join hands, keeping their eyes lowered and their backs straight, no spine sagging, no muscle moving. The slightest disturbance was observed; the mere shuffling of one's feet could merit a bad point at the weekly evaluation of each girl's conduct. The morning prayers were always said in Latin, beginning with the Pater, ending with the Confiteor. At the final amen, chimes announced the morning Mass, "the most saintly action of the day." With long black veils over their heads, the girls walked in step in ranks of two and two into the chapel.

The ordered silence continued after the Mass as the moving procession of girls marched back to their rooms to lay down their veils and then to the refectory, where breakfast was served. At all meals the girls were expected to be models of politeness and manners. "It is especially at the table," the regulations emphasized, "that a young person well brought up distinguishes herself from those who have not received the same education." At every meal either a lecture was delivered, usually on some aspect of character formation, or there was a reading in German or in French which the girls were expected to listen to without speaking. "The hardest thing in the beginning," Rose later recalled, "was to learn all the small gestures which took the place of speech—the raising of the hand to ask for juice, the lowering of the middle finger to say, 'Napkin, please.' What a great relief it was to hear the gong which ended all these gestures by allowing us to speak for the last few minutes of the meal, and, oh, how we chattered away, our voices bursting forth into the air."

The class hours were long and the nuns were demanding, but with this aspect of convent life Rose had at least some familiarity, since the curriculum at Blumenthal was the same as it had been at the convent in Boston, "only here naturally we recite and learn things in German instead of English." In the first semester, besides the courses required of all students at her level, she took up modern history, astronomy, literature and the history of art, along with German and French. "The French is in the afternoon," she wrote home, "and the girls speak very well. Just the same as it was last year, only harder."

"Even the time of private study was carefully mapped," Mary Colum explained, "fifteen minutes for this, ten minutes for that . . . at ten minutes to three I had to study French irregular verbs every day until I knew them and could repeat all the moods and participles without a mistake, and at half past one I had to practice embroidery stitches on a piece of cotton."

There was no escape from the community; you might long to curl up on a bed and read a novel or take a walk through the woods with a friend, but this could never be. Even during the hours set aside for recreation—"the only hours of the day where the rules permitted talk in order to form the art of polite and sensible conversation"—it was forbidden "to gather without permission in the garden, to sing or play games which haven't got the approval of the mistress, to climb benches etc." The regulations seemed to take it for granted that learning to live with oneself was more important than learning to make friends, that the "joys of solitude" were more valuable than organized activities. The major recreational activity was "the promenade"—a half hour's walk up and down the terrace which provided time to be alone and to meditate. "Without these moments," Janet Erskine Stuart wrote in explanation of the Sacred Heart emphasis on silence and rest, "the conditions of life at present will give us tempers and temperaments incapable of repose and solitude."

For healthy, robust girls like Rose and Agnes, who had been swimming and skating, riding horses and playing tennis since they were very young, this concept of recreation was difficult to understand. In an early letter to her mother Agnes lamented that they played "only one game at recreation and this is not very exciting." Then in another letter she reported, "Rose and I have been running around in slippers for the last week. The doctor said that we didn't exercise here as much as at home and that our feet became swelled and too large for our own shoes."

On Sundays the rule permitted sisters and cousins to take their recreational promenades together, but since these moments were so rare and since the girls were expressly told to avoid all familiarity, the strolling girls soon became as uncommunicative as the chestnut trees beneath which they strolled. Because ideas, feelings and moods could not be shared with others in ordinary conversation, Rose found little to talk about except the future or the past. "During these promenades," she reported, "we usually plan what elite clubs we shall join when we arrive home or else we describe some distractingly pretty ballgown our mother has had in the past."

At the time the Fitzgerald sisters were at Blumenthal, there was a convent rule against "particular friendships": the girls were forbidden to go off and speak or play with one another without permission; they were warned against demonstrating too much affection with one another and expressly told to avoid "throwing themselves spontaneously on one another with familiar manners which did not conform to the reserve of persons well brought up."

It was this aspect of convent life, the rigid surveillance which denied all spontaneous attachments, that proved the most troubling to Rose. "It gets a little mite lonesome," she conceded, her rebellion always below the surface, "especially when we hear about other girls having so much fun at home. The girls are lovely here but so quiet, no life or excitement. It is hard to make friends because we have little opportunity to talk with them and friendships among the girls are not encouraged by the mothers at Blumenthal." Agnes put the matter even more forcefully: "I tell you frankly," she wrote to her mother, "you can't make what you call a friend in school."

Yet if the grueling routine was the most exasperating challenge Rose had ever experienced, it was also the most compelling. For beneath the strict code of discipline lay a definite system for training in moral conduct, self-control, respect for authority and polished manners—a system which depended on spurs and baits, punishments and rewards to set the will in motion. Every Sunday morning the entire school assembled in the chapel for a public examination of each girl's conduct the week before. The dramatic ceremony began as the meticulously dressed girls —their shoes shined, their stockings straight, their white gloves spotless —marched down the aisle and formed a semicircle facing the altar. In front of them, in a straight line, stood the mother superior with a set of colored notecards in her hands, the mistress of discipline holding a large black notebook, and all the teaching nuns.

All during the week the girls had been watched over carefully for the slightest imperfections—for walking too impetuously or forgetting to pass things at table, for being late for dinner or failing to curtsy in front of the religious statues, for talking together in recreation in a way that excluded others, for leaving their chapel veils in the wrong place, or for talking during a period of silence. Each imperfection, depending upon its seriousness, counted for a certain number of "negative" or "bad" points on the master list which the mistress of discipline kept in her big black book. On the other side of the ledger, each student received a certain number of "good" or "positive" points for poise and politeness, for assisting at Mass, for good use made of study halls, for unselfish service to others and for flawless recital of their lessons in class. At the end of each week, the inspectors and the teachers got together to determine a composite score for each girl. This score was then used to determine the girl's ranking in the "weekly primes."

The proclamation of the weekly primes always began with the names of the students who had the lowest scores, which meant that as each name was called every girl agonized, fearing that it would be hers. Then there was the additional mortification of the ceremony itself, which required each student, when her name was called, to walk up to the altar, curtsy before the mother superior and then stand on display in front of all the others as the list of her faults was read aloud.

Yet, for all its harshness, the Sacred Heart system relied on pride more than shame, on emulation more than admonition, on encouragement more than criticism. It is worth remembering, too, that for every girl who found herself at the bottom of the weekly evaluation, there was another girl who came out at the top, who glowed with pleasure as she heard her named called to accept the coveted blue card signifying that her performance all week long had been *très bien*. Those who regularly received *très biens* at their weekly primes were eligible for the next round of prizes—the blue ribbons distributed three times a year to the top fifteen girls. And beyond ribbons there were medallions; and beyond medallions, sodalities. In this well-articulated system of inducements and rewards there was always a higher prize to reach for, a higher standard to meet, a better person to emulate.

Moreover, strict as the code of discipline was, there were enough moments of release, on Sundays and holidays, to keep the girls trudging through the rest of the weeks. "Today . . . is the Feast of All Saints," Agnes explained to her mother in a letter on November 1, "and . . . so we have a little extra time for writing. . . . I suppose Rose has told you about the great preparations they are making for the feast next Sunday" (the Feast of Saint Nicholas). The first week in December brought another great feast—the Feast of the Immaculate Conception, at which time, as Rose explained, "we wear our white dresses and form a procession after Mass. We receive a lily in the chapel and then we pass through nearly the whole house singing hymns."

On feast days the girls were allowed to sleep fifteen minutes later than usual; they were given a free study period, an extra half hour for recreation, a treat with their afternoon tea (cake or cookies), and the freedom to put out their own lights at night. On certain holidays they were even allowed to dance and play games, to read novels and poems. In the intensity of the convent's regular routine, these small privileges were experienced as moments of pure pleasure, which added to the strength and the power of the festivals themselves.

And still there was more. On festival days there was a real beauty in the convent: in the ancient rituals and practices, in the great poetic liturgies, in the deep and subtle music, in the intoxicating smell of flowers and in the rich luxury of colors—a mysterious beauty which surrounded the place and made the experience one to hold on to forever. For the American girls, in particular, less familiar as a group with ancient Gregorian hymns and the mighty antiphons, less accustomed to such elaborate, triumphant processions, the convent festivals were unforgettable. "The Midnight Mass was beautiful," Rose exclaimed in a letter to her mother, "and we shall always remember it." The same with Holy Week, with Good Friday and Easter Sunday. "It was all so new and lovely to me," Agnes wrote, "that you may be sure it made an everlasting impression." After the bareness and austerity of the ordinary daily routine, the splendor of the festivals had an astonishing impact on the girls, providing the kind of total experience that no one fails to remember. "We had the loveliest feast day on the feast of Corpus Christi," Rose told her parents. "We wore our white dresses and veils and had a long procession through the garden, followed by the priest with the Blessed Sacrament."

·  ·  ·

The particular interest of Rose's experience at Blumenthal lies not simply in seeing the days as they passed, but in understanding the gradual
turning that took place in the young girl's vision of herself and of her
place in the world—a turning that would have the deepest significance
for the character of the mature woman Rose would become. Something
happened to Rose during these long months of detachment from the
bustle and activity of modern life; something which brought her face to
face with her inner, silent self; which allowed her to find within herself
what she later called "the gift of faith."

Up until now, though she had been born into a family that was certainly pious by most people's standards, there is no evidence that Rose
differed from any number of Catholics for whom churchgoing was essentially a participation in a social and cultural phenomenon rather than
a religious experience. "While I had always believed in God," Rose later
said, "and had faithfully gone to church and confession, this was not
really the same as the living faith I acquired at Blumenthal."

"For me," she explained in her autobiography, "faith means the continual awareness of the existence of God, not in some far off and unrelated manner, but as an object of spiritual existence in which I am
personally involved." Faith, she wrote, is not "something we are born
into, a kind of family legacy in the spiritual realm"; nor is it something
"we can simply talk or reason ourselves into possessing; the truth is that
just as it centers upon God, so too it comes from Him to those who seek
it."

That Rose was not yet possessed of this wholehearted, unquestioning
response to faith when she first entered Blumenthal is suggested in any
number of her early letters home, which reveal an easygoing, almost
nonchalant attitude toward her religion. While there is no doubt of her
intellectual assent to all the traditional doctrines of Catholicism, she
somehow manages to project the stance of a sympathetic bystander, a
person standing outside and looking in. Describing a feast day in late
September on which the girls entertained the sisters with five or six
plays, she writes that she "played the part of a child who did not want to
go to church." And then, in a mood of evident good humor, she adds,
"I told the girls that it was mean to 'give me away' like that."

In another letter, written a few weeks later, a similar tone is conveyed
as she explains to her parents that she has become an "angel"—a neo-
phyte in a sodality, which means she has to get up fifteen minutes earlier
than the others and go to meditation nearly every morning. "So you
see," she reports, "my piety is increasing. If I am extremely angelic, I
may become an aspirant for the Children of Mary; later, I may become
a Child of Mary. That is the highest honor a child of the Sacred Heart

can receive. So I shall have to be a model of perfection for the next few months." Missing here in Rose's lighthearted talk of "the next few months" is the energy of affirmation ordinarily called for by those who aspired to become members of the Children of Mary, which was supposed to embrace a commitment for life, a deep personal resolve to attend Mass, not just once a week, but every day; to say the Rosary regularly; to make an annual retreat, to go to special Masses and to renew one's religion daily so that it becomes inseparable from one's life.

Further evidence of Rose's relaxed attitude toward her religion in those early convent days can be found in her memory of being "startled and amused"—an attitude hardly consistent with impassioned faith—when she first encountered a detailed list of all the books on the Index of Forbidden Books, an index published by the Vatican which proscribed the reading of different categories of "bad books."

When we understand that excommunication was the punishment reserved for those who knowingly violated the Index laws, Rose's recollection of being "amused" when she first encountered the list becomes even more interesting to note. So, too, the wry detachment she manages when she shares her newfound knowledge with her parents in a letter written on November 24:

> When we were speaking about French books the other day, my teacher told us that Les Miserables is on the Index and that it is a frightfully wicked book. I knew that we had an English translation of it at home, and so I thought perhaps you would want it destroyed. It might not look well to have it in our library. There are two volumes with a sort of brown mixture color. They are not very large books. The story deals with exaggerated social conditions and that is why it is wicked. You see I am more or less acquainted with the book. Fortunately I did not inquire what grade of excommunication would come to individuals who had already read the book. There are some circumstances where ignorance is bliss. Please do not make any illusion [sic] to the book in your letters because the nun who reads the letters would be shocked. I am going to ask permission to send this letter sealed, it will not be read like most of my letters are.

Taken as a whole, Rose's letters during the autumn months show her at open war with herself, struggling terribly hard to preserve a certain detachment from the molded community, pleading with her parents to keep her in touch with everything that is happening out in the world; yet, all the while, gradually sensing within herself a stealing allegiance to the Sacred Heart standards, a growing commitment to the silent world of prayer where all external things recede into the distance.

There is a restless tension in her letters. On the one hand, the logic of the convent life functioned in complete opposition to the logic of the world in which she had grown up. From her earliest childhood years her father had taken immense pride in her ambition and in her accomplishments; he had wanted her to look and be the best in any situation, to stand out in any group. Yet here at Blumenthal the constant preoccupation was to look and act like everyone else. In this community there was no room for singularity. The attributes the nuns held in high esteem —humility and patience, contrition and obscurity—were the antithesis of everything she had been taught. To give in and become the kind of young woman the nuns wanted her to be was to let a vital part of herself go, to surrender the uniqueness she valued the most. On the other hand, the inducements for adapting herself to the convent standards were overwhelming.

The early months were the hardest: in proportion as the news and desires and appetites and conflicts of the world filled her mind and her heart, she found it difficult to experience the joy of interior silence. There is a frantic quality in her repeated requests for news from home, a constant striving to fill the silence with sound. We see her in mid-September imploring her parents to send her *The Republic* and *The Transcript* once a month along with copies of the latest songs wrapped inside, including "Take Me Out to the Ballgame" and "Are You Sincere?" Then, in early November, she entreats them to let her know as soon as possible who has won the presidential election; when she finally learns of Taft's victory, she regretfully replies: "Bryan has tried so many times that I wish he had gotten it."

But the news from home, coming as it did only once or twice a month, could not begin to fill all the empty corners of the days she had to spend behind the enclosed convent walls. Still chafing under the strict discipline and worried about what she was missing in life, she turned her mind to the romance of travel; through all of November and December her letters were filled to the brim with intricate and ever changing travel plans for the chaperoned trip she and Agnes were planning to take during Christmas vacation.

When the holidays finally arrived, Rose and Agnes set forth on a two-week journey that took them all over Germany. The trip afforded the Fitzgerald girls a glimpse of the splendor of the Old World: of kings and czars; of grand dukes and crown princes; of plumed helmets and spheres of influence. Arriving in Leipzig, they went immediately to a concert which was "perfectly glorious"; then they went to Berlin, which Rose found to be "almost as good as New York." New Year's night in Berlin, with all the court in attendance, the girls heard the opera *Tannhäuser*. "It was truly wonderfully beautiful," Rose exclaimed. "We had to wear 'decolleté' gowns and you should have seen us. We took the yokes out of our light dresses and threw veils on our heads and there we were. The Kaiserin and Crown Princesses as well as other members of the royal family had a loge directly below us."

For Agnes, the European idea of hereditary power, fascinating as it seemed, still paled before the American idea of democratic power. After seeing the Kaiser in his full regalia, Agnes sent her little brother Fred, then aged six, a card with a picture of the little Crown Prince of Germany, "a little boy who will some day be the Kaiser of Germany if he lives . . . Never mind, Fred," Agnes continued, "you may be President of the USA someday which is far better." For Rose, the spectacle of European royalty seemed to provide a substitute for the life she had left behind. In letter after letter she revealed a keen interest in the life of the nobility. At the news of the birth of Princess Juliana to Queen Wilhelmina of Holland, she could barely contain her excitement: "We sang the Dutch national song and made speeches at dinner, telling how glad the representatives of the different nations here were that the Queen had a successor." Coming as it did at such a vulnerable time in her life, the pageantry of the Old World had a tremendous effect upon Rose; indeed, from her convent days she developed a romantic attachment to the "idea" of royalty which stayed with her for the rest of her life.

The start of the second week of January 1909 found Rose back once more behind the hushed convent walls, facing a long stretch of at least six months without a break, plus the prospect of another whole year as a boarder. Decades later Rose could recall the conflicting emotions she experienced as she began her second semester at Blumenthal. "I realized when I came back after my vacation that I had not yet fully committed myself to the life of the convent, that my mind all fall long had been filled with external things, with news from home and thoughts of travel. But it was not in my nature to remain an outsider for long. All my life I had responded vitally to everything I did. It came to me that I must try harder to dedicate myself to the standards of the convent life, that I must take more seriously my commitment to becoming a Child of Mary. So I searched in my heart for a steady resolve, and little by little I found it. I found in myself a growing desire to pray and a new understanding of the purpose of silence."

While Rose was moving closer to her religion, the convent was preparing for its annual retreat, a period of four days during which the ordinary school schedule stopped completely to allow each girl to examine the state of her conscience, to reflect on why she had been sent into this world and to meditate on her eternal destiny. Though the girls had been conditioned to silence at meals and at different periods during the day, during the retreat the silence was supposed to be complete, uninterrupted and kept for four days straight. "You can imagine me keeping still for three minutes much less almost four days," Agnes wrote to her mother on the eve of the retreat. ". . . I am positively looking on the occasion with white face and chattering teeth for I just know I can't make my mouth behave."

For some of the girls, the strain of the prolonged silence, the meditations and the sermons on hell proved too much, provoking attacks of hysteria and anxiety. Yet, according to their letters home, both Agnes and Rose emerged from the retreat happy and full of satisfaction. Despite her initial fears, Agnes found the retreat "very beautiful and instructive" and was even "a little sorry to have it ended." As for Rose, who had already resolved to commit herself more fully to God, the retreat "laid a permanent foundation" to her religious life.

"As I look back now," she said some seventy years later, "to that long distant experience, I look back with thankfulness to God for having granted me the occasion for shaping a lasting covenant with Him. Freed from all distractions and from all worldly thoughts, I was able to find in myself the place that was meant for God. The silence spoke to me of a different kind of happiness, a happiness that never wears out, a happiness that consists in knowing and loving God. Deprived of everything else, I became intensely aware of all the things I had taken for granted —the beauty of the sky and the stars at night, of the birds singing and the trees in bloom. And with this heightened awareness of God and of His world, I emerged more at peace with myself than I had ever been before."

The first outward signs of Rose's growing piety were not taken too seriously by her Blumenthal friends. "I used to be behind her in confession," Margaret Finnegan reported to one of Agnes' friends when they all returned home. "My God, I used to have to wait an hour," she said in a tone suggesting it was all a bit funny, "waiting for her to come out of the confessional box." But if Agnes and some of their friends thought it was funny, Rose was intensely serious. As wholeheartedly and as persistently as she had once pursued her academic ambitions, she was now determined to be all that the nuns wanted her to be. Imposing an armistice on the inner struggle that had occupied her during the fall, she allowed herself to be drawn more and more into the convent's daily routine. From now on, she would be circumspect in everything she did; from now on, self-control and faith would be the guiding principles of her life. Moreover, the more she submerged herself in the healing silence of the religious life, the more her religious horizons expanded. The process had a momentum of its own that took her beyond where even she could have guessed she would go.

Sociable as Rose had always been, she found at Blumenthal that she also had a strongly introverted side that could draw vast pleasure from solitude and silence. Step by step, the young girl who a few months earlier had scarcely known how to respond to the unending, unchanging routine found all the tormenting variety and choices of her old life cut away. Once she had committed herself to secure a religious basis for her life, the firm structure of the convent, with almost every moment of the day accounted for, felt supportive and consoling. She now became fully absorbed in the quest to become a Child of Mary.

Still, even with this commitment, it remained a difficult struggle; becoming a Child of Mary had little to do with the familiar benchmarks of academic success; nor was it simply a quest for perfect behavior, for absolute adherence to the rules. The goals to be met were nothing less than the conquest of pride and self-will, the achievement of interior silence. "Sometimes," Rose later recalled, "it seemed that the harder I tried, the more imperfect I became." Though she was seldom penanced for the same fault twice, there were always others. The last days of winter and the early days of spring telescoped into one long battle in the formation of character.

Eventually the discipline showed, and on May 22, 1909, Rose Fitzgerald was offered membership in the Children of Mary. Recording the dramatic event in a letter to her mother the following day, Agnes reported: "Rose was named last night as a Child of Mary. I was so glad she got it because she tried so hard. Two other girls were also named, an Irish girl and a German girl."

At the initiation ceremony each aspirant was asked to make a number of personal promises along with the basic commitments to attend daily Mass, go on special retreats, etc. Among her pledges, Rose made two which she returned to time and again in her long life: the first, "to make the effort necessary to practice those family virtues suited to my position as daughter, wife, mother, such as kindness, gift of self, abnegation and evenness"; the second, the promise "in the face of changes of fortune, to hold my soul free," and "in difficult moments, to obtain from Our Lady of Sorrows the courage to suffer as she did, standing at the foot of the Cross."

In becoming a Child of Mary, Rose let a part of herself go, that part of herself that had originally conceived of independent ambitions and career accomplishments, that part of her that had once wanted so fiercely to go to Wellesley College. The convent had done its work on Rose; the long silences, the immutable routine, and the daily lessons of the Sacred Heart curriculum had readjusted her vision of the world. When she looked out now from her new vantage ground, the old world she had known, the world of personal ambition and success, seemed shallow compared with the challenge of motherhood and the lifelong tasks of forming a child and building a family. "If Papa runs for mayor next fall," she wrote to her parents toward the end of May, "perhaps you would prefer to have us home. I might be able to be a little company for mother. I would not feel badly for my own sake if he were not successful. I am just as proud and happy to be his daughter today as I was two years ago when he had the highest position in the city. I suppose I could help the boys and Eunice in their studies too."

On the other hand, if she was not needed at home, then she would like to go to school somewhere, to have another year at her books. "I realize more and more every day how much I have to accomplish." In saying this, she did not mean going to a college, but instead choosing between two Sacred Heart schools, Montreal and Manhattanville. "College is out of the question," she suddenly announced in her letter of May 23. "The convent girls may not know as much Greek etc. as the college girls, but I think in general they can hold their own, in the positions to which they are called."

She continued in another letter written the same week:

> You see, one year at day school and one year at a foreign boarding school is not quite enough to give me all the little charms and graces of a Sacred Heart girl. . . . I am so ignorant compared with some of the girls who have been in convents all their lives and who have been free from all the distractions of the theatres. The people over here do not have to show off their knowledge like we Americans. They are so refined and cultured . . . Really I never felt quite so stupid in all my life . . . There are lots of things I could learn at home. For instance how to receive, how to write an archbishop, etc. By the way, Miriam [Finnegan] tells me you must have a special kind of paper on which to write him.

Abandoned by her parents to the harsh and lonely routine of convent life, Rose had to find some way to sustain herself. As she herself said, she was not the kind of person who could be an outsider for long. Surrounded by the beauty of the Church and the convictions of the nuns, she turned to God for consolation, finding in the self-denial of the convent atmosphere the healing substance of religion. From here on, Rose would later say, she would never be alone again, for she had found in God someone she could always love and trust.

Had she been allowed to go to Wellesley College, perhaps it all would have been different; perhaps she, as someone later suggested, might have become the first Catholic President instead of her son. Some might say it was fate which diverted her path, the result of a chance encounter between her father and the Archbishop of Boston. Yet the forces that drove her resided within her; it was she who decided to become what the nuns of the Sacred Heart wanted her to be. It was she who trod the path toward her religion which would give her life a new and irrevocable direction.

Having decided that it was time to bring his daughters home and that he himself would sail across to get them, Fitzgerald had no intention of letting the pressures of politics spoil his trip. No sooner had he reached Blumenthal than he set off with the girls for a gay sightseeing tour that took the three of them to Amsterdam, The Hague, Brussels, Paris, Portsmouth, London and Edinburgh. "We are certainly having a royal time," Agnes wrote to her mother on August 5, 1909; "how we wish you were with us. Oh, why didn't you come? Never mind, a week from today [we] sail on the *Cymric*. What a fine time we will have when we get home again."

The *Cymric* docked in Boston on August 20. "Our mother greeted us with tears in her eyes," Rose reported. "She had been terribly lonely." It was decided that the girls would not go so far away again; Agnes would continue her studies at the Sacred Heart Convent at Providence, Rhode Island; Rose would enroll at the Sacred Heart Convent in the Manhattanville section of New York City.

# CHAPTER 12
# THE
# MAYOR'S
# DAUGHTER

As the autumn of 1909 approached, political observers naturally began to speculate as to the effect Mitchell's trial and conviction would have upon the political fortunes of John Fitzgerald, who remained the most visible Democratic contender for mayor. The position of the Democratic Party bosses was simple. They did not think, with all the baggage he carried, that Fitzgerald could be reelected, and had it been left to them to choose the nominee, as it had been for decades under the reigning system of party government, Fitzgerald would have had little chance. But, by an ironic twist of fate, the same Finance Commission which had collapsed Fitzgerald's chances of winning the support of the regular Democratic politicians opened a backdoor to his election, by providing a new method of nomination in the charter reform package it successfully presented to the electorate in November 1909.

After eighteen months of hearings, the Finance Commission had come to the conclusion that Boston's corruption and graft could be significantly reduced only with basic structural reforms in the city's electoral system. Grouped together under the label "Plan Two," the reforms called for abolishing primaries and removing the party label from the ballot, extending the mayor's term to four years, and subjecting the mayor's departmental appointments to the approval of the Civil Service Board.

The party leaders fought hard to defeat Plan Two, but their efforts failed to match the crusading zeal of the reformers, whom Lincoln Steffens likened to "a group of schoolboys turned loose in an apple orchard." When the referendum votes were counted, the proponents of reform emerged victorious and a new city charter came into being. Vastly encouraged by the popular vote for the charter reform, the Good Government Association was convinced that the time had come for all the forces in the community desiring better government to unite upon a single candidate for mayor and to make up their minds to fight for him with every resource they possessed.

And this time they believed they had the ideal candidate in James Jackson Storrow, a blueblood patrician descended from the best of the old Yankee stock, from the Higginsons, the Cabots, the Jacksons and the Lees, families which for generations had been associated in important ways with the Boston community. Tall and handsome, a predestined Harvard man, Storrow had captained a crew that beat Yale and had earned his law degree from Harvard Law School. Partner in the great banking firm of Lee, Higginson and Company, with a sumptuous town house on Beacon Street and a rambling country estate in Lincoln, he was said to be one of the richest men in all New England.

As president of the Chamber of Commerce and an overseer of Harvard College, Storrow projected the perfect Republican propriety. But, while the Republicans supported him, he was in fact a Yankee Democrat, a community benefactor who believed that a city should be something more than a collection of buildings for the convenience of people engaged in money-making, a man with more conscience than most of his background. He had served as chairman of the Boston School Committee, president of the Boy Scouts of America and chairman of Boston's relief committee to minister to the needs of those stricken by the San Francisco earthquake. He had founded the West End Club for newsboys, provided the town house of the Boston City Club and given a quarter of a million dollars to turn the Charles River mud flats into a beautiful esplanade.

Storrow's announcement that he would run for mayor produced widespread enthusiasm, and all but one of Boston's newspapers lined up behind him. But those who believed he would coast in to victory underestimated the formidable powers of John F. Fitzgerald, whose intuitive understanding of the popular mind still remained unequaled in all of Boston.

Long before he announced his candidacy, Fitzgerald had planned his strategy. From the outset, he recognized that his biggest liability was the taint of corruption which the Finance Commission and the Mitchell trial had spread over his first administration. At the same time, he understood that denials of specific charges would be fruitless, that factual rejoinders would only implant the charges more deeply in the voters' minds. Moreover, the mere process of responding to accusations would put him in the fatal position of being on the defensive, responding to the moves of the opposition and never moving on his own. Therefore, the first and indispensable step was to find a wholly different issue which would allow him to take the offensive.

Fitzgerald found his issue in Storrow's enormous wealth. On the day the campaign opened, Fitzgerald addressed a public letter to Storrow in which he proposed that each candidate agree to limit his campaign expenses to $10,000 and to publish the contributions and expenditures before election day. In his carefully worded letter, which appeared in all the newspapers the next day, Fitzgerald said:

> The growing cost of political campaigns is recognized by all thoughtful observers as a serious evil, tending to limit candidates for high office to men who are rich enough to pay out large sums from their own pockets.
>
> I recognize that you can raise $10 for every $1 which I can raise. I believe in asking you to forgo this advantage I am in accord with the public sentiment of the voters and if you agree we will make a notable contribution to the cause of cleaner politics and a better government in this city and Boston will be far in advance of other great cities.

Even before he made the offer, Fitzgerald understood that Storrow would never accede to any such scheme; as the lesser-known candidate and the less effective speaker, Storrow needed the exposure that money could buy—the newspaper ads, the billboards and the posters. Yet, by making the dramatic pitch at the outset of the campaign and then following it up relentlessly day after day, Fitzgerald managed to simplify the election into a contest between "an Irish boy from the slums and a wealthy encrusted Harvard blueblood." In speech after speech, Fitzgerald sounded the theme that "no man, no matter how wealthy he is, can put a price on City Hall." And to illustrate this point, he papered the walls with large photographs of City Hall on which was inscribed: "NOT FOR SALE, MR. $TORROW." The pervasive theme was reinforced in a campaign poster showing a photograph of Fitzgerald with his family, his wife, his three girls and his three boys, with the caption "MANHOOD AGAINST MONEY."

At this juncture, the money issue was the politician's dream. At the national level, the battle cry had already been sounded against the use of money to buy elections, and Theodore Roosevelt had even gone so far as to propose an appropriation from the public treasury to meet the proper and legitimate expenses of the national parties. More specifically, the issue had great advantages for Fitzgerald. It allowed him to appear as the representative of the common man, a symbol to "every father and mother that their boy needn't be a millionaire in order to be mayor of Boston." At the same time, the spending issue enabled Fitzgerald to deflect attention from the substance of Storrow's messages to the cost of Storrow's ads. "Of course," *Practical Politics* observed, "the sympathetic electorate did not stop to reason" that Fitzgerald himself was far from helpless in the matter of financial resources, for "the sympathetic electorate rarely stops to reason when once its sympathy is aroused."

In spite of Fitzgerald's best efforts, Storrow's money had a devastating impact in the form of a brutally effective series of half-page ads which were all grouped under the common heading "Fitzgeraldism" to suggest the presence of "a Fitzgerald ring" behind all the scandals uncovered by the Finance Commission. Carried in all six of the daily papers in bold three-quarter-inch type, the ads forcefully awakened all the unanswered questions regarding the flagstone contracts and the coal frauds, leaving the clear impression that Fitzgerald and his friends had walked away with considerable cash.

Coming from a man of Storrow's esteemed reputation, these sensational accusations aroused substantial public attention and submerged the entire Fitzgerald family in a new round of anguish and embarrassment. "I would awaken practically every morning," Rose recorded, "to find my father accused in headlines of being guilty of nearly every sin short of murder. . . . My instinctive reactions were shock and outrage; I seethed." Yet, Rose recalled in amazement, her father "seemed to take it more or less for granted. Some of the accusations and personal slurs undoubtedly angered him, but outwardly, at least so far as I could see, he was unperturbed. I remember bringing the morning papers in to him. . . . He would sit up in bed and go through them with great interest, and now and then would reach for his penknife and excise an item he wanted to make use of or to rebut, but with no more visible emotion than my mother might display when, for instance, cutting out a recipe or an advertisement for a bargain at Filene's department store."

Whether Rose realized it at the time or not, her father's apparent objectivity masked the formulation of a bold and brilliant response to Storrow's accusations, a deliberate plan to identify the vilification against him with a more general prejudice against Irish Catholics. Behind this strategy stood the recognition that Catholics in Boston were still uneasy about their status in the city; if they could be brought to feel that the attacks on Fitzgerald were really aimed at them, it really wouldn't matter what was being said. Thus began what Storrow later described as "an underground campaign" in which men were sent "to hundreds of little gatherings in barrooms, hotels, clubrooms and other places" to say that they knew all about Storrow, that he was a religious bigot, a prejudiced man, a Harvard snob who was anti-Catholic, anti-Negro and antilabor.

In an effort to counteract the effect of this underground campaign, Storrow issued a passionate statement which openly accused Fitzgerald of "blowing the bellows of religious, racial, and social animosities, of striving with might and main to sow hate and distrust between different groups of our citizens." But Fitzgerald had no intention of admitting that he had had anything to do with such scurrilous tactics; on the contrary, he now took the high road with an immediate reply that, in his view, "religion should not be an issue in this campaign." Indeed, Fitzgerald went on, knowing full well that the message of Storrow's intolerance had already been soaked up, "if he wants a certificate from me that I know of no reason which should lead any citizen of Boston, whether Catholic, Protestant, or Hebrew, to withhold a vote from him on any religious grounds, I now cheerfully give it to him."

As the campaign progressed, Fitzgerald sensed that he had to do more than attack, that the voters had to be convinced that he was *for* something as well. So once again he began to talk of all the things he would like to do for the people of Boston, advocating many of the same proposals he had made four years before. But this time he injected a new technique designed particularly to counter Storrow's ads. Using the same-size type for his heading and setting the copy in the same style as the Storrow display, Fitzgerald appropriated the phrase "Fitzgeraldism" for himself by linking it in the voters' minds with all the progressive programs he stood for: "FITZGERALDISM IS CONSTRUCTIVE," the headlines read; "IT MEANS BETTER SCHOOLS, BETTER STREETS AND BETTER HOSPITALS."

As the contest drew to a close, Fitzgerald's greater experience showed up in the human dimension he was able to give to every issue. Responding to Storrow's criticisms about the inefficiency of his administration, he claimed "he was proud of having kept the old men of the street department at work on the ledges during the seasons when the ground was frozen and the street work stopped, rather than discharging them." And as for that heartless Finance Commission, "Can you conceive of anything more inhuman," he would ask, "than their position that a city employee should not be able to attend the funeral of a relative without loss of pay?"

Nor, as an experienced campaigner, did Fitzgerald ever forget his paramount issue—Storrow's wealth, Storrow's connections, Storrow's spending.

> The great issue in this campaign [he wrote in a campaign ad] is my record as a public official as compared with Storrow's record as a director in trusts and corporations. . . . I am willing to accept blame if blame belongs to me, but I will not allow any man who has been identified with the United Shoe Machinery Company, the greatest monopoly in the US, a man identified with the United Fruit Company, which company has destroyed thousands of acres of plantations in order to keep up the price of fruit, or a man identified with J. P. Morgan and the entire State Street ring, associates of the notorious Ice Trust, Sugar Trust, copper combine . . . to censure me before the people of Boston. The people did not vote to exclude political parties with any idea that the power taken away from them would be turned over to State Street. They did not look for a campaign of money spending upon a large scale to inaugurate the better conditions of politics and government promised by the new charter.

Time and again, Fitzgerald's dramatic oratory produced its desired result—tumultuous cheers of commendation from the audience. Indeed, as one reporter observed, everywhere Fitzgerald went, his reception was "as vociferous and as boisterous as strident voices, heavy shoes, muscular arms and hands and formidable canes could make it. The approving thousands followed him closely through the defense of his conduct of the city, applauded his statement of what he had endeavored to accomplish for the city, laughed at his thrusts at the Finance Commission and agreed with his portrayal of Storrow's business affiliations."

Then, typically, before the shouts had died down, Fitzgerald would ask the crowd to join him in singing a rousing melody such as "The Wearing of the Green," "When Johnny Comes Marching Home Again" or "Sweet Adeline." Through his association with St. Stephen's Church, he had seen the effect of music upon a crowd, and now, during this most important campaign of his life, he incorporated music and song into each of his rallies. It was at this time, in fact, that the legend of Honey Fitz, the man with the golden voice, was born.

In marked contrast to Fitzgerald's emotional appeal, Storrow had "a simple unaffected conversational method of putting things," and "no one would accuse him of being an orator." While his proposals were carefully reasoned, his language lacked all natural ease; it scarcely moved or breathed, and "he deliberately denied to his speeches many qualities by means of which appeal is usually made to the voters."

As the day of the election—January 11, 1910—approached, it was generally believed by most seasoned observers that Storrow was holding a slight lead. "It looks as if my candidate for mayor might win Boston," Lincoln Steffens told his sister Laura on January 4. "He is James Jackson Storrow, the leading banker of the city." Six days later, George Nutter registered a similar mood of hope. "The whole town is ablaze with excitement," he wrote in his diary the night before the election. "Everybody talking about the contest on the streets. The general impression is that Storrow will pull through, though the betting is even and the contest will be close."

When the official results were calculated, however, Fitzgerald emerged the winner by a plurality of 1,402 votes.

Not surprisingly, in a battle so intensely emotional as this one, the results were deeply felt. "It certainly is a public calamity," George Nutter recorded, "that such a discredited man should get back. This is the disastrous end of all the hard work of a year." Moreover, the defeat in Boston was only part of a tide of reform defeats across the nation. That November, Tom "Golden Rule" Johnson had been defeated in Cleveland, as had Francis J. Heney in San Francisco. Reform candidates were beaten in Jersey City and Philadelphia as well. "All my friends who ran this year were beaten," Steffens lamented.

For his part, Fitzgerald called it "the greatest triumph" of his political career. "No man can ask for a greater victory," he said. "My family appreciated the triumph especially because there had been so much injustice in the attacks made on me—so much misrepresentation and vilification. For the sake of my boys and girls I wanted to win the election as a vindication."

As a vindication of Fitzgerald the victory was complete, and it was savored all the more as it helped Mitchell to secure an early release from jail. But for Mitchell there was no vindication. Although he was reported to be all smiles on his return to his Charlestown home, he was still privately tortured with sorrow. His sisters found him a changed man. As the months went by there were signs that the pain inside him was increasing rather than diminishing. "He lived only a short time after that," Julia Hill recalled. "And when he died, everyone said he had died of a broken heart."

With the mayor's triumphant return to power, a golden era dawned for the members of the Fitzgerald family as each in turn felt the glow of Fitzgerald's renewed energy and vitality. This time around, with the experience of his first term behind him, the mayor was more clearly in control of his position: he was in complete possession of all of his forces, secure in the knowledge that he was indeed equal to the task of governing his city—a task that, ironically, would be easier his second term, as a consequence of the reform legislation he had so vigorously opposed. By providing limits to the frenzied patronage-seeking which had undermined his first term in office, the new city charter protected Fitzgerald from some of his own greatest vulnerabilities and allowed him to concentrate on the ends as well as the means of government.

From the outset, Fitzgerald made it clear that he intended to judge his second term by one standard alone: by his ability to advocate legislation and enact programs that would make the life of the average citizen more worth living; measures that would improve the moral and physical welfare of the people of Boston, measures that would give the citizens easier access to parks and recreational facilities, museums and libraries, schools of learning and other institutions that, taken together, would produce a happier and better common life. And this time around, as Rose Kennedy pointed out in her memoirs, there was sufficient time to carry out these goals, since the charter change had doubled the mayoralty term from two to four years. As a result, she wrote, "my father could relax a bit, which relaxed us all."

For Rose especially, as her father's favorite child and chosen companion, the years from 1910 to 1913 brought high adventure and glowing happiness. When, in June of 1910, she received her graduation certificate from Manhattanville, along with the gold medal for general excellency, she was finished with her formal schooling and therefore free to spend most of her days in the company of her father, who took her with him wherever he went—to "dedications, cornerstones, receptions, banquets, picnics, parades, orations, rallies, greetings, grand marches and ceremonies."

Throughout this period, Rose accompanied her father on all manner of official trips as well. She was with him in Chicago for an international meeting of municipal executives and in Baltimore for the nomination of Woodrow Wilson at the Democratic national convention in 1912. "He loved to travel," Rose explained, "and as mayor he could always find a good reason for a jaunt of some sort, and at least a plausible reason to take me." So when he journeyed to Panama to ponder the possible effects on Boston of the recently opened Panama Canal, Rose went along as "hostess-companion-helper." And when he led a Chamber of Commerce delegation aboard the Cunard steamship *Franconia* to visit the industrial cities of Hamburg, Brussels, Munich, Berlin and Paris, she put to use her fluent German and French and became the interpreter for the group.

It was a special time, Rose recorded in her memoirs, "a time to laugh and a time to dance." She was "the mayor's daughter again" but now old enough to participate in all the pleasures that came her way. Having abandoned her earlier strivings to go to college and to realize independent ambitions for herself, she devoted all her powers and her energies to her father, secure in the belief that her experiences with him would be as fulfilling and as challenging as any she had ever known. Under his encouragement, she began to read and clip the daily newspapers, a habit which developed in her an awareness of the importance of current events which was far from customary among young women in the early years of the century.

Fitzgerald delighted in the good looks of his daughter, in her intelligence, her presence of mind and her superb social skills. Always at her best when surrounded with people of high vitality, she proved to be her father's equal in conversation, curiosity, dancing, athletic ability and powers of endurance and even in the capacity for fascinating reporters. On their return from Europe after the Chamber of Commerce tour, Rose's vigorous comments on "the inferior position of women abroad" in comparison with America merited front-page news. Father and daughter, people said, were cut from the same mold. Strikingly handsome, alike in their habits of reading and their ways of talking, they were both true Fitzgeralds. If one were to set them on opposite sides of the earth and observe their behavior for a single day, it would be absolutely clear that they belonged together. Each understood the other thoroughly. And they adored each other.

All the while, according to Rose, Josie Fitzgerald remained contentedly at home, watching her husband and her daughter with pleasure and pride. "For reasons not only of temperament but of time," Rose explained, "Mother had a limited capacity for the official social whirl." With two children under the age of ten still at home and with no natural inclination for social life, she declined most invitations and sent her willing daughter in her place. It was, in Rose's words, "a perfect arrangement" for everyone concerned.

Yet one wonders if this was really so. For, in delegating the role of companion to her daughter, Josie was giving up a part of her marriage, detaching herself from the essential identity of her husband and reducing their common life to those select moments when the political warrior chose to bring his tired body home. Perhaps Fitzgerald wanted it this way and perhaps Josie did, too, preferring the absolute control she enjoyed of the little kingdom on Welles Avenue to the confusion of sharing in her husband's larger world. However, it is hard to dispel the thought that under her stoic acceptance Josie was also experiencing deep resentment and hostility toward both her absent husband and her vibrant daughter who had all the charm and all the social skills she herself lacked.

For each time she chose to stand aside, failing to assert herself, she seemed to register within herself an explosive and uncontrolled bitterness which would periodically erupt, driving her, against her conscious self, to seek revenge and humiliation on both her husband and her child. Then, just as swiftly as it came, the violence of her vindictive outburst would begin to abate and her habitual good manners would return. Just such an outburst took place early one evening when Fitzgerald arrived at his home with a reporter from the *Post* who had been assigned to write a feature story on the mayor and his family.

"I did not know you were coming, Miss Burt," Josie said by way of introduction, "or I would have been prepared. Mr. Fitzgerald never told me a thing about it until the last minute. That is just like him." It was plainly a sore spot and bothered her deeply, for all the while she spoke she could not repress a slightly sarcastic smile.

At that uneasy moment Fitzgerald jumped up and said, "Turn on the phonograph, Rose, and we will liven things up a bit."

The machine was started, Miss Burt reported, and "in less than no time" the mayor was on his feet dancing an old-fashioned waltz with his daughter. No sooner was the music finished than Rose approached the piano, announcing that she had a new song, "Row, Row, Row," for her father to try, which, of course, he willingly did, cheerfully singing the chorus in his "clear, well-placed," albeit out-of-key voice.

When the ballad was done, Fitzgerald sat down once more to talk with Miss Burt. "Every evening when I am home—" he began, but no sooner had he said this than the children—all six were present—cried out in a body, "Every evening!" Then the mayor resumed, "Every evening when I'm home we play Tom Jenkins Says Hand Down. It is a fine game.

Clear the table and we will start it," he commanded. And "in no time," Miss Burt reported, "the game was in full sway."

All the while, Josie had been sitting close by, watching the mayor. "John," she said with a curious smile on her face, "it does indeed seem refreshing to have you here. I am not sorry that you are to have photographs taken to mark the evening. I am going to frame one and place a card over it on which I will write: 'Taken on his one evening at home.' "

The tone of Josie's indiscreet remark—suggesting perhaps a measure of suspicion about his frequent absences—stunned her husband, who had all he could do to collect himself and carry on. "Now you will make Miss Burt think that I neglect my family if you keep on," announced the mayor. "I spend every Sunday with them, Miss Burt, and I have them each in town at least once a week. I am a family man. And the reason I am such is because I was one of many children. I cared for my brothers . . . , did all the buying for the family and was father and mother in one." Even now, he went on, "I think nothing of buying the girls' hats and coats. Just a little while ago I happened to see two coats that I thought were quite attractive, so I bought them."

"They were perfect fits," said Agnes in an obliging tone, which somewhat reduced the mounting tension. Rose, meanwhile, had gotten up from her chair, unable to watch her mother attacking her father in front of this woman. For nothing in the world would she have allowed her father to be hurt like this, but her mother's unrestrained bitterness was beyond control. Years later, Rose spoke with a measure of sympathy toward her mother's position that night, recognizing that while Josie could deal with the fact that her husband was rarely at home, she could not pretend to portray a family togetherness that simply did not exist at that time. But at the moment the encounter took place, all Rose could feel was shame for her mother and tenderness for her father. The anger she saw in her mother's face frightened and surprised her. A lump rose to her throat as she struggled unsuccessfully to understand, and all that night she could not sleep.

When morning came, neither parent said a word to the children about the events of the night before, nor did the family ever speak of the interview again. That Sunday the article came out in the feature section of the *Post*, and, fortunately for the harmony of the Fitzgerald family, the overall tone of the piece was decidedly favorable. While Josie's words were repeated verbatim, the wrathful tone behind her statements was not described, allowing the unsuspecting reader to imagine that her comments were meant only in jest. Yet the felicitous result could not erase for Rose the haunting image of her mother's "stern face, cold eyes and peculiar smile" as she carried out her relentless attack.

Beyond the events of that particular night, there must have been more general anxieties and guilts in Rose attached to the awareness that, in many ways, she was usurping her mother's role. This is not to say that Rose ever had conscious knowledge of the possibility that her relationship with her father was hurting her mother. In her mind, she may well have believed that the curious triangular relationship was indeed "the perfect arrangement" for everyone.

Moreover, while her father's position brought Rose power and prestige at an early age, it also distanced her from many of her young girlfriends who enjoyed a less purposeful and more carefree existence. Sharply aware of the criticism that might be leveled against her as the mayor's daughter, she never allowed herself to engage in any unconventional or even frivolous activity. Nor did she indulge in the trading of confidences and gossip that often binds young girls together. More than one friend remembers her as so attached to her father that she was undemonstrative toward everyone else; indeed, so often did she quote her father in her daily conversation that her friends began to call her "Father says." But if she resented their teasing, she never let them see her resentment. Even then, her biographer Gail Cameron asserts, she had "that control of her emotions for which a nation later held her in awe."

A vivid portrait of this intensely serious, self-reliant, enchanting young girl at the age of twenty has survived in the newspaper accounts of her spectacular debut, which was held in her parents' home on a winter evening in early January 1911 and was considered "one of the most elaborate coming-out parties ever conducted in Boston." A girl's debut in that era was a rite of passage, a ceremony performed to introduce her as a prospective bride into the world of society, allowing her to join in the steady round of balls, assemblies, ballets, opera, theater and cotillions which structured the social life of the wealthy, the prominent and the fashionable.

It was a dark and cloudy evening, but the large white house was "ablaze with lights" as the long line of covered carriages and motorcars arrived at the door, depositing the more than 450 guests into a walkway covered on all sides with flowering plants. "As the guests entered," the *Globe* reporter observed, "they found themselves confronted by a beautiful young woman whose frank, smiling face bade them welcome before they had hardly crossed the threshold." Wearing a simple gown of the finest white chiffon traced with Italian embroidery over yellow silk ribbon, the debutante "stood revealed" as a natural beauty. "Not a jewel did she wear, not even a necklace or armlet of gold; only in the dark of her hair a silver ribbon had been twisted."

Her thorough training in manners and poise came together in this moment of social testing, enabling her to do exactly what was expected of her, to smile, to talk, to dance. But there was something more in her that reporters saw—something in her bright appearance, her "dancing eyes," her friendly handclasp and her "complete absence of cant" that had an immediate effect on those she met and won for her not only the affection but also the respect of the entire gathering. "As score after score of people trooped in and met her," the *Globe* reporter wrote, "she never lost her self possesion or gave the least indication of being tired or bored. She had pleasant words for all and a laugh that was musical."

Amid all the front-page descriptions of the party, from the preparations beforehand to the reception in the drawing room to the dinner dance held later in the evening for a small group of Rose's closest friends, one curious image stood out: the image of Fitzgerald wandering aimlessly about the house, his head slightly bowed, his countenance betraying anxiety. On his face there was not a trace of that animation which generally sparked his eyes and his smile. On the contrary, the spirit in him seemed suddenly quenched; there was about him an air of melancholy, a sense of impending loss. His little girl was entering adulthood and would soon be gone from him forever.

The debut and all the months of planning for it seemed to have had just the opposite effect upon Josie Fitzgerald, whose irritable shyness appeared to have completely vanished for the occasion. Dressed in an exquisite black dress which served as a frame for her stunning figure, with her luxuriant black hair done up in a pompadour, she "wore the look of one who has done what she could and is satisfied with the result." Greeting everyone with an easy affability foreign to her temperament, she introduced her daughter to the long list of guests with an extraordinary "delicacy and tact that prevented hurry, banished uneasiness and yet swept things along." It was as if a fresh current of energy came into her being now that her daughter was about to embark upon a full social life that would eventually lead to a marriage of her own.

It was an unusually cosmopolitan gathering, including men and women prominent in both Catholic and Protestant circles. As mayor, Fitzgerald had friends and connections belonging to several different social sets; the guest list embraced the new Governor, two congressmen, leading bankers, doctors, lawyers and priests, the district attorney and the entire Boston City Council, which had closed its doors for the day in order to attend the event. But if the adults reflected a mixing of religious circles, the young people were almost entirely Catholic, for in those days, as Rose recalled, "there were two societies in Boston," one of them Protestant, the other Irish Catholic, and the young people in one society had nothing to do with the young people in the other. Indeed, so separate were these two societies in the first decade of the twentieth century that the newspapers carried two separate social columns on different pages, "one about them, one about us," Rose recalled.

"As the leader of the young Catholic set in Boston," Rose considered herself very lucky and never "bemoaned the fact" she was not a proper Bostonian. "The comment that I could not get into Boston society irritated me," she later wrote, "because I never expected to mingle with that group nor did I have any desire in that direction." Having known since young girlhood about the social division, she simply accepted it as "one of those elementary facts of life not worth puzzling about."

Moreover, Rose asserted, there were some advantages to the arrangement, for "it helped prevent romances leading to mixed marriages with the eventual unhappiness that sometimes awaited such a marriage in the world as it was." Not once, for instance, did she recall meeting a Protestant boy at a single one of the big subscription dances held three times a year at the Somerset Hotel. The only Protestant boys she knew were those she had met in the public schools in Concord and Dorchester, and, as the years went by, these friendships invariably perished under the heavy pressure of parental disapproval. "On the one or two occasions when a Protestant beau appeared on the threshold, my parents greeted him coldly, discouraging him. They felt the Church would blame them if there were a mixed marriage and they wanted no responsibility in that regard."

In Rose's era, people belonging to the same social set met most frequently in clubs. Here the young debutantes launched their social careers under the guise of organizing benefits, bazaars and charity balls. To be anyone in Boston society, you *had* to belong to the most prestigious clubs. "They had their Junior League," Rose recalled, "we had our Cecilian Club," both organizations equally dedicated to performing good works. With her high standing in the Catholic community, Rose had no problem being elected to any Catholic club she wanted to join. But as she surveyed the clubby atmosphere in 1910, the year before she came out into society, she decided to found a club of her own geared more to educational purposes than to straight charity work. Composed of young women who had been to school abroad and were interested in studying and discussing world history and current events, the Ace of Clubs, as Rose called it, soon became "*the* club for Catholic women in Boston." With Rose as their first president, the Ace of Clubbers met regularly every Tuesday afternoon in the Rose Room that Fitzgerald arranged for them at the Hotel Somerset. There, in the luxurious atmosphere of rich carpets, silver tea sets and comfortable sofas, they listened to an impressive selection of lecturers corralled by Fitzgerald to address the young women on the leading topics of the day.

For all her self-assurance about the rising gentility of the Irish society in Boston, Rose was not quite prepared for the agitation she experienced on the night of October 17, 1911, when she attended the opening performance of Irish playwright John Millington Synge's *Playboy of the Western World* at the Plymouth Theatre. As this was the most famous of the plays which Dublin's Abbey Theatre was putting on during its month-long stay in Boston, it was not surprising that it opened to an overflow crowd.

Looking back years later on the events of that dismal night, Rose recalled the tremendous pride and excitement with which she had initially greeted the news of the visit of the Abbey Players to America. "It was considered a time of the Renaissance of Irish literature," she observed, "and a most auspicious moment for Irish culture. In Boston, the Irish deeply resented the feeling of inferiority which had been foisted upon them by the so-called Yankee element and they were aspiring to achievements in fields of culture and learning and refinement. When they heard of the proposed visit of the Abbey Players they welcomed the news and thought the ancient culture of the Ireland of literature and poetry would be brought to the public and would bring to light and prove the culture and erudition of the Irish people."

Just three weeks earlier, in fact, Rose had accompanied her father to the impressive ceremony which had attended the arrival in Boston of William Butler Yeats, the famous Irish poet and playwright, who was directing the Abbey's productions, and the distinguished Lady Gregory, the Abbey's patroness and the author, with Yeats, of *Kathleen ni Houlihan*, which was one of the dozen or more plays being presented by the Abbey Theatre. On that occasion, before what the press described as a huge and brilliant audience, Mayor Fitzgerald had officially welcomed the Abbey Players with a graceful statement, delivered in an exultant mood. "It has been my privilege," he began, "to read some of the works issuing from [this] remarkable group of Irish writers who . . . have resurrected the ancient genius of Ireland and struck a new note in modern poetry. We who are of Irish blood should offer the welcome of kinsmen to the members of the Abbey Theatre company . . . , proud that the creative and interpretative powers with which they are blessed have carried their movement far beyond the boundaries of race and made it one of the most significant literary movements of the age."

Yet, on the morning of the day that was to see the opening of *The*

*Playboy*, Fitzgerald had warned Rose that in choosing to go she might be placing herself in an ugly situation. Apparently the storm of criticism and discussion which had first greeted Synge's controversial play in Dublin, branding it as indecent, immoral and salacious, had reached across the ocean, and trouble was anticipated. Unwilling to see the play as a work of satire which targeted the habit of accepting appearances for reality and the tendency to romanticize criminal behavior, dozens of Irish organizations in Boston had already called upon the mayor to ban its showing. Characterizing the work as a degrading spectacle which profaned the Irish character, several prominent Irish associations had publicly announced their intention to disrupt the performance should it be allowed to go on the stage.

For these reasons, the mayor himself had declined to attend, sending in his place William Leahy, the city's official censor, whose task it was to determine if the play was in fact "obscene." And, in anticipation of trouble, he had also asked the police commissioner to have a full complement of policemen in and around the theater. Knowing all this, Rose still wanted to go. "I considered myself above all those narrow viewpoints," she later recalled, "and I really wanted to see the play for its literary qualities."

Rose knew in advance that the action of the play centers on a young man, Christie Mahon, who has sliced open the head of his tyrant father in a sudden burst of rage. Thinking he has murdered him, Mahon goes to a neighboring village, where he boasts of the deed, telling the story so many times that it is eventually seen as a great romantic tale. The poor inhabitants, hungering for excitement, make the lad a hero and shower him with gifts and attentions, and the prettiest girl in the village bestows her heart upon him. Then the old man appears with a bandaged head. The worshiping villagers, finding the story a hoax, viciously turn on the young man.

But knowing the general outline of the play did not prepare Rose for the emotional reaction she experienced in seeing it performed. No sooner had the first act begun than she found herself "blushing and squirming" in her seat. No matter how hard she tried, she could not help but feel embarrassed by the coarse dialogue and the sordid portrayal of the Irish people "as drunken sods and quarreling fools." Startled at the intensity of her anger, she reproached herself for bearing witness to this "horrible slur against the Irish character." Nor did the satirical intent comfort her. As she later said, it had been "heralded as a distinctly Irish play which captured the common language and actual behavior of the peasant class, [so] it was inevitable that the audience take it as a characterization of the Irish people." And worse still, she noted, "it had been just those qualities of poverty, dirt and sloth which the Yankees had always accused [the Irish] of having and there they were, depicted as characters of the old country—unvarnished and naked to the eye."

If she felt quietly offended by some parts of the play, however, she was far more embarrassed by the tasteless response of many of her kinsmen in the audience who, in their anger, began throwing tomatoes and eggs at the stage and hissing and booing loudly. (This was, a veteran drama critic said, the first time that the peculiar English custom of booing as an indication of one's disapproval had been heard on this side of the Atlantic.) At one point it even seemed that a riot was about to erupt as policemen began ejecting the protesters, some of whom were brandishing golf clubs and baseball bats.

Not knowing how to respond, Rose turned her eyes from the stage to the orchestra below, where Boston's grande dame Isabella Stewart Gardner was seated, surrounded by a circle of her society friends. More than any other woman in high society at that time, Isabella Gardner was regarded as an arbiter of taste. Never lacking for money—she had inherited nearly three million from her father and several million more when her husband died—she had through the years procured a magnificent and highly regarded collection of European paintings, including Rembrandts and Raphaels, Whistlers and Degases. And then, to house her splendid treasures, she had bought a Florentine palace abroad and had it shipped, piece by piece, to the Back Bay. One had only to look at her, from the high cheekbones of her face to the slimness of her curvaceous figure to her expensive clothes, to understand the meaning of elegance and grace.

As the tension and tumult mounted, the people sitting with Mrs. Gardner were overheard discussing the advisability of retiring before the hostilities opened. "If they start throwing things," said one, "we'll get it right in the heads. Perhaps it would be better for us to move back." But Mrs. Gardner insisted on remaining in her proper seat, and to every boo and hiss that floated down from the balcony she responded with a clapping of her hands in praise of the performance. And when the curtain closed she led her friends in a standing ovation, making it absolutely clear that she, for one, believed it was a "splendid" play. "It was a great success," she announced in the lobby, her face wreathed in smiles. "I enjoyed every minute of it."

Years later, Rose confessed that in her mind she knew Mrs. Gardner was right, that Synge's work was indeed a work of art. Yet whatever her intellect told her, she could not control her instinctive recoil from the sordid image it left of Irish life. While something told her that out of respect for art she should join in the applause, she found herself as incapable of clapping as she was of booing. Belonging neither to the world of the proper Bostonians in the orchestra nor to that of the jeering Irish in the balcony, she drew away from the milling crowd without saying a word to anyone. Throughout her life the memory of that night would produce in her a feeling of sadness, a feeling of being caught between two worlds and not knowing which way to turn.

# CHAPTER 13
# HARVARD
# COLLEGE
# '12

For the most part, Rose Fitzgerald had everything before her. Respected by the leading members of the community, surrounded by ardent admirers, she moved with elegance and ease wherever she went. Furthermore, she lived with the secret knowledge that the first love she had ever felt, for the handsome Joe Kennedy, was still the strongest love she had ever known. From that romantic summer at Old Orchard Beach when she was sixteen, through all her years in the convent schools and all her adventures with her father, she had remained irrevocably drawn to the ambitious son of P. J. Kennedy. More commanding by far than all the other boys she knew, he was now a Harvard student, filled with ambitious dreams of glory, wealth and success.

Harvard College in the four years Joe spent there from 1908 to 1912 was a school in transition. While its undergraduate life was still controlled by a select group of rich and fashionable families whose sons merely arrived when they were due to fill the places that had been waiting for them from the day they were born, it was, at the same time, opening its doors to a more cosmopolitan student population and beginning to take the first tentative steps toward mitigating the evils of a pyramidal social system that concentrated all its social honors upon the rich and the wellborn.

It was not as simple as to say that Harvard was a rich man's college. Of the total of nearly six hundred young men entering with Joe in the class of 1912, more than 60 percent had graduated from a public high school, and fewer than 25 percent were the sons of college graduates. And for every millionaire's son who arrived with his trunks, his servants and his yearly allowance of $10,000, there was another fellow who was making his way through school with no allowance at all. Yet the tone of college life was set by the enviable few: the golden boys who came to Harvard from Groton, St. Mark's, St. Paul's and Middlesex, the ones who knew one another by instinct and breeding, who always seemed to be disappearing behind the charmed threshold of some handsome club-house where they could associate in peace and quiet with men of their own kind.

The chasm that cut through Harvard's social life was apparent the first day the freshmen arrived. Joe Kennedy and others like him, the gradu-ates of the public schools and the boys of modest means, were herded together in the only living quarters the college provided, a drab and dreary set of "highly unattractive" dormitories—some of which, accord-ing to Harvard historian Samuel Eliot Morison, still lacked central heat-ing and had no plumbing above the basement. The sons of the well-to-do, however, found themselves situated in luxurious private suites with baths, steam heating and handsome chandeliers in one of the half-dozen elegant residential halls which had been built by private capital on a scale of outward magnificence recalling the splendor of a Venetian palace. Clustered along Mt. Auburn Street and designed specifically to cater to the needs of the wealthy, these expensive dorms—which carried the names of Beck Hall, Claverly, Apley Court, Westmorley, Randolph and Dunster—allowed the sons of the rich to live in their own "Gold Coast" world completely out of touch with the body of their class as though they attended another university.

A vivid portrait of this exclusive Gold Coast world as it appeared to an outside observer is preserved in an article written by reporter Owen Johnson for Collier's Weekly in 1912. It is a wonderful piece, evincing a genuine attempt to understand how the system of social segregation at Harvard came to pass and what it would take to restructure it. But the most unforgettable images are the satirical accounts of daily life as it was lived then in these luxurious halls, where, Johnson reports, everything was provided for the smallest desires of the patrician boys, and every-thing was structured to minimize the need for any exhausting physical effort.

At Dunster an elevator obligingly saves them the agony of toiling up fati-
guing flights of stairs . . . ; When they rise in the morning they go down
to their own private swimming pool, which, as at Westmorley, with its
marble surfaces and elaborate scheme of decorating, with gracefully distributed plants and twin fireplaces, with comfortable wicker chairs to
lounge in . . . , has a Roman luxuriousness. Private squash courts, not
too far removed from the swimming pools, exist to spare them the shock
of the weather which would be met in going to a gymnasium . . . Each
dormitory has its uniformed servants on watch at the door—butlers ready
to receive a card on a tray or ready to run the minor annoying errands.

Joe would long remember his first encounter with the Gold Coast
crowd. On a crisp autumn day when the leaves were just beginning their
splendid turn, he was walking down Mt. Auburn Street when three
young men approached. Dressed alike in white pants and blue jackets,
their faces browned from rowing with the crew, they sauntered along
the tree-lined street, their arms resting on each other's shoulders. Joe
could see in the smug expressions on their faces that they were not the
men who made up the steady stream that poured into dinner at Memorial Hall. Fine-shouldered lads with high cheekbones and healthy outdoor skin, they seemed to look out at the world from an eminence of
their own. Joe wondered at once who they were. Not a single face in
this jaunty threesome looked familiar to him, although the Boston papers regularly reported the activities of the most prominent Gold
Coasters. In Joe's years, these included Kermit Roosevelt, Theodore
Roosevelt's son; Vincent Astor, son of John Jacob Astor IV and heir to
the greatest fortune in America; Herman Caspar Schwab, son of the
steel magnate Charles Schwab; and Edward Atkins, whose father was
the Atkins of Westinghouse Electric.

When Joe passed by, they took no notice; indeed, so caught up were
they in the pleasure of their own conversation that they never stopped
laughing and talking even as they turned into Claverly Hall and closed
the door behind them. Why Joe remembered this incident so vividly is
not clear, for as the tale was told, nothing happened; there was no
engagement of any kind. Yet perhaps that is the point. For in his conclusion to the story he said he felt a strange longing when he watched the
threesome go by, as if he were glimpsing a world he would never really
know, a world that was going on all around him but that he would never
touch. It was a melancholy feeling he would experience again.

It must not be supposed from this, however, that Joe was lost or lonely
at Harvard. On the contrary, he was better situated than a good number
of his classmates. Having come from Boston Latin, which traditionally
sent a large percentage of its graduates to Harvard, Joe arrived with his

own circle of friends—including three other Joes, Sheehan, Donovan and Merrill—which cushioned him against the feelings of loneliness described by Harvard man John Reed, '10.

"I went up to Harvard almost alone," Reed wrote in an unpublished essay he completed shortly before sailing in 1917 to Russia (where he would find material for a best-selling book on the Russian Revolution and where three years later he would lose his life), "knowing hardly a soul . . . for the first three months it seemed to me, going around to lectures and meetings, as if everyone . . . had friends but me. I was thrilled with the immensity of Harvard . . . but desperately lonely. I didn't know which way to turn, how to meet people." Reed's perceptions about the impenetrability of the social structure at Harvard were underscored by Owen Johnson. "Those who come to Harvard unknown," he reported, "are amazed at the difficulty of making friends." The man who comes unheralded is "appalled" by the "aloofness" of the individuals he meets. "Knowing no one when he arrives, he continues to know no one, after eating his heart out in loneliness."

For a warm and confident young man like Joe, however, whose reputation as a school leader and a champion ball player preceded him to Harvard, the opposite pattern developed. Secure in the friendships he already had, he reached out to create more. In his freshman German class he made friends with Tom Campbell, a football player and fellow Catholic from Lowell whose spontaneous and original wit would long be remembered by all his classmates.

Through Campbell, Joe met Bob Fisher, from Dorchester, a magnificent athlete who had taken a postgraduate scholarship year at Andover and would go on to become an all-American right guard on Harvard's varsity team. When Joe met him, Fisher was living at home and commuting to school in order to save money. Recognizing at once how difficult this situation was for the gregarious Fisher, who loved to be in the middle of things, Joe invited his new friend to share the room he had taken, and which his uncles were paying for, at Perkins Hall. Fisher happily took up Kennedy's offer and the two men became the closest of friends. The next two years they roomed together in Holyoke House, and for their senior year they moved into Hollis Hall in Harvard Yard, where they were joined by Campbell. It was, Campbell observed, the start of a triple friendship that was to last until the first of the three, Fisher, died in 1942.

Joe's circle of friends at Harvard was an act of his creation. It was not, as other college circles were, simply an association of men of the same class and background. Unafraid of being rebuffed, Joe crossed lines he was not supposed to cross. Through the freshman baseball team, which

Joe easily made, he met Robert Sturgis Potter, a scion of an old Philadelphia family, a graduate of St. Mark's prep school and a resident in
Randolph Hall, which was perhaps the most sought-after dormitory
along the Gold Coast. Charming, well bred and Protestant, Potter was
one of those happy few who had entered Harvard by right and were
automatically eligible for the highest social honors Harvard provided.
Yet when Joe approached him at the start of their friendship, Potter
responded. After baseball practice, they began spending some hours
together, taking walks, telling stories, arguing and laughing. Joe had a
rich, contagious laugh that left those in his presence feeling merry. Soon
Potter became a regular visitor to Joe's quarters at Perkins Hall, and in
time, since Joe wanted all his friends to like each other, Potter developed
close ties with Campbell and Fisher as well.

Looking back on Joe's social success at Harvard, Campbell observed
that Joe had "tremendous charm" and that "his charm made him friends
easily." But it was more than that. Charm may create the initial desire
for friendship, but the ability to develop and deepen friendship is a rarer
gift which people possess in varying degrees. Fifty years later, when an
imposing assortment of men whom Joe had known in all stages of his
life were asked to sort out their personal recollections of him for a
privately printed book, *The Fruitful Bough*, the quality they most frequently emphasized was his capacity for friendship.

Rejoicing in the company of his friends at Harvard, Joe was the one
who took the time and the pains to keep the circle together. Instinctively
understanding that friendship finds reinforcement in tradition, he engaged Campbell, Fisher and Potter in a ritual excursion every Sunday
afternoon to his family's home in Winthrop, six miles away from Cambridge, about an hour's journey by trolley car and the narrow-gauge
railroad. The Kennedy house was huge and rambling, surrounded by a
wide porch which fronted on a large green lawn and backed on Boston
Harbor. Here, for six hours or more, Joe and his companions were able
to enjoy the comforts of a warm and welcoming home in an atmosphere
of intimacy and relaxation which stood in sharp contrast with the institutional coldness of dormitory life.

For Joe's family, his sister Margaret recalled, these Sunday visits were
always "the climax of the week." While the boys greatly enjoyed themselves walking along the beach or reading the papers or playing ball,
Mrs. Kennedy and the girls prepared huge and sumptuous dishes of
"baked beans, homemade bread and slathers of butter, platters of cold
baked ham and sliced chicken," enough to serve a festive supper for
what usually amounted to nearly twenty people, including one or two of
the neighbors and the young girlfriends of Joe's two sisters. Then, after

supper, Margaret recalled, everyone would gather around the grand piano for a spirited evening of music and song. With Loretta at the piano, Joe would lead his house guests, their voices joined in simple harmony, their bodies swaying with the music, in a lively medley of songs ranging from old-time favorites "Danny Boy" and "Molly Malone" to Harvard's fight song and the latest Broadway hits. These jovial nights would long be remembered by all the participants for the sweet and unaffected pleasures they afforded. "Even as a youth," Margaret concluded, "Joe understood the meaning of life and loved it."

In their sophomore year, Joe and his friends emerged as leaders of their class; whenever committees were appointed to organize the class smokers or dances, whenever nominations were announced for the student council, the names of Kennedy and Potter, Fisher and Campbell headed the lists. So it came as no surprise when all four young men were tapped, early in the fall of their sophomore year, for membership in the Institute of 1770. Closely allied with the Hasty Pudding Club, to which nearly all its members were eventually elected, the Institute was not really a club in the sense of a group of persons organized for specific activities; it was, rather, a badge of honor, an essential first step if a young man hoped to be considered for one of the seven coveted final clubs, the small exclusive clubs which stood at the summit of Harvard's social hierarchy, commanding the lion's share of social distinction both within the college and to the outside world.

Since the point of belonging to the Institute was simply to belong, the order in which a man was selected was of paramount importance. Indeed, up until 1904 the entire list from one to one hundred was printed in the Boston papers as an index of a man's standing in his class. While this practice had disappeared by Joe's day, there remained a special honor in being chosen early. The Institute conferred its membership in ten series of ten: the whole membership from the junior class chose the first ten sophomores, the first ten chose the next ten and so on until the limit was reached. If a man was elected in the first four or five tens, he was admitted to an inner club within the club, known as the ΔKE or the Dickey. It was a mark of distinction for Joe Kennedy that he and his three friends made the Dickey together.

Speaking more than half a century later, Rose Kennedy saw it differently. "It's a curious thing," she said, "but I am now convinced that being selected for the Dickey was the worst thing that could have happened to Joe, for it spawned in his heart the illusory hope that it qualified him as a good bet for membership in one of the exclusive final clubs. To be sure, he understood that even with the ΔKE designation the odds of making a final club were tremendously against him. Still, he somehow believed he would. It would have hurt him less, I believe, if he had accepted the social divisions at Harvard from the very start, just as I accepted them in Boston, as elementary facts of life not worth worrying about."

In figuring that the clubmen would be won over to him in spite of themselves, Joe failed to understand that for many of these men the decision to choose a member meant a lifetime commitment to seeing the man in a corresponding club in Boston or New York. Those who made the Porcellian or the AD Club at Harvard, for instance, generally succeeded to the Somerset and Union Clubs in Boston, and from there they typically went on to join one of the prestigious brokerage houses, which were likewise organized along the lines of congeniality, common interests and class. So the question of being club material at Harvard was not simply a question of having a jovial personality which would provide good fellowship for the other club members during their college years; it was a question of having come from the right family and the right school, of being drawn from the same station in life, so that the similarity of past associations and experiences would render those chosen mutually agreeable comrades for years to come.

Still, Joe persisted in believing that for *his* class and with *his* friends it would all be different. Was it not true, after all, that change was in the air? Just months before, indeed, a new president had been inaugurated at Harvard, a large and forceful man by the name of A. Lawrence Lowell who had called in his inaugural for a broader conception of class association. As Harvard was now structured, he had argued, by basing its social life upon divisions of wealth and family, it was failing to fulfill its natural mission of throwing together youths of promise of every kind from every part of the country. And even as Lowell was issuing his challenge, a progressive movement was under way to bring all the seniors back into the Yard for their final year in a vigorous attempt to dissolve the invidious distinctions between the Gold Coasters and the dormitory men under the banner of class solidarity.

Nor had Joe experienced anything in his life up to that point that could make him believe that the lottery of his destiny would forever bar him from entry into the world of the clubs. On the contrary, both at Boston Latin and at Harvard his gregariousness had allowed him, time and again, to cross the borders of class, wealth and standing. If he could create a circle of friends which included a Main Line Philadelphian, a middle-class Protestant from Boston and a fellow Catholic from Lowell, and if he could be admitted into the Institute of 1770, why couldn't the next step be taken as well, allowing him to penetrate the highest social circles on the strength of his personality?

Joe's illusions were finally dispelled in the late winter of his sophomore year, that raw, nondescript time of year when the final clubs held their first round of elections for new members. For weeks there had been avid speculation over who would be taken by which of the seven clubs.

It was the custom in those days for the entire membership of each club, as soon as its new members were chosen, to march together through the streets with the treasured invitations in their hands while all the hopeful sophomores remained anxiously in their rooms, waiting for a tap upon their door. Then, as each new member was informed, he would join the others in a dancing serenade as they wended their way to the quarters of the next person chosen, until all the men on the list had been notified. Everywhere was the sound of excitement, a holiday spirit that finally crested and died down as each of the snakelike processions returned to its own clubhouse, where the members settled down to a long evening of food and drink.

All that day, as Rose heard the story told, Joe had remained in his quarters at Holyoke, his proud soul undaunted as the hours slipped by. Earlier in the afternoon he had shared in his roommate's excitement as a singing procession of Digammas had burst in upon their room and carried Fisher off into the street. Taking comfort in Fisher's good fortune, Kennedy redoubled his belief that it was only a matter of time until one of the clubs came for him. But by the end of the afternoon, as the light of day faded, he was forced to acknowledge to himself that no one was coming. Not knowing how to respond, he stood for an additional hour helplessly staring out the window into the black night.

In the distance, Joe heard sounds coming from the square, whereupon he put on his coat and went out of his room. Walking mechanically through the Yard, he found himself on Massachusetts Avenue across the street from the most coveted of all final clubs, the Porcellian. In the middle of the afternoon Joe had learned that his good friend Potter had been one of the happy few, along with Kermit Roosevelt, Theodore Frothingham, Jr., Arnold Welles Hunnewell and several other Groton boys, to make the Porcellian. Drawn like a moth to the lighted window above, Joe tried to imagine what it was like inside. Like the other clubs, the Porcellian did not stand isolated behind walls and gates but merged naturally with the other buildings on the street. Its rooms consisted simply of a bar, a dining room and a library warmed by a roaring fire, with a thick rug, a rack of newspapers and a number of aging leather chairs. Yet for all its simplicity, the Porcellian Club would remain forever a thing of mystery and fascination to Joe, as its tradition dictated that no Harvard man who was not a member could ever step across the threshold.

Standing there on the street, he later told Rose, Joe suddenly realized that Harvard was a tougher place than he had previously understood, that the conventional ideal of college life was merely a pretense, the ideal that a multitude of young men could all be linked together by the indissoluble bonds of collegiate unity. What he had mistaken for a progressive campus was in fact a bastion of a bygone era, an intolerant island on which the religion of the fathers was laid upon their sons. Was it sheer coincidence that Fisher and Potter, the two Protestants, were both taken into clubs while he and Campbell were not? The more he thought about it, the more he realized that not a single one of his Catholic friends had been asked to join a final club—neither Joe Merrill nor Joe Donovan nor Joe Sheehan. More than he had realized, there were things here that were not in his power to bring to pass. It was a moment of high emotion, a moment he would remember all his life.

By a tremendous effort of will, Joe forced himself to accept the idea that there were dozens of places in *his* school where, no matter what he did, he would never be welcome. But in his resigning himself to this fact of life, that part of his personality that had once been able to commit him unquestioningly to Boston Latin was forever buried, that part of him that had once imagined a long and lasting relationship with the class of 1912 died. While his great common sense precluded his degenerating into rebellion or withdrawal, Harvard had hurt him more than anyone knew. It had ripped something out of him that night; never again would he experience loyalty to any institution, any place or any organization. And in the place of that loyalty, resentment had crystallized out hard as rock; whether he knew it or not, his siege against the world had already begun.

In order to place Joe's feelings of rejection in perspective, one must remember that rejection was part of the game in a system which accepted less than 12 percent of the student body. And while this rejection left an indelible mark on some, it was barely felt by a great many others who were aware from the start that the life of the clubs could never be theirs. Not surprisingly, the greatest sufferers on election day were those whose experience had led them to believe they could be accepted anywhere.

Like Joe, the journalist Walter Lippmann, '10, had been born into a sunny world, a world of privilege in which everyone he knew was wealthy, Jewish and of German background. Assuming he would scale the social peaks at Harvard as easily as he had at his preparatory school in New York, Lippmann was stunned when he first encountered the exclusion of the club system (the doors of the clubs were closed more tightly against Jews than they were against Catholics)—so stunned, indeed, that he could never bring himself to speak of it openly to his friends.

In time, Lippmann found his voice in a savage article he wrote about a fictitious clubman, "Albert the Male." "In college," Lippman wrote, "Albert achieved the right club after many nights of worry, and a rather strenuous campaign conducted by his mother. I saw something of Albert in those days when we were freshmen together and he was always cordial when we were alone. In public he did not know me so well and there were times in the month before his election when he did not know me at all." The article went on to argue that it was the Alberts of the world who had brought Europe to ruin, the Alberts of Eton and Oxford who had compelled England to muddle in blood, the Alberts of Prussia who thought blood and iron were the instruments of destiny. The essay was his "belated revenge," Lippmann biographer Ronald Steel observes, "against the Alberts, people who had hurt him more than he was willing to admit."

A similar story of rejection and revenge has been offered to explain the hostility President Franklin Roosevelt directed toward Wall Street and the Morgans and the Whitneys. When Roosevelt entered Harvard in the class of '04, the adored son of a doting mother, nothing had prepared him for the personal sense of failure he would experience when he was not taken into the Porcellian Club. Indeed, for a boy like Franklin, born into the right family, baptized in the right church, educated in the right schools, the rejection could not be mistaken for a hereditary fault. Not being tapped for the Porc, he later admitted, was "the biggest disappointment" in his life—a bitter moment made all the more bitter by the fact he was living at the time at Westmorley Court, a luxurious Gold Coast dormitory whose hallways were as thoroughfares for the final clubs. Living side by side with all the most eligible clubmen, acutely aware of who had been chosen for which club, Roosevelt derived little comfort from his ultimate election to the Fly Club, which was viewed only in comparison with the Porcellian.

All these months while Joe was finishing up his freshman and sophomore years at school, Rose Fitzgerald had been away—first at the convent school in Holland, then at Manhattanville in New York. If John Fitzgerald had hoped that distance would dampen his daughter's romance with Joe he was wrong, for the time apart only seemed to increase their eagerness and affection for each other. But now that Rose had settled back into Boston for good, Joe could no longer tolerate merely carrying the relationship along. The time had come to get his girl.

And he did. In the late 1970s when Rose thought back on Joe's final years at Harvard, she remembered them happily as the time she fell "more and more in love." After two years apart, they were together again and this time they were much closer than they had ever been, for the time they spent together was so much greater.

In the afternoons they would meet on the steps of University Hall with the beautiful expanse of the college grounds stretching before them. They took hundreds of long walks together from this meeting place—past the sitting statue of John Harvard, past the vine-covered walls of Harvard's venerable buildings, through the imposing gates leading out of the Yard to the surrounding streets of Cambridge. Their wanderings took them to the triangular Cambridge Common, to the site of the old Washington elm, "a worn and broken veteran, its limbs shorn and shattered by its weight of years," under which George Washington first took command of the Continental Army on July 3, 1775. From there, in a scene strangely reminiscent of the courtship days of Josie Hannon and John Fitzgerald, they would wander through Mt. Auburn Cemetery, the beautiful burial ground of Longfellow, Lowell and Holmes, or they would stroll up stately Brattle Street, also known as Tory Row for its succession of splendid mansions dating back to the royalist era.

In the late-afternoon sunlight one of their favorite rambles took them over the Lars Anderson Bridge with its shining Norse helmets to the opposite bank of the winding Charles River, where, with a stirring vista of Harvard before them, they would have "long and affectionate" talks about their future pleasures and the eventual life they would lead together. There, as twilight descended, they enjoyed "a perfect privacy," unspoiled by parental demands or social obligations. These languid strolls brought with them a closeness so binding that it would last a lifetime; for the rest of their time together, intimacy and nature would be so joined in their minds that whenever they needed to replenish or restore their relationship, they instinctively set out together for a long walk.

But always in the days of their courtship they came back to the Yard, the heart of Harvard's college life, where the seasons cycled round from the invigorating coolness of autumn to the snowy months of winter when the great quadrangles were blanketed with geometrical precision, from the abounding vitality of spring to the full bloom of summer. For it was there, Rose remembered with special delight, there in the Yard with its crisscrossing footpaths and its ivy-covered buildings, that she and Joe first steeped themselves in "the joy of being seen by others for what we really were—a young couple in love." While it was true that anyone who knew anything about Rose or Joe could tell they were in love, it was also true that for years the seriousness of their relationship had to be kept camouflaged because Fitzgerald objected so strenuously to Joe. In Harvard Yard, however, where the protective conspiracy of youth could be counted on, they could enjoy their romance in the full light of day.

It has been written that Fitzgerald objected to Joe because he did not believe the son of P. J. Kennedy was good enough for his treasured daughter. Others have suggested that Fitzgerald had his heart set upon a different suitor, a sensible, well-mannered young man by the name of Hugh Nawn. The Nawn family lived within a short walk of the Fitzgeralds' home, in a baronial mansion which was a testimony to the triumphant success of the Nawn Construction Company founded by Hugh's father, Harry Nawn. As one of the wealthiest Catholic contractors in the city, Harry Nawn was naturally involved in politics; over the years his company had been awarded major contracts for the building of the city subway system and the metropolitan water supply system, and in this time a steady friendship had evolved between Fitzgerald and him. In Nawn, Fitzgerald had a friend much like himself: charming, nervous, energetic, chatty and warm. Late at night Fitzgerald would often be found at the Nawn house, where he and Harry would sit together for hours, eating and talking. Seeing young Nawn over these years, as he prepared at Roxbury Latin and entered Harvard College in the class of 1910, Fitzgerald believed he was just what a young man ought to be, solid, well-bred and considerate. Between Hugh Nawn and Joe Kennedy there could be no comparison, in Fitzgerald's eyes.

Perhaps Fitzgerald truly did believe that Nawn would make the better husband for his daughter. Though he was not half so handsome nor half so good-humored and high-spirited as Joe Kennedy, the bespectacled Nawn was indeed an extremely agreeable man with a "fine" future before him as the heir to his father's firm. But from all we know of the powerful bonds which held Fitzgerald to his favorite child, it is more likely that the shrewd and clever politician sensed in Joe Kennedy a formidable rival for his daughter's heart, a dark threat to his exclusive attachment to her, whereas with a suitor of his own choosing their relationship could go on as always.

After all, Rosie had been "his girl" from the first moment he saw her. If it is always difficult for a father to let a daughter go, it is easy to imagine how intolerable it must have been for Fitzgerald to detach his feelings from his "wild Irish rose," as he sometimes called her, for she was not simply the little girl who still adored him; she was his traveling companion and his political hostess, more of a wife than Josie. How much easier the thought of separation must have seemed if the entire courtship could be subject to *his* design.

In choosing Nawn, Fitzgerald never spoke disparagingly of Joe Kennedy. "There were no scenes and no lectures," Rose recalled. Observing in his daughter's eyes the love she felt for Joe, Fitzgerald was too clever to provoke her into open rebellion. The war he waged was a more subtle one. While he denied permission for her to accept most of Joe's invitations, he would relent on others. And whenever the question of her going somewhere with Joe came up, Fitzgerald would focus on Rose and her youth rather than on Joe, pointing out that she was still far too young to commit herself to any one man, for if she did so she would miss out on a great many adventures in life. Not wanting to forfeit her father's good opinion, Rose would often agree to go to the assembly or the cotillion with someone else—most likely Hugh Nawn—knowing that once she got there she could dance with Joe. Still, the lack of her father's encouragement regarding Joe was hard for Rose to endure.

Moreover, while letting Rose know that Joe was not a welcome guest in their house, Fitzgerald cheerfully invited young Nawn to join the family on their outings to dinner, to the theater or to the symphony. And in the autumn, when the wind was swirling the leaves everywhere beneath the trees, Nawn was a regular member of Fitzgerald's party at the Harvard football games, where, with Rose by his side, he cheered on his alma mater and then accompanied the mayor and his party to the traditional after-football dinner at the Hotel Touraine. One summer, Fitzgerald even arranged to have Nawn meet up with his touring party in Europe so that he and Rose could sail back to America together on the liner *Franconia*.

Fitzgerald's maneuvers created an insoluble dilemma for Rose, made all the more agonizing by the fact that her mother sided with her father in cautioning her against an early commitment to Joe. "I adored Joe," she later wrote. "I also adored my parents and knew how much I owed them. I didn't want to be ungrateful and certainly didn't want to offend or deceive them." Her heart divided between her love for Joe and her love for her father, she felt frightened and confused. Until now, the pattern of her life had been set by her father. Until now, with the major exception of her wish to go to Wellesley College, her desires had closely coincided with her father's. Yet, facing her father's disapproval, she was powerless to break away from Joe. Seized by anxiety, she felt "wobbly" much of the time. Sometimes the struggle haunted her, kept her awake at night and made her weep profusely.

But, more than she may have realized at the time, she had a will of her own; despite the intensity of her attachment to her father, she would not allow his will to dominate her completely. Caught in the tide of young love, she was determined to do what she wanted to do, even if her actions brought her into conflict with the voice of duty. Moreover, she had romantic notions of her own gleaned from all the books she had read which "praised the girl who listened to her heart and not her head and then lived happily ever after with her true love." So it was "with pangs of conscience" that she began to see Joe more often than she was supposed to, more often than her father knew. Acting by design, she would meet Joe at lectures or in the library and then walk part of the way home with him. Enlisting the family chauffeur in her cause, she would have him drive past a certain corner where Joe happened to be standing, on her way home from one of her many club meetings. And, more and more, she took to visiting her good friend Miriam Finnegan, who happened to live in Cambridge just down the street from Harvard Yard.

For his part, Joe was at his best in a situation like this. Fitzgerald's opposition only sweetened the prize, strengthened his determination and forced him to fight, with patience and skill, for what he wanted. The need for conspiracy gave ordinary conversations an air of mystery and romance which materially increased Rose's desirability in Joe's mind to the point where his love and need for her became as much a part of him as his ambition for wealth and his hunger for success. His imagination fired by the intrigue, Joe devised all manner of means by which he and Rose could spend more time together.

It was customary in those days at all the important dances and assemblies for young girls to carry dance cards which their partners had to sign before each dance began. Recognizing that Fitzgerald would ask to see the card when Rose arrived at home, Joe resorted to what Rose called "a bold and elegantly simple solution—forgery." With lighthearted abandon, he blithely made up names and initials he liked and then managed to dance dozens of dances with Rose under the guise of these invented characters; his favorite personage, Rose remembered fondly, was Sam Shaw, or S.S. for short. Looking back, Rose relished the memories of these evenings, of "music floating in the night air and the distant sounds of gaiety and laughter" while she and Sam Shaw strolled hand in hand along the hotel verandas or out along the terraces and paths.

But Fitzgerald's was an obdurate kind of tenacity which did not surrender easily. A week or so after his daughter's coming-out party, he arranged for Rose to meet him for lunch at the Somerset Hotel. When she arrived at the table, she remembered years later, he presented her with a beautiful new hat, which he proudly fixed upon her head, and then told her to prepare herself for an exquisite surprise. Caught up in the contagion of her father's high spirits, Rose listened with rapturous delight as he detailed his plans to take her with him on a winter vacation to Palm Beach in honor of her new status in the world. While her mother would remain at home with the rest of the family, she and her father, together with several of his political friends and a girlfriend of her own choosing, would board the *Federal Express* for the two-day journey through New York, Washington and all the Southern states to Palm Beach, where they had reservations for a two-week stay at the luxurious Breakers Hotel. Moreover, he said, since Palm Beach was known in the highest circles of New York society as a center of style and fashion, she must begin at once to shop for a new wardrobe of summer frocks and evening dresses. Never to be outdone by anyone himself, he had already fixed his eye upon a classy white broadcloth suit, designed in the newest "Mark Twain" style, which he wanted her to take a look at after lunch. Dazzled and excited, Rose jumped up from her seat and threw her arms around her father, whose answering smile, she recalled, lighted up the entire restaurant.

Within minutes, however, Rose realized with "a sinking feeling" in her heart that the Southern trip conflicted with the Junior Dance at Harvard which she and Joe had been looking forward to for weeks. As one of the fourteen members of the Junior Dance Committee, along with Bob Potter, Ralph Lowell and John Hoar, Joe was responsible for selling the four hundred or more tickets to this most important class celebration, which was to be held in the large and comfortable living room of the Harvard Union under a maze of multicolored lights. And this time, since the Junior Dance at Harvard stood high on Boston's social calendar, Rose had managed months before to secure her father's permission to accept Joe's invitation. For a dreadful moment, as she looked across the table at her father's still smiling face, Rose had a sudden conviction that he had known of the conflict all along, but this thought she quickly dismissed with the recognition that "as mayor he was far too busy to keep track of his own engagements, much less of hers."

Acting on instinct, Rose simply blurted out, "Oh, no, Daddy, I can't. I just can't go. I promised Joe Kennedy I'd go with him to the Junior Prom and I just can't break that promise now." As he heard this, Fitzgerald's sunny mood instantly darkened and his voice took on a "cold-hearted tone" as he flatly told Rose that he would hear of no such thing; she was his daughter and she was coming with him to Florida and that was that. Hardly had he finished speaking than he rose to greet some friends at a neighboring table, leaving Rose to collect her emotions. "Never dreaming of arguing" with her father, she choked back a dry sob and tried to overcome her dejection, but through all the preparations for the trip she remained "visibly upset, downcast, teary and melancholy."

Rose was not one to sulk for long periods. Although she had every intention of remaining in ill-humor throughout the entire trip, she could not dwell incessantly on her sadness; by the time the *Federal Express* reached Washington, where she and her father had a private meeting with President Taft, she had already made the transition from cheerlessness to exuberance. After all, no one could be better company on a trip than John Fitzgerald; no one knew better than he how to heighten the pleasure of every event or how to draw everyone about him into his good spirits. And surely it would be a memorable experience to see Palm Beach for the first time, with its white sandy beaches, aquamarine waters, palatial hotels and fashionable people.

The two weeks at Palm Beach turned out to be one of the most enchanting vacations Rose had ever taken with her father. Away from the daily rigors of his work, the mayor thoroughly relaxed, delighting in the pure and uninterrupted pleasures of swimming, eating and dancing. Shortly after they arrived, the *Boston Post* reported a typical day which began at dawn when Fitzgerald and Miss Rose "breasted the rough tide," which few others had dared to do that day, and then went up to the hotel pool, where "some fine dives" brought them great applause. Then, while two to three hundred people looked on from the hotel balcony, the mayor and his athletic daughter put on a thrilling swimming race up and down the pool which the mayor won only after "a decided spurt" at the end. Over to the dining room next for lunch and a concert on the spacious veranda, followed by an afternoon of spirited athletic contests, high tea at the elegant Coconut Grove and dinner at eight. In the evening, Fitzgerald escorted his daughter to "the greatest ball" ever, he said, a dazzling affair whose guests included the wealthiest people in the country, the Vanderbilts, the Searses and the Whitneys, dressed in the handsomest gowns and wearing the richest jewelry he had ever seen. Not surprisingly, Rose agreed that "she was having the time of her life."

So the precarious balance in the struggle for Rosie's heart seemed to tip temporarily toward her father. But in the end, for all his contagious charm and his magnetic warmth, Fitzgerald was up against a will far stronger and far more singleminded than his own. When he chose, Joe Kennedy could be as captivating and as warmhearted as Fitzgerald; and toward the people he loved he exhibited great gentleness and untold kindness. Unlike Fitzgerald, Kennedy did not honestly care for a single soul beyond the circle of his friends and his family. If he found it convenient he could be as tactful and as dignified as the next man; yet, if it suited his purposes, he could be brutal, relentless and cunning. In a world which he saw as a never ending battleground, he could plot and make use of people without compunction. Whereas Fitzgerald was divided by the conflicting desires of pleasing thousands and winning approval of far distant crowds, Joe Kennedy stood all of a piece: his character, his qualities, his talents were all subordinated to his ambitions. When he set his wits on getting something, no one could stop him.

If Fitzgerald was unaware of the giant resolve resting in Joe, he should have been forewarned by the droll scene he witnessed from the grandstand at Soldiers' Field Stadium on June 23, 1911, when Harvard's varsity baseball team defeated Yale for the Crimson Nine's first championship since 1908. In that era, the final goal of the Harvard teams in all sports, in baseball, in football, in rowing and in hockey, was to win from Yale. As a measure of the importance of the rivalry with Yale, tradition dictated that only those players who played in the Yale game, regardless of their record in the regular season, were entitled to the varsity H, the dream of every young athlete from the day he entered Harvard.

Because of several injuries, it was not until the start of Joe's junior year that he finally made the varsity team. He had been maintaining a respectable .285 average until he was hurt once again, in a game against Navy, and from that day until this, the final game of the season, he had seen little action. It followed, then, that the game this day held a special meaning for Joe, heightened all the more by the knowledge that his best girl and her father were among the thousands of spectators in the overflowing crowd.

Harvard bolted from the mark in the first inning when Potter singled to right, bringing Charles McLaughlin, Harvard's captain and starting pitcher, to the plate. Playing the last game of his triumphant college career, the quiet, likable team captain was given a rousing ovation, to which he responded with a long double to left which brought Potter home for the first run of the game. Yale tied the score in the top of the third with a sacrifice fly, but in the bottom of the same inning Harvard scored two more runs to take the lead, and from then on it was all McLaughlin's game. As the cheers of the crowd grew more and more insistent, McLaughlin set down the visitors inning after inning, adjusting every pitch to the situation and the batter at hand. It was an elegantly pitched, intelligent performance, his finest of the year.

As the game dwindled down to the final inning, however, the tension mounted on Harvard's bench, where Joe Kennedy and two of his teammates, Rogers and Kelly, had been sitting all afternoon, anxiously waiting to be put in so that they could claim their coveted H. The ninth inning opened with Harvard leading 4–1. After retiring the first batter, McLaughlin gave up a bloop single to Yale's catcher, who then advanced to second when the next batter grounded weakly to the plate. It was here, with two outs and a runner on second, that McLaughlin turned to the umpire and asked for time so that Coach Sexton could send Kelly to center, Rogers to right and Kennedy to first, assuring all three their varsity letters. With the crowd on its feet, it fell to Kennedy to figure in the last play of the season, as Yale's next batter, Corey, came to the plate. Hunching his shoulders, McLaughlin delivered the ball, which Corey grounded to the shortstop, whose throw to Kennedy at first base beat the Yale man to the bag for the final out.

There is no good explanation for what happened next. As the story is told, while the rest of the Harvard team gathered joyously on the mound to congratulate McLaughlin, Kennedy began walking off the field, the game-winning ball in his hand. Not quite believing what was happening, McLaughlin ran to catch up with Joe. Surely if anyone deserved the game ball as a treasured souvenir it was the team's captain, whose college career had come to an end with his fine performance that day. But when McLaughlin finally caught up with Kennedy and asked him for the ball, Kennedy simply shook his head, stuffed the ball into his back pocket and walked away.

It was, apparently, a sight to remember—so much so that years later several of those who had been present volunteered the incident to Kennedy's biographer, Richard Whalen, as a startling illustration of the fact that if Joe Kennedy wanted something badly enough, he didn't care how he got it. And over time, conjecture has thickened to produce a variety of motives for Joe's unthinkable behavior. The common view suggests that his insensitivity was born of his earlier resentment against McLaughlin for beating him out in the quest for a regular position on the varsity team, a feeling that was compounded by the humiliation of being kept on the bench all afternoon, in full view not only of Rose and her father but of all the members of his own family; in this view, Kennedy simply reached out in retaliation to restore his wounded pride. Others have suggested a more elaborate scenario which unites both McLaughlin and Kennedy in raw self-interest. As this version is told, McLaughlin was visited several days before the game by a friend of Joe's father who knew that McLaughlin was interested in a license to operate a movie theater in Boston. If he wanted his license, the stranger warned, he had better see that young Kennedy won his letter. In other words, what appeared at first as an act of generosity on McLaughlin's side was simply part of a trade to which Kennedy responded in kind. The spectacle has also been cited to suggest a deeper well of resentment in Joe: the contempt of the Irishman for the conventions of the establishment.

The interest excited by this incident is understandable, for it does indeed suggest a striking portrait in which Joe's want of common decency, his utter indifference to everything but his own self-will, and his hardened insensibility to the feelings of others are marked in strong, bold lines. Yet, in the end, it is no fairer to characterize him solely by this display of pure selfishness and lack of concern for all external considerations than it would be to characterize him solely by the openness and generosity he exhibited toward his friends. The truth is that he united in his person both inexorable self-will and the capacity for deep attachment, both appalling ruthlessness and unswerving fidelity; the images jostle one another, yet are part of the same complicated character. Deficient in civility, he could be the most disagreeable man in the world; unbounded by convention, his crudeness would betray others again and again. However, when the gates of his passions were opened for those he loved, the love he received in return was past the size of dreaming. Let the world classify him a blackguard, so long as his family and his friends ranked him a king.

Much of young Joe at Harvard was pure P. J. Kennedy. He had his father's shrewd intelligence, his organizational ability and his good common sense. All his working life, P.J. had moved cautiously from one step to the next, never expanding his enterprises beyond his capacity to control them, always preparing his way carefully for the next move. It was a prudence rooted in his early life. While P.J. was still an infant, his thirty-five-year-old father had died from cholera, leaving P.J.'s mother, Bridget, nearly destitute with four small children to support. The family had survived with the help of the neighbors, who provided the bread and soup while Bridget Kennedy went to work in a small notions shop at the foot of the ferry landings in East Boston where her husband had worked as a cooper. A strong-willed woman, Bridget kept her family together and eventually became the owner of the tiny shop. As the only son, P.J. had grown up faster than many children, leaving school to take a job loading and unloading cargoes on the docks when he was only fourteen. Yet, even in these difficult circumstances, he had managed to keep his eye on the future, dividing the wages he earned between his family's needs and a small savings account. When the time was right, he used his savings to purchase a modest tavern in Haymarket Square that had come onto the market at a low price because its owner had fallen on bad times.

With hard work, P.J.'s tavern prospered, and within several years, while he was still in his early twenties, he was able to buy into two more —one by the docks, the other in a famous Boston hostelry, the Maverick House. Once again his willingness to work hard and his attention to detail paid off: before he was thirty, by pooling all his resources he established his own business enterprise, a liquor-importing business which brought in fine liquors from Europe and South America. Bearing his name, P. J. Kennedy and Company was the perfect business venture for him, for it absorbed all his previous experiences, putting to good use his familiarity with ships and dockworkers as well as his operational knowledge of saloons and hostelries. From this clever and cautious man, young Joe learned at an early age the value of looking forward before acting in order to provide against all possible contingencies.

But heredity had infused into Joe a more adventurous and more defiant strain. Joe's mother, Mary Augusta Hickey, had been born in circumstances far more comfortable than his father's. As the daughter of a successful businessman and the sister of three men prominent in the community—the oldest a police lieutenant, the next a physician who had graduated from Harvard Medical School, and the youngest a funeral director—Mary Hickey was a prize catch for P. J. Kennedy. "She was an amazingly quick-witted woman," her granddaughter Mary Lou McCarthy recalled, "with an exceptional mind capable of perceiving humor in almost any situation and of expressing herself in a clever and amusing way. If, for example, one of her children came home feeling that the end of the world had come because he or she had failed an exam, she would immediately gather the family together to plan a wake to mourn the failure." From this woman Joe inherited his ability to recognize incongruities and absurdities in situations and people which allowed him to laugh at himself even in the most trying of circumstances. Under her imaginative guidance, his mind developed an irreverent and fanciful quality which provided a rich counterpart to the sensible, conservative streak inherited from his father.

As a small child Joe had proved himself stormier and more willful than his father, and as he grew older, surrounded by the love of his family and the warmth of his upbringing, his resolution to do things his own way only increased. As the firstborn, Joe had always held a special place in his mother's heart. This position of privilege was substantially fortified when his younger brother Francis died from diphtheria at the age of two. "The death of the baby was so unexpected and so senseless," Mary Augusta's granddaughter said, "that her only way of coping was to pour even more love onto Joe."

The death of young Frank affected P.J.'s relations with his only son as well. "However busy P.J. was with his work or his politics, he always found the time to spend with Joe," his granddaughter said. An avid baseball fan, P.J. shared his love for the game with his son, playing ball in the yard with him for hours each day and taking Joe with him to all the games of the Boston Red Sox. As Joe grew older, Mary Lou Mc-

Carthy said, "the two of them were inseparable." He took Joe with him everywhere—to his political meetings, his bank offices and his importing company. Nor, it seems, did Joe ever suffer jealousy from his two younger sisters, Loretta and Margaret, who responded to his primacy by "adoring him all their lives, taking great pride in his accomplishments and talking always about him as 'my Joe.' "

In light of his upbringing, it is no surprise that Joe walked through Boston Latin and Harvard with an assured step and that he expected things generally to go his way. This self-confidence found its expression at the end of his Harvard schooling when the moment came to choose his career. It was the conventional wisdom of the day that politics provided the surest road to power for an ambitious Irish youth. Constituting close to 40 percent of Boston's population in 1912, the Irish had entrenched themselves in city government, where they held a majority of the elected positions and controlled almost all the manual laboring jobs on the city's payroll. And beyond the loyalty of their own ethnic group, the experienced Irish bosses had captured the loyalty of many of the newer immigrants as well, most importantly the Jews and the Italians, who, taken together, accounted for another 20 percent of the population. Indeed, by the second decade of the twentieth century, as Joe was finishing up at Harvard, the Irish machine was beginning to gain real power in the state government too, promising the young generation of Irish politicians vaster fields of opportunity than ever before.

In addition to the advantage of being an Irishman, there would have been, for the son of P. J. Kennedy, the inestimable benefit derived from the extended network of personal relationships which had been developed over the years by the sturdy old boss's unremitting efforts to provide jobs, favors and assistance to all the thousands of men and women who had passed through his fiefdom.

Yet, when Joe looked upon his father's world, built up as it was, family by family, block by block, district by district, it seemed an unduly circumscribed world that he would never have the patience to build or maintain. "I never felt I had the temperament to be a politician," Joe told his friend Clem Norton. "Though I loved going with my father to the precinct caucuses and the torchlight parades, I couldn't stand to watch the incessant demands that were continually being placed on my father's time. Never was there a single moment when someone didn't want something from him; never was there a single stretch of peaceful time when he could thoroughly relax and totally enjoy a good meal or a good book."

Every hour of every day, it seemed to Joe, there was yet another searching soul who appeared at the family's doorstep, invariably disturbing the household routine with a request for "just a word with Mr. Kennedy." As Joe's sisters remembered it, their mother instinctively recoiled from these unwanted intrusions upon her family's privacy, and her eldest son seemed to follow her lead. Mary Augusta believed that people were sponging on P.J. because he was known far and wide as a soft touch for anyone with a hard-luck story. Wincing when the doorbell rang, she would have to fight back her anger as she watched her husband rise from his place at the head of the table and attend to the needs of whichever unfortunate person had wandered into their home, for she knew that the encounter taking place would most likely result in P.J.'s giving away either his time or his money or both. An East Boston resident remembered his father saying that "everyone who ran for any political office would get fifty or seventy-five dollars from P.J. though he could have used it himself."

Yet, to P.J., personal generosity was simply part of his job as the boss of his district; in giving what he could to his neighbors, even at the expense of his family, he felt he was doing the right thing. Having received the support of his neighbors when he was a fatherless child in desperate need, he retained forever a profound feeling of indebtedness to others which he continually worked out during his long political career. Years later, P.J.'s daughter Loretta still remembered the plaque that hung above her father's desk in his book-lined study. "I shall pass through this world but once," it read. "Any kindness I can do, or goodness show, let me do it now—for I shall not pass this way again."

In this regard, father and son bore little resemblance to each other, though their polarities created an odd balance. Whereas P.J. took deep pleasure in supporting others and helping his neighbors, Joe's more calculating mind always placed himself and his family first. Nor did Joe possess the temperament that suffered fools or weaklings well. In these daily pilgrimages to his home Joe frequently saw the same people returning again and again, never able, it seemed, to make their own way without his father's repeated help. "I remember looking into the eyes of the hundreds of pleading people who came into our house," Joe told Eddie Gallagher, "knowing that my father saw only the gentle appeal of honorable men and women, but, all too often, all I could see was their predatory stare."

As an illustration of Joe's attitude toward such favor-seekers, classmates of Joe's at Boston Latin liked to quote a certain financially irresponsible youngster who would borrow from everybody except Kennedy. One day when the youngster was trying to raise a nickel for pastry, someone said, "Ask Joe Kennedy. He'll lend it to you. He always has money." The perpetual borrower shook his head gloomily. "Nope.

If I got it from Kennedy, he'd expect to be paid back." This is not to say Joe was a miser, wanting in feelings toward others; on the contrary, when he later became a rich man he too derived heartfelt pleasure from giving his money to people he believed in. But, unlike his father, he was never, in Richard Cardinal Cushing's words, "an open handed Santa Claus." "Toward his close friends Joe was as soft as his father," Joe's friend George Pumphret observed, "but he never ran around with his heart on his sleeve. And almost always, he insisted upon keeping his contributions anonymous, believing that charity was the last basis on which to build a personal relationship."

Joe's rejection of politics as a young man, however, sprang from a source still deeper than his temperamental dislike for the daily traffic with people in need. Impelled by an irresistible longing for power and prestige, Joe might well have been able to accommodate his personality to the demands of the political trade had he truly believed that politics was the surest route to real power. But from his personal observation it was not. "It doesn't make any difference," he told a reporter in 1914 when asked why he had decided not to enter politics, "how high a young man may rise in politics, nor how brilliant his future may seem, his ultimate defeat is inevitable."

Whether Joe fully comprehended the profound meaning of what he was saying when he forecast bitter endings for all those who entered political life—a searching observation suggesting the eventual power-lessness of the politician since, dependent as he inevitably is upon the fickleness of public favor, he can never be his own man—we cannot know. We do know, however, that Joe had seen his father deeply hurt by a stunning defeat and that years later that experience was still in Joe's mind as distinctly as it had been the day the defeat had been rendered.

The sudden upset had occurred in the fall of Joe's freshman year at Harvard. All through the previous decade, after serving eight successive terms in the state legislature, P.J. had left elective office to others, preferring to wield his substantial influence indirectly through his powerful position as the unquestioned boss of his local ward. But then in the middle of October 1908, at the urging of both Mayor Fitzgerald and his lifelong friend Judge Corbett, the old warrior had reluctantly agreed to become a candidate for the influential position of street commissioner. His decision to run was taken by the local press as tantamount to his nomination and election, and the more he threw himself into the race, committing himself unreservedly to win, the more certain his victory seemed. For P. J. Kennedy was at this time a significant figure in Boston politics. Tall, lean and gentlemanly, with a smooth-cropped mustache, a long, straight nose and bushy eyebrows, he projected at all times a cultivated and honest appearance. He had about him an air of wisdom and dignity which distinguished him from most of the more rough-and-tumble politicians of his day.

It was this expectation of sure triumph that made P.J.'s defeat—at the hands of a little-known claims agent in city government whose candidacy was never taken seriously—so startling in its impact. For the most part, the political insiders responded with bewilderment and regret. "There was no reason why P. J. Kennedy should not have been nominated," *Practical Politics* concluded. "He is a man of standing in the community and he was backed by various faction leaders." Even the Brahmin paper, the *Boston Evening Transcript*, expressed sorrow at the results: "The Democrats made the poorer choice between candidates, for while Mr. Kennedy is an active politician, he is a man of experience in city affairs and bears a fairly clean record of public service." In the end, two contradictory explanations emerged. Either Fitzgerald had double-crossed Kennedy by urging his candidacy simply as a means of keeping others out of the race, and then not backing him up with enthusiasm, or the power of the old-style bosses and their machines was declining, signaled by the striking fact that only half of the enrolled voters had come out to vote.

P.J. faced his defeat as he seemed to face almost everything in his life, with gentle dignity and good-humored complacency. "No doubt you take it in your usual philosophical way," P.J.'s friend Richard Sullivan wrote, "but as a friend I can't take it that way." Upon hearing the final tally, which showed him trailing by three hundred votes, P.J. issued an artful statement in which he simply thanked "most heartily" the friends who had been kind enough to vote for him and the newspapers which had consistently accorded him such "fair treatment."

From that moment on, P.J.'s political ship remained permanently moored within the confines of his old world; never again would he seek adventure in the larger political world. Becoming circumspect in everything he did, he settled down to an even more prudent existence, devoting more and more of his time to his local business.

All this and more the perceptive young Kennedy saw in the elder Kennedy's tired eyes. Years later, Joe told Eddie Gallagher that while his father succeeded in persuading everyone else that the loss meant little or nothing to him and that everything was just as it had been before, he could see that, underneath, his father was grieving like a child who had been unjustly punished. To Joe, the experience suggested that nothing wears out faster than generosity; that, in the end, political loyalty and gratitude were simply commodities, easily bought and easily sold. "After seeing the thanks his father got," George Pumphret suggested, "Joe decided to stay away from politics. Here was a man, he reasoned, who had given all he had twelve months a year for twenty-five years to the people of Boston, and yet in six short weeks a totally unknown candidate could come out of nowhere and defeat him."

It was then and there, it seems, that Joe determined to lay his foundation on what was under *his* control. The only way to guarantee power was to establish a base of financial success, and then from that base the man of wealth could do as he pleased. "Joe Kennedy saw early what made the power and gentility he wanted," a friendly critic commented. "It wasn't talent, it was ancient riches. Power came from money. Joe had a keen mind; it was honed against the great cynicisms underlying rank and station in Brahmin Boston."

Beyond the impact of his life experience which channeled him away from politics toward the world of business and finance, one can almost say of Joe Kennedy, as of Frank Cowperwood, the buccaneering hero of Theodore Dreiser's *Trilogy of Desire*, that he was born a financier, "with all the knowledge that pertained to that great art, . . . as natural to him as the emotions and subtleties of life are to a poet." From the very first, young Kennedy, like young Cowperwood, had known how to make money. As a child Joe sold candies and peanuts to excursion boat passengers on the docks near his house, at the age of ten he entered and won a soap-selling contest, and as a teenager he organized a circle of his friends into a profit-making baseball team.

Propelled by a conquering will as well as by the urgency to escape the embarrassing identification with his softhearted father, Joe seemed to know instinctively how to use money to make money. While he was still a student at Harvard, he used the money he had accumulated from his smaller enterprises to venture into his first real business, the ownership and operation of a sightseeing motorbus. One afternoon when he and his friend Joe Donovan were riding on a tour bus from Boston to Lexington and Concord over the Paul Revere route, they learned from the lecturer that the owner was going out of business, and they decided, on the spot, that if they could buy the bus cheap they would go into the sightseeing business themselves, with Donovan as driver and Kennedy as lecturer. Kennedy recognized that beyond the novelty of motor driving, the passengers would be interested in history, and he was determined to "let them have it." But when they approached the owner they found that his lowest price was double the six hundred dollars in capital they possessed between them. Abandoning hope, they readied to leave, but the owner surprised them by offering to take the payments in installments, six hundred down and six hundred more over the course of their first full season.

It was a shabby bus, but the enterprising partners made it look distinctive by painting it cream and blue, with the name "Mayflower" written across its side in bold black letters. Having gathered the whole situation in his mind as a general grasps the plans of his campaign, Kennedy immediately understood that the location of the bus stand, more than anything else, would determine the number of its passengers. The buses with the choicest stands—such as the stand outside South Station—made the best profits. It was as simple as that.

Shooting for the best, the boys put in an application for the South Station license. The real force behind the licensing board was the mayor —a situation which should have ended all possibilities for Joe, since Fitzgerald was still set against his romance with Rose. Undaunted by this consideration, Joe decided to go directly to Fitzgerald. Never deluding himself concerning the motives of others, Joe intuitively recognized —with a brassy kind of courage that would forever mark his character— that if he approached the mayor and asked right out for the South Station stand, the mayor, wanting Joe in his debt, would grant his request. For a man like Fitzgerald, Joe reasoned, there would be great pleasure in the idea of locking his daughter's favorite suitor into an obligation, assuming that when the right time came he could use the leverage he had gained in the larger struggle for Rose's heart.

Fitzgerald's assumption was one that would have worked with most men, but not with Joe. For when Fitzgerald granted Kennedy the license, the clever young man simply took it and ran, not feeling for a moment that in accepting the favor he had done anything that might jeopardize his relations with Rose. On the contrary, he believed that by outsmarting the mayor he was gaining an edge on the older man. And he was right. With the best location in the city, the Mayflower prospered; in its two seasons of life, which stretched from late spring to early fall, its operations were so successful that Kennedy and Donovan cleared a spectacular profit of $10,000.

# CHAPTER 14

# "BANKING . . .
# COULD
# LEAD
# A MAN
# ANYWHERE."

By the time Kennedy graduated from Harvard on the sunny morning of June 23, 1912, his mind was made up: he wanted to be a businessman, and he intended to start out in the field of banking. Though he was graduating with no academic honors—indeed, the story has been told and retold of all the troubles he had with an accounting course which he eventually had to drop—he had learned that he could manipulate his environment to create and operate a successful business. And, more than that, he had learned how to multiply the money he made. In the winter of his senior year at Harvard, he had invested his profits from the Mayflower in a small real-estate operation which, he later said, gave him an important insight into the world of business.

"I saw, even in my limited dealings, that sooner or later, the source of business was traced to the banks," Joe later recalled. Fascinated by the mystery of mortgages, liens and credit negotiations, he concluded that "banking was the basic business profession" which "could lead a man anywhere, as it played an important part in every business."

In his belief in the paramount importance of the banker, Joe was not alone. Indeed, the turn of the century was the age of the banker, so much so that the leading bankers of the day had become legendary figures in the public imagination—vast, overshadowing behemoths whose colossal power seemed to reach everywhere. "These bankers," Louis D. Brandeis wrote at the time, "bestride as masters America's business world, so that practically no large enterprise can be undertaken successfully without their participation or approval." At a time when the economic resources of the country were being increasingly concentrated in the hands of newly formed trusts and giant corporations, the bankers had become the central force in promoting new industries and reorganizing old ones, in directing railroad corporations, insurance companies and public utilities. "Access to other people's money," Brandeis argued, was the key which enabled these individual bankers to take "so large and so controlling a role in every aspect of American economic life."

And the bankers lived on a scale appropriate to their power. John Pierpont Morgan, the most towering of them all, possessed a luxurious mansion on Thirty-sixth Street in New York as well as two or three sumptuous apartments in the best hotels in other leading cities of the world; he spent his summers in his country house on the Hudson, and his winters—in the company of a continuous stream of friends—aboard his lavish three-hundred-foot yacht; he entertained in a baroque style; he courted beautiful women and owned a magnificent collection of English portraits and landscapes, rich porcelains, bronzes, Bibles, miniatures, precious manuscripts and jewelry which was considered the greatest collection in the modern era and earned him a comparison with Lorenzo de' Medici. And although Morgan was indisputably the king of the financiers, his partners and allies also moved in an extravagant world of mansions and yachts, servants and secretaries, nannies and tutors, a world of conspicuous prosperity.

Oddly enough, the same public attention that imbued the bankers of the era with their crimson glory was also the portent of their decline.

With the new century came a new spirit of criticism, a rising public awareness that control by the few was destroying opportunity for the many. Spurred on by the muckraking press, there arose a clamor for reform which, in the spring of 1912, culminated in the formation of the Pujo Committee to Investigate the Concentration of Control of Money and Credit. Headed by Samuel Untermyer of New York, the Pujo Committee translated the suspicion of concentration into a devastating set of figures which made plain the means by which an inner group of bankers had gained control of America's economic life. This "tumbling cascade of facts" stirred the public and its legislators to a series of reforms which, taken together, meant that after J. P. Morgan died, there would never be another banker like him. Indeed, his death in 1913 would mark the end of an entire era in high finance.

Still, there remained something irresistibly attractive about the image of the banker to a young man of Joe's immense ambitions. For in Boston, even more than in New York, the leading circle of bankers monopolized not only power but prestige and privilege as well. Recruited almost exclusively from the oldest Brahmin families, they occupied what was clearly the most favored place in Boston's social and cultural life. Indeed, a list of the directors of the city's largest banks in 1912 reveals the names of many of the most prominent families of the day: Higginson, Amory, Thayer, Storrow, Ames, Gardner, Choate, Coolidge, Draper, Gaston, Lyman, Sears, Shaw, Saltonstall and Lawrence.

Having long shared the same clubs, the same schools and the same church, and frequently related by marriage, Boston's financial elite had succeeded by this time in concentrating banking capital even further than its counterpart in New York. Over 90 percent of the banking resources of the entire city of Boston was held by the two largest international banking houses, Lee, Higginson and Company and Kidder, Peabody and Company—both long established and rich and each possessing an extensive, wealthy clientele—and the two largest banks, the National Shawmut Bank and the First National Bank of Boston, and the twenty-one other banks and trust companies in which their directors were also directors. There appeared to be only six banks in all Boston, representing less than 5 percent of the banking resources, that were free from interlocking-directorate relations cemented by mutual stock holdings, codirectorships and family ties.

The very existence of this closed economic circle suggests the enormity of the task confronting young Kennedy in his desire to become a banker. For those in control, it was so much easier and more natural to bring in a relative, even one of modest abilities, whose "ties of blood and sentiment would guarantee a degree of application, loyalty and honesty not always assured in unrelated hands." As a consequence, in 1912 there was not a single Irishman who sat on a single board of a major Boston bank. So, by choosing the less traveled road of banking over the populous route of politics, Joe was choosing "an occupation where his Celtic name and church would always make him a stranger."

It was an act of foolishness, it was an act of courage—it all depended on the outcome. Never sentimental in analyzing his future prospects, Joe recognized from the start that the odds were against him. Yet, though the initial obstacles to success appeared so much more formidable, and though the climb to power would be more difficult to negotiate, the sun at the summit, should it ever be reached, promised to rise so much more brilliantly that, to Joe's adventurous mind, the steeper hill was well worth the challenge.

Joe's initial advance into the world of banking was made possible by his father. The week before he graduated from Harvard, he secured a position as a clerk in the counting rooms of a small East Boston bank, the Columbia Trust Company. P. J. Kennedy was one of the original founders of the Columbia Trust, which had opened its doors for business at 20 Meridian Street in 1895 as a people's bank—an institution dedicated to the small businessmen of East Boston. "Its birth was humble," the *East Boston Leader* recalled on the occasion of Columbia's golden anniversary, "for its founders were men of limited means." But, by mingling on its board old Yankee, Irish, Jew and Italian, reflecting the highly cosmopolitan makeup of East Boston's population, it managed to build an institution which grew steadily each year, with assets totaling nearly $700,000 by 1912. This was small, perhaps, compared to the tens of millions of dollars in assets controlled by the large downtown banks, but it was a good place for Joe to begin, nonetheless.

As a new clerk, Joe was apprenticed to Alfred Wellington, the man upon whom the institutional life of the bank depended. Balding and fifteen years older than Joe, Wellington had started as a clerk himself on the day the bank had opened and had risen by slow but steady promotions to the position of treasurer. He was a kindly, honest man who had attained a genuine excellence in his craft. As treasurer, he was completely reliable, a bulwark of order, ready to protect the bank against danger of any kind.

Had he searched the city, Joe could not have hoped to find a man in banking who was better suited as his first teacher. From the start, Wellington took a keen interest in this shrewd and clever young man. Joe's whole manner suggested an eagerness to learn and a willingness to work diligently at the smallest task assigned to him. Every day he came into the bank with his active mind full of more and more questions, until he gradually began to envision the larger network in which the work of the men in his community was transformed into a circulating currency that moved in and out of the bank in the form of deposits and loans.

For eight weeks, through the sweltering days of July and August, Joe worked side by side with Wellington, their relationship gradually taking on a lasting significance for both men. The master gave his protégé the best of himself, so much so that the time spent with Wellington remained printed on Joe's memory; years later he would still speak of Alfred Wellington with great affection as the man who first set him on his way. Throughout his life, from that summer on, Joe would show an uncanny faculty for making friends with older men and being introduced into new realms.

By summer's end, Joe's unbounded ambitions had already outstripped his mentor's imaginings. For all his honorable dedication to the bank, Wellington was not a man of broad vision—a man like, say, Amadeus Peter Giannini, founder of the Bank of America, the largest bank in the world, who was not only able to dream up an entirely new transcontinental system of branch banking but was also able to execute his master plan. An instinctive settler, the stalwart Wellington took only one day at a time.

Nor could Joe fully understand the meaning of the word "loyalty" as applied to an institution. Such loyalty was a positive sentiment, no doubt, but if the bank failed or if it changed hands, where would Wellington be? Not now nor ever would Joe trust his ventures to one place or to one person; having seen the meager return his father had received for his own unflinching loyalty to his constituents, and having been hurt by the club system at Harvard, Joe was determined to keep his own life sacred to himself, his family and a few friends. This did not mean he was lacking in sentiment with respect to the bank. Later, in fact, he referred to the Columbia Trust as his "first love." Yet, for him, there would never be the same wedding of man and institution as there was with Wellington—a wedding which would allow Wellington to wait patiently for thirty-five years before he would finally be appointed president of the bank.

It was a mark of Joe's temperament that he understood even then, as a young man, the limiting dimension of routine and the hazards of institutional loyalty. Speaking to a reporter when he was only twenty-five, he emphasized the vast difference between those who "made their jobs routine" because they let routine entrap them and those who made "routine a part of their education for better jobs." So deeply did Joe fear such entrapment, in fact, that over time his career would take him through a dizzying variety of institutions in banking, shipping, brokerage, movies, liquor, government and real estate.

To be sure, by refusing to stay in any one place long enough to develop an attachment to it, he would never allow himself the satisfaction of creating a little institutional world for himself. Nor would he know the pride of building an organization or the security of being fully accepted by the insiders in any single field. On the other hand, his succession of jobs would allow him always to see things from a different angle; by continually moving on, he was forever freed from the limitations of customary thought and conventional wisdom—a freedom that would save him from destruction in the crash of 1929 when the whole world of finance collapsed around him.

Yet, in spite of his awareness of Wellington's limitations, it never seemed to occur to Joe to thereby judge his mentor adversely. He simply accepted Wellington for what he was. As a consequence, Joe's growing restlessness at the bank managed to win Wellington's support rather than his antagonism. Indeed, it was Wellington himself who first recognized that Joe needed to find a new channel for his budding financial talent. Seeing infinite possibility in the young man, Wellington suggested that Joe take the civil-service examination to become a bank examiner; the best way to master the intricacies of banking was to be a student of all banks and not a minor functionary in a single bank. As Wellington laid it out, the job as an examiner would supply Joe with his traveling papers for the future, a map allowing him to make ready for his fantastic journey.

With Wellington as his tutor, Joe passed the examination, which put his name upon the official list from which the Governor would choose three examiners and twenty-two assistant examiners to work in the bank commissioner's department the coming year. But Joe was not willing to leave his appointment to chance. According to George Pumphret, he went to see Mayor Fitzgerald, armed with a chart demonstrating that over the years there had not been a single Irish Catholic bank examiner. Spurred by the evidence Joe had produced, Fitzgerald then reportedly went to see the Governor, Eugene Foss, and threatened to make a public issue of discrimination unless Joe was appointed. The appointment came through on September 12, 1912, at a salary of $1,200 per year. Later, when he was asked how Joe Kennedy had made his millions, Fitzgerald would say, "It was easy. I got him a job as a bank examiner. That gave him an entree to the whole financial world. And it was simple from then on." But when the story of Fitzgerald's intervention was repeated in the initial draft of the exhaustive *Fortune* article on Joe Kennedy in 1937, Joe reacted strongly: "John Fitzgerald may think he secured this position, but it was really Wellington."

The bank commissioner's department, located on the first floor of the State House, comprised a suite of three main rooms, a large safety vault and some small anterooms. Under Commissioner Augustus Thorndike, the department's work load was staggering; in Massachusetts in 1912 there were 549 banking institutions under state supervision, including 162 cooperative banks, 65 trust companies and 194 savings banks, each of which, according to law, had to be examined at least once a year "to establish its solvency, to determine the legality of its transactions and to ascertain its ability to fufull its obligations to its depositors." These inspections, of course, varied in intensity over time, but in 1912, more than ever before, with the structure of the banking system a primary topic of the day, the public clamored noisily for more frequent and "more searching investigations of banks and banking operations."

As a consequence, Joe spent most of his eighteen months as a bank examiner on the road engaged in actual investigations. "Inspection work took me to all parts of the state," he later recalled, "and gave me an opportunity for a field course in banking of many kinds: in mill towns, fishing towns and the bigger multiple industry cities. I learned that . . . we make a mistake when we call money hard cash. It's lively and fluid— the blood of business."

The beginning of each inspection would be announced by the sudden arrival of a crew of examiners, bursting through the doors in the style of an old Western movie. The most critical part of the examination was to descend "without previous notice" and "at irregular intervals." For if the officials were given even one hour's time, they could cover up almost anything. Upon entering the banks, the examiners took immediate possession of all cash, notes, securities owned, collateral securities, necessary books of accounts and the like, permitting no release of any part until they were satisfied that a complete check or record had been made.

Joe turned out to be one of the most industrious bank examiners the state banking commission had ever known. Within a matter of months, he knew the financial structure of many banks even better than the bankers. He knew which banks had made loans subject to criticism and which ones had failed to comply with the provisions of the law. He knew from what types of people different banks drew their depositors, and to which businesses they gave their loans. He knew which banks were expanding and which were retrenching and why.

"That bank examiner's job laid bare to Joe the condition of every bank he visited," banker Ralph Lowell suggested. "He learned as much in two years about the business of banking by examining the structure and securities of the state banks as he'd have learned in ten years on a banking job." From their ledgers alone, Boston reporter Bill Duncliffe observed, "he learned far more than he ever could have learned at Harvard."

In the course of his examining journeys, Kennedy showed such uncommon intelligence and financial skill that a circle of Boston men became convinced that here was a great financier in the making. His indomitable spirit and the intensity of his personality made an immediate impression on everyone he met. As a result of these contacts, Joe would later be given access to money and resources which his own purchasing power could never have landed, and which he would then multiply still further through his exceptional capacity to make the money he had work to make more money.

Of equal importance to his future success, his experience as an examiner served to discipline still further his already disciplined mind, reinforcing his analytical capacities and confirming his ability to make decisions unswayed by sentiment or desire. Through the science of dissection, he had found weaknesses and shortcomings in even the most established institutions. Never would the gleaming beauty of a bank's marble floors blind him to the possibility that the structure below might well be unworthy of the public's praise. Never would he delude himself with the ornamental appearances of institutions or people. "There are no big shots," he determined, coining an aphorism which guided him through the rest of his days as he brought his analytical skills to every business enterprise with which he became associated.

# CHAPTER 15
# THE
# BALANCE
# SHIFTS

While Joe was becoming a familiar figure in the banking district, preparing the ground for all the dazzling conquests he would eventually make in the world of finance, the fortunes of John Fitzgerald were moving in the opposite direction. His was not a sudden, surprising collapse, but rather a gradual decline in political power and prestige, the seeds of which were sown in the last quarter of 1913. Viewed from the perspective of a giant measuring scale with two trays hanging from a crossbar, each side representing the two contenders in the contest for Rose Fitzgerald, we can identify the late autumn and early winter of 1913–14 as the time when the balance shifted once and for all from John Fitzgerald to Joe Kennedy.

Ironically, when he entered the final months of his mayorship John Fitzgerald appeared more popular with the people of Boston than he had ever been before. Much had been accomplished in his second term; indeed, there were many who credited the energetic mayor with the commercial revival of the city and the rebirth of its harbor. And the public monuments to his resourceful leadership—the new playgrounds and baths, the new high school of commerce, the new consumptives' hospital, the municipal athletic meets, the Franklin Park Zoo, the City

Aquarium—and the host of public holidays sponsored by the city were to be enjoyed by the community at large.

"And why should not the parks echo with children's voices and the strains of music?" the mayor had asked in lobbying for legislative sanction for the use of parks for games and sports and concerts. "Sometimes," he argued, "such things as playgrounds, parks, recreation piers, museums and libraries, school lunches, municipal theatres, model tenements, social centers have been discussed as if they were frills and furbelows. As a matter of fact they come very close to the real objects for which cities exist."

Indeed, so successful had his second term in office been that the mayor nourished visions of a contest against Henry Cabot Lodge two years hence for the first United States Senate seat in Massachusetts to be filled by popular election.

For months, all through the summer and the early fall, Fitzgerald had been saying he would not be a candidate for reelection to the mayor's office. The time had come, he repeatedly made clear, to turn his attentions to his family before his children had all grown up and gone away. Behind these statements of personal desire, however, lay the public recognition that the last thing he needed if he was going to mount a successful campaign for the U.S. Senate in 1916 was another bruising and exhaustive campaign for the mayor's job in 1914. Better to leave all that battering to others while he moved on to crown his career with election to the United States Senate.

Taking Fitzgerald at his word, Roxbury's Congressman, James Michael Curley, began planning his own campaign for mayor halfway through Fitzgerald's second term. Possessed of gigantic strengths and unpardonable faults, Curley had burst upon the Boston scene in the early 1900s, and nothing in the city would ever be the same again. After a term in the Common Council and a stint at the State House, he had made his name a household word when he was elected to the Board of Aldermen from the Charles Street Jail, where he was serving his sixty-day sentence for taking the civil-service exam in place of a friend. With his blustering demeanor and his superb oratorical skills, Curley had turned his disgrace into a political blessing by defending his crime as an act of heroism in overcoming a system which gave the fortuitously better-schooled Yankees discriminatory advantages over the Irish.

Curley's secret charm lay in his developing legend: the more indecorous and outlandish his actions seemed, the more the Irish loved him. He excited people and he excited emotions; from his earliest days in politics through the unparalleled length of his spectacular career he provided his supporters with vicarious pleasures in his tempestuous battles, his unconventional tactics and his gorgeous flights of oratory. Elected to the Congress in 1910, he made it clear to anyone who would listen that his real goal was to be the mayor of the city. Having waited hungrily through six years of Fitzgerald's reign, he defiantly announced for mayor in November 1913, warning the bosses that his candidacy would be exotically different from any they had ever seen. Refusing to solicit the help of a single boss, he threatened that when he became mayor he would put an abrupt end to the outmoded system of ward bossism.

Curley's announcement sent a shiver through the spines of the ward bosses, who had grown accustomed to Fitzgerald's more conciliatory style, his softer humor, his more relaxed temper and his definite capacity for compromise. Indeed, much of the success of Fitzgerald's term had been attributed to his increasing urbanity, his growing respectability among the lace-curtain Irish and his reconciliation with Martin Lomasney, the shrewd old boss who still controlled the balance of power between the Irish and the Yankees. In contrast, the more roguish aspects of Curley's cruder personality reflected the attitudes of a newer generation of American-born Irish who no longer viewed the sturdy ward bosses as father figures, a more rootless generation anxious to express its resentments against all forms of established rule, Irish and Yankee alike.

Whereas Fitzgerald had idolized the North End boss Matt Keany, Curley's experience with the boss of his own district had been grotesquely different. Curley was only ten when his thirty-four-year-old father died lifting a heavy stone on a construction job, but he never forgot that at a time when his family desperately needed help they received absolutely nothing from the boss of Ward 17, Pea Jacket Maguire —not a basket of food, not an article of clothing or even a visit to the house. Nothing. "I can't remember a time when I didn't have to fight for what I got," Curley later said, in a tone suggesting the enormity of the struggle he was willing to wage if he succeeded to his desired position as mayor of his city.

Sensing that Curley meant what he said about dismantling the entire system, the frightened bosses put great pressure on Fitzgerald to stand for reelection one last time. While they appreciated his genuine reluctance to become a candidate, they also knew he was a man who succumbed easily to flattery and praise. They speculated that in the face of an orchestrated draft urging him to run again, he would change his mind. So the word spread that the future of the Democratic machine, nay, even more, the future of the entire city, was hanging on Fitzgerald's decision. At meetings and forums all over the city, unanimous resolutions were adopted calling on Fitzgerald to become a candidate.

In deciding to pursue Fitzgerald, the bosses left no stone unturned: half a dozen editorials suddenly popped up in the city papers urging the mayor to run, and colorful Fitzgerald badges and buttons instantly sprouted on thousands of loyal chests.

The breadth of the organized campaign threw Fitzgerald off balance, especially when his own group of trusted friends reported back to him "a remarkable condition as far as his strength was concerned." Never before, he was told, had he enjoyed such a widespread popularity with the people of Boston. While he had experienced bruising campaigns in the past, this one promised to be just the opposite. After all, they said, Curley was too much a realist to fight against Fitzgerald and Lomasney and all the other bosses too. The sheer weight of Fitzgerald's announcement would end Curley's campaign, and Fitzgerald could look forward to a relatively uncontested nomination.

Responding as the bosses thought he would, Fitzgerald announced on November 28, 1913, that the period of uncertainty was over. "Boston has done much for me," he told the press, "and I am led to believe by the petitions that have come to me that I owe it to Boston to run again."

It was a calamitous decision, one he would regret for the rest of his life.

For despite all the comfortable assurances Fitzgerald had received that his announcement alone would bring an immediate halt to Curley's candidacy, Curley defied the conventional wisdom by redoubling his resolution to remain in the race. Within hours of the mayor's announcement, the word spread that Curley was more determined to run for the mayoralty than ever before. "The stories that have come to his ears from the mayor's friends threatening him with political extinction if he did not retire have aroused his fighting blood," the Boston Evening Transcript reported, "and made reconciliation impossible."

Speaking before the members of the Tammany Club, Curley revealed the brutal directness of the approach he intended to take. "For one hundred or more times in the last two years," Curley said, "the mayor has told me that he would not be a candidate for reelection. I entered the campaign three weeks before Mayor Fitzgerald announced his candidacy. I am not opposing him. He is opposing me. I had supposed Fitzgerald would keep his word, although I knew he had broken his word with others; but I supposed he would keep his promise with a tried friend." Curley ended his address by promising that he was in the contest to stay and would get out for no man. At this point, only death, he dramatically concluded, could draw him from the contest.

Curley's surprising obstinacy created a sensation along Newspaper Row as seasoned observers predicted the most vicious and brutal campaign in the history of the city. Yet it is unlikely that anyone, least of all Fitzgerald, could have imagined the ugly turn the struggle would take, threatening to undo everything the mayor had accomplished.

There was at this time another man in the city who had his own reasons for coveting Fitzgerald's defeat. This was Daniel Coakley, the small handsome lawyer who had vowed years before to take revenge upon Fitzgerald for the remorseless role the mayor had played in the shattering downfall of the undertaker Michael J. Mitchell. All these years, as the story is told, the thought of Fitzgerald's treachery "had gnawed at Coakley," and nothing would content him until the score was evened.

Stories differ as to when Coakley first approached Curley with the astounding piece of information on which the election would turn. Some say that Coakley had imparted his mischievous knowledge immediately after Fitzgerald's announcement, in the hopes that it would encourage Curley to stay his course. Others say that Curley had already taken his stand to remain in the race before he received the startling news. Whichever version is correct, it is clear that Curley listened with greedy interest as Coakley unburdened himself of his tale.

It seemed that sometime earlier that fall Coakley had been visited in his law offices by a triumphantly beautiful young woman named Elizabeth Ryan. Acting on the advice of a friend, she had come to ask Coakley to represent her in a $50,000 damage suit she wished to bring against a Mr. Henry Mansfield, the proprietor of the popular Ferncroft Inn in Middleton, for his alleged breach of promise to marry her.

According to her story, she was a good girl corrupted by a bad world. She had grown up with eleven sisters and brothers on a small farm in Connecticut, where she had lived a wholesome life until one luckless day when she saw the bright lights of New York City for the first time. As she portrayed it, she learned her first lesson in misplaced ambition sitting at a table in a restaurant in New York. Surrounded by glimmering lights, good music, fine food and wonderful service, she suddenly felt out of place in her simple clothes, and all at once a host of burning desires kindled within her heart, desires for expensive dresses and fancy hats, for sparkling pendants and diamond rings. Leaving her country ways and her religious scruples behind her, she painted her lips, reddened her cheeks and found herself a job as a cloak model in a department store. And then came the day when she was invited by a group of friends to join them on a weekend jaunt to Boston. She traveled on a sleeper train for the first time, then attended the traditional Harvard–Yale football game and stayed the night at the Lenox Hotel. The following day the entire party journeyed together by auto to the Ferncroft Inn, where "the event of her life" occurred: she met the man of her dreams whom she "intended to live with forever"—Harry Mansfield.

At the time of their first meeting, in the fall of 1907, the forty-year-old Mansfield was an agreeably wealthy man, owner of a shellac business and a wholesale drugstore as well as the Ferncroft Inn. While the truth of his long relationship with Elizabeth Ryan will never be known—the testimony at the subsequent trial on the central question of whether he ever promised to marry her was sufficiently contradictory as to produce a hung jury—all the witnesses agreed that Mansfield was instantly taken by Miss Ryan's beauty. All that first night, they said, he held her hand and kept his arm around her, and in the course of the following years she spent months at a time at the Ferncroft Inn, where he showered costly gifts upon her. She was variously employed there, under the name of Toodles, as a cigarette girl, a cashier and a professional enter-tainer whose job it was to lure selected guests from the restaurant into the upstairs gambling room, where roulette was illegally played.

The importance of all this was intensified for Coakley when Toodles listed the names of various other admirers she had attracted while she was there, among them the mayor of the city, John F. Fitzgerald. Viva-cious and cheerful, he would always tell her how rich in beauty she was and would often invite her to join his party, where he would pull her close to him and flirt with her for hours. Proud of their friendship, he pursued her shamelessly; when they danced, he would press her tightly against his chest and smother her with kisses.

No sooner had she volunteered this information than Coakley knew he had his weapon. The only question was how to use it. It is difficult to make clear what a subtle and significant power this story suddenly placed in the hands of the scheming Coakley, who was an acknowledged master at the technique of insinuation, of distilling the poison of scandal drop by drop, of hinting obliquely at evil doings. (All this would be made clear in the decade ahead when Coakley would be disbarred from practicing law for participating in a conspiracy known as "the badger game." As the clever intrigue was later described in the Suffolk County Court, a man of some substance would be led by a young woman in Coakley's employ to a hotel bedroom. Sometime later, when the two were in a clearly compromising position, their room would be broken into by a policeman who was also being paid by Coakley. Charged with fornica-tion and contributing to the delinquency of a minor, the man or his attorney would soon come to know that Mr. Dan Coakley had a remark-able relationship with the district attorney, Joseph Pelletier—who would also be disbarred—which, for a substantial fee, he would be willing to use in order to get the charges nol-prossed, or dropped.)

Had he searched the world, Coakley could not have found a more fitting revenge, one entrapment for another. While there was nothing in Toodles' testimony on Fitzgerald that would stand up in a court of law, the mayor lived in a world where people thought he was a certain kind of man. Just one cartooned image of "the Little Napoleon" kissing the voluptuous Toodles—with her enormous chest daringly revealed, her painted cheeks and her huge brown eyes—would be enough to transform this pillar of the community into a fool. Interestingly enough, there was no evidence that Fitzgerald had anything to worry about beyond his kisses. For her part, Toodles was clearly consumed by her passion for Mansfield. And though the subsequent trial, which took place in January of 1915, received full and lurid treatment in the city press for over a month, producing front-page headlines ("FITZ KISSING RYAN," "TOODLES COLLAPSES ON STAND") larger than the latest reports of the raging war in Europe, Fitzgerald was mentioned only once, in the testimony of a seventy-two-year-old man who claimed that he had seen the mayor kissing Toodles on a September night in 1912. Yet, if Fitzgerald was an innocent victim being drawn into a trap, it was, Coakley argued, precisely what he deserved for the unforgivable sin he had committed against poor Michael Mitchell by letting that honest man fall into the snare of a conviction *he* did not deserve.

In deciding to go to Curley with his information about Fitzgerald's flirtation with Toodles, Coakley gambled wisely. There were not many politicians who would have been willing to employ such crass political pressure. While the personal attack was one of the oldest of political strategies, it was generally assumed that these attacks would be kept within the bounds of understood rules. But Curley was not a man to be limited by convention. Master of the unorthodox technique, Curley distinctly appreciated that the only chance he had of besting Fitzgerald, who would clearly beat him at the polls, was to match his stronger will against the other man's fear of humiliation and *force* him to withdraw from the race. It was a risky maneuver, for if Fitzgerald called his bluff and stayed the course, Curley might well have foundered on the rock of bad taste, losing not only the election at hand but even more, his chances for the future.

On the first day of December, Curley had a black-bordered letter delivered to the house on Welles Avenue, informing Mrs. Fitzgerald that unless the mayor withdrew from the race the family's reputation would be exposed to the scandal of her husband's relationship with a twenty-three-year-old cigarette girl named Toodles. From that moment on, everything was in confusion in the Fitzgerald household. While the Fitzgeralds had weathered storms before—popular rumors had long asserted that John Fitzgerald chased after pretty women—this time Josie took it into her head that the only way to avert public humiliation was for her husband to get out of the race.

For Fitzgerald the situation was hopeless. On the one hand, he believed he was being unfairly accused and the sense of injustice rankled. As he later confided to Clem Norton, it was the worst moment of his life when he walked into the house and found his wife standing in the hallway with an expression of furious indignation on her face and the infamous letter in her hand. Worse still was the look of pain on his favorite daughter's face as she stood in silence behind her mother. Still hoping he could ride out the storm, Fitzgerald tried to persuade Josie that if only she could pull herself together they could stand their ground with pride and call the blackmailer's bluff. To back away now would be to cut himself off forever from the respect of the bosses; it would be a cowardly surrender to an unscrupulous villain.

Fitzgerald's arguments might have persuaded Josie at an earlier moment, but this time was different. From the first, she had been strongly opposed to his running again, and now, with this ugly threat before them, there was no doubt in her mind. For years now he had left her to manage the house and the children while he gave himself entirely to his political ambitions, begrudging even the time he had to sleep. In return, his hard-earned success had provided her with a luxurious household and all the servants she needed to manage it. It was a bargain, and for the most part she had accepted her position without complaint. But public humiliation was the one thing she refused to risk. For if the aura of respectability within which the family moved was dissipated, then everything they had built would be lost.

The hopelessness of the situation kept Fitzgerald from sleeping. Haunted by the knowledge that he was caught in a trap with no escape, he felt, he told his private secretary, Eddie Moore, as if he were walking in a nightmare. And all this time, life had to be lived and engagements kept until he decided once and for all how to respond to Curley's threat. Finally, his body betrayed the siege against his mind: the pressure was too much, even for a man of his strength, and he literally collapsed.

On the day before his collapse he was roused from his bed at 3 A.M. by the news that a devastating fire was raging at the Arcadia lodging house on the corner of Laconia and Washington streets. Trapped in the six-story brick structure were 170 lodgers who had been sleeping when the flames seethed through the old building, barring all the means of exit. Among the first to enter the building when the flames had burned themselves out, Fitzgerald was "visibly shocked" at the scene of horror: twenty-four men were lying dead in the ruins, the bodies of four others were splayed upon the sidewalk, where they had been killed in an attempt to escape by jumping, and more than two dozen others were badly injured.

Appalled by the deplorable conditions he found—"scores of unfortunate men sleeping in double decked beds in dimly lighted rooms that were not provided with adequate means of escape"—the mayor issued a passionate protest against the private owners of the Arcadia and announced that he would immediately undertake a personal inspection tour of all the other cheap lodging houses in the city. By the end of the all-day tour, Fitzgerald's worst fears were confirmed; so bad were the conditions he saw that he ordered several of the biggest lodging houses closed and promised that in their place the state would provide decent and safe sleeping quarters for all the poor and unfortunate men and women who had been forced to live amid such squalor.

All the next day, Thursday, December 4, the mayor worked with the district attorney and the fire authorities on the investigation of the Arcadia fire. By nightfall, reporters observed, the fifty-year-old mayor was feeling unusually weak and was advised by his secretary to go home, but he insisted on making a second tour of the worst lodging houses to ensure that his orders were being carried out. It was at one of these dingy places, the old Union lodging house on Washington Street, that his body finally gave way. Since they were traveling with him on the tour, the reporters on the scene were able to describe his collapse in elaborate detail, though they had no idea of the mental anguish that had preceded the physical strain.

"Mayor Fitzgerald collapsed and narrowly escaped serious injury," the *Boston Herald* reported, "when he fell headlong down a flight of stairs" and "came within an ace of falling over the railing to a narrow hallway 20 feet below." He was just about to start down from the fourth floor when he suddenly succumbed to his exhaustion and fell. "This would have meant serious injury if not death," the *Herald* went on, had the mayor's secretary, Edward Moore, not caught him before he fell over the rail. As it was, "he struck his head heavily against the rail and his helpless body crashed against the brick wall and then fell limp into the arms of a reporter."

"For several minutes," the reporter from *Practical Politics* wrote,

Secretary Moore feared that the city's chief executive was going to die in harness. It was not until he was well on his way home in the auto that there were any signs of recovery and an examination by his physician, Dr. Gannett, showed that the mayor had overtaxed his brain and body to such an extent that he must temporarily quit his activities if he wishes to fully recover.

In the days that followed, reporters and politicians alike monitored Fitzgerald's condition closely, but information on the mayor's health proved as elusive as predictions on his plans for the campaign. To the surprise of those who had known him over the years "as a man of iron constitution," he seemed to be rallying slowly. For days, no one beyond the immediate family was allowed to see the patient and the bulletins issued were not encouraging. Finally, in answer to the many callers who were telephoning in to ask after her father's health, Rose admitted, said a reporter, that

> on account of the Mayor's failing to get his natural rest, he had not improved so rapidly as had been expected. From the start, she said, the Mayor had had great difficulty in sleeping, both on account of his illness and also owing to the fact that the Arcadia tragedy and the horrible sights he witnessed while investigating the lodging house conditions were preying on his mind.

In this unquiet time, not knowing that his goal had largely been effected by the letter alone and the paralyzing breakdown it had produced, Curley determined to shed some further blood. According to his own account, he decided to deliver the first of three public lectures which he had previously planned as a means of contrasting Mayor Fitzgerald and certain famous men in history. Prepared with the help of a noted Fordham University professor, James Walsh, the first of these was entitled "Graft in Ancient Times versus Graft in Modern Times." The lecture opened with the tale of the Finance Commission's investigation of the mayor's brother, James T. Fitzgerald, "who for years had been spared the expenses of paying his water bills to the city" by the simple but illegal act of removing the water meter from his three-decker home. Thereupon Professor Walsh related an analogous tale about a great public fountain in ancient Rome. Trying to discover why the huge fountain's flow had been reduced to a trickle, an investigation revealed that for years some of the leading Roman tribunes had been stealthily tapping for their private use an aqueduct leading into the fountain. So, the lecture concluded, history keeps repeating itself.

If Curley seemed to be simply toying with Fitzgerald, the intensity of his purpose was fully revealed when he announced the titles of his next two lectures. The second, he said, would be "Great Lovers in History: From Cleopatra to Toodles," while the third would deal with "Libertines in History from Henry the Eighth to the Present Day."

As it turned out, Curley found it unnecessary to deliver these other two lectures, for on December 18, reluctantly and with a great sense of melancholy, Mayor Fitzgerald announced that he was withdrawing from the race on the advice of his physician, who had urged upon him the absolute necessity of a prolonged rest.

The news of the mayor's withdrawal created a sensation. Coming at a time when his reelection was considered "as certain as anything in politics could be," his action took the city by surprise, leading reporters to accept his word that health and family considerations had prompted his withdrawal. "Boston is deprived . . . but the city's loss will be his family's gain . . ." the *Herald* wrote. And from the *Boston American* came the suggestion that the big reasons for his withdrawal could be found in the "petticoat element," in the women of his family, in particular his wife and eldest daughter, who had finally put their feet firmly down and said he could not risk the strain of another campaign.

With Fitzgerald out, Curley's dominance was assured, and he went on to become the thirty-eighth mayor of Boston and from there to forge an astonishing political career which saw him elected mayor three more times, congressman twice and governor once. What might have been can, of course, never be known. But if Fitzgerald had stood his ground and accepted the risk to his reputation, it is possible that he rather than Curley would have emerged the victor; and had he continued his successful career, it is possible that he, rather than Curley, would have been immortalized as the hero of Edwin O'Connor's *The Last Hurrah*. Just as conceivably, Fitzgerald's reelection to City Hall in 1914 might have given him a stronger base from which to launch his next campaign against Henry Cabot Lodge for the Senate in 1916, an election he would come within 33,000 votes of winning. And if Fitzgerald had become the Senator from Massachusetts in 1916 instead of Lodge, the history of the country and indeed of the entire world might have been different, for it was from that very Senate seat that Lodge played his decisive role in the crushing defeat of the Covenant of the League of Nations, the defeat that, in President Woodrow Wilson's words, "broke the heart of the world."

As it was, however, Fitzgerald's withdrawal from the race at the height of his power cost him the esteem of his fellow politicians and left his name forever under a cloud of gossip. For eventually the word spread that Fitzgerald had lacked the capacity to stand up to his enemies, that he had been frightened away by "the woman question" and that he had lost the will to wield his power. And then, having lost the respect of his peers, Fitzgerald lost his confidence in himself; despite a number of comeback attempts in 1916, 1918, 1922, 1930 and 1942, he never won an election again.

The Toodles incident seems to have affected relationships within the Fitzgerald family as well. As Mary Heffernan heard the story told by

Emily Hannon, Josie's sister, Rose was profoundly disturbed, far more than her mother, by the revelations about her father and some beautiful young girl who was, after all, only twenty-three years old, the same age as Rose. While Josie had long since made her peace with Fitzgerald's passionate nature, exacting her own penance in her own way, Rose had continued to idolize her father, never even allowing herself to imagine in him the existence of human weakness. But in the aftermath of the withdrawal, although she felt sorry for her father for losing his kingdom over what seemed to be simply a kiss, she also felt angry. While to Fitzgerald his flirtatious relationship with Toodles was doubtless quite apart from his far deeper love and need for his daughter, signifying nothing more perhaps than a chase after beauty and youth, it was hard for Rose to see it that way.

In the long run, however, the tawdry incident had a positive influence on Rose, for it left her freer to shape a life of her own. For seven years she had been struggling with the weight of her father's displeasure with Joe, powerless to break away from either man. But now, having seen her father so completely caught up in his own concerns, the whole question of her marriage presented itself in a different aspect. "Though she still did not conceive of any behavior toward her father that was disrespectful," Mary Heffernan suggested, "she began at this time to realize that the choice of a husband was ultimately *her* choice and not her parents', since *she* would have to live the marriage and not they. While she had given up Wellesley College for her father, she would not give up Joe Kennedy as well."

A confirmation of these speculations presented itself in the shape of a small article which appeared in the Boston papers eleven days after Fitzgerald's withdrawal. Under the caption "The Mayor's Daughter Is to Wed," the article reported that the many friends of Mayor Fitzgerald were discussing the rumors of the engagement of his daughter, Miss Rose, suggesting a direct connection between Rose's acceptance of Joe's proposal of marriage and her father's fall from grace.

While the Fitzgeralds were absorbed in their own affairs in the fall of 1913, Joe Kennedy was deciding on the course of his career. The time had come, he determined, to leave his job as an examiner so that he could get "a start on his life work." While he found all the various aspects of the job "fascinating," he longed for an opportunity to be on his own, in a position where he could decide policies and direct others.

The opportunity came in the fall of 1913 when P. J. Kennedy's bank, the Columbia Trust Company, found itself threatened by a hostile take-over by the First Ward National, the largest bank in East Boston. According to Rose Kennedy, the First Ward offered Columbia's stockholders "a good price" and "most of them—holding a majority of the stock—wanted to accept." For P. J. Kennedy and Alfred Wellington, however, the takeover presaged the end of a dream, the dream of a thriving neighborhood bank run in the best interests of the local people. But with the president of the bank, Frank Wood, lined up on the side of the merger, and without enough money of their own to buy out the others, there seemed little hope of blocking the deal. Still wanting to try, however, and believing it would be a good experience for his son, P.J. called upon Joe to organize the fight. It was the perfect situation for Joe, allowing him to protect his father and his friend from being hurt while at the same time affording him the chance to advance his ambitions.

Reckoning he would need at least $100,000 to stave off the takeover, Joe set to work with animating spirit, turning first to his Hickey relatives, his three favorite uncles, Jim, John and Fred, who had adored him from the day he was born, and his spinster aunt, Katie, who kept house for his Uncle Jim. From there he made the rounds of his neighbors and his friends, slowly building up the war chest he would need to mount his resistance. At the same time, he approached every person who held stock in Columbia and tried to persuade each to change his mind. In many cases he was unsuccessful, but he did manage, by appealing to local pride and ethnic identity, to collect the proxies of a small group of Irish stockholders.

After two weeks of unremitting effort, however, he was still far short of controlling a majority, since the largest block of stock remained in the hands of the Sullivan family, the descendants of Columbia's first president, John H. Sullivan.

Joe calculated that he would need $15,000 additional in order to buy out the Sullivan shares at a better price than the First Ward was offering. Having exhausted every source he knew, he turned to a man he had met only two or three times, Eugene Thayer, the young president of the prestigious Merchants National Bank, one of the largest financial organizations in the city.

Born into one of Boston's oldest Brahmin families, schooled at Groton, Harvard '04, member of the Somerset Club, Eugene Thayer seemed at first an unlikely target for the young Irishman's appeal. But Thayer was one of the bankers whom Kennedy had impressed in the course of his examining days. Priding himself on his judgment of men, Thayer had decided the first time he saw him that Kennedy was an exceptional young man.

The Merchants National Bank was a handsome stone building located on the corner of State and Congress, across the street from the Old

State House in the center of Boston's financial district. Years later, Joe would recall the apprehension he felt, his body shivering from the cold January day, when he entered the magnificent main banking room of this newly built structure, its walls lined with Botticino marble, and stepped behind the rail which led to the president's quarters. In his heart, he knew that the entire future of the Columbia Trust Company had come down to this single moment: if he was unable to persuade Thayer to lend him the bank's money, he had nowhere else to turn and time was running out. It was now late in the day on Thursday, and the showdown meeting at Columbia had been called for the following Tuesday, January 20, 1914.

For all his nervousness, Joe maintained a remarkable outward dignity, and after he had crisply explained the situation to Thayer, Thayer held out his hand and smiled broadly. "The money is yours," Thayer said. "Come back tomorrow morning and it will be here on my desk waiting for you."

On Monday morning, January 19, 1914, both the First Ward National and Columbia's president Frank Wood, aware they had been outmaneuvered, retired from the battle. From that moment on, Joe's election to the presidency was assured. In the eyes of both P. J. Kennedy and Alfred Wellington, the only other contenders for the position—as P.J. was vice-president and Wellington the treasurer—Joe was the one who had single-handedly saved the bank; if he wanted the office, it should be his. And all the rest of the shareholders present at the annual meeting on Tuesday agreed; by a unanimous vote Joseph P. Kennedy was elected to the presidency of the Columbia Trust Company.

Then the young man to whom all eyes now turned stood up and presented his slate for the new board of directors. There remained only the tricky problem of providing a promotion of some kind for Alfred Wellington, lest he feel a relative loss of stature with the sudden change in young Joe's position. This difficulty was resolved with ease when P. J. Kennedy declined reelection as vice-president, opening the door for Joe to recommend Wellington to the double role of vice-president and treasurer, a promotion which was heralded within the banking world as deserved in every way.

The next morning Joe awoke to find himself the subject of admiring articles in all the Boston papers. Struck by the fiery vehemence of Kennedy's youth, the reporters hailed his election as making him "the youngest man to hold the presidency of a banking house in the state of Massachusetts." At a time when most bank presidents were perceived as snowy-haired figures long past their prime, young Joe's triumphant struggle for control captivated reporters and readers alike. In the handsome picture which accompanied the stories, Joe seemed to glow with intensity. He was wearing a brushed-wool suit and a round-collared shirt; his eyes were shining and his hair was combed smoothly back from his forehead. While the caption identified him as the new president of a bank, the wide-eyed innocence he projected seemed more befitting a young priest newly ordained.

Nor did the publicity stop in Boston. The large green family scrapbook contains over two dozen clippings about "the youngest bank president," collected from remote papers all over the country. Oddly enough, the farther away from Boston the story spread, the more distinctive young Joe's accomplishments became. From being hailed in Boston as the youngest bank president in the state, he went on in Cedar Rapids, Iowa, to become the youngest bank president in the country, and by Sidney Falls, South Dakota, he had become the youngest bank president in the world. In the same westward movement, the Columbia Trust Company grew from a small neighborhood bank to one of the largest and soundest institutions in the country.

What had begun as a straightforward local news story became, in the hands of the Hearst Company, which distributed it through its national service, an inflated feature article, the first in a long series of features that would follow the lives and careers of generations of the Kennedy family. Having to justify their focus on Joe to a national audience, the Hearst writers simply called into being the national qualities they wanted Joe to possess. What did it matter if in their enthusiasm certain extravagant claims were made? After all, it was a good story—even if, in the span of time it took for the series to appear, it became an anachronism. Published in the fall of 1916, over two years after Joe's accession to the presidency, when he was twenty-eight years old, the Hearst series still presented "the boy banker" as twenty-five, as if time had somehow stopped on the day he became Columbia's president.

Apparently, Joe took the national publicity in stride and was even able to laugh a little at himself. His friend Tom Campbell long remembered that "the story contained a statement that he worked 14–16 hours a day at the bank. A bank clerk from Brooklyn wrote him and said that he had looked up the statement of the bank and if it took him 14 to 16 hours a day to manage that bank, he must be either 'stupid or dumb.' Telling this story, Joe laughingly said, 'Of course, he was dead right.' "

Still, however exaggerated the facts were, the story remained a good story of youth replacing age, though the more significant transition went unrecognized by every reporter at the time, for it involved a shift in the inner balance of the Kennedy family which could be understood only with the passage of time. Looking back now, we can see that when P.J.

offered and Joe accepted his resignation as vice-president of the bank, a reversal was taking place in the relations between father and son. From that moment on, Joe would be the guiding force in the family, while his father, having labored hard and long, would stand by, his pipe in his mouth, admiring but never interfering.

There is not the slightest shred of evidence that P. J. Kennedy was embittered by this transition; on the contrary, his being eclipsed by his son only made him feel proud, and his pride only deepened as his son's fame increased.

While young Kennedy had walked through the double glass doors and up the marble steps into the handsome brick structure more than a hundred times before, his first entry as the bank's president made a firm impression on his mind. He later recalled "the deep satisfaction" he took in "watching the figures of all the men and women as they moved about the floor in the course of their jobs." Along the wall stood the tellers' cages behind which both the tellers and the bookkeepers stood as they counted the cash, posted the people's accounts and labored over the bank's ledgers. To the right, their desks slightly raised above the floor by a small platform, sat the officers of the bank, talking with clients, opening new accounts and making loans. As he stood in the center of the floor, with the wintry sun streaming in through the tall bubble-glass windows, Joe was much affected by the bustling spirit of the place and by the curious realization that all these people scurrying busily about were now working for him.

The new president's first task was to make his presence felt in all the decisions of the bank and in the community at large. He had learned a great deal about the running of banks through his experience as a bank examiner, and he recognized that the Columbia Trust was a highly personal banking institution whose success depended upon the intimate relationship with the people it served. Over the years the bank had built for itself a solid reputation as a people's bank where every person would receive good and sympathetic treatment. Now the time had come to build this strength; the new president's first goal was to increase the number and the amount of bank deposits. To this end, Kennedy made himself accessible to anyone who walked inside the door; he deliberately adopted a hard-working, down-to-earth style which contrasted sharply with the reserved image of the typical banker. He would reach the bank no later than eight o'clock and would lunch at his desk on crackers and milk, his sleeves rolled up, and there were many nights when the light from his desk could be seen from the street, welcoming late callers.

Joe also understood that a bank's deposit business is generated by the loans it makes, since every time a bank makes a loan to a customer it creates a demand deposit for him. With his subtle mind, Joe realized early on that the key to his success as a banker would depend almost entirely on increasing the number of good loans the bank made—a good loan defined simply as a loan that was paid back. Recognizing that the basic judgments a banker makes are based as much upon the character of the borrower as upon a list of his assets, Joe prided himself on the strength of his ability to gauge a man's potential.

At the same time, his experience as a bank examiner had lessened his willingness to take risks. As he studied the ledgers of the bank, he found too many uncollected loans still on the books; many of them, he discovered, had been arranged through his father's goodwill. Approaching the task of lending from the perspective of a ward boss, P.J. was not as good at collecting his loans as he was at making them. As a consequence, the bank was suffering. Joe maintained a more cynical attitude toward his customers: he kept close tabs on all his borrowers, he checked out their businesses, he asked around, and he listened to the local gossip.

Nor did Joe cringe at the prospect of calling a loan, as he later made clear in a blunt letter to his father.

> Some immediate steps should be taken on the question of getting additional collateral from John Bates. My own feeling is that Bates is not on the level about paying these loans or reducing them. He owes everybody and unless we go after him very hard, the first thing we know he is going into bankruptcy or is going to die and we are going to take very heavy losses. I have some inside information on this.

During his three-year tenure at the bank, Columbia's deposits increased from $580,654 to $1,055,759, while the amount of money Columbia loaned out went up from $516,112 to $822,109. And when the bank examiners came in to evaluate the bank in 1918, they discovered only three small loans which merited a negative rating as being "of doubtful value" or "secured by collateral of doubtful value."

With Joe's striking change in status, Fitzgerald finally consented to his daughter's marriage. Though he was still troubled by the match, prudence now required that he gracefully yield. In full possession of his conciliatory powers, he conceded that his only hope in preserving a close relationship with his favorite child lay in accepting her desire to marry this remarkable young man. So on June 13, 1914, "the Honorable John F. Fitzgerald and Mrs. Fitzgerald announced the betrothal of their eldest daughter Rose to Mr. Joseph P. Kennedy, Harvard '12."

Now that she was officially engaged, Rose sent off a round of letters to her friends and acquaintances telling them the long-expected news. From the wistful responses she received, it is clear how absolutely central marriage was in those days to the deepest dreams of the young women who made up the circle of her friends. "I hope the next best man . . . is waiting for me," Eleanor King wrote in a letter filled with yearning for the expected completion that only marriage could bring. A similar craving characterized the response of Cecile Murray, a classmate of Rose's at Manhattanville, who conjectured how "perfectly wonderful" it must feel to be engaged:

> You are the first of the famous 1910 graduates to become engaged and announced so you have upheld the honor of this class. We all had been fearing that Manhattanville had sent forth into the world of 1910 not very interesting girls. Now we know that 1910 is all right for dear Rose is engaged. All is well.

The languid summer months that followed were a special time for the young couple, a time for blending anticipation and recollection, a time for bridal showers, bachelor parties and the mutual avowal of love. "In those days," Rose recorded in her memoirs, "we unquestioningly believed that life was meant to have certain basic forms and structures. We felt that 'To everything there is a season, and a time for every purpose.' There was courtship, there was the discovery of love, there was engagement, there was marriage, there was parenthood: Each in its season and marked by traditions and rituals which, believe me, were sources of strength for young people."

The period of the betrothal came to an end on October 7, 1914, when Rose Elizabeth Fitzgerald became the wife of Joseph Patrick Kennedy in a traditional Catholic ceremony performed by William Cardinal O'Connell in his exquisite private chapel. Only the immediate families of the bride and groom were present at the early-morning Mass, which was followed by a wedding breakfast at the Fitzgerald house for about seventy-five guests. For a young couple descended from two prominent families, whose marriage was said to have excited "much interest throughout the city," the wedding was startlingly simple. This, after all, was the young lady whose debutante party had been heralded as the event of the year and been attended by more than 450 persons. And this was the first marriage in either of the two families. Was it simply, as Rose suggests, that neither the bride nor the groom wanted "a public fiesta"? Or did the plainness of the event reflect a lingering political shame on the part of Fitzgerald?

The young couple took their departure in the early afternoon under a bright autumn sky and traveled to White Sulphur Springs, West Virginia, where Joe had made reservations at the majestic Greenbrier Hotel. Surrounded by splendid mountains, winding streams and flowering meadows, the Greenbrier was distinguished for both the natural beauty of its setting and the scientific quality of its baths, which were said to rival the best of the European spas such as Aix-les-Bains and Baden-Baden.

For the next three weeks, Joe and Rose would spend hardly an hour apart. In the crispness of the early-morning air, they would stroll along one of the dozens of picturesque paths which led off from the hotel and took them over the rolling hills to the edge of the mountain streams below, where they would sit on a stone and wait for the sounds of the birds and the rustle of the trees. After breakfast on the terrace, they would head out once more, two athletic figures with their golfing bags, heading for a course which was considered one of the most beautiful in the world. And for a couple who enjoyed playing cards there were always people gathered in the card room, which was connected by a crossway to the billiard room, the gentlemen's writing room and the central lobby of the hotel. Then, at night, when the light gradually faded, dinner was served in a magnificent dining room finished in Caen stone and illuminated by hundreds of candles. And later on one of these nights, from the best we can tell by the timing of the birth, the first of their nine children was conceived.

On returning to Boston, the young Kennedys settled into a modest gray house with clapboard siding which stood on a shaded street in the suburb of Brookline and which Joe had purchased the month before the wedding. While most of their young friends were starting their married lives in rented apartments, Joe decided that his first home had to be a house. "From the very beginning," Rose later asserted, "home was the center of his world and the only place that really, finally counted in his plans. Moreover, . . . he had a strong need for privacy, for independence, for being able to choose the people he wanted to be with in close association." And in choosing Brookline, Joe was choosing a predominantly middle-class and overwhelmingly Protestant suburb.

It was early November when Joe and Rose moved into their new home. The swing of the winter social season in Boston had just begun, but with Joe working at the bank twelve hours a day, six days a week, there was little time for socializing. There were, to be sure, weekly visits to the symphony, and Sunday dinners with the P. J. Kennedys in Winthrop, but if Rose had envisaged her early married life as a continuation of her girlhood days, filled with parties and balls, first-night boxes at the theater and trips to all parts of the world, she must have been sorely disappointed. For while she continued to see her girlfriends at various luncheons and at the Ace of Clubs, the life she was leading was undoubtedly quieter and more solitary than the life she had known in the white mansion on the hill where she had reigned as the daughter of the mayor and the belle of Catholic society.

There was little time to dwell on these matters, however, for Rose soon discovered she was going to be a mother, the "sacred role" for which she had been systematically trained for years by the nuns of the Sacred Heart. As the spring turned into summer, Joe rented an airy gray house in Hull on a sandy hook of land that curved far out into Massachusetts Bay. There, surrounded by the fresh sea air, and by her parents and a number of their friends who had also rented houses at the beach, Rose awaited the birth of her first child, due at the end of July. In those years, Hull's Nantasket Beach was one of the most beautiful summer resorts in the state, a blend of Monte Carlo and Coney Island, with the gleam of a thousand lights shimmering from the dozens of hotels, restaurants and gambling rooms which adjoined Paragon Park, and with the sky and the sea around and beyond.

In common with the way most women gave birth in those days, Rose had her baby at home with the help of attendants, in her case two doctors, a trained nurse and a housemaid. The moment the first contractions were felt, the nurse came to the house to prepare all the paraphernalia and supplies that the doctors would need—"the fresh sheets, towels, ice bags and pots and kettles of hot water." Then, when the labor was well established, the doctors arrived to administer the ether which would put Rose to sleep through all the final phases of her delivery. It was also in keeping with the custom of the time that Joe did not participate in his wife's childbirth, either by lending her support during her labor or by being present during her delivery. At that incredible moment when his own child was emerging from the birth canal and taking its first breath of air, Joe was doing what most expectant fathers were expected to do: he was pacing the floor in a separate room. Finally, on the morning of July 25, just as the clock sounded the last stroke of the hour of ten, the doctors stepped out into the sitting room to announce the event. "A boy," they said to the father. And a rugged little boy he was, weighing in at nearly ten pounds. He was handsome and alert, his eyes "bright blue, his complexion . . . fair and there were dimples in his cheeks."

If reporters failed to record the father's response to the newborn child, it was because their eyes were fixed upon a different star. "It's Grandpa Now," the *Boston Post* announced, setting the tone for a spate of stories which detailed everything John Fitzgerald felt about the birth of the boy as if he were the one who had done all the work. As the story was told in the leading paper, Fitzgerald was out on the beach playing with his son Fred and a score of other children when a messenger came running across the sands and the breakers with the news "It's a boy, it's a boy," at which point Grandpa was off for the house "with the speed of a crack sprinter."

No sooner had he reached the house and confirmed the news than he called the press to announce that he was quite "the happiest man" in the world. "Feeling fine and just as young as ever," he chuckled, "though of course I'm another generation removed now. No, I don't know what we'll make of the youngster. . . . He can yell all right and I'm sure he'd make a good man on the platform some day. . . . Is he going into politics? Well, . . . of course he *is* going to be President of the United States, his mother and father have already decided that he is going to Harvard, where he will play on the football and baseball teams and incidentally take all the scholastic honors. Then he's going to be a captain of industry until it's time for him to be President for two or three terms. Further than that has not been decided. He may act as mayor of Boston and governor of Massachusetts for a while on his way to the presidential chair."

If we are accustomed to such assertions by proud parents and grandparents at a time such as this, the remarkable thing is that the reporters seemed genuinely struck by the radiant happiness they saw on Fitzgerald's face that day. And the best was yet to come. For, strangely enough, while nothing had prepared him for the way he would love and be loved by his grandchildren, he would be remembered all his life as "the best grandfather a grandchild could ever have." Having grandchildren seemed to speak to his need for affirmation and renewal, allowing age and youth to blend together in joy and celebration. By recovering what it meant to be a child, Fitzgerald was able to retain his capacity for growth through all the years of his long life.

Compared with the unbroken pleasures of grandfathering, the experiences Fitzgerald had with his own children, particularly his sons, were filled with frustration. In his own household, "the Little Napoleon" was an overwhelming figure, whose sons would remain "Honey Fitz's boys" all their lives: one would eventually drink himself to death, another would stay at a low-level job with the Boston Edison Company and the third would serve as a toll collector on the Mystic River bridge as his nephew prepared for the presidency of the United States.

But as the demands of his own life subsided, something gave way in Fitzgerald's heart which allowed him to let go and love his grandchildren with that kind of nonjudgmental love that was impossible for him as a parent. And the love he gave was returned with overflowing affection as all of his grandchildren spoke of him in glowing terms as "the warmest and most wonderful friend," "the best pal a kid could have," and "the greatest storyteller we ever heard." One by one, they would remember all the things he had taught them when they were young: how to make a snowman, how to build a castle in the sand, how to swim and how to skate. "With Grandpa, everything was special," one of his grandchildren recalled. "With each of us he would mark off special times and special rituals—a fishing trip for one, a baseball game for another, a train trip for a third." And with the magic of his companionship would come all his wonderful tales of the past, communicating to his young admirers a sense of continuity with the mystery of life as it sweeps from generation to generation.

All this, of course, was still to come on that cloudless Sunday in July when the new grandfather held his newborn grandson in his arms. At the time of the birth, none of the family would say what the name of the infant would be, leaving reporters to speculate that he would be named John Fitzgerald Kennedy after his maternal grandfather. But if Fitzgerald was still the more powerful figure on the Boston scene, his son-in-law was indisputably the power in his own family. And Joe Kennedy wanted his firstborn son to carry his own name—Joseph Patrick Kennedy—which in turn would link this golden child of the bright-blue eyes with three generations of Josephs and Patricks, stretching back to the homestead in Ireland whence the first Patrick had come.

# BOOK TWO

# THE KENNEDYS

## (1915-1940)

# CHAPTER 16

# A STRANGER
# AMONG
# FRIENDS

So gentle was the surf along the white sands of New England's shore that tranquil summer of 1915 that the happy young parents of Joseph P. Kennedy, Jr., could not possibly have comprehended the unremitting slaughter of the bitter war that was raging across the Atlantic among all the great powers of Europe, a catastrophic war which would mark the end of one period of history and the beginning of another.

When the first dispatches of the war came to the United States, accompanied by photographs of uniformed soldiers marching to the front, most Americans viewed the struggle as just another in Europe's endless progression of internecine squabbles, far away in distance and even farther away in spirit from the primary concerns of their daily lives. The early inclination of the typical American was to turn his back on what seemed to him a barbaric conflict, a senseless quarrel that would surely come to an end before the first winter's snow. "We assumed it would all be done with," Rose Kennedy recalled, "peace restored, before it could possibly affect our own life together in any direct way."

But with each passing month, as the combatants widened the battle lines and the engagements grew more bloody and more intense, the

European crisis began to dominate the American headlines, and, inevitably, more and more Americans became emotionally involved. From the early stages, the disposition of the American people was to favor the Allied cause, a disposition which was unquestionably shaped by the effective ways in which British propaganda played upon the common heritage of Anglo-Saxon culture in most of the American citizens. But as Harvard historian Donald Fleming has argued, it was not so much "what Englishmen said which made the Americans pro-Ally," it was "what the Central Powers *did*"—the Austrian ultimatum to Serbia, the hasty German declarations of war and the flagrant invasion of neutral Belgium.

Then came the succession of German submarine sinkings, culminating in the torpedo attack on the great British liner *Lusitania*, with a loss of nearly twelve hundred lives. Among those who perished were 128 Americans, including the millionaire Alfred Gwynne Vanderbilt and the theatrical producer Charles Frohman. For a people who still thought of war as a limited exchange between fighting men, the image of women and children drowning at sea stirred an emotional outcry against Germany which became strident.

Moving against the mounting fervor, Joe Kennedy refused to be swayed by the sound of the drum. Others might wish to talk of nothing but battles and guns, but as for him, he preferred to concentrate his attentions on his developing career and his growing family. While the American people gradually came to accept the inevitability of American involvement, Joe, according to Rose, refused to waver in his conviction that the terrible conflict would only bring far-reaching misery upon all its participants.

"Through all the early years of the First World War," Rose recalled, "Joe could never accept the idea that war had a nobility of its own. He could never understand how anyone could really believe that all that killing and bloodshed could ever settle anything. As he saw it, the essence of war was waste and destruction—the destruction of wealth, the destruction of order, the destruction of property and the destruction of lives. And nothing, he believed, could ever be worth all that destruction."

Perhaps a part of Joe's detachment can be explained by his Irish heritage. There were, indeed, quite a few Irish Americans who found it hard to sympathize with Britain's ringing defense of small nations like Belgium, given Britain's treatment of Ireland. And there were other Irish nationalists who went so far as to see in the defeat of Great Britain the shortest route to Ireland's independence. But from what we know about Joe, it would seem that his negative attitude toward the war had roots far deeper than his politics.

As we have described, during the years in which Joe was growing into his manhood he had come to the determination that he would keep his life sacred to himself, his family and his few friends. Having seen the pain his father suffered by sacrificing his personal interests to those of his community, Joe had decided early on that he would build his life on his own foundation without depending on the loyalty of any place or any institution. This conviction was strengthened by his experience at Harvard, an institution which had almost managed to command his loyalty in spite of himself until it rejected him from the inner circle of the life of its clubs. Never making the same mistake twice, he left Harvard with a redoubled determination to forge his own way in his own world, keeping his eye focused more and more sharply on what was of advantage to *him*. Expecting no one beyond his family to sacrifice anything on his behalf, he had no illusions about the glory of sacrifice when the war came. Cool and mature at the age of twenty-six, he was too realistic and too absorbed in his own ambitions to be swept away by a sentiment as vague and remote as patriotism.

A dramatic insight into Joe's early vision of the war comes down to us through an embattled conversation between him and three of his buddies which left such an indelible mark upon Rose that she was still able, sixty years later, to vividly remember the main threads of the prolonged argument. The occasion was a gathering with his friends Bob Potter, Tom Campbell and Bob Fisher on the long holiday weekend which preceded the Fourth of July, 1916. As Kennedy was the only one of his group who was married at the time, it was he who generally took the initiative to bring them together either for dinner at his Brookline home or, as it happened on this occasion, for a weekend stay at his parents' house in Winthrop.

From the affectionate way the four young men greeted one another at the start of the weekend, Rose was certain it would be a joyous reunion. Campbell had spent the past few years at the University of North Carolina, where he was coaching football. Fisher too had received some coaching offers after graduation, but instead he had taken an executive job with a Boston department store, where his advancement had been steady and his future seemed bright. But, of the four classmates, it was Potter, not surprisingly, who stood the farthest along in his career. Like Joe he had entered the world of finance, but, with his family background and his Porcellian connections, he had moved almost immediately into the center of Boston's financial world, landing a plum job with the prestigious National Shawmut Bank, the third-largest bank in Boston, where he was certain to be chosen a vice-president within the year.

There was much for these four old friends to talk about, but, as it happened, the beginning of the great Allied offensive at the Somme

River in France, which was reported in the press all weekend long in spectacular detail, eclipsed all argument about the relative merits of the Boston Red Sox versus the Boston Braves or Woodrow Wilson versus Charles Evans Hughes. Describing it as by far the most extensive military action ever taken since the beginnings of civilization, the early accounts were filled with glowing expectations that this huge offensive, which the British staff had spent six months preparing and which was considered "the last word in scientific warfare," would be *the* decisive battle of the war. Spoken of even before the fact as a historical moment comparable to the Battle of Waterloo, the Battle of the Somme promised once and for all to break through the bloody deadlock in the bitter trench warfare which had absorbed hundreds of thousands of lives and frustrated both the Allies and the Germans since the winter of 1914.

The most important element of the British plan was an immense and "sophisticated" artillery attack against the German front-line trenches which was designed to destroy the German barbed wire, batter their machine guns into silence and force their troops to surrender or to evacuate their positions, so that the main task of the Allied infantry would be merely to walk across "no man's land," go through the breaches in the wire and occupy the deserted trenches. Then, from the safety of the German front-line trenches, the Allies would renew their artillery attack, driving the enemy back from their second trench line to their third, until they were finally forced to evacuate France entirely.

For this tremendous offensive England had prepared nearly two million soldiers, the vast majority of whom had volunteered for service in the autumn of 1914 when, in the words of military historian John Keegan, "an extraordinary enthusiasm to enlist" had seized the male population of the British Isles—from the sons of the nobility and the upper middle class, who deserted the rugby fields of the great public schools of Eton and Harrow and the classrooms of Cambridge and Oxford in such numbers that "emptiness" and "silence" reigned everywhere, to the sons of the miners in the Scottish Lowlands, the furnacemen in Yorkshire and the riveters at Clydeside. Innocent of all experience of war—not for a hundred years had England fought in a Continental war involving all the great powers—and trained in a tradition that translated unpleasant realities into romantic ideals, a generation of England's best young men rushed to participate in this "greatest of all adventures" which held the promise of glorious sacrifice, great marches, happy comradeship and thrilling danger. "It was," Keegan wrote, "a time of intense, almost mystical patriotism," a time of sublime faith and unthinking confidence, a time of innocent love that would never come to England again.

Joe's friends arrived in Winthrop on Friday night, June 30, filled with news of the preliminary artillery bombardment which the British had been concentrating upon the German trenches for an entire week, a bombardment so unprecedented in its degree of fury, its monstrous guns and its huge number of exploding shells (more than a million shells had been fired each day) that clouds of smoke and dust were said to be hanging over the entire field of battle as far as the eye could see. The great offensive was expected to be launched at any moment.

Saturday morning, July 1, dawned hot and steamy in Winthrop, the warmest day of the year, sending the Kennedy party to the beach, where, Rose remembered, "the boys had a wonderful time swimming, playing ball and joking around as if they were still eighteen." Then, just as they were planning to go boating, they saw a crowd of people gathering about a young newsboy. The reason for the flurry of excitement soon became clear, for in the boy's hands were extra editions of the evening *Globe* announcing that at seven-thirty that morning, English time, the great Allied offensive had officially begun. With several copies of the paper under their arms, the men walked back to the house, where their conversation inevitably turned to the one subject where Joe would find himself deeply at odds with his friends, so much so that a barrier would develop between them which would not be lifted for several years.

To a man, Joe's friends, including the Irishman Tommy Campbell, were deeply moved by the stirring accounts of the British offensive. As the story emerged in the papers, the sun had just lifted the morning clouds at 7:30 A.M. when "great waves of men," the finest body of soldiers England had ever produced, "sprang from the trenches" and rushed forward toward their goal, singing "the tunes they used to sing on the drill grounds at home after they responded to Kichener's call." Tearing across the uneven ground to where the first line of German trenches stood, they were met with an unexpected hurricane of German shells, but still they advanced, "cheering through the machine gun fire as if it were just the splashing of rain." So violent was the German resistance that many thousands of young Britons dropped on the field, but the others went on, "with a spirit of self sacrifice beyond the ordinary courage of men," *The New York Times* reported. In the words of one wounded soldier, "they went across toppingly"; wave after wave advanced until a score of soldiers finally converged upon a German hole, leaping into the enemy trench with fixed bayonets and "with a whoop on their lips."

It was a scene of "terrible beauty," the *New York Times* correspondent reported. "There was a thrill in the air, a thrill from the meaning of attack." The *Boston Post*, while admitting that the German resistance was far more intense than the British staff had expected, reminded its readers that the British authorities were prepared to face an immense roll of dead and wounded, possibly running into the hundreds of thousands, "if they could achieve their object and drive the Germans from France and Belgium."

As Rose remembered the conversation at the house, at first Joe just listened to the enthusiasm of his friends and didn't say much. "He merely shook his head with sadness." But as the hours went by, and the fortunes of the British Expeditionary Force became the only topic of conversation—intensified perhaps by a pouring rain which kept the four friends cooped up in the house over the third and the Fourth—Joe finally turned to them all and said their "whole attitude was strange and incomprehensible to him." As he saw it, "thousands of young men were dying out there on that bloody field, cut off from the world of their parents and their memories, cut off from their dreams of the future." In his heart, he could not believe that "all those men would go to their deaths singing and laughing, fearlessly charging ahead into a torrent of bullets." No matter how the correspondents tried to romanticize it, Joe said, "dying out there on that scarred land had to be intolerably painful and horribly lonely."

Nor was Joe swayed by the British argument that even staggering losses would be acceptable so long as the military objective was reached. "The immense figures being bandied about struck Joe as barbaric and monstrous," Rose recalled. "In his mind, no amount of recaptured territory could ever atone for the lives of hundreds of thousands of dead young men." Worse still, he warned his friends, "by accepting the idea of the grandeur of the struggle, they themselves were contributing to the momentum of a senseless war, certain to ruin the victors as well as the vanquished."

The vehemence of Joe's outburst placed such a strain on the gathering that Rose heaved a sigh of relief when the long weekend finally came to an end. "I can still remember how quiet the house seemed after Joe's friends had gone," Rose recalled. "When I went upstairs, I could hear only the even breathing of our baby in his crib. Just then, Joe too came into the bedroom and looked down at our sleeping child. 'This is the only happiness that lasts,' he said softly, and then he walked away."

Afterward, it became clear that the great Somme offensive was an immense human tragedy, "the single worst day in the entire military history" of Britain, darker and more devastating than Joseph Kennedy in his most melancholy pessimism could ever have imagined. "We can see now," Keegan wrote, that the week-long bombardment "for all its sound and fury, was inadequate to the task those who planned it expected from it. The shells which the British guns fired were the wrong

kind, falling short of the German trench line and the wire entangle-
ments." As a result, neither the German dugouts nor the German guns
were destroyed, allowing the Germans, once the bombardment had
ceased, simply to carry their machine guns upstairs, ready to mow down
the attacking waves of British soldiers.

Unaware of the unsatisfactory result of the shelling, the doomed British infantry marched to their deaths, stumbling across no man's land
with no means of replying to the heavy fire which they inexplicably
encountered within seconds of leaving their trenches. Pinned in the
open with no support, they were hit and hit again; they were "practically
annihilated and lay shot down in waves." Better and more professional
troops would have given up, but these men were idealists, "volunteers
who had willingly, eagerly answered the call to defend their country."
So they kept moving forward, heroically and trustingly, only to find
themselves trapped in the end by German barbed wire which in too
many places had been left intact by the inadequate bombardment. Out
of the 110,000 British troops who attacked on that first day, 60,000 were
killed or wounded and of that number perhaps 20,000 had been killed in
the first hour or even the first minute of the attack. By sunset of that
first day on the Somme, writer Paul Fussell observed, only one thing
was clear, "the *war* had won and would go on winning."

Once the great offensive had been declared, however, it had to go on.
To pull back after all those valiant young men had lost their lives on a
single day was altogether impossible. So the British attack on the Somme
continued for five more treacherous months until, mercifully, the autumn rains made all further offensive action impossible. By this time,
however, the British casualties had reached the astounding total of
412,000, spelling the end of an entire generation of the nation's most
promising men.

By Christmas of 1916 the war had lasted twenty-nine months, with no
appreciable shift in the battle lines. A terrible gloom overcame the entire
Continent as the realization set in that millions of lives had been lost to
move the front a few hundred yards here or there. In both Germany
and Russia, more than two million men had already died, in France the
casualties totaled nearly 700,000, while in England whole families had
been terminated in the male line after hundreds of years. Still the dying
went on. The more the war cost, the more desperately both sides clung
to the belief that they would win if only they could hold on long enough.
And from the Allied side, in particular, there was an additional reason
for hanging on—for as 1916 gave way to 1917 it became obvious to all
that sooner or later "the Americans were coming."

·  ·  ·

When the United States entered the war in April of 1917 in order to make the world "safe for democracy," Rose Kennedy was in her eighth month of pregnancy with her second child. It had been an easy pregnancy; now, in these last languorous weeks, there was no way to shorten the time it would take for the baby to assume its birth position. However listless she might feel, the young mother had no choice but to trust in the slow rhythms of nature.

In a vivid contrast to the natural cycle of birth moving slowly to a close, the machinery of war and destruction was being mobilized throughout the country at a speed so phenomenal, as *The New York Times* reported at the time, that "a vast transformation of the whole nation's activities and modes of thought" was taking place. For a nation which had studiously disengaged from the affairs of Europe for more than a century, there was much to be done to make ready for a Continental war.

At the outset, with an army numbering only 212,000 men, there was general agreement that "only the draft system could furnish the enormous number of men required." So the Congress set to work at once, speedily enacting a selective-service law on May 18, 1917, which authorized the President to conscript hundreds of thousands of men between the ages of twenty-one and thirty into the military forces. While this vast machinery for registering, examining and classifying what eventually amounted to ten million men was being organized, the Kennedy household witnessed the birth of a second son.

Born in the master bedroom of their Brookline house at three o'clock in the afternoon of May 29, 1917, the small blue-eyed boy was named John Fitzgerald Kennedy in honor of his maternal grandfather. "It is needless to say," the *Boston Post* reported, "that Grandpa Fitzgerald, the former Mayor Fitzgerald, is wearing a pleased smile."

It was also reported in the Boston papers that the baby had appeared on a day that was "certainly a bright one" in the life of his father, for, in addition to being presented with a second son, Joseph Kennedy was "elected a trustee of the Massachusetts Electric Company to succeed Richard Olney," the powerful Attorney General and aggressive Secretary of State under President Cleveland. With this election, the *Post* reported, "Kennedy is now said to be one of the youngest trustees of a big corporation as well as the youngest bank president in the country."

Twice before, according to writer Joe McCarthy, the name of Kennedy had been suggested as a member of the Massachusetts Electric board, but twice before it had been turned down. "The company's president admitted to [Kennedy]," McCarthy wrote, "that he had been rejected earlier only because he was an Irish Catholic and apologized to him for the company's discrimination." When asked later why the election meant so much to him, Joe Kennedy reportedly said, "Do you know a better way to meet people like the Saltonstalls?" And surely he was right, for sitting with him on this board was as fine a collection of Boston's leading Brahmin figures as an Irishman was likely to meet, including Galen Stone of the brokerage house of Hayden, Stone and Company, Gordon Abbot, chairman of the powerful Old Colony Trust Company, Charles Francis Adams, the great-grandson of John Quincy Adams, and Philip Saltonstall.

Despite Joe's pleasure at his elective honor, the circumstances surrounding the birth of this second child were very different from those attending the first. Joe Junior had made his appearance on a summer morning in an airy beach house full of light and life. Having set aside this time as his vacation, Joe Senior had been freed from the rigors of his workaday world, a happy respite affording him the chance to build the early bonds of what would later become an intense attachment to this firstborn son.

The new baby, by contrast, arrived at a melancholy moment in his father's life, a time of emotional distress brought about by the coming of the war that Kennedy feared would shake the foundations of the world in which he and Rose had grown up. War was the single subject that was able to destroy his peace of mind. In the unquiet weeks preceding the birth of young Jack, as the baby was soon to be called, Joe Kennedy had stood helplessly by as first one and then another of his friends had voluntarily given up their careers to enlist in the fighting forces of their country. Feeling empty of such patriotism and still believing the war to be an enormous void of "wasted efforts and wasted lives," he felt himself becoming "a stranger in his own circle of friends."

In the depths of his heart, Rose later said, Joe "believed he was right in not volunteering for the war, but, given the views of the circle he lived in, he could not feel good about his decision." Among all his close Harvard group, he alone failed to respond to the stirring summons which was being issued all over the country to Harvard graduates to join the regiment at Plattsburgh, New York, where thousands of Harvard men were training to become the officers of the new draft army. Not surprisingly, in light of the enthusiasm they had expressed toward the war effort the year before, Campbell and Potter had been among the first to enlist, arriving in Plattsburgh in the early days of May. By the middle of May they were joined by Joe Sheehan, Kennedy's boyhood companion from East Boston who had gone to Boston Latin with Joe before he entered Harvard. And before long, Bob Fisher, Joe Donovan and Joe Merrill would also enlist, contributing their part to the total number of 11,319 Harvard men serving in the war. From the class of 1912 alone, the military drew an astonishing ratio of three men for every five graduates.

On June 5, one week after the new baby's birth, every man in the United States between the ages of twenty-one and thirty was required to register for military service. On that day Joe was among the millions of young men whose names and newly assigned serial numbers were transmitted to the provost marshal in Washington, where a massive lottery was being prepared to determine which of them would be called up and in what order.

Joe Kennedy was not chosen in this first lottery, a luck of the draw that should have made him happy. And yet, as the days and weeks skipped by, Rose recalled, Joe began to feel "a sameness to his life," and a "feeling of sadness" stole into his heart. While citizens all over the country were geared into the immensity of things, as industries of every imaginable sort were converting their plants to the production of the materials of war—from corset factories which were using their plants for the making of grenade belts to typewriter companies which were furnishing signal pistols, to firms manufacturing caterpillar tractors which were now making tanks—Joe's humdrum life at the bank was simply repeating itself. Cut off from the pace and fervor of the war, he increasingly began to feel "a desire for action," as Rose put it, and "a sense of regret" welled up within him. Since the war was now here, he began to argue, perhaps "there was nothing to do but accept the situation and turn all his efforts to winning it."

As Joe began to cross the bridge from opposing the war to embracing it, he was following a well-worn path outlined by the pacifist Randolph Bourne in his classic essay *War and the Intellectuals*. In this shrewd work, Bourne attributes the gradual coalescence of the intellectual classes in support of a war they initially abhorred to "the itch to be in the great experience which the rest of the world was having," a craving for action so irresistible that "the task of making our country fit for peace was abandoned in favor of a feverish concern for the management of war." Unable to bear the pain of standing apart from the central action of the day, thousands of would-be dissenters decided to float with the current, drowning all their ideals, their consciences and their hesitations "in the elemental blare of doing something." With the acceptance of action came the end of anxious and torturing attempts to reconcile their ideals of peace with the fact of an entire world caught up in a colossal war, "a crowning relief of their indecision."

As it happened, several things combined to provide Kennedy with the ideal opportunity for joining in the action without having to subject his life to the course of a stray bullet. From the moment the United States entered the war, the primary need was for ships. With Germany staking everything on the hope of severing Britain's maritime arteries and starving her out of the war before America could mobilize and transport an army across the ocean, victory would turn on whether the Allies could beat the German submarine, the U-boat, or whether it could beat them. And in 1917 the balance was in favor of the U-boat, which was destroying Allied shipping twice as fast as new ships were being built. The most direct reply was the construction of destroyers, armed warships designed to destroy the U-boats and protect the merchant ships. At the same time, it was necessary to build hundreds of carrier vessels to ferry the American army three thousand miles across the ocean and then keep that army supplied with food, rifles, ammunition, shells, guns, trucks, locomotives and railway lines. "We are in a crisis," reporter Mark Sullivan wrote at the time, "where there is no such thing as enough ships."

In the context of this urgent need, contracts worth hundreds of millions of dollars were awarded to the various shipyards already in existence, a number of which were owned by the giant Bethlehem Steel Corporation. While these contracts were being let, and in consultation with the Navy Department, Bethlehem Steel responded to the challenge by centralizing the management of its separate plants. As a consequence of this reorganization, Bethlehem's large Fore River plant in Quincy, Massachusetts, found itself in need of an entirely new administrative team.

At the recommendation of Guy Currier, a shrewd and successful lawyer who was the attorney for the Fore River Corporation, Kennedy was invited to a conference at Young's Hotel, a dining place much frequented by Boston's businessmen, on Saturday, September 29, 1917. There he was interviewed by Joseph Powell, who was to be Bethlehem Shipbuilding's new vice-president, and by Samuel Wakeman, a Cornell graduate who had spent nearly all his life in shipbuilding and was soon to become the general manager of the Fore River plant. While Kennedy had, as he later admitted, "absolutely no knowledge of shipbuilding," he did possess ripe experience in the world of finance which Powell considered essential for the position he was seeking to fill—the office of assistant general manager. A decisive man himself, Powell was quick to embrace the vigor of Kennedy's temperament, and before the lunch had ended he determined that of all the candidates he was considering, Kennedy was the one "who combined the qualities and experience that best fitted him for the work." Impressing upon the young man that it was "a patriotic duty for him to help in an undertaking of such national importance," Powell offered Kennedy a salary of $15,000 and asked him to report to work two days later.

Accepting the offer without hesitation, Kennedy agreed to start as soon as he could wind up his affairs at the Columbia Trust—which he did in a most advantageous way by having his father elected to succeed him as president of the bank. It was, it seemed, the best possible situation for Joe, allowing him to feel, as he later wrote, that he "was doing something worthwhile for his country" while at the same time affording him participation in the one form of warfare which *The Nation* described at the time as "an investment instead of a waste," since the United States would be building not only for the war but for after the war as well.

The main administration building at the Bethlehem plant, where Kennedy's office was located, was an old brick one with small-paned windows, standing in the shade of a tree-lined street, surrounded by a picket fence. Behind this simple facade there arose what must have seemed to the people of Quincy a giant industrial fairyland, an immense plant stretching over hundreds of acres of ground, encompassing nearly eighty buildings and employing over seventeen thousand workers. The original shipyard had been constructed decades earlier on what was then fertile farmland by a young man named Thomas Watson with the money he had earned from assisting a friend, Alexander Graham Bell, in the invention of the telephone. But the spirit of Watson's small and struggling company was now wholly submerged in the mighty and clamorous industry Bethlehem had developed, a shipyard which was soon to earn the honor of being called one of the most efficient shipyards in the world.

No sooner had Kennedy arrived at the Fore River plant than he found himself caught up in the exhilarating atmosphere. The air was full of the heterogeneous sounds of thousands of workers laboring to subjugate tons of resistant steel into all manner of shapes toward the common goal of building more ships in less time than ever before. All over the landscape, all the way down to the river, men were calling out to one another as huge cranes hoisted and lowered the flat plates of steel into the various shops where they would be sorted out, marked and molded into shape. The entire place vibrated with the challenge of the war; in each building, teams of workers—draftsmen, machinists, riggers, riveters, electricians, plumbers, carpenters, joiners and painters—competed with one another to finish their work in record time.

As assistant general manager, Joe had occasion to involve himself in widely varied aspects of the shipyard's work, from the management of the plant railroad and the preparation of the bills of sale to the supervision of the plant's emergency hospital and the settlement of accident claims. During his years at Bethlehem, there were more than 150 injuries per month caused by falling machinery and by rivet heads breaking off and flying at people, resulting, in this era before the wearing of goggles, in the loss of at least one eye per month. Kennedy later acknowledged that he worked harder during his eighteen months at Bethlehem than ever before in his life; indeed, so hectic was the pace that he would pass many nights in his office, catching only an hour or two of sleep before morning.

Kennedy arrived at Bethlehem just in time to participate in the first stage of the construction of a second shipyard just two and a half miles away from Fore River, in Squantum. With the balance of power still weighted in favor of the German submarine, the Emergency Fleet Corporation commissioned Bethlehem to build a separate shipyard solely for the construction of destroyers. It was a monumental undertaking, necessitating as it did the filling in of seventy acres of soggy marshland, the building of a dozen huge construction sheds, a warehouse, a storehouse, a main office building, a service building, ten wooden ways and four wet docks. It fell to Kennedy to supervise the construction of the restaurant at the new plant, which could accommodate nearly fourteen hundred people at one seating in its main dining room while also providing both a cafeteria service and a luncheon counter service. Kennedy was also charged with the tasks of laying out new streets and railways and with building a large complex of dormitories, rooming houses and private homes which, taken together, could meet the needs of the nine thousand men and women expected to work at the new plant. The housing project alone, it was later said, "was equivalent to building practically overnight an entire, self-sustaining township."

Always at his best in situations which demanded quick action and an orderly procession of thought, Kennedy threw himself into his new duties with good temper and disciplined vigor. "The contractors began work on the 7th of October, 1917," reported the plant newspaper, *The Fore River Log*, and from that time on, things happened so fast that in spite of having to contend with the "unparalleled severity" of one of the worst winters this section had ever known, the new "Victory" plant, complete with railroad tracks, streetcar tracks and roadways, was ready to lay the keel of its first destroyer by the early spring of 1918. As to the work of the plant itself, it was worthy of history's notice: more destroyers were launched at Squantum more quickly than anywhere else in the world. "It was," Navy Secretary Josephus Daniels told a cheering crowd of Bethlehem workers, "substantial proof that the age of miracles has not passed."

While Kennedy was immersed in his new duties at the shipyard, the Army was in the process of substantially revising its draft regulations in preparation for its second huge draft call. Under the new system which was anounced in mid-November 1917, the procedure for making deferments was reversed. Under the original procedure, the first step was the calling up of all those chosen by lot before their local draft boards for their physical examinations. Those who were found physically qualified for military service were then given an opportunity to submit claims for exemption on the basis of their providing the necessary support for their family or their employment in a necessary industry. It was a cumbersome method, compelling the boards to examine an average of five men for every one obtained for service.

Under the new system, all registrants were required within seven days of December 15, 1917, to file answers to an extensive questionnaire, which the local boards then used in order to place each registrant in one of five classes, ranging from those considered most fit for service to those whose drafting would strike at the roots of industries essential for the war effort. Since it was the best military opinion that none of the classes except Class 1—which embraced all single men without dependent relatives and all married men whose families were supported by income independent of their labor—would be touched, the new procedure allowed the local boards to limit their physical exams to the list of men in Class 1, thereby reducing 95 percent of the work of the old system and resulting in the certification of four out of five men who were called up.

The evidence suggests that Kennedy initially approached the matter of the new classification in a cavalier manner, assuming that the conditions of his employment were so intricately tied to the heart of the war effort that his claim for a deferment on industrial grounds would automatically be granted. Only the month before, indeed, recognizing that the numbers of men working in shipbuilding were still not sufficient to meet the critical need for ships, the provost marshal had granted a special deferment for all registrants "engaged in building and manning ships." But Kennedy's local board, apparently concluding that he had no technical knowledge of shipbuilding and was therefore not essential to Bethlehem's program, rejected his deferment claim and placed him in Class 1, which made him subject to immediate certification, pending the results of his physical exam.

The unwelcome news of his status came as a shock to Kennedy. Writing on February 18, 1918, he begged the district board to recognize that his employment at Bethlehem had not come about by his own design but rather at the strong request of Bethlehem's top executives Joseph Powell and Sam Wakeman, that the original invitation had been issued way back in early October, and that his responsibilities were important to the war effort. Powell backed him with a strongly worded letter to the board detailing the conditions under which Kennedy was originally employed and saying that his services were indeed essential. "To draft him to other service," Powell wrote, "would . . . place a man eminently fitted for the difficult administration work he is now carrying on into another line of work, where his services to the U.S. could not compare in value to those he is now rendering."

Despite these efforts, the district board flatly rejected Kennedy's appeal, upholding the local board's determination that he belonged in Class 1, liable for immediate military service. It was at this point that Powell reached out to his political connections in Washington, sending a telegram to Meyer Bloomfield at the Emergency Fleet Corporation in which he outlined the situation and argued: "There are not over six men in this establishment whose loss at this time would be felt as much as Kennedy's and for him to be put in Class 1 is inexcusable from any point of view. What can you do to help us out?"

This produced the desired result. Kennedy was not bothered again by his local board and was allowed to remain at his desk at Fore River throughout the entire war.

Though Kennedy achieved what he wanted at the time, there is reason to believe he felt a measure of guilt in response to his dealings with the draft, for in his later accounts of his early life he had a disposition to replace the actual date when he began his work at Bethlehem, October 1917, with a much earlier one; he was even capable of stretching it back into 1916, the year before America entered the war. It is, of course, possible that the mistaken date was simply a matter of forgetfulness, but the false recollection obtrudes itself with such tenacity as to suggest the possibility that, consciously or even unconsciously, he substituted the earlier date as a means of avoiding the unpleasant memories associated with the charge that he had joined Bethlehem to evade the draft.

It was, all in all, not an easy time for Joe. While he should have been able to take great pride in the phenomenal job Bethlehem was doing, the truth is that his accustomed self-possession was increasingly disturbed by the growing gulf which divided him from his friends. It was not just that he was no longer able to spend time with his comrades; it was that their way of life now was so different from his that he feared they would remain forever apart from him even when the war ended. Some of the loneliness he was feeling is apparent in the stream of letters he wrote to his soldier friends during the spring and summer of 1918.

Writing on April 15 to Joe Sheehan at Camp Devens, in the hills of Massachusetts, where graduates of the Plattsburgh officers' training camp were teaching tens of thousands of recruits the techniques of trench warfare, Kennedy acknowledged feeling that Sheehan was fortunate to be working side by side with Campbell and so many other old friends.

> I have been up to Devens a couple of times with John F. but I guess both days I have been up there have been your days off. At least when I go down to Mother's they tell me that you had been in Winthrop. I am glad you are enjoying it there and are getting along so well. I have not seen any of the fellows myself, Tommy Campbell and Arthur Kelly, and feel that I have gotten horribly out of touch with everybody.

There is a similar tone of loss in a letter written to Bob Potter in Washington, D.C., where the soon-to-be major had joined the Aviation Signal Corps after his graduation from Plattsburgh.

> I have written you two or three letters in the last couple of months and as I have never heard from you I thought there was a possibility that they might have gone astray. . . . I was in Washington about a month ago and tried to get you at your office, but you were reported out every time I tried . . . let me know what you are doing as I am more than anxious to find out how you are getting along.

They had all become soldiers in such a short time, and as such they had worries, aims and desires which Kennedy could never understand in spite of his efforts to stay in touch. And the feeling of alienation would grow stronger still in the summer of 1918 when Campbell and Potter and hundreds of thousands of American doughboys finally put their months of maneuvers and training behind them and sailed away for the bloody battlegrounds of France, where fierce combat awaited them in the trenches of the Somme, along the plains of the Marne and in the Argonne Forest.

There is a fascinating letter from Chris Dunphy, a good friend Joe had recently made in Boston, written sometime in the late summer of 1918 from the French front. It responds to a letter in which Joe had apparently expressed such keen regret at not being in the service that Dunphy figured he was about to volunteer:

> Well, old top, I read your great letter yesterday and it was a joy untold. . . . Take my advice and stick to building those ships. You are of better service to the country right there. You could come over here and not be half as much use to the Country. We occupy most all of France and you might be miles from the firing line and not see any excitement.
>
> I've been up to the Fighting Zone just before we started our big drive at St. Mihiel and they are certainly boxing the Huns and making them look

silly. They are OK in waves but when it comes to open war and courage
they fall a way short of the American boys. I have been in two air raids
. . . I have seen every bit of France except what the Hun still holds but I
think I will see that soon. I am in great health and could bat above 300.

It is a mark of the strong affection Dunphy held for Joe that he is the
one providing solace to his homeside friend rather than the other way
around. For, after all, Joe had been given ample opportunity to join the
service, either as an officer or as an enlisted man, had he truly wanted
to fight in the war. The truth is that his abstract feelings of patriotism
and justice were simply not as strong as his fundamental principle of
self-interest and his passionate desire for the aggrandizement of his family. Yet, while he did not care to be a soldier himself, he was greatly
moved by the abundant stories of death and injury which he could not
dismiss from his mind as part of the inevitable legacy of war. "He always
knew," Rose later said, that "but for the grace of God and the powers of
Washington" he too might have been among the hundreds of Harvard
men killed in the war—men who had lived and loved and dreamed much
as he.

While the Great War spelled the end of life for millions of young men,
Joseph Kennedy made a rapid advance in the world of wartime shipping,
where his capacity for decision and his meticulous attention to detail
elicited great praise from all his superiors. Indeed, for an ambitious man
like Joe, who thrived upon his labors and possessed a genius in the twin
realms of making money and controlling costs, there was probably no
better place in all the country than Bethlehem.

Founded in 1904 through the vision and daring of Charles M.
Schwab, a woolen worker's son who began his meteoric career driving
stakes in the engineering department of the Carnegie Steel plant at
Braddock, Pennsylvania, at a dollar a day, the Bethlehem Steel Corporation was put together with the idea that a giant firm could be successful only if its workers and managers had a direct share in its profits. The
cornerstone of the Bethlehem system, which Schwab had adapted from
a similar system at Carnegie, was the idea of allowing each individual a
share of the profits that resulted directly from his personal efforts. Cou-
pling low salaries with large incentive bonuses, Schwab worked out a
system which measured each man's results and paid him accordingly.
If, for example, a riveter could drive more rivets a day or a reamer could
enlarge more holes a day than the company's average, the extra work
would be reflected in an extra payment in his weekly pay envelope. So,
too, if a team of riggers completed its work ahead of schedule, each man
on the team would receive a bonus. At the executive level, the bonus

system included a share in the profits: each administrator was allotted an interest in the company according to his record.

Under Schwab's philosophy, Bethlehem's steel production soared, bringing the company to the top of the steel industry, second only to the gigantic United States Steel. As for its shipbuilding interests, so capable did Bethlehem become during the war that it turned out more ships than any other company in America or Europe. In a system which promoted from within and gave its executives a free hand, Schwab's eminent talent lay in his judgment of men.

Clearly, in an organization like this, Kennedy's conspicuous talents did not go unnoticed. Encouraged by Wakeman, a boss who prided himself on giving his men unbridled freedom of action and thought, Joe plunged into his many projects with an almost boyish enthusiasm. Raw as he was in his knowledge of shipbuilding, the key to Kennedy's success at Bethlehem lay in his ability to give heightened significance to ordinary projects. Always thinking ahead, his mind instantly comprehended future opportunity even while he was enmeshed in present tasks. While conducting negotiations with the government for the wartime restaurant which the United States was to build at the Squantum plant, Kennedy began designing a larger restaurant at Fore River which he proposed to operate himself for a healthy profit.

Even in the most routine of his assignments, administering the company's insurance program, Kennedy forged a creative policy which sought to restore injured men to work as soon as possible lest they become permanent objects of company charity. Under his guidance, the Fore River Insurance Company was the first in the country to fully embrace the advantages furnished by the Red Cross Institute in New York, a program of intensive training designed to develop new skills in crippled men so that they could return to work in a different area. The big obstacle until Kennedy came along had been the matter of the employee's support while being trained, the expenses for his transportation, boarding and food. Kennedy led the insurance company to undertake these additional costs while still paying the family its regular compensation, knowing that, in the end, when the worker was returned to work, the company would profit.

The summer of 1918 was to see the turning point of the war. After four years of an exhausting struggle in which the forces of both sides had been so nearly equal that their armies on the western front had swayed back and forth over a scarred and bloody zone only a few miles in width, the fresh American troops had finally tipped the scale. Numbering over two million men, healthy and strong, the Americans added the decided strength the Allies needed both to repel the last, convulsive

German offensives at Amiens and the Marne and to launch a counter-offensive of their own, a continuous series of successful blows which would drive the Germans farther and farther back. By September, the Germans had reached the limit of what they could do. Back at home, war weariness, food shortages and subversion were undermining morale; at the front, German desertions were skyrocketing. But some of the fiercest fighting lay ahead before this suicidal war would finally come to an end.

While few people took notice, preoccupied as everyone was with the war, a deadly new virus was invading the United States. Known to us now as the great influenza epidemic of 1918, it would encircle the entire globe with such frightful speed that it would single-handedly kill more people in less time than any other catastrophe known to man. It was the tremendous sweep of the disease that made the death totals so high; before its course was run, a quarter of the world's population was affected and 22 million died, twice as many people as died in combat on all fronts in the entire four years of the war. In America alone 675,000 people would die from the flu in less than a year. It was, in the words of one noted doctor, "the medical catastrophe of all time."

Boston was the first city in America to be struck by the flu. On August 27, 1918, two sailors at the Commonwealth Pier reported to sick bay with a sudden illness, the passage from apparent health to near-prostration having taken only one or two hours. Bearing fevers running up to 105 degrees, the sailors complained of severe aches in their muscles, joints, backs and heads. On the next day eight new cases were reported, on the following day fifty-eight. Within two weeks two thousand officers and men of the First Naval District had contracted the flu. From Boston the disease moved inland thirty miles to the troops at Camp Devens, where it spread explosively, striking 17,000 men and leaving 789 dead. At first, no one understood why these robust young men were becoming so sick and dying. "After all," Alfred Crosby wrote in his study of the epidemic, "influenza, flu, grippe, grip—whatever you called it or however you spelled it—was a homey, familiar kind of illness: two or three days in bed feeling downright miserable, a week or so feeling shaky, and then back to normal." Death for some of the victims could be explained by the propensity of this particular flu to develop into pneumonia. But in the victims who died within forty-eight hours of the first ache or cough, autopsies determined that the air passages were clogged with a strange bloody fluid, something doctors had never seen before, which they thought must be some new kind of plague.

As the doctors stood helplessly by, faced with an illness as inexplicable as the war itself, the killer flu spread through all the cities and towns of Massachusetts; by the end of September 85,000 citizens were sick, and 700 died in the last week of the month alone. As a rule, influenza kills infants and old people more readily than young adults; but the most extraordinary feature of this flu was that half the deaths were in the twenty-to-forty age group, young men and women in the prime of their lives, and this was the pattern throughout the world.

By early October, the epidemic reached its peak in Massachusetts. The week before, Boston's mayor, Andrew Peters, had issued an order closing all theaters, schools, churches, dance halls and other places of public assembly; in the same week, the Governor had sent an emergency request for help to Washington, which the authorities responded to by sending five hundred doctors and a thousand nurses to Massachusetts from the Midwest. But still the sick came searching for aid; they over-flowed the hospitals and poured into the makeshift emergency hospitals until there were no hospital rooms and no ambulances left. The Brook-line Board of Health reported "whole streets where every house has illness." Everything was in such a state of confusion, with funeral bells tolling all day long, that few people were able to keep their senses. "I tell you, they must come for her *now*, or I'll put her on the sidewalk," screams the terrified landlady in Katherine Anne Porter's *Pale Horse, Pale Rider* upon hearing that no ambulances are available to take away the sick young heroine, Miranda. "I tell you," she goes on, "this is a plague, my God, and I've got a household of people to think about."

The Bethlehem shipyard, now with 26,000 men working together in close quarters and living together in crowded dormitories, became a breeding ground for the disease. One reporter estimated that over five thousand of the workers were stricken as the epidemic swept the yard "with the suddenness of a simoom." Within days, even the most vigor-ous of the men, the ones "who had been in the best of physical condition and freest from previous disease," were unaccountably ill. "They'd be sick one day—gone the next, just like that, fill up and die," said the physician and poet William Carlos Williams. And all the while, the ur-gent work of building ships had to go on. Before a week had passed, the officials of the company recognized the desperate need for immediate action. On September 21, 1918, an emergency task force was named to coordinate the plant's response to the crisis, and Joseph Kennedy was put in charge.

There was much for him to do. The first task was to convert one of the large dormitories into an emergency hospital. It was a staggering job, requiring the installation of utilities, the gathering of large quantities of beds, linens, medical supplies and surgical equipment, and the recruiting of a large staff of doctors and nurses—at a time when the flu had laid a withering hand on all essential services and when shortages of hospital supplies were endemic. Kennedy was not to be thwarted, however, and before he went to sleep that first night the first patients had been admitted to the hospital. To staff it he was fortunate to secure the services of a highly respected physician, Dr. Stowe, who was able, in turn, to detail a continuing stream of naval doctors and hospital apprentices to Quincy. That settled, Kennedy transformed the Fore River Club into a nurses' home with an up-to-date commissary department which was put into operation overnight and was capable of cooking a thousand meals a day.

The doors of the hospital were open twenty-four hours a day. Everywhere nurses and doctors were running, their bodies bent as one toward the common task of healing. There were times, *The Fore River Log* reported, when as many as thirty of the one hundred nurses at the hospital were sick with the disease, but still the work was carried on "with a remarkable degree of efficiency." In this scrambling time, the plant guards were called out as ambulance drivers, stretcher bearers and gravediggers. However, it soon became clear, as the *Boston Evening Transcript* reported on September 25, that the deaths in Quincy had become so numerous that burial facilities were inadequate.

At the height of the epidemic, Kennedy's body began to register the strain he was under, and he fell victim to a severe attack of ulcers. On a special visit to Fore River to study the methods Kennedy had employed to meet the crisis, Charles Schwab beheld "a drawn young man nervously smoking more than was good for him." His face was pale and there was an unnatural fire in his eye which showed plainly that he was exhausted. Upon his review of the conditions at the plant, Schwab determined that with the hospital now in full working order and with doctors predicting that the worst was over, Kennedy had to leave the shipyard at once in order to restore his health. Telling him that large possibilities awaited him at Bethlehem's headquarters as soon as the war came to an end, Schwab arranged for Kennedy to go to a health farm and made him promise to stay there until his body returned to its original strength.

All the while, Kennedy had his own private worry. When the flu first broke out in Boston, Rose was in her final weeks of pregnancy with her third child. With only one set of lungs to handle the affairs of two bodies, women in the late stages of pregnancy were particularly susceptible to the complications of the flu. Indeed, so serious was the epidemic in Boston in the week the baby was due that the Boston City Hospital announced it would soon be obliged to refuse the admission of new patients. Fortunately for Rose, she had already planned to have the baby at home, and on September 13, 1918, she was delivered of a girl, Rosemary, born in the same master bedroom at the Beals Street house in which her brother Jack had been born sixteen months before. It was, Rose later reported, "a normal delivery," and the baby was "a beautiful child."

Nonetheless, a thick brown leather book at St. Aidan's Church in Brookline speaks to the continuing anxiety the family must have felt even after the child was born. For, as against the twentieth-century custom, fruit of modern medicine's advance, of waiting at least three weeks to baptize children, the Kennedys decided to have Rosemary baptized when she was only six days old. It was as if the flu and the helplessness the doctors were experiencing in the face of it had turned the clock back to the previous century, propelling families once more to grasp at familiar supports. Stripping the modern world of its rational base, the flu provided a link between this little girl and another little girl whose ancestry she shared, Ellen Rosanna, the infant daughter of Tom and Rosanna Fitzgerald, who had died in another epidemic fifty years earlier at a time when all kinds of diseases produced the same anxiety that the mysterious flu was now generating in the world of 1918.

Before the winter months set in, however, the flu epidemic subsided and the Great War came to an end. On the eleventh hour of the eleventh day of the eleventh month, an official German delegation met with representatives of the Allied powers in a railway car in the Forest of Compiègne, and there, by the signatures of six men on a white piece of parchment, four years of some of the worst fighting the world had ever known were finally brought to an end.

# CHAPTER 17
# LEARNING
# THE TRICKS
# OF THE
# TRADE

With the ending of the war, the master spirit which had guided the work of the Quincy shipyard disappeared and the pace of the great shipbuilding machine slackened. Gazing one wintry evening over the deserted yard, Kennedy was struck with the stillness of the place: all the riveters, riggers and machinists had departed. The building sheds which had swarmed with life and bustle through many a long night were now sullenly shut, the walkways empty. In all the crowded hours he had spent at his wartime desk, Kennedy had never experienced a time when the plant was absolutely quiet. Now, however, with demobilization rapidly under way and with scores of superfluous ships rotting at their wharves, there was, Kennedy later recalled, a bleakness in the air, an awful silence which allowed him to hear the sounds of his own footsteps echoing hollowly behind him.

With the common challenge of beating the German submarine gone, the work force cracked into numberless parts; increasingly, the workers refused to take on extra work. "As soon as the signal sounds," *The Fore River Log* lamented in an editorial in 1919, "everyone rushes for the clock to see who will get there first." To Kennedy's astute mind, the unwonted stillness of the plant seemed a warning knell, an indicator that the spectacular productivity he had seen at Fore River he now would see no more. Aware that nothing short of another war would bring back the hour of splendor shipbuilding had enjoyed, Kennedy determined then and there—in spite of the promising offer Schwab had made to him the previous autumn—that the time had come for a new adventure.

With the arrival of the world's first peacetime spring in four years, Kennedy's mind was already stirring with an uncannily intuitive sense that a new economic age was in the making—a wildly prosperous era expressly inviting his exploration and conquest. "The key to Kennedy's spectacular financial success," said his friend and longtime associate John Ford, "was his anticipation of the future. On a day-to-day basis, his guess was as good as the next man's, but his vision of what lay down the road, a vision that was always there, sustaining him and guiding him —that vision was simply phenomenal." Waiting to declare itself behind the riddles and confusions of the postwar era, Kennedy's vision determined that things were shaping up for a great boom in the stock market; he saw an epic phase in the history of the American economy in the making, and he resolved to be at the center of the action in the dominant passion of his age.

Kennedy could not have entered the stock market at a more auspicious time. The war which had impoverished Europe had greatly stimulated industrial productivity and efficiency in the United States, bringing America to the threshold of the twenties, a golden decade when the American people would enjoy the highest standard of living any people had ever known. Moreover, as a consequence of flourishing innovations in the techniques of mass production, the twenties marked the first time when productive volume rose not at a cost of more labor but less, expanding leisure time and starting a whole new social era in American history—an era when, for the first time, men and women of moderate means were able to buy a dizzying multitude of consumer products similar in quality and even in styling to the products owned and used by the well-to-do. Purchased on the installment plan, these material goods—automobiles, radios, vacuum cleaners, washing machines, iceless refrigerators, sewing machines, electric ranges and more —would spread pleasure, save labor and transform daily life in millions of households. At the same time, by supporting the belief that anything was now possible, the materialist standard evoked by these shared possessions exerted a profound effect upon the stock market. Stimulated by the optimism of the decade, people in all walks of life who had never dreamed of entering the market began now to buy and sell shares on margin. Never before in the financial history of the country had a speculative boom engaged so many people or permeated the life of the nation so deeply. Never before had there been so good a time for getting rich in the market.

With the deliberateness that was his mental habit, Kennedy carefully charted his course, anxious before severing relations with Bethlehem to find the most fitting entrance into the mazed world of buying and selling securities. Recognizing that a professional knowledge of market operations would be highly important if he was seriously to engage in stock trading, he became more and more certain that he wanted to join a brokerage house. He determined that the firm of Hayden, Stone and Company, a venerable brokerage house with an impressive list of wealthy customers, was the firm he most wanted to join. This clarity of view was unusual for a man so young, for while there were other houses where he might have made more money more quickly, there was probably no better place in the entire city for him to learn about the mysterious inner workings of the market, no better place for him to test all the expressions of human avarice, confidence, duplicity, decency, judgment and luck.

At the time of its founding by two Boston men, Galen Stone and Charles Hayden, in 1892, Hayden, Stone and Company was distinctly a commission brokerage house, engaged in buying and selling securities and commodities on all the principal exchanges. Solidly established by the turn of the century, the firm gradually expanded its operations until it became a leading investment banking institution, specializing in finding companies in the early stages of their development when they needed additional capital. "The peculiar genius that Hayden, Stone possessed," the founder's grandson David Stone concluded in his history of the company, was "the ability to sense inherent growth potential."

There is a legend in the Kennedy family that one day in the late spring of 1919, while Joe was still at Bethlehem trying to dispose of surplus ships, he set up an interview with Galen Stone in order to persuade Stone, as chairman of the board of several steamship lines, to buy Bethlehem's ships. When Kennedy arrived at Stone's office, the story is told, he discovered that Stone had just set off for an unexpected trip to New York. Undaunted, Kennedy departed at once for South Station, where he secured a seat next to Stone on the New York–bound train. By the time the train approached the journey's end, Kennedy had established a warm relationship with the older man, which resulted, within a fortnight of the trip, in his being offered a job as a customers' man at the firm of Hayden, Stone and Company.

The story is believable, though the impression it creates of a fortuitous shift in Kennedy's career is misleading. Kennedy's first acquaintance with Stone dated from his own appointment to the Massachusetts Electric Board two years earlier. As a fellow trustee, Stone had impressed Kennedy profoundly with his quiet wisdom. Indeed, observed Kennedy's biographer Richard Whalen, Stone was one of the few men who produced in Kennedy a permanent feeling of awe. Anxious to find a mentor in the market who could teach him to be more than he was, knowing there was nobody in the world he would rather work for, Kennedy more likely brought himself to Stone's attention deliberately, using the conversation about the ships as a means to an end.

Having accomplished his mission, Kennedy prepared to leave Bethlehem Steel. At first, the news of his intention to resign was received with nervous misgivings. At a time when the plant was moving through its blackest days, with only 25 percent of its steel ways in operation, his decision reflected grimly on those who had decided to stay, those who had locked their careers into the fickle fortunes of the industry and were trying hard to restore confidence in the shipbuilding business. For a man like Kennedy's immediate boss, Sam Wakeman, Kennedy's resignation must have been demoralizing, undermining still further the morale of the already dispirited plant.

Yet, in his final week at Fore River, Kennedy received both a warm letter of praise from Bethlehem Shipbuilding's vice-president, Joseph Powell, and a bonus check "for services rendered at a time when no one else could have done what you did" from Wakeman. Later, in the months ahead, when relations between Kennedy and Bethlehem turned bitter, this friendly leave-taking seemed premature.

The source of the trouble lay in a proposal Kennedy had made before leaving, to set up a private organization to take over the management of the Fore River restaurant. Kennedy agreed to supply both the management and the food and to assume all losses, if any, and Wakeman promised to pay Kennedy $15,000 a year. The understanding was to cover a period of two years, but, for reasons now unknown, Bethlehem abruptly terminated the contract at the end of six months. Blazing with frustration and anger, Kennedy feared there was no course open to him but to bypass Wakeman and take his grievance directly to Bethlehem Steel's president, Eugene R. Grace. But this he knew would only arouse hard feelings on all sides and possibly make him look trivial in Grace's eyes. Suppressing the temptation to rush into action, Kennedy wisely chose instead to share his dilemma with the goodhearted banker Eugene Thayer, who was now president of the Chase National Bank in New York. Thayer listened attentively to Kennedy's tale, asked him a few questions, and then immediately went into action.

Working as only an insider could work, Thayer used his membership on Bethlehem Steel's board as his point of access to discuss the situation with Grace, casually observing that from all he could find out about the matter, Kennedy was absolutely justified in his bitter feelings about the manner in which his relations with Bethlehem had been severed. Thayer's casual remark accomplished all that Kennedy could have hoped and more; the following week he received a warm personal letter from Grace which, in effect, apologized for any hurtful actions on the part of Bethlehem's people and offered Kennedy a generous settlement amounting to $12,500 in lieu of the canceled contract. In a letter to Thayer openly expressing his gratitude, Kennedy wrote: "I don't know when I will be in a position to repay all the favors you have granted me for the past six years but if you feel that my very best efforts are of any value to you at any time, they are yours to command."

The chance to repay Thayer came sooner than either Thayer or Kennedy could possibly have imagined at the time. Less than four weeks later, Albert Wiggin, a Chase director who, in recent months, had taken up a cold and even antagonistic attitude toward Thayer, was elected chairman of the board, and from that moment on Thayer labored under tensions so severe that he suffered a nervous breakdown which forced him to take an indefinite leave of absence from the bank and ultimately to resign his presidency in favor of Wiggin. "I can't tell you how sorry I am," Kennedy wrote to Thayer, and he went on to tell him that he had reached the point where he could lay his hands on $50,000 to $75,000, all of which he could get to Thayer on seventy-two hours' notice. "I mean this, Hughie," Kennedy affirmed, "because I figure that the start you gave me at the Columbia Trust Company has made all the rest of the things possible . . ." As it turned out, while Thayer did not need Kennedy's money, he would always remember that at that bitterest moment in the life of an ambitious man, the moment when his upward career came to a full stop, Kennedy had offered to come to his aid without waiting to be asked.

It was early in July of 1919, when the long, hot summer days had just set in with short sultry nights, that Kennedy began his labors at the prestigious Hayden, Stone and Company, and once the change from Bethlehem was made he was convinced the new work was suited to him in every way. In the first place, the old Yankee firm, unlike the Fore River plant or the Columbia Trust, was located in the heart of the financial district, in a handsome white granite building at the corner of Milk and Congress. Here, within easy walking distance, were all the great institutions of Boston's financial world: the First National and the National Shawmut, the private banking house of Kidder, Peabody, the investment firm of Lee, Higginson and Company, and the Boston

Stock Exchange. Here, Kennedy could see in a moment, was the economic life of the city, a whirling mass of brokers, bankers and customers whose conflicting judgments and combined actions in the stock market would serve, in the words of financier Bernard Baruch, as "a total barometer" for the city and the nation alike, a daily register of "anything and everything that happens in our world, from new inventions and the changing value of the dollar to vagaries of the weather and the threat of war or the prospect of peace."

At that time, the offices of Hayden, Stone and Company occupied three floors, connected by an old-fashioned rope elevator, of the seven-story New England Mutual Life Insurance Building, which dated from 1874 and boasted a huge bronze emblematic statue on its top. Entering from the street, the visitor was drawn at once into the large and tastefully furnished customers' room, which resembled a gracious library in an exclusive men's club more than a business office. There, surrounded by such plentiful reminders of opulence as thick Oriental rugs, brass spittoons, fine wooden benches arranged like pews, and costly paintings on the wall, Joe Kennedy executed buy and sell orders for his customers, arranged for bank loans to cover the securities which were held in a grated stock cage in the basement below, and looked after all the other details associated with the brokerage aspects of the firm's business.

In the adjoining room, reaching across an entire wall, was a large board containing movable blocks of figures representing the ever changing prices of dozens of key stocks and commodities on the great market. To keep the prices up-to-date, the firm employed a crew of board boys, dressed in white shirts and dark trousers, whose job it was to keep posting and reposting the kaleidoscopic quotations as fast as they came out over the ticker. Then, at the end of the trading day, the board boys would make a record of the highs and lows in each security to be sent to the bookkeepers, stiff-looking men in stiff white collars and prim ladies with neatly combed buns and white blouses, who sat in high-backed chairs and recorded figures in large leather ledgers under the light of overhanging lamps. "It was a very elegant place," veteran stockbroker Edwin Hodder recalled, "from the polished marble table in the bond department to the arched windows in the margin department, and all the people working there reflected that elegance in their appearance and their manner."

Throughout the war Kennedy had been dabbling in stocks, maintaining a small margin account with Richardson and Hill on Congress Street. In those years, the small investor had only to put up 10 percent of the price of his stocks "on margin," with the broker carrying the balance of the cost, a dangerous practice which allowed the lucky few with rising stocks to pyramid a small amount of money into a fortune while leaving tens of thousands of others vulnerable to losing everything if the prices of their stocks dropped—for the moment a customer's account seemed in jeopardy, the brokerage house would protect itself by selling out the stocks unless the customer could hastily scrape together enough money to maintain his margin.

Operating on his own, Joe had had mixed experience in the wartime boom market. While his purchase and sale of one hundred shares of Carbon Steel netted him a profit of $2,096, and his participation in the Waldorf Systems Syndicate, a restaurant business, credited his account with $2,730, his losing investments in a widely scattered group of other corporations, ranging from a manufacturer of die-casting machinery to a mining syndicate in Utah, exhausted his margin to the point where he was asked in May of 1919 to promptly send in additional cash.

His employment at Hayden, Stone marked an important change in his approach to speculation. In the course of his first months as a customers' man it became abundantly clear to him that the only way of making real money in the market was to concentrate all his time and energy on a limited number of prospective companies, studying every demonstrated fact and every imaginable contingency that might affect the value of the stock before he bought even a single share—the soundness of the management structure, the usefulness and appeal of the product, the level of leadership talent, the nature of the competition, the impact of the political and economic climate. Striving to find four or five stocks at most on which to focus his attention, the budding financier could be seen many late nights through his lighted window, surrounded by reading material ranging from the *Financial Chronicle* and *Poor's Manual* to the weekly newsletters of every brokerage house in town, his head bent over some thick volume on his desk, engaged in a ruthless search for the facts upon which all his future judgments would turn.

Yet, while he was becoming a student of the market, absorbed in the facts and figures revealing company earnings, he never made the mistake of thinking that his subject was a bloodless science. Guided by a man no one "could help liking to work with," as Kennedy later described Stone, he learned that buying and selling stocks was also an art, demanding a skillful interpretation of the changing moods and emotions of the hundreds of thousands of individual investors scattered in all parts of the country. For, at any fixed moment in time, Kennedy came to understand, the strength of a company's stock was dependent solely upon the numbers of people willing and anxious to buy its shares, a phenomenon often unrelated to the strength of the company itself. By the same token, Kennedy came to recognize that the forces which drove the prices of stocks down were not the impersonal forces of science nor the changing events of politics but the human reactions to those happenings. Indeed, as the maddeningly human aspects of the entire craft unfolded before Kennedy's curious eyes, there formed in his mind an even greater certainty that the game of speculation was precisely the one he most wanted to play at this stage of his life.

The position at Hayden, Stone placed a subtle and significant power in Kennedy's clever hands. While he was paid only $10,000 a year for his work as a customers' man, and while in those days the man whose business it was to produce clients for the firm was not entitled to added income on a commission basis, his compensation came in other ways. What made his experience at Hayden, Stone so valuable was the opportunity, in the wild, unregulated market of the twenties, to be numbered again and again among the insiders—the charmed circle of men who won their fortunes by exercising the prerogatives of insidership: by using confidential information of the internal conditions within a company to speculate in the market; by being awarded large blocks of common stock in return for services rendered; by sitting on boards of directors at a time when it was a common practice for management pools to manipulate the market in order to make money at the ordinary shareholders' expense.

The world in which Kennedy found himself at the gateway to the twenties was one in which groups of insiders all over the country were able to alter artificially the supply and demand of chosen stocks in so many ingenious ways that the uninitiated speculator was left in a position similar to that of the infantry in war, who often had great difficulty knowing what was really happening on the battlefield in consequence of the vast amount of smoke by which they were surrounded. If one looks at any of the celebrated traders in the twenties—from Jesse Livermore and Arthur Cutten to Bernard Baruch and Percy Rockefeller—one can see that all of them were profiting in one way or another from access, connections and inside information. What was more, the acquisition and use of such information was taken as a matter of course at a time when the investment bankers who sold security issues for a corporation were expected to take a controlling voice in the affairs of that corporation in order to protect their investors. There was, for instance, nothing unusual in the fact that Galen Stone sat on the boards of twenty-two companies whose securities he sponsored, including such major companies as Amoskeag Mills, Chase Securities, Pond Creek Coal, Anaconda Copper, Eastern Steamship, Mathieson Alkali, Pierce-Arrow, International Harvester and Atlantic Gulf West Indies (AGWI).

From the first, Kennedy realized that his association with Stone, if properly used, would give him the purchasing power of a dozen times as much as his original capital would have brought him. While the shrewd old man was not given to long speeches, he taught by the power of example, and the observant Kennedy was an apt student. The art of Stone's teaching was not to give Kennedy information but to teach him how to acquire it and to make him estimate it for what it was worth. Recognizing that Stone never went into battle without some part of his forces held back, Kennedy set the building of a strong cash reserve— both to protect himself from ruin and to be able to take immediate advantage of opportunity—as an indispensable first step before he could begin speculating in earnest. Toward this end, he decided to make his first moves with the soundest securities he could find, steadily rising ones that would unquestionably be accepted as collateral at any bank, allowing him to pyramid his unrealized paper profits into lines of credit at various banks which he could then use to purchase additional, more speculative stocks.

At this very time, Stone was concerned with four or five ventures which seemed to meet Joe's demand for security while yielding fine profits as well. The first company which fascinated Joe was Eastern Steamship, a young and flourishing company which operated eighteen passenger steamships from Maine to Boston and from Boston to New York. Having taken the New York steamer himself on many a warm summer night, boarding at the foot of Lewis Wharf at 5 P.M. to enjoy an excellent dinner and a comfortable sleep before arriving just after dawn in New York City, Kennedy had seen for himself just how successful and popular these luxury steamships were. Moreover, with Stone as chairman of the board, he knew he would be privy to any changes in the company's structure which might affect the earnings.

As it turned out, Kennedy could not have chosen better. In the summer of 1919, when he bought his first thousand shares, Eastern Steamship preferred was selling at 48. By September the stock had risen to 58, and it kept rising, reaching 68 in November and 75 in February of 1920. And all the while it was rising, Kennedy parlayed his earnings to buy more stock until he had accumulated several thousand shares. Now the advantages of leverage seemed to play into his hands. Owing to the shrewdness of his mental calculations and his ready access to the banking world, Kennedy knew how to make his stocks work for him to secure the loans he needed to buy other securities which would pay him more in earnings than the loans would cost him. In the space of several weeks, he was able to borrow a sum of nearly $60,000 from three different banks simply by depositing a maximum of three hundred Eastern Steamship shares at each bank. By this means, he was afforded the opportunity to pick up shares in several other companies with which Stone was closely associated—Amoskeag Mills, AGWI and Mathieson Alkali—so closely associated that when Stone died, six years later, flags at each place were flown at half mast.

Then, in August of 1921, when Eastern Steamship crossed the line at 77½, Kennedy decided to sell off one thousand of his shares, realizing $77,500 on his initial investment of $4,800, which represented the 10 percent margin he had to pay for his first $48,000 worth of stock. With a sizable block of Eastern Steamship left on his account, as well as the additional stocks he had accumulated with the cash that his original Eastern holdings had generated, there seemed no limit now to the resources of which Kennedy found himself possessed.

Still, success did not pile on success as fast as Joe had anticipated. The tricky postwar boom market had come to an end by November 1919, followed by a sharp recession that lasted for nearly two years and had a shattering impact on many industries which were caught by surprise and failed to adjust their inventories quickly enough to handle the slackening of demand. At the bottom of the downward cycle, the steel industry operated at only 18 percent of capacity. As prices tumbled, interest rates climbed to the highest levels since 1907 and the Dow Jones Index fell from a high of 119 in November 1919 to a low of 63 in August 1921. These were heartbreaking years for many traders on Wall Street, among them William Crapo Durant, president of General Motors, who within the space of six short months lost both $90 million and control of the company as GM's stock plummeted from 40 to 28 to 12.

It was during this "dark and dreary" period, as Kennedy described the recession in a letter to his friend Chris Dunphy, that the young financier made his first bad mistake. Yielding to an unreasoned impulse, he followed what he considered a straight tip on a stock that was selling at 160, only to watch it plunge rapidly to 80, taking with it a substantial portion of his cash reserve. It was an agonizing experience for Kennedy, all the more so because in buying the stock on an outside tip, without seeking corroborative advice or making his usual investigation of the company and its prospects, he had gone against all the lessons his knowledgeable tutor had been preaching for months.

Years later, Kennedy could still recall the wounding shame he endured when the moment came to admit the crushing mistake to his mentor. Walking slowly into Stone's gracious office, the young man felt that a black curtain had gone down upon a sunny period in his life. But before his cheerless tale was fully told, Stone rose from his chair and placed his aging hands on Joe's shoulders. "He who has never failed somewhere," Stone said, his face breaking into a kindly smile, "that man cannot be great. In any business, failure is the test of a man, but especially so in the market; for if you've never lost money in the market, you've never played the game." Stone went on to say that Kennedy's hope for the future lay not in humbling remorse but in a shrewd analysis of his mistakes, an understanding of why, in this instance, he had selected badly so as not to fall into the same situation again in a similar circumstance.

Under Stone's patient guidance, Kennedy learned to formulate which stocks were worth fighting for and which were not. Accepting the inevitability of mistaken judgments, Stone told him, the professional trader must learn to minimize his losses by relinquishing his position if he determines that the reasoning behind his investment was unsound in the first place. Galen Stone was speaking from experience. In 1920, the year of the great deflation, his own losses were so immense that he had no taxable income—this in striking contrast to the previous year, when his income was so large that his tax bill was $1.5 million.

What makes the ability to sell so difficult, Stone explained, is the admission of failure. So long as one holds on to the plunging stock, there is always hope, hope that a magical turnaround will prove the investor right. But such hope can be fatal, the great trader Jesse Livermore once explained: "When I see a danger signal handed to me, I don't argue with it. I get out . . . I figure it out this way. If I were walking along a railroad track and saw an express train coming at me 60 miles per hour, I would not be damned fool enough not to get off the track and let the train go by. After it had passed, I could always get back on the track, if I desired."

As Kennedy watched and learned, Stone skillfully steered the firm through the recession, never losing his basic confidence that industrial recovery would soon be on its way and that once the market started up it would not sink back soon again. In this optimistic judgment, Stone was fundamentally correct. On August 26, 1921, the Dow Jones Index started to climb up from 63, and but for a few small dips it continued to climb through all the golden years of the twenties, soaring higher and higher until, in September of 1929, it finally reached the dizzying height of 381, bringing business, in the words of journalist Frederick Lewis Allen, to "a perfect Everest of prosperity." Setting the stage for this unparalleled boom, Stone had never made the mistake, even in the midst of the collapsing prices of 1920 and 1921, of selling off his good investments along with his bad ones. The value of a good investment, he would repeatedly say, is like character in an individual: it stands up in adversity. Recession might bring a temporary fall in the market price of the stock, but if the company meets a genuine economic need and is under good management, it is bound to recover.

While striving to understand the broad swings of the market, Kennedy learned from Stone to make his buying and selling decisions stock by stock, regardless of the rest of the market. So long as he remained confident in the judgment that carried him to a particular stock in the first place, he must have the courage to stick with that stock, no matter how wildly his stomach was churning. "Whatever money I have made," Stone publicly observed, "has been in staying with a property and not regarding fluctuations." Drawing upon this splendid advice, Kennedy accepted in advance that he would have to endure many despairing days when even his soundest stocks—Eastern Steamship, Amoskeag, Mathieson Alkali and AGWI—went down, but if he stuck with them patiently and let them run their natural course, he stood to realize great profits.

What a resource Galen Stone was for a man of Kennedy's ability! At an age when many of his counterparts had stopped learning, Kennedy's mind was still being stretched the way a young student's mind is stretched by working under a master teacher. By spending hours with the master himself, listening to his discussions and watching him make decisions, Kennedy acquired a decade of learning within the space of thirty months. It was as if a rare and priceless book, laying out the mysteries of the exchange, had suddenly fallen on Kennedy's lap, allowing him each day to turn one leaf after the other until the moment came when it was no longer possible to tell where Galen Stone left off and Joseph Kennedy took up.

As early as August 12, 1920, Kennedy was offering the same advice to his friend Chris Dunphy that Galen Stone had consistently given to him. "Eastern may look tough," Kennedy wrote, "but it's better than I ever told you it was. Keep up your courage! Some day you will make plenty on that." This was disconcerting advice coming as it did in the midst of the recession when blue-chip stocks, including Eastern, were collapsing, but it was soon demonstrated that Kennedy was right. For no sooner had recovery set in than Eastern began a sharp upward movement that carried its common stock all the way up from 28 a share, where it stood when Kennedy urged patience, to a remarkable high of 127 a share in 1923. The maturing apprentice was unmistakably on his way.

# CHAPTER 18
# SEPARATION
# AND
# RESOLVE

While Joe's world was lustily expanding, his wife's was substantially contracting. From her earliest childhood Rose had been taught to believe that marriage was to be her great adventure, her journey's end. But, as the days and weeks went by, with three children under five and a fourth baby expected in the late winter of 1920, she began to feel, she later recalled, that her entire life was contained in the small rectangular rooms of the wood frame house in the quiet suburb of Brookline, that the world outside was receding before the relentless demands of her growing family. While she reluctantly accepted her husband's need to be away from home much of the time, working long days, nights and weekends to provide for his family, her social nature was unprepared for the isolation of suburban life, where her days were coming to resemble her mother's more than her father's. Nor, cast adrift as she was in a largely Protestant neighborhood, had Rose anticipated the separation she would feel from the richly textured world of the Boston Irish, where family traditions, political events, social gatherings and religious celebrations connected every man and woman with the rest of the community.

By comparison with the tight little Catholic world contained in Dor-

chester and in the North End, the social structure of suburban Brookline in the 1920s was as scattered and as fragmented as the motives of
the different groups of people who had come to live there. To be sure,
there were substantial families in Brookline still and some gracious old
mansions, remnants of the days when rural Brookline had been the
favorite resort of wealthy Boston merchants seeking nearby country estates in lush settings surrounded by trees and ample grounds. And in
the 1920s there were still many shaded streets like the one where the
Kennedys lived, where each house stood apart from the next, separated
by a fenced-in yard. But since the turn of the century, when Brookline
was invaded by the builders of apartments and was sold to the public as
the ideal "bedroom community," situated within easy commuting distance of Boston, the residents had tended increasingly to be apartment
dwellers whose interest in the community where they came only to sleep
was not the same as the interest of families who had a stake in the land.
Replanted in this unfamiliar ground, very few of the strong, collective
bonds which, in Boston, had kept Rose tied to her Irish heritage were
able to survive.

The impact of the separation from the world of her girlhood was all
the greater for Rose because there had earlier been such a glorious
vitality to her communal life. To live in Boston as the daughter of the
city's most celebrated mayor was to be constantly surrounded by the
signs and symbols of her family's position and power. Whether walking
with her girlfriends down the city's cobblestone streets, so old, so
crooked and so rich in their history, or wending her way past the old
City Hall, possessed by her father for nearly a quarter of her single life,
Rose would invariably be recognized by scores of her father's friends, by
fellow members of the Democratic Party or by associates of one of the
many Irish organizations to which her family belonged. Moreover,
growing up in an age when the activities of the Church penetrated all
relations in life, Rose had grown accustomed to an uncommonly vibrant
social life, filled with pageantry and parades.

Now, however, as she approached her sixth year of marriage and her
thirtieth birthday, an oppressive sense of isolation welled up within her.
With so many of her old roots sundered, she felt, in her own words, that
her "life was flowing past" her. It was not that she was idle. On the
contrary, in spite of the help she received with the household chores
from a cook and a nursemaid, she was always doing something in relation to the children. In the early twenties the child-rearing books
stressed the importance of bringing children out of doors every day,
regardless of the weather. At the same time, considering the cleanliness
of the child a cardinal command, the entire first chapter of L. Emmett

Holt's best-selling book on children is devoted to establishing the supreme importance of the daily tub bath, which should be omitted only in the case of very feeble or delicate children. When she tried to follow these twin commands, Rose discovered that even with help there were never enough hands to dress and undress, wash and dry, button and unbutton a family of three toddlers three or more times a day. Yet, even as she kept herself energetically busy, Rose no longer felt she was moving forward, and at each year's end an emptiness remained. In the stark routine of her existence, she no longer felt she stood for anything which lasted over time. If she straightened up the house, it would soon get messy. If she laced up the children's shoes, they would soon be taken off. For a vibrant young woman who had been brought up to believe she had a great purpose in life, the repetitiousness of her life in the suburbs was hard to accept.

Even harder to accept, Rose admitted long afterward, was the feeling she had in the early years of her marriage that she was growing more and more distant from Joe. Through so many years of courtship, she and Joe had shared so many dreams, so many conversations about their future. Now that their future was upon them, however, she was more separated from him than ever before. Though her father's vigilant eye no longer played a role in keeping the two of them apart, the realities of Joe's long days at work and his distaste for speaking about business at home took him away from her even more. Over time, it had become increasingly clear that for Joe work existed in a special department of his mind into which he was unwilling to admit his wife. And while Rose would brush off her ignorance of Joe's work as an inevitable consequence of his fast-moving pace—"My husband changed jobs so fast," she liked to say, "I simply never knew what business he was in"—and while she would frequently argue that their marriage was all the better for their not interfering in each other's work, nevertheless there loomed within her an ancient fear: the terrible knowledge of the disintegrating effect on her parents' marriage of separate interests and concerns.

It is also possible, as some Fitzgerald relatives have suggested, that Rose was suffering at this time from the awareness that Joe enjoyed going out with his bachelor friends, often in the company of other women. "Even in the early years of their marriage," one relative recalls, "Joe had a reputation for being a ladies' man, and some of this gossip must have caught up with Rose."

At the very least, it is clear from Kennedy's private papers in the early twenties that he enjoyed being seen by others as a fun-loving, red-blooded male. There is, for instance, a letter to Vera Murray, a woman who worked in New York with the theatrical producer Charles Dillingham, just as Joe was beginning to make his first forays into the world of the theater:

> Dear Vera:
>
> Jack Potter said you were coming up with Mr. Dillingham . . . [N]ot knowing what the functions are of the right hand man to the powers that be, I don't know how close you will be obliged to stick to your boss tonight. I know how close you would have to if I were your boss. However, Messrs. Conway, Moore and Kennedy will arrive at the Plaza at 7 to take you to dinner . . . At this dinner you might state what is your pleasure for the balance of the evening, and the three Boston youths will try, in so far as they can, to make things pleasant for you during your stay.

There is a similar tone in a letter written to Arthur Houghton, a young theatrical manager connected with a musical-show company who eventually became a lifelong friend of Joe's:

> I hope you will have all the good looking girls in your company looking forward with anticipation to meeting the high Irish of Boston because I have a gang around me that must be fed on wild meat. Lately they are so bad. As for me, I have too many troubles around to bother with such things at the present time. Everything may be better, however, when you arrive.

Whether Joe's jaunty tone in these letters was simply talk and nothing more, we cannot know. We only know that the loneliness and the isolation Rose felt during this same period brought upon her a moody unhappiness which she vividly remembered many years later.

The hardest part for Rose was that she couldn't admit that she felt cheated and disillusioned in any way. For years she had been told that motherhood would be her principal work and glory, that when she advanced to motherhood she would be reaching "the most beautiful station" in her life. And she still believed this to be true. How, then, to explain this aching desire for something more, this craving for movement which found no satisfaction in her quiet life? It had all been so different in her youth when she had been continuously exposed to high-spirited talk about the central issues of the day, when she had been afforded the privilege of sharing fully in her father's adventurous world. Taught to make the most of every advantage that life had to offer, she had traveled to such new and delightful places as western Europe and South America; having experienced the pride of knowing that her entry at a ball attracted all eyes, she had come to believe that she was meant to live at the center of glitter and excitement.

Remembering all this one long wintry weekend in early 1920 when two of her three children, who now ranged in age from five to one, were sick and Joe was away from home, Rose suddenly wanted to be with her father again, to be with him as she had been when she was a little girl. In a state of fatigue made worse by her pregnancy (her fourth child was due in February), she decided that after the children got well she would pack up some of her clothes and go back to her girlhood home on Welles Avenue, back to the stately white house which had gleamed its welcoming lights to all the gathering guests on that sparkling night of her brilliant debut years earlier. There, in the big house where she had danced and dreamed when her life was all before her, there, surely, she could figure out what to do.

Later, Rose described her return to Welles Avenue as nothing more than "a needed rest," but relatives recall it as a serious, if temporary, break in her marriage. After three weeks at home, however, sleeping in the same room where she and Agnes had whispered together in better, happier days, she understood that she no longer belonged in her parents' home, that she could never again lie down as a child, secure beneath her father's roof.

Curiously enough, when Rose first arrived home she found the old house much as it used to be. For one thing, all her sisters and brothers, ranging in age from twenty-eight to fifteen, were still single and still living at home. And while her father had failed in his most recent attempt to return to political life—in November 1918, he had narrowly beaten incumbent Congressman Peter Tague, only to be unseated three months later on charges of illegal registration and ballot stuffing—he remained as exuberant as ever, emerging once again from disgrace like a duck from water, and the local newspapers still considered him the leading citizen of Boston. Radiating health and vigor, John Fitzgerald was a man of such overwhelming personal force that even out of office he was able to keep a bold stamp on the consciousness of the public.

An uncontestable measure of Fitzgerald's formidable popularity at this time can be judged by the tremendous outpouring of public sympathy he received following press reports of his being run over by a two-ton truck while he was sitting on the first-base line watching his sons play ball at a ballfield in Nantasket. As the story was told and retold in the Boston papers, Fitzgerald, his back to the truck, failed at first to hear the crowd's warnings when the driver of the truck lost control at the top of an adjacent hill, causing the big vehicle to careen wildly toward the crowd. When the shouts finally reached him, Fitzgerald acted quickly, pushing out of the way dozens of children, several of whom, the *Boston Post* reported, "would probably have been severely injured if it were not for the prompt action of 'Mayor' Fitzgerald." Unable to get out of the way himself, Fitzgerald was trapped as the truck ran over his legs, lacerating his right leg badly, tearing the muscles of his left and fracturing his kneecap to the point where an operation was called for. Yet even as he lay on the field to be taken to the hospital, he told the shaken crowd not to worry, and to prove that he was all right he began singing his old campaign song, "Sweet Adeline." With this, the *Boston Globe* reported, "the crowd cheered and the trip to the Sturgis Hospital assumed the form of an ovation." Such were the symbols from which Fitzgerald's continuing popularity was forged.

As a young girl in her father's house Rose would lie awake at night knowing she was the center around which this great man's affections revolved. But now, as she tried to recover that irretrievable feeling, she noted how attentive and affectionate her father had become to her youngest sister, Eunice, who seemed, in turn, to know his every state and every shade of feeling. Eunice had been only fourteen and positively ungainly when Rose was married, but at twenty she was, in Rose's opinion, "a beautiful young girl, intelligent as well as attractive, with very lively ways, much of the spunk and spirit and wit of my father." Her skin was creamy white and pink and she had soft curly brown hair and large, expressive eyes. It was on this young girl, after Rose was married, that Fitzgerald had concentrated his whole affection, constantly singing the praises of her gentleness, her sympathy and her acute intelligence. Having graduated from the Henry Pierce Grammar School in Dorchester at the age of eleven, a record for the school, Eunice had completed her education at the Sacred Heart academies in New York and in Boston, where she earned a prize for the best literary essay. Then, when the Great War broke out and her favorite brother, Tom, was shipped to France, Eunice became a member of the Red Cross, working day and night in the cottage on the Common, refusing to yield to fatigue even as the dreaded disease of tuberculosis began destroying her health.

Though Eunice was already desperately ill by the time Rose returned home in the winter of 1920, neither she nor her father had given up hoping; on the contrary, both father and daughter were possessed with the same boundless spirit, the same determination to fight a winning battle to regain her health. That battle would later take Eunice to Montreal for two lung operations by the foremost surgeon in Canada and later still to Saranac Lake, a sanitarium in upstate New York, where she would stay for weeks and months at a time. No one in the family spoke much of the illness, but it was plain to Rose that, in her courageous struggle to live, Eunice had penetrated into her father's soul in a way that no one else, not even she herself at the peak of their intimacy, had ever done. As the days went by Rose observed the inexpressible delight on her father's face whenever Eunice came into the room, and somehow everything that had once been familiar to her suddenly seemed strange and unnatural.

Still Rose remained in her old home, until one snowy night when, as she remembered the encounter sixty years later, her father came into her room and told her sternly that he believed the time had come for her to return to her family. "You've made your commitment, Rosie," he said, "and you must honor it now. What is past is past. The old days are gone. Your children need you and your husband needs you. You *can* make things work out. I know you can. If you need more help in the household, then get it. If you need a bigger house, ask for it. If you need more private time for yourself, take it. There isn't anything you can't do once you set your mind on it. So go now, Rosie, go back where you belong."

Galvanized by the authority in her father's voice, Rose began thinking more sharply than she had done for weeks. Of course she could make things work. She always had managed and she always would. It was just a matter of accepting her own needs and then reorganizing the household so that she could create definite goals for herself *and* have a clear vision of what she hoped to accomplish with her family. It was a question of accepting that her own desire to grow and learn deserved expression just as surely as that of her children. There must be a way, she determined, of doing with the children what she herself enjoyed, of sharing with them her love of history and travel, of politics and ritual; there must be a way to encourage the children into activities which would allow her to grow as well.

In her new resolve, not surprisingly, it was to the Church that Rose turned as the one remaining tower of strength in the landscape of her life; in particular, she decided before going home to attend a religious retreat, a series of days passed in solitude and prayer, which the Boston diocese regularly sponsored as a means of inducing its parishioners to withdraw from the rush and tumult of the world in order to draw more readily toward God and to reflect on the purpose of their lives. At these retreats, Rose later wrote, the participants would gather together in the quiet of a religious house and listen to talks by priests specially trained for this kind of work. Through these talks, which provided practical as well as spiritual advice for the daily problems people faced, the participants were encouraged to look back on their lives without intrusion and to cleanse their bodies and minds of bad habits and crippling thoughts. Later in her life, Rose considered her lifelong habit of making retreats one of her greatest blessings, one that helped her keep calm during upheavals, poised during confusion and confident during trage-dies.

From this retreat, Rose vividly recalled, she brought home with her a renewed understanding of the ideals of Catholic womanhood and an altered recognition that while the theater, the cotillion and the dinner party all had their proper place in refined social life, all these things were good only if one undertook something else, some work, some duty, some mission. And her mission, she now emphatically realized, was to create a family: to provide her husband and her children with a feeling of belonging to something greater than themselves. Moreover, at a time when the modern American family was seen to be in a state of collapse, having lost its traditional functions to the triumphant industrial order, Rose understood that the kind of family life she desired would not simply happen. It would have to be constructed by conscious effort, by instill-ing values and traditions so strong that every member of the family would know what to do and what to expect without having to ask.

Once Rose had determined that her aim in life was to re-create the strong family unit which had existed in the past, strong enough to with-stand the disintegrating forces of twentieth-century life, then she was able, as she later wrote, to look on child-rearing not simply as a work of love and duty but as "a profession that was fully as interesting and challenging as any honorable profession in the world" and one that demanded the best that she could bring.

From this point on, Rose rejected the role of the martyred wife. In contrast to her mother's pattern of keeping the family and the home as an embittered bastion against the outer world, relishing the power she exercised in her own domain, Rose decided to encourage her husband to become more actively engaged in their ongoing family life. Together, she determined, they would establish a joint scale of priorities for the kind of family they wished to create.

Fortunately for Rose's plans, the separation had jolted Joe substan-tially, uprooting him from his preoccupation with his work and propel-ling him more closely into the emotional center of his family's life. To be sure, Joe had always believed strongly in family life, having received some fixed ideas on the importance of family from his own father and mother; but at the feverish pace he was working in the early years of his marriage, his engagement with his family was at best that of a typical father who willingly concedes to his wife the overwhelming responsibil-ities for bringing up the children until they are teenagers, when it is often too late to reenter their lives.

Then, within weeks of Rose's return, there followed a second emotional crisis which would shake Joe even more—the near-death of his second son, Jack, from scarlet fever in February 1920. A disease especially of young children, scarlet fever is characterized by a sudden high fever, often rising to 105 degrees in the first few hours, accompanied by a deeply red congested throat, swollen tonsils, a puffy face and a scarlet rash spreading over the entire body and legs. In ordinary cases, the rash begins to fade after four or five days, followed by a two-week period during which the skin peels off in large flakes from the entire surface of the body. But with Jack, right from the start, the disease assumed an intensely virulent form; and when nearly a week had passed, neither the rash nor the fever had diminished, raising the serious danger of life-threatening complications.

Jack's illness plunged the Kennedy household into a state of what Rose later described as "frantic terror." At the time the first symptoms of the disease erupted, Rose was just hours away from the delivery of her fourth child, and women during and after childbirth were known to be particularly liable to contract the disease. Moreover, as scarlet fever is highly contagious, there were also fears that Joe Junior and Rosemary would get it, and even the new baby, a little blue-eyed girl who was born at home on February 20 in the midst of all this confusion, and who was named Kathleen. In the fear of contagion, nerves became frayed, sleep was fitful and nothing could go on as usual. Nor was there anywhere Jack could be taken to receive the proper care. In the 1920s, Rose explained later, Brookline's hospital did not admit patients with contagious diseases, and the Kennedys weren't eligible to use the Boston hospitals because they didn't live in the city.

Indeed, so frightful and so contagious was scarlet fever in those days before the introduction of penicillin that the Brookline Board of Health prescribed that all persons ill with the disease remain isolated for at least five weeks, and that no well child from a house where there was a case of scarlet fever be allowed to mingle with persons of any other house until after the removal, recovery or death of the patient and the disinfection of the premises. The regulations also obligated every affected household to refrain from sending exposed articles of clothing to a laundry, to keep all waste materials in a separate receptacle, to send all library books used by the patient to be disinfected before returning them, and to affix on the front and rear doors a card stating the disease to be avoided.

With Rose convalescing from childbirth, the colossal responsibility of caring for Jack fell upon Joe, who immediately determined that the only hope for his little boy, whose condition was worsening each day, lay in his being admitted to the South Department of the Boston City Hospital. Opened in 1895 as the first separate contagious-disease hospital in the country, the South Department had achieved a worldwide reputation for its progressive treatment of diphtheria and scarlet fever. Moreover, if Jack could be admitted as a patient, he could be placed under the care of the great Dr. Edwin Place, perhaps the nation's leading authority in the field of contagious diseases. Educated at the Harvard Medical School, the bespectacled Dr. Place was considered one of the finest clinicians in the country; he was also known as an indefatigable worker who inspired great loyalty and dedication on the part of his staff.

The more Joe learned about Dr. Place and the Boston City Hospital, the more obsessed he became with getting Jack in. For several days he pressed his case, mobilizing every source of influence at his command, including that of his father-in-law, until finally—in spite of the fact there were only 125 hospital beds available for the more than six hundred children in Boston suffering from scarlet fever at the same time—the hospital bent its rules and admitted young John Kennedy.

By this time, as Rose recorded in her memoirs, Jack was a "very, very sick little boy," burdened not only with the wretched discomfort of his physical condition but also with his first separation from his home and his family. Years later Joe vividly recalled the distressing experience of leaving his two-and-a-half-year-old son in the small square sterile room, which doctors, nurses and attendants could enter only after thoroughly scrubbing their hands and putting on a specially disinfected gown. He looked at his son's thin little form tossing about in the large white impersonal bed, knowing by instinct that the boy was far sicker than they dared tell him, and he suddenly felt he would strangle at the pain welling up in his throat.

"I had never experienced any very serious sickness in my family previous to Jack's," Joe wrote later to Dr. Place, "and I little realized what an effect such a happening could possibly have on me. During the darkest days I felt that nothing else mattered except his recovery."

From this moment on, Joe's conduct was puzzling to many and he upset many settled notions about himself. Every morning he went to church to pray, promising in his prayers that if Jack was spared he would give half of all his money to charity. Every afternoon, he left his office earlier than he had ever left any job in his life and journeyed to the hospital, where the love and attention he brought were no doubt magic to the child. Seated for long periods on the edge of his boy's bed, Joe realized now that no amount of money could recompense him for a death in his family. And with that realization, the world suddenly looked smaller.

For Jack, the convalescence was slow and painful. Day after day his misery lasted, prompting one of the nurses assigned to him after his first week in the hospital to record how sorry she was that "Jack has had to have these ill turns. But we must just hope for the best and not lose courage." Finally, in the third week of March, the illness began to subside and slowly he began to feel better. Still, it would be a long time before Jack would be allowed to go home; he would spend another four weeks in the hospital plus two additional weeks recovering at the Mansion House in Poland Springs, Maine. By the time he was returned to his family, it was already May and spring was in the air. Nearly three months had passed since that dark and dreary February week when he was first taken ill—a significant passage of time in the mind of a small child.

Throughout the long ordeal of his separation from his family, young Jack displayed a remarkable character trait which served to lessen his emotional loss and which stayed with him the rest of his life. The portrait of the little boy that emerges from the letters of the hospital nurses is that of an irresistibly charming child with an uncommon capacity to stir emotions in people, creating in each of them the feeling that he and they somehow shared a special bond.

"He is such a wonderful boy," Nurse Sara Miller tells Joe in the middle of Jack's hospital stay. "We all love him very dearly." In a similar tone, Nurse Anna Pope comments, "Jack is certainly the nicest little boy I have ever seen." Surely some of this emotion can be explained by the embattled atmosphere generated within the contagious pavilion of the hospital. Because it was a self-contained unit and quite isolated, hospital historian John Byrne writes, "there was an unusual spirit of friendliness and intimacy, almost a sense of family, that pervaded the institution." And in Jack's case there was, of course, the attractive vulnerability of his extreme youth, his thatch of chestnut hair, his bright-blue eyes and his irrepressible smile.

But the affection Jack inspired in his nurses was special; it continued even after he had left the hospital, and two of the women made visits to his house to see him. In a letter to Jack's Aunt Loretta written after her first visit, Sara Miller says: "I enjoyed seeing *my Jack* again so much. Mrs. Kennedy has a wonderful family I think. And she is such a little girl herself. But of course none of them is as nice as my Jack." And Nurse Pope, noting sadly that she fears Jack will soon forget her, writes to Joe: "I am afraid I asked for too much when I asked for Jack's picture but he was so lovable and such an excellent little patient, everyone loved him. I felt very lonesome when I left him. I was glad I had a little girl whom I could go to."

Younger and smaller than his favored brother Joe Junior, Jack perhaps had learned at an even earlier age how to reach out beyond his parents, to his aunts and his uncles, his maids and his governesses—and now to his nurses—for the affection he craved. For him, reaching out to others in the larger world promised salvation; yet even as he charmed people one by one, drawing friends to his side as if by magic, he would retain a measure of reserve, an avoidance of easy intimacy, which, in the strange alchemy of his relationships, served only to increase his attraction to others.

When Jack was fully recovered, his grateful father wrote an emotional letter of thanks to Dr. Place, concluding with "My only hope is that you might always feel that I am indebted to you." To all appearances, Joe fulfilled his pledge to God as well, by giving a check to the Guild of St. Apollonia, an organization of Catholic dentists committed to providing dental care to children in Catholic schools. With Joe's check, the guild was able to purchase a motor van to transport the parochial-school children to and from its dental infirmary. The amount of the check was $3,750, which, according to Rose, was exactly half of Joe's "fortune" at that time. How close she is in her estimate we cannot say, though it is hard to imagine, from the large amounts of money Joe was then juggling in the stock market, that he was worth only $7,500. Unless, of course, in making up his balance sheet for God he donned his bank examiner's garb and considered only those assets which could be immediately converted into cash!

The importance of this dramatic family crisis lay in Joe's developing sense of fatherhood. From this time forward, according to Rose, he took to coming home earlier in the evenings and he gave his children the best part of himself. From this moment on, the governesses were told never to hesitate to interrupt him, whether he were in a conference, or visiting with friends, if they wished to consult him about his children.

"Joe was absolutely devoted to his children," Rose wrote in her memoirs. "He loved them and let them know it . . . in the most outgoing demonstrative ways. In business and politics people found him hardheaded and tough, but they should have seen him at home, warm and gentle with the little ones. He would sweep them into his arms and hug them and grin at them and talk to them and perhaps carry them around . . . Also, as each one became old enough to talk . . . he would want that child in bed with him for a little while each morning. And the two of them would be propped up on pillows with perhaps the child's head cuddling on his shoulder and he would talk or read a story or they would have conversations."

Yet Joe's commitment to his children at this juncture was still conditioned by his primary commitment to making money, a goal he and

Rose jointly shared. While his wife's separation and his son's near-fatal illness heightened his resolve to spend more time with his family, his business activities still consumed most of his waking hours. To Rose's mind, however, there was a definite change. "After Jack's illness, Joe was determined to keep up with every little thing the children were doing," she recalled. "Every night we would spend hours together talking about the family and going over the children's activities. It made me feel that I had a partner in my enterprise."

With Joe's vigorous backing, Rose dedicated her intelligence, her energy and all her talent to the tasks of bringing up her children and making a total family life. Indeed, so strong was her determination to mold her children's characters and encourage their ambitions that she felt absolutely no guilt in asking for additional household help. If she was putting all her energies into educating the children, she should not be expected to handle the material details of the household as well; taking care of the physical needs of her husband and children must not distract her from the larger goal. Many young women in Rose's position might have had difficulty accepting the idea of having others serve them, but the daughter of Mayor Fitzgerald had no difficulty whatsoever taking on the accoutrements belonging to the upper class. Nor did Joe object to Rose's spending money to ease the daily burden of cooking, cleaning and physically caring for the children. In Joe's eyes, Rose was an excellent manager—indeed, the more involved Joe became with his family, the more respect he developed for the orderly manner in which the household was run: from the servants down to the food, the clothing and the children's manners, there was a general solidity in the household, an old-fashioned discipline which inspired his lifelong respect and admiration.

Joe also backed up his wife in her desire for a larger house, and in August 1920 the papers were signed for the purchase of a two-and-a-half-story residence two blocks away, on the corner of Naples Road and Abbotsford Road. The new residence boasted twelve rooms, a porch that stretched halfway around the house, and, most important, enough extra space—even with the rooms set aside for the additional live-in help —that Rose could have a room of her own when she wanted to think, read, sew or be alone, a door to shut between her and the children when she wanted peace and privacy. All her life Rose would insist on such a place for herself, a place where she could assert her own needs and not feel she was continually sacrificing herself for the children. All her life she would hold a part of herself back from the children—keeping intact a mysterious region of her soul into which she did not consider it necessary to admit them. By having her own space, Rose never had to suffer from the notion that she was on call every hour for her family; rather, she was working with her husband and her children on an enterprise of their joint creation.

The Kennedys took possession of their new home on October 1, 1920, after weeks of shopping together for new rugs and additional furniture. In contrast to the decorating of the Beals Street house, which Rose undertook mainly on her own, this time Joe was intimately involved in the selection of the furnishings, the rugs and the draperies. In the midst of his business correspondence from Hayden, Stone on stocks and bonds, there are a number of letters to Paine Furniture, Palais Rugs and other stores which, taken together, reveal that Joe was the one who was actually making the final decisions on the Oriental rugs, the wall coverings and the antique furniture. And, as further evidence of his increasing role in the life of his family, his private papers reveal a number of occasions when he canceled business engagements because of conditions in the family. On January 5, 1921, for example, his secretary reports that "Kennedy could not get to New York because his boy is ill. He can't go until the boy is a great deal better." (The sick boy is probably Jack, who, in the months after his recovery from scarlet fever, suffered whooping cough and mumps.) Then on June 21, 1921, Joe wrote to his friend Chris Dunphy to cancel plans for a golfing trip to Bretton Woods. "Nothing I'd rather do than spend the three day holiday on the 4th at Bretton Woods but on account of Mrs. Kennedy's condition I do not feel I would want to be away from home at this time." On July 10, 1921, Mrs. Kennedy's "condition" resulted in the birth of her fifth child, a daughter whom she named in honor of her dying sister Eunice.

Seen from a distance, the structure of the family life the Kennedys created can be judged harshly, as hobbled by an excess of prescribed behavior and regulated activity. Yet, living in the shadow of the disintegrating twenties—the dizzying decade of flappers and bootleggers, of sensuous music, scandals and fads—Rose believed that adherence to daily ritual offered the best hope for the family's survival. At a time when many "nice" girls were smoking and lifting their skirts, when age was imitating youth instead of youth modeling itself on age, the only way to hold a family together, Rose believed, was to impose upon all the children unchangeable ideals and fixed routines which would enable them to resist the pressures of moral and social drift. So, from the start, even when the children were still toddlers, Rose established certain times of day as constants, including family meals eaten together, shared religious exercises and daily excursions, all of which she deemed essential for the maintenance of a secure, ongoing home life.

Every morning when the domestic chores were getting under way,

Rose would take the children for a long walk or for a visit to a historic place, the Bunker Hill Monument or the *Constitution*, Old North Church or the Boston Common. Remembering how her own love of history had been fostered by the many wonderful expeditions she had taken with her father, she wanted her children to be able "to know and feel the past," to walk the streets of the present in a timeless proximity with the heroic figures of Boston's past.

At the same time, she wanted her children to have a sense of the vitality of the politics she had known as a child, when the gay jingle of bells announced a street-corner speech, when entire neighborhoods would become involved in political events, when the attachment to political parties, based as it was on the innate sentiments of fidelity and fellowship, still had an emotional character. Recognizing that the spontaneous life of the Democratic Party could never be the same in the suburbs as it had been in the crowded wards of the city, Rose took every occasion she could find to bring her children back into Boston for political events. Invited to a banquet given by the city of Boston for General Jacques of Belgium, she let Joe and Jack accompany her into Boston so that they could see the splendor of the banquet table before being sent home with the nursemaid. Acquainted with the political calendar from her own childhood, she brought her children into the city for all the most festive parades, processions and public ceremonies.

Later, as she looked back on those early years in Brookline, Rose described herself as feeling suddenly out of joint with the politics of the times and its dominant notes of cynicism, conservatism and indifference. Disillusioned by the pointless slaughter of the war which had decimated an entire generation in Europe and had returned men to a medieval sense of man's wickedness, the new generation had turned its back on the Democratic Party and on public life in general, preferring to concentrate its energy on private affairs. "The great problems of the world . . . do not concern me in the slightest," wrote the drama critic George Jean Nathan in a representative opinion. "What concerns me alone is myself and the interests of a few close friends." It was an age in which money was the measure of the man, a period that witnessed an almost complete collapse of the movement for a broader social justice which had dominated the nation for the first fifteen years of the century.

Succumbing to both the temper of the times and the interests of his financial career, Joe Kennedy indulged himself for a while in an open flirtation with the Republican Party. For him, as for many traditional Democrats engaged in banking and business, the Republican Party offered the key to the infectious prosperity of the decade. In the 1920s the association of business and politics took on a new dimension: with the

Democrats in flurried retreat, government became so completely fused with business that the two became synonymous. In the context of this situation, it is not surprising that Joe seriously considered taking the step of joining the Republican Party, even though it meant repudiating the party he had belonged to since the day he was born. "We welcome you with open arms," Republican leader Louis Coolidge wrote on October 18, 1920, when Kennedy accepted his long-standing invitation to join the Middlesex Club, the oldest Republican club in New England.

For several years, Joe's sympathies had been moving in an increasingly conservative direction. When the mostly Irish Boston police force went out on strike in September of 1919, Joe lent his name to the Fund for the Defenders of Public Safety, an association which labeled the striking policemen as deserters and called upon the citizenry to recognize the few policemen who remained on duty as the real heroes of the crisis. Miserably underpaid and overworked in station houses which were dilapidated, crowded and dirty, the police had voted in the summer of 1919 to affiliate with the American Federation of Labor. Policemen in thirty-seven other cities had taken such action without arousing public concern, but, in a year when dozens of strikes had paralyzed industry and commerce across the nation, the decision of the Boston police to join a union was seen as proof of labor's increasing radicalism, as "a first step toward sovietizing the country," in the words of Henry Cabot Lodge. The city's conservative police commissioner responded to the fledgling union by suspending its nineteen leaders, an arbitrary action which provoked the policemen to vote a strike, 1,134 to 2. The first night of the strike, mobs took control of the streets, smashing windows and assaulting women. Chaos reigned until the Governor, Calvin Coolidge, finally mobilized the State Guard, which, together with a citizens' guard made up mostly of Harvard students and former Harvard athletes, restored order to the city. After the rioting, the striking police voted almost unanimously to return to work, but the vengeful police commissioner issued an order, backed by the Governor, directing that not a single one of the strikers ever be allowed back on the police force.

It was a difficult event for the Kennedy family. Joe's favorite uncle, Jim Hickey, had been a policeman for thirty years and was now a captain in charge of the East Boston station house. Though men at the level of captain were not involved in the union, Hickey's sympathies for his men were clear from the outset. On the eve of the strike he expressed his sorrow that such a thing should happen and told his men, "You are levelheaded and you know what you are doing."

In addition to his uncle, Joe had another relative on the police force, a father of two young children. He went out on strike and never regained his job, spending the rest of his days sitting on his front porch with a lost and vacant look in his eyes. Yet, when the issue was drawn between chaos and order, Joe turned his back on the grievances of the striking policemen and chose to support the forces of order. It was the close of an era.

Joe's shifting sympathies were further solidified by his narrow escape from injury in the Wall Street bombing of September 16, 1920. He had been only a few hundred feet from the point of the frightful explosion (which killed thirty persons instantly and injured some three hundred more, of whom ten died later). On his way to a noon meeting of the stockholders of the Todd Shipbuilding Company, he had just turned the corner of Wall and Broad Streets when, he later told the *Boston Herald*,

> I felt a sudden shock to my entire body and found I had been knocked down. Because I was stupefied rather than because I was overstocked with courage, I jumped up, turned, and ran back to Wall Street. As I did so I saw a cloud of flying glass falling. I saw men and women with their heads split, with blood streaming down their faces everywhere. I heard cries on every side of the street.

Breaking virtually every window in the immediate vicinity and covering the streets with shrapnel-like fragments of brick and stone blasted from the walls of the skyscrapers, the explosion emanated from a point directly beside J. P. Morgan & Company, the geographical and metaphorical center of financial America. The front of the Morgan building was demolished, but J. P. Morgan himself was on holiday in an English country house and all of his partners who were in the building at the time escaped serious injury. Indeed, as it turned out, not one of the dead was a king or a general of finance; those who died in the blast were Wall Street's attendants and privates—the stenos, clerks, bookkeepers, messengers and porters who had stepped out of their buildings a minute or two before noon on their way to an early lunch.

The government never found the bombers, but few people doubted at the time that the bomb had been planted by radicals of one stripe or another, as part of the general pattern of industrial unrest that accompanied the dislocation of the postwar period. Whatever the meaning of the mysterious explosion, it confirmed for Joe and for thousands of others like him the importance of strong governmental action to quell disorders.

But if there was a moment in the early twenties when Joe officially considered becoming a Republican, that moment passed when Rose brought all her persuasive powers to bear upon the decision. Later, Rose recalled the argument about party affiliation as one of the few occasions when she talked politics with her husband. Believing strongly in the family's connection with the Democratic Party as a legacy to pass on to the children, Rose was convinced that changing parties would be a terrible mistake. As it turned out, Joe himself was becoming disillusioned with the state Republican Party over what he saw as a continuing failure to appoint Irish Catholics to various positions. In an angry letter to the president of the Middlesex Club, he said that the Republican Governor had made a big mistake in failing to reappoint one William Maguire as clerk of the court.

> I realize that you are anxious to get the Republican party as representative as you can; to do this, people like myself must be made to feel that there is a chance in the Republican party to at least see that Irish Catholics are not discriminated against just because they are Irish Catholics. I think the success of your idea to enroll a number of Irish Catholics in the Republican party will meet with success only when instances like the failure to reappoint Maguire are entirely eliminated.

But Rose did not rest content with Joe's temporary pique. On the contrary, she used the occasion to drive home her point by mobilizing the most effective ally she could find—Joe's soft-spoken father, P. J. Kennedy. Calling one day upon P.J., Rose simply mentioned her concern about Joe switching parties, knowing that loyalty to the Democrats would find resonance in P.J.'s heart. Her strategy worked. From then on, while Joe occasionally voted Republican, he no longer talked about joining the party.

If Rose found the old rituals of the political party weakened in the twenties, the vitality of the Catholic Church suffered a double assault under the dispersion of the middle-class Irish to the suburbs and the enactment of restrictive laws against immigration which reduced the foreign flood of new Catholics to a trickle. The Church of the immigrants in which Rose had grown up had been one in which God was a living force; to an immigrant population seeking security, survival and hope, the parishes were seen as the center of their social and emotional lives.

By comparison, the Church of the twenties was no longer as encompassing as the immigrant Church had been. On weekdays at St. Aidan's Rose encountered no more than a dozen worshipers; this in contrast to the hundreds and thousands of people in the North End for whom St. Stephen's Church had been a second home.

Struggling against odds to counter the rapid secularization of society and save something of the old ways, Rose determined to *make* the Church a vital element in her children's lives. While many of her Irish friends, reaching toward ease and comfort, found themselves in the position of wanting to shed some of the Old World attachments and customs in order to become more American, Rose embraced the ancient rituals, finding deep pleasure in the doing of things as they had always been done. If traditional faith was losing its cutting edge, she would find a way to bring her children to a continual awareness of the existence of God. Every morning on her way home with the children from their daily walk, she would stop in at St. Aidan's, where they could immerse themselves for a moment in the beauty of the rustic stone church with its low walls, high-pitched roof and English Gothic design. "I wanted them to understand that Church isn't just for Sundays and special times on the calendar," she wrote in her memoirs, "but should be a part of life."

While for many Catholics religion was becoming peripheral rather than central to their way of life, Rose insisted on the recital of grace at every meal, the saying of the Rosary as a family event and the practice of nightly prayer. While interest in Catholic traditions was withering in the society at large, she took it upon herself to teach her children about the meaning of Shrove Tuesday and Palm Sunday. And when the religious holidays came, she would, whenever possible, bring her children back to St. Stephen's Church in the North End, where the feast days were still celebrated in the old-fashioned way, with all the pomp and pageantry of great spectacles.

Beyond the morning walks, the historical expeditions, the daily visits to church and the saying of nightly prayers, Rose insisted on the regularity of family mealtimes, so that dinners and weekend lunches could become a time for communication and not simply a filling up of plates and a moving away. By establishing a fixed time every day for the major meal and by demanding adherence to that schedule, she made her children coordinate their engagements around the family instead of vice versa. While she appreciated the importance of school, sports and other outside activities, she wanted none of these involvements to take precedence for her children over their family life. At the same time, by organizing daily topics for the mealtime discussion—usually geared to the religious calendar or to current events—she encouraged an exchange of information and ideas in which even the younger children learned to speak up for themselves.

Though the institutions of the Church and the family were failing others, Rose was determined to adapt them to her own life in her own way so that they could serve *her* needs and *her* ambitions. It took a determined spirit—a spirit as determined as Joe's had been when he first decided to challenge the prevailing wisdom of the day which cautioned any Irish Catholic in Boston against entering the field of finance.

As both Rose and Joe became increasingly involved in sustaining the family life, their marriage seemed to settle on a different plane. With such intense concentration on the children—who now numbered five with the birth of Eunice in 1921—the old excitement of their forbidden romance diminished; in the regularity of their daily life, the spontaneity of their early meetings became an irrecoverable remembrance. But, at the same time, their powerful feelings of love for their children and their respect for each other as parents seemed to lay the foundation for a new life and a quite different happiness. From here on, Rose and Joe appear less like lovers than like partners in the common enterprise of welding their children together into a family group with its own standards, its own language and its own traditions. Refusing to use the children as a means of getting back at each other, as Rose's parents had occasionally done, they made the family the object of their concord, the instrument of their togetherness.

Instead of living for each other as they had done as young lovers, they now lived for the children and for themselves. Having been hurt twice by the men she loved, first by her father and then, it seems, by Joe as well, Rose was determined not to let her life and her love be one. Henceforth Joe had his world of business and his golfing buddies, a world she did not try to enter, while she had her clubs, her girlfriends and, most important, her love of travel.

If Joe went off golfing, as he did once or twice a year, to Florida or to Hilton Head, Rose knew that once he returned she would have a trip of her own, accompanied by someone she wanted as a companion, to a place of her own choosing, and that while she was gone Joe would arrange his business plans to be home with the children. For her part, Rose was eager to travel to other parts of the country or of the world— "I would have been bored by going to the same place every year for a holiday," she confessed—while Joe preferred the regularity of sun and golf in Palm Beach. The mutual acceptance of this arrangement is reflected in the lack of bitterness each of them showed when the other was away; unlike many a wife or husband who feels compelled to tell the missing partner all the grisly details of all the household troubles, neither Rose nor Joe engaged in the infliction of guilt. When an epidemic of measles hit the Kennedy household while Rose was in California on a six-week trip with her sister, Joe never said a word about it, not wanting her to cancel the trip; similarly, when Rose took a phone call from Joe from the West Coast minutes after she arrived home from a car accident that had put a gash in her forehead large enough to require stitches, she pulled herself together and spoke as naturally as she could lest his worry about her and the children spoil his trip.

"Each time of life has its own kind of love," Tolstoy writes. If the excitement of the conquest was over, there was, it seems, an ease in the Kennedys' relationship which developed into a different kind of love.

# CHAPTER 19

# "THE
# WALL
# STREET
# RACKET"

On the third Sunday in June of 1922, Joe Kennedy motored to the Hotel Pilgrim in Plymouth, Massachusetts, where he joined over two hundred of his Harvard classmates for their tenth reunion. There is a picture of Kennedy taken on the first full day of the celebration which shows him standing arm in arm with Bob Fisher, Ralph Lowell, Oscar Haussermann and Hugh Gaddis. They are all dressed alike, wearing white shirts, bow ties and crimson cardigan sweaters with floppy pockets edged in white with a lettered white square over the left breast which signaled to all who could see that they were the men of 1912. Looking merry and a little foolish, just as one might expect a group of college reunioners to look, they spent their first morning engaged in field sports, stunts and sightseeing. The feature of the sunny afternoon was a burlesque boxing bout on the lawn, during which someone turned the lawn hose on the contestants, producing a general commotion which ended with the drenching of nearly half the class.

In the programmed days that followed there were a host of activities, including luncheons and clambakes, movies and entertainment and a class parade in which the ten-year men, arrayed in flaming-red coats with white trousers and farmer hats and led by Bob Fisher, marched under a variety of colorful banners.

It must have been a happy reunion for Joe. In the crowd of young men milling around and greeting one another with forced bonhomie, he stood out as one who had done exceptionally well in the ten years since graduation. Considering where he had started from, he had made more money than most, and if a man is known by the company he keeps, Kennedy's association with the prestigious firm of Hayden, Stone added to his luster. Yet he wore his success lightly and he threw himself heartily into all the activities. "Joe loved fun," said one of his classmates. "He was a leader at the reunions." Having served, along with journalist Frederick Lewis Allen, on the subcommittee on entertainment, Joe had pulled off a coup by obtaining copies of the newly released films of the Dempsey–Carpentier heavyweight boxing bouts—a coup which earned him the lasting gratitude of the decennial committee.

But for Joe, according to Rose, the best parts of the reunion were the relaxing hours he was able to share with his three college buddies, Fisher, Campbell and Potter. With the return of peace had come an end to the tensions which had estranged Joe from his soldier friends during the war. Once the slaughter had been brought to a halt, it dawned on perceptive men and women everywhere that the war fought to save the world for democracy and to abolish all war had ended in a peace which laid the foundations for new dictatorships and for future conflicts. Seen after the fact, it was America's most disillusioning experience—a dirty, unheroic struggle which few soldiers remembered with any emotion save distaste. In his class report Fisher admits that his war record was certainly nothing he could boast of, while a disenchanted Campbell speaks sarcastically of "the apparently unsuccessful attempt to save the world for democracy" which demanded his time for a few years. "My military career aroused no cheers," Campbell quipped, "and fortunately for me caused no tears." Such reactions as these—and there were many such—brought an end to the prewar idealism which had made Joe a stranger in his own circle of friends. Considering that Joe was the only one of his group who had spoken out against the war at the beginning, it was ironic that he should be the one whom the war benefited the most. For Fisher and Campbell, and even for Potter, the war came as a major interruption in their lives. Before the war, Fisher had begun a promising career in the department store business, but upon returning to Boston he found that his experience in the war had made his interest in the business ebb and he decided instead to accept the position of head football coach at Harvard. Not long after this, Campbell also left the world of business, which he had just entered before the war, to become assistant graduate treasurer of the Harvard Athletic Association, where he coached the freshmen and, as he put it, used all the influence he had with the ticket office to see that "no 1912 man sat in the wooden stands."

To be sure, it was an exciting time to be associated with the Harvard football team. With Fisher at the reins, the 1919 team was not beaten once during the entire season and went on to win the Rose Bowl at Pasadena in January 1920. With the championship teams he was fielding as head coach, Fisher not surprisingly enjoyed a special prominence among his classmates at the tenth reunion. What man was there to whose mind the reunion scrimmages did not conjure up the old green playing fields of his own days—where everything wore a cloak of fertile promise and boyish dream?

Nevertheless, as John P. Marquand observed in *The Late George Apley*, "There are certain persons of whom it has been said that their clock struck twelve while they were undergraduates at Harvard and that in the interval remaining to them between youth and the grave their personalities underwent no further change." If this is an unfair indictment of the lives of Fisher and Campbell taken as a whole, it does perhaps stand as a portrait of the image they projected at their reunion, where they seemed to have fallen back on the triumphs of their youthful past.

So for Kennedy it was Potter rather than Fisher or Campbell who served as the most exacting measure of his own relative success. Living in a luxurious town house in an elegant section of the Back Bay, Major Robert Sturgis Potter had returned from the war to the National Shawmut Bank, where he had been made a vice-president, a position superbly suited to a man of his talent and background. Married to the former Dorothy Tweedy of New York and the father of two small children, Potter spent much of his leisure time at the club—the Somerset Club, that is, to which his election had been assured almost from the day he made the Porcellian at Harvard. Loyal to its old standards, the Somerset Club remained the most elite club in Boston, still consisting only of those people whom all the members would immediately understand and instinctively like.

Yet, of the two rising young men, it appears that Kennedy was the one with more ready access to cash. In Kennedy's papers there are dozens of 1920s notes to Alfred Wellington at the Columbia Trust in which Kennedy informs the bank's treasurer that one or another of his friends is in need of a loan and requests that the bank act promptly and favorably on the matter. Among these notes, at the bottom of a descending scale of urgency, is a cool letter informing Wellington that Bob Potter wants to borrow $3,500. "It is all right to give it to him," Kennedy states, "if you can get collateral accepted in the savings department. Otherwise, just tell him that you have not got the money."

Kennedy had come by his money through his own efforts and he prized it all the more highly. Yet, with all his growing success in the world of business, he was still denied the taste of the full sweetness of social acceptance. Later in the summer of 1922, the Kennedys rented a large shingled beach house with a rambling porch overlooking a wildly beautiful rock-studded beach at Cohasset. In contrast to the more raucous Nantasket, which had become an Irish enclave years before, the heavily Protestant Cohasset remained a private preserve of the old Boston families. From the porch, where the interloping Kennedy children rode their tricycles, talking and laughing all day long in voices so loud that the neighbors took notice, one could see the Boston Light, the oldest lighthouse in the United States, sentinel of the days long gone by when Boston's commercial trade stood first in all the nation.

Like most of his friends and acquaintances who summered at Cohasset, including Bob Fisher and Dudley Dean (the treasurer of a land association which had its offices in the same building as Hayden, Stone), Kennedy looked forward to the long summer on the South Shore as a time for playing golf as well as relaxing with his family. For this purpose he made what should have been a routine request for a summer membership in the Cohasset Golf Club. But in the atmosphere of 1922, when Irish Catholics were still looked down upon by the reigning Protestant establishment, the application proved anything but routine. The first hint of trouble occurs as early as May 7, 1922, in a long letter from Dean to Fisher on the subject of "Mr. J. P. Kennedy's summer membership in the Cohasset Golf Club."

"I had a chat with Hugh Bancroft Saturday A.M.," Dean reports. (Bancroft was one of eleven members of the golf club's election committee.)

> Bancroft is not the controlling spirit and he knows of Mr. K. very favorably; but he emphasized that a great many of the members regarded the outfit as a rather close corporation in a social way because of long acquaintance and not very heavily on the golf end per se. In other words, those having that special regard wanted to see old faces, continually . . . it looks as tho it wouldn't be as easy sailing as I imagined when you broached the matter. However . . . I will gladly see it to a conclusion and do all I can.

In the long and often confusing struggle that followed, Dean remained true to his word. On June 2, 1922, he wrote to Mat Luce promising that he would personally see any of the members of the election committee with whom he had influence, and reminding Luce that he, in turn, had promised to see three others.

Six days later Dean followed up with a note to Bancroft notifying him that he had that day filed Kennedy's application for membership with the secretary, G. Glover Crocker.

> I propose, Luce seconds. I shall appreciate it as a personal favor if you see your way clear to vote for Kennedy and, if consistent, say any necessary word that way to any other member of the Election Com. In interesting myself in this particular application I would say I am under no obligation of any kind or sort to Kennedy. I like his cut and his attitude.

But as the hot summer days passed by, with June and July giving way to August, Kennedy's application remained in limbo, and the time came when even Dean was wearied by the game the election committee was playing.

> Your were going to let me know quite a number of days back about the case of Mr. J. P. Kennedy [Dean wrote to Bancroft on August 14]. You said, for instance, one day that the committee was to meet the following day and you would advise thereafter. I should appreciate it very much if you would drop me a written line on the outcome. I think it is only fair to Kennedy to see the thing through to an entire conclusion, even if his application was not found acceptable.

This note was followed four days later by a scribbled note to Kennedy: "Trying hard to get your death warrant in writing so you can have it framed . . . Haven't even gotten it verbally yet! But be patient."

"It was petty and cruel," Ralph Lowell later said. "The women of Cohasset looked down on the daughter of Honey Fitz and who was Joe Kennedy but the son of Pat, the barkeeper."

We can easily imagine the embarrassment Kennedy must have suffered all summer in knowing that his candidacy to the club had become a cause célèbre. Having wandered successfully through the maze of the thick and pathless financial woods, he could no longer disguise from himself the melancholy fact that no matter what he accomplished in Boston, he was still unable to secure the unrestricted access and the social acceptance he craved. While in later years he denounced all social clubs as stupid and tiresome, there remained in his soul a bitter feeling which he would always associate with Boston. Indeed, through many years some strange chords in Kennedy's heart would vibrate to the slightest circumstance reminiscent of his mortifying club experiences at Cohasset and Harvard, leading him one day to make his departure from

Boston, uprooting his entire family from the city which had been their home for three generations.

Had Joe Kennedy started his career in a different, less stratified city, the social acceptance he desired might have come much earlier and therefore meant much less. But as it was, he was deeply hurt by his double rejection from the final club at Harvard and the country club at the shore. To strive so hard and reach so far and still be unable to get where one wanted to go seemed insupportable to him, so much so that he became all the more determined to live by his own standards in a world of his own making.

From 1922 to 1929, the nation witnessed a dynamic surge of productive effort, bringing nearly seven years of unparalleled prosperity to the American people, with the notable exception of those who were living on farms. As the recession of 1920–21 gave way to a rushing revival, spectacular advances were registered in dozens of new industries, ranging from the manufacture of electrical machinery and household appliances to the development of plastics, celluloid, rayon and the radio. But the key industry of the twenties, and the one indirectly destined to mark a significant increase in Joe Kennedy's fortune, was automobile manufacture. More than any other industry, it symbolized the striking technological advance of the twenties; indeed, the astonishing growth of the automobile alone was sufficient to account for the industrial prosperity of the decade. Before the war, motorcars were largely restricted to the wealthy and to the upper middle class; in 1916 there were only 4 million registered cars on the road. By the middle of the twenties, with nearly 4 million cars being produced each year, ownership was no longer a class distinction. With the mass production of the cheap and sturdy Model T, fruit of Henry Ford's vision of the auto as an engine of democracy rather than a hallmark of aristocracy, its use spread to the lower middle class and the wage earner, and with its spread came a boom in highway construction. By 1928 there were over 24 million cars touring the nation's newly paved roads, remaking the face of America itself, spreading the old cities out into new suburbs blooming with garages, filling stations, hot-dog stands, traffic lights and blinkers; making the American people more than ever a migratory folk.

Galen Stone supplied the lucrative connection between Kennedy and the soaring auto industry. In 1922 Stone was chairman of the board of Pond Creek Coal, a company which held the mineral rights to 22,000 acres of land in Kentucky and was in the business of producing soft coal for the manufacture of illuminating gas. Pond Creek had been in business for eleven years, performing admirably though not brilliantly. Judging from the moderate volume of trading in its stock and its stability over a long period, there was no reason to anticipate any great change in the price of its stock, which had settled in the $15–$20 range. Then, suddenly, in the month of December 1922, the trading volume increased to around 25,000 shares a week, more than ten times the average of recent years, and the price of the stock jumped dramatically from $18 to $31 in the space of four weeks. Its steady rise then enlisted more traders, and the price continued to climb; a sense of urgency for ownership had developed.

While these dramatic changes in the affairs of Pond Creek were going on, Joe Kennedy was sitting nervously with the knowledge that tens of thousands of dollars, by far the largest amount he had yet gambled in the market, were riding on the continuing upward movement of this stock. For as it happened, months earlier, taking the word of Galen Stone, Kennedy had borrowed to the limit to purchase some fifteen thousand shares of Pond Creek, then selling at about $16 a share. Knowing that Kennedy had taken some hard losses during the recession, Stone had privately shared with him the privileged information that, as Pond Creek's chairman, he had entered into secret negotiations with Henry Ford to integrate the coal company with Ford's automotive operation. Recognizing the fashionable appeal of automobile stocks, the mere sound of which had a magic effect on investors, who were willing to pay dear for the opportunity of joining in the astronomical growth of that industry, Stone understood that all he needed to do was drop a hint or two about the possibility of a merger with Ford in order to attract a large following of new investors.

As the negotiations dragged on through the months of October and November, Kennedy grew more and more anxious, knowing that if Ford changed his mind and decided to back away, the value of his Pond Creek stock could tumble and he would have to pay dearly. As it turned out, however, it was one of those times, Kennedy later said, when luck turned his way, for by the third week of December Ford and Stone reached a final agreement on the integration. Just before this agreement was reached, when *The New York Times* carried a story suggesting the possibility of a merger, Pond's stock jumped seven points, and the actual announcement of the sale in the last week of December 1922 prompted the trading of 39,500 shares, which pushed the stock up to a new high of 39. The following week Kennedy sold his entire block at approximately $45 a share, realizing $675,000. Since in those years one had only to put up 10 percent of the price on margin, the Pond Creek transaction enabled Kennedy to realize a profit of more than $650,000 on his original investment of $24,000.

In the course of this single deal, brought to a close within eight or nine months, Joe Kennedy had amassed nearly three quarters of a million dollars, more than his father and his grandfather had accumulated in the course of two lifetimes.

On January 1, 1923, a day so unseasonably warm that all the windows at 87 Milk looked out upon a steady rain, Galen Stone retired from the partnership of Hayden, Stone and Company. After thirty years of unremitting labor in which he had amassed almost as many millions, he was determined to grow old at a more leisurely pace, filling his days with less work and more rest, with nature, sailing, music, books and family.

With Stone gone, Kennedy's prospects with the firm, which had once seemed so bright, were now considerably dimmed. Aware of the fact that the Brahmin-born Hayden, whose ancestry traced back to the Revolution, had originally opposed his hiring ostensibly on the ground of inexperience but more likely because of his ethnic background, Kennedy recognized that the chances of his becoming a partner in the firm were slim. While his unusual talents had carried him from the post of customers' man to head of the stock exchange department of the Boston office, he knew that so long as he was not a partner he would be forced to listen while others spoke and he would never feel like the master of his affairs. While Kennedy would remain loyal to Galen Stone, proclaiming to anyone who listened that this was one man in a thousand, "one of the noblest figures in American business," his loyalty to the firm—having been encompassed all along in his personal bond with Stone—ended the day Stone retired. The time had come for him to travel his road alone.

Kennedy elected to set up his private office in the familiar corridors of 87 Milk Street, connected by a short flight of stairs to the quarters of Hayden, Stone and Company. There, in a small office which he furnished in simple good taste, behind a door lettered JOSEPH P. KENNEDY, BANKER, the thirty-four-year-old Irishman went into business for himself, free now to do as he pleased, to jump in and out of the market at will, without having to consider the impact of his actions on anyone.

In choosing to call himself a private banker as opposed to speculator or trader—a privilege of the man in business for himself—Kennedy was choosing a title still considered the crown of the social system, a title of honor implying membership in an exclusive club. The word "banker" served an additional purpose as well: it sent a signal to the financial community that he stood ready, on the basis of the training he had received at Hayden, Stone and Company, to offer his technical experience in a wide range of market operations—ranging from directing pool operations to managing syndicates—in return for a heavy price.

Kennedy had been installed in his new office scarcely six months when opportunity beckoned, allowing him to proclaim to the financial world that he was a man of considerable subtlety, craft and vision. On a moonlit night early in April, Kennedy was awakened from sleep by someone repeatedly ringing the doorbell of his Brookline home. Coming downstairs with a robe thrown over his pajamas, he opened the front door to Walter Howey, the mercurial editor of Hearst's *Boston American*. Considered the greatest city editor of his day, the man responsible for printing the country's first movie column, first radio column and first medical column, Walter Howey would later in life pass into American folklore as the model for Walter Burns, the uncouth and unpredictable editor in the smash Broadway hit *The Front Page*: a fantastic character, half myth, half maniac, the caricature of a dying breed of newspaper editors who fought savagely for circulation, with cunning and ferocity, with spies and saboteurs and kidnappings, using all the techniques of open warfare.

A proud man, Howey was reaching out for help in an uncharacteristic manner. But the stakes for him were very high, facing, as he believed he was, the prospects of financial ruin. Before coming to Boston, Howey told Kennedy, he had invested nearly all his life's savings in the stock of the Chicago-based Yellow Cab Company, whose founder, John Hertz, he had known since they were young newsmen together on the Loop. In January 1924 the stock had been trading at 63; by the end of March it had slipped to 60; and by now, the end of April's second week, it was falling off nearly half a point each day, with no end to the heavy trading in sight. In the same period a similar fate had befallen the stock of the Yellow Cab Manufacturing Company, which Hertz had created to produce the taxis and buses needed to keep his various transportation systems running. Opening the year at 90, Yellow Cab Manufacturing had dropped into the 70s by early April and was now declining at an even more rapid rate than Yellow Cab.

Yet the profits and earnings of both companies were up from the previous year and stood to increase still more in the coming year, inasmuch as Hertz was negotiating a merger with New York's Fifth Avenue Coach Company, which would allow him to expand his operations into New York. Watching the ticker, both Howey and Hertz had concluded that a pool of New York operators was deliberately attempting to force the Yellow stocks down. While the identity of the raiders could not be proved, it was believed that the Checker Cab Company was behind the attack, with the goal of thwarting Hertz's entry into New York by sabotaging his negotiations with the Fifth Avenue line.

Howey's call for help came at a difficult moment in the Kennedy household. His tired host was suffering from neuritis, a painful and debilitating condition. Additionally, Rose was expecting another baby within a few weeks. Still, it seems never to have occurred to Kennedy that he could turn his back on a man whose friendship he had come to treasure. The two men had met two years earlier when Kennedy successfully persuaded the newly arrived editor of the *Boston American* to support his father-in-law, John Fitzgerald, in his bid for governor against Channing Cox. While Fitzgerald lost the race, Kennedy did not forget the favor, and in the months that followed he developed a warm friendship with Howey, a friendship which Howey was now calling on by asking the ailing Kennedy to journey by sleeper train to New York later that night so that he could meet with Hertz in the early morning at the Waldorf-Astoria to formulate the plan for Yellow's defense. "I can never forget," Howey told Kennedy decades later, "that while a child was being born in your household, through sheer friendship for me you went to New York and saved my tiny fortune from financial ruin."

When Kennedy arrived at the reception desk of the Waldorf, he was told by the clerk that Mr. Hertz was expecting him immediately in the popular men's restaurant, the North Café. Weary from the pain of his illness, he wished only to fall into bed, but the sight of the pulsing lobby with knots of people engaged in all the shops and booths, purchasing theater tickets here, sending telegrams there, with porters, bellboys and messengers rushing about in rapid commotion—that singular sight, he told Rose when he met her for dinner that weekend at the Duck Inn in Providence, filled him with such electric excitement that his lethargy instantly lifted.

In the early years of the twentieth century the Waldorf-Astoria enjoyed the patronage of the world's most fashionable people. An international hotel with a cosmopolitan atmosphere, an oak reading room containing a large selection of foreign newspapers, and a score of employees able to converse in French, German and Spanish, the Waldorf was also a first-class hotel for business, equipped with its own brokerage offices, a corps of efficient stenographers always on duty in a corner of the reading room, and a telegraph office open from seven in the morning until midnight, with wires and cables reaching to every corner of the civilized world.

But what interested Kennedy most that day, caught up as he was in the panorama of the lobby, was an intense awareness of his own ambition for power and wealth, an ambition which Rose later said he described to her that same weekend as "the desire for the freedom which money provides, the freedom to come and go where he pleased, when he pleased and how he pleased." Poised on the threshold of what he considered the most difficult challenge of his financial career ("If ever I was scared," he later admitted, "it was then"), Kennedy was propelled forward beyond his fatigue by the force of his desires, desires which mingled indistinguishably with the current of his blood.

He entered the North Café at the height of the breakfast commotion while waiters were busily scurrying to and fro with platters of food and steaming pots of coffee. Craning his neck, he soon spotted Hertz, his face buried in the depressing market figures of the previous day, which revealed an additional three-point drop in Yellow's stock, plunging it to a new low of 57 with a trading volume of over seven thousand shares. Shaking Kennedy's hand and introducing him to Yellow's vice-president, Charles McCulloch, Hertz started at once into an explanation of his plan for bolstering the collapsing market, calling upon Kennedy, with the backing of a vast treasure chest of $5 million, to begin immediately a process of accumulating large holdings of the stock all over the country, on the theory that the renewed confidence evidenced by the numbers of shares being bought would make the bidding competitive again and drive the price up. For nearly three weeks now, Hertz confided to Kennedy, he had been trying on his own to beat the raiders back by purchasing large blocks of his own stock, with the intent of eventually reselling these shares at a stabilizing price to his own employees. But in spite of his best efforts the situation was steadily deteriorating, and he now knew he was incapable of winning the battle without professional help. While he and his fellow directors would remain behind the lines supplying the strategy and the ammunition, they needed Kennedy as their battlefield marshal.

As the hour of the battle approached, one thing was certain: after ten years of striving to create the first great public fleet of taxicabs to operate on city streets, Hertz was not the type of man to accept defeat without a memorable fight. Born in a remote hamlet in the Tyrolean Alps, John Hertz was brought to America as a small child and grew up in the slums of Chicago under conditions so destitute that he left school in the fifth grade and ran away from home. In his flight from poverty, the young Hertz turned to a variety of enterprises, including newspaper peddling, exhibition boxing, sportswriting, selling automobiles, and finally using surplus cars from auto dealerships to take passengers where they wanted to go for a fee.

From this modest beginning in the taxi business Hertz moved on to create the Yellow Cab Company, which was destined to change the face of the entire taxi industry in America. Before he entered the field, taxi companies had been operating on the luxury principle, sending out big limousines on call to wealthy customers with charge accounts. It was this system that Hertz altered. The key to reducing costs, Hertz believed, was to reduce the habit of calling for a cab, so that the company could operate on a more strictly cash, not charge, basis. "It was ridiculously simple," he said later, referring to his patentable idea to make all his cabs a uniform shape and to paint them a color so easy to recognize that people would ordinarily find it easier to hail one from the streets than to call for one from their home. When a lab test proved that yellow was the most easily recognized color by day and by night, the Yellow Cab Company was born, with the first fleet appearing on the streets of Chicago on April 2, 1915. This was the remarkable achievement Joe Kennedy was called upon to preserve.

Kennedy heartily agreed to accept the combat assignment, on the condition that Hertz abandon his conventional plan of attack in favor of a radically different strategy which he had been evolving in his own mind in the course of the preceding twelve hours. Gathering his thoughts like a lecturer preparing to speak before the public, Kennedy argued that by demonstrating uncontrollable panic at the center, the absurdly expensive plan envisioned by Hertz as a means of bolstering his stock against further collapse would have just the opposite effect. In Kennedy's mind the Yellow's raiders were like vultures preying upon weakness; the moment they scented blood, as they surely would in Hertz's transparent effort to corner his own stock, they would swoop down for the final kill.

With characteristic boldness, Kennedy suggested that as far as he could see a fateful war was in the making which could be met only by a frontal assault launched directly at the enemy. Believing that fear was the only language the raiders would understand, he proposed to turn the tide and force the shorters onto the defensive, placing them in the fatal position of responding to *his* moves instead of moving on their own. To carry out his plan, Kennedy demanded full authority to buy *and* sell Yellow stock all over the country, pushing it up suddenly here, pulling it down swiftly there, thrusting and twisting it in a manner so bewildering that the parties now selling it short could no longer anticipate the future. Threatened with substantial losses if they guessed incorrectly, the raiders would have to halt their attack. Then and only then, Kennedy believed, the time would be ripe for taking positive steps to restore confidence among the ordinary stockholders.

The longer Kennedy spoke, the more Hertz was attracted by the force of his delivery and the sheer effrontery of his plan. Before the meal was ended, he gave Kennedy unquestioned authority to go ahead, promising him all the money and stock he needed to carry on. Exhilarated and exhausted, Kennedy took his leave, and promptly collapsed into bed.

While Kennedy was meeting with Hertz, Edward Moore, a family friend and intimate associate whom Kennedy had brought along as his secretary, was making all the arrangements for a special suite of rooms equipped with its own automatic ticker and a bank of phones. Uncomplaining and zealous in discharge of his duties, Moore was one of the few men in the world, Rose later observed, whom her husband "trusted implicitly in every way and in all circumstances." Kennedy had first met Eddie about a dozen years before, back in 1912 when Moore was serving as chief secretary to Mayor Fitzgerald, a position he would retain in the succeeding administrations of Curley and Peters. Educated in the public schools of Charlestown, Moore was an affectionate man with a face that was always crinkling in a smile, a warmhearted Irishman whose salty sense of humor produced an immediately favorable impression on Kennedy. When Mayor Peters left office, Kennedy invited Moore to come to work with him on a full-time basis as his confidential adviser, and from that day forward the bond between the two men proved inseparable.

With Moore, there was no confusion in ambition—all his thoughts and feelings were directed with one accord toward Joe; but, at the same time, the dignity of his person was never impaired by thwarted efforts on his part to maintain it. In time, it was apparent to all who could see that neither man could have functioned as well without the other. Indeed, so completely were they identified the one with the other that Moore would follow Kennedy all his life, moving with him from city to city, from one job to the next, from Fore River to Wall Street to Hollywood; from the Securities and Exchange Commission to the Court of St. James's to the precincts of Massachusetts politics, until his final infirmity in the summer of 1952 rendered him incapable of working.

For the next four weeks, with Eddie Moore constantly at his side to take calls, admit visitors and order meals, Kennedy grappled with the "bears" from his Waldorf suite. Staying on the telephone for hours at a time, he placed calls to different brokers all over the country, some of whom he instructed to buy and others to sell, naming the price in each case. Wishing, for example, to give Yellow stock the appearance of strength in a particular market on a particular day, he would buy thousands of shares at a good price early in the day and then, when the activity generated by his buying had attracted a following on the bullish side, he would turn around and sell an equal amount of the stock. If, on another day, however, he desired to produce weakness in the stock, he would simply open the market by selling thousands of shares and then, as soon as that order was executed, repurchase an equal amount of the same stock. In other words, instead of simply trying to support prices by buying millions of dollars of stock on a sliding scale downward, he would often sell a block of the stock first and then be able to buy it back at a lower price, thus providing even more support with the same amount of money.

Covering his tracks skillfully, Kennedy moved with such quickness of mind and subtlety of idea that not even the brokers who found themselves stationed at Yellow's posts on the floors of the various exchanges, yelling out his contradictory orders, could be certain what his true position in the market was. Kennedy was convinced that he could beat the raiders at their own game so long as no one could tell when he was accumulating stock and when he was unloading. So he shrouded his movements in absolute secrecy, leaving his room at the Waldorf only upon absolute necessity.

It took Kennedy more than a month to accomplish his goal, but by the second week it was plainly apparent that his ingenuity was producing widespread anxiety in the other camp. Unable to determine why the stock was jumping up and down from 57 to 52, from 46 to 53, from 51 to 48, the raiders found themselves in the position of reluctant riders on a sharply banked roller coaster, forced by the whim of an unseen operator to remain in their seats while their open cars sped steeply up and down a narrow, winding trestle. Never knowing what had hit them, they finally gave up, leaving the market to find its natural level once again.

But Kennedy's assignment was not yet completed, for there remained the problem of the larger community of Yellow stockholders, thousands of ordinary men and women who, knowing nothing of the inner manipulations of the market, had grown increasingly nervous in recent weeks as they watched the value of their stocks continue to slide. Recognizing the importance of moving quickly to dissuade them from selling their stock the moment the first steady rise took place, Kennedy advised Hertz to launch a public-relations effort to help the original investors regain their confidence in the value of Yellow's stock.

As part of this deliberate strategy, numerous favorable articles began appearing in the press: the first announcing that the negotiations with New York's Fifth Avenue line were proceeding satisfactorily and approaching a conclusion; a second discussing plans for expansion of Yellow Cab Manufacturing; and a third giving prominence to Yellow Cab's most recent quarterly report, which showed net earnings for the first quarter of 1924 up 25 percent from the corresponding quarter in 1923. If the purpose of this publicity was to surround the stock with an aura of stability and prestige so that the original investors would be dissuaded from selling, it was splendidly achieved; for by the middle of May, while Kennedy was still controlling affairs from his suite at the Waldorf, the descent was halted, the heavy volume of trading tapered off and the price slowly began to climb up to the point where Hertz wished it.

With his triumph in beating back the bears, Kennedy achieved a victory as complete as anyone could have won; for not only had he accomplished everything he had been asked to do—in seven weeks he had preserved both the fortune of a friend and the life of a company—but at the same time, since his elegantly providential scheme called for all his purchases to be offset by sales, he was able to bring the campaign to a close with Hertz's $5 million still intact. The strain had been immense, as Kennedy's own words attest: "I woke up one morning, exhausted, and I realized that I hadn't been out of that hotel room in seven weeks. My baby Pat had been born and was almost a month old and I hadn't even seen her."

In the years to come, the story of his homecoming would become one of the stories Joe loved most to tell. Though Rose was still recovering from the May 6 birth of her baby Patricia, the five older children insisted on journeying to the train station to greet their father. So there they all were as he came out onto the platform, two boys aged nine and seven and three little girls aged four, three and one, all waving and yelling and laughing, "Daddy! Daddy! Daddy! We've got another baby." As Joe told the story, the other arriving passengers found the scene a curious one: "They were smiling . . . but with a touch of perplexity and sympathy, as if they might be thinking to themselves, 'What that fellow there certainly doesn't need right now is *another* baby.' "

While the returning father was indeed a tired man, he woke to find himself, in return for his manipulative skill, if not yet a multimillionaire, at least a very wealthy man. For his services in halting the raid, Kennedy was given not only a large sum of cash and a fair proportion of Yellow's stock but also the lucrative opportunity to get in on the ground floor of Hertz's expanding operations. Indeed, if any action was designed to melt away the weariness of Kennedy's recent months, it was the offer Hertz made in June 1924 to join with him in his newest and potentially most lucrative project—the Hertz Drive-Ur-Self System, a far-reaching system of rental cars and licensed stations which a later age would come to know as Hertz Rent-A-Car. The grateful Hertz also brought Kennedy into the Omnibus Corporation, the flourishing new holding company that resulted from his successful takeover of the Fifth Avenue line, a merger which enabled Hertz to provide New York with the same inexpensive bus transportation he had secured for Chicago while still managing to double the company's annual earnings.

From the narrow standpoint of money earned on an hourly basis, one would be hard put to find in Kennedy's career a more lucrative assignment. But the significance of his victory went further still in identifying him to the inner circle of Wall Street observers as a financial genius.

Surely his participation in the brokerage house of Hayden, Stone and Company had been critical to his education, but now he had come into his own.

Dealing now from strength, Kennedy came to know fairly intimately, as far as commercial relationships went, some of the shrewdest men of the steadily enlarging financial world. One of these was Matthew Brush, president of the American International Corporation, one of the largest investment trusts in the country. Considered "the prince of speculators," Brush was said to have made more than $15 million in his personal market trading between 1919 and 1929.

In an unchronicled time when the concentration of information in the hands of insiders had the effect of setting apart a special economic class bound together by common affiliations, Brush found in the vital yet discreet Kennedy a man whose judgment he considered astonishingly sound. In the rich correspondence between the two, there is a strikingly frank exchange of confidential information which each man turned to his own advantage. "I bought some AGWI Common around 48," Brush told Kennedy in a letter written from New York, "and still have what for me is a substantial block of it. Based upon all the dope that I can get, plus the fact that Mr. Stone is the Czar in this picture . . . , I am going to hold this for over 100. Am I not sound in my judgment?" Kennedy's scribbled answer was a definite yes—intelligent advice considering that before the year was out AGWI nearly doubled in price.

Knowing that Stone was also running Eastern Steamship, Brush went on to tell Kennedy that he understood Stone had in mind a plan whereby Eastern would be able to use part of the equipment under the Clyde Line management in order to operate a line between New York and Florida in the wintertime. "If this is so," Brush wrote, "Eastern Steamship a year or two years from today ought to be worth considerably more money. I have in mind to put away a little bit of this and would appreciate your judgment." In reply, Kennedy told Brush he expected to see Stone on Monday morning and would probably be in New York on Tuesday, at which time he would come in to share the latest information with Brush.

It is obvious from the unselfconscious tone of these letters that it never occurred to either man that in sharing their access to private information they were doing anything wrong. On the contrary, the big operators took pride in having built up connections and sources of information that could generally be relied upon. At a time when insiders routinely operated with little regard for the effect of their actions on the ordinary stockholder, the only question—as Kennedy once put it to a friend—was how long the unregulated market would last "before they pass a law against it." Speaking with similar directness, Brush later admitted that "the Wall Street racket made Al Capone look like a piker."

The more Kennedy moved into this world, the farther he moved from the values and principles which had guided his father's life. Throughout the old man's long political career, P. J. Kennedy had given both his time and his resources to the ordinary man, even to the point where his generosity depleted his own savings and irritated his wife and family. To be sure, such a genuine love of humanity is rare indeed, but it is hard to imagine a more striking contrast than that between P.J. and his son. For in the business code Joseph Kennedy was developing in the 1920s—a code perfectly suited for the materialistic decade—nothing assumed greater primacy than self-interest.

# CHAPTER 20

# "THIS
# IS . . .
# A
# GOLD MINE."

From his early forays in the stock market, Kennedy accumulated a small fortune, estimated at about $2 million by the middle of the twenties. But all along he had his eye on a different target: the burgeoning motion picture industry, dominated at that time by a special group of sharp and unschooled immigrants, most of them first- or second-generation Jews from central and eastern Europe.

Growing up with the youthful industry, Kennedy had followed the transition from the simple chase scenes and the comic sequences depicted in the early twelve-minute one-reelers to the rich plots and dramatic spectacles presented in full feature-length silent films. For the masses of the people, particularly the tens of millions of non-English-speaking immigrants who had settled in the United States at the turn of the century, the silent film provided a magnificent world of dreams, allowing them to break away from the toil and drudgery of industrial labor that remained alien and pitilessly hard. Indeed, for many working men and women who could afford neither to vacation in a hotel nor to eat in a fancy restaurant, the hours spent in the great picture palaces afforded the most sublime luxury they would ever enjoy.

By the middle twenties, with an investment of nearly $1.5 billion, with eight hundred feature pictures made annually and with as many people permanently employed in it as in the automobile business, the American film industry was the sixth largest in the country and one of the most profitable. Yet, in several respects, the business was unique; for in spite of its proven success—by 1926 there were 21,000 movie theaters in operation, with an attendance of more than sixty million people a week—its financing remained almost.entirely on a personal basis, forcing all but the largest motion picture companies to rely on certain individuals, known as bonus sharks, who loaned money at excessive interest rates or participated in the profits. Most banks were dismayed by the huge inventories motion picture companies carried (Samuel Goldwyn, for example, had enough properties and equipment to shoot eleven pictures at a time), by the incredible salaries (reaching to $15,000 a week) which the stars received, and by the lack of tangible assets. Only a half-dozen banks in the entire country, most notably the Bank of America under Amadeus Peter Giannini, were willing to issue extensive credits to the movie industry.

Here, Joe reasoned, taking note of both the spectacular profits and the primitive state of financing, was an industry in which a fortune could be made. "This is . . . a gold mine," he would often say. "In fact, it looks like another telephone industry." But gaining a foothold in the movies was not as easy as Kennedy imagined; indeed, seven years would pass—from 1919 to 1926—before his repeated efforts met any substantial success.

The first operation with which he became associated was the Maine–New Hampshire Theatres, a chain of thirty-one small movie houses in northern New England. Beginning in 1919 as a financial adviser to the general manager, William Gray, a former jockey who had made a fortune in real estate and lived with all the trappings of a movie mogul in Lewiston, Maine, Kennedy bought a controlling interest in the tiny chain and then attempted to expand his base into the more populous cities of Massachusetts. In this attempt, however, he was repeatedly foiled by the dominating influence of the giant theater chains such as

Loew's or Paramount. In frustration, Kennedy appealed to motion picture czar Will Hays.

Kennedy had first come into contact with Hays during the all-important battle against censorship in Massachusetts—a battle which proved to be a turning point in the industry's national struggle against a rising tide of public criticism. In 1922, censorship bills had been introduced in thirty-six states. The biggest test was Massachusetts, where for the first time public opinion on censoring films was to be tested by referendum. During the struggle, Kennedy introduced Hays to a number of newspaper editors and helped to sway the opinion against censorship.

Now the time had come to call in his chips. In his appeal to Hays, Kennedy argued: "In New England, practically no political or banking influence is behind any phase of the picture industry"—a consideration that should warrant theater owners' selling their properties to him at a fair price. "I feel I can start the right people in the industry," Kennedy promised.

It is unclear whether or not the powerful Hays, head of the industry's self-regulating association, intervened on Kennedy's behalf. We know only that on December 1, 1922, after a string of unsuccessful negotiations with theater owners in various cities, Kennedy finally acquired his first movie house in Massachusetts, in the town of Stoneham. But as the years went by, according to one associate, "Kennedy learned [that] from the theater side of the business, Hollywood could wring you dry. He wanted to get where the wringing was done."

He found the opportunity he sought through a connection he had forged at Hayden, Stone with one of the largest trading houses in the British Commonwealth, the Grahams of London, which had a substantial investment in an American motion picture firm, the Robertson-Cole Company, producers and distributors of nearly fifty films a year. With thirty-three offices throughout the United States plus an extensive network of offices in Europe, the R-C Company and its operational subsidiary, FBO (Film Booking Offices), had established a national reputation for producing action-filled, fast-paced melodramas and adventure films aimed at the less demanding patrons of small-town movie houses. The FBO company was also noted for its shrewd moves in capitalizing on popular sentiment. Not long after the sudden death of the famous actor Wallace Reid from a drug overdose, his widow was persuaded by FBO to produce *Human Wreckage*, a film on the evils of drugs. Released at a time when public sympathy had been aroused to an acute degree, the picture was a great money-maker. A similar coup was scored following the separation of Rudolf Valentino and Natasha Rambova, when FBO signed the wife of the sheik to star in *When Love Grows Cold*.

Yet, for all its success in making and distributing movies which Main Street America wanted to see, FBO, as a small, privately held company with a weekly payroll of nearly $60,000, was forced to borrow its working capital from private individuals at ruinous interest rates of up to 18 percent. As a consequence, the company was losing money and its English owners reluctantly decided to sell off the entire business to an American buyer. Arriving in New York in 1921 to effect the sale, Sir Erskine Crum of the Grahams headed first for the venerable banking house of Hayden, Stone, where he was introduced to the one broker in the firm who followed the movie industry religiously—young Joseph Kennedy. After several days of discussion with Hayden, Stone, an agreement was reached whereby Kennedy was given an exclusive option as a broker with the promise of a $75,000 commission if he sold the business for the sum of $1.5 million. And while he was endeavoring to make the sale Kennedy was to serve FBO as an adviser, for a fee of $1,500 a month.

For several months, Kennedy tried to interest various film companies, including William Randolph Hearst's, in buying FBO, but nothing came of his efforts and after a while the English owners gave up their hopes of unloading the company at a fair price.

All along, from his first meeting with Crum, Kennedy had harbored the dream of buying FBO for himself, but it was not until the summer of 1925 that he was able, with the help of Boston attorney Guy Currier and Boston businessman Louis Kirstein, to put together the capital to make a serious offer. Traveling to Europe in August, he offered the Grahams $1 million for a controlling block of FBO's stock. But by this time, five years after the original decision to sell had been made, the Grahams had sunk over $7 million into FBO, against which the $1 million offer seemed far too small.

Arriving back in Boston in late September, a disappointed Kennedy decided to relinquish his long-frustrated plans for entering the moving-picture industry. As the air grew chill and the leaves on the trees began to fall, he settled back into the familiar world of stocks and bonds, and made plans with three of his golfing buddies for a long midwinter vacation in Palm Beach.

It was a cold and blustery February day in Manhattan, a day on which everything that could be seen—the people, the automobiles, the mailboxes—was covered with snow. It was just the right time of year to be heading south, as Kennedy and his three friends were preparing to do. Having assembled in New York the night before, the four young men had stayed at the Harvard Club on Forty-fourth Street while they readied themselves for their long-awaited Florida vacation. Emerging from the porch of the club into a driving wind which hurled snow into their faces, the men stepped into a cab headed for Grand Central Station, where they were to catch the *Havana Limited* to Palm Beach. A mood of good cheer surrounded the foursome as they watched the porters pile their luggage and their golf bags into the trunk. Then, just as the cab started to pull away from the curb, a bellboy rushed out. "Phone call for Mr. Kennedy—they say it's important." Kennedy stopped the cab and went back into the club. A few minutes later, he returned and told his friend Eddie Moore, "Sorry, but you fellows will have to go to Florida without me. I'm going to Boston tonight. I seem to have bought a moving picture company."

As it happened, the English owners of FBO, having arrived at that psychological moment when they wished simply to unload their property, had suddenly decided to accept the offer Kennedy had made the previous August. In order to raise the money he needed, Kennedy sold part of his little theater chain to a subsidiary of Paramount.

In putting together the capital to consummate the deal, Kennedy went, as he often did on his various deals, to his irrepressible father-in-law, John Fitzgerald, whose connections in the worlds of banking and politics remained unbroken. For several years, these two strong-minded men had enjoyed a surprisingly good working relationship; for his part, Fitzgerald was convinced that Kennedy was a born financier, as shrewd and as talented a man as one could meet, while Kennedy deeply admired the high-spirited personality which seemed to keep Fitzgerald forever young.

So it happened that when the deal was forged for buying FBO, with Guy Currier assuming the role of Kennedy's major partner, John Fitzgerald was invited into the group as a small investor. But Fitzgerald was as talkative with the press as Kennedy was uncommunicative, and on the weekend of February 7 he leaked the story of the deal to the Boston papers while Kennedy sat on a train headed back for New York, where he was to assume official control of the company on Monday morning.

Told in the spirit of the booster who, in his enthusiasm, confuses his dreams with reality, Fitzgerald's account made the FBO deal sound far larger than it really was. "FITZGERALD A FILM MAGNATE," the *Post's* banner headline read in big block letters, under which came the explanation: "Ex-Mayor, with son-in-law, Joseph P. Kennedy, buys big producing company and will become actively engaged in motion pictures game—deal involves $10,000,000." If Fitzgerald's own role was not really as large as he was making it seem, then he would simply expand that role over time to fit the picture he was painting. If the deal was not really a $10 million deal, why, it would become one by the time he and Kennedy got through with it. The truth was that John Fitzgerald was as incapable of not blowing himself up to the press as he was of not being an enthusiast.

Nevertheless, when the other Boston papers followed the lead of the *Boston Post* and hailed Fitzgerald as the prime mover of the deal, it was not easy for Kennedy to take. Never, it seemed, no matter what he did, was it possible for him to receive the full measure of recognition he deserved in the city in which he'd been born. In his mind, it was Boston once again that aroused his anger, Boston that saw him not as the fabulously successful businessman he was but only as the son-in-law of a colorful Irish politician.

The moment was played out without incident, however, for Kennedy was too caught up in the pleasure of owning his own movie company to let his mind dwell on the peculiar problems of Boston.

In many ways, the challenge at FBO was ideally suited for a man of Kennedy's acumen. Having studied the company as an adviser for seven years, he recognized that while it was losing a good deal of money, the situation appeared worse than it really was, since the problem lay not in the company's productivity but in the shakiness of its financial structure. Surely a banker with Kennedy's accumulated experience could place the company's financing on a sounder footing. Before a month had gone by, Kennedy had set up an affiliate organization, the Cinema Credits Corporation, which succeeded in raising substantial capital for FBO by issuing preferred-stock certificates.

It was Kennedy's well-grounded idea that in a time of prosperity such as America was enjoying, people would readily swap cash for stock certificates, particularly with such respected men as Kirstein and Currier already on board. At the same time, Kennedy persuaded railroad magnate Frederick Prince, the son of the former mayor of Boston, to purchase a large block of CCC stock. Prince was also persuaded to lend FBO a half million dollars through his Chicago Union Stockyards Company. Beyond this, Kennedy used his contacts in the financial community to establish a half-million-dollar line of credit at four banks—the First National of Boston, the National Shawmut, the Old Colony Trust Company and the Bank of Italy. With these considerable resources at Kennedy's command, FBO's credit squeeze was ended, and, from that point on, the company never lost money again.

While keeping a few of the professionals from the former management such as Joe Schnitzer, FBO's vice-president in charge of production, whom Kennedy immediately reassured with a written expression of "the greatest confidence in the world" in his ability, he ultimately brought in his own team to run the company, men whose loyalty ran first and foremost to him. It has been said of Kennedy's men, several of whom moved with him from job to job, that they were tight-lipped cronies who watched over the organization with the sharp-eyed vigilance of private detectives guarding the silver at a splashy Irish wedding. Yet these men, Eddie Moore, Pat Scollard, Charlie Sullivan, E. B. Derr and Johnny Ford—all of whom had worked with Kennedy at Fore River—were more interesting individuals than the image of the crony suggests. Good-humored and affable, they were also the bearers of considerable talents, not unlike Kennedy in the discipline and subtlety of their minds but different in the depth of their ambitions. As private secretary to three mayors, Eddie Moore was considered one of the most popular figures at City Hall, "quite in a class by himself," the *Boston Post* suggested. So, too, was Johnny Ford, whose first-rate work as an accountant at Fore River during the war had earned him the personal commendation of Charles Schwab. Between Kennedy and these old friends, there was no beating around the bush; on the contrary, a kind of animal coarseness prevailed which precluded false flattery.

A letter written by Eddie Moore to Kennedy not long after Kennedy assumed control of FBO captures the unceremonious and good-humored tone that characterized their lifelong relationship. Writing from the Blackstone Hotel in Chicago, where he was working on FBO business, Eddie reflected:

> Little did we think when you were treasurer of the John F. Fitzgerald clothing company (with a salary of $25 per week, a salary you voted yourself unknown to one of the three directors, namely Mr. Fitzgerald) and I was general manager, janitor and elevator man for the same company and also a stock holder with stock in escrow, that one day we would be big movie men weighing 190 and 155. Wasn't it lucky we didn't go into the unrefillable bottle business and lose all our money now that prohibition is with us? . . . Yes, sir we got lots to be thankful for. . . . We will soon prove to the industry we are not looking for the easy money and once we do that we'll have the field all to ourselves and then you can just sit in your New York office on your fat fanny and fight like a bastard and I can fulfill the wish and dream of a lifetime, i.e. to go prancing around the country with a dress suitcase, a new pair of shoes and a can of bandits for a pillow when I ride on sleepers.

With FBO's finances and personnel in order, Kennedy bent his eyes to the place where the money was made—the production studios in Hollywood. In the middle of March 1926, when the weather on the East Coast still hovered between winter and spring, he boarded the *Twentieth*

*Century Limited* for the first leg of what was then a three-night-and-two-day journey to California. Celebrated in story and song as one of the classiest trains on earth, the *Century* provided the railroading public with such unheard-of innovations as a barbershop, valet and maid service, a secretary, and twin dining cars complete with dinner-jacketed maîtres d'hôtel and subdued string music.

Never in his business life had Kennedy been farther west than Chicago. His financial adventures, far-reaching as they were, had been almost exclusively confined to a narrow corridor up and down the East Coast. But by entering the movies he was forced to shift his vision to southern California, whose continuous sunshine and boundless variety of natural scenery had destined the once sleepy community of Hollywood to achieve a stunning domination of the movie industry. "Never before or since," D. J. Wenden wrote in *The Birth of the Movies*, "have a few square miles gained complete supremacy in the manufacture of a product."

For a man who enjoyed life as much as Kennedy did, his first transcontinental journey must have been a fascinating experience, though one wonders why Rose did not accompany him. Granted, he was heading west on business, but surely Rose would have enjoyed the opportunity to participate in the high emotion which the trip promised. Granted, too, there were children to consider; in their interest their parents had embarked upon the habit of taking separate vacations so that one of them could always be at home. Nevertheless, the fact that Joe and Rose rarely traveled together during these years must have diminished their intimacy.

FBO's headquarters were at 780 Gower Street in Hollywood. Framed on both sides by long retangular arched buildings which were partitioned into stages, the administration building, looking out as it did on Beverly Hills, enjoyed one of the better views in the movie capital. Kennedy's offices, situated on the second floor, would later be seen by the moviegoing public as the offices of Monroe Stahr in the filmed version of F. Scott Fitzgerald's *The Last Tycoon*. At night from these rooms could be seen the famous thirteen-letter HOLLYWOOD LAND sign, studded with four thousand 70-watt light bulbs spaced every eight inches around the perimeter of each letter. A beckoning call to some, the dazzling sign became a symbol of despair for others when Lillian Entwhistle, a noted actress who failed to repeat in films her spectacular success on the stage, started a trend by climbing to the top of the glittering "H" that had grimly mocked her for months and jumping to her death fifty feet below.

It was often said of Kennedy, with some degree of accuracy, that his success was due to his exquisite indifference to the business he was engaged in, in consequence of which he was never carried away by rash enthusiasm nor made foolish mistakes. Yet there is an unmistakable tone of excitement that runs through Kennedy's letters at the time of his first visit to California, when he took his first tour of the studio's back lot—thirteen acres of fairyland filled with fragments of locations ranging from a boxing ring to Broadway to a college football field. The studio was an arena always alive with activity, as Kennedy discovered when he walked past the cutting rooms, the rehearsal halls, the prop departments and the commissary and suddenly came upon an entire Western village —a permanent set, complete with houses and stores and roads, which was used again and again in the score of Western movies FBO produced.

While Kennedy was touring the studio, he came upon Ralph Ince engaged in directing a scene in *Bigger than Barnum's*, a melodrama of circus life. As Kennedy watched, an acrobat on a high trapeze swung and leaped and missed his hold three times in a row. "It was more than the efficient banker could endure," Hollywood chronicler Terry Ramsaye reported. Approaching the director, Kennedy asked, "Why don't you get somebody who can do that stunt?"

"I can," Ince replied, "if you insist—but, you see, it would spoil the story, which calls for a flop. I've been two days getting this fellow to fall."

As it turned out, *Bigger than Barnum's* was the first picture FBO completed after Kennedy became president of the company, and to celebrate his debut as a movie man he arranged for a preview to be held in his home city of Boston. Speaking at a luncheon for reporters on the day the film was released, Kennedy offered *Barnum's* "as an example of the sort of entertainment FBO believes the average person wants and likes." Stating his company's policy as one of producing pictures for the entertainment of Main Street rather than for the more sophisticated taste of Broadway, he promised to eliminate all plots which depended for their popularity upon sex appeal, so that all of FBO's movies would be worthy of being witnessed by every member of the American family. "We can't make pictures," Kennedy later argued, "and label them 'For Children,' or 'For Women' or 'For Stout People' or 'For Thin Ones.' We must make pictures that have appeal to all."

"It is out of the question," Kennedy admitted, "for us to attempt to compete with the big motion picture concerns in the matter of salaries or in the expense of production and we are not entering the field as competitors of theirs, but seek rather to develop and to fill a field of our own. In other words, we are trying to be the Woolworth and Ford of the motion picture industry rather than the Tiffany."

Under Kennedy's astute leadership, FBO concentrated on low-cost productions (the average negative cost of an FBO film was around $50,000) consisting of a dozen Western pictures with lots of "action, riding and manly stuff," a dozen dog pictures and twenty-five or more assorted features each year. "Melodrama is our meat," Kennedy admitted, but, he said, it was "high-class melodrama" which allowed the public to weep and to sympathize with the handsome hero and the beautiful heroine. Appealing to the exhibitors in small towns who changed their pictures three times a week, Kennedy established a definite niche in the film industry for FBO's films. This strategy enabled FBO to carry on a business generating nearly $9 million worth of income in the first year of his presidency and producing splendid profits for years to come.

Among the Kennedy children Joe Junior was the model child, the one to whom the parents looked as an example for the younger children. Yet as the two brothers pose together in 1921, a close look reveals that Joe Jr. is squeezing Jack's hand so hard that Jack is grimacing.

*J*oe Junior with his father and paternal grandfather at Nantasket Beach.

*J*oe Senior with Joe Junior and Jack at Nantasket Beach.

*J*ack and Rosemary during summer vacation in Cohasset, Massachusetts, in 1923.

*P*. J. Kennedy, Rosemary, and Jack, who is pretending to smoke a cigar.

Within the family, Jack was the Pied Piper who won the hearts, if not the minds, of his siblings with his humor and his pranks. Shown here standing with his medals at Cohasset with Kathleen, Rosemary, Eunice, and Joe Junior.

*Once the Kennedys recognized that Rosemary was retarded, they hired a score of private tutors to teach her how to print, play tennis, ride a bike, dance, and read. And for a few years, these ceaseless efforts seemed to work. She is shown here sledding with her godfather, Eddie Moore, and riding her bike.*

*J*oe Junior caught in a moment of fun; four young ladies dressing up. From left, Pat, Eunice, Kathleen, and Rosemary.

*R*ose in posed shot with Joe Junior, Kathleen, Eunice, Rose-mary, and Jack; Jack at his confirmation in 1927.

*R*osemary, Jack, Eunice, Joe Junior, and Kathleen in Hyannis Port.

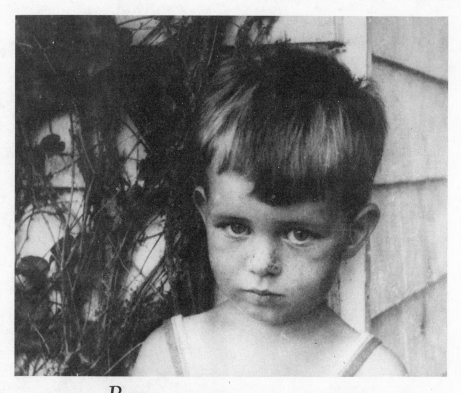

*B*orn into the household after a quartet of baby girls, Bobby had a hard time asserting himself. He was small, rather shy and uncertain, and his grandmother feared that he would become a sissy.

*J*oe Senior as husband, father, and public servant, shown here with his fellow SEC Commissioners.

*Rose geared the children's activities to the rhythm of the seasons —"to the strength of the wind, the salt of the sea, and the excitement of the snow."*

*Pat, Bobby, and Teddy on horseback.*

*Kathleen, left, and schoolmates at Noroton.*

*Bobby adjusting his roller skates.*

*Winter fun with Ted, Pat, Eunice, Jean, Bobby, and Joe Junior.*

*Teddy in the middle of a boxing class.*

*Bobby and Teddy in an affectionate moment at the beach.*

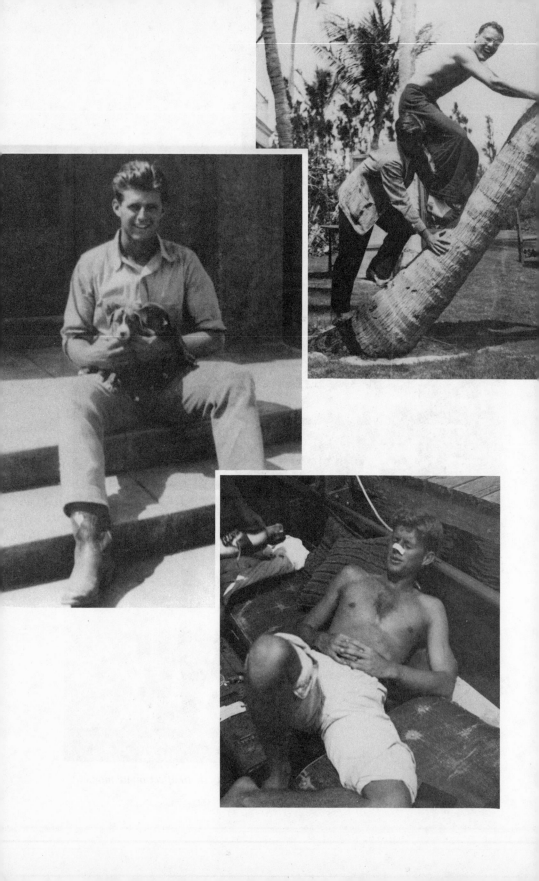

*By the time Joe Junior, Jack, and Kathleen had reached their teens in the middle of the 1930s, they were welded together into an elite family, sharing intense loyalties and myriad connections that would bind them tightly in future years. From top left, Jack and his lifelong friend LeMoyne "Lem" Billings fooling around; Joe Junior with dogs; Jack stretched out in the sun; Jack and Kathleen dancing; Joe Junior and Kathleen in Scotland.*

When Joe Kennedy became Ambassador to Great Britain in 1938, Rose and the children enjoyed some of the most exciting and stimulating experiences of their lives. From top left, the new Ambassador presents his credentials to the King; Joe Junior sits with Teddy; Kathleen plays tennis at the Queen's Club; Kathleen, Rose, and Rosemary are presented to the Court of St. James's; and the entire family, except for Joe Junior, who is in Spain, attend the coronation of the Pope.

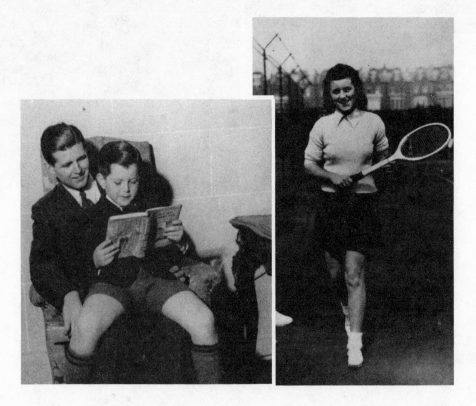

S.FELICI-ROMA

Joe Junior, Kathleen, and Jack en route to the Palace of Westminster, September 3, 1939, to hear Great Britain declare war on Germany. Little could this golden trio have imagined, as they walked into the House of Commons, how much each would lose by the war that was about to begin.

# CHAPTER 21
# GROWING
# UP
# KENNEDY

While Joe was developing his movie company, Rose cared for the children, now numbering seven with the birth of a third son, Robert, on November 20, 1925. Looking back on this period when her husband was away more than he was home, Rose claims that she never once felt that she was being unfairly burdened by Joe's frequent absences; on the contrary, since she had made her resolve in the early twenties and "since it was Joe's duty as the head of the household to do whatever he must to support the family, it was my responsibility to take charge of the day-to-day activities." Moreover, she added, since she had grown up in a household where her own father was away much of the time and her mother never complained, she had a familiar role to play.

Yet one wonders if it really was as easy as Rose makes it sound for her to forsake the role of companion she had once enjoyed with her father. For a woman who had loved nothing more than the chance to participate in Fitzgerald's adventurous world, there must have been some measure of loss in her growing distance from the exciting new world into which her husband was moving.

For the Kennedy children, the immediate effect of Joe's journey to Hollywood was to add a touch of magic to the worshipful love they already felt for their powerful father. Through the children's earliest letters, the figure of Joe Senior strides with a masterful step; here was a man standing at the center of so many fascinating worlds, and yet this same man was unfailingly interested in the smallest things they did in their own small lives, from their swimming meets and their football games to the movies they saw and their work in school.

At the impressionable ages of eleven and nine when their father shifted his career to Hollywood, young Joe and Jack were perhaps the most vividly aware of the glamorous life their father was leading, all so new and various. What boy was there in whose mind the prospect of meeting face to face with cowboy movie star Tom Mix or baseball great Babe Ruth or football hero Red Grange, all of whom were negotiating with Kennedy for different FBO movies, would not conjure up irrepressible feelings of awe and delight at the richness of their father's world? "It was very exciting to know Joe in those days," Rose's lifelong friend Marie Greene recalls. "He was so young and successful, with friends as varied as Red Grange, Irving Berlin and Bernard Baruch."

When Joe was at home, the boys would listen intently to his every word; to be with him, to talk with him, to do things with him—all that was pleasure beyond imagining. And while he was away, they would write him spirited misspelled letters in which the details of their daily lives are suffused with powerful feelings of affection. And almost always, reserving the warmest side of his character for his family, Joe would respond by return mail to each letter from every child.

Writing to young Joe at Camp Wyanoke in Wolfeboro, New Hampshire, where he was spending the summer of 1926, Joe assured his firstborn son that he was getting busy at once on the project they had discussed on parents' visiting day the week before—to produce a special Krazy Kat cartoon which would incorporate some of the funny things that happened that summer to Wyanoke counselors and boys. "Tickled to death with the way you seem to be getting along," Joe wrote, and "I certainly think you were wonderful to Mother to remember her on her birthday and to show her such attention at Camp . . . it made me very happy indeed."

Again and again in his letters to his children, Kennedy emphasized the importance of respecting their mother. Yet, curiously, this generalized family value was the only value Kennedy openly avowed. Taken as a whole, his letters to his children represent a guidance in manners, not morals. Not once in more than two hundred letters did he put forward any ultimate moral principles for his children to contemplate. On the contrary, he stressed to his children the importance of winning at any cost and the pleasures of coming in first. As his own heroes were not poets or artists but men of action, he took it for granted that his children too wanted public success, and he confined himself to advising them how they could get it. All too often, his understanding about their desires and his practical advice were fruits of *his* experience and *his* dreams, not necessarily theirs.

From his Hollywood trips, Joe would return with a special present for each of his children. Years later Rose remembered "the look of wonder" on the faces of her two oldest boys when they tore open a large package from their father to discover inside two small pairs of chaps, just like the ones Tom Mix wore to protect his legs against rope burns when he rode his famous steed, Silver King, across every movie screen in America. For days, Rose recalled, "Joe and Jack ran around with those chaps on and all the neighborhood boys . . . were very envious of them."

For all the material benefits the boys derived from their father's access to Hollywood, however, the fact remained that he was away from home now far more than ever before. On many occasions, Grandpa Fitzgerald stepped in, faithfully appearing in the stands for their games in school and taking them out on weekends to Fenway Park. Yet, in spite of his long absences, Kennedy managed, just as Fitzgerald had done in the previous generation, to make his children feel they were always on his mind; somehow he was the one—being all the more idealized, perhaps, in his absence—who held the enchantment for them. Indeed, Joe Kennedy, having achieved an almost primitive dominion over his children's youthful souls, would rule his boys and girls for the rest of their lives.

Within the family, Joe Junior, as the eldest son, was accorded an initial position of primacy which he then built upon as a consequence of his temperament. To all appearances, young Joe was a child gifted by the gods. He seemed to have come directly out of Ireland, strong and glowingly handsome with his dark-blue eyes and his sturdy frame, filled with vitality, health and energy. In the small circle of his household he emanated power, passion and promise. Even as a child he possessed a conquering poise that made him seem older than he was. At the sheer sound of his voice calling or talking, the faces of both Rose and Joe Senior would break into radiant smiles; from all accounts, this was clearly a child of love. Emotions resonated between young Joe and his parents that none of the others would ever know, that none of the others would ever forget.

From his earliest childhood, Joe tried in everything he took up, from throwing a ball to riding a bike, to attain success and perfection. A perceptive child, he grasped at once the central importance to his parents of the family bond and the critical role he was meant to play as the model son. "If you bring up the eldest son right," Rose later wrote, "the way you want the others to go, that is very important because the younger ones watch him. If he comes in and shakes hands with the guests, the others will watch him in the doorway and they'll come in and do the same thing. If he works at his studies and his sports until he is praised, then the others will follow his example."

"I have always felt," Jack later wrote,

> that Joe achieved his greatest success as the oldest brother. Very early in life he acquired a sense of responsibility towards his brothers and sisters and I do not think that he ever forgot it. . . . He would spend long hours throwing a football with Bobby, swimming with Teddy and teaching the younger girls how to sail. . . . I think that if the Kennedy children amount to anything now or ever amount to anything, it will be due more to Joe's behavior and his constant example than to any other factor. He made the task of bringing up a large family immeasurably easier for my father and mother for what they taught him, he passed on to us and their teachings were not diluted through him but strengthened.

There were times, no doubt, when Joe Junior's attitude toward his brothers and sisters seemed patronizing and overbearing. Taking it upon himself to act as first sergeant when his parents were away, he often found himself in the role of disciplinarian. A quick-tempered youth, his heart often ruling his head, he could as easily hurt the feelings of a younger sibling as he could gather them up in his arms after a nasty fall. "It wasn't the father they were afraid of," said one family friend, "it was Joe Junior." Yet there was love and caring as well. When Joe came home from camp or school, the younger children would come running to him, hugging and kissing him as if he were their father instead of their brother.

But in the process of his acting as the little adult, a part of Joe's childhood was lost. It seems that one consequence of Joe's early maturity was the impossibility of consciously experiencing certain feelings, anxiety, rage, impotence or jealousy, fearful perhaps that if these feelings surfaced he would lose his parents' love. Knowing that his mother, especially, depended on him to act in a particular way, he learned to suppress his spontaneous reactions. "I never heard him utter a foul word," Jack recalled. But as he suppressed his feelings, he walled off a part of himself as well. "I suppose I knew Joe as well as anyone," Jack wrote shortly after his brother's death, "and yet, I sometimes wonder whether I ever really knew him. He had always a slight detachment from things around him—a wall of reserve which few people ever succeeded in penetrating."

Throughout his childhood, Jack grudgingly accepted Joe's primogeniture, his occupying a place to which Jack could not aspire. The younger boy had early wisdom. He could not disguise his eager desire for his parents' praise and affection, yet he could be complacent about his own role within the family as the warm and playful brother, the "Pied Piper" who won the hearts if not the minds of all his brothers and sisters. According to Lem Billings, Jack's oldest friend, Jack found it easy to pardon his father's preference for Joe because he believed his father always behaved fairly toward him and because he valued the space and obscurity that his status as the younger brother provided. But toward his mother, who found his irreverent and playful demeanor almost intolerable, he developed a lifelong detachment. As Lem described Rose, she was "a tough, constant, minute disciplinarian with a fetish for neatness and order and decorum. This went against Jack's natural temperament —informal, tardy, forgetful, and often downright sloppy—so there was friction, and, on his part, resentment."

There is evidence in a diary Rose kept in 1923 that Jack's unorthodox attitude toward his religion was also something of a trial to his devout mother. Apparently while Rose was at church with her children on Good Friday, she urged them all to wish for a happy death; the others complied, but Jack rebelled, saying that he would like instead to wish for two dogs. Three days later, Rose left with her sister Agnes for a three-week journey to California. As all the children gathered on the front porch to say goodbye only Jack spoke up: "Gee, you're a great mother to go away and leave your children alone."

Never understanding why his mother took so many trips away from home, Jack told a friend he used to cry every time she packed her bags until he realized that his crying irritated her no end and only made her withdraw from him even more. "Better to take it in stride," he said.

Perhaps the warmest moments little Jack spent with his mother were when he was confined to bed by the frequent bouts with illness which plagued him through his growing years. On these occasions, when Rose would spend an hour or more reading books to her bedridden son, Jack found a world he could happily inhabit for the rest of his days, a world of kings and queens, of heroes and adventures. Gifted with a fine intelligence and an active imagination, he laughed with Peter Pan and cried with Black Beauty; he followed Sinbad the Sailor on all seven of his voyages through the Persian Gulf and tracked Billy Whiskers across the Pacific to the Sandwich Islands.

Confident within himself that he surpassed Joe in one area alone, in mental ability, he delighted in the look on his mother's face when he asked an intelligent question or showed a deep understanding of the story they were reading. As his own reading abilities developed, he turned more and more to stories of adventure, to King Arthur and the Round Table, *Treasure Island*, John Bunyan's *Pilgrim's Progress* and Rudyard Kipling's *Jungle Books*.

Through his sensitivity to books, Jack developed an intellectual maturity which set him apart from his brothers and sisters and proved especially irritating to Joe, who was accustomed to being the best. Of all the children Jack was the only one who ever tried to challenge Joe. Refusing to stay out of Joe's way or to heed his commands, Jack was always full of mischief, provoking Joe and catching him off guard. As a result, the two brothers stalked each other from the earliest age, and while Joe's greater strength would win out time after time, Jack kept coming back for more. Later, Robert Kennedy remembered cowering with his sisters upstairs while his older brothers fought furiously on the first floor. With Jack, Joe often turned bully, exercising far less patience with his closest brother than he exercised with others in the family. Although with Bobby he would gently throw a football for hours, gradually building up the speed of his throw as the younger boy learned how to catch the ball, with Jack he "would often find an excuse to slam the ball into his stomach and walk away laughing as his younger brother lay doubled up in pain." With Jack far more than with his other siblings, Lem Billings recalled, Joe's attitude was "sarcastic and overbearing and disapproving and challenging," almost as if the young Kennedy heir already sensed an implicit challenge to his throne.

In later years, one encounter stood out above the others in Jack's mind as a symbol of the heavy-handed approach Joe had used with him. On a sunny afternoon one spring, Joe suggested a bicycle race, with each going around the block in the opposite direction. Approaching each other head on at the final corner, neither boy swerved. The collision left Joe unhurt, but Jack was thrown from his bike into the air, coming down on the ground in a bloody heap that it would take twenty-eight stitches to put together again.

Feeling "frustrated and domineered" by his older brother, as Lem described it, Jack adopted Joe as a model in reverse: whereas Joe was impulsive and feverish in his enthusiasms, Jack developed a more cautionary approach to life which inclined him to look at a situation from all angles and to contemplate his action. While Joe was an orderly child at home and a serious student at school, even tackling things he did not like, Jack was unpardonably sloppy at home and lazy at school, interested only in the things that pleased him. When Jack was small, Rose later recalled, he was "invariably late" for meals despite the household rule that whoever came late could eat only what was being served at the moment and would have to miss all the previous courses. "So he would take . . . the last spoonful of dessert or whatever it was," Rose recalled, and then "he would promptly go to the kitchen, where the cook, who loved him very much, would serve him his meals, and I'm afraid that was the way he was the greater part of his life. He would charm people into giving in to him."

Yet, for all the difficulty between the two brothers, they shared a common vitality and an essential closeness. When Joe first went away to sleepover camp in the summer of 1926, Jack initially rejoiced in the freedom he felt from his brother's continuing harassment, but before two weeks had passed, as Joe Senior reported to Joe Junior, Jack was "really very lonesome for you and he wants me to be sure and promise him that he will go to camp next summer." After Joe's death, Jack would confess that in all his experience, he didn't know anyone with a better sense of humor or anyone with whom he would "rather have spent an evening or played golf or in fact done anything."

During their first years in school, Joe and Jack attended a public elementary school on Harvard Street in Brookline. Known as the Devotion School in honor of one of Brookline's early benefactors, Edward Devotion, the school was located in an old gambrel-roofed house with a large central chimney and a fine pedimented door. With its high academic standards and its proximity to the Naples Road house, it seemed an ideal place for the Kennedy children. Had Rose had her say, she might well have kept the boys in the public system—her only concern about Devotion was that it let the children out too early, freeing up too many hours for mischief—but by the fall of 1924 Joe Senior had a different plan in mind. The time had come, he believed, for his sons to meet the sons of Beacon Hill, and the perfect place for that introduction would be the Dexter School, a six-year elementary school for boys, of the country day type.

Serving originally as the lower school for the prestigious Nobles and Greenough School, Dexter provided early training in the mores of private-school life for those born to positions of wealth and influence. At Dexter, unlike Devotion, the day extended from eight-fifteen in the

morning until four forty-five in the afternoon. At the close of the morning session, a hot dinner was served, after which, until two-thirty in the
afternoon, there was a rest period for the younger boys and a supervised
study period for the older ones. The rest of the day was devoted to
organized sports—football, tennis, soccer, field and ice hockey, baseball
and track—played under the direction of trained instructors who had
the luxury of spreading their teams over four and a half acres of well-
graded playing fields.

Comprising a social register of the area, Dexter at the time included
James Jackson Storrow III (grandson of the Yankee politician who lost
the mayoralty to John Fitzgerald in 1910), Francis Appleton III, Francis
Stanley Parker, Thomas B. Hunnewell, Leverett Saltonstall, Jr., and the
two Bundy brothers, William and McGeorge.

Looking back later, Jack thought of Dexter as a sort of "junior-grade
Groton" and realized that he and Joe were probably the only Catholics
in the school. Yet, at the time, because they lived near the school and
walked home every day in familiar surroundings, he was only "slightly"
aware of being different. More memorable to Jack than the sensation of
being an outsider was the experience of competing with Joe for the
various athletic honors the school passed out. Though Joe was by far
the healthier, the stronger and the more intense of the two, Jack seemed
to possess a somewhat greater athletic ability, which enabled him, by
the time he reached the fourth grade, to be chosen both captain and
quarterback of the school's football team—an honor his older brother
had not yet been accorded. It was a victory which would not come to
Jack easily again, for Jack's ill health would create a fundamental want
of balance in the physical competition between the two.

Rosemary had followed her two older brothers to the Devotion School
for kindergarten, but when the year drew to a close her teachers could
not recommend her for the first grade. While she had an uncommonly
sweet and gentle disposition, she seemed unable to grasp even the sim-
plest tasks—the making of potholders or the folding of papers—which
the other children in the class were routinely able to accomplish. The
teachers' report confirmed in her mother all the lurking suspicions she
had harbored about her five-year-old daughter from the first year of her
life.

Born at the height of the flu epidemic of 1918, Rosemary had seemed
to all appearances a normal baby. As an infant, she had soft brown hair,
high coloring and clear blue-green eyes which seemed to look out upon
the world with "a steady and peaceful gaze." "She was a very pretty
baby," Rose recorded in her memoirs, "and she was sweet and peaceable
and cried less than the first two had, which at the time I supposed was

part of her being a girl." As the months went by, however, symptoms of trouble began to appear. Slower to crawl, slower to walk and slower to speak than her brothers, Rosemary had problems managing her baby spoon and her porringer and she was unable to put on or take off her clothes without help. Still her mother remained patient—"concerned" and "beginning to be a little apprehensive," but not really worried, because she had persuaded herself that all babies have their own individual rates of growth and of acquiring skills and that it was only a matter of time until Rosemary caught up.

Yet all the time the worry was there, like a dark cloud streaking across the summer sky, and as a consequence Rose spent more time with her firstborn daughter than with any of her other children. Knowing that Rosemary was unable to steer a sled skillfully enough to get her safely down the hill, Rose would arrange for the governess to take the other children coasting while she took Rosemary for a special walk to Coolidge Corner. There, holding hands with her mother, the winsome little girl took delight in gazing at all the new dresses in the department store windows, developing a love for pretty clothes which stayed with her into adulthood. Recognizing this love, Eddie Moore, whose intense affection for his godchild far exceeded the ordinary responsibility of the godparent, developed a tradition of buying Rosemary a new dress for every holiday. Among the early family letters Eddie's letters to Rosemary shine through with loving care. "My dear Rosemary," Eddie writes when she is only four and a half, "This season they are showing such wonderful and pretty little frocks for little women that I regretted not having you with me to help me choose. However I feel had you been along we both would have decided on this little party dress so I am sending it to you with love and Easter greetings."

"Rosemary was constantly on my mind," Rose recalled, "so much so that I probably didn't spend as much time with the others as I should have, particularly Jack, who was so ill so much of the time as a little boy that he needed a lot of attention. But I could never tell what she was going to do." If Rosemary saw the other children going out in a rowboat, Rose remembered, she would insist on going, too, but of course she couldn't manage the oars. If the others took a walk by themselves to the post office she would impulsively decide to go with them, but then once she was there she would just as impulsively decide not to come home. "So it was a great worry," Rose admitted.

Still, nothing prepared Rose for the heartbreak she would experience when she finally had to admit to herself that her beautiful daughter was retarded and had probably been so since birth, though no one understood exactly why and how it had happened. "I went to the head of the psychology department at Harvard," Rose recalled, "I went to a priest from Washington who had made a study of retarded people, Father Moore. They all told me she had a low IQ, but when I said, 'What can I do to help her?' there didn't seem to be very much of an answer." As the awareness of Rosemary's retardation deepened, the search of both parents for hope grew more frantic. "We went from doctor to doctor . . . From all, we heard the same answer: 'I'm sorry, but we can do nothing.' For my husband and me it was nerve-racking and incomprehensible."

One look at the dismal state of the literature on mental retardation in the 1920s and 1930s suggests a measure of the frustration the Kennedys must have experienced. For classification and management, "defective" children were divided into three groups—idiots, imbeciles and feebleminded. At the lowest end of the scale, the term "idiot" was given to describe those whose mental development never reached beyond that of a two-year-old baby. Unable to wash, to dress themselves or to form sentences, this group was believed to constitute 10 percent of the mental defectives. The next group, the "imbeciles," were considered capable of developing in a more or less irregular fashion until they reached the degree of intelligence possessed by the average child ranging in age from three to seven, and there they remained: able to read and spell simple words, to count on their fingers and to name common objects, but unable to care for themselves, to concentrate their thoughts upon a particular subject or to carry out sustained work.

In her day, the best hope for Rosemary lay in being considered a "feebleminded" child, in contrast to an imbecile or an idiot. By far the largest group of defectives, feebleminded persons, or "morons," as the American Association for the Study of the Feeble Minded had recently elected to call them (from the Greek word for "fool"), were considered just mentally competent enough to pass for pretty fair imitations of men and women although their mental development generally stopped at somewhere between ages eight and twelve. In the early years, the literature suggests, they are scarcely distinguishable from the normal child of their age, although their progress in every area is always slower than that of normal children. To the untrained eye, they could talk like anybody else as long as the conversation didn't get too complicated, and they could even jog along after a fashion for several grades in school, learning to read and write and to do simple sums.

But be not misled, *Good Housekeeping* warned in 1915, just three years before Rosemary was born. The morons, readers were told, were the greatest menaces of all the defectives.

> They are born of and will breed nothing but defective stock. From this class seven-eighths of our criminals are recruited. Take care of the morons

and crime will take care of itself. The cruelest and the unkindest thing that can be done to these perpetual children is to leave them out in the world, exposed to the competition and the impositions, too often the teasing, cruel treatment and exploitation of their normal fellows. They are awkward, grotesque and clumsy and their foolish speeches provoke ridicule, mockery and jeers.

Nor, it was believed at the time, could feebleminded children ever be anything different from what they were—or produce any other kind of offspring than their own type. In a progressive age when the remarkable discoveries of science had begun to sweep away the vast majority of diseases known to man, and when it looked as if man would soon be able to take life into his own hands to mold, model and improve at will, the group of defects associated with feeblemindedness, imbecility and idiocy seemed to be the one intractable, pathetic and pitiful exception in the otherwise triumphant advance of modern medicine. Worse still for the Kennedys, the established wisdom held that the prognosis for improvement of any kind was favorable inversely as the child was comely to look at. In other words, a stunted, misshapen victim of morbid heredity was likely to be more responsive to training than their lovely, placid daughter.

But when the day came to make the decision to send Rosemary to an institution—a decision recommended by the psychologists and routinely practiced at that time by many families—both Joe and Rose rebelled against the thought of their daughter living and sleeping away from home, forced to grow up in a world of strangers. "What can they do in an institution that we can't do better for her at home—here with her family?" Joe questioned, with the tone of his voice providing the answer.

So the Kennedys made the decision not only to keep Rosemary at home but to shoulder themselves a large part of her unequal struggle for happiness. Determined to develop her capacities to the utmost, Rose hired a special governess as well as a score of private tutors to teach her how to print, play tennis, dance and read. And for a few years these ceaseless efforts seemed to work. In the Kennedy papers there are a number of Rosemary's childhood letters; the printing in them is that of a child, but the simple thoughts are clear and perfectly understandable. "Dear Santa Claus," she writes when she is living in Brookline and probably about six or seven, "i am writing to you i want a doll, and doll carriage and some paper doll block boad little set of dishes. Your friend Rose Kennedy 31 Naple rd." As time goes by, moreover, the spelling improves and the letters grow longer and more descriptive.

An even more astonishing sign of progress can be found in several of the arithmetic papers which Rosemary completed and the family saved.

In one of those papers, dated February 21, 1927, the nine-year-old Rosemary correctly and neatly computed several problems in multiplication (428 times 32; 693 times 65) and several more in division (3924 divided by 6; 4634 by 5) to earn the high praise of her tutor at the top of the sheet: "a very nice paper."

In these years, Rosemary also learned how to dance and play tennis. While her basic coordination remained weak, and while she always seemed heavy on her feet, nevertheless, after hundreds of private lessons, she was able to waltz, to do the fox trot, and to hit a ball across the net. Years later, her younger sister Eunice remembered watching their mother play tennis with Rosemary for hours. Even though Mother never played with the rest of the children, Eunice wistfully recalled, she would play with Rosemary.

Every effort was made to see that she was always one of the family, and it was accepted by the other children that whatever they did Rosemary would also do, even if it meant providing her with special assistance. At the dining table she was unable to cut her meat, so it was served to her already cut. In the sailing races, she would always be taken along as a member of the crew and she could usually work the jib so long as she was told what to do. When all the girls were dressing up to go out, she too would get dressed up, with the help of one of her sisters who would then keep a watchful eye on her throughout the night to make sure she didn't spill things on her clothes or try to put on fresh lipstick herself. "She loved compliments," Eunice recalled. "Every time I would say, 'Rosemary, you have the best teeth and smile in the family,' she would smile for hours." And from her mother she would eagerly respond to the slightest attention: "Even if I said to her no more than 'Rosemary, that's the most beautiful hair ribbon,' she would be thrilled," Rose recalled.

In a family governed by the desire to be extraordinary in everything they chose to do, Rosemary was a constant reminder of the arbitrariness of destiny. Speaking about mental retardation in the fall of 1968, Rose Kennedy said that she believed God sent these children for a special reason—"to do a work he cannot do through any other child . . ." "Our family was the perfect family—boys brilliant, girls attractive and intelligent, money, prestige, a young father and mother of intelligence, devoted exemplary habits and successful in the education of their children. . . . But God or 'destiny' just does not allow a family to exist which has all these star-studded adornments." So he left them with a retarded child, Rose concluded, "who must receive benefits rather than bestow."

Rose's equanimity about Rosemary came much later in life, however; when Rosemary was still a child, Rose continually wondered why this one child alone had been given so few natural gifts while the other members of the family had been so abundantly endowed. Searching for an explanation, Rose was haunted by the fear that the retardation was the consequence of her parents' once forbidden marriage, the genetic fruit one generation later of second cousins bearing children. Easier to accept was the thought that Rosemary's mind had been damaged in the process of delivery; perhaps the forceps used to help her emerge had penetrated her soft skull to damage the brain. Other family members offered additional explanations. Helen Barron remembered a summer vacation at Winthrop when Rosemary was only four or five. In the middle of the night the family doctor arrived to treat the little girl, who was suffering from convulsions after a high fever, and the following day the doctor confided to Helen's mother that he hoped to God no permanent damage had been done.

But, after all the searching questions, there was never a conclusive answer. Living in an era when mental disability was regarded as shameful, the Kennedys decided to keep the nature of Rosemary's "condition" within the family. Surrounding her with the mantle of family affection, they projected Rosemary as a sweet but bashful little girl who was simply quieter than her rambunctious brothers and sisters. One adult friend of Rose's, observing Rosemary standing in the background while the other children were laughing and playing, attributed her difference to the vibrant presence of her younger sister Kathleen, an especially charming little girl who was clearly the "pet" of the family. Another relative remembers seeing Rosemary for years as part of the family group and thinking of her only as very pretty and very quiet. "Then, one day," Marnie Devine remembered, "we were all in the same car on a long train ride from Boston to Palm Beach, and after watching her and listening to her for a while I could see that something was wrong, and I came home and asked my mother."

Undoubtedly, the denial of Rosemary's retardation had much to do with the ethos of the times, but it also seems to represent a dominant motif in the Kennedy family—the tendency to deny the dark and unpleasant aspects of reality by continuous movement, by striving against odds and working against hope to achieve victory in everything they did. Just as young Jack was rewarded by the family for fighting his way through the chronic illnesses which plagued him, so Rosemary was rewarded for trying to improve, for trying, as much as she could, to look and to act like the rest of them. In a family of such strong characters and high ambitions, it must have been terribly wearisome for Rosemary to keep on striving, but she had no choice.

For the rest of the Kennedy children, Rosemary became an instrument of their togetherness. All of them, at a very early age, acquired a sense of responsibility for their sister which served to open their eyes to the difficulties and the drudgery of the workaday world. In a family cushioned by wealth and privilege, Rosemary's endless troubles provided a bridge of understanding to the ravages of everyday life. Years later, Rose maintained that the key to her children's compassion for the poor and the underprivileged was unlocked by their sister's struggle for the smallest victory.

Because of Rosemary's handicap, Kathleen enjoyed the status of eldest daughter in the family. Five years younger than Joe and three years younger than Jack, Kathleen had curly reddish-blond hair, deepset eyes, rosy skin and a playful, energetic disposition. As a small child she was like a high-spirited pony, so uncomplaining, unafraid and full of fun that her family gave her the nickname "Kick."

Twenty years later, thinking about the different personalities of her children, Rose reserved her warmest feelings for Kathleen, who seemed in so many ways an uncanny reincarnation of Rose herself as a young girl. "Never was there a girl," Rose marveled, "who had so many gifts lavished upon her . . . with life geared to make her extravagantly happy if life ever was." As a youngster, "she was lovely to look at, full of *joie de vivre* and so tremendously popular." Clever and effervescent, she was also a good athlete who could ski, sail and play tennis as well as her brothers. At the same time she was a great dancer and she had excellent taste in clothes, meeting her sisters and her brothers at a kind of intersection between masculinity and femininity.

Kathleen was "the sunshine" of her family, one of her friends, Dinah Bridge, maintains. "Wherever she stood, there would be warmth, fun, gaiety and charm." Happy and carefree, she had a wonderful smile and an infectious laugh that projected a kind of tinkling sound, like the bells on the cows in a mountainside field. Carrying within herself a secure sense of being loved by her parents, knowing that she was her brother Jack's favorite companion, Kathleen developed an extraordinary ability to get along with everyone. Neither moody nor snobby, she could fit into all situations with all kinds of people, making friends everywhere.

But what set Kathleen apart from her siblings was the fact that she more than they maintained a sense of wonder at how lucky she was to be born who she was in her family and in the world. "All her life," one friend recalled, "Kathleen would say she didn't know why she deserved such a wonderful life and she didn't know how it could possibly last."

Forming a family within the family, Joe Junior, Jack and Kathleen were the golden trio who shared all the inestimable advantages of being wealthy, good-looking, confident and intelligent. "They were the pick of the litter," says one Kennedy friend, "the ones the old man thought would write the story of the next generation." And, Rose recalled, "beyond all their advantages of temperament and personality, they were just at the right age to enjoy and participate in all the glorious, exciting adventures which their father's world opened up to them."

Standing at the crossroads of the two clusters within the family, Eunice veered more toward the younger children, Pat, Bobby and eventually Jean and Teddy. From the beginning, Rose later noted, Eunice was aware that she could not compete with her older brothers or her sister Kathleen, and while she idolized them she spent most of her girlhood in games and sports with the younger ones rather than trying to connect herself with the older, more sophisticated group. Born three years after Rosemary and one year after Kathleen, Eunice as a youngster was, in Rose's words, "rather pale and of a nervous, highly conscientious demeanor." Suffering from her own bouts of ill health, which included chronic stomach troubles, Eunice early on assumed a leadership role in relation to her younger siblings. "If anyone in the family wanted to do something but was afraid to ask, Eunice was the one who would jump up and say, 'I'll speak to Dad about that, don't worry.'" Unafraid of arguing, she possessed an infallible sense of knowing when and where to make her case. Nor was she reticent about using her authority to keep the little ones in line, often serving as the female counterpart of Joe Junior.

Eunice was also the child within the family who developed the strongest bond with Rosemary. From her earliest years, Eunice seemed to possess a deep understanding of Rosemary which none of the others fully shared. She always seemed to know what Rosemary wanted or required without having to be told and never needed to be asked to take her shopping or for a walk. "Somehow," a family friend remarked, "Eunice seemed to develop very early on a sense of special responsibility for Rosemary as if Rosemary were her child instead of her sister. There was an odd maturity about Eunice which was sometimes forbidding but which clearly set her off from all the rest."

As the sixth and seventh children, Patricia and Robert must have experienced a trickling down of parental attention, and as a consequence the two of them shared a special kinship. Looking back, Rose confessed that it seemed so important for her to spend her time and energy on the older ones—whose problems seemed more serious at the time—that the younger ones tended to be left more to fend for themselves, "free from moral and physical harm, so long as they had a competent, pleasant governess of high moral standards."

Of the five girls, Pat was considered by many to possess the best physical features: taller than her sisters and taller even than Bobby, she carried herself with an aristocratic poise reminiscent of her grandmother Josie Hannon Fitzgerald. Gifted with natural grace, she was also, as a youngster, the best athlete in the family. But while the others seemed to take delight in the competitive spirit within the household, Pat never seemed, in her mother's words, to be "particularly ambitious or enthusiastic or keen about anything." Although she had a good mind, a fine physique and a beautiful face which could easily have led her to excel in school, in sports or in appearance, Rose contended "she would never make the effort to achieve distinction" in any of these areas. Nor was she interested in social distinction, Rose recalled. "She thoroughly enjoyed her own school, her own friends and her own sphere and had no inclination to change any of them."

Born into the household after a quartet of baby girls, "Bobby had a lot going against him," Lem Billings noted. "He was small, rather shy and uncertain and lost, as he was in the middle of a flock of sisters; lacking in identity, he had a hard time asserting himself." With his father away much of his early childhood, and his older brothers off in school, his grandmother Josie feared that he would become a sissy, "stuck by himself in a bunch of girls." "The gentlest and the shyest in the roaring family," he was, as well, the most open with his affections, unafraid to close his letters to his mother, to whom he was extremely close, with "oodles of love" and hundreds of Xs for kisses. Protected and consoled by his mother, he had a more difficult time with his father, who, according to historian Arthur Schlesinger, was "on occasions impatient and rough with him."

But neither Josie nor Joe needed to worry for long about Bobby's becoming a sissy. As he grew, he developed an external toughness which sustained him in his struggles. "I was," Robert said, "the seventh of nine children and when you come from that far down you have to struggle to survive." And struggle he did, possessing within himself that same drive, sense of purpose and will to win that had propelled his father to success. Slow at swimming, he threw himself off a small boat in Nantucket Sound as if resolving to learn all at once or to drown. His brother Joe pulled him out. Afraid of being late for dinner when he was four years old, he ran into a heavy glass door, leaving several deep gashes in his face. Feeling, in Billings' words, "the least loved" of the sons, he became "a devoted observer of all the clan rules," turning out to be the best behaved, the most punctual and the most religious of the boys.

Yet, beneath the image Bobby projected, there remained a fullblooded youngster who looked to his brother Jack for mischief and fun as if they were members of some forbidden society. Though Joe Junior probably spent more hours with young Bobby than Jack ever did, teaching him all the things an older brother was supposed to teach—how to sail, how to ski and how to play football—Jack seemed to meet Bobby at a deeper level of his soul. Each afternoon when Jack returned home from school he found Bobby waiting anxiously in hopes that his brother would take him for a walk. And in these walks the shy youngster would open up, asking Jack to tell him stories of heroes and adventures which Jack had learned from the many books he read. Not then a reader himself, Bobby delighted in the imaginative journeys his brother's stories afforded, while on Jack's part there was something special to him about Bobby's feeling that his older brother knew everything.

It has been said that aspirations are not inherited. When a man forces his way to the top his most precious asset is his drive, his will, his indomitability. Yet that is the one asset he cannot easily pass on to his children. He can pass on his wealth, his knowledge and his influence, but he cannot pass on the memory of hardships, the will to win and the fierce determination born of struggle. Indeed, the easy conditions of his children's lives, sitting at the top simply because they were born into the right family, do much to ensure that they will be less highly motivated than their parents.

The experience of the Kennedy children seems to run counter to this trend, perhaps because, as Bobby recognized, the sheer size of the family created a miniature struggle for survival within the household itself. It must also be recognized that Joe and Rose Kennedy consciously chose to create an atmosphere pervaded by high expectations. But part of the continuing drive for success which the children so clearly projected must be attributed to the peculiar conditions of life in Boston, where, for all of Joe Kennedy's wealth and accomplishment, the Kennedy family was still unable to penetrate the inner sanctums of Boston's insular society.

In other large cities, surrounded by large numbers of different ethnic groups, Joe Kennedy's Irishness would have been much more easily blurred and diffused. As former U.S. ambassador to Ireland William Shannon has observed, the Irish who went to Chicago and St. Louis and to other cities of the Midwest had the advantage of growing up with their city, while those who went to New York found themselves trying to join wealthy classes that were at once fluid and diverse in their makeup; but in Boston, where, for more than four decades, the Irish were the only major immigrant group in the Yankees' midst, all social encounters were played out against a two-dimensional backdrop—the Irish versus the Yankees. As a result, social antagonisms were not easily diverted and the scars of prejudice remained forever open, like festering wounds. Moreover, since the city was already more than two centuries old when the Irish arrived, there seemed to be no way for the accomplishments of the newcomers to match those of the earlier settlers. At every turn the old Yankee society seemed to be looming up and asking, What could you people possibly accomplish to compare with what we have done, we whose ancestors started the movement toward the American Revolution in the eighteenth century, we who produced such a large explosion of genius in the nineteenth century?

Joe Kennedy believed he deserved better from the city of his birth. Yet, time and again, just as he was beginning to feel some sense of progress, he was again administered a curt rejection. After the insult of his experience at Cohasset, he decided to move his family to Cape Cod, and in the summer of 1925 he rented a gracious white house known as the Malcolm Cottage at the end of Merchant Avenue on the beach at Hyannis Port. Here, he believed, in a new house in a new town, he could start afresh. But no sooner had the family settled in than Rose began to hear snide comments from the neighbors—scathing talk about the noisiness and the gracelessness of the children, unpleasant mutterings about the way the Kennedys pushed too hard to win.

Surely the Kennedys' style contributed to some of their social difficulties. From dawn to dusk both house and lawn resounded with the yelling and laughing, the pushing and pulling of active children at play. From the earliest ages, the children were entered in all the town's swimming and sailing races, and from the beginning, Eunice recalled, they were always taught that "coming in second was just no good." Moreover, an extraordinary intimacy seemed to band the family together: they unashamedly hugged and kissed one another and they preferred each other's company to anyone else's. One childhood playmate recalled the intense loyalty the children showed toward each other: "No matter what anyone else had done, the Kennedy children always praised each other's accomplishments to the skies. While it was amusing and touching for a time, it got to be rather tiresome after a while."

In a sense, the Kennedys were caught in a cycle: rebuffed by the Brahmin world, the family closed up within itself; but the more they banded together, the greater the anger and the envy they aroused. "Years ago," Rose wrote, "we decided that our kids were going to be our best friends and that we could never see too much of them. Since we couldn't do both, it was better to bring up our family than to go out to dinners. My husband's business often took him away from home and when all of us had time to be together we didn't want to share it with outsiders." As a result, the Kennedy children became natives of the Kennedy family, first and foremost, before any city or any country.

Finally the time came, in the fall of 1927, when Joe Kennedy evidently wearied too much of the frustrations he was still experiencing in Boston. While his phenomenal success compelled an unqualified respect in both New York and Hollywood, he found no similar satisfaction in Boston. The time had come to move his family to New York.

Years later, in an interview with Kennedy, a reporter asked, "I've seen you quoted as saying that the reason you moved your family out of Boston in the 20's was the anti-Catholic and anti-Irish prejudice in Mass. Is that so?"

"That's exactly why I left Boston," Kennedy responded. "I felt it was no place to bring up Irish Catholic children. I didn't want them to go through what I had to go through when I was growing up there. . . . They wouldn't have asked my daughters to join their deb clubs; not that our girls would have joined anyway—they never gave two cents for that society stuff. But the point is they wouldn't have been asked in Boston."

Apart from his concern for his children, however, it was also true that in moving to New York Joe Kennedy was simply doing what many a successful businessman in the same position would have done—moving to the place where the action was. In moving from Boston to New York, Kennedy was leaving behind a city whose days of glory seemed to have passed. "Poor old Boston does not want in the least to be a real city," journalist Elmer Davis argued in *Harper's* in 1928. "It lives in terror, shudders in its bed at night," fearing that if it moved forward into the future it would lose the identity of its past and would be no more. The very look of Boston in the 1920s, genteel but shabby, seemed to confirm the view that the Athens of America was suffering. While New Yorkers were overreaching themselves, throwing upward new skyscrapers whose towers testified to the vast energies released by the city, Boston was moving in a different direction, becoming the first city in the United States to secure the enactment of a comprehensive law to limit building heights. For decades, 125 feet was the limit in Boston and that limit was strictly enforced. Many a Bostonian remembered the case of a hotel whose owners had to knock off the top story which they had put on apparently in confidence that they could get away with it on the payment of a small fee, as they probably could have almost anywhere else.

If anyone in the family was reluctant to leave Boston, it was Rose, whose roots in the city of her birth ran the deepest, but even she did not expect the effect the actual move would have upon her. "It was like a blow in the stomach," she recalled later. "For months I would wake up in our new house in New York and feel a terrible sense of loss."

For Joe there was less to leave behind. While he would miss the tradition he had established of bringing his children every Sunday to his father's house in Winthrop, the house itself was no longer the same since the death of his mother from stomach cancer in 1923. And while he would never forget the loving sympathy and interest of a number of older men in his career—including some of the crustiest old Yankees— he believed the time had come to move on to higher ground. Nevertheless, he too would admit, in a letter tendering his resignation from the board of the Dexter School, that he certainly had "many regrets in pulling out of Boston, but there doesn't seem very much else for me to do."

In order to make the departure easier for Rose, Joe sent Eddie Moore to New York to scout the area for a house to rent until a proper mansion could be found. Heeding Rose's desire to live in a neighborhood with good schools, Moore produced a thirteen-room house in the exclusive Riverdale community on the Hudson just north of Manhattan. Then, when the time came to depart, Joe hired a private railroad car for his family so that all his children, his servants and his possessions could leave Boston in sumptuous splendor. And at the same time, to make his departure less total, he purchased the white house in Hyannis Port to allow his family to keep at least part of its roots in Massachusetts. Still, the move must have been a difficult one for everyone: in the health cards Rose religiously kept for each of her children, it is recorded that on the day they actually left, September 26, 1927, Eunice, who was then six years old, had a bad stomach upset; perhaps the tension of the family's move was making itself visible in the body of this sensitive little girl.

But even as Kennedy made his plans to leave behind the city of his birth, he was concocting an ambitious project that would bring him into an intense working relationship with Harvard College.

# CHAPTER 22
# THE
# YOUNG
# MOGUL

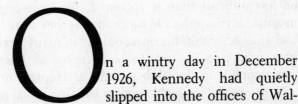

On a wintry day in December 1926, Kennedy had quietly slipped into the offices of Wallace B. Donham, dean of the Harvard Business School. The young producer had a bold plan for a series of lectures on the motion picture industry, to be given by the heads of the largest companies and other major figures in the business and to form an integral part of the school's curriculum. As one of the largest and fastest-growing industries in the country, Kennedy argued, the film industry could no longer be ignored by serious students of industrial conditions. By sponsoring the series, Harvard could carry forward the exploring tradition of New England pioneers and prove itself the home of fresh ideas; by responding to the overwhelming approval of the movies by the people at large, whose daily attendance ran into the tens of millions, Harvard could be the first university to place the stamp of legitimacy on an important new industry that was likely to have a major influence on American life for decades to come.

As a self-appointed mediator between Hollywood and Harvard, Kennedy had chosen an opportune moment. Five years earlier, Hollywood had suffered under the backlash of several notable scandals: the trial of

Fatty Arbuckle on a charge of manslaughter after a wild drinking party at a San Francisco hotel, the drug-related death of leading actor Wallace Reid and the unsolved murder of director William Desmond Taylor, which was all the more shocking because he was considered a man of high culture and refinement. The appointment of Postmaster General Will Hays as head of the Motion Picture Producers and Distributors of America had done much to quell the emotions of the public, but abroad in the land there still remained a widespread impression that the entire world of Hollywood was synonymous with immorality and riotous living. It was this impression Kennedy hoped to counter by engaging the most distinguished leaders of the most successful movie companies in a series of seminars with some of the best young minds in America.

Before approaching Harvard, Kennedy had discussed the idea with Will Hays, who was so enthusiastic about the opportunity it provided to enhance the dignity of the movie industry that he offered to put the full resources of his office at Kennedy's disposal. The first step was to ensure that all the top leaders, the men in commanding positions of authority, agreed to come. This, Kennedy believed, with unerring intuition, would be less difficult than it appeared, for he recognized in many movie moguls, as triumphantly successful as they were, the same longings that had gnawed within his own soul for so many years—the longings of the immigrant and his sons to be accepted as Americans. From his own experience with the club systems at Harvard and Cohasset, Kennedy had developed a valuable insight into the mood of an insecure industry, an acute understanding of Hollywood's need for legitimacy and acceptance. And where better to be accorded that acceptance than on the hallowed ground of Harvard, the oldest and most venerated university in the country, the symbol of light and learning for people all over the world?

From the first instant, the idea of the new course which Kennedy suggested as a required subject for all second-year students at the business school appealed to the imaginative dean. But, unfortunately, Donham's excitement was not shared by all the members of the community, some of whom believed that the prestige of Harvard would be impaired by its association with something as venal as the motion picture industry.

In a long, angry letter to Harvard's President Lawrence Lowell, William Marston Seabury, a great-great-grandson of Dr. Samuel Seabury, first bishop of the Protestant Episcopal Church in America, argued that the entire industry was in the hands of "approximately four men, two of whom are alleged to have been born in Hungary, one in Germany and one in New York," and that "to place the formative minds of students at the instructional mercy" of such men was an outrage. Furthermore, Seabury continued,

> in the opinion of many thoughtful people, the pictures made by the so-called American industry which are absorbing as much as 90% of the screen time of many countries of the world are doing incalculable harm to America in parading our riches before the people of the world, in stimulating animosity rather than friendship, and in falsely representing our national ideas, manners, and customs, and in indicating that we have no such thing in America as culture but that large numbers of our people pursue lives of violence and crime.

It would be a terrible pity, Seabury concluded, to allow this proposed connection with this corrupting industry to destroy the reputation of one of America's greatest national institutions.

In spite of the protests, Harvard decided to go forward, no doubt strengthened in its resolve by the pledge Kennedy made to contribute $30,000 for the establishment of a film library to be located at the university's Fogg Museum.

As it turned out, all the men Kennedy approached, from Jesse Lasky and William Fox to Harry Warner and Cecil B. De Mille, were thrilled at the prospect of receiving recognition from Harvard; the unexpected obstacle was not desire, but fear—fear of coming forward in person and talking to a class of graduate students.

"It's all right for you to tell me not to get nervous," Robert Cochrane, Universal's vice-president and one of the most powerful men in Hollywood, wrote to Joe.

> And it's a comforting thing to know you will be at Harvard to hold my hand, but this thing is getting my official goat just the same. I am such a rotten talker! Maybe it will help me a little if you will give me a little atmosphere . . . Do I have to stand up on some damned stage, or do I get down and mingle with the proletariat? Do I have to wear anything? I'll tell you here and now I will NOT wear a Prince Albert, first because I don't like 'em, second because I look like hell in 'em.

But when Cochrane finally stood before the class of over five hundred in the large hall of Baker Memorial Library, he proved himself a master of the crowd, which responded with great warmth to the mood of nervous excitement he projected. It was for Cochrane an openly happy moment.

> I told you at the station [he wrote to Joe] I had no intention of trying to find words to express my sentiments about Harvard and what happened

there. I am still in the same hopeless condition, for the words simply won't come. As I found myself getting more miles away from Harvard, I found, to my amazement, that instead of lessening my enthusiasm it became greater than ever. I don't believe you realize now, or will realize for some time to come, what a great big thing you have started and how far reaching it is bound to be. . . . When I think back on the light of zeal and almost fanaticism that I saw in your eyes, I am satisfied that pretty soon you will be dropping all of your business connections, taking the veil, and becoming a real Harvard Professor which, by the way, would be a corking good thing for Harvard.

Among the distinguished group of speakers, which, Dean Donham observed, included "almost the entire inner cabinet of the industry," Adolph Zukor and Marcus Loew were "the elder statesmen, the pioneers who saw the possibilities of the motion picture when everyone else was blind, adventured their capital and energy into the future and reaped great reward as the infant grew to a giant."

A tiny man of enormous ability, Adolph Zukor had been born in the village of Ricse, Hungary, where all the males of his line except his merchant father were rabbis. In his seventeenth year he walked out of Castle Garden in New York among a batch of immigrants from central Europe and ended up in Chicago. Beginning as a cutter of furs for actresses' coats, while learning English at night, he saved enough money to start a penny arcade. Then it occurred to him that people would rather pay five cents to sit down than a penny to stand; so, in collaboration with Marcus Loew, whose parents had immigrated to America from Vienna, he built up a chain of nickelodeons which eventually developed into the largest theater chain in the country. Convinced that he needed a higher-quality product to keep his customers satisfied, Zukor created a new company, the Famous Players Film Company, which recognized the importance of finding serious plots for its movies and understood the appeal of the star system in attracting large audiences. In the palmy days of Famous Players and its successors, Famous Players–Lasky and Paramount Pictures, all the most glittering stars—names like Pickford, Fairbanks, Swanson, Valentino and Negri—were on Zukor's payroll.

Yet when Zukor stood on the platform at Harvard, ready to start his lecture on the origins and growth of the industry, he was so excited and nervous that he could barely control the shaking in his voice. "To a man like myself who never had the chance of a college education," Zukor began, "this is a rare opportunity and if I am a bit nervous it is not because I am not glad to be here. Even if it should be an ordeal to talk to you I do it with pleasure and I hope it may do you some good. . . ."

For Marcus Loew, who was suffering at the time from a chronic heart ailment which would lead to his death just six months after the course, the excitement of coming to Harvard to lecture had so overpowered his reason that he chose to ignore his doctor's prophetic warnings against making the strenuous trip. Born in humble circumstances on New York's Lower East Side, and with no formal schooling beyond his tenth year, Loew had had a phenomenal rise to power which had taken him from penny arcades and peep shows to the consolidation of a vast theater chain and after that to the purchase of the Metro Picture Corporation, which he eventually merged with the firms of Sam Goldwyn and Louis B. Mayer to form the celebrated Metro-Goldwyn-Mayer (MGM).

On the day of his lecture every seat in the auditorium was taken and hundreds of students were turned away from the door. When the time to speak came, the old man, holding himself erect, moved in front of the audience and, with pride in his voice, said, "I cannot begin to tell you how much it impresses me, coming to a great college such as this to deliver a lecture when I have never even seen the inside of one before. Yesterday morning before I left the doctor thought I shouldn't, but . . . I do not know what I should ever have done if I neglected this opportunity . . ."

In the days before and after the lectures of Zukor and Loew, the motion picture industry was subjected to a thorough analysis which included the points of view of the producer, the director, the actor, the distributor and the banker. "Assembling all these men at Harvard was no mean feat," Richard Whalen observed; "many were suing one another and they had to be assured that process servers would not confront them at the lectern."

Once there, however, each lecturer seemed to find pleasure in the new world that was opened to him, a world of notebooks and learning, of libraries and books having little in common with his past.

Perhaps the most thoughtful lecture in the series was delivered by the silent screen star Milton Sills, a graduate of the University of Chicago and a fellow in philosophy before he took up acting. "We are beginning to recognize," he told the students,

> that amusement satisfies a fundamental human appetite, that it is a commodity as essential to the physical and mental health and well being of the human animal as lumber, wheat and oil. Particularly is this so today . . .
> In modern life very few of the men and women who carry the burden of the world's work find a compensating joy in that work. The bulk of it lacks intrinsic interest. Some compensation for the miseries and boredom of existence is necessary . . . For an hour or two the spectator identifies himself with the hero or heroine; potential adventurer at heart, he becomes

for the moment an actual imaginative adventurer in a splendid world
where things seem to go right.

For Kennedy, the Harvard project was immensely beneficial. For one
thing, it placed him on personal terms with all the leading figures of the
industry. Hearing from Jesse Lasky that it was "the best day he had had
in a good many years" and from Cecil B. De Mille that he was still
thrilled over his "very wonderful day in Boston," Kennedy recognized
that with this one project he had made more of an impact on his standing in the Hollywood community than he could have made with years
of hard work.

"It was not so long ago," the movie critic "Mac" observed in the
*Exhibitors' Daily Review*, "that the picture industry and Joseph Kennedy
were strangers. . . . [Now] this industry owes a great deal to Mr. Kennedy. The fact that Harvard College has taken such an interest in the
motion picture industry lifts the entire standing of the industry to greater
heights." A similar tribute was offered to Kennedy by the *Canadian
Moving Picture Digest*: "Kennedy should be tendered a banquet by the
industry as a testimonial for his most valuable service to the motion
picture industry."

Six months later, with the publication of the lectures in a book, *The
Story of the Films*, Kennedy received additional honors from major
newspapers all over the country. Writing in the *New York Herald Tribune*, Harriet Underhill decided that with this book Kennedy belonged
on the movie industry's "White Hope" list, a short list with severe tests
for inclusion. No less enthusiastic was the reviewer for *The New York
Times*, who said:

> The most ingenious maker of tales of magic or of fairy stories has never
> written, and perhaps none could ever spin out of his imagination a more
> marvelous yarn than this plain, simple truth of the birth and growth of the
> motion picture art and industry. The serious, unadorned, businesslike
> presentation of the different phases of that story given in this volume by
> men who speak with authority shows . . . that this young Cinderella of
> the Arts has won her place in the royal circle and that her title, whether
> as art or industry, is no longer to be questioned.

As the most essential preliminary to the establishment of his future
empire, Kennedy moved first in the direction of acquiring his own capacity for producing "talking movies," the wondrous new invention
which Warner Brothers had unveiled with the release of *The Jazz Singer*
on October 5, 1927. In addition to the Vitaphone sound system which
had brought Warner Brothers to its triumphant peak of success, there

was another system, called Photophone, which was being perfected by the Radio Corporation of America, in collaboration with General Electric and the Western Electric and Manufacturing Company. Believing that Photophone excelled all previous efforts toward sound reproduction and synchronization, Kennedy opened negotiations with RCA's president, David Sarnoff, in the fall of 1927 which eventually resulted in a linkage between RCA and FBO, the first combination between the rival industries of radio and pictures. For both Kennedy and Sarnoff, each as shrewd and ambitious as the other, the partnership was eminently satisfactory. Providing Kennedy with his entry into the world of sound, and Sarnoff with his entry into film, the deal gave FBO the services of the technical staffs and the use of all the present and prospective patents for sound devices developed by RCA in return for RCA's acquiring a substantial interest in FBO.

The next step in the Kennedy-Sarnoff strategy called for FBO to take over a chain of theaters to form an initial market for the Photophone system. Inquiring after the condition of one company after another, Kennedy concluded that the Keith-Albee vaudeville circuit, representing more than three hundred beautiful and commodious theaters scattered all over the country, and recently expanded through a merger with the Orpheum chain to become the Keith-Albee-Orpheum circuit, or KAO, would be the choicest acquisition he could make. It was a fortuitous choice, for, as it happened, the general manager of KAO, John J. Murdock, had just arrived at that moment in his own life when he too was wishing that some such merger opportunity might come along. Early in 1927, Keith-Albee had merged with Pathé–De Mille pictures, making Murdock the president of Pathé in charge of its lavish forty-acre studio in Culver City. A theater man with no experience in producing pictures, the canny Murdock recognized in Kennedy the strong, efficient executive he needed to bring Pathé's soaring costs under control.

But the daring dreams of Kennedy and Murdock encountered a formidable obstacle in the initial unwillingness of old Edward Albee, the founder and nominal boss of KAO, to allow a substantial share of his stock to be sold. Having grown up in Boston, where his father worked as a shipwright, Albee had risen from the position of shill in a traveling circus to become the absolute ruler of vaudeville. An autocratic man, he bristled at the thought of losing some of his power to the aggressive Kennedy. While he unfalteringly trusted Murdock and appreciated that Murdock would be pleased beyond measure to bring young Kennedy in, Albee sensed a danger for himself in connection with Kennedy.

So when Kennedy first approached Albee with an offer to buy 200,000 shares of common stock in KAO for the healthy sum of $4.2 million, raised by a syndicate of bankers including Elisha Walker, president of the Blair Company, the Lehman brothers and Jeremiah Milbank, Albee refused to sell. In the days that followed, however, the pressures on Albee mounted as he was brought to realize that Kennedy's offer would bring him $21 a share for his stock, compared with $16 quoted on the market, an opportunity that might never come again. Albee finally accepted the offer on May 10, 1928.

Albee would soon come to regret this decision more than any other he had made. While the public announcement of the deal called for Kennedy and Albee to work together in a new and ambitious program of expansion for the KAO circuit, assuring the stockholders that with this injection of "new blood and financial interest into the business," KAO would prosper beyond imagining, the private manipulations of power were such that within a matter of months Murdock and Kennedy, as the chairman of the newly created board of directors, were able to force Albee to resign from the presidency. As the story is told, Albee's illusion that he was still the boss finally came to an end one day when he entered Kennedy's office to make a suggestion. The conversation, according to associates, was short and blunt: "Didn't you know, Ed?" Kennedy asked. "You're washed up. You're through."

Feeling bewildered by Kennedy and betrayed by Murdock, Albee involuntarily retired from the organization he and B. F. Keith had founded more than forty years earlier. Consumed with bitterness, he was dead within sixteen months.

With the KAO merger, Kennedy also assumed the position of special adviser to Pathé films, and it was widely assumed that it would be only a matter of time until FBO absorbed Pathé, thereby eliminating one producer in the vastly growing combine. For years Pathé had enjoyed a near monopoly in the making of short comedies and newsreels, but, with the coming of sound, many of the large film producers were setting up their own newsreel departments, and Pathé was losing money.

Living up to the reputation he had achieved at FBO for his administrative efficiency, Kennedy boosted the company's sales $70,000 a month while cutting the weekly overhead costs by more than $30,000. Explaining his success, he later said, "Employees [in motion picture companies] were vastly overpaid. It was no uncommon thing for accountants to receive $20,000 a year, when in other businesses they graded from $5,000 to $10,000. [I] changed that."

With Cecil B. De Mille's half of the Pathé operations, however, Kennedy moved with unaccustomed slowness, reluctant to take a step that would cause the flamboyant director to leave the studio. Having been forced by the bankers several years earlier into a merger with Pathé, De

Mille lived with the continuing fear that the ever-increasing involvement of Wall Street would eventually destroy the entire picture industry.
"When the banks came into pictures, trouble came," he liked to say.
"When we operated on picture money, there was joy in the industry;
when we operated on Wall Street money, there was grief in the industry." Knowing Kennedy personally gave De Mille a measure of security,
but with each new organizational layer built upon the next, the brilliantly individualistic De Mille felt more and more uncomfortable.

For his part, Kennedy genuinely appreciated the trail-blazing role De
Mille had played in the development of the movies. A pioneer in the
technique of filmmaking, and the virtual inventor of the epic film, De
Mille possessed an uncanny foresight into the temper of the public mind
which the equally prescient Kennedy valued. From his 1914 production
of *The Squaw Man*, one of the first feature-length films to be shot in
Hollywood, to his most recent epic, *The King of Kings*, a film about
Christ, De Mille had given the movie public what they wanted to see.
With war clouds gathering in 1916, he deftly turned out a series of
stirringly patriotic films, including the celebrated *Little American*.
Then, even before the armistice, he cast about for a new genre and
came up with a series of sophisticated comedies about love and marriage
in which the heroes and heroines moved in a materialistic world of sex
and motorcars, steamships and elegant homes. Understanding the wish
of many people to imitate the manners and customs of the rich, De
Mille opened up to the shopgirl and the factory worker the fashions, the
furnishings (lavish bathrooms were his trademark) and the foibles of the
fabulously wealthy. Then, when the voices of reform began to be heard
across the land in opposition to sex and sin on the screen, De Mille
turned around once again, to initiate a series of Biblical extravaganzas
beginning in 1926 with *The Ten Commandments*, which remained
among the top-grossing films for many years.

Kennedy had been forewarned by critics that the studio was being
bankrupted by De Mille's grandiose style, lavish costumes and spectacular sets, but he saw the genius in the man and was determined to come
to terms with him somehow.

Years later, Kennedy would remember the sunny afternoon in the
spring of 1928 when he strolled the back lots of the Pathé studio with De
Mille. Dressed in his customary director's garb—wide-brimmed hat,
open-throat shirt, riding breeches and leather puttees—De Mille
proudly recalled the venerable history of the studio, the days of Thomas
Ince, Hal Roach, Harold Lloyd and the early Will Rogers, and the joy
he had felt when he first moved into his office, built as a replica of
George Washington's Mount Vernon.

Behind the mansion was an impressive forty-acre layout which included a swimming pool (or Venetian plunge, as it was called), eight or ten immense stages with canvas panels, superb drapery and property departments, a large commissary, dozens of small editing rooms, a meandering ravine and some sensational standing sets—most notably those representing old Jerusalem, built for *The King of Kings*. For the huge set of the Praetorium of Jerusalem, the judgment seat of Pontius Pilate, one whole wall of a stage had been removed. Around it, the entire governmental district of Jerusalem had been miraculously recreated, with Corinthian columns perfect in every detail. But the most celebrated feature of the set was the colossal wall, seventy-five feet high, which was actually a ceilingless outdoor set surrounding the palaces, the council chambers and the streets of Jerusalem.

There are many magical things about Hollywood, but none more so, perhaps, than the wondrous variations of atmosphere achieved by the alteration of the sets from one movie to the next. Five years later the colossal Holy Land wall had become the site of Skull Island's ruined city in RKO's weird and wonderful movie, *King Kong*. The huge opening where the bronze gates and Corinthian columns once stood had been replaced with a massive double door, constructed of vertical planking and equipped with a gigantic wooden bolt, used to "protect" the natives from the jungle. And covering the entire wall, which originally took hundreds of carpenters working day and night over a month to build, "grew" an impressive array of primitive carvings and jungle undergrowth. Five years more, and the great wall was being prepared for its final and most impressive use—the burning of Atlanta in David O. Selznick's *Gone with the Wind*. Suitably camouflaged to project the rows of elegant homes on the major streets of the city, the wall was laced with pipes filled with thousands of gallons of oil ready to send tongues of flame two hundred feet into the air. When the signal was given, the flow of oil began, and within six minutes every particle of the wall crumbled into ashes, producing one of the most spectacular scenes in movie history.

Kennedy was impressed by the history of the Pathé lot. His inclination was to preserve De Mille's autonomy, leaving him to produce his incomparable epics while casting about elsewhere for another producer to combine with FBO. The company which interested Kennedy the most was First National Exhibitors' Circuit, a production and distribution group. In January of 1927 he had received a confidential telegram from fellow banker Motley Flint urging him to attempt a takeover of the disorganized company.

"Deeply appreciate your wire," Kennedy responded. "Have already been approached by bankers of that company with idea of going in. Have had several conferences but as Stanley Company holds the key, situation does not look inviting as they have problems of their own at present time."

So the matter stood until the summer of 1928, when Kennedy was asked by the still ailing First National to take charge of all production and distribution for five years for an annual salary of $150,000, with an option to purchase 25 percent of First National's stock at any time during that period. Kennedy's move "stirred an air of expectancy in the industry," Richard Whalen writes. It was widely predicted that Kennedy was engineering the biggest deal yet, with KAO taking over the Stanley Company's theater chain while First National, Pathé–De Mille and FBO all became one giant producer. "The pieces of the big deal appeared to be falling into place," observed Whalen. "Then, with stunning swiftness, everything collapsed." After six days of deliberation, First National's board of directors refused to ratify Kennedy's contract, and Kennedy had no choice but to resign.

In part, the failure of the deal can be attributed to Kennedy's unrelenting insistence on absolute authority in his new position; apparently, a majority of the board preferred to have at least some control over the sweeping powers of their new executive. But there were whispers that Kennedy's lack of discretion also played a role in destroying the deal. As the story was heard by Judge Charles Wyzansky, Kennedy went to dinner with a beautiful girl one night in the midst of the negotiations. Surveying the situation with haughty insolence, believing he was cleverer by far than all his rivals, Kennedy boasted to the girl that within a matter of hours he would be the new ruler of one of the largest motion picture companies, having wrested control from a dumb and ignorant Jew. Unfortunately for Kennedy, the story went on, the girl happened to be the mistress of the company's head, and when she revealed Kennedy's sentiments to her lover, the deal collapsed.

Defeat—whatever its true source—broke Kennedy's stride only momentarily, however, for his mind was already spinning with the pieces of another deal. In August 1928, De Mille signed an agreement to make three pictures at MGM and, with his staff, moved out of Mount Vernon; selling his Pathé stock at a handsome profit, he parted on good terms with Kennedy, who was freer now than before to merge Pathé with another company. All the elements of Kennedy's most fabulous Hollywood deal came together in October. In a banner headline in *Variety* it was announced that Joseph P. Kennedy and David Sarnoff would be the active heads of a huge new combination, bringing RCA together with FBO and KAO to create Radio-Keith-Orpheum, a new holding company with assets of more than $80 million. In this new combination, RCA was to supply the facilities for broadcasting the production of talking pictures for the movies and eventually for television; KAO was to provide a large chain of theaters and a selected staff of entertainers; and FBO (and eventually Pathé, which was brought into the merger not long afterward) was to supply the facilities for making motion pictures. So for the moment, an exhilarating but fleeting one, Kennedy stood astride one of the largest mergers in the history of film. It was a moment history would record as the birth of RKO.

With the creation of RKO, Kennedy reached the full height of success in the Hollywood world; for the next few months he enjoyed more adulation in the press than ever before. National fame, at last, was knocking at his door. Reporters were struck by his youth, his exuberance, his confidence and the contrasting image he projected from that of the typical film mogul, who was small, dark-haired and eastern European. With his blue eyes, his freckled face and his enormous family, he was considered a new type of movie man.

"The most intriguing personality in the motion picture world this autumn," Thomas Carens wrote in the *New York Herald Tribune* in 1928,

> is not some newly discovered beauty from the corn belt, a new Valentino rescued from the obscurity of a tentshow in Czechoslovakia or some hatchet faced actor with the voice of a Barrymore. . . . The person who now monopolizes conversation in the studios and on locations is . . . Joseph P. Kennedy.
>
> Half a dozen years ago, whenever the Boston newspapers had occasion to report the sayings or doings of a hustling young banker named Joseph Kennedy, it was an invariable office rule that he should be identified as the son-in-law of former Mayor John F. Fitzgerald. In Boston, where politics has always seemed a lot more important than it really is, that appeared to be Joe's chief claim to fame. . . . Now all that has changed. A new order of things has arrived . . . Joe is going so fast just now that before another year it may be necessary to identify John Fitzgerald's name in the newspapers with the phrase, "father-in-law of Joseph Kennedy."

# CHAPTER 23
## "GLORIA NEEDS HANDLING..."

Joseph Kennedy first met film actress Gloria Swanson in the Renaissance Room of the elegant new Savoy Plaza Hotel, which stood on Fifth Avenue diagonally across from the lower end of Central Park. It was an unseasonably warm day, the eleventh of November, 1927, a day when thousands of New Yorkers, through services and ceremonies, were commemorating the ninth anniversary of the signing of the armistice which had ended the First World War. The meeting that would alter the lives of both Gloria Swanson and Joe Kennedy had been arranged by First National's Robert

Kane. Swanson, who was probably "the most talked-of star in all of Hollywood," had turned down a million-dollar salary with Famous Players–Lasky in order to set up her own producing company under the banner of United Artists. Aware that the new company was struggling and that Gloria was suffering serious financial troubles, Kane had asked Kennedy as a special favor to meet with her in New York.

Gloria needs handling [Kane advised Kennedy], needs being properly financed and having her organization placed in proper hands, and I have taken the liberty of asking her to see you, and am writing you now asking you to see her and find out if there is some way that we can get together on taking her over as a producing asset. Regardless of what anybody says, Gloria was the biggest thing that Famous Players ever had . . . So won't you please see Miss Swanson; have a talk with her; and for the love of Mike, don't be guided by what some of the wise-crackers tell you about her value . . . As you will see, she is in better shape physically and mentally than she has ever been, and is now prepared to place herself in proper hands and to become the artist again and stop trying to be a business woman producing her own pictures.

When two days passed without a reply from Kennedy, Miss Swanson took matters into her own hands. "Arriving New York Friday Century," she notified Kennedy in a telegram. "If you have heard from Kane shall appreciate a wire from you Blackstone Chicago advising whether you can see me Friday afternoon. Stop. Shall be at Savoy Plaza. Regards. Gloria Swanson." Sealing the bond in an exchange of telegrams which remain today amid the private papers which he kept all his life, Kennedy replied: "Will be very glad to see you Friday afternoon. Please telephone me Bryant nine four six naught after you arrive New York. Kindest regards."

For Joe, Gloria Swanson must have been, on first meeting, an enigma. To a man who defined himself mainly in terms of his increasing financial stability and his growing family, Gloria's headstrong spirit, her careless disregard for money and her three marriages must have seemed strangely out of place for a woman. At the time they met, Miss Swanson was twenty-eight years old, with more than a decade of successful films behind her. Radiant with a passion to take from life every opportunity brought to her by her looks, her charm and her intelligence, she was a deceptively small woman, with bright eyes, high cheekbones and a large sensuous mouth. Her skin was pale, her cheeks were painted red and her hair was dark. The excessive contrasts were a little too odd, a little too striking to be considered natural beauty, but she had a gift for throwing a romantic glamor over herself which produced a remarkable effect upon everyone she met.

Having risen to the top in the mad, lush years of the twenties, Gloria Swanson had decided early on that while she was a star she would be "every inch and every moment a star" so that everyone "from the studio gateman to the highest executive will know it." The only child of an alcoholic father and an ambitious mother who loved to dress her up in fancy and unusual clothes, Gloria was chosen at sixteen by the casting director of the Essanay Studio in Chicago for the role of the young girlfriend to child actor Bobby Vernon in a series of light, homespun comedies centering on "the boy next door." Very much in command of herself, the stage and the situation, she rose quickly through the ranks, growing from a simple Essanay ingenue to a spunky Mack Sennett comic star to a glamorous woman of the world in a series of Cecil B. De Mille's sophisticated marital melodramas. In an age when women in the movies were the vessels of both men's and women's fantasies and the barometers of changing fashion, Gloria was one of those emblematic and aggressively adaptable figures in whom the changing tastes of the decade were reflected. In particular, the films Swanson made with De Mille, *The Affairs of Anatol, Male and Female* and *Why Change Your Wife?*, deliberately designed as they were to indulge the audience in the lavishness of gigantic fourposter beds, marble bathrooms and spectacular clothes, established Gloria as the all-time prototype of the movie star —temperamental, extravagant, dramatic, exciting and sensual.

Twice divorced by age twenty-three—first from actor Wallace Beery and then from restaurateur Herbert Somborn—Gloria bought one of the largest homes in Beverly Hills for herself and her four-year-old daughter. Built by razor-blade-millionaire King Gillette, the cream-colored two-story mansion stood at 904 Crescent Drive, just above Sunset Boulevard and opposite the main entrance to the celebrated Beverly Hills Hotel. With its sweeping lawns, iron-railed terrace, twenty-two rooms, private elevator and five baths, Gloria's great home soon became an inspired stage set that gave architectural shape to her personality and her well-publicized private life. She draped the enormous reception room in peacock silk, hung tapestries and paintings on the walls of the elaborately furnished living and dining rooms, painted the breakfast room cream and gold, turned one room into an intimate movie theater, and next to her bedroom installed a black marble bathroom with a golden tub.

A self-invented queen, Gloria hired four butlers and staged elegant dinner parties with a liveried footman stationed behind each guest's chair. "There is no star in Hollywood who lives in such gilded luxury as

Gloria Swanson," proclaimed Adela Rogers St. John in the September, 1927, issue of *Photoplay*. "Gloria's home is the home of a great lady." Swanson argued later: "In those days the public wanted us to live like kings and queens. So we did—why not? We were in love with life. We were making more money than we ever dreamed existed and there was no reason to believe it would ever stop."

Yet it almost did. In the two years since she had turned down Jesse Lasky's million-dollar offer, Gloria had made only two films on her own, *The Love of Sunya*, which took nine months instead of six weeks to make and which was not well received by either the critics or the public, and *Sadie Thompson*, a daring and expensive adaptation of Somerset Maugham's celebrated story about a missionary who falls in love with a harlot. After investing $200,000 in *Sadie Thompson*, Gloria was met with a concerted protest against its release by all the big studios on the grounds that the original story, "Rain," had been previously banned by the Hays organization and that to allow Swanson to release an adaptation, even with the changes she made, was to destroy "the Formula."

Gloria eventually received permission to release her film, but the months of litigation involved cost her thousands of dollars more. By the time Joseph Kennedy came upon the scene, she was in a perilous situation.

For her part, Gloria knew almost nothing about the attractive-looking man with sandy hair and bright-blue eyes who was now seated across the table from her. Advised by Kane that he was a banker who could help her solve her financial problems, she found that he "didn't resemble any banker" she had ever known. There was a bluster and a boyishness in him which most successful bankers had long since shed. Moreover, with his solid build kept in good shape by regular exercise, his winning smile and his tendency to break into peals of laughter and whack his thigh when something funny was said, he proved himself, from the start, a most pleasing companion. Apart from his manner and his accent, Swanson recalled, his hands were the most noticeable thing about him. "They looked unused to work," she recorded in her memoirs, "and there were wide spaces between his fingers. He gestured often and animatedly with them when he talked."

In the course of their first conversation, which was to continue that night over a sumptuous dinner at an elegant restaurant on Long Island, Joe freely mixed together all kinds of talk, from personal observations about his children, his father and his father-in-law to brainstorming about the pros and cons of establishing prizes for the best motion picture and the best performance of every year, from technical explanations of the accounting methods in the film industry to detailed discussions of various directors and studios. Finally, Swanson recalled, he "even dared to ask" if she minded telling him why she had turned down a million dollars a year from Jesse Lasky, and "his enthusiasm was so direct and open" that she had no qualms talking about it, even to the point of admitting that since that day she had passed many an anxious moment. But, she bravely concluded, she would do it again tomorrow. "I would have been the second or third person in movie history to sign a million dollar contract, but I was the very first to turn one down." At this remark, Joe laughed so merrily and so unaffectedly that Swanson found herself deliberately saying more clever things just to entertain him.

But, amusing as their conversation was, Joe was unable, as he confessed in a letter to Kane several days later, to find out if there was "any possibility of doing business there." As Swanson herself was not clear about her various obligations and agreements, Joe suggested that she grant him permission to look at her relevant papers and files so that he could see for himself if he could be of any help. Swanson agreed at once, feeling in her bones, as she later described it, that she had just passed a significant evening and that this man might be "the right business partner" to straighten out her career.

The situation Kennedy uncovered when his men went swooping down upon Gloria Swanson's files, in a swashbuckling manner reminiscent of his days as a bank examiner, was far more desperate than even Swanson recognized at the time. Unless she made a number of changes at once, Kennedy concluded, there was a strong likelihood of bankruptcy. The bottom line was simple: while she had made hundreds of thousands of dollars in the course of her acting career, she had consistently spent more than she made, and then, as Kennedy put it in a note to Kane, "she got herself all spread out with debts and told too many people about it."

Gloria Swanson was not alone in her predicament. According to a contemporary article in *Variety*, the film industry in the twenties had "more million dollar a year people and less millionaires than any of the large industries in the country." Despite the huge weekly salaries the big stars commanded, ranging from $5,000 to $20,000, only about ten actors and actresses—including Harold Lloyd, Mary Pickford, Tom Mix and Charlie Chaplin—could be considered millionaires. For the rest, *Variety* argued, a number of factors contributed to prevent the steady accumulation of money. First and most obvious was the expensive front the stars felt they had to maintain: as Hollywood became synonymous with glamor and luxury, stars competed with one another for the most elegant houses, motorcars and wardrobes. Beyond this, *Variety* observed, "the gambling fever inherent in almost all those connected with the picture industry has depleted the capital of at least one hundred near the million mark who attempted to go into business on their own after success in either directing, acting, or producing under salary."

To make an awkward situation even worse, Swanson was in serious trouble with the Internal Revenue Service. It seemed, as Kennedy discovered when he investigated her files, that a number of warrants had been signed against her for unpaid taxes totaling $102,743.36, covering the years 1921–26. While Gloria had filed a tax return for each of these years, she had apparently deducted extraordinary expenses for clothing, trips and entertainment; she claimed that they were essential to her because they generated publicity that increased the box office value of her pictures. It was an argument the IRS agents failed to appreciate.

Swanson was under contract at the time with Famous Players–Lasky at a salary ranging from $2,500 to $7,000 a week. Although the contract called for her to appear in public, whenever possible, "in attractive and fashionable costumes," the Commissioner of Internal Revenue ruled that because the studio agreed to pay for apparel worn in connection with her services before the camera, all other moneys expended for apparel represented personal rather than professional expense and were not deductible. Similarly, the Commissioner ruled, though the contract required her to entertain, the entertainment expenses she claimed (over $18,000 each year) were purely personal and therefore merited no deduction. Indeed, going back over all of her returns for the period 1921–26, the Commissioner determined that she had deducted more than a quarter of a million dollars more than she was entitled to.

For the historian, Gloria Swanson's financial returns, crammed together in a brown cardboard box among Joseph P. Kennedy's personal papers, provide a window on the glittering world of the twenties. For 1922, a year in which the twenty-three-year-old actress received a salary of over $231,000, her disallowed deductions alone came to a total of $87,730.73. And these, at a time when the average net income was $5,497, consisted of the following:

| | | |
|---|---|---|
| Apparel | $11,055.94 | |
| Appearance | 26,932.39 | (jewelry, makeup, manicuring, masseuse, hairdressing, perfumes, etc.) |
| Entertaining | 10,594.62 | |
| Musicians | 1,290.65 | |
| Shoes | 735.61 | |
| Automobiles | 6,810.47 | (Pierce-Arrow, Cadillac) |
| Supplies | 6,390.54 | |
| Insurance | 4,321.35 | |

| | |
|---|---|
| Maids, chauffeurs | 5,404.84 |
| Studio charges | 1,085.75 |
| Manager and secretary | 6,500.00 |
| Photos and mailing | 1,233.88 |
| Rent | 3,943.59 |
| Legal expenses | 1,828.10 |
| | $87,730.73 |

Since the listed expenses represent only what Swanson thought she could get away with, we can begin to imagine how much money she actually spent each year.

Kennedy's financial solution for Gloria called for the replacement of her existing production company with a new one, Gloria Productions, Inc., which, for tax purposes, would have its principal office in Delaware and which would be run as a company should be run, by financial experts. "My only job was to forget everything and let them set up a proper company for once and for all," Gloria recounted in her memoirs. "Once I signed a single power of attorney made out to EB, EB would handle everything." (E. B. Derr had been the works accountant at Fore River when Kennedy invited him to Hollywood.)

"You're offering me all I've wanted for two years," Gloria told Joe, "freedom from the hassle of business worries. It's worse for me than for most star producers, because I'm a woman and I'm alone."

Next, according to Swanson, Kennedy proposed "a whopping deal" that would set all her finances straight: if Gloria would give Joe Schenck at United Artists the full distribution rights to both *Sunya* and *Sadie*, Schenck would not only agree to wipe out her substantial debt to United Artists for all the monies advanced in the making of the two pictures, but he would allow her to use more than six thousand shares of her United Artists common stock to liquidate her most pressing obligations.

While taking steps to stabilize Gloria's overall finances, Kennedy also moved quickly to cover her short-term debts. With a loan of $20,000, he set up a special account for her at the Columbia Trust Company which was to be used to pay off her outstanding obligations. Fully aware of her extravagant ways, Kennedy made certain that his money was used for the purposes for which it was lent, by having Eddie Moore hold the check in his possession until Gloria's assistant, Miss Crossman, working from a list Kennedy prepared, had actually delivered all the checks to the various tradespeople. Once the deliveries were made, Moore was allowed to deposit the money in the bank as protection against those checks.

From Kennedy's point of view, it was madness for Swanson to live so wastefully. Distressed to find that she was paying out over $900 every week to people in her employ, he asked E. B. Derr for suggestions on which ones could be cut. "Ruthlessly speaking," Derr began, starting from the top, her production manager, P. A. Bedard, was "not essential"; eliminating him would save $250 weekly. "I know she has a very warm spot in her heart for Bedard, and she will take a personal dislike to anybody who causes any unpleasant situation for Bedard. I am ready to be elected, even though Bedard is a peach of a fellow, but I know lots of peaches I can't pay $250.00 weekly to, and some of them I would like to give it to." After Bedard, Derr recommended replacing I. R. Wakoff, Gloria's accountant, who was making $75 a week. "Wakoff is a very industrious, good clerk but his work is not worth over $45.00 a week." Beyond these, "Mrs. Morgan, the dressmaker, is not necessary between pictures, which would save $125.00 a week until the next picture as well as the $25.00 a week which is currently being paid to the seamstress, Miss Evers."

Moving to reorganize without considering the feelings involved, Kennedy produced a host of bitter reactions. Pete Bedard, venting his feelings in a long telegram to Gloria, wrote:

I PRESUME YOU KNOW I AM SUPPOSED TO BE NO LONGER IN YOUR ORGANIZA-
TION BUT AFTER YOUR ASSURANCES THAT MY POSITION WITH YOU WAS SE-
CURE WHEN I REPEATEDLY ASKED YOU WHAT WAS TO BECOME OF ME IN YOUR
NEW SET UP THIS COMES AS A DISTINCT SURPRISE. CANNOT BELIEVE THAT
AFTER OUR CLOSE ASSOCIATION AND FRIENDSHIP YOU WOULD TREAT ME WITH
LESS CONSIDERATION THAN THE MOST MENIAL EMPLOYEE. NO WORD FROM
YOU OF ANY SORT AT THIS TIME HAS CERTAINLY NOT HELPED ME IN AN
EXTREMELY HARD SITUATION.

An even harder loss for Swanson was that of her personal lawyer, Milton Cohen, who had volunteered his services after her divorce from Somborn five years earlier and who had helped her arrange for the adoption of a baby brother for her little girl. Apparently angry at being left out of the detailed negotiations for the new company, Cohen wired this message to Swanson: "A real friend should never be destroyed. Regret your attitude exceedingly. Wish always to be your friend but never your lawyer. Please arrange immediately for other counsel."

As all these far-reaching changes were taking place, Gloria Swanson grew more dependent upon Joe. Reaching her where she felt most vulnerable, her inability to control the financial base upon which her luminous image and vaunted lifestyle depended, Joe swiftly took over her entire life, and, as she later put it, she had little choice but to trust him to make the most of it.

As for Joe, his new relationship with Gloria, who was considered by many to be Hollywood's reigning sex goddess, must have served to swell the triumphant intoxication of days when he was flush with his own success and was more and more conscious of being admired and respected. In the weeks that followed their first meeting, their acquaintance ripened fast. With Rose safely ensconced in Boston awaiting the birth of their eighth child—for the last month of her pregnancy, Rose had returned to Boston so that she could be under the care of her regular obstetrician—Joe felt free to spend as much time with his new client as he wanted.

Looking back at the frequency of Joe's absences at the moments when she was about to give birth, Rose laughingly claimed that giving birth was the one area where Joe had absolutely no expertise, so why should he feel compelled to stay at home? "Besides," she added, "he always knew I'd be all right." Yet, for a man who professed such a deep devotion to his family, this rationalization seems to go a little too far. While Rose clearly accepted Joe's frequent need to be away from home on business, it seems that his definition of "business" was rather broad.

It happened that in the first winter of her relationship with Joe, Gloria was still married to her third husband, Henri de la Falaise de la Coudraye, a French marquis whom she had met in Paris three years earlier when she was filming *Madame Sans-Gêne*, a funny story about a washerwoman who is elevated to the nobility by Napoleon. So strong was her initial feeling for the handsome Marquis that Gloria decided to stay in France until her divorce from her second husband became final, so that she could come back to America as the Marquise de la Falaise. "For the first time ever," Gloria recalled, recounting the early months of her romance with Henri, "I was in love with a man quite near my own age and he happened to be a handsome, gallant French nobleman, the kind every woman dreams about."

It was a modern marriage, separated often by an ocean and sealed by a written marriage contract in which each party retained "ownership of all the property which belongs to him or her," while neither party was to be held responsible for the debts of the other. There was also, as Gloria confessed in her memoirs, a child conceived in the months before the marriage which, without telling Henri, she decided to abort, knowing that if she had the child the film industry and the American public would reject her "as a morally unsound character, unfit to represent them." In those days, the Hays office ruled Hollywood with a rigid code of censorship and an equally rigid code of behavior—a code which would never tolerate the idea of pregnancy outside of marriage. So Gloria had gone ahead with the abortion, consoling herself with the thought that she and Henri were young and could have other children together.

But, in the three years of their marriage, Henri and Gloria had been unable to produce another child. Nor had Henri found it easy to stand in the shadow of his wife's cresting career. While his noble ancestors had once lived as noblemen should, enjoying the pleasures and sports of a titled life, Henri had little money of his own and found himself in the awkward position of working in Gloria's employ, splitting his time between the Continent and the United States.

The Christmas holidays found Joe Kennedy in Riverdale with his family while Henri and Gloria headed west for California. "As soon as the holidays were over," Gloria recounted, "the funny voice from Boston, the voice I had imitated so often for Henri, was on the phone almost every day. He wanted Henri and me to meet him in Palm Beach . . . He said there was lots to be settled, including an important place for Henri with an office in Paris."

For several winters, Kennedy had been regularly visiting Palm Beach, joining what was considered at the time to be "the greatest aggregation of rich and fashionable notables" that had ever gathered in a single place in America. Regarded as "the winter counterpart of Newport," Rhode Island, Palm Beach attracted a cosmopolitan fragment of the wealthiest international society seeking the pleasures of warm June days in the middle of winter and the prestige afforded by being in the right place at the right time. In January the weather was fair and dry, perfect for the playing of golf, which Kennedy did every day, usually in the company of three or four of his golf buddies from Boston. Settling in for three weeks or more, he generally stayed at the Royal Poinciana Hotel, a six-story building that looked like a skyscraper lying down, which had been built by Henry M. Flagler at the turn of the century and was said to be the largest resort in the world. For those who could afford the accommodations, the Poinciana was an elaborate stage set, an odd mixture of more than a thousand rooms and a great veranda, facing magnificent gardens and double rows of delicate palm trees which stood like sentinels against the pale-blue sky.

As Swanson later described her Sunday-morning arrival at the train station in Palm Beach, Henri was making arrangements with Eddie Moore for her seventeen pieces of luggage to be sent to the Poinciana when "Joe Kennedy came charging down the narrow aisle from the other end of the car like a cyclone." Away from her for several weeks,

Joe had apparently been preoccupied with thoughts of her. If it wasn't love, it was the kind of profound interest people feel in things seemingly out of reach, yet actually within reach if only they dare to act on their feelings. The moment he reached Gloria Joe pushed her back into the drawing room, said a few excited words and then kissed her twice. Just as quickly he released her, but as he straightened up to his full height he scraped his head on an overhead rack and knocked off his spectacles. "I missed you," he said, with no embarrassment at all. "And I wanted you to know."

"I missed you too," Gloria said, managing to keep her voice steady although her body was shaking as though the train were still in motion. "Come out and meet my husband. He's there, beside Eddie Moore. Do you see?"

There followed from this first stolen kiss a momentous shift in Gloria and Joe's relationship. What only weeks earlier had been a business partnership now gave rash promise of being much, much more. For three full days, however, the two would-be lovers were so caught up in a crowded schedule of business discussions, teas, receptions and dinner parties that they had no time to be together alone. It was odd how, without any admission that their feelings were joined, everything was changed. From here on in, their meetings generated an air of electricity, and a sense of silent complicity grew between them. When the affair was finally launched, during an afternoon when Henri had gone off deep-sea fishing with Eddie Moore, Gloria realized that ever since the kiss on the train she had known it would happen.

In her memoirs, the only eyewitness account history possesses, Gloria tells the story of their first encounter. Having arrived at her hotel room just as the maid was leaving, Kennedy stood silently in the open door, staring at her for a full minute or more before he entered the room and closed the door behind him. "He moved so quickly," Gloria recounted as she journeyed back fifty years in her memory, "that his mouth was on mine before either of us could speak. With one hand he held the back of my head, with the other he stroked my body and pulled at my kimono. He kept insisting in a drawn-out moan, 'No longer, no longer. Now.' He was like a roped horse, rough, arduous, racing to be free. After a hasty climax he lay beside me, stroking my hair. Apart from his guilty, passionate mutterings, he had still said nothing cogent."

For the thirty-eight-year-old Kennedy, the affair with Gloria was a relentless pursuit of more, a quest to have it all, to live beyond the rules in a world of his own making, a world filled with excitement, stimulation and novelty. For the most part, he and Rose still had a strong and satisfying relationship, better indeed than many of the couples they knew. There was true intimacy in their long talks about their children and their future, and there was comfort and tradition in the many rituals they shared. From all accounts, neither partner had any complaint or at least any they gave voice to. The marriage was stable and traditional.

Yet, from everything we hear about Joe's frequent involvements with other women, it is clear that his sexual drives were not satisfied within his marriage. There is a story told by Marie Greene which strongly suggests that Rose held a very circumscribed view of what constituted proper sexual behavior for a practicing Catholic. With her husband, Vinnie, Marie spent many Friday nights playing cards with Joe and Rose. As she tells the story, Joe would often take these Friday-night gatherings as occasions to tease Rose about the narrowness of her views about sex. "Now, listen, Rosie," he would say to her, his blue eyes twinkling. "This idea of yours that there is no romance outside of pro-creation is simply wrong. It was not part of our contract at the altar, the priest never said that and the books don't argue that. And if you don't open your mind on this, I'm going to tell the priest on you." But, ac-cording to Marie Greene, Rose remained firm in her beliefs and years later, after her last child was born, she simply said, "No more sex." From then on, she and Joe had separate bedrooms.

Rose seemed to have accepted an earlier and outdated Catholic code at face value. According to the strictest interpretations set forth by Saint Augustine and Pope Gregory the Great, pleasure was not a fit purpose for intercourse; at all times, the sexual organs were to be used only for their primary, essential purpose—the propagation of the species. Con-sequently, in using her sexual faculties, a woman must open herself at all times to the possibility of having a child, acting not for the transient good of the individual but for the collective good of the species in accor-dance with divine plan. Just as it was forbidden to place a direct obstacle to prevent the natural process of procreation from attaining its life-giving character (birth control), so it was wrong, if one did not want a child, to perform the act simply to satisfy one's own physical pleasures. It followed that sex was forbidden during pregnancy or menstruation or in old age.

Yet, to attribute Rose's sexual attitudes wholly to Catholicism is to short-change the analysis which suggests that Catholic ideology may have served as a cover for a dislike of sex on Rose's part, stemming perhaps from the complicatedly intense relationship she had experi-enced with her father so many years before. In contrast, Gloria Swanson was the forerunner of the far more liberated woman who was emerging in the 1920s. An adventurer by nature, determined to live her life as fully as she could, Gloria had early on become an outspoken partisan of the revolution in manners and morals which was promising to bring about fundamental changes in the relationships between men and women.

Gloria's flirtatious temperament naturally allied itself with the sophisticated views of marriage, divorce and desire which were beginning to imbed themselves in the American mind. As the Freudian gospel circulated throughout the country, producing in its wake a "pervasive obsession with sex," Gloria opened her mind to all the new and dangerous currents of thought. Among the papers which Joe Kennedy kept is a bill of Gloria's from Brentano's bookstore on West Forty-seventh Street in New York detailing the purchase of three new books: *Sex and the Love Light, Psychoanalysis and Love* and *The Art of Love.*

After a series of casual encounters with a variety of women, Kennedy's relationship with Gloria seems to have been his first fully sustained affair. In yielding to his wishes and acting them out in the cloistered circumstances in which an affair normally develops, he must have been reminded of the days of his courtship with Rose, when love and romance, intensity and insecurity, secrecy and excitement were one. It was twenty years since that day when he had first met Rose at Old Orchard Beach, the day when he first determined that she would be his wife. With Gloria, Joe could still feel young, he could retain all the romantic dreams and pleasures of his adolescent days without forfeiting a single one of his adult privileges. It was an exciting thing to do so long as it was skillfully managed and kept suitably hidden from view.

From the outside, Joe had everything a man needed to be successful with a mistress—a great deal of time on his hands, considerable money, a guilt-free conscience and a capacity to live an almost schizophrenic existence. (Though it does seem that with Gloria, given the intensity of his feelings for her, Joe did experience some guilt.) To make everything simple, Joe rented a house in Beverly Hills so that he would have a place where he and Eddie Moore could stay on their increasingly frequent trips to California. Located on Rodeo Drive, five minutes away from both the Beverly Hills Hotel and Gloria's house on Crescent Drive, the house allowed Joe to maintain a certain decorum in his relationship with Swanson. "There is no question they had an affair," film director George Cukor recalls. "We all knew of it, that's all. But that doesn't mean they went around walking openly on the boulevards holding hands or linking arms. They never defied society like Marion Davies and William Randolph Hearst; indeed, Joe even found a great job for Henri as head of Pathé's European studios which kept him away half the year and provided an extra umbrella of legitimacy for all of them. But if anyone saw the look on Joe's face when he was with Gloria, it was clear that he was infatuated."

"In those days," film writer Cy Howard acutely observes, "Hollywood was the perfect place for an Eastern banker to have an affair. Separated from the East Coast by three days on a train, there was little worry of the accidental encounter between a wife and a mistress in a restaurant or on a street corner. Beyond that, there was the nature of the film industry, which provided dozens of Hollywood producers just like Joe with the perfect cover for spending their time with any number of beautiful actresses who just happened to work for them. You see, the film industry was actually the cover, allowing men to take their mistresses to dinners or even to parties, providing a form of legalized whoring."

Nor in those days, Howard argues, would the press ever talk to the detriment of an insider. "If an important producer or director had a paternity suit filed against him, then Louella Parsons, by a single phone call from the head of a studio, would simply stand up and say she knew exactly how it happened: why, this voracious girl with two sets of breasts had forced this poor man's body to go down on her and ejaculate his semen left over from winter!"

Under these conditions, Joe had the opportunity to enjoy his affair with Gloria for many months without feeling the need to choose one relationship or the other. The old love was home, family, security and shared experiences. The new love was romance, intensity and youth. And surely that part of Joe Kennedy that still yearned for acceptance must have been immensely flattered that Gloria Swanson, the most celebrated actress of the day, cared for him.

During Gloria's first trip to Palm Beach, Joe arranged for a welcoming party in her honor to be held at El Mirasol, the famous forty-two-acre estate belonging to the Stotesburys of Philadelphia. For many years Mrs. Stotesbury was considered the leading Palm Beach hostess, and her lavish parties, planned with the help of seventy-five servants, enjoyed the reputation of being the most sought-after affairs on the entire Palm Beach social calendar. Enclosed by a buff stucco wall which also contained the Stotesburys' private zoo complete with monkeys, parrots, parakeets and lovebirds, the Stotesbury mansion was a showplace in Spanish style. "There were great paintings on the walls," Rose Kennedy later recalled, "there were tapestries, there were velvet coverings on the tables."

"People will be arriving from all up and down the Eastern seaboard" for the party, Joe proudly announced to Gloria, leaving no doubt that Mrs. Stotesbury was definitely the big fish, the unquestioned leader of Palm Beach society. "That's right," Eddie Moore said; "anybody who didn't get an invitation has just one week to commit suicide or leave town."

As all of Palm Beach scrambled to meet the Marquis and the Marquise, Joe, according to Gloria, "manifested an endearing, boyish pride in himself" as if he were challenging "all the swells to remember that he was the saloon keeper's son who was providing them with the thrill of their social life." On the evening of the grand party, even Gloria seemed excited as she pinned red carnations on both Henri and Joe in the lobby of the Poinciana and journeyed forth into the moonlight in a magnificent blue-gray gown designed by René Hubert. As the handsome trio arrived at the arched Moorish gateway of the Stotesburys' house, Joe must have been extremely pleased with himself for the social victory he had achieved. It is hard to imagine a more glittering occasion on which to show off his famous prize.

Yet, for Joe, the affair with Gloria was something more than a badge of social acceptance. At a time in his life when he was away from his family for weeks and even months, Gloria answered his need for companionship. Unlike Rose, she was fascinated by the smallest details of his business dealings, and since she walked in the same world, she was able to ask questions that engaged his mind and activated his talent. At the same time, the warmth of their affair was kindled by Gloria's keen sense of humor, merry wit and sharp tongue. "In an era of wonderful nonsense," George Cukor recalled, "Gloria was always full of hell, always playing practical jokes, always able to find amusement in the most difficult situations."

Soon Gloria and Joe started writing funny telegrams to each other. "Everything all right now," she wired him upon arriving back in California after a journey to the East, "you don't have to have Campbells [funeral parlor] meet body. I had twelve hours sleep."

How much Rose knew about Gloria remains an interesting question. At the age of ninety, Rose was still outspoken in her assertion that she never worried, not even for a day, about Joe's relationship with Gloria. Journeying back in memory to discover what she wanted to believe, she recalled simply that Gloria needed Joe desperately to straighten out "the financial morass" she had created for herself; unable to cope anymore on her own, she had reached out to Joe as the one man who could keep her from going bankrupt. Seen from the distance of time, the image of Gloria which Rose called back to her mind was the image of a talented but lonely woman for whom love and marriage were very complicated matters. Indeed, throughout her life Rose spoke about Gloria with a strange solicitude, never publicly giving the slightest hint of jealousy, fear or rage.

Yet is is impossible to believe that Rose did not know. And there is at least one story which gives evidence that she did. According to this story, Fitzgerald had come to his own understanding of the situation months earlier but had preferred to take on Joe first before telling Rose. Geraldine Hannon, Rose's niece, vividly recalls overhearing a loud argument one summer afternoon at the Fitzgerald house in which Fitzgerald told Joe straight out that unless he stopped the affair with Gloria immediately, he would tell Rose. Undaunted, Joe threatened in turn that if Fitzgerald did tell Rose he would simply marry Gloria. That's all there was to it.

In the first round Fitzgerald backed down, but apparently some weeks later Josie decided to take the matter into her own hands by forcing Rose to see what everyone else knew. If this is true, it leads one to wonder how much of Josie's telling reflected true concern for her daughter and how much a subliminal desire to retaliate against her for the special love she had always received from her father. There is something about the manner of telling that suggests "You see, you fool, your beloved husband is no different from your beloved father. Now you finally know what men are really like!"

Even supposing Rose was told to her face about the affair, it seems, from all accounts, that she willed the repugnant knowledge out of her mind. After all, Rose seemed to have what she wanted in her marriage: children, wealth and privilege. At the same time, the marriage satisfied what may have been her own desire for sexual distance. Better perhaps to follow the pattern set by her mother long ago: to suffer in silence rather than take the enormous risk of shattering the entire family and bringing public disgrace upon herself and her husband. So long as she felt secure about remaining Mrs. Joseph Kennedy, what did the rest really matter? In this attitude Rose was not alone. According to Cy Howard, if you looked closely at the marriage of almost any Hollywood producer in those days, you'd find a similar story. "No matter what the mistress has," Mrs. Zanuck would say, "she's not Mrs. Zanuck, so why should I worry? So long as I've got the house and the name and the position, that's all that counts."

And what a position Rose had to protect! With the birth of her eighth child, Jean, on February 20, 1927, she was already becoming a celebrity in her circle of friends and acquaintances. From Hollywood to New York to Boston, she received hundreds of flowers and cards, including a large bouquet from Gloria Swanson de la Falaise. "My road to fame is now clear," the actor Fred Thomson wrote. "In future years I will be able to say I knew Joe and Rose when they had only 7 children." And from the respected producer William Le Baron came a special request: "Are you ready to consider a 5 year contract for the new Miss Kennedy?" Nor were the telegrams of praise limited to the secular world. "I have followed the growth of your interesting family," Father William Toohig wrote from his parish rectory in Dorchester. "It is couples like yourself who give priests much consolation in their work, make them feel that in a world which shirks labor and seeks only pleasure, there are still many souls who allow conscience to have its say and accept the burdens that go with the use of privilege."

Moreover, there followed for Rose a magnificent diamond bracelet selected by Joe and a month's rest in Boston while Eddie and Mary Moore took care of the children in Riverdale. "Everything is going smoothly and well along the Hudson," Mary wrote to Rose.

All the little Kennedys are well and steadily growing up and across. Joe is doing remarkably well in French. Jack is surely doing his bit too. Getting along splendidly in school and looks so much better. He shall surely get that trip to Washington. Eunice looks very well too. She is just as clever as ever and certainly is there with the punch . . . The other three little girls are in good form. Rose is just as husky, Kathleen just as wise and Pat just as smart as ever. Your son Bob is just one tough guy. He is untiring and plenty of "It" . . . I can tell you we miss you so much and shall receive you and that darling baby with open arms.

"How I envy you," Fred Thomson's wife, Frances, wrote to Rose after visiting the Riverdale house.

Those darling children—when they came trooping in I didn't know whether to laugh or weep. I wanted every one of them and I felt as if my life were such an insignificant gesture when I spoke about my one chick. They were all so sweet and well behaved. You can be so proud of them. Fred would have the time of his life with the boys and I hope their father will let them come to meet us this summer.

With all this at stake, it is little wonder that Rose never publicly let on that she knew what everyone around her knew. So long as her marriage remained secure, the pretense allowed her to keep intact the one thing that was sacred to her: the institution of the family.

# CHAPTER 24
# THE
# QUEEN KELLY
# CURSE

Twenty-seven miles southwest of Los Angeles Harbor, in the dark-blue waters of the Pacific Ocean, rise the mist-blown peaks of Santa Catalina Island. Twenty-two miles long, the island looks from the mainland as if a tiny section of the Coastal Range, with all its mountains and valleys and luxuriant foliage, had been transplanted to the open ocean. The beaches are narrow and pebbly, but the clear waters of the many bays and coves make them highly popular for swimming and yachting. For centuries, the island remained largely undeveloped; then in 1919 William Wrigley, Jr., invested millions of dollars to create a romantic town at the mouth of a large canyon complete with sumptuous hotels, a lush casino, grassy squares and sparkling fountains. Overnight, the island became a favorite haunt of wealthy Californians.

It was here on Catalina Island, on a bright Sunday afternoon in the middle of March 1928, that Gloria and Joe talked for the first time with the director Erich von Stroheim about the possibility of the three of them working together on the film that was destined to change all of their lives. For weeks Joe had been harboring a dream of creating a great movie for Gloria, an artistically ambitious movie that would leave an indelible imprint upon the film industry. Moving against the logic of his whole life, he kept insisting to Gloria that this time he wanted to take a big risk; he wanted to move beyond the mediocre movies he was turning out and produce a great one. "That's precisely what all the people you got to speak at Harvard would advise you not to do if you want to make money," Gloria warned.

"Well, they're wrong," Joe insisted, reminding Gloria that she had once said that her work on *Sadie Thompson* was her best so far because the Somerset Maugham story was the best she had ever had; if that was true, why consider anything but the next big artistic step forward, a great story *and* a great director? "Isn't that what you turned down a million dollars to be able to do, Gloria?"

In his selection of director Erich von Stroheim, Joe could not have chosen better. "Von Stroheim," Louis B. Mayer once said, "was the greatest director in the world. That's a fact and no one who knows pictures would dispute it." Like Griffith and Chaplin, he was an original, a pioneer who led silent pictures beyond the range and power of the industry as a whole. Though he had directed only five films when Joe first met him, his reputation as a genius was clearly acknowledged. All of his films were counted among the best of their day, and one of them, *Greed*, based upon Frank Norris' gripping naturalistic novel *McTeague*, still ranks among many critics as one of the ten best films ever made.

Throughout his meteoric rise, critics remarked upon the impeccable detail which Stroheim lavished upon his films: the careful attention to costumes and scenery, the glances and gestures that indicated the depth of the characters, the intimations of the psychology that motivated them. Stroheim was said to have delayed shooting on *Foolish Wives* for a full day because the gold rims on a thousand champagne glasses were a quarter of an inch too narrow, and in *The Merry Widow* he insisted that all the soldiers wear silk underdrawers with the monogram of the Imperial Guard. A passionate believer in authenticity as an inspiration to his cast and crew, he sought out a house in which a man had actually murdered his wife to use as the home of Mac and Trina in *Greed* and then he compelled his actors to live in it while shooting the scenes of their total estrangement. Obsessed with attaining perfection, Stroheim spent days trying to photograph a group of pigeons flying in from the sea. Undeterred by nature—the wind blew constantly from the Pacific and the pigeons flew against the wind only—he kept the camera rolling until the birds finally achieved the flight pattern he sought.

For all his brilliance, however, Stroheim was a strange man, embarked, it seemed, upon a curious pattern of self-destruction. He was determined to give the public what *he* wanted, regardless of the money it cost or the mores of the time, on the theory that no director can ever turn out an artistic work if he is conscious of money or morality. Habitually flaunting instructions, contracts and censors, he shot reels and reels of material that by virtue of length and content could never survive a first cut. He had some streak in him that compelled him, time after time, to the filming of wild scenes of sex and decadence that no censor in the country at that time would ever have passed, almost as if he *had* to slip something offensive into every picture so that the world would know it was his. At the same time, he was embroiled over and over in stormy battles with every one of his producers, who refused to believe, as he did, that the American public would willingly sit for eight or ten hours at a good film. Refusing to yield, Stroheim consistently placed himself in a situation where he had to be taken off the set so that the final editing could be completed.

In choosing Stroheim, Kennedy was aware of the older man's reputation for being, as Gloria warned him, "an undisciplined spendthrift, a hopeless egotist and a temperamental perfectionist." But, Joe told Gloria, "I also know he's our man. I can handle him." To Kennedy's mind, the problem with Stroheim was that he had beguiled too many producers into giving him too much rope, for, once his self-destructive pattern set in, he invariably used whatever rope he had to hang himself. So long as he could be kept under tight control, Kennedy believed, everything and everyone would be fine.

In the magical atmosphere peculiar to Catalina, Stroheim began telling Gloria and Joe the curious melodramatic story he had in mind for Gloria's film.

Providing an escape into the life of a European court in the lavish and romantic days before the Great War, the tale involves an imaginary German kingdom, a mad queen, a dashing prince and an innocent convent girl. When the prince falls in love with the convent girl, the queen places him under arrest and throws the girl out of the palace. The girl then journeys to German East Africa, where she becomes the proprietress of a low-down dive and the wife of an evil planter. In the midst of the worst sin-drenched surroundings, she manages to retain her grace, charm and virginity, and she becomes known far and wide as Queen Kelly. Meanwhile, back in Germany, the prince finally manages to escape from the queen, and he sets out at once to find the girl. A violent struggle erupts; both the evil planter and the mad queen die. In the final scene, the prince is crowned king and Queen Kelly becomes a genuine queen.

Listening to this improbable tale which reminded her of nothing she had ever heard before, Gloria was suddenly seized by a premonition that this was the film that would change her life. She saw the role of the convent girl as a once-in-a-lifetime role which would allow her to portray both youthful innocence and more mature scenes of dramatic conflict. Beginning as a young girl, smiling and eager, she would gradually pick up assurance and flair. She would be both beloved and feared, and her commanding personality would inspire stories told throughout the jungle and on all the high seas. And, Gloria recognized, beyond the role as it was written lay Stroheim's unparalleled capacity for bringing out hidden depths in his actresses, one of whom, Mae Murray, had given the single substantial performance of her career under his demanding direction.

For his part, Kennedy imagined that a powerful movie lay before him. With this story, he thought, and with a director who was an acknowledged genius, a star who was considered by many the best actress of her day, and plenty of money, he now had everything he needed to enter the temple of art. All afternoon, as he listened to Stroheim speak, he smiled so broadly that he reminded Gloria of a proud little puppy who had run up from the garden with a choice bone in his mouth, as if to say, "What do you think of that?"

While Stroheim returned to the work of finishing the script, Kennedy negotiated with lawyers for weeks to produce an ironclad contract. "Be sure your advance payment on story is very low," Kennedy aide Charley Sullivan counseled, "so that after script is completed if too expensive to shoot you are not left with expensive story on your hands which only Von Stroheim can shoot." In the best of circumstances, it was difficult to wrestle with Stroheim on the conditions of his employment, but, coming at a time in his life when he was particularly sensitive to his contractual relations, these negotiations were very, very hard.

During the negotiations, Sullivan reported, Stroheim thought that "they were putting a striped suit on him" and "had a God d— sword hanging over his head." Things got so heated, in fact, that on several occasions punches were almost thrown.

Nevertheless, a workable contract was signed between Gloria Productions and Erich von Stroheim on May 9, 1928, calling for Stroheim to receive the bulk of his money only after the actual filming had begun. In addition, there were built-in bonuses worth tens of thousands of dollars, provided Stroheim did not fall behind the time schedule or exceed the estimated cost by more than 15 percent. And if he did fall behind schedule or run over budget, then he could be terminated at once.

With the signing of the contract, a great mood of euphoria settled over the project, which was named *Queen Kelly*.

By the middle of the summer, all that Kennedy had wished had been realized. While the actual writing of the script had taken longer than anyone thought, even with the intervention of Ben Glazer to supply some new ideas, the final product was pronounced by Robert E. Sherwood, then the film and drama editor of *Life* magazine, "the best film story ever written." As it now stood, Kennedy's producer Bill Le Baron told him in a letter on September 25, the script was in 735 scenes and "we are having a final all-night session tonight to cut it down to actual shooting length. . . . With Von actually working day and night as hard as any human being could work, the script will be in more perfect condition than any script I have ever seen."

Feeling relaxed enough about the situation to leave Stroheim in Le Baron's capable hands, Kennedy sailed for Europe in August to take a six-week vacation with his wife at Biarritz, Deauville and London. While he traveled through Europe, Gloria remained on the West Coast, bombarded with party invitations from people curious to know what Stroheim, the mad genius, was up to. In Kennedy's private papers there is a series of telegrams from Gloria during this period, one of which reveals the good-humored, confidential tone their relationship had assumed. "Don't see why I should pay twenty five dollars to read cable just received," Gloria writes to Joe in London's Carlton Hotel. "Very well then am going to tell my mother on you. The very nicest kind of regards."

When Kennedy returned to America, he was greeted with a present from Stroheim, a final copy of the completed and revised script, carried to his office on a silver platter by two black men clad as Nubian slaves in lion's skins. That night, bursting with excitement, Joe handed a copy of the massive script to Gloria. "Oh, I tell you, Gloria," he said, pressing her hand tightly, "this is going to be a major, major motion picture."

In the meantime, Stroheim was at work completing the cast. It included Walter Byron, a young English actor, as the wild and romantic Prince Wolfram; Seena Owen, one of Stroheim's favorite actresses— whom he had met during the making of *Intolerance* more than ten years before—as the jealousy-crazed queen; and Tully Marshall as Kelly's loathsome planter husband, Jan. For the principal cinematographers, Stroheim chose Gordon Pollock, Paul Ivano and Gregg Toland, whose work would later be seen in *Wuthering Heights* and *Citizen Kane*. Capable of doing the most startling things in his quest for perfection, Stroheim insisted that the cinematographers help him supervise the construction of the sets so that they could plan the lighting properly.

And the sets, which took months to build, were something else again. Surviving pictures suggest an unrestricted scope and a detailed decoration rarely seen in film. For the European sequences, six different sets were constructed, including a royal palace complete with corridors filled with marble statues, a sweeping staircase with curved banisters and a sumptuous banquet room. Before the first shot had been taken, the cost of construction and props reached more than $81,000, followed by a similar outlay for the elaborate costumes required for the palace scenes, which included hundreds of uniforms for the palace guards and the palace servants.

Once the German sets and costumes were under way, Stroheim turned his attention to the preparations being made for the second sequence, in German East Africa. Dominating his cast and crew at every stage, he insisted on going over the preliminary sketches for every set, from the saloon-hotel known as the Swamp to the streets of Dar-es-Salaam, from jungle swampland to native huts. In Stroheim's original conception, the jungle and swamp scenes called for tidal waters, rain effects, tsetse flies and crocodiles. Dissatisfied with the animals obtainable in Hollywood, evidently believing, as one reporter put it, that they "wouldn't have the right vibrations to play in jungle scenes," Stroheim ordered a whole shipload of monkeys, crocodiles and snakes from Africa, where, the reporter suggested, "the fauna still are free, elemental souls."

The filming of the European sequence of *Queen Kelly* began at the FBO studios in the first week of November. "Never," Swanson says Stroheim confided as he walked her proudly through the sets, "had he felt so utterly confident in the rightness of every detail in a project as he sensed around him with *Queen Kelly*. For the first time in his career, absolutely nothing was wrong; everything worked." Declaring that he would complete the film in ten weeks of camera work, putting all the controversy of his previous pictures behind him, Stroheim claimed he had changed his attitude. "One naturally does as he grows older. I am more philosophical about the making of pictures. I am, so to speak, aged in wood, mellower."

Though Gloria's scenes were not scheduled to begin for a week or more, she met with Stroheim each night to look at the rushes from the shooting that day. As the lights in the screening room went down and Stroheim's first images flickered across the screen, she reported, the result was breathtaking. "Every scene was alive with glowing light play and palpable texture. You could almost smell the thin Havana cigars and taste the Viennese coffee and feel the dew on the grass."

Gloria's state of euphoria about the film remained through the first month of shooting; indeed, the feeling of working with Stroheim took hold of her with such power and joy as to produce in her a belief that this film would prove the beginning of a new phase in her career. "The experience of working with him was unlike any I had had in more than fifty pictures," Gloria recorded in her memoirs. "He was so painstaking and slow that I would lose all sense of time, hypnotized by the man's relentless perfectionism. A scene that Allan Dwan or Raoul Walsh would have wrapped up in an hour might take Von Stroheim all day, fondling and dawdling over the tiniest minutiae, only to announce late in the afternoon that he would like to try it once more the following day. But his exactitude always paid off in the rushes, and it was a course in the art of filmmaking to hear him defend his choices and explain his reasons."

Never before, observers reported, had Gloria Swanson looked more arrestingly beautiful. An image of health, vitality, ambition and love, she projected an aura of innocent beauty that made her look a dozen years younger than she was. In a beautiful prayer scene in a church, the camera photographed her face through the light of several candles from different angles, to achieve an unforgettable effect.

For all the élan generated in the early weeks, however, there remained the desperate pressures of time, which operated in Stroheim like a clock ticking in his heart. Determined to finish the picture within his allotted schedule, the director pushed his cast and crew into fourteen-hour days, forgetting that his own unmeasured powers for work and concentration were not evenly shared. When Kennedy arrived upon the set in the second week of November, he found the entire troupe overworked and deathly tired, walking wearily around in that dreamy, sluggish state equivalent to being drunk. Reacting at once to quell an incipient revolt, Kennedy issued an immediate order forbidding the excessive overtime and requiring a day off every time the troupe was called upon to work late into the night. He then moved to placate his director by securing an extension of Stroheim's time from Pat Powers of Celebrity Pictures, with whom Stroheim had a previous contract that would have required him to start a new picture in November. How different all this was from Stroheim's previous experience! In Kennedy, it seemed, for the first time Stroheim had found a producer who knew how to marshal his incredible talent.

The fruitful working relationship between the two continued through the month of November and into December, when it became clear that Stroheim's original fifty-two-day shooting schedule could never be met, as he was shooting at the rate of only four and eight-tenths script scenes per day, at which pace it would take 103 days to shoot, at a cost of at least $5,000 per day. Determined to control the budget, Kennedy worked on Stroheim to eliminate nearly a half-dozen scenes. With Glazer's help, a new ending was written to supplant the original jungle-and-swamp version, which would have required an extraordinary number of special effects to produce the tidewaters, the rain effects and the tsetse flies. Then, to eliminate the expense of the coronation scene, it was suggested that the prince should go to Africa but abandon Kelly at the very end when he hears he is to be crowned king, in fear that she will not make a suitable queen, at which point Kelly would have a breakdown and end up in an insane asylum.

Somehow, in the clash and strain of many personalities fighting for their ideas, Kennedy managed to keep an open line with his director. Agreeing with E. B. Derr that the original hope of shooting several sequences on Catalina Island must be given up, he persuaded Stroheim that the same sequences could be shot on the studio lot with a trick water background. When Derr also insisted upon eliminating some palace scenes, more compromises were called for, as he reports in one of a series of telegrams:

HAD SESSION LAST NIGHT WITH VON. NEW ENDING NOT ALL WRITTEN BUT SLOWLY WORKING OUT IN VON'S MIND. HOWEVER UNQUESTIONABLY STORY IS A PICTURE AND A HALF AND VON KNOWS IT. HE MUST CUT FOUR OR FIVE REELS OUT OF STORY AND EVERY THING SUGGESTED HE CALLS MILESTONES. I WISH HE HAD ONE AROUND HIS NECK. VON HAS AT LAST ABANDONED QUEEN LYING IN STATE BUT HE CALLS BANQUET MILESTONE . . . VON NOT GIVING UP CORONATION AS HE DOES NOT WANT TO END AN EPIC ALONGSIDE BOX SET IN HOSPITAL . . .

Gloria too began worrying about the slow pace of the shooting—according to her calculations, it would take another four months to complete the remaining two thirds of the film—but so long as Kennedy and his assistants held their peace and Stroheim continued to purr through the rushes, she assumed they would speed up once they reached the Pathé studio where the African sequences were scheduled to be shot.

While the silent sequences were being shot, Kennedy was making his own preparations to place dialogue and songs in the final two reels. He engaged a dialogue instructor from New York to come to Los Angeles to give Gloria daily vocal lessons, and at the same time he opened negotiations with Irving Berlin to do the scoring for *Queen Kelly* and to write a theme song for Gloria to sing. Convincing Stroheim of the possibilities of sound was more difficult, for the limitations of the early talkies were enormous, but even Stroheim finally agreed that sound could be introduced in at least a part of the film. "When Kennedy saw the first sound film," Stroheim later reported, he realized at once that it was "the death knell of silent pictures. His exact words to me were: " 'Von, the lousiest sound film will be better than the best silent film.' "

Succeeding this first wave of exhilaration, which carried into the new year, there came a period of restlessness, dissatisfaction and anxiety. It began, as so many troubles with Stroheim began, with his obstinate unwillingness to speed up the pace of his shooting—a dispute which gradually brought about a radical change in the good working relationship between Stroheim and Derr, who was able to figure the mounting costs in his head with dazzling speed and accuracy. But the troubles deepened beyond control as the action of the film shifted from the imaginary kingdom in central Europe to the streets of Dar-es-Salaam in eastern Africa. In this second sequence, which was meant to comprise two thirds of the film, Gloria was called upon to shift her character from the young innocent maiden who falls in love with the prince to the hardened, sophisticated madam who comes into daily contact with men from the roughest and lowest walks of life. Yet in spite of her capacity to run an establishment catering to flesh and the devil, she would not, as Stroheim described her role, seem immoral. Retaining her virginity and her personal chastity, she would evolve her own code of morality which would permit her to flourish without losing her essential sense of self.

It was not an easy role to play, however, and during the filming of the African scenes something was set in motion which undermined the trust and confidence Gloria and Stroheim had originally placed in each other. What this dynamic was is still not clear, though the papers in Kennedy's files suggest that under the weight of Stroheim's demanding style of direction Gloria simply collapsed.

Perhaps part of the problem was the well-grounded respect and affection Stroheim held for Seena Owen, the young actress who played the role of the mad queen. From all accounts Miss Owen's performance was extraordinary, and it was later whispered around Hollywood that she was the one, rather than Gloria, who romped away with the honors in *Queen Kelly*. Unused to sharing center stage, Gloria may well have reverted to her prima-donna stance, only to find that Stroheim had absolutely no toleration for the fancies of a foolish star. It is also possible that the anxieties of introducing even the small measure of sound that was contemplated caused both Stroheim and Swanson to fly apart, losing their habitual assurance.

As the situation deteriorated, Kennedy tried, from a distance of three thousand miles, to keep things under control, and for a while his efforts proved successful. With characteristic insight, he suggested that Gloria speak with her mentor, Cecil B. De Mille, and at the same time he ordered E. B. Derr to keep a closer watch on Stroheim. The intervention seemed, at first, to work. "E.B. successful," Gloria telegraphed to Joe on January 21, 1929. "Von toeing the mark. De Mille inspired confidence and courage. Watch my smoke."

But the process set in motion by Kennedy's orders to Derr proved irreversible. With two consultants, Ben Glazer and Edmund Goulding, already employed, Derr hired a third man, named Eugene Walter, to look at the reels Stroheim had already shot and report on the picture "without prejudice." Failing utterly to appreciate either the fairy-tale quality of the film's beginning or the sordid realism of poverty, drunkenness and racial mingling which Stroheim wanted to project in the African scenes, Walter concluded that "in an attempt to be bizarre and unusual" Stroheim had been "vulgar, gross and fantastically impossible in the conception and execution of situations, characters and the incidents of narrative." By way of reporting "without prejudice," Walter took especial exception to

the revolting spectacle of the Madam of a whore-house on her death bed [Kelly's aunt] . . . being given the last rites by a shiny, sweating nigger priest . . . [who] enters with his vestments trailing through the slimy gaudy-house with his nigger acolytes bearing the host and the chalice in what was evidently intended to be an impressive procession and this continues without reverence, is revolting and smacks of sacrilege. . . .

Beyond the racial mingling and the problem with the Church, Walter questioned

the ethics of a convent girl, who wants to keep herself clean for her Prince, if he should ever come trotting along, becoming Queen Kelly and living off the earnings of prostitutes and running a house of ill fame. . . . To my mind, a woman who takes the profit from a bawdy house could scarcely be credited with possessing any of the higher virtues of her sex. . . . The production is magnificent and the composition may be noteworthy and commanding, but in my humble opinion it is mostly gilding the manure pile.

Walter's report apparently undermined whatever confidence Derr still had in Stroheim, and a fierce battle developed. According to a story in *Variety* on January 30, 1929, Derr had become increasingly concerned about the number of shots Stroheim had taken that could not pass the censors. In the Hays-approved original script, for example, the Swamp was a dubious hotel; now, in the shooting, it had become a brothel. The argument became quite heated, *Variety* reported, and Derr fired Stroheim. "The latter walked on a set filled with people waiting to work and then left the lot. Efforts were made to bring about a peaceful settlement to the battle, but both Derr and Von Stroheim were obdurate. Each got hold of Kennedy at Palm Beach. Phone conversations continued for three days with Kennedy but nothing was accomplished. Then Goulding was assigned."

On reflection, however, Kennedy decided that despite all the unpleasantness he still wanted Stroheim as his director, and he came up with an ingenious plan. Stroheim would be reassigned to complete the silent version of the picture—a version which could be shipped to all the foreign markets—while Ben Glazer would direct the talking version for the American audience. To be sure, Stroheim had shot far too many irrelevant reels, but, just as *Greed* had emerged from the cutting room an acknowledged masterpiece, so *Queen Kelly* could still be edited into greatness, Kennedy thought. Meanwhile, Stroheim too was coming to his senses. For all his arrogance, he seemed to understand that the effect of another firing would be immeasurable. For years he had seen his beloved movies cut, dismembered and finished by others, but this was different. This was to be his pride and joy, and if this one failed it would be very hard for him to work again.

So production resumed at the point in the script where Kelly was being married off to the planter Jan. By this time Gloria's confidence in Stroheim was almost totally destroyed, but for Kennedy's sake as well as her own she agreed to continue. For weeks, she too had listened to the gossip in the studio about the various lewd scenes Stroheim had shot. One day, back in the European sequence, her seamstress had come to her dressing room to alert her to something she thought Gloria had missed in that day's shooting: apparently in between a scene where young Kelly throws her fallen panties at the laughing prince and a scene where the prince playfully flips them back to her, Stroheim had inserted an extra scene in which the prince specifically puts the panties up to his face and then fondles them in his hands. At that time, however, since Gloria believed everything else was so beautiful, she had decided to hold her veto for later.

That time arrived with the shooting of the scene of Kelly's marriage to the repulsive planter. According to Gloria's account in her memoirs, "Mr. Von Stroheim began instructing Mr. Marshall, in his usual painstaking fashion, how to dribble tobacco juice onto my hand while he was putting on the wedding ring. It was early morning, I had just eaten breakfast, and my stomach turned. I became nauseated and furious at the same time."

"Excuse me," Gloria said to Stroheim, and she turned and walked off the set. Once she reached her bungalow, she says, she slowly took off her makeup and costume, and then she called Kennedy and demanded that he come to California at once.

"I'll be there as soon as I can," he said. "I'll leave tonight or tomorrow."

When Kennedy arrived, as he told Gloria's husband Henri in a long and surprisingly intimate letter, Gloria was "in very bad shape in the hospital, as the result of practically a nervous collapse. She was down to 108 in weight and her attitude towards the picture, and everybody connected with it, was quite hostile."

Leaving Gloria in the hospital, Joe returned to Pathé, where, for ten hours, he sat in the screening room, watching the lengths of film taken over the past several months, knowing that these twenty-one reels represented nearly $800,000 of his own money. As he sat back, the European sequences flashed before his eyes with all the splendor and magnificence he had come to expect in Stroheim's work. But then, as soon as he saw the African sequences and especially the scene of the black priest carrying the sacrament to the madam of a brothel, a scene which he knew "would offend millions of Catholics," he agreed that the picture could not be released in its present form and he decided to get another ending.

Still unwilling to abandon his original director, Joe offered Stroheim the opportunity to direct a new silent ending written by Ben Glazer. But this was something Stroheim apparently found it impossible to do, as it was not his own story. So Joe was left with no choice but to fire Stroheim. Moreover, Gloria now insisted that she would work only with Goulding, whose relaxed directorial style was far less threatening to her shattered self-esteem than Stroheim's dictatorial control.

> We worked on this for ten days [Joe reported to Henri] and it was a seemingly impossible task. Goulding was hopeless and Gloria suggested four or five other people who seemed equally hopeless on this problem.
>
> There is no need to go into the personal reaction of Gloria toward owing me considerable money on the picture but it was far from a pleasant one. She went so far as to see Lasky with the idea of doing pictures there. I think her entire attitude was due to her overwrought condition and the discouragement over the whole situation. We had a very drastic showdown after the Lasky incident, and I insisted that some sort of a finish must be made because there was too much money at stake and too much loss of prestige if the picture was not finished.

All that spring, however, while everything was falling apart, Kennedy was unable to return to Hollywood, for his father was seriously ill with a progressive disease of the liver. For six years, since the death of his wife, Mary, in 1923, P. J. Kennedy had been living with his married daughter Margaret and her husband, Charles Burke, in the family home in Winthrop, across the harbor from East Boston. While Joe was still in Brookline he would see his father regularly, driving his children out every Sunday to visit the old patriarch. And even when he moved to New York, according to Rose, Joe had never let a week go by without talking to his father. Now, with the old man in critical condition in the Deaconess Hospital, Joe put aside all matters of business in both New York and California and boarded a train for Boston.

At seventy-one, P.J. remained an exceptionally considerate and affectionate man. He saw life steadily, without bitterness and with a grace of spirit. For all his shyness with outsiders, he was, toward his family and friends, genuinely warm. No one, Joe later said, had a more various range of loving relationships, deepened over the years by continual contact. Each time he came back to Boston, Joe was reminded anew of the astonishing measure of respect his father had engendered in the course of his long lifetime of public service. Indeed, throughout his life it was almost impossible for P.J. to reject a plea from someone in trouble. He had an instinctive sympathy for anybody who was in need of something. And now, as his own strength was diminishing, P.J. was rewarded for all his giving by a constant stream of visitors and a continuing current of concern.

From his hospital bed, P.J. made a single request, directed toward his daughters Loretta and Margaret. "Go into my rolltop desk," he told them. "In the drawers you will find all sorts of papers and ledgers. I want you to take them all away and burn them. Do you understand?" Following their father's orders, the two girls sorted through what turned out to be hundreds of slips of paper and several large ledger books representing thousands of loans made to as many poor people in East Boston. Worried that someone might come forward to collect these IOUs for his estate, P.J. wanted them destroyed so that all the loans could die with him. In view of Joe's feeling about his father's tendency to give away his money too freely, it is little wonder that, in this instance, P.J. turned to his daughters instead of to his favorite son.

In Joe's absence from California, the *Queen Kelly* situation deteriorated rapidly. Without Stroheim's directorial style, the sets were empty and uninhabited, the film lacked a unifying element. For months, Stroheim had carried the passion and excitement for all the cast and crew. With his firing, one director after another was assigned, but no one was able to do what Stroheim could have done. Waiting on the East Coast, Kennedy realized this and decided that as soon as he got to

California he would try to bring Stroheim and Swanson together again. But in the meantime things were going from bad to worse, and he was unable to leave because his father's illness was dragging on.

Then, in the middle of May, P.J.'s condition suddenly seemed to improve. He appeared more chipper and contented than he had been for a long time, and the doctors agreed that the crisis had passed. Taking advantage of the respite, Joe decided to leave at once for California, telling himself that if he compressed all his business activities into twenty-four-hour days he could return to Boston within three weeks.

But on Saturday morning, May 18, just a day after he had arrived in Hollywood, he received word that his father had died. Caught in California, three thousand miles from home, Joe suffered what Rose later described as a "sea of despair." For days, he would walk round and round the studio trying to come to grips with his guilt about having been so far away at the moment of death. His telegrams of response to some of the hundreds of messsages of sympathy he received betray that desperate sense of guilt. "You can't realize," he wrote to banker Attilio H. Giannini, brother of the Bank of America's head, A. P. Giannini, "what a shock it was not to return before this thing happened. He was a great man and a great father." "I had hoped to be able to get back," he writes in another telegram. "They told me I could and the shock out here is tremendous."

Among the letters Kennedy preserved in his papers was a long note from his friend Chris Dunphy:

> I know the great loss that you have just had and the love you had for your Dad. But that ought to be compensated for by the great pleasure and pride that your Father has enjoyed in the past years in being able to enjoy your wonderful success with you. You too have a great example before you in . . . the number of wonderful friends he had during his time. A lot of people I know that don't know you have often said in speaking of you, "If he is anything like his Father he is alright."

Yet, while sympathizing with Joe for the fate which destined P.J.'s death at a moment when his son was on the opposite coast, it is difficult to understand why Joe did not drop everything and return to Boston in time for the funeral, which could easily have been delayed a day or two. It can only be surmised that in the choice between leaving Gloria in a distraught state, perhaps even on the verge of breakdown, and returning to Boston, he chose to stay in Hollywood with Gloria. It was a haunting choice, reminiscent of the one James Tyrone, Jr., makes in Eugene O'Neill's *Moon for the Misbegotten* when he wrongs his dying mother and then wrongs her again a thousand times over by entertaining a prostitute in his drawing room while escorting her body home on the train.

The funeral of P. J. Kennedy was held on Tuesday morning, May 21, 1929, in the Church of St. John the Evangelist in Winthrop. It was, the *Boston Globe* noted, an impressive gathering, proving what P. J. Kennedy "meant in life to his legion of friends." In addition to family, the mourners included every prominent name in Boston politics from governors and mayors and congressmen to state legislators and city councilmen. And there were delegations representing the various political, social and fraternal organizations of East Boston. But beyond all this there were hundreds of poor people who would have been unrecognized by P.J.'s own children but who had been the recipients at one time or another of P.J.'s largesse. "With Mr. Kennedy," the *Post* reported, "public service meant public trust. . . . No man ever left his door in want or distress."

From the church, the body was carried in procession through Winthrop to East Boston. When it passed the quarters of Engines 9 and 11, the fire apparatus was pulled outside the doors while the bells tolled and all the firemen stood at attention. "Despite the rain," the *Globe* reported, "hundreds of men, women and children stood bareheaded as the body of the beloved P.J. moved through the streets of East Boston. Stores and shops were closed during the funeral. Flags were placed at half-staff. Grief was in evidence all through East Boston, where Mr. Kennedy was best known and loved."

In Joe's absence, the decision was made to let young Joe, aged thirteen, stand in his father's place. Joe Junior escorted his mother to the wake at the Washington Street house and, according to Rose, behaved with incredible dignity. Whatever discomfort he felt at the sight of what was probably the first dead body he had ever seen, he retained his poise throughout the difficult evening and proved a great comfort to his mother. "I have heard such lovely reports about you at Grandpa's funeral," Joe Senior wrote on June 3. "I am more than proud to have you there as my representative. Help mother out and I'll be with you as soon as possible."

At his death, P. J. Kennedy left an estate valued at less than $55,000, consisting mostly of several savings accounts, shares in Columbia Trust and stock in the coal company he had helped to organize. In his curious will, he bequeathed half his estate, including his stocks, his gold watch, and his ring with the diamond in it, to his immensely wealthy son (whose own estate would be valued at $250 million forty years later), while dividing the balance between his two daughters, Loretta and Margaret.

. . .

After his father's death, Kennedy tried to resume production on *Queen Kelly*. For some months now he had been living with the possibility that without Stroheim nothing could be done to save the film. While one new director after another was brought in to reshape and re-edit the forty-two completed reels, it was impossible for anyone to recapture the original vision. But to deal with Stroheim at this point, given Gloria's excessive sensitivity about him, would have required in Joe a health and vitality for the project he no longer possessed. For weeks, Gloria wrote, Joe was like "a beached whale." He took no interest or pleasure in any of his business enterprises; he wanted only "to fall asleep and dream again."

In the final go-round on *Queen Kelly*, a new ending was devised and the Polish director Richard Boleslavsky was brought in to shoot additional scenes with dialogue and music. With Walter Byron, Tully Marshall and Seena Owen reassembled at Pathé, Gloria's enthusiasm for the picture began to return. But, she later recalled, as soon as the first rushes were seen "all the accumulated excitement evaporated. The new scenes didn't look like Von Stroheim's work or have the same mood or texture. The actors, too, were responding differently to Boleslavsky; they seemed like different people. Even the sets clashed."

Two days later, Kennedy sent the actors home and suspended production. "Kelly started and stopped again after three days," Joe wired Henri, "Gypsy curse still on it." This time, however, Gloria recorded in her memoirs, Joe was not in despair. "He was resigned. He said there was no sense in throwing more good money after bad on a project that now seemed in every way behind the times. After the holidays, he would have editors piece Kelly together as best they could and we would release it." The time had come to cut his losses. (In the thirties, a truncated version of *Queen Kelly* would be released in Europe and South America, but Stroheim was able to prevent its release in the United States.)

Not a man to brood on failure, Kennedy hired Edmund Goulding to direct Gloria in her first talkie, an original story about a young stenographer in Chicago who is "destined by fate to be lifted out of a prosaic existence and plunged into a life that encompasses the loftiest heights and the bitterest depths of the mortal scheme of things." Employing all the old formulas of popular entertainment—poor girl meets rich boy only to lose him when rich boy's father intervenes; poor girl bears rich boy's child only to renounce the child years later following a tragic auto accident—*The Trespasser*, as the film was called, was completed in three months' time, the least expensive film Gloria had made since becoming a star.

When the United Artists sales force in New York screened the picture and predicted that it would be a great box office hit, Joe decided, Rose recalled, "on a campaign of international publicity and successive premieres in Paris, London, New York and Los Angeles, building to a tremendous climax when the film was released to the general public."

There followed from this business decision a personal one which brought Gloria and Rose together for the first time. Filled with excitement, Joe decided that he and Rose would accompany Gloria at *The Trespasser's* European premieres in Paris and London. In her memoirs, Gloria claims that she resisted at first, appalled by the boldness of the scheme, but that once Joe's mind was made up "there was not a big enough lever in the world to move him."

Kennedy booked passage on the luxurious liner *Île de France*, the flagship of the French Line and the largest postwar ship of any nation. In her memoirs, Gloria states that she and her friend Virginia sailed with Joe and Rose to Europe. Indeed, she describes the five-day voyage in vivid detail. From the first day, Gloria claims, "Virginia grasped the curious situation in which she was taking part," a coming together, on the same voyage, of the wife, the husband and the mistress, but whether Rose understood this or not Gloria says she couldn't tell.

Never once, Gloria claimed, did Mrs. Kennedy treat her with anything but respect and friendship. "If she suspected me of having relations not quite proper with her husband, or resented me for it, she never once gave any indication of it. In fact, at those times during the voyage when Joe Kennedy behaved in an alarmingly possessive or oversolicitous fashion toward me, Rose joined right in and supported him." Was Rose a fool, Gloria asked herself, or a saint? Or just a better actress than she was?

Vivid as her description of the voyage appears, Gloria was imagining a sailing which did not take place. The records reveal that when the Kennedys left New York on August 20, 1929, Gloria and Virginia had already departed, ten days earlier, on a different ship. Sailing lists published in *Variety* at the time provide the first clue to the misrecollection: they place Gloria and Virginia in the company of the Busby Berkeleys and Emily Stead Mestayer on the *Olympic*, while Joe and Rose were joined by Mr. and Mrs. Maurice Chevalier and Colonel and Mrs. J. B. Dodge on the *Île de France*. But the conclusive argument is contained in a telegram dated August 16 from Kennedy to Gloria at the Plaza-Athénée in Paris. "Hope you had a fine trip," Joe wires from New York four days before his own departure.

That this misrecollection is caused merely by Gloria's mistaking the return trip, when they all did travel together, for the voyage over is, of course, possible; elsewhere in her memoirs details and chronology are misleading. But it seems more likely that as she journeyed back in thought Gloria was groping, even in her memory, for a mastery over the pain of her sudden discovery in Europe that her husband was having an affair with the actress Constance Bennett. For Gloria, it seems, it was essential to believe that at every step she had control over her own life. Better to lose Henri because of her affair with Joe, which she claims had become obvious to Henri during the trip, than to lose him to another woman. In her memoirs, she even goes so far as to claim that it was only after this fateful trip that Henri met Constance Bennett and became involved in a romance that eventually led to marriage.

Rose remembered the drama of those weeks quite differently. While both couples were together in Paris, Rose recalled, Gloria received an envelope meant for her husband but mistakenly using the feminine form of his title instead of the masculine. When she opened the envelope, she found inside a love letter from Constance Bennett which made it abundantly clear that she and Henri were having an affair. Furious at the discovery, Gloria announced that she intended to seek a divorce at once, and she told Joe she would not go to any of the premieres with Henri.

"Joe was flabbergasted," Rose recalled in her memoirs. "Hank retreated to other quarters in the hotel. Gloria's attitude was one of cold, regal rage. . . . When emotions had cooled enough, we began to take stock. Joe had a lot of money in the movie, and of course so did Gloria . . . So we sat around for long hours discussing the problem. Would it be better 'box office' if Gloria were involved in a sensational divorce (as this was bound to be) or would it cause a boycott of the movie? . . . Joe finally brought everything back into focus by declaring that he had put money and time and effort into this picture, and so had other people, and these were not going to be lost just because of a disagreement between a husband and a wife. He proposed that Hank and Gloria act out the relationship they had before the trouble began. Until the premieres were finished they were to appear in public as a devoted, happy, and glamorous couple. And that's what they did."

"Poor Gloria," Rose said on looking back. "It was a very difficult time for her and I felt very sorry to see her so hurt. But Joe was right in forcing her to go on with the show and to pretend at least for the moment that everything was fine. It was not easy to calm Gloria down but since Joe had a bit of control over the situation, as Gloria and the Marquis *and* Connie Bennett all worked for him, his will prevailed."

How ironic it is to hear the phrase "Poor Gloria" coming from Rose to describe the woman who was sleeping with her husband and who, at this point, now that she was on the verge of leaving her own husband, must have presented at least some threat to the Kennedy marriage. The only explanation lies in the firmness of Rose's belief that no matter how involved Joe might be with Gloria, he would never leave his wife and children. And so long as that was true, Rose could afford to impose her own version of the facts on the world at large. If she said that nothing happened between Gloria and Joe, then nothing it was!

The London premiere of *The Trespasser* at the New Gallery Theatre —to which Gloria, Joe, Rose and Henri made their way surrounded by a roaring mob of enthusiastic fans—was a smashing success. "The crowd gave Miss Swanson a great welcome when she arrived," the United Press reported, "and cheered her again when she left. . . . Some critics said it was her best picture."

In preparing for the openings, Gloria and Rose went shopping together at the salon of the leading couturier in Paris, Lucien Lelong. This was Rose's first full exposure to the *haute couture*, and the experience created in her a special interest in clothes which remained with her. Feeling that she couldn't compete in natural beauty with the movie stars who surrounded Joe on a daily basis, Rose decided that she could keep her figure trim, her complexion good and her grooming perfect. And so, with Joe's endorsement, she began spending more time and more money on clothes, until she eventually landed on the lists of best-dressed women.

When the whirlwind days of the openings came to a close, Rose recalled, she and Joe sailed back to New York with Gloria. In a letter to Henri written at the end of the voyage, Joe reported that Gloria was not at all well and that she had remained in bed the whole trip with the exception of one night. But, once again, when the ship docked Joe insisted that Gloria hide her despondency and rise to the occasion of facing the hundreds of fans and reporters who were awaiting her arrival. "Gloria did a magnificent job," Rose recalled. "I was tired from all the emotion of the trip, so I stayed in my stateroom while the boat was docking, but Gloria went out with Joe, holding her head high and waving to all her fans. But then, because she and Joe were together on deck and I was nowhere to be seen, reporters mistakenly decided that something was going on between the two of them, and from that moment on all sorts of rumors began to fly. But I knew I never had a thing to worry about and I only felt sorry for poor little Gloria."

In a letter to Henri upon returning to America, Joe speaks of both Constance and Gloria in telling Henri: "*Variety* today carries an article that there is a rift between you and Gloria. Can't imagine where they got the information, unless somebody in Paris talked." So Rose was probably correct in fixing Paris as the place where Gloria uncovered Henri's affair with Constance Bennett. But her further suggestion that the joint appearance of Joe and Gloria on the deck sparked all the rumors about her own husband's affair provides testimony to the plasticity of her memory as well. How fascinating it is to compare these contrasting recollections of two older women, equally proud and equally determined to assert their own views of an incident that happened more than fifty years earlier.

Back home, Gloria remained dispirited for weeks. "In fact," Joe reported to Henri on October 2, 1928, "she is in bed now and will probably remain there for the balance of the week." While the New York opening of *The Trespasser* was considered a "triumph" and her performance was hailed as "brilliant," she was unable to cope with the loss of her husband to Constance Bennett.

During this period, Gloria claims, she was summoned by Cardinal O'Connell to talk about her relationship with Kennedy. According to her account, he informed her that Kennedy had sought official permission to live apart from his wife and maintain a household with Gloria. She claims that the Cardinal explained to her that this was impossible and pleaded with her to recognize there was no way Kennedy could be at peace with his faith and continue his relationship with her.

To accept Gloria's account here is to deny everything that is known about Cardinal O'Connell, a proud and imperious man who held himself aloof from the everyday problems of his parishioners. Nor is there any indication in the archives of the Boston Archdiocese that the Cardinal was in New York at the time Gloria claims to have met him. Even granting that such a meeting took place, it is difficult to imagine that Kennedy would have been willing to trade not only his wife but his entire family for the chance to live with Gloria Swanson. For a fleeting moment, perhaps, in the aftermath of the breakup of Gloria's marriage, Kennedy may well have suggested that they find a house together on the West Coast. But the strength of the suggestion pales beside the actual commitment he made in these same months to purchase a new family home in Bronxville, New York, a large brick Georgian mansion surrounded by five acres of landscaped grounds.

Indeed, by the fall of 1929 the sun of Joe's romance with Gloria was setting. While they would still make one more movie together, a light comedy called *What a Widow*, and while their working relationship would continue for another year, Joe was already beginning to disengage himself from Hollywood, and with that disengagement his days with Gloria were numbered. Prompted perhaps by the guilt of being so far away from home at the moment of his father's death and by the added

pressure now that Gloria was free of her husband, Joe decided to liquidate all his movie holdings and return to Wall Street.

Gloria Swanson was not so fortunate. Kennedy's departure left her
with monumental losses on *Queen Kelly*. In time, Kennedy would re-
coup his *Kelly* losses with the profits from *The Trespasser*, but Gloria
would remain in debt for years. Then, too, Gloria had lost her husband.
"It was," Gloria recorded in her memoirs, "as if two men—my ex-
husband and my ex-paramour—had in some mysterious way, through
me, cancelled each other out and moved on. I was completely on my
own again, without love and without money."

How different it all was from what Gloria and Joe had planned in the
heady days when both *Queen Kelly* and their romance held such wondrous promise. But the *Queen Kelly* story had a special sequel years
later when Swanson and Stroheim were reunited in a classic film, *Sunset
Boulevard*, which provided Gloria with the best role of her long career.
Considered by many the finest movie about Hollywood ever made, the
film featured Gloria as a once adored aging star obsessed with achieving
a return to glory. In a barren mansion, the great ex-star lives with her
male servant and former director (Stroheim), who has devoted his
wrecked life to mending the leaks in her delusions. Playing his role
magnificently, Stroheim joins Swanson in a lonely New Year's Eve party
at which she is watching clips of her old movies, one of them an actual
cut of *Queen Kelly*, the film that effectively ended Stroheim's directorial
career. Only in Hollywood could an event fraught with such sadness be
transformed, as Rose put it, into an "inside joke."

# CHAPTER 25
# RIDING
# THE
# ROOSEVELT SPECIAL

While Joseph Kennedy was winding up his affairs in Hollywood, a frenzied trading on the stock market was making prices soar out of all relation to the country's economic reality. With the election of Herbert Hoover to the presidency in November 1928, the nature of the speculative boom had changed. Believing there would never be a better time to get rich, tens of thousands of new customers had entered the stock market by trading on margin. "Never before," business journalist Albert Atwood wrote in January of 1929, "has a stock market boom engaged so many people, permeated to such an extent the life of the nation or loomed up so portentously alongside the structure of industry, commerce or finance."

By the spring of 1929, the rise of stock values no longer reflected the rise of earning power generated by advances in technology and expansion of consuming markets. Buying on expectation rather than realization, the American public was escaping into a world of make-believe. To be sure, there were a few voices—most notably Paul M. Warburg and Alexander Noyes—who warned that the market was too high, but at a time when the mood of the public was one of invincible optimism, pessimistic comments were seen as attempts to discredit American prosperity, and skepticism was dismissed as sandbagging. "A few gloomy souls had warned of impending danger," veteran reporter John Flynn later wrote, "but those who dared to suggest there was a ceiling to America's soaring radius and that the curve of the business cycle would cease its upward sweep until it had curled over the moon were brushed aside as croakers."

Cautious and questioning by nature, immune to most enthusiasms, Joseph Kennedy decided, in the spring of 1929, to begin to liquidate his stock holdings and gradually get out of the market. The lessons Galen Stone had taught him a decade earlier on the importance of judging every stock by the true value of its earning power and dividend returns were too deeply imbedded for him to be fooled by the wildly inflated prices. Actually, Kennedy had already reduced his portfolio by more than half in the period from 1926 to 1928, as he found himself too involved in Hollywood to concentrate sufficiently on the market. Yet, if his instincts smelled trouble, his judgment told him he should consult with some of the old pros before betting against the crowd.

So, in February of 1929, Kennedy decided to pay a visit to J. P. Morgan II. "It was a move he must have been planning for some time," journalist John Brooks later wrote. "He must have believed his influence had reached the point where Morgan would be curious to meet him or failing that would judge he could no longer afford to snub a man of such stature." But, for once, he had miscalculated. When he stepped through the double doors at 23 Broad Street and announced who he was, he was told simply that Mr. Morgan was too busy to see him.

Fortunately for Kennedy, Morgan's rebuff sent him back to his old friend Guy Currier for advice. For Currier, unlike Morgan (and so many other members of the establishment who were blinded to the truth by their institutional complicity in the creation of the sham), saw that the spiraling market prices were unconnected to business conditions. "It looks to me," Currier wrote to Boston businessman Louis Kirstein on April 1, 1929, "that there is about an even chance that we are in for some degree of business depression. Present money conditions are slowing up building and will restrict public works. How far it will affect the auto industry I don't dare to guess. On the whole it is not an attractive time to go into new matters."

Beginning that month, and continuing throughout the summer, Kennedy began to sell his remaining shares in Eastern Steamship, Anaconda Copper and many other stocks. Taking cash for some, he purchased municipal bonds with others. As the market rallied still higher in the summer of 1929, many of Kennedy's friends questioned his judgment. Journeying to "the Street" himself on a hot July day in 1929 to get his own feel of the situation, Kennedy was assailed on all sides by optimism. Still, his cold professional judgment told him no. Later, Kennedy liked to tell the story of his encounter that day with a talkative shoeshine boy whose sophistication about the market and ready knowledge of inside tips stunned him. "When the time comes that a shoeshine boy knows as much as I do about what is going on in the stock market . . . it's time for me to get out."

So it happened that Kennedy was standing at a safe distance in September 1929 when the great bull market finally began to crack. As prices fell, and more and more margin calls went out, the smaller investors were hurt first. There followed weeks of uncertainty during which the market seemed to rally, giving rise to hopes that this was only another break before an even larger upturn. But then, on October 24, as millions of orders to sell pounded the exchange, plummeting prices to all-time lows, a general panic set in.

It was in this context, as stunned, silent crowds gathered in the streets, that the establishment decided to step in. Meeting in the offices of J. P. Morgan and Company, diagonally across Broad Street from the New York Stock Exchange, a half-dozen of the top bankers, including Charles E. Mitchell, Albert H. Wiggin and Thomas W. Lamont, agreed to create a pool of $240 million to support the market. Their plan was to shore up selected stocks and so rally the rest. For several days, the medicine seemed to work. As word of the bankers' pool spread, the market steadied. At the same time, President Hoover issued a statement declaring that "the fundamental business of the country" was "on a sound and prosperous basis."

But words of reassurance were no longer enough; once the basic confidence was lost, the crash was inevitable. It came on October 29, a "Black Tuesday" that would haunt the dreams of a generation. On that day, the most devastating day in the history of the New York Stock Exchange, sixteen million shares changed hands, crushing all the marginal traders and subjecting thousands of the wealthy and the well-to-do "to a levelling process comparable in magnitude and suddenness to that presided over by Lenin a decade before." For days, the press focused on dramatic accounts of the suicides of fallen financiers.

For his part, Joe Kennedy was "sitting pretty" in the Bronxville estate he had purchased the previous June from Joseph A. Goetz for $250,000. Having never been a member of the inner circle, which in 1929 was still run by the white Anglo-Saxon Protestants, Kennedy felt no constraints now to save the system. Operating from a desk at Halle & Stieglitz, he coldly calculated which stocks to sell short and why, turning the devastating situation to his own advantage. Like his friend Ben Smith, who became known on Wall Street at this time as "Sell-'em Ben," Kennedy was unfettered by loyalty to old school or class or even country. Driving the market down still further, his membership in the fraternity of bears left him an even wealthier man after the crash than he was before.

Yet, as 1929 gave way to 1930, Kennedy still had one tricky financial problem to solve. When he merged FBO and KAO and RCA to form RKO in 1928, he had retained his interests in Pathé and the company was not doing well. To be sure, he had inherited a situation where Pathé was in the red, but in the three years he had guided Pathé the situation had only gotten worse. Despite glowing public-relations reports in *Variety* which repeatedly claimed that his brilliant stewardship was turning things around, the company's costs were exceeding sales by a greater margin each year. And during this time the common stock ceased earning anything and the preferred stock earnings were cut in half.

This unusual failure on Kennedy's part was explained by Walter Brooks in a letter to Hiram Brown, the head of RKO, as a consequence of the "almost absent treatment" Kennedy had given Pathé. "The Swanson pictures always had precedence over Pathe's interests," Brooks suggested, "even on Pathe's own grounds. The majority of Pathe's values are being neglected and lost under present circumstances."

Never one to compound his losses, Kennedy decided to sever his last remaining link with Hollywood. Throughout the spring and summer of 1930 he negotiated with Howard Hughes to take over Pathé, but the deal fell through when Hughes joined up with Joseph Schenck at United Artists and Schenck advised against it. Then, to Kennedy's great fortune, Pathé came through in the late summer of 1930 with three big-money pictures. Acting at once on the momentary good news, Kennedy worked out a deal whereby RKO bought all the assets of Pathé, including all the buildings, land and equipment, the Pathé news service, completed films, story rights, contracts and laboratories for a purchase price of less than $5 million, with $500,000 in cash and the rest in notes.

> I can't tell you [Kennedy wrote to J. J. Murdock on December 9, 1930] what a relief it is to me to get this cleaned up. It was so loaded with dynamite over the last three or four years that anything could have happened at any time. . . . I believe this has probably taken another five years off my life. I am going to stay around until the stockholders meeting in January and if there is anything left of me then, I am going away for three or four months.

If Kennedy felt relief at getting out of Pathé with a substantial amount of cash, many of the stockholders, whose stock had reached a low point at the time of the sale, felt otherwise, and a lawsuit was instituted against him on the grounds that the sale defrauded the stockholders. The lawsuit dragged on for years, but at a time when the unregulated market was still tilted so tremendously toward the insiders, nothing came of the suit. It was yet another case where the rules of the game allowed the insiders to take their spectacular profits on the backs of the unsuspecting public.

There are in Kennedy's papers several letters from individual Pathé stockholders which give evidence to the anguish Kennedy caused in deciding to sell out. "I purchased twenty shares of Pathe at $14 a share," Anne Lawler writes from Jamaica Plain, Massachusetts, "and my sister the same at $12 a share." (By the time of the sale, the value of the common stock had fallen to $1.50 per share.)

> To you this sum may seem small [she continues] but to us it was a life's savings. . . . Knowing your father and father-in-law, I put my money in your enterprise, only to see where you are willing . . . to pass it over to another concern for almost nothing. This seems hardly Christian like, fair or just for a man of your character. I wish you would think of the poor working women who had so much faith in you as to give their money to your Pathe.

Another letter, handwritten on plain folded notepaper and unsigned, reveals even more clearly the extent of the bitterness which Kennedy and his fellow insiders engendered among ordinary people:

Mr. Kennedy

> We are going to put you on the spot. You have fair warning. We are not going to be like you, sell Pathe inc. out on the stockholders and then push them out with nothing.
> We are not going to plug you or we are not going to stick you in the back, but we are going to cut your throat from ear to ear as a warning to others what pulls the same deal. Now you may go to Florida, Europe or any other place but we will get you anyway when you least expect it, you know Kennedy the stockholders of pathe are all poor people and nothing else and you ruined them to make youself more richer than what you are. You have Roals Royce cars a house full of servants, all with your crooked work but you are at the end of your roap. This is one time you made a mistake, we were very careful and went and found out who who sold out the stockholders and pushed them out with only a piece of paper to hold and we found out that you are the one that pulled a deal. Well so long til we see you the sooner the better.
> You will have a note pinned on your cloth to tell why you passed out.

Why Kennedy kept this letter (it was hidden in a brown folder labeled "Bronxville House") or how he responded to the threat, if he did, is not known, but its desperate tone is a harsh reminder of the fundamental unfairness of the market of that era.

The times were desperate. The crash had brought an end to a prosperous era, one blighted by the uneven distribution of the wealth created. For eight years, as production steadily grew, the disposition was to inflate profits and maintain prices, piling up wealth in the hands of the few, while holding down wages and raw material prices so that workers and farmers were denied the benefit of increases in their own productivity. The result was a steady decline in mass purchasing power which remained hidden only because Wall Street had invented so many devices for getting easy credit that it was possible to go on raising new money for expansion long after the need for expansion was exhausted. With the collapse of the market, the slowdown accelerated. By the spring of 1930, over four million Americans were unemployed and millions more were working only two or three days a week. And with each succeeding season, the productivity of the economy continued to decline.

Across the country, a dismal era was beginning as unemployment and homelessness began to settle into a way of life. Night after night, once proud men found themselves huddled together on bread lines, waiting patiently for a piece of bread and a cup of coffee, while their families pawned everything of value they owned to stay alive. And every day, every week, more factories and stores were shutting their doors, leaving more and more people out of work.

While millions of Americans were being introduced to a new and humiliating mode of existence, the Kennedys were experiencing what Rose later described as "a golden interval" in their lives, a time of family peace and economic security. Returning home from Hollywood, Joe Kennedy had become his old self again, warm, happy, and content to pour his affection and vitality upon his family. Spending hours of his time on the furnishings of the new house in Bronxville, Kennedy infused every space with his overpowering presence. And with his return, his summer house in Hyannis Port was also infused with a new life. Outwardly, the only change was the installation of a talking-picture apparatus in the basement, but inwardly, Rose later recalled, "the same spacious rooms, the same grassy lawns and the same ocean vista took on an entirely different tone with my husband home to stay."

For her part, Rose apparently accepted her husband's return with no questions asked, rejoicing in the joy and cheer his presence brought.

Perhaps it was not so much a hardening of her emotions—though surely some hardening did take place—as a conscious choice, a recognition that her commitment to marriage, family and the Church was so deep that she would not only stay with the marriage, she would simply not allow herself to worry about other women.

For Rose, it seemed, Joe's interest in Gloria Swanson was little different from the interest of a boy in going to a strip house. In her mind, a woman like Gloria had nothing to do with her marriage. "But if he took out a good Irish Catholic girl from Boston or Chicago," Cy Howard observed, "now *that* would have been a threat." But as it was, Rose's attitude seems best expressed by the comment of a beautiful woman about her playboy husband: "He worships in many churches but only one cathedral."

"I think," Eddie Gallagher speculated, "that when Joe realized how close he had come to destroying his family, he determined that from there on in, he would keep his encounters with women at a more casual level. I think he simply decided that he would never again get so deeply involved with anyone, and as far as I know he never did."

In her memoirs, Rose describes this period as one of the happiest of her married life, a period when her marriage entered yet another phase as she and her husband spent long hours with each other, walking hand in hand along the ocean shore at the Cape or through the Bronxville woodlands, while all the children stayed behind. If their love had come to a standstill in the twenties and ceased to grow, now a renewed commitment to their marriage seemed to take possession of their souls, bringing with it an absorbing affection for each other.

Joe's niece Mary Lou McCarthy remembers visiting the Kennedys about this time and watching a happy banter between Joe and Rose, filled with taps and winks and teasing. "Joe always had a sweet tooth," Mary Lou recalled, "and he especially loved Fanny Farmer candies, which he kept in a box locked up in the buffet in the dining room. At the end of the meal he'd say, 'Now it's time for my Fanny Farmer candies.' 'Oh, really, Joe,' Rose would counter. 'You know it's no good for your fine physique and what's going to happen to that smashing grin of yours if all your teeth fall out?' It was delightful banter, like watching a tennis match. But in the end, of course, she'd take out the key and hand him the box of candy with an affectionate tap on his shoulder."

In her letters in the early 1930s, Rose revealed a host of warm feelings toward her husband. In a postscript to a letter that eleven-year-old Kathleen had written to her father in January of 1932, when he was away on a business trip, Rose wrote: "Joe dear—I love you very much and would like to see you this minute."

Yet there is little denying that the Swanson affair had a permanent effect upon the Kennedy family, for history would later record a connecting link between the risks Joseph Kennedy took with Gloria Swanson and the sexual daring that would be observed again and again in his sons. It would seem almost as if, in repeating their father's behavior, they were unconsciously trying to gain some sort of mastery over this early trauma that had nearly destroyed everything they had.

The year after Joe's return to the East, Rose gave birth to their ninth child, a sturdy little boy whom they named Edward Moore after Joe's faithful friend and companion. Making his way into the world on February 22, 1932, the baby was in momentary danger of being called George Washington Kennedy—his fourteen-year-old brother Jack's suggestion—but in the end he became simply Teddy.

With their twentieth anniversary approaching, Rose must have realized she was living a life of great privilege in comparison with the meager existence of most Americans as the nation staggered into yet another year of the depression. At a time when the average American had used up not only his life's savings but his access to loans from relatives and friends, until, as Arthur M. Schlesinger, Jr., put it, "the lines of friendship and compassion . . . snapped," Joe Kennedy was negotiating a business loan from the National City Bank for $1.5 million. At a time when the average American was struggling to save the family homestead from foreclosure, Joe Kennedy was purchasing his third estate, a magnificent ocean villa, built by the most celebrated architect in Palm Beach, Harry Mizner.

Even with the birth of the new baby, it was understood that whenever Rose wanted to travel she was free to leave for weeks and even months at a time. "Joe didn't like traveling unless he had to," Rose later explained. "But he was glad that I enjoyed it so and he never objected to my getting away, even if it meant arranging his schedule to be home with the children."

In honor of their anniversary, Joe presented to Rose the gift of a European vacation, including a sojourn in Paris to see all the new fall fashions and the leeway to buy whatever clothes she desired. From the elegant Ritz in Paris on the actual date of the anniversary, Rose telegraphed to Joe in Bronxville: "Thank you. Twenty years. Rare happiness. All my love always. Rosa."

For his part, Joe sent a long, loving cable to his wife which, despite his philandering, suggests the continuing presence of a deep familial bond.

DARLING

THIS IS YOUR TWENTIETH ANNIVERSARY. I CANNOT TELL YOU HOW HAPPY
THESE YEARS HAVE BEEN FOR ME AND WHAT A MARVELOUS PERSON YOU HAVE
BEEN THROUGH IT ALL. THE THING THAT MAKES THIS SO TRUE IS PROVEN BY
THE FACT THAT I LOVE YOU MORE NOW THAN EVER. I HAVE TAKEN THE
CHILDREN TO LUNCH AT THE PLAZA AND MOVIES AND THEY ARE ALL IN FINE
SHAPE. . . . I WISH I WERE WITH YOU IN PARIS TODAY TO CELEBRATE OUR
ANNIVERSARY.

Impressed by the length of Joe's cable, Rose wired back at once to say
she loved every word of it. "I had counted my words very carefully as
you saw," she confessed. "I just wished I might have been with you
today darling . . . I ordered a lace dress good for New York and Palm
Beach and may get a coat or I may go to London Wednesday . . . Much
much love to you—my dearest. Rosa."

Contented as he was, Kennedy could not rest secure so long as the
staggering losses of the depression continued to spread, threatening
eventual ruin for everybody. In the face of the continuing economic
decline, the machinery of civilized life was breaking down. A widespread
feeling of helplessness was crippling the capacity of the country to organize and distribute the daily necessities of life, crushing rich and poor
alike.

Driven by a fear that paralyzing disorder could break out at any moment, Kennedy saw with prescience that the leaders of the business
community could no longer cope with the situation. While most of his
business friends continued to believe, with Hoover, that recovery would
come in time so long as America remained patient, Kennedy understood
that without substantial political intervention the situation would only
get worse. Fearing that his own fortune would be unsafe so long as
conditions remained as they were, Kennedy accepted the need for a
fundamental shift in the political order. "I am not ashamed to record,"
he later confessed, "that in those days I felt and said I would be willing
to part with half of what I had if I could be sure of keeping, under law
and order, the other half."

Having forsaken politics for business three decades earlier out of a felt
sense of the uncontrollability of the electorate, he now returned to
politics in the belief that strong political leadership was the only solution
to the uncontrolled economy. As he looked ahead, Kennedy foresaw
that the center of gravity in America would shift from big business to big
government. "In the next generation," he told his friend the singer
Morton Downey in the 1930s, "the people who run the government will
be the biggest people in America." So, just as he had resolved in the

1920s to be at the center of action by becoming a businessman, so now he saw politics as the only means by which he could remain inextricably involved in the dominant passion of his day.

Searching for a leader who could lead, Kennedy found his candidate in Franklin D. Roosevelt, the popular Governor of New York, whose vitality, affability and charisma were unmatched by any other contender for the White House. Kennedy's first contact with Roosevelt, back in the days of World War I when he was building ships for the government at Fore River and Roosevelt was the Assistant Secretary of the Navy, had been an adversarial one, marked by frustration and anger. But their renewed acquaintanceship in the 1930s quickly blossomed into a fascinating friendship that would continue to deepen throughout the tumultuous decade. Recognizing the need for strong leadership to combat the nation's paralysis, Kennedy believed that FDR, more than anyone else in the country, had the resources, talent and personality to bring it about. What Kennedy hoped might result from a Roosevelt presidency was the creation of a positive governmental force strong enough to demonstrate to both the radicals and the ultraconservatives that capitalism could be saved so long as it was transformed.

"I was really worried," Kennedy later confessed. "I knew that big, drastic changes had to be made in our economic system and I felt that Roosevelt was the one who could make those changes. I wanted him in the White House for my own security and the security of our kids—and I was ready to do anything to help elect him."

The first public indication of Joe Kennedy's evolving sympathies came with his journey to Warm Springs, Georgia, on Sunday, May 8, 1932, in the company of Eddie Moore. Initiated by Roosevelt's aides, the visit was intended to bring the wealthy Kennedy into the Roosevelt camp. But so new was Kennedy as a national public figure that when the Associated Press first reported the visit it mistakenly identified Kennedy and Moore as John Fitzgerald and James Michael Curley. Once Kennedy was correctly identified, the press found particular significance in the fact that he was just returning from a trip to California, where he had visited William Randolph Hearst, his friend from his Hollywood days, whose delegate control extended beyond his own state of California to the state of Texas as well.

As it happened, Hearst was destined to play a pivotal role at the Democratic national convention in 1932. When the convention opened in Chicago in mid-June, Roosevelt was clearly in the lead, holding a majority but not the necessary two thirds of the delegates. Supporters of Roosevelt worried that unless the uncommitted delegates could be swung over in the first two or three ballots, a deadlock could result, ending with the nomination of a dark-horse candidate, possibly Newton D. Baker, the Secretary of War in Woodrow Wilson's Cabinet. In this situation Hearst's support was crucial, since the delegates he controlled could swing the tide to Roosevelt. Hearst, relishing his role, had originally decided to hold out until the seventh ballot, a decision which a half-dozen people, including Joe Kennedy, tried desperately to change. Never one to pull his punches, Kennedy spoke bluntly to W.R., as he called him. "Do you want that man Baker running our country," Kennedy asked, "that great defender of the League of Nations, that ardent internationalist whose policies you despise? No, of course you don't. But that's just who you're going to get if you keep holding out your delegates from Roosevelt, for if the convention cracks open, it'll surely be Baker. And then where will you be?"

To be sure, Kennedy's call was only one of many Hearst received, but when the publisher finally fell in line for Roosevelt, setting in motion a bandwagon effect that resulted in Roosevelt's nomination on the fourth ballot, Kennedy claimed full credit, boasting proudly that his call was the one which brought Hearst around.

Following a night of wild celebration, Kennedy set to work raising money for the campaign, a task at which he proved himself eminently suited. Beyond the $50,000 he himself contributed, it is said that Kennedy raised over $150,000 for Roosevelt in the space of four months. Little wonder, then, that his relationship with the candidate grew warmer and warmer.

Beyond Kennedy's political and financial contributions, Roosevelt's attraction for the Boston Irishman was obvious. Joe Kennedy was intelligent, high-spirited, gregarious and affable—the kind of person FDR, delighting in hearty souls, loved to have around him. Moreover, the two men shared a strong sense of humor, born of an intense vitality and a rich appreciation of the wonder and variety of life. Late at night, when the two of them would get together to talk, the sound of their laughter would float through the halls.

For all their similarities, however, there were as many contrasts. FDR was gracious and indirect, whereas Joe Kennedy was blunt and painfully direct. And on a more fundamental level the differences were even greater. At bottom, for all his warmth and capacity to make friends instantly, FDR was a man without a deep commitment to anyone. He enjoyed people, they gave themselves to him time and again, but he rarely gave himself to them. Below the cheerful strength that radiated from him there was a final melancholy, a deep loneliness that even his children and his wife could not reach.

In contrast, Joe Kennedy was a man so deeply committed to himself and his family that everything else took second place. He too enjoyed meeting people and they enjoyed him, but in the end none of them really mattered to him compared with his family and his few close friends. With FDR, detachment provided a liberation, a freedom from idealism as well as cynicism, a capacity to devote all his considerable energies to his public life, to consider every action in terms of his own best interests and those of his country. Yet, as long as Kennedy's narrower sense of self-interest coincided with Roosevelt's broader vision, their friendship would remain on solid ground.

In the fall of 1932, FDR invited Kennedy to accompany him aboard his campaign train on its thirteen-thousand-mile journey from the East Coast to the West and back again. Against the advice of his more conservative advisers, who believed that the Democratic nominee should stay at home and deliver a series of set speeches, FDR was determined to spend the month making a whistle-stop tour through more than twenty states. In doing so, he was as much intent on obtaining firsthand data on conditions in various parts of the nation as he was on expounding his views. It was a brilliant strategy, for it gave Roosevelt his first opportunity to project his contagious warmth, vitality and confidence to the great mass of the American people.

Accompanied by the amiable Eddie Moore, who soon became a favorite of the entire Roosevelt entourage, Kennedy boarded the *Roosevelt Special* at midnight on September 13, 1932, in Albany for the first leg of its journey through Missouri, Kansas, Utah, Montana, Washington, Oregon and California. Many years later, as Joe Kennedy talked with his son on the eve of Jack's own campaign for the presidency, he was to remember this cross-country trip. Indeed, even after his friendship with Roosevelt ebbed, Kennedy would remember the candidate as he saw him those weeks, sitting in his car amid dozens of local visitors who were picked up at every stop—bankers, newspaper owners, politicians, manufacturers; standing on the rear platform of the train waving to the thousands of people gathered by the tracks; electrifying the crowds with his deep, resonant voice.

The *Special* had nearly a dozen cars. After the dining car and the lounge car came a car for the candidate and his family (which included twenty-six-year-old James Roosevelt and his young wife Betsy Cushing, the daughter of the eminent Boston physician Harvey Cushing, and Anna Roosevelt Dall, thirty and married to stockbroker Curtis Dall). There were two cars for cameramen, radio announcers and representatives of the telegraph companies, and a separate car for the newspapermen—a colorful bunch including James Hagerty of *The New York*

*Times*, Ernest Lindley of the *New York Herald Tribune*, Robert Allen of the *Philadelphia Record*, John Boettiger of the *Chicago Tribune* and Louis Ruppel of the New York *Daily News*. There was a special car for what Raymond Moley called "visiting firemen"—those dignitaries whose status called for one or two days of jaunting with the candidate as compared with the four- or five-hour allowance accorded the lesser bandwagon riders. And there were two cars for the more or less permanent members of the troupe. These included Kennedy and Moore; Raymond Moley, Columbia professor and head of the Brain Trust which gathered data for the Governor's speeches; Missy LeHand, Roosevelt's secretary; James A. Farley, the campaign manager, who joined the party in Salt Lake City and left in Los Angeles; Charles Pettijohn, a veteran of the movie industry who made contacts with motion picture distributors at every stop; Senators Key Pittman of Nevada, Thomas J. Walsh of Montana and George W. Norris of Nebraska; old Jack Cohen, veteran newspaperman, and Breckinridge Long, Assistant Secretary of State under Wilson, both splendid entertainers, possessed of an incredible stock of anecdotes, whose role was simply to surround the visitors with a friendly, all-embracing spirit of welcome. And there was Judge Robert Marx of Cincinnati, taken along as a good-luck charm because he had traveled with FDR in the latter's campaign for the vice-presidency in 1920.

Later, Rose recalled the intense pleasure Joe experienced when he discovered that he and Eddie had been placed in Car D, the car carrying all the candidate's closest advisers and friends, including Moley, Farley, Long and Marx. Kennedy, whose energy was the match of much younger men, found the camaraderie of the train an experience he would not forget. Midnight would invariably find a dozen or more of them gathered together, regaling one another with tales, their voices breaking frequently into explosive laughs. To speechwriter Ray Moley, an affable square-shouldered man with an engaging smile and a professor's heavy dark pipe, these gay voices were tantalizing sounds as he struggled in his own drawing room over the texts for the next day. Feeling at times as if he were a virtual prisoner of his own compartment, which was piled high with reference books and memoranda, Moley looked with longing at the late-night conviviality that went on in the other rooms of Car D.

In this gathering of vigorous, talkative men, Kennedy fit in perfectly: merry, provocative and colorful, his unusually warm personality shaped a number of instant friendships. To young Jimmy Roosevelt, Kennedy stood out as "a rather fabulous figure," a man of many parts whose contacts in the varied worlds of film, sports and finance provided a fascinating stream of insights as well as a number of practical bonuses: when the party reached Williams, Arizona, Kennedy chartered a fleet of buses to take everyone to the Grand Canyon. Then, when the returning train happened to pull into Chicago on the third day of the World Series between the Cubs and the Yankees, Kennedy managed, perhaps from Cubs owner Wrigley, his friend from the days when he saved Hertz, to corral a block of tickets which allowed everyone on the train to see Babe Ruth and Lou Gehrig lead the Yankees to a 7–5 victory over the Cubs. It was in Chicago that Kennedy met for the first time the *New York Times* reporter Arthur Krock, who found him "a remarkably handsome and charming man," sowing the seeds for a friendship that would last for twenty-five years.

As the train sped west, Kennedy might have thought back to the first cross-country trip he had made in the mid-1920s when the nation was sitting in the midst of the most prosperous era in its history. How much had changed in the course of a single decade! Now one out of four people was out of work, factories that had once darkened the skies with smoke stood ghostly silent, families waited for hours on bread lines and scavenged for food in city dumps.

At every stop, the routine was basically the same. First, the indefatigable Roosevelt, his legs under his steel braces so thin that they could not even match the size of Kennedy's arms, would make his way to the back platform, accompanied by the strains of "Happy Days Are Here Again." Then he would smile his magical smile and say a few words of greeting to the gathering crowd. At Paris, Illinois, where no stop was even scheduled, more than five hundred men, women and children stood on the track and forced the engineer to bring the train to a sudden stop. There they remained until Governor Roosevelt appeared and waved his hand in greeting. At Mattoon, Illinois, at least two thousand people gathered and as the brass band blared away a man yelled out, "When do we get beer?" "I hope pretty soon," the Governor replied. "We want jobs too," shouted another. "I hope you get jobs soon, too," the Governor replied.

It wasn't so much what he said as the spirit of affirmation in which he said it. Believing that the people *had* the will to go on, if only they had the confidence, Roosevelt saw his task as that of waking up their souls, retrieving the spirit of American initiative which had almost disappeared, pulled away by the fever of fear. "For Roosevelt," Arthur Schlesinger has written, "the faces before him were an unforgettable experience—the great mass of Missourians under the lights before the Capitol at Jefferson City, the Kansans listening patiently in the hot sun at Topeka, the Nebraska farmers in the red glow of sunset at McCook, the stricken but dauntless miners of Butte." Sometimes the faces seemed to him "happy in great hope," other times they had "the frightened look of lost children."

But through it all, the candidate, wearing the same battered felt hat every day as a symbol of luck, never wearied or lost his good humor. Campaigning was for him "an unadulterated joy," and the people responded in kind. At Laramie, Wyoming, two members of the Laramie Post of the American Legion, wearing sombreros, chaps and purple silk shirts, came to the platform and presented a horned toad to Roosevelt. The Governor laughed and with a merry glint in his eyes handed the toad to his daughter, Anna, who received the sinister-looking but harmless creature with a slight shudder but smiled gamely all the while. As Roosevelt rode in a parade through the main streets of Denver, the crowds lining the curb on each side were three or four deep; some were shouting, "Hurrah for Franklin, our next President," others, too wearied by the daily struggle for survival, stood silently and stared.

The crowds, responding with increasing warmth to Roosevelt's confidence and hope, grew larger and more enthusiastic at each stop. In Butte, Montana, seven thousand people gathered in front of the courthouse to hear the Governor speak; in Seattle, a wildly cheering audience of sixteen thousand packed Auditorium Hall; in San Francisco a crowd of 100,000 lined the streets to cheer him as he proceeded from the ferry station to the Palace Hotel. The enthusiasm reached a climax on the return trip in Chicago as the candidate received what reporters described as "one of the greatest demonstrations ever accorded a candidate." Riding in an open auto with Mayor Anton Cermak at his side, Roosevelt was cheered by crowds estimated at more than 200,000. And behind the cars in which the Governor's party rode, with kerosene torches lighting the way, marched members of the Democratic clubs from all of Chicago's wards bearing banners and placards after the manner of an old-time parade.

In each city, while dinners and speeches were going on, Kennedy slipped away from the official party to wander the streets on his own, seeking out local financial leaders to explain why Roosevelt was the man who could save capitalism and to solicit pledges from them. Sauntering into drugstores and barbershops, he also sought to find out in his own way what the people were thinking and talking about. With his mind vitally open to experience, he found these sorties invaluable, allowing him to bring back to the train at night fresh ideas and phrases that would sometimes get incorporated into the speeches the following day.

In the course of the trip, Roosevelt delivered sixteen major speeches as well as sixty-seven second-string ones, all of which, taken together, provided a preview for the program of action he would create in the historic Hundred Days, when fifteen major laws, including the Emergency Banking Act, the National Industrial Recovery Act and the Farm Credit Act, would be enacted by Congress. According to Moley, the great majority of the work for the major speeches had been completed before the tour began, but with each day's experience continual additions and revisions were made, and the evenings often found the inner circle wrapped in heated discussions about various policies. In these arguments, Kennedy never hesitated to clash with others, though when he lost he accepted defeat good-humoredly. And if, on occasion, his bluntness hurt the feelings of others, Eddie Moore was always there to smooth things over for the boss. As Moley put it, Eddie Moore's "infinite capacity to make friends" made up for many of Kennedy's shortcomings.

While he was on the train, Kennedy received a number of letters and telegrams from business friends filled with advice for the Democratic candidate. Writing almost daily, Herbert Bayard Swope, former executive editor of the *New York World*, suggested that FDR must prove that liberalism was not radicalism, that reform of the capitalist system did not mean its abolition.

> Capitalism is the wagon in which we ride to such measure of happiness as it is possible to humanly achieve [Swope wrote]. It has been a reasonably good vehicle for several hundred years, and in it we have gone ahead. Now it is creaking and in places worn out. This does not mean we must abandon the wagon; that we must climb out and destroy it and then search for another conveyance or travel through the bogs afoot. It means we must repair it; that we must replace the worn out parts with new ones; that we must continue to make the wheels go round; that we must see that those riding in it are given reasonably good chances at good seats. After all, capitalism is not an end in itself, but the means to an end.

Of all his speeches, the one Roosevelt delivered at the Commonwealth Club in San Francisco on September 23 best captured the mood of the early depression. It was a powerful speech, carrying his audience on a journey through American history with the argument that for too many decades financial titans, unethical competitors, reckless promoters and giant corporations had been allowed to work their will unrestrained by government, with the consequence that the rights of the many were being crushed. "We have no actual famine or dearth," he argued, "our industrial and agricultural mechanism can produce enough and to spare." But in the relentless process of concentration, equality of opportunity to share in that production no longer existed. "Our government owes to everyone an avenue to possess himself of that plenty sufficient for his needs through his own work," he said.

We know that individual liberty and individual happiness mean nothing unless both are ordered in the sense that one man's meat is not another man's poison. . . . We know that the liberty to do anything which deprives others of [their] elemental rights is outside the protection of any compact and that government in this regard is the maintenance of a balance within which every individual may have a place if he will take it, in which every individual may find safety if he wishes it, in which every individual may attain such power as his ability permits, consistent with his assuming the accompanying responsibility.

On the train, "time never stopped." Despite the cumulative fatigue the trip provoked, it provided for everyone a rare experience of intense camaraderie and a sense of participation in the great currents of the day. Exhausted by the work and the strain, each responded to the energy of crowds with a renewed energy of his own. Little wonder, then, that when it was finally over, nostalgia set in, a feeling that something mysterious had occurred that would not come easily again.

As the train climbed over the hills that surround the State Capitol at Albany and pulled into Union Station at the end of the journey on Monday morning, October 3, Joe Kennedy felt suddenly sad. For the first time in his life, he had experienced a group camaraderie akin to that of soldiers in a war. And now it was over. Writing later to one of his reporter friends, Louis Ruppel, he said that of all the experiences in his life this was surely one of the best. "I have had a lot of fun in my life and met a lot of fine people, but none finer or a greater crowd than I met on that train."

On election night, Kennedy celebrated Roosevelt's victory over Hoover as though it were a personal triumph, staging a lavish party that spilled through two floors of New York's Waldorf-Astoria. In the hotel where he had first come to meet John Hertz in 1924, where he had pledged himself to achieving power, he now returned in a mood of exhilaration and triumph matched by the familiar strains of "Happy Days Are Here Again."

The merrymaking continued in Florida as FDR took a post-election cruise aboard Vincent Astor's yacht with his top backers and associates, including Kennedy. At night, lovely parties were prepared on shore; at one of these Honey Fitz and Josie were among the guests. Even Josie was caught up in the mood of excitement. "Isn't it wonderful," she exclaimed while waltzing with actor-producer Eddie Dowling, "my son-in-law Joe Kennedy has made FDR President."

Having tasted the pleasures of the campaign, Kennedy now looked forward to an even greater excitement ahead. Surely, if anyone was assured of an important administrative post, it was Joseph Kennedy.

# CHAPTER 26

# POLICING

# WALL

# STREET

ne by one, week by week, the men who had contributed to FDR's victory were offered a place in the Administration—all but Joseph Kennedy, who spent the winter in Palm Beach waiting for a phone call which never came. Mystified by the sudden change of heart in a man whom he had judged a friend, Kennedy considered filing a lawsuit against the Democratic National Committee for repayment of his campaign loan. But even as he prepared for battle and took to criticizing FDR openly, he continued to seek a path to the Administration, through Ray Moley, Bernard Baruch and Herbert Bayard Swope.

Later, Rose remembered a sultry evening in Palm Beach when the house was unusually empty and she and Joe were sitting alone in the living room. "All night," she recalled, "Joe kept trying to figure out what had happened to keep FDR from contacting him. Having been brought up by his father to believe in loyalty as the cardinal principle of politics, he simply did not understand why he alone had been left out. For months, he had given his full time and energy to the campaign, to say nothing of the money he had contributed, and now, for some inexplicable reason, FDR saw fit to ignore him. And then to make matters worse, there were all these stories in the press speculating on his possible appointment to this or that, as well as dozens of phone calls from friends asking when he'd be leaving for Washington. It was pretty humiliating and he was pretty hurt and angry."

As it turned out, unbeknownst to Kennedy, Roosevelt was caught in a conflict of loyalties, for Louis Howe, his best friend and closest assistant, was unalterably opposed to appointing Kennedy to any position. Apparently, the sixty-two-year-old Howe was opposed in principle to including a man with Kennedy's speculative background in an administration dedicated to reforming speculative greed. From his first meeting with Kennedy, when the brusque and diffident Howe had refused to be taken in by the Irishman's personal charm, the relationship between them had been cool and distant. But during the campaign, knowing that the "Boss" needed Kennedy's money, Howe kept his own counsel, and Kennedy assumed that Howe's gruffness was simply temperamental. Matters worsened, however, as reports filtered back to Howe at campaign headquarters in Albany of the friendship that seemed to be developing on the train between Kennedy and Roosevelt. As Rose later heard the story told, Howe was particularly upset by reports of the easy banter between the two men, the shared interests in movies and sports, the friendly competition for outdoing each other in telling great stories, the pleasure taken in laughing aloud. Jealous of anyone with whom FDR had a special relationship, Howe was determined to keep Kennedy out of the Administration.

Howe had first met Roosevelt in 1911 when Howe was forty-one years old, a newspaper reporter in Albany, and Roosevelt was a young man of thirty, a member of the New York legislature. After watching Roosevelt in his first term in the State Senate, Howe decided that he ought to be President of the United States, and from that moment on, to Howe politics was one man.

For over two decades, from when Roosevelt was Assistant Secretary of the Navy through his comeback from polio to his successful campaign for governor, Howe had committed his life to Roosevelt. The two men were strikingly different in temperament. Whereas Roosevelt was a large, cheerful, social person, a man who was happiest in public life, Howe was a small, shy man, secretive and abrupt by nature. An ugly man, his face pitted with scars, his nose bulbous, his clothes rumpled and dirty, Howe often joked about how children fled from his protruding eyes, and he sometimes likened himself to a character out of Dickens. Howe had been frail as a boy, the victim of asthma, bronchitis and a persistent heart murmur, and looked all his life like a shriveled old man who needed six months' rest in Florida. But beneath his shell of weariness lay a tremendous hidden energy which he focused solely on the interests of his hero and friend. Working sixteen hours a day, he seldom went out in the evening; he never went to the theater, to the movies or to any sporting event. Yet, in spite of his obsessive personality, or perhaps because of it, he remained, in the opinion of many observers, the only man who could persuade Roosevelt to change his mind.

"Looking back now," Rose later said, underestimating the role that devotion to principle played, "I can see why Howe was threatened by Joe, for while Joe too could be brusque and abrupt, he could also be absolutely charming and his sense of humor perfectly coincided with President Roosevelt's. I just wish we had known at the time what was going on, for those months after the election seemed very long indeed."

A proud man, Kennedy did not find it easy to initiate contact with Roosevelt, but in the spring of 1933 he sent the President several letters, all of which received polite replies but no mention of an appointment. To Missy LeHand, Roosevelt's secretary, he revealed a measure of his longing. "I read and hear about you all of the time," he told Missy on May 19, 1933, the day after legislation to create the Tennessee Valley Authority was signed into law, "and know that you must be terribly happy to think that things are going so well for your Boss and the country. I do miss seeing you and having a laugh, but maybe that will come one of these days."

In his letters to William Randolph Hearst, however, Kennedy was equally capable of speaking about the President and the state of the Union with disdain, knowing that the influential publisher had grown increasingly disillusioned with Roosevelt. "My interest in politics and national affairs has not ceased," Kennedy telegraphed to Hearst in December of 1933.

MY CONTACT CEASED FROM THE DAY WHEN A CERTAIN GENTLEMAN NEGLECTED TO SEND A TELEGRAM TO YOU URGING YOU TO COME TO NEW YORK WHICH HE TOLD ME HE WOULD DO. IN SPITE OF MY VERY CLOSE CONNECTIONS DURING THE CAMPAIGN I HAVE NEVER SEEN HIM FROM THAT DAY TO THIS. I AM VERY HOPEFUL THAT YOUR STAND ON PUBLIC QUESTIONS WILL IN THE NEXT YEAR AS IT HAS SO EXTENSIVELY IN THE PAST YEAR KEEP THE SHIP ON AN EVEN KEEL. IT IS THE ONLY INFLUENCE LEFT IN AMERICA THAT CAN TAKE A DEFINITE STAND.

After many months, Kennedy finally learned that Louis Howe was the source of his undoing. That knowledge gave him some measure of optimism, for at least now he could begin working around Howe to influence Roosevelt. Writing to his reporter friend Louis Ruppel, Kennedy was even able to joke about Howe in telling the tale of a broken leg he had received from a fall off a horse.

> By a strange coincidence, the horse's name was "Louis," named after you I hope, not after the President's secretary, Mr. Howe. But then, after all, I have been thrown pretty consistently by Louises this year. I will recover, however, and press on to greater efforts. Moore suggests that I ride one of those horses that they put in swimming pools, and when I fall off, I can only get wet.

While he waited to hear from Roosevelt, Kennedy returned to Wall Street and his old ways. Why fight for reform when he was excluded from the reformist spirit of the Hundred Days? While recognizing that the system itself would soon be changed, Kennedy was not about to become a preacher without a pulpit. Besides, there was still good money to be made in the market, particularly if one felt no compunction about selling short or joining in pools, the very activities the reformers were determined to terminate. As he resumed his trading, Kennedy joined hands with Henry Mason Day, a senior partner of Redmond and Company, a long-established brokerage firm with offices on Broad Street. It was a strange choice, for while the firm had a good reputation, Day himself was still tainted by an old scandal stretching back to the Teapot Dome which had landed him in jail. For a man who dreamed of entering public life, the association with Day was risky, but, as always, Kennedy knew how to lessen his risks: the name that appears on all the accounts of the company records is Edward E. Moore, not Joseph P. Kennedy.

There is no way of knowing the full extent of Kennedy's complicated maneuvers in the market of 1933. But, from the financial statements which still remain in his private papers, it is clear that he was dealing in hundreds of thousands of dollars and that most of his profits came from driving various company stocks down by selling short. (A "bear" borrows stock for a time from a broker for a fee. He then delivers these borrowed shares to the buyer, collects payment and waits for the price to fall. Once it does, he buys shares at a lower price and gives them back to the broker to replace those he borrowed. The bear makes his profit on the difference between the price at which he sells the borrowed shares and the replacement cost.) In one account, labeled "Edward E. Moore, Esquire," there is recorded a credit of $308,277.50 of a short sale of 4,000 shares of National Distillers as well as a credit of $40,648.55 for a short sale of 974 shares of Auburn Auto. In another account, simply labeled "Account Number 96," in the space of one week in February a credit of $23,750 is given for a short sale of 400 shares of American Can, $27,300 for a short sale of 700 shares of Du Pont de Nemours, $51,875 for a short sale of 2,500 shares of Loew's and $27,562.50 for a short sale of 900 shares of Westinghouse Electric.

As he made himself hundreds of thousands of dollars, Kennedy displayed an extraordinary lack of concern for the effect of his profiteering on the continually declining market. All through the campaign, his voice had been clear on the need to reform the speculative system in order to protect the ordinary man. Yet now that he was being snubbed by Roosevelt, he was capable of ignoring everything he had said in order to act in his own self-interest.

And all these sales were taking place at a time when both Republicans and Democrats were joined in a full-scale attack against those who were profiteering from the depression. Indeed, only the year before, Herbert Hoover, believing that the bear raiding tactics of professional stock manipulators were to blame for the depressed market, had launched an investigation into short selling. Had Kennedy tried, he could not have chosen a riskier time to reenter the market, for if his extensive short selling had been uncovered his name would probably have carried too much odium for public office.

As it was, the only activity from this period that would later come back to haunt Kennedy was his participation in an immensely profitable pool in the stock of the Libby-Owens-Ford Glass Company. In the atmosphere of excitement which surrounded the anticipated end of Prohibition, the hottest stocks on the market were those which related in any way to liquor. Recognizing the intensity of the "repeal stocks," Mason Day came up with an idea of boosting a stock that only appeared to be caught up in the coming liquor boom. With the help of Elisha Walker of Kuhn, Loeb and Company, Day hit upon the idle stock of the Libby-Owens-Ford company, a manufacturer of plate glass. While in fact the company had nothing to do with making bottles and its business was in no way enhanced by the repeal of Prohibition, its name could easily be confused with the Owens-Illinois Glass Company, which was a bottle manufacturer, especially when the operators of the pool, by their active buying and selling, fomented a deceptive appearance of genuine demand for the stock. As the price of the dormant stock began to rise, thousands of unsuspecting people scrambled to get in on the ground floor, driving the price way up from $26 to $37, at which time, exactly three weeks after their initial purchases, the members of the pool pulled out with a profit of $395,238, leaving the public to cope with the sudden collapse. As a partner with a one-sixth share, Kennedy made a profit of $60,805.

While he was exploiting the liquor mania, Kennedy was also establishing himself as a major player in the emerging liquor industry. Having been aware since the summer of 1932 of Roosevelt's deeply critical attitude toward Prohibition, Kennedy had given much deliberation to the question of where and how he should enter the industry. With Roosevelt pushing for repeal, he correctly figured, it was only a matter of time until the required thirty-six states ratified the Twenty-first Amendment, which called for repeal of the Eighteenth and thus would bring about the demise of the notorious Volstead Act—the law that for more than a decade had held legal drinks in America to less than one half of one percent alcohol.

All through the "dry" twenties, Kennedy had been surrounded by rumors suggesting his involvement in the illicit liquor trade. For one thing, he seemed to have easy access to large private supplies of liquor whenever a festive occasion demanded it. It was Kennedy who supplied the liquor for his tenth reunion at Harvard; it was Kennedy who repeatedly arranged to sell liquor at cost to a large circle of his friends and acquaintances. In the early twenties, some of this supply undoubtedly came from P. J. Kennedy's private stock, stored in the cellar of his Winthrop home during the last days of legal liquor in January 1920. Interviewed later, Helen Barron still remembered "the hectic rush in those last days before Prohibition to get all the remaining liquor from the shelves of P. J. Kennedy's retail store into the basement of his home. Everyone was involved in the carrying and the storage, even Joe's sisters, Margaret and Loretta." While P. J. stored the hard liquor, Joe filled his Brookline cellar with bottles of wine which he later valued at thousands of dollars in reporting a robbery at his Brookline home in November 1922.

At the same time, Kennedy had personal access, through his father, to a Mr. Dehan who was considered one of the best distillers in the Boston area. In a letter to Matt Brush written on June 26, 1922, Kennedy noted that Brush was interested in getting hold of some gin.

Before selling it to you I would like you to get the whole story on it. The committee on our Decennial at Harvard bought 190 proof alcohol, and had it blended and fixed up by a Mr. Dehan, who formerly worked for my father, and who really is one of the best men on this in this part of the country. The stuff turned out very well, indeed, and was perfectly satisfactory to all the fellows in the class who are, of course, used to the best— and the worst. Twenty-five dollars is the actual cost of the stuff and I would be very happy to have you have it, if you think it would be satisfactory.

Beyond his father's supply of liquor, Kennedy also seemed to have access to a large supply of whiskey (eight hundred bottles) which had been stored in the Quincy Cold Storage Warehouse and which the Columbia Trust Company bought in 1925. According to a letter in Kennedy's papers, the deal was arranged by Honey Fitz's brother, James T. Fitzgerald, who earned $8,000 for making the sale. For James Fitzgerald and his younger brother Edward, both of whom had been profitably involved in the liquor business all their lives, Prohibition was a shattering experience. In the days before the First World War when James owned the Van Nostrand brewery, on the road to Everett, he had so much money that he would walk around with hundreds of dollars crunched in his pockets. In those same years Edward was the proprietor of the Hotel Warren in Charlestown as well as the owner of three successful bars in Boston.

Knowing no other business when Prohibition came, the two Fitzgeralds naturally drifted into the illicit liquor trade. With $40,000 of his own money, James bought a building on Atlantic Avenue in Boston which he turned into a speakeasy drugstore, containing a soda fountain, a magazine stand and a corner where medicinal prescriptions for liquor could be filled. Like thousands of its counterparts springing up all over the country, Fitzgerald's drugstore profited from a major loophole in the Volstead Act which provided that doctors and druggists could legally prescribe liquor to patients for all manner of curious illnesses. During the fourteen years of Prohibition, historian Andrew Sinclair points out, ten million doctors prescribed more than one million gallons of liquor each year to soothe the ailments of sick Americans.

Beyond the liquor legally dispensed by prescription, the Fitzgerald drugstore also provided a back room, hidden from view, where liquor was illegally sold at high prices. During the twenties, the number of such speakeasies reached an estimated 219,000, only slightly less than the number of saloons on the eve of Prohibition. "The drugstore and soda fountain were located right on Rose Wharf," James's nephew Tom later recalled, "and the layout of the building was such that the back room stretched out over the harbor. It was rigged so that if it were raided, they could pull a lever and the whole thing would go into the sea. He kept it going this way for years until Deputy Wall finally got him."

With Rose's uncle as a built-in market, it is possible, as some people have claimed, that Joe Kennedy got involved in financing illegal shipments of liquor from Canada or the Bahamas. Over the years, countless stories have surfaced from people who claim to have seen Joe Kennedy standing on the rocky Gloucester shore, watching for his boats to come in, a romantic image of derring-do which links him with the old Yankees whose original money came from the opium trade with China. If the stories are true—and no hard evidence has yet been produced—it is most likely that Kennedy was involved in the early twenties, when a host of small bootleggers and rumrunners competed for the profits of the trade. Mobster Frank Costello, just before his death, claimed that early in his own career he had been a partner of Kennedy's in the liquor trade.

It is harder to imagine Kennedy still involved during the middle to late twenties, after the large criminal gangs had taken over and fundamentally changed the nature of the illicit trade. For one thing, he could scarcely have had time to compete with the big liquor bosses when his mind was as preoccupied as it was by Wall Street and Hollywood. For another, when the Wall Street racket was working as well as it was, why should a man of Kennedy's strengths risk all his gains on a venture he could never hope to control without full-time involvement? "Talk about liquor, textile, taxicab or other rackets," A. P. Giannini wrote to Joe Kennedy after the crash, "none in the world can compare with the Wall Street racket. It is the most ruthless and destructive racket in the world." But it was also, as Kennedy had learned, a racket in which great riches could be made.

If history fails to record the full measure of Kennedy's involvement with the illicit liquor trade in the twenties, we do know that his intimate familiarity with medicinal permits, sources of supply and distributorships provided him with a substantial advantage in the thirties as the end of Prohibition grew near. Determining that his best entry into the liquor trade lay in securing the American distributorships for high-class English liquors, Kennedy decided to make a trip to Europe in September 1933 with the purpose of negotiating a deal with Haig & Haig, Dewar's and Gordon's. Knowing that the competition for these franchises would be intense, since they were virtually licenses to become rich, Kennedy invited President Roosevelt's son Jimmy and his wife, Betsy, to travel with him and Rose to London.

Since the days of the campaign in 1932, Jimmy Roosevelt and Joe Kennedy had become close friends. Roosevelt, a spirited and ambitious young man, was determined to make it on his own in business, and in this effort he frequently sought out Joe Kennedy's advice. Working as the representative in Boston for the Travelers Insurance Company, Roosevelt managed, partly through Joe, to persuade the top officials at Hayden, Stone, the National Shawmut Bank and the First National Bank to switch their insurance to Travelers. For these and other favors, including several loans, Roosevelt was most thankful. "I can't tell you how much I appreciate what you did for me," Jimmy wrote to Joe on May 19, 1933, after receiving a check, "and anyway words mean so little that I hope that my actions will sometime make you realize how really grateful I will always be."

The favor was returned when Jimmy agreed to accompany Kennedy to status-conscious London, where the President's son was viewed as America's Prince of Wales. There Kennedy and Roosevelt met with the top men in the British liquor trade, and within two months Kennedy was able to close a deal which would be worth millions of dollars in the years ahead. Writing to his son Joe Junior on December 4, 1933, Kennedy revealed that he had closed "with the Englishmen for the distribution of Haig & Haig & Dewar." Speaking especially warmly of Tom Wilkinson on the Haig side and William Harrison of Black and White, Kennedy informed his son that he was creating a new importing company in New York and putting Ted O'Leary in charge. The name of the firm was to be the Somerset Company—an intriguing choice, suggesting the continuing presence in his mind of the old Somerset Club, that powerful Protestant enclave on Beacon Street which still prohibited Catholics from entering its front door.

Correctly anticipating the success of his negotiations, Kennedy had moved, weeks before the franchise was secure, to obtain two huge medicinal permits from Washington which allowed him, even before Prohibition ended, to bring in one large shipment of Haig & Haig "medicine" and another of Dewar's "medicine." His supplies stockpiled in warehouses, Kennedy was in an ideal position on the night of December 4, with legal liquor sales only a matter of hours away. As the nation prepared for the end of Prohibition—which officially arrived on December 6 when Utah, the last of the necessary thirty-six states, furnished by vote of its convention the constitutional majority for the ratification of the Twenty-first Amendment—the newspapers warned that a drastic shortage of everything was probable for the next few days. "Cocktails will be a quarter almost everywhere," the Boston Transcript predicted. "Wines will be fantastically high. Scotch whiskey is virtually unobtainable." What pleasure Joe Kennedy must have received from reading these predictions, knowing that even at that moment thousands of bottles of the best British whiskey were making their way from his warehouse into the hands of hundreds of retailers, where they would soon be sold at a great personal profit to him!

While Kennedy was becoming richer and richer through his dealings in liquor and stocks, the Senate Banking and Currency Committee was just beginning its historic investigation into the whole pattern of stock exchange activity which allowed the few, time and again, to take advantage of the many. Spurred on by a growing mood of resentment toward "the Street," the Senate investigation attracted hundreds of reporters each day to the Senate Caucus Room, where, under the tall windows and the glittering crystal chandeliers, a small Italian with flashing black eyes by the name of Ferdinand Pecora, the investigating subcommittee's counsel, was calling many of the nation's most prestigious financiers before the public. For more than a year, these sensational hearings would continue, producing amazing admissions of wrongdoing from a parade of leading bankers and brokers—admissions of the taxes they had avoided (in 1931 and 1932 neither J. P. Morgan II nor any of his fabulously wealthy partners had paid any income tax in America), the pools they had rigged, the holding companies they had launched and the bad investments they had passed off time and again upon an unsuspecting public.

Pecora had been born in Sicily, the first child of a poor shoemaker. He was an indefatigable worker who examined witnesses all day and then stayed up half the night in his rooms at the Mayflower Hotel with his devoted staff to prepare for the next day's session. Brilliantly suited to the task at hand, the short, cigar-smoking immigrant with dark curly hair provided a striking contrast to the tall silver-haired bank officials who paraded through the Caucus Room, accompanied by their retinues of lawyers and accountants.

The great success of Pecora's investigation—which resulted eventually in the Truth-in-Securities Act of 1933 and the Securities and Exchange Act of 1934—came primarily from his uncommon skill at collecting, analyzing and assimilating large quantities of data concerning his witnesses' activities. Speaking without notes, he amazed even his own talented staff with his photographic memory. "I looked with astonishment," wrote John Flynn, the financial editor of *The New Republic*, who served on Pecora's staff, "at this man who, through the intricate maze of banking syndicates, market deals, chicanery of all sorts and in a field new to him, never forgot a name, never made an error in a figure and never lost his temper." Retaining his own dignity and composure at all times, despite numerous attempts on the part of the witnesses to patronize him, Pecora so dominated the proceedings that *his* name rather than the committee chairman's became irrevocably identified with the hearings.

Since Pecora generally knew ahead of time, from the work he and his staff had done, the answers he could expect to elicit from the testimony of almost every witness—ranging from J. P. Morgan II of Morgan and Company to Richard Whitney, president of the New York Stock Exchange—and since he had proof to challenge any witness who lied, he could proceed in a genial fashion, inexorably drawing forth the disclosures he wanted. As a consequence, the American public was treated to a shocking series of revelations about the country's banking and securities practices, involving practically all the important names in the financial community.

At the same time, the Senate subcommittee amassed an enormous store of information about what was wrong with the stock market, which the Roosevelt Administration put to immediate use in calling for a new regulatory commission to compel disclosure of information, force investigations and control margins. The legislation, drafted by a talented group of New Dealers, originally called for specific prohibitions against all forms of stock manipulations, such as short selling, pools and wash sales, but in the give-and-take of a Congress still responsive to the outraged cries of Wall Street, the bill that emerged eschewed flat prohibitions and left almost everything to the discretion of the new Securities and Exchange Commission.

Even with the compromises made, the new law represented a definite advance. For the first time, the authority of the federal government was asserted over the whole field of security markets. After sixteen long months of exhaustive work, Pecora could rightly take pride in the accomplishments of his dedicated staff as he stood in the Oval Office on June 6, 1934, and received a presidential pen at the signing of the law. Even at the signing, knowledgeable observers were already predicting Pecora as the obvious choice for the new chairman. During the entire investigation, Pecora had been living on a meager salary of $225 a month. Clearly, his work had been a labor of love, but at this point, many felt, the President owed him something substantial in return. Moreover, given the wide discretion granted the newly created commission, it was obvious to all that with the President's appointees rested success or failure of the law. Pecora dropped a hint to that effect at the signing ceremony. "Ferd, now that I have signed this bill and it has become law, what kind of a law will it be?" the President asked. "It will be a good bill or a bad bill, Mr. President, " Pecora replied, "depending upon the men who administer it."

In the days that followed the signing, there was much talk in the press about the possible makeup of the commission. While it was taken for granted that Pecora would get the chairmanship, the names mentioned for the other four positions included James Landis, a member of the Federal Trade Commission, who had been involved in the drafting of the law; George Matthews, another trade commissioner; Robert Healy, a justice from the state of Vermont who had been made chief counsel of the FTC; and Frank Shaughnessy, president of the San Francisco Stock Exchange.

But, while the press focused its light on Pecora, Roosevelt was considering a very different man, a man recommended for the chairmanship by Raymond Moley—Joseph P. Kennedy. Asked by the President to make a list of possible appointments to the SEC, Moley, who was now chief of Roosevelt's academic advisers, placed Kennedy's name at the top. "The best bet for Chairman," he wrote, "because of executive ability, knowledge of habits and customs of business to be regulated, and ability to moderate different points of view on Commission." To Roosevelt's mind, the suggestion of Kennedy was an excellent one. Having roused the financial community by the passage of the law, he now hoped to assuage it with the appointment of a man they could trust.

As word of Roosevelt's thinking drifted out, however, a storm of criticism built up and the President began to waver. Louis Howe complained that assigning Kennedy to police Wall Street was like setting a cat to guard the pigeons. Friends of Pecora tried to talk the President into making Kennedy simply a member of the commission while reserving the chairmanship for Pecora. On the afternoon of June 28, Roy Howard of the Scripps-Howard newspaper chain came into the Oval Office to offer the opinion that Kennedy's appointment would be disastrous. Unsatisfied by Roosevelt's response, Howard rushed to his Washington paper, the *News*, to dictate an editorial for the late edition. "The President," the *Washington News* declared, "cannot with impunity administer such a slap in the face to his most loyal and effective supporters as that reported to be contemplated in the appointment of Joseph P. Kennedy."

Confused about which way to go, Roosevelt sent for Kennedy, Moley and Bernard Baruch. The three men arrived at the White House on Saturday evening, June 30. It was a hot, muggy night in Washington, the start of a record heat wave in which the temperature in some of the old government buildings reached 110.

According to Moley's account, Kennedy arrived at the White House in an unusually pensive mood. While he had been warned by Roy Howard, whom he knew and even liked, that he would be torn to pieces in the paper if he took the job, he was not prepared for the bitter tone of Howard's editorial. Surely if Howard felt so strongly against the appointment, the criticism was just beginning. Already there had been talk of his involvement in the Libby-Owens-Ford pool, for this was one of the pools which the Senate investigation specifically condemned, and Kennedy recognized that once the appointment was made official the stories and investigations would multiply a hundredfold.

"Mr. President," Kennedy began, "I don't think you should do this. I think it will bring down injurious criticism." At this point, Moley, familiar with the workings of Kennedy's mind, interrupted. "Joe, I know darned well you want this job. But if anything in your career in business could injure the President, this is the time to spill it. Let's forget the general criticism that you've made money in Wall Street."

Kennedy reacted then precisely as Moley had anticipated. "With a burst of profanity," Moley recalled, "he defied anyone to question his devotion to the public interest or to point to a single shady act in his whole life. The President did not need to worry about that, he said. What was more, he would give his critics—and here again the profanity flowed freely—an administration of the SEC that would be a credit to the country, the President, himself and his family—clear down to the ninth child."

Kennedy's emotional outburst sealed the appointment in Roosevelt's mind. Saying all along it would take a thief to catch a thief, Roosevelt believed, against Howe's advice, that only a man who knew Wall Street from the inside could put a clamp on its illicit practices. At the same time, with his great intuition at work, Roosevelt assumed that, having made his pile, Kennedy would now like to make a name for himself for the sake of his family. Telling Kennedy that the appointment was set, Roosevelt relaxed in his chair, called for a round of beer, and settled in for a late night of easy talk which kept Kennedy, Moley and Baruch in his office until well past midnight.

The decision to make an insider the first chairman of the SEC seemed to some a brilliant stroke, the perfect way of giving those on Wall Street who were friendly to the purpose of the regulatory law an opportunity to prove their willingness to cooperate. But to ardent liberals who had followed the hearings for sixteen months and had placed great hope in the new commission, the appointment of Kennedy was seen as an act of betrayal. Writing in *The New Republic*, John Flynn expressed the anger and shock of many New Dealers: "Had FDR's dearest enemy accused him of an intention of making so grotesque an appointment as Joseph Kennedy to the Chairman of the SEC, the charge might have been laid to malice. Yet the President has exceeded the expectations of his most ardent ill wishers."

"Of course," Flynn continued the following week, "I did not in my wildest dreams imagine he [FDR] would appoint a speculator as Chairman." There were various groups on Wall Street, he went on; at the bottom were the speculators. "Who, I ask, would have believed, as Pecora last February unfolded the sorry tale of repeal pools, that the President of the US would have gone to this class? I say it isn't true. It is impossible. It could not happen."

For Pecora, the makeup of the commission posed a difficult problem.

Upon first hearing not only that Kennedy was Roosevelt's choice for chairman, but that Kennedy had been given the longest term, five years, while he himself had been accorded the shortest, one year, Pecora had considered refusing the appointment. But he knew that his refusal to serve would undermine the commission before it even began to function, thereby undoing all the hard work of so many months. On the other hand, he found himself in a particularly embarrassing situation, for he had been so certain of being chosen as chairman that he had already wired the Senate investigating subcommittee announcing that he would proudly accept.

The swearing in of the new commissioners was scheduled to take place at 3 P.M. on July 2, 1934, in the old gray stucco building on Connecticut Avenue which housed the Federal Trade Commission. But when the time approached, the commissioners were still sitting behind closed doors, locked in an argument over who should be chairman. By law, though FDR had already made known his own preference for Kennedy, the five commissioners were technically responsible for electing one of their number as chairman. And that morning, as Pecora boarded the train in New York, he had let it be known that he intended to be chairman or he would resign.

Never one to leave anything to chance, however, Kennedy had arrived in Washington the night before and had spent all morning—while Pecora sat on the train—preparing the ground for his election. Stopping first at the White House, he picked up from Marvin McIntyre, secretary to the President, a scribbled note which Roosevelt had written earlier informing Landis, Matthews and Healy that he wanted Kennedy as chairman. Armed with the note, Kennedy walked directly to the office of James Landis at the FTC. Robust, self-confident and anxious to win approval, Kennedy took care to show the proper respect for Landis' talents. "After that morning," Landis later commented, "I came out with the conclusion that . . . he was the best man." With Matthews and Healy already on board, there remained only the problem of Pecora.

When Pecora finally arrived, minutes before the scheduled 3 P.M. swearing-in ceremony, the temperature had hit 93 degrees outside, and in the hot stucco structure, put up for temporary quarters during the First World War, it was probably ten degrees hotter. In the corridor, anxious reporters, assuming that a major battle was about to begin, mopped their brows as Pecora, his face grim and beaded with perspiration, walked by headed for Landis' office. Emotions heightened further when Pecora and Landis remained alone in the room behind closed doors, while Kennedy, Matthews and Healy were huddled in Matthews' office four doors away. As three o'clock came and went, the two groups remained in separate offices, with Landis continually in motion from one to the other. "He looked very solemn as he passed back and forth," the reporter for *The New York Times* observed, "and refused to answer any questions." Finally, when more than an hour had elapsed, Kennedy emerged from Matthews' office and was escorted by Landis to the office containing Pecora.

Another hour passed. Then, suddenly, the door of Landis' office opened and Kennedy, Landis and Pecora emerged and proceeded down the hall to Matthews' office. They were smiling, reporters observed, with Pecora and Kennedy marching side by side and in perfect step, "as chipper as two long-parted and suddenly reunited brothers."

With Pecora won over, Kennedy was unanimously elected chairman and at last, under flashing bulbs, the five members of the new Securities and Exchange Commission took their oath of office. Answering questions later that day, both Pecora and Kennedy smilingly shrugged off queries as to the subject of the two-hour meeting, and Kennedy had nothing but praise for Pecora and Landis. "I'm no sucker," he told reporters. "They know more about this law than I ever hope to know. They put their blood into it." As for his own participation in the very activities the new SEC was created to abolish, he simply said, "I am what I am." But, he went on, there was a long time between then and when the Congress would meet again the next January to confirm the appointment. "I believe that between now and then there will be plenty of time for me to prove whether I'm worth keeping on the Commission. I know that if I am, I will be kept."

With the press prepared for war, Kennedy then disarmed his critics with a reference to his family. "Boys," he said, "I've got nine kids. The only thing I can leave them that will mean anything is my good name and reputation. I intend to do that and when you think I'm not doing so, you sound off."

Building further on the foundation of his impressive start, Kennedy managed to secure Pecora's high praise before two weeks were out. When asked about the initial rift between the two, Pecora spoke in glowing words of his faith in Kennedy's leadership. "I think Kennedy brings to the commission a knowledge of Wall Street," he said. "He has experience which is far better than any knowledge from intense study. I like him immensely . . . I think the man is of sound judgment and he knows how to do things."

During his days at the SEC, Kennedy lived with Eddie Moore in a lavish 125-acre estate deep in the Maryland countryside, which he rented for a year with the assumption that his entire family would move to Washington. But as Joe and Rose talked the situation through, rec-

ognizing that Joe intended to stay in Washington only until the SEC
was put on its feet, they both decided it made little sense to uproot the
younger children from their schools, their parish, their doctors and their
dentists. So Kennedy and Moore lived like potentates at Marwood, the
thirty-three-room French Renaissance mansion built on the Potomac
by Samuel Klump Martin III, heir to one of Chicago's great retailing
fortunes. A beautiful gray-and-green château, Marwood could pass for
a small hotel, with a living room the size of a lobby, a dining room
replicating one in which King James I sat in England, a large library and
twelve master bedrooms complete with dressing rooms and baths. In the
basement there was a recreation room large enough for several billiard
tables and three Ping-Pong tables, and below the recreation room was a
movie theater with seats for a hundred guests. Set against a dense green
background, Marwood was flanked by a large swimming pool with guest
bath houses.

Living in the countryside suited Kennedy well, for he was able to
direct his energies as he chose, steering clear of the dinner parties in
Washington while making his home a place of great warmth, relaxation
and pleasure for his friends and, occasionally, his female companions.
"Joe took good care of himself," said a friend. "He didn't smoke or drink.
He ate well. He slept. He exercised. You have to admire the organized
human material—not a bit of waste." In the mornings he rode his horse
for a half hour before work. After dinner, he liked to relax by listening
to classical records. Throughout his life, Joe's love of classical music
would confound his friends, who relentlessly teased him to put on some
livelier tunes. "You dumb bastards," he retorted, "you just don't appreciate culture."

While he lived at Marwood, Kennedy played host on several occasions
to President Roosevelt. As the President's confidence in Kennedy's ability deepened, the friendship grew stronger. And Marwood proved the
perfect place for the President to relax in. The splendid château seemed
centuries removed from the daily demands of everyday life, but the drive
from the White House took less than half an hour. An account of one
of these festive evenings at Marwood was provided by *New York Times*
reporter Arthur Krock.

Krock had been invited to Marwood as a guest for the last weekend in
June 1935. The lazy hours of sun and talk were interrupted at Sunday
noon by a telephone call from the White House. It was the President,
inquiring if he could drive out that evening for cocktails and dinner.
Consenting at once, Kennedy forgot to mention that Krock was in the
house, a presence that might prove awkward for Roosevelt, as Krock had
just that week taken the President to task for his manner of dealing with

Congress. Not wanting to intrude, Krock offered to leave, but then, "the day being intensely hot," he decided instead to stay in his quarters upstairs, "a voluntary prisoner."

A limousine drew up at seven o'clock with the President, his secretaries Missy LeHand and Grace Tully, John Burns, general counsel of the SEC, and Tommy Corcoran, the colorful presidential assistant, who arrived with his famous accordion in his hand.

"The party soon became very merry," Krock recorded in his memoirs; "it was impossible not to hear much of what went on." Apparently, the design of the house was such that the sounds from the terrace echoed clearly into the second floor, where Krock remained throughout the evening hidden from both the President and the five Secret Service men who accompanied him.

> The President's laughter rang out over all, and was most frequent. After a reasonable number of mint juleps, which the President (when they were proposed) said would be "swell," they dined in the same mood. At dinner, though I was trying not to listen, the President said one thing so loudly it was impossible not to overhear him. "If I could," he said, "the way I'd handle Senator Huey Long would be physically. He's a physical coward. I've told my fellows up there that the way to deal with him is to frighten him. But they're more afraid of him than he is of them."

After dinner, Kennedy had a projector and a screen set up on the lawn. The film was *Ginger*, a sentimental story which the President judged to be "one of the best in years." "Then," Krock recorded, "Mr. Corcoran took out his accordion and the real merriment began. The President joined in all the songs, in a rather nice tenor-baritone, and finally he took the instrument and performed creditably for one unfamiliar with it."

"The singing and talking went on until well after midnight," Krock observed, with Roosevelt seeming all the while—despite having been battered all week by Congress and the press—as if he had not a care in the world. Finally the eavesdropper fell asleep, "pondering the paradoxes of the men who occupy the highest office in the land."

During the early months of Kennedy's tenure as SEC chairman, Wall Street remained apprehensive, regarding him fearfully as "an erstwhile alley gamin eager to display and expose his old haunts and tricks to his newly found friends from the other side of the financial community." But, in speech after speech, Kennedy showed that his first priority was to bring about a resumption of new financing, promising that governmental supervision would be no hardship except to the crooked. "We of the SEC," he announced, "do not regard ourselves as coroners, sitting on the corpse of financial enterprise. On the contrary, we think of ourselves as the means of bringing new life into the body of the securities business." In the end, he predicted, if the new agency was able to protect the honest businessman from fraudulent dealers and stock swindlers, then "a New Deal in finance will be found to be a better deal for all."

Until the enactment of the Securities and Exchange Act, the stock exchanges had operated completely on their own. Despite a rising chorus of criticism over the years, their members had steadfastly refused to consider that the mechanics of exchange operations were matters of public interest. It was Kennedy's complex task to get all the various exchanges, including the New York Stock Exchange, to register with the SEC and make themselves subject for the first time to governmental regulation. Nine exchanges that refused to meet this requirement were closed, including the California Stock Exchange, the Boston Stock Exchange, and the Denver Stock Exchange.

From the start, Kennedy outlined two goals for the commission. The first was the adoption of laws, regulations and enforcement proceedings to abolish the major evils of the exchanges, such as wash sales and matched orders, both of which had been commonly used to give false pictures of stock activity. At the same time, false and misleading statements by brokers, dealers, sellers or buyers became a penal offense. During his first months as chairman, Kennedy tried to get the exchange to take care of such flagrant abuses on its own, but when the exchange dragged its feet the commission instituted proceedings against dozens of firms and individuals suspected of stock manipulations. In the first year alone, these proceedings led to the issuance of more than fifty injunctions.

But, even as he sought the goal of "full and adequate disclosure of relevant information for the investor," Kennedy never forgot that his prime goal was the resumption of capital investments essential to recovery. To achieve this latter goal, he had to walk a fine line between the liberals on the commission, who were out to punish business with what he considered unduly harsh restrictions, and the conservatives in the business community who defiantly refused any sort of cooperation. Defining his task as that of making Wall Street legitimate again to the American public, Kennedy insisted that the commission aim its rules at the most flagrantly dishonest practices, saving the rest for another day after normal business had resumed. In this way, he argued, he could rally to his side all those "good" financiers who wanted to separate themselves out from the "bad."

Once again, as in the successful mediating role he had played in the movie industry in the backlash of several scandals, Kennedy displayed a special insight into the national mood, an acute understanding that the financial scandals had produced a crisis of legitimacy for the entire brokerage industry. Though he himself had stepped over the ethical line hundreds of times in the preceding decade, he was now willing to change the rules, even if it meant a short-term loss of profit, in order to preserve what he already had. Deeply affected by the fear that uncontrolled economic individualism would topple the entire capitalist structure, Kennedy finally came down on the side of the ordinary stockholder.

As it turned out, Kennedy's chairmanship of the SEC would comprise his finest hours in public service. "It was a real achievement," the *Kansas City Star* wrote, "for the administration to find a wizard who was able to take what was regarded as an unworkable act and make it work and make the moneyed interests like it." And while he sustained the confidence of the business community, he also earned the strong support of reformers, displaying a remarkable political acumen that allowed him to adapt himself to various warring groups while affecting their reconciliation in the process.

Working day and night, Kennedy assembled an uncommonly talented staff, including John J. Burns, former judge of the Massachusetts Superior Court, Yale Professor William O. Douglas and New Deal lawyer Abe Fortas. "You are such a swell administrator," Douglas later wrote, "that all of us have felt we were working for you personally." Writing in a similar tone, Fortas admitted he was sort of "an old timer (as things go with the administration), but I never dreamed it possible that work for the government could be as pleasant and unfettered as it has been under you and Landis. I believe you have done an unparalleled job of setting up an organization in which men can breathe and work with a minimum of the tapes that bind."

"It was significant," SEC historian Ralph de Bedts observed, "that only fifteen months after the first commissioners of the new agency had taken their oath of office, spokesmen for the business world could say 'the SEC was generally considered the New Deal's most significant reform.' At the same time, it was noted that the 'SEC has drafted its administrative rulings so meticulously that it has thus far been challenged in the courts far less than any other New Deal agency.'"

Having promised Roosevelt that he would stay only long enough to get the commission on its feet, Kennedy decided to resign in September of 1935. "I'm proud of you," Clem Norton wrote from the Boston City Council. "You're quitting at just the proper time. No big man stays too long in a job. Your resignation increases your stature ten times. And it is all done with such finesse, such tact . . . You handled yourself better than any Irish American of our day to hold high office. You made the way easier for others of your kind who will come after you."

When news of his resignation hit the wires, Kennedy received glowing editorial tributes in papers and magazines all across the country. But no words could have pleased him more than the public apology he received from John Flynn, his harshest liberal critic at the time of his appointment. "When Joseph Kennedy was named by President Roosevelt as a member of the SEC and in effect made its chairman," Flynn admitted in the October issue of *The New Republic*, "I expressed in this department a sharp criticism of the appointment . . . I ventured some criticisms of his record in a business which, I thought, made his appointment unwise. Now Mr. Kennedy has resigned as Chairman of the Commission. And I think it but fair to him to say that he disappointed the expectations of his critics. He was, I firmly believe, the most useful member of the Commission."

# CHAPTER 27
# THE
# MODEL SON
# AND THE
# PIED PIPER

By the time Joe Junior, Jack and Kathleen had reached their teens, in the middle of the 1930s, they were welded together into an elite family, sharing intense loyalties and myriad connections which would bind them tightly in the years ahead. Strikingly good-looking, with their high cheekbones and their gray-blue animated eyes, the three Kennedys were alike in their vitality, their sensuality, their cleverness and their particular brand of humor. Born within a five-year span, the three of them were enrolled in nearby boarding schools at about the same time, with Joe and Jack attending the Choate School in Wallingford, Connecticut, while Kathleen was at the Noroton Convent of the Sacred Heart not more than thirty miles away.

Had Rose had her way, the boys would have gone to parochial school or, failing that, to public school. A number of years later she confessed that this was one of the few areas where she and Joe had a serious disagreement. "If Joe wouldn't accept a Catholic school," Rose recalled, "I thought they should go to public school, where they'd meet the grocer's son and the plumber's son as well as the minister's son and the banker's son. They could have seen that some of those boys were even brighter than they were. But as it was, Joe took responsibility for the boys while I took charge of the girls." To Joe's mind, the advantage of the predominantly Protestant Choate lay in the social contacts it would offer. And beyond the contacts, he wanted his sons to walk in a world where preference and priority were assumed.

Having scrambled for his wealth, Kennedy wanted his children to start life on the heights to which he had lifted them. Freeing them from material concerns, he hoped to instill in them that natural confidence possible only to people who never had cause to doubt their social position. With three mansions and a retinue of servants and cooks, he hoped to create in his children that aristocratic ease of manner which he had first observed among the Brahmin students at Harvard when he was a freshman.

But, even as he treated his sons as princes and patterned their education after that of the Yankee gentleman, he insisted they work hard at what they did. The sense of privilege he inculcated in his children did not allow for laziness or lack of effort. If they were to move into the ranks of the most successful, they had to become a tiny aristocracy of talent, they had to *keep* striving so that the family victories could grow larger and larger. "It was an astonishing act of will," Garry Wills observed, "to create a kind of space platform out of his own career, one from which the children could fly out to their own achievements and come back for refueling."

People did not always take to the young Kennedys, feeling at times that they were centered in upon themselves and unappreciative of others. Living in a world so secure and so pleasant, they tended to take its fundamental values for granted. In the midst of the depression Jack confided to his father that he had not even learned about the market slump until months after it happened. Trained to do equally well in sports and in school, they were not able to endure the discipline necessary to really become masters of any one thing; preoccupied with their practical achievements, they could not achieve a full intellectual life. Yet their weaknesses came from too much exuberance, not too little. At all times they threw themselves into their opportunities with zest and vitality. If it was possible to dislike them, it was impossible to ignore them. For wherever they went, their high spirits created an immediate impression.

Still setting the pace, as he had done throughout their childhood, Joe Junior became a model student at Choate, respected by teachers, coaches and classmates alike. Choate, founded in 1896 by Episcopalians and modeled after Eton College, was situated in the beautiful rolling countryside of central Connecticut, with a spacious elm-shaded campus, large playing fields, eighteen tennis courts, stables, a gymnasium, an infirmary, a chapel, a library and a half-dozen or more classroom buildings of the Georgian type. In Joe's entering class there were only a scattering of Catholics and even fewer Jews. In those days, the standard application form included among its first dozen questions "Is the boy in any part Hebraic?" And among the regulations spelled out in the school's catalogue was the requirement that every boy, whatever his religious affiliation, attend a daily service in the school chapel.

In the thirties, the headmaster was George St. John, a tall, severe-looking man with hollow cheeks and a balding head, who, after more than twenty years at his post, still presided over the students and faculty with a strong, authoritarian hand. Demanding total loyalty from his faculty, who were expected to live in houses on the campus and perform triple duty as teachers, housemasters and coaches, St. John considered marriage an outside threat to the integrity of the school and required that faculty members receive his special consent if they wished to marry. Promising parents that the school would provide "efficient teaching, manly discipline, systematic exercise and association with boys of purpose," St. John instituted a system by which the average grades of each boy's work in his studies were given at the end of each fortnight, providing the basis for a biweekly talk by the housemaster with the student, analyzing causes of any failures and making constructive suggestions.

For young Joe, it must have been a little unnerving at first, having never been separated from his parents and siblings for more than a month, to find himself on his own in an entering class of 125 boys. The rules at Choate were strict: serious study was expected, and the work was difficult. Moreover, Choate was a school founded upon hierarchy, with the older boys—the sixth formers—enjoying many privileges, such as being first on all lines, skipping study hall and being allowed to leave assembly and prayers before the rest of the school.

Having always commanded his younger brothers and sisters, Joe found it difficult in the beginning to accept his subordinate position. On his first trip home, his younger brother Jack reported gleefully to their father, who was in California: "He was roughhousing in the hall a sixth former caught him, he led him in and all the sixth formers had a swat or two. Did the sixth formers lick him. O Man he was all blisters, they almost paddled the life out of him. What I wouldn't have given to be a sixth former. They have some pretty strong fellows up there if blisters have anything to do with it." Before long, however, Joe came to an understanding of the rules, and by the middle of his freshman year he had earned the respect of the older boys. At fourteen, Joe was physically sturdy, standing five feet six inches tall and weighing 130 pounds, and was considered "one of the most promising" of Choate's younger athletes. The physical director reported that he would be "watching his development with special interest."

The work was not easy for Joe, and his grades the first half of the year were poor. Yet, in all his letters to his father, there was such an earnestness in his approach that one imagined him doing far better than he actually was. In letter after letter, Joe reported that he was studying hard, going every Sunday to Mass and staying out of trouble. And when his grade in history slipped to seventy, he joined the Book-of-the-Month Club in an attempt to enlarge his vocabulary. "Mr. Hemenway says that is why I don't get very good marks in history," he explained to his father. "They have some swell books."

Eventually, young Joe's persistence paid off. "It is rare that quarterly grades come in climactic order," one of Joe's teachers commented on his report card for the last quarter of his freshman year. "Joe is better than ever." In every subject, his marks went up, bringing his average from fourth group to second. "Joe's determination has answered the problem of his failure for the first half of the year," his Latin teacher wrote, "and he has rightfully earned promotion." In English, the teacher commented, "Joe deserves a great deal of credit for turning defeat into victory," and his algebra teacher rated him "one of the ablest boys in my classes." From his housemaster as well, Joe received a glowing report. "He has been one of the most liveable boys in the whole house," Ben Davis wrote, "and he accepted discipline—not nearly as frequently necessary the latter portion of the year—with more grace and manliness than any other boy."

By the headmaster's standards, young Joe was an ideal student, a hard worker, a fine athlete and a good companion. Writing to Kennedy Senior during Joe's first year at Choate, St. John described Joe as "one of the most worthwhile people in the world. He has a high Academic Quotient, big heart and a young boy's way of doing things. I am betting on him 100%."

In time, young Joe fulfilled everyone's hopes. Possessed of an astonishing self-control and a practiced eye capable of discerning how best to meet the expectations of others, he soon became a dominant power on campus, winning varsity positions on the football and hockey teams, becoming the editor of the yearbook and accepting the vice-presidency of the Andrews Society, a student association devoted to charitable works.

Yet, for all his involvement with Choate, Joe was never so enmeshed with his friends or his activities that he lost sight of his dominant interest, his family. As the carrier of his family's ambition, he seemed to identify his whole being with his family's well-being; in his young soul, the desire for power and fame attained a force so intense that it tended to set him off from easygoing relations with his fellow students. At school, he talked about his family constantly, and to one or another of his sisters and brothers he wrote almost weekly. When he came home, where he was greeted by his younger brothers and sisters as a conquering hero, he headed straight for the nursery to lift the baby, Teddy, into his arms. Between the youngest and oldest sons there developed a special bond of love. Remembering a trip with Joe Junior to the Cape one weekend, a friend recalled, "The minute we got out of the car, Teddy came running up. Joe grabbed him and kissed him like a father would and hoisted him up to his shoulder. They were like father and son." When, after much lobbying with his father, young Joe got his first boat, he named it the *Teddy.*

Heading directly home on his vacations, Joe Junior established a family tradition of inviting schoolmates for visits, making the Kennedy household a lively center of activity which drew every child home as soon as school was out. "All day long, wherever the Kennedys were," Lem Billings recalled, "there was something going on. In Bronxville, we'd play touch football on the lawn; in Hyannis Port we'd go sailing or play tennis; in Palm Beach we'd gather by the swimming pool, where we'd talk and fool around for hours. Mr. Kennedy wanted his children with him as much as possible and he realized that unless he welcomed their friends, there might be countervailing pulls on them to go elsewhere for their vacations. Not that he paid that much attention to the friends, his mind was always on his own children. But so long as that splendid villa in Palm Beach was open to their friends, why should the kids choose to go elsewhere?"

Jack arrived at Choate in the fall of 1931 after a difficult year at Canterbury Prep, a Catholic school in Rhode Island, from which an undiagnosed illness had forced him to withdraw before the end of the term. Having spent the summer restoring his health and studying Latin with a tutor, he was, his family hoped, ready to take up the challenge of Choate. Eager to prepare the school for her second son's arrival, Rose informed Mr. St. John that while Jack hated routine work, history and English were subjects which fired his imagination. "He has a very attractive personality—we think—but he is quite different from Joe, for whom we feel you have done so much." It is a strange note, no doubt sent with the best of intentions, and yet, given St. John's obsession with making students understand what it meant to learn thoroughly and to take pains with even the most routine assignments, it must have sent a warning signal to the headmaster to beware of an indolent aspect of Jack's personality.

For years, it seems, faced with an eldest son who answered a mother's dream, handsome, neat, studious, and self-possessed, and a second son who didn't, who remained sloppy, irritating and undisciplined, Rose had a hard time hiding her preference, and this only exacerbated the advantage of age that Joe already possessed. Wherever Jack went, Joe had arrived before him and had already attained a stage of such successful control over his environment that Jack could not believe he would ever catch up. The frustration he must have experienced is described in another family by Henry James, who wrote that his older brother, William, "had gained such an advantage of me in his sixteen months' experience of the world before mine began that I never for all the time of childhood and youth in the least caught up with him or overtook him." Now, as the two boys were about to be pitted against each other in a school where Joe Junior was already one of the acknowledged kings, it should have been a time for Rose to sing Jack's praises and hope for the best.

When Jack arrived at Choate, skinny and tall for his fourteen years, Joe was already a fifth former, "one of the big boys of the school," as Mrs. St. John put it, with all the special privileges that went along with this second-to-highest ranking. To Jack, who had already grown a shell of detachment to protect himself from his exacting parents, the hierarchy at Choate was no different from the one he had experienced at home, and he responded in the oddly appealing way in which he had responded to similar challenges before—by refusing to emulate Joe, and by using his charm to build a cadre of loyal friends with whom he could shape his own path in his own way. It was a strategy which brought him freedom and independence, but the price was high, for by taking himself out of the academic competition he became accustomed to sloppy work, and once the habit of not working hard was deeply set it was hard to break, even when he later tried.

For his parents, Jack's nonchalant attitude toward his responsibilities was a source of constant frustration. Informed by Jack's teachers at Choate that he was intellectually bright but undisciplined, his father tried everything he could, from pressure to praise, to mobilize his second son. But the pattern continued: the resolutions Jack solemnly made to try harder were all too quickly broken, and his freshman grades found him in the second-to-last grouping. His reports picture him dropping his clothes on the floor wherever he took them off and flinging his wet towel onto the nearest table or chair with no regard for neatness.

On the playing fields, it was a different story. For here Jack *did* drive himself with everything he had, trying especially hard to excel in football, the area of his brother's greatest fame. Fighting hard, he was considered by his coach "a tower of strength" on the line, but, given his frail physique and his continual health problems—which caused him to make frequent visits to the infirmary for overnight stays—his best was good enough only for the junior squad. Nevertheless, he fought hard, going out also for baseball and basketball, as well as crew and golf, and his father respected his fight.

It was Jack's lack of organization that raised his father's ire and prompted him, at times, to write nagging letters to his son. "In looking over the monthly statement from Choate," Kennedy wrote in the spring of 1932, with an oblique reference to the notorious messiness of Jack's dormitory room, "I notice there is a charge of $10.80 for suit pressing for the month of March.* It strikes me this is very high and while I want to keep you looking well, I think that if you spent a little more time picking up your clothes instead of leaving them on the floor, it wouldn't be necessary to have them pressed so often."

Above all, Kennedy worried about his son's detached attitude toward his academic responsibilities. After a weekend visit to Choate in the fall of 1932, Kennedy expressed his feelings to Mr. St. John. Telling the headmaster he believed Jack was at a critical stage in his career, "that it would be quite easy for him to go ahead and be very much worthwhile or else slide off and get in with a group which regarded everything as a matter of fact," Kennedy confessed that after seeing him he feared he was *not* on the right track. While he did exceptionally well the work he wanted to do,

> he seems to lack entirely a sense of responsibility.
> The happy-go-lucky manner with a degree of indifference that he shows towards the things that he has no interest in does not portend well for his future development. I feel very, very sure that if responsibility can be pushed on his shoulders, not only in studies, but in other things, that he

* In the thirties, most students were able to get by with spending under ten dollars for dry cleaning for the entire school year; $8.50 was advertised as the total cost of picking up, pressing and delivering 120 pieces.

may decide to observe them. He has too many fundamentally good qualities not to feel that once he got on the right track he would be a really
worthwhile citizen.

At the same time, Kennedy wrote to Joe, asking him to help his
brother.

> Mr. Ayres told me that he has one of the few great minds he has ever had
> in history, yet they all recognize the fact that he lacks any sense of respon-
> sibility and it will be too bad if with the brains he has he really doesn't go
> as far up the ladder as he should. If you can think of anything that you
> think will help him, by all means do it.

This could not have been an easy letter for Kennedy to write. Nor was
it easy for him to admit, as he did in another letter to Choate, that some
of Jack's problems may have been rooted in the family. "We have possibly contributed as much as anybody in spoiling him by having secretaries and maids following him to see that he does what he should do,
and he places too little confidence on his own reliance."

In fact, the more likely source for Jack's irresponsibility lay in his
attempt, however misguided, to preserve his individuality amid the tremendous family pressures.

Yet, the strain between father and son never became an open break,
primarily because they both continued to entertain the hope that great
change was just around the corner. After a poor set of grades for one of
the quarters had been posted, Jack wrote a long letter to his father, more
direct and open than any written by Joe Junior, telling him that he had
definitely decided to stop fooling around; that he really felt, now that he
thought it over, that he had been bluffing about how much real work
he'd been doing.

Responding by return mail, Kennedy told his son he had gotten a
"great satisfaction" out of the letter.

> In fact, I think the improvement started when you made up your mind to
> write and there seems to be a forthrightness and directness that you are
> usually lacking. . . . [Y]ou know if I didn't really feel you had the goods I
> would be most charitable in my attitude toward your failings. After long
> experience in sizing up people I definitely know you have the goods and
> you can go a long way. Now aren't you foolish not to get all there is out
> of what God has given you and what you can do with it yourself.

Yet, in ways that neither Joe Kennedy nor the headmaster yet recognized, Jack was already leaving his mark on Choate, using the one

already emerged talent he had inherited from his father: the capacity for making friends. Right from the start, among a group of boys who were all new to one another in their freshman year, Jack was afraid of no one and held no one in awe. Operating from an inner core of deep self-confidence in his personality, he was able to form large numbers of friendships, some of which lasted weeks, others years and a few through-out his life. "When he flashed his smile," the headmaster's son, Seymour St. John, later recalled, "he could charm a bird off a tree."

Most of the students at Choate came from relatively affluent families living in New York, Connecticut, Massachusetts or Pennsylvania, with a scattering of scholarship students from a dozen other states. From the beginning, Jack developed a loyal following, but his most enduring friendship was formed with Kirk Le Moyne Billings, or "Lem," a warm, bearish boy with large features, unkempt blond hair and pale-blue eyes. They met as sophomores going out for the student yearbook, and, as Lem later described the relationship, "it was the closest friendship either of us ever knew." Although Lem was a scholarship student, he was descended from a family of Mayflower aristocrats and throughout his childhood, until his father lost a fortune in the stock market crash, he had lived a rich boy's life. Things were tougher after that, but as his father remained a noted physician in Pittsburgh, there was still money. Then, not long after Lem met Jack, his father died, leaving his mother without income and forcing Lem to rely on scholarships.

"I was immediately captivated by Jack," Lem later recalled. "He had the best sense of humor of anybody I had ever met and in his company I had more fun than I had ever had in my whole life. No matter where we went he knew how to make the outing a special occasion: if we were at a show together, he'd somehow manage to sneak backstage to see the leading singer, if we were eating out he'd be so charming to the waitress that we'd end up with an extra dessert. He enjoyed things with such intensity that he made you feel that whatever you were doing was abso-lutely the most wonderful thing you could possibly be doing."

They became Johnny and Billy or sometimes Ken and Le Moan, and in time their friendship became an essential in each of their lives, though Lem, as the more involved of the two, was more easily hurt by his friend's occasional aloofness. Never had Lem been taken over by anyone as much as he was by Jack; as the relationship developed, Jack would tell him when and where they were to meet and what they were going to do. Yet so completely was Lem lacking in guile and so warm and forthright was he in his affections that in time Jack came to count on the friendship almost as much as Lem did. Games, girls and sports, they approached every pleasure with equal zest, though in some ways their styles were very different, as Jack was the more spontaneous and uninhibited of the two. Undertaking the adolescent rites of passage together, they went one night to Harlem—in full evening dress—so that they could lose their virginity to the same prostitute.

Comfortable in the knowledge that he had a best friend, Jack reached out for other close friends as well, among them Ralph Horton, or "Rip," the son of a wealthy dairyman in New York. Soon Jack began to feel, as Lem later put it, "that Choate was *his,*" irrespective of his brother's considerable presence there, for he knew that behind all of his brother's accomplishments there remained a certain loneliness in him, an absorption so deep in the future and in his father's great plans for him, that "he could never fully enjoy the present."

For all Jack's bravado and his real social success, there was no question that his failure to keep up with Joe, academically or athletically, hurt. One of Lem's most poignant memories of Jack revolved about the Prize Day exercises in 1933, a warm and rainy Friday afternoon at the end of May when parents and students gathered in the school chapel to honor the graduating sixth formers. Earlier that morning Joe and Rose Kennedy had arrived in Wallingford, along with Grandpa and Grandma Fitzgerald, to enjoy Joe's moment of triumph.

Conducted in the same manner each year, with the singing of the same songs and the same hymns, the Prize Day exercises carried a special weight not only for the graduating seniors but for all the younger students as well; for, as Lem explained, "as we sat in our seats, we'd all be imagining ourselves standing up there two or three years later, and we'd wonder what if any prizes we would win." In the Choate handbook, there is a list of the coveted prizes the school conferred: a special prize for the highest rank in the sixth form; prizes of books for doing best in each of the departments of study; an award for excellence in public speaking, in music, in athletics and in Bible study; a prize for earnest and persistent effort; and one for leadership in clean sport.

Sitting next to Lem, Jack listened as each award was given out, predicting that before the ceremony ended his brother would receive a major award. And he was right. To the great applause of the entire student body and the faculty, Joe was awarded the Harvard Trophy, a small bronze statue of a football player given to the graduating sixth former who best combined scholarship and sportsmanship. As Lem tells the story, Jack was "very pleased for his brother," but at the same time, "when he saw the look of pride bursting from his father's face, he felt a little sad." It was a feeling Lem fully understood, for three years before, at another Prize Day ceremony, Lem's older brother Josh, who was the president of his class and the captain of the football team, had also walked away with all the honors. And Lem would always remember the look of happiness on *his* father's face, a look he rarely saw directed at him.

After the ceremony there was a concert by the glee club on the chapel steps, followed by supper under a large tent on the lawn. Wishing suddenly to escape the crowd, Jack led Lem on a long walk across the muddy campus to the athletic field, where they sat together for several hours under a large tree and talked openly, for the first time, about the pain they each experienced on account of their older brothers. "This was the first time Jack ever admitted to me that underneath it all he believed he was smarter than Joe but that no one understood this, least of all his parents. His intelligence, he believed, simply worked along different lines—more questioning perhaps, and more imaginative, but less organized. Nor did he really believe that Joe was the better athlete. To be sure, Joe had, by far, the healthier body but he was not necessarily more coordinated. Yet whatever internal confidence Jack possessed, it had been shaken that day as he watched his parents race up to Joe with arms outstretched and a look of wonder on their faces. Nor could he help but wish that someday the roles would be reversed, that someday he would achieve supremacy in a family in which he had for so long felt himself in a subordinate role."

While Jack was wandering through the campus with Lem, Joe was basking in his parents' affection. He had worked hard, and now, after four years, he had the reward he wanted—his parents' respect.

Mother and I are very proud of the whole job you have done at Choate [Joe Senior wrote upon returning home], as I feel that you have accomplished certainly more than I had hoped you would and the awarding of the prize on Friday is a fine finish . . . I know that the attitude that has made a success of your Choate career will make one of your College career. There is not much that a father can do to make his boy's career a success—it rests entirely upon the boy. You can look for help and suggestions—that you know I am prepared, willing and anxious to give at all times. All the family are terribly proud of you.

In saying there was not much he could do to make his son's career a success, Kennedy was downplaying the substantial role he had already played in young Joe's achievements. For years, Kennedy had studied Joe Junior's disposition, fostered his talents, applauded his triumphs and kept up with his interests. Now the time had come to shape the boy's character with a new experience. Even before young Joe had graduated his father had gone to Harvard law professor Felix Frankfurter for advice. In a warm letter, Frankfurter had responded with the suggestion of sending Joe to London to spend a year with Harold Laski, whom Frankfurter called "the greatest teacher in the world."

To Rose Kennedy, the idea of sending her favorite son to London to study under a socialist professor, whose wife was an ardent supporter of the movement for birth control, seemed "a little wild and even dangerous." It was unsettling enough, she told Joe, to have compromised on sending the boys to a Protestant prep school, but this suggestion simply went "beyond the pale." But the more Joe Kennedy thought about it, the more captivated he became by the idea of exposing Joe Junior to an important strain of political thought that was bound to have an impact on the social order for years to come. With the United States and most of the Western world in the grip of a depression that was testing the staying power of the free-enterprise system, and with many revolutionary currents and ideas in the air, he wanted his son to understand what the have-nots were thinking and planning.

It was a year young Joe would not soon forget, for it was the year in which his intellect caught fire, enabling him to take full advantage of the extraordinary opportunity Professor Laski provided for seeing the world from another perspective. Described as the most articulate human being who ever lived, Harold Laski was known widely for the quality of his teaching. He was a small man with a large mustache, large round glasses and a penetrating mind which contained an apparently limitless repertoire of anecdotes, an inexhaustible stream of learned information and a vital interest in the relationship of current problems to different theories of government. Able to recite long passages of poetry and prose from a large field of literature, Laski looked upon teaching as both a vocation and an avocation. Wherever he went, he was met by his former students, many of whom considered their relationship with him the highlight of their university days.

Arriving in London with an introduction from Frankfurter, Joe found himself queuing up with a large group of students waiting outside the professor's door to consult him about everything from Marxism and socialism to constitutionalism and democracy. At his lectures, crowds jostled for seats and large numbers stood up in the back trying to take notes with nothing to lean on but the crook of their arms. A less confident boy might have found the whole situation greatly intimidating, but, as it turned out, Joe became one of Laski's favorite students, someone Laski vividly remembered ever after. Joe's relationship with Laski was quite an accomplishment for an eighteen-year-old whose mind was not half as sophisticated or half as well trained as those of the great majority of his fellow students.

Explaining his abiding affection for Joe Junior, Laski said that he had

had innumerable students over the years, plenty of them far abler than Joe, but not many who had either "his eager zest for life or his gift of winning one's affection instantly. He was always anxious to know. He repaid one's efforts with a fidelity of heart that was deeply moving." Above all, Laski recalled, what stood out about Joe was his astonishing vitality and his capacity for enthusiasm. "What he liked, he liked with all his heart. He had nothing of the cynic's pose which sometimes affects the undergraduate. He gave all of himself to what he did with immense energy and eagerness." Then, too, Laski continued, there was his profound interest in politics. "He had set his heart on a political career and yet, with a smile that was pure magic, he was willing to submit to relentless teasing about his determination to be nothing less than the first Catholic President of the United States."

Laski's real teaching took place at his celebrated Sunday teas, which he hosted for his students in the small book-lined study in his London flat. "Joe would always come to the teas," Mrs. Laski later remembered. "He was tall and very good looking and argumentative and very bright . . . " At these teas, Joe Junior's biographer Hank Searls has written, "students would sprawl on the rugs and the air would grow heavy with pipe smoke and dreams of a world in which all men owned all things." If it wasn't easy for Joe, who was basically conservative by temperament, to answer all the socialist arguments put forth by Laski and his friends, he never failed to join in the conversation, struggling with the issues raised until he had come up with an answer. "I am a socialist," Laski would say, "though from time to time I shall prescribe other books as an antidote to my poison. If you disagree, come along to my study and tell me where I am wrong."

Speaking later of Joe's magnetic presence in these gatherings, Laski said:

He was with me during a year when the three outstanding students in my department all happened to be at once Socialists and poor Jews from the East End of London. Nothing was more admirable than Joe's attitude toward them, a deep respect for their ability, an ardent promise that one day he would know enough to argue with them on equal terms and his keen satisfaction and obvious affection for them. . . . His mind was only just beginning to discover the enchantment of thought.

While meeting with socialists during the week, Joe spent a number of his weekends with the English aristocracy. "I'm at Sir James Calder's country home," he wrote to his father in the autumn. (Sir James, head of the largest whiskey concern in the world, did business with Somerset.)

"The house is like a great castle, with very attractive lawns outside with yew and holly trees. All over the house there are great open fires with blazing logs . . . Have a huge room and bathroom with a valet turning on my bath and laying out my clothes. They even put a hot water bag in your bed. You are awakened by having the curtains drawn back and a pot of tea is placed before you." Another weekend was spent in a place near Southampton with a married actress whose husband, Joe reported, was a Jew and owned a Rolls. "My taste seems to go for actresses," Joe confessed to his mother, "don't know whether that's very good or not. The little I go out, I go out with this other actress and I have some interesting information for you. She went to a Convent and naturally is a Catholic."

Felix Frankfurter attended one of Laski's Sunday teas and was so impressed with Joe Junior that he wrote a letter to his father commenting on the boy's "solidarity, his real niceness, his sense of what is important and unimportant and his capacity to assimilate experience wisely." Commenting also on a remarkably mature letter he had received from Joe, Frankfurter said he was particularly pleased with the kind of dad that was behind such a letter. "Really," he concluded, "you have every right to have confidence in the boy and every reason for believing his year in London is one of those durable investments that neither managed currency nor a Wall Street boom can touch."

For his part, Joe Junior wrote long, detailed letters to his father almost every week.

Am getting along fine in school and am learning a great deal [he wrote on November 6, 1933]. Read two newspapers in the morning, The "Times" and the Manchester "Guardian," a socialist paper, so I get both points of view: also read the "NY Herald" and "The Evening Standard"; so you see I'm getting pretty well posted. Besides read "Literary Digest" and "The Nation," "What Everyone Wants to Know About Money," by Cole, "Tract on Monetary Reform," by Keynes, and am in the midst of many books on economics, international relations and British politics. Taking another course of Laski on politics and another on "Economic effects on Western World in 19th Century." Have 12 lectures a week . . . Have met quite a few boys during my different athletics and they all seem darn nice. It is more interesting to talk to them than an American boy, because they talk about important things and not on dances etc. and it gives me a chance to get their point of view. I am just getting to the point where I can discuss matters intelligently and not be like a dumb ham.

For a man who was so tough-minded in his business affairs, Joe Senior's reply to his son's letter was filled with emotion and bursting with pride.

I can't tell you how pleased I was with your last letter. I have great admiration for your capacity at all times to assume a job and then see it
through, but the way you have taken hold of this situation abroad was
beyond my fondest expectations. . . . I feel definitely sure that this year
may be the turning point in your whole life and getting what you are out
of it will have great effect on your future judgment.

During Joe Junior's breaks from school, he traveled to various parts of
the Continent, journeying over Christmas vacation with his adviser,
Harry Greaves, to observe the Disarmament Conference in Geneva.
"Would like very much to have you make Geneva trip at my expense,"
Joe Senior had wired to Greaves earlier that December, "advantages
accruing to Joe will way overshadow cost." While he was in Geneva, Joe
spent his days reading in the League of Nations library and came away
with a paper on the League which pleased his adviser very much. It was,
for Joe, an excellent opportunity to gauge the prevailing mood of the
European democracies, where the general revulsion against war was still
running so deep that disarmament, abandonment of conscription and
arms limitation had become the dominant issues of the day.

Then, in the spring of 1934, Joe traveled with his roommate, Aubrey
Whitelaw, to Germany, where Adolf Hitler was moving at an astonishing
speed to recruit millions of volunteers into a new German Army and to
bring all of German life under the single control of the Nazi Party.
Having acceded to the chancellorship in January 1933, just two months
before Franklin D. Roosevelt was inaugurated President of the United
States, Hitler had succeeded in establishing himself the complete master
of the German government. In 1934 the open contempt for justice and
order that the Nazis regularly employed was considered by many Germans a necessary part of the revolutionary movement, a movement
which produced a feeling of exhilaration and anticipation after years of
hopelessness. "Hitler recognized this mood," historian Alan Bullock
wrote, "when he told the German people to hold up their heads and
rediscover their old pride and self-confidence. Germany, united and
strong, would end the crippling divisions which had held her back, and
recover the place that was her due in the world."

It was this spirit of pride and the accompanying pageantry which most
captured Joe Junior's imagination as he toured Germany, causing him
to miss completely the pernicious connection between that newfound
pride and the brutal expressions of racial hatred and prejudice which,
even then, were more than evident to the observant eye or the sensitive
heart.

"One is struck by the number of people marching," Joe reported in a long, revealing letter to his father on April 23, 1934.

They march to their celebrations, the children march to school. They seem to love it. The troops seem to have a great spirit and they sing songs as they march. Just to watch them one feels he would like to join them, so it is not strange that the small boy wants to be a soldier. In all parts of the country, as in Italy, the children give you the Hitler salute as you pass, thus showing the appeal even to children. Nobody is required to salute, but nearly everybody does, and I'm sure if I was a German and valued my health I would expend that slight effort which is required to raise my arm.. It is almost comical the number of times the two words, "Heil Hitler" are used. Before a brown shirt speaks to another he says "Heil Hitler" and always he ends by this expression. Many people talking to each other use it, and it means "Hello, How are you, Goodbye"; in fact, it can mean nearly anything. Hitler's pictures fill shop windows . . . The German people are not allowed to forget him for a minute.

Before starting his trip, Joe told his father, he had heard the greatest condemnation of Hitler and his party. "I had been to Laski's many times to tea, and had heard him and many German socialists tell of the frequent brutalities in Germany." But now that he had had the opportunity to talk with Germans who continually stressed what it was like before the coming of Hitler, he had, he thought, reached a better understanding of the situation.

They had tried liberalism, and it had seriously failed. They had no leader, and as time went on Germany was sinking lower and lower. The German people were scattered, despondent, and were divorced from hope. Hitler came in. He saw the need of a common enemy, someone of whom to make the goat. Someone, by whose riddance the Germans would feel they had cast out the cause of their predicament. It was excellent psychology, and it was too bad that it had to be done to the Jews. This dislike of the Jews, however, was well-founded.

Betraying a terrible insensitivity to the plight of the German Jews, who were even then being purged from the civil service and from all work in journalism, theater and radio, Joe Junior absorbed malignant German arguments as plausible rationales for Hitler's increasingly systematic oppression of the Jews.

They were at the heads of all big business, in law etc. It is all to their credit for them to get so far, but their methods had been quite unscrupulous. A noted man told Sir James the other day that the lawyers and prominent judges were Jews, and if you had a case against a Jew, you were nearly always sure to lose it. It's a sad state of affairs when things like that can take place. It is extremely sad, that noted professors, scientists, artists, etc. so should have to suffer, but as you can see, it would be practically impossible to throw out only a part of them, from both the practical and psychological point of view. As far as the brutality is concerned, it must have been necessary to use some, to secure the whole-hearted support of the people, which was necessary to put through this present program. I can see how a great deal of brutality was on private lines, as those supporters of Hitler felt so strongly that they lost their heads over the non-supporters. It was a horrible thing but in every revolution you have to expect some bloodshed.

Hitler is building a spirit in his men that could be envied in any country . . . This spirit would very quickly be turned into a war spirit, but Hitler has things well under control. The only danger would be if something happened to Hitler and one of his crazy ministers came into power, which at this time does not seem likely. As you know, he has passed the sterilization law which I think is a good thing. I don't know how the Church feels about it but it will do away with many of the disgusting specimens of men who inhabit this earth.

I am sending this to you, Dad, to see how you think I have sized it up. It is not taken from any reading, but from what I have actually seen and heard. I would not like to discuss it with Laski, or with Greaves as a matter of fact, as it might hurt their feelings. Laski would probably give me examples which might change me back again. Anyway I'm sending this to you.

One might attempt to excuse Joe Junior on the grounds that he was nineteen years old and that countless others, with far more experience, also misunderstood the malignant nature of the Nazi phenomenon in its early years. But the letter reveals such a complete acceptance of the stereotyped image of the Jew as driving, unscrupulous and unethical that it betrays in young Joe a certain grounding in anti-Semitism that can only have come from his family background.

Surely it was not uncommon for Irish Catholics in America to join Anglo-Americans in disparaging the Jews. Founded in orthodoxy, in the fixing of Jewish responsibility for the Crucifixion, the Irish Catholic prejudice was reinforced by the perception that the Jewish immigrants as a group were achieving financial and intellectual success more rapidly than they were. The very rapidity with which the Jews adjusted to the economic conditions of life in America became a major handicap to Jewish acceptance. For many of the Irish, it was easier to explain the greater success of the Jews by pointing to Jewish pushiness, clannishness and unscrupulousness than by looking inwardly at their own failure to adapt to the competitive American culture.

John Fitzgerald reflected some of these prejudices when he told Clem Norton that he was folding up his small-time clothing business because he "couldn't compete with the unscrupulous methods of the Jews." And Joseph Kennedy reflected similar prejudices when he first went to Hollywood and discovered, in his words, that "a bunch of ignorant Jewish furriers" were running the entire movie industry, "simply because they had unethically pushed their way into a wide-open virgin field."

Yet, if some of the nativist anti-Semitism in America represented jealousy of Jewish financial success, Joseph Kennedy enjoyed the same form of success. Indeed, it can be argued that Kennedy embodied many of the traits traditionally associated with the Jews. It was said that the Jews did not cultivate the earth or work at mechanical trades, preferring to live by their cunning and wit in the "unproductive" roles of creditors, speculators and middlemen. It was said that the Jews were unscrupulous profit-takers who made their gains from the labors of others. It was said that the Jews were pushing for social acceptance too hard and too soon, while their voices were still uncouth and their sense of tact still in the stage of the pushcart peddler. All of these charges could be equally laid against Joseph Patrick Kennedy.

Moreover, as a "money man" himself, Kennedy could hardly have accepted the distinction between the "productive laborer" and the "unproductive middleman." Nor, with his experience in the stock market and in banking, could he have seriously entertained the image of a vast international Jewish conspiracy dominating the financial world. It seems more likely that the roots of Kennedy's attitude toward the Jews lay in the social sphere.

By the turn of the century a remarkable number of Jewish people had prospered mightily and were pressing heavily upon a limited field of social opportunity, demanding entrance into prestigious clubs, exclusive summer resorts and a small number of Eastern prep schools and colleges. For a man who had been held back all his life in this very sphere, Kennedy was not about to give up his own sense of possession and preeminence to yet another ethnic group. In this regard, several of Kennedy's friends remember his arguing vociferously against letting too many Jews into Harvard on the ground that they would soon take over the school, while other friends remember his disparaging remarks against letting Jewish families into Christian country clubs. (In later years, however, Kennedy would join a Jewish club situated near his home in Palm Beach.)

All these attitudes, casual as they may have been, Joe Junior must have absorbed to the point where he knew that in his father, unlike Laski, he had a willing listener for his negative observations on the Jews. Not once in his single-spaced four-page letter did Joe Junior feel compelled to moderate his astonishing observations. Nor, from what can be discerned from subsequent correspondence, did Kennedy Senior ever attempt to correct or soften Joe Junior's tone. On the contrary, the only question Kennedy seemed to ask regarding the situation in Germany concerned the tense relationship between Hitler and the Church.

Had Kennedy seen his role as one of inculcating ethical standards in his nineteen-year-old son, he should have met this blatantly bigoted letter with a long letter of his own. But for a man whose dominant ideology was achievement, the importance of Joe Junior's experience abroad lay not so much in the substance of the beliefs he was acquiring as in the capacity he was developing to express them. When the Laskis invited Joe Junior to travel with them to Russia after school was out in May, Kennedy wired his enthusiastic approval, knowing what a great experience it would be for his son. And so it was. "We arrive tomorrow," Joe wrote his to father from the ship, the S.S. *Rykov*.

> There are no deck games, but most of the day is occupied by discussions on Marx, Communism, etc. There are several Americans, young fellows who are going to Russia for a job because they can't get anything at home. It's a pretty disgraceful state of affairs. Everybody is either a bolshevist or a communist and I'm all alone. I wish you could hear some of their conversations. It is really an education and an enlightenment. Laski is very amusing and some other people are screams, so it's darn good fun.

After three weeks of seeing Russia through Laski's eyes, Joe returned to Hyannis Port immersed enough in the ideals of socialism to be able to argue with his father on the comparative merits of capitalism and communism. In this discussion, in which Joe Junior took the socialist side of the argument, Jack sided with his brother, hinting that Joe Junior understood the situation better than his father. According to Rose, this did not bother her husband at all. "If I were their age I probably would believe what they believe, but I am of a different background and must voice my beliefs," he said. "I don't care what the boys think about my ideas. I can always look out for myself. The important thing is that they should stand together."

# CHAPTER 28
# CHILDREN
# OF
# PRIVILEGE

I n the autumn of 1934, Joe Junior began his freshman year at Harvard. It was a different college from the one his father had entered three decades before. In the early 1930s, a revolutionary "house" plan had been inaugurated whereby all the students, from their sophomore to their senior year, would live in one of seven new houses modeled after the colleges at Oxford. Beautifully constructed with large living quarters for both students and resident tutors, elegant dining halls, spacious common rooms and comfortable libraries, the houses were intended to provide a home where young men of all strata and conditions could mingle, work, eat and sleep. Through these houses—which eliminated the luxurious Gold Coast and provided a vast improvement in living conditions for the majority of the students—it was hoped that a new and freer social pattern would gradually evolve.

But at a place like Harvard the ties of background would never be eliminated, and to some extent the class structure simply transferred itself to the houses, each of which acquired a certain character and admitted a certain "kind" of boy. Eliot House became known as the aristocratic house, the home of unfriendly socialites; Lowell attracted grinds and academic highbrows; Kirkland, Midwestern hustlers; Winthrop, jocks. According to economist John Kenneth Galbraith, who was a tutor at Harvard in the 1930s, "applications for entry into the houses were cleared more on past status than on present achievement and all the prestige was still associated with the white shoe people from good families, the boys who were casual of dress with an easy association with alcohol, athletics and sex, the passively anti-intellectual ones."

As Galbraith explained it, "Each student's application for a house was charted on a large form. To the left was 'S.P.' for St. Paul's or 'S.A.' for St. Albans. Then 'M' for Middlesex or 'G' for Groton, and 'OP' for other private schools. Then, finally, 'HS' for public school. Then religious preference, Protestant, Catholic and Jewish. If 'Jewish' was checked, all the rest was irrelevant, for the Jews were still a class unto themselves in those days; indeed, the university still had a quota. Nor had the Irish emerged into full respectability. True, the angry discussions about the Irish in the twenties, when it was feared the Irish would take over the college, crowding Harvard men out of both athletics and social life, had died away. For by the thirties it was clear that the Irish still had not laid claim to social leadership as against the old Boston families, so they were less feared. No longer actively discriminated against, they were just lower in the social hierarchy. Nor did they have the disadvantage of excessive intellectuality as the Jews did. In other words, if a student checked 'Jewish,' most of the houses were closed to him, whereas he still had a chance if he were Irish, but in all cases the checks were counted in order from left to right, with all the weighting on the left checks."

Nor did the house structure eliminate the disproportionate role the clubmen still played in setting the tone for undergraduate life. "Nowhere else in the world," Benjamin Welles wrote in an article about Harvard in the thirties, "except in the Third Reich, does a small minority impose its stamp so strongly on a great sprawling majority." Though only 10 percent of the undergraduates were accepted into one of the eight exclusive clubs, the clubmen still remained the special few whose antics were watched and condemned and secretly envied by all the rest.

And still the Porcellian held sway as the most exclusive and most awesome of all the clubs. Boasting a total of nine Adamses, seven Lowells and eleven Cabots in its 150-year history, the Porcellian remained an object of fascination on initiation night as the newly chosen members, escorted blindfolded through the streets, were admitted into the inner sanctum. A system that had been ingrained for generations could not be easily undone by change from the top.

Having graduated from a private prep school and come from a background of great wealth, Joe Junior started his Harvard career with far more social leverage than his father had enjoyed. While Choate was not St. Paul's, it was a good private school which gave Joe a significant head start over his fellow students from public high schools. "Still, it was not easy for him to get into the house of his choice," Galbraith recalled. "On the chart, Choate fell into the OP category, way behind St. Paul's, St. Albans, Middlesex and Groton. But in selecting Winthrop, Joe chose wisely, for Winthrop was the first house to go from the anti-Irish attitudes of the twenties to the anti-Semitism of the thirties and on the strength of his OP, he barely made it."

Joe also had the advantage of entering Harvard as "the son of a famous father." In an article on Harvard in late September of 1934, Joe Junior "of Bronxville and Choate" was pictured along with two other entering freshmen as a young man who had a reputation to uphold. "In those days," Galbraith recalls, "even though the students were overwhelmingly anti-New Deal, the faculty was so centered on Washington that it used to be said you could house a faculty meeting on the *Federal Express* to Washington every Friday night. The association between Harvard and Washington was closer then than ever before or since. And in the New Deal, Joseph Kennedy was obviously a big figure. As a result, all the tutors and young faculty were interested in talking with young Joe to find out what he knew from his father."

Then, too, there was his appearance and his athletic ability. Standing almost six feet tall at around 175 pounds, "he was so handsome," his cousin Charles Burke said, "he could have been in the movies." Joining the freshman football squad, he quickly made friends in the athletic crowd, and when the time came for the clubs to choose their new members he was invited into both Hasty Pudding and the Spee Club, a club that stood just below the top echelon of Porcellian, A.D. and Fly.

But to Joe, unlike his father, the social life of the college mattered very little. While he formed close friendships with Ted Reardon and Tom Bilodeau, he essentially operated alone, preferring to spend his nights at the movies or the dog races at Revere in the company of his father's friend Boston Police Commissioner Joe Timilty. And while he often attended debutante balls in order to partake of the fancy spreads of food, his tastes in girls, as he had admitted to his mother, ran to show girls and actresses.

"For Joe," Lem Billings observed, "Harvard was simply a way station, for he already had his heart set on a political future and he was so closely tied with his father's ambitions for him that there was little room for anything else." There is, indeed, an extraordinary warmth and intimacy in the letters between Kennedy and young Joe during this period, evidencing much careful thought about the future. "I have doubts about the value of a course in Philosophy your freshman year," Kennedy wrote to his son soon after the school year started. "I think true values can be had out of courses of this kind after you have had a chance to set yourself in the University atmosphere. As to whether they [the courses] are too hard, . . . Felix's judgment on the whole layout would be invaluable." But remember, he concluded, speaking about the freshman football team, "being out for the team gives you a great chance to meet a lot of fellows, and after all, that is the first requisite of a successful college education—learning how to meet people and getting along with them."

Then to Felix Frankfurter, Kennedy wrote:

> The assistant graduate manager of athletics sent me word that he thought Joe was taking a much too difficult course and his Mother received a letter from the Passionist Priests with whom Joe had made a retreat, stating that his point of view was not what they had hoped it would be and his Mother became unduly concerned. Judge Burns said that the philosophy course in his first year might not be the best thing. I wrote him and told him all these facts, but said, of course, I would be governed by his decision and made no suggestions as to what I thought he should do. He told me he was going to consult with you the minute he had time . . .

In his letters to his son, Kennedy shared the latest news on FDR and the New Deal. "I stopped in and spent an hour and a half with the President this morning," Kennedy wrote on December 7, 1934, "and he is looking very well and is feeling quite optimistic about conditions. I am very hopeful that if we get set to a good start when Congress comes in we will be well on our way toward recovery." In his responses, young Joe revealed a serious interest in public affairs. "The S.E.C. decision last week seemed fair enough to me," he wrote to his father. "It looked like [Judge John] Burns just wanted to get Jones [J. Edward Jones, chairman of the National Petroleum Council] behind the bars so badly that he wouldn't stop. Supposing a person had applied for registration and then found something wrong which he hadn't known of before, he wouldn't be able to withdraw. What do you think? . . . "

"Joe talked about his father a great deal," Galbraith recalled. "He would invariably introduce his thoughts with the words 'Father says.'" (The same expression Rose frequently used in relating her own father's thoughts!) "But we were always glad to see him because he had such fascinating information and insight from Washington. Now, there were times when I thought he took himself too seriously and times when I found him a bit humorless and too somber, but he *was* seriously concerned with issues, which was far more than you could say for most undergraduates."

And in his studies, he was, as he had always been, a hard worker. "I congratulate you on your excellent report," Kennedy wrote during Joe's sophomore year. "I think it would be most creditable to get on the Dean's list. Besides doing a good job it means additional prestige and that all helps in the long run." That "the long run" was meant to include politics is clear from another letter, in which Kennedy suggests that it might be a "very good experience" for Joe to get himself signed up and make some speeches in the presidential campaign throughout Massachusetts. "It would be a very interesting experience and you could work up two or three subjects you wanted to discuss and go out through the state."

In coaxing young Joe to consider the future, Kennedy never pressured him to the point where his son rebelled. He didn't have to, for Joe Junior had already internalized a lifetime of pressure to the point where he saw his father's goals as his. As a result, Joe Senior could afford to stand back a little and offer a sense of perspective. For instance, even as he suggested the idea of campaigning, he recognized that, with football, Joe might not have enough time. And when Joe Junior missed the Dean's list by one point, he received a warm note of consolation from his father. "It really was tough luck to miss the Dean's list by such a close call," Kennedy wrote, "but it was a real worth while effort and I am sure you will make it later on. Incidentally, it is much closer than your father ever got."

For his part, Joe Junior apparently felt free enough about his relationship with his father to tease him about his reputation with women. "By the way," he wrote during his sophomore year, "Barbara Cushing and a friend of hers who was out with you in New York hearing Toscanini, Persian Room etc. till 3 o'clock were up here and gave me the low down on you. They said they nearly went South." (Barbara Cushing was a Boston socialite and the sister of Jimmy Roosevelt's wife, Betsy. Apparently, Kennedy had spontaneously invited the two girls to Palm Beach.) "I think Mother ought to keep a better eye on you!" Joe Junior concluded. Responding by return mail, Kennedy told him not to worry too much about Barbara Cushing and her pal, "as 21 or 22 is still a little too young for me. I still play nursemaid for Jimmie."

And always there was talk of football, though here too the image of Joe Kennedy constantly pressuring his sons to outdo themselves on the athletic fields is simply not correct. On the contrary, from the letters between father and eldest son it seems that Joe Junior was the one, far more than his father, who insisted on playing sports, despite repeated injuries to his body, including a broken arm his freshman year and an injured knee his sophomore year, which necessitated an operation in the fall of his junior year. Writing to a friend, Jim Reilly, at the time of Joe Junior's operation in October of 1936, Kennedy predicted that the operation would "certainly put an end to all football activities, but that fact does not bother me at all," he added.

> Strange [Kennedy continued] how one's point of view changes. As you and I know, during undergraduate days making the team is of importance second to none other and we would never stop to reckon any price too great to pay for that honor. . . . When we reach maturity, we realize that a bum nose or lame leg is not worth the coveted letter. I shall never have any regrets if none of my boys get mixed up in inter-collegiate football. I have tried to impress these thoughts on the boys, but I am somewhat doubtful as to my success.

The operation on Joe's knee was complicated, and his recovery was retarded when he fell in the shower while he was still in the hospital. For months afterward he was unable to walk correctly, and his weight dropped to a point where the doctors considered him underweight. Writing to Dr. Sara Jordan, Kennedy asked her to prescribe something that would start to fill him out. "After all, he is only eight pounds more than Jack and that's not very encouraging."

Yet, when spring training came around, young Joe's thoughts turned once again to football, and his father was worried.

> I am still a little concerned about your going back and trying football [Kennedy wrote]. I know how anxious you are to make your letter, but after a fellow has been banged up the way you have and as you have only one more year to go before you go out in the world, you should think very seriously whether it is worthwhile or not. I do not want to be in the position of telling you not to, but all my judgment urges me to at least ask you to give it grave consideration. I would by all means talk to Dr. Richards before I made any plans, because in his conversations with me he thought the knee should be taken care of still some time to come.

Despite his father's urgings, however, Joe decided to go out for football one more time, not because he lacked respect for his father's judgment, but just the opposite. Since he was a toddler Joe had been taught to strive for everything with every resource he possessed; for years, his father had carefully nurtured the habit of competition. And now that habit was so deeply set in his own heart that, even as his father cautioned him to take it easy, he could no more stop striving than he could stop breathing. What the father had forged over a lifetime could not be altered overnight.

With his older brother away at college, Jack felt an enormous sense of release. "When he came back to Choate his junior year," Lem recalled, "he was really ready to give himself to his work and he even began to enjoy some of his subjects." In his English class that year, his teacher, Harold Tinker, reported that "he had a very definite flair for writing" and advised a literary career. When a subject aroused Jack's interest, his lounging manner would suddenly give way to ardent excitement and his mind would become totally engaged. The only student who subscribed to *The New York Times* (and read it every morning from front to back), Jack was also the acknowledged champion at *Information Please*, a popular radio program which purported to measure encyclopedic knowledge.

But once again illness returned to curb whatever strides Jack might have taken. In the winter of his junior year he returned from the Christmas holidays looking especially pale. By February his body was covered with hives, and he was removed to New Haven Hospital, where a monitoring of his blood count revealed a serious condition which was probably hepatitis. At the time, however, the nature of his illness remained a mystery, no doubt compounding the worry on all sides and leading the family to bring Jack home in March for the rest of the term. And when he returned to Choate the following autumn, he was prohibited from engaging in strenuous athletics and forced to return periodically to the infirmary. Indeed, before he graduated his record showed more class absences for illness than that of any other boy in the school.

Despite his poor health, however, Jack enjoyed his final years at Choate tremendously. In an atmosphere of friendship and conviviality, his natural gregariousness and his spontaneous humor made him extremely popular with everyone. And even at sixteen he was beginning to develop a winning way with women that would last throughout his life. "The girls really liked Jack," Lem recalled. "I hated to admit it at the time, but it was true. In fact, he was even more successful with girls than his brother Joe. Though Joe was bigger and better-looking, Jack knew better how to handle girls and they mattered more to him. Even when we were young, he spent a lot of time thinking about girls and he was incredibly successful with them. Yet none of them could ever match up in his mind with his sister Kathleen."

"God, was Kathleen a great girl," Lem recalled. "I can still remember how happy Jack was when she came to the convent at Noroton. The first week she was there he insisted we sneak up and visit her, and what fun we had! I think I probably fell in love with her right then and there. She opened up a side of me that no woman ever reached. Kathleen and Jack—they were the two people I loved more than anyone else in my life, and they in turn loved each other as much as any brother and sister I have ever seen."

Throughout their childhood, Jack and Kathleen had been especially close. Sharing the same sense of humor, the same irreverence and the same vital curiosity about people, the two of them could talk for hours on end. "After parties," one friend recalls, "Kathleen liked nothing better than to sit up in her bathrobe with Jack, talking into the middle of the night about the personality of everyone who was there. They were so close at times I thought of them as twins."

Kathleen looked extraordinarily like her mother. Her features were the same as Rose's and the structure of her brow and her nose was hereditary; but in Kathleen's case all was illumined by her radiantly joyous, self-confident sense of life and youth. Wherever she went, she gave excitement with her lithe figure, her violet-gray eyes, clear and quick, and her rosy complexion. Here was beauty allied with animation. In the case of her mother, the face, though essentially the same, had acquired a more limited range of expression, a formal gaze and a circumscribed smile, suggesting a subtle mask of control shaped and molded over the years. In contrast, Kathleen's range of expressions was as vast as a blue sky on a cloudless day.

Brought up in an atmosphere of affection and privilege, Kathleen carried within herself a great fund of life; for sheer vitality and curiosity, she was hard to match. Moreover, she had in the depths of her nature an unquenchable desire to please, a magnetic quality which attracted varied personalities to her. It was a quality Rose deeply admired; at the same time, when Kathleen turned thirteen she worried that her popular daughter, who was living at home and attending the Riverdale Country Day School, was spending too much time with boys. "She was on the telephone with them for hours at a time," Rose recorded in her memoirs, "and was being distracted from her schoolwork and other duties by boys inviting her to the Saturday-afternoon movies and so forth." Rose's solution was to send her daughter to the same kind of convent school that she herself had attended. There, under the strict routine prescribed by the Sacred Heart nuns in a boarding school situated in Noroton, Connecticut, on a ten-acre estate surrounded on three sides by the waters of Long Island Sound, Kathleen would better train her mind and her body.

Noroton in 1933 retained essentially the same philosophy which had guided all Sacred Heart schools for more than a century. Although the plan of studies had been revised since Rose's day, freeing the students somewhat from the conformity of former years, the seventy-five girls wore the same brown wool uniforms, endured the same weekly primes and took the same pink and blue ribbons. In the center of the campus, surrounded by grassy lawns and a circular drive, stood the main building, a stately mansion once belonging to the Stokes family and then to the official greeter for the city of New York, Grover A. Whalen. With classrooms situated on the ground floor, and big beautiful bedrooms with four to a room on the upper floor, Noroton offered its boarders a much warmer and cozier atmosphere than the perpetually chilly one Rose had encountered in the gray stone building at Blumenthal.

The beauty of the surroundings belied the austerity of the daily regime. The girls were awakened at six each morning to attend Mass, shrouded in black veils. Lights went out at nine. Silences were imposed at regular intervals during the day; mail, even from families, was censored. No jewelry was allowed, and baths were permitted only twice a week.

Strangely enough, this strict routine did not appear to produce any open rebellion in Kathleen. Recognizing that most of her girlfriends, even her Protestant ones, were attending equally strict boarding schools, Kathleen decided to adapt as best she could, working hard and doing well (in her first semester she achieved an average of 87), while looking to her vacations in Palm Beach and Hyannis Port for all the freedoms and adventures she was denied at school. Moreover, in contrast to the sedentary life Rose and Agnes had led at Blumenthal, the Noroton girls participated enthusiastically in sports. "In Kathleen's day," Sister Gabriella recalled, "the girls would play field hockey like fiends. Bursting with health, they'd be out on the fields for an hour and a half each day, regardless of the weather."

While Kathleen was at Noroton, she became good friends with Charlotte McDonnell, a pretty blond girl who was as animated and as headstrong as she. One of fourteen children of a wealthy New York Irish Catholic family, Charlotte was a well-suited companion for Kathleen. "The two of them were always in the midst of everything," Sister Gabriella recalled. "They were much too spirited to win a ribbon for good conduct, yet their sense of fun was always humorous and almost always innocent. One day one of the girls had a spot on her uniform. Kathleen and her friends said, 'Give it to us, we'll get it out.' The next day, the unsuspecting student got her uniform back with a hole in it."

Even at Noroton, where the rules prescribed that the girls entertain boys only at formal Sunday teas in the presence of the mother superior, Kathleen retained her amazing popularity with boys. "There were more boys who thought they were in love with Kathleen than you can possibly imagine," one friend recalls. "First there were boys she had known from New York, then there were boys she met through her friends at Noroton and finally, of course, there were all those friends of her brothers, boys like Lem Billings and later Torbert Macdonald, both of whom fell hard for her."

While she was at Noroton, Kathleen wrote to Lem every week, beginning a monumental correspondence that would stretch over three continents before being bound into a scrapbook which Lem kept until he died. There is a gentle teasing in all the early letters, representative of the way so many teenagers hide their feelings behind banter and jokes, but the warmth and affection of these two young people is obvious on every page. Using nicknames like "Dear Picklepuss," Kathleen shared with Lem her feelings about school, her observations on mutual friends and even, on occasion, her feelings about herself. For his part, Lem gave Kathleen long and detailed descriptions of all the funny things he and Jack were doing and what the other boys were saying about her.

"How about going up to the Harvard game with Rip and I," Lem wrote on a crisp October day. "We're going up Friday afternoon. You could stay at your grandmother's Friday night and go to the game with me Saturday. We could also step out a bit Friday night. We'll be going right through Noroton and could pick you up and bring you back Sunday. I hope Mother Superior still enjoys my letters."

"Am afraid I couldn't work it," Kathleen replied, "much as I'd love it. In fact, Mr. Billings, I don't know where I'd have a better time. The only hitch being we have absolutely no weekends except at Thanksgiving. Why couldn't that game have happened then."

With all the restrictions Noroton placed upon her social life, it is little wonder that Kathleen spent much of her time in school anticipating the pleasures of her next vacation. As her mother had done in her convent school years before, Kathleen filled her letters with hopes for future trips and memories of the past. "How is everything in Palm Beach?" Kathleen asked her mother after returning to school from Christmas vacation.

I miss you all like anything, in fact, worse than I ever have. Everyday this week I'd sit in the study hall and think a week ago today I was basking in the sun and now I am in a firetrap trying to study. It's a great life if you don't weaken. . . . Yesterday was the Committee of Games congé. We had quite a bit of fun and listened to the radio . . . We had a little play which won the prize out of six others. I was the hero and Ann was the villain whom I killed. I had ski pants on and Mother Fitzgerald wouldn't let me appear without a coat over the pants. She thinks pants are immodest. Ski pants, mind you. If she only knew. I cannot wait until Easter when I will be back in the Sunny South.

P. S. We get up at 6:30 now as it is too dark and cold at 6:00. Nice, isn't it?

In the large cloth scrapbook, held together with black string, which Kathleen religiously filled with clippings and mementos of her girlhood, there are countless descriptions of parties at the Kennedy villa, but always these parties are the children's rather than the parents'. One clipping read: "Kennedy's Palm Beach villa was the setting for one of the most enjoyable parties given for members of the visiting school set when John, Kathleen, Rosemary and Joe Junior were hosts at a buffet supper for a large group of their school and college friends. Tables were set for six and later motion pictures were shown. Guests included Charles Amory, Lem Billings, Randolph Hearst and Jeffrey Roche."

In her second year at Noroton, in the fall of 1934, Kathleen's asthma, which had been fairly mild throughout her childhood, flared up, making it difficult for her to sleep at night. Writing to Jack, Joe Senior confided that he was not at all sure Kathleen would be able to stick it out, because of the climate. Worried about his favorite daughter, he tried to get permission to take her out of school on a Saturday for the Harvard–Princeton game. But, for all his power as the chairman of the SEC, he was unable to move Mother Fitzgerald. "I am awfully sorry," Kathleen wrote, "but I won't be able to go on Saturday as Mother Fitzgerald says she just cannot give me permission. None of the girls are allowed to go and it is hard to make an exception. Ann and I were just crazy to go but we just cannot be different from everybody else."

When the asthma attacks continued into October and November, the doctors recommended that Kathleen take the winter semester off to spend in Palm Beach. But like her brother Jack who had battled against far worse health problems all his life, Kathleen was determined to beat her affliction and to make the best of it, a quality that made her father love her all the more. "I was very proud of you in our talk the other night," he wrote, "when you were so serious about continuing at Noroton when you had a chance to spend the winter at Palm Beach. It demonstrated a very fine spirit."

The affection Joe Kennedy gave, Kathleen more than returned in kind. Addressing him in her frequent letters as the "dearest, darlingest daddy," she is so warm and affectionate that one senses immediately an unusual bond between father and daughter. "I don't know when I have ever had so much fun as Wednesday night," Kathleen tells her father. "It was such fun being home and it was awfully swell of you and Mother to go and see that show again . . . Thanks again for the vacation."

And if, at times, Kathleen's high spirits led to defiance of family rules and regulations, she was quick to apologize. "Dearest daddy," she wrote after another vacation at home, "I didn't have any time to see you before I left but after thinking about Saturday night I realize what a low trick it was, after you and Mother had done so much for me already. I'm sorry it had to happen at the end like it did, as it rather left a very unpleasant blot on the holidays. . . . Love from a daughter who needs more sense. P. S. Got third place in my history test."

Joe Senior took a special pride in the extraordinary closeness between Jack and Kathleen. "We had lunch with Kathleen Sunday," Kennedy wrote to Jack at Choate at the start of February 1935.

> She really thinks you are a great fellow. She has a love and devotion to you that you should be very proud to have deserved. It probably does not become apparent to you, but it does to both Mother and me. She thinks you are quite the grandest fellow that ever lived and your letters furnish her most of her laughs in the Convent. She is coming up on the 16th February and I told her if you and LeMoyne or another of your gang can get off, I will blow you all to a party.

As it turned out, however, the plans for the party were forgotten in the wake of Jack's near-expulsion from Choate the following week. This time, the problem was not his grades, but a club formed by Jack, Lem, Rip and ten other boys which had just come to the attention of Mr. St. John. In his scrapbook, Jack noted that the object of the club was to "put over festivities in our own little way and to buck the system more effectively." Innocent enough in its function as a loose gathering of high-spirited friends, the club had deliberately chosen to call itself the Muckers Club, appropriating a word the headmaster frequently used in chapel to epitomize the bad elements of the school, the boys who weren't trying hard enough to obey the time-honored rules of Choate, the goof-offs who were not diligent enough about their studies. To enhance their camaraderie, each Mucker obtained a special badge of membership, a small gold charm in the shape of a shovel with "Choate Muckers Club" engraved upon it.

Regarding the Muckers Club as a serious challenge to his authority, St. John decided the time had come to lay down the law to Jack and his friends. As a first step, he called all the members into his office and threatened them with expulsion unless the club was disbanded. Then, to make sure the rest of the school understood the seriousness of the offense, the headmaster devoted an entire chapel to the Muckers Club, specifically naming all the members and characterizing their leaders as "public enemies" of the Choate community. "They weren't wicked kids," St. John later admitted, "but they were a nuisance. At one time, it came to the point where I was saying to myself, 'Well, I have two things to do, one to run the school, another to run Jack Kennedy and his friends.' "

As a more intuitive headmaster might have predicted, the public sermon in the chapel only enhanced the feelings of self-importance the boys already had. Still thinking of the whole incident as a big joke, Jack called up Kathleen to let her know he was now public enemy number one. Responding in kind, Kathleen sent a funny telegram to Jack and Lem in which she teased them about their new status as public enemies. Unfortunately, St. John intercepted the telegram and became even more furious at the boys for turning his sermon into a joke. The time had come, the headmaster decided, to notify Mr. Kennedy and make him come to Choate for a talk. "I was angry," St. John admitted. "I couldn't see how two boys from the same family as were Joe and Jack could be so different."

Kennedy arrived at Choate at noon the following Sunday, February 17, having left the SEC to board a sleeper train the day before. It was a cold day, cloudy and overcast, with a light snow falling. Earlier that morning, as Lem later told the story, Jack was in a state of considerable agitation. "It was one thing to take on St. John, it was quite another to confront his father. For hours, he just kept pacing around the room, unable to sit still. While he knew that in the end he hadn't really done anything seriously wrong—hell, the worst things we did were to sneak out for milkshakes and to play our radio when we weren't supposed to— he was terrified that his father would lose confidence in him once and for all."

When Jack walked into the headmaster's study at the appointed hour, his father was already there, seated in a large black rocking chair beside St. John's desk. Recounting the incident later that day to Lem, Jack admitted that he felt a lump in his throat when he saw the two of them sitting together, for he feared that his fate had already been decided. Greeted coolly by his father, he prepared himself for the worst. But then, as Jack described it, an amazing thing happened. The phone rang for St. John, and in that moment Joe Kennedy leaned over to his son, winked and whispered, "My God, my son, you sure didn't inherit your father's directness or his reputation for using bad language. If that crazy Muckers Club had been mine, you can be sure it wouldn't have started with an M." The moment Jack heard this, his whole body relaxed; it was as if a secret had passed between the two of them, breaking the crust of his fear. And from then on, though his father officially backed up St. John in everything he said, Jack knew that in the end his father would be with him no matter what.

Skillfully treating the incident with all the seriousness St. John believed it deserved, Kennedy listened carefully to the tale and then began to speak to Jack, essentially repeating all the things he had been saying to him for years about the importance of developing a sense of responsibility. "In fact, he spoke very very strongly," St. John proudly recalled, "supporting the school completely. I've always been very grateful to him. There are lots of boys who go through a period like that, and the greatest kindness is some severity. Jack's father didn't hold back."

With the headmaster satisfied, Kennedy took his son to lunch, where once again he mixed together serious warnings with a quick wit. Astonished to discover that Jack had never even recognized that the word "muckers" had a particular meaning in the history of the Irish in America—it was the name of derision given to the sons of Irish construction workers in the days of their snowball fights on the Common—Kennedy wondered aloud if the proper Mr. St. John himself was aware of the previous usage of the word when he used it so regularly in his chapels.

Yet, while extending his warmth and wit to his son, Joe Kennedy did not in any way condone his foolish behavior. Even Kathleen came in for a scolding for her role in the affair. "I know you want to do all you can for Jack," Kennedy wrote to her the following day,

> but I think I should tell you that one of the serious difficulties he found himself in was his characterization of public enemy and that group of his with the frightful name muckers. I really don't think there is anything smart about it and I hope it won't be the cause of having him expelled from the school. Therefore, I want to urge you to stop all this talk in letters and telegrams . . . The Headmaster told me of the wire you sent him last Sunday and it merely added fuel to the fire. It has all been smoothed out temporarily, but have this in mind.

At the same time, Kennedy wrote a letter to Dr. Paul O'Leary at the Mayo Clinic in an attempt to reverse the original decision made against Jack's participating this last year in athletics. "I went up to see Jack yesterday," Kennedy relates, treating the visit as an ordinary one, and he seems to be looking very well; but I feel that he has so much time to himself, being out of athletics, that his tendency is to get into trouble. I have suggested that he start going in for athletics to see what effect it has on him. I am afraid a boy with Jack's ideas, with too much time on his hands, could have a much more serious breakdown than a physical one. We will watch him closely and if we see anything happening physically we will stop him at once.

As it turned out, Jack was not expelled. Once he agreed to disband the club, he and his group were simply kept over on Easter vacation for three or four days while the rest of the students went home. Gossip has it that soon after the incident Kennedy donated two movie projectors to Choate, but in fact the donation was made two years earlier. In her memoirs, Rose Kennedy sees the silly episode as "a turning point" in Jack's life. "Something certainly soaked in and deeply. There would be no way to measure the influence of this embarrassing necessity to talk things out—and to have a good talking-to, in open forum, from his father."

Yet the incident brought Jack triumph as well as defeat, for once again he discovered the depth of his father's support. Having come to the edge where he almost lost that support, Jack was determined not to risk it again, and his father realized this. As Jack headed into his final exams, Kennedy wrote: "Don't let me lose confidence in you again because it will be pretty nearly an impossible task to restore it—I am sure it will be a loss for you and a distinct loss for me."

Under this impetus, Jack came through all his exams with passing grades, graduating in the middle of his class, with a record decent enough to afford him the chance to follow in his brother's footsteps and spend a year abroad at the University of London. And, in a final joke, he helped to manipulate the class elections, trading votes among his friends so that he was awarded the distinction "most likely to succeed."

When the time came for Jack to study with Professor Laski at the University of London, Rose decided to send Kathleen to Europe as well. Recognizing their closeness, she thought that if Kathleen was in school in France she could meet Jack during the holidays and they could exchange visits during the year. At the same time, Rose wanted Kathleen to benefit, as she had, from a year's experience in a convent where she could absorb a European culture and language.

So in September 1935 Joe and Rose, with Jack and Kathleen, sailed on the *Île de France* to Europe, traveling first to northeastern France, where "Kick" was scheduled to begin her studies at a Sacred Heart convent. Within days of her arrival, Kathleen was certain she would hate the place—the rules were incredibly severe and the convent was so remote from general life that she felt terribly forlorn. Trusting her immediate impression, she contacted her mother and begged for a change of schools. As Rose listened to her daughter, a part of her thought Kathleen should try to stick it out, enduring the privations just as she had done at Blumenthal, but when she heard the sadness in Kathleen's usually vibrant voice she agreed to let her transfer at once—to a more sophisticated convent school in the Parisian suburb of Neuilly.

Jack, settling into his quarters at the London School of Economics, had little time to get to know Harold Laski, for within weeks of his arrival he was once again seriously ill, this time with an attack of jaundice. Fortunately, Joe and Rose were still in London at the time, and Joe made immediate arrangements, through Ambassador Robert W. Bingham at the American Embassy, to get Jack good medical care. By the third week of October, however, it became evident that Jack would have to interrupt his studies and go home. Writing to Bingham on October 21, 1935, Kennedy expressed his "heartfelt appreciation" for all Bingham had done, but, he said, "I have found it necessary to send my boy home and Mrs. Kennedy and I are leaving on the Berengaria on Wednesday."

Arriving back in the States, Jack felt better and thought he could manage at an American university. The place he wanted was Princeton, because Lem Billings and several other good friends from Choate were there, and perhaps because his brother was *not* there. According to Rose, Joe would have preferred his going to Harvard with his brother but finally acceded to Jack's desire and, through Herbert Bayard Swope, managed to get him admitted for the fall term even though classes had already begun. But no sooner had Jack arrived at Princeton than his old hepatitis flared up again, sending him back once more to the doctors. Wishing to remain in school, he never admitted how sick he was, but his father knew.

"I had a nice talk with Doctor Raycourt," Kennedy wrote to Jack on November 11, 1935,

and we have decided to . . . see how you get along until Thanksgiving. Then if no real improvement has been made, you and I will discuss whether or not it is best for you to lay off a year and try to put yourself in condition. After all, the only consideration I have in the whole matter is your happiness, and I don't want you to lose a year of your college life (which ordinarily brings great pleasure to a boy) by wrestling with a bad physical condition and a jam in your studies. A year is important, but it isn't so important if it's going to leave a mark for the rest of your life.

An even truer measure of Kennedy's concern for his son can be seen in a letter he wrote to Ambassador Bingham the following day. "Jack is far from being a well boy," Kennedy wrote, "and is giving me great concern with the result that my time for the next six months will be devoted to trying to help him recover his health with little or no time for business and politics."

Soon even Jack could no longer keep up his pretense of health. A few weeks after Thanksgiving he withdrew from Princeton, and he spent nearly two months in the hospital. Then, through Arthur Krock, Kennedy arranged for Jack to go to the Jay 6 Ranch in Arizona, where the sunny and dry climate was said to be good for health. There Jack gradually regained his strength, and by the fall of 1936 he was finally ready for college, though this time around he decided to go to Harvard instead of Princeton.

Jack's illness had a dampening effect on Kathleen's year abroad. While she found her first Solemn High Mass at Notre-Dame "the most impressive thing I have ever seen," which she wouldn't have missed for the world, she felt utterly alone and didn't know whether she could make it through a month, "let alone nine of them." Missing Jack terribly, she bought him a Tyrolean hat but could express her feelings only in her typically humorous style. "Am rather sad at the prospect of Xmas in Switzerland without any of the family," she wrote. "Every time I think of that darn brother of mine I burn. He certainly was a bum to go home."

But, once she recognized she had no choice but to stay, she made the best of the situation, throwing herself into her reading of *The Three Musketeers* in French, immersing herself in the great art exhibitions in Paris, and attending operas and balls. For no matter how strange the routine of the school seemed, there was always the opportunity to travel, the escape her mother had discovered a generation earlier. Traveling to Gstaad in Switzerland for Christmas and New Year's, she found she enjoyed skiing Swiss style, in which the skis were strapped to one's feet and it was necessary to have animal skins on the bottom of the skis. "The best part of all," she wrote Bobby, "is when the snow is very deep and you fall in a nice, soft, white bed." Then, at her March break, she went with four other girls and a chaperone to Rome, where she heard Mussolini speak and had an audience with the Pope, arranged through her father's friend Enrico Galeazzi, the Vatican's financial adviser.

Still, there remained an emptiness in her soul which she could not fill without her family. Anticipating her spring break, she begged her mother to come for a visit. "Mother, please please come over because it does get kinda lonely here . . . I'm sure I could stand saying goodbye after you came as I would realize I will be home in three months which isn't long compared to the six months I've gotten through." And, writing to her brothers and sisters, she kept repeating that she could not believe how long it had been since any member of her family had seen her. "Do you realize," she asked Bobby, "I haven't seen any beautiful Kennedy faces for seven months, such a long, long time?"

Finally, in the middle of April she received word that her mother was sailing on the *Île de France,* and she counted the days. Years later, Rose would remember Kathleen's face when they met at the Ritz in Paris. "She looked so pretty and so sophisticated in her new suit and hat, which she had bought just for my visit, but the moment she saw me she dissolved in tears of happiness as if she were still a little girl. I will never forget what I felt when I saw her. I realized so clearly how lucky I was to have this wonderfully effervescent, adorably loving and extremely pretty child as my daughter and friend."

They were indeed friends, sharing a love of clothes, a love of travel and a thirst for adventure. Through Kathleen, a social side of Rose that had been long dormant was brought to life once more and she felt almost as if she were seeing Europe for the first time. After spending a week in Paris, Rose decided to take Kathleen to a place where neither one of them had ever been before—Russia. Having received so many varied impressions from young Joe after his own trip to Russia with Laski the previous spring, Rose thought it would be an exciting idea to go and see for themselves. But in those days, Rose recorded in her memoirs, since to most people "the Soviet Union seemed as remote and mysterious as the other side of the moon," everybody seemed to think she was slightly out of her mind when she made arrangements for the two of them to travel there on their own.

As it turned out, they had a most enjoyable trip. With Ambassador William C. Bullitt as their host, they saw "everything there was to see" in Moscow and Leningrad: the ballet and the museums; schools and hospitals; the famous private apartments of Nicholas and Alexandra; and Lenin's tomb, where, well preserved, he rested on a red cushion in a glass case.

Indeed, it was such a wonderful trip, and Kathleen felt so happy being with her mother again, that when it was over she wasn't sure at first if she could make it on her own until the end of the term in July. "When we first got back to Paris," Rose recalled, "Kathleen couldn't imagine returning to the convent, but after we talked it over she agreed she should finish what she had begun."

In the springtime of their adult relationship, Rose and Kathleen were so close that many thought they were sisters. As Kathleen emerged into young womanhood, there was no one whose companionship Rose enjoyed more. "Traveling with Kathleen was such a joy," Rose later recalled, "it reminded me of all the wonderful trips I had taken with my sister Agnes."

Sailing home on the maiden voyage of the *Queen Mary* on May 27, Rose penned a loving letter to her daughter:

> My dear Kathleen,
>
> Here I am aboard, sailing over to Cherbourg—so near and yet so far from you, my pet. We went off with the band playing the English national anthem, and there were dozens of small craft and large excursion boats in the harbor and many yachts . . .
>
> Well, darling, I miss you and wish you were along, but I am so glad you decided to stay. You are a great joy to us both.

# CHAPTER 29

# TEMPTING

# THE

# GODS

These were good years for Joseph Kennedy. After his successful tenure at the SEC, everything he touched seemed to become gold. In the spring of 1936, Paramount Pictures hired him as a special adviser to analyze why the company was failing; in the second quarter of 1936 it had reported a deficit of nearly $6 million on operations alone. Kennedy's report took less than a month to complete, but it was so helpful to Paramount executives that Adolph Zukor tried to persuade Rose to let her husband stay in Hollywood a bit longer. "I am sure you will be interested to know of the splendid work Joe did while he was here . . ." Zukor wrote to her on May 28, 1936. "He was very reluctant to make any commitments or promises as he feels it would prevent him from spending the summer with his family which is so important to him, to you and the children. His understanding of the industry and its problems is so very valuable and important to us at Paramount that we all feel it would be a great loss if he did not remain with us."

Performing similar work for RCA at a fee of $150,000, Kennedy had become one of the highest-paid financial consultants in the country. His return to business did not diminish his closeness to FDR, however. On the contrary, their friendship remained strong, as evidenced by numerous invitations to the White House from the President and his various aides. "I am asking a little group of old friends of the President to have dinner with me," Jim Farley wrote on June 11, 1936. "We are planning to make the night on which the President accepts the nomination the greatest night of his life and I want your help and counsel on the best way to bring this about."

Then, as the '36 campaign got under way, Kennedy volunteered to put together a defense of Roosevelt's policies in a small book which he called *I'm for Roosevelt*. Starting with an outline which he sent to the White House for Roosevelt's suggestions, Kennedy enlisted Arthur Krock to write the book. "I wonder if you could give me some of your time each week for, say the next five weeks, to help put it in shape," Kennedy wrote to Krock on June 24. "I shall like to make a deal with you for $1000 a week for 5 weeks, if that is worth your while. Your time and efforts are worth a lot to me and if you can see your way clear to doing it, I should love to have you." Krock agreed at once to work on the book, though he made a note for his own files that he was doing it gratis. "I haven't done much playing since you tossed this batch of literature at me," he wrote to Kennedy on July 3, "but I enjoyed the labor and do not begrudge the time, only hoping you are pleased."

Published in September, the book was a curious product, an embrace of the New Deal so uncritical that "it ventured perilously out on a limb to applaud its hero." Arguing that "an organized functioning society requires a planned economy," the book said nothing about the limits, if any, of government planning. In his emotional loyalty to Roosevelt, Kennedy credited the Administration with every improvement in the economy since 1933. "Roosevelt must be gratified by the publication of this book by Mr. Kennedy," *The Saturday Review of Literature* noted, adding that Kennedy was a man who commanded widespread confidence in the public's mind.

Kennedy also made a number of speeches for Roosevelt that fall, as well as a highly publicized radio address. Directing his comments to businessmen, he spoke clearly and effectively. "As an American citizen," he told the Democratic Business Men's League of Massachusetts, "I resent the efforts which are now being made for low, political purposes to confuse a Christian program of social justice with a Godless program of Communism. It is a cowardly trick of discredited Republican politicians to play upon religious feelings and patriotic impulses in a desperate attempt to evade the real issues of the campaign. There has scarcely been a liberal piece of legislation during the last sixty years that has not been opposed as Communistic . . . Those who battle for truth, for social justice, must of necessity follow a thorny path but even if he were vilified one thousand times worse, he is vindicated in the righteousness of his cause and will be compensated in the sweetness of victory."

With the incontrovertible completeness of Roosevelt's victory over Alfred Landon in November 1936, Kennedy's power increased. In an article entitled "Who's Who at FDR's Ear," *Business Week* noted: "Joseph Kennedy has grown tremendously in Roosevelt's esteem. His voice will be potent on any question in respect to the handling of business, corporations and taxes."

In this happy and fulfilling time, sorrow arrived unexpectedly with the sudden death of Agnes Fitzgerald, Rose's younger sister. Throughout her twenties and most of her thirties, Agnes had remained single, living with her parents in their Dorchester home. A pretty woman with blond wavy hair and skin as clear and soft as it was when she was a girl, Agnes had attracted many suitors, among them Joe Kennedy's friend Chris Dunphy. But it was not until she met Joseph Gargan, a young lawyer who had been a football hero at Notre Dame and a captain in the Marine Corps, that she decided to marry. Becoming pregnant for the first time at thirty-seven, she gave birth to a son, Joey, in a difficult cesarean delivery. "In those days," her son later recalled, "the theory was that a woman should not have her first child after twenty-six because it was thought that the pelvic area was no longer stretchable, that it turned to bone. So Mother had a cesarean with me and then two more cesareans with my two sisters, Mary Jo and Ann, born when she was thirty-eight and forty-two."

The late summer of 1936 found Agnes at home in Boston with her three children, having just returned from a family vacation in Maine. Her husband was away on a business trip. On the evening of September 17, she talked with her father on the telephone around nine o'clock, making preparations for the party the next day to celebrate Mary Jo's fourth birthday. The next morning, when six-year-old Joey came running into his mother's room he could not rouse her from sleep, and he knew at once that she was dead. At the young age of forty-three, Agnes had suffered an embolism, experiencing the same fate that had felled her grandmother, Rosanna, some sixty years before. It was the third death in the Fitzgerald family; Eunice was first, dying of tuberculosis at twenty-three, then Fred, who drank himself to death at thirty-one, and now Agnes.

For Rose, Agnes' sudden death came as "a terrible blow," the most serious loss she had yet sustained in her life. For months she was unable to leave her home, finding solace only in the extended visit of Joe Gargan and the three small children Agnes had left behind. As the year came to an end, she was still in mourning, still not recovered enough to attend a dinner at the White House. "As I told you last night on the phone," Joe Kennedy wrote to Missy LeHand, "Rose and I regret exceedingly that we are obliged to decline the President and Mrs. Roosevelt's invitation to attend dinner on January 5. The real reason is since Rose's sister's death two months ago she has been terribly upset and has not gone out publically [sic] at all . . . She feels bad about it . . . but I am sure it is for the best that she should stay here for awhile longer. She is not well by any means."

In these difficult months, Rosemary provided an additional source of sorrow. While the early reports from her tutors suggested that, given her limitations, she was doing exceptionally well in her class work, having reached about a fourth-grade level in reading, spelling and arithmetic, her progress from then on seemed to stop, frustrating her teachers, her parents and, most of all, Rosemary herself. "I had a firm talk with Rosemary," Kennedy wrote to Miss Newton, her teacher at the special convent school in Providence where she had been sent at sixteen, "and told her that something must be done and I am sure she really wants to do it. It is something else besides herself that must be blamed for her attitude. By that I mean, it is her inherent backwardness, rather than a bad disposition."

Rosemary never stopped trying even though her fear of failure was very great. Writing to her parents about a Latin test, she asked them to "pray very hard that I will get someplace." Then, after seeing her father one weekend at school, she wrote, "I would do anything to make you so happy. I hate to disapoint [sic] you in anyway. Come to see me very soon. I get lonesome everyday."

As the years went by, Rosemary's problems increased dramatically. "I have had from 15 to 20 years experience with retarded children," Helen Newton told Rose in 1936, "and Rose is the most difficult child to teach so that she may retain knowledge that I have ever encountered." At the age of eighteen, she had reached only a fifth-grade level in English, and in math she was unable to move beyond the fourth-grade problems she had originally learned at nine or ten. Even her dancing was becoming difficult for her. "Am wondering if Mrs. D working her too hard at dancing," her tutor Amanda Rohde wrote to Rose. "She seems especially irritable the day after her lessons.

"It appears to me," the tutor went on, "she has taken advantage of her weakness and has used it as a weapon to have her way too much. . . . Now she makes herself unpleasant when she finds herself in a situation in which she has to think. If she is allowed to continue in this, she will become more and more difficult to live with. Little by little she must be brought to face reality . . . day-dreaming allows her to brood too much about herself." In attributing Rosemary's problems to a spoiled childhood, Miss Rohde failed to understand that the problem was just the opposite: born into an uncommonly achieving family, Rosemary never stopped trying to improve, but no matter how hard she tried she could never catch up with her sisters and brothers, and, as the years went by, her frustration deepened.

Still, Rose and Joe tried to include her in as many family activities as possible, and they repeatedly urged Joe Junior and Jack to take her to dances, to call her up and to write to her. "Rose will be in Boston around Wednesday or Thursday," Kennedy wrote to Joe Junior, "so give her a ring and tell her you understand she was swell down South." To these requests both Joe and Jack usually responded at once, and their correspondence with their sister is sensitive and warm. "Received your very nice letter this morning," Joe Junior writes, "and was delighted to notice how good your writing was. It will be very much better than mine as I didn't try to write well until I was your age, so now I am sorry. Keep up the good work."

For Rosemary, it was a special treat to be taken to lunch or dinner by her handsome brothers. "Rosemary had a marvelous time," Kennedy told Jack after one of these occasions, "and really does not require many gestures like this to make her life worthwhile."

In January 1937, the Kennedy family traveled to Washington for the second inaugural of Franklin Roosevelt.

> We arrived in Washington D.C. about 6:30 January 19 [twelve-year-old Bobby recorded]. On Wednesday we went to the luncheon in the Ballroom of the White House . . . We talked with the President's secretary, Mr. McIntire and Jimmy Roosevelt who took us in for an interview with his father. President Roosevelt said, "It is about time you came. How is your father? How can I put my arm around all of you? Which is the oldest? You are all so big?" At five o'clock we all went to the reception in the Grand Ball room in the White House. Mrs. Roosevelt and some others were in the receiving line. Mrs. Roosevelt did not realize who we were until we had almost gone by. She spoke to us and said, "This is the Kennedys, isn't it?"

The President's reelection brought Kennedy an offer of a job, but not the Treasury post he desired. "I am very anxious to have the U.S.

Maritime Commission appointed and functioning at the earliest possible date," Roosevelt wrote to him in February. "I am naturally anxious that in its organizing stage the commission shall have the advice and help of the most outstanding person available. My thoughts have turned to you and although I know that you are not anxious to return to public service, I am writing to ask your favorable consideration of my desire to appoint you as Chairman of the Commission."

At first, Kennedy expressed reluctance about accepting the assignment. "To be very honest with you," he wrote to his friend Senator James F. Byrnes of South Carolina, "I had great hesitancy in taking this job. I had received a couple of large assignments which were along the lines I like and they would have proved very profitable but the President made his appeal on such a personal basis that there was nothing for me to do but go back into government service."

His hesitancy was merely a pose, however, a desire to appear in public as a reluctant maiden, for in fact, as Rose herself later admitted, "he wanted nothing more than to return to the stimulation of public life." Telling Roosevelt he was "deeply honored by the suggestion," Kennedy prevailed once more upon his old friend Eddie Moore, and the two of them returned to Marwood, the same house they had rented during their days at the SEC. And this time Kennedy's appointment was met with praise from all quarters. "I am delighted that you are back in the official family," Secretary of the Interior Harold Ickes wrote. "That the President should have made you Chairman of the Maritime is the highest possible compliment." Always sentimental at moments like this, Kennedy thanked Ickes profusely for his note and told him "it would go down in the archives with the three or four I have from the President for my children and grandchildren."

As soon as he was settled back into Washington life, Kennedy met with the Society of American Newspaper Editors and delivered a remarkably straightforward speech which set him off on just the right footing. Conceding at the start that his only experience in maritime matters was his work at Bethlehem during the war, he said, "I will not try your credulity by posing as an expert in the matters which are the concern of the Maritime Commission. In fact, I feel a good deal like the English judge of probate who, although completely ignorant of admiralty law, because of the illness of a colleague was pressed into service to handle a crowded session in admiralty. As he ascended the bench, he looked very sorrowfully at the assemblage of admiralty lawyers and dolefully remarked, 'And may there be no moaning of the bar when I put out to sea.'" The editors loved the speech, and for months Kennedy received nothing but the most positive press.

But his success with the press did not come without a great deal of planning on his part. Indeed, the desire to enhance the Kennedy image was a driving force in this complicated man, and the skill he evinced at creating just the right image was phenomenal. In his private papers there are countless letters to individual reporters; whenever a favorable article reached his attention through his private clipping service, he wrote to the reporter and thanked him; and at every holiday he lavished expensive gifts on dozens of journalists. "Just arrived home after a brief trip," Drew Pearson wrote in 1937, "to find your very lovely present awaiting me. It is most beautiful and I shall wear it with great relish and with many memories of a very swell friend."

In the world of journalism, there was no man closer to Kennedy than *New York Times* columnist Arthur Krock. Since their first meeting during the 1932 campaign trip, the two had come to share each other's ambitions and disappointments to the point where each instinctively moved to help the other out. Perhaps it was merely a relationship of convenience, as Krock suggested years later after the friendship had turned sour, but in the thirties, when they were working together on a number of projects and sharing vacations at Palm Beach, there was an intimacy between these two powerful men that can be described only as a friendship.

> I have just finished reading your article in the *Times* this morning [Kennedy told Krock on July 1, 1937]. Three years ago this week you started me on my way with another article in the *Times*. I am practical enough to know that the help you have given me beginning with that article three years ago and all those in between and today's have been the real reason that the Press of the country have given me all the breaks. So Arthur, my father taught me, "be grateful and be loyal at whatever cost." I am most appreciative and will never forget it.

Krock diplomatically countered: "I may have lighted your federal path . . . [but] I never started you on it. Every inch of the way you won yourself and splendidly."

From the start, Joe understood that the image a man projects to the public is not something that simply happens but something which can be shaped in large part by the man himself. Operating his own public-relations office, he took pains to have himself portrayed in public the way he wanted to be portrayed—as a brilliant businessman whose first love was his family, a reluctant public servant who heeded his President's call at the sacrifice of his private interest. Throughout the twenties and thirties, Joe's efforts at his own image making proved remarkably successful, so successful that in September 1937 *Fortune* magazine decided to devote its cover story to Joseph Patrick Kennedy.

When he first heard the news, Rose recalled, "he was thrilled, for he knew that *Fortune* was one of the most prestigious magazines in the country and that this story would spark many more." As it happened, however, the reporter assigned to the project, a young man named Earle Looker, did not come away with a glowing opinion of the feisty Irishman. The article was one of the least favorable pieces ever written about Kennedy, portraying him as a man driven by his own ambitions with little regard for the institutions he touched, a profiteer willing to take money wherever he could find it. Fortunately for Kennedy, an agreement had been forged which gave him access to an advance draft of the article, and the moment he finished reading it he prepared for battle.

The first step was a long letter to the managing editor of *Fortune*, Russell Davenport, which began in a tone that made Kennedy's feelings unmistakably clear:

> Generally, my comment on this article is that it is permeated with distrust of my character, dislike of my occupations and social prejudice against my origin. If this is the kind of attitude *Fortune* wants to reflect, the choice is within your right to make. If, however, you prefer to have the article written objectively, without precise aspersions and nasty insinuations, I have marked 54 inaccuracies in as many places. These I should be glad to point out to you if and when you come to see me on that understanding.

A reading of the "54 inaccuracies" suggests that in many cases Kennedy was right. But in other cases his objection was more a matter of not liking to see in print what Looker had to say.

> I have no trouble in trusting you [Kennedy wrote to Davenport in a follow-up letter]. The trouble is with Looker whose presentation of me is so cheap and tawdry that a rereading of the script sickened me. There are so many deliberate misrepresentations that I believe that either Looker has an ingrained hatred of the Irish or a resentment against me personally. The only basis for personal antagonism I could think of might be Looker's anger at my failure to arrange for him a sale of his book to a motion picture company . . . If such is the explanation for the article, the word blackmail despite all its ugly imputations is not too extreme a characterization. After consulting with some friends in Washington, I am convinced that it would be useless to attempt to revise a draft so permeated with bias and incompetence.

In response, Davenport arranged for Kennedy to meet with one of his top editors to voice his critique in person. At that meeting, the editor apparently assured Kennedy that the tone of the article did not reflect *Fortune*'s attitude toward him but was simply the personal opinion of the author. "I am convinced after talking with your Mr. Wood," Kennedy wrote to Davenport, "that it is just the brainchild of a psychopathic case."

But he wanted more than personal satisfaction: he wanted the article killed. And, astonishingly, after a meeting in Washington with Davenport, this was precisely what happened. At great trouble and expense, *Fortune* agreed to assign a new writer, Robert Cantwell, to the story, and the article he produced, after weeks of exhaustive research, presented Kennedy in a very favorable light and became the foundation for much that was later written about him.

It was, for Joe Kennedy, a clear-cut triumph. But his experience in this instance, confirmed by the generally positive press that followed him through the rest of the decade, generated in him a characteristic arrogance toward the press that would lead inexorably to a celebrated interview which would bring his public career to a humiliating close.

While concentrating during the week on maritime business—which involved instituting a new subsidy program to revitalize the shipping industry—Kennedy spent his weekends working as a consultant to the debt-ridden Hearst organization. For the leader of the world's greatest publishing organization, the day of reckoning had come. After years of spending more money than he had—in the support of unprofitable papers and the purchase of castles, Old Masters, antiques and other treasures—the seventy-four-year-old Hearst was so burdened with debt that he was no longer able to borrow new money to service the old. The only alternative to avoiding bankruptcy was to begin liquidating his assets by selling off the losing papers (including the *Washington Times-Herald*, the *New York American*, the *Boston American* and the *Chicago Herald*) and putting his treasures up for auction. It was a difficult period for the old warrior as he was "forced to do a thousand things he did not want to do." In distress, Hearst turned to Joseph Kennedy for advice.

From the correspondence in Kennedy's papers, it is clear that Kennedy took a hard line from the start, advocating the sale of a major asset, such as the newspapers. "We all realize this necessitates a frightful sacrifice in the value of this property," he concluded, " . . . but facing the problem tonight it is the only move to be made." But in 1937 Hearst was unwilling to make this choice. Explaining this to Kennedy, his aide Arthur Poole wrote: "While it will be all right to sell antiques or real estate it would be harmful to have people know that any public properties are for sale. People are so accustomed to Mr. Hearst's boast that he does not sell publications, that they would be startled by the offer of several of them for sale and would infer that his cash position was weak."

Still, Kennedy insisted that the fight against insolvency required something more than the sale of antiques, which he correctly predicted would be a slow process at best, and in June of 1937 he offered to purchase the two Boston papers, the *Daily Record* and the *Evening American*, himself for cash. This was not an offer of charity. For several weeks he and his friend Walter Howey had been talking about buying the papers, and Howey was convinced that "should these properties come into our hands I can turn their small loss into a profit of a half million dollars the first year. . . . This apparent miracle will be accomplished by turning the evening paper, which now is a white elephant, into a tabloid."

But even as conditions worsened, the same old Hearst weakness, the refusal to face up to an unpleasant reality that was a part of his megalomania, came into play and Kennedy was unable to get a straight answer from him. "I am receiving little information," Kennedy telegraphed to Hearst on August 19, 1937. "I am not at all happy over the situation as I know it. I am informed that you are not directly available by telephone. I believe it highly desirable that you be so located as to be open to telephone communications immediately when required."

On the days when Hearst was willing to face the staggering nature of his problem (the organization's debt totaled $126 million to sixteen different banks), he considered placing Kennedy in legal control of his finances. "Don't be surprised if Kennedy becomes Hearst's general manager," *Newsweek* predicted on August 28. But the process of liquidation was ultimately so complicated and so painful for a man of Hearst's vulnerable ego that hard decisions took months and years to make. And in the meantime Kennedy had a great many other projects to keep him busy.

Curiously, the more Kennedy's national stature grew, the more he turned his attention back to the city of his birth, as if he could now *will* Boston into giving him his proper due. Invited to give the major address at the fifty-fourth annual St. Patrick's Day dinner, sponsored by the Irish Clover Club, at the Hotel Somerset in Boston, Kennedy delivered a strange speech in which he conceded that too many of the Irish in Boston had suffered under the handicap of "not possessing family tradition adequate to win the respect and confidence of their Puritan neighbors." Still possessed, as was his father-in-law, John Fitzgerald, of a positive image of the old Yankee forebears who had passed their power and resources down through the ages to their children, Kennedy seemed to be arguing that the Irish must follow in their footsteps. A sensible argument, perhaps, encapsulating what he himself had tried to do, but not one calculated to win the support of an Irish people still sensitive to criticism and, in particular, to comparison with the Yankees.

"It was with astonishment," a bitter Francis O'Hara wrote to Kennedy,

> that I read your address . . . to the effect that our people had not tradition sufficient to satisfy our Puritan neighbors. What tradition had they? Descendants of people who abandoned their faith in time of adversity and whose chief claim to fame is an ability to accumulate money? A race who have stolen the lands and the property of weaker peoples all over the world? . . . When you stated our traditions were not sufficient for these Yankees it made me and many of my friends sorrowful that you, who represented us in high positions, should be so unaware of our great traditions and present such shallow thoughts on a day dedicated to the Patron Saint of Ireland.

In response, Kennedy tried to assuage O'Hara with the argument that newspaper reports had been misleading about the tone of the speech and that he had never for a moment intended to endorse the superiority myth of *The Late George Apley;* but the incident reflected a confusion in his mind as to where he belonged. Wanting to prove he was above the ordinary Irishman, Kennedy found it necessary at times to disassociate himself from Irish ways, yet try as he might he could never escape the fact that his emotional roots were deeply sunk in the old Irish sections of Boston. It was a confusion that he would never resolve.

But, for Kennedy, the continuing pull of Boston was also explained by the presence of his two oldest sons at Harvard. In the fall of 1936, while Joe entered his junior year, Jack had become a freshman. Recovered from his illness but still not robust, Jack was a lank, bony six-foot-tall youth who looked even lighter than his 149 pounds. Harvard had not been an uncomplicated choice for him, for as he settled into Room 32 of Weldon Hall he faced the same situation he had faced when he first entered Choate: his own presence on campus was distinguished mainly for his relationship to his older brother, who was steadily emerging as one of the stars in the class of '38.

It could not have been easy for Jack that first year, when the pages of the *Crimson* were filled with his brother's political triumphs. In the early spring, Joe Junior was elected chairman of the Winthrop House committee. Then, in May, he beat out Caspar Weinberger, Nathaniel Benchley and thirteen other juniors to win a position on the student council. The following week he was selected as an usher for Class Day, and the week after that he was named business manager of the class album. In contrast, Jack failed to finish among the top six out of twenty-nine candidates vying for the freshman slots on the student council, and so he was not in the runoff election.

Nor did Jack achieve the success he wanted in sports, though his failure was certainly not for lack of trying. While he survived all the early cuts on the freshman football squad, and while he was single-minded in his efforts to get his body in shape, his low weight proved an insurmountable obstacle. "It was a matter of determination," Jack's friend Harvard football hero Torbert Macdonald recalled. "After practice was over he'd have me throw the ball for him and he'd practice snagging passes for an hour at a time, hundreds of passes."

Years later, Macdonald recalled a tense scene after practice one day. Joe Junior came up to Jack and offered advice: "Jack, if you want my opinion, you'd be better off forgetting about football. You just don't weigh enough and you're going to get hurt." Jack's face flushed with anger, but he did not respond. At this point, Macdonald decided to get involved. "Come off it, Joe," he said. "Jack doesn't need any looking after." But, to Macdonald's surprise, Jack whirled on him, saying, "Mind your own business! Keep out of it! I'm talking to Joe, not you!"

As it happened, Joe Junior showed prescience in his advice, for the following year, in a scrimmage against the much heavier varsity squad, Jack was thrown to the ground and ruptured a spinal disc. It was an injury that was to plague him the rest of his life.

In swimming, Jack had better luck. As a backstroke artist, he helped to lead his undefeated freshman team to victory in the relay against Dartmouth and he stood a good chance of qualifying for the starting position against Yale. But once again, illness intervened. Three weeks before the Yale meet, he was confined to the campus infirmary with yet another undisclosed ailment. Determined to keep practicing, he managed, with the help of Torby, to sneak into the pool for an hour a day. His best effort fell short, however, when Richard Tregaskis, later to become famous as the author of *Guadalcanal Diary*, came in three seconds ahead of him in the qualifying heat, undoing his chance to compete against Yale.

In spite of his difficulties with athletics and his failure in campus politics, Jack managed to create his own world at Harvard, just as he had done at Choate. Within months he had created a loyal cadre of friends, and in Torby Macdonald he found a best friend who was for him the counterpart of Lem Billings at Choate. Also a second son, also having had to fight to win recognition from his family, Torby intuitively understood Jack's personal struggle. And, like Lem, Torby also fell in love with Jack's sister Kathleen.

Toward the end of his freshman year, Jack joined the committee that sponsored the annual freshman smoker, a rowdy corncob-pipe affair that attracted more than a thousand freshmen. Agreeing to provide the entertainment, Jack knew he could count on his father, and his father came through. Through Joe Kennedy's contacts in Boston, Jack managed to get Gertrude Niessen, the throaty New York stage and concert singer, and baseball stars Dizzy Dean and Frankie Frisch. Writing to Joe Conway just before the smoker, Kennedy Senior said: "I had no idea I was wishing such a tough job on you when I suggested to young Jack that he get in touch with you to have Dizzy Dean and Frankie Frisch for his smoker . . . you have done your usual job." When the night of the smoker arrived, young Jack was in his glory. With Memorial Hall filled to capacity, he was remarkably funny as master of ceremonies and the smoker was considered one of the most sparkling in many a year.

After this wildly successful performance, Jack's stature in his class increased. When the time came to apply for admission to a house, he had no trouble gaining acceptance into Winthrop House, where he was ranked as "one of the most popular men in his class."

Academically, Jack's record the first year remained mediocre, but his grades told only part of the story of a rapidly maturing mind. Tutors recall him as a vital student who thought deeply about political issues, who probed, read and asked questions. Then, in the summer of 1937, after his freshman year, a summer when Joe Junior and Kathleen traveled together on the Continent, Jack set off for Europe with his friend Lem Billings on a voyage that would hasten still further the growth of his political insight. While his letters to his father during the trip reveal a young man's perspective on complicated events, his understanding of the situation in Europe proved far more sophisticated than the analyses his brother Joe had made on his trip three years before.

From Spain, where the battle between supporters and opponents of the newly established Spanish republic had erupted into a bloody civil war, Jack wrote to his father about "the almost complete ignorance 95% of the people in the US have about situations as a whole here. For example, most people in the US are for Franco, and while I felt that perhaps it would be far better for Spain if Franco should win—as he would strengthen and unite Spain—yet, at the beginning, the Government was in the right morally speaking as its program was similar to the New Deal." Able to view the Spanish situation in its international context, Jack concluded that the crux of the situation lay in the extent to which the intervening powers—Germany, Italy and Russia—would go "in trying to secure victory for themselves."

. . .

It was a time, indeed, when Joe Senior could rightly be proud of both his sons just as they were terribly proud of him. In the fall of 1937, Joe Junior, as chairman of the Winthrop House committee, invited his father to be a guest speaker in the Thursday-night speaker series. Thirty years later, the head of the Winthrop House dining hall, a warmhearted woman named Mrs. de Pinto, could still recall the entire evening as if it had taken place the week before. Both Joe and Jack arrived a few minutes late, she recalled, having rushed in from football and swimming, and they wanted very badly to speak to their father but felt they had better wait. But then, as Winthrop's housemaster, Dr. Ferry, stood up to introduce Kennedy, he saw the boys standing in the back and invited them to come up and say hello to their father before the speech began. With that opening, the two boys happily ran up to the front of the hall, and without any apparent embarrassment, in front of all their friends and teachers, they embraced their father warmly and kissed him on the lips.

At the time of the speech, Joe Senior was the chairman of the Maritime Commission, but he chose to speak about his days at the SEC, giving what John Kenneth Galbraith, who was then a tutor at Winthrop House, recalls as "an absolutely wonderful talk, filled with anecdotes about his days in the unregulated stock market, telling what he personally knew of bucket shops, wire houses and pools." It was a speech, Galbraith observed, "ideally calculated to a young audience, ending with himself leading the raid as the SEC policeman." And beyond the speech, Galbraith recalls his vivid impression of Kennedy as "a buoyant, enormously self-assured man, greatly given to showmanship and filled with an extraordinary vitality." Indeed, Galbraith concluded, "Kennedy was so ebullient and so successful in his presentation that even if his son had not become President, I would have remembered that night."

That same vitality could unleash an extraordinary anger when Kennedy believed one of his children had been given an unfair deal. Within a month of his appearance at Winthrop House, Kennedy was back at Harvard again, this time for the Harvard–Yale game on November 20, 1937. Seated next to his old friend Tommy Campbell (who was then vice-president of the Norfolk Trust Company in Boston), Kennedy was there to watch his son Joe become eligible for his football letter. All through the fall, despite his bum knee, young Joe had traveled with the team, shivering on benches from West Point on the Hudson to Dartmouth in the mountains of New Hampshire, seeing little action but knowing that so long as he was put in for but a few seconds of play at the Yale game, he would win his H.

The day of the big game had dawned cold and cloudy, but the dismal weather failed to diminish the enthusiasm of the more than 58,000 fans who crowded into the stadium. While Harvard had not beaten Yale since 1933, this team, under Coach Dick Harlow, was considered "the hardest hitting, best coached and most spirited Crimson eleven in many years," and was given a good shot at beating the unbeatable Blue and restoring Harvard's pride.

As it turned out, Harlow's team performed better than even Harvard's most fervent rooters had expected. As the halftime break approached, with the fat-bellied clouds beginning to unleash a steady stream of snow, Harvard was ahead of Yale 6–0. On the bench, the graduating seniors began to shift impatiently, knowing that by tradition the minutes before the halftime gun were when the coach was likely to play his substitutes and thus assure every member of the squad his letter. But at this juncture Yale threatened a return touchdown, and Harlow made no move to send in his second string.

When the teams returned to the field after the half, Yale took the kickoff and marched straight for a touchdown in seven plays. There was a dramatic tension in the cold stadium air as the crowd watched Yale miss the extra point, leaving the score tied at 6–6. There it remained until the last quarter of play, when Harvard's Francis Foley swept the Yale left flank to score a touchdown standing up in the corner of the end zone. This time the conversion was made, putting Harvard ahead by a score of 13–6.

With less than six minutes left, the Harvard bench found it almost impossible to keep their seats. Surely now, with a seven-point lead, Harlow would begin to make substitutions. But, as the minutes flew, with Yale threatening the entire time, the coach sat impassively in his seat, deciding, against tradition, to keep the first team on the field to ensure a victory. "Some seniors stayed tight-faced," Hank Searls reports; "some, like Joe, fought tears; some could bear it no longer and begged" to be put in. The clock moved forward, and sometime in the last moments young Joe had to face the fact that his fondest dream, the dream for which he had suffered a broken arm and an injured knee, was dead.

As the final whistle blew, signaling a Harvard triumph, thousands of joyful spectators raced onto the muddy gridiron, "like schoolboys released for a recess period." Joe Senior, still seated in the stands, turned helplessly to Tommy Campbell, then fought his way through the hysterical fans to provide solace to his son. In the melee, the story is told, Kennedy ran into Harlow, but what was exchanged can only be imagined, for in one stroke Harlow had ruined the hopes Joe Junior had entertained for four long years. Nor was Kennedy alone in his bitterness. In the *Crimson* the following day, Harlow was asked to defend his refusal to give the subs a chance. "Our first debt is to Harvard football," he replied. "We needed our strongest defensive combination up to the closing whistle."

Victory at any cost: it was an attitude Joe Senior would have respected under different circumstances. But when the cost was pain to one of his own, he was unforgiving. Branding Harlow's action an unthinkable breach of tradition, he vowed never to contribute another cent to his alma mater.

As it turned out, Kennedy's resentment toward Harvard was soon forgotten in the wake of a great triumph for the entire Kennedy family. For, in the second week of December 1937, Joseph Patrick Kennedy was appointed ambassador to the Court of St. James's, the first Irishman ever appointed to that position.

According to Arthur Krock, the then Ambassador, Robert Bingham, had long been anxious to resign. Plagued by ill health, he had returned to America for treatment in the spring of 1937, at which time Roosevelt had begun considering the possibility that Kennedy might succeed him. Then, in November 1937, Bingham was again hospitalized and this time his condition looked critical. Knowing that the ambassadorship to Great Britain was the one post Kennedy could never turn down, for it was the most prestigious of all diplomatic posts, Roosevelt called him into the White House in early December and offered him the job. To Roosevelt, the appointment seemed ideal. While Kennedy merited a place in the Administration, he was of too independent a temperament to be considered for the Cabinet; the London post, however, was a great plum and it was far away. As for Kennedy's reaction, Roosevelt knew his man. "The moment the appointment was proposed," Rose later admitted, "Joe accepted. It was the kind of appointment he had been waiting for all along."

The press reaction to Kennedy's appointment was overwhelmingly favorable. In paper after paper, the story was told of the East Boston lad who had worked his way through college to become the youngest bank president in the country and a millionaire by the time he was thirty. Seen as the Irish-American Rockefeller, the Frank Buck of the business jungle, the country's number-one financial doctor and a social reformer with a King Midas touch, the image of Irish Joe in England delighted reporters all across the land. Concentrating on his immigrant forebears, the press portrayed the appointment as the fulfillment of the American dream.

From dozens of friends and acquaintances, Kennedy received an additional battery of praise. "I am tickled to death that our country is going to send a good man to England," Leverett Saltonstall wrote, "as we need him over there." And speaking simply as Mike from East Boston, an old friend of P. J. Kennedy's wrote, "I thank God I have lived long enough to see Kennedy's name spread all over the world the way I like it."

But the letter that touched the deepest chord in Kennedy came from Joseph Tumulty, a fellow Irishman and Woodrow Wilson's former secretary.

> As in your case [Tumulty wrote, referring to his own appointment to the White House twenty-four years before], for the first time in the history of the U.S. a man of my faith and my race was appointed to this important post. Upon taking the oath of office, I entered into a solemn covenant with myself that . . . I would strive to conduct myself so that no member of my faith or race would regret my appointment, otherwise I would disappoint every Irish lad in the world. Then too there was a feeling in my heart that I must not disappoint my dear father and mother who had struggled to make it possible for me . . . You will not only be the American Ambassador to Great Britain, but in your actions as you go across the sea, you will be the trustee of the hopes and dreams of every Irish lad in America.

In an emotional response, Kennedy told Tumulty, "I do not expect to get a letter from any one in this country that will move me as much as your letter has done . . . I, too, have a hostage to the future in my large family, as you have and my only personal satisfaction is that I will leave the heritage to them that I did the best I could for a great nation."

At this glorious moment of unprecedented publicity and pride, it was perhaps not surprising that Kennedy failed to absorb the one countering message, received in a long, remarkably thoughtful letter from his reporter friend Boake Carter:

> You are a sincere man, Joe. You are a man of courage. You possess that great faith that so many Irishmen have—the faith that no matter what he tackles, he can't be licked. You are an honest man. But the job of Ambassador to London needs not only honesty, sincerity, faith and an abounding courage—it needs skill brought by years of training. And that, Joe, you simply don't possess. Do not think me unkind in saying that. On the contrary, I'm trying to save you some heart aches. I don't condemn the trolley car driver because he cannot pilot a plane off the ground . . . I do not condemn Kennedy, the organizer, the businessman, because he is not a trained diplomatic surgeon. But, I say this to you in all sincerity from the bottom of my heart—it takes a mighty big man to know when a job is too big for him—or let us say, when there is a job before him which he knows is not his type of job.

You've got enough horse sense to know that with the experience you've had, and the experience that this sort of job demands, in view of the fact that the probable welfare of 130 million lives may hang on the results of the conduct of that post, you tempt all the Gods of the world in diving into the Court of St. James as an expert. Joe, in so complicated a job, there is no place for amateurs . . . For if you don't realize that soon enough, you're going to be hurt as you were never hurt in your life. . . .

Seen in retrospect, in view of how far Kennedy would fall from this height of earthly greatness, how calamitous the ambassadorship would turn out for both the country and the man, Boake Carter's warnings give the Kennedy story the aura of dramatic tragedy. Indeed, had Kennedy been able to say no, the entire history of the Kennedy family might have been different. Had he remained in the States to finish up his work at the Maritime Commission and then returned to private life, there is no reason to believe that Kennedy would not have been tapped for yet another challenging assignment at home. Had he been able to say no and made it very clear, as Carter suggested, that he was doing it "on behalf of the people," his no could have become "a centurion shout" on behalf of finding the most highly skilled diplomat for this most sensitive post.

But as it was, Kennedy was unable to consider the possibility that any job was beyond his range. Standing at the summit of his powers, he was revealed as a man whose source of greatness, his absolute confidence in his ability to tackle anything, became his fatal flaw. Built on a grand scale, possessed of great passions and desires for his family, he would carry abroad his fatal tendency to identify his country's well-being with that of himself and his own immediate family. And when it was all over, his failure would not be something which simply happened to him as a consequence of events beyond his control, it would be something he brought about by his own actions. Borne as he was on an irresistible tide of ethnic pride, Joseph Patrick Kennedy could not have refused the opportunity to become the first Irish-American appointed to the court of St. James's.

# CHAPTER 30
# ARRIVAL
# IN
# LONDON

Joseph Kennedy took possession of the American Embassy in London on a brilliant afternoon in the first week of March 1938. The day was cool but sunny, a promise of the coming of spring, whose wonder and enchantment never failed, in the words of British travel writer H. J. Massingham, to take London by storm, "soothing our sickness, recharging our sap, meeting our unbelief."

Situated in the heart of the great Grosvenor Square, an elegant section of London originally built in 1725 as a series of connecting Georgian town houses surrounding a spacious central garden, the newly reno-vated brick embassy stood at the corner of Broad Street. The United States had an association with Grosvenor Square dating back to the late eighteenth century, when John Adams, the first U.S. Minister to the Court of St. James's, lived in the house at the corner of Brook and Duke Streets. Adams later became President of the United States, as did four other ministers who served in London: James Monroe, John Quincy Adams, Martin Van Buren and James Buchanan.

In the months preceding Kennedy's ambassadorship, a decision was made to bring together under one roof all the embassy staff that hereto-fore had been scattered throughout the city. For this purpose, three town houses were purchased and renovated by the U.S. government. In the process, it was decided that the upper floors, approached from an entrance at No. 3, would be occupied by flats leased out to private individuals, while the ground floor, the first floor and part of the base-ment and the second floor would be used for the American Embassy. This rather surprising arrangement, built on the last horizon of an end-lessly retreating vision of innocence about security matters, was in keep-ing with the hitherto unpretentious diplomatic tradition of the American republic. (In contrast, the present U. S. Embassy, which takes over the entire west side of the square, is raised and protected on a gently sloping hill and is set slightly back from the square, projecting in its islanded integrity a marked change from the relatively relaxed accommodations taken in 1938.)

The Ambassador's office was large and airy, but its décor left Kennedy with "a mixture of amusement and chagrin." In his first letter to Jimmy Roosevelt he notes, "I have a beautiful blue silk room and all I need to make it perfect is a Mother Hubbard dress and a wreath to make me Queen of the May. If a fairy didn't design this room I never saw one in my life."

The first days on the job were ones of becoming familiar with the lay of the land and with the twenty officers and seventy-five staff people currently at work in the embassy. As was his usual custom, Kennedy surrounded himself with a few of his faithful friends and associates, in several cases supplementing the governmental salary with money of his own. Not surprisingly, Eddie Moore was his first choice for chief secre-tary, though the gentle Irishman stayed in America until May so that he could accompany Rosemary and Eunice, who had to stay in school longer than the other children, to England. Besides Moore, Kennedy enlisted the aide of Jim Seymour, who had been with him on and off since his Hollywood days, and Harvey Klemmer, a speechwriter at the Maritime. Then, as his personal assistant, he hired Page Huidekoper, an intelligent, high-spirited young woman from Baltimore who secured her job through Jimmy Roosevelt and later became a good friend of Kathleen's. And, as his comrade in pleasure, he brought along Arthur Houghton, the handsome silver-haired old Irishman whom he had known since his earliest days in the movies. At the time, Houghton was working for the Will Hays organization, but Kennedy persuaded them to transfer him to London. "I am planning to take that Irishman [Houghton] out there away from you," Kennedy wrote to Joseph Breen, the director of the Motion Picture Association, as soon as he learned of the appointment, "to be sure I have somebody over there I can have a laugh with. I hate like hell to take him away from you but, my God, London is cold, dreary and foggy during the winter."

Page Huidekoper later recalled the stunned look on the face of the prim Foreign Service officer in charge of the embassy when he first met the Kennedy crowd at the boat. "You see, Herschel Johnson came from a distinguished South Carolina family and he was frightfully proper and wildly protocol conscious," Page laughingly recounted. "Having received a cable that all these Irish characters were turning up, he was terrified that they'd all be chewing gum."

In addition to Moore, Seymour, Klemmer and Huidekoper, Kennedy brought with him Harold Hinton, a staff reporter on *The New York Times*, to serve as his liaison with the press. "There is little doubt," the British chancery in Washington cabled to the Foreign Office in London, "Hinton has got his job through the influence of Arthur Krock . . . It is given out that he is going to write the Ambassador's speeches and keep contact with the press. From what he himself hints it will appear that he will have other jobs to do in the Embassy. This is however none of our business." Moreover, the report continued, "if Mr. Hinton is representative of his paper's views, he will be welcomed, for the New York Times is as reasonable and as Anglophile as any paper in the United States."

Kennedy was scheduled to receive his formal accreditation as ambassador at 11:30 A.M. March 8, 1938. While the ceremony was to be carried out at Buckingham Palace, the home of the royal family since 1850, the official title of Kennedy's position remained "Ambassador to the Court of St. James's" in honor of the days when the court was situated at St. James's Palace, the splendid Tudor structure built by Henry VIII.

Earlier that morning Kennedy had found himself in a state of unconcealed excitement. "It's a quarter past nine on Tuesday morning," he wrote to Senator Byrnes, "and I am sitting in a bathrobe at the Embassy and am supposed to dress in about an hour to get ready to be drawn to the Palace in a carriage with white horses to present my credentials to the King." At the appointed hour, three state carriages arrived at Grosvenor Square, complete with coachmen, footmen and outriders in top hats and long scarlet cloaks. After entering the gates at Buckingham Palace, Kennedy and his entourage were cheered by the crowds as they filed between the lines of the yeomen of the guard. "We were ushered into the forty-four room (the audience chambers)," Kennedy recorded in his unpublished memoirs,* "where stood Lord Halifax [the Foreign Secretary] and the King, straight and almost boyish looking in his uniform as an Admiral of the Fleet." The ceremony itself was short and simple, after which Kennedy chatted with King George VI, who expressed a wish to see all the Kennedy children when they arrived.

Ignorant of court protocol which called for visitors to the palace to refrain from ever quoting what the King said, the new Ambassador immediately launched into talks with reporters, telling them proudly that the King was particularly interested in meeting his family. Later that day, deeply conscious of the great adventure that lay before him, he wrote his first letter as ambassador to his friend and supporter Arthur Krock.

"I have just been received by the King and found him much more nervous than I was," Kennedy wrote. "He was most gracious . . . a very pleasant chap who acts to me like a fellow that was doing all he could to keep the people loving the 'King.' " As for Halifax, Kennedy noted, he "looks and acts like a Cardinal or Abraham Lincoln (without a beard)." But mainly Kennedy wanted Krock to know how grateful he was for all the help and support Krock had supplied over the years. "Your persistent urging me to come here and your holding my hand during the uncertain days will always remain in my mind and heart . . . If all my experiences in Washington leave me nothing, meeting you and being with you has been worth it all."

During the days that followed, Kennedy carried out a ritual which custom demanded, calling on all the ministers of government and on all the resident foreign representatives of equal rank, including the Spanish, Brazilian, French and Russian ambassadors. Most of the previous American ambassadors, taking their cue from their surroundings, had tended to affect the stiff and pretentious manners of English gentlemen. But Kennedy insisted, in all his dealings, in retaining his usual straightforward and relaxed carriage. "You can't expect me to develop into a

---

* During his years at the embassy, Kennedy kept diary notes, which, along with his diplomatic dispatches and correspondence, he intended to use as the basis for a memoir on his ambassadorial career. In the 1940s all this material was given to James Landis, who prepared a first draft. The completed draft, after it was edited by Kennedy, stretched to forty chapters, but the project was abandoned, apparently because Kennedy concluded that its publication might embarrass Jack.

statesman overnight," he said engagingly, propping his feet up on his highly polished desk to the great satisfaction of Americans and Britons alike, who believed that for too long American ambassadors to England had mistakenly tried to adapt to English standards.

Standing always for the American, his face fixed in a ready smile, with an attitude of general hospitality to the chances of life, Kennedy had an initial advantage in his robust, masculine appearance. He appeared to possess that kind of health and strength which figured in the ideal image the English already held of Americans at their best. Friendly, frank and well disposed, he created an immediate sensation in the press when, playing his first round of golf in England, he lofted an iron shot off the tee and into the cup for a hole in one. Back at Harvard, reading of their father's exploit, Joe Junior and Jack sent a cable, "Dubious about the hole in one." Responding with equal humor to all the fuss, Kennedy was widely quoted as saying, "I am much happier being the father of nine children and making a hole in one than I would be as the father of one child making a hole in nine."

Even before he arrived, Kennedy announced that he would not follow the traditional court procedure, prescribed over centuries, which required that all men wear silk stockings and knee breeches in their formal presentations at court. Refusing to let himself appear foolish in the eyes of the world, he was granted official permission to wear a tailcoat and long trousers instead. Having been warned over and over by his friends against the tendency of American representatives to ape European mannerisms, Kennedy was determined to remain at all times a powerful specimen of an American. "When you feel that British accent coming upon you," President Roosevelt quipped, "and your trousers riding up to your knees, take the first steamer home for a couple weeks' holiday."

In the same spirit, Kennedy determined at once to do away with the traditional practice of presenting American debutantes to the King and Queen. For years, the American Embassy in London had been caught in the impossible position of selecting thirty young women from among more than three or four hundred applicants, all of whom were endorsed by long batteries of senators, congressmen and governors. "The spectacle seemed to me a sorry one," Kennedy recorded, noting that for every woman chosen ten others were rejected. "Surely the time of the Ambassador and his staff could be better employed than acting as a social secretariat for ambitious hostesses and their ambitious charges. Moreover, this race to gain social prestige at home by having the opportunity, for no particular reason, to bend the knee abroad, had the makings of what we Americans know as a 'racket' without any real purpose or real benefit." Securing the President's approval, Kennedy announced that from here on, the presentation of American ladies to the British court would be limited to immediate families of American officials in London or to immediate families of residents of the United States who were residing in England for a long period.

Seen in some quarters as the rebuke of a democratic Irishman against the snooty pretensions of the Four Hundred, the decision was generally hailed in Britain and in America, where, in the midst of the gloomy political situation in Europe, it received front-page coverage.

Had Europe remained in a state of peace during Kennedy's tenure, it is possible that he could have come and gone, leaving behind a reputation as a vigorous ambassador, capable alike of providing acute observations on the European scene, of negotiating treaties of trade with skill and finesse and of representing America to the British people at large. It was his own and his country's tragedy that he became ambassador at a critical hour in Europe's history, a time, more than any other since 1914, which demanded an uncommon understanding of history, a profound judgment of men and affairs, and a broad vision of responsibility— qualities of mind and spirit which Joseph Kennedy, shrewd as he was in business affairs, simply did not possess.

In the spring of 1938, just as Kennedy arrived in England, "the curtain was rising on the final act of the tragedy of appeasement." For years, Germany's Adolf Hitler had been putting Europe on notice that he saw himself as the protector of tens of millions of Germans who had been cut off from the German Reich by the Treaty of Versailles and that he intended, by force if necessary, to bring all these people back into a new and remilitarized Reich. As early as July of 1934, a group of Austrian Nazis had murdered Austria's Chancellor in an attemped coup which was meant to open the door to Austria's annexation by Germany, but when Mussolini imposed restraint, Hitler temporarily shelved his "Anschluss" plans. A year later, however, it was a different story. Moving cautiously into the Rhineland, where he expected to meet French resistance and where he was prepared, if necessary, to retreat, Hitler was surprised to find that neither France nor Britain, so obsessed with peace that they had deliberately failed to rearm, was willing to lift a finger to stop him. Success bred success, and by March 1938 Hitler believed the time had come to reactivate his plans for the Austrian Anschluss.

During this critical time, the British Prime Minister was the aging Neville Chamberlain, tall and lean, with graying hair, his entire figure molded by his seriousness of purpose and his strength of personality, a stern, morose and humorless man whose inner life remained largely hidden from his friends and associates.

Having settled into his job as the Prime Minister of Great Britain on May 28, 1937, Chamberlain convinced himself that if he had been put into office for a single purpose it was to keep the European peace, and that the best and only way to keep that peace was to maintain a policy of appeasement toward the fascist dictators, a policy which required taking positive steps toward conciliation and avoiding any action likely to offend Hitler or Mussolini. A man of passionate rigidity, profoundly affected by the First World War, which he regarded as a fiery holocaust with no winners and no losers, Chamberlain believed that if the alternative to coming to terms with Hitler and Mussolini was another war, a war even more horrible than the last, then almost any act of political accommodation was fully justified. And, good businessman that he was, Chamberlain could not believe that in bargaining with Hitler and Mussolini mutually satisfactory compromises were impossible. Mistakenly convinced that the aims of the fascist dictators were limited to redressing specific grievances and that once these were reasonably conceded they would settle down peaceably, Chamberlain proceeded with a policy which merely strengthened both their appetites and their means of satisfying them.

Masterful at the art of internal politics, Chamberlain exerted a strong measure of influence upon his entire Cabinet, forming a government that looked more and more like a one-man affair. Only days before Kennedy's arrival, Anthony Eden, the handsome young Foreign Secretary, had resigned his position, concluding that the policy of appeasement would lead ultimately to disaster. Eden's resignation was a tremendous blow to the small body of resisters who saw the peril of Hitler for what it was and were prepared to meet the challenge before it grew even more formidable. Winston Churchill later confessed that his heart sank when he heard the news of the resignation and for a while "the dark waters of despair" overwhelmed him. "During all the war soon to come and its darkest times," he wrote, "I never had any trouble sleeping . . . But now, on this night of February 20, 1938, sleep deserted me. There seemed one strong young figure standing up against the long, dismal, drawling tides of drift and surrender, of wrong measurements and feeble impulses . . . he seemed to me at this moment to embody the life hope of the British nation. Now he was gone."

Arriving in England after Chamberlain had replaced Eden with Lord Halifax, a diplomat of the old school who viewed loyalty as a paramount virtue, Kennedy tried at first to steer clear of all the confusing political currents.

The more I talk with people in the City [he wrote to Krock], with diplomats and with British Cabinet members, the more convinced I am in my own mind that the economic situation in Europe, and that includes Great Britain, is the key to the whole situation. All of the playing house they are doing on the political fronts is not putting people back to work and is not getting at the root of the situation. An unemployed man with a hungry family is the same fellow, whether the swastika or some other flag floats above his head.

Judging each development in Europe by the single yardstick of its possible effect upon America, Kennedy confessed that in spite of all the emotions surrounding Hitler and Mussolini, he could not see how "the Central European developments affect our country or my job." He seemed at first to agree with Churchill, after lunching with him, that the worst result of Eden's resignation was the impact it was having on the smaller countries of Europe, which were being led to believe that Hitler and Mussolini, in their growing strength, had forced Eden out and that the time had come when everyone should play ball with the dictatorships. But he remained thoroughly convinced, he wrote to FDR, "with all due respect to these ideas . . . that the US would be very foolish to try to mix in."

As it turned out, events in Europe were moving too rapidly for the United States to stand aside. For on the night of March 11–12 the country of Austria ceased to exist. Earlier in the month, Austrian Chancellor Kurt von Schuschnigg had announced a plebiscite through which the Austrian people could express themselves on the question of unification with Germany. Furious at this attempt of Schuschnigg's to strengthen his hand against the Austrian Nazis, Hitler decided upon an immediate military occupation of the country. In preparation, Austrian Nazis took to the streets to seize control of government offices, demanding that the Nazi leader Artur von Seyss-Inquart be made chancellor. Within hours, Schuschnigg had resigned and the plebiscite was canceled. Even so, on the morning of March 12, German troops crossed the border. Decrees passed that night proclaimed the end of the Austrian republic, making it a province of the German Reich. Two days later, Hitler made a triumphant return to Vienna, the former capital of the native land which he felt had rejected him in his youth. "I believe," he said at the time, "it was God's will to send a youth from here into the Reich, to let him grow up, to raise him to be the leader of the nation so as to enable him to lead back his homeland into the Reich."

In taking this aggressive action, Hitler knew, from his repeated experience with Britain and France, that neither country would make a move to stop him so long as they themselves were not directly menaced. And he was right. At the critical moment of the Anschluss, France was without a government and Britain effectively decided to do nothing.

"The hard fact is," Chamberlain told the House of Commons, "that nothing could have arrested what actually happened in Austria unless this country and other countries had been prepared to use force." Hitler's only serious worry had been over Mussolini's reaction, but when Mussolini held aloof, evoking an emotional telegram from Hitler, "Mussolini, I will never forget this," Hitler knew at once that he had achieved a great victory. Adding seven million subjects to the Reich without firing a shot, he had gained a strategic position of immense value.

Within hours of the Anschluss, the arrests began—more than seventy thousand in Vienna alone. "For the first few weeks," journalist William L. Shirer reported from Austria,

> the behavior of the Vienna Nazis was worse than anything I had seen in Germany. There was an orgy of sadism. Day after day large numbers of Jewish men and women could be seen scrubbing Schuschnigg signs off the sidewalk and cleaning the gutters. While they worked on their hands and knees with jeering storm troopers standing over them, crowds gathered to taunt them. Hundreds of Jews, men and women, were picked off the streets and put to work cleaning public latrines and the toilets of the barracks where the S.A. and the S.S. were quartered. Tens of thousands more were jailed. Their worldly possessions were confiscated or stolen.

Unaccountably in retrospect, the Western democracies let the matter pass without incident—a decision with which Kennedy, concerned first and last with what he perceived to be America's national interest, wholeheartedly concurred. In a phone conversation with Secretary of State Cordell Hull on March 15, Kennedy urged him to keep America out of the Austrian affair and to refrain from making any speeches on the subject, inasmuch as nothing the United States might do would reverse the fait accompli. In time, his isolationism would produce a storm of criticism, but in the spring of 1938, a time when the vast majority of people still supported Chamberlain's quest for peace, Kennedy's position found widespread understanding and support.

As the Austrian crisis unfolded, Kennedy found himself in the midst of preparing his first major public speech, which was scheduled to be delivered March 18 at the Pilgrims Society, an organization to promote good fellowship between citizens of the United States and Great Britain. "The Pilgrims' dinner," Kennedy noted, "is traditionally to a new Ambassador what a 'coming out party' is to a debutant girl. That is where he will meet his real test." Working hard on the speech with a battery of speechwriters, he submitted a draft to the State Department for clearance on March 10. Determined not to deliver just another statement of meaningless amenities, Kennedy decided to tell the English frankly and forcefully what they might expect from the United States in the event of another war, letting them know that if they got themselves into a mess beyond their capacity, they should not count on America to bail them out. "We might, but then again, we might not."

Reading the first draft in his office in the Department of State, Secretary Hull feared that, given the critical nature of the moment, the tone of the speech was a little too rigid and a little too isolationist. As things now stood, Kennedy had written, the United States had "no plan to seek or offer assistance in the event that war—and I mean, of course, a war of major scope—should break out in the world." After conferring with the President, Hull wired Kennedy to delete that statement and to soften a host of others. Yet, even after the revisions, what was left remained a strong statement which made a deep impression on journalists and spectators alike.

"It must be realized," Kennedy warned the British, "that the great majority of Americans oppose any entangling alliances. Most of our people insist that their country retain its independent and unmortgaged judgment as to the merits of world crises as they arise." In some quarters, he said, the American attitude had "been interpreted to mean our country would not fight under any circumstances short of actual invasion. That is not accurate, in my opinion," he declared, "and it is a dangerous sort of misunderstanding to be current just now." At these words, self-contained though British audiences usually are, the applause was particularly vehement, suggesting a wave of tremendous relief.

But when Kennedy went on to project the other misconception, the belief that the United States would never remain neutral in the event of another war, the applause subsided and the audience remained perfectly still. "That, I believe, is just as dangerously conceived a misapprehension as the other," he warned. The United States would be glad, he declared, to join in a peace program based on economic recovery, but on the question of war the American people would *not* commit themselves in advance and the government would "pursue whatever course we considered best for the United States."

In its treatment of the speech, the British press omitted any reference to this statement and made much of the other—that no one should assume that America would fight only if invaded. Coming at a time when war clouds were threatening all over Europe, these were precisely the words of support the British wanted to hear. Indeed, one London paper went to far as to say that the American Ambassador had clarified the entire diplomatic situation with respect to the European crisis, and that it was unfortunate that England could not have as forthright and clarifying a statement of policy from His Majesty's Minister.

For all the pleasure he felt at being met by the English with such affection, Kennedy missed his family badly. "Hurry that boat up," he cabled to Rose on March 12, "terribly anxious see all especially you." Joe had originally planned to have Rose and the children travel with him to England, but in late January Rose had suffered an attack of appendicitis and been hospitalized for an operation, so he had had to precede them. Plans were made to bring the children over in three installments. As soon as she was well, Rose would bring Kathleen, Pat, Bobby, Jean and Teddy; two months later, once Rosemary's term at the special school was finished, she and Eunice would come, accompanied by Eddie Moore. Then, as soon as Joe had graduated from Harvard and Jack had completed his sophomore year, the two boys would come.

But in the meantime, while Joe awaited Rose's arrival on the sixteenth of March with the first five of the children, the faithful Eddie Moore sent him long, richly detailed weekly letters, keeping him informed about the smallest happenings in the children's lives.

> Jack has had intestinal flue [sic] after the grippe. He went to see Doctor Jordan and she put him in the Baptist hospital. He has been there for four or five days and will be there a couple more. I have talked with him and with Doctor Jordan and he's okay—honest he's okay. If I didn't think so you know that I would be up there. His swimming is out for the year, and naturally, he was disappointed, but is all right about it now.
>
> Joe is studying very hard and putting in unlimited time on his thesis [a study of the "Hands Off Spain" movement, an isolationist group arguing against intervention in the Spanish Civil War]. Judge Burns told me that he was in to see him in Boston the other day to talk over with him some information that he wanted. Rosemary is fine. She spent last Sunday, as Rose arranged before leaving, with Mrs. Waldron [the housekeeper] . . . The papers are filled with news from abroad and not much else, but I won't go into that. The most important thing to know is that Jack, Joe, Rosemary and Eunice are all right—nothing else matters. I hope the children had a great trip and I hope that you are fine and happy.

To Kennedy, even in the middle of his responsibilities in London, nothing mattered as much as the news of his children. For all his toughness, he was basically, hopelessly sentimental about his family. Writing to his sister Loretta in the spring of 1938, Kennedy tells her the "pictures of mother and dad did not arrive until yesterday, but I was tickled to death to get them and don't know of anything that would have pleased me half as much. I will have them hanging in my room tonight."

When Rose finally arrived in the middle of March with Kathleen and the four youngest Kennedys, the British reaction was extraordinary. For the weeks preceding their arrival, the London newspapers had published dozens of pictures and stories of the Kennedy family, involving their readers in the Kennedys in a manner usually reserved for accounts of the royal family. But when Rose and the children actually reached London, the warmth of their welcome exceeded all expectations. Londoners smiled and waved at the children "as though they had become national property." Hardly a day passed without a newspaper photograph of little Teddy taking a snapshot with his camera held upside down, or the five Kennedy children lined up on a train or on a bus.

If Joseph Patrick Kennedy ever got to be President, *Life* magazine predicted, he would owe almost as much to his children as to the abilities which had earned him $9 million.

His bouncing offspring make the most politically ingratiating family since Theodore Roosevelt's. Whether or not Franklin Roosevelt thought of it beforehand, it has turned out that when he appointed Mr. Kennedy to be Ambassador to Great Britain he got eleven Ambassadors for the price of one. Amazed and delighted at the spectacle of an Ambassadorial family big enough to man a full-sized cricket team, England has taken them all, including extremely pretty and young-looking Mrs. Kennedy, to its heart.

The day Rose and the children arrived, Joe moved into the palatial thirty-six-room embassy residence, the gift of J. P. Morgan to the U. S. government, which stood at 14 Princes Gate in fashionable Knightsbridge. Located thirty minutes by foot from Grosvenor Square, the residence stood six stories high and was part of a long row of similar, connecting houses which shared a large enclosed expanse of lawn and garden almost opposite beautiful Kensington Gardens. There, along a regal bridle path which had supported the coaches of many a king, Joe got into the habit of horseback riding each morning, often accompanied by one or more of his daughters.

Rose later recalled the intense pleasure Joe took in living in a house originally owned by the man whose son had snubbed him on Wall Street just nine years before. But, turn the clock ahead nearly half a century and the visitor to 14 Princes Gate will find a blue plaque on the front door signifying that the building has been chosen for the prestigious Historic Register, based not on its connection with J. P. Morgan or with Joseph P. Kennedy—neither of whom could have qualified as "a person voted eminent in his sphere by a majority of the members of his profession, who made some important positive contribution to human welfare and whose name is well known to the informed passerby"—but on the fact that a young Harvard student named John Fitzgerald Kennedy stayed there for ten months during his father's residence as ambassador.

In the weeks that followed Rose's arrival, she and Joe were invited everywhere, sharing in the gaieties of the most fashionable families in English society. As the American ambassador, Kennedy was automatically made an honorary member of all the most exclusive clubs in London, including the Royal Thames Yacht Club, the Athenaeum, the Harlequin Football Club, the Queen's Club, the Monday Luncheon Club, the Sunningdale Golf Club, the Phyllis Court Club and the International Sportsmen Club. "Look at this, Rosie," Rose later remembered him saying as he pointed proudly to the list, "according to my count I am now a member of at least six exclusive golf clubs. I wonder what the people in Cohasset would think if they saw me now. It sure shows that if you wait long enough, the wheel turns."

If Rose's smile in these early weeks was larger than usual, it was not surprising. Finally, after nearly twenty-five years of marriage during which her social life had markedly diminished from the glittering days of her girlhood in Boston, she had what she wanted—a calendar filled with all kinds of exciting activities. Never before, she confessed, had the savor of social success been so sweet or been associated with so much that was so entertaining. The parties, the dinners, the weekends, the invitations and the fancy clothes all were vivid reminders that the Kennedys finally belonged, and, even more, they were an assurance to her that she was still young and still able to look forward with pleasure to new experiences. Having meticulously kept her weight down and her face moisturized and protected from the sun, she looked much younger than her forty-eight years, so much younger, indeed, that several reporters failed to recognize her as the Ambassador's wife and mistakenly identified her as one of her daughters.

> And Mrs. Kennedy [a reporter for *Vogue* asked], how has this charming, unaffected, and typically American woman struck London? First, as a phenomenon. Those nine children must be changelings, adopted, borrowed . . . but not hers . . . or how to explain that lithe grace, that slim hipless elegance; that calm, unruffled gaiety; that dark Irish hair and those absurdly debutante blue eyes? For Rose Kennedy, time has indeed marked time.

Responding joyfully to every social occasion, Rose was clearly in her element. Friends had never seen her more radiant. Since her trip to Paris with Joe and Gloria Swanson, she had developed impeccable taste in clothes, a flair which she now displayed again and again, revealing her face and figure in the best possible light. Under her dark curly hair, her blue eyes stood out, and in the excitement of social conversation she regained the girlish charm and the ease of manner that she had begun to lose after so many years of being at home.

By the time the London "season" officially started in the spring, the Kennedys were firmly entrenched upon the scene, having triumphantly risen to the surface of the "new people." It was, many have said, a particularly brilliant season, almost as if the British aristocracy foresaw that with the coming of the war its days would be numbered. There was a steady round of parties tied to the great events of the social year—the Derby race at Epsom Downs with its Royal Derby Ball, the Royal Ascot race at Ascot Heath with its Gold Cup Day, the tennis championships at Wimbledon, the Henley Rowing Regatta, the Goodwood Races, and the Yachting Regatta at Cowes. To all these events the Kennedys received the most select invitations: on the train to Epsom Downs for the Derby race, they rode in the car with Lord Derby himself, whom Rose found to be the jolliest and most cordial of all the Englishmen she had met; at Ascot, they were told to enter the royal box after the first race so that they could dine with King George, Queen Elizabeth and assorted dukes and duchesses. "It was a wonderful time for the two of us," Rose later recalled, "so much excitement, so much anticipation, so much fun."

But the high point of the Kennedys' social life in 1938 was the April weekend they spent with the royal family at Windsor Castle, an experience Rose long considered to be "one of the most fabulous, fascinating" events of her life.

Joe and Rose motored down to Windsor in the late afternoon on the ninth of April. It was just before sunset when they reached the bridge separating the castle from Eton College, from whose famous playing fields, Joe remarked to Rose, so many hundreds of young men had marched to their deaths in the World War. Approaching the castle from the main processional avenue which leads to the center of the Great Park and up to the castle walls, they arrived at seven o'clock and were led to their rooms by the Master of the Household.

The accommodations consisted of two bedrooms and two bathrooms joined by a lovely sitting room done in green. In an embrasured window overlooking the well-kept lawns there was a desk fitted with a blotter, an inkwell and a pen. In the drawers of the desk, Rose found stationery embossed with the royal arms. "Look, Joe," she exclaimed delightedly. "Let's write to each of the children on it tonight. They will be so surprised and pleased." Joe was as excited as she. Seated in a comfortable chair in front of a cheery fire blazing upon the hearth, he turned to his wife and said, "Rose, this is a helluva long way from East Boston."

At 8:20 P.M. the footmen came to escort the Kennedys to the Grand Reception Room, a magnificent golden room created by Wyatville for King George IV as a place of assembly for guests before a function in one of the adjoining rooms. Hung with Gobelin tapestries and decorated in Louis XV style, the room betokened splendor and beauty in all its aspects. It was there, waiting for the King and Queen to arrive, that Rose and Joe first encountered the other weekend guests, Prime Minister and Mrs. Chamberlain, Lord and Lady Halifax, and Lord Elphinstone and his wife, who was Queen Mother Mary's sister. At eight-thirty the King and Queen arrived and passed along the line of guests, while all the women, wearing formal dresses and long white gloves, curtsied, and the men, dressed in the Windsor *tenue* of black suits with red collars, shook hands with the royal couple.

A sumptuous table was laid for ten in the Garter Throne Room, where three dazzling chandeliers filled the table with reflected light. The King and Queen sat opposite each other in the middle of the table, with Rose on the King's right and Mrs. Chamberlain—described by Rose as a "matronly-looking" woman with "a wonderfully fresh complexion"—on his left. The Ambassador sat on the Queen's right and the Prime Minister on her left.

During dinner, Joe told the Queen that President Roosevelt was one hundred percent behind Chamberlain's drive for peace. "What the American people fear more than anything else is being involved in a war. When they remember 1917 and how they went in to make the world safe for democracy and then they look now at the crop of dictatorships, quarrels and miseries arising out of that war they say to themselves, 'Never again!' And I can't say I blame them. I feel the same way myself."

"I feel that way, too, Mr. Kennedy," the Queen replied. "But if we had the United States actively on our side, working with us, think how that would strengthen our position with the dictators."

Joe later recorded that he was struck by the earnestness with which she spoke. "Fired by an idea, speaking rapidly, her face acquired a charming animation that never shows in photographs." Suddenly it occurred to him that relations between Britain and the United States could be vastly improved if the King and Queen made a personal visit to America. "You would charm them as you are charming me," Joe suggested, and the Queen was instantly taken with the idea.

Turning then to Lady Halifax, who said she understood that President Roosevelt was a personal friend of his and that she had always wondered what he was really like, Kennedy attempted to describe the President's freedom from constraint, his warmth and his sudden flashes of humor.

"If you want him in one word," he finally concluded, "it is gallantry. The man is almost paralyzed, yet he ignores it and this forces others to overlook it. He dominates a room. I have seen him, when he is determined to win an argument, rise to his full height and, bearing his weight solely upon his arms braced against the desk, make the point to bring him victory. This always brings a lump to my throat, although I consider myself pretty hardboiled."

As the dinner came to an end, a Scotch bagpiper walked through the room piping, and later the women followed the Queen into a drawing room. Years later Rose would still recall the emotions she felt upon seeing for the first time the famous Vandyke portrait of the five eldest children of Charles I, painted for their father in 1637: "It was so incredibly beautiful. There was young Charles with his enormous black eyes, dressed in red satin, with his hand on the head of this huge dog. And then next to him his brother James, his sister Mary and two little girls, Elizabeth and Anne. There they stood, looking as if they had not a care in the world, and yet before their childhood was finished, two of them would die and the other three would be left to struggle for the crown in the wake of their father's beheading, an event which would bring upon their country a reign of terror and confusion beyond imagination. There was something about seeing those children frozen for that moment in time, blissfully ignorant of all the pain of the years ahead, that made me shudder inside and suddenly feel afraid."

The following morning, Palm Sunday, Rose and Joe attended a late Mass in the town of Windsor. Located in a cobblestone alley, the small Catholic church stood in marked contrast to the gorgeous Anglican chapel, St. George's, where the King and Queen, along with all the palace guests save Rose and Joe, were present at the morning's service.

Arriving back at the castle for lunch, the Kennedys found themselves talking with the two princesses, Elizabeth, aged twelve, and Margaret Rose, eight, for it was their custom to lunch with their parents on Sunday. Always at ease with children, Joe struck up a conversation with Princess Elizabeth while Margaret Rose sat across the table, very serious, not saying a word and eating as fast as she could. "We all began laughing at her mixture of solemnity and haste," Joe recalled, "and the Queen explained that the reason for it was that the grown-ups always finished first, which embarrassed the little princess." Upon hearing this, Joe brought a wide smile to Margaret's face by telling her that he had a young son, Teddy, who suffered from just the opposite problem—at every meal, he ate so fast and so much that he was rapidly becoming a butterball and everyone was desperately trying to teach him to slow down.

After lunch it was arranged that the guests would take a walk and everybody changed into comfortable shoes and tweeds. It was during the leisure of that Sunday afternoon that Kennedy had his first chance for a lengthy discussion of politics with Chamberlain and Halifax. The imagination, stimulated by Kennedy's diary notes, takes flight in picturing this first prolonged meeting between this fateful trio whose mutual support and mysterious unity would keep Britain on its tragic road of appeasement.

First, the image of Chamberlain, his dour personality in sharp contrast with the gregarious Kennedy. Yet, tramping through the fields together, they were a strangely complementary pair, bound by a shared sensitivity to their common social origins, a sensitivity which the born aristocrat Lord Halifax would never understand. Like Kennedy, Chamberlain, for all his political and financial success, suffered throughout his life from the feeling that he would never receive the social acceptance he deserved.

Then the image of Lord Halifax, tall and handsome, with an intelligent face, an aristocrat who moved with the grace of a tall water bird wading in the shallows. Impeccably dressed in well-cut clothes which bore the unmistakable mark of a country squire, Halifax was, in Joe's words, "a scholar, a sportsman and everything that an upper class Englishman who gives his life to public service ought to be." Having graduated from Eton and from Oxford, where he took a first class in history, Halifax could have led a life of tranquil scholarship had he chosen to stay in his family's country estate in Yorkshire. But politics was in his blood—his great-grandfather was Lord Grey of the Reform Bill—and as a young man he had relinquished the tranquil beauty of the Yorkshire moors to stand for Parliament, eventually rising to become the Viceroy of India, the Lord Privy Seal and now, with Eden's resignation in February, the new Foreign Secretary.

They were an oddly matched trio, poles apart in temperament and personality, yet united in an abiding hatred of war, a revulsion so deep that it brought all three to the same belief in appeasement. Chamberlain's hatred of war was born with the First World War and the death in action of his cousin Norman Chamberlain, a dashing and ebullient figure who had become Neville's protégé in Birmingham and was said to be one of the very few persons with whom Chamberlain had established relations of personal intimacy. Halifax's hatred of war, like Kennedy's, stemmed more from a sense of war's profound stupidity and waste than from a previous loss. With his limited experience in foreign affairs, Halifax was so frightened by the prospect of another world war that he was willing to secure peace at almost any price. But even in his most pessimistic moments he could not possibly have imagined the devastating personal toll that war would impose upon his family in the years ahead, bringing death to his second son, Peter, and the loss of both legs to his youngest son, Richard.

During their long conversation, Chamberlain recounted for Kennedy the discussion that had taken place the previous month when British Ambassador Sir Neville Henderson met with Hitler and heard the Führer's demand for self-determination for the German peoples.

"It seems to me," Kennedy observed, "that the big question is whether Hitler means to limit his activities to helping his Germans or whether he has further objectives that will violate the self-determination of other nations."

"That is the important point precisely," replied Chamberlain. "Yet the only way we can find the answer is to wait and see. Up to now every one of Hitler's demands has concerned Germans and he undoubtedly has a majority of his people behind him. In *Mein Kampf* he writes that Germany's future sphere of expansion lies in southeast Europe and the Ukraine. If he means economic penetration without force, we cannot very well object. Besides, war wins nothing, ends nothing. In a modern war there are no victors."

"Do you think a failure to reach an agreement with Germany will mean war?" Kennedy asked the Prime Minister.

"No," Chamberlain responded, "for we are convinced that Germany is in no position as regards resources or reserves to go to war. Germany is like a boa constrictor that has eaten a good meal and will have to digest the meal before it can take on anything else. Meanwhile we shall have an opportunity to attempt pacification, which, if we can persuade Italy and Germany to realize the fact, will be far more to their advantage than a general war and the collapse of civilization."

With these sentiments Joseph Kennedy wholeheartedly agreed, so much so that in the weeks ahead, despite his intention to steer himself clear of British influence, he became more and more involved in Chamberlain's efforts to keep the peace. "I'm just like that with Chamberlain," he gestured to Bernard Baruch. "Why, Franklin himself isn't as confidential with me." Anticipating the terrible pressure that could be brought to bear on the United States if a major war broke out in Europe, Kennedy concluded that there would be no war only "if Chamberlain stays in power with strong public backing, which he seems to be acquiring day by day." With Halifax, too, Kennedy grew closer and closer. When the British Foreign Office, much to the distaste of British liberals, decided to go forward with an Anglo-Italian agreement which implicitly renounced the principles of the League of Nations by recognizing Italy's conquest of Ethiopia, Kennedy promised to help Halifax sell the treaty to Washington. Making good on his promise, he not only urged compliance but went so far as to supply Roosevelt with a draft for a statement which acknowledged the treaty as "proof of the value of peaceful negotiations."

As reports of Kennedy's growing intimacy with Chamberlain filtered back to America, many Washingtonians were surprised. "Who would have thought," Roosevelt jokingly said to Treasury Secretary Henry Morgenthau, "that the English could take into camp a redheaded Irishman?" Assuming that the new Ambassador had fallen under the sway of parliamentary oratory, Walter Lippmann gently warned Kennedy that he was showing "some of the same symptoms which have appeared in every American Ambassador . . . since Walter Hines Page, namely the tendency to be overenthusiastic about the government of the day."

Yet this reading, as Arthur Schlesinger observes, does Kennedy an injustice. It was not because he was unduly influenced by Chamberlain's personality that he felt at home with him. Had the power of personality been the motivating factor, then surely the huge, fascinating figure of Winston Churchill would have been more to Kennedy's liking. It was because he believed that he was buying peace for America that he chose Chamberlain over Churchill. The choice would come back to haunt him in the years ahead, but for now, in the early months of his ambassadorship, it was a choice with which the overwhelming majority of people in both Britain and America agreed.

# CHAPTER 31
# AT THE
# COURT OF
# ST. JAMES'S

In June 1938 Kennedy requested permission to return to the United States to attend his son Joe's commencement at Harvard. From all indications, it promised to be a wonderful trip, an occasion of great pride for the popular Ambassador—pride in his cherished son, who was graduating with honors and had been selected chairman of the Class Day committee, and pride in his own accomplishment, which, the papers predicted, would earn him a coveted honorary degree from Harvard.

"Plenty of excitement over here," Mayor Fitzgerald had written to Kennedy in the middle of May, "as to whether you are to get a degree. The newspapers call me up and I say I do not know but they all believe you deserve it and will get it." By long tradition, the names of the recipients of honorary degrees from Harvard, chosen in secret sessions by the seven members of the Harvard Corporation, were withheld from public knowledge until commencement. As a result, the popular pastime of Boston newspapers in May and June was guessing who the recipients would be.

By the ninth of June, the week before Kennedy set sail on the *Queen Mary* for America, rumors centered upon two men, Walt Disney, the celebrated creator of animated films, and Joseph Kennedy, class of 1912. "When Joe heard he was being considered along with Walt Disney, he was thrilled," Rose recalled, "for the two awards taken together confirmed his long-held insistence that Harvard accord proper recognition to the motion picture industry." The *Boston Globe* noted that both Kennedy and Disney had been powerful influences in the movies and that when the awards were given on Commencement Day the two men could speak the same language.

For Kennedy, the award held a special meaning apart from its national prestige. In the city of his birth, an honorary degree from Harvard symbolized acceptance into the most select circle of Bostonians, an acceptance which had eluded Kennedy all his life. "It was an honor he wanted for the entire family," Rose explained, "for it meant yet another door that would be opened to his sons and his daughters."

Nor was Kennedy alone in the high value he placed upon Harvard's honorary degree. For thirty years the Archbishop of Boston, William Cardinal O'Connell, had waited in vain for a call from the president of Harvard offering him such a degree. When the call finally came, in the spring of 1937, shortly after his seventy-seventh birthday, the Cardinal had lost the use of one eye and had an advanced cataract on the other. For months he had hesitated about undergoing surgery for removal of the cataract, but when he heard the long-awaited news from Harvard President James Conant he decided to go through with the operation—because otherwise, he confided to his doctor, his chances were high for stumbling on the platform when he received the degree.

The *Queen Mary* arrived in New York Harbor on Monday, the twentieth of June. "I'm just the same—you won't find me changed a bit," Kennedy had assured a welcoming newspaperman over the ship-to-shore telephone as the liner neared the harbor. Upon disembarking, Kennedy was met by Jimmy Roosevelt, Rear Admiral Emory Land, his successor as chairman of the U.S. Maritime Commission, and a host of reporters all pumped up by a recent story suggesting Kennedy's candidacy for the presidency in 1940.

The idea of Kennedy being nominated had first been mentioned in late May in an article by Ernest K. Lindley in *Liberty*. While admitting that the odds were against him at this stage, Lindley suggested that "a few connoisseurs of Presidential material" were willing to make "long shot bets" that Kennedy would be the next Democratic nominee. His assets were "brains, personality, driving power and the habit of success," plus "an athlete's figure, a clean-cut head, sandy hair, clear straight-shooting eyes, a flashingly infectious smile and faultless taste in dress." In 1940, Lindley concluded, "both the Democratic politicians and the country at large may demand a man who can make business and progressive reform pull together toward sound prosperity."

Once suggested by a prominent journalist, the idea was picked up by a number of newspapers, including the *Boston Post*, the New York *Daily News* and the *Washington Times-Herald* (where columnist John Lambert reported that college graduating classes throughout the country were voting Kennedy their overwhelming choice for President in 1940). Acknowledging that Kennedy had an excellent chance to be the first Catholic President, *Washington Post* columnist Harlan Miller observed that of all the contenders Kennedy had "the nearest to a Rooseveltian personality," and what was more, "all the kinetic Kennedys (and especially the beautiful Mrs.) would be a tremendous asset in a campaign." He concluded, "A mental picture of the White House with nine or ten Kennedys galloping about is most beguiling."

Despite this sudden flurry of interest in his potential presidential candidacy, Kennedy was a realist who understood that many factors, including his Catholicism, mitigated against him. "I knew the time was not propitious," he recorded in his memoirs.

> I knew that many of [Roosevelt's] closest advisors were urging him to break with tradition and run for the third term in 1940. There was little doubt that he had the matter under consideration. Mr. Roosevelt also had a quality—a failing, some have called it—of resenting the suggestion that he was to be succeeded and cooling perceptibly towards a man who might be considered, by his friends, a worthy successor. For many years Mr. Roosevelt had been my chief; he still was. I wanted no such false issue to arise between us and endanger both an official relationship of some importance and a personal association which to me had been heavy with meaning.

So Kennedy greeted reporters at the dock with a flat statement that he would not consider any presidential boom in 1940. "I enlisted under

President Roosevelt to do whatever he wanted me to do," he told report-ers. "There are many problems at home and abroad and I happen to be busy at one abroad just now. If I had my eye on another job it would be a complete breach of faith with President Roosevelt." This matter out of the way, he relaxed and accepted questions about his experi-ences in London, including the inevitable knee-breeches question. Had he worn long trousers to hide something? he was asked. Smiling broadly, Kennedy pointed to a pretty woman reporter in the crowd and offered to show her, privately, that he was neither knock-kneed nor bowlegged.

The following morning, after spending the night at the Waldorf-Astoria, Kennedy traveled to Hyde Park to talk with the President. Dur-ing their meeting, which took most of the day, Kennedy gave his personal reactions to the English scene, and the ever-curious Roosevelt soaked up every available tidbit of information. What particularly cap-tured Roosevelt's imagination was Kennedy's observation that he had met the same kind of perpetual complainers in London that he used to meet in America, people who wailed that the world was coming to an end and they would have to sell their Rolls-Royces; the only difference was that in Britain they did not blame it on their government. After laughing heartily at this "grand line," as he called it, Roosevelt came back to serious matters and asked Kennedy to tell Chamberlain that he was ready, when the time came, to place the moral authority of the American presidency behind a British plea for peace.

Staying late to share a dish of strawberries with Mrs. Roosevelt, Ken-nedy left that evening on the overnight train, the *Owl*, scheduled to arrive in Boston at 6:30 A.M. "It was on that train," Rose was later told, "that Joe heard for certain that he was not going to receive an honorary degree after all." Apparently some of the stories had been generated by several of his well-intentioned friends who hoped that by saying it would happen they could actually make it happen. By one account, the nomi-nating committee had considered Kennedy but decided that the rumors about his bootlegging activities in the days of Prohibition made it impos-sible to confer upon him such a distinguished award. "There were some people who were convinced Kennedy had been a shady character in the twenties," Oscar Handlin observed. "And when the Yankees turn on the freeze they never turn it back." By another account, the committee considered the award premature, telling Kennedy, in essence, If you're a good ambassador, we'll consider it.

The truth was probably a mixture of these accounts, along with a continued prejudice against Irish Catholics.

"It was a terrible blow to him," Rose later confessed. "After all those expectations had been built up, it was hard to accept that he wasn't really even in the running. All that night as the train headed for Boston his mind ranged back and forth over the years and suddenly he felt as if he were once again standing in front of the Porcellian Club, knowing he'd never be admitted."

Considering the personal toll the disappointment took, Kennedy initially handled the matter with surprising grace. When confronted by journalists at the Ritz-Carlton with reports about his honorary degree, he stated simply that there would be but one honor degree in the family, and that was "pretty good for one family, I think."

He then spent the rest of the afternoon with young Joe at the Class Day festivities, a colorful mix of activities which Joe had helped to organize, including a mile-long parade of Harvard alumni, three or four thousand strong, with each class dressed according to its own theme, from silk hats and spats to Scotch kilts; a hilarious Ivy oration delivered by Nathaniel Benchley, son of the humorist Robert Benchley, who had been the Ivy orator for the class of 1912; a burlesque radio skit organized by the twenty-fifth-reunion class; and, finally, the customary confetti battle between a swarm of Harvard men standing on the stadium field and thousands of girls, wives and children in the stands.

But when Class Day was over, Kennedy chose to retreat to his summer home at Hyannis Port, where he planned to meet young Joe the following afternoon, once the official commencement exercises had drawn to a close. Though he had come all the way across the Atlantic to see his son graduate, he now told the press he would spend the day instead with his second son, John, who was suffering from a stomach malady.

In fact the nineteen-year-old Jack was not really ill; indeed, he was well enough to participate that same afternoon as a member of Harvard's seven-man sailing team in the McMillan Cup races, which were being held that year at the Wianno Yacht Club. But somewhere along the way Joseph Kennedy must have decided that it would be too painful for him, after his hopes for the award had been raised so high, to witness the stately pageant during which Walt Disney and twelve other distinguished men, including writer John Buchan, Yale President Charles Seymour and Williams President James Phinney Baxter III, would be awarded the crimson hood.

History does not record how Joe Junior felt about his father's sudden decision to forgo the graduation. After all the time and effort his father had put into his education, even to the point of helping him with his various school papers, it must have been painful to realize that at the last minute Kennedy was unable to rise beyond his own personal disappointment to enjoy this day with him. How many memories it must have recalled of his early childhood when his father was away from home for weeks and months at a time! Nor could Rose make up for Joe Senior's absence, because weeks earlier it had been decided that she would stay in England while her husband traveled to Cambridge. Thus no member of the Kennedy family was present when Joe Junior received his Harvard degree.

While Disney was basking in glory and Kennedy was preoccupied with his latest slight from Harvard, an incident occurred which, according to Kennedy, "heralded a beginning to a series of misunderstandings" that was to plague his relationship with Roosevelt. On June 22, as the story is told, the President's secretary, Stephen Early, gave out a story to the *Chicago Tribune*'s Walter Trohan to the effect that the President was annoyed with Kennedy, partly because of his presidential boomlet and partly because Kennedy had chosen to send a series of confidential letters to his friends in the press before sending them to the White House. Trohan's story appeared in the paper the following day. It spoke of "the chilling shadow of 1940" falling across the friendship between Roosevelt and Kennedy and argued from unimpeachable sources that the Hyde Park conversation had been carried on in a frigid atmosphere. "Joe Kennedy never did anything without thinking of Joe Kennedy," a high Administration official was quoted as saying. "And that's the worst thing I can say about a father of nine kids."

When Kennedy saw the story and learned that Early was the source, he was furious. During the first years of the New Deal he had been drawn to Early and had even offered to supplement his salary at the White House so that Early could afford to live in a proper style. But now, in the midst of bureaucratic infighting, that friendship had obviously come to an end. "It was a true Irish anger that swept me," Kennedy remembered. "An angry interview with Early brought a half-hearted denial, and a further interview with the President, with whom it was not my habit to mince words, brought a denial that he had had anything to do with it. In his way he assuaged my feelings and I left again for London, but deep within me I knew that something had happened."

While Joe was in the United States, Rose was entertaining her parents in London. At seventy-five, the indomitable Fitzgerald had been looking forward to the ocean voyage from the moment he heard about Joe's appointment. All spring long he had sent a series of letters to the embassy on behalf of various friends who were traveling to Europe—such as Kelly, the "big dry goods man," and Bayard of the *Malden News*, "a great scout." As May turned into June he decided the time had come to enjoy for himself the perquisites of embassy life, and on June 16 he and Josie set sail for England on the S.S. *Manhattan*.

From the moment of their arrival at the plush Knightsbridge residence, the Fitzgeralds were caught in a busy round of social invitations, including a visit to the Astors' estate, Cliveden, a meeting with Dowager Queen Mary at Wimbledon, and tea at the residence of the Prime Minister, where Fitzgerald had a long talk with Mrs. Neville Chamberlain about their common Irish heritage. "It was for Father a fabulous trip," Rose recalled. "Still possessed of an extraordinary vitality, he threw himself completely into every new experience and he absolutely charmed everyone in sight. It made me so happy to be able to open social doors for my father just as he had done for me all my life."

Only one problem arose during the otherwise idyllic visit. Still thinking as a ward boss after twenty-five years away from public life, Fitzgerald went down one day to a secretary's office, helped himself to engraved ambassadorial invitation cards—which had blank spaces to be filled in with the occasion and the hour people were to arrive—and mailed over a hundred of them to his pals in Boston, inviting them to a fancy tea at the embassy five days later. Knowing perfectly well, according to Rose, that by the time the guests received the invitations it would be difficult for them to make arrangements to get to London, he felt it was a nice, harmless gesture which would make a lot of people happy, and he was quite proud of himself for thinking of it. But Joe Kennedy did not quite see it that way. Finding out that a hundred official embassy invitations were crossing the Atlantic, he was "considerably annoyed."

Nevertheless, it was, all around, a successful visit, summed up best by Eddie Moore in a letter to Joe Sheehan: "John F. had a great time while he was in London. He has seen more of this Island than the fellow who invented it. He has seen more places and talked with more people during the time he was here than any visitor in the last ten years."

When Kennedy returned to London, he brought young Joe and Jack with him. It was planned that Joe would stay for the year and work as his father's secretary, while Jack would remain for the summer and then, at a later point, take a semester's leave of absence. The idea of finding work for his sons at the embassy had evolved from a suggestion made by Felix Frankfurter, who reminded Kennedy that two of his predecessors, John Adams and Charles Francis Adams, had brought their sons with them to the London embassy, where they had enjoyed "an unparalleled post-graduate education." The Kennedy boys arrived just in time for the annual American society ball held at the Dorchester Hotel on July 4, 1938.

No sooner had Kennedy settled back into London than he and Joe

Junior set off for Ireland, where the Ambassador was to be awarded an honorary degree at the National University. After the disappointment of the degree episode at Harvard, the news of Ireland's award "came at just the right moment," Rose recalled, and he chartered a special plane so that his wife, his eldest son and Eddie Moore could all come with him. The day was a miserable one for flying, however. Throughout the morning there was a heavy downpour, and at the last minute Rose, who was still somewhat afraid of airplanes, decided not to go. "It was about as rough a trip as we ever had," Eddie Moore wrote to a friend, "rain, cloudy, and bumpy," but well worth it, for once the trio alighted from the plane at Baldonnel Aerodrome they were treated with such warmth and friendliness that Moore recalled the brief trip as one of "the most enjoyable and interesting" he had had in his life.

For Kennedy, it proved to be an emotional journey to the homeland of his ancestors. Smiling broadly from the moment he set foot on Irish soil, he found his Irishness welling up within him, and throughout the entire trip, his first to Ireland, he was observed to be "in the best of spirits."

Officially it was the first time an American ambassador to Great Britain had visited Ireland, and as a result all the preparations were finely tuned. At the ceremony for the conferring of the degree, the Irish Prime Minister, Eamon de Valera, in black-and-gold robes, presided and a large number of the university senate were present. From a seat nearby, Joe Junior heard his buccaneer father described as a man devoted to civic service by sea and by land, a man ever prompt in forward action at his country's call.

But the most emotional moment came at the state banquet given in Kennedy's honor at Dublin Castle on July 8. "We welcome you," the Prime Minister toasted Kennedy, "for yourself and for your race. We are proud that men like you not merely do honor to your country, but honor to our race."

In reply, Kennedy spoke with unusual eloquence, fearful all the while that he might burst into tears. "Perchance," he began, "my thrill and emotion are the greatest because this is the first visit I have paid to the land of my forefathers. . . . My parents and my grandparents talked ever of Ireland and from my youth I have been intent upon this pilgrimage. I did not dream I should come as I came today, tendered the laurel of an old and eminent university, the supreme honor of a state banquet and the warm handclasps of the great men of my own blood."

As Joe Junior and Jack settled into the embassy residence, Rose took great joy in the thought that the entire family was together once more.

For the past nine years, ever since young Joe had gone away to Choate, the Kennedys had been scattered except on vacations. But now, with all the younger children in school in and around London and the older boys working for their father, the family was able to spend considerable amounts of time together. Little wonder Rose Kennedy later described the embassy years as "by far the happiest years of my married life."

Echoing the same sentiment, the Kennedys' nurse Luella Hennessey recalled the embassy years as "wonderful years for all the children." Rosemary was happily situated at a special school in the country. Eunice, Pat and Jean attended a convent school at Roehampton but came home on the weekends. Bobby and Teddy went to a day school in London. "I used to meet the boys at their school and walk them home," Hennessey recalled. "We'd walk through Hyde Park and they'd kick pebbles, the way boys do. Teddy was always so bubbly and happy, always wanting to talk. If I were with him alone, he'd hop and skip to get to the outside of the sidewalk so he could act like the man protecting the woman. If they were together, Bobby was always the more serious one, always explaining in detail what had happened that day."

For the younger boys, Hennessey recalled, the greatest moment of the day came when they were allowed to visit their father for an hour alone in his room while he was preparing for the evening's events. "As a psychologist," Hennessey observed, "Joe Kennedy had them all beaten. He understood the importance of being with each child separately, so he let Bobby in first and then Teddy. He was a man who cared more for his children than any man I've ever seen. Since Bobby was less outgoing, they tended to have quiet conversations. Even at thirteen and fourteen, Bobby was a deep-thinking boy and very close to his mother. Whenever we'd be flying anywhere, he'd say, 'I'll go over and sit with Mother.' But that hour with his father was perhaps his greatest treasure. Then Teddy would come in and the atmosphere in the room would completely change, for Teddy was like the sunshine, lighting up everything in sight and keeping his father young. Through the corridors, you could hear them laughing as Teddy jumped up and down on his father's bed until he was exhausted. After that, he'd go to see his mother, who would calm him down by telling him where they were going that night and get him ready for bed. The Kennedys had such different personalities, but it all evened out so well for the kids."

In London even more than in New York and Boston, Joe Junior, Jack and Kathleen set the pace for the younger generation. At twenty-three, twenty-one and eighteen, they were just the right age to appreciate the richness of the cultural experience and to enjoy the heady social life into which they were immediately plunged. Among London's aristocracy the Kennedy children were accepted without question, accepted far more easily than they had ever been at home. They were invited to country houses for the weekends, Lady Astor's, the Duke of Marlborough's and Sir James Calder's; they were asked to teas, balls and dances; and they were given special badges for all the regattas and the races.

But London was, above all, Kathleen's town. At eighteen she had an exceptional look—the air of a happy temperament joined by high intelligence. Her youth and freshness made heads turn, but more than that it was her vibrant personality which captured British hearts. Brought up to value the art of conversation, she found in London, more than in contemporary America, the social texture which allowed her best qualities to shine. In talking with people from all walks of life, from lords and ladies to the household servants, she was able to focus completely; her movements never betrayed an inconsistency of attention, and her answers to all questions were uniformly genial and charming. She was always in the mood for liking everything, her sheer enjoyment of life was taken as a tribute to others, and the beaux began pursuing her more than ever before. "It was," Rose said, "as if everything that made Kathleen what she was came together in London."

When Kathleen first arrived in London, she and her mother investigated a couple of colleges for her, but, as Rose notes in her diary, the problem was that "so very few English girls went to college then . . . This was especially true of the girls of the upper classes and the aristocracy."

From the start, Kathleen's social life was dictated by the hectic activities surrounding the debutante season. By making the decision to bring her and Rosemary out in London instead of waiting until the family returned to America, Rose made it possible for Kathleen to join in with the "best" young crowd at the lavish balls and dances that were being held nearly every night between April and August in honor of one or another of the coming debutantes. Protocol required that Mrs. Kennedy meet the mother of any debutante before Kathleen could attend her party, so Rose was soon having tea parties at the embassy with Lady Mountbatten, whose goddaughter, Sally Norton, was considered one of the year's outstanding debs, and Lady Redesdale, the Mitford girls' mother, whose youngest, Deborah, was also coming out.

Perhaps the most splendid party of the season was the ball given by Lady Baillie for her daughter Pauline at 25 Grosvenor Square. For the occasion, an entire dining room in gold and silver was built in the garden and two ballrooms, illuminated by hundreds of candles, were set aside for different types of dancing—the first for the Lambeth Walk and the Big Apple so popular with the younger crowd, and the second for the foxtrot and other less strenuous dances preferred by their elders. With a celebrated singer and a supper described as one "to arouse the envy of gourmets," it was not surprising that the party went on until dawn.

> Certainly everyone seemed to enjoy it [the society reporter for the London *Times* observed], nobody, I'd guess, with more lively appreciation than Miss Kathleen Kennedy, looking charming in her pink taffeta dress. The whole family is taking to London life with the ease of the proverbial ducks to the pond. But it is Kathleen especially who is about everywhere, at all the parties, alert, observant, a merry girl who when she talks to you makes you feel as if you were seeing it all for the first time too.

The British had seldom seen a girl with such vitality and informality, so brash, so outspoken and so obviously American. At weekend parties in country houses, she would bound in from playing tennis, kick off her shoes and immediately join in the conversation, cheerfully expounding on any number of topics. Having joked with her brothers for years, she felt no constraint about teasing the British aristocracy about anything. "When she came into a room," Lady Astor's niece Dinah Bridge recalled, "everybody seemed to lighten up; she made everyone feel terribly happy and gay."

> Spent Easter weekend at Lady Astor's [Kathleen reported to Lem], and it was really wonderful. She invited me through Dad and of course I was scared to death not knowing any of them. . . . All the guests turned out to be very nice and the other four girls were really the best English girls I've met. The Duke and Duchess of Kent came for dinner one night. She is lovely but he is very disappointing. We all played musical chairs and charades. Very chummy and much gaiety. Dukes running around like mad freshmen.

To impress the beautiful Lady Astor—as Kathleen did at once—was quite an accomplishment, for Virginia-born Nancy Langhorne Astor was considered one of the leading hostesses in England. Having succeeded her husband, Waldorf Astor, in Parliament to become the first woman MP, she had a knack for becoming close friends with the notable personalities of the moment, including George Bernard Shaw, T. E. Lawrence and Mahatma Gandhi. She insisted that she entertained not simply for pleasure but for the opportunity to bring people together, Americans and English, Conservatives and Labourites, and by so doing she made Cliveden, the Astors' palatial Victorian estate in Buckinghamshire, the scene of some of the most memorable parties of the prewar era.

"Nancy Astor developed a special liking for Kathleen the minute she saw her," Rose later recalled. "And as they got to know each other better, they became extremely close. I think Nancy thought of Kathleen as a kindred soul, a younger version of herself. And in many ways they were alike. They both had an amazing energy, they could both talk about anything with great spirit and intelligence, and they were both great fun to be with."

"Aunt Nancy really loved Kick," Dinah Bridge remembered. "They shared a sort of 'nous,' a special sensitivity that allowed them to fit in wherever they went. They could talk with cab drivers and secretaries as easily as they could converse with kings and queens. Remember, this was a time of complete leisure, of friendship and wit, a time when every kind of young talk had wonderful ground from which to spring. It was a structured form of social life which Kick had never really experienced before, and in that glittering world she reached the optimum moment of her life."

Through the endless rounds of parties and dances Kathleen gradually shaped her own circle of friends, many of whom stayed close to her for the rest of her life. One of these was Sissy Thomas, daughter of Hugh Lloyd Thomas, the former private secretary to the Prince of Wales. So close did they become that when Sissy's father was killed in a steeple-chase accident Kathleen invited her to come live at the embassy residence. Through her, Kathleen met the young Oxford student whom Sissy eventually married—David Ormsby-Gore, the heir to the Harlech barony, who became a close friend of Jack's. Also studying in England that year at the London School of Economics was David Rockefeller, then twenty-three, a confident young man whom Kathleen frequently dated. Additionally, there were William Douglas-Home, later to become a celebrated British playwright, who reportedly asked Kathleen to marry him, and the young Earl of Rosslyn, who fell madly in love with her.

Kathleen pasted into her scrapbook hundreds of clippings detailing her social life, as well as dozens of letters and cards from her various boyfriends. "Darling Kick. When—oh when," reads one note from "Your devoted lover, Prince Ahmed Husain, Oxford." "You'll always mean everything to me," reads another, signed "Peter," while someone named Charles writes to his "darling Kick" on the program from the Ascot races. Amid the notes there are pictures and ticket stubs, race cards and calling cards, colorful jigsawed mementos of all the events she attended.

With so many boyfriends crowding around her, it was inevitable that some should find out about the others, but apparently Kathleen treated them all so openly that no one felt betrayed. "Everyone is talking about you and Grace," Lem writes to Kathleen just after she arrived in London, referring to Peter Grace, heir to the shipping fortune of W. R. Grace. "What is the true story about this guy, according to Pete Gorman's brother who works in the bank with him Grace is wildly in love with you and is heading for England this summer in order to clinch the romance—so watch it, Kick."

Kathleen shared with Lem her opinions about everyone she met, from Henry Page, a Princeton graduate who invited her to Oxford for a weekend but was "rather too polite and too sweet," and Byron "Whizzer" White, who would eventually become a U.S. Supreme Court justice and who, Kathleen argued, "should have gone to an Eastern college" to overcome his small-town background, to George and Lizzie, as she irreverently referred to the King and Queen. And always Lem responded with humor and warmth. "I miss you an awful lot over here," he admitted. "I don't seem to have a quarter as good a time with anyone else I go out with."

The high point of Kathleen's social season came at Buckingham Palace when she, her sister Rosemary and her mother were presented at court. "Have to practice up on the curtsey left over from convent days," Kathleen confessed to Lem in the weeks before the event, knowing that many English girls were tutored by dance mistresses in the art of curtsying. In preparation for the event, Rose took her daughters to Paris, where Kathleen selected a white net Lelong dress trimmed with silver while Rosemary chose a Molyneux. On the evening of the presentation (with Rose secretly worried that Rosemary might not be able to carry it off despite hours of practice), the palace was illuminated, the guards resplendent and the Beefeaters in uniform with maces. As it turned out, everything went splendidly and the British press complimented Mrs. Kennedy on her two beautiful daughters, Rosemary's retardation having gone unnoticed.

Several weeks later Rose held a coming-out party for Rosemary and Kathleen. After a dinner for eighty young people, the two girls and their mother received more than three hundred guests in the paneled French ballroom, where one of the most popular English swing bands played into the night and singer Harry Richman gave a rendition of "Thanks for the Memory" that brought down the house. All evening long Kathleen changed partners among noblemen and royalty, including Prince Frederick of Prussia, the Earl of Chichester and Viscount Newport. It was a great social triumph for Kathleen. With every man in the ballroom seemingly captivated by her, she had become the most exciting debutante of 1938.

Part of Kathleen's great charm was her capacity to laugh at herself even as she was achieving the very position in society her father had longed for all his life. "Our brawl," she wrote Lem, "went off very well. Tried to get everyone to cut in but it was the most terrific effort. They all acted as if it was absolutely the lowest thing in life to tap someone on the shoulder . . . but otherwise everything was wonderbar."

How Rosemary felt about Kathleen's astonishing popularity can only be imagined. Though she too was invited to many of the same parties, her mother never dared let her go unless she could be there to protect her and make sure that she had someone to dance with. "This is where Kathleen was so special," Rose recalled. "In the midst of her own excitement, she never forgot about Rosemary. In fact, she somehow managed to juggle her own suitors around so that one of them was always dancing with Rosemary."

Moving about in a world that was overwhelmingly Protestant, it was perhaps inevitable that Kathleen would fall in love with a non-Catholic man. But at the time Rose was not concerned, for she judged correctly that Kathleen was more in love with the season and with life in general than with any young man in particular. If she worried to herself on occasion that Kick was meeting too many Protestants, she figured there was safety in numbers. Amused, proud and happy with her daughter's overwhelming popularity, she trusted that before Kick allowed anything romantic to go forward she would instinctively ask herself what the future would bring and would conclude that a mixed marriage could lead only to unhappiness. Besides, she was only eighteen, and before the time came for her to settle down the Kennedys would be back in America, where the number of eligible Catholics was far greater.

It all might have worked out as Rose Kennedy imagined had Kathleen not met William Cavendish, the Marquess of Hartington, known to everyone as Billy.* Billy was the heir to the Duke of Devonshire, one of the wealthiest, most powerful men in England, a member of the old landed aristocracy that stood like a massive block in the heart of English society. For hundreds of years, the Devonshires had been one of the strongest pillars of the English aristocracy; Billy's great-great-uncles included the eighth Duke of Devonshire (the man who, as Lord Hartington, had been the leading member of Gladstone's Liberal Party in the late nineteenth century) and Lord Frederick Cavendish (the Chief Secretary for Ireland who was brutally assassinated in Dublin's Phoenix Park). On his mother's side, Billy was descended from the Cecils, an-

---

* English aristocrats use their titles as surnames. When he was a marquess Billy was known as Hartington; when he succeeded his father he would have been known as Devonshire even though his actual name was Cavendish.

other of England's grandest families, which included the earls and marquesses of Salisbury.

Kathleen and Billy first met at the annual garden party given by the King and Queen on July 18, 1938. "The little Princesses were there," Eddie Moore reported to his friends at home, "the Duke of Kent and his wife, all of the Ambassadors, and all told, there were about 12,000 people. It was very brilliant. The gardens of Buckingham Palace are beautiful. There is a small lake with swans and the tent that the tea was served in was lovely—not just a big white tent, but all different colors."

The warm summer breeze filled the air with the scent of flowers as Kathleen arrived in the company of her friend Sissy and her two older brothers, Joe and Jack. Earlier that day Jack had gone to Angel's to rent a gray suit which he wore to the party along with Arthur Houghton's gray vest and his father's gray topper. Kathleen, in a new pastel summer dress, looked especially beautiful, Rose recalled. With all the debutantes of the year eligible to attend, the garden party was considered a high point of the social season.

Only special guests, including the Ambassador and his family, were invited to tea in the royal enclosure, the section under the striped canopy noted by Eddie Moore, which had been presented to England by India at the time of Queen Victoria. It was there, as she was strolling with Sissy and David Ormsby-Gore, Sissy's boyfriend, that Kathleen encountered Billy, David's cousin and best friend. From the first moment, Kathleen later told her mother, she realized she had never encountered a more substantial and interesting figure. Billy had a well-bred air, a quiet ease that covered his handsome face and lent a certain grace to his tall, lanky frame. For nearly an hour the two stood talking amid a constant swirl of activity, and when the conversation was over they both knew, Kathleen later said, that something special was going to happen.

Billy was undoubtedly amused, perplexed and decidedly charmed. He had never before heard a young girl express herself so openly on so many issues in just this fashion. Throughout his years at Eton and now at Trinity College, Cambridge, where he was studying for his B.A. in history, Billy's dates had been largely confined to the well-bred daughters of the highest aristocratic circle. Considered one of the most eligible young noblemen in all of England, even to the point of being mentioned as a possible suitor for the hand of twelve-year-old Princess Elizabeth, he had been romantically linked with a variety of young women, including Lady Irene Haig and Lady Mary Rose Fitzroy.

But Billy was also a man of imagination and sensibility, and he knew from the first how extraordinary Kathleen was. There were many pretty women in the world, but she knew how to think and she knew how to feel. If he said to himself that she was too uncultivated and too provincial, he must have recognized that she carried within her a defiant and passionate streak which lent a romantic air to everything she did.

As for Kathleen, she was carried away, for the first time in her life, by Billy Hartington. Accustomed to juggling the attentions of most of her men, who invariably liked her more than she liked them, she found in Billy the perfect challenge. While he listened with interest to her remarks, and while his sensitive face registered his liking for her, he treated her initially (as he had treated all the women in his life) in an offhand way—which only made her romantic feelings for him all the greater.

The week after they met, Billy invited Kathleen to his coastal home, Compton Place in Eastbourne, for the Goodwood races. The lovely ivy-covered house with comfortable furniture was only one of eight great Devonshire houses. There were Holker Hall in Lancashire, a magnificent villa at Chiswick just outside London, Bolton Abbey in Yorkshire and Lismore Castle in Ireland, to say nothing of the family's three magnificent estates in Derbyshire, the idyllic heart of the English countryside and the seat of the Devonshire family. First of these was Churchdale Hall, where Billy had been born and raised, a modest estate compared to Hardwick Hall, where Billy's recently widowed grandmother, the dowager Duchess, now resided, or to Chatsworth, the greatest of all the Devonshire estates—a breathtaking 150-room mansion set against dark, dramatic woods and precipitous hills and facing a sweeping, rippling river and terraced gardens, the work of England's outstanding landscape artist of the eighteenth century, Capability Brown.

It is interesting to imagine Kathleen's first meeting with Billy's parents, Lady Mary Alice Gascoyne-Cecil and Edward William Spencer Cavendish, the tenth Duke of Devonshire. The Duke's father, Victor Cavendish, the ninth Duke, had died at Chatsworth only two months earlier. The fifty-year-old Edward had been a member of the British delegation at the Paris Peace Conference in 1919 and a member of Parliament from Derbyshire for fifteen years, and was now the Under-Secretary of State for Dominion Affairs. It has often been said that the grander the English family, the more democratic they are about accepting outsiders, and with the Devonshires there was already precedent in the marriage of Edward's younger brother Charles to the American dancer Adele Astaire, sister of Fred Astaire. But with Edward himself and with his elder son, Billy, the rules were different. The succession was at stake.

Yet, if by the Duke's judgment Kathleen Kennedy was certainly no figure for marriage, he seemed to have little objection to his son's initial interest in her. Trusting Billy as he would trust himself in the same situation, he undoubtedly considered the relationship a novel friendship and nothing more. In London society, the Duke's anti-Catholicism was legendary. He was a leading figure and a future grand master of the English lodge of Freemasons, a powerful Protestant secret society used to maintain class and Commonwealth interests.

Even so, Kathleen was hard to resist; she was so animated and she had such a charming personality that Billy's parents could not help liking her. So long as the relationship remained casual, as it gave every promise of doing, there was no great need to lay down the law. And in the meantime, there was much to be enjoyed about this vital young girl. During the weekend, Kathleen attended all the races with Billy, along with his younger brother, Andrew, who was dating Debo Mitford. In Kathleen's scrapbook there is a picture of the group with a big wicker basket at a picnic lunch, a picture which serves as a window on a world of aristocratic ease and pleasure.

After the weekend, Kathleen's state of mind struck her friends as unprecedented. She collected every newspaper picture of Billy she could find, including one of Lady Irene Haig and Billy sitting on a bench and another of Billy dancing with Lady Mary Fitzroy. But so much experience had she had with men that she knew better than to let Billy know how she felt, and she made sure to continue accepting the invitations of other men so that Billy would know she was still in demand.

For the month of August the Kennedy family had taken a house in Cannes on the French Riviera, and Kathleen was scheduled to fly from London on August 3. As August was a month when the English scattered in different directions, Kathleen looked forward to spending time with her brothers and sisters, finding once again her deepest pleasures in her family life.

# CHAPTER 32

# "PEACE
# FOR OUR
# TIME"

While the Kennedys were relaxing at Cannes, playing in the blue Mediterranean waters and lying on blankets in the sun-drenched sands, the situation in Europe was moving steadily toward the crisis that would soon culminate in the infamous Munich Agreement. For years, Hitler had been stirring up trouble in Czechoslovakia, claiming that the Treaty of Versailles had wrongfully and maliciously given Czechoslovakia the Sudetenland, the rich mountainous region bordering on Germany which contained three million Germans. Employing the same technique against Czechoslovakia he had employed against Austria, Hitler had long been encouraging the Czech Nazi Party to exploit the grievances of the Sudetens and to agitate for increased local autonomy. When Britain and France made it easy for him to subjugate Austria in March, Hitler was encouraged to pursue his designs more sharply against Czechoslovakia.

In late May 1938, the situation had moved further toward its climax when reports of menacing German troop movements led to a partial mobilization of the Czech Army. Since then, through all the summer months, negotiations had been conducted in Czechoslovakia, but by late August no agreement had been reached and Germany placed one and a half million soldiers upon a war footing. Germany's action produced headlines in all the London papers and forced the British Cabinet into a series of tense secret meetings. As the situation stood, France was committed by treaty to come to the aid of Czechoslovakia if Germany invaded; and if France stepped in, Britain was bound to follow. On August 28, Winston Churchill attacked Germany's mobilization as a threat to peace and said proudly that if it were necessary, England was still capable of defending the "title deeds of mankind."

For Kennedy, tanned and rested, "the holidays were clearly over," as he recorded in his memoirs. Leaving Rose and the children at Cannes, he flew back to London, arriving at the embassy on the afternoon of August 29. There followed the toughest six weeks of his ambassadorship, a time of crisis which would require him to be in his office until three or four in the morning; a time of crisis which would test his mettle and find him wanting.

On the night of August 30, Kennedy met with Chamberlain at 10 Downing Street just after the close of a long Cabinet meeting held to discuss the increasingly explosive situation. The question before the Cabinet was whether or not Britain should repeat the warning it issued back in May, a warning which some believed had deterred a German invasion of Czechoslovakia. Both Chamberlain and Halifax argued against a new warning on the grounds, as Chamberlain put it, that "no state . . . certainly no democratic state ought to make a threat of war unless it is both ready to carry it out and prepared to do so," and that given Britain's military weakness, she was neither ready nor prepared. To his friend Kennedy, Chamberlain admitted there were some in his Cabinet who strongly believed that unless Hitler was stopped now his prestige would so increase that it would soon be impossible to halt him. With this Chamberlain disagreed. "It is quite easy to get into war," he said, "but what have we proven after we are in?"

To make the decision to lead his country over the brink was something Chamberlain could not bring himself to do. Neither, for that matter, could his colleagues in the Cabinet, who decided in the end not to issue a new warning to Hitler.

With his own strong predilections against war, Kennedy was relieved to find Chamberlain still standing firm against allowing the Czechoslovakian situation to embroil England in a European conflict. "Today," he concluded after the conversation, "Chamberlain is still the best bet in Europe against war. It is my impression that even if Hitler strikes . . . his opinion will be to keep the French out," and "if the French do go it will be some time before he goes." In this line of thinking Kennedy wholly concurred, for he feared that if Chamberlain was overruled and

Britain went to war, the event he most dreaded, the involvement of the United States, would inevitably come to pass.

Over the weekend, Kennedy was scheduled to travel to Scotland to dedicate a memorial to Bishop Samuel Seabury. On August 31 he submitted to the State Department a draft of the speech he intended to deliver in Aberdeen. In the middle of it were two fiery paragraphs:

> I should like to ask you all if you know of any dispute or controversy existing in the world which is worth the life of your son, or of anyone else's son? Perhaps I am not well informed of the terrifically vital forces underlying all the unrest in the world, but for the life of me I cannot see anything involved which could be remotely considered worth shedding blood for.
>
> Whether our counsel and our aid will be accepted by men already immersed in the heat of quarrel we cannot tell. We can only hope that reason will carry the day . . . For we shall have to stand for judgment before our children and their children for the manner in which we regulate the world's affairs just now.

Admirably humane as these statements might have been in another context, they did not sit well with Roosevelt or Secretary Hull, both of whom were privately troubled over Chamberlain's increasing dedication to the proposition of "peace at any price." Though Roosevelt was unwilling to commit the United States to anything other than an observer's role, he did not want his ambassador to England making a speech which sounded as if he were saying "I can't for the life of me understand why anybody would want to go to war to save the Czechs." Kennedy was told to exorcise the two offending paragraphs. Speaking to Henry Morgenthau about the episode, the fifty-six-year-old Roosevelt said of the almost fifty-year-old Kennedy, "That young man needs his wrists slapped." Kennedy was probably unaware of Roosevelt's privately held negative sentiments about Chamberlain. Knowing Kennedy's strong feelings about war, Roosevelt undoubtedly exercised considerable caution in expressing his own emerging views—views which allied him far more closely with Churchill than with Chamberlain.

After an August 31 meeting with Halifax, Kennedy wired a report that Halifax was interested in possible American reactions in the event Czechoslovakia did explode. In retrospect, it is clear that the British bid for guidance was a way of shifting at least part of the awesome decision to others. Kennedy fell for this, but the State Department did not. Angry at being placed in a situation where any response would make the United States a party to Britain's decision, Secretary Hull wisely elected to send a general message which merely repeated an earlier statement.

Yet neither Hull nor anyone in the State Department warned Kennedy directly about getting too involved in the details of the unfolding crisis. On the contrary, as events heated up, the State Department consistently praised the full and rich reports Kennedy was sending, reports which were possible only because of his closeness to the British government. "I can't tell you how admirably you have been keeping us informed," Undersecretary Sumner Welles told Kennedy. "It couldn't be better."

On the sixth of September, Kennedy celebrated his fiftieth birthday with a party at the embassy. At the time Rose was in Paris with Kathleen and Joe Junior; at his father's suggestion, young Joe was just beginning a two-month stint with Ambassador Bullitt in the spacious American Embassy overlooking the Trocadéro. When Rose had first arrived in Paris she had gone to Cartier's and bought her husband a pair of "terrifically expensive" diamond cuff links for his birthday, and on the evening of the sixth she and Kathleen talked with him on the phone. (Curiously, for all their clannishness, the Kennedys did not seem to regard birthdays as special occasions. Perhaps, with both parents traveling as much as they did and with eleven different birthdays to celebrate, it was just too complicated to organize special birthday events.) The two women were filled with tales of their daily trips to museums, dog races, the fountains at Versailles and a small café in Paris that Kathleen remembered from her convent days. But when Joe spoke, Rose recalled years later, there was a solemn timbre to his voice, a terrible fear that Europe really was on the brink of war and that if war came everything he had worked for would be lost.

There was in Kennedy's thinking about the war an apocalyptic tone strangely at odds with his fundamental pragmatism. With huge leaps of the imagination, he convinced himself that the chaos of war would bring the end of civilization. Holding a narrowed view of cultural life which equated civilization with the accustomed economic system, he argued that if war came, the entire network of commerce and finance between New York, London and the markets and trade centers of the Continent would be destroyed, and that under the collectivist demands of modern war the capitalist system could not survive. When it was all over, Kennedy feared, Europe would be reduced to rubble, preparing the way for the triumph of Communism. And given the unhappy choice between Nazism and Bolshevism, Nazism—with all its objectionable features— was, to him, preferable.

Beneath these global fears, however, Kennedy was motivated by the far more personal fear that the coming of war might bring an end to his family's financial security. Speaking about this fear to the private citizen Henry L. Stimson that July, he admitted that a few years earlier he had thought he had made enough money to provide for his children, but now he saw it likely to be all gone and he lay awake nights over it.

On the evening of September 12, people all over Europe, politicians, ambassadors, journalists, soldiers and ordinary families, sat close to their radios, awaiting news of Adolf Hitler's speech at the Nuremberg party rally. For days, the question of Czechoslovakia had played a central role in Nuremberg as hundreds of thousands of Nazi followers, including party wardens from all towns and villages, storm troopers, elite guards and forty thousand members of the Hitler Youth, had gathered in the huge stadium for a week-long program of pageantry, songs and speeches.

On Monday, Hitler's chief minister Hermann Goering had set the tone of the party congress with a bellicose statement on Czechoslovakia. "A petty segment of Europe is harassing the human race," he said, referring to the Czechs. "This miserable pygmy race without culture— no one knows where it came from—is oppressing a cultured people, and behind it is Moscow and the eternal mask of the Jew devil."

Fearing that Hitler's speech on the final day of the congress would be a declaration of war, all Czechoslovakia was tense; in Prague, the streets were deserted from eight to ten as people huddled inside by their radios. In London, Chamberlain and his ministers were gathered at 10 Downing Street, and at the embassy Joe Kennedy sat with Eddie Moore and several of his aides. "The shrill, almost whining, German was, of course, unintelligible to me," Kennedy wrote in his memoirs, "but there were shortly translations furnished that enabled us to grasp the substance of what Hitler was saying."

Hitler took the offensive immediately, with not a moment's small talk.

Since the days when we took over the government, the united front against Germany is standing against us. Today we again see plotters, from democrats down to Bolsheviki, fighting against the Nazi state . . . But it becomes unbearable for us at a moment when a great German people, apparently defenseless, is delivered to shameless ill-treatment and exposed threats. I am speaking of Czechoslovakia . . . Among the majority nation-alities that are being suppressed in this State there are three million five hundred thousand Germans . . . The Almighty . . . has not created seven million Czechs in order that they should supervise the three million five hundred thousand Germans or act as guardians for them and still less do them violence and torture. I can only say . . . that if these tortured creatures cannot obtain their rights and assistance by themselves they can obtain both from us.

As Kennedy interpreted the speech, it was "boastful, offensive, and threatening," which indeed it was. In the opinion of foreign correspondent William L. Shirer, "the Adolf" had never been "quite so full of hate, his audience quite so on the borders of bedlam." But at least Hitler did not, as was expected, demand that the Sudetens be handed over to him outright. He did not even demand a plebiscite, voicing instead a passionate argument for self-determination, coupled with a strong intimation that, as Kennedy put it, "he would brook no interference with its realization." But at the same time, Kennedy recorded in his diary, "Hitler held out to the democracies the hope that, this issue being settled, European peace was a possibility."

Later that evening, Sir Alexander Cadogan, the British UnderSecretary for Foreign Affairs, reported to Kennedy the reaction of the Prime Minister and his Cabinet: "They thought the speech was highly offensive in tone but not as bad as it might have been." In their judgment, Hitler had "neither closed the door entirely nor yet put his hand to the trigger." (We now know from captured German documents that, even as he spoke, Hitler had already set October 1 for an attack across the Czech frontier.)

Seizing as usual the slightest opening to peace, Chamberlain rushed in the door—with a stunning decision to seek a personal interview with the Führer. Without consulting the members of his Cabinet other than Halifax, Home Secretary Sir Samuel Hoare and Chancellor of the Exchequer Sir John Simon, Chamberlain sent a personal note to Hitler asking him to suggest the time and place for a meeting. Hitler, says Shirer, was

> astounded but highly pleased that the man who presided over the destinies of the mighty British Empire should come pleading to him, and flattered that a man who was sixty-nine years old and had never traveled in an airplane before should make the long seven hours' flight to Berchtesgaden, at the farthest extremity of Germany. Hitler had not had even the grace to suggest a meeting place on the Rhine, which would have shortened the trip by half.

The reaction of a large part of the world to Chamberlain's decision was, as Kennedy described it, one of "profound admiration and relief." And in Paris, where she was preparing to head back to London with her children after a worried phone call from her husband, Rose recorded in her diary: "everyone ready to weep for joy and everyone confident that issues will be resolved." But in Czechoslovakia, where the people rightly suspected a sellout, the news was received without enthusiasm. "Extra! Extra!" the newsboys in Prague shouted. "Read all about how the mighty head of the British Empire goes begging to Hitler!"

On Tuesday morning, September 15, Chamberlain's plane left Heston airport for Germany, and for two days, Kennedy reported, "we awaited anxiously to learn what was occurring at Berchtesgaden." Chamberlain arrived home on Friday night and the following day Kennedy went to see him. At this meeting, Chamberlain told Kennedy that he had agreed in principle to the idea of self-determination, which in this case would involve a transfer to Germany of all areas in which ethnic Germans constituted a majority. Chamberlain told Kennedy that Hitler did say he did not feel it right for an old man to make such a long journey, but apart from this remark, he came away disliking Hitler intensely. On the other hand, Chamberlain was convinced that in spite of a certain cruelty in Hitler's manner, the German leader was, in the final result, a man of his word.

Sunday, the eighteenth of September, was devoted completely to discussions between British and French ministers for the purpose of preparing a joint communiqué specifying those German districts within Czechoslovakia which should be given to the Reich. The Anglo-French proposals were then presented to the British Cabinet, where, Chamberlain confided to Kennedy, they were strongly objected to by some of the members. In talking with Kennedy, Chamberlain said he appreciated that the rape of Czechoslovakia was going to be put on his shoulders but, since war was the only alternative, he was willing to take the responsibility.

The following day the Anglo-French proposals were presented to the Czech government, which immediately rejected them with a dignified and prophetic note saying that to accept them would put Czechoslovakia "sooner or later under the complete domination of Germany." But the British and the French were in no mood to allow the Czechs to interfere with the course of peace they had laboriously set. No sooner had the Czech letter been received than the Czechs were told that if they persisted in holding out, they would have to fight Germany alone, without the aid of Britain or France. On the other hand, if they agreed to the transfer, both Britain and France would guarantee the borders of the new Czechoslovakian state. Deserted by its allies, the Czech government "had no other choice," an official communiqué stated, but to accept the Anglo-French proposals. "The Czech government, constrained by great pressure put to bear by the British and French governments, sadly agrees to accept their proposals for the transfer of Sudeten German districts to Germany on the supposition that the two powers will stand by for the protection of Czechoslovakia if her territory is invaded."

Once the press was apprised of the exact terms of the Anglo-French proposals, the reactions were mixed. In England, not surprisingly, the

Conservative papers heartily applauded the plan, while the opposition paper the *Manchester Guardian* said that Great Britain had accepted "a moral defeat which will have consequences beyond our present range of vision." Winston Churchill deplored the complete surrender by the Western democracies to the Nazi threat of force. "The belief that security can be obtained by throwing a small state to the wolves is a fatal delusion," he warned. But as Joe Kennedy saw it, "there was little doubt the country as a whole stood behind Chamberlain. It was evident in the throngs gathered in Parliament Square and in the streets converging on Whitehall."

Having persuaded all the parties to accede to Hitler's demands, Chamberlain departed on September 22 for what he expected to be an easy second meeting with Hitler, using the proposals as the basis for a final round of discussions. On that same day, Kennedy was lunching at the embassy with Colonel Charles A. Lindbergh, whom he had met at the home of the Astors the previous spring. The two men had taken an instant liking to each other. "He is not the usual type of politician or diplomat," the famed aviator had observed. In her diary that night, Anne Morrow Lindbergh recorded that her husband had so enjoyed talking with Kennedy she could barely pull him away.

At the luncheon, Lindbergh gave Kennedy his firsthand appraisal of the relative strength of the air forces of western Europe and Russia. Several months earlier he had visited German airfields and installations at the invitation of Goering and had come away convinced that "without doubt the German air fleet is now stronger than that of any other country in the world." Kennedy was so impressed by Lindbergh's observations that he asked him to dictate a brief summary of them, which he gave to the British government the next day and put on the wire to America for the President and the State Department. In his report, Lindbergh wrote: "Germany now has the means of destroying London, Paris and Prague if she wishes to do so. England and France together have not enough modern war planes for effective defense or counter attack . . . " Nor did he have much confidence in the Russian air fleet, whose great weakness, he observed, lay in inefficiency and poor organization. "German military strength," Lindbergh concluded, "now makes them inseparable from the welfare of European civilization, for they have the power to preserve it or destroy it." Today, historians conclude that Lindbergh's evaluation was unrealistically bleak, the consequence of effective German propaganda. But the dismal picture he painted provided a convenient rationale for the no-fight policy to which Chamberlain and Kennedy had already committed themselves on other than military grounds.

On the afternoon of September 22, as the Swastika and the Union Jack flew side by side in the lovely Rhineland town of Godesberg, the second meeting between the Prime Minister of England and the Führer of Germany took place. In a mood of great satisfaction, Chamberlain began by recounting his complicated but successful efforts at convincing first his British colleagues, then the French and finally the Czechs themselves to accept the principle of the Sudetenland transfer, with an international commission to supervise the entire process. With Hitler's Berchtesgaden demands acceded to in full, Chamberlain expected that the two could move on to the real goal he hoped to accomplish, the formulation of a plan for world peace. But, to Chamberlain's astonishment, Hitler responded by saying that the plan was no longer of any use, that he had since decided that Czechoslovakia must hand over the Sudetenland by October 1 with no nonsense of an international commission, and that the other nationalities within the Czech state must receive satisfaction as well.

"It seems that Hitler has given Chamberlain the doublecross," Shirer observed from the Hotel Dreesen, where the meeting took place. "And the old owl [Chamberlain] is hurt. All day long he sulked in his rooms at the Petershof up on the Petersberg on the other side of the Rhine, refusing to come over and talk with the dictator." Finally at 10 P.M. the two men met, but the meeting broke up without much agreement and "now it looks like war."

When Chamberlain returned to London, very tired and worn, he attempted to do the very thing he had informed Hitler he would not do: persuade the British Cabinet to accept the new Nazi demands. But this time he ran into strong opposition, not only from those who had been wary the first time, like Alfred Duff Cooper, the First Lord of the Admiralty, but even from Lord Halifax, his own faithful lieutenant. Nor could he persuade the French government, which both rejected the Godesberg memo and on the same day ordered a partial mobilization. Then from Czechoslovakia came the news that the Czech government had flatly rejected the German proposals, which they said would "deprive us of every safeguard of our national existence." "Finally cornered, . . . Chamberlain agreed to inform Hitler that if France became engaged in war with Germany as a result of her treaty obligations to the Czechs, Britain would feel obliged to support her."

"The Cabinet finally swung around," Kennedy told Secretary Hull, "to the point that they would go through with the French and fight. Chamberlain would give up the idea of battling any further and running the risk of losing the country. This was definitely decided at the meeting this morning. They are all one unit. Even the dissenting members agreed to go along."

As Chamberlain reached the limit of his ability to maneuver between Hitler and the British Cabinet, the specter of war loomed larger and larger. "All over London," Kennedy recorded in his memoirs, "people were being fitted for gas-masks. In the churches, in the theatres, at the sportsmatches, announcements were made of the depots to which they should go. A motor van slowly cruised through Grosvenor Square with a loud speaker attachment urging people not to delay in getting their masks. It carried posters pleading for more recruits for the air protection services."

As war drew nearer, and with it the consensus that London would be subjected to very severe attacks from the air, hundreds of families began leaving the city. "For a few days," Eddie Moore reported to a friend, "nobody knew what was going to happen. Mary's trunks and bags were packed and I could have moved her out of the city on short notice. The basement windows of the Chancery were protected with sandbags and in Hyde Park, 200 yards from where I live, the men were at work digging trenches night and day."

On the night of September 26 Hitler delivered another of his impassioned speeches, to a cheering crowd of fifteen thousand party workers at the Sportpalast in Berlin. Shouting and shrieking in the worst state of excitement correspondent Shirer had ever seen him in, he stated that he would have his Sudetenland by October 1 no matter what. If Beneš, the Czech President, didn't hand it over to him, he would go to war. Conservative MP Leo Amery described the speech in his diary as "the most horrible thing I have ever heard, more like the snarling of a wild animal than the utterance of a human being."

But those who wanted to find hope even in the darkest of Hitler's pronouncements found it. After hearing Hitler's speech, the financier Elisha Walker wrote to Kennedy that he was more optimistic than he had been for several days. "It seems to me that he left the door open enough for a settlement but in any event I can hardly believe that England and France will go to war when Hitler states publicly that this ends his ambitions for further territory in Europe. . . . Naturally this whole situation has created quite a shock and undoubtedly has had some effect in holding up business. On the other hand if peace should rule I still look for business to improve here for a few months to come."

Late that night Sumner Welles called Kennedy from Washington to say that the President had a few suggestions to make to Chamberlain with regard to the radio speech the Prime Minister was to make the following evening. The first was to suggest to Hitler a widening of the scope of the negotiations to include all nations directly interested in the present controversy. The second was for Chamberlain to make a personal appeal to Hitler to resume the negotiations. Kennedy delivered the suggestions to Chamberlain, who said he would consider incorporating them into his speech.

There were now fewer than thirty-eight hours remaining before the German deadline. It was therefore not surprising that Kennedy was profoundly depressed. In a letter to Arthur Krock written on September 26 he confessed that he was feeling "very blue" because he was "starting to think about sending Rose and the children back to America and stay here alone for how long God only knows. Maybe never see them again."

It was a melancholy Chamberlain who spoke to the British people on the night of September 26 and said:

> How horrible, fantastic, incredible it is that we should be digging trenches and trying on gas masks here because of a quarrel in a far-away country between people of whom we know nothing. It seems still more impossible that a quarrel which has already been settled in principle should be the subject of war . . . I am myself a man of peace to the depths of my soul. Armed conflict between nations is a nightmare to me; but if I were convinced that any nation had made up its mind to dominate the world by fear of its force, I should feel that it must be resisted. Under such a domination life for people who live in liberty would not be worth living; but war is a fearful thing, and we must be very clear, before we embark on it, that it is really the great issues that are at stake, and that the call to risk everything in their defence, when all the consequences are weighed, is irresistible. . . .

Listening to Chamberlain's speech from Scotland, where she had come to attend the launching of the *Queen Elizabeth* in the presence of the Queen and the two princesses, Rose heard "his voice filled with sadness, with loathing of war, with discouragement as to result of his efforts." And the following day she recorded in her diary that the "individual, brooding silence was as general as un-smiling, unemotional faces. Everyone unutterably shocked and depressed feeling from the prime minister's speech that his hopes for peace are shattered and that a war is inevitable."

Joe Kennedy found at least one glimmer of light in the Prime Minister's words which recalled the President's suggestion of the night before. "I shall not give up the hope of a peaceful solution," Chamberlain had concluded, "or abandon my efforts for peace, as long as any chance for peace remains. I would not hesitate to pay even a third visit to Germany, if I thought it would do any good. But at this moment I see nothing further that I can usefully do in the way of mediation."

In the wake of the Prime Minister's speech, the country quickened its preparations for war. An SOS call was issued for every able-bodied man to report to the nearest labor exchange to help dig trenches. Many of the city schools were closed to facilitate the distribution of gas masks to the lengthening queues of applicants. And in all sections of London, hospitals were emptied to accommodate the estimated fifty thousand casualties which were expected in the first few days of air attacks.

At the embassy, Kennedy had the children's belongings packed, and placed an urgent phone call to Rose in Scotland telling her to come home at once to make plans. No one wanted to leave, Joe admitted, except Teddy, "who wants to go to North America to have his tonsils out because he thinks if he does he can drink all the Coca-Cola he wishes and all the ice cream."

An oppressive gloom hung over Europe as "Black Wednesday," September 28, dawned. At 2 P.M. Hitler's time limit for Czechoslovakia's acceptance of the Godesberg proposals would run out. War seemed inevitable. In London, Parliament was scheduled to convene at 2:45, and in anticipation of the historic event the galleries had been filling up with dignitaries of every sort. The Queen Mother and other royalty were present as were Winston Churchill, former Prime Minister Lord Baldwin, leading members of the clergy and a full contingent of ambassadors. Everyone waited in dread anticipation that Chamberlain would deliver an ultimatum which would plunge the country into war. "It was impossible," historian John Wheeler-Bennett has noted, "not to recall a parallel event on August 4, 1914, when Sir Edward Grey had addressed the House on a terribly similar occasion."

Just before Kennedy left the embassy to ride to the House of Commons, he received a personal cable: "I want you to know that in these difficult days I am proud of you. Franklin D. Roosevelt." Stuffing it into his pocket, he hurried to Parliament Square, where he encountered masses of people milling about in the expectation that something big was about to happen. "Narrow lanes for the movement of traffic were being kept clear by the police," he recorded. "The crowds were silent and unsmiling, though now and then a cheer went up as a Minister or a well-known member of Parliament went by."

Seated in the tight-packed diplomatic gallery near the ambassadors of France, Italy and Czechoslovakia, Kennedy watched as Chamberlain entered the chamber, spread his speech on the lectern before him and began to speak in calm and measured tones. "Today," he began, "we are faced with a situation which has had no parallel since 1914." Slowly, step by step, he proceeded to trace at length the melancholy course of hope and disappointment which Britain had plodded in her desperate effort to settle the Czech dispute, up through the ill-fated meeting at Godesberg. "As he passed from that part of the story that everyone knew," biographer Larry Fuchser wrote, "to the part that had not yet been divulged, the entire House leaned forward in silent anticipation."

The Prime Minister then told the House that just that morning he had directed a "last, last" appeal to Hitler. His tired face twisted with emotion, Chamberlain read to the Parliament the contents of that message, which essentially said he was ready to come to Berlin at once to discuss arrangements for the Sudeten transfer with representatives of Germany, Czechoslovakia, France and Italy. "The House," according to the *Daily Mail*, "poised so long between war and peace, listened intently to this, admiringly but without much hope." Then, at about twenty minutes to four, after Chamberlain had just finished describing his recent communications with Mussolini, "the supreme thing happened."

While the Prime Minister was speaking, a messenger ran up the steps to the peers' gallery, pushing peers to one side and audibly crying that he had an important letter for Lord Halifax, the Foreign Secretary, who was sitting between the Duke of Kent and Lord Baldwin. The letter was passed over the heads of the peers and noisily torn open by Halifax, who beamed as he read it, held it for a moment before Lord Baldwin's face and then rose to push his way out. "Sorry, excuse me," he said as he trod on peers' toes on his way down to the floor of the House, where he handed the message to Lord Dunglass, Chamberlain's private secretary, who read it, looked astonished and thrust the contents into Sir John Simon's hands. Sir John took one rapid glance and tugged the Prime Minister by the coat. Chamberlain, at a loss, turned around. Simon ran a finger along the salient lines of the message. Sir Kingsley Wood, the Secretary of State for Air, who had also had a quick look at it, piped in, as though fearing that Chamberlain, in the sway of his speech, might not at once take in the great news and would keep the House waiting. "There it is," Wood seemed to be saying.

In all the commotion, there had been a pause of at least a minute. As Chamberlain read the message, some believed they saw a smile cross his face and color return to his cheeks. "Shall I tell them now?" he asked in a whisper. When Simon nodded, Chamberlain turned to the House and began to speak again, his voice strained and hushed, "That is not all," he said. "I have something further to say to the House yet. I have now been informed by Herr Hitler that he invites me to meet him at Munich tomorrow morning. He has also invited Signor Mussolini and Monsieur Daladier. Signor Mussolini has accepted and I have no doubt Monsieur Daladier will also accept." He paused for a moment. A stiff smile creased his face. "I need not say," he added, "what my answer will be."

From the back benches someone said, "Thank God for the Prime

Minister!" With that, a roar of approval, "like the biggest thunderstorm you ever heard," swept over the House. The government ranks rose and raised hearty voices, the ambassadors clapped, the opposition clapped, and almost to a man the entire House stood and cheered in a tribute more overwhelming than any the majestic old chamber had ever before witnessed.

Then, speaking in a thin tone, Chamberlain said, "Mr. Speaker. All of us are patriots and there cannot be any member of this House who did not feel his heart leap that the crisis has been once more postponed, to give us once more an opportunity to try what reason and goodwill and discussion will do to settle a problem which is already within sight of settlement." At this his voice faltered, and there were some in the House who believed that he would break down. "Mr. Speaker, I cannot say any more," he managed. "I am sure that the House will be ready to release me now to go and see what I can make of this last effort."

With this the House adjourned and Chamberlain was at once surrounded by members admiring and praising him. From the gallery Kennedy was grinning broadly and cheering loudly. Amidst the rejoicing, only a few members understood the critical fact that while Chamberlain had originally asked for a five-party meeting, Hitler had pointedly invited him to a gathering of four. Though the conference would decide the destiny of the Czech nation, the voice of the Czech people would not even be heard. Recognizing this at once, Anthony Eden walked out of the chamber pale with shame and anger, and from his seat in the diplomatic gallery Jan Masaryk, the Czech Minister, the son of the founding father of the Czechoslovak republic, looked down at the cheering throng and could scarcely believe what he was seeing. "Was it possible that at this eleventh hour Britain and France had completely abandoned Czechoslovakia?"

As the happy throng in the galleries clambered to move below, Masaryk stood for a moment alone, silently mastering his emotions. He then left the House of Commons, not to enter it again for four years. On the street he encountered Joe Kennedy, and the two shared a car back to their respective embassies, which stood near each other at Grosvenor Square. "I hope this doesn't mean they are going to cut us up and sell us out," Masaryk said to Kennedy, who had no response. Reaching the embassy, Kennedy ran in smiling and grinning. "Well, boys," he said, "the war is off."

Masaryk decided later that afternoon to seek an explanation from Chamberlain and Halifax at the Foreign Office. He was told that Hitler had consented to a conference only on condition that Czechoslovakia and the Soviet Union not be represented. For a moment, Masaryk said nothing. Then he faced the two Englishmen across the table and said, "If you have sacrificed my nation to preserve the peace of the world, I will be the first to applaud you. But if not, gentlemen, God help your souls."

After the drama of the House of Commons speech, Kennedy wrote, "Munich itself was an anticlimax." Without the Czechs present, the substance of the deal was already settled; it was only a matter of packaging. There was no attempt to return to the Anglo-French plan which had been accepted by the governments of Britain, France and Czechoslovakia; discussion turned instead on modifying the most unacceptable terms of the Godesberg memorandum. For Chamberlain, the only real victory was a debating point, the idea that settlement should precede action, that the terms of the agreement should be accepted before Hitler moved into the country. Only in this way could the all-important principle of peace by negotiation be upheld. In substance, when it was all over, Hitler had gained everything. He had threatened that his troops would enter the Sudetenland by October 1, and so they still would—the only difference being that now they would not have to fight their way in. Without firing a shot, he had destroyed the Franco-Czech alliance, driven the Soviet Union out of the European alignment and paved the way for his next step: the total destruction of Czechoslovakia.

As the four-power signing was being completed, a popular Czech poet, Josef Hora, spoke the mood of the Czech people: "In the days of our sorrows when others, more powerful, have decided to beggar our ancient country, lift up your heads, all of you, in pride and calmness. It is not we who should be ashamed."

But so relieved were the British people at not having to go to war that Chamberlain was treated, upon his return from Munich, as a conquering hero. To the tens of thousands of cheering people who lined the streets as the Prime Minister made his way to see King George, Chamberlain was very much the man who had saved the peace. The crowd's enthusiasm reached its highest pitch when Chamberlain reached his official residence at 10 Downing Street. From the windows on the first floor he showed himself to the crowd and uttered the now famous phrase. Saying he believed he had come back from Germany with peace with honor, he concluded, "I believe it is peace for our time." At this, the street below rang with cheers of "Good Old Neville" and a loud chorus of "For he's a jolly good fellow."

Rose later recalled that Joe was so happy when Chamberlain returned from Munich that "he kissed me and twirled me around in his arms, repeating over and over what a great day this was and what a great man Chamberlain was." Across the Atlantic, wiser heads prevailed. The day after Munich, Roosevelt sent Kennedy a cable for delivery to Chamberlain: "I fully share your hope and belief that there exists today the greatest opportunity in years for the establishment of a new order based on justice and on law." But then, recognizing that even this carefully worded cable might come back to haunt him in the months ahead, Roosevelt instructed Kennedy to deliver the message orally to the Prime Minister.

In the contrast between Kennedy's wildly emotional response to Munich, based as it was on his perception of his own parochial interests, and Roosevelt's cautious expression of hope lay the fundamental difference between the two men. Though Roosevelt was severely limited as to what he could say and do about Hitler by the strong isolationist sentiments within America, his mind had already comprehended the nature of Hitler's threat and he was determined that America should come down on the right side.

When Parliament reassembled on Monday, October 3, 1938, the mood of the British people was rapidly changing. Over the weekend, Wheeler-Bennett observed, "the country had slept off its debauch of emotion" and had now awakened "with something of a bad taste in its mouth." As the threat of personal danger, made so vivid the week before by the digging of trenches and the distribution of gas masks, gradually receded, many in Britain began to remember the Czechs and to recognize that the "very deliverance from war which they had celebrated on Friday with such rejoicing had been purchased with the sacrifice of Czechoslovakia." By Monday morning, the thought of Munich began to provoke feelings of guilt, humiliation and shame. And the turnabout was even more marked in the United States, where the citizens had not viscerally experienced the fear in the first place; "within a few days," Kennedy recorded, people in all quarters "began to turn against [Munich] and those who had any part of it."

Both Rose and Joe Kennedy were present in the gallery as the great debate on the Munich policy took place. "The House was crowded," Kennedy reported, and Chamberlain, who had lost thirteen pounds during the crisis, "looked thin." As expected, Alfred Duff Cooper, the First Lord of the Admiralty, who had announced his resignation from the Cabinet the day before, was the first to speak. In a moving speech of high oratory and courage, he gave the reasons for his resignation.

Explaining that the Prime Minister believed in addressing Hitler through the language of sweet reasonableness while Hitler was open only to the mailed fist, Cooper argued that the issue was not simply Czechoslovakia but whether one power should be allowed "in disregard of treaty obligations, of the laws of nations and the decrees of morality, to dominate by brutal force the Continent of Europe. . . . I have forfeited a great deal," he concluded. ". . . I have ruined, perhaps, my political career. But that is little matter: I have retained something which is to me of greater value—I can still walk about the world with my head erect."

Over the next few days, these same doubts were echoed by others, but it was Winston Churchill who, in gloomy and unforgettable eloquence, proclaimed for history the meaning of Munich. "We are in the presence of a disaster of the first magnitude," he began. "Our brave people should know that we have sustained a defeat without a war . . . that we have passed an awful milestone in our history, when the whole equilibrium of Europe has been deranged." And one should not suppose, he concluded, that this was the end. "This is only the first sip, the first foretaste of a bitter cup which will be proffered to us year by year unless, by a supreme recovery of moral health and marked vigor, we arise again and take our stand for freedom as in the olden time."

Listening without objectivity to the arguments put forward over a three-day period, Kennedy recorded merely that "the climax of the debate came with the vote that sustained Chamberlain by a majority of almost three to one." Having staked so much on the destiny of Chamberlain's mission, he was in no mood to allow any scoring of points for the opposition. On the contrary, characterizing the opposition's presentation as ordinary and mediocre, he went so far as to make the questionable claim that there were "men in every house of representatives in the United States that could make better arguments and advance their cause in a much better shape." Rose, however, was able to respond more honestly to the quality of each orator, and in her diary she confessed that she found the brilliant Winston Churchill "fascinating, delightful and easy to follow."

After the debate, the outline of Munich appeared suddenly more striking. The contrast between those who applauded the agreement and those who criticized it, between the appeasers and the anti-appeasers, seemed more clearly marked. As men on both sides became convinced of the rightness of their position, an atmosphere of passion and morality enveloped the British scene. From this point on, each speech, each event, each gesture was interpreted from one side or the other. At a luncheon at Lady Asquith's, Rose heard the observation that "the pros and cons regarding Munich were dividing English people into two camps, almost as much so as the Dreyfus case, the Irish question."

In this highly charged atmosphere, Kennedy made the great error of committing himself fully and unequivocally to Chamberlain's policy.

Having stood by the Prime Minister through all the ups and downs of the Munich negotiations, he now continued to stand by him as the flames of hatred and invective rose up everywhere. As soon as the parliamentary debate was concluded, the exhausted Prime Minister prepared to go to Scotland for a short vacation, but not before calling in Kennedy to thank him for all the help he had given during the crisis. "He was kind enough to add," Kennedy recorded in his memoirs, "that he had depended more on me than on anybody for judgment and support."

Drawing closer and closer to Chamberlain, Kennedy had failed to maintain the traditional diplomatic reserve which protects ambassadors and their countries from becoming too deeply involved in local partisan politics. As a consequence, the man who had once enjoyed the most flattering press any American ambassador to Britain had ever known began to find himself the subject of open attack and unfriendly gossip. As an increasingly high degree of irritability came to characterize the times, stories about Kennedy's various indiscretions became rampant. Among those which received wide circulation and did great damage to his reputation was a tale told by Jan Masaryk, who, a few days after Munich, was walking through Hyde Park when he encountered Joe Kennedy riding in a car.

"Hi there, Jan. Want a lift?" Kennedy asked. Masaryk got into the car, and Kennedy slapped him on the back. "Oh, boy! Isn't it wonderful!" Kennedy said.

"What is?" Masaryk asked.

"Munich, of course. Now I can get to Palm Beach after all."

If the story is accurate, it reveals a remarkable insensitivity on Kennedy's part to Masaryk's feelings, for surely he must have recognized that to a man like Masaryk, whose entire life was wrapped up in the history of the young Czech republic, the Munich Agreement represented the beginning of the end. Indeed, those of Masaryk's friends who saw the fifty-two-year-old Czech minister after September 1938 scarcely recognized him, for his pallid face and sunken eyes made him look years older. And while his spirits would return during the war when he assumed a leading position in the exiled Czech government, he would experience such pain at the postwar settlement and the resultant Communist takeover that he would end his life by jumping, so it is believed, from the window of his apartment in the Foreign Office. But then, Kennedy, having ducked the draft in 1917, was never a man who appreciated the sentiments attached to nationalism, arguing again and again that the only lasting emotions were those attached to family and friends.

Perhaps the most controversial speech Kennedy made during his ambassadorship came at the Trafalgar Day dinner of the Navy League, held on the evening of October 19, barely three weeks after Munich and in the midst of the rising national debate on the results. Intending to give the British government a vote of confidence for having spared Europe the catastrophe of war, he launched into a plea for coexistence with dictatorships, hoping that in an atmosphere of tolerance the policies of the Munich declarations could work themselves out:

> It has long been a theory of mine that it is unproductive for both democratic and dictator countries to widen the division now existing between them by emphasizing their differences, which are self-apparent. Instead of hammering away at what are regarded as irreconcilables, they can advantageously bend their energies toward solving their remaining common problems and attempt to reestablish good relations on a world basis. The democratic and dictator countries differ ideologically, to be sure, but that should not preclude the possibility of good relations between them. After all, we have to live together in the same world, whether we like it or not.
>
> The nations of the world have always embraced many forms of government, races and religions. Surely we should be able to surmount a difference in political philosophy.

In another context, the counsel of coexistence might have seemed ordinary common sense. But in the passions of the moment, with the extremeness of the threat Hitler represented, the speech provoked a storm of criticism on both sides of the Atlantic. Within hours, telegrams were flooding the White House and the State Department asking whether American policy toward the dictatorships, outlined a year earlier in Franklin Roosevelt's electrifying "quarantine" speech, had been suddenly changed. "For Mr. Kennedy," the New York Post editorialized, "to propose that the U.S. make a friend of the man who boasts that he is out to destroy democracy, religion and all the other principles which free Americans hold dear . . . that passes understanding."

Only after the speech was so roundly criticized did the State Department recognize its fundamental error in originally approving the text—an error directly attributable to the large ambiguities in American foreign policy. But now that Kennedy had spoken, something had to be done. While FDR was desperately trying to walk a delicate line between expressing his growing distaste for the fascist dictatorships and bowing to the isolationist sentiments of the large majority of the American people, his Ambassador to Great Britain was now creating the impression that all the ambiguities had been resolved in favor of living with the dictatorships, "whether we like it or not."

In the wake of the controversy, the State Department hurriedly prepared a radio speech for President Roosevelt sharply critical of the dictatorships. Delivered within days of the Trafalgar speech, Roosevelt's statement was considered a public repudiation of his Ambassador, and Kennedy described it as a stab in the back.

As reaction to the Munich crisis deepened, more people began to question Kennedy's judgment. Writing to President Roosevelt on October 27, 1938, Felix Frankfurter observed, "I wonder if Joe Kennedy understands the implications of public talk by an American Ambassador, and realizes the discouragement to right things and the encouragement to wrong things that he may, however unwittingly, give. . . . Such public approval of dictatorships, in part, even, plays precisely into their hands in that it helps to debilitate confidence in the democratic way of life . . ." There is a note of sadness in this first critique, but in time Frankfurter's tone became bitter, and by the following year there is scarcely one friendly or generous word about the Ambassador in his letters.

In this tense period, Kennedy's friendship with Lady Astor was also called into question. In the London papers, the people whom Lady Astor regularly gathered in her magnificent country home were characterized as having pro-Nazi leanings and dubbed "the Cliveden set." In the fancy of the press, a "second Foreign Office" of pro-appeasement leanings functioned under the Astors' roof, with leading ministers in tweeds and riding gear deciding policy while seated in great leather chairs sipping whiskey and soda. In fact the collection of guests at Cliveden was a heterogeneous one, ranging from Oxford dons to diplomats, from men of affairs to women of society. But the image was otherwise, and Kennedy was caught in the image. In a nationally syndicated column, Drew Pearson and Robert Allen, both of whom Kennedy had once counted as friends, accused him of having been taken in by the Nazi sympathizers in the Cliveden set.

While Kennedy was prepared for the accusation of being pro-British, he was "hardly prepared," he said, "despite years in public life, for the full viciousness" of the post-Munich onslaught. Looking back later, he claimed he could understand the position of Jewish publishers and writers. "After all," he later wrote, "the lives and futures of their compatriots were being destroyed by Hitler. Compromise could hardly cure that situation; only the destruction of Nazism could do so. To that end they therefore bent their energies, and Munich, increasing as it did the misfortunes of their fellows, offered no hope to Jewry."

But at the time, as Kennedy increasingly found himself an object of attack in papers that previously had praised him, he instinctively turned against his attackers, claiming that they were distorting every move he made and that when the facts did not permit distortion they were simply making up the facts to suit their ends.

Amid the critical onslaught, Kennedy received a word of support from his son Jack, who had just returned to Harvard to begin the first semester of his junior year. "While it seemed to be unpopular with the Jews etc.," Jack told his father, referring to the Trafalgar speech, it "was considered to be very good by everyone who wasn't bitterly anti-fascist."

And from John Boettiger, the President's son-in-law, came another heartening letter, telling Kennedy he had been doing a grand job. "There are plenty of brickbats flying around," Boettiger wrote, "but that is an old-fashioned American custom that always comes as a reaction to anything unpleasant." Before Munich, he continued, people had been unanimous for preventing a war with Germany; now they behaved like the fellow who ran away after someone twice his size threatened to punch him in the nose—and later declared he should have hit the bully himself. "Out here in the wide open spaces, people are tremendously relieved . . ."

But whatever support the theory of coexistence might have received quickly evaporated on the night of November 9–10, when Hitler carried out his terrible pogrom against the Jews, throwing into stark relief the nature of the fascist dictatorship. Later known as Kristallnacht, the night of the broken glass, the Nazi rampage through the Jewish ghettoes of Germany was "provoked" when a seventeen-year-old Jewish boy, whose father had been among ten thousand Jews deported to Poland in boxcars, took revenge by murdering the third secretary of the German Embassy in Paris. The murder furnished the Nazis with a pretext for "spontaneous demonstrations" against the 600,000 Jews in Germany. Gangs of Nazis swept through Jewish neighborhoods, burning, looting, raping and murdering. Thousands of Jewish shops and homes were destroyed, some two hundred synagogues were set on fire, thirty-six deaths were reported and twenty thousand Jews were arrested. Much worse was to be inflicted on the Jews by this man and this state, William L. Shirer wrote, but on this flaming riotous night "the Third Reich had deliberately turned down a dark and savage road from which there was to be no return."

As the Western world recoiled in horror, in the words of Franklin Roosevelt, that "such things could occur in a twentieth-century civilization," the Munich Agreement was in danger of falling apart. For years, the appeasers had managed to avert their eyes from Germany's treatment of its Jewish population. Fearing that any official statement on behalf of the Jews might break the tenuous link with Hitler, the Chamberlain government had repeatedly chosen to remain silent about the evils being done inside Germany. For some, the official silence no doubt represented anti-Semitism; for others, it was simply a price they were willing to pay for peace.

While we may never know the true nature of Joe Kennedy's feelings toward the Jews, one thing is clear. In the late thirties, his passion for peace—and with it his perception that peace provided the only protection for himself and his family—was so overriding that he was willing to sacrifice almost anything to achieve it.

In the summer of 1938 he had a series of conversations with the German Ambassador to London, Herbert von Dirksen, in which Dirksen quoted him as saying "it was not so much that we [Germany] wanted to get rid of the Jews that was so harmful to us, but rather the loud clamor with which we accompanied this purpose. He himself understood our Jewish policy completely; he was from Boston and there, in one golf club, and in other clubs, no Jew had been permitted for the past fifty years."

Surely, even discounting for the fact that Kennedy had a penchant for telling people what they wanted to hear and that Dirksen had an interest of his own in portraying Kennedy's remarks in the most sympathetic light, there is little to be admired in a public servant whose vision was so narrow-minded that he was willing to write off the Czechs and the Jews and almost anyone else to achieve peace.

Judging every course of action by its effect on keeping the peace, Kennedy took a new tack after Kristallnacht. Fearing that Nazi excesses toward the Jews were shaking the world's confidence in Munich and endangering the prospects of appeasement, he became a leading advocate for a massive resettlement plan to rescue hundreds of thousands of Jews from Germany, in the hope that once the Jews were removed from the spotlight the prospects for peace would be restored.

"This last drive on the Jews in Germany has really made the most ardent hopers for peace very sick at heart," Kennedy wrote to Lindbergh, who had just returned from another visit to Germany. "Even assuming that the reports from there are colored, isn't there some way to persuade them it is on a situation like this that the whole program of saving western civilization might hinge. It is more and more difficult for those seeking peaceful solutions to advocate any plan when the papers are filled with such horror."

The resettlement scheme, quickly dubbed "the Kennedy Plan" by the generally admiring press, called for transporting massive numbers of Jews from Germany to sparsely populated regions in Africa and South America. "The problem seemed to me essentially a simple one," Kennedy recorded in his memoirs, missing the moral point entirely by starting from the mad premise that Hitler had the right to confiscate Jewish property and kick the Jews out of Germany.

> If a reasonably good area for settlement could be made available some-where in the world [Kennedy suggested], the problem of financing the immigration of Jews to that area could be put as a challenge before those persons of Jewish and non Jewish extraction who felt sufficiently touched in their pocketbooks as well as in spirit to make possible at least some degree of immigration. A fund of 50 to 100 million dollars, I thought, would make a significant dent in the problem. . . . Assuming Germany's desire to get rid of her Jews, their acceptance in the countries of settle-ment hinged upon their ability to have sufficient financial resources to permit them to contribute to the economy of that country and not as paupers to lower its standard of living.

It would require a huge fleet of ships and the erection of massive refugee camps at points of embarkation, but to Kennedy's entrepreneur-ial mind it all seemed possible so long as there was a will to do it. "What Mr. Kennedy has managed to do," reported *The New York Times* in November of 1938, "is the talk of diplomatic circles in London at the moment." Echoing this sentiment, *Life* magazine predicted that if Ken-nedy's plan succeeded it would "add new luster to a reputation" which might well "carry Joseph Patrick Kennedy into the White House."

But in the end, Kennedy discovered what George Rublee and the Intergovernmental Committee on Refugees had discovered months be-fore in working on a similar scheme: that while many countries ex-pressed sympathy with the problem, very few were willing to make any specific commitment for the future. "It was plain," Kennedy recorded, "that most of them, including us, were afraid of acquiring a minority problem of their own. In the US, the Department of State argued there was little hope of effecting any change in the immigration laws involving larger quotas," while in Latin America, where "the greatest possibility for emigration lay," restrictions on immigration were actually tightened as the Jewish persecution persisted. Only Santo Domingo, Kennedy recalled, showed any generosity, offering to provide a haven for 100,000 Jews. Nor would France cooperate, declining to open her colonies to any refugees of German origin. As for the British, Kennedy observed, they initially were very coy. While Chamberlain's survey of the British colonial empire indicated that small-scale settlements were possible in Kenya, Northern Rhodesia and Nyasaland, and that in Tanganyika some fifty thousand acres could be made available, he stipulated that further study was still necessary before a commitment could be made;

in the meantime, the British were admitting into England almost as many refugees as were entering the United States (which wasn't very many), "but they did not wish to have this fact generally known because of the anti-Semitic pressures that it might arouse."

So the "problem" of removing the Jews from Germany dragged on until the war intervened and Hitler devised his own catastrophic solution.

After the furor over Kristallnacht had died down, an illusory optimism prevailed, and as 1938 gave way to 1939 the hope for peace returned. But try as he might, Kennedy found it difficult to share in this hope. "In spite of the complacency of the British at the moment," he cabled to FDR in February of 1939, "the topside men in the Government ask themselves every night, if the Germans continue to arm and it is becoming more and more difficult to stop arming and make the transition to a peaceful economic basis, what can Herr Hitler do? Rather than assume the burden of a new economy for Germany it would seem easier to continue warlike methods. Whatever way you look at it, it seems to me that the long pull outlook is exceedingly dark for England."

But even in his most pessimistic moment Kennedy did not predict the turning point that would be reached on March 15, 1939, when Hitler's armies invaded Czechoslovakia. Here, less than eight months after the Munich Agreement was signed, amid repeated assurances that the cession of the predominantly German Sudetenland represented his last demand in Europe, Hitler was setting out to conquer non-Germanic lands. The German troops met no resistance, and by evening Hitler was able to make a triumphant entry into Prague, choosing to spend the night in Hradschin Castle, high above the River Moldau, where the Czech patriots Masaryk and Beneš had lived and worked for the first democracy central Europe had ever known. Within forty-eight hours the Czechoslovakian nation had ceased to exist.

"The destruction of Czechoslovakia struck Britain," historian Wheeler-Bennett observed, "with all the suddenness of a clap of thunder in a blue summer sky." To those who had been critical all along of the government's policy, it came as a confirmation of their worst fears; to those who had believed in the durability of the Munich Agreement, it came as a hideous disillusionment. Now no one, not even Chamberlain himself, could ignore the fact that Hitler had broken the pledge he so solemnly made at Munich. "Chamberlain felt," Kennedy recorded, "not only a sense of national but also of personal grievance against Hitler for these evidences of his perfidy."

Finally Chamberlain made up his mind to act. Indeed, faced with a storm of criticism from the press, with an impending revolt in the House of Commons, and with Hitler now making ominously familiar threats against Poland, he had little choice but to reassess his position. In an abrupt and fateful turning point, on March 31, 1939, sixteen days after Hitler entered Prague, the Prime Minister told the House of Commons that if Poland was attacked "His Majesty's Government would feel themselves bound at once to lend the Polish government all support in their power" and that he had given the Polish government an assurance to this effect.

"That statement marked a new shift in British policy," Kennedy recorded in his memoirs. "Never before had England guaranteed any borders [east] of the Rhine; never before had she so phrased her guarantee that the issue of peace or war was no longer in her hands. I talked about it that night to President Roosevelt. 'Chamberlain's plan,' he said, 'is a good one, but it probably means war.' "

In this prediction Roosevelt was correct, for with the British pledge to Warsaw less than six months remained before the outbreak of the Second World War.

Still, Kennedy continued to advocate political and financial appeasement of Germany. In this position he was joined by a host of powerful bankers and businessmen in both England and America who believed that continued economic relations with Germany were essential to the maintenance of a stable world order in which their own enterprises could flourish. As chronicled by Charles Higham in *Trading with the Enemy*, this group included key executives in General Motors, Ford, Du Pont, Standard Oil, Chase Manhattan and the Bank of England. Speaking for the group, General Motors' James Mooney argued, "We ought to make some arrangements with Germany . . . There is no reason why we should let our moral indignation over what happens in that country stand in the way."

In April of 1939, Mooney journeyed to Germany to discuss Hitler's request for a massive American gold loan to provide the basis for his New Order. There he met several times with Emil Puhl of the Bank for International Settlements and the Reichsbank and Helmuth Wohlthat, Goering's American-educated right-hand man in the Four-Year Plan. Wildly enthusiastic about the scheme, Mooney traveled to London to enlist Kennedy's aid. On hearing the plan, Kennedy agreed at once to meet with Puhl and Wohlthat in Paris, but when the White House heard about the trip he was told not to go. Undaunted, Mooney suggested that Wohlthat come to London, where he met with Kennedy on May 9. In his diary, Mooney noted that the Nazi economist and the American Ambassador got along very well, seeing eye to eye on everything. And indeed, fifteen years later, in a letter to Morton Downey, Kennedy mentioned that while he was in Paris he had seen his "friend Wohlthat, the German who was Hitler's Minister of Economics whom you probably heard me speak about," and that he was planning to travel to Düsseldorf that September to see him again.

But in the spring of 1939, with the specter of war on the horizon, Roosevelt was strongly opposed to letting his Ambassador make any deals with Goering's right-hand man, and after hearing of the London meeting he forbade Kennedy to have anything further to do with the arrangement.

Unlike Kennedy, FDR understood that there was a limit to the price that democracies would pay to avoid war. And with the destruction of Czechoslovakia in flagrant violation of the Munich Agreement, that limit had been reached. From here on, the views of the President of the United States and his Ambassador to Great Britain would dramatically diverge.

# CHAPTER 33
# THE
# LONG
# WEEKEND

In Europe's last remaining year of peace, Rose Kennedy and her children enjoyed some of the most exciting and stimulating experiences of their lives. Speaking to reporters as she arrived at Saint-Moritz with the children for a skiing holiday at the turn of the new year 1939, Rose said, "We hope to stay in England for a long time, perhaps years. We like England and we just love the English. I've had some of the happiest times of my life in England." During the following week, as the children enjoyed "one of the loveliest vacations they ever had," Rose wrote to the President, who was just then meeting with her husband in the United States, thanking him, on behalf of herself and the children, for having made the enriching opportunity possible.

Indeed, in reading Rose's diaries for 1938 and 1939, it seems impossible to imagine the awful calamity toward which Europe was heading. For throughout the events leading up to Munich in September and the invasion of Czechoslovakia in March, the events of the social world continued as regularly as the changing seasons, almost as if the upper class, filled with so many painful memories of the First World War, was deliberately trying not to think about the future. At a lunch with the

Duke of Sutherland at Hampden House, Rose records, the conversation centered on the impact of divorce on English and American politics. The Duke was interested to know whether divorced people could hold office in the American government, as it was impossible to do so, practically, in England. "In fact," Rose learned, "you cannot go in the Royal Enclosure at Ascot if you are the guilty party."

Preoccupied with the smallest details of proper etiquette while Europe was beginning to crash around her, Rose was terrifically upset one day when, mistaking her signal, Joe improperly took Lady Airlie down to lunch ahead of the Archbishop of Canterbury. For most functions, she was meticulously prepared, expressing anxiety only when the unexpected occurred. When, for instance, Queen Maud of Norway suddenly died, ushering in a six-week period of court mourning, Rose found it difficult to plan her clothes, for she had many parties to attend and only a few black dresses. Yet, in spite of her social obligations, she still managed, as she always had before, to find her own peace and serenity. On many mornings, she stayed in her room until noon, writing and reading. And then, for weeks and months, she occupied herself with the task of filling the embassy bookcases with old and valuable books, all of which she had specially bound in soft, restful browns and beiges.

While Rose was enjoying her social life, young Joe was traversing the Continent from one crisis spot to another. Like his father, he had developed early on a remarkable instinct for being in the right place at the right time. But in Joe Junior this tendency was edged with a certain rashness: climbing mountains or skiing down slopes, he seemed always to take unnecessary chances, acting as if he were invulnerable. Like his father, Joe rarely spent a directionless day. He surveyed the American Embassy in Paris "from top to bottom" in a matter of three weeks and then prepared to leave for a sixteen-day journey to Prague, Warsaw, Moscow, Leningrad, Scandinavia, Berlin and the Hague. Writing long reports to his father which contained perceptive summaries of the situation in eastern Europe and Russia, he pushed his way into the center of things wherever he went. Back home, the Ambassador would tell his friends he expected to get a few gray hairs before his son's journeying was over, but to Rose he confided that Joe's courageous spirit made him immensely proud.

That Christmas, while the Ambassador was on leave in America, Joe traveled with his mother and his brothers and sisters to Saint-Moritz, where he discovered on the Cresta Run a new sport exactly suited to his taste. "They have a small sled," he wrote to his friend Tom Schriber, "steel-enforced weighing about ninety pounds. You go down on your stomach and reach a speed of about seventy-five miles an hour. It's a terrific thrill, going around the corners at that speed only a few inches above the ice." Bobsledding as a novice on a daring run, he came within seconds of the world's record. But on the ski slopes the following day his speed and daring caught up with him. Skiing alone down a steep trail, he fell, lacerating and breaking his arm. Using his scarf as a tourniquet, he skied back to the Subretta House, where the family was staying, and from the desk called Luella Hennessey to say he needed a Band-Aid. Hennessey took one look and called Eddie Moore, and within minutes the three of them were off in a sleigh for the nearest hospital, three hours away.

Speaking later of the scene in the operating room, Hennessey marveled at Joe's high threshold of pain. "He never complained," she remembered, except afterward, when he said with a smile, "Look at this! It sure looks awful, doesn't it?" The next day Joe was out on the skating rink, his arm in a sling, and when he returned to London he reported to his father simply: "Everybody got pretty good on skiis including Teddy who was going along splendidly til he hurt his leg. However, he recuperated in a few days and was out showing everyone how it should be done."

Back in London for a crash course in international banking, Joe spent three days each in Bankers Trust and National City Bank and two days in a brokerage house, all of which enabled him, he told his father, to get "a pretty good general idea of foreign exchange, the discount market and the different types of bills." But then his restlessness returned and he set his heart on traveling to war-torn Spain, where the long civil war was finally coming to an end. Ever since completing his honors thesis at Harvard on the Hands Off Spain Committee, Joe Junior had dreamed of traveling through Spain, but each time he suggested the trip his father had vetoed the idea.

To Kennedy's mind, there were two problems with the trip. One was the fact that Joe Junior was traveling through Europe on a diplomatic passport, which meant that if he got into trouble it would involve the American State Department. More important, Kennedy was afraid for his son's safety. While the world had concluded by the early months of 1939 that the Spanish Civil War was over and that it was only a matter of time before Franco's insurgent Nationalist armies emerged victorious, the republican government, backed by a combination of liberals and Communists, still held a third of the country, including Madrid and Valencia, the two cities where Joe wanted to go. The civilian population was starving and the Loyalist armies possessed very little war matériel, but the policy of continued resistance, urged most strongly by the Communists, was still being followed. And the situation was complicated further by internal fighting between the Communists and the other republicans. Kennedy feared that if his son were caught in Madrid or Valencia at a time when the Communists were in control, his name could mean imprisonment.

Years later Rose recalled a long discussion on the subject of Spain between her husband and her eldest son. "It was just before Joe set off for America at Christmastime in 1938, and young Joe badly wanted his father's permission to go to Spain before the boat left for America. But Joe was adamant, arguing that because he himself had intervened in the situation the year before by taking a stand against the repeal of the Embargo Act,* young Joe would be persona non grata in republican Madrid. And beyond the internal political situation was the constant shelling from fascist air raids and the whole problem of the passport. It was just too dangerous, he concluded. Besides, there were plenty of other countries for Joe to visit, why not just leave Spain out for now?"

But Joe Junior did not give up so easily. While his father was still in the States and his mother was preparing for a six-week cruise to Cairo and Rome, he procured a regular American passport and left for Madrid, figuring that he had taken care of at least one part of his father's objections. On February 16 the Ambassador arrived back at Prince's Gate, accompanied by Jack, who had taken the semester off from Harvard so that he too could enjoy the opportunities the ambassadorship provided. At the door of the residence, the Ambassador was greeted by a cable from his eldest son: "Sorry I missed you. Arrived safely Valencia. Going to Madrid tonight. Regards Joe." "And that," he remarked to a reporter, "is the reception I get after being away for two months . . . I wish he would stay out of the firing line. His mother will die when she hears he is in Madrid."

But, at the same time, Kennedy was pleased with his son's high spirits, and, with pride in his voice, he told the press of Joe's visit to Prague during the crisis six months earlier. Overnight, young Joe became the "Crisis Hunter" in the London papers and "Don José" in the New York Herald-Tribune. When Kennedy received the first of a series of vivid letters from Joe, he allowed his pride in his son to become apparent to all who would listen. These included the Astors, the Lindberghs, London Times editor Geoffrey Dawson and his wife, and Lord Lothian—to all of whom Kennedy read the letter aloud after tea at Cliveden when he spent the day there on February 25.

From the shattered city of Madrid, where there was no heating, hot

---

* This was a reference to the Neutrality Act, which was preventing help from going to the legitimate government of Spain.

water, medicines or surgical dressings, and where the people had existed all winter long on a daily issue of two ounces of lentils, beans or rice, Joe Junior wrote that what impressed him most was the magnificent spirit of the people.

> The theatres are packed, for people don't know what to do with their money. They can't buy anything they need and besides it's a relief to get their minds off everyday facts. . . . There was an occasional shelling while we were in there. Not enough to interrupt the performance. . . .
>
> This morning I went to a private residence to Mass. There were only about nine people there and the priest was dressed in ordinary civilian clothes. There is no public celebration of Mass in Loyalist Madrid and people are still very much afraid of letting their religion be known.
>
> I talked with the priest, who formerly—for thirty years—studied at the Quirinal. He told me that ninety-four priests were killed there, mostly the savants who were great experts in different lines. Almost all the priests were thrown into prison. Now he travels around in plain clothes and even the people with whom he stays have no idea he's a priest.
>
> Many priests, he explained, are working for the State, some at the Front and others at the roads. He is at a loss as to how to explain the fact of the people's having turned so against the Church. But now, he says, they have realized the error of their ways and will return once again to the fold.
>
> I hope—for Spain's sake—he is right. In this upheaval of their lives, their horror and suffering, the people need something to which they can turn and cling for sustenance. What is there left—except a faith and a religion to lift them up. Yet, today, here in this shattered city, religion must hide and be furtive in disguise, hemmed in by fears on every hand. I imagine that today many prayers were breathed all over the world for these poor war-trodden human beings as they blindly try to find existence again.
>
> Good night, Dad, and much love to all of you. Somehow, this must be prevented from happening to any of you.

In saying that he was impressed with the people's spirit in the face of terrible conditions, Joe fails to mention that these conditions were imposed by Franco and his insurgents, who were shelling and starving them into submission. He speaks of the murder of priests (which was not condoned by the Spanish government) but not about the atrocities committed by the Franco forces, including the Moors, and not about the centuries of well-known oppression by the Church, which was supporting Franco.

But Joe's one-sided letter gave precisely the slant the crowd at Cliveden wanted to hear. Anne Morrow Lindbergh recorded in her diary that the letter was "very vivid and balanced and yet young too. I am surprised at a young person seeing so clearly and recording so well, in the middle of such moving times."

The Astors' guest of honor, Neville Chamberlain, arrived later. At dinner that night, Kennedy sat between Lady Astor and Anne Lindbergh, near Chamberlain and the Duke of Devonshire. "Kennedy can hardly talk to me," Mrs. Lindbergh recorded in her diary that night, "from wanting to talk to Lady Astor and Mr. Chamberlain, though when he does I am touched by what he says. He talks about their [the Kennedys'] life together. How in Boston they had never in twenty years (before coming to England) given as many as twenty dinner parties, or been to twenty. They had decided that the most important thing in their lives were their children and giving them a family life and they couldn't 'go out' and do this at the same time, so they just took the choice."

After dinner, Lady Astor rounded up all the guests to hear Kennedy read Joe's letter again. They sat around quietly, Mrs. Lindbergh reported, and when Kennedy was done, knowing the impression the letter had made, he took off his glasses and suddenly looked "like a small boy, pleased and shy, . . . like an Irish terrier wagging his tail (a *very* nice Irish terrier)."

The Prime Minister turned to Mrs. Lindbergh and said, "It *must* end soon," and went on to say, apropos of Joe Junior's comments on the bombing, that Franco had probably been very clever about his method of dropping bombs—"a few every day on Madrid, wearing people's morale down." Then very quickly, perhaps fearing his enthusiasm for the bombing sounded strange from a man who was supposed to hate war so much, he added, "But I think that was undoubtedly the most humane method he could take, the most saving of lives."

While the men and women at Cliveden were discussing Joe's letter, the last tragedy of the civil war in Spain—the war within the war—was just beginning, as a group of Loyalist officers who believed it madness to hold out any longer carried out a coup d'état against Juan Negrin, the Prime Minister. One month later, General Sigismundo Casado, the leading spirit of this group, surrendered to Franco without conditions. During this time, Joe stayed in Madrid, a witness to the final agonies of a struggle which later would be considered one of the most passionate wars of all time. At the embassy in London, Kennedy received a letter from his son almost every other day and with each letter his fatherly pride swelled still further. Carrying a batch of these letters with him wherever he went, he ended up quoting aloud from them, this time at Chamberlain's urging, at a small dinner at 10 Downing Street.

While Joe Junior was in Spain, Pope Pius XI died and Eugenio Cardinal Pacelli was elected as Pius XII. Two years before, Pacelli had been a guest of the Kennedys at their Bronxville home, and so when President Roosevelt decided to send an official American representative to the coronation—for the first time in history—Kennedy was the natural choice.

The coronation was set for March 12, 1939. Rose, who had immediately journeyed to Rome from Egypt upon hearing the news, was determined that all the children be there for the historic occasion. Kennedy agreed and, to the amusement of others, chartered a whole *wagon-lit* on the Rome express, for, in addition to the children, he brought along the governesses, as well as Mary and Eddie Moore and Arthur Houghton. Riding on the same train with the Kennedy family was the Duke of Norfolk, the leading Catholic peer of the realm, whom King George had designated as England's representative to the coronation.

When the train pulled in, Rose was at the station to greet her family. Years later, she recalled her disappointment at discovering that young Joe was not among the children as they trooped off. When she questioned her husband, he said he had sent a cable to Madrid but apparently, in the chaos of the situation there, Joe had not received it. In her diary Rose repeats the story, saying that when she finally talked with Joe Junior after it was over, he said he had never received his father's message but "had heard on the radio that we were all there except him."

From papers in the Ambassador's private files, this story appears to have been concocted by Kennedy and his son to allow Joe to stay in Madrid without raising his mother's ire. For on March 9, the day before Kennedy left London for Rome, he responded by cable to a request by Joe to stay in Madrid a little longer: "Wire received. We are attending Pope's coronation Rome Sunday representing President. Stay Madrid if you think safe. Nothing here. Good luck and love."

The coronation of Pope Pius XII was a splendid event, made more special for Joe and Rose because they considered themselves personal friends of the new Pope. There was an added specialness, Rose reported, in spending time with Cardinal O'Connell, the aging prelate who had married them a quarter of a century before.

On the morning of the great pageant, a bright, crisp, sunny day, the Kennedys were up at dawn. They drove to St. Peter's flying the American and papal flags through streets crowded with people and lined with troops in olive-green uniforms.

The great square in front of St. Peters was packed, and some 70,000 people had crowded into the church [Kennedy recorded in his memoirs]. . . . We sat directly before the altar and heard the Pope celebrate the Mass. It was essentially the same Mass that is said everywhere in every Catholic

Church, but the beauty of it that day was beyond belief. To us kneeling in the hollow of the Dome, the intonation of the Kyrie and the Gloria by the Pope and the responses of the Sistine Choir were a never to be forgotten experience.

The following morning, the Pope received the Kennedys and their eight children in private audience. Reminiscing about his visit to Bronxville, he seemed especially pleased to see Teddy, whom he remembered as the little boy who had sat on his lap and been so curious about the large crucifix hanging from his neck. Two days later, the seven-year-old Teddy received his first communion from the Pope, the first American ever so honored.

Writing from Madrid, Joe told his parents he had listened every night on the radio to hear the news of the coronation. "It must have been a wonderful sight and it certainly was a great honor. At the same time everything was popping here," as the Casado men were fighting in the streets with the Communists. "We could see men hit right outside the house and be carried out by the Red Cross. Many civilians hit as they would be walking along the street when the shooting would begin . . . Do you think that an article on this trip would be interesting or do you think it would be bad politics. I think it could be made politically impartial."

Kennedy advised his son not only to publish an article but to write a book, for, as he confided to Rose, a person who has written a book gains a certain prestige. To help Joe in this effort, Kennedy enlisted the skills of embassy aide Harvey Klemmer with the promise that he would send Klemmer's children through college in return. As it turned out, while Joe did publish a letter in *The Atlantic Monthly*, he never completed the book. Perhaps he never sat still long enough to finish a draft, or perhaps the decision was made that it *was* bad politics. But, with this extraordinary experience under his belt, as correspondent George Bilainkin observed in London's *Evening Chronicle*, he emerged "a different Joe from the young man I knew a few months ago. There is the same smile, the friendly winning way, but he is now much older than 23 . . . Already with his knowledge of the world and the incomparably rich experience of meeting all the celebrities the world sends to the Metropolis, he stands assured of a place in the hierarchy of the US of tomorrow."

While Joe was laying the groundwork for his place in the future hierarchy of the United States, Jack was just arriving in England, having completed the first semester of his junior year at Harvard. In the early fall he had worked out an agreement with Harvard that if he took six courses instead of the customary four, he could take a leave of absence in the spring and still graduate with his class in June 1940. And that fall at school, with Joe Junior gone, Jack demonstrated a greater sense of purpose and self-confidence than ever before. Despite his heaviest course load, he received his best grades, high enough to warrant a place on the Dean's list.

After visiting Jack at Harvard on a weekend in October, Lem wrote Kathleen to say:

> Brother Jack is certainly doing well up there. He's really terrifically popular and I feel sure if he wasn't taking this half year off he'd be pretty much of a power to contend with up there. That Spee Club is really something . . . Jack has gotten himself a new sweetie far superior to any he has had before. In fact this is really a damned attractive girl—Frances Anne Cannon—you probably know her because she used to go to Sarah Lawrence. She's going to school up in Boston somewhere . . .
>
> We got back to Princeton to find the college practically in flight due to an invasion of rocket-ships from Mars—who supposedly had landed in Trenton—from which monsters had poured that were laying havoc to the land and heading for Princeton. It was in reality all a hoax—it was a play given over the radio* that many people had happened upon after it had started and since it was done in a very realistic manner, by news flashes and talks from Secretary Ickes pleading with the country to be calm in the grave disaster—you can't imagine the consternation caused in New Jersey.

Jack spent the Christmas holidays with his father in Palm Beach— where the Ambassador had gone after his meetings with Roosevelt—and then sailed with him for London on February 10, 1939, aboard the *Queen Mary*. In his luggage Jack carried a pile of books which he was reading in preparation for his senior honors thesis on Great Britain's lack of preparation for war. During the fall term, in the aftermath of the Munich Agreement, Jack had hit upon the preparedness topic, which earned him the enthusiastic approval and support of his teachers, Bruce Hopper and Payson Wild. It was indeed a good idea for a thesis, especially since he could spend his semester in England gathering firsthand information. Moreover, the very fact that Jack had come up with a topic so early showed a certain diligence and forethought not previously noted in his character.

"Jack arrived looking much too healthy," Kathleen reported to Lem. "Gosh it was good to see him again." No sooner had he arrived than he

---

* This was the famous Orson Welles radio play "The War of the Worlds."

journeyed with his family to Rome for the coronation. Then in April he set out on a fact-finding tour of eastern Europe, following an itinerary carefully prepared by his father.

Jack started his odyssey with a month's stay in the American Embassy in Paris, where Ambassador Bullitt's assistant, Carmel Offie, recalls him "sitting in my office and listening to telegrams being read or even reading various things which were actually none of his business but since he was who he was we didn't throw him out."

From Paris, Jack went to Poland, Lithuania, Latvia, Russia, Turkey, Palestine and the Balkans, sending detailed reports of his observations to his father from each. Taken as a whole, his letters reveal the working of a shrewd, perceptive, detached mind. From Poland, for instance, he sent a long letter analyzing the prospects of war and peace. Writing at a time when the future of the Continent depended upon Germany's decisions about Poland and Poland's response, Jack correctly observed: "Probably the strongest impression I have gotten is that rightly or wrongly the Poles *will fight over* the Question of Danzig." The Soviet Union, Jack concluded after covering a great deal of its vast territory by airplane, was "a crude, backward, hopelessly bureaucratic country."

He returned in June to London, where he enjoyed an active social life for a month before heading back to the Continent with his Harvard friend Torby Macdonald. After traveling through Germany Jack wanted to visit Czechoslovakia. But with the Prague government under Nazi control, and the city itself in turmoil, such visits were forbidden. "Yet in the midst of this confusion," Foreign Service Officer George F. Kennan recalled, "we received a telegram from the embassy in London, the sense of which was that our ambassador there . . . had chosen this time to send one of his young sons on a fact-finding tour around Europe, and it was up to us to find means of getting him across the border and through the German lines so that he could include in his itinerary a visit to Prague." The embassy staff was furious that they should have to waste their time on this "upstart ignoramus," but they did as Ambassador Kennedy asked and Jack was shown what he wanted to see in Prague.

For Jack, the tour was an extraordinary educational experience. Not only did he get the chance to witness the final rumblings of an entire continent moving toward war, but his numerous contacts helped in the gathering of information that would make substantial contributions to his thesis on preparedness.

While her brothers were touring the Continent, Kathleen was more than contented to stay in London. Indeed, following in her mother's footsteps, she absorbed herself so fully in her rich social life that the impending war intruded only rarely into her conversations and her letters. Back in the days of Munich, Kathleen had complained to Lem Billings that "all you can hear or talk about at this point is the future war which is bound to come. Am so darn sick of it." Afterward, however, even after the Munich Agreement was shattered by the invasion of Czechoslovakia, the talk of war never returned to the fever pitch it had reached before Munich. During weekends at country houses, the imminence of war was discussed with a certain detachment, as though it were merely a topic of intellectual interest. It was not British, one writer observed, to voice one's private terrors.

In America, by contrast, according to Lem Billings in a letter he wrote to Kathleen three weeks after Hitler's invasion in March, the consciousness of war was growing stronger and stronger.

> You'd be surprised to see the difference between the feeling against Hitler now and the way everybody felt during the Munich peace. At that time we all didn't care what happened—we weren't going to war—but Hitler and the big Moose have to be stopped now and it certainly seems that war is the only way to do it . . . Last night at the movies they showed in the newsreel pictures of our air force and army maneuvers and everyone hysterically got up and cheered—even brother John's flat feet and bad stomach won't keep him out of this one.

In reply, Kathleen wrote: "It really is amazing that you can sound so pessimistic about the war etc. People over here are absolutely calm compared to Americans. It's rather odd as England is so near and exposed and America so far away and comparatively safe." Having thus dealt with her thoughts on the war, she went on to describe in detail a "very exciting" weekend spent with her family and the Astors at Cliveden, special excitement having been provided by a surprise visit of the Queen and the two princesses. Then, she told Lem, as soon as she returned to London she attended the premiere of *Wuthering Heights*, coupled with a large party thrown by Jimmy Roosevelt. Spencer Tracy was over as well, she reported, and he got a gigantic reception. "Eunice and I played tennis with him yesterday morning."

Most of Kathleen's English friends were probably terribly confused about the coming war. On the one hand, as young people they had to come to terms with the terrifying prospect of being drafted. And they must have known, from the stories they had heard from their parents and from the countless memorials in their public schools and colleges, the disproportionate price the Great War had exacted from the upper class. On the other hand, boys like Billy Hartington and David Ormsby-

Gore, coming as they did from families filled with soldiers in each generation, believed it was their duty to fight, no matter what the odds.

Sometimes, as Rose recorded in her diary after a conversation with Kathleen, the British boys were willing to admit their anxiety about the war news, telling Kathleen she was lucky to be an American. In the next breath, they would playfully offer to shoot her or one of her family and make it look like the result of a supposed German air raid, "as they could not imagine USA not in war if American Ambassador or some of his family were shot."

One evening during this time, while Joe Kennedy was showing a film about the Great War, Billy Hartington and several other young Englishmen who were guests of Kathleen's talked almost eagerly about getting into battle. In reaction, the Ambassador kept up a running antiwar commentary throughout the film and became especially heated during a scene showing English soldiers being slaughtered in the trenches. "See that?" he said. "That's what you'll look like if you go to war with Germany." Though he was undoubtedly voicing the silent fears of the boys themselves, it was not something the young people wanted to hear. For no matter what their parents told them about the horrors of war, they, like generations before them, were beginning to feel the stir of excitement at the prospect that their country's destiny lay in their hands. In the awkward silence that followed the Ambassador's outburst, Kathleen sat red-faced. Afterward she apologized to Billy. "You mustn't pay attention to him. He just doesn't understand the English as I do."

In late July 1939, Kathleen traveled with her brother Joe and their British friend Hugh Fraser to Spain, where, for the first time, she saw the results of war. Though the Spanish Civil War had been over for four months, Kathleen reported to Lem that everything was still in a chaotic state and "they are just getting back on their feet. The outskirts of Madrid are mere ruins and thousands are homeless. One can also see the first line trenches of both the Reds and Franco's troops." She told of meeting the Nationalist General Mossarch, the man who had held the command of the famous Alcázar fort for three months with very little food until reinforcements arrived from Franco.

It was his son the Reds seized and forced to speak into the phone to his father saying if the General did not give up the fort the Reds would kill him. Needless to say the General told his son to die like a Spaniard.

It really is impossible to believe that such things occurred in this present day civilization and that the boys we see walking in the streets have just come out of trenches . . . It seems funny to hear of a war just over when one has heard so much of the war to come outside of Spain.

When the Spanish trip was over Kathleen joined her family in Cannes, where they had once again taken a house for the month of August. "It was good to get away from the bustle of London," Joe Senior admitted, exhibiting a certain gift for escapism. "In Cannes it was possible for me really to see my children again and have close at hand the kind of world that some men were seeking to destroy and others were too divided to preserve."

While the Kennedys were in France, Billy Hartington celebrated his coming of age at a party in the garden at Chatsworth. It was the first majority celebration to be held at the historic mansion since 1811; his father had reached his twenty-first birthday during the First World War, a time when all great parties were suspended. For the entertainment of their 2,800 guests, Billy's parents had hired an entire circus. It was one of the "greatest events" of the year, if not the decade, and Kathleen was hundreds of miles away in France!

Years later, Rose recalled Kathleen pleading with her to let her go back to England in August so that she could attend the party, but despite a vivid memory of a similar confrontation with her own father over conflicting plans for a vacation in Palm Beach and the Harvard junior prom, Rose remained adamant. Vacations were times for the family to spend together and that was that. Kathleen acquiesced, as she usually did. Once she got settled in Cannes, she relaxed into the family routine, knowing that as soon as she returned to London in September a new round of parties would begin and that at all these events she was bound to be thrown together with Billy Hartington.

Though Kathleen was absent from Billy's party, her closest friends assumed she and Billy were semi-engaged. On the day of the party, reports of a secret engagement were published in the Boston papers with the tantalizing headline "Kennedy Girl May Wed Peer." Both families immediately denied the rumor, and the truth was that the young couple had reached no such agreement. While they had been seeing each other regularly ever since their first meeting at the royal garden party, and while Kathleen had been a frequent weekend guest at Billy's various homes, religion remained an insurmountable obstacle. But, for Kathleen, the romance with Billy was definitely the most intense relationship she had ever experienced, lending a vitality to her life in England which made her, like Rose, wish that the ambassadorship would never come to an end.

With the announcement of the Nazi-Soviet Pact on August 21, Europe moved yet another step closer to war. Journeying at once back to London, Kennedy found Chamberlain "more depressed and more downcast" than he had ever seen him before. "I have done everything that I can think of, Joe," he said, "but it looks as if all my work has been of no avail. I can't fly again; that was good only once . . . The thing that is frightful is the futility of it all. The Poles can't be saved. All that the English can do is to wage a war of revenge that will mean the entire destruction of Europe."

The waiting was over on September 1, 1939, when Hitler moved against Poland. "The news . . . came with a rush," Kennedy recorded, "like a torrent spewing from the wires—German troops had crossed the border; German planes were bombing Polish cities and killing civilians; the Germans were using poison gas." Some of the accounts were exaggerated, but the central fact was true: the German Army was on the march against Poland. By the pledge Chamberlain himself had given back in March, Britain was bound to come to Poland's aid.

Later that day, in a last attempt to avoid the inevitable, Chamberlain dispatched a message to Berlin informing Hitler that unless Germany withdrew its troops from Poland, Britain would go to war. At the same time, knowing what was to come, parents placed thousands of children, many of whom had never left their homes before, on trains and boats to be taken to rural areas as part of a vast evacuation plan.

Saturday, September 2, was, Kennedy wrote, "a day of ominous waiting silence." In the House of Commons Chamberlain was greeted with anger and frustration. "There shall be no more devices," Labour MP Arthur Greenwood said, voicing the sentiment of the majority, "for dragging out what has been dragged out too long."

Finally, on Sunday morning, with no answer from Hitler, the government had to make good on its word. In his office at the embassy, Kennedy cleaned up his desk and had a small radio brought in so that he could listen as Chamberlain spoke to the British people. "We were all terribly moved by the solemnity and tragedy of the occasion," he recorded. "The tears came to my eyes as I heard Chamberlain say that 'all my long struggle to win peace has failed.'"

As soon as Chamberlain stopped speaking, Kennedy picked up the telephone and asked for him. To his surprise, the Prime Minister came on the line at once. "We did the best we could," Chamberlain said, his voice still quivering from the emotion he had showed in the broadcast, "but it looks as though we have failed."

At the embassy residence at Prince's Gate, Rose, Joe Junior, Jack and Kathleen were leaving for the House of Commons, which was scheduled to meet at twelve o'clock. There is a remarkable photograph of the three young people en route to the Palace of Westminster. Captured in arrested movement, they have a look of high adventure, almost a jaunty appearance. To the left is Joe Junior, handsomely dressed in a pinstriped suit, with a white handkerchief carefully tucked into his pocket. To the right is Jack in a light jacket and striped tie, his left hand in his pocket. And in the center, wearing a simple black dress, white pearls and white gloves, her pretty face framed by a large black hat, is Kathleen. Walking swiftly toward the Houses of Parliament, past the memorial to the sons who had given their lives in the First World War (a memorial that reads in part, "Happy was your death. You paid for your father and the common debt that all men owe to nature . . ."), this golden trio could not have imagined how much they each would lose by the war that was about to begin.

Shortly after noon, from their seats in the Strangers' Gallery of the overflowing House chamber, the young Kennedys witnessed the dramatic moment when Chamberlain, after telling the Commons that the German government had failed to respond to Britain's ultimatum, finally said, " . . . consequently, this country is at war with Germany."

At this point, the entire chamber broke into sustained applause. In an uncharacteristic move, the Prime Minister pounded the lectern as he delivered his final line. "I trust I may live to see the day when Hitlerism has been destroyed and a liberated Europe has been reestablished."

When Chamberlain finished speaking, other members took the floor, including Churchill, who said, "The Prime Minister said it was a sad day and that is indeed true, but . . . there is a feeling of thankfulness that if these great trials were to come upon our Island, there is a generation of Britons here now ready to prove itself not unworthy of the days of yore and not unworthy of those great men, the fathers of our land, who laid the foundations of our laws and shaped the greatness of our country. This is not a question of fighting for Danzig or fighting for Poland. We are fighting to save the whole world from the pestilence of Nazi tyranny and in defense of all that is most sacred to man."

In the midst of this patriotic fervor, which Joe, Jack and Kathleen heartily embraced, only one member, the son of a Glasgow steelworker, spoke the words the senior Kennedy privately felt. Confessing that he could not take the road of public opinion, John McGovern said he could only regret that on this Sunday morning mankind found itself in the position where "men are on the eve of having to live like beasts, with lice and vermin crawling over them, grubbing for food, blinding and tearing bodies apart and blowing limbs asunder."

But these were not the words that the Parliament wanted to hear that day, and the session ended with a blazing peroration by the old statesman Lloyd George: "The Government could do no other than they have done—I have been through this before and there is only one word I want to say about that. We had very bad moments . . . [but] we won a victory for right. We will do it again."

And so on a clear, bright Sunday morning, the Second World War began. The time had come for Rose and the children to go home.

# CHAPTER 34

# "HOSTAGES

# TO

# FORTUNE"

The Kennedys returned to America as they had come to England—in stages.

Rose, Kathleen, Eunice and Bobby have gone back [the Ambassador wrote to Arthur Krock on September 15, 1939]. Joe went yesterday on the Mauretania. Next week the rest of them will go home and some time later on Eddie and Mary Moore in order to be back with the Kennedys. So from then on it promises to be rather a lonesome spot . . . I don't want Rose to get lonesome so call her up occasionally and tell her the American news because, while she will be all right with all the children, after a while she is bound to get a bit depressed.

Actually, it was Joe Kennedy who suffered the most from a prolonged feeling of exile. Though he would have liked to resign his ambassadorship as soon as the war broke out, he knew this was impossible, so he settled in for what would be one of the most difficult periods of his life. Throughout the previous year, as tensions mounted and divisions sharpened, Kennedy could always count on his friendship with Chamberlain as a strong anchor in the political sea. But once Chamberlain became the leader of a nation at war, he could no longer acquiesce in the unrelenting pessimism which Kennedy continually expressed about the course of events. While Joe was saying nothing different from what he had said before, his bluntness about England's weaknesses built a wall which eventually cut him off from almost all his English friends. At this early stage in the war, anyone who was well informed about the relative strength of England and Germany was bound to be pessimistic; but, while the British soberly acknowledged the tough odds and were inspired to fight harder, Kennedy was simply a defeatist. Believing that the only chance for Britain's victory lay in the thing he feared most, America's intervention, he gradually reined in his feelings for a country he had come to love, refusing to let emotion cloud self-interest.

This was not the first time Kennedy had been separated from his family, but in the past any loneliness had been compensated for by his ever-increasing sense of accomplishment. Now he was facing just the opposite situation. The longer he stayed in London, the more he witnessed a diminution of his power. Where once he had been deluged with invitations, now he found himself spending more and more time alone in the embassy. Where he had once been Roosevelt's right-hand man, now he was being bypassed by the White House and the State Department. (The week after the war began, FDR had opened his famous secret correspondence with Churchill, who had been brought into the War Cabinet as head of the Admiralty.)

Having said repeatedly that England had little chance of winning the war and that he did not want his country involved, Kennedy should not have been surprised to discover a certain cooling toward him in London. But, even as he placed himself on a collision course with the British, he never understood that no matter how many of his British friends had argued before the war that Britain should stay out, once His Majesty's Government was in the war, everything was different. To Lord Halifax, for instance, the declaration of war brought unexpected relief. "My feelings," he told Kennedy the next day, "reminded me of a dream I once had in which I was being tried for murder. I was finally convicted and, to my surprise, a feeling of relief rather than fear swept over me." Even Chamberlain, Kennedy admitted, "was now committed," and in his prosecution of the war he needed America's help. Speaking of the current battle in America for repeal of the Neutrality Act, Chamberlain observed, "If it failed to pass it would be sheer disaster for us." Kennedy listened to his arguments with sympathy, and in fact he himself was in favor of lending Britain as much aid as possible. But in his mind always was the fear that at a certain point American aid would lead to American involvement in the war.

The war itself, in those early months, was "a queer war," in the words of the writer Janet Flanner, "a phony war" as described by the American press. There were no marching soldiers, no brass bands, no great battles being fought between the Franco-British and German forces. Were it not for the piles of sandbags on the streets, the eerie silence of the blackout at night and the knowledge that it was against the law to go onto the street without a gas mask slung over the shoulder in its khaki case, it would have seemed, Flanner observed, a beautiful Indian summer. "The only thing that does get our goat is the blackout," Eddie Moore wrote to Missy LeHand, "and it is perfectly terrible. It is not much fun prowling around after it starts in, for taxis and buses can still hurt a lot if they creep up and nudge you." Before the war, author H. V. Morton wrote, "no one could have believed" that London could be "utterly abandoned to the dark." So frightening was it at first that "even burglars stayed at home." But after a while the people got used to it and began venturing forth into the night, walking splay-footed and with their elbows out as buffers. Walkers groped with their hands for the sides of the houses and were told to blow their noses frequently as a means of adjusting the nerves of balance just behind the ears.

In his memoirs, Kennedy painted a picture of England in the last months of 1939, "girding herself for war, trying to make up for lost time, yet fumbling so frequently . . . Officialdom worked hard. Behind blacked out windows the lights burned nightly at Whitehall and across the street in the War Office." But in Kennedy's estimate it was too late, Germany was too far ahead and it was only a matter of time until the real war began. As the weeks went by, the intensity of the work at the embassy began to affect Kennedy's health. Every day the lines at the American Embassy of refugees trying to leave Europe grew longer. Kennedy was also charged at this time with representing American interests in the complicated problem of Anglo–American trade, disrupted now by the war. And he was, of course, continuing to send his daily dispatches on the evolving situation to the State Department. "In slightly over two months," he recorded, "I had lost some 15 pounds. Sleep was at a premium; the telephone rang at all hours with its insistent demands."

Increasingly depressed by the situation, Kennedy derived comfort from sharing his dismal thoughts with other worriers. During this period he turned increasingly to Montagu Norman, the director of the Bank of England, who like Kennedy held a bitterly bearish attitude. In the preceding two decades, believing that continued economic relations with Germany were paramount to the maintenance of a stable world order, Norman had opposed forcing her to pay her debts and had come to the rescue of the Reichsbank with a large credit. Now, with the onset of war, everything he had worked for was shattered.

In Norman's opinion, Kennedy wrote to FDR, England was broke already and could go on spending for only two more years at most. "If this struggle goes on," Norman had told Kennedy, "England as we have known her is through. Twenty-five years ago Germany was her customer, but now Germany is lost and others as well. Without gold or foreign assets England's trade is going to be forced to narrow itself more and more until she will be forced to trade with what is left of her dominions and colonies and the US will drop out as a substantial customer. The end is likely to be that . . . the Empire will contract in power and size to that of other nations."

Telling Roosevelt that he was in complete accord with Norman, Kennedy went on to say that he had yet "to talk to any military or naval expert of any nationality who thinks that, in the present and prospective set-up of England and France on one side and Germany and Russia and their potential allies on the other, England has a Chinaman's chance." As Kennedy saw it, England was fighting for her possessions and "place in the sun," just as she had done in the First World War, and the results would be equally catastrophic, not only for England but for the cause of democracy in general; for after the centralization of power required by war, "democracy as we now conceive it in the US" would not exist in Europe, regardless of which side won.

In his predictions about the effect of the war upon England's empire, Kennedy showed remarkable prescience. But in believing that England had a genuine choice about whether or not to go to war once the menacing nature of Hitler's Germany became clear, he showed once again his blindness to the profound threat which Hitler posed. Moreover, by forecasting democracy's end Kennedy failed to appreciate its resilient capacity to absorb centralized controls during war and then throw them off again once peace returned.

During these dark days, Kennedy turned to the one member of his family who was left in England—his nineteen-year-old retarded daughter, Rosemary. When the rest of the family sailed home, the decision had been made to leave Rosemary in the school where she was making more progress than she had made in many years—a convent school deep in the Hertfordshire countryside and safe from the bombing, at least for the moment. It was run by a nun named Mother Isabel, and as a special companion for Rosemary Joe had secured the services of an extraordinary woman named Dorothy Gibbs. After so many bad experiences with schools at home, Rosemary finally seemed to have found a place where she could relax and feel accepted. "It is now possible,"

Dorothy Gibbs wrote to Joe several months after Rosemary's arrival, "that we have her surrounded by the right people in religious surroundings to give her the happy feeling of freedom and a certain independence . . . At last she really seems launched."

The key to Rosemary's happiness seems to have been that the school, a training center for Montessori teachers, gave her the opportunity to read to a group of small children every afternoon; the experience apparently did wonders for her. One of the big difficulties with Rosemary in the past had been getting her to take a rest when her anxiety level was high. But now, as Dorothy Gibbs wrote to the Moores, "she willingly puts herself to rest for an hour in the afternoon, saying 'It will be good, won't it, as I shall be refreshed to read to the children afterwards.' With all the quiet around her she seems to choose things that are best eventually. She has decided (we had a little quiet talk together) that she will not be 'fierce' with the children whatever happens because it is not 'Montessori' . . ."

In her own letters to the Moores, Rosemary spoke all the time of her father. "I see in the papper where Daddy . . . attends to leave for London . . . There was a pice about him in the sketch. I have ordered it for myself. I have heard Daddy name on the radio. About world affairs." The letters, printed neatly on notebook paper, suggest the intensity of her attachment to her father during these months. With all the rest of her family gone, she took it upon herself, as best she could, to be his companion and to follow his activities.

Ever so pleased to see his daughter making progress, Kennedy visited her regularly and had her come to stay with him on occasional weekends at the embassy's country lodgings in Windsor. He made Mother Isabel promise not to be afraid of asking for anything the school needed for Rosemary, even another house, furniture, servants, etc., and Mother Isabel responded with a long list of needed improvements.

Still, the Kennedys were determined to keep the true nature of Rosemary's condition from the press. In November 1939, two reporters from the *Boston Globe* learned that Rosemary had remained in England to "housekeep" for her father and wrote her a letter requesting a short interview. In response, Eddie Moore prepared a letter which Rosemary then copied over. "When my mother and the rest of the children left England, I thought it my duty to remain behind with my Father," it began. "I have always had serious tastes and understand that life is not given us just for enjoyment . . . For some time past, I have been studying the well known psychological method of Dr. Maria Montessori and I got my degree in teaching last year. Although it has been very hard work, I have enjoyed it immensely and I have made many good friends."

Apparently the letter satisfied the reporters, and the request for an inter-view was withdrawn.

But even with Rosemary as his companion, Kennedy felt increasingly isolated from everyone else he loved, and by the end of November he felt the pull of his family so strongly that "he couldn't stand it anymore." Just in time, Roosevelt decided to call his Ambassador home for a round of consultations. On November 29 Kennedy left London for Paris, and from there he went to Lisbon, where his trans-atlantic flight was to originate. But at Lisbon there were no planes available, and he had to wait three additional days. "Hopelessly impatient and disappointed," he cabled to Rose, "but nothing I can do so eager to get home."

The eventual trip home was a much needed tonic. "It was a treat to see New York again. There was a gaiety to it that was missing in wartime England. Even the lights of Times Square seemed to blaze more bril-liantly as I thought of the blackness of London."

On December 10, accompanied by his two older sons, Kennedy returned to East Boston for the seventieth-anniversary banquet of the Church of Our Lady of the Assumption. Here, in the church where he had served as an altar boy, he made his first speech since the start of the European war. "As you love America," he declared, "don't let anything that comes out of any country in this world make you be-lieve that you can make the situation one whit better by getting into the war. There's no place in the fight for us. It's going to be bad enough as it is."

Perhaps Kennedy did not realize that his extemporaneous comments in his hometown would be carried in British newspapers, but they were and when he returned to England after the holidays his reception was so chilly that he found it "a little difficult" to take up his work again. In the records of the British Foreign Office for this period there is a re-markable memorandum explaining Kennedy's attitude on the war as a product of his political position. "One of the most important problems which Mr. Roosevelt has had to face during his eventful tenure of of-fice," the memo begins, "has been the inefficiency and even dishonesty of many American civil servants, executive officers and politicians." This difficulty, the memo goes on, had been aggravated by the spoils system of appointment in which top jobs were farmed out among groups with whom the Administration wished to stand well.

> The East Coast Irish are such a group and are of great importance to a Democratic Administration—at the same time they represent about the most dirty group of politicians in the country.
> To pacify the East Coast Irish Mr. Kennedy was given his present ap-

pointment. From Mr. Kennedy's point of view he owes his position to the fact that he represents a Catholic, Irish, anti-English group. . . .

Worried that Kennedy's negative attitude would affect American opinion, the Foreign Office began collecting a file of "Kennediana"—a miscellaneous collection of public statements, newspaper articles, reports of private conversations, anecdotes, rumors and even Kennedy's private telegrams. The government hesitated to take him on directly, fearing that an open confrontation with the American Ambassador could provoke difficulties with its once and future ally, but with each passing week the British resentment of Kennedy grew until it finally spilled over into the public press.

When he reached London in late February 1940, Kennedy was asked by reporters to assess the strength of the isolationist mood in America. "If you mean by isolation a desire to keep out of war I should say that it was even stronger during the last two months I was there," he said. "People understand it less and less. They don't understand what it is all about."

In reply to this statement, a prominent member of Parliament, Beverly Baxter, wrote an open letter to Kennedy in the *Sunday Graphic*:

> With the greatest respect and even with some claims as a personal friend I feel constrained to ask, My dear Ambassador, Why didn't you tell them? There is no living man in a better position to tell the people of the USA the truth about the war . . . You have a large and young family. Your interest in their careers and your unqualified joy in their companionship won the hearts of all of us over here. We realize the loneliness you are feeling now at being separated from them . . . And why is this war being fought? In order that your children and my children and the children of every country may live in a world where there is decency and light instead of the darkness of war and scientific barbarism. Because of the sacrifice of the young men of France and Britain our sons and daughters shall not see the Gestapo or the concentration camp, the fouling of the young mind, the setting of son against father, the enslavement of the soul and the end of individual liberty. They shall not see the night replace the day nor civilization turn back to the ages of cruelty and ignorance . . . That is what this war is about.

In April 1940, London was, in the words of American visitor Clare Boothe Luce, "lovely beyond even an Englishman's belief. There were bright azaleas in the window-boxes of hotel and home windows and tulips in the court of Buckingham Palace." But London's peaceful spring came to an abrupt end with Hitler's sudden invasion of the neutral countries of Denmark and Norway. The daring of the plan, in defiance of Britain's superiority in seapower, staggered the Allies and brought "the phony war" to an immediate end. "The news is stupefying," William L. Shirer wrote in his diary, "Copenhagen occupied this morning, Oslo this afternoon . . . All the great Norwegian ports, Narvik, Trondheim, Bergen, Stavanger, captured. How the Nazis got there—under the teeth of the British Navy—is a complete mystery."

In his memoirs, Kennedy recorded that the brutal invasion shocked the conscience of the world, and that in its wake "a revolution in British government broke with all its fury." In Parliament the call for a new Government was sounded with bitter intensity. The time had come, Lloyd George said in the last great parliamentary speech of his long career, for the Prime Minister himself to give an example of sacrifice, "because there is nothing which can contribute more to victory in this war than that he should sacrifice the seals of office." Still, Chamberlain tried to hold on, calling on "my friends in the House—and I have friends in the House" for support. "So difficult," Chamberlain biographer Larry Fuchser observed, "had been the upward climb, so staggering the view from the top, that a descent from those giddy heights proved all too difficult to contemplate."

At the parliamentary "division," or voting, Chamberlain retained an eighty-one-vote majority, but forty-four Conservatives voted against him; and even more devastating, some sixty others abstained, including Lady Astor. Profoundly shaken, Chamberlain agreed to resign, calling Churchill and Halifax into private conference. In a later conversation with Kennedy, Chamberlain said "he wanted to make Halifax Prime Minister, but Halifax didn't think he could handle it, being in the House of Lords." As a member of the Lords, Halifax would be cut off from the House of Commons, always living, as he put it, in a kind of twilight just outside the things that really mattered. Hearing the hesitation in Halifax's voice, Churchill drove the nail into the coffin. "I don't think you could," he said, and that, according to Chamberlain, settled it. "Chamberlain said he would serve under either but wanted Churchill to have Halifax as Foreign Minister instead of Eden. And so Churchill succeeded him."

Less than twenty-four hours later, Hitler's forces broke through the defense of the West, leading in short order to the occupation of Belgium and Holland, the fall of France and the isolation of Britain. On May 13, Churchill appeared in Parliament as Prime Minister for the first time and made his historic "blood, toil, tears and sweat" speech. "You ask, What is our aim? I can answer in one word: It is victory, victory at all costs, victory in spite of all terror, victory however hard and long the road may be, for without victory there is no survival."

Sounding an entirely different note, Kennedy wrote to Columbia

Trust President Drew Porter, "All I can say is the longer it goes on, the worse it will be for everybody . . . I suppose there is always some personal satisfaction in being able to say 'I told you so,' but while people thought I was unduly pessimistic when I was home, it has now turned out that I was probably too optimistic."

The surrender of the Belgian Army after eighteen days of fighting left tens of thousands of members of the British Expeditionary Force trapped in northeastern France. On May 29, Churchill approved preparations for the risky operation that would be known to history as the miraculous evacuation from Dunkirk. At first it was not expected that more than a fraction of the 350,000 troops could be saved, but in less than a week a "Mosquito Armada," as Churchill named the collection of over eight hundred small boats, ferries, tugs, fishing craft, barges and pleasure craft, managed to shuttle almost the entire army across the Channel to safety.

Churchill never lost faith that victory was possible, and he imposed that faith on the less confident. From a distance, he looked extraordinarily old-fashioned in his black coat, his winged collar and his bow tie, but his understanding of the Nazi threat was more profound and more precocious than that of any other politician. Scion of a famous house with a long line of distinguished ancestors behind him, Churchill appreciated the romance as well as the horrors of war. "He had a real zest for war," historian Robert Rhodes James has written. "If war there must needs be, he at least could enjoy it."

Perhaps in a different decade Kennedy would have appreciated Churchill's strength and inner vitality, but as events were unfolding in this momentous year of 1940 he perceived Churchill as a mortal threat to America's noninvolvement in the war, and Churchill, fearing that Kennedy's pessimism would undermine the British cause in America, returned the suspicion in kind. As the weeks went by, Kennedy found himself increasingly cut off from 10 Downing Street. "I resented this," he recorded in his memoirs, still missing the message, "because I felt that it was personal . . . Beaverbrook [the Conservative newspaper publisher] told me that Randolph Churchill had poisoned his father against me . . . I told Beaverbrook to hell with Churchill."

The fall of France on June 17 was the culmination of a bewildering period for the British people. Stunned by the brilliant speed and organization of the German drive, they took refuge in what journalist Mollie Panter-Downes has called "the classic national formula for disaster," their calmness, and in their increasingly dogged determination to hold back the juggernaut. Though Britain had now lost her closest ally, the nation with whom she had expected to fight until the bitter end, "London was," Panter-Downes observed, "as quiet as a village. You could have heard a pin drop in the curious, watchful hush. . . . It would be difficult," she concluded, "for an impartial observer to decide today whether the British are the bravest or merely the most [unimaginative] people in the world . . . The individual Englishman seems to be singularly unimpressed by the fact that there is now nothing between him and the undivided attention of a war machine such as the world has never seen before."

All through the summer of 1940, when the threats of invasion, aerial bombing and brutal warfare loomed so large, so terrible and so imprecise, the British went about their business as if nothing untoward were happening. Their isolation seemed to them to simplify the struggle, and the people became "both gaier and more serene than they had been at any time since the overture to Munich struck up in 1937." Throughout this period, Kennedy recorded, the high British officials were so certain Hitler would invade England that they even picked the date. "In fact betting on just when the invasion would come became an indoor sport. Always it seemed the Germans were coming 'within the next 72 hours.' "

For their fantastic courage, Kennedy admired the British people greatly, but in his judgment, qualities of the human spirit could not be measured against Britain's lack of planes, tanks and guns to meet the invading Germans. In cold, hard terms, he argued, Britain simply did not have the resources to hurl back the Germans, and he predicted she would collapse that autumn just as France had collapsed the previous spring.

"The finish may come quickly," Kennedy wrote to Joe Junior that summer. "The British of course will fight, but only through pride and courage. With the French out of the way and the Germans in control of all the ports I can see nothing but slaughter ahead. I am arranging to send everybody away with the exception of about ten of us."

With each dismal prediction, Kennedy's popularity fell still further. "Yet, to be fair to Kennedy," John Kenneth Galbraith later observed, "it should be understood that anyone reporting on Britain after the fall of France who didn't say there was little hope would be doing a bad job of reporting. In purely rational terms, Kennedy's dim assessment of British prospects was correct. Yet this was one of those rare occasions in history when romantic and heroic optimists managed to be right. Why? Because Hitler didn't realize his full strength after Dunkirk. Because he turned on the Soviet Union first before finishing Britain off. Because Churchill's rallying of the intrinsic strength of the British was remarkable. And, of course, because the U.S. finally got involved."

Sitting alone in London, unable to figure out a way of making a graceful exit, the much criticized Ambassador found his only solace in the hope that his experience in holding such a critical post at such a memorable time like this would somehow, someday, benefit his family. Even in the midst of the invasion scare, Kennedy collected original posters for his children and sent them on to the Prime Minister to autograph. "I realize it is an imposition," he apologized, "but I know that unless I give one to each of the children I will get into plenty of trouble. It's bad enough having to explain an Ambassador's stray remarks, let alone try and defend myself to my own family."

All that summer, Kennedy kept up with the smallest details of his children's lives, savoring each piece of news about their swimming races, their sailboat races and their social life. Indeed, the more depressed he felt about his falling prestige, the more solace he found in his children's accomplishments. Little by little, starting slowly in this period and multiplying in the years ahead, he began to live vicariously through his children, counting their successes his own, as if he were resurrecting his injured love of self through them.

Back in Boston, young Joe had enrolled as a first-year student at Harvard Law School, preparing, slowly and methodically, for the day when he could begin his assault on the world of politics. Every Sunday, he would journey into Boston to have dinner with his grandfather, gradually absorbing the old man's understandings of a lifetime in Massachusetts politics. "Joe absolutely adored his grandfather," Rose later said. "He used to say he could listen to his stories for hours and there was nothing he liked better when he was at law school than to put his books aside and come in to the old Bellevue Hotel, where my parents had a live-in suite. Situated right across from the State House, the Bellevue was the perfect place for Father, for it allowed him to keep abreast of everything that was going on."

As 1940 was an election year, Fitzgerald suggested that Joe take his first political step by running for delegate to the presidential convention to be held that summer in Chicago. The idea appealed at once to Joe, and he told his grandfather he would relish the opportunity. His desire catapulted the seventy-seven-year-old Fitzgerald into immediate action. As it happened, William Burke, the chairman of the Massachusetts Democratic Committee, lived in the hotel, too, and he and Fitzgerald breakfasted together almost every day. Over the months, Burke had come to know Joe fairly well, so when Fitzgerald went to him to ask that his grandson be put on the slate, Burke was more than glad to oblige.

"Burke just phoned me about being a delegate," Joe cabled to his father on February 14, 1940. "As you know the delegation is pledged to Farley. Do you think it's all right?"

The district from which Joe was running ranged from the upper-middle-class wards of Brookline, Newton, Waltham and Wellesley to the apartment-house districts of Brighton and down to the poorer "Brick Bottom" wards of Cambridge. Ordinarily, Democratic Party endorsement would be tantamount to automatic victory, but this year a group of able young state legislators and politicians wanted to run, too, and Joe was worried. "I've got to figure some way to prevent myself being last on the ballot," he wrote his father later that spring. "Was some criticism of me not being on voting list but that was straightened out okay and protestor finally got only consolation in stating it was sending a child on a man's job!"

Two weeks before the election, Joe confided to his father that Fitzgerald "thought he could arrange something with the ballot commission so I could get a good vote. He said there would be nothing crooked in it because there was no contest. However, I think he will have a bit of trouble arranging it." Hearing this, the Ambassador immediately wired to his son, telling him to have nothing to do with any such arrangements and urging him instead to get out on the streets and stump for the seat.

So the grandson of Boston's Honey Fitz took to the neighborhoods, knocking on doors, walking into saloons and barbershops. "I'm Joe Kennedy, Jr. I'm pledged to Postmaster General Farley. I'd like to represent you at the national convention." Handsome and warm, Joe made an immediate impression on everyone he met, and as April 30, the day of the election, approached, his confidence increased.

On the ballot, Joe Kennedy, Jr., was pitted against five candidates for two seats. The day of the voting was clear and sunny, and more than 8,000 ballots were cast. When the tally was made, John Brennan, Joe's running mate on the endorsed slate, came in first, while young Joe came in a strong second, thus assuring him a seat at the convention.

"Grandpa thought I did quite well," Joe told his father in a triumphant letter, "so I guess the Kennedy name is a pretty good vote getter. I came second about 100 votes behind Brennan who got 2250. I beat a State Senator by 200 and old Dan Coakley was way behind. They say he was pretty broken up about doing so badly."

For John Fitzgerald, young Joe's victory over his old nemesis, Dan Coakley, was especially sweet. Writing to the Ambassador, he boasted that "if it were not for one Cambridge ward [Joe] would have led the list. Coakley was a very bad fourth. He has not been seen at the State House since and this morning's paper says he is going away for a much needed rest."

On foreign-policy issues, Joe had followed his father down the line, becoming a founding member of Harvard's Committee Against Military Intervention in Europe. Viewing the situation as his father did, in terms of dollars and cents, Joe argued that America would be better off striking a trade bargain with Hitler than bankrupting its economy in a total war. But during the spring of 1940, as the war in Europe heated up with Germany's invasion of Scandinavia and the Low Countries, he saw the writing on the wall. "Overnight," he warned his father, "the people have turned strongly sympathetic to the allies and now many, many people are saying they would just as soon go to war, that they will have to go anyway and why not now. Also feeling here that we are bound to be in the war, like a mysterious force which is bringing the country closer."

As involved as Joe Junior was in politics, he continued to work hard at his studies. "I can't tell you how pleased I have been with your super-lative effort this year at the law school," Kennedy wrote to his son at the beginning of June.

> It was a terribly tough thing to go back to that kind of work after a year in Europe and the fact that you stuck with it is a great tribute to you. Hoping and praying I would be back so that I could be with you on your 25th birthday, because on that day you take over your interest in the Trust and you become owner of a considerable amount of securities and money. In addition, you are now arriving at the point where you have responsibilities to the family. Of course, I am completely confident nothing is going to happen to me in this mess, but one never can be sure and you don't know what satisfaction it is for me to know that you have come along so well and I have such confidence that come what may, you can run the show.

By providing his children with independent shares in the family trust, instead of forcing them to come to him each time they needed money, Joe Senior liked to claim he was giving them the chance to spit in his eye if they wished. And to some extent this was true. But, at a deeper level of consciousness, the trust was a mechanism for binding his children permanently to his own dreams for the Kennedy family.

In reminding his son that he was reaching the point where he had family responsibilities, Joe Senior made explicit what Joe Junior must have known all along: that his financial freedom carried with it an implied obligation to enter public life in one form or another so that he could carry the Kennedy name to further heights. Having been given so much by his family over the years, Joe Junior had absorbed a large measure of the family's dreams and values. None of this was ever pushed on him in a harsh way. But, in the loyal individual, internalized expectations and injunctions provide psychological forces which can coerce just as strongly as external pressure.

· · ·

The summer of 1940 was a good one for young Joe. When the first-year grades were posted, he made a general average of 72 on a scale where the highest grades were in the low eighties; it was "an excellent grade," Jim Landis told the Ambassador, "putting him in the first eighth of his class." And then there was the wild experience of the Democratic national convention in the middle of July.

When the convention opened in the old Chicago stadium on July 12, 1940, there was considerable confusion among the delegates, since Roosevelt had not yet announced whether he was running for a third term. All spring long, Jim Farley, the warm and personable Postmaster General and Democratic National Committee chairman, who was loved throughout the party, had sought repeatedly to elicit from Roosevelt his plans for running. But he was unable to get Roosevelt to commit himself, and as a consequence the popular party chairman began to think about running himself. By the time the party faithful began gathering at the Blackstone and Stevens hotels, Farley had garnered a substantial number of delegates, though everyone, including him, recognized that if Roosevelt should enter, Farley's support would quickly crumble.

But Roosevelt's last-minute entry into the race put many of Farley's delegates on the spot. Some of them had already reserved the right to vote for FDR if his name was placed in nomination; others, like William Burke, the chairman of the Massachusetts delegation, felt a higher loyalty to Roosevelt and simply made the decision to bolt Farley despite their pledge to him. It was, moreover, a matter of some urgency, for Harry Hopkins, Roosevelt's chief operative at the convention, feared that unless the President was nominated unanimously on the first ballot, the inviolate third-term prohibition would defeat him at the polls in November.

The pressure on Farley was increased, but still he refused to move out of the way until after the roll call was taken. In the Massachusetts delegation, people were switching from Farley right and left and Chairman Burke wanted to make it unanimous for Roosevelt. But Joe Kennedy, Jr., refused to go along, believing that since he had pledged himself to vote for Farley, he should keep his word. Clem Norton went up to Joe and told him that if he refused to switch he would wreck his own political career and would bring the wrath of the President down upon his father's head. And later that night one of Roosevelt's men phoned the Ambassador in London and told him to straighten out his son. "No," Kennedy responded, perhaps working out his own growing hostility to Roosevelt through his son, "I wouldn't think of telling him what to do."

As it happened, Joe himself had called his father for advice and was told that if he intended to go into public life he might as well find out whether calling the play as he saw it was going to cause him difficulty; in other words, if he believed he had made a commitment to Farley, he should stick by it and take the consequences as they came. So when the time came for the delegates from Massachusetts to cast their votes, Joe Junior stood up and said firmly, "I was pledged to Farley and I vote for Farley."

When the first roll call was completed, the vote stood at 946 for Roosevelt and 72 for Farley, at which point Farley did what he had promised to do all along: he stood up and moved that Roosevelt be nominated by acclamation.

As Joe headed west for a vacation, a score of people wrote to his father commending his son's performance. "He seemed to gain the respect of everybody there," Joseph M. Patterson, publisher of the New York *Daily News*, wrote. "I am sure he can have a political future if he wants one." And from Jim Farley, Kennedy received the following cable: "I will ever be grateful to your son Joe for his manly and courageous stand at last night's convention." To which Joe Senior proudly replied: "As you can imagine I had heard about the struggle to get him to change his vote and was delighted he took the stand he did. After all if he is going into politics he might just as well learn now that the only thing to do is to stand by your convictions. Am most happy to say he needed no prompting in this respect."

For Jack too, the summer of 1940 was a good time to be alive. Throughout the spring he had worked hard on his honors thesis, harder than he had worked on anything in his life, and the final product had earned him a magna cum laude. Originally conceived as "England's Foreign Policy Since 1731," it had evolved into a thesis called "Appeasement at Munich," a paper which argued that British weakness in response to Hitler's moves in Europe was not the fault of the rulers—Prime Ministers Stanley Baldwin and Neville Chamberlain—but rather a failure of the democratic system, whose slowness to rearm left the leaders little choice. In his conclusion, young Kennedy expressed considerable anxiety about the limitations of democracy for national security. While he argued that democracy was a pleasanter form of government because it allowed for the full development of man as an individual, he feared that democratic governments did not have the intensity or the long-range view afforded to dictatorships and that, as a result, democracy suffered in dealing with world problems.

"Finished my thesis," Jack had written to his father back in March. "It was only going to run about average length, 70 pages, but finally ran to 150. Am sending you a copy . . . I'll be interested to see what you think of it, as it represents more work than I've ever done in my life."

As it turned out, the Ambassador not only thought it a "swell" job but suggested that Jack send it on to Arthur Krock to see if he felt it could be published. Always ready to aid the Kennedys, Krock offered to help put it into shape for publication and suggested the title *Why England Slept*, as a contrast to Churchill's *While England Slept*. The timing could not have been better, for the submission of the manuscript to the publishers coincided with the Nazi invasion of Scandinavia and the Low Countries, obvious proof, if any more proof was needed, that the theory of appeasement had been wrong.

Once publication was arranged, but before Jack set to work polishing the manuscript, the Ambassador wrote to his son that he had shown it to "various people around here," and that "one or two" of them thought it had "gone too far in absolving the leaders of the National Government from responsibility for the state in which England found herself at Munich. These people," Kennedy wrote, "agree that no good purpose can be served by making scapegoats out of Baldwin and Chamberlain; on the other hand, they feel that you have gone too far in putting the blame on the British public."

In response to his father's letter, Jack shifted the entire tone of his conclusion, adopting large portions of the letter almost verbatim. But probably the most significant difference between the thesis and the book related to the problem of democracy's response to crisis. Whereas the thesis had speculated that democracy might be an unaffordable luxury, the finished book included lyrical endorsements of democracy and viewed its preservation as the very reason for rearming. At a time when the Western democracies were becoming more imperiled and as the United States was beginning to be drawn more and more to the Allied cause, Jack Kennedy's final paragraph proclaimed ultimate faith in democracy: "We should profit by the lesson of England and make our democracy work. We must make it work right now. Any system of government will work when everything is going well. It's the system that functions in the pinches that survives."

When the book was published in July, the young author became an instant celebrity. Within weeks it was appearing on the best-seller lists across the nation, and eventually it sold over forty thousand copies. Writing from London, a proud father told his son that Chamberlain, Halifax, Montagu Norman and Harold Laski had all asked about it. "So, whether you make a cent it will do you an amazing amount of good. You would be surprised how a book that really makes the grade with high class people stands you in good stead for years to come. . . . Now that you've got the book off, get a good rest. You have the brains and everything it takes to go somewhere, so just get yourself in good condition so you can really do things."

That summer, even as he continually laughed at his own surprising success, Jack did everything he could to promote the book—giving newspaper and radio interviews, autographing copies, checking bookstores. And he was good at it; indeed, as his biographer Herbert S. Parmet observes, "young Jack was finding the limelight to his liking."

Visiting the Kennedys in Hyannis Port that summer, Jack's friend Charles Spalding was impressed by the vitality of the entire household. "Jack was autographing copies of *Why England Slept* while Grandfather Fitzgerald was reading to him a political story from a newspaper. Young Joe was telling about something that happened to him in Russia. Mrs. Kennedy on the phone with Cardinal Spellman. Pat describing how a German Messerschmitt had crashed near her father's house outside of London. Bobby trying to get everyone to play charades. Next thing all of us choosing sides in touch football, Kathleen calling the plays on our side. Conversation at dinner ranged from war and Washington politics to books, sports and show business."

For Kathleen, who had loved England the most of all the Kennedy children, the adjustment to life in the United States was difficult. In the course of eighteen months, she had bloomed into a woman with her own heart and mind. She had fallen in love for the first time. And for the first time, she told Lem, she felt she was "a person in her own right, not simply a Kennedy girl." "It all seems like a beautiful dream," she had written to her father in September 1939 as the S.S. *Washington* docked in New York. "Thanks a lot Daddy for giving me one of the greatest experiences anyone could have had. I know it will have great effect on everything I do from here on in."

Upon her return to America, Kathleen enrolled in Finch College, a popular finishing school in New York, to study art and design, but she lived mainly for the weekends when she could visit her brothers in Cambridge or travel with them to various social events in New York and Baltimore. As always, the young men flocked around her. Both Lem Billings and Torby Macdonald were still "crazy" about her, as was Peter Grace (who, Billings finally admitted, after riding with him one night into the city, was "a hell of a nice guy"). Then there was Johnny Coleman, or Zeke, whom Kick also liked. "Everyone likes him a great deal," Eunice reported to her father. "In fact first boy completely approved of by all the Kennedys."

Yet her heart was still in England, and Kathleen was unable to commit herself to any of the American boys who fell in love with her. Occasionally, Jack felt obliged to lecture her about her "insincerity" with his friends, but it was difficult for her to take her brother's counsel seriously when he himself was juggling any number of girlfriends. And when they really talked, as they often did, Jack understood the intensity of Kick's desire to return to England. Intervening on his sister's behalf, he wrote to his father in the spring of 1940, telling him that Kick was very keen to go over to England, "and I wouldn't think the anti-American feeling would hurt her like it might us—due to her being a girl, especially as it would show that we hadn't merely left England when it got unpleasant."

But Joe was adamant about keeping his children safe from the certain catastrophe he saw descending. Receiving Kathleen's first request just as France was about to fall to the Nazis, he predicted that England would be finished within a matter of months. With this sentiment Kathleen strongly disagreed.

> I still keep telling everyone [she wrote on May 21] that British lose the battles but they win the wars. There was a vote taken last week as to whether we should go into the war. I and other girl were the two yeses. All the rest voted no. I have received some rather gloomy letters from Jane [Kenyon-Slaney] and Billy [Hartington]. Billy's letter was written from the Maginot line. Daddy I must know exactly what has happened to them all. Is Billy alright? Hugh Fraser, the Astors, David Gore and the rest?

As it turned out, at the time Kathleen was writing to her father Billy and his Coldstream Guards battalion were on the French coast, where they narrowly escaped the invading Nazis just a few days before the Dunkirk evacuation. After the fall of France, Kathleen tried again. "I wish I could come to England to keep you company," she wrote to her father on August 6. "Is there any chance of it? I should so love it."

Lonely as he was, especially after Rosemary and the Moores had left the previous May, Kennedy could not consider Kathleen's ingratiating request. Her letter arrived in London just as the Battle of Britain was about to begin. In the middle of July Hitler had issued his Directive 16 calling for a full-scale air offensive against England, with the goal of driving the Royal Air Force from the skies in preparation for his projected invasion that September. "As to what is going to happen here," Kennedy wrote, "I haven't the slightest idea. If Hitler has the strength he says he has in the air, England should feel it pretty soon and we may get a quick answer to the whole war."

The Battle of Britain began on September 7, 1940. In the first phase, the Germans sought to engage the RAF in battle over the Channel, and then they planned to destroy British airfields and radar stations in Kent and Sussex. According to the German plan, the RAF was to be crippled and driven out of the sky over southern England within four days and to be out of the fight completely in four weeks. But for every plane the RAF lost the Germans lost two, and in many instances RAF pilots who were shot down in the morning were flying combat missions that same afternoon. "In spite of everything," Kennedy told Kathleen, "I do not think that Hitler will make an attempt at invasion unless his air force is strong enough to knock off the British air force."

> As far as I can see [he told Jim Landis the same week], the crux of the situation is whether the Germans have the air force they think they have or at least that they tell us they have. . . . It is ghastly to think of and yet I know that 5000 first class airplanes in the hands of the British last year would have stopped the war. It is staggering to think that the whole face of civilization may be changed as the result of a failure to expend over a period of years the amount that the British Empire is now spending every week.

By the end of August, the strain on the RAF was tremendous and Hitler was within measurable distance of achieving his objective of superiority over southeast England. Then, inexplicably the whole character of the German offensive was altered. Goering publicly assumed command of the air battle and turned from the fighter airfields of Kent and Sussex to the city of London. For fifty-seven nights, during the period known to history as the Blitz, the bombing of London was unceasing and tens of thousands of British citizens died. The aim was to break the spirit of the Londoner and to render uninhabitable the world's largest city. But in these new purposes Hitler did not succeed.

In the early days of the Blitz the heaviest attacks were concentrated on the thickly populated east side of the city, but in the weeks that followed more than a million houses and cottages and buildings in all parts of the city were damaged or destroyed, including the British Museum, the Tate Gallery, the Tower of London, the Bank of England, Buckingham Palace, the Treasury, Westminster Abbey and St. Paul's Cathedral.

Writing to eight-year-old Teddy about the raids, Kennedy said:

> I am sure, of course, you wouldn't be scared, but if you heard all these guns firing every night and the bombs bursting you might get a little fidgety. It is really terrible to think about and all those poor women and children and homeless people down in the East End of London all seeing their places destroyed. I hope when you grow up you will dedicate your

life to trying to work out plans to make people happy instead of making them miserable, as war does today.

And to Eunice:

Last night they dropped one in the pool at Buckingham Palace; one back of Lansdowne House; one at Marble Arch; and Piccadilly is all blocked off today. . . . I don't know where it is all going to end but everything I see confirms what I always thought, that it ought never to have started. The unfortunate part of this war is that poor women and children are getting by far the worst of it. I can't tell you what my state of mind would have been if any of you had been over here. I think I should have gone mad.

During the nights, there was no pretense of normality. Except in the depths of the London underground, no one escaped the noises of the Blitz: the warbling of the alert, the howling of dogs, the swish of the falling bombs, the clatter of incendiaries on roofs and pavements, the dull thud of walls collapsing, the crackle of flames and the bells of the fire engines. It was said that a bomb falling half a mile away would give you ten seconds' warning, but the one which would kill you or bury you alive could be heard only when it was almost upon you.

Still the British did not waver. And after the first week of terror they adapted themselves to the fear, calmly lining up for the public shelters late each afternoon. Gradually it became a sort of war cry, a common affirmation of faith, to arrive on time for work in the morning no matter how little sleep had been achieved the night before. "You get experienced," the film director Paul Rotha wrote. "A plane overhead, a scream, you count one-two-three-four, they either get closer or get distant. If closer, you seek handy shelter. . . . If distant, you go on doing what you are doing. . . . It's remarkable how sensitive your ears get."

The shops in the heart of the city became a symbol of defiance. Big and small, they had their windows blown out, but business continued as usual the following day. "More Open Than Usual" was a common sign, while one pub advertised: "OUR WINDOWS ARE GONE BUT OUR SPIRITS ARE EXCELLENT. COME IN AND TRY THEM."

Kennedy expressed astonishment at the ability of Londoners to withstand the prolonged assault. Visiting bombing sites during the day, he confessed: "I did not know London could take it. I did not think any city could take it. I am bowed in reverence."

For months Kennedy had wanted to go home, but he knew that so long as the invasion was imminent he could not leave his post. By the end of

September 1940, however, with the RAF still functioning effectively, the threat of invasion had substantially subsided. The time had come, Kennedy believed, for him to resign and return to America.

On October 16 he sent a cablegram to the President insisting that he be allowed to come home. That same day, anticipating that FDR might prefer to keep him in England until after the November election, he telephoned Undersecretary Welles and said that if he did not get a favorable reply to his request he was coming home anyhow. For months, he told Welles, he had been ignored by an Administration which had sent envoys to London without informing him in advance and had completed the destroyer-bases deal despite the worry he had expressed that American ships would fall into German hands if the British surrendered. He told Welles he had written a full account of these facts to his secretary in New York, Eddie Moore, with instructions to release the story to the press if the Ambassador was not back in New York by a certain date. A few hours after this telephone conversation, the cabled permission to return was received.

Keeping his intentions about the resignation shrouded in mystery, Kennedy made a round of farewell visits, calling on the King and Queen, Churchill and Chamberlain. He found Chamberlain propped up in bed with a small bed table at his side. The seventy-one-year-old former Prime Minister was dying of cancer, but his countrymen, who regarded him now with derision and contempt, were not interested. Kennedy was profoundly saddened by the pathetic condition to which he had been reduced, believing Chamberlain to be "one of the most misunderstood and unappreciated men ever to occupy a commanding place in world affairs."

The two men had passed through much together in the preceding two and a half years, from the triumphant signing of the Munich Agreement to the bitter recognition of its failure. After speaking of old times, Chamberlain told Kennedy he didn't expect to live much longer. Having seen his father, Joseph Chamberlain, linger in pain for nine years after a stroke, he said he preferred the thought of death to that of continued incapacity. Kennedy agreed. "I haven't had many successes in my life," Chamberlain said, "but I've made real contributions." Then, clasping Kennedy's hand, he added, "This is goodbye. I remember that you always said you would stay after me. But we will never see each other again." They never did. Chamberlain entered the hospital for surgery three days later, and in less than three weeks he was dead.

Kennedy arrived on October 27 at New York's La Guardia Airport, where he was embraced tearfully by Rose and four of the girls. For days the press had been speculating about his return, with some reporters suggesting that his fear of war was now so great that he was about to endorse the Republican presidential candidate, Wendell Willkie. Surely something dramatic was about to happen, for, as one newspaperman observed, "he looked for all the world like a man bursting with things to say."

But the President had long since anticipated Kennedy's arrival and, guessing his intent, had sent a wire to the plane inviting Joe and Rose to the White House that night for dinner. Knowing how much influence Kennedy could have if he turned against him ten days before the election, Roosevelt was determined to win back his Ambassador's support. And with Rose present, Roosevelt shrewdly understood, Kennedy would be forcefully reminded of all the benefits the White House had provided for the Kennedy family over the preceding decade. (Indeed, Kennedy later found out that the stage for this dinner had been carefully set days before when it was determined that he could play an essential role in saving the Catholic vote that was rapidly deserting Roosevelt.)

During the flight to Washington, acting almost on cue, Rose pleaded with her husband not to turn against the President. "The President sent you, a Roman Catholic, as ambassador to London, which probably no other President would have done. . . . He sent you as his representative to the Pope's coronation . . . You would write yourself down as an ingrate in the view of many people if you resign now." Against this appeal to political loyalty, Kennedy weighed the consideration that if he were free to speak, his voice could be an important one in keeping America out of the war.

When the Kennedys reached the White House, they were joined by Senator Byrnes and his wife, "proving," Kennedy believed, "that Roosevelt didn't want to have it out with me alone." As the guests entered the upstairs room, Rose recorded, the President was seated at his desk, "shaking a cocktail shaker and reaching over for a few lumps of ice with his powerful hands." As they sat down to a Sunday dinner of scrambled eggs, toast and sausages, the Ambassador reported on conditions under the Blitz and his final visit with the dying Chamberlain. The talk moved on to other things, and then Byrnes, "acting as though a wonderful idea had just struck him," said he thought "it would be a great idea if I would speak on the radio on behalf of FDR's reelection."

The President affirmed that such an address could be critical to the success of the campaign, but Kennedy, still feeling that he had been treated terribly his last months in London, gave no direct reply. Undaunted, the President turned to Rose and, in his most charming manner, regaled her with a succession of stories about her father, claiming that on a recent trip to South America he had met dozens of people who still remembered the last visit of Honey Fitz there, when he had sung "Sweet Adeline."

All the while, Joe Kennedy was keeping his peace, assuming that the President would ask him into another room for a private talk. But finally it became obvious that Roosevelt had no intention of leaving the dinner. "Since it doesn't seem possible for me to see the President alone, I guess I'll just have to say what I'm going to say in front of everybody," Kennedy burst out. As her husband spoke, Mrs. Kennedy felt butterflies in her stomach and she observed that Roosevelt looked "rather pale, rather ashen."

"In the first place," the Ambassador began, observing that Byrnes was aghast, "I am damn sore at the way I have been treated. I feel that it is entirely unreasonable and I don't think I rated it." He said that whenever the President had got into a jam or his family had got into a jam it was Kennedy to whom he had turned. He then went on, using "many words not found in dictionaries" to denounce the State Department in blistering language, citing chapter and verse on the treatment he had received, including not being informed on vital matters and being consistently bypassed. The President listened closely, nodding occasionally as was his habit when he wanted those who poured out their hearts to him to feel that he was taking in all they said.

When Kennedy finished, concluding that under these conditions he would not go back to London, his wife tactfully suggested that perhaps the difficulty in communication was due to the distance of three thousand miles. But, to everyone's surprise, the President offered no rebuttal to Kennedy's diatribe. On the contrary, he said that as far as he was concerned, Kennedy was being charitable. The officious men at the State Department should not be allowed to treat a good friend of his with such callousness. Had he known, and he hadn't because of the pressures of the European crisis, he would have put a stop to their behavior earlier. And surely after the election there would be a real housecleaning to ensure that a valued public servant like Joe Kennedy would never again be so abused.

Totally disarmed by the President's words, Kennedy unwittingly relaxed. Once the tension had dissipated, Roosevelt turned the conversation to the subject of Kennedy's extraordinary sons Joe and Jack. Clearly having been filled in on all their accomplishments, he congratulated both Kennedys on having produced such fine young men. "I stand in awe," he told Joe, "of your relationship with your children. For a man as busy as you are, it is a rare achievement. And I for one will do all I can to help you if your boys should ever run for political office."

Then, sensing that the right moment had arrived, the masterful Roosevelt once again asked Kennedy if he would deliver a speech endorsing his reelection. "All right, I will," Kennedy replied. "But I will pay for it myself, show it to nobody in advance and say what I wish." No sooner had he agreed than Missy LeHand telephoned the Democratic National Committee to ask that radio time be turned over to Kennedy the following Tuesday night.

As it turned out, Kennedy's speech to a nationwide audience was a great success and a great boost to the President. Since the papers had been speculating for days about the rift between the President and his Ambassador, Willkie supporters confidently predicted that Joe Kennedy would speak his mind. When the news came that Kennedy was paying for the special CBS hookup himself, at a cost of more than $20,000, the hopes of the Willkie backers soared. Reveling in the melodrama, Kennedy deliberately refused to travel with Roosevelt on the presidential train and even declined an invitation to attend a large rally at Madison Square Garden where FDR was scheduled to speak. The suspense continued to build, and by the evening of the twenty-ninth no one really knew what he was going to say.

He began by saying that after his experience in war-torn Europe he had returned to the States "renewed in my conviction that this country must and will stay out of war." To be sure, he admitted, there had been some disagreements between himself and the President, but on the momentous issue of war or peace he totally supported the President's decision to continue aid to Britain while keeping America out of the war. And in this time of crisis, he argued, when the decisions of the President would seriously affect every man, woman and child in the country, the question of opposition on principle to a third term paled to insignificance in light of the experience, wisdom and talent, diplomatic foresight, courage and great ingenuity required by the President in the next four years and possessed by FDR.

"My wife and I have given nine hostages to fortune," he concluded. "Our children and your children are more important than anything else in the world. The kind of America that they and their children will inherit is of grave concern to us all. In the light of these considerations, I believe that Franklin D. Roosevelt should be reelected President of the United States."

Listening from the White House, FDR was absolutely delighted, and Kennedy received praise from all over the country. "As a vote getting speech," commented *Life*, "it was probably the most effective of the campaign. For more than anything else it allayed fear that Mr. Roosevelt would 'take this country into war.' "

On November 5, the American electorate went to the polls and gave

FDR a third term by a narrow margin. The following day Kennedy celebrated by tendering his resignation. Roosevelt agreed to the resignation but asked that Kennedy keep the title of ambassador until a successor could be found, hinting that during the interim he would have a chance to find something else for Kennedy to do in Washington.

Delighted with the happy turn of events, Kennedy planned to make a trip to California, but first he journeyed to the Lahey Clinic in Boston for a physical. While he was in Boston, he agreed to talk with three newspapermen in his suite at the Ritz-Carlton. It was a casual appointment that was to have disastrous consequences for Kennedy's reputation.

It started innocently enough when *Boston Globe* reporter Louis Lyons left a note for Kennedy at the Ritz on Friday morning, November 7, saying: "The Globe hopes I can persuade you to talk to me a little for our people—just as a traveller home from the wars, not political talk. You will recall a most interesting interview you gave me in 1936. Any time, anywhere . . ."

Kennedy agreed to meet with Lyons at his hotel suite on Saturday afternoon. He also agreed to see two journalists who had asked only for a background briefing for future editorial guidance—Charles Edmondson of the *St. Louis Post-Dispatch* and the latter's boss, Ralph Coglan, who was in Boston to appear at a Nieman Fellows dinner at Harvard. "It so happened," Nieman Fellow John Crider later wrote, "that Kennedy's secretary let the three in at the same time, figuring, I suppose, that since they were all newspapermen it made no difference."

The three journalists found Kennedy relaxing in his shirtsleeves eating apple pie, his suspenders hanging loosely around his hips. In an expansive mood, he spoke with startling candor, saying outrageous things, apparently forgetting that even though Edmondson and Coglan had requested an off-the-record exchange, Lyons had originally asked for an interview on the record. Or perhaps, in speaking freely, he assumed that once again, as before, his "friends" in the fourth estate would edit out his worst remarks.

Kennedy spoke with the newspapermen for an hour and a half, sharing with them all his pessimistic feelings about democracy and war. "I'm willing to spend all I've got left to keep us out of the war," he said. "There's no sense in our getting in. We'd just be holding the bag . . . People call me a pessimist. I say, What is there to be gay about? Democracy is all done . . . Democracy is finished in England. It may be here." As for England, "It isn't that she's fighting for democracy. That's the bunk. She's fighting for self-preservation, just as we will if it comes to us."

In the informal context of the appointment, Ralph Coglan understood that Kennedy's comments on democracy referred to the general impact of a centralized bureaucracy on any country during a war. "They tell me that after 1918 we got it all back again," Kennedy said. "But this is different. There's a different pattern in the world." Listening to Kennedy, Coglan found him "sound, realistic and reasonable." Writing to Arthur Krock two days after the celebrated interview, Coglan said Kennedy's way of putting things made complete sense. "He is for unlimited aid to Britain but against American entrance into the war."

But Kennedy's comments did not stop with democracy and war. He went on to speak about the President's wife, Charles Lindbergh, the British Cabinet and the stammering King of England. "Now, I will tell you," he declared, "when this thing is finally settled and it comes to a question of saving what's left for England, it will be the Queen and not any of the politicians who will do it. She's got more brains than the Cabinet." As for Eleanor Roosevelt, "She's another wonderful woman. And marvelously helpful and full of sympathy . . . she bothered us more on our jobs in Washington to take care of the poor little nobodies who hadn't any influence than all the rest of the people down there together. She's always sending me a note to have some little Susie Glotz to tea at the embassy."

When the sensational interview was over, Lyons and Coglan rushed for a cab to get to an office where they could compare notes and save every crumb they could of Kennedy's extraordinary talk. "I wouldn't be in your shoes," Coglan told Lyons. "How do you know what you can write? He just puts it up to you to follow your own conscience and judgment and protect him in his diplomatic capacity."

"Well," Lyons responded, "last time I interviewed him in 1936, he poured himself out like this, without laying any restrictions on me, and I wrote every bit of it and it went all over the country—the interview in which he said why he was for Roosevelt. And he said it was the best interview he'd ever had. But he wasn't an ambassador then."

"It all depends on how you handle it," advised Coglan. "Any story can be told if it's told right."

Lyons resolved his dilemma by printing practically everything Kennedy had said while casting the story in the soft form of a feature which deliberately downplayed the sensational news aspects of the piece. But so provocative were so many of Kennedy's statements that the interview created banner headlines in newspapers all around the world. Picked up by the Associated Press and quoted out of context, his unguarded statements seemed even worse than they were. In place of prescient ruminations on the impact of war on democracy, he was quoted as saying simply, "Democracy is finished in England." And his comments on Mrs. Roosevelt, shortened by omission of his praise of her kindness and sympathy, came out as: "She bothered us more on our jobs . . . than all the rest of the people down there together."

On or off the record, ambassadors are not supposed to speak so bluntly. For weeks Kennedy was subjected to an intense barrage of criticism. After six years in public service, his unguarded talk had finally done him in. While the interview did not actually cost him the ambassadorship—since he had already resigned—it did prevent him from finding the graceful exit he had been seeking for months, bringing his ambassadorial career to a humiliating close.

For years journalists would debate the ethics of the Lyons interview. Ralph Coglan believed that Lyons had done Kennedy an injustice, as he told Krock:

> It is true Kennedy said most of the things Lyons quotes him as saying, but the total effect, as Kennedy says, is to create a false impression. Kennedy was talking in shirtsleeves and should have been protected. . . . Kennedy was highly informal and did not pretend to round out his thoughts and Lyons was very hazy about what he meant in various instances when Lyons and I compared notes. So was I, because we did not have a chance to question him fully. The more reason for going back to Kennedy to clear things up . . . it was a question for a reporter's judgment as to what to use, and Lyons showed bad judgment.

The day after the story appeared, Kennedy issued a statement repudiating the interview with the argument that he had cautioned Lyons that the entire conversation was to be off the record. He also asserted that Lyons had taken no notes during the interview and had written the piece entirely from memory. This last assertion was true but irrelevant, since no one present, including Kennedy, ever claimed that the statements themselves were incorrect.

When the news of Kennedy's interview crossed the Atlantic, the British people were angry but not surprised. "It is all to the good," British columnist A. J. Cummings wrote,

> the British people now know just where Kennedy stands. His suspicion that his standing in London is gone is justified. While he was here his suave monotonous style, his nice over-photographed children and his hail-fellow-well-met manner concealed a hard-boiled businessman's eagerness to do a professional business deal with the dictators and he deceived many decent English people.

"Don't mind the attacks," Kennedy cabled to Jim Seymour, "but resent personal observations on family." But he did mind the attacks. In the weeks that followed the Lyons interview, his bitterness increased and he took every opportunity to speak out against England and the war. In the files of the British Foreign Office there is a report of a vitriolic speech Kennedy made at a meeting of some fourteen film producers and executives in Hollywood in which he warned that "there was very strong anti-Jewish activity in England and that they had better not make any more pro-British pictures or even anti-Nazi pictures."

Indeed, were it not for his family, one friend observed, Kennedy might have become totally withdrawn and hostile. As it was, however, his pride in his children once again kept him going, and when the crisis died down his spirits began to return.

In February 1941, Kennedy's resignation as ambassador became official. Writing to a friend that week, he declared: "Having finished a rather busy political career this week, I find myself much more interested in what young Joe is going to do than what I am going to do with the rest of my life."

BOOK THREE

# THE GOLDEN TRIO

## (1941-1961)

# CHAPTER 35
# THE
# CIRCLE
# IS BROKEN

At twenty-five, Joe Junior was a handsome young man, driven by a fierce ambition. "There was something in his presence," Rose later claimed, "that created an immediate impression. He had such a strong personality that anyone who met him knew at once that he was destined for great things." Allowing for a mother's pride, it does seem that even as a law student at Harvard Joe was making his mark upon the local political scene, but guided always by his father's hand. During this period Kennedy arranged for him to sit down with Bill Mullins of the *Boston Herald* to discuss his future, and Mullins was so impressed that he wrote Kennedy a long letter, offering to help in any way he could.

"I am more grateful than I can tell you," Kennedy responded. "I think Joe has a tendency towards public life and by that I mean, I think he would like to be a candidate for public office. . . . Of course, to make any plans today is just a complete waste of time, but when this mess is over—at that time we'll have to consider what is the best advice we can give young Joe."

But in 1941 the "mess," as Kennedy called the war, was still very far from being over and it was only a matter of months until the United States would officially enter. Having registered for the draft the year before, Joe Junior knew that unless he volunteered for the Navy or the Air Force he would have to enter as a private once the anticipated compulsory military service arrived. He made his decision in May 1941, when, having completed his second year of law school, he signed up for the naval aviation cadet program and was assigned to Squantum Naval Air Facility in Quincy, Massachusetts.

In choosing naval aviation, Joe had chosen one of the most difficult programs in all the military services. Naval pilot training held coldly to the premise that it was best to remove those who couldn't conquer the tensions of flying early, before too much time and money had been wasted on them. As a consequence, the attrition rate of entering cadets was 50 percent. Joe Senior heard the news, pleased and worried at the same time. "Wouldn't you know," he complained to all who would listen, "naval aviation, the most dangerous thing there is."

At Squantum, Joe Junior found himself tested to the limits of his physical endurance, courage and aggressiveness. The ground portion of the preflight program was run by "commandos" who forced the young cadets through both a grueling physical regimen of push-ups, rope climbing, marching and running and a tough academic course in navigation and flight theory. Fortunately Joe had kept himself in good shape, and as a result he suffered less than some of his classmates.

After several months of hard work, his reward finally came. In late July he was told to report to the naval air station in Jacksonville, Florida, for the next stage of his training. There, at the great sprawling base with green lawns and alabaster buildings, he remained in primary flight training for ten difficult months. In Jacksonville the ground school program was even tougher than it had been at Squantum. In courses on aircraft engines and structures Joe had to compete with classmates who held engineering degrees, but by the end of the program he was one of the top three in his class. He also excelled in indoctrination courses, coming out fourth in his class.

The flying was another matter. In the air, where he was faced with a frustrating mix of instructions and counterinstructions, academics didn't count, and in fact the mental habits of law school, where Joe had been taught to question every ruling, were a detriment. Flying with an instructor at dual control, Joe was trying so hard at first to maintain the proper altitude, compass heading and air speed that he could not relax and let his instinct take over. He was concentrating so much on the individual tasks at hand that he was forgetting the whole. "Student flies with head in cockpit too much," his instructor wrote. But there were good days too, and Joe's instructor finally admitted that he was developing a feel for flying. His anxiety seemed to have died down and he began to relax.

With news of the Japanese attack on Pearl Harbor on December 7, however, the pace of the training intensified. "I saw young Joe in Jacksonville last week," Joe Senior wrote to his reporter friend Tim McInerny on January 26, 1942. "They are working them frightfully hard and he's quite thin, but he seems to be very happy and is anxious to do his bit."

A natural leader, Joe was elected as his class representative on the board of governors of the cadet club, a lively institution which served beer and liquor and was the hub of social life. Within his barracks he developed a reputation as a top card player, an easygoing friend and a champion of his fellow classmates.

During his time at Jacksonville, Joe developed a lasting friendship with the chaplain, Father Maurice Sheehy, a priest who was also the public-relations officer of the base. As president of the Holy Name Society on the base, Joe was responsible for waking up the Catholics in the barracks for the chaplain's early Mass; but the friendship with Father Sheehy grew mostly on the golf course, where they became regular companions.

For the graduation exercises on May 6, 1942, the base commander, G. R. Fairlamb, had invited Ambassador Kennedy to come up from Palm Beach to address the cadets, so it happened that Joe Senior was able to pin the coveted golden wings on his son. It was a proud moment for the Ambassador. Although Joe Junior was twenty pounds thinner than he had been when he started, he had survived the ordeal better than most of the others. When the time came for Joe Senior to speak, he took a long time to get out what he wanted to say and his eyes became moist with emotion. "The sight of those boys moved me so deeply," he wrote the base commander, "that I am afraid I did not do what I consider my customary job of speaking. It made me realize how unimportant everything and everybody is today compared to them."

Joe was sent next to Banana River, Florida, for operational training. "We might just as well be in the middle of Africa as here," he wrote to his parents during his first week at the new base. "We are fifteen miles from the nearest town. The weather has really been tropical . . . It looks, however, as if it will be a good healthy life and a life without women."

On the night before his first flight, Joe wrote to his father saying he thought he should make some kind of will. Responding that it was a good idea, Joe Senior decided the time had come to let his son know exactly what he was entitled to under the family trust. Kennedy aide Paul Murphy drew up a statement showing that as of his twenty-fifth birthday young Joe personally owned $31,728.53 in cash plus a vested interest in his full share of the cumulative income of the family trust, which came to $127,315.85 as of May 31, 1942. Then beyond his share in the income of the trust he was also entitled, when he reached fifty, to his share in the corpus of the trust, which had a market value of approximately $250,000.

"My own suggestion," Joe Senior wrote to his son, "is that you let your interest that you haven't withdrawn from the trust, remain in the trust for the benefit of your brothers and sisters . . . I should like to protect the children as long as I could with whatever there is in the trust." In responding, Joe wrote directly to his father, with a postscript regarding his mother at the end: "I didn't want to address this to her, for she might get disturbed about the will situation."

In the middle of July, Joe reported that he had been out on several night patrols and that the place was shaping up better all the time. Some girls had come down from Jacksonville during his free days, and he had gone to Jacksonville one Sunday to play golf with Father Sheehy.

> I was duty officer of the squadron about a week ago, and everything possible happened. One man got hit on the head with a depth charge as they were loading planes; an army plane forced a landing next to the hangar . . . Later, after night flying, in bed three hours, and heard crash. One of the planes taking off about 4:30 in the morning hadn't gotten off the water in time and hit a building. The engine caught fire, but thrown free of the plane by a miracle, both men are alive.

While Joe was in Florida with his squadron, his father conducted a running correspondence with Father Sheehy as a means of keeping tabs on his activities. Everywhere his children went, it seems, Joe Senior managed to find someone—a friend, a local journalist, a teacher or a superior—who was willing to keep him informed about the smallest details of his children's lives, so much so that over time an elaborate network of "spies" emerged. The astonishing thing about this was not simply the intrusive control that such a network suggested, though intrusive it surely was, but rather the seeming acceptance of the whole system by the children. From all accounts, they not only knew that all this exchange of information was going on but were able to treat it as "Daddy's prerogative."

At some point, rumors must have reached the family that Joe was seriously involved with a Protestant girl. Rose hurriedly sent him a year's subscription to *The Catholic Digest*, but Father Sheehy apparently assured Joe Senior that it was just a passing romance. Getting wind of the rumors, Joe wrote to his parents that "regardless of reports to the contrary, my heart belongs to Daddy, and there is no great love within my vista at present." But Joe Senior evidently decided that no chances should be taken, for he told his son in a long letter that one of the Democratic-primary candidates for the Senate seat from Massachusetts that summer, Joe Casey, was encountering a great deal of criticism from Catholic women because he had married a Protestant (and become the father of a baby five months later).

> You wouldn't think this was very important but it definitely is, and I am thoroughly convinced that an Irish Catholic with a name like yours and with your record, married to an Irish Catholic girl, would be a push over in this state for political office. They just wouldn't have anything to fight about. It seems like a silly thing, but I can't impress it on you too strongly . . .

As it happened, Casey's opponent in the primary was none other than the indefatigable John F. Fitzgerald, who at seventy-nine was running an energetic campaign that surprised the entire state. It is said that Joe Senior was behind the move to find an opponent to run against Casey, a down-the-line supporter of Roosevelt. Earlier that summer Kennedy had contacted Ed Hanify, a young Boston lawyer working for Ropes & Gray, and asked him to help prepare speeches for Fitzgerald. "Joe was anxious to show FDR there was a Kennedy stronghold in Massachusetts," Hanify recalled. "As Casey was an all-out New Deal congressman who went along with the White House on everything, Kennedy figured we could capitalize on the growing sentiment against the New Deal, and by running Fitzgerald we were beginning with a man whose name alone was worth fifty thousand votes before he said a word.

"And, of course, John F. loved it. Every morning he would come into Joe's suite at the Ritz and start off like a champ. His unfailing zest was really something to see and he was still a splendid speaker. And Joe would sit back and chuckle at his enthusiasm. They seemed very close.

The way it worked was like this. Joe would give me all the material, clippings, statistics and quotes I needed and then I'd produce a speech which we'd give to Fitzgerald not too much in advance of delivery so as not to ruin the spontaneous nature of his speaking style. And through it all John F. always remained cheerful and vital."

"We've had more fun than a barrel of monkeys," Joe told a friend in Washington. And the enthusiasm Fitzgerald generated was contagious. "What a great old guy he is," Kathleen wrote to Billings on August 6, 1942. "He's up against Casey in the primaries and if he gets that he will run against Lodge in the final poll. Everyone thinks that if he wins the primaries he is all set."

Joe Kane, Kennedy's cousin, was also involved in the campaign. A colorful figure in Boston politics, Kane had an "office" at Walton's lunchroom on School Street. One day, according to Hanify, Kane came into the Ritz with a cartoon about Casey's somewhat belated war service; evidently Casey had presented himself to the public as a war veteran when in fact he had been in the service for only a few weeks before the armistice. But, to everyone's surprise, Joe said he considered the idea of the cartoon a low blow and rejected it at once. "Look," he said, "I've got two boys in this war. When they come back I don't want there to be anything in this campaign they can reproach me about." Then, as Hanify tells the story, Joe went over to the fireplace and sobbed. "It seemed as if something had suddenly hit him inside," Hanify recalled, "as if he were having a premonition about the fate of his own boys."

But Joe Kennedy was operating on more levels than the idealistic Hanify understood, for even as he was claiming to Hanify that he would never play dirty politics with Casey's war record, he was doing precisely that behind the scenes. "Here is one of the things about which we had the most fun," Kennedy told his newspaper friend Frank Waldrop. "For weeks Casey had been telling how as a World War veteran he understood the rigors of war and the lonesomeness of the boys at the front . . . accusing Lodge [the Republican candidate] of being a faker in that he had never seen action. Well, John F. looked up his record and found that he entered the service on October 10, 1918 and spent the four weeks until [the] Armistice . . . as a student at B.U. and he was mustered out on the 23rd of November, two weeks after the Armistice."

"I think John F. will make a great showing," Kennedy predicted right before the vote. "WR [Hearst] went through 100% for him and turned the papers over lock, stock and barrel the last four days."

As it turned out, while Fitzgerald lost to Casey, he made a very respectable showing, polling about 82,000 votes against 106,000 for Casey. "From John F.'s point of view," Hanify later observed, "his last campaign finished his career on a dignified, substantial basis, while from Joe's point of view the campaign had also been a success, clearly achieving the goal of showing that FDR was not impregnable in Massachusetts and that the Kennedys had a power base there which could not be ignored. All in all, it was a totally engaging experience for all of us."

When the primary results were tallied young Joe wrote to his father, "I am awfully sorry to hear that Grandpa got beaten . . . Maybe I'll get a shot at Casey when this thing is over."

While Joe was gradually accumulating the six hundred hours of flying time that would allow him to qualify as a patrol commander, Jack had enlisted in a naval officers' training course, and on September 25, 1941, he had received his commission as an ensign. On the first go-round he had failed the physical, but the initial failure only made him more determined to enter the Navy. After a summer devoted to back-strengthening radial exercises he tried again, and this time, with the help of his father's friend Captain Alan Goodrich Kirk—who arranged for Jack to see a medical friend of his in Boston to retake the physical—he made it. "I am most deeply grateful for your help and cooperation," Joe Senior wrote to Kirk. "When I get out of a place or retire from a job I find that a surprisingly large number of people find it very difficult to do favors . . . but you've been most kind and I'm deeply grateful."

With Kirk's added assistance, Jack was assigned to the Office of Naval Intelligence in Washington, where he was given the task of preparing daily and weekly bulletins that distilled information from various foreign sources. It was not the kind of romantic job a young man dreams of in a war situation, but it allowed Jack to be reunited with Kathleen, who had recently moved to Washington to work as a reporter on the *Times-Herald*, a conservative newspaper published by the eccentric Cissy Patterson. Finding an apartment at the Dorchester House, just a few blocks from Kathleen's apartment on Twenty-first Street, Jack became an instant member of her lively social circle.

The social ambience in Washington in those days was relaxed and collegial. "Everything was done in groups," one of Kick's fellow reporters recalled; "whole households of boys would take out whole households of girls. Part of it was economics: a group of young bachelors would live together in an apartment and tend to go around together; the same was true of the girls. And there were so many parties to go to that everyone just traveled in groups. Indeed, you were almost looked at askance if you tried to get someone off by yourself."

Included in Kathleen's group were several friends from the past— Dinah Bridge, Nancy Tenney, Betty Coxe and Page Huidekoper (who was now a *Times-Herald* reporter)—and two new friends she had made on the paper: John White, the star feature writer, and Inga Arvad. White, a handsome blue-eyed North Carolinian, the son of an Episcopal minister, had gone to Harvard four years ahead of Joe Junior and had come to the *Times-Herald* after several years on a Boston paper. A freethinking spirit, he found a congenial atmosphere under Frank Waldrop, the *Times-Herald*'s executive editor. "The only problem with the paper was its politics," White would recall, "but no one dreamed of making you write anything you didn't believe in."

Years later, White could still remember the day, a warm one in mid-September, when Waldrop brought Kathleen into the office to meet him. "I liked pretty girls," White confessed, "and here was one pretty girl. I didn't really know much about her except that her father had been ambassador to England, but I found her so attractive and so much fun, I asked her to go to the movies that very night."

Thus began a warm, argumentative relationship which brought both Kathleen and White much pleasure and much grief. Considering himself wiser and older than Kathleen, as indeed he was by eight years, White was alternately attracted and appalled by the naive sexual outlook which brought Kathleen to fend off even the most innocent advances with the automatic responses she had been taught as a girl. Although she had had dozens of boyfriends, it was immediately obvious to White that she was totally inexperienced sexually, a condition he blamed on the Catholic Church. "Bickered with KK," White wrote in his diary on October 16, 1941, "foolish Irish Catholic girl. She is best fun to argue with of any girl because she is always wrong—even called me up at home to say birth control is murder. I said it was the Catholic Church's way of keeping up its membership."

"KK and I here and eat," White recorded in his own form of shorthand in his diary two weeks later, "make up my bed and to ice follies. Very little hanky panky for long time. Not sure why. Not so much passes fended off as passes not made. Yet that wasn't me." But two weeks later White reported proudly: "Tonight for first time I held the hand of KK on way back from Baltimore and did feel very friendly toward her and do now wonder what will become of us."

As the weeks went by, Kathleen and White spent more time together. He began inviting her for suppers at the "cave," White's basement apartment in the Georgetown house owned by his older sister Patsy and her husband, the anthropologist Henry Field. Both movie buffs, Kathleen and White would sneak off from work for matinees. On weekends they would spend time walking together around Haines Point or Arlington Cemetery. And almost every night there would be some sort of party or gathering, where White was a master at the wide assortment of word games the young people liked to play.

Yet, beneath the surface of their friendship, they were impossibly matched, for despite his uncommon intelligence and his sharp wit, White at thirty admitted to no ambition other than maintaining a string of girlfriends and a reputation as an eccentric. And while he was definitely a good-looking young man, he refused to fuss over his appearance, tending to arrive at most social occasions in a rumpled jacket without a tie. Embarrassed by his constant state of dishevelment, Kathleen would argue with him about the importance of social conventions, after which he would retaliate by deliberately putting together even more garish combinations of clothes.

On the other hand, White correctly guessed that part of the attraction he held for Kathleen was the very unconventionality she deplored, that beneath her "soap-and-water" appearance there lay a rebellious streak of her own which was not yet quite strong enough to break through all her years of training. And as time went by, she began to get better about putting up with his unconventional ways, even to the point of staying at his side as he walked barefoot through museums. But no matter how close they became, she refused to give in on the matter of sex. "Took her to Haines Point on pretext of gathering willow bud," White recorded on January 23, 1942. "She tells me what priest told her not to do. I ask her to get dispensation."

"Another fight," White recorded ten days later. "This is intolerable and I'm sick of it. Too many words and no action. For two weeks as of this day I shall not see her alone . . . My God, that does sound terrible . . . but do it I shall to see if I can't get some sort of control of myself. I'm behaving terribly." The great resolve lasted only a matter of days, however, and soon White was once again telling Kathleen she was undersexed and her friends were "empty weeds." Finally he came up with a plan for ending all strife. "I would not plague her for kissing on condition she ask me to, over reasonable periods of time . . . All depends on her interpretation of reasonable." For a while the plan seemed to work, but then White once again began to despair. "I want a business of fire and freezing and she wants this placid agreement."

For all their feuding, there were many tender moments, the best of which generally came at the end of evenings after he had escorted her home. Great talkers, they would chat in her room until she grew tired, and then she would run into the bathroom and return in her flannel nightgown. "She to bed," White described the ritual in his diary. "I rub her back and put cream on her face. Observe her put hair in pins and net. Prayers." Many nights, performing a curious ritual in which Kathleen appeared like a little girl wanting nothing more than a mother to put her to bed, White would stay at her bedside, reading aloud until she drifted off to sleep, and then let himself out the door, completely disarmed by the sight of her innocent face above her long flannel nightgown.

While her relationship with White was wending its rocky course, Kathleen developed a close friendship with another fellow reporter, Inga Arvad. Inga wrote a daily feature, "Did You Happen to See . . . ," that ran on page two of the *Times-Herald*, introducing government officials and newcomers to Washington readers. A graduate of the Columbia School of Journalism, she was considered one of the best writers on the paper. According to Frank Waldrop, she could present in three hundred words "an insight into character and personality as good as anyone today could do taking up half a page of newsprint."

At the time Kathleen met her, Inga was in her late twenties, though no one knew for sure since her past was shrouded in mystery. There were stories that she had been Miss Denmark, and indeed she was a stunningly beautiful woman. A full-bodied blonde with large blue eyes and a healthy, glowing skin, she was so magnificent, according to Frank Waldrop, that "no photograph then, before, or after, ever did her justice." There were hints that she had led an exotic life in Europe, though she talked very little of her past. It was known only that she had been married twice, first at sixteen to an Egyptian foreign-service officer and then to a Hungarian film director named Paul Fejos.

If Kathleen was the original sweater-and-socks girl, Inga exuded sexuality. But in other ways the two young women were very much alike, Inga being as outspoken, warm and effervescent as her younger friend. Soon Inga and Kathleen became inseparable, swapping necklaces and trading confidences. It was only natural, then, that Jack and Inga should meet, and somewhere along the way Jack fell into a passionate affair with her. According to White, "Papa Joe" found out about Inga the first time Jack dated her—suggesting the extraordinary efficiency of his spy network—but at the beginning "he decided it was fine because she could properly initiate him into the mysterious ways of sex, in the fashion of some older, marvelous practitioner." But, as Inga was not yet divorced from her second husband, the affair had to be kept a secret so that Rose Kennedy would not find out. Relishing the clandestine atmosphere, Jack covered his tracks by double-dating with Kathleen and White.

"Supper at Inga's," John White recorded in his diary November 24, 1941. "K and J Kennedy, Inga and I . . . leave them together. Join at end." As far as anybody would know, they had all been together all evening. For her part, Kathleen was amused by her brother's romance; while she knew that she would never indulge in sex before marriage, she evidently had no qualms about her brother's affair. White's diary contains entry after entry about suppers at Inga's after which he and Kathleen willingly exited, leaving Jack and Inga alone, and then returned only at the end in order to maintain an appearance of propriety.

How much "Papa Joe" knew about Inga's mysterious past is not clear. If he had conducted his customary search into her life, as he did with the lives of all his children's friends, there would have been much to find out. But unlike John White, whose past was relatively easy to check out, Inga was a foreigner. Years later, John White remembered the shock he had experienced on his second date with Kathleen when she suddenly began asking him questions about his life in North Carolina, dropping bits and pieces of knowledge about his record in school and his family that he was certain he had not given her. Finally he had to ask, "How the hell do you know all these things about me?" Her reply left him speechless. "Every time one of us goes out with somebody new, we have to call our father," she told him in a matter-of-fact tone that suggested that she had long since resigned herself to this arrangement. "Then he puts his people onto it and tells us if it's all right to keep going out with that person. They are very efficient people, so the reports are very complete."

"Then how on earth can he let you go out with me?" John asked. Kathleen laughed. "Oh, he considers you frivolous but harmless." After she had described her father's operating procedure, White had a fantasy of Mr. Kennedy "lying in bed in some luxury hotel far from home, his nine children all obliged to know his exact whereabouts so that they could check in at the end of the evening."

If Joe Senior was fully aware of Jack's involvement with "Inga Binga," as Jack playfully called her, Rose was kept blissfully in the dark. In his letters to his mother during this period, Jack maintained a lighthearted, easygoing attitude which made it seem as if he had nothing on his mind but his work and his family.

> I enjoy your round robin letters [he wrote in November 1941]. I'm saving them to publish—that style of yours will net us millions. With all this talk about inflation and where is our money going—when I think of your potential earning power—with you dictating and Mrs. Walker beating it out on that machine—it's enough to make a man get down on his knees and thank God for the Dorchester High Latin School which gave you that very sound grammatical basis which shines through every slightly mixed metaphor and each somewhat split infinitive. . . .

My health is excellent. I look like hell, but my stomach is a thing of beauty—as are you, Ma,—and you, unlike my stomach—will be a joy forever.

Jack's romance with Inga took place at a difficult time in the nation's life, in the midst of the trauma over the Pearl Harbor attack and the U.S. entry into the war against Germany, Italy and Japan. It was a time of rumor and suspicion, a time when enemy sympathizers were believed to be everywhere. It was in this atmosphere that Inga's past became a subject of investigation by the FBI.

The suspicions about Inga were born one morning in the morgue of the *Times-Herald* when a fellow reporter called out to Page Huidekoper, "Hey, have you seen this picture of Inga with Hitler?" It showed a smiling Inga in a box with Hitler at the 1936 Olympics in Berlin. On seeing the photograph, Page felt compelled to report the discovery to Frank Waldrop, who suggested she go directly to Inga with her worst fear, the fear that Inga was a German agent, and then bring the information to the FBI. Upon hearing the news, Inga had simply shrugged. "I'm not a bit surprised," she said. "I hear this all the time."

As Inga told her story, her association with Hitler coincided with the start of her journalistic career. On a visit to Germany in 1935, she said, she had heard a rumor that Hermann Goering was engaged, and posing as a reporter, she had managed to get an exclusive interview with him which she then sold to a Danish newspaper. Impressed by her initiative, the newspaper made her its correspondent in Berlin, where she met Adolf Hitler while covering Goering's wedding. Hitler was apparently much taken with Inga, referring to her in a much-quoted remark as the perfect example of Nordic beauty. After the wedding he granted her an interview and invited her to view the Olympic Games with him as a member of the press.

As it happened, the FBI had been watching Inga from her first year in America, when a classmate at the Columbia School of Journalism advised them that she might have been sent by the Germans to influence American morale. Her friendship with Hitler was noted by the FBI's New York office on June 7, 1941. But when the same information was relayed to the FBI by the *Times-Herald*, the Washington office stepped into action. Unbeknown to Jack Kennedy, the FBI began charting his romance with Inga, on the grounds that he had access to secret information in the Office of Naval Intelligence. A confidential report was entered on Jack's file confirming that he had been "playing around" with Inga and "apparently spending the night" with her.

Still, the affair continued its course, until the publication on January

12, 1942, of a sensational item in Walter Winchell's column in the *New York Mirror*. Apparently Winchell had a source in the FBI and, on the basis of the bureau's fragmentary reports on Inga and Jack, had gone ahead to exploit the great case of the Ambassador's son and the beautiful blond spy. "One of ex-Ambassador Kennedy's eligible sons is the target of a Washington gal columnist's affections," Winchell had written. "So much so she is divorcing her explorer-groom. Pa Kennedy no like."

"All manner of to do" in the office, John White recorded the following day. "J. Kennedy in, evidently discussing story with Waldrop," who was furious to learn that Winchell's source had been the FBI. According to Waldrop, Winchell hated the publisher, Mrs. Patterson, and this was simply an attempt to embarrass the paper. By this time, Waldrop was convinced that Inga was surely not a spy. After discussing the situation with Mrs. Patterson, he considered writing a violent castigation of the bureau. "Must say," White recorded in his diary, "Inga looking her very best" as all this was going on.

Joe Kennedy, now in Washington, went to dinner with Jack and Kathleen, and the next morning Kathleen told White that her father thought the great Inga scandal was very funny and had told Jack to do as he wished. But according to Waldrop, Joe Senior's reaction was far different. "Old Joe had learned by then to mask what he was doing. He was smart enough to know he didn't want to make a big thing about it in front of the children for fear his disapproval would backfire, but he certainly wasn't going to just sit back and let Jack's reputation be hurt by a misguided relationship with a woman."

As it happened, Jack was in real danger of being cashiered from the Navy as a result of his affair with Inga. At the Office of Naval Intelligence, an assistant director, Howard Kingman, was extremely upset by the situation. Fearing that Inga was a Mata Hari who was using Jack to find out all she could about what was going on in the Navy Department and ONI, Kingman wanted to get rid of Kennedy as soon as possible. There are some who believe that at this point Joe Kennedy intervened to prevent his son from being thrown out of the service, persuading the Navy brass to simply reassign him. However it happened, Jack was suddenly transferred, receiving orders to go to Charleston, South Carolina, two days after the appearance of the Winchell column.

In his diary on January 17, 1942, White recorded that Inga was very gloomy about Jack going to Charleston and that Jack too seemed very sad. The next day Inga and Kathleen helped Jack pack up his belongings, and the day after that he left for the Charleston Navy Yard, where he remained for six long months before he finally got the sea duty he had wanted all along. There were some who believed that Joe Senior was also the force behind Jack's eventual assignment to the Pacific, that all along he was moving behind the scenes against Jack's will, manipulating the changes of duty in order to separate him from Inga. This reading seems to do an injustice to both Joe Senior and Jack. Just before the Inga scandal broke, Joe had told his friend Arthur Houghton that Jack had a very responsible position in Washington, but, "like all kids, wants to get out on a destroyer in the Atlantic. It makes me sick to think of it."

To be sure, Kennedy probably was far more agitated about the affair than he let on, particularly when all the rumors about Inga's past were made public, but if he did pull strings to have Jack transferred to sea duty it was most likely at his son's request. Writing to Joe Junior in June of 1942, Joe Senior reported that Jack had been to Washington and had asked for an assignment at sea. "He has become disgusted with the desk jobs," Joe wrote, "and as an awful lot of the fellows that he knows are in active service, and particularly with you in fleet service, he feels that at least he ought to be trying to do something. I quite understand his position, but I know his stomach and his back are real deterrents—but we'll see what we can do."

In his offhand use of that phrase, "we'll see what we can do," Kennedy reveals the extraordinary extent of his involvement with his children, an involvement so intense at this stage of his life that it is hard to distinguish where his needs begin and his children's needs leave off. Was it simply, as he liked to say, that he enjoyed being with his children and doing things for them more than anything else in the world, especially now that his public career had been brought to a halt? This was probably part of the motivation, but not all of it, for it would seem that by investing in his children's future as deeply as he did, Kennedy was able to balance the frustrations in his own life and to hide the fact that he had nothing else to do. Now that he was no longer traveling the world in pursuit of his own affairs, Kennedy looked upon his grown-up sons as if they were still children living at home.

On July 23, 1942, Jack finally got his chance for action when he was told to report to the United States Naval Reserve midshipmen's school at a branch of Northwestern University in Chicago, where he would learn the rudiments of seamanship in preparation for active duty.

In the six months since he had left Washington, Jack had seen Inga several times—visits which were well monitored by the FBI. It was at this point that Joe Kennedy stepped in, telling his son it was one thing to have a fling and quite another to continue a relationship with a non-Catholic divorcée under investigation as a Nazi spy. Jack's future, Joe argued, would be permanently damaged and the scar of the scandal would affect the entire family.

The father's arguments must have sunk in, for on March 6, 1942, White recorded in his diary that Inga had "parted forever from JK due to the argument they might get in trouble." Five months later, Inga decided to leave Washington for New York. "She is going to marry a Dane," Kathleen reported to Lem, "she admits that Jack was the only person she cared for really and when she couldn't have him there was no sense to sit around waiting for someone else who might never come."

For his part, Jack was very lonely after he and Inga split. White remembers many phone calls from Charleston when Jack would talk with Kathleen for hours about Inga. Yet to the rest of his family he appeared his same debonair self. Writing to his mother on official Navy stationery, Jack displayed his customary playfulness:

> Thank you for your latest chapter on the "9 little Kennedys and how they grew" by Rose of Old Boston. Never in history have so many owed so much to such a one—or is that quite correct? If you would look in that little book of yours under Churchill Winston—I imagine you can check it.
>
> They want me to conduct a Bible class here every other Sunday for about ½ hour with the sailors. Would you say that is un-Catholic. I have a feeling that dogma might say it was—but don't good works come under our obligations to the Catholic church. We're not a completely ritualistic, formalistic, hierarchical structure in which the Word, the truth, must only come down from the very top—a structure that allows for no individual interpretation—or are we? However, don't worry about this—just send me Father Conway's Question Box as I would like to look through it.

Had Rose known what was really going through Jack's mind when he thought about his religion, she would have worried a great deal. For on May 8, John White recorded in his diary that at supper Kathleen had confided to him that Jack seemed to be on the verge of renouncing his Catholic religion. Whether these feelings of rebellion were connected to Jack's thwarted romance with Inga it is impossible to say. Perhaps it was just a matter of doubt accumulating over time as his adult mind tried to reconcile and understand some of the illogical teachings he had learned as a child. Or perhaps it was a matter of having too much time on his hands to think while he sat at his desk in Charleston; for, once he was settled at Northwestern enjoying the companionship of new buddies and the excitement of knowing he would soon be shipping out, the deep concern with religion seemed to vanish as suddenly as it had arrived.

With America in the war and two of his boys in the Navy, Kennedy decided to put his doubts behind him and offer his services to the President. "In this great crisis all Americans are with you," he wired to FDR minutes after the attack on Pearl Harbor. "Name the battle post. I'm yours to command." But after the difficulties he had had with Kennedy at the Court of St. James's, Roosevelt was not about to bring him back. For months, Kennedy waited for a reply, always assuming that the problem was not the President but his aides. "I am afraid the influences around Roosevelt are stronger in this case than his own desires," Kennedy wrote to a friend, "as I still think he'd like to have me back."

So masterful was FDR that he somehow managed to make Kennedy believe that in the chaos of the days following Pearl Harbor he had not seen Kennedy's telegram, though his assistant, Steve Early, had responded to it at the time by saying that the President was very pleased. In March 1942 Kennedy sent Roosevelt copies of the telegram and Early's answer, writing, "I don't want to appear in the role of a man looking for a job for the sake of getting an appointment, but Joe and Jack are in the service and I feel that my experience in these critical times might be worth something in some position."

With this letter, Kennedy believed the ice had broken, but as the months went by and nothing happened he grew more and more depressed, finding it so painful to be out of favor that he couldn't stand going to Washington; when he had to go there on business, he came and went as quickly as he could, hesitating to see anybody except friends like Arthur Krock and Justices Frank Murphy and William O. Douglas. "I am so damn well fed up with everything . . . ," he wrote to a friend, "and so disgusted at sitting on my fanny at Cape Cod and Palm Beach when I really believe I could do something in this war effort that it is better I don't see anybody."

In truth, Kennedy was not simply waiting to hear from Washington, for he had a number of business deals in the works to keep him busy. In a letter to Jack, he reported that the family trust had bought a couple of very interesting blocks in New York on Lexington Avenue, at Fifty-first Street and Fifty-ninth Street, "which should turn out to be very good after the war," and that he was negotiating a deal to introduce Coca-Cola to South America. "Mother insists that the South Americans won't like Coca-Cola," Kathleen told Lem, "but Daddy's cry is 'I'll make 'em like it.' " At the same time, he agreed to meet with a rising young restaurateur named Howard Johnson to see if some kind of working relationship could be established. But none of these projects, exciting as each one would have seemed to the ordinary businessman, was able to fully engage Joe Kennedy's mind, once it had been so richly expanded by his experience in public service.

Nor was the Kennedy household ever the same after the golden trio left home. In 1941 Kennedy made the decision to sell the Bronxville estate, preferring to divide his time between his two other homes in Palm Beach and Hyannis Port. The decision made sense for the elder Kennedys, but it was tough on the children—particularly the younger ones, who no longer had a fixed base during their school years. For Eunice, aged twenty, the loss of the Bronxville home had little impact, for by then she had graduated from Noroton and was studying at Stanford University for a degree in social work. But for all the younger ones it was a disorienting experience to lose the only home they had ever really lived in for months and years at a time.

Looking back later, Luella Hennessey claimed that with the sale of the Bronxville home there was "a loss of stability" in the Kennedy family, almost as if a dividing line had been drawn and the younger children fell on the wrong side. "After England," Hennessey recalled, "Mr. Kennedy began to withdraw more and more into himself. He was not as outgoing or as happy as he had been before, and the kids felt it. Still, he tried as best he could to keep his spirits up whenever they were around and he still enjoyed their company more than anything else in the world."

During these years Pat graduated from Rosemont College, Jean followed her older sisters to Noroton, and Robert was sent to Portsmouth Priory in Rhode Island, where he struggled to do well. "As a child," Lem Billings recalled, "Bobby was the smallest and least articulate of all the boys. Nothing came easy to him, but he never stopped trying. He *willed* himself into the water to learn to swim, and he willed himself onto the football field. And where Jack rebelled against his parents' obsession with punctuality, Bobby was always on time for everything—for meals, church and school. Yet the funny thing was that while he secured his mother's love by being so good, so gentle and so religious, it made him even more invisible to his father."

"While they all knew what was expected of them," Rose recalled, "Bobby really worked at it." And for this persistence Rose was forever grateful. In her letters to her seventh child, she displayed a special warmth. She called him her "little pet" and she took it upon herself to monitor his schooling, in contrast to the situation with Joe Junior and Jack, where her husband had assumed responsibility for their sons' education as soon as they reached prep school.

Writing to the headmaster of Portsmouth Priory, Rose urged that Robert be encouraged to write up his experiences at the embassy. "Unfortunately, none of us Kennedys seem to have a gift for writing," she admitted. "However it would please me very much if you would encourage Bobby to do something with the wonderful material which he has on hand and which so few of his generation have had an opportunity to enjoy."

"I was so disappointed in your report," she wrote to Robert at the priory. "The mark in Christian doctrine was very low . . . certainly in a Catholic school you should be taught that above everything else you should apply yourself to that subject. Please get on your toes . . . I do not expect my own little pet to let me down."

Part of this shift in parental roles can be explained by the fact that the Ambassador was across the Atlantic during Bobby's first years in boarding school. But even when Joe returned, though he quickly shifted his third son from the Catholic priory to Milton Academy, his letters reveal a subtly different set of expectations from the consistently high standards he had demanded of Joe and Jack.

Kennedy's mellower attitude had a paradoxical effect on his son, making Bobby struggle even more to win his father's attention and respect. By this point, the drive to come in first had long since been engraved in the Kennedy family tradition and Bobby was keenly aware of the pride his father had taken in the accomplishments of his older brothers. "I wish Dad," the boy wrote, "that you would write me a letter as you used to Joe and Jack about what you think about the different political events and the war as I'd like to understand what's going on better than I do now." When Kennedy responded with a two-page single-spaced letter outlining his views on Europe and the Far East, Bobby was very pleased. "Thanks very much for your letter, Dad, which is just what I wanted," he wrote.

It was Teddy who was hurt the most by the loss of a permanent home. From all accounts, he was a cheerful, loving child, but his cheerfulness was in part a protection against the tension of constantly being thrust into new situations and new schools. Before he reached the age of thirteen, biographer Burton Hersh observes, he had attended ten different day and boarding schools as his parents alternated their summers and winters at the Cape and in Palm Beach. For any child, this constant transplantation would be hard. For young Teddy, unsure of his intellect and so overweight at the time that his brothers called him "fatstuff," it was extremely damaging.

Years later Rose understood that it had been a serious mistake to send Teddy away to boarding school when he was only eight or nine, but since their living pattern was the one both she and her husband wanted, she felt that there was little else she could do. She had tried one year, she said, to keep Teddy in a day school in Palm Beach, but since the family didn't come to Florida until November and left in April, it proved impossible. (With this second tier of children, the needs of the parents for mobility assumed a clear precedence over the needs of the children for stability.)

Yet through it all Teddy remained a good-natured, lovable child, adored and teased by his sisters and brothers. After a visit to the Fessenden school, Kennedy Senior reported that Teddy was "a riot, as usual," that the consensus was that he had "a fine head," though "he goes off half-cocked when anybody asks any questions and he gives them an answer even though most times it is wrong . . . so if he isn't a bright student, he is a good salesman."

During these years, Rose continued to travel as much as she could, journeying to South America with Eunice and Jack in 1941 and to California in 1942. Now past her fiftieth birthday, she was an amazingly handsome woman and was still gripped by her youthful enthusiasm for seeing new places and learning new things. Traveling away from home she experienced a sudden revival in her intellectual powers, feeling once more a link to the vital young woman who had stood at the top of her high-school class. To her friend Mother Patterson Rose confessed that she had kept a diary during her trip to South America and was hoping to publish it—possibly in *The Ladies' Home Journal*—and give the money to the English orphans. "Please do not mention this to anybody," she warned, "as my sons and my husband scoff at the idea, in fact, you are the only one who has ever given me any encouragement."

If Rose was not confident that her husband respected her intellect, she must have known that he held her in great esteem for the job she did in bringing up the children and organizing their complicated household. In his letters to his wife when she was away and he was left to run the house, Joe reveals a keen appreciation for his wife's skills and he makes an honest effort to let her thoroughly relax.

> Don't go bothering your head about anything around here [he tells her when she is in California], because everything is moving along and it is certainly no bother for me. I'm not giving it your thorough handling but we'll be all right . . . So darling . . . take it easy now and don't bother your head about Eunice's lunch and Pat's schooling. [Like Jack, Eunice suffered from a bad stomach, and her parents constantly worried about her weight.] Neither of them is going to die and neither of them is going to be very badly off and you just make yourself miserable by worrying about them, so you will be doing the best thing for us and in the long run for them, if you will just go to the courses and take it easy.

In Joe's letters to Rose during this period there is evident an extraordinary level of intimacy regarding family matters, a sharing of the details of daily life so intense that the typed words on the page read as if they were being spoken to a best friend. Yet it was during this period that Joe took it upon himself, without telling Rose, to make a devastating decision about Rosemary that he would regret for the rest of his life.

In the eighteen months following Rosemary's return from England, there had been a marked deterioration in her mental skills. After she was forced to leave the only school where she had been happy, the only situation where she had been able to contribute to others, her customary good nature had given way to tantrums, rages and violent behavior. Pacing up and down the halls of her home, she was like a wild animal, given to screaming, cursing and thrashing out at anyone who tried to thwart her will. No one fully understood what had happened, though some experts traced the violent shift in mood to the belated sexual changes that were bringing the twenty-one-year-old Rosemary into womanhood.

"It had never been easy for Rosemary," Lem Billings observed, "but when she returned from England she became aggressively unhappy, irritable and frustrated at not being able to do all the things her siblings could do. All through her childhood she had fought against her limitations by never giving up and by retaining the sweetest nature you could ever imagine. But now she seemed to realize that no matter how hard she tried she would never even come within sight of her Harvard-educated brothers and her glamorous journalist sister. And once she recognized this, her level of frustration grew so high that she became almost impossible to handle. Every day there would be one terrifying incident after another: physical fights where Rosemary would use her fists to hit and bruise people, long absences at night when she'd be out wandering the streets and violent verbal exchanges."

Something had to be done, not only for Rosemary but for her mother, who could not rid herself of the fear that something terrible was going to happen to her daughter. "I was always worried," Rose later noted, "that she would run away from home someday or that she would go off with someone who would flatter her or kidnap her, as the kidnapping craze was on then." And beyond these concerns, there was the deeper fear that Rosemary would get pregnant. At twenty-one she stood five feet seven inches tall, with a full rounded figure, a clear complexion and excellent features. "She was the most beautiful of all the Kennedys," Ann Gargan recalls. "She had the body of a twenty-one-year-old yearning for fulfillment with the mentality of a four-year-old. She was in a convent in Washington at the time, and many nights the school would call to say she was missing, only to find her out walking around the streets at 2 A.M. Can you imagine what it must have been like to know your daughter was walking the streets in the darkness of the night, the perfect prey for an unsuspecting male?"

While Rose prayed to God that her daughter's violent moods would come to an end, Joe took matters into his own hands. When he was in

England he had talked with doctors about a pioneering operation called a prefrontal lobotomy, in which a hole about the size of a dime was drilled in the skull and a knifelike instrument inserted into the front part of the brain to sever the connecting fibers and disconnect the lobe areas from the rest of the brain centers. In the early 1940s the operation was considered a miracle treatment for sufferers from certain types of hopeless insanity characterized by worry, depression, intense frustration and violent behavior.

To us today, the idea that one part of the brain could be improved by destroying another sounds like the suggestion that the functioning of an automobile can be improved by smashing the engine. We now understand that the frontal lobes are where man's personality lives, that while an individual may appear to function without them, it is precisely his individuality which disappears. He is simply a zombie going through the motions of life, without the capacity to coordinate his daily tasks into any kind of integrated whole. But in 1941 it was widely believed that for an extremely agitated person for whom no other treatment had proved successful, severing of the frontal lobes promised the only hope.

"Few surgical events can top the dramatic simplicity of a typical frontal lobotomy as performed in an up to date hospital," Marguerite Clark reported in *The American Mercury* in 1941. "Until about seven years ago the pre-frontal lobes of the brain were the least understood region of the cerebral hemispheres. Today it is a different story. Scientists have learned that the frontal lobes are the organs of imagination and anticipation." In a healthy brain, the theory held, these frontal lobes enabled man to envisage great things for the future and to anticipate them pleasurably, but in an unhealthy brain they became the breeding ground of worry, causing the sufferer to experience intense frustration as his perception of things as they were clashed with his conception of things as he thought they should be.

"These unfortunates may, in some cases, be brought back to useful life by the surgical removal of the frontal lobes of the brain," Marguerite Clark wrote. "When worry leads to agitated depression, violence or gloomy silence, surgeons can remove the patients' cares . . . by removing that part of the brain concerned with the future."

The first lobotomy for the relief of mental disorder was performed in 1935 at the University of Lisbon by Dr. Egas Moniz, who later won a Nobel Prize for his work. The patient, a young man of twenty, who had suffered for five years from agonizing apprehension, was regarded as hopeless, but just minutes after the sharp knife was inserted into his brain and twirled around, it was claimed, he made a remarkable recovery. "The stark fears from which he suffered were relieved by cutting down the many pathways in his brain by which ideas, whipped furiously by his unruly imagination, crowded in too closely and painfully upon one another."

Word of the new operation quickly spread. In America, Dr. Walter Freeman and Dr. James Watts of the George Washington School of Medicine were the first to report successful operations on the frontal lobes to the American Medical Association. Freeman later calculated he had performed over four thousand operations in the 1940s, using a gold-plated ice pick which he carried with him in a velvet-lined case. Boasting that there was less pain after a lobotomy than after a dental extraction, since the brain, the ultimate seat of consciousness, has no local consciousness of pain, Freeman developed a new technique that kept the skull intact while the ice pick was plunged through the base of the upper inner angle of the eye socket, severing the frontal nerve connections within seconds.

To Joseph Kennedy, the lobotomy was an obvious solution to the debilitating frustrations Rosemary was experiencing as she tried to find a place for herself in her hard-driving family. If, as the doctors claimed, the frontal lobes could be severed without impairment of Rosemary's capacity to function on a daily basis, then she could only find relief by discarding that part of her brain that produced her painful self-consciousness and her abnormal capacity to worry. With her frontal lobes inoperative, she would no longer have to worry about her future; she could simply live day to day without suffering invidious comparisons with her ambitious brothers and sisters. If everything worked, if her sexual drive was calmed down and her violent moods were contained, she could remain with her family for the rest of her life.

The family archives do not record where Rosemary had her lobotomy, for Joe kept it a secret not only from Rose but from the entire family. We know only that something went terribly wrong during the operation and that Rosemary emerged far worse than she had ever been. "They knew right away that it wasn't successful," Ann Gargan later said. "You could see by looking at her that something was wrong, for her head was tilted and her capacity to speak was almost entirely gone. There was no question now that she could no longer take care of herself and that the only answer was an institution."

Knowing nothing about the operation, Rose was simply told that the time had come for her daughter to be put into an institution and that for both their sakes she should not visit for some time. The place Kennedy chose, on the recommendation of Archbishop Cushing, was St. Coletta's in Jefferson, Wisconsin. Among friends and relatives the word was spread that the family couldn't take care of Rosemary anymore, and, not knowing what had happened, Joe's sister and Rosemary's god- mother, Margaret Burke, offered to take her in. "For Joe," Ann Gargan said, "it was an absolutely devastating thing, but once it was done he decided that he had to protect Rose from the heartbreak, believing it would shatter her to see her daughter that way while it would do Rose- mary no good at all, since she no longer realized who she was."

This explanation is hard to accept. Even granting that at some level Joe *was* trying to protect his wife from heartbreak, it is also likely that he was protecting himself from her legitimate wrath at not having been consulted before the decision. For twenty years Rose had devoted her- self to the task of "making Rosemary a Kennedy," and now, with one movement of one sharp instrument, all that work was forever destroyed. Even granting that Rose too was feeling the same mixture of love and frustration, sorrow and rage that led Joe to decide upon the lobotomy, there is no way of knowing how *she* would have decided had she been given the chance to express her opinion. By playing God with his family, Joe had prevented her from having her rightful share in this fateful decision.

For years, in an astonishing act of control, Joe kept Rose from know- ing the truth. It was only after he suffered a stroke in 1961 that Rose took it upon herself to go to St. Coletta's. "Then she knew," Ann Gargan said, "though she had to piece the story together chapter by chapter." Approaching her friends one by one, she would ask why they hadn't told her, but as it turned out none of them knew any more than she did. "Why didn't you advise me?" she repeatedly asked Luella Hennessey. "Because I didn't know," Hennessey responded.

In the years ahead, there would rise in Rose's voice an uncharacteris- tic bitterness as she spoke about the operation. "He thought it would help her," she said when she was ninety, "but it made her go all the way back. It erased all those years of effort I had put into her. All along I had continued to believe that she could have lived her life as a Kennedy girl, just a little slower. But then it was all gone in a matter of minutes." Yet even then Rose refused to dwell upon her bitterness and was able to rationalize that "St. Coletta's was a wonderful place, that the nuns there were marvelous and that at least there was always the knowledge that she was well cared for."

For Joe too, the excellence of the institution would provide a certain measure of solace. Writing to Sister Anastasia of St. Coletta's in 1958, he would say, "I am still very grateful for your help . . . after all, the solution of Rosemary's problem has been a major factor in the ability of all the Kennedys to go about their life's work and to try to do it as well as they can."

In the years ahead, prompted perhaps by his guilt over Rosemary, Joe would devote a substantial amount of his money to research on the retarded, and his daughter Eunice would become a pioneering force in the field, but in 1941 the failed operation had to be one of the most heart-wrenching failures Joe Kennedy had ever experienced.

For Rosemary's sisters and brothers, her sudden disappearance must have been met by dozens of questions that were never fully answered, surrounding the incident with the aura of forbidden mystery. To be sure, the older children must have seen that their parents were deeply worried about Rosemary's behavior, but why, after all these years, did she have to be institutionalized now? And why couldn't any of the family see her? And most ominously, why wouldn't anyone really talk about what was happening?

# CHAPTER 36
## "HERO
## IN THE
## PACIFIC"

I t was while Rosemary was being moved to her permanent home at St. Coletta's that Jack received his orders to report on July 27, 1942, to midshipmen's school at the downtown branch of Northwestern University in Chicago, located about five blocks from the famous Drake Hotel. During the ten-week program, Jack lived in Abbott Hall, a fourteen-story office building which had been converted into dormitories and classrooms. It was a crash program, with courses in navigation, gunnery, semaphore and seamanship, designed to teach college graduates how to become sea-going officers.

While Jack was at Northwestern, the campus was visited by two naval officers, John Harlee and John D. Bulkeley, whose early exploits with PT boats, considered the most versatile of the Navy's small combat craft, had been celebrated in a best-selling book called *They Were Expendable*. Harlee had just been named the executive officer of a new PT school that the Navy had established at Melville, Rhode Island, and he and Bulkeley were visiting colleges and universities to find the reserve officers to man a new fleet of PT boats that were being equipped for operation in the southwest Pacific. Smaller than destroyers, engined for speed and designed for deadliness, the PT boats had already played a major role in the Mediterranean and in the fight for the seas off the east and south coasts of Britain, but they would earn their greatest prominence in the closely fought battles of the Pacific and the Far East.

More than any other branch of the Navy, the PT service tapped a corps of wealthy and aristocratic young men, disproportionately Ivy League, whose families owned motorboats and cabin cruisers. Having spent their summers around marinas and yacht clubs, these men were considered especially capable of handling the small, maneuverable PTs. From the moment Jack heard Harlee and Bulkeley talk, he knew that he wanted to command a PT boat, and in the interview with the two officers he sold himself hard, expressing a "great enthusiasm and desire to get into combat." Harlee and Bulkeley were favorably enough impressed with both his attitude and his experience as an intercollegiate sailing champion to recommend him for the service. Had either officer known that Jack suffered from a bad back it is unlikely that he would have been accepted, for these boats were so sensitive to every movement of the sea that "even when they are going at half speed it is about as hard to stay upright on them as on a broncho's back." And when they moved at full speed, planing over the water at forty knots and more, with bows lifted, slicing great waves from either side of their hulls, they gave their crew "an enormous pounding."

As it happened, Jack's back had been bothering him terribly all summer long, so much so that he had to sleep on a table instead of a bed. Worried that he would be unable to get through the grueling regimen of calisthenics and athletics at Melville, he sought his father's advice on the advisability of having an operation before entering the school. As the PT-boat course was scheduled to begin on October 1, Jack traveled directly to the Cape as soon as his officer's training at Northwestern was over. There, with Kathleen also at home, he spent three days in consultation with his father.

"Jack came home," Joe Senior confided to Joe Junior, "and between you and me is having terrific trouble with his back. . . . I don't see how he can last a week in that tough grind of Torpedo Boats and what he wants to do, of course, . . . is to be operated on and then have me fix it so he can get back in that service when he gets better. This will require considerable manipulation and I have given up the idea of going to California with mother to see if I can be of any help to him."

When Joe spoke with the doctors, he discovered that any operation was risky at best and would probably take Jack out of active duty for at least six months. So the decision was made that he should enter the school and keep at it until it became physically impossible to continue.

Fortunately, except for his back, he appeared to be in better health than he had been for years. "You cannot believe how well he looks," Rose reported to Joe Junior, "and how he has improved in his general attitude towards the ordinary conditions of life . . . You can really see that his face has filled out. Instead of it being lean, it has now become fat."

From the first week Jack arrived at Melville, he was, Kathleen reported to Lem, "crazy about the school." For one thing, he shared his Quonset hut with his old friend from Harvard, Torby Macdonald, whose presence at Melville was the result of the Ambassador's intervention. In addition to Torby, he met someone else who was to become a lifelong friend, Paul "Red" Fay, a big Irish Catholic athlete whose father owned a construction company in San Francisco. In his courses, including those in torpedoes, gunnery and firefighting, Jack performed excellently, but his back continued to give him trouble. One of his classmates recalls that he now had to sleep with a piece of plywood under his mattress.

How much Harlee knew of this is uncertain, but when Jack graduated on December 2, it was decided to assign him to a training squadron as a teacher instead of sending him overseas. Not surprisingly, Jack was sorely disappointed. All his friends were going overseas and that was where Jack wanted to be. He argued with Harlee about it, but Harlee insisted that he would be more valuable as an instructor. So Jack remained at Melville, an unhappy warrior.

On December 9, 1942, Jack was granted five days' leave. He went to Palm Beach, where he hoped, as always, to get some help from his father in pulling strings to allow him to see combat. Jack's desire for action put his father in a difficult situation. When he first joined up with the Motor Torpedo Division, Joe had confided to Father Sheehy that Jack's decision was "causing his mother and me plenty of anxiety . . . I suppose that I should be proud that my sons should decide to pick the most hazardous branches of the service in this war, and of course, there is pride in my heart but quite a measure of grief in my mind." Nevertheless, he promised to do what he could.

During his five days in Palm Beach, Jack was joined by Joe Junior, who was stationed then in Puerto Rico, assigned to fly Navy patrol planes on antisubmarine missions. At their mother's insistence, the two young men posed for a photograph in their Navy uniforms. In the handsome picture, both are smiling broadly, looking straight into the camera. Joe Junior, wearing a single gold ensign stripe, is, for once, the junior man.

After Jack returned to Melville, Joe Senior got in touch with Massachusetts Senator David I. Walsh, chairman of the Senate Naval Committee and easily, in Harlee's words, "the most powerful man in the

Senate as far as the Navy was concerned." Over the years, both Fitzgerald and Kennedy had done a number of favors for Walsh and now the time had come to cash in. An arrangement was made for Walsh to meet with Jack, and the Senator came away from the meeting highly impressed. "Frankly," Walsh wrote to Fitzgerald, "I have not met a young man of his age in a long time who has impressed me more favorably. He has a fine personality, energetic and outstanding qualities of leadership, and with all a becoming modesty."

After the meeting Senator Walsh wrote a letter to the Navy Department requesting that John F. Kennedy be assigned to a war zone. Within weeks, Jack received the news he had wanted to hear all along: he was ordered to report to the Solomon Islands as soon as possible.

Jack sailed to the South Pacific aboard the *Rochambeau*, a French liner which had been converted into a transport ship. When he reached the Solomons on March 28, 1943, the war in the Pacific had been in progress sixteen months, and despite two substantial Allied victories in 1942—the Battle of the Coral Sea and the Battle of Midway—the Japanese were still in control. In early August 1942 the U. S. Marines had landed on Guadalcanal, beginning a bitter and bloody engagement that had dragged on for five months at the expense of many American casualties. But by January of 1943, two months before Kennedy's arrival, the Japanese had finally given up trying to reinforce Guadalcanal, and a five-month lull in the Pacific was about to begin.

Kennedy arrived at Tulagi on April 14 and headed for PT headquarters at Sesapi, a primitive scattering of thatched-roof huts for living and dining, machine shops, an officers' club and a cluster of PT boats nestled along makeshift docks. "As to conditions," he wrote to his parents,

they are not bad here, though if this is the dry season the wet season must be considerably damp. Rains every day for four or five hours—solid rain —everything gets soaked and on my blue uniform a green-mold has grown almost one quarter of an inch thick. However, the food isn't bad at all and the waters are very calm, which makes it ideal for the boats. . . . We go out on patrol every other night and work on the boats in the day time. They get us up at 5:45 and the black-out begins at 6:30. The blackout is total as the huts we live in have no sides. They have just opened up an Officer's Club which consists of a tent. The liquor served is an alcoholic concoction which is drawn out of the torpedo tubes, known as torp juice. Every night about 7:30 the tent bulges, about five men come crashing out, blow their lunch and stagger off to bed. This torp juice, which is the most expendable item on the island, makes the prohibition stuff look like Haig and Haig but probably won't do any one any permanent harm as long as their eyes hold out.

In another letter, written to his parents on May 10, 1943, Jack reported that he had learned that

what they say about Japs is true—or at least in one case. The other day we went to pick up a Jap pilot that had parachuted into the water. We pulled alongside of him to a distance of about 20 yards. He was young looking, powerfully built—short black hair. He suddenly threw aside the life belt he was wearing, pulled a pistol and started firing. We let go with everything but he didn't seem to get hit until finally an old soldier aimed with his rifle and took the top of his head off. He leaped forward and sank out of sight. That I understand is the usual story with the officers. With the men, however, there would seem to be no such desire for the glorious death.

As the commander of his own boat, the *PT 109*, Jack had his first real experience as a leader, and from all accounts it seems that his men respected him. His "exec" and roommate, Lennie Thom, a 220-pound tackle from Ohio State, wrote to his fiancée that he liked Jack the minute they met, almost as if their two personalities meshed into one. A second roommate, Johnny Iles, remembered: "Jack was a big letter writer. He got a lot of mail from everybody in his family. We [all] used to read our family letters aloud to each other. So I really got to know his whole family this way." Joe Atkinson, a fellow graduate of Melville, also hung around Jack's hut. "He was very brilliant," Atkinson recalled, "and had a way of really picking your brain if you knew something he didn't. He had everything going for him, personality, money, connections." Yet he apparently wore his celebrity lightly, for a roommate named Foncannon, a young man from the Midwest, never knew that he was the son of an ambassador. "He just seemed like the ordinary young fellow—just like Lennie and Johnny."

The men stationed in the Solomons at the time agree that Jack didn't like to drink or play cards, preferring either to sit around and chat or to lie on his bunk reading and writing letters. And the letters he wrote were uncommonly thoughtful and rather eloquent. "Going out every other night for patrol," he told his parents on May 14.

On good nights it's beautiful—the water is amazingly phosphorescent— flying fishes which shine like lights are zooming around and you usually get two or three porpoises who lodge right under the bow and no matter how fast the boat goes keep just about six inches ahead of the boat. It's been good training. I have an entirely new crew and when the showdown comes I'd like to be confident they know the difference between firing a gun and winding their watch.

No one here has the slightest interest in politics—they just want to get home—morning, noon and night. . . . As far as Joe wanting to get out here, I know it is futile to say so, but if I were he I would take as much time about it as I could. He is coming out eventually and will be here for a sufficiency and he will want to be back the day after he arrives, if he runs true to the form of everyone else.

Feeling OK. The back has really acted amazingly well and gives me scarcely no trouble and in general feel pretty good. Good bunch out here, so all in all it isn't too bad, but when I was speaking about the people who would just as soon be home I didn't mean to use "They"—I meant "WE."

Never one to romanticize his situation, Jack wrote to Kathleen on June 3, 1943, that the "bubble" he had had about

lying on a cool Pacific island with a warm Pacific maiden hunting bananas for me is definitely a bubble that has burst. You can't even swim—there's some sort of fungus in the water that grows out of your ears—which will be all I need, with pimples on my back—hair on my chest and fungus in my ears I ought to be a natural for the old sailors home in Chelsea, Mass.

I read in Life magazine an article by Johnny Hersey on PTs out here. It didn't have the wild west stuff of "They Were Expendable," but it was a much truer picture. The glamour of PTs just isn't except to the outsider. It's just a matter of night after night patrols at low speed in rough water— two hours on—then sacking out and going on again for another two hours. Even with that however it's a hell of a lot better than any other job in the Navy . . . As a matter of fact this job is somewhat like sailing, in that we spend most of our time trying to get the boat running faster— although it isn't just to beat Daly for the Kennedy cup—it's the Kennedy tail this time.

Speaking of Johnny Hersey I see his new book "Into the Valley" is doing well. He's sitting on top of the hill at this point—a best seller—my girl [Frances Anne Cannon]—two kids—big man on Time—while I'm the one that's down in the God damned valley. That I suppose is life in addition to fortune knows God, say I.

As life and fortune had it, however, Jack Kennedy was just then poised for a series of adventures. In June, the long lull in the Solomons came to an end as the major staging bases in the South Pacific—Guadalcanal, Tulagi and Nouméa—began preparations for the first major Allied offensive in the Pacific war. Suddenly the night patrols took on a new meaning, for if the Allies were able to invade the Japanese strongholds in New Georgia, the ability of the small PT boats to prevent Japanese reinforcements from getting through would be critical.

Writing to his family as Japanese aircraft from Rabaul and Bougainville were striking almost every day, trying to destroy Allied ships and bases, Jack playfully claimed that "to know that all nuns and priests along the Atlantic Coast are putting in a lot of praying time on my behalf is certainly comforting. Kathleen reports that even a fortune-teller says that I'm coming back in one piece. I hope it won't be taken as a sign of lack of confidence in you all or the Church if I continue to duck."

The question of faith appears again and again in Jack's letters from the Pacific, though it is generally disguised in a humorous manner. At Easter, Jack assures his mother that he had gotten to church even though the service was held in a native hut with enemy aircraft in the vicinity. Then on June 24 he tells her, "You will be pleased to know that there is a priest nearby who has let all the natives go and is devoting all his energies to my salvation. I'm stringing along with him—but I'm not going over easy—I want him to work a bit so he'll appreciate it more when he finally has me in the front row every morning screaming halleluyah."

Jack's roommate Johnny Iles remembered very clearly that Jack was going through a troubled time in the South Pacific with his religion. "We were both Catholics and we talked about it a lot. I can clearly recall sitting in a jeep one night on Tulagi, having a long discussion. Jack had lost his religion . . . He said he'd work it out someday. He told me he'd go see Fulton Sheen when he got home."

Speculation about what this religious struggle meant to Jack leads to the recognition of the absolute irreconcilability between the contrasting messages the Kennedy children received from their parents. From their mother they were told: Be Irish, be Catholic, follow the rules, live by the limits. Yet to accept their mother's conscious message was to deny the unconscious message suggested by every contour of their father's life, which told them never to let themselves be limited by anything, not by their Irish Catholic background, nor by convention, nor even by the rules of the game. Perhaps in trying to sort out his feelings about religion Jack was trying to shape his own identity within the family structure.

Once again, however, the pace of events overtook Jack's concern with religion. On the night of July 17–18, a Navy patrol bomber picked up the "Japanese express" in nearby Vella Gulf. According to the dispatch from Admiral Halsey, it was reported to be three cruisers, six destroyers and two transports. By radio, Commander Warfield ordered the *PT 109* and two other PT boats to go into the waters in search of the express. No doubt the crew of the *109* was tense, for this expedition promised to be their first direct confrontation with the enemy.

But, though Jack kept the *PT 109* in the water until three hours after midnight, neither he nor his companion boats were able to make any contact with the express. The decision was made to turn back, but just at that moment a Japanese plane came over and dropped a flare right above the boat. Two large bombs fell on either side of the 109. Kennedy unmuffled his engines at once and slowly pushed the throttles wide open, zigzagging and laying smoke. It was the nightmare of every PT commander to be hit by Japanese fire, for each boat, when fully fueled, carried three thousand gallons of gasoline held behind a thin plywood edge, rendering it a floating firebomb. Two of Jack's men were hit by shrapnel, Maurice Kowal in the leg, Leon Drawdy in the arm. Seeing them fall, Kennedy turned the helm over to his exec, Lennie Thom, grabbed a first-aid kit and attended to their wounds. At 4 A.M. the 109 returned to base.

"We had a letter from Jack the night before last," Kennedy Senior told his golf partner, Jerry O'Leary, "and evidently he's had a few close calls, a couple of his boys having been wounded and the ship shot up a number of times . . . he assures us that he is all right, except of course, there is a note that he's seen what he went out to see and he'll be glad to come home but I hate to mix into any of his business for fear I'll do the wrong thing." (Perhaps the failure of Rosemary's operation was placing a temporary brake on Kennedy's interventions in his children's lives.)

Jack later told his family that one of his men, Andrew Kirksey, a married man with three children, had been badly unnerved by the bombing. He had been with Jack for as long as Jack had been in the Pacific, but evidently the closeness of the bomb had come as a great shock.

> He never really got over it, he always seemed to have the feeling that something was going to happen to him. He never said anything about being put ashore—he didn't want to—but the next time we came down the line—I was going to let him work on the base force. When a fellow gets the feeling that he's in for it—the only thing to do is let him get off the boat—because strangely enough they always seem to be the ones that do get it. I don't know whether it's coincidence or what.

As it happened, Jack was unable to accomplish Kirksey's transfer, and Kirksey was one of the thirteen men aboard the 109 on the night of August 1–2. In the late afternoon of August 1, Commander Warfield received word that the enemy express was expected to run that night, with the Japanese base at Vila Plantation on southern Kolombangara as its destination. Shortly after the message arrived, a fleet of eighteen Japanese dive bombers attacked Rendova in a daring effort to destroy the PTs, many of which were just then in the process of refueling there in preparation for their nightly patrol. Fortunately, only two PTs were hit and demolished by the bombs. All that day, Jack had been trying to get the 37-millimeter gun properly mounted on the forward deck of the *109*. But with the interruption of the air raid the job was still not complete by nightfall, so he had his men simply lash the gun to a makeshift mount with line.

At 6:30 that night, fifteen PTs, including the *109*, left the base to patrol the Blackett Strait. Collectively, it was by far the greatest lineup of firepower the PT force had ever deployed against an express. If they made contact with the enemy destroyers and fired, even if only a few of the torpedoes hit, the effect would be devastating.

It was a starless night, black and overcast. From Rabaul, as expected, the express was barreling southward. It was composed of four first-line destroyers: *Amagiri*, *Hagikaze*, *Arashi* and *Shigure*. The first big express the Japanese had mounted in many days, it carried nine hundred troops. At midnight, the *PT 159* picked up five pips on its radar, indicating the near presence of four destroyers. With the *PT 157* following, the *159* fired four torpedoes, but in the process its torpedo tube caught fire, lighting the sky like a beacon and giving the Japanese a fine point of aim. After firing her own torpedoes, the *157* swung between the *159* and the destroyer to lay a smokescreen so that the Japanese couldn't see the fire. Then, with shells from the destroyer being fired all around, the two PTs moved quickly away, zigzagging and laying smoke.

Patrolling nearby, the *109* saw gunfire and a searchlight in the direction of the northern coast of Kolombangara. Kennedy called general quarters, and the crew went to battle stations. Unable to ascertain whether the searchlight came from shore or from ships close in, Kennedy intercepted the *PT 162* and was incorrectly informed by the commander, John Lowrey, that it was apparently from shore batteries. Then, suddenly, Kennedy intercepted a terse radio message: "I am being chased through Ferguson Passage! Have fired fish!"

At this point, in what naval officer Robert Bulkeley later called "the most confused and least effectively executed action the PTs had been in," both the *109* and the *162* made a hasty withdrawal, fearing that in the glow of the strong searchlights they could easily have been shot. Had the two skippers recognized the lights for what they were, enemy destroyer fire, they might have trailed the source of the light and found a golden opportunity to engage the enemy. But as it was, both Kennedy and Lowrey sped off into the blackness until orders were received to resume their normal patrol station.

It was now about 2:30 A.M. In formation with two other PTs, the *109* was patrolling on one engine at idling speed. Ross was on the bow as lookout, Thom was standing beside the cockpit, Kennedy was at the wheel, and with him in the cockpit was Maguire, the radioman; Marney was in the forward turret; Mauer, the quartermaster, was standing beside Thom; Albert was in the after turret; McMahon was in the engine room; Kirksey was lying down on the starboard side. The location of the other four crew members at that moment is unknown. Suddenly a dark shape loomed up on *PT 109*'s starboard bow at a distance of two to three hundred yards. The man in the forward turret shouted, "Ship at two o'clock!" The dark shape was the destroyer *Amagiri*, bearing down at high speed and heading straight for the *109*.

Kennedy spun the wheel to the left in preparation for firing torpedoes. But the *109*, running on only one of three engines so as to make a minimum wake, answered sluggishly. Kennedy again whirled the wheel to port, and Ross went through the motion of slamming a shell into the breach of the 37-millimeter antitank gun. But then, before the PT had turned thirty degrees, the huge destroyer rammed directly into it, crunching across the bow with a tremendous force that split the boat in two. Traveling at an estimated speed of forty knots, the *Amagiri* vibrated sharply but continued right on course.

At impact, Kennedy was thrown hard to the left in the cockpit and he thought, This is how it feels to be killed. In a moment he found himself on his back on the deck, looking up at the destroyer as it passed through his boat.

Down below, in the engine room, McMahon was thrown painfully against the bulkhead, landing in a sitting position. A tremendous burst of flame came back at him from the exploding gas tanks, and he put his hands over his face, waiting to die. Then suddenly, just after the flames reached his body, he felt a cold splash of water hit him. His half of the PT was sinking, and he was being sucked downward into the sea. Struggling upward through the water, he saw a yellow glow—gasoline burning through water. He broke surface again, trying desperately to keep away from the fire.

Standing in the forward turret at the time of the crash was nineteen-year-old Harold Marney, who had just come aboard the *109*. The first one to sight the destroyer, he was never seen again after the crash. Nor was Kirksey, the father of three who had been living with the fear of death ever since the bombing incident two weeks before.

In all, scarcely ten seconds had elapsed between the sighting of the dark shape and the crash. As the destroyer rushed off into the darkness, there was an eerie silence broken only by the sound of gasoline burning. As it happened, Kennedy's half of the PT had stayed afloat, and when he shouted "Who's aboard?" feeble answers came from five men clinging desperately to the hull—Maguire, Ross, Thom, Mauer and Albert. But there was no time to rejoice in being alive, for at that moment a fire ignited only twenty feet from the boat, and Kennedy, thinking it might reach the hull, ordered all hands to abandon ship. Then, when the danger had passed, they all scrambled back aboard.

Once again Kennedy shouted for survivors, and from the darkness in the distance came the cries of the five men who had survived the sinking of the other half of the boat. "Mr. Kennedy! Mr. Kennedy!" Harris shouted. "McMahon is badly hurt." "Pappy" McMahon, the engineer, was forty-one and a favorite of all the men in the crew. Kennedy took off his shoes and his shirt, then dived in and swam toward the voice. Meanwhile, Thom and Ross struck out for the others. When Kennedy reached Harris and McMahon, he found the latter suffering from serious burns on his face and his hands. As McMahon was unable to swim because of his burns, Kennedy towed him back toward the boat, working against a current so strong that it took forty-five minutes to make a hundred yards. He then returned for two other men. It was 5 A.M. before all the survivors were gathered together on the tilted deck of the sheared PT.

Stretched out on the deck, the men rejoiced at being alive and speculated on how long it would take for the other PTs to come back and pick them up. But as it turned out, the other boats, having seen the fiery collision from a distance, assumed that no one had survived, and back at the base, services were held for the souls of the thirteen men of the 109. As the day of August 2 dawned, a message was working its way across the ocean to the home of Joseph P. Kennedy in Hyannis Port, informing him that his son Jack was missing in action.

By 10 A.M. of the crew's first day in the water, it became obvious that the *PT 109* would soon sink, so Kennedy decided to abandon ship for a small island, Plum Pudding Island, which could be seen to the southeast about four miles away. At 2 P.M., once again taking McMahon in tow, he started out. Clenching the ties of the wounded man's life jacket in his teeth, thereby converting the kapok into a towline, Kennedy faced down into the water while McMahon floated along above him on his back. The other swimmers followed, the stronger pushing and towing a float, rigged from the makeshift gun mount, to which two nonswimmers were tied. It took five hours to reach land.

When the exhausted men arrived on shore, they discovered that the island was even smaller than they had realized, only seventy yards wide, with six coconut trees and some brush. And to their dismay they realized, once they got their bearings, that the island was south of Ferguson Passage, the only place where there was much hope of meeting other PT boats. Kennedy decided to swim out into the night over the reefs to the edge of Ferguson Passage in the hope of flagging a passing PT boat. The men objected and tried to dissuade him, arguing that he was too tired to negotiate the unknown currents. But within thirty minutes of his arrival on the atoll, Kennedy was gone.

Making his way along the reefs, he reached Ferguson Passage by 8 P.M., and there he remained, hugging his lantern, for four hours. But that night, for the first night in many, the PT boats had decided to go patrolling west toward Vella Lavella instead of east through Ferguson Passage. Giving up hope, Kennedy started back, but as he swam through the darkness he got caught in a fast-moving current that swept him right past the little island. For hours, his body drifted. His mind was a jumble. He thought he had never known such deep trouble. But finally he bumped up on a reef, crawled ashore on a sand spit and passed out. Later he awoke and made his way back to the island, arriving about noon. The other survivors, who had given him up for dead, were overjoyed. He was vomiting, feverish and exhausted, when they reached him. "Ross, you try it tonight," he said. Then he passed out again. That night Ross swam into the darkness, but he too encountered nothing.

The following day Kennedy decided to change islands, hoping to get closer to Ferguson Passage. With the uncomplaining McMahon once again in tow, the eleven survivors made their way to Olasana Island, a larger island which, it was hoped, might even have water. For by now, not having had a good drink of water for three days, the men were suffering acutely from thirst. But when they reached Olasana the only source of water they found was rain, which they tried to catch in their mouths as they lay on their backs during a storm.

The next afternoon Kennedy asked Ross to swim with him to an island called Nauru, even nearer Ferguson Passage. Near the center of that island they found a treasure chest: a one-man dugout canoe, a fifty-five-gallon drum full of fresh water, and a crate containing crackers and candy. Leaving Ross on Nauru, Kennedy paddled the canoe back to Olasana in order to distribute the crackers and water to the men. When he arrived he found a fire going and two friendly islanders helping the survivors. Returning to fetch Ross the following morning, Kennedy picked up a coconut with a smooth shell and scratched a message on it with a jackknife: "Eleven alive Native knows Posit and reefs Naura Island Kennedy." Then he said to the islanders, "Rendova, Rendova." They seemed to understand.

All that day Kennedy and Ross "lay in a sickly daze," and that night, fearful that the natives might not reach Rendova, Kennedy persuaded Ross to go out with him once more into Ferguson Passage. Caught in a sudden rainsquall, they were swept up against a reef on Cross Island, where they remained the rest of the night. The next morning the two officers were wakened early by the sound of four approaching islanders.

"I have a letter for you, sir," one of them said, in an excellent English accent.

Kennedy tore the note open. It said:

> On His Majesty's Service
> To the Senior Officer
> Nauru Island
> I have just learned of your presence on Nauru Island. I am in command of a New Zealand infantry patrol operating in conjunction with US Army troops on New Georgia. I strongly advise that you come with these natives to me. Meanwhile, I shall be in radio communication with your authorities at Rendova and we can finalize plans to collect balance of your party.
> Lt. Wincote

Reading the formal message, beginning with the words "On His Majesty's Service," with a six-day growth of beard, half naked and sick, Kennedy turned to Ross and smiled. "You've got to hand it to the British," he said.

They all shook hands and the four islanders took Ross and Kennedy in their canoe back to Olasana to tell the others the good news. There they built a lean-to for McMahon, whose burns had begun to rot and stink, and for Ross, whose arm, lacerated by coral from the swim along the reef the night before, had swelled to the size of a thigh. Then, in the middle of the night, moving under cover in darkened canoes, the eleven survivors made a successful rendezvous with a PT boat from Rendova. Kennedy jumped aboard first and hugged the men—all of them his friends. The boat roared back to the base, where the eleven survivors were given brandy sent by the squadron surgeon to revive them.

Meanwhile, halfway around the world, Joe Kennedy had been living with the knowledge that Jack was "missing in action" for four days. Having heard the news from unofficial sources, most likely through his connections with Navy Undersecretary James Forrestal, he had decided not to tell Rose anything about it until he was absolutely certain. In her memoirs Rose seems grateful to her husband for saving her from an unnecessary torment, yet once again, as with Rosemary, one wonders about the continued intimacy of a marriage in which one partner could keep such fateful knowledge from the other. According to Rose, the first news she heard was a radio announcement reporting that the missing John Kennedy had been found. At that moment Joe was in his car returning home from an early-morning horseback ride in Osterville.

Listening to the same radio bulletin, he momentarily lost control of the car and drove off the road. When he returned to the house, he told Rose the entire story and the two of them fell into each other's arms.

The news of the *PT 109* affair made the front pages of the major newspapers. In all the accounts the focus was on Kennedy, if only because his name was the best known. In *The New York Times* of August 20, 1943, the headline read: "Kennedy's Son Is Hero in Pacific as Destroyer Splits His PT Boat," while the *Herald Tribune* spoke of Kennedy's son writing a "blazing new saga in PT boat annals." In the years to come these heroic versions of the incident, magnified by an account written by John Hersey in *The New Yorker* and republished in *Reader's Digest*, would become an important element in the development of John Kennedy's early political career. Yet critics would argue that there was nothing heroic about the incident in the first place and that Kennedy was deliberately exploiting his own role at the expense of the real contributions made by his fellow crew members.

There is obvious truth in the argument that the incident itself, the ramming of the *109*, was anything but heroic. Indeed, in a general history of torpedo boats, Bryan Cooper argues that the whole engagement that night was a great failure for the entire PT squadron, "their least effective action since the beginning of the Solomons campaign." Here was an opportunity for directly engaging the enemy that would not come easily again, yet, against all their training, "the boats attacked independently, without informing the others when they located the enemy." As a result, only half of the fifteen PTs fired off their torpedoes and none of the torpedoes fired could be confirmed as hits.

Yet, if young Kennedy could take little pride in the humiliating moment when his boat was unexpectedly rammed by the *Amagiri*, it seems unjust to deny him praise for his part in the rescue of his crew. Nor does it seem fair to blame Jack for the attention that was focused on him. Indeed, through it all he seemed somewhat embarrassed by the fuss that was being made over him, stating right from the start that he never considered himself a hero. And much later, when asked at a press conference how he became a hero in the South Pacific, he simply smiled and said, "It was easy. They cut my PT boat in half."

As the news of Jack's heroic rescue spread from America to Europe, Joseph Kennedy received dozens of congratulatory letters. "What a splendid story it is of your son John's gallantry," Beaverbrook wrote. "How proud a father you must be . . . I am so glad for you." In response to this and other letters, Kennedy penned an ingenious reply which managed to link Jack's bravery with the best of America's national character: "It certainly should occur to a great many people that although a boy is brought up in our present economic system with all the advantages that opportunity and wealth can give, the initiative that America instills in its people is always there. And to take that away from us means there is really nothing left to live for."

Yet, even as he waxed eloquent about America's destiny, Joe Senior was pulling every string he could, as he admitted in a letter to Joe Junior, to bring Jack home from the South Pacific because, he wrote, "I imagine he's pretty well shot to pieces by now." "I'm sure if he were John Doake's son or Harry Hopkins' son he'd be home long before this," he told Arthur Houghton. Never, it seems, did Kennedy's pride in his son's adventure catch him up in a spirit of patriotism that diminished for a moment his basic horror of war.

Nor is there any indication in the letters Jack wrote to his family after the incident that it had changed any of his own feelings about war. On the contrary, in responding to the news that his brother Bobby wanted to get into PT boats, Jack emphatically advised that he was "too young to be out here . . . To try to come steaming out here at eighteen is no good . . . It's just that the fun goes out of the war in a fairly short time and I don't think that Bobby is ready yet to come out. I also think Joe is nuts to come. He's doing more than his share by merely flying, but I suppose he wants to get away."

Then, in a letter written on September 12, Jack expressed his deep sadness at losing his two men.

It certainly brought home how real the war is—and when I read the papers from home—how superficial is most of the talking and thinking about it. When I read that we will fight Japs for years if necessary and will sacrifice hundreds of thousands if we must—I always like to check from where he's talking—it's seldom out here. People get so used to talking about billions of dollars and millions of soldiers that thousands dead sounds like drops in the bucket. But if those thousands want to live as much as the ten I saw —they should measure their words with great great care. Perhaps all that won't be necessary—and it can be all done by bombing.

After the 109 was destroyed, Jack was given command of another boat, the PT 59. It was a new type of boat, with guns replacing torpedoes, and Jack was excited about his crew. Still, he told his father, he had finally learned the wisdom of the old naval doctrine of keeping his bowels and his mouth shut and never volunteering. Writing to Inga Arvad at this same time, he confessed that he used to believe that no matter what happened he would live through it.

It's a funny thing that as long as you have that feeling you seem to get through. I've lost that feeling lately. As a matter of fact, I don't feel badly about it. If anything happens to me I have this knowledge that if I live to be 100 I could only improve the quantity of my life, not the quality. This sounds gloomy as hell but you are the only person I'd say it to anyway. As a matter of fact, knowing you has been the brightest part of an extremely bright 26 years.

# CHAPTER 37

# FORBIDDEN
# ROMANCE

During the time Jack was missing in action Joe was in North Carolina learning to fly a new and strangely menacing plane, the B-24 Liberator. Considered "fast and dangerous," the Liberator was "a stable plane in firm hands," but in uncertain ones "it flew like a boxcar and landed like a weary truck." The pilot and co-pilot sat a yard apart "in low seats sunk below the long and bulbous nose"; its four big engines were mounted so low that "a tall man could peer into the cockpit by chinning himself." Loaded, it weighed more than thirty tons. Though Joe had never flown anything larger than a twin-engine seaplane, he managed to "check out" in the Liberator in six days.

In learning to fly the Liberator, Joe was preparing himself for a new assignment for which he had volunteered in the middle of the summer. On July 15, Jim Reedy, who had been Joe's executive officer during his training, had been picked as commanding officer for a new squadron, VB-110, which was scheduled to leave for England in September to join the RAF patrols searching the English Channel and the Bay of Biscay for German U-boats. The moment Joe heard about the dangerous assignment at a meeting called by Reedy, he volunteered. "The most excited man in the room was Joe Kennedy," a fellow officer recalled. "He was bursting with enthusiasm." As it happened, a great but deadly adventure awaited all the men who volunteered that day and those who joined them later. It was, indeed, an extraordinary group: they would win two Navy Crosses, four Distinguished Flying Crosses, twenty-seven Air Medals and two Purple Hearts. They would lose twelve planes. And sixty-eight of them would die in action.

As soon as he had tested out on the plane, Joe was given the task of ferrying new Liberators back to Norfolk from the factory in San Diego. It was during a hectic period when he was making five cross-country trips in eight days that the news of Jack's encounter with the enemy broke. Arriving in San Diego, Joe met Nancy and Ned Burke, friends from home. Ned had just received a letter from a boy in the Pacific saying that Jack was missing. "I read this about three hours before I saw the papers," Joe later wrote to his family, "and got quite a fright." But apparently he didn't call his parents at the time, for the following week Joe Senior wrote to his son that he had been "considerably upset that during those few days after the news of Jack's rescue we had no word from you. I thought that you would very likely call up to see whether we had any news as to how Jack was."

Explaining his silence as a consequence of his grueling schedule in ferrying the Liberators across the country, Joe wrote a long, jaunty letter to his family on August 29, 1943. "With the great quantity of reading material coming in on the actions of the Kennedys in various parts of the world," he began, "and the countless number of paper clippings about our young hero—the battler of the wars of Banana River, San Juan, Virginia Beach . . . will now step to the microphone and give out with a few words of his own activities."

A week later Joe was granted a few days' leave, and he arrived in Hyannis Port in time for his father's fifty-fifth birthday. He brought his commanding officer, Jim Reedy, with him, and Police Commissioner Joe Timilty was down from Boston. So, too, was Judge John Burns. At a festive dinner that night, while Joe sat at his father's right, the judge proposed a toast: "To Ambassador Joe Kennedy, father of our hero, our *own* hero, Lieutenant John F. Kennedy of the United States Navy." According to Timilty, that was the end of the toast. The judge sat down and Joe lifted his glass to his father and his absent brother, a tense grin plastered on his face. But Timilty claims that that night, lying in his bed, he could hear young Joe crying, unable to hold in his frustration any longer.

If Joe was feeling hurt, his mother did not see it. "Joe Darling," Rose wrote a few days later. "It was wonderful last week to have seen you looking so well and feeling full of pep and it was great luck to have had you home on your father's birthday." And with her letter she sent along a silver medal which had been blessed by a priest and which she wanted Joe to take with him to England.

When Joe arrived in England, Kathleen was already there, having left America in June to work for the Red Cross. Through the fall of 1942 and the spring of 1943, she had been trying to figure out a way of getting overseas. Though she was doing very well on the *Times-Herald* (she had successfully taken over Inga's column), Kathleen still wanted to return to England, and her longings grew stronger as she watched many of her friends leave home.

In May 1942 John White had enlisted in the Marine Corps, bringing to an end their year-long romance. Just before he left, White finally mustered the courage to tell Kathleen that he loved her. It was at the end of the evening, and as he was rubbing her back he was suddenly overwhelmed. "Feel all kinds of affection for the little girl at such times," he confided in his diary, "what a sweet, sincere, good-hearted little thing she is." "I love you, Kathleen," he whispered before she drifted off to sleep. The following day, nervous about his admission, White took her directly home after dinner and said a quick good night. He started down the hall, but she came running after him, crying.

"Did you mean what you said last night?" she asked. He nodded.

"I love you too, John," she said.

The next day White headed off for Marine boot camp at Parris Island, South Carolina.

Lem Billings was the next to go, leaving in July for North Africa, just in time for the Battle of El Alamein, which was the beginning of the Allied march to Tripoli. "Here we are on the high seas at last," he had written in July. "All I can say is that whole set up is far better than I possibly imagined. I'm really enjoying every minute of it."

From Tripoli, Lem wrote to Kathleen about a strafing attack on the hospital unit to which he was attached. During the bombing a wounded officer was brought into the hospital.

> He had been leaping feet first into a slit trench when Jerry was bombing —a bomb hit very close to his trench and got him in both legs. There was a wonderful surgical team attached to the outfit—but they couldn't save his legs—they had to amputate both of them. It was Lord Halifax's son [Richard Wood]. I understand one of Halifax's sons had been killed in action previously. It certainly is a tough break. I wonder if you knew this one.

As it happened, Kathleen not only knew the handsome Richard Wood, but even as she received Lem's letter she was spending a lot of time with him in America, where he had come to get his wooden legs fitted; at the time, Lord Halifax was the British Ambassador to the United States. Richard and Kick became very close in Washington, so much so that he reportedly fell in love with her. "He is the most amazing young man," Kathleen wrote to Lem. "I've never seen such spirit in my life. He has told me long stories about life in the desert and it just amazes me that anyone who has been through such experiences can go back and live a normal life."

Then that summer, in August 1942, came the first death among Kathleen's friends. She and George Mead, son of the founder of the huge Mead Paper Company in Ohio, had been friends ever since they met as children on Cape Cod. When he was in Marine officer training at Quantico, Virginia, he would often come up to Washington on weekends to visit Kathleen and Jack. George was killed on Guadalcanal in the first American offensive there. "He died trying to rescue the body of one of his men," Kathleen wrote to Lem. She had learned of his death through a valiant letter from his mother which so impressed her that she wrote back, prophetically, "Future days may bring bad news to us all, but remembering your words and the way you have acted, one cannot help but feel—Please God, let me act in a similar fashion."

Both Kathleen and Jack were profoundly moved by George's death, and it may have prompted Jack's desire to go to the Solomons. When he did get to Guadalcanal, he visited George's grave and wrote to his parents about it. "He is buried near the beach where he fell—it was extremely sad."

With George dead, her brothers away and so many of her friends leaving, Kathleen was more determined than ever to get to England. When she was finally accepted by the American Red Cross, to serve in one of the rest-and-recreation clubs it was setting up all over England for American servicemen on leave, she was overjoyed. Installed generally in hotels, the clubs provided a cafeteria, a snack bar, showers, a barbershop, a tailor shop, a shoeshine parlor, games and other recreation, reading and writing rooms and a first-aid room, in addition to sleeping quarters. One of the greatest attractions was a large map of the United States labeled "Is there someone here from your home town? Watch the flag." The map was dotted with tiny red flags with the names and home addresses of GIs using the club at the moment. This device led to many happy reunions.

The young American women whom the Red Cross recruited to staff the clubs were expected to live in the club to which they were assigned and provide various services to the GIs, which included greeting the boys, directing them to the club's facilities, dancing, playing cards and other games, providing help in writing letters, and listening as they talked of their hopes and fears. In signing up for the program, Kathleen was taking a chance. Though she specified London as her first choice for assignment, she could just as easily have been placed in a remote area of the English countryside, and in fact for a while there was a danger of her being sent to Australia. But, with her father on her side, pulling strings with the higher-ups as he always did, she figured it was worth the gamble.

And she was right. For when Kathleen arrived in England she found herself assigned to the Hans Crescent Club, one of the most sought-after posts in the entire country, located in the heart of London in an old Victorian hotel just one block from Harrods. The assignment took a little doing, as Joe Kennedy's friend Tim McInerny, who was posted at U.S. Army Headquarters in London, explained. "I consider ourselves most lucky that we were able to keep her in London," McInerny wrote to Joe, "as they generally farm out these girls to air fields and camps in the country for about six months til they get seasoned and forget about the States. But by putting the squeeze on a few people and with . . . [Admiral Harold R.] Stark's aid I think we were able to get over the worst part of the job. She is really a delight and a real Kennedy, straight and true, in every sense of the word and I can assure you that any little thing that I can do for her is amply repaid by gaining her friendship."

While he was paving the way for her assignment by using his contacts with the Army, the Navy and the Red Cross (through Harvey Gibson, its head) Kennedy also tried to prepare Kathleen for the anti-Kennedy sentiment she was bound to run into in England. "Don't get too upset if you hear the British talking about your Dad," he warned her on July 3, 1943. "After all, the only crime I can be accused of is that I was pro-

American instead of pro-English. I don't blame them for being mad at me . . . I don't care what they say, so don't let it bother you."

As it turned out, the job was a little more than Kathleen had bargained for, since it allowed her only a day and a half off each week—usually not weekends, as they were the busiest times. "I'm not sure yet but I don't think this is what I was born for," she admitted to Frank Waldrop after her first weeks of jitterbugging, playing gin rummy, Ping-Pong and bridge and just being an American girl among fifteen hundred GIs far from home. Her schedule made it difficult for her to spend time with her friends, the very reason she had wanted to come to London in the first place. At the start, trying to see as many people as she could in the narrow time allotted, she was allowing her social life to spill over into the club. "The director . . . just had a little chat with me," Kathleen confessed to her parents; " . . . the first complaint was that I had too many phone calls. Second, I should cut down on my personal life. I don't see how I could possibly do it any more than I am already doing."

After receiving a long letter from Kathleen detailing her social life, her brother Jack teasingly observed, "I don't know how much of the big personality the Americans are getting as she seems to be doing a good deal of crossing with Billy of Hartington and Tony [Earl of Rosslyn] . . . There is only so much butter and a good deal of bread and she seems to be spreading it pretty thin, but I imagine she'll manage OK . . . It's great that she can be over there."

In her first months on the job, Kathleen also confronted a certain measure of resentment toward her on the part of her fellow workers. To their mind, she was always receiving preferential treatment. Indeed, when she arrived another young woman was summarily dispatched to Londonderry in order to make room for her. And during her first week in London, Mrs. Harvey Gibson gave a tea in her honor to introduce her to some of the other girls—hardly a routine practice for new recruits. Then there was all the publicity about her, some of which, of course, was generated by her father. One summer day, a photographer on the *Daily Mail* in London photographed Kathleen in her blue-gray uniform on a bicycle pedaling to work. The photograph was snapped up by the *Boston Globe* and reproduced all over the States as a symbol of the all-American girl coming to the aid of the GIs abroad.

"I judge . . . that you are not especially happy with your post there," Kennedy wrote to her,

so I've asked Tim and I'm asking you to let me know exactly what I can do to help you. I don't want to stick my oar in and mess it up for you . . . You must remember that those pictures of you in the paper and the fact that everybody in England who is worthwhile is on your team is bound to affect a lot of those pompous bosses of yours as well as doing something to your associations. It is human nature—always has been . . . and is definitely no reflection on you . . . Do let me know about your job there and whether I can help you.

Kathleen replied that she would much prefer a job in public relations, but when this proved impossible (Red Cross policy required that British citizens be hired for such positions) she made up her mind to make the best of the situation. "What a woman that gal is, Joe!" Tim McInerny wrote. "She has this town under control with a vengeance."

"Aren't you longing to hear about a day in the life of the Red Cross girl," Kathleen wrote to Lem:

Live here in the Club where I work. Am on the job at ten. There are always boys wanting information of various sorts—books out of the library, ping pong balls, etc. If there isn't too much doing I may sit down and have a chat with one of them or more . . . In the evening we might be having a dance which begins at 7:30. I check the girls in and after the intermission go in and have a few merry dances . . . You wouldn't recognize old Kick who used to walk around with her nose quite far in the air if she had to go in the subway to get to the Automat with you. I'd give my two tiny hands, covered as they are with warts for a meal in the Automat and I wouldn't care if I had to sit with two dirty truck drivers. As a matter of fact they are probably the only people I know how to charm now.

And limited as her nights off were, Kathleen still managed to lead an active social life. "I am really so pleased to be back," she wrote to her family, "I've never been so happy about anything. Sometimes I feel I have more good, close friends here than in America." No sooner had Kathleen arrived in England than Lady Astor once more took her under her wing, inviting her to Cliveden on weekends and to dinner parties in London. "She has gone very far out of her way to be kind to me," Kathleen told her parents. "I think in a way I remind her of herself when she first came to England."

In a letter to Joe Kennedy, Tony Rosslyn wrote that Kathleen was surrounded by her old friends and declared that she was exactly his ideal of what he wanted for a wife, though he would never let her know that as he didn't suppose she would ever have him. Then there was William Douglas-Home, who squired her about, but while Kathleen found him "very good company," she told Jack that that was as far as it went. And there was Richard Wood, who had returned to his family's estate in Yorkshire and was trying out yet another new pair of legs.

But, of all the men in her life, Billy Hartington remained the one she cared about the most. Billy was stationed in Scotland with the Coldstream Guards when Kathleen arrived in England, but as soon as he heard she was back he traveled all the way down to London, and on July 10, 1943, they saw each other for the first time in four years. Kathleen later told her mother that they both knew that night that they still loved each other, more than they had ever loved anyone else, but until they could figure out some solution to the problem of religion there was nothing they could do about it. In the meantime, Kathleen was determined to project a nonchalant air so as not to make her family worry.

"It really is funny to see people put their heads together the minute we arrive any place," she wrote to her parents after her first date with Billy.

> There's heavy betting on when we're going to announce it. Some people have gotten the idea I'm going to give in. Little do they know. Some of those old Devonshire ancestors would jump out of their graves if anything happened to some of their ancient traditions. It just amuses me to see how worried they all are.

Two weeks later, Billy invited Kathleen to his seaside home at Eastbourne, where she spent a wonderful weekend with his parents, who could not help but enjoy her lively company despite their worries about the future.

> For 24 hours I forgot all about the war [Kathleen wrote to Jack]. Billy is just the same, a bit older, a bit more ducal but we get on as well as ever. It is queer as he is so unlike anyone I have ever known at home or any place really. Of course I know he would never give in about the religion and he knows I never would. It's all rather difficult as he is very, very fond of me and as long as I am about he'll never marry. However much he loved me I can easily understand his position. It's really too bad because I'm sure I would be a most efficient Duchess of Devonshire in the postwar world, and as I'd have a castle in Ireland, one in Scotland, one in Yorkshire, and one in Sussex, I could keep my old nautical brothers in their old age. But that's the way it goes. Everyone in London is buzzing with rumors, and no matter what happens we've given them something to talk about. I can't really understand why I like Englishmen so much as they treat one in quite an offhand manner and aren't really as nice to their women as Americans, but I suppose it's just that sort of treatment that women really like. That's your technique isn't it?

Securing another leave two weekends later, Billy came down to visit Kathleen at Lady Astor's, where he had to sleep on the floor. "I wish his father could have seen him," Kathleen joked with her family. "Of course on Sunday morning there was the great problem of my going to church, four miles away, but finally I hopped on a bike." Writing to Rose after the weekend, Nancy Astor reported how happy Kathleen was to be back in her spiritual home and how pleased all her friends were to have her back again. "She talks a lot about you and the family," Nancy concluded, deliberately omitting any mention of Billy.

Whether Rose was kept in the dark about the seriousness of Kathleen's feelings toward Billy, or whether she simply preferred not to see, Joe recognized the true situation almost immediately. Hearing regularly from his faithful correspondent Tim McInerny, he knew all he needed to know about Kathleen's social life in England. Right from the start of the difficult courtship, he let Kathleen know that he would support her no matter what she decided. "As far as I'm concerned," he wrote on September 8, 1943, displaying a greater flexibility with his daughter than with his sons, "I'll gamble with your judgment. The best is none too good for you, but if you decide it's a Chinaman, it's okay with me. That's how much I think of you."

While Kathleen was "absolutely thrilled," as she put it in a letter to Lem, "to be back in my old stamping grounds," she never for a moment lost touch with her family. As busy as she was, she managed to write to her parents and her siblings almost every day. "Of course the news about Jack is the most exciting thing I've ever heard," she wrote to her parents as soon as the first stories about the *PT 109* appeared in the London papers. When Joe Junior arrived on the southern coast of England in September and called her while she was having lunch with Clark Gable and former actress Virginia Cherrill (then the Countess of Jersey), she described his call as "the biggest event of the week." And whenever she received a letter from her younger brothers and sisters, she would read it aloud to all her friends.

In the middle of October, Joe Junior managed to secure an assignment that would take him to northern England to pick up some matériel, and en route, by what he described to his parents as "some deft arranging," he landed at an airfield near London so that he could see Kathleen. For three weeks now he had been flying under the RAF, and while he noted that the night life on the Cornish coast consisted only of a few local pubs which ran out of beer at nine o'clock, he was finding it a great pleasure to work with the British airmen. "They are so far ahead of the US in the work which we are doing," he reported to his parents. "Also they have a much better general attitude and don't try to make things as difficult as possible."

As soon as he set foot in London, Joe headed for the Hans Crescent Club, where he surprised Kathleen with a crate of eggs brought all the way from home. Finding her surrounded by GIs who thought she was "easily the nicest girl there," he sat down to play gin rummy with her, to the sound of American songs blaring from the jukebox in the corner. That night, after having dinner together, they went to the 400 Club, the plush nightclub which was still "the place to go." Despite the blackout, the same crowd sat at the same tables, including the "Dukie Wookie" of Marlborough, as Joe and Kick called him, and the Argentine ambassador's daughters Bebe and Chiquita Carcano.

The next night Joe had dinner with his friend Bill Hearst, W.R.'s son, who was stationed in London as a war correspondent. Dining at the Savoy, they were joined by one of Joe's old girlfriends, Virginia Gilliat, who was now Lady Sykes, and by Patricia Wilson, a beautiful young woman with dark curly hair and deep-blue eyes. Seated next to Pat Wilson, Joe was immediately intrigued by her warm, open manner and her infectious laugh. He soon found out that she had been born in Australia, the daughter of a sheep rancher, but had come to London with her mother when she was seventeen and there had met and married the wealthy twenty-one-year-old Earl of Jersey. Theirs had been the "dream match" of the year, with a spectacular wedding in St. Margaret's, Westminster, but within two years the Earl had taken up with Virginia Cherrill, and the year after that he and Pat were divorced. When she was twenty-five Pat had remarried, this time to a banker in his late thirties named Robin Wilson. From her two marriages she had three small children. At the time Joe met her, Wilson was a major in the British Army stationed in Libya and had been away from home for over two years.

Joe learned that Pat was living in a tile-roofed cottage called Crastock Farm in Woking, about one hour south of London. Woking, as it turned out, was on the same train line as Dunkeswell in Devon, where Joe's squadron was soon to be moving. Before the evening ended, Pat had invited him to visit her on one of his leaves. A few weeks later, Kathleen reported to her father that Pat particularly wanted to be remembered to him; apparently Pat and her banker husband had spent some time with the Ambassador three years before.

As much as Joe enjoyed the flying, he greatly anticipated his weekend leaves, for the conditions at Dunkeswell, as he described them to his parents, were like "living in a mud hole." The sixty-four officers and 106 men of his squadron had arrived at "Mudville Heights" in the middle of the wettest fall that Devon had experienced. All day and night, the base seemed to float in a sea of mud. "We hopped, skipped and jumped," radioman Dee Vilan remembered, "like a troupe of Martha Graham dancers executing a fertility rite." The men lived in primitive Nissen huts, with two pilots to a room. Sharing his hut with Mark Soden, Joe said his tiny space smelled forever of pipe smoke and soggy woolen socks. And in the perpetual dampness it was impossible to stay warm. "A small stove which takes about an hour to get going serves as the only means for keeping us from catching pneumonia," Joe reported to his parents. "For a bath you have to go several miles and you must make it in the morning for all the hot water has been taken by evening . . . So at long last, I'm really beginning to fight the war." But, he jokingly told his mother, there was no sense in worrying about him. "If I can keep my feet dry, the greatest hazard will be overcome."

After several hard weeks of straight flying on cold and miserable patrols that were ten to twelve hours long, Joe put in for a week's leave for his entire crew. With Jim Reedy, their commanding officer, joining them, they all went up to London, where Kathleen threw a big party for them, complete with a band, at the home of Marie Bruce, a woman her mother had grown very close to during the ambassadorship. "It was the first party London had had for the young for two years," so the people swarmed in, Kathleen excitedly reported to her parents. Among the guests was Irving Berlin, who played his new piece "My British Buddy" and then, while everyone sang along, a lot of his old songs ending with "Over There."

"Kick handled herself to perfection as usual," Joe wrote to their parents, "and made a terrific hit all around. The girls looked very pretty and made quite an impression on the love-lorn sailors whom I brought." Kathleen had also invited a group of Billy Hartington's friends from the Coldstream Guards, as well as a number of political figures, including Alfred Duff Cooper. But if Hartington or Pat Wilson was there, neither Kathleen nor Joe mentioned it to the senior Kennedys. By this point, the two siblings had become quite diplomatic in their relationship with their parents, sharing their secrets with each other and not with the rest of the family.

In the weeks that followed, Kathleen and Joe grew closer than ever. From his base at Mudville Heights, Joe would call two or three times a week, and whenever he had a leave they would arrange to be together. Many a weekend they would meet at Pat Wilson's cottage, which was conveniently located for everyone—including Hartington, now stationed at Alton in Hampshire. Other frequent guests were Bill Hearst and his wife, Lorelle, who would describe the tile-roofed cottage as "charming beyond belief." None of Kathleen's friends was scandalized about the growing relationship between Joe Kennedy and Pat Wilson.

By 1943 many young married women whose husbands were away had taken up with American soldiers. In the chaos of war, everyone was in love with someone.

Still, Joe felt compelled, knowing all too well how his parents would respond to news of his affair with Pat, to mention other girls in his letters and to state specifically that romance was "unknown in the life of this romantic, dashing naval airman." Over New Year's, he reported, he stayed with the Carcanos and "they couldn't have been nicer . . . I met the daughter of the Duke of Alba and under Spanish law I would become the Duke if I married her, so I am toying with the idea. Wouldn't you like to have a Duke in the family?"

Kathleen mentioned *her* potential duke, Billy Hartington, in almost every letter to her parents, though she constantly reassured them that she understood she could never marry him. "Next Saturday is Elizabeth Cavendish's dance," she wrote on January 2, 1944, "which should be great fun with all the relatives giving me a good going over . . . Don't worry about me. I'm not going to make any wrong decisions. Each day I feel luckier and more broadened from this experience. What a lot of things have been packed into my life from 1938 to 1943." A few days later she reported that the Duke's Christmas present had arrived, a lovely pair of pearl and diamond earrings to match the cross the Duchess gave her. "Mother will long for them."

In her letters to her parents during this period, Kathleen seems so happy and full of life that it must have been impossible for Joe and Rose not to sense she was in love with Billy. Nor, apart from religion, could they possibly have chosen a better suitor for her. In the five years since Hartington had met Kathleen, he had grown into an intelligent, handsome, responsible young man, faced with a limitless future. And he could not have come from finer stock. Describing a dinner party the Devonshires had at the Connaught Hotel before the aforementioned party for their daughter Elizabeth at their Eaton Square home, Kathleen waxed lyrical about the conversations she had had with all the distinguished guests, including Evelyn Waugh, the writer, and Lord David Cecil, Billy's uncle, whose conversation made her realize how much she had to learn.

In the same letter, she teased her father about a newspaper article on the Florida Gold Coast which referred to him as the playboy of Palm Beach. "I think it shows there's a lot of life left in that old man of ours if he can start being a playboy at his ripe old age! I wouldn't have been a bit surprised if they had named Grandpa, but I didn't expect Daddy to have the title."

Kathleen reported in the middle of January that Billy had been granted leave from the Coldstream Guards to stand for Parliament from the Derbyshire seat that had been occupied by Cavendishes for all but five of the past two hundred and ten years. At any other juncture, Billy's election would have been almost automatic, but, at a time when Conservative candidates in other districts were suffering surprising setbacks, the family recognized that it would be a difficult battle. His opponent was Charles White, a fifty-three-year-old alderman who was running on an Independent Socialist ticket in breach of the political truce between the principal political parties, whereby the seat in wartime should have remained in Conservative hands.

Capitalizing on Billy's youth and inexperience, White turned the focus of the race into a contest between a ducal heir and a cobbler's son. It was the common man against the "Palace on the Peak," the culmination of a family feud between the Cavendishes and the Whites which had lasted half a century. In the middle of the campaign, Billy received a warm letter of support from Churchill in which the Prime Minister traced the great heritage of the Cavendish family and personally appealed to the people of the district to make Billy their member of Parliament. As it turned out, in a harbinger of the defeat Churchill himself would suffer the following year, the letter probably worked to Billy's disadvantage.

Kathleen spent most of her weekends and her leave time in Derbyshire campaigning with Billy, and she loved every minute of it. Riding with him through the countryside in a pony cart covered with ribbons the colors of the Union Jack, she discovered in herself the same love of campaigning that her mother had experienced years before as the mayor's daughter. And through all the handshakes with thousands of farmers, the dozens of trips to market and the hundreds of speeches, Kathleen's genuine warmth proved an invaluable asset. In the end, though Billy lost, it was said that he had done a wonderful job and predictions were made that he would surely win the next time around.

"I saw a by-election and how it really works," Kathleen reported enthusiastically to Lem. "Billy made about ten speeches a day and did very well with all the odds against him. However it was a good experience and it won't hurt him to get beaten. I think it threw his father the Old Duke back a few paces."

Once the election was over, Billy had to return to his regiment, but after spending so much time with Kathleen he was more in love with her than ever. Still, it seemed impossible to imagine how they could marry without destroying their families. It was a particularly difficult situation since Billy could not bring himself to agree to bring up his children as Catholics—the only way that Kathleen could marry him and still stay within the Church. Aware of his father's deep alarm over the prospect of a Catholic heir, he felt he could not go against his family. The only hope, it seemed, lay in a special dispensation—"some stretch of the rules," as Rose described it—by which the marriage "could be sanctioned or at least tolerated by both the Roman Catholic and Anglican churches."

In a letter written to "mother and daddy only," Kathleen reported that the Duchess had brought an Anglican priest, Father Ted Talbot, to explain to her what the Cavendish family stood for in the Church of England and the impossibility of Billy permitting a son of his to be brought up a Roman Catholic.

> He took the trouble to explain to me the fundamental differences between Anglican and Roman Catholic. Of course I explained that something one had been brought up to believe in and which was largely responsible for the character and personality of an individual is a very difficult thing for which to find a substitute. Further, I explained that I had been blessed with so many of this world's goods that it seemed rather cheap and weak to give in at the first real crisis in my life . . . both the Duchess and Talbot don't . . . want me to give up something. They just hoped that I might find the same thing in the Anglican version of Catholicism.
>
> Yesterday I felt most discouraged and rather sad. I want to do the right thing so badly and yet I hope I'm not giving up the most important thing in my life . . . Poor Billy is very, very sad but he sees his duty must come first. He is a fanatic on the subject and I suppose just such spirit is what has made England great . . . If he did give in to me his father has told him he would not be cut off, in fact, nothing would happen . . . . This Friday going to see Bishop Mathew about a dispensation. I suppose it will be practically impossible. You two have been wonderful and a great strength.

As Kathleen had predicted, it was practically impossible to secure a dispensation. When she went to see Bishop Mathew, he had nothing to offer her and went so far as to say that in a big public case like this the Church would have to be very careful so as to avoid all criticism—that, in fact, it would probably bend the other way about making any concessions. "Please," she begged her father, "try and discover loopholes."

Joe Kennedy did everything he could. He went to see Francis Spellman, the Archbishop of New York. Spellman, a powerful prelate, was a longtime friend of Kennedy's, and together they worked out a means of reaching the Vatican. But it was soon clear that even with this intervention nothing could be done. Admitting to Kathleen that his efforts were not proving successful, Kennedy tried to reassure his daughter. "As I've told you lots of times, you're tops with me. I'll bet on your judgment anytime for any amounts." Later that day he wrote to Joe Junior, asking him to give his sister "the benefit of your counsel and sympathy because after all she has done a swell job and she's entitled to the best and with us over here it's awfully difficult to be as helpful as we'd like to be. As far as I personally am concerned, Kick can do no wrong."

Rose, for her part, was supportive of her daughter so long as she believed that in the end, if a dispensation could not be found, Kathleen would renounce her love. "Daddy . . . feels terribly sympathetic and so do I," Rose wrote on February 24, "and I only wish we could offer some suggestions. When both people have been handed something all their lives, how ironic it is that they cannot have what they want most. I wonder if the next generation will feel that it is worth sacrificing a life's happiness for all the old family tradition."

Sensing that this was not the all-out support she was getting from her father, Kathleen solicited the help of Marie Bruce to persuade Rose that even if the technicalities could not be resolved, the marriage would still be a match of great love. "Dear Rose," Marie wrote, "suppose I better write to you about Billy. I like him very much indeed. He is a very nice young man and I think he will make her very happy . . . He is a grown up man now, good war record, great sense of responsibility and he loves little Kick very much . . . of course there is big difficulty about the religion. She thinks you would not approve. I think if you saw the pair of them together you certainly would."

Kathleen was right to worry, for when her mother received Marie's letter, with its implied acceptance of the marriage even if a dispensation could not be found, Rose was furious. Writing to her parents on March 4, Kathleen reported, "Marie Bruce hasn't heard from Mother and is scared to death you might be upset with her . . . I think something will have to be decided one way or another before we both go nuts . . . Somehow I can't make myself see that the Lord in Heaven (not the one in question) would make things so difficult."

In late March, Joe Junior came up to London, bringing Kathleen a sailor coat like the ones the Navy boys wore. While he was there, he went to see the bishop on her behalf, as Kathleen reported:

Billy also went to see him. Bishop told me it would put church in a very difficult position for us to get a dispensation and would be better we went ahead and got married and then something might possibly be done afterwards . . . Of course Dukie is very worried about having a Roman Catholic in the family . . . In their eyes the most awful thing that could happen to our son would be for it to become a Roman. With me in the family that danger becomes immediate even though I would promise that the child could be brought up as an Anglican. The Church would not marry us and the result would be that I would be married in a registry office. I could continue to go to Church but not Communion.

While Rose was becoming more and more distraught at the possibility that Kathleen might go ahead and marry Billy, Joe kept reassuring his daughter that he would stand behind her no matter what she decided. Telling her that in the end she and Billy would just have to work it out themselves and "let all the rest of us go jump in the lake," Joe jokingly told her that he had heard reports that she was making converts. "Maybe if you made enough of them a couple of them could take your place. If Mother ever saw that sentence I'd be thrown right out in the street . . . I'm still working for you so keep up your courage."

Kathleen hated the idea of getting married in a civil ceremony. In England civil weddings had an unsavory connotation as the last resort of divorcees and others who could not receive God's blessing. Writing sadly to Lem, Kathleen recalled the conversations and daydreams she used to have as a young girl about her potential wedding and all the bridesmaids she was going to have, and now she could look forward only to a ten-minute ceremony in a registry office. For a time she thought it might be better to convert to Anglicanism so that she could be totally accepted by Billy's church instead of simply living in lifelong estrangement from her own. At least this course of action would make one set of parents happy. While she was exploring this possibility the Duke presented to her a lovely old leatherbound copy of the Book of Common Prayer of the Church of England, and arrangements were made for her to discuss the possibility of conversion with an Anglican monk. But in the end, Kathleen realized that a conversion would hurt her mother even more than a registry wedding. At least with a registry wedding she could still hope for an eventual redemption if Billy were to die before her; then the fact that she had not been married in a Protestant church could be used in her favor if she wanted to return to the faith.

In the last week of April, after spending three days with Billy in Yorkshire, enjoying lobsters and champagne every night, Kathleen finally consented to marry him on what were essentially his terms, though they agreed to have a civil ceremony. As soon as she said yes, making them officially engaged, Billy wrote a long letter to Mrs. Kennedy.

I have loved Kick for a long time [he told her]. After Xmas I realized that I couldn't bear to let her go without asking her . . . I know I should only be justified in allowing my children to be brought up Roman Catholic if I believed it desirable for England to become a Roman Catholic country. Therefore, believing in the National Church of England as I do very strongly and having so many advantages and all the responsibilities that they entail I am convinced that I would be setting a very bad example if I gave in.

I do feel terribly keenly the sacrifices I'm asking Kick to make but I can't see that she will be doing anything wrong in the eyes of God . . . I shall never be able to get over my amazing good fortune in being allowed to have Kick as my wife, it still seems incredibly wonderful. Please try not to think too harshly of me.

Later that week, Kathleen had dinner with Tony Rosslyn and told him she was engaged. "She said she would be perfectly happy if she had but one week with him," Rosslyn wrote to Joe, "and she felt she was fated to be his wife, as he had wanted it to be this way for six years and if you wanted something badly enough you eventually were sure to get it. I pointed out the fallacy of this argument but she said she loved him and that was all there was to it."

Hearing the news of Kick's engagement, Rose was, in her own words, "heartbroken and horrified." She had given her life to bringing up her children as good Catholics, and now, to her, this marriage proved that her job was not very well done. Beyond this, she worried that Kathleen would set a precedent for her brothers and sisters and, even more, for every young Catholic in the country. "I thought it would have such mighty repercussions in that every little young girl would say if Kathleen Kennedy can, why can't I . . . Everyone pointed to our family with pride as well-behaved, level-headed and deeply religious. What a blow to the family prestige."

So, in a move that would bring great sadness to Kathleen, Rose cabled to her daughter: "Heartbroken. Feel you have been wrongly influenced —sending Arch Spellman's friend to talk to you. Anything done for Our Lord will be rewarded hundred fold."

If Rose's attitude toward her daughter's marriage appears harsh or uncompromising, it must be remembered how much she herself had sacrificed to become a good Catholic and how much effort she had put into bringing up her children Catholic. At the same time, she truly believed that no finite happiness on earth could possibly be worth what she saw as the sacrifice of one's eternal life in heaven. "I can't help admiring Rose for her convictions," Kathleen's friend Dinah Bridge said. "So many others would have thought, oh how great, my daughter is marrying into nobility, what a splendid match! It shows how deeply grounded she was in her convictions about the Church."

Although Kathleen had expected her to be upset, she had held on to the hope that once she finally decided to do it her mother would back her up, right or wrong. Now, with the arrival of Rose's cable, she became terribly agitated and even a little afraid. In her turmoil she turned to her brother Joe, and in him she found her best ally. "Once she had definitely made up her mind to do it," Joe later wrote, "I did the best I could to help her through. She was under a terrible strain all the time and as the various wires came in she became more and more upset."

Though he surely understood that his support of Kathleen's marriage would not sit well with his mother or with his potential Catholic constituency back in Massachusetts, Joe Junior was able on this occasion to move beyond his own ambitions to help his sister. Perhaps his deepening involvement with Pat Wilson made the decision easier, but his courage in standing up for Kathleen at this critical juncture should not be underestimated. All his life Joe had been held up as the model child, the one who would set the example for all the rest, yet when the moment came for him to choose between his allegiance to the family's religion and the happiness of his sister, he was able to support his sister.

"Billy is crazy about Kick," young Joe wrote to his parents,

> and I know they are very much in love . . . I think he really has something on the ball . . . he is ideal for Kick . . . As far as Kick's soul is concerned, I wish I had half her chance of seeing the pearly gates. As far as what people will say, the hell with them. I think we can all take it. It will be hardest on Mother and I do know how you feel Mother, but I do think it will be alright.

In the difficult days before the wedding, which had to be held almost immediately since Billy's unit was scheduled to take part in the Normandy invasion in June, Joe came up to London to help Kathleen. He went over to see the Devonshires' lawyer and read over the marriage settlement and he convinced the Devonshires that while she had given Billy her promise that she would bring up the children as Anglicans, she should not be forced to sign a paper to that effect. "Never did anyone," Kathleen later wrote, "have such a pillar of strength as I had in Joe . . . He constantly reassured me and gave me renewed confidence in my decision. Moral courage he had in abundance and once he felt that a step was right for me, he never faltered, although he might be held largely responsible for my decision."

The wedding took place on Saturday morning, May 6. Escorted only by her brother Joe, Kathleen walked into the small red brick building of the Chelsea Register Office at a few minutes before ten o'clock. She wore a pale-pink street-length dress with a little half hat made of two pale-pink ostrich feathers. At her throat she wore a diamond brooch, and in her hand she carried an old gold mesh bag and a new posy of pink camellias, both contributed by Marie Bruce as "something old, something new." Ushered into a small drab room, the bride met the groom, who was wearing his Coldstream Guards uniform. Representing Billy's side were his parents, the Duke and Duchess of Devonshire, his aunt Lady Salisbury and his sisters Anne and Elizabeth. His best man was an old friend, Charles Manners, the Marquess of Granby, son of the Duke of Rutland. Besides Joe, Kathleen was represented only by Mrs. Bruce and Lady Astor.

During the ten-minute ceremony, Joe gave away the bride and Billy slipped a small eternity ring on Kathleen's finger. Joe and the Duke of Devonshire signed as witnesses. But in spite of the austerity of the occasion, "everything was wonderful," Joe reported. And in a cable to Rose, Marie Bruce wrote: "You would rejoice in their young happiness. Only grief your sorrow. Kathleen looked lovely."

After the ceremony, the Devonshires received two hundred guests at a relative's town house in Eaton Square. Then Kathleen and Billy boarded a train for Billy's home at Eastbourne, where they received a private Anglican blessing and spent a week's honeymoon.

The day after the wedding, Joe Junior sent a cable to his father: "The power of silence is great." Back in the United States Joe Senior was in an extremely difficult position. Because everything had happened so fast, he had had no time to prepare Rose. When Rose finally received Kathleen's letter informing her of the upcoming marriage, she lost her composure and retreated to her room, refusing to talk with anyone but her husband. To complicate matters further, the newspapers headlined the story with pictures of Henry VIII, "Protestant," and Catherine of Aragon, "Catholic." For days the press barraged the Kennedys with questions: "How do you feel about your daughter renouncing the Catholic religion?" and "Do you favor the marriage of your daughter outside of the Church?" At the same time, letters began pouring in from various priests and nuns commiserating with the Kennedys on their great misfortune. "May the Blessed Mother give her the necessary grace to see the error of her ways before many weeks have passed," the Reverend Hugh O'Donnell wrote. In a similar spirit, the president of Manhattanville College wrote to Rose that she was praying each day that God would give Kathleen the opportunity of repairing in full measure "the mistake into which a human love had led her."

Rose was inconsolable for days, and Joe Senior felt for her and tried to give her all his support. On the other hand, he understood that Kathleen also needed his support, and so after several days of silence he finally sent her the cable she had been waiting for all along. "With your faith in God," Joe wrote, "you can't make a mistake. Remember you are still and always will be tops with me." Then he arranged for Rose to enter a hospital for a checkup so that she could be kept safely away from reporters.

Kathleen received his cable on the second day of her honeymoon in Eastbourne and was so overjoyed that she ran to the telegraph office at once to send a reply: "Your cable made my happiest day. Most distressed about mother. Please tell her not to worry." The following day, May 9, seated at a desk in the library of her honeymoon home, she wrote a long letter to her mother:

> I was very worried about a newspaper report here that you were very ill. They made out that it was because of my marriage. Goodness mother I owe so much to you and Daddy that nothing in the world could have made me go against your will. However, I felt that you expected the action I took and would judge that it was the course to take under the circumstances . . . [Now] every morning letters arrive condemning my action. They don't bother me at all and I only hope and pray that things will not be too difficult for you and the rest of the family with the McDonnells etc. Please don't take any responsibility for any action which you think bad (and I don't). You did everything in your power to stop it. You did your duty as a Roman Catholic mother. You have not failed, there was nothing lacking in my religious education.
>
> Not by any means am I giving up my faith, it is most precious to me. Billy wants it to remain as such. We would have been married in the Church if they had consented to perform the ceremony without Billy signing the paper. This they would not do . . . . Fifteen years ago our marriage could have been solemnized in the church, the boys being brought up in the father's religion, the girls in the mother's. However then a rule was made like the one in our country which put a stop to those marriages. Bishop Mathew . . . told me that perhaps at a later date our marriage could be made valid. Until that time I shall go on praying and living like a Roman Catholic and hoping. Please, please do the same.

Concluding on a lighter note, Kathleen shared with her mother all the details of the wedding and told her that "Joe was absolutely wonderful." Through it all he was in "tremendous form" and, after seeing his face plastered all over the papers, quite aware that he was "finished in Boston." "I never realized how many friends I had in this country (some of them are just impressed but most of them are genuinely pleased)."

While Rose was in the hospital, Joe talked with Archbishop Spellman about the situation, and Spellman assured him that Rose was being much too hard on herself. "She has done the best she could and that's all her worry should be," he told Joe. When Joe reported this to Rose she felt better; indeed, according to Joe, the Archbishop's words "carried her over the tough time." Then, when the papers finally quieted, she began to assume a more peaceful outlook on the situation and she let Joe telegraph Kathleen to say that she was shopping for clothes for her. That same day she asked Joe to send a cable to Marie Bruce saying that everything was fine.

Relieved, Kathleen relaxed for the first time since the wedding. As she described her situation to her mother on May 8, things were still not easy on the religious front, but "now I feel I can stand anything." At the moment she was living in a small country inn in Alton near where Billy was stationed.

It's very comfortable and we have the prize suite . . . Billy is their first Marquess and they all take the greatest delight in calling him that at the top of their lungs on every occasion. He has a motorbike to go back and forth to camp and I have my bike to get around on during the day.

In the same letter Kathleen spoke honestly about Billy's father. He was

very nice but very difficult in ways. The funny thing is that he thinks Billy has given in as the one thing he always dreaded is that one of his sons should marry an R.C. Even though his present daughter-in-law has acquiesced to his demands he always sees within me a sort of evil influence. I shall just have to prove myself over a period of years I suppose.

It took Kathleen only a matter of months, not a period of years, to prove herself to Billy's father. Writing to Joe Kennedy only three months after the marriage, the Duke confessed that everywhere Kathleen went she managed to win everyone's heart. "Just lately she had been doing some functions in Derbyshire," he commented. "My old political agent wrote to me she has won golden opinions everywhere and I am sure that if Hartington cannot win the seat back for himself, his marchioness will win it for him."

"Billy and I talk a lot about going to America immediately after the war," Kathleen wrote to her parents. "I have already told him what each relative will say to him. He had a bit of it at the wedding when an American sargeant [sic] came up to him and said, 'Listen, you God damn limey, you've got the best damn girl that America could produce.' "

With the immediate crisis resolved, Joe Senior wrote a long letter to his eldest son, going over the whole situation and thanking him for everything he had done for Kathleen. "I'm delighted that you were there and in her letters to us she always said what a tower of strength you were for her. I've got great respect for your judgment and I'm sure you advised her as I would have if I had been there . . . and I agree with you that if any of our chances of getting into Heaven are 25% as good as Kick's are, I'll settle today."

After Kathleen and Billy had spent four weeks together at the country inn in Alton, where they were treated like royalty by the staff (including a bellboy who was, Kathleen described in her diary, "as Irish as paddy's pig"), Billy received his orders to participate in the Allied invasion of Europe.

"Although I've been expecting it daily," he recorded in Kathleen's diary, "it is a shock now that it has come. I shall always remember this month as the most perfect of my life. How beastly it is to be ending things. This love seems to cause nothing but goodbyes. I think that that is the worst part of it, worse even than fighting."

"Oh my darling," Billy wrote to Kathleen from his new headquarters. "It went so quickly and I do miss you so terribly. I can't help feeling sorry for myself, stuck in this dump, but I do really feel that now I have got you, nothing really matters to me."

*T*o all appearances, Joe Junior was a child gifted by the gods. In the small circle of his household, he emanated power, passion, and promise. From top left, at St. Moritz in 1939; as a delegate to the 1940 Democratic Convention; with his girlfriend, Pat Wilson, in England.

$K$athleen *was the sunshine of her family. All her life, one friend recalled, Kathleen would say she didn't know why she deserved such a wonderful life and she didn't know if it could possibly last. Here she is shown, from top left, in a portrait; with the Red Cross in England; at her wedding to Billy Hartington, with the Duchess of Devonshire and Joe Junior behind her; and with Mr. and Mrs. Winston Churchill. In contrast, nothing ever came easily to Rosemary, shown here in an uncharacteristically light moment; and as she grew older, her level of frustration grew so high that she became almost impossible to handle.*

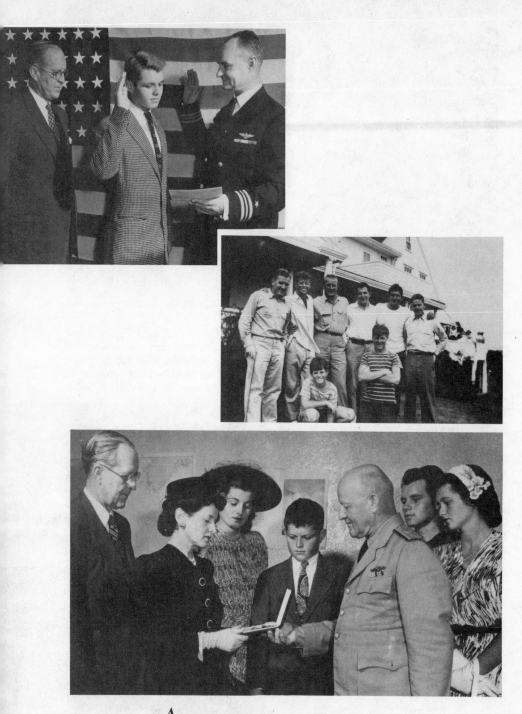

$A$t the top, nineteen-year-old Bobby is being sworn into the Navy's V-12 program in the presence of his father. In the center, Jack gathers with his PT-109 buddies in front of the Hyannis Port house one month after Joe Junior's death. At the bottom, in 1945 Rose receives Joe Junior's posthumous Navy medal while Joe Senior, Pat, Teddy, Bobby, and Jean look on.

$B$y Thanksgiving of 1948, when this family picture was taken at Hyannis Port, both Joe Junior and Kathleen were dead and Rosemary had been permanently institutionalized. As the surviving brother, Jack, shown below in 1946, felt an "unnamed responsibility" to his family. And once he decided to enter politics, his parents backed him up at every turn. Here Rose is shown speaking at a tea in Worcester in 1952.

What Jack and Jackie, shown here as a young girl, had in common had less to do with the wealth and privilege of their backgrounds than with the loneliness that each of them had experienced as a child.

By the late 1950s, the balance of power between Jack and his father was shifting; but within the family, Joseph Kennedy, shown here with Ted, Jack, and Bobby, remained the dominant force.

Now the story of the Fitzgeralds and the Kennedys, the century-long ascent from the immigrant slums of Boston's North End, was to become something different: the personal and political journey of John Fitzgerald Kennedy. And that journey would reach its goal on January 20, 1961, as the family, shown here at the inaugural ball at the armory, gathered to celebrate Jack's inauguration as the 35th President of the United States. Despite the bitter weather, the new President enjoyed himself immensely, especially when the PT-109 float came by, carrying his wartime crew.

A t John Kennedy's inaugural, the old Fitzgerald Bible, its frayed pages standing witness to the lives of three generations, was brought from Boston to Washington to be used in the swearing-in of the first Catholic President of the United States.

# CHAPTER 38

## "NOW
## IT'S
## ALL
## OVER."

Throughout that spring of 1944, while Kathleen was making her decision about Billy, Joe was flying his regular patrols. By the third week of March he had flown twenty-four missions, which left him only six more before he was supposed to be relieved. But in a letter to his parents on March 24 he reported that he might have to stay on for forty missions. "I don't mind much as I would just as soon be here as any place." In reply, Joe Senior wrote that while he understood that Joe wanted to be there for the Allied invasion, "I sincerely hope that they'll call it a day at 30."

As it turned out, the U.S. Navy and Royal Navy planners had big plans for the squadrons at Dunkeswell. For over two years, the architects of D-Day had been haunted by the vision of German U-boats suddenly emerging in the waters of the Channel as Eisenhower's vast armada approached the coast of France with tens of thousands of men and millions of tons of equipment. The specter made Pearl Harbor look like a minor embarrassment. To prevent this dreadful possibility, an ambitious plan was conceived, calling for hundreds of planes to fly hourly patrols over the Channel during all the days of the invasion. As soon as he heard about Operation Cork, as it was called, Joe volunteered to extend his stay.

"I have finished my missions and was due to start back in about two weeks," he told his parents on May 8, "but volunteered to stay another month. I persuaded my crew to do it, which pleased me very much. We are the only crew which has done it." Explaining further in another letter, written the following week, Joe said that while most of the boys were leaving, it seemed rather silly to him to land in the States a few days before the invasion occurred. "In any case I am giving it another month, and if nothing happens by then, I will probably come home. There's no use in tempting fate."

As D-Day dawned on June 6, Joe Junior took off from Dunkeswell, heading toward Cherbourg. His patrol that day was northwest of the invasion beaches, but the invasion force was so large, larger than any force ever assembled in history, that he could actually see some of the outlying ships. Flight duration was eleven and a half hours, which allowed each plane to make a dozen circuits during a working day. It was an exhausting flight pattern for all those who participated, but in the end Operation Cork worked. In the entire month of June, not a single ship of the invasion fleet was lost to a German U-boat.

For young Joe it was a heady time. Though he recognized that his own role had not been a sensational one, he knew that he and his crew had done what was expected. "I am delighted that I stayed for the Invasion," he wrote to his parents.

> I stayed with Pat Wilson for my day off and Kick had been staying there for a couple of days . . . I have been having a wonderful time when I could get away from this place so all and all it is pretty pleasant foreign duty. . . . I now have 39 missions and will probably have about 50 by the time I leave. It is far more than anyone else on the base, but it doesn't prove a hell of a lot . . . Don't worry about me. I don't think I am in as much danger now as I was (knock on wood).

As a second-tour man, Joe had more leave time, which he regularly spent at the cottage with Pat. It was, of course, an impossible romance, far more so that Kathleen's, for, even assuming that Pat secured a divorce from her second husband, it was inconceivable that a man with Joe's political ambitions could marry a twice-divorced Protestant. But there was no denying that Joe was deeply in love, probably for the first time in his life. "Rumor hath it," his mother wrote on July 19, "that you are very much in love, but we have not had any of the details." (Had she had the details, Rose's tone would probably have been very different!) In the squadron, there was talk that Joe and Pat were engaged, and for some reason Joe let it spread, perhaps because he so wished it were true that he could not bring himself to deny it.

In his letters to his parents, he said very little about Pat, but when he did bring her up his involvement was obvious. In the week following his twenty-ninth birthday he wrote:

> I had a wonderful birthday party, I stayed with Pat Wilson and Kick was there. She had some people over for dinner including Rothmere, the newspaperman. There was champagne, and a delicious dinner, so I really enjoyed it. It wasn't at all like a birthday at home, but if I were going to have it any place but home again, I would take a duplication of last night.

At the end of his letter, however, Joe deliberately changed the subject, telling his mother, as he often told her, that she had better get someone lined up for him when he got home, for the big thing in his life at present was that he was starting to get gray, so "I had better get a gal while there is some life in the old boy."

While the Kennedys were eagerly awaiting Joe's arrival in Hyannis Port at the end of July or the first of August, a lone plane, like those Joe had been flying, was making its way across the ocean from Norfolk, Virginia, to England in the first stage of a top-secret mission. Since midnight of June 13, a week after D-Day, London had been subjected to a terrifying barrage of V-1 flying bombs, Goering's last-bid effort to regain the prestige he had lost by his failure to break the British will during the Battle of Britain. Launched from giant concrete bunkers constructed all along the French coast, the V-1's were "unmanned jet aircraft, gyro-controlled and loaded with dynamite." While the first V-1's launched were clumsy and inaccurate, the buzz bombs or doodlebugs, as they were variously called, were now dropping on London with horrifying speed, producing a greater panic than all the piloted bombers together had produced at the start of the war.

In her diary, Kathleen reported many sleepless nights on account of "the doodlebugs" and suggested that the eeriness and "the inability to hit back at a human target" made them much more frightening than regular bombs. "People are absolutely terrified and one senses that they are always listening first for them to arrive and next for the sound that the dreaded engine has stopped." Perhaps, too, it was that the war was now five years old and a general exhaustion had set in, but whatever it was, British morale was being seriously affected and something had to be done. Civilian casualties from the new bomb were immense: in the month of July alone, nearly 2,500 persons were killed and over 7,000 wounded.

As soon as the PB4Y plane landed in Dunkeswell, its insides were gutted; it was emptied of all but minimum radio and radar and stripped of guns and even the co-pilot's seat. Then into the belly, stowed on the flight deck where the radioman and the navigator usually sat, lashed even into the tunnel leading to the turret, boxes and boxes of explosives were loaded, more tonnage of explosives than was ever gathered in a single plane until the atomic bomb was launched. The plan was for two pilots, a pilot and a standing co-pilot, to take the sacrificial plane into the air and then guide it toward its target—a gigantic concrete bunker set into the hills of Calais which was believed to be the launching site for Hitler's V-1 rockets (and the laboratory for an even more deadly rocket known as the V-2, which would travel so fast, at a speed greater than sound, that no defense was considered possible). While the bunker had proven invulnerable to ordinary bombs, the combined explosives in this mysterious plane promised to do the job. According to the top-secret plan, the PB4Y was to be piloted across the Channel toward Calais until a designated moment when its controls would be switched to remote and picked up by the mother plane flying nearby. At that point, the two pilots were supposed to parachute out while the mother plane guided the suicide plane toward its target.

When Commander Reedy first heard about the secret mission, he volunteered himself to be the pilot, but he was considered too senior for the job and another candidate had to be found. From the first it was clear that the mission was exceedingly dangerous. The week before, the Army had tried a similar maneuver; not a single one of the Army missions was successful, and of the six pilots who tried, one was dead and two were severely injured, making it a 50 percent casualty rate. Yet, not surprisingly, as soon as Joe Kennedy heard about the mission, he begged Reedy to let him go. Believing Joe to be his best pilot, Reedy reluctantly gave his assent.

"I am going to do something different for the next three weeks," Joe wrote to his parents on July 26. "It is secret and I am not allowed to say what it is, but it isn't dangerous so don't worry . . . I imagine you are a bit disappointed that I haven't gone home, but I think when I tell you the whole story, you will agree with me."

"I can quite understand how you feel about staying there," Joe Senior wrote in reply, "but don't force your luck too much."

But by the time Joe Junior received his father's warning he had already committed himself to an assignment so hazardous that its successful completion would have been one of the two or three greatest feats in the war. It would have made him perhaps a greater hero than his brother Jack had been painted to be. This was not the first time Joe had pushed himself forward. "There was never an occasion for a mission that meant extra hazard that Joe did not volunteer for," his squadron mate Louis Papas later wrote. "He had everybody's unlimited admiration and respect for his courage, zeal and willingness to undertake the most dangerous mission."

It can be argued that in taking these risks Joe was simply responding to a lifetime of pressure, to the constant demand to be the best at everything he did. Now, try as his father might, it was too late to call the demons back. Perhaps beneath the surface of Joe's self-assurance there existed the precarious feeling that because he had not yet become a war hero he had failed to live up to some ideal image or measure. Having been admired all his life for his success and achievements, he could not bear the collapse of self-esteem that accompanied a less than spectacular performance, especially in comparison with his brother Jack's.

But given all the bright promise of a political future that Joe Junior had to look forward to, the nature of his risk-taking was so extreme that it suggests a different explanation. Perhaps beneath the surface of his "model child" behavior there existed a rebellious streak, a need to belong to himself before he belonged to his father's dreams. Perhaps, in this light, his high-risk behavior can be seen as a desperate attempt to shape his own life in his own way.

For several days, fog and rain had brought a postponement of the secret flight, but finally the weather cleared and takeoff was scheduled for sunset on August 12. On the evening of the eleventh, after the briefing was completed, Joe had pedaled his Raleigh bike to the airfield to make a final inspection of his plane. The evening was warm, and in the late-summer sun the bomber took on a golden color as she sat, huge and clumsy, on the field, her body already so crammed with explosives that she seemed about to squash her tires. After talking for a while with Red Bradfield, the plane's mechanic, he pedaled back to base, scrambled some eggs for his roommate and himself, and then, as he always did before turning in, he knelt on the floor to pray.

On the day of the mission, the flight plans were reviewed again and again. Joe, along with his co-pilot, Wilford Willy, was to take the drone plane up to two thousand feet and then head toward the target. In the meantime, the mother plane would begin to establish control. Flying as a mere passenger, Joe would remain in the drone for another twenty minutes, checking everything, until the designated moment when he and his co-pilot were supposed to bail out. But just before doing so they were to make an electrical connection to the arming solenoids so that the plane, heading straight for the bunker, would explode upon impact. In addition to the drone and the mother plane, sixteen Mustangs were going along, to provide fighter cover, as well as a Mosquito plane from which photo-reconnaissance officer Elliott Roosevelt, the President's son, was supposed to take pictures.

In front of his crew Joe displayed surprising calm throughout the entire day, but there must have been a moment of fear, for on a last-minute impulse he put in a call to Lorelle Hearst at her apartment in the Claridge Hotel. "I'm about to go into my act," he told her. "If I don't come back, tell my dad . . . that I love him very much."

At eight minutes to six, Joe Kennedy sat in the plane with Bud Willy standing behind him. Pushing her throttles gently forward, he lifted her into the air. Eighteen minutes later, at the designated altitude of two thousand feet, he trimmed the aircraft and engaged the autopilot. He then picked up the microphone and called the mother ship, which was flying at his stern. Anderson, the pilot of the mother ship, then turned Kennedy left, and he and Joe began to check out the individual controls. From his photo plane, Elliott Roosevelt caught a picture of Joe in the cockpit and Willy in the bubble. In the clouds nearby, an Army B-17 was preparing to land near Dover in order to pick up the parachutists at the spot where they were to land.

Seated at the controls, Joe had only ten minutes more in the air before his part of the mission would be completed. At 6:20 P.M., Anderson directed Joe into a gentle left turn, and then suddenly, with no warning or explanation, Joe's plane exploded in midair.

It was "the biggest explosion I ever saw until the pictures of the atom bomb," said Wherry, a pilot in the mother ship. At the force of the explosion, Colonel Roosevelt's Mosquito ship was slammed almost to its back. On the ground, in Newdelight Woods, a small town near the east coast of England, fifty-nine buildings were damaged from the blast as the local people stared in wonder at the flames in the sky. Not a single part of Joe Kennedy's body was ever found.

It was early Sunday afternoon in Hyannis Port when the message reached the Kennedy family at their big white house at the breakwater. It was a warm day, so the family had taken their lunch outside on the porch, picnic style. After lunch, Joe Senior had gone up to his room for his customary nap. The children were all gathered in the big living room, chatting quietly so as not to disturb their father. Rose was in a chair reading the newspaper. There was a knock at the front door, and when Rose answered it she found two priests, one of whom, a Navy chaplain, Father Francis O'Leary, asked to see Mr. Kennedy. Thinking it was simply a routine matter, Rose invited the priests in and suggested that they join the family for a short time until Joe finished his nap. "No," Father O'Leary said. "This cannot wait. It concerns your son Joe Junior, who is missing in action."

Rose ran upstairs and burst into her husband's room. Waking him, she stood for a few moments, her mind half paralyzed, trying to speak but stumbling over her words. Then she managed to blurt out what the two priests had said. Joe Senior rushed down and escorted the priests into a small room off the living room. There he and Rose heard the story which made it clear that there could be no hope. Their eldest son was dead.

When the priests left, Joe held on to Rose for a moment and then went into the living room to break the news to the others. "Children," he said, "your brother Joe has been lost. He died flying a volunteer mission." Then, with tears in his eyes and his voice cracking, he said, "I want you all to be particularly good to your mother." And with that he retreated into his bedroom and locked the door.

Back in London, the RAF, unable to locate Kathleen, called Virginia Sykes and told her about Joe. She, in turn, broke the news to Pat Wilson, who was staying at her house awaiting Joe's arrival. The following day, Pat wrote a long and touching letter to Rose Kennedy:

. . . loving him as much as I did, I can understand a little the agony you, as his mother must be going through. Although Joe would hardly ever admit anything at all flattering to himself he did once tell me that he thought you loved him the best of your sons maybe—so I can truly realize how unhappy you must be and I long to be able to give you comfort. My thoughts and my deepest heartfelt sympathy are with you and because I loved him so much and we were so happy together I pray and believe that they will reach to your heart from mine.

I know you so well from things he said like "Mother always liked us to do this or that"—"Mother always sends me this buttercrunch and boy isn't it good" (eating 5 bits before breakfast!) . . . I want you to know all the five months we loved each other it was complete happiness and brought nothing but happiness to those near and dear to us . . . all what Kick calls "the gang at Crastock" . . . I shall always think of him bursting into the nursery for breakfast before catching the early train and saying "Hi ya Saarah" (my baby of 2 who was his favorite).

Our love was strong, true and unspoilt—please forgive me even if you blame me for loving him so much that he wanted to stay here and took this job. He would have taken some job anyhow and the only way I could have made him go back to America would have been to say I didn't love him—which he would not have believed. Here are some photographs [and letters] . . . perhaps, if you would like it, I will write to you again and send you more. I feel that you will understand when I say that I want to so much. I now realize more than ever before how lucky I was to have been loved by someone so perfect as Joe and I thank God for the lovely times we had together.

While Rose never acknowledged Pat's letter, Joe sent a cable in which he gently suggested that her mementos would not be welcomed at this time by Mrs. Kennedy. "I do not understand completely about the letters," Pat responded. "It was just a thought that Kick and I had that Mrs. Kennedy might like bits of them."

Kathleen was staying with the Devonshires in London when the RAF finally reached her with the news of her brother's death.

Dear Kick has been splendid and very brave [the Duke wrote to Joe Kennedy]. She was with us when the sad news came which was perhaps better than if she had been alone and her first thoughts were of her mother and you and not of herself. She is a really fine girl and I cannot begin to tell you how much we think of her and what a joy and comfort she has been during this anxious time . . . I am afraid she will feel the loss of her brother terribly and that it will add to the burden of her husband's absence in France, but we will do the best we can to find a home life for her.

Kathleen did indeed have a very hard time accepting Joe's death. In the last months, through so much turmoil, he had been her closest friend. Though she was determined to be brave, she found herself unable to control her emotions, and when Joe's roommate, Mark Soden, called her to extend condolences she sobbed at the other end of the phone. Later that night, however, she pulled herself together and wrote a letter of apology to Mark. "I'm so sorry I broke down tonight. It never makes things easier."

As she tried unsuccessfully to fall asleep that night, Kathleen realized that she had to get home right away. It was the only answer. Through her father, she made arrangements to fly to the States on an Army transport plane. When she landed in Boston, her brother Jack was there to greet her. He had been back in the States for six months, spending most of his time in the Chelsea Naval Hospital, where an operation on his back had been a failure. That evening in Hyannis Port, after seeing their parents, Jack and Kathleen decided to take a walk to St. Francis

Xavier, the little church on the corner which they had attended since they were children. Somehow, no matter how many difficulties they both were having with Catholicism, they were still able, kneeling in the familiar pews, to find some measure of solace in their church.

For Rose, the first weeks after young Joe's death were "the blackest hours" she had ever known. In her room she wept shamelessly at the thought that her son's magnificent body and smiling face had "splintered into a thousand pieces." And at night she could not sleep for imagining the terror he must have experienced in that single moment before his body yielded to death. Over and over, she kept remembering the days when he was a young boy, "running into my arms and snuggling into my lap." For so many years Joe had been the one child to whom she had given her unrestricted warmth and her deepest love, and in return he had been the perfect model for all the others, always reliable, always working hard at everything he did, always respectful to his parents. All his life, Joe had filled her with an indefinable sense of comfort; simply thinking of him could produce a happy feeling in her heart.

But now he was dead, and for weeks all that Rose could do was stay in her room, saying her rosary again and again, leaving it up to her husband to handle the arrangements, the letters and the telegrams. Indeed, years later she confessed that because she was so consumed by her own grief and because Joe was so immediately mobilized into action, she failed to realize how completely devastated he was at the death of his son.

In the first weeks, it is true, Joe Senior did seem to take great comfort in reading and responding to all the letters that kept pouring in, especially from people who had known Joe Junior in school or in the Navy and invariably spoke of his special radiance. "I have never known a gayer, more confident and adventurous fellow," Mark Soden wrote, "always looking for something more exciting and more dangerous to do . . . We've been together since Joe joined VP-203 in San Juan and our friendship has been one of the most treasured experiences of my life . . . I personally feel as grieved as if I'd lost my own brother." And from squadron mate Louis Papas came the following: "I hope it will help you somewhat to know that in his 29 years Joe was more of a success than most men ever are who live to a ripe old age. He was loved and respected by all who knew him—what more can a man ask."

In a letter to the Duke of Devonshire, Kennedy spoke of the comfort he was finding in the praise of Joe's squadron mates. "Their words," he wrote, "created a sense of nearness" to Joe and through them he was beginning to see the events of the past month in a pattern. It was also, he wrote, a great consolation to have Kick at home, for she could talk to him at length about all the things Joe had said and done in his last months in England. Then, diplomatically, he told the Duke he appreciated how difficult it was for Kick to be so far away from her husband, as the increased distance only seemed to heighten her anxiety about the dangers of war. "You have no idea how your letter seemed to bridge the distance between her and Billy at a moment when she is so distraught and craves some words of Billy's hazards. God grant that he will continue as you put it 'to come through.' "

The external composure Joe seemed at first to have achieved was shattered on a warm Cape afternoon in late summer when he received the last letter Joe had written to his family. "There was something about receiving that letter," Rose later recalled, "that simply tore Joe apart." In it, Joe Junior told his parents that while he could not yet share with them the secret details of his upcoming mission, he was sure that when he did they would understand why he had volunteered. "Don't get worried about it," he signed off, "as there is practically no danger." On reading those words, Rose recalled, "Joe threw the letter on the table and collapsed in his chair with his head in his hands, saying over and over that nothing would ever be the same again, that the best part of his life was finished." Until that letter came, Rose observed, Joe had been able to block the death from his mind, basking in all the wonderful things being said about his son as if he were simply delayed in coming home, but "when he read Joe's final letter and he knew he would never again be able to hear his voice or to read his words, he was suddenly hit with the finality of the loss."

There followed for the Kennedys a reversal in their initial reaction to Joe's death. Whereas Rose now grew stronger, Joe seemed to sink into a deeper gloom with each passing day. As the weeks wore on, the religious passion that had once allowed Rose to come to terms with her difficult experience at the Blumenthal convent now worked on her to forsake her grief and return to life. "As soon as I fully accepted that God had his reasons for taking Joe," Rose said later, "I began to recover. And my recovery was speeded up by all the wise and wonderful letters I received from various priests and nuns I had known over the years."

"I had been longing to write," the mother superior wrote to Rose from the Convent of the Sacred Heart, "ever since your letter in May [at the time of Kathleen's marriage]—and now another sorrow. I was going to say 'stunning blow' but anything God permits in this world is not meant to stun but to educate in supreme trust. We can never have too much confidence in an infinitely good God . . . Part of one's first pain is the thought of a splendid life cut short. But there's such a thing as 'living a great space in a short time.' And God asks not a finished work but great desire."

Joe's religious friends tried to console him in a similar manner, but as Joe himself admitted, his faith was not rooted deeply enough to bear the burden. "When young Joe was killed," he wrote to a friend years later, "my faith, even though I am a Catholic, did not seem strong enough to make me understand that after all, he had won his eternal reward without having to go through the grief of life. My faith should have made me realize this and I should not have indulged in great self-pity the way I did." But at the time, as he confessed to Father Sheehy, the Navy chaplain, he could not regard his personal tragedy in its "greater light," as Sheehy was urging him to, and he feared it would take him a long time to place the death in any kind of perspective.

For this man whose involvement with his children had become the primary motive of existence, the death of his firstborn son left a scar that could never be healed. "It was one of the most severe shocks . . . that I've ever seen registered on a human being," Arthur Krock wrote. "I still can't read about that boy," Kennedy wrote to Choate headmaster George St. John in December, "without it affecting me more than I ever thought anything could affect me in this life." For months he stopped reading the papers and listening to the radio, shutting himself up in his room for hours playing classical music. "I just can't get in the mood" to do much of anything, he told Sir James Calder. "You know how much I had tied my whole life up to his and what great things I saw in the future for him. Now it's all over." And writing to his friend Arthur Houghton, he said he recognized that he had better interest himself in something pretty soon lest he go mad, "because all my plans for my own future were all tied up with young Joe and that has gone smash."

In these letters, the love Kennedy felt for young Joe is clear and powerful. But the letters also suggest that more was at stake than the loss of a son. In his open admission that all his own plans for the future had been demolished, Kennedy reveals the single-minded nature of his ambition, an ambition that called for Joe Junior to make restitution for all that he himself had been unable to accomplish. It was as if Joe Junior's life belonged to Joe Senior as a second life for himself, a second chance to bring the name of the Kennedy family to the heights of national greatness. With Joe Junior's death, all these plans seemed forever destroyed.

Nor did Joe Kennedy's pain ever go away. "When the young bury the old," he explained to his friend Bunny Green, "time heals the pain and sorrow; but when the process is reversed the sorrow remains forever." And writing to his old friend Walter Howey years later on the occasion of Mrs. Howey's death, Joe said he understood a little of the pain Howey was feeling because of his own experience with young Joe's death. "After almost nine years," he confessed, "I still can't talk about him without softening up in an almost childish manner. Rose, on the other hand, with her supreme faith has just gone on and prayed for him and has not let it affect her life."

Of all his children, Kathleen seemed to provide her father with the most comfort. Staying with him into the middle of September, she would sit with him for hours, helping him respond to all the letters about Joe. Unable to relax with her mother, who seemed to be holding herself aloof on account of Kathleen's marriage, the daughter directed her warmth toward her father, even as she worried herself to sleep each night thinking about Billy.

While Kathleen was in Hyannis Port, Major William Cavendish was advancing with his company through the Low Countries, heading toward France. Forced to sleep in slit trenches with the ever present sound of shells falling overhead, Billy was determined to observe certain social niceties wherever he could. Each night he insisted on spreading a white tablecloth on his mess table, no matter where he set up camp. And wherever the company went, a table and a chair would be carried for Billy so that when he set up the company office, even in the midst of abandoned, ransacked buildings, it could be properly furnished. Maintaining a sense of humor about military life, Billy would deliberately go through an elaborate ritual each time the company set up a new camp. "Now," he would say in mock deliberation as he surveyed a green field or the rubble of a town, "where is the company office going to be?" Then, taking his table and chair to a section of the land, he would grandly announce, "Ah, we'll have it *here*."

Nevertheless he was "brave and fearless," as one of his men later wrote, "and as a company commander, just and fair, as a result of which he was admired and respected by all whom he commanded."

By the end of August, with the Germans inexplicably in retreat, the Fifth Battalion made spectacular progress. "The last six days have been truly incredible and unforgettable," Billy wrote to Kathleen on September 4. "We have advanced and advanced and advanced." Indeed, encountering only an occasional skirmish, Hartington's men took only a few hours to cross the Somme River, the site of the mass slaughter in the Great War. Then in one day the battalion pushed forward an incredible distance of nearly one hundred miles, marching all the way from Douai to Brussels, where they were greeted by cheering crowds of liberated citizens who surged forward as the British tanks rolled by, clambering onto the vehicles and embracing the men. "They were deliriously happy," wrote the battalion's intelligence officer, "and we were happy too; it seemed there had never been such happiness, nothing like this had ever happened before or could ever happen again." All along the route, the townspeople tossed apples and plums to the British soldiers and draped garlands around them, singing "It's a Long Way to Tipperary" at the top of their voices.

> The reception we have had makes me want to cry [Billy wrote to Kathleen], it is so touching. I now realize what a really horrible time these wretched people have had under the Huns and how deep is the loathing for them . . . There is nothing, absolutely nothing in the world they would not do for us. I would not have believed the human race could be capable of such emotion and such gratitude and one feels so unworthy of it all, living as I have in reasonable safety and comfort during these years while they have been suffering such terrible hardships under the Germans. I have a permanent lump in my throat and I long for you to be here as it is an experience which few can have and which I would love to share with you.

But the euphoric mood of the Fifth Battalion was suddenly shattered the following day on the road to Louvain and Tessenderloo, where they encountered a large German contingent comprised of fanatical soldiers determined to fight with everything they had. "That night," the historian of the Coldstream Guards observed, "a sharp dose of shell fire recalled the realities of war." On the morning of September 8, Billy's Number Three Company set off to capture the village of Beverloo. It was a miserable day, with gray skies and pouring rain, and the Germans inflicted heavy losses, making it one of the worst days in the entire war. But the company made steady progress, climbing over factory walls and through railway yards, and as dusk began to fall they reached their objective.

Company Three's objective on September 9 was to capture the village of Heppen, where they were to join up with Company Two. The morning dawned bright and sunny; nevertheless Billy was wearing his white mackintosh, an odd choice of clothing, his platoon commander thought, because it made him such an obvious target. Accompanied by his batman, Ingles, Billy headed out in front of the tanks, completely calm and casual, calling back to his men, "Come on, you fellows, buck up," trying to sustain morale in a unit that had lost a quarter of its men the day before. Walking briskly, with a huge pair of wire cutters in his hands, he had progressed just a few hundred yards when he was shot by a German sniper. The bullet pierced his heart, and he died instantly.

The terrible news reached Kathleen on September 16 in New York, where she and her family had gone on a shopping expedition. She was trying on dresses at Bonwit Teller's when Eunice appeared with a message that they must return to the Waldorf immediately to talk with Daddy. At the hotel, Joe was waiting at the door of his suite when Kathleen arrived. Placing his arm around her, he ushered her into the suite and behind closed doors told her that Billy was dead.

For the next few days, hearing nothing official from London, Kathleen clung to the slim hope that the news was untrue. But all along she knew in her heart that Billy was dead, and as soon as she could make arrangements she left for Quebec, where the British government sent a plane to bring her back to England. The same compulsion that had made her return to Hyannis Port to see her family of birth as soon as young Joe died worked now in the opposite direction to take her back to her new family, the Devonshires.

"So ends the story of Billy and Kick," Kathleen recorded in her diary on September 20. "I can't believe that the one thing I feared might happen should have happened . . . Life is so cruel. I am on my way to England. Writing is impossible."

For weeks, Kathleen was unable to sleep in a room by herself. She stayed for a time with the Devonshires at Compton Place and then moved in with Billy's aunt Anne Hunloke in Westminster. And in her extreme grief—for days on end she wept in her room—she spent most of her hours with Elizabeth Cavendish, Billy's favorite sister, who was said to be the most like him of his siblings. On September 30, 1944, Kathleen joined the Devonshire family for a simple memorial service held in a little church in Edensor, the village near Chatsworth. Since the fourteenth century many of Billy's ancestors had been laid to rest in the grassy plot behind the country church. "He loved his Derbyshire home and everything connected with it," his fellow guardsman Charles Waterhouse wrote. "He had a great place to fill in England and his character, inclination and training fitted him to fill it."

With the memorial service over, the Kennedys assumed that Kathleen would soon return to the States, but she elected to stay in England. Though she had lost her legal claim to Chatsworth or to any portion of the Devonshires' vast holdings when her husband died without a male heir, she still retained her title as Lady Hartington, and, as she and the new Duke-to-be, Billy's younger brother, Andrew, were very close, she knew she could use all the family's homes as her own. More important, with the religious problem now moot, the Devonshires opened their hearts completely to their spirited daughter-in-law, emphatically encouraging her to stay in England.

Returning to the Church, which welcomed her back once her Protestant husband was dead—"I guess God has taken care of the matter in His own way," she remarked bitterly—she also returned to the Red Cross, where her work now became vital to her existence. It took time, but gradually her native love of life reasserted itself and Kathleen began to be herself again.

"This is a very hard letter to write," she confessed to Lem Billings on November 29,

> because it's hard to explain to anyone I know so well as you and yet have not seen for such a long time, exactly what Billy meant to me. I thought so much before we got married about what it would be like, living in England away from home and living with all the difficulties. Then I made up my mind and nothing could budge me . . . And then suddenly one morning I wake up and find everything gone . . . I still can't believe it. And then suddenly someone says "you've got to think about what you have, not what you haven't got. And one thing you can be sure of life holds no fears for someone who has faced love, marriage and death before the age of 25." It's hard to face the future without someone who you thought would always be there to help and guide and for whom you'd sacrificed a lot.
>
> Luckily I am a Kennedy. I have a very strong feeling that that makes a big difference about how to take things. I saw Daddy and Mother about Joe and I know that we've all got the ability to not be got down. There are lots of years ahead and lots of happiness left in the world though sometimes nowadays that's hard to believe.

Back in the United States, Joe Kennedy received a new round of condolence letters, including telegrams from FDR—"Please tell Kathleen I am thinking of her in her crushing sorrow"—and Winston Churchill. "Thank you for your comforting message," Kennedy cabled to Churchill in return. "Repeated blows are bewildering but inspiring tributes to both boys from those who were with them afford helpful consolation."

"For a fellow who didn't want this war to touch your country or mine," Kennedy wrote to Max Beaverbrook on October 23, "I have had rather a bad dose—Joe dead, Billy Hartington dead, my son Jack in the Naval hospital. I have had brought home to me very personally what I saw for all the mothers and fathers of the world. The more I read of young Hartington and hear about him from Kathleen, the more I realize what a fine boy he was. His marriage to Kathleen was a real love match."

# CHAPTER 39
# SHADOWBOXING

For Jack, who felt, in Lem Billings' words, "completely powerless to comfort his inconsolable father," the months after his brother's death were a difficult time. For as long as he could remember, he confided to Lem, "his competition with his brother had defined his own identity." Now Joe was gone and Jack did not know where to turn.

Evoking a powerful mix of love and loss, rage and sorrow, Joe's death came at a particularly hard moment for Jack. After years of being the underdog, Jack had just begun to outperform his brother—first at Harvard and then in the Navy. But now the possibility of eventual victory was forever closed, for in his heroic death Joe was invulnerable, "his superiority sealed forever in his father's heart." "I'm shadowboxing in a match the shadow is always going to win," he told Lem.

In the early months after Joe's death, Jack described himself as feeling "terribly exposed and vulnerable." For twenty-seven years he had lived with a protective shield, since everything was expected of his older brother. So long as Joe was there to attract the force of the family's intense ambitions, Jack could move about more or less freely, focusing on what *he* wanted to do. But with Joe's death came an abrupt removal of the protection he had enjoyed and he felt an "unnamed responsibility" both to his parents and to his brothers and sisters.

But, with his father locked in his room, grieving for a part of himself as well as for Joe, it was not immediately clear what Jack was now expected to do as the eldest surviving son. Waiting for a sign that something different was demanded, he came up with the idea of putting together a small memorial book about Joe to present to his parents at Christmas and invited about twenty friends and family members to contribute recollections and reminiscences. Serving as the editor for the little volume, which he called *As We Remember Joe*, Jack also wrote the introductory essay. In it he spoke without embarrassment of the great promise Joe's life had held for all those who knew him. "His worldly success was so assured and inevitable," Jack wrote, "that his death seems to have cut into the natural order of things."

While the Ambassador found the book so sad that he "could read only one article at a time," he told Arthur Krock, he nonetheless judged it "a splendid piece of work" and was very grateful to Jack for producing it. It was at this point, as legend has it, that Joe consciously turned to Jack and ordered him to take Joe's place as the champion of the Kennedy clan in politics. The Ambassador was now fifty-five years old, and there was little time to waste if his dream of creating the first Irish Catholic President was still to be realized. The whole family would unite to help him, Jack was told. And then and there, the story is told, in spite of a welter of confusing emotions Jack answered his father's call, drawn into politics by circumstances beyond his control.

In fact the process which allowed Joe Kennedy to see Jack as a surrogate for young Joe was a much more complicated one for both father and son than legend has made it out to be. For so many years Kennedy had been so focused on young Joe's political talents that he had never really evaluated the considerable potential that Jack too possessed for public life. Speaking about the two boys later, Kennedy admitted that "Joe used to talk about being President some day, and a lot of smart people thought he would make it. He was altogether different from Jack —more dynamic, sociable and easygoing. Jack in those days . . . was rather shy, withdrawn and quiet. His mother and I couldn't picture him as a politician. We were sure he'd be a teacher or a writer."

There is in Kennedy's papers a revealing correspondence with his second cousin Joe Kane, the clever old-school politician who had been involved in Fitzgerald's campaign for the Senate in 1942. Smart and cunning, with the composure of a sphinx and an ever present fedora pulled down over one eye in the manner of Edward G. Robinson, Kane was considered one of the most knowledgeable men in Boston politics.

In the spring of 1944, when Joe Junior was still in England and Jack had just returned from the South Pacific, Kennedy had asked Kane to evaluate the possibilities in Massachusetts for both boys, though it is clear from his letters that with Jack he was thinking more along the lines of public service while Joe was the one who would run for political office.

As it happened, however, Jack was in Boston in the hospital at this time, so Kane got to know Jack much better than Joe. "There is something original about your young daredevil," Kane told Kennedy on February 14, 1944, after several encounters with Jack. "He has poise, a fine Celtic map. A most engaging smile." At a dinner at his grandfather's, "he spoke with perfect ease and fluency but quietly, deliberately and with complete self-control, always on the happiest terms with his audience. He was the master, not the servant of his oratorical power. He received an ovation and endeared himself to all by his modesty and gentlemanly manner."

Yet, when Kane raised with Jack the question of a political career, arguing that there wasn't any reason why a young man of means, well educated and with a fine family background, couldn't, like Thomas Jefferson, place politics among the fine arts of human relationships, Jack said simply and clearly, "My brother Joe has priority in aspiring for public office." "I think," Kane concluded, "he prefers a position on a governmental commission."

Now that young Joe was dead the question of priority was removed, but for both father and son the struggle to create a place in each other's heart was far more complex than the decisions about politics. And before any political decisions could be made, Jack's health had to be restored. For nearly six months, throughout the summer and fall of 1944, he had been in and out of the Chelsea Naval Hospital with severe and disabling pain from the gaping hole in his back left from the failed operation he had endured immediately after his return. Upon his release in early January, Jack promised his father that his first priority was to rebuild his health. And for that purpose he journeyed to the Hot Springs Hotel near Phoenix, Arizona, where he planned to stay until he had brought his body back into shape.

While Jack was in Arizona, Kennedy did everything he could to make sure that his son had all the care he needed, but, since Jack rarely admitted how bad he was feeling, it was hard to know what to do. On the phone Jack was "still his gay self," Kennedy told Red Fay in a letter, "but Dr. Lahey saw him in Phoenix and didn't think he was getting well at all." Admitting his discouragement to his son Robert, Kennedy voiced the fear that at some point Jack would have to return for another operation on his back. (In the spring of 1944, with the help of his father, nineteen-year-old Bobby had entered the Navy's V-12 training program at Harvard.)

Through the months Jack remained in Arizona, his father called him every day at 5 P.M. and gradually the two of them began to talk more fully and freely. "You could set your clock by it," recalled Pat Lannan, a new friend of Jack's who was in Arizona at the same time, also recuperating from an illness. "It was a wonderful relationship, I thought. He was always asking if there was anything he could do for Jack." For his part, Jack had long relished talking with his father about national issues, but never before had he had so much time to read during the day and then express his ideas to his father at night. Years later Rose recalled how impressed Joe was when he came away from these conversations—"it was the one thing that seemed to make him brighten up."

Even as they circled closer, neither Jack nor his father was able, in the spring of 1945, to focus on whether Jack really could pick up his brother's mantle. When Pat Lannan asked Jack what he was going to do when he returned home, Jack said that "his father had set up a trust for him, and he, Jack, didn't see any point in making any more money, or going into business, so he said he thought he'd go into public service." It was the first time Lannan had ever heard the term, so he said, "You mean politics?" But Jack wouldn't say "politics" to save his life, insisting that it was "public service."

Franklin Delano Roosevelt died in Warm Springs on April 12, 1945, in the final weeks of the war in Europe. While he had not been well for a long time, his death came without warning.

For Joseph Kennedy, the news brought mixed emotions. In the early days of the New Deal they had spent many happy hours together, but when Kennedy moved on to the Court of St. James's and separated himself from the President's policies a permanent rift had developed, which Kennedy preferred to blame on various White House aides but knew in his heart was due to Roosevelt. Then, when Joe Junior died in the war Kennedy had never wanted, his bitterness was sealed.

Kennedy had last seen Roosevelt six months earlier, in the final weeks of FDR's fourth presidential campaign, when the old warrior, anxious to pull in all the help he could, invited him to the White House. "If I hadn't been warned by the stories of his illness," Kennedy recorded in his diary, "I would have been shocked beyond words. He sat behind his desk and his face was as gray as his hair . . . He is thin. He has an unhealthy color. His hands shake violently when he tries to take a drink of water."

Kennedy noted that about ten percent of the time Roosevelt was talking his words were not clearly enunciated and when he spoke about Kathleen's husband he mistakenly referred to him as "Billy Harkshire," and *that* for Roosevelt was unheard of, since "his memory was his greatest asset next to his charm." At this point, Kennedy wrote, "the terrible realization came to me that the Hopkins, Rosenmans and Frankfurters could run the country now without much of an objection from him." But when the conversation moved on to the election Roosevelt proved that he was still a master at assessing public reaction, and Kennedy came away feeling that while the President had lost some of his old-time pep, he still had "a great deal of his old charm."

In the end, Kennedy never fully comprehended the nature of the man who had led his country through two of the most traumatic events of its history, never losing his faith in human nature, "a huge and unprovable faith in the possibilities of human understanding, trust and love." To examine Roosevelt closely, his biographer James MacGregor Burns has written, is to see failings and deficiencies interwoven with huge capacities. "But to stand back and look at the man as a whole, against the backdrop of his people and his times, is to see the lineaments of greatness—courage, joyousness, responsiveness, vitality, faith."

For weeks before the formal end of the war in Europe on May 8, 1945, the papers had been filled with speculation about the United Nations Conference scheduled to convene in San Francisco on April 25. Anticipating what an important event it would be, Joe contacted his friend Louis Ruppel, executive editor of the Hearst *Chicago Herald-American*, to suggest his sending Jack as a correspondent. Immediately taken with the idea of sending a PT-boat hero to cover the conference from a GI viewpoint, Ruppel reached Jack, who was then at the Mayo Clinic, and Jack enthusiastically embraced the idea.

Making his way among twelve hundred journalists—six for every delegate—Jack remained for a month, filing sixteen stories of about three hundred words each. The dispatches are interesting for their unsentimental awareness of the basic realities that were likely to torpedo the efforts to create a meaningful international organization. While he did not say so outright, almost every story reflected disillusionment with the raw power politics he was witnessing among the participating nations.

Responding more openly to one of his PT-boat friends who asked for his opinion on the conference, Jack wrote:

> It would be very easy to write a letter to you that was angry. When I think of how much this war has cost us, of the deaths of Cy and Peter and Orv and Gil and Demi and Joe and Billy and all those thousands and millions

who have died with them—when I think of all those gallant acts that I have seen or anyone has seen who has been to war—it would be a very easy thing for me to feel disappointed and somewhat betrayed . . . You have seen battlefields where sacrifice was the order of the day and to compare that sacrifice to the timidity and selfishness of the nations gathered at San Francisco must inevitably be disillusioning. . . . Things cannot be forced from the top. The international relinquishing of sovereignty would have to spring from the people—it would have to be so strong that the elected delegates would be turned out of office if they failed to do it. . . . We must face the truth that the people have not been horrified by war to a sufficient extent to force them to go to any extent rather than have another war. . . . War will exist until that distant day when the conscientious objector enjoys the same reputation and prestige that the warrior does today.

Reading his son's column in Hearst's *New York Journal-American*, Joe Kennedy was very pleased. "I think your column is doing very well," he wrote to Jack at the San Francisco Palace Hotel, "and I think you're particularly fortunate in getting such fine representation everywhere." For Joe Kennedy, the art of writing was always something of a mystery, something that never came easily to him, so it made Jack's success more impressive to him. And when Jack told him he had been asked by the Hearst organization to go to London to cover the British elections in June, his heart swelled with a pride that, according to Rose, he had not thought he could ever feel again.

Before setting off for London, Jack spent a few days on the East Coast visiting family and friends. During this time, Joe Kennedy confided to Vice-Admiral Russell Willson, Jack talked with Secretary Forrestal, who "offered him quite a responsible position in the Navy department. If it's open when he returns the latter part of July, I'm sure he would like to take it."

While he was in England, Jack made use of Kathleen's contacts to give him a rich perspective on the English political scene. "Will see Eden Friday, Crowther of *Economist* Friday afternoon," he reported on May 28 to his father. "Had dinner with the Duchess . . . Lord Brand and Elizabeth Cavendish tomorrow and lunch with Hugh Fraser and Dinah Brand . . . I shall not really come to a conclusion about things until I have covered most of my trip."

In his first dispatch, dated June 23, he displayed a certain prescience in predicting, against all the opinion of the day, that Churchill might lose the election. Arguing that the British people were tired of ten years of Conservative government and wanted change, he wrote that Churchill "was fighting a tide that is surging through Europe, washing away monarchies and conservative governments everywhere." In his memoirs, Arthur Krock stated that Jack's performance in England persuaded him that "this boy had the makings of a very good political observer." In his dispatches and even more in two private letters which Jack wrote to Krock, "he was the only source of my expectation that Churchill would be turned out of office." Yet, on the day of the election, Jack hedged his bets and predicted that the voting would be close and that this time at least the Conservatives might win. History records, of course, that his first prediction was the correct one—for the Labourites defeated the Tories in a landslide, turning Churchill out of office.

Once again, Joe Kennedy was very pleased with his son's performance. Writing to thank Louis Ruppel at the *Chicago Herald-American* on August 7, he noted that Jack was due back that day. "He's planning to go back into the hospital and have the operation he was going to have when you yanked him out and sent him to San Francisco and I believe, did him a real, real service. I think if the operation turns out successfully, he'll really start to settle down and go places."

His spirits partially restored by his renewed faith in his second son, Kennedy purchased the Merchandise Mart in Chicago, the world's largest privately owned structure, second in area only to the U.S. government's Pentagon. Built by Marshall Field in 1930 at a cost of $30 million, the huge, sprawling twenty-four-story building had been losing money for Field for years, and Kennedy was able to purchase it for $12.5 million. Speaking of the deal years later, Rose observed: "Joe had a genius for seeing something and knowing it would be worth something more later on. And with the Mart he was absolutely right, for once he turned it around, with physical changes and spectacular merchandising, it skyrocketed in value and became the basis for a whole new Kennedy fortune. For years afterward, he liked to brag that a Jewish group had seen the Mart before him and done absolutely nothing about it, which was unusual, he would say, since the Jews have such great heads for business. Then along comes an Irishman from Boston who bought it and realized its potential worth."

At the time of Kennedy's purchase, over 40 percent of the rentable area of the Mart was filled by various government agencies—the worst tenants, in Kennedy's mind, as they were paying submarginal rates on short-term leases. Determined to replace the government leases with more lucrative corporate leases, Kennedy embarked on a major renovation of the building, investing over $5 million in air-conditioning. "At that time," Wally Ollman, manager of the Mart, recalled, "air-conditioning was a comparatively new development. Few if any major Chicago properties offered this much needed service but Mr. Kennedy foresaw its potentialities and realized that within a comparatively short time air-conditioned space would be a 'must' in a prospective tenant's list of requirements." Within ten years, Kennedy was clearing more profit on the building each year than he had put down for its purchase.

Kennedy was also buoyed up by the country's response to President Truman. "Harry Truman has taken the public fancy in a wonderful fashion," he wrote to Sir James Calder in August 1945. "One never hears the name Roosevelt mentioned and I am thoroughly convinced that if Roosevelt had remained alive, we would have been in the worst mess that anyone could have imagined. There was such a feeling of antagonism toward him and his theories that I doubt if we would have ever started on a peacetime plan, and so on the whole God was again good to the US."

God was also good to Joseph Kennedy, for during these last weeks of summer Jack agreed to run for public office. Arriving home from England on the day after the United States dropped the atomic bomb on Hiroshima, Jack spent "hours on end," according to his mother, discussing his future with his father. "He was still pretty unsure at that time whether politics was the right thing for him to do, but his father had enough enthusiasm for the two of them."

By this time, nearly a year after young Joe's death, Kennedy was finally able to look more clearly at his second son. And he liked what he saw. Though he still harbored the fear that Jack did not have "a temperament outgoing enough for politics," he had come to a deeper appreciation of his second son's intelligence and charm. Perhaps, with a little luck and a lot of hard work, the dream could be realized after all.

Once Joe determined that Jack "had the goods," the pressure on Jack was fierce. "It was like being drafted," Jack later told reporter Bob Considine. "My father wanted his eldest son in politics. 'Wanted' isn't the right word. He demanded it. You know my father." According to Arthur Krock, Jack was very reluctant at first to take up the challenge. Politics was not the career he would have chosen. But the shifting of attention "was almost a physical event," Krock maintains, and Jack had no way to escape. That August he made the decision to stay in Massachusetts and pursue a political career.

It was a family in which sorrow could be healed only through action, a family in which each member was coerced as much by internalized expectations as by direct pressure. Indeed, so powerful were the family bonds of need and desire, love and respect, that the question of who was using whom for what would soon become very hard to judge.

"Jack arrived home and is very thin," Kennedy wrote to Sir James Calder on August 22, 1945, "but he is becoming quite active in the political life of Massachusetts." And then, using words that would have seemed impossible to voice a year before, he concluded: "It wouldn't surprise me to see him go into public life to take Joe's place."

When Jack Kennedy made his entry into Massachusetts politics in the fall of 1945, he was, in some ways, "a stranger in the city of his birth." He had been six when his family moved to New York, and after that, until the war, he had spent most of his life in exclusive schools and in comfortable accommodations on trips abroad, with winters in Palm Beach and summers in Hyannis Port. He had lived in Cambridge for four years while he was attending Harvard, but the world of Harvard was as remote from the working-class districts of Cambridge as Palm Beach was from Boston. The only person he knew in Boston, he would later recall in a half-joking manner, was his eighty-two-year-old grand-father, so it was no accident that he set up his headquarters in a two-room suite at the Bellevue Hotel, just down the hall from the suite where Fitzgerald and his wife had been living for nearly a decade.

The idea was to move around the state, meeting people and making speeches, while avoiding as long as possible a declaration for a specific office. In this way, Joe Kennedy assumed, young Jack could capitalize both on his own reputation as a war hero and on his relatives' status as Boston's leading celebrities, developed over the years through a combination of real accomplishment and clever public relations. As it happened, at the very time Jack was settling in, Joe Kennedy was crisscrossing the state himself, having been assigned by Massachusetts Governor Maurice Tobin to conduct an economic survey of the state. It was a fortuitous assignment, for it allowed the Ambassador to rehabilitate his reputation in Massachusetts while meeting every person of consequence in state government, politics and the media.

Setting up his own headquarters at the Ritz-Carlton, Kennedy arranged to meet his son at the end of each day in order to analyze the events of that day and to plan for the next. In these early months, most observers agree, public speaking did not come easily to Jack. While he was able to speak clearly and effectively when he had time to prepare and when he knew a lot about his subject, he found it difficult to simply stand up and make extemporaneous speeches on local political issues. As a result, his early speeches tended to focus more on international issues where he could draw upon his wide-ranging travels. Asked to address the members of an American Legion post on September 10, 1945, Jack shrewdly chose to speak on the status of postwar Europe, a topic which allowed him to tell personal stories of his various meetings with leading European politicians and statesmen. The speech was a success, and when the Ambassador arranged to have it carried over the radio by the Yankee Network it generated over 130 requests for copies and a large number of congratulatory notes. "It was a most interesting talk," a typical letter began, "more especially as the young officer had visited those countries."

But as the momentum picked up and Jack found himself—with his father's help—invited to speak before an increasing number of organizations, ranging from Holy Name societies to Kiwanis clubs to women's clubs, his speeches had to be varied in content and hurriedly prepared, and on these occasions he lacked confidence in his delivery. Years later, Eunice recalled her brother's discouragement. "Many a night when he'd come over to see Daddy after a speech, he'd be feeling rather down, admitting that the speech hadn't really gone very well or believing that his delivery had put people in the front row fast asleep. 'What do you mean,' Father would immediately ask. 'Why, I talked to Mr. X and Mrs. Y on the phone right after they got home and they told me they were sitting right in the front row and that it was a fine speech. And then I talked with so and so and he said last year's speaker at the same event had 40 in the audience while you had 90.'

"And then," Eunice continued, "and this was the key, Father would go on to elicit from Jack what *he* thought he could change to make it better the next time. I can still see the two of them sitting together, analyzing the entire speech and talking about the pace of delivery to see where it had worked and where it had gone wrong. Now, to play that role Daddy had to be on the phone gathering facts from the minute Jack left till the minute he returned. But once he had those facts he was able to use them to criticize Jack's performance and stretch his ability at the same time."

Looking back later on his early days in politics, Jack liked to say that if he initially lacked confidence, his father had confidence enough for them both. "If I walked out on the stage," he once told a friend, "and fell flat on my face, Father would say I fell better than anyone else." But Joe Kennedy's technique was more subtle than sheer flattery. In politics there are always plenty of people to say a candidate has performed well no matter how badly he has done; with Kennedy, the flattery was only a means to improvement. The praise he gave his son was always based on bits and pieces of facts which he had garnered from someone present. And then once the compliment was delivered, the Ambassador could go on to shape a critique without ever putting Jack on the defensive, a critique that involved his son in a joint enterprise of evaluation.

Nor did Jack find it easy to approach people on street corners and strike up a conversation, the very failure his father had feared. But in the hurly-burly of Massachusetts politics his reticence worked like a charm, setting him off favorably from the typical backslapping Irish politician. "He never once said to anybody," his aide Billy Sutton recalled, " 'How's Mother? Tell her I said hello.' And he never went to a wake unless he knew the deceased personally."

"There was a basic dignity in Jack Kennedy," another aide, Dave Powers, observed, "a pride in his bearing that appealed to every Irishman who was beginning to feel a little embarrassed about the sentimental, corny style of the typical Irish politician. As the Irish themselves were becoming more middle-class, they wanted a leader to reflect their upward mobility."

It was, curiously enough, Joe Kane, a prototype of the older Irish politician if ever there was one, who first recognized the potential of a new kind of appeal to a new generation of Irish men and women. Responsible for coining the slogan "The New Generation Offers a Leader," Kane had written to Joe Kennedy back in 1944 that "in a state where money as well as public office is handed down from generation to generation, where a Lodge succeeds a Lodge, a Weeks a Weeks, a Saltonstall a Saltonstall," a brand-new appeal could be made to the newer arrivals to find a leader of their own who could carry on in the same high-minded, aristocratic way as the Lodges and the Weekses. "Brother," Kane concluded, "would they puff and go for that line."

"Your Jack is worth a king's ransom," Kane had told Joe Kennedy even before Kennedy fully recognized Jack's political potential. A unique figure in Boston politics, Kane united in himself all the experience of the old ward days—complete with a gruff manner, long cigars and a fantastic storytelling ability—with an uncommon feel for the future. "Joe Kane had such wonderful stories," Jack later said, "that you could listen to him for hours without ever thinking of anything else." When the Ambassador first brought Jack together with Kane, he was surprised by Jack's reaction. "I thought Jack wouldn't last five minutes with him," Kennedy said, "but I was wrong, for he not only stayed for over four hours but he loved every minute of it."

"It was a strange thing," Dave Powers later observed, "while Jack Kennedy was a completely new type of Irish politician himself, having come from such a different background, he was, at bottom, very Irish and he could never hear enough of the old Irish stories. So many times when we'd be together in a group he'd turn to me with a grin and say 'Now, Dave, tell that story about Paddy,' and so I would. And it would always be some funny old story which we had heard a hundred times growing up but which he was just hearing now for the first time."

When Jack first started moving around the state, his father believed that his son's best shot would be to run for lieutenant governor on the

Democratic ticket with the incumbent Governor Maurice Tobin. A friend of Kennedy's, Tobin made it abundantly clear that he would welcome the addition of the young PT-boat hero to the ticket. To the Ambassador, nothing else looked as positive as the idea of Jack starting his political career as lieutenant governor and then moving from there to higher office. Promising as this strategy was, it never appealed to Jack, who knew that his greatest strength lay in his ability to charm people one on one and feared a diminution of this strength if he had to spread himself all across the state the first time out. At the same time, Jack's interest in national and international issues far outweighed his interest in local issues, so he would much prefer an office with national responsibility.

While Jack and his father were discussing the lieutenant governorship, a congressional seat from the Eleventh District, the same polyglot district Fitzgerald had represented at the turn of the century, opened up. It was a gift from a most unlikely donor, James Michael Curley. In November 1945, Curley ran a victorious campaign for mayor, and as a result his congressional seat was suddenly open, to be filled by election in November 1946. To Jack, the race for Congress seemed far more manageable even though he would face a large number of opponents. At the same time, it provided the rare opportunity to enter politics at a national rather than a state or city level.

The Ambassador was not immediately convinced, preferring the lieutenant governorship. The decision was put off for several months. Then, on March 7, 1946, a month before the filing date for the congressional vacancy, Joe Kane finally spoke his mind in a frank but thoughtful letter to Joe Kennedy. "Give the kid a break!" he began, stating at the outset:

> A Tobin-Kennedy victory, with a chance of [Senator] Walsh dying, Tobin taking the Senate seat and Jack moving up, is a big lure and a gamble that fascinates you. . . . Has it ever occurred to you Tobin might be licked and Jack win . . . Do you realize Jack at 28, as a candidate for Lieutenant Governor, would be exposed to Republican party and press attacks where he is the most vulnerable without any public record.
>
> On the other hand, Jack, seeking seat in Congress in district where Republican party and press cannot hurt him and where his political strength is greatest, would only have to overcome opposition of his opponents. . . . As outstanding Congressman with national and international reputation he would be in demand as public speaker while as lieutenant governor he would be simply a silenced political priest. Walsh is the only lieutenant governor in 32 years to make Governor. . . . At the moment, the boys helping Jack only to see him win are for Congress. Greedy boys, who want to cash in, are for lieutenant governor.

Responding four days later, the Ambassador confessed that while he would still rather see Jack as lieutenant governor he was feeling less happy about the run for that office, understanding now from Kane's letter how lack of experience would play on a state level. "Therefore," he concluded, "since he would have an easier chance to win in Congress, I believe I am inclining more toward that idea."

On a warm spring day in the third week in April, Jack Kennedy formally announced his intention to seek Mayor Curley's old seat in the Eleventh Congressional District. "The temper of the times," he declared, sounding a theme of public service that would one day become permanently associated with his name, "imposes an obligation upon every thinking citizen to work diligently in peace as we served tirelessly in war. . . . Everyone who is able should do his utmost in these days of world and national progress to contribute his talents in keeping with his abilities and resources."

The primary race for the Eleventh District seat soon developed into a "wild free-for-all" with a field of ten candidates vying against one another. At the outset, Mike Neville, the mayor of Cambridge, was the clear favorite. Formerly the Speaker of the House of Representatives in Massachusetts, Neville, according to one observer, was "probably the most powerful fellow" in Boston's public life at that time. Another strong contender was John F. Cotter of Charlestown, an old politician with deep roots in his city. Having served as Curley's secretary in Congress and before that as Representative Higgins' secretary, Cotter knew the district better than anyone else and was already considered by many voters a sort of unofficial congressman. Also in the race were Catherine Falvey of Somerville, a Women's Army Corps major known for dressing in her whites; Joseph Lee, a Yankee patrician; four Bostonians of Italian origin, including two Joseph Russos; and an idealistic schoolteacher.

At first, the rest of the candidates laughed young Kennedy off. "The poor little rich kid," Catherine Falvey dubbed him. "Carpetbagger," others cried, "an outsider trying to buy the election with his father's money." "During the bitter months of the worst winter, I was side by side with Curley," Cotter proclaimed. "My multimillionaire opponent was basking at Hialeah and the sunbaked sands of Palm Beach." "People said he was simply a millionaire's son," Dave Powers recalled, "who would never get ten votes in the tough working-class districts of Boston, Charlestown, Somerville or Cambridge." Perhaps he'd win some votes at Harvard, others taunted, but pristine Harvard was but a small corner of a sprawling district which enclosed a score of immigrant groups packed into three-decker houses sandwiched between smoking factories, oil tanks, elevated railways, dumps and freight yards.

Recognizing the narrow, localized strengths of the other candidates, the strategy was for Jack Kennedy to become the number-two man in all sections. For this, Joe Kane argued, would be "almost victory—politically speaking." But in order for Jack to run strongly throughout the entire district, he would need a large volunteer organization, which, in turn, would depend upon a strong cadre of loyal workers at the center. So the heavy emphasis in the early months went to the development of a highly visible, idealistic group of committed workers—a group that eventually included Dave Powers, Billy Sutton, Mark Dalton, Billy Kelly, John Droney, Tony Galluccio, Tom Broderick and Teddy Reardon. All of these "amateurs" had deep roots in their own communities, but, once recruited into Jack's campaign, they developed a great feeling of comradeship and fellowship toward one another. "We few, we happy few, we band of brothers," Jack Kennedy liked to quote years later in talking of all those who were with him during this first tough struggle.

If Joe Kane deserves credit for suggesting the names of many of the original cadre, Jack Kennedy was the one who drew them all in. "There was something about his personality," Dave Powers observed, "that made you want to drop whatever you were doing and go to work for him." Years later, Dave would remember in vivid detail the night when Jack Kennedy climbed the stairs to the top floor of his Charlestown three-decker and knocked on the front door. "There was only a twenty-watt light bulb in the front hallway, and I could barely make out this tall and thin handsome young fellow standing alone in the semi-darkness," Dave recalled. "He stuck out his hand and said, 'My name is Jack Kennedy. I'm a candidate for Congress.'" Kennedy went on to tell Powers that his name had been suggested as someone who might be able to help him in Charlestown. Straightaway, Powers told him that he had known John Cotter over many years and in fact had just had a beer with him, but this did not discourage Jack; instead, he just continued asking Dave's advice about Charlestown. "I remember saying to him," Powers recalled, "that the people in Charlestown were only looking for a decent place to live, an opportunity to give their children an education, and knowing where their next buck was coming from. He took that in as if he were trying to memorize it. He said, 'You know, that sounds about right.'"

When Jack was leaving he casually told Dave that he was planning to attend a meeting of the Gold Star Mothers two days later in Charlestown. Would Dave go with him? Figuring it wouldn't do any harm simply to attend the meeting, Powers agreed.

Jack's talk at the meeting two nights later centered on the sacrifices of war and the need to keep the world at peace. All the women in the room were mothers who had lost a son in the war. As he ended his speech, Jack paused, looked at the women and then said hesitantly, "I think I know how all you mothers feel because my mother is a Gold Star Mother, too." At that moment, Dave recalled, Jack forged some sort of "magical link" between himself and everyone in the room. By revealing himself as a person who shared their suffering, he bridged the distance between the candidate and the crowd.

"Suddenly, swarms of women hurried up to the platform," Dave continued, "crowding around him and wishing him luck. And I could hear them saying to each other, 'Isn't he a wonderful boy, he reminds me so much of my own John' or 'my Bob.' It took a half hour for him to get away. Now I'd been to rallies since I was ten and had always measured everything by Curley's masterful performance, but this reaction was unlike any I had ever seen. It wasn't so much what he said but the way he reached into the emotions of everyone there."

When Jack finally made his way out of the hall he turned to Dave and asked him how he thought the speech had gone. Caught off guard, Dave confessed that he had never seen such a crowd reaction in all his life. "Then do you think you'll be with me?" Jack asked. "I'm already with you," Dave responded, putting out his hand.

John Droney, another young veteran like Dave, recalled a similar experience. Asked by his friend Tony Galluccio to see Jack, he went to the Bellevue. When he got out of the elevator he saw quite a few generals and captains and other brass going into the apartment. Disgusted, he pressed the elevator button to leave, but just as he was about to step in he found himself facing a tall, slim fellow in shirtsleeves who introduced himself as Jack Kennedy and asked him why he was leaving before his appointment. Droney said he had had enough of the brass during the war and thought he'd just drop the idea of the campaign. At this, Jack laughed and said, "John, I feel the same way, but Tony thinks you can help me a great deal in Cambridge and I'd like to sit down and tell you my plans. I can take you into another room and we won't be bothered." In the conversation that followed, Jack perceptively sensed that Droney was hesitant about politics in general, seeing himself headed for a career in law, so he shared with him some of his own hesitations about political life, telling him that he had originally wanted to be a newspaperman. "But," he concluded, making an argument on the need for changing things in the country, "if we're going to do the things we like to do we have to do many things that we don't care about doing." This personal approach appealed to Droney strongly, and he agreed to sign up that day.

With both Powers and Droney, however, as indeed with every alliance

Jack made, nothing was final unless the Ambassador approved. The following day, Droney recalled, Jack phoned to ask him if he'd be willing to go over to the Ritz to see his dad, because he had to clear everything with his father. Droney agreed and met with the Ambassador and Eddie Moore. Within a half hour of the meeting Jack called to say that his dad had approved of him and everything was fine. "This was how we started," Droney said.

To the outsider, Jack's acceptance of his father's absolute control must have seemed extraordinary, but it was a matter of course to Jack and the other members of his family, who were long accustomed to needing and seeking Daddy's approval.

Powers recalled a similar experience. After working for Jack a day or so, he received a note asking him to go to the Ritz to see the Ambassador. He was dressed in suntans and a T-shirt, and he asked the secretary if he should go home and change. "Oh no," she replied, "when the Ambassador wants to see you, he wants to see you." During the meeting, Kennedy asked Dave how many votes there were in Charlestown. "Oh, about ten thousand," Dave answered. "I know about," Joe replied sharply. "I want to know exactly." "Was he scary!" Dave recalled. "Yet the next morning when I saw him again and told him the figure was 10,637, he patted me on the back and made me feel great. And from then on I always made sure I had my numbers straight. He was so good at making you feel that if you didn't do something right you were letting him down."

According to Powers, the Ambassador also controlled the disbursement of all funds. Each month when he needed the forty dollars to cover the rent for the Charlestown headquarters, Powers had to see Eddie Moore. "It was the strangest experience," Powers recalled. "I would meet Moore at the campaign's central headquarters at 18 Tremont Street and he would then lead me into the men's room, where, putting a dime into the slot, he would take me into a closed toilet. There, with no one able to watch us, he would hand me the cash, saying, 'You can never be too careful in politics about handing over money.' "

Nor was Joe Kennedy's influence limited to approval of staff and money outlays. "Joe Kennedy was the mastermind of all Jack's campaigns," Joe Timilty once said. "He was completely in charge of everything, every detail." With this assessment Mark Dalton agreed. "The Ambassador was the essential, real campaign manager," Dalton recalled. Though he remained, as Rose put it in a letter to Kathleen, "behind the scenes so whatever success there is will be due entirely to Jack and the younger group," his influence could be felt from wherever he was, from the Ritz, from Hyannis Port and even from Palm Beach.

Writing to Kane from Palm Beach on February 11, 1946, the Ambassador said he had heard that Jack was working "like a beaver" but "I hear from some other people up there that they think he should visit more Jewish organizations." Less than two weeks later, Kane reported that Jack would be addressing three Jewish organizations within a short period.

And, on a strategic level, there was no one whose ideas held more weight than the Ambassador's. It was the Ambassador who hired the John Dowd Advertising Agency to do Jack's public relations. And it was the Ambassador who embraced the concept of having Jack run primarily as a young veteran, recognizing, after a private poll had confirmed greater interest in Jack as a PT war hero than as a political candidate, that the links forged by the common experience of fighting a war could bring Jack together with thousands of young men who might otherwise feel a sense of distance from a millionaire's son.

So, with the Ambassador's prompting, the veteran angle appeared in almost every press release issued by the Kennedy for Congress headquarters. A typical release read:

> Men who pushed back the Japs, island by island in the Pacific, men who stormed into blazing Normandy on D-Day and who hammered their way across France and Germany to blunt the Nazi military might are now fighting a different kind of campaign—a political battle on behalf of a young man who at one time during the war was reported missing in action. . . . One of the impressive features of his campaign has been the manner in which veterans of all branches have rallied behind his candidacy. . . .

For Jack, it had never been easy to wear the mantle of war hero—perhaps, as we have seen, because he never believed that his actions had been heroic. The PT incident became still more embarrassing during the campaign as it became more and more embellished. "My story about the collision is getting better all the time," Jack observed to a war buddy one day in the course of the 1946 campaign. "Now I've got a Jew and a Nigger in the story and with me being a Catholic, that's great."

In the end, however, Jack agreed with his father that his experience in the war gave him a special bond with all manner of men whom it otherwise might have been difficult to reach. "After he'd been in a bar," Dave Powers recalled, "I'd stay back and listen and get a sense of what the longshoremen thought. And invariably they'd say the same thing in a different way, all boiling down to something like 'Now, that guy has balls.' "

Still, Jack found it more comfortable, when talking about the war, to speak of himself in the third person or to stress the heroism of his crew. In a speech delivered to a number of veterans' organizations, he dwelt at length on the courage of Pappy McMahon, the forty-one-year-old engineer who was so badly burned. "I felt that his courage was the result of his loyalty to the men around him," Kennedy said. "Most of the courage shown in the war came from men's understanding of their interdependence on each other. Men were saving other men's lives at the risk of their own simply because they realized that perhaps the next day their lives would be saved in turn. And so there was built up during the war a great feeling of comradeship and fellowship and loyalty."

It was a feeling, Kennedy observed (speaking perhaps to his own loneliness), which thousands of soldiers returning home desperately missed. "They miss the close comradeship . . . that sense of working together for a common cause." The challenge of politics, as young Kennedy saw it, was to build that sense of participation in peacetime, to make people recognize they were as dependent upon each other in civilian life as they were in war, to get people mobilized into a common effort.

As the weeks passed, Jack's speaking ability steadily improved, and though he never overcame his discomfort with strangers he forced himself into firehouses, police stations, post offices, saloons and poolrooms. Fascinated by the richness of the political experience, which brought him up rickety stairs into crowded apartments for the first time in his life, Jack found himself enjoying the process of campaigning far more than he ever could have imagined.

Years later, Joe Kennedy told the story of a day in East Boston in 1946 when he happened to be talking with a friend in front of the Columbia Trust Company. Suddenly, his eye caught a glimpse of Jack standing across the street shaking hands with a group of longshoremen, asking each one for his vote. "I remember saying to the man who was with me that I would have given odds of five thousand to one that this thing we were seeing could never have happened. I never thought Jack had it in him."

In his daily rounds through the sprawling district, Jack received a special boost from his grandfather. Whenever he could, particularly when Jack was going into the North End or the West End, Honey Fitz would accompany him, serving as a visible link to the days when the ward politicians were involved in the lives of families in the neighborhood. "Fitzgerald was a cheerleader with the elderly," Billy Sutton recalled. "Still a Sunday parishioner at St. Stephen's, he had a remarkable memory for names and faces and he was able to introduce Jack to hundreds of people. Watching his grandfather, Jack made up his mind to memorize as many names and faces as he could." The discipline obviously worked, for, according to one of Kennedy's aides, Jack was brilliant about picking up names and even remembered nicknames. "All he had to do was see you once," the aide recalled, "and he'd remember you the second time."

Because Jack was already a celebrity in his hometown, there were people all over the district who wanted to meet him. For thousands of people coming out of the depression and war, the Kennedy name meant success, power and wealth, the fulfillment of the American dream. It seemed almost as if everything had come full circle. Whereas politics had provided the first generation with their first boost up the ladder, Joe Kennedy's wealth had given the family a social status which Jack Kennedy was now able to translate back into political power.

While he never once denied his Catholic faith or his Irish heritage, it was clear to the voters that John Kennedy had lived his life in a different world from theirs. Yet, because he was able to treat those differences with humor and grace, he turned his wealth into an asset, making it something to aspire to rather than be angry about not having. At one gathering, at which each of his opponents was introduced as the son of a poor man, Jack won over the crowd by saying, "I seem to be the only person here tonight who didn't come up the hard way."

Early in the campaign, the decision was made to spend considerable time and money trying to attract campaign workers who had never before been in public life and to meet people who ordinarily weren't interested in politics. For this purpose, an elaborate series of house parties was planned as a way of bringing the campaign directly to the voters in their own neighborhoods. While house parties had been used before in other campaigns, they had never been planned as carefully as these nor scheduled on a scale so ambitious that the candidate could cover at least half a dozen in a single evening.

Run with the help of Jack's sisters Eunice and Pat, who coordinated the volunteer hostesses, providing them with cups and saucers, coffee and cookies, silver and flowers, each party accommodated between twenty-five and seventy-five people. On party nights, Eunice and Pat would start off in one location and then move to the next, with Jack following shortly behind. Generally the party would begin with a special newsreel or some brief entertainment, followed by a general circulation of the guests. Then Jack would arrive, make a short speech and afterward open himself for questions and answers.

"Kennedy was at his best at these affairs," James MacGregor Burns reported, "coming in a bit timidly but with his flashing picture magazine smile, charming the mothers and titillating the daughters, answering questions with a leg draped over the arm of his chair, wandering into the kitchen for a word with proud grandparents about news from the 'old country,' a final round of handshaking before leaving for the next affair."

"The older ladies seemed to mother him," John Droney recalled; "all the young ones fell in love with him."

After the party, the name of every person who attended was forwarded to headquarters, and within a matter of days a volunteer would call and solicit the help of each. The Kennedys instinctively understood the importance of attending to the smallest detail. Indeed, so finely was the campaign tuned at the individual level that it was said to be a throwback to the days of machine politics. Having missed a house party in the middle of May because his flight from Washington was delayed by stormy weather, Jack wrote a note of apology to every invited guest, ending with: "Miss Kirby and Miss Norton were kind enough to say they were planning to give another house party and were going to invite you. I hope most sincerely that you will be able to attend. My warmest thanks to you for your nice reception of my sister Eunice and Mr. Mark Dalton and . . . hope I shall meet you soon."

Before the campaign ended, the entire Kennedy family with the exception of Kathleen (whose marriage to Hartington was still considered a political liability in this largely Catholic constituency) had joined in the fight, as had a number of Jack's friends including Lem Billings, Torby Macdonald and Red Fay. Arriving in his sailor suit, twenty-one-year-old Bobby, just back from a tour of duty on the U.S. destroyer named after his brother Joe, went around with Jack at night, meeting quite a divergent group of people, he wrote to his mother, "from Irish bartenders to Negro members of the VFW." He then stayed for several weeks, working in three wards of East Cambridge, where he was remembered years later for joining up with the neighborhood kids in pickup basketball and football games.

But, to the surprise of everyone except perhaps John Fitzgerald, who knew all along that politics had been in his daughter's blood since the day she was born, Rose Kennedy proved to be the most effective campaigner of them all. Joining only in the last few weeks, which qualified her as a "hot weather campaigner," Rose brought a special glamour and style into the campaign. "Had she started early," Billy Sutton observed, "the glamour would have worn off. But as it was, she represented an unreachable dream to thousands of Irish matrons. Women came as much to see her and her clothes as they did to see Jack." Refusing to deliver a political speech on the grounds that her audience wanted something different, Rose shrewdly talked instead about her family, telling stories about her children and the challenge of raising a large family, while at the same time sharing with the audience a glimpse of her glamorous life at the Court of St. James's, complete with word portraits of the King and Queen.

The story is told of an occasion when Rose was one of a number of speakers warming up an audience before Jack arrived. Walking in far later than expected, Jack flashed a grin at his mother and pointed proudly to his hat. Throughout his campaign, all the older advisers, including his mother and Joe Kane, had been after him to wear a hat both to cover his tousled shock of hair and to make him look older. But the younger staff felt, as Dave Powers later put it, "if you put a hat on a Kennedy, you lose three quarters of the head and all the charisma." And besides, Jack simply did not like wearing a hat. Nevertheless, for this event, knowing that his mother was going to be there, Jack was wearing a hat.

As he walked up to the stage, still grinning at his mother, Jack said, "Well, Mother, how do you like my hat?"

"Dear," Rose responded, to the delight of everyone present, "it would have looked a lot better two hours ago!"

In the final weeks of the campaign, in an irony of fate that only Joe and Rose Kennedy could fully appreciate, "everybody wanted to be in high society with the Kennedys." To the socially conscious Irish, the Kennedys had now emerged as the "first Irish Brahmins," a position worthy of emulation. By simply being with the Kennedys, the Irish could imagine that they too would one day walk in a world of wealth and privilege. The mere association made them feel better about themselves. In recognition of the potential power of this social phenomenon, the idea was put forward to stage a huge formal reception at a fancy hotel in Cambridge, with engraved invitations sent to women voters in the name of the Ambassador and Rose.

The idea polarized the staff. Who, the critics demanded, had ever heard of asking the voters to dress up to be presented to a candidate and his family as if they were royalty? John Droney argued that it was "too effeminate," that it would make the Kennedys a laughingstock if their fancy tea party failed to attract a crowd. Others argued that it was a great waste of money and effort, since it would bring out only those who were going to vote for Jack anyway. And the old pols claimed they could make far better use of the money on beer busts. But Eunice took to the idea at once and, with her support and her willingness to coordinate the enormous task of addressing thousands of invitations, the decision was made to go ahead.

The reception was scheduled in the grand ballroom of the Commander Hotel in Cambridge for Saturday, June 15, three days before the primary. It was a warm night, and the mood at Kennedy's headquarters all afternoon had been high. But the fantastic success of the event went beyond all imaginings. At least fifteen hundred women came, all dressed in their finest clothes. At the head of the receiving line, making his only public appearance on behalf of his son, stood the former Ambassador to the Court of St. James's.

"It created a gigantic traffic hazard," Kennedy worker De Guglielmo recalled. "No one could get into Harvard Square." The reception line was a block long and veteran journalists were amazed. "The crowd swelled onto the streets," observed one reporter, "in a demonstration unparalleled in the history of Congressional fights in this district," as hundreds of women unable to gain entrance to the ballroom waited patiently for a glimpse of young Kennedy.

After everyone had gone through the receiving line, Rose gave her little talk and then the entire family circulated around the room shaking hands. The next day the Sunday papers carried spectacular stories of the event. The old pols admitted they had never seen anything like it. "Every girl there was gonna be Mrs. Kennedy, for crissakes," Patsy Mulkern said. "There was a storekeeper tol' me, 'I let out more gowns this week than in a whole year before. I wish he'd run forever.' " And looking at the turnout, a veteran politician from Cambridge said, "This kid will walk in."

Still, Joe Kennedy left nothing to chance. Through his many contacts in the publishing industry, he arranged for a well-illustrated article on Jack in *Look* magazine to appear on the newsstands the final week of the campaign. Supplied with favorable material from the Kennedy family, it led off with a large picture of Jack, his father and Honey Fitz; below that was a small picture of the handsome war hero in naval dress uniform. In the text, which began with the question as to why a young and wealthy man would run for Congress, Jack was quoted as saying the answer was simple, "I have an obligation as a rich man's son to people who are having a hard time of it," and he noted that he had another more personal reason: to do the job that his dead brother Joe would have done.

> He has guts and brains [the text of the article read], a war career, an intelligence and a personality which should satisfy the most exacting constituency. His Navy record is a source of envy in politics . . . Most important, Kennedy has the looks and Irish personality which often combine in Massachusetts politics to sell a candidate to the voters . . . Jack Kennedy if he goes to Congress won't be in anybody's pocket. He will be neither pro nor anti administration. He doesn't hesitate now and he won't hesitate in Congress to say what he thinks.

It was rumored during the campaign that Kennedy spent nearly $250,000. This figure was vigorously denied by the Kennedy family but if one considers Joe Kennedy's celebrated capacity to leverage his money in all manner of ways, the total was probably even higher. During these months, for instance, he worked out a deal with the archdiocese in which he pledged a contribution of $600,000, the largest family contribution in the archdiocese's history, to erect a convalescent home for poor children in Brighton. The home would bear the name of his eldest son, but when the time came for the public ceremony Kennedy arranged it so that Jack handed the check to Cardinal Cushing.

In the closing days, the Ambassador also provided the money for 100,000 reprints of John Hersey's "Survival" article to be mailed out to the voters, coupled with a special press release consisting of a tribute by William Johnston, one of Jack's crew on the *PT 109*:

> I'm not a politician and I don't know much about politics. But, if the people of this district want a congressman with real abilities, with great qualities of leadership and with unusual courage, then John Fitzgerald Kennedy is their man. . . . Somebody has talked about the need for a seasoned congressman. Kennedy was seasoned enough to command a PT boat in action. He was seasoned enough for the lives of his crew to be entrusted to him . . . We may not know too much about politics, but we know a lot about John Fitzgerald Kennedy.

On the morning of the primary election, June 18, Jack went to vote with his grandparents. Then he went from ward to ward, thanking his workers. That evening, as the returns came in, it soon became clear that he had won a smashing victory. And when the votes were all counted, he had taken more than 40 percent of the ballots cast, an astonishing feat in a ten-man race.

It was a jubilant group of supporters at Kennedy's headquarters at 18 Tremont that night. When the triumphant candidate entered in the company of his parents and grandparents, the crowd went wild. It remained only for the irrepressible Honey Fitz, with tears in his eyes over the young man's sensational victory, to jump on a table to dance a jig and lead the crowd in a rousing chorus of "Sweet Adeline," the swan song of a passing era in Boston politics.

In the weeks that followed the stunning victory, Kennedy received a great deal of attention in the press. "If Mr. Kennedy lives up to his present prospects," the *Boston Globe* predicted, "the sometime Ambassador to the Court of St. James and the eternally young statesman emeritus of the Boston and Commonwealth Democracy will be identified in a decade or less as the father and grandfather of the young man elected to the high state or federal position of—oh well, let the political prophets supply the title of the office."

In November, as expected in a district where the Democrats held an overwhelming majority, the Republicans offered only token opposition, and John Kennedy won in a landslide. The die was cast, Joe Kennedy wrote to an acquaintance. "I find myself with a new occupation—that is, furthering young Jack's political career."

How far Jack's career would go no one could know, but Joe's friend Herbert Bayard Swope had great expectations. "My crystal ball reveals you," he wrote to Jack on November 4, 1946, "as the centre of a fascinating drama—one that carries you far and high."

# CHAPTER 40
# THE
# YOUNG
# CONGRESSMAN

When Jack first arrived in Washington, he rented an attractive three-story town house on Thirty-first Street in Georgetown, where he lived together with his aide Billy Sutton, the Kennedy cook Margaret Ambrose, and his twenty-six-year-old sister Eunice, who, thanks to their father, had a job as executive secretary to the Juvenile Delinquency Committee of the Justice Department. In 1947 the government was just beginning to deal with the problem of juvenile delinquency. Speaking with reporters as she began her job, Eunice said that "substantial efforts must be made to keep adolescents from quitting school at fourteen or fifteen and to give them a chance to learn a trade or develop special skills."

Tall and thin, with copper hair and high cheekbones, Eunice had been subject to a series of illnesses throughout her life, but, like Jack, she had willed her way through the pain. "Eunice was born mature," Rose later said, "and because she was so close to Rosemary a special sense of responsibility developed within her, which later showed up when she went to Harlem to do social work. Then, from that experience, she became convinced that something had to be done about juvenile delinquency and she went to work in Washington. And once she got there no one could stop her. Her political skills, even then, were extraordinary." Speaking in the same vein but putting it more crudely, the Ambassador said of Eunice, "If that girl had been born with balls she would have been a hell of a politician."

"Of all the kids in the family, Eunice was far and away the strongest-minded," Jack's fellow Congressman and friend George A. Smathers of Florida observed. "Sort of the leader of the clan. Very tough when she wanted to be. Eunice would have loved to be the one the father picked to run in the Eleventh Congressional District in '46. If she'd been a little older, and if it had been today, when a lot of women are running for office, I suspect the history of the Kennedy clan would have been quite different."

The Georgetown house was a lively, friendly place, with guests likely to pop in unpredictably at any moment to stay for days or weeks at a time. On almost any night, a small group of people could be found at the dinner table with Jack and Eunice, including Smathers, Representative Henry M. Jackson of Washington state and R. Sargent Shriver, a handsome Yale graduate who had joined the Ambassador's staff after working at *Newsweek*. During these days, Jack also spent time with fellow Congressman Joseph R. McCarthy of Wisconsin. A popular bachelor on the Washington cocktail circuit, McCarthy shared with Jack a sense of fun and a love of women. In later days, Jack's friendship with McCarthy would become a serious political liability, but in 1947 McCarthy was a young congressman whom all the Kennedys, including Joe Kennedy, liked very much.

The women in Jack's life during this period, including actress Gene Tierney, model Florence Pritchett and British tennis star Kay Stammers, fell into a pattern—all of them bright, beautiful and amusing, but all of them "safe" girls he could not or would not marry. "He was young, rich, handsome, sexy," recalled reporter Nancy Dickerson, who also dated him, "and that's plenty for starters. But the big thing about him was that he was overpowering—you couldn't help but be swept over by him."

"I could walk with Jack into a room full of a hundred women," fellow Congressman and friend Frank Thompson said, "and at least eighty-five of them would be willing to sacrifice their honor and everything else if they could get into a pad with him." And he loved it, spending more of his time and energy on his women in those early days than he did on his congressional duties.

Jack's Choate friend Rip Horton remembers what the Georgetown bachelor pad was like: "I went to his house in Georgetown for dinner. A lovely-looking blonde from West Palm Beach joined us to go to a movie.

After the movie we went back to the house, and I remember Jack saying something like 'Well, I want to shake this one. She has ideas.' Shortly thereafter another girl walked in. Ted Reardon was there, so he went home and I went to bed figuring this was the girl for the night. The next morning a completely different girl came wandering down for breakfast. They were a dime a dozen."

"Jack liked girls," George Smathers explained. "He liked girls very much. He came by it naturally. His daddy liked girls. He was a chaser."

Jack seemed to be imitating the pattern his father had established after the near-disaster of his affair with Gloria Swanson, a pattern of keeping his relationships with women both superficial and numerous. It appears that the Kennedy children not only knew about their father's womanizing but fully accepted it, so long as their mother was protected from public embarrassment.

"I was at some posh restaurant in Washington," said Washington socialite Kay Halle, "and the waiter brought me a note inviting me to join friends at another table. It was Joe and his two sons, Jack and Bobby. Jack was a congressman then. When I joined them the gist of the conversation from the boys was the fact that their father was going to be in Washington for a few days and needed female companionship. They wondered whom I could suggest, and they were absolutely serious."

The older he grew, it seemed, the more Joe Kennedy craved the presence of women. As he approached his sixties, he was still a remarkably handsome man. His reddish hair had silvered, but his blue eyes remained bright and his freckled face retained its look of vibrant enthusiasm toward life. But, beneath his healthy appearance, Kennedy was suffering mysterious pains in his stomach—pains so intense that he feared the onset of cancer. Perhaps, with the beauty of a young girl beside him, there was something to live for which stirred him to anticipation and made him feel young again.

With Jack too, a connection can be drawn between his problems with health and his obsession with women. Perhaps, as Garry Wills suggests, "his continual, almost heroic sexual performance [was] a way of cackling at the gods of bodily debility who plagued him," as if to say, 'I'm not dead yet.' "

In that regard, Chuck Spalding observed, Jack was fascinated by Byron. "He'd read everything about him and read most of the poetry too. There were a lot of similarities. Byron too had that conflict between irony and romanticism; he too wanted the world to be better than it was; he also had the disability—the clubfoot—and the conviction of an early death; and most of all he had the women . . ."

Yet, with Jack, something different was at work than a liking for women. So driven was the pace of his sex life, and so discardable his conquests, that they suggest a deep difficulty with intimacy.

"The whole thing with him was pursuit," said one of the women Jack courted. "I think he was secretly disappointed when a woman gave in. It meant that the low esteem in which he held women was once again validated. It meant also that he'd have to start chasing someone else . . . I once asked him why he was doing it—why he was acting like his father, why he was avoiding real relationships, why he was taking a chance on getting caught in a scandal at the same time he was trying to make his career take off. 'I don't know, really,' he answered. 'I just can't help it.' He had this sad expression on his face. He looked like a little boy about to cry."

Jack Kennedy never came into his own in the United States Congress. Assigned to the Education and the Labor Committee, he proved himself an able questioner at the hearings held to revise the National Labor Relations Act of 1935, and when the Taft-Hartley bill was reported to the floor he gave a ringing dissent, suggesting that the bill "would strike down in one devastating blow the union shop, industry-wide bargaining and so strangle collective bargaining with restraints and limitations as to make it ineffectual." As a House member Jack favored federal aid to education and was a strong supporter of housing legislation, introducing a measure which authorized up to $1 billion annually in federal loans to families of moderate means for housing projects.

But basically he was in a role he did not relish, one where the greater part of his time had to be spent servicing the mundane needs of the Eleventh District of Massachusetts, while his real interest lay in national and international matters. To be sure, a number of national and international situations did arise, in the debates over President Truman's plan to aid Greece and Turkey and over the Marshall Plan, where he found the opportunity to voice his larger concerns, but the everyday work of the House required Jack to engross himself so deeply in the rough-and-tumble politics of Massachusetts that he had little time for world affairs.

"While he loved the process of campaigning more than he ever imagined he would," Billings observed, "since it allowed him to talk to all different kinds of people from all walks of life, he found most of his fellow congressmen boring, preoccupied as they all seemed to be with their narrow political concerns. And then, too, he had terrible problems with all the arcane rules and customs which prevented you from moving legislation quickly and forced you to jump a thousand hurdles before you could accomplish anything. All his life he had had troubles with rules externally imposed and now here he was, back once again in an 'institutional setting.' "

His first secretary, Mary Davis, said that he seemed rather lost in those early years in the Congress. "I don't think he really knew if he wanted politics, if he was going to remain with it, or what politics was going to do with him."

"I think time was heavy on his hands," William O. Douglas later recalled. "I'd see him at Palm Beach or Hyannis or Washington and he never seemed to get into the mainstream of any political thought or political action or any idea—nothing. He was sort of drifting."

Jack's drifting was concealed from his constituents by an excellent staff in Washington, which was aided by all the resources and talent of Joseph Kennedy's headquarters on Park Avenue. But local issues could be tricky as well as mundane, as Jack soon discovered when, half a year into his first term, he found himself in a complex, career-threatening political situation brought about by Boston's Mayor James Michael Curley.

Eighteen months earlier, just after the people of Boston had voted him back into office for a fourth term as mayor, Curley had been indicted by a federal grand jury for participation in a fraudulent organization which had misrepresented its resources to obtain wartime contracts for clients. While his involvement had been limited primarily to the use of his name on the organization's letterhead, the jury found him guilty of using the mails to defraud, and subsequent appeals failed to reverse the original decision. So in June 1947 a federal court moved for Curley's immediate commitment to jail to serve a sentence of six to eighteen months.

Receiving the news in a hospital in Cohasset, where he was undergoing treatment for diabetes and high blood pressure, the seventy-two-year-old Curley announced that he would go to Washington on June 26 to request a suspension of his sentence because of his "most serious and precarious condition." "This trip may mean his death," his doctor said, adding, ". . . if he goes to jail, I don't think he'll last long."

Curley's daughter Mary, who accompanied the mayor on the twelve-hour trip to Washington, said upon their arrival that there was a new numbness in her father's left arm and leg which had the whole family terrified that he was about to suffer a cerebral hemorrhage. Nevertheless, federal judge James Proctor peremptorily denied his plea for clemency, and four hours later, claiming he was being sentenced to die, Curley was on his way to the federal prison in Danbury, Connecticut, where it was made clear to him that he was just another prisoner and would be treated as such.

During his incarceration, Curley's visitors were limited to two a month and his correspondence to four letters every seven days. It was therefore impossible for the Boston mayor to conduct municipal business from his new dwelling place. It was a humiliating time for the man who had wielded more power in his city and state for more years than anyone else in the commonwealth's history.

Through it all, the people of Boston continued to support their colorful old mayor. On the day the indictment was handed down, more than a thousand men and women had turned out in the streets, with horns and cheers, to let Curley know they still loved him. Then, as the date of the sentencing drew near, over 172,000 people, representing a quarter of Boston's population, had signed a petition requesting clemency from the judge. And now, with the mayor in jail, Massachusetts Representative John W. McCormack, Democratic whip of the House, was circulating a petition for Curley's pardon which he intended to give to President Truman after securing the signatures of all the members of Congress from New England.

Calling the sentence "cold" and "amazing" in light of Curley's ailing health, McCormack undertook a personal crusade to get the Boston mayor released from jail. When nearly the entire Massachusetts delegation had signed, the pressure on Jack grew intense. From the start, most of his advisers, particularly Joe Kane, had been urging him to sign, arguing that it would be political suicide to go against the old man in a district that had supported him overwhelmingly for over thirty years. Then, too, they argued, it was bad politics to buck McCormack on something that obviously mattered to the Democratic floor leader, for McCormack was the main channel of Massachusetts patronage.

"I don't know how many people he consulted on the Curley pardon," recalled Mark Dalton, one of the few advisers who urged Kennedy *not* to sign. "I was furious that he had been asked to sign . . . here was a young man starting his political career, just on the threshold of it, and I thought that the older people who were putting the pressure on him to sign this petition had a terrible nerve . . . "

The Ambassador's position on the pardon changed as the days went by. In the beginning he sided with Joe Kane, believing that it could damage his son fatally in his district if he refused to sign, particularly if Curley's physical condition worsened. Reflecting Kane's position, he implored Jack to find out everything he could about the real state of Curley's health. After checking with the Surgeon General, they concluded that Curley was not as ill as he was claiming to be, that his condition could easily be treated in the penitentiary hospital. Once the Ambassador was convinced that Curley was unlikely to die in jail, he began to think more carefully about the changing nature of Massachusetts politics, where, he concluded, a permanent association with an unsavory character like Curley would damage Jack down the line. "I think they were so farsighted," Massachusetts politician Garrett Byrne later observed, "they were anticipating what effect it might have on them fifteen to twenty years afterward."

Then, beyond all these rational calculations, there was the issue of the long-standing feud between Curley and Fitzgerald. "If Jack signed," Billy Sutton said, "how could he face his grandfather?" For over thirty years, John Fitzgerald had been forced to stand on the political sidelines while his old nemesis Curley managed, time after time, to retain his hold on center stage. "It was not easy for my father," Rose Kennedy later said, "for all along he believed he was just as talented and just as charismatic as Curley and that if it had not been for Curley, *he*, John Fitzgerald, would have been the major Irish figure in Massachusetts politics. I thought about the question of timing when I read *The Last Hurrah*, for if Curley hadn't come along when he did, John Fitzgerald would have been *the* central character in all the Irish novels of the age. And how that would have pleased my father."

Weighing all these factors, Jack decided not to sign even though his decision singled him out in the press as the only Massachusetts Democrat who refused to support Curley. Ted Reardon remembers the scene as Jack walked back into his office after making his decision public. "Well, I'm dead now," he announced. "I'm politically dead, finished."

With this sentiment veteran political observer Daniel O'Brien agreed. "I thought he made a hell of a mistake politically when he refused to sign that Curley pardon, because if there was one fellow who was entitled to a pardon, it was Curley, who had done so much for the people he represented here in that particular district, which was the congressional district Jack was representing."

Five months later, when Curley's sentence was finally commuted by President Truman, Jack was vindicated in his initial suspicions about the gravity of his illness. Curley, met by scores of jubilant supporters at his home, announced that he was feeling better than he had felt in the past few years and would be at his desk the following morning to resume his duties as mayor. And when he did return to City Hall, his return provoked negative editorials all over the country, as in the *Washington Post*: "We do not begrudge the former prisoner a new lease on life. What really bothers us is the failure of the citizens of Boston to rise in wrath and demand the retirement to private life of an official who is a disgrace to any self-respecting community."

So while Jack's decision to separate himself from Curley may have caused some political grumbling at the time, it served, in the long run, to enhance his reputation as a new breed of Irish politician, able to get around without the telltale hat and the telltale political retinue to lead the way, a cut above his predecessors in background, education and style.

During the 1947 summer recess, Jack journeyed to Europe as part of a congressional fact-finding committee "to study education and labor conditions" in Western Europe and Russia. Earlier that spring President Truman and Secretary of State George C. Marshall had urged the Congress to save postwar Europe from being overrun by Communism by enacting what became known as the Marshall Plan, a program of financial aid on a scale unprecedented in the history of mankind. With hearings scheduled to begin once Congress returned, dozens of senators and congressmen flocked to Europe during the recess to see for themselves whether Truman's gloomy warnings of imminent collapse were justified.

Leaving Boston on Sunday, August 31, Jack stopped first in Ireland for a prolonged visit with Kathleen, who was staying at the Devonshires' Lismore Castle in County Waterford, southern Ireland. Rose described Lismore in her diary as "a picture book castle" with its gray walls covered on one side with soft green moss and on the other with reddish ivy. Then "the steep straight down drop to the quickly running stream . . . the artistic bridge over the stream with a few figures fishing and the winding road beyond where the children walk along from school in their bare legs and shabby shoes and torn coats but shining rosy faces." When Billy was a young boy he had loved to come to Lismore in August and September to fish, and as Kathleen considered it "the most perfect place" in the world, the Devonshires encouraged her to stay there as much as she liked.

In preparation for Jack's visit, Kathleen had invited a special group of her friends, including Tony Rosslyn, then a member of Parliament; Charles Johnson, later British High Commissioner in Australia; Hugh Fraser; Sean Leslie, an Irish writer; Anthony Eden; and Pamela Churchill. "Anthony Eden arrives today for five days," Kathleen wrote to Lem on September 3, "so by the end of the week he and Jack will have fixed up the state of the world."

It had not been easy for Kathleen to make her peace with Billy's death. It was particularly hard for her as the war drew to an end, when she confided to Lem that she was "rather depressed," as she kept thinking about all those who weren't coming back. And when Billy's younger brother, Andrew, came home to England from Italy in March 1945 she fell into another depression. "It nearly kills me to see him," she wrote to her parents, "not that he is really at all like Billy but the whole idea of seeing Andy makes Billy's absence so much more noticeable. However, it is just another one of those things that must be borne." Then, two months later, as the time of her first wedding anniversary approached, she again admitted feeling "a bit sad," but she told her family with characteristic spirit, "I try and do lots and that makes the days pass quickly."

Reading between the lines of Kathleen's determined effort to appear strong, the Ambassador wrote to her nearly every week and indulged her with unusually expensive gifts. "Just got Daddy's letter about my diamond and sapphire watch," Kathleen wrote to her family on her twenty-fifth birthday. "There is no doubt . . . I LOVE large expensive gifts." And in the first week of May as her memories turned to the excitement of her wedding day the year before, she received a thoughtful telegram from her father. "Thinking of you with love and affection on May 6," it read.

Joe Kennedy never fully understood why his beautiful daughter elected to live in war-ravaged England when she could have had everything she wanted at home. Speaking in his typically blunt style, he asked her friend Pamela Churchill, "Why does that daughter of mine want to stay in that goddamn country of yours with all those goddamn snooty Englishmen? Why, when she's got everything in America should she throw in her lot with a country that's in trouble and a continent that's on the decline? It just doesn't make sense." But, according to Pamela, Joe so admired and loved Kathleen that he finally accepted her decision.

Once Kathleen made up her mind to live in England, she bought herself a house in London at 4 Smith Square—a charming white town house which Rose Kennedy would later liken to one of "those attractive old brick houses at Louisburg Square." "I feel that I have absolutely terrific roots here," Kathleen told Lem in a letter just after she had purchased the house, "and for the rest of my life I shall be torn in two. Daddy writes that he has bought an airplane which will span the Atlantic so we shall all be set for transportation."

As her spirits returned, Kathleen found herself once more surrounded by admiring beaux, including Richard Wood, who had learned to walk awkwardly with the aid of a cane, Seymour Berry, the wealthy thirty-seven-year-old son of Lord Camrose, and Anthony Eden, whose friendship she relished. "I love your letters," Eden wrote to her when he was traveling in the Middle East, "especially when you write as you talk, for then I can imagine that you are here. How I wish that you were . . . But if one has not the delight of your company it is a joy to imagine it."

As Kathleen had expected, Jack got along famously with all her friends, and the month at Lismore they spent together turned out to be one of the most enjoyable in her life. "We have a varied group and the various people couldn't have mixed better," she wrote to her father, adding that Jack ended up liking Anthony Eden "enormously." As for Eden, "he arrived loaded down with official looking conservative documents but when he had been here only a few days got into the Irish spirit and was reading 'No Orchids for Miss Brandish.' "

One morning while Jack was at Lismore, he approached Pamela Churchill, "rather quietly, rather apologetically," as she remembered it, and asked if she would mind coming with him on an expedition to look for his ancestors in a town called New Ross, fifty miles east of Lismore. He was carrying with him a letter from his Aunt Loretta which directed him to the old family home. It was a beautiful day and all the others had gone off to play golf, but Pamela and Jack set off in Kathleen's station wagon, a huge car imported from America which was considered the height of luxury at the time. As they left, Jack was obviously excited, Pamela recalled, but he asked her not to make a big thing of it to Kick.

They motored through the soft green countryside along the southeastern coast of Ireland and across the bottom of Kilkenny County, past wooded valleys and ruined castles, along roads so bumpy that it took more than five hours to reach the little market town of New Ross, settled on the banks of the Barrow River. At the outskirts of the town Jack stopped the car and asked a man where the Kennedys lived. "Oh, now, and which Kennedys will it be that you'll be wanting? David Kennedys? Jim Kennedys?" a very Irish voice replied. Jack explained about being from America and looking for his relatives, and the man told him to drive to a little white house on the edge of the village.

"We found the house," Pamela recalled, "a small white house with a thatch roof and with chickens and geese all in front spilling out the door, and a tough-looking woman came out surrounded by a mass of kids, looking just like all the Kennedys. Jack said he was from America looking for Irish relations, but she didn't seem at all convinced at first and sent one of her kids up the mountainside to fetch her husband. When the husband came down, she suddenly got warmer and invited us in."

After much conversation about various Kennedy relatives who had emigrated to America, it was still not clear how, if at all, Jack was related to the Irish family (later he figured they were third cousins), but as the minutes passed, everyone relaxed and Jack was "enjoying himself thoroughly." Pamela was "very impressed" by the dignity of the man and his wife. "I would have thought, given that we clearly looked rich with our clothes and our gleaming station wagon, that they would have immediately latched on to us as relatives, but they wanted to make sure. I remember they made us tea and offered us butter and eggs, very difficult to come by in 1947. And they never could figure out who I was. Wife? they'd ask. I'd say No. And they'd say, 'Ah, soon to be, no doubt!' "

Before they left, Jack asked if there was anything he could do for them. Finally they broke down and said he could do one thing: drive the children around the village in the station wagon. So they piled the children into the wagon and Jack paraded them, their faces lit with pleasure, through the half-dozen little roads of the village.

When the station wagon pulled into the grounds of Lismore Castle, Jack was still excited and was anxious to tell Kathleen about his visit, but dinner was ready and Kathleen was angry because he was late. "Well," Kick said, failing to understand the magic of the afternoon, "did they have a bathroom?" The answer was no.

In the days that followed, however, Kathleen and Jack spent a lot of time together. In the mornings they took long walks together through the Irish countryside, and in the afternoons they liked to stretch out side by side on the rocks by the edge of the Blackwater River. It was during one of their long talks by the river, according to Lem, that Kathleen confided to her brother that she had fallen in love with a married man. It was a secret that must be kept from their parents for the time being, but she wanted Jack to know.

His name was Lord Peter Fitzwilliam, and he was a war hero and one of the wealthiest peers in England. He was not really handsome—his arresting face was a little too long—but women seldom realized it when caught by his charm, as so many women were. Like the Devonshires, the Fitzwilliam family owned enormous estates scattered in various parts of England and Ireland, including Wentworth Woodhouse, a magnificent mansion with a room for every day in the year. But unlike so many of England's cash-poor aristocrats who were forced to dismantle their great estates after the war, the Fitzwilliams had aggressively invested their money so that they were able to live their lives on the same grand scale they had enjoyed before the war.

Peter had grown up believing there was nothing in life he couldn't have. In his early childhood he developed a passion for horses, which deepened as the years went by until he became the owner of one of the finest stud farms in all England and was voted president of the Racehorse Owners' Association. Attracted to danger, speed, and pretty women, Peter was something of a rake; even as a university student he had the reputation of a playboy who would flirt with any woman who caught his eye. He was famous for his Irish charm, and it was said that he could talk anybody, man or woman, into doing anything. Married at twenty-two to Olive Plunkett, the beautiful heiress to the Guinness family fortune, Peter was ill equipped to assume the responsibilities of marriage, and over the years Olive became an alcoholic and the marriage broke down irretrievably.

Kathleen first met Peter in June 1946 at a ball held in honor of the Commandos, the elite operational unit set up by Churchill in 1940. Earlier that spring, finding it easier to keep her mind off Billy if she kept busy, she had agreed to chair the committee responsible for organizing the ball. It was a large undertaking but, under Kathleen's leadership, all the tickets were sold and Princess Elizabeth agreed to come as a special sponsor. In the days before the event, Kathleen must have heard again and again about the dashing Peter Fitzwilliam, for he was one of the stars of the occasion, having earned the Distinguished Service Cross, Britain's second-highest military honor, for his exploits during the war.

On the night of the ball, Kathleen looked particularly radiant. Slimmer than she had ever been and dressed in a pale-pink gown which set off her honey-colored hair, she immediately attracted Fitzwilliam's attention. "Peter and Kathleen sort of eyed each other awhile," one friend commented, "and then they were together." Another says, "It was overnight and it was the real thing—illicit, passionate, encompassing. One gets the impression that she'd discovered something she didn't really plan to experience in life."

"Peter had all the charm in the world," his close friend Harry Sporberg said, "to a rather dangerous extent really." And while he was not interested in politics or public service as Billy had been, he possessed a boldness in business affairs that must have reminded Kathleen of her father. Kathleen's friend Jane Kenyon-Slaney made the comparison overtly, finding Peter "like Joe Kennedy himself—older, sophisticated, quite the rogue male. Perhaps in the last analysis those were the qualities required to make her fall deeply in love."

Always something of a romantic, Kathleen told Jack that in Peter she believed she had found her Rhett Butler, the dark, handsome man who could tell her the most ribald stories and make her laugh, appealing to an Irish coarseness which lay within her. In Peter she had found a man who knew how to play and who swept her along with him. For too many years life had been too sad, filled with sacrifices and preoccupation with war. But now, with Peter, she had found a man's man and she could have fun again, more fun than she had had since the last summer before the war.

And yet, for all the passion they shared and the tremendous fun they had together, it was a love affair filled with even more complications for Kathleen than the one with Billy had been, since Peter not only was a

Protestant but was married. And even if he did secure a divorce, as he was planning to do, there was still the fact that his carefree, irresponsible nature was the very antithesis of everything Kathleen had been taught to value in terms of public service and sacrifice. But Kathleen was blindly, recklessly in love.

All this, according to Lem Billings, Kathleen shared with Jack that September at Lismore, and Jack was a bit envious, admitting later to Lem that in all his relationships with women, except perhaps with Inga, he had never lost himself as Kathleen appeared to have done. He promised to keep Kick's secret from the family and he did, for when Rose Kennedy arrived in Paris at the end of September she had no idea of the depth of her daughter's involvement. Indeed, joining Rose for a shopping spree at the fashion salons of Paris, Kathleen had a wonderful time, laughing with her mother as they had not been able to do for many years. Then Rose returned with her daughter for a fortnight's stay in London, where, she wrote to Joe, "she has all her friends (all of whom I like) dropping in and so it is very pleasant."

While Rose was in London, she spent a good deal of time with the Devonshires. With the religious problem removed by Billy's death, she could now give full rein to her great admiration and respect for the Devonshire family, and her affection was returned in kind. Writing to Lem after her mother's visit, Kathleen reported that her in-laws "got on terrifically well with mother so wasn't that good?" All in all, Kathleen later told Lem, evidencing once again her family's startling capacity to lead compartmentalized lives, it was the happiest time she had spent with her mother in years.

While Kathleen and Rose were together in Paris, Jack was seriously ill in London, where he had collapsed with acute nausea and low blood pressure. Rushed to the London Clinic, where he was placed in the care of Lord Beaverbrook's doctor, Sir Daniel Davis, he was diagnosed a victim of Addison's disease, an illness characterized by a failure of the body's adrenal glands and resulting in general weakness, poor appetite, loss of weight, nausea, vomiting and circulatory collapse. When first discovered by British physician Thomas Addison, the disease was considered fatal, as it gradually destroyed the body's resistance to infection, but with the development of adrenal-hormone extracts in the 1930s the mortality rate fell dramatically. Even with the new drugs, however, it was a serious illness, and the examining doctor told Pamela Churchill, "That young American friend of yours, he hasn't got a year to live."

When the Boston papers broke the news of Jack's illness, there was no mention of Addison's disease. Ever skillful in their handling of public relations, the Kennedys managed to characterize the illness as simply a recurrence of the malaria Jack had suffered in the South Pacific. Since a common symptom of the two diseases is a brownish-yellow pigmentation of the skin, the story was never questioned until years later, during the height of the 1960 presidential primary campaign, when Lyndon B. Johnson's workers charged that Kennedy was suffering from Addison's disease.

Aside from his adrenal problem, Jack was still suffering from his unstable back, whose vulnerability to injury subjected him to periodic episodes of excruciating pain. "At least one half of the days that he spent on this earth were days of intense physical pain," Bobby later wrote. Through it all, however, Jack refused to act like a sick man. "He went along for many years," Rose recorded in her memoirs, "thinking to himself—or at least trying to make others think—that he was a strong, robust, quite healthy person who just happened to be sick a good deal of time." "Those who knew him well," Bobby said, "would know he was suffering only because his face was a little whiter, the lines around his eyes were a little deeper, his words a little sharper. Those who did not know him well detected nothing."

This was a family which prohibited self-pity, in which disability had been overcome again and again by energetic action from the days when John Fitzgerald first forced himself to become a champion sprinter. Of all the family members except Rosemary, Jack had the hardest battle to fight. It was a battle more heroic than the American people ever knew, for the Kennedys were a family in which secrets were closely held.

For nearly twenty years, Rosemary had been put forward as a shy but serious girl committed to the teaching of young children. And the deception had worked, conceived as it was at a time of monumental public ignorance about mental retardation. With Jack's health, the Kennedys engaged in a similar deception. Fearing that the public would recoil from an aspiring leader with a life-threatening disease which required daily medications, they invariably described Jack's ailments as war-related diseases, with each episode a discrete illness temporarily invading an otherwise healthy body.

Jack remained under the constant care of doctors for months at a time, and as a result his attendance record was among the worst in the House. With the help of his father's entire administrative apparatus, however, and buoyed up by the recent addition of Jim Landis and the hard work of his own able staff, he was able to educate himself sufficiently on the issues and to serve his constituents adequately enough to earn plaudits from the local papers.

It was a bitter winter in the Northeast, and more than twenty-five snowstorms fell upon Boston, but by the beginning of March all the members of the Kennedy clan—including Kathleen, who had arrived home on February 19 in the company of her sister-in-law Elizabeth Cavendish for a two-month stay—were happily ensconced in their sunny villa on Ocean Boulevard in Palm Beach. All winter long Kathleen had kept her relationship with Peter from her family, but she was so in love by the spring of 1948 and so determined to marry Peter that she spent much of her vacation at home gathering her courage to tell her parents. The confrontation finally took place during her last weekend with her family before returning to England.

The Kennedys had been invited to White Sulphur Springs, West Virginia, for the reopening of the Greenbrier Hotel, where Rose and Joe had spent their honeymoon in 1914. Promising to be *the* social event of the spring, it drew three hundred guests, who had traveled in planes, automobiles and fourteen private railroad cars from all over the country to join in the festive schedule of dining, dancing and golf.

Kathleen waited until the last evening at Greenbrier to tell her parents, hoping against hope that once they recognized how happy she was they would accept her decision. After all, her mother had finally come to terms with her marriage to Billy and had eventually come to appreciate the Devonshires. But in this hope Kathleen underestimated the depth of her mother's feelings about the sacrilegious nature of divorce. Having structured her whole life on the concept that a marriage, once made, could not be unmade no matter how difficult things were, Rose was not about to sanction her daughter's marriage to a divorced man. Speaking in stronger tones than she had ever used before, Rose told Kathleen that if she went ahead with the marriage she would be disowned by the family and as far as her mother was concerned she would be regarded as dead.

This time the Ambassador was silent. Perhaps this time he sensed danger. Kathleen's marriage to Billy had not taken her from him, but her involvement with Peter was altogether different. And then, too, there was Jack's political future to worry about. In the end, perhaps even Joe could not have explained the origin of his misgivings, but his wife was vocal enough for them both. So he remained quiet, a silent partner-in-arms against an unknown peril.

Profoundly shaken by her parents' reaction, Kathleen went to Washington, where she spent a final weekend with her old friends Patsy Field and John White. Unable to sleep, she came into Patsy's bedroom and lay down beside her. "I don't know what to do," she confided, telling Patsy that Eunice had made an appointment for her to see Monsignor Fulton Sheen in New York the following day but that she really didn't want to go because she knew she wasn't going to change her mind about Peter and she feared it would only make things harder for everyone.

Hesitating a moment, Patsy said, "I'd call Bishop Sheen and cancel the appointment."

"You're right, really, it's my life," Kathleen replied, voicing almost the same understanding her mother had come to more than three decades earlier when she made up her own mind to marry Joe despite her father's opposition. "There's no point going through catechism all over again. I'm going back to England and do whatever I have to do so I can be with Peter."

On April 21, the day before she sailed on the *Queen Elizabeth*, Kathleen had lunch with Joe Junior's old friend Tom Schriber in New York. "She looked really alive," Schriber remembered. "She was revved up, ready to go. She had written off her mother but not the old man. She said, 'I'd like to get Dad's consent. He matters.' "

Back in England, Kathleen and Peter were together constantly. With the plans proceeding for his divorce, they decided to announce their engagement in the middle of May. Anticipating the tremendous coverage the press would give the announcement, Kathleen came up with a plan which, years later, Marie Bruce disclosed to Joe in a letter. "I was going to take a small house somewhere abroad in my name," Marie wrote, "to hide her from the reporters when the story broke, as I hid her once before. And I thought it would be wiser for him to see her chaperoned at home in the eyes of the world, and not against a background of hotels, night clubs and cagey weekends. It was important. He was an Englishman and their kind of a man, and what man is not when he chooses a wife."

Still, Kathleen desperately wanted to get her father's blessing before making her decision public. As it happened, Joe Kennedy was scheduled to be in Paris on the weekend of May 15 on a fact-finding tour for the Marshall Plan. Kathleen called him and asked if she could bring Peter to meet him. When she hung up the phone, Kathleen's housekeeper recalled, she looked absolutely "radiant," announcing happily that her father had agreed to meet them for lunch at the Ritz Hotel on Saturday, May 15.

To strengthen her position, Kathleen asked Jane Kenyon and her new husband to come to the lunch. Jane had recently divorced Peter Lindsay and married Max Aitken, the son of Lord Beaverbrook. As one of Peter's closest friends, Max could serve as a character reference for him. But in the end Kathleen must have hoped that Peter himself, with all his charm, would be his own best advocate. Anticipating the meeting, Peter laughingly told his cousin he was going to do all he could to try to bring the old boy around. "If he objects, I'll go to see the Pope and offer to build him a church."

On Thursday, May 13, Kathleen and Peter climbed into a De Havilland Dove eight-seat plane at an airport just outside London and took off for Cannes, where they were planning to spend two days alone before going to Paris for the big meeting. Arrangements had been made for the private airplane to land in Paris for refueling, but when the Dove arrived at Le Bourget, Peter impulsively decided to telephone a few of his racing buddies for lunch so that they could meet Kathleen. Returning to the airport three hours later than scheduled, they were met by Peter Townshend, the pilot, who announced that if they took off now for Cannes they would be flying over the Rhone Valley at precisely the time a thunderstorm had been predicted. All commercial flights were being canceled and this flight was far too risky. But Fitzwilliam was so insistent—arguing that if they didn't get to Cannes that evening there would be no sense in going at all, since they had to be back in Paris to meet Kennedy on Saturday—that the pilot found himself giving in.

The plane took off at three-twenty and climbed to a cruising altitude of 9,500 feet. Landing time at Cannes was scheduled for six-thirty. But by late afternoon, just as the weather service had predicted, the small plane found itself at the edge of a violent thunderstorm. Struggling against the treacherous winds and unable to see through the heavy rain, Townshend headed straight into the eye of the storm. Suddenly the Dove began tossing wildly for thousands of feet in different directions.

For twenty minutes the pilot desperately tried to regain control. With the rain obscuring all visibility and the instruments spinning uselessly, they thrashed up and down with no conception of where they were until the plane shot out from the bottom of a cloud, headed straight for a mountain ridge. The pilot and the co-pilot stuffed handkerchiefs into their mouths, a standard procedure in a crash landing to avoid biting through the tongue. For about ten seconds Peter and Kathleen must have realized they were going to die.

In the tiny town of Privas, a farmer named Paul Petit heard the explosion and he and his father scrambled up a stone trail, to find the wrecked body of the plane, nose down, against a ridge near the top of the mountain. Hours later, several gendarmes followed the farmers up the mountain to the wreckage. The pilot and the co-pilot lay crumpled against the cockpit; Peter Fitzwilliam's crushed body lay beneath his seat; Kathleen, who had been sitting in the rear to balance the plane, was lying on her back still fastened into her seat, her body askew, her jaw and pelvis broken and a deep gash on the right side of her face. On the ground nearby lay her high-heeled shoes, knocked off by the force of the impact. The four bodies were placed in a farm cart and pulled down to the village.

Word came first to Jack Kennedy's office at the Capitol and then to the Georgetown house, where Jack had just returned from a dinner engagement with his aide Billy Sutton. A *Washington Post* reporter, hearing a report from the wires in Britain that a Lady Hartington had been killed in a plane crash, phoned after midnight. Getting Eunice on the phone, he relayed the information and asked if Lady Hartington was her sister.

"I'm not sure," Eunice answered. "There are two Lady Hartingtons." Please let it be Debo, she thought (referring to Debo Mitford, who by then was married to Andrew Hartington, Billy's younger brother), even though she knew it was a terrible thing to wish. The reporter said the passport of the victim showed "Kathleen" as the Christian name.

While Eunice was on the phone, Jack was lying on a couch listening to a recording of the musical comedy *Finian's Rainbow*. Hearing the terrible news from Eunice, he immediately got on the phone to Ted Reardon, his executive assistant, and asked him to check the story out. When the call came a short time later saying Kathleen's body had definitely been identified, "How Are Things in Glocca Morra," was playing. Ella Login had a sweet voice, he said to Billy Sutton. Then he turned his head and began to cry.

Ambassador Kennedy heard the news from a *Boston Globe* reporter at 6:30 A.M. at the George Cinq Hotel in Paris. Saying he would not give up hope until the last possible moment, he rushed to the airport to fly to Lyon and then travel down the Rhone to Privas. He had to see for himself that it really was Kathleen. When he arrived in Privas, the gendarmes escorted him to the town hall, where flowers covered four makeshift coffins. He was led to Kathleen's coffin and was obliged to identify her disfigured body.

When asked about his plans for the burial, Kennedy was unable to respond. "I have no plans," he said, his voice broken, "no plans." The following day Kathleen's body was taken to Saint-Philippe-du-Roule, a Catholic church in Paris, where the order of the Sisters of Hope watched over the bier until the decision was made whether to bury Kathleen in England or on Cape Cod.

Meanwhile, all the far-flung members of the Kennedy family were gathering in Hyannis Port, drawn to the sheltering protection of the big white house. After flying up to Boston with his sister Jean, Jack drove to the Cape, picking up Teddy at Milton Academy on the way. Rose was at the Homestead in Hot Springs, Arkansas, when Jack called her to relay the news. Arriving in Boston, she was met by Eunice and Pat, and then the three women drove together to Hyannis Port. Only Robert, in Italy on a tour with a friend, was unable to join the family, as he was sick in bed with jaundice.

When Joe Kennedy called home after his journey to Privas, he said nothing about Kathleen's mangled body. He told the family only how beautiful and peaceful she looked, lying on her back as though she were asleep. This description made its way into the press along with a totally false account of the purpose of the trip. According to the New York *Daily News* (published by Joe Kennedy's friend Joseph Patterson) in a story which was widely reprinted, Kathleen was on her way to Cannes alone when she met Lord Fitzwilliam by chance in the Ritz Hotel in Paris, and the Irish peer told her he was leaving for Cannes that very afternoon in a chartered plane and offered her a ride.

Subsequent features on Kathleen's life published after the crash focused only on her undying love for Billy, avoiding all mention of Peter Fitzwilliam. Suggesting that it was to be near Billy and "only near him that she remained in England and visited frequently in France," the *Boston Post* observed in a front-page story that had Billy lived, "Lady Kathleen would have become, next to the Queen, the most powerful woman in England . . . His tragic death ended the speculation about the possibility of a Boston-born girl of Irish ancestry rising to such a position of social authority in the British Isles."

As the days went by, with Joe Kennedy hidden in his hotel, unable to decide what to do with his beloved daughter's body, the Devonshires finally helped him to a decision by strongly suggesting that Kathleen be buried in the family plot near Chatsworth. Though she was planning to marry someone else, she had died as Billy's widow and they had loved her as their own daughter. And, more important, since she herself had so loved her life in England, there could be no more beautiful resting place than the quiet graveyard at Chatsworth set deep in the Derbyshire countryside. To the Devonshires' surprise, the Ambassador consented immediately.

So Kathleen's burial finally took place on May 20. Earlier that day a High Mass was sung for her at the Farm Street Church in Berkeley Square, London, and then some two hundred of Kathleen's friends, including Anthony Eden, William Douglas-Home, the Earl of Rosslyn, Seymour Berry, Randolph Churchill, Evelyn Waugh, Pat Wilson, Nancy Astor, Lady Harlech, Max and Jane Aitken and David and Sissy Ormsby-Gore, crowded into a special train and accompanied the coffin to Derbyshire.

"I can still see the stricken face of old Joe Kennedy," Alistair Forbes recalled nearly thirty years later, "as he stood alone, unloved and despised, behind the coffin of his eldest daughter amid the hundreds of British friends who had adored her and now mourned her." Among the wreaths which covered the casket was one with a handwritten note from Winston Churchill.

As the coffin was lowered into the ground, Kennedy put his arms around Kathleen's housekeeper, Ilona Solynossy, the warmhearted woman who had seen the intense joy in Kathleen's face just days before when she had learned of her father's willingness to meet Peter. It was the Duchess who chose the epitaph for Kathleen's tombstone: JOY SHE GAVE / JOY SHE HAS FOUND.

# CHAPTER 41
# THE
# LONE
# SURVIVOR

Of the brothers and sisters, Jack was perhaps the most powerfully affected by Kathleen's death. For months afterward, he was a wounded man who refused to show anyone, except perhaps Lem Billings, the depths of his despair. "He was in terrible pain," Billings recalled. "He told me he couldn't get through the days without thinking of Kathleen at the most inappropriate times. He'd be sitting at a congressional hearing and he'd find his mind drifting uncontrollably back to all the things he and Kathleen had done together and all the friends they had had in common. He thought of her now as his best friend, the one person in the family with whom he could confide his deepest thoughts, his complex feelings about young Joe, his questions about God and his doubts about the future. And now she was dead."

"How can there possibly be any purpose in her death?" he asked Billings again and again as if Billings could somehow provide an answer. His Catholic faith had taught him there was a purpose to everything that happened in the universe, and perhaps a strongly religious person like his mother could see in Kathleen's death a means of saving her from a sacrilegious marriage. But all that Jack could see was a vital, high-spirited woman, cut down in her fullest flowering. Once again, as with Joe, the timing seemed so incredibly unfair.

"The thing about Kathleen and Joe," Jack later said, revealing a measure of guilt at being alive, "was their tremendous vitality. Everything was moving in their direction—that's what made it so unfortunate. If something happens to you or somebody in your family who is miserable anyway, whose health is bad, or who has a chronic disease or something, that's one thing. But for someone who is living at their peak, then to get cut off—that's the shock."

In retrospect, the deaths of his brother and sister in quick succession, coming as they did on the heels of the discovery that he had Addison's disease, marked the beginning of a terrible period of confusion for Jack in which established landmarks of thought and ambition were displaced. Suddenly, the safety of "we three" had become the isolation of I, for now he was the lone survivor of the golden trio. His emotions raw, his body weary, he thought and talked constantly about death in these months, as if he were promising Joe and Kathleen that he too would be dead in a little while.

He told columnist Joseph Alsop that his disease was "a sort of slow-motion leukemia" and that he doubted he would live past the age of forty-five. Lem Billings remembers him preoccupied by what "runs through your mind in the moments before your death. Would you really think about all the good things that had happened to you, as some believed, or would you be filled with regret at all the things you hadn't done?" And Ted Reardon recalls a strange conversation about death which Jack initiated one spring day during a walk around the Tidal Basin. "Tell me, Teddy boy," Jack began, "what's the best way to die?" When Reardon replied that he thought old age was probably best, Jack emphatically disagreed. "You're wrong, wrong as hell. In war—that's the best way to die. The very best way. In war."

"After Kathleen's death," Billings recalled, "Jack had terrible problems falling asleep at night. Just as he started to close his eyes, he would be awakened by the image of Kathleen sitting up with him late at night talking about their parties and dates. He would try to close his eyes again, but he couldn't shake the image. It was better, he said, when he had a girl in bed with him, for then he could fantasize that the girl was Kathleen's friend and that when morning came the three of them would go for breakfast together.

"In a family that considered grief a weakness, Jack felt trapped and betrayed," Billings continued. "For Jack, losing Joe and Kathleen was losing a part of his past, his common experiences, his identity. Yet there was no one in his family with whom he could share this huge loss. As a result, he seemed to lose his *raison d'être*. He just figured there was no sense in planning ahead anymore. The only thing that made sense, he decided, was to live for the moment, treating each day as if it were his last, demanding of life constant intensity, adventure and pleasure."

For those around him, Jack's intensity was contagious, transforming ordinary events into special occasions. "There was something about time," Chuck Spalding recalled, "special for him, obviously, because he always heard the footsteps, but also special for you when you were with him. Death was there. It had taken Joe and Kick and it was waiting for him. So whenever he was in a situation, he tried to burn bright, he tried to wring as much out of things as he could. After a while he didn't have to try. He had something nobody else did. It was just a heightened sense of being; there's no other way to describe it."

In the long run, however, the only resolution to Jack's grief was to forge a new identity shaped around his own plans for the future. Within a year of Joe's death he had plunged himself into the challenge of running for the United States House of Representatives. But the compulsion to keep moving could not hide the fact that in many ways his actions had been a charade, a means of healing his father's sorrow rather than his own. For while his entry into politics was able to create a new bond of love and affection with his father, he must have realized all along that victory within the family was the one thing he could never achieve so long as his brother's memory remained alive. Now, with the shock of Kathleen's death, this mistaken loyalty to the past was snapped.

As the months went by, Jack gradually began to accept his new situation. As the sole survivor of the golden trio, he felt he was a different person. "Slowly," Billings recalled, "he began to fight back, knowing that to stand still was to stay in sorrow, that to live he had to move forward. He recognized he could never return to what he was—the younger brother of Joe and the older brother of Kathleen. So he began to establish a new and separate personal identity. He came to a point in his grief where he decided to help himself, and the interesting thing is that once he focused on what *he* really wanted to do with his life, he realized that it really might be politics after all."

As 1949 gave way to 1950, Jack's physical condition also took a marked turn for the better, due to the discovery that cortisone could be a "miracle drug" for Addison's patients, allowing them for the first time to lead fairly normal lives. The discovery set off a great stampede for the drug, a supply of which the Kennedys quickly stored away in safe-deposit boxes around the country so that Jack would never run out. Patients treated with cortisone, clinicians found, generally experienced "a markedly increased sense of well-being approaching a state of euphoria accompanied by a real increase in energy, concentrating power, muscular strength and endurance."

For years, Jack had struggled against a series of mysterious illnesses, including high fevers and hepatitis, jaundice and malaria, acute gastroenteritis and an absolute inability to gain weight. These illnesses had preyed upon his energy, leaving him tired and weary, without his ever understanding what was wrong. It was only in his thirties, with the diagnosis of chronic Addison's disease, that he was finally able to understand why he was so vulnerable to infection.

"When he was first told about the Addison's," Lem Billings recalled, "it only seemed to increase his sense of personal doom. But after he got used to the treatment and especially after cortisone came into use, he experienced a whole new lease on life. It was at about this time that we all noticed in him a new seriousness, a greater thoughtfulness about public life and a renewed commitment to politics."

Ironically, these positive feelings about politics were reinforced by a bizarre tragedy in the family of James Michael Curley.

Through the years, death had claimed Curley's wife and five of his nine children. Now, on February 11, 1950, forty-one-year-old Mary Curley, his only surviving daughter, who had served as his first lady when he was mayor and governor, died suddenly of a cerebral hemorrhage while talking on the telephone in her Beacon Street apartment; and on the evening of the same day, in the same room and at the same phone, her brother Leo, thirty-four, collapsed and died from the same cause.

"Stunned by the news of the double tragedy," the *Boston Globe* reported, people all over the city "could talk of little else." Having heard the news of Mary's death earlier that day, "men and women of all ages huddled in little groups to catch further news of the second death."

In the course of the next two days, while the two bodies lay side by side in the large hallway of the red brick Georgian house on the Jamai-caway, the Curley family received over fifty thousand visitors from all over the state. In the face of bleak winds and in freezing temperatures, the callers, including Congressman John F. Kennedy, waited outside the house for hours, forming long serpentine lines around the block.

It was for John Kennedy, in the words of Dave Powers, "an incredibly moving experience" to see the extraordinary outpouring of people representing every element in the community, come to show their sympathy for James Michael Curley. There Curley stood in the main hallway, at the head of the receiving line, his aging face ashen white, his eyes sunken and outlined in red, but his will so strong that it enabled him to shake hands with and personally address every one of the thousands of people who filed past the biers.

"The man must be made of iron," Powers said. "No matter what you say of him," Jack replied, "you have to admire him for his great courage." It was, perhaps, a mark of Jack's recovery from his grief that his attention was seized by Curley's strength. Just months before, it seems, he had been fantasizing that he could die in order to be reunited with his sister, but now it was the survivor with whom he identified.

Later that night, Jack paid a visit to his grandfather at the Bellevue Hotel. The old man had visibly aged—his hair was now white and his face deeply lined—but he was still possessed of his full faculties and his phenomenal energy. Having followed every word of the Curley tragedy in the papers, Fitzgerald was filled with genuine sorrow for his lifelong rival. In times like this, he told his grandson, "you realize how fleeting our small political battles are compared with the enduring legacy of family." For now Curley had no successor to carry on his name. Only two sons remained, one a Jesuit and the other temperamentally unsuited to politics. There would be no one to keep the political tradition alive.

All his life, Fitzgerald had sought to blend his twin loves of politics and family to a single use. There were times, he confessed to Jack, when politics had burned within him so fiercely that it consumed all his need for family, but now, in his advancing age, he found himself sustained most of all by the daily warmth of his family. To be sure, not all his dreams for acclaim had been realized. Despite many tries he had been unable to forge a political comeback after his withdrawal from the race against Curley in 1914. Yet, far from condemning the political process as malicious and fickle, he openly encouraged his grandson to carry on in political life.

Indeed, what Jack remembered most about this last, long conversation with his grandfather was how the old man's eyes still burned when he talked of the incomparable richness of political life. He had wanted

Boston to be a better place, he told Jack, and he had wanted the people of Boston to lead better lives, and if the means he had chosen to bring this about had sometimes failed, he knew that his intentions were good and that most people understood this. In his final years he had been much caressed by the public. In the year he turned eighty-five there had been an all-day celebration in his honor, and the newspapers invariably spoke of his famous energy and his generosity of spirit.

Jack could see that his grandfather was tired, but there was some need of his own that kept the conversation going until well into the night. For the experience of the Curley wake had had a deep impact on Jack. When he had looked about the room and seen the astonishing variety of faces crowded together to lend support to an old politician who had been variously acclaimed and reviled, he had suddenly appreciated the indestructible rapport that springs up in political life. And now his grandfather, having achieved an unmistakable presence from the cumulative effect of his days in public life, was passing on the same message. "You are my namesake," Fitzgerald told his grandson that night, describing for him one last time the long road that had taken him from the tenement on Ferry Street to the happy years he had spent in political life. "You are the one to carry on our family name. And mark my word, you will walk on a far larger canvas than I."

Eight months later, with his wife and two of his sons at his bedside, John Fitzgerald died. Though he had been virtually bedridden in the hotel for the preceding several months, no one could believe that his native vigor would give out, so his death came as a shock. This was the first time in his superactive life, the *Boston Post* observed, that he was unable to make his rounds of the city carrying on his lifelong campaign for a "Bigger, Better and Busier Boston." He was, the *Post* concluded, "one of Boston's most beloved figures . . . his vitality in his advanced years was a constant source of amazement and delight to his friends and acquaintances."

He had outlasted all his brothers except the youngest, Henry, who would live for another five years. Twelve years earlier Edward had suffered a fatal heart attack, and Jim had died the previous February. John Fitzgerald had not had an easy family life. He had buried three of his six children and had lived to see ambition's death in his two older boys. But there was always Rose, his favorite child; her accomplishments had given him more pleasure and lifted his own name to greater heights than he could have imagined.

But at the time of his death his "rambling Rose" was in Paris. "Griefstricken" by the news, the *Post* reported, she was "distraught because she could not arrange immediate plane passage home . . . in time for the funeral." Years later, suffering the same guilt that Joe had felt about his father, Rose would deeply regret the passion for travel that had taken her thousands of miles from her father just at the moment he had finally yielded to death. "In spite of his age," she said, "it was impossible to conceive of life without him."

The day of the funeral, October 5, more than 3,500 persons crowded into the Cathedral of the Holy Cross for the services.

> Bankers knelt side by side with laborers [the *Post* reported]. State and national dignitaries, men high in public life shared the same pews in the church with unpretentious housewives from the North End, South End, Dorchester and Roxbury . . . . Secretary of Labor Maurice Tobin, former Ambassador to Great Britain Joseph Kennedy, former Secretary of the Navy Charles Francis Adams and Robert Cutler, president of the Old Colony Trust Company, were but a few pews removed from a delegation of Boston longshoremen who knew, admired and loved John F. for his efforts to promote the Port of Boston.

Seated next to his sisters Eunice, Pat, and Jean, Jack saw the funeral as "the final triumph" of his grandfather. "All his life he had loved his city of Boston," Jack later told Clem Norton, "and now Boston was returning that love." The indomitable spirit of the man had called forth a remarkable array of people from all walks of life, "the great, the near great and the humble." It was a magnificent tribute to the old warrior before he was laid to his final rest, in a flower-banked grave on a tiny knoll at St. Joseph's Cemetery in West Roxbury.

Jack Kennedy later told Lem Billings that he decided to stick with politics and go for statewide office at just about this time and that the solidarity and good feeling evident at both the Curley wake and his grandfather's funeral had played a significant role in leading him to that decision. If this is so, there is nothing that would have pleased old John Fitzgerald more.

"There was something in the pageantry and the richness of those two occasions that really got to Jack," Billings recalled. "It made him realize the extraordinary impact a politician can have on the emotions of ordinary people, an impact often forgotten in the corridors of Capitol Hill. It was as if he were seeing for the first time that he really might be able to touch people as a politician and that if he could, then they could give him something back—something to make up for his terrible sense of loneliness and loss."

While Jack's new resolution about politics was probably influenced just as strongly by the successful treatment for his Addison's disease, it does seem that he found in his final conversation with his grandfather a way of living that promised to transmute private loss into public gain. If victory within the family was forever denied to him, there was out there an entire world to be charmed, cajoled and conquered.

# CHAPTER 42
## "SHOOTING
## FOR A
## STAR"

Now the story of the Fitzgeralds and the Kennedys, the century-long ascent from the immigrant slums of Boston's North End, was to become something different: the personal and political journey of John Fitzgerald Kennedy. The family was to become celebrated as never before, the focus of a public interest of unmatched intensity. His parents and siblings were to play a large and well-publicized role in John Kennedy's success, but in the largest sense it was his own triumph. For his capacity to arouse the questing imagination of his fellow citizens, and of much of the world beyond America's borders, was to elevate the family saga past the borders of mythology.

By the beginning of the fifties he already contained all the elements from which his leadership was to be compounded, forged in tumultuous experience, anchored and given direction by his often resented but always unbreakable links to his extraordinary family. Emotionally and materially John Fitzgerald Kennedy was always a Kennedy. Yet there was also a sense—especially as he neared the summit—in which he needed no one else at all. Because he was so much his own man, so armored in his solitude, he could belong—if not to anyone, to everyone. Resentful of his mother's distance and jealous of his father's preference for his older brother, he transformed his youthful rebellion into a powerful independence. Instead of rupturing less than perfect family ties, he reforged them, and then used them to strengthen his own purpose.

Of all the Kennedy children, Jack was the one to notice that "the idea of the family" served to substitute for his parents' absence. There was nothing dearer to his parents' hearts than their children, yet both Rose and Joe spent substantial amounts of time away from home, leaving it to Eddie and Mary Moore and the family governesses to give daily evidence to the family values of warmth and togetherness. The children were given a lot of affection by various surrogates, but they never enjoyed the security of the continuing presence of the two people who stood at the center of their lives.

Lying ill for months at a time, Jack developed what Lem Billings called "an inner eye" which he focused on the gap between his parents' ideals for the family and the reality of their daily life. While Joe Junior and Kathleen seem to have been too busy with their activities to look below the surface, Jack developed an acute sensibility to everything that was going on around him. Even when his mother was home, Jack was only one of many children competing for her time and attention. Years later, Rose admitted that it must have been tough for Jack, since so much of her own time was taken up either with Joe, whom she had chosen as her model for the younger children, or with Rosemary, whose needs were so obvious. "In the process," Rose said, "I'm afraid poor little sickly Jack was left on his own too much of the time."

Yet, precisely because he was left alone so much of the time, Jack had the freedom to be a child. By contrast, Joe Junior developed early on "the perfect personality." Reliable, convenient and well-behaved, he revealed only what was expected of him. And in the process he was never quite a child.

Indeed, the very hopelessness of Jack's situation—the clear recognition that he would meet with continual frustration if he tried to compete with his model brother—gave him the possibility of developing his own emotional life with his siblings, his governesses and his nurses. Within the family he became the warm and playful brother, the Pied Piper whose humor and vitality aroused an answering chord among his sisters and brothers, and made him, at least for some of his family, the center of attention.

From his first recorded encounter with the world beyond his family circle—as a small boy consigned to the hospital surroundings he would come to know well—we see signs of his recognition that personal charm, the capacity to warm and please others, could win the loving admiration which was not, as Joe's, his by right of birth. "He is such a wonderful boy . . . we all love him very dearly," reported the nurses who had been skillfully seduced by the precocious child. His desire to charm had an intensity, a singleness of purpose, that came from his own vulnerability—a dimly felt, perhaps unconscious, almost insatiable need for warmth, approval and love.

He seemed to emit some part of his own vulnerable intensity, transmitting a force which bound others to him. It was a process that drew both individuals and crowds into his orbit. "Even in a crowded room," an aide reported, "when he talked to you, asking questions, responding with unfeigned interest, it was as if there was no one else in the world, just the two of you." His self-assured manner concealed a more explosive insecurity. It was not the confidence of one who had inherited the world, but of a man who believed he could win it if he tried.

He was gifted with intelligence and imagination which flourished in the isolation of his childhood. The books his mother read him during his days of youthful illness—those rare times when he alone occupied the center of Rose's attention—were absorbed and charged with high intensity. Camelot, or the concept of a Camelot, the joys of adventure, the glory of high deeds, were conceived in the fevered brain of a sick child. "When we were reading *Lives of the Saints*," his sister Eunice remembered, "Jack was reading Carlyle." As he became older, books took on another life-enhancing function. They were his retreat from the continual rivalries and tensions of his family surroundings; a world to which he could withdraw, where he could be, not a Kennedy—not just a Kennedy—but Jack.

He was not "bookish," not a scholar by temperament. He liked competition and action, hungered for the pleasures of the sensual life so often denied him by illness. Yet his reading provided him with an inner life from which he drew vitality. And from the worlds of adventure, history and biography which were his favorites he was giving form to the values and ambitions that were to guide him as he entered more seriously into public life.

His struggle for independence within the family was also reflected in the almost complete lack of ideological commitment or public philosophy with which he entered public life. "Some people have their liberal-ism 'made' by the time they reach their late twenties," he told James MacGregor Burns. "I didn't. I was caught in cross-currents and eddies. It was only later that I got into the stream of things."

The statement is both revealing and misleading. John Kennedy was never to subsume himself under a coherent political philosophy, liberal or conservative. He never fully identified himself with a cause or an institution except in pursuit of goals. In his early years as a congressman, his position on issues reflected a mixture of his father's conservatism, the liberalism of his district, and the fierce and not wholly altruistic populism of his namesake, John Francis Fitzgerald.

These were not insubstantial sources of public philosophy. But nei-ther the political attitudes of his family nor the historical discourses of Carlyle nor the legends of King Arthur constituted an adequate guide to the national problems or political issues of postwar America. Lacking a coherent intellectual and moral commitment, John Kennedy was forced to find his compass in personal experience. How ironic, in retrospect, seem the concerns of those who feared the influence of the Catholic Church on this most secular of leaders.

This lack, the absence of a principled consistency to guide his re-sponse to public issues, was a source of his largest failings as a political leader, blinding him, for example, to the large moral issues raised by the anti-Communist witch-hunts of the 1950s. He consistently voted to fund the House Un-American Activities Committee, he joined in Republican criticism of Truman for the "loss" of China, and he would refuse to join the Senate censure of Joe McCarthy.

Yet this failing was also the root of his greatest strengths as a leader. His vision, unobstructed by ideological preconception, was continually reformed by experience; his mind welcomed and absorbed divergent views. He had the capacity to admit mistakes and, if possible, reverse them, and the strength to surround himself, not with sycophants, but with men of intelligence and strong convictions.

People who knew him were struck by the impersonality of his attitudes and his ready grasp of the views and interests of others. In his discussions of people and issues he was often candid about himself, wryly humorous and dispassionate in his judgments. In another man the absence of systematic ideological commitment might have allowed irrationally de-structive actions, reflecting the dominance of ego over facts, arguments and the lessons of experience. John Kennedy, however, possessed an intellectual self-confidence which allowed him to modify his approach to public problems, to reform even the firmest opinions, to entertain divergent possibilities, without feeling personally threatened. It was through his superior intelligence and imagination, his curious, questing relationship to language and ideas, that he had been able to establish a unique position in a largely nonintellectual family so preeminently dedicated to action and achievement. Whether he was reading alone, in a sickbed or seated apart from the frenzy of family activities, or, later, writing books and articles, his mounting confidence in the powers of his own mind became the most important component of his defense against the most basic insecurities of his relationship to parents, family structure and life itself.

"The world breaks every one," wrote Hemingway, "and afterward many are strong at the broken places." John Kennedy appears to have been one of the fortunate ones strengthened by the potentially destructive encounters of childhood.

To describe these qualities is not to summarize the man. There is always something more—an indescribable compound of self drawn not simply from his own experiences but from the experiences of the generations who lived before him.

From his namesake, John Fitzgerald, Kennedy inherited a driving will, a determination to overcome sorrow and disability through perpetual motion. As a young boy Fitzgerald had reacted to the death of his sister by forcing himself to become a champion swimmer, and in the years after his father's death he had driven himself to become the first son of immigrant parents to reach the office of mayor in the city of Boston. Kennedy also shared with his grandfather a radiant warmth which he was able to project onto crowds and individuals alike. Yet beneath his gregarious exterior he carried within him his grandmother Josie's coldness, a psychic pain brought about by unforgiven grievances.

From his grandparents on his father's side, he inherited a certain self-possession and dignity of bearing which his father never achieved. Like P. J. Kennedy, John Kennedy commanded respect and attention from all who came in contact with him. And Joseph Kennedy, recognizing this quality in his son as the one thing he had always desired for himself, was very impressed.

John Kennedy himself thought that the best quality he inherited from his family was curiosity. Having taken several trips with his mother, he had seen her face light up as she allowed herself to become a part of every new city into which she stepped. "Whenever Mother traveled anywhere," Jack told Lem, "her eyes were so bright and so gay and her enthusiasm so contagious that she could not help but attract everyone who came in contact with her."

With his family's wealth, Kennedy was able to travel extensively as a young man. He had lived in England and served in the wartime South

Pacific. He had traveled through eastern Europe and South America, met most of England's ruling class, talked with Third World leaders and seen some of the poverty and discontent which surrounded the world's tiny islands of extravagant wealth.

He discovered through his own observations that foreign leaders were, in particular ways dictated by their own circumstances, bound by the universal imperatives of politics; that they had interests and constituencies which limited their actions and determined the realistic opportunities for American foreign policy. Sukarno of Indonesia and the ward boss of East Boston, Nasser of Egypt and Daley of Chicago, were subject to the imperatives of political power, and once this was understood, then conversation was possible and deals could be struck.

If his approach to America's domestic problems was slower to mature, it was largely because his travels outside his congressional district had been largely confined to the vacation resorts of Palm Beach and Hyannis Port. It was not until later, when his campaigning would take him through the deprived areas of Massachusetts, the coal mines of West Virginia and the slums of Detroit, that he would become aware of the injustices of poverty and of the heroism with which many endured misfortune.

But of all the influences that shaped John Kennedy, his father's absolute commitment was probably the most important. For the first time in his life Jack was now experiencing the full strength of all the insight, understanding and affection that had once been focused on Joe Junior. It had been a long time in coming, but precisely because it had taken so long Jack was able to absorb the force of his father's personality without losing his own.

Whether he decided to run for governor or the Senate—a question still unresolved—Jack Kennedy, in the spring of 1951, began a ceaseless, grueling pursuit of the statewide constituency either office would require. Every Thursday, he flew to Massachusetts for a three- or four-day "weekend" of speaking engagements, communion breakfasts, political and social meetings and church socials. "Jack told me," Dave Powers recalled, "to let everybody know he was available as a speaker on weekends, and I talked to the local Elks, VFWs, Amvets, Holy Name societies and volunteer fire departments wherever I went. No town was too small or too Republican for him. He was willing to go anywhere and every group was glad to have him, not only because he was an interesting political figure, but because he never charged a dime for expenses."

Accompanying Jack were Frank Morrissey, Bob Morey, John Galvin and Dave Powers, all of whom he drove as relentlessly as he drove himself. Rising before dawn, riding in a car for hours in rain or snow or over bumpy roads, they usually ended up, Galvin recalled, "sleeping in a crummy small-town hotel with a single electric bulb hanging from the ceiling over the bed and a questionable bathtub down at the far end of the hall." On a good day for Jack, Powers had him scheduled for a dozen speeches in three or four different towns, which meant racing from town to town, grabbing malteds and cheeseburgers on the run, and all this with a continuous pain in his back which grew so bad as the months went by that after each appearance he would sink into the back seat of his car, grit his teeth and close his eyes.

At the same time, the Ambassador, with the help of two advance men, was working to establish a statewide organization far broader than the traditional Democratic structure. Leland Bickford, editor-in-chief of the Yankee Network News Service, journeyed across the state for more than a year and a half, making contacts with town and city clerks, local editorial writers, independents and Republicans, gathering opinions on Jack's performance and compiling a list of potential supporters.

Operating from Palm Beach and Hyannis Port, the Ambassador was so involved in this preparatory phase of Jack's campaign that he turned most of his business affairs over to his New York office, which allowed him, he wrote to his English friend Jim Calder, to step aside from his enterprises except in a very supervisory capacity. "As far as I am concerned," he wrote to Calder in November of 1951, "I am interesting myself in Jack's candidacy."

From the start, Joseph Kennedy was of the opinion that Jack should run against the incumbent Henry Cabot Lodge II—grandson of the isolationist who had defeated John Fitzgerald for the Senate thirty-six years earlier—for the Senate. "When you've beaten Lodge," he said, "you've beaten the best. Why try for something less?" But, characteristically, he insisted on facts to support his intuition, taking a number of private polls, which, to everyone's surprise, showed that Jack had a fair chance of toppling the Yankee giant. "You wonder why we're taking on Lodge," Kennedy later confided to an old classmate. "We've taken polls. He'll be easier to beat than Saltonstall." (Leverett Saltonstall was the senior Republican Senator from Massachusetts.)

For Jack too, the Senate seat had much more appeal. It was an office that would allow him to focus on foreign affairs and international relations. "He asked me what I thought," William O. Douglas recalled. "I told him I believe in every young man shooting for a star and this was a star."

But Jack Kennedy was not the only Democrat interested in the Senate seat. During 1951 and into the spring of 1952, Paul Dever, the state's very popular Governor, was also considering a Senate race. If he decided to go ahead, Kennedy would either have to change his plans and run for governor or take on Dever in the primary, a risky move at best.

So the Kennedys waited from January until April 1952, while Dever was making up his mind, an uncomfortable position for a family accustomed to taking control. "It really was the Governor's choice," Dever aide J. John Fox explained. "If Dever had decided to go for the Senate, his decision would have been controlling and Jack would have run for governor."

Finally, Dever agreed to meet with Jack Kennedy on Palm Sunday to disclose his plans. "We will all be anxiously waiting for the results of Sunday's momentous meeting," Bickford wrote to the Ambassador on April 3. There is no record of the meeting, but the results were as the Kennedys wished. "I've just talked to Dever," Jack told his aide Lawrence O'Brien that afternoon. "He's running for governor again. Here we go, Larry—we've got the race we want!"

To some, even among those in the Kennedy camp, the quest seemed impossible. At the start of the campaign, John Kennedy was known to only 35 percent of the voters in Massachusetts, while 68 percent knew Henry Cabot Lodge. For nearly two decades the handsome blue-eyed Lodge had dominated political life in Massachusetts, having soundly beaten three of the most popular Irish politicians in the history of the state. At the age of thirty-four, in his first Senate race, he had defeated Curley by 142,000 votes in a tough campaign during which Curley persisted in calling him "Little Boy Blue" as a reminder of his aristocratic background. Six years later he won reelection against Joe Casey, then resigned from his seat in 1944 for military service during the final stages of the war in Europe. In 1946 he was triumphantly returned to the Senate by defeating the "unbeatable" David I. Walsh.

Born in a cavernous gray clapboard house set amid the coves and jagged rocks of Nahant, a lean peninsula ten miles north of Boston, pointing toward Europe, Henry Cabot Lodge had been christened in honor of his grandfather. Like Kennedy, Lodge had graduated from Harvard and dabbled in journalism before settling into a career in politics. And like Kennedy, he was a decorated war hero with a reputation for appealing to the women's vote.

"Rarely in American politics," James MacGregor Burns observed, "have hunter and quarry so resembled each other. Not only were they both tall, young, handsome and winning, each a Brahmin in his own way, but their careers were remarkably parallel."

Lodge had no illusions about the strength of the challenge Kennedy posed. "From the beginning," he said, "I knew it would be much harder than it had been against Curley, Casey and Walsh, for the people had nothing against Kennedy as they did against all the others. All along, I always knew if there came a man with an honest, clean record who was also of Irish descent, he'd be almost impossible to beat."

Even before John Kennedy's announcement, Lodge saw that his own success in 1952 would depend on the ability of the Republicans to field a powerful presidential candidate. "From the start," he said later, "I believed that the Republican front-runner, Senator [Robert A.] Taft, could not possibly be elected nationwide and that his defeat would hurt all Republicans in Massachusetts. As a party, our only chance was to go with Eisenhower, whose broad appeal could take him way beyond the conservative dominions represented by Senator Taft."

In September 1951 Lodge visited Dwight D. Eisenhower at NATO's Paris headquarters. Reviewing the deterioration of the Republican Party's moderate faction, he told the General he was the only moderate who could be elected to the presidency. "You must permit the use of your name in the upcoming primaries," Lodge told him. Finally, after much discussion, Eisenhower said he would "think the matter over," and he recorded in his memoirs that from that time on he "began to look anew" at himself and politics.

Two months later, it was announced that Lodge would be the manager of the draft-Eisenhower movement. "It is a dangerous gamble that could backfire against Lodge," Boston columnist James Colbert observed, recalling that a similar action by Massachusetts Governor Robert Bradford in 1948 on behalf of Thomas E. Dewey had aroused conservative Republican animosity which cost Bradford his reelection.

Through the winter of 1952, while Lodge worked tirelessly on Eisenhower's behalf, Joe Kennedy worked to exploit the mounting resentment of the Taft conservatives. Through the years, his own isolationist leanings had drawn the Ambassador close to Senator Taft and a number of his key supporters. Now, as the Taft camp began to turn against Lodge for deserting "Mr. Republican," the Ambassador began the effort which would, in time, allow Jack to inherit the votes of the disaffected Taft supporters, votes which tended to be concentrated in the large ring of Republican suburbs surrounding Boston. In his letters to Bickford, Joe Kennedy repeatedly stressed the importance of creating a new organization which could penetrate these old Republican bastions.

During the campaign, Joe Kennedy rented an exclusive apartment on Beacon Street, just a few blocks away from Jack's Bowdoin Street address. There, seated at a desk overlooking the Public Garden, the Ambassador mobilized his own circle of aides—a group of men he had known for a long time, including Jim Landis, Lynn Johnston, Ralph Coglan, John Harriman and John J. Ford.

Only Eddie Moore was missing from the Ambassador's inner circle. At seventy-seven years of age, Joe Kennedy's partner was largely confined to his bed on the Cape, struggling to close his life in the same spirit he had lived it. Radiating cheer, Moore insisted on keeping up with all the details of the campaign, hoping, as he put it to Rose, "to be right in the swing of things as long as these pesty doctors let me." He had witnessed many Kennedy triumphs and endured many heartaches, a silent partner moving with the family wherever it went. Their secrets, traditions, resentments, hopes, dreams were his delight, his life, beyond which there was only his wife, Mary Moore.

Dave Powers later recalled the valiant struggle Eddie Moore put up to do his bit in the campaign. "We had a beautiful brochure made up, a twelve-page colored brochure with a series of pictures of Jack, and we wanted to get it delivered all over the state. But instead of mailing it, knowing that in a campaign people often empty mailboxes, we decided to get it hand-delivered, and Eddie volunteered to take responsibility for the Cape. I was afraid it was too much work for him, but he wouldn't admit it, until one day I got a call asking me to come down and help. I went at once, and I can still remember the smile on his face when we finished. Then that night he was so proud to call headquarters and give the report that the Cape had been completely covered."

It was no secret that Joe Kennedy was providing money for his son's campaign. It was expensive to spread the young Congressman's name across the state, to hire the cars and charter the planes that allowed the candidate to cross the state in a single day, to print the engraved invitations for the dozens of teas attended by more than fifty thousand women.

On May 13, Jim Landis suggested to Joe Kennedy that he should contact every state Democratic senator and representative and make small contributions to their respective campaigns. "This is one way to get right down to the local level and have these people battle for Kennedy." Two weeks later, the Ambassador wrote to his lawyer, Bart Brickley, for a legal opinion as to whether the owners of the Mart or of the Columbus Avenue building could make donations, "because, after all, they are the ones from whom we expect to get the most money." In response, Brickley wrote a long, complicated letter which basically argued that there was apparently "no limit on the number of different candidates or different committees to which a contribution of $1000 may be made."

Moving quickly, Joe Kennedy set up a variety of committees—committees for "Improvement of the Massachusetts Fish Industry," for "Improvement of the Shoe Industry," for "Improvement of the Textile

Industry," along with "Citizens for Kennedy and a More Prosperous Massachusetts," to which the family gave a total of $70,000, topped only by the Ambassador's friends and acquaintances, who contributed more than $200,000.

With the money came power over campaign decisions, and in the early days of the campaign Joe Kennedy wielded his power with a heavy hand. At strategy sessions, an insider reported, "the father was the distinct boss in every way. He dominated everything, even told everyone where to sit." Kennedy aide De Guglielmo remembers an early session at Hyannis Port when the talk centered on the comparative strengths of Kennedy and Lodge. "I told Jack's father that in my judgment Jack would get the bulk of the women's vote. Hearing this, the old man pooh-poohed Jack's appeal and said that only *old* ladies like him. Jack got embarrassed as hell." Later, when the talk shifted to assigning roles in the campaign, Jack evidently felt the need to reassert his authority. Running down a list of assignments, he came to a task called "making all the money." "We concede you that role," he said to his father.

The tension between father and son was illustrated most damagingly in the callous treatment of Mark Dalton, the quiet and intelligent young man who had managed Jack's previous campaigns for the House. By 1952 Dalton's law practice had grown to where he could no longer afford the sacrifice of working as an anonymous, unpaid volunteer, and so John Galvin was instructed to draw up a press release announcing that Dalton was the full-time campaign manager. Of the men around Jack, Dalton was the one who could speak the most honestly to him; there was something in his relaxed, bookish demeanor which touched the concealed sensitive side of Jack Kennedy. But if Jack trusted Dalton completely, Joe Kennedy did not, perhaps finding Dalton's relaxed style *too* relaxed. Or perhaps, as some observers have suggested, the old patriarch could never place anyone except a Kennedy in a position of authority. For when the time came to release Dalton's appointment to the press, the Ambassador held it up.

It came as "a grave disappointment" to Dalton, made even harder to accept by the fact that Jack would tell him only that there were three reasons why he couldn't release the statement, refusing to explain any of them. "After all the years of work for John," Dalton lamented, "all the years of advice and help and everything else, when he wouldn't announce that I was campaign manager, it was a very grave blow to me."

Still, he stayed on until a hot afternoon in the late spring. "Dalton was at his desk, smoking a pipe," a witness recalled, "when Joe Kennedy breezed in. The old man spread all the books on the desk in front of him, studied them for about five minutes without saying a word, then shoved his finger in Dalton's face and yelled, 'Dalton, you've spent ten thousand dollars of my money and you haven't accomplished a damn thing.' "

Dalton said little at the time, but as soon as the Ambassador had left he took his coat and hat and left the campaign for good. Finding him later in the quiet reading room of the Boston Athenaeum, Beacon Hill's stately private library, Kenny O'Donnell tried to talk with him, but the decision was already made.

"The whole affair really hurt Jack," John Galvin observed. "He felt a great affinity toward Mark. They respected and admired each other very much. But I think Jack determined it would take too much to resolve the whole matter. He was too busy, there was too much momentum. So he just dropped him."

With Dalton's departure and the staff leaderless, morale weakened and the campaign, O'Donnell thought, was headed toward "absolute disaster." In the midst of the chaos, O'Donnell decided that unless Jack's brother Robert took over, the fight would be lost. Calling Robert in New York, where he was working for the Justice Department on a federal case, O'Donnell pleaded with him to take a leave from his work and return to Massachusetts. "Don't drag me into it," Robert responded, explaining in an angry tone that he loved what he was doing in the Justice Department and didn't know anything at all about Massachusetts politics. "I'll screw it up," he warned, "and . . . I just don't want to come." But when O'Donnell said, "Unless you come, I don't think it's going to be done," Robert agreed that he would at least talk to his father.

In the years after the war, Robert had gradually attracted his father's attention and respect. His academic record at Harvard had been undistinguished, but he had "willed himself," to use Lem Billings' phrase, onto the varsity football squad and emerged from the Yale game with his Harvard letter, something neither of his older brothers had accomplished. After his graduation, he had journeyed to Europe for a long trip meticulously planned for him by his father. "He is a remarkable boy," Lord Beaverbrook had written to Joe after meeting Bobby. "He is clever, has a good character, energy, a clear understanding and a fine philosophy." The letter pleased Joe very much. "He is just starting off," Joe explained to Beaverbrook, "and has the difficulty of trying to follow two brilliant brothers, Joe and Jack. That in itself is quite a handicap and he is making a good battle against it."

While Bobby was in Europe, the Ambassador made arrangements for him to publish a series of articles in a Boston paper. "I am very grateful to you for doing the job," Kennedy wrote to the editor of the *Boston*

*Advertiser.* "Bobby has a lot on the ball. In fact I think he writes better than Joe or Jack, but as a third son, he has had a lot of trouble basking in the reflected glory of Joe and Jack."

Through his years in law school and his marriage to Manhattanville graduate Ethel Skakel in 1950, Bobby's modest store of self-confidence began to grow. Nevertheless, he never strayed far beyond his family orbit. A few days after talking with his father, Robert Kennedy gave up his job in the Justice Department and headed for Massachusetts, where, most observers agree, his entrance into the campaign proved to be a decisive turning point. "Bobby could handle the father," said O'Donnell, "and no one else could have . . . Those of us who worked with him over the next few months are convinced that if Bobby had not arrived on the scene and taken charge when he did, Jack Kennedy most certainly would have lost the election."

Bobby's first crisis concerned Jack's relationship with Governor Dever. In the spring Dever and Kennedy had agreed that each would work separately within his own statewide organization. But during the Democratic national convention in Chicago, Dever's stock fell badly. Asked to deliver the convention's keynote address, Dever, his aide J. John Fox recalled, "prepared a magnificent speech, and he was so excited about it that he spent the entire day before the convention's opening ceremonies practicing it in the Chicago Coliseum, where a dozen workmen stopped their work of preparing the empty hall to listen and shout their approval. But in the process Dever strained his vocal cords, and the next day, his voice already hoarse and raspy, he spoke louder and louder, trying to will the milling delegates to attention, until his voice completely cracked. In short, it was disastrous." Soon after he began to speak, it was reported, "rivulets of sweat were streaming down his face," which he repeatedly tried to wipe away with his handkerchief. Facing the largest audience of his life—seventy million television viewers—Dever looked like a beaten prize fighter.

Many of Dever's aides were convinced that the Governor's only hope of recovering from this political disaster was to ally himself with the popular young Kennedy. The Kennedy campaign had no objection at first to closer ties, but when huge Dever-Kennedy signs appeared all over the state a number of Kennedy workers feared that the integrity of their operation would be blown apart. "Every afternoon Dever's people would come over with these big signs and stickers," recalled Phil Fine, a lawyer and Kennedy worker, "and every night we'd tear them down." But others within the Kennedy camp, most notably the Ambassador, argued that an open fight with Dever would bring about a damaging split in party ranks. Forced to resolve the issue, Jack decided he should disassociate himself from Dever, but without letting Dever know that the decision was his. It would be made to appear that Bobby was insisting on the separation. "Don't give in to them," Jack told Bobby. "But don't get me involved in it. Treat it as an organizational problem."

Bobby went to Dever's office and told him in flat, undiplomatic terms that there would be no joint Dever-Kennedy headquarters. Furious, Dever sent word to the Ambassador that henceforth all relations between the two camps would have to go through him, as he would have nothing more to do with that fresh young kid. It was through incidents like this that the impression of Bobby's ruthlessness was created. With Bobby to play the role of opportunistic enemy, Jack could avoid an open personal confrontation with Dever, and the two camps maintained an uneasy peace throughout the campaign.

The more Kennedy's advisers studied Lodge and his record, the more they despaired of drawing a line on issues which could win the support of the party's indifferent and suspicious liberal wing. Both men were internationalists with a heritage of isolationism, both were liberal conservatives who veered back and forth on domestic issues. The decision was to have the candidate take strongly liberal positions, while his father would work to attract conservative support.

Particularly disturbing to liberals were the known views of the omnipresent father—in particular, his reputation as an anti-Semite. "We were in a real bind with respect to the Jewish people," said Phil Fine. "At first we didn't have a soul with us." With time and work, the situation improved as Jack slowly and methodically met with key Jewish leaders all over the state. Then, at the Boston Club, speaking to a dinner meeting of three hundred prominent Jews, Jack decided to confront the problem directly. After a long and forceful speech on Israel, he sensed a lingering doubt in his audience. "What more do you want?" he finally asked, revealing once again his gift for articulating people's unspoken thoughts. "Remember, I'm running for the Senate, not my father." This frank declaration was just what his listeners wanted to hear, and they applauded warmly.

While Jack was moving to secure the liberal vote, his father was mounting a campaign against Lodge's right flank. When the Republican convention nominated Eisenhower, the Ambassador moved at once to convert the embittered Taft contingent to Jack's candidacy. His efforts centered on Taft's precampaign manager, Basil Brewer, the powerful publisher of the New Bedford Standard Times.

"I can still remember Brewer's press conference in September," Lodge recalled, "when he announced that he was lending his wholehearted support to Jack Kennedy and hoped that all of Taft's supporters would do the same. It was a great blow, for all the station-wagon Republicans in the suburban towns west and south of Boston had been with me for decades. Even there, I'm not sure they meant to defeat me, for after the election I got hundreds of apologetic notes from Republicans saying they didn't really mean to send me out of office, they just wanted to punish me by lowering my vote. Imagine that! What childishness!"

Despite the strenuous efforts of the dual Kennedy campaign, Lodge began to gain momentum as the election neared. "There was so little to get Kennedy on," Lodge recalled, "so I decided to go with his absentee record. Now, my attendance record wasn't so great either, because of the traveling I was doing for Eisenhower, but it was better than his, so we could go with it. And as it happened, when our big advertisements on the absentee problem hit the papers, it struck a raw nerve, a submerged feeling that Jack Kennedy was not taking his job seriously, that it was only a way station from which he could move on to bigger things. Now, I knew that he'd been sick a lot and I didn't like capitalizing on that, but I also knew that he had traveled a lot all over the world, so I didn't feel too guilty about it."

Many years later, Lodge recalled "a growing feeling of confidence as the election approached. I recognized that I had started campaigning too late, but I really felt that with Eisenhower's growing momentum and with my own attention now back on Massachusetts, I could pull it off. There were only three worries I had. The first was the Brewer situation, but even though I lost him I didn't believe that all those suburbanites who supported Taft would really go after me. I was wrong. My second concern was to hold a substantial vote in the city of Boston. In 1946 I had actually carried Boston. No Yankee ever forgets such a thing, it's like Calais on Queen Elizabeth's chest. I knew it would be much harder this time, but I figured if I could get the endorsement of the *Post*, which in those days was worth forty thousand votes, I could hold my own in Boston. I didn't get it. And the third worry was the women's vote and those spectacular teas the Kennedys were sponsoring."

The episode of the *Post* endorsement was a critical turning point. "I will never forget as long as I live," Lodge recalled, "the night I went to see John Fox, the publisher of the *Post*. It was very difficult for me to do, since he was furious with me for supporting Eisenhower and made his anger very obvious. But I knew the managing editor, Ed Dunne, and I knew that over the years the *Post* had supported both my grandfather and me. Anyway, there are a lot of things you're willing to do in a campaign that you really hate to do. So I said, 'I know how you feel about Taft and about my support for Eisenhower, but if you look to the future and all the issues you care about, you'll see they are far more likely to be secured by a Republican than a Democrat.' He remained silent for a long while, deliberately keeping me hanging, but he finally said, 'OK, I've decided to support you even though I don't like you.' I came home that night, wrote him a note of thanks and went to bed thinking that I had won the election."

But, unknown to Lodge, Fox soon received another visit from Joseph Kennedy, and that changed everything. By 1952 the flamboyant Fox, a self-made millionaire who speculated in oil and gas properties, was desperately short of cash. He had bought the faltering *Post* the year before and transformed it from a Democratic sounding board into a passionate anti-Communist Republican paper, but the expensive deal had left him in a difficult financial situation. How much Joe knew about this when he went to plead Jack's cause remains unclear, but the Ambassador was celebrated for his extensive sources. At any rate, Fox abruptly changed his mind, and two days later the powerful paper printed a ringing editorial endorsement of John Kennedy's candidacy.

Years later, Fox admitted that, about the same time, he had obtained a half-million-dollar loan from Joseph P. Kennedy. Joe Kennedy himself characterized the loan as an ordinary business transaction, agreed to only *after* Fox had decided to back his son. He was so grateful to Fox when he heard that the paper was about to support Jack, he said, that he told Fox if he needed anything all he had to do was to ask. It was at this point, and this point only, both Fox and Kennedy later insisted, that money was discussed. "Oh yes," Lodge laughingly recalled, "I've heard that story, too. And it continues to relate that it was Brewer who changed Fox's mind, not Joe Kennedy. But I've never doubted for a moment that Joe Kennedy was the one who turned Fox around, though I imagine he handled it pretty subtly, with all sorts of veiled promises and hints rather than an outright deal. Still, even with the loss of both Brewer and Fox, I think I could have made it if it hadn't been for all those fancy tea parties the Kennedys sponsored all over the state."

The idea of the tea parties was a masterstroke, for it brought the entire Kennedy family into direct contact with tens of thousands of women who looked upon them as royalty and saw their own dreams of success mirrored in the Kennedys' achievement. "At one of these teas," Lodge remembered hearing, "John Kennedy spoke directly to the past, arguing that his grandfather had lost to mine by only fifty thousand votes in a close election which could have gone the other way if women had been allowed to vote. But now they could vote, he concluded, and this election could well turn on their decision. What a great pitch! And beyond the votes they gained, the teas served as a brilliant means of bringing new people into politics."

In all, there were thirty-three teas, with the success of each tea multiplying the number of women attending the next one. From the start, recalled Polly Fitzgerald, who organized the teas, "we decided to rent the fanciest rooms in the nicest hotels and to set up the rooms with lace tablecloths and silver candelabras. We wanted the setting to be beautiful, as if it were an exclusive party in someone's estate instead of a political reception in a hotel."

The entire Kennedy family stood in a receiving line while the guests poured in. "For approximately two hours," Cabell Phillips observed in a piece published in *The New York Times Magazine* right before the election, "an unbroken line of women filed slowly across the stage, shaking hands with each of the Kennedys, mumbling confused introductions and pleasantries, and pushed on through a side-door into the lobby, still packed with those waiting their turn to go through the receiving line."

"Mrs. Kennedy was a key element in our success," Polly Fitzgerald reminisced, "known for her style in clothes and her rich experiences in travel; all the women wanted to meet her, and she was the reason they all came in their best dresses. And I must say she was a master at knowing how to turn an ordinary event into a special occasion. And what a terrific speaker she turned out to be."

Writing to his British friend Calder, Joe Kennedy proudly described the ease with which Rose delivered remarkable speeches to crowds of people. It was all the more amazing, he commented, "because she had always felt she would get so nervous speaking to even a small group that she never attempted it." In this campaign she was now speaking "before thousands," looking beautiful and doing extremely well. Before a group of Italian women in the North End, she presented herself as the mother of nine children who had grown up in the neighborhood and attended St. Stephen's Church. Then, in her limousine en route to a gathering of Beacon Hill matrons, she would adorn her simple black dress with expensive jewelry and put on her mink coat. "Now," she would say, after speaking a few minutes about her son, "let me tell you about the new dresses I saw in Paris last month."

Throughout the campaign, frequent reference was made to Jack's heroism in the South Pacific. And in one of those fortunate "coincidences" that were so often to mark Jack Kennedy's swift rise to power, a dramatic letter from Japan arrived a few weeks before the election. It was written by Kohei Hanami, commander of the destroyer *Amagiri* which had split Jack's boat in two. In an August issue of *Time* magazine Hanami had read an interview in which Kennedy told of having gone to Japan after the war in an unsuccessful search for the destroyer's commander, and he sent a warm letter to Kennedy which (in earnest if not perfect English translation) said, "I am firmly convinced that a person who practice tolerance to your former enemy like you, if elected to the high office of your country, would no doubt contribute not only to the promotion of genuine friendship between Japan and the United States but also to the establishment of the universal peace." Kennedy's head-quarters immediately released the letter to the press, accompanied by pictures of the *Amagiri* and the *109*, providing, as the release said, "a pleasant echo from the desperate sea battle" that had almost taken Kennedy's life.

On election eve, General Eisenhower, moved by his friendship for the beleaguered Henry Cabot Lodge, made his final speech of the 1952 presidential campaign at Boston Garden, carried nationwide on televison and radio. He was the first Republican presidential candidate to end his campaign in Boston, and the capacity crowd greeted him with a tumultuous demonstration. Eisenhower urged his listeners to reelect Lodge, "one of the very first to seriously suggest to me that I might undertake this great crusade. . . . I consider him," Eisenhower proclaimed, "a man of courage and conviction, a vigorous opponent of the menace of godless Communism . . ."

On a cool, windy election day, the early returns foretold an Eisenhower sweep over Governor Adlai E. Stevenson of Illinois and a close, uncertain contest between Kennedy and Lodge. The uncertainty continued until the early hours of the next morning, when Jack began to pull ahead. "At five A.M.," Powers recalled, "we could feel victory in the wings as our headquarters began to fill up with smiling faces waiting for the final count." At 7:34 A.M., Lodge conceded. "I extend my congratulations," he wired to Kennedy, "and express the hope that you will derive from your term in the Senate all the satisfaction that comes from courageous and sincere efforts in public service."

When this telegram was read, the tumultuous crowd at Kennedy headquarters burst into cheers, shouts, whistles and enthusiastic applause. It took Jack a long time to make his way through the milling mob to the platform to speak. He began by expressing special gratitude to his brother Bob. "Until then," Lem Billings said, "I don't think Jack had been aware that Bobby had all this tremendous organizing ability. But during the campaign Bobby had proved himself again and again, forging a blood partnership that would last until the two of them died."

For the entire Kennedy family, Jack's victory was a great triumph. "This is probably one of the jobs I thought Joe would have filled," the Ambassador confided to Calder after the election, "but we are more than fortunate to have Jack come along with the same hopes and ideals."

For Rose, the victory brought back a different memory. "I kept thinking about my father," she recalled, "and what this victory would have meant to him. In my mind, I kept picturing him as a little boy, huddled in the servants' quarters at old Henry Cabot Lodge's home as he warmed his shivering body from the cold of his newspaper route. In his wildest dreams that winter's night, could he ever have imagined how far both he and his family would come?"

# CHAPTER 43
# TRIUMPHANT
# DEFEAT

On the night of January 20, 1953, the new Senator from Massachusetts attended President Eisenhower's Inaugural Ball with Jacqueline Bouvier. Twenty-three years old, she had dark, luxuriant hair and wide-set deep-brown eyes which seemed black under long lashes, and an open gaze that looked upon the world with alarming candor.

They had met in 1951 at a dinner party given by Jack's old friend Charles Bartlett. "From the beginning," Lem Billings observed, "there was a playful element between them. Jackie gave him a good match: that was one of the things Jack liked. But there was a serious element too . . ."

Born in fashionable Southampton to New York Stock Exchange member John Bouvier III and Janet Lee Bouvier, Jackie had attended Miss Porter's School in Farmington, Connecticut, before spending two years at Vassar, one year at the Sorbonne in Paris and a graduating year at George Washington University in Washington, D.C. When she met Jack in 1951, she was working as the "Inquiring Photographer" for the *Washington Times-Herald*, the paper where Jack's sister Kathleen had first worked a decade before.

"I knew right away," Lem Billings recalled, "that Jackie was different from all the other girls Jack had been dating. She was more intelligent, more literary, more substantial. And her mother's second marriage, to Hugh Auchincloss, carried the family into *The Social Register*, which gave Jackie a certain classiness that is hard to describe. All her life she had moved in a world of privilege, shuttling between family estates in Newport, Long Island and New York, much as Jack had moved back and forth between Hyannis Port, Bronxville and Palm Beach. All these things combined, I think, to make her a challenge for Jack, and there was nothing Jack liked better than a challenge."

In fact what Jack and Jackie had in common had less to do with the wealth and privilege of their backgrounds than with the loneliness that each of them had experienced as a child. Jackie was six when her parents first separated and nine when they divorced. A vulnerable and sensitive child, she was left from this trauma with feelings she could not easily share with anyone else. Trusting less in people than in animals and in nature, she sought her deepest pleasures in solitary acts: riding a horse, reading a book, listening to music or taking a long walk on the beach. Jack's loneliness was more subtly shaped, less visible to the naked eye, born, as we have seen, of continuing illness and the preeminence of his older brother in his parents' hearts. But Jack had so successfully surrounded himself with friends and acquaintances, extending an instinctive sympathy to everyone he met, that it took a practiced eye to see the reality beneath his gregarious exterior.

Jackie possessed such an eye. As she looked at the exuberant man she saw "the little boy, sick so much of the time, reading in bed, reading history, reading the Knights of the Round Table," and his vulnerability aroused her deepest interest. For his part, Jack saw in the aloof young woman the little girl who adored her handsome father and was inconsolably crushed by the breakup of her home. "They were kindred souls," Lem Billings romantically observed, "two halves of the same whole."

By the time they met, both Jack and Jackie had invented attractive personas to present to the world. "They had both taken circumstances that weren't the best in this world when they were younger," Lem observed, "and learned to *make themselves up* as they went along. . . . They were both actors and they appreciated each other's performance."

They shared an intelligence that worked along different lines—imaginative, disinterested, questioning. And they shared as well a biting wit, a tough-minded and detached outlook on people that in many ways solidified their bond. With Jackie, as earlier with his sister Kathleen, Jack found intense pleasure in gossiping about the personalities and eccentricities of their various friends.

Yet if these shared understandings promised intimacy and genuine companionship, patterns of behavior from the past hampered them both. Having been so private for so long, they did not find it easy to give of themselves, especially at a time when Jack was so totally absorbed in his race for the Senate. "It was a very spasmodic courtship," Jackie said, "conducted mainly at long distance with a great clanking of coins in dozens of phone booths."

Nevertheless, by the spring of 1953 Jack's romance with Jackie had progressed further than any of his other relationships. And in May, while Jackie was in London photographing the coronation of Queen Elizabeth II, Jack proposed by telegram. By this time, Betty Spalding recalled, Jack was in his mid-thirties and "his chariness of marriage was being superseded by the political need for a wife."

The wedding was scheduled for September. Jackie busied herself with her trousseau and with the lavish preparations for the large reception which was to be held at Hammersmith Farms, the magnificent estate in Newport, Rhode Island, owned by her stepfather. "For the Kennedy family, it was a strange summer," Lem Billings recalled. "Ever since Joe Junior's death, Jack had been the focal point of the family's ambition, and now that he was marrying they feared that he'd be drawn away from them, taking away the center from their lives. It wasn't true, of course, but they didn't know that at the time, and as a result they perceived Jackie as a threat. This was especially true for Jack's sisters, who called her 'the Deb,' made fun of her babylike voice and worked relentlessly to engage her in the family's physical activities, where they knew she could never excel. And it was even true for many of Jack's friends, who saw in Jackie a serious rival for his time and affection."

If Jackie was intimidated by the raucous atmosphere of Hyannis Port, she never let on, determined to hold her own against the almost overwhelming pressures to become a Kennedy. It could not have been easy to refuse to take part in the ritualistic games of touch football, but after trying once and breaking her ankle she simply sat on the sidelines and watched. Nor did she feel compelled to sharpen her tennis so that she could beat her future sisters-in-law. "It was enough for me to enjoy the sport," she commented, "it wasn't necessary to be the best." Years later, after having watched Teddy's young wife, Joan Bennett Kennedy, go through the same struggle, Jackie wished she could have given her advice. "In the beginning Joan was so happy with Ted. Whenever we were all in Hyannis Port you could see the pride on Ted's face when she walked in the room with her great figure and her leopard-skin outfits. If only she had realized her own strengths instead of looking at herself in comparison with the Kennedys. Why worry if you're not as good at tennis as Eunice or Ethel when men are attracted by the feminine way you play tennis? Why court Ethel's tennis elbow?"

Of all the Kennedys, Joe Kennedy Senior appreciated Jackie the best, finding in her display of independence a quality he much admired. Accustomed to deference from his children and their mates, he enjoyed Jackie's teasing way of giving him the needle. "I used to tell him he had no nuances," Jackie later recalled, "that everything with him was either black or white, while life was so much more complicated than that. But he never got angry with me for talking straight to him; on the contrary, he seemed to enjoy it." So while others played football on the lawn, Joe and Jackie would sit on the porch, "talking about everything from classical music to the movies."

During the first week of July, Joe went to Newport to meet the Auchincloss family. "They are very nice," he reported to his friend Bernard Gimbel in a tone suggesting his approval of the social status of the family, "and we are all crazy about Jackie. I think Jack is a topside fellow but he certainly is very fortunate to get as lovely a girl as his bride."

If Joe became Jackie's secret ally within the family, Rose was, at first, her most open antagonist. To Rose, who wanted everyone in the household to occupy a carefully arranged structure, Jackie's independent spirit was as hard to accept as Jack's had always been. Angered at Jackie's habit of sleeping late, Rose let it be known that participation at meals was expected; irritated with Jack's continuing messiness, Rose tended to blame Jackie instead.

For her part, Jackie was so drawn by the pull of Joe Kennedy's formidable personality that she failed at first to appreciate the indomitable will that had allowed Rose to survive and even to triumph through so much sorrow and pain. It was only later, Jackie admitted, that the two women came to understand the true measure of each other's strengths.

The spectacular wedding of Jacqueline Bouvier to John Fitzgerald Kennedy took place at St. Mary's Roman Catholic Church in Newport on September 12, 1953. Almost three thousand people, *The New York Times* reported, broke through police lines outside the church, "nearly crushing the bride," a striking contrast to the small private ceremony that had joined Joe Kennedy and Rose Fitzgerald almost forty years before.

The first year of marriage was very difficult for Jackie. Night after night Jack arrived home from his office tired and ready to sleep. But it was above all on weekends that the pain and the separation were most acute—when she sat alone in their small Georgetown house while Jack was traveling through Massachusetts. "I was alone almost every weekend," Jackie recalled. "It was all wrong. Politics was sort of my enemy and we had no home life whatsoever." Withdrawing more and more into herself, she turned increasingly to the world of things—to furnishings and clothes, constantly decorating one room or another in an almost obsessive fashion.

Jack never seemed to comprehend the invidious effect his continuing absences were having upon his marriage. After all, he told Lem, his parents had experienced even greater separations when his father was making his fortune, and their marriage had endured. In making this comparison, however, he failed to appreciate that his parents had been in love for eight years before they married, eight years during which a companionship had been developed, and, even so, that companionship suffered a serious strain from the long separations in the early years of their marriage, and, to some extent, they had gone their separate ways.

Nor, it seems, did Jack understand the devastating effect on Jackie of his continuing involvement with other women. "Jack kept assuring us that she didn't suspect," Jim Reed said, "when it was obvious that she knew exactly what was happening. He was so disciplined in so many ways. Discipline was, after all, the secret of his success. But when it came to women he was a different person. It was Jekyll and Hyde."

He was following a pattern established by his father. But, in Rose, Joe had a woman who had willfully turned her attention from her husband's dalliances, knowing that her first priority was to keep her marriage alive. Rose had grown up in an age when a popular woman's magazine could write without hesitation that a woman must never forget two things: first, that a man is paying her "the highest honor" when he marries her; and, second, that while fidelity is "a natural state" for the woman, it is not so for the man, who has to fight against his natural instincts to succeed in being faithful. "A woman may not have married the right man," Elinor Glyn argued in 1913, writing in *Good Housekeeping* magazine, "but if she is sensible, she will make the best of it, realizing that the welfare of the home for which she is responsible is of far more consequence than her personal emotions."

And beyond the reigning concept of marriage, there was for Rose the force of her deeply held religious beliefs, which called for a marriage to last "until death do us part." "A woman cannot live alone," Cardinal O'Connell had observed a few years before Rose's marriage. "It is against every law, human or divine." If she forgets, "she has lost the last vestige of womanhood."

Jackie belonged to a different generation in which one marriage out of every five was ending in divorce. Moreover, having suffered through the breakup of her own parents' marriage, she could not rely on the permanency of the marital bond as either a rationale or a salve for the disappointments in her relationship with her husband.

"While on one level," Billings observed, "Jackie must have known what she was getting into by marrying a thirty-six-year-old playboy, she never suspected the depth of Jack's need for other women. Nor was she prepared for the humiliation she would suffer when she found herself stranded at parties while Jack would suddenly disappear with some pretty young girl. Before the marriage, I think she found Jack's appeal to other women tantalizing—I suspect it reminded her of the magic appeal her handsome, rakish father had had with women all his life—but once she was married and once it was happening to her, it was much harder to accept. Perhaps if Jackie had had children right away it would have been different, for children would have provided the separate bond both she and Jack really wanted, but as it was it would be four years before the first child was born."

During the spring and early summer of 1954 Jack had been having increasing trouble with his back, suffering from pain even more acute than he had experienced just before entering the training school for PT-boat officers back in 1943. "This time," Lem Billings said, "the pain was so bad that he could no longer disguise it from his close friends, and the toll it was taking on his mind and body was tremendous." He was forced to use crutches, and the daily routine of answering quorum and roll calls became an agonizing ordeal as he willed his thin frame along the long corridors of the Senate with their hard marble floors.

After Congress adjourned on August 20, Jack headed straight for the Cape, where a team of specialists from the Lahey Clinic came to see him. According to his doctors, Jack's best hope was a complicated operation, a double fusion of spinal discs. But because of the Addison's disease, which left him with a lowered resistance to infections, the operation was deemed extremely risky. That same year, in fact, in the same hospital where Jack would be admitted, a forty-seven-year-old man with Addison's disease underwent an appendectomy and died three weeks later from a massive infection that antibiotics were unable to treat.

When the doctors left the Cape, Jack closeted himself with his father. "Jack was determined to have the operation," Rose recalled. "He told his father that even if the risks were fifty-fifty, he would rather be dead than spend the rest of his life hobbling on crutches and paralyzed by pain. Worried about the high risk, Joe first tried to convince Jack that even confined to a wheelchair he could lead a full and rich life. After all, he argued, one need only look at the incredible life FDR had managed to lead despite his physical incapacity. But even as Joe spoke, seeing that Jack was determined to go ahead, he finally told his son he'd do everything he could to help. 'Don't worry, Dad,' Jack replied. 'I'll make it through.' "

All that night, Rose recalled, Joe was unable to sleep. "He went to bed around midnight, but then at one A.M. he was up again and he couldn't get himself back to sleep. He sat for hours in the small library off the living room, and his mind kept wandering back to the last letter he received from Joe Junior, the letter written right before his death, assuring his father that there was no danger involved and that he would be sure to return. The memory was so painful that Joe actually cried out in the darkness with a sound so loud that I was awakened from sleep."

Jack entered the New York Hospital for Special Surgery on October 10, 1954. *The New York Times* reported the next day that he would undergo a spinal operation "to clear up a wartime injury" and was expected to stay in the hospital about six weeks. Over the next ten days the operation was postponed three times, as a team of endocrinologists and surgical physiologists insisted on a special program of treatment before submitting the patient to the severe trauma of surgery. Finally, on October 21, the long operation began. Thirty-seven years old, a United States senator with a limitless future before him, he succumbed to the anesthesia knowing he had only a fifty-fifty chance of ever waking up again.

The operation lasted more than three hours, during which he received four pints of blood to compensate for the blood loss produced by the double fusion. That night he was returned to his own room in fairly satisfactory condition, but before three days had passed he developed a urinary-tract infection which proved resistant to antibiotic therapy. He was placed on the critical list, and his secretary, Evelyn Lincoln, was told during the night that the doctors did not expect him to live until morning. With the family present, the decision was made to call in a priest to administer the last rites of the Church.*

For Joseph Kennedy, the days passed with agonizing slowness. Wandering into Arthur Krock's office one afternoon, he dropped into a chair and began to cry. To Joe, Rose recalled, "it seemed inconceivable that he could once again be losing his eldest son, and his entire body shook with anger and sorrow, but I remained calm, telling myself over and over that God had his reasons for everything."

For days, Jack's condition fluctuated, but finally he rallied. "The doctors don't understand where he gets his strength," Evelyn Lincoln was told.

By late December, however, eight weeks after the operation, Jack

---

* As is customary in English-speaking countries, the anointing of loins was omitted from the last rites—an omission which Jack laughingly discussed with Lem Billings after the fact, arguing that for him the anointing of the loins and the corresponding remission of all his carnal sins would have been worth the price of his illness.

remained in extremely poor condition. Hoping that a change of environment would hasten his recovery, doctors advised that he be removed to his father's home in Palm Beach, where an entire wing of the sprawling ocean villa was converted into a makeshift hospital suite. There, though Jackie tried to keep his spirits up by reading to him every day, the weeks passed with little sign of recovery. The doctors could not say whether he would ever walk again, let alone walk without crutches. Exhausted from the constant pain—the scar on his back was over eight inches long—Jack began to lose the optimism that had carried him through ever since he was a small boy. "It was a terrible time," Lem Billings remembered. "He was bitter and low. We came close to losing him. I don't just mean losing his life. I mean losing him as a person."

"By February," Rose recalled, "Joe came to the conclusion that something had to be done, so he flew to New York to see the doctors, and came back with a recommendation for a second operation. He recognized the high risk involved, but now he understood what Jack had meant in the beginning about not wanting to live unless he could really live." So on February 15, 1955, a second operation was performed. This time Jack began to mend.

During the long convalescence at Palm Beach, Joe Kennedy arranged for regular visits from Jack's friends, and Lem Billings took a leave of absence from his marketing business to spend a month with him. "The whole time I was there," Billings recalled, "Mr. Kennedy was so warm toward me that for the first time in twenty years I felt as if I were a part of the family. It was as if my decision to stay with Jack provided proof of my loyalty and once that loyalty was shown, a door opened up in Mr. Kennedy's heart."

Jack recovered enough to return to the Senate on May 23. "Aside from experiencing some difficulty in walking," the *Boston Post* reported, "the Senator looked to be in excellent shape. His face was fuller than it was last summer when he was in almost constant pain," his features were tanned "a golden brown" and his hair was bleached by days spent in the healing Florida sunshine. Walking without crutches, he made his way into his office, where he received a warm welcome from his fellow senators, including a huge basket of fruit from the Vice-President, accompanied by a card: "Welcome home. Dick Nixon."

From here on, Billings observed, "there wasn't so much talk about death. Jack had grown up thinking he was doomed. Now he had a different view. Instead of thinking he was doomed, he thought he was lucky."

Jack had spent part of his convalescence working on what the *Boston Globe* referred to as "a history of the Senate." The book, which was finally published under the title *Profiles in Courage*, was not a history but a collection of stories about eight political leaders—from John Quincy Adams of Massachusetts to Edmund Ross of Kansas to Thomas Hart Benton of Missouri—whose political courage had led them to defy their constituents and their colleagues in order to serve the national good. Each story reinforced the confident belief that one man counted, that one man could change the course of events.

Written in clear, dramatic language, the book found a responsive chord in the "silent generation"—the generation that had seemingly opted for conformity and success. Within weeks of its publication, it became a smashing best-seller, a literary triumph with excellent reviews all across the nation. In a major front-page article in *The New York Times Book Review*, Cabell Phillips wrote that it was "the sort to restore respect for a venerable and much abused profession." Apparently, the ancient ideal of individual courage was like a beacon of light in the mass society so scathingly portrayed by David Riesman in *The Lonely Crowd* and by William Whyte in *The Organization Man*.

In choosing to write about the moral courage of others, Jack Kennedy may well have been trying to sort out his thoughts about his own courage. Of all the virtues, Robert Kennedy later wrote, Jack Kennedy admired courage the most. Yet, while his physical courage was undeniable —courage under enemy fire, to endure illness and pain with silence and good humor—it is less clear that he possessed the kind of moral courage he enshrined in his book, the willingness to risk position, power, career for the sake of some abiding conviction. One imagines he would have answered by saying that he could not change the world or make it a better place without power, without being, as he put it, "at the center of the action." It is a rational answer. And it is true, as far as it goes. But there are limits, a place where the public man must confront the deepest roots of the private person.

In the years to come, questions would arise about the extent of Jack's authorship of the book, given the substantial help and guidance he received from staff members and historians who prepared the material on which the book was based and who wrote drafts for most of the chapters. "This kind of political production is normal," Garry Wills has observed, "not only for an officeholder's speeches but for his books. There is no deception in this, because there is no pretense that the man signing his name did all or even most of the writing." But in Kennedy's case things were complicated by the fact that he allowed his father's friend Arthur Krock to lobby the Pulitzer advisory board for a *writer's* prize.

In the first round of the selection process, *Profiles in Courage* was not even mentioned, as the jury for biography nominated Alpheus T. Mason's *Harlan Fiske Stone: Pillar of the Law*, James MacGregor Burns's *Roosevelt: The Lion and the Fox*, Irving Brant's *James Madison: The President, 1809–1812*, Samual Bemis' *John Quincy Adams and the Union* and William Chambers' *Old Bullion Benton*. But at the advisory-board level the jury was overturned, and the prize was awarded to Kennedy for what the board termed "a distinguished American biography . . . teaching patriotic and unselfish service to the people." Without question, the prestigious award provided a great boost to Jack Kennedy's growing national reputation; it helped to shape an image of a young senator distinctively different from the conventional politician. But in accepting the prize as if the work were wholly his own, Jack aroused suspicions about the extent to which his substance was fabricated by illusion, suspicions which would linger for most of his life.

Jack Kennedy would remain in the Senate for only eight years, spending at least half of that time campaigning for national office. He realized, almost from the moment of his election, that the road to the summit did not lie through Washington, that establishing a reputation as a hard-working, achieving senator was not the way to win a nation. The Senate could be a useful platform, little more, for a man with presidential ambitions.

From his earliest days in the Senate, Kennedy recognized that in order to become a national figure he had to create an image of himself as a broad-gauged politician whose concerns transcended the parochial interests of Massachusetts. Had he been able at the start to secure a seat on the Committee on Foreign Relations, he could have more easily begun to shape that broader image he desired. But, as it was, he was appointed to Government Operations and to Labor and Public Welfare, committees which forced his attention to the complex domestic issues of labor reform, unemployment compensation and the minimum wage. Yet, even within the limited leeway his committee appointments provided, Kennedy was able to keep his eye on his larger goal.

"The gold ring doesn't come around very often," he liked to say, "and when it does, you better be ready to grab it." Fortified by the belief, deeply imbedded in his family heritage, that swift and decisive action was the key to success, he was able to create his own opportunity with a determined daring that few other politicians possessed.

His first opportunity came during the Senate debate on a bill to support the St. Lawrence Seaway project. The bill had been opposed by the overwhelming majority of politicians in New England, who were fearful of sacrificing the interests of Boston's port for those of the Great Lakes region. Indeed, Kennedy's grandfather John Fitzgerald had long been one of the most articulate opponents of the project. To Kennedy's shrewd mind, however, the issue transcended local politics, providing him with the perfect opportunity to show that he was able to put the interests of his nation above those of his own region. He decided not only to vote for the bill but to make a major speech on the issue. Pointing out that no member of the Massachusetts delegation had voted in favor of the Seaway in over twenty years, Kennedy argued that he could not accept such a narrow and destructive position. The United States, he concluded, quoting from Daniel Webster, is "one country," with "one Constitution" and "one destiny."

His family's money created other opportunities. Despite his initial failure to secure a seat on the Foreign Relations Committee, he kept his interest in foreign affairs alive by traveling abroad as often as he could. He took a five-week trip to Europe to analyze the inner workings of NATO, he journeyed to eastern Europe to study the effects of totalitarianism on everyday life, and he made an extensive tour of the Far East. Returning from southeast Asia to an intense debate on the French struggle in Vietnam, he became a widely publicized spokesman against channeling American men and machinery into what he publicly described as a "hopeless internecine struggle."

For all his cleverness in cultivating his national image, however, Kennedy made a major mistake in his failure to recognize the moral issue at stake in the Senate censure of Joseph McCarthy. For years, the Republican Senator from Wisconsin had bedeviled both the Truman and Eisenhower Administrations with his self-appointed crusade against Communism and, in the process, had jeopardized the careers and reputations of thousands of Americans.

When the Senate finally got around to censuring McCarthy on December 2, 1954, Jack Kennedy was in the hospital recuperating from the first operation on his back. He was, however, in communication with his Senate office and, under the rules, could have put himself on record by pairing his vote with that of another absent senator who opposed the censure. He failed to give instructions either way, making him the only Democrat who neither voted against nor paired against McCarthy. Whatever the reason—preoccupation with his health, his father's influence, his own loyalty to McCarthy or political calculation—it was a decision he would live to regret, for it deepened and solidified the suspicions of the party's liberal wing, which would prove the greatest obstacle to his pursuit of the presidency. More than an error of political calculation, and in startling contrast to the actions of his heroes in *Profiles in Courage*, the unwillingness to take a stand against McCarthy suggests a moral lapse we have seen earlier in the history of this family, from John Fitzgerald's betrayal of Michael Mitchell to the Ambassador's half-sympathetic blindness toward the evils of Nazi power.

In an earlier era, Kennedy's national ambitions might have been brought to a halt by his failure to take a stand against McCarthy. But so strong was the young Senator's growing national image in the middle of the fifties that doubts about his substance were increasingly pushed aside. It was a decade marked by the decline of political parties, the rise of television and the transformation of politics into public relations—a decade perfectly suited to the engaging personality of John Fitzgerald Kennedy. In an era dominated by Dwight David Eisenhower and the restrictive symbols of Midwestern morality, Kennedy projected a counterimage of youth, glamour and excitement. With his open smile, his careless perfection of dress and his self-deprecating humor, he was fast emerging as the most sought-after speaker on the national scene.

"It was the goddamnedest thing," Senate Majority Leader Lyndon B. Johnson later said, "here was a young whippersnapper, malaria-ridden and yellah, sickly, sickly. He never said a word of importance in the Senate and he never did a thing. But somehow with his books and his Pulitzer Prizes he managed to create the image of himself as a shining intellectual, a youthful leader who would change the face of the country. Now, I will admit that he had a good sense of humor and that he looked awfully good on the goddam television screen and through it all he was a pretty decent fellow, but his growing hold on the American people was simply a mystery to me."

Johnson was correct in emphasizing the importance of television in John Kennedy's rise to power. Just as the amusing novelty in the living room was beginning to dominate American life, Kennedy was described by New York TV critic Jack Gould as "the most telegenic person in public life." With his handsome face and his laid-back approach, he required little adaptation to fit into the new TV-dictated way of presenting oneself.

Throughout his life, the secret to Jack Kennedy's success had been his ability to break the walls which separated him from his various audiences so that he could create an illusion of intimacy with almost anyone —from his nurses in the hospital to the crowds of men and women he encountered along the street. Now, with the phenomenal growth of the television industry, this ability to create intimacy with strangers assumed an entirely new dimension.

Still, there was something else. "I used to think," Lyndon Johnson admitted, "that old Joe Kennedy had a lot to do with it, pouring his money in strategic places all over the country and getting the press out front on his son's behalf, but I've finally come to realize there was something in John Kennedy himself, some sort of dignity that people just liked when they saw it, for without that his incredible rise to power simply makes no sense at all."

As the election year of 1956 approached, the press speculated that the young Massachusetts Senator might find himself a place on the national ticket as the vice-presidential nominee. "He has youth and good looks, an engaging personality, a quick mind and a fluent tongue," reporter Cornelius Dalton wrote. As the speculation increased, Joe Kennedy tried to hold his son back, arguing that Adlai Stevenson would be badly beaten in his second run against Eisenhower in the November election, and if Jack was on the Democratic ticket the defeat would be blamed on his Catholicism, damaging the hopes of all Catholics who might want to run for high national office. Sailing to the Riviera at the end of May 1956, Kennedy dictated a letter to Jack, detailing a long conversation with Clare Boothe Luce in which she had argued that "defeat would be a devastating blow to your prestige, which at the moment is great and non-partisan. She has many good arguments and many hopes for your future. I think definitely you should see her if you can . . . This I assure you is very, very important."

In reply, Jack assured his father that despite all the talk, he himself had done nothing to try for the vice-presidency, "although if it looks worthwhile I may have George Smathers talk to some of the Southern Governors. While I think the prospects are rather limited, it does seem of some use to have all of this churning up."

But as the convention drew nearer, Jack was irresistibly caught up in the excitement of hearing himself continually described as a leading candidate for the vice-presidential nomination. Moreover, the nomination suddenly seemed more valuable when, in early June, President Eisenhower was stricken with an attack of ileitis and forced to undergo major abdominal surgery. At news of Eisenhower's illness even Joe Kennedy began to reconsider. "With Eisenhower running as a sick man," he wrote to Morton Downey from the Riviera in July, "I may go back for the convention for a week. This, however, is still very uncertain . . . If [Jack] really intended to get into the fight one of the fellows I would want to contact would be Jimmy Byrnes* because in the present set-up, as I read it, I doubt if he has anybody he would prefer over Jack. But we'll watch it from the sidelines for another week or ten days and if you get any real news, let me know."

---

* Since the days when Joe Kennedy had first met the then Senator from South Carolina, Byrnes had gone on to become a Supreme Court justice, Truman's Secretary of State and the Governor of South Carolina.

When the convention opened in mid-August, however, sentiment in Stevenson's headquarters favored either Senator Estes Kefauver of Tennessee, who had battled Stevenson in the primaries, or Senator Hubert H. Humphrey of Minnesota. While Kennedy's name remained on the list of possible running mates, Kefauver appeared the likely choice.

Jack Kennedy arrived in Chicago on Sunday, August 12, accompanied by his pregnant wife and his entire family with the exception of his father, who had stayed on the Riviera, and his sister Pat, who was eight months pregnant. By the summer of 1956, all the Kennedy children except Teddy were finally married, and most of them had children of their own. "It was as if Jack's marriage opened the door for the rest," Rose observed, "for within the next few years they all seemed to follow each other down the aisle." In fact Eunice had preceded Jack to the altar by four months, having married Robert Sargent Shriver in May 1953 after a seven-year courtship. While Sarge was managing Joe Kennedy's Merchandise Mart in Chicago, the couple had their first son, Robert, and their first daughter, Maria.

Pat Kennedy's marriage to actor Peter Lawford had taken place in June 1954, when Pat was thirty. Their first child, Christopher, was born the following year. In 1955 the youngest daughter, Jean, married Stephen Smith, an executive for a New York transportation firm founded by his grandfather. With Ted's marriage two years later to Joan Bennett, a Manhattanville girl whom he would meet at her school when he dedicated a new gymnasium in honor of his sister Kathleen, the Kennedy family would be complete.

On the night of Monday, August 13, the opening day of the 1956 Democratic national convention, eleven thousand delegates watched as a giant movie screen unrolled for the presentation of a skillful propaganda film on the history of the party, produced by Dore Schary and narrated by Jack Kennedy. Schary later recalled that "the personality of the Senator just came right out. It jumped at you on the screen. The narration was good, and the film was emotional. He was immediately a candidate. There was simply no doubt about that because he racked up the whole convention." Reporters agreed, observing that with this single appearance Kennedy had dramatically improved his chances for the vice-presidential nomination. "Senator Kennedy," *The New York Times* reported, "came before the convention tonight as a photogenic movie star."

Kennedy became an instant hero in Chicago. He was surrounded by crowds, on the streets, in the lobby of the hotel and on the convention floor. But if he hoped to turn the crowd's enthusiasm into a vice-presidential nomination, he received a double setback the following day when Eleanor Roosevelt refused to support him, declaring that "Mc-Carthyism was a question on which public officials must stand up and be counted" and that on this issue she had never heard Senator Kennedy express his convictions. Later that day, the word came from Stevenson's headquarters that the Governor wanted Kennedy to deliver his nominating speech. Believing the invitation to be a consolation prize, Jack assumed that Kefauver was Stevenson's choice.

Unexpectedly, however, Stevenson made a decision that would stun veteran politicians. (Lyndon Johnson called it "the goddamned stupidest move a politician could make.") He declined to name his running mate and left the vice-presidential choice to the delegates. The would-be candidates had only about twelve hours to fight for the nomination. Jack immediately decided to run, delegating Bobby to call his father on the Riviera and "tell him I'm going for it." When the connection was made, Dave Powers recalled, the Ambassador argued passionately that since Eisenhower had recovered, the Republicans would certainly win and Jack would ruin his political career. "Whew, is he mad!" Bobby said as he hung up the phone.

Jack later told a friend that he experienced "a momentary paralysis" after the phone call to his father. For so many years, he had listened to his father's advice on so many things, and now, confronted with a decision that could shape his entire future, he was about to move in exactly the opposite direction from the one his father wanted him to take. It was a chilling moment, but when it was over Jack regained his confidence and decided "to go for it" as planned. And with this decision, "a sudden warmth" radiated through him as if he had drunk "an entire bottle of wine."

"The next twelve hours were a nightmare," Evelyn Lincoln recalled. " 'Where do we get a printer this time of night?' someone asked." They finally found one who would work all night printing banners, buttons, leaflets, placards, noisemakers—the necessary armament of a candidacy. All night long Jack, Bobby and their friends went from one hotel room to the next persuading, appealing and making the case for Jack's candidacy.

Mistakes were made. According to one old pro, "they kept Carmine de Sapio [a New York politician] outside Jack's hotel room for a half hour at 1:30 in the morning, while he was waiting to deliver ninety-two New York votes. Nobody knew it was de Sapio." And later, when the tide was turning against Humphrey, thus freeing the votes of the Minnesota delegation, Jack mistakenly approached Humphrey through an aide while Kefauver, hat in hand, called on Humphrey himself.

Still, the hastily assembled Kennedy campaign achieved remarkable results. On the first ballot, Kefauver, with 483½ votes, led all contenders, but Kennedy's strength of 304 votes was the big surprise. On the second ballot, New York came through for Kennedy, and then, to the surprise of many observers, Lyndon Johnson stood up to announce, "Texas proudly casts its vote for the fighting sailor who wears the scars of battle."

Though the Texas delegation was voting against Kefauver more than for Kennedy, one detects in Johnson's decision the fine hand of Joseph Kennedy, to whom he wrote just after the convention:

> I've been thinking of a lot of things, one of them being the phone call from you in October last year. You said then that you and Jack wanted to support me for President in 1956, but that if I were not interested, you planned to support Adlai Stevenson. I told you I was not interested and it occurs to me that you may be somewhat mystified about my activities in Chicago last week. When I see you, I will explain how they involved a local political situation here in Texas and were not inconsistent with what I told you last October. But this note, Joe, is being sent your way to tell you how proud I am of the Democratic Senator from Massachusetts and how proud I am of the Texas delegation and other delegations from the South for their support of him in Chicago last Friday afternoon.

With the support of Texas and New York, Kennedy shot ahead, outdistancing Kefauver 618 to 551½. By the end of the second ballot, Kennedy needed only 33½ votes to win, and the convention was in a tumult. It was an unprecedented drama that kept forty million television viewers in alert suspense until it was over. Kefauver's strength in the Midwest and the Rocky Mountains proved amazingly solid on the third ballot, however, and a number of Southern delegations began to shift back. Watching from his suite, Kennedy recognized that he had peaked on the second ballot and Kefauver would win. "That's it, let's go," he said, heading for the amphitheater, where his personal appearance electrified the noisy crowd. As he made his way to the rostrum, he received a long and emotional ovation. Then, in graceful, controlled tones, flashing his infectious grin, he moved that Kefauver be nominated by acclamation. And then he was gone, the underdog candidate who had intrigued and captivated the hearts and minds of millions of Americans.

"This was his great moment," James MacGregor Burns observed, "the moment when he passed through a kind of political sound barrier to register on the nation's memory. The dramatic race had glued millions to the TV set." Kennedy's near-victory and sudden loss, the impression of a handsome vigorous young man who fought valiantly and accepted defeat with a smile—all this touched the hearts of people in living rooms across the nation. "In this moment of triumphant defeat," Burns wrote, "his campaign for the presidency was born."

Even more to the point, Jack had followed his own instincts against his father's advice, and it was clear that he had been absolutely correct in his decision. It was an important rite of passage. But no sooner had the convention ended than Jack flew to Paris, from there to join his father on the Riviera. Now that the battle was over, an exhausted son needed comfort and affection, and, as always, there was no better place to get it.

The trip was poorly timed. Jackie was in the final months of her second pregnancy—she had had a miscarriage in the first year of their marriage—and she too needed a rest after the hectic week of the convention. Unable to leave her doctors, she asked Jack not to go, to spend the time instead with her, but he elected to go nonetheless.

"Jack arrived here very tired," Joe Kennedy wrote to his friend Morton Downey, "but I think very happy because he came out of the convention so much better than anyone could have hoped. As far as I'm concerned you know how I feel—if you're going to get licked, get licked trying for the best, not the second best. His time is surely coming!"

After long talks with his father, Jack left the Riviera for a week-long sailing trip with his brother Teddy and George Smathers. The chartered yacht was sailing off the coast of Elba, the island of Napoleon's exile, when Jackie, back in the States, began to hemorrhage and experience severe cramps. Rushed to the hospital in Newport, she underwent an emergency cesarean operation, but the baby girl was stillborn. It must have been a terribly lonely moment for the twenty-eight-year-old Jackie as she faced the death of her child without even knowing where to reach her husband. For three days the Kennedy family tried desperately to locate the chartered yacht, but it was not until Jack docked at Genoa and called home that contact was made.

As soon as he heard the news, Jack flew back to the States. A front-page story in the *Washington Post* headlined, "Senator Kennedy on Mediterranean Trip Unaware His Wife Has Lost Baby." The publicity only added to the sorrow. For months, Jackie had been planning and decorating a nursery in the big house she and Jack had bought in Virginia the previous year. Now that the baby was dead, she could no longer bear the sight of the house. Four months later, the young couple sold "Hickory Hill" to Bobby and Ethel and moved back to Georgetown.

For Jack too, the loss of the baby was a wrenching experience. Writing to a friend, Joe Kennedy confided, "Jackie losing the baby has affected him much more than his illness did during that bad year . . ." Children evoked in all the Kennedy sons the strongest emotions they would ever know. "This was true for Bobby and Teddy as well as for Jack," Lem Billings observed. "They were all oriented toward their kids far more than toward their wives."

"The death of the baby produced a real strain on Jack and Jackie's marriage," Billings recalled. "Jackie worried about whether she'd ever be able to have a baby, and she blamed her problem on the crazy pace of politics and the constant demands to participate in the endless activities of the Kennedy family. The only answer, she decided, was to separate herself even more from the rest of the family, insisting even in the summer months that she and Jack have dinner by themselves instead of gathering at Joe Senior's house as everyone else in the family did."

It was a wise position for Jackie to take, for it allowed her to keep a part of herself intact. Years earlier, in much the same manner, Rose Kennedy had insisted on a small beach house of her own so that she too could retain her sense of self apart from her raucous family. But within the Kennedy family Jackie's increased withdrawal was taken as a sign of aloofness, and for a while there was considerable tension in the household whenever Jackie was around.

Unaware of all these complicated private troubles, the American people responded simply and sympathetically to the baby's death with an outpouring of letters. And these letters came on top of thousands of other letters written to Jack Kennedy in response to the Democratic convention. "People wrote of how they cried and how their children cried and how they prayed for him," Evelyn Lincoln recalled. It was certain proof, if proof were needed, that something had taken place that night in Chicago, that Jack Kennedy had made the difficult, mysterious transition from a promising young senator to a potential national leader.

# CHAPTER 44

# BURYING THE
# RELIGIOUS
# ISSUE

On November 25, 1956, surrounded by his wife, six children and a dozen grandchildren, Joseph Kennedy presided over the traditional Thanksgiving Day feast at Hyannis Port. It was a crisp autumn day on the Cape, a day that would long be remembered by the family as the day Jack decided to run for President.

"After dinner," Rose recalled, "Jack and his father went into the little study off the living room to talk about the future. Their conversation started with Jack presenting all the arguments against his running in 1960, knowing that his father would break them down. I remember thinking it was like a minuet with each partner anticipating the steps of the other.

"To each argument Jack presented—his youth, his lack of support from the party's established leaders, and his religion, Joe responded with a counterargument. 'Just remember,' Joe said in closing, 'this country is not a private preserve for Protestants. There's a whole new generation out there and it's filled with the sons and daughters of immigrants from all over the world and those people are going to be mighty proud that one of their own is running for President. And that pride will be your spur, it will give your campaign an intensity we've never seen in public life. Mark my word, I know it's true.' "

With this, Rose recalled, Jack's face broke into a huge grin. "Well, Dad," he said, "I guess there's only one question left. When do we start?" In answer, Joe grinned back and threw his arms around Jack.

The decision at this time was an act of daring. John Kennedy was less than forty years old, inexperienced in party affairs, by far the junior in the group of Democratic hopefuls already beginning to prepare to seek the 1960 nomination. Few political experts would have given him much of a chance; but they could not be aware of the impatient urgency which would compel a young man who had lived much of his adult life accompanied by a dread expectation of the nearness of death. Nor could they know that the young Senator had become a far more serious politician than the lighthearted, casual person who had come to Washington a decade earlier.

John Kennedy was finally at ease with himself, more, at least, than he had ever been before. He had triumphed over a mortal threat to existence and, with the help of cortisone, had pushed back the danger of his life-threatening Addison's disease. He would soon have a family of his own. And he had in a moment of high drama become a national figure, acknowledged and admired in his own right. No longer a surrogate for his brother, he was ready to shape his own destiny, ready to choose from the elements of his lineage those most appropriate to his own temperament and the political ambience of the time to forge, in the fire of his ambition, a campaign of unprecedented duration, single-mindedness and popular appeal.

From his grandfather's mastery of precinct politics, and his father's command of pragmatic, worldly skills, he drew the abilities necessary to build and sustain an efficient, dedicated organization of national scope. The sloppy, chaotic behavior which had been a foil against his family was replaced by an intense appreciation for the values of organized effort, and for the values—ambition, self-interest, loyalty—which are the binding force of a personal political machine. To the proven techniques of his heritage he added the unique contributions of his own personality and the access to wealth, privilege and celebrity which his generation of Kennedys and Fitzgeralds was the first to receive by right of birth. To his understanding that the delivery of jobs and favors was crucial to maintain the allegiance of skilled followers there was an added psychological dimension—the sense, carefully cultivated, that others could be drawn into his orbit by the ambience of his vitality and his rank among the wealthy and famous, finding in that identification, in the awareness, perhaps the illusion, of social acceptance, a further spur to their loyalty and commitment. "He brought the old ward boss and the bright ambitious kids into his home," explained a friend, "and made them feel a part of all that luxury. After that it was hard for them to let go." Nor was it merely calculation. John Kennedy was intensely interested in other people. From the first meeting he would inquire into their interests, values and background. This seductive intensity, a natural attribute, would now also be used to measure and enlist others in his cause.

John Kennedy also possessed a profound respect for the power of symbolism—the appeal of pageantry, ritual and outward show. That understanding had its antecedents in the slums of his grandfather's youth, where the rituals of the Catholic Church and the saints' day parades were a welcomed and adored relief from the drab struggle of daily life. It came also from Hollywood, where his father had discovered that the power of images to entertain and exhilarate could be the source of immense worldly success. The sense of occasion, of display, as a tool of leadership was never absent from his thought or action, and was to become an important source of his political success and his achievements as a national leader.

From 1956 forward all his actions would be designed to fortify his drive for the presidency. The campaign itself would be constructed within the tacit limits imposed by the Eisenhower presidency: the General's immense personal popularity made it difficult to articulate the underlying discontent, the vaguely sensed stagnation.

John Kennedy understood that Eisenhower's popularity was not merely a tribute to his past valor or his person, that it reflected the always present desire for a measure of security and tradition in an uncertain and dangerous world. The conservative Eisenhower faithfully reflected a dominant conservative strain in the nation as a whole which coexisted uneasily with the desire for great achievement—for success and even daring—which was also rooted in the American story. In response, John Kennedy would adopt a relatively cautious and moderate approach to domestic affairs, being careful in the process not to alienate the traditional elements of the Roosevelt coalition.

In foreign affairs, where traditional liberal and conservative divisions were confused and intermingled, he would use the Senate as his forum to speak out for a strong and benevolent American leadership against decaying colonialism and expanding Soviet totalitarianism. In this arena, he could establish that he was neither a dilettante nor a playboy, but possessed of qualities of statesmanship that entitled him to seek the highest rank of public office. It would not be until 1960, and the debate with Nixon, that old impressions would be eradicated. But it was on his mind from the beginning, and he knew that a seat on the Senate Foreign Relations Committee would provide him with a matchless platform. That assignment, however, could be bestowed only by the formidable Senate Democratic leader, Lyndon Johnson.

"All of a sudden," Johnson later recalled, "Joe Kennedy bombarded me with phone calls, presents and little notes telling me what a great guy I was for going with Jack during the vice-presidential fight. But I knew all along there was something else on his mind, and sure enough one day he came right out and pleaded with me to put Jack on the Foreign Relations Committee, telling me that if I did, he'd never forget the favor for the rest of his life.

"Now, I knew Kefauver wanted the seat bad and I knew he had four years' seniority on Kennedy. And I would have preferred showing preference for Tennessee over Massachusetts. But I kept picturing old Joe Kennedy sitting there with all that power and wealth feeling indebted to me for the rest of his life, and I sure liked that picture."

On January 8, 1957, at a closed session of the Democratic Steering Committee, Senator John Kennedy won the nomination to the Senate Foreign Relations Committee, described in *The New York Times* as "one of the highest honors granted by the Senate."

From his position on the committee, Kennedy delivered a blistering attack against the Eisenhower Administration for supporting France's Algerian war. No attempt to incorporate Algeria into France would succeed, he argued, since "colonies are like fruit which cling to the tree only till they ripen." The only solution for the United States was to put its influence behind an effort to reach a settlement which would recognize "the independent personality of Algeria."

The speech provoked an enormous reaction. Described by *The New York Times* as "perhaps the most comprehensive and outspoken arraignment of Western policy toward Algeria yet presented by an American in public office," it produced strong editorial comments from virtually every paper in the country. The Ambassador told Jack he was a "lucky mush" who would eventually be proved right on everything he said. "You don't know it and neither does anyone else, but within a few months everyone is going to know just how right you were on Algeria."

Taking a more cautious approach to domestic affairs, Kennedy voted with the majority to include a jury-trial amendment in the Civil Rights Act of 1957 even though liberals passionately argued that requiring cases arising from violation of the new act in the South to be heard by Southern juries would effectively gut the bill. Displaying an equally moderate stance toward labor affairs, he used his position on the Labor subcommittee to pilot through the Senate a series of bills requiring improvements in unemployment insurance, regular union elections and full disclosure of financial reports. During this same period Bobby Kennedy was also involved in labor affairs, as chief counsel of Senator John L. McClellan's select committee investigating rackets in labor and management.

It is reported that at the beginning both Jack and his father were opposed to Bobby's determination to take on Jimmy Hoffa and the labor unions, fearing it would lose support for 1960. But, as it happened, the widely televised Senate hearings provided the tousle-haired Bobby with a national audience who, by and large, liked what they saw. Though "a little more rumpled and rough-hewn, a little more brusque in manner than his brother," Bobby appeared on the screen as an upright and intelligent young man.

"This is the first time I have ever written to someone whom I don't know," a woman from Indiana addressed Mr. and Mrs. Kennedy. "However, I just had to tell you what a wonderful job you have done in raising your children. I am now watching your son Bob on TV [the Senate hearings] and you both must have a good warm feeling of accomplishment."

Less detached than Jack, Bobby fought through the jungle of labor racketeering with uncanny skill, impressing even his adversaries with the passion of his convictions. "I find Bobby a most lively character," Beaverbrook wrote to Joe in 1957 after spending a week with him in Nassau, "with an exceedingly aggressive mind, well-balanced, clear in statement, powerful in argument, well-read and bound to do a great deal in life. Possibly much mischief if he becomes President. For my part I expect the Kennedys to equal the record of the Adams family."

In the summer of 1957 Jack and Bobby were the subject of an eight-page illustrated feature in *Look*. Called "The Rise of the Brothers Kennedy," the article included sixteen photographs of the two brothers at their jobs, with their families and with the public. And this was just the beginning of an astonishing outpouring of stories on "the Amazing Kennedys," the title of a lead article in *The Saturday Evening Post*. Written by Harold Martin in September 1957, "The Amazing Kennedys" contended that Senator Jack Kennedy was not the only member of the family with talent, looks and a private fortune. Starting with Joe Kennedy Senior, Martin detailed the accomplishments of every child from the heroic Joe Junior to Edward, the youngest of the clan, "the biggest and best-looking of the Kennedys with the outgoing amiability of a handsome Irish cop."

"Fervent admirers of the Kennedys," Martin concluded, "profess to see in their national prominence the flowering of another great political family, such as the Adamses, the Lodges and the La Follettes. They confidently look forward to the day when Jack will be in the White House, Bobby will serve in the Cabinet as Attorney General, and Teddy will be the Senator from Massachusetts."

These were prescient words in 1957. Yet few would deny that even at this early date the Ambassador harbored just such a dream for his three surviving sons. As he approached his seventieth birthday, his sandy hair had silvered and he was balding on the top, but his fair complexion still retained a healthy glow. There was still the pain of young Joe's death, a pain he would continue to feel until the day he died. "You never really accept it," he told Jack Knight of the *Miami Herald* in March 1958, just after Knight had lost his own son. "You just go through the motions . . . you think of what he might have done with a few more years and you wonder what you are going to do with the rest of yours. Then one day, because there is a world to be lived in, you find yourself a part of it again, trying to accomplish something—something that he did not have time enough to do. And, perhaps, that is the reason for it all."

The Ambassador candidly likened his son's popular appeal to that of Hollywood stars. "Jack is the greatest attraction in the country today," he said in an interview in the late fifties. "I'll tell you how to sell more copies of a book. Put his picture on the cover. Why is it that when his picture is on the cover of *Life* or *Redbook* they sell a record number of copies? You advertise the fact that he will be at a dinner and you will break all records for attendance. He can draw more people to a fund-raising dinner than Cary Grant or Jimmy Stewart. Why is that? He has more universal appeal. That is why the Democratic Party is going to nominate him. The party leaders around the country realize that to win they have to nominate him."

No one could doubt that Jack's popularity was rising. "Seldom in the annals of this political capital," Marquis Childs reported in May 1957, "has anyone risen as rapidly and as steadily as Senator John F. Kennedy in the ten years since he came to the House from Massachusetts. While all the precedents are against him—the fact that the Democrats have not in a century selected a Senator as their Presidential nominee, his youth, the fact that he is a Roman Catholic—there is nevertheless more and more talk of Kennedy as a candidate in 1960."

In November 1957, Jackie gave birth to a seven-pound baby girl. Born in the Lying-In Hospital in New York City, the baby was named Caroline Bouvier Kennedy after Jackie's sister, Caroline Lee. Having a baby seemed to complete Jackie's life. "That child made all the difference in the world to her," said a Georgetown friend. "She had tried so hard to have a baby before and had taken such good care of herself to insure a safe delivery with Caroline that I think she would have had a nervous breakdown if anything had gone wrong. It also gave her more acceptance with the rest of the Kennedys, who produced children so effortlessly and thought seriously that something was wrong with Jackie because she always had so much trouble."

For Jackie, being a mother seemed to validate her sense of self. It gave her an inner peace and security which nothing else ever had. It opened her heart.

In the forty-year-old father the baby girl produced equally strong emotions. "Jack was more emotional about Caroline's birth than he was about anything else," Lem Billings observed, "and I had seen him respond to a hell of a lot of emotional occasions over the years. I remember how his voice cracked when he called to tell the news, and when he showed me the baby he looked happier than I had seen him look in a long time. With this child, he finally had a family of his own."

John Kennedy was up for reelection to the Senate in 1958. His Republican opponent was Vincent Celeste, an Italian American from the North End who lived on the top floor of a three-decker in East Boston's waterfront district. This was no fight at all, most observers agreed. Yet the Kennedys set to work, running so hard that it seemed that Jack's entire future turned on the margin of his victory. Precisely because Celeste was such a weak opponent, Kennedy believed that only a majority of at least half a million votes would constitute a clear enough victory to boost his chances for the presidency.

Once again the Ambassador was behind the scenes, supervising, manipulating and spending an estimated $1.5 million. By late summer, it was clear that everything was falling into line, so clear that for the first time Rose Kennedy was not called into action. "Shall await the big putsch—1960," she wrote from Eden Roc, where she had gone to spend the summer and the early fall.

On November 4, a record turnout gave Kennedy 73.6 percent of the total senatorial vote, the greatest margin ever recorded in the history of Massachusetts. "The vote was beyond our fondest dreams," the Ambassador told his friend Joe Conway. "Keep in shape—there may be more work to be done."

That night, a dying James Michael Curley was following the returns from his bed at the Boston City Hospital. For weeks he had been failing, suffering from an obstruction in his large intestine. His lucid moments came only when he talked about the elections. "How's Kennedy doing?" was his question to every visitor, almost as if he wanted a glimpse into the future even as his own era was ending. When the doctors decided to operate, the indomitable Curley remarked that it was "just another campaign," and for a few days he seemed to be mending. But a week later, just sixteen days short of his eighty-fourth birthday, he lapsed into a coma and died. His death signaled the beginning of the end of an era in American politics—the colorful era of professional bosses and political machines built to satisfy the survival needs of the immigrant population.

John Fitzgerald Kennedy was forever linked to this stormy and memorable era by the life histories of both his grandfathers, but he himself had long since transcended the limitations of the ward politician. While he would still need to deal with those bosses who remained in power, he was already playing in a different league.

On January 20, 1960, Senator Kennedy entered a crowded press conference in the Senate Caucus Room. "I am announcing today my candidacy for the presidency of the United States," he began, projecting from the start a tone of confidence that America was entering a new era of forward movement in sharp contrast to the Eisenhower years of passivity and acquiescence.

John Kennedy realized that to succeed he would have to wage two distinct but closely related campaigns. Many of the most important delegations at the Democratic national convention would be controlled by powerful political bosses—men like Governor David L. Lawrence of Pennsylvania, Chicago Mayor Richard J. Daley, California Speaker Jesse Unruh. Even in states which lacked a single dominant leader, a variety of local officeholders and ranking politicians would influence or control the delegates, who were, for the most part, creatures of established political structures. It was not until the following decade that the spread of the primary system finally eliminated the decisive power of local leadership to select the presidential nominee.

During the past three years John F. Kennedy had flown tirelessly across the country to attend hundreds of political functions, Jefferson-Jackson Day dinners and public rallies on behalf of the Democratic Party and its local candidates; campaigning as if the entire continent were a magnified version of his Massachusetts constituency. The goal was to establish ties with future delegates and their leaders—to impress them with his qualities, make alliances, incur debts, come to understand their personalities, concerns and ambitions. This effort was enormously successful, and would be handsomely repaid in Chicago. But it was not enough. And he knew it was not enough.

Many of the most important political leaders were ambivalent, even hostile, toward his candidacy. Some were friendly toward other potential candidates. Governor Lawrence, for example, had been one of Adlai

Stevenson's most vigorous supporters for the 1952 and 1956 nominations. Many, perhaps most, thought that Kennedy's youth and religion might be an insurmountable obstacle to a Democratic victory. They had to be persuaded that his victory was not only desirable but politically possible. And Kennedy's only chance to demonstrate his potential appeal to a national constituency was through victory in the important presidential primaries.

The primaries could not directly determine the outcome—too few delegates were chosen through them. But they could test a candidate's ability to reach the ordinary voter, serving as a kind of litmus test of popular appeal. In John Kennedy's case, they were the only vehicle which would allow him to show apprehensive political leaders that his inexperience and Catholic faith would not lead to a decisive rejection by the voters. After eight years of Eisenhower, the Democrats wanted a winner. And, despite growing respect and even affection for the young Massachusetts Senator, they had serious doubts about his ability to win.

In 1960, as in 1958, 1952 and 1946, campaigning was a family affair. Once again Bobby was drafted as campaign manager. Steve Smith was assigned to coordinate Jack's schedule, while Teddy was given the Rocky Mountain states to organize. And through it all, balancing their commitments to their own children, Eunice, Pat and Jean put in weeks at a time. Over the years, all the children except Pat, who was based in California, had purchased homes near their father and mother at Hyannis Port so that they could spend their summers and holidays together. At one of these gatherings, Joe Kennedy looked at them all—sons, daughters, in-laws and grandchildren—and said, "This is the most exclusive club in the world."

For the kickoff of the New Hampshire primary, the campaign sent Rose Kennedy into the state several days ahead of Jack as an advance guard. Appearing at four or five gatherings a day, her youthful appearance giving the lie to her seventy years, Rose once again proved herself to be the daughter of Mayor Fitzgerald. At each appearance, she delivered a remarkably effective personal speech that included comments on Jack's youth, his dislike of war, his early training and success. Sparing no sentiment, she observed, "Jack knows the sorrow, the grief, the tears and the heartbreaking grief and loneliness that come to a family when a mother has lost her eldest son and a young bride has lost her bridegroom. So I know that Jack will never get us into war."

"Rose is sensational in New Hampshire," Kennedy's investment advisor Jim Fayne wrote to Joe. "She will be worth 100,000 votes in Wisconsin."

From his command post at Hyannis Port, where he remained in self-imposed exile through most of the primary season, Joseph Kennedy took great pride in his wife's ability to campaign so effectively. "Whenever Uncle Joe would hear someone describe Aunt Rose's activities on the campaign trail," Ann Gargan recalled, "his face would light up like a little boy and for a moment I felt I was catching a glimpse of the young East Boston boy who fell in love with the young Rose Fitzgerald more than half a century ago."

In many ways, the years had not been kind to Joe and Rose; beset by devastating personal losses, they had gradually moved apart, with Rose taking spiritual solace in her Church while Joe committed himself to the secular success of his family. While Joe continued to enjoy a wide-ranging set of friendships, from Baltimore Colts owner Carroll Rosenbloom to Lord Beaverbrook, Rose was retreating more and more into her own world. Drawing her pleasures from the starry sky and the ocean breezes, she spent long hours by herself walking along the beach or reading in her little shack trying to keep alive that intellectual side of the self so undervalued in her active family. Her old curiosity had not passed away; it had merely cordoned itself off into her books and her Church.

Preoccupied with fears that some "forbidden books" had made their way into her library, Rose wrote to Father Cavanagh of Notre Dame University an urgent letter requesting his advice. In response, Cavanagh informed her that Hugo's *Les Misérables* and Zola's works were on the Index along with several of the publications of Rousseau. "What to do with books on the Index which you have on hand? I suggest you send them to a library conducted under Catholic auspices so they will be read only with the proper permission of the Church authorities."

But once Rose was out on the campaign trail, her vision suddenly expanded, as if she possessed a buried chord of vitality that needed only to be struck. "I loved all the villages and the stores and the crowds," she said, "remembering as though it were yesterday the chill nights in late autumn when I was a young girl and when the great torchlight parades for my father had swept out from the North End with hundreds of men and women yelling and screaming."

While she was campaigning, it seemed to her that she was bred for this very thing. In every appearance, she betrayed her political origins —the perfect use of a phrase, the perfect sense of timing, the perfect choice of dress. Over a long lifetime she had known betrayal, defeat, unhappiness and despair. But here, in this hotel or that, as she thought over the past, each reflection was filled with the happy memory of a different child, and now one of these children was running for president.

Even while Rose Kennedy was enjoying the march toward a Kennedy victory in New Hampshire, the campaign was moving on to Wisconsin, the first real test. Jack would have preferred a showdown with Humphrey almost anywhere else in the nation. "The Wisconsin farmer is a very reserved person," *Washington Post* reporter Carroll Kirkpatrick observed. "Day after day, Kennedy would walk along the street and shake hands with the people, but their response was never very enthusiastic. It was pleasant but just a sort of grunt and a nod of the head."

More than one day started at five-thirty in the morning and ended at one-thirty the next—an exhausting routine for a man with a bad back and with Addison's disease. In Hyannis Port, Joseph Kennedy, continually worried about his son's health, worked out an arrangement with Dave Powers to report to him every evening between six-thirty and seven to tell him about Jack's health, checking to see whether he took his vitamins, ate his prescribed New York–cut sirloin and drank his orange juice. "Dave, if you want him to win, keep him healthy," the Ambassador implored night after night.

As the weeks went by, the momentum had clearly shifted to Kennedy, and the press, charmed by his humor and attracted by his confident manner, gradually fastened on the Massachusetts Senator as the sure winner in Wisconsin.

Then, the Sunday before the Tuesday primary, the *Milwaukee Journal* published a large color map of the state, broken down in a number of ways, including religious lines. Kennedy was furious, fearing it would bring religious prejudice to the surface. On primary night, his fears were realized. Although he won the state, his narrow margin came almost entirely from four heavily Catholic areas, while Humphrey swept the vote in four of the predominantly Protestant districts. Realizing that the vote would be interpreted as a Catholic–Protestant split, he lashed out once more at the religious map, as if it alone were the cause of his trouble. Asked what the narrow victory meant, Kennedy responded biterly, "It means that we have to do it all over again. We have to go through every one and win every one of them—West Virginia and Maryland and Indiana and Oregon, all the way to the convention."

Meanwhile, Hubert Humphrey, interpreting his narrow loss as a moral victory, impulsively decided to take on Kennedy in West Virginia. "Here is where fate intervened," Pierre Salinger has observed, "for had Humphrey given up the campaign then and there and not run in West Virginia, Kennedy might never have been able to demonstrate that he could overcome the Catholic issue. Had he faced no opposition, any victory there would have been meaningless in terms of bargaining with big-city bosses."

"We have a few troubles in West Virginia," the Ambassador confided to his friend Beaverbrook. "Only about three percent of the state is

Catholic, probably the smallest percentage in America. And they are passing out religious leaflets up and down the line. The Baptists are the most bigoted group."

Although the issue of his Catholicism was the greatest menace to Kennedy's dream, a number of influential Kennedy aides believed it was best left untouched and undiscussed, that the risks of attacking the issue directly outweighed the possible gains. But in West Virginia it soon became clear that old fears remained alive—fears that a Catholic President would report to the Pope, fears that the Catholic religion did not respect civil liberties, fears that America would become a Catholic country. There is in Joseph Kennedy's private papers a copy of a cartoon from a Baptist paper. Under the title "Big John and Little John," the cartoon depicts Pope John XXIII on the throne with his hand on John Kennedy's head. Underneath is the caption "Be Sure to Do What Poppa Tells You."

The abstract debates of many years about the wisdom of raising the religious issue were resolved in West Virginia. At the end of the very first day of campaigning, Kennedy was standing on the steps of a building with a microphone in his hand, talking to about four hundred people. Suddenly someone in the crowd asked him an unexpected question about the religious issue. "I am a Catholic," Jack responded, always at his best in impromptu situations, "but the fact that I was born a Catholic, does that mean that I can't be the President of the U.S.? I'm able to serve in Congress and my brother was able to give his life, but we can't be President?" Standing in the middle of the crowd, Kennedy's coordinator in the state, Robert McDonough, could feel the crowd respond. The reaction he got, McDonough recalled, could actually be felt. It made Jack realize that he shouldn't wait for the religious issue to come up, that he should bring it up himself, and from then on he did, repeating again and again that he "would not take orders from any Pope, cardinal, bishop or priest," while asking the voters in return to exercise fair play.

Still, the early weeks were tough for Kennedy. West Virginia was an extremely poor state and Humphrey was the natural workingman's candidate, having fought all his life for liberal measures to care for people in distress. There was no way Kennedy could match Humphrey's long record of accomplishment, but in a sense he didn't have to, for his emotional response to his first encounter with hunger and misery— many of the Appalachian children had never enjoyed a glass of milk— was so genuine that it touched a chord in everyone he met. And from here on, whenever he spoke of the need to protect the common man against the ravages of poverty, hunger and ill health, his voice was alive and his speech was infused with passion.

From Hyannis Port, the Ambassador suggested that FDR's son Franklin D. Roosevelt, Jr., should be sent to West Virginia to campaign for Jack. It was, everyone agreed, a brilliant stroke. "There were more monuments to Roosevelt in West Virginia than perhaps anywhere else," journalist Peter Lisagor observed. "By monuments I mean bridges, structures that were built in Roosevelt's time. And you'd go to some small mountain cabin, and about the only picture on the wall would be a picture of FDR. While Kennedy went up through the valley, Roosevelt was with us. He would make remarks on the back of a truck. You could see in the people when he started hammering away that they were quite fascinated and intrigued, that this was the son of their great idol."

Franklin Roosevelt, Jr., did not confine his role to nostalgia. A tough politician himself with considerable experience on the stump, he carried with him a series of documents which proved that during World War II Humphrey had sought deferments from the military and implied that he was a draft-dodger. No sooner had Roosevelt made the charge, as the campaign had planned for him to do, than Kennedy angrily disavowed it. "Any discussion of the war record of Senator Humphrey was done without my knowledge and consent, as I strongly disagree with the injection of this issue into the campaign." But as Kennedy perfectly understood, the deed was already done, the contrast had been drawn between a young decorated veteran and a politician who didn't even want to be a soldier. It is interesting to remember that back in 1942, in Fitzgerald's campaign for the Senate against Joe Casey, the Ambassador, having evaded the draft himself in 1917, had sanctioned a similar tactic while continuing to insist all the while that he would never stoop to such low-down behavior.

The voters in West Virginia went to the polls on May 10, a raw, drizzly day. By 10 P.M. it was clear that Kennedy had defeated Humphrey by a large margin. Hearing the returns in his Georgetown home, Kennedy called his father at the Cape and then set off for West Virginia. After assembling his plane crew sometime after midnight, he arrived at the Kanawaha Hotel in Charleston shortly before 3 A.M. There, to the jubilant throng gathered in the large ballroom, he happily—though, as it turned out, mistakenly—claimed, "The religious issue has been buried here in the soil of West Virginia . . . ," promising, "I will not forget the people of West Virginia, nor will I forget what I have seen or learned here."

From West Virginia on, the primaries went as Kennedy had hoped. The country had heard "the unmistakable sound of a bandwagon calliope," *The New York Times* reported as Kennedy added sweeping victories in Nebraska, Maryland and Oregon to his previous triumphs in New Hampshire, Indiana, Wisconsin and West Virginia. "Well, the seven primaries are over," Joe Kennedy wrote to Beaverbrook on May 27, "and we won an overwhelming victory. If we can get a break at all in Pennsylvania and a reasonable break in California, we're home. . . . The only thing that will make it possible for Nixon to win is if they steal the nomination from Jack."

By the time the convention opened in Los Angeles in the second week of July, Kennedy had some 550 publicly pledged votes. But even as his victory seemed close at hand, Adlai Stevenson was emerging as the candidate of a growing and impassioned movement. And behind Adlai Stevenson stood Lyndon Johnson, who was hoping that if Stevenson could prevent Kennedy's nomination on the first ballot, Kennedy's strength would crumble, leaving the door open for Lyndon Johnson.

Desperately Johnson lashed out at Kennedy for his inherited wealth and his support from the leaders of the big political machines. "I haven't had anything given to me," Johnson told delegates. "Whatever I have and whatever I hope to get will be because of whatever energy and talents I have." At the Washington state caucus he went even further, attacking the Ambassador himself. "I wasn't any Chamberlain umbrella-policy man," Johnson claimed. "I never thought Hitler was right."

The high point in the Stevenson–Johnson drama came on Wednesday evening, July 13. When Stevenson's name was placed in nomination by Senator Eugene McCarthy, the galleries erupted. It took the convention chairman twenty-five minutes to ease the stamping, shouting crowd back to order.

The emotions belonged to Stevenson, but the votes were Kennedy's. While Stevenson had been passively awaiting a spontaneous draft, Kennedy had been adding to his roster of committed delegates. All spring long the Ambassador had been pressing Mayor Richard Daley to deliver Stevenson's home state of Illinois for Jack. Skillfully timing his move, Daley waited until the opening of the convention to caucus his delegates and announce the results—59½ votes for Kennedy, 2 for Stevenson and the rest scattered. Hearing these results, Stevenson had only one remaining hope: he asked his old friend Daley whether the lack of support for him was merely because the delegates believed he was not a candidate or whether it meant he simply had no support. Daley said he had no support. "With that," Theodore White wrote later, "the hope of a real Stevenson candidacy" came to an end.

The balloting began at 8 P.M. on Wednesday. Earlier that day Kennedy had successfully eluded the press, slipping away unnoticed from his headquarters to pay a private visit to his father, who was staying at the Beverly Hills home of Marion Davies. Never leaving anything to chance, the Ambassador had stopped in Nevada on his way to the convention and placed a substantial amount of money on Kennedy for president to ensure that the gambling odds on the nomination would come out in favor of Jack. At the whitewashed Spanish-style Davies villa, he and his son enjoyed a long afternoon together, feasting on a hearty Irish stew. Ann Gargan, witness to the afternoon's events, recalled that "there was no question that day of the strength of the bond between these two men. They both understood how long they had worked together for this and now the pieces were all falling in place. It was an incredible moment of high anticipation, an intimate moment in which Jack understood so clearly everything his father had done."

But even as the family prepared to go to the Sports Arena for the long-awaited moment of triumph, the Ambassador elected to stay home, still fearful that his controversial presence would detract from his son's night. Rose later recalled trying to persuade her husband to go with the family, but he was adamant. The thing to do, he believed, was to play as subdued a public role as possible until everything was set in place.

Try as he might, however, Joe Kennedy was too large a figure for the press to ignore. In a *Time* cover story issued the week of the convention there was a picture of the entire Kennedy clan striding forward together, with the caption "Handsome as thoroughbreds in a meadow," and in the story that followed Joseph Kennedy was unmistakably depicted as "the dominant force in making the remarkable Kennedy family what it is today."

Although the patriarch stayed away, the rest of the Kennedys with the exception of Jackie (now five months pregnant) attended in full force. Wearing a dress of brilliant red, Rose Kennedy dominated the family box, surrounded by all her children and her grandchildren. In later years a shift would occur in the public perception of Rose and Jackie's relationship that would make Jackie the more dominant force, but during the presidential campaign it was clear to everyone that Rose projected the best public image the family could have.

"It's just like the circus to the Kennedy youngsters," a *Boston Globe* reporter wrote, commenting on the extraordinary number of lively children scurrying in and out of their seats. Clearly, both an exquisite sense of public relations and the pattern of early political involvement that Rose had begun with her own children so many years before was now being transmitted to the next generation. "Box 22B on top of the first balcony is typical of any family with mothers and their youngsters at the circus. Kids spilling Cokes on their pretty dresses and blue top coats and empty paper bags and broken balloons under their chairs."

The candidate himself was watching the scene on television, positioned far away from the crowd. By the time the state of Washington was called, Kennedy had already accumulated 710 votes, and then, as anticipated, the rush of other delegations began. When the nomination became official with Wyoming's announcement that its fifteen votes belonged to "the next President of the United States," the candidate prepared himself to drive to the arena. Before his entrance, Jack met Bobby outside the convention hall in a special area so that they could celebrate the triumph in private. "They walked off into the corner," reporter Hugh Sidey observed, "Bob with his head bowed as he usually did. And I remember . . . the only show of emotion was [Bobby] hitting the open palm of his left hand with the fist of his right hand repeatedly and a kind of smile on Jack Kennedy's face: the ultimate satisfaction."

The nomination decided, attention turned to the vice-presidential choice. Before the victory night ended, Kennedy had decided to make the first offer to Lyndon Johnson. For several days now, according to Rose, the Ambassador had been arguing that the Majority Leader was the natural choice. As Joe Kennedy saw it, simple arithmetic was decisive: add the votes of New England to the votes of the solid South and only a small percentage more was needed to carry the election. Even the harsh remarks Johnson had made about the Ambassador's role with Chamberlain mattered little compared with the prospect of victory. "Lyndon Johnson and Joseph Kennedy understood each other as kindred souls," Ann Gargan observed. "They recognized power blocs, they each knew the other was always up to some mischief."

Early Thursday morning, Kennedy telephoned Johnson and said he would like to call on him. The Texan replied that he would go to see Kennedy at Kennedy's convenience, but in the exchange of courtesies Kennedy prevailed, and he knocked at the Majority Leader's door two floors below forty-five minutes later. The meeting was not long, but it was long enough for Kennedy to make the offer and long enough for Johnson to startle the political world by accepting it.

After his acceptance speech, Jack flew from Los Angeles to his home on Cape Cod. Visiting him that summer, while both Joe and Rose were on the Riviera, Lem Billings recalled that Jack seemed "incredibly happy, not simply because he had won the nomination, but because *he* had done it. While he knew he could never have done it without his family, he also knew that only he could have done it."

For two months, beginning just before Labor Day, Kennedy journeyed through every section of the country, carrying with him the slogan of his campaign, the need "to get the country moving again" after its long period of stagnation and drift. But no sooner had Jack begun to articulate his hopes for a new defense policy and a new economic policy than it became clear that the religious question had *not* been buried in the West Virginia primary, that, on the contrary, echoes of old fears and bigotries were being amplified. In the first weeks of September, the Baptist state convention in Arkansas approved a letter saying: "We cannot turn our government over to a Catholic President who would be influenced by the Pope and the power of the Catholic hierarchy." It was the first of many attacks.

The Kennedy camp decided to meet the religious issue head on with a major speech to a group of Protestant ministers in Houston, Texas, on September 13. Working round the clock, Kennedy brought in several Catholic thinkers for help, among them John Courtney Murray and John Cogley, an editor of *Commonweal.*

If Kennedy was nervous before what many considered the most important speech of his campaign, he gave no sign of it. Looking across the sea of three hundred faces, many of them hostile, he began by saying that because the religious issue was obscuring all other issues in the campaign, he recognized the necessity to state once again, "I believe in an America where the separation of church and state is absolute . . . that is officially neither Catholic nor Protestant nor Jewish . . ." His speech was patient, good-tempered and unfailingly clear, punctuated by the dramatic statement that he would resign the office of the presidency before he would allow religious pressures to violate his conscience or the national interest.

Although anti-Catholic prejudice remained an important factor in the election, the Houston speech made it difficult for well-intentioned individuals to believe that Kennedy's Catholicism represented a threat to America's separation of church and state. And it lifted the spirits of the candidate, who always felt better when he could confront a crisis directly.

Kennedy's first debate with Richard Nixon came on the evening of September 25, 1960. When the networks first suggested a televised debate, Kennedy accepted without hesitation, realizing that since his major handicap was the impression that he might be too young, too immature and too inexperienced for the presidency, he need only prove himself Nixon's equal to gain political ground. When the debate concluded, that was precisely what Kennedy had accomplished. "Neither man fell flat on his face," columnist Joseph Alsop wrote. "Neither even stumbled . . . Both were, in fact, enormously impressive, each in his different and characteristic way. For this very reason, it is hard to believe the debate was at all decisive."

But it had been decisive. A new type of politician—a new politics— had emerged: one able to distill the high drama of political theater—

rallies, parades, music, torchlight processions—into the shrunken compass of a television screen.

Only a few columnists realized, as Ralph McGill put it, that "maybe the audience looked more than it listened," and that in the battle of appearances Kennedy had scored a triumphant victory. Nixon, McGill observed, looked sick. He appeared sad. The camera betrayed the nervous awkwardness of his movements. The heavy makeup Nixon applied to conceal his jowls and his heavy beard, a thick theatrical cream, caused his face to sweat terribly under the hot lights. In contrast, Doris Fleeson observed, Kennedy looked charming. "His movements have a patrician grace and the cruel cameras are kind to his rounded face, which refuses to betray campaign fatigue." Moreover, throughout the debate Kennedy's stage personality was in perfect control and he spoke forcefully, precisely and coolly, whereas Nixon's private self, nervous, sweaty and edgy, kept poking through no matter how hard he tried to conceal it.

Seventy million Americans received their first exposure to Jack Kennedy as a presidential candidate during that debate. And from that point on he was met by huge, wildly enthusiastic crowds at nearly every stop. The entire campaign took on an air of confidence and goodwill. "To be transferred from the Nixon campaign tour to the Kennedy campaign tour," Theodore White observed, "meant no lightening of exertion or weariness for any newspaperman, but it was as if one were transformed in role from leper and outcast to friend and battle companion."

In Boston, election day was crisp and clear. Accompanied by Jackie, Jack descended to the basement of an old branch library in the West End, Martin Lomasney's old domain, to cast his vote. The papers reported that the candidate whispered to his wife just before she entered the voting booth. "I told her how to operate the machine," Kennedy laughingly explained. From Boston the two flew to Hyannis Port, where the rest of the clan was gathered—Joe and Rose, Bobby and Ethel, Teddy and Joan, Pat and Peter, Jean and Steve, Eunice and Sarge.

There the long wait began. Jack spent the afternoon walking between houses, casually dressed in a sweater and slacks. Dinner was served at the Ambassador's house for the entire family, along with Joe Kennedy's friends Arthur Houghton, Father Cavanagh and Carroll Rosenbloom. "It was a festive meal," Ann Gargan recalled, a meal complete with a barrel of Maryland crabs flown up specially by Rosenbloom. "It was still Joe Kennedy's house," Ann observed. "There was no changing of the guard yet."

After dinner, most of the crowd went to watch the returns at Bobby's house, which had been established as a command post with direct access to operators at Jack's headquarters in Washington. At various intervals, Jack and his father strolled across the back lawn between their own houses and Bobby's, a stroll taken so many times over so many years that it must have felt eerily familiar on a night as portentous as this one.

The early returns brought elation to the Kennedy compound, but by midnight the shape of the election was not as the Kennedys had anticipated. Apparently, Catholics had not voted in the numbers expected; the election was much closer than privately predicted. At two in the morning, four states held center stage: Michigan, Illinois, Minnesota and California.

Many observers felt that the key state was Illinois, the flat sprawling state in which two cultures merged uneasily into each other: one of the big city, crowded with minorities, immigrants and their offspring, the other of rural America with small towns and prairie farms. Downstate Illinois was as Protestant and Republican as Cook County was Democratic and Catholic: their alien ways of life fixed in suspicious confrontation across the borders of Cook County. And Cook County Democratic leader Richard Daley knew that the Republican precinct workers downstate were just as capable of playing with the vote totals as he was. Indeed, in previous elections both sides had used the tactic of holding back a portion of their votes until they determined how many were needed to supply the margin of victory.

Late in the afternoon Daley was informed that the downstate precincts had stopped counting. They had taken their ballots home, they said, and would not be able to report the totals until after midnight. At this point Daley decided to hold back an even larger portion of his votes than he figured the Republicans were holding back (twice as many, in fact).

Even with these votes withheld, however, it was clear by early evening that Daley had achieved a smashing victory in Chicago. An unprecedented 89.3 percent of the eligible voters in the heavily Democratic city had gone to the polls, compared to a national turnout of 64.55 percent. However, although the Kennedy vote reported in Chicago so far was huge, it was still not enough to offset the overwhelmingly heavy Nixon vote in the downstate counties, which was finally reported in around 4 A.M., sending Illinois into the Republican column.

Just before four, when it had become clear that the election would not be decided for hours, Jack Kennedy decided to go to bed. When he awoke, he discovered that Michigan had come over to him at 5:45 A.M. but that the results from Illinois and California were still not in. At eight-thirty he called his father's house to ask if Ann Gargan could take Caroline riding. When Ann arrived, she found the candidate still sitting in bed, dressed in his pajamas.

"I've brought a message from your father," Ann told Jack. "He says not to worry, you've got Illinois."

"Who says so?" Jack wanted to know. "Did I miss it on TV?"

"No," Ann replied, "your father says so."

With that, Jack cursed and grinned at the same time.

Sometime after 4 A.M., after the downstate Illinois totals had been stamped as final, Daley had brought in the block of votes he had withheld the night before, and when these were counted Illinois had reentered the Democratic column. Daley had successfully outwaited the opposition, delivering his state to Kennedy just as Joe Senior had promised he would. And by 9 A.M. the news from other undecided states was equally positive. After twenty-four hours of waiting, victory was certain.

The time had come for Jack to go to the armory in Hyannis Port, where television cameras were waiting, to acknowledge his triumph to the country. Ann Gargan recalls that he tried to persuade his father to come, only to have the Ambassador refuse. Piling into the car without the patriarch, the family started for the armory, until Jack ordered the car stopped so that he could make one last appeal to his father. When Jack appeared at the armory as the new President-elect, his father was by his side, their first public appearance together in over a year.

In the weeks between the election and the inauguration, almost as if he were making up for lost time, Joe Senior seemed intent on drawing his family around him at every opportunity, and Jack willingly complied by making Palm Beach his headquarters for the transition planning. During this time Jackie remained in Washington, for her baby was due in mid-December. Flying back and forth between Palm Beach and Washington, Jack was returning to Florida aboard the *Caroline* on November 25 when he received word that his wife had gone into early labor and had been taken by ambulance to Georgetown University Hospital. "I'm never there when she needs me," he said, recalling his trip to the Riviera, when Jackie delivered a stillborn baby girl in 1956. As soon as the *Caroline* set down in Palm Beach, he boarded a faster plane to head back to Washington. During his flight, word arrived that Jackie had given birth by cesarean section to a baby boy. This time, however, the premature baby survived, and when the President-elect arrived at the hospital it was announced that both the baby and the mother were doing fine. The following day the smiling father made three visits to the hospital to see his wife and his son, who was given the name John Fitzgerald Kennedy, Jr.

In the weeks that followed, Jack split his time between Palm Beach and Washington. While in Florida he spent many hours with his father, playing golf and taking walks. But the Ambassador recognized that these were only the transitional months, and that once the inauguration took place everything would be different. Speaking to reporter Hugh Sidey in early December, Joseph Kennedy sadly admitted, "Jack doesn't belong anymore to just a family. He belongs to the country. That's probably the saddest thing about all this. The family can be there, but there is not much they can do for the President of the United States."

But there were some things the President of the United States could do for his family. And Joe Kennedy knew exactly what he wanted. And he knew he had to move quickly, for with each passing day Jack was becoming more and more his own man. As the patriarch saw it, the victory was a victory for the entire family, and all the brothers and sisters had a right to share the spoils. From all accounts, it was Joe Kennedy who insisted that Jack appoint his brother Bobby to the post of attorney general, arguing that the President needed someone in his Cabinet whom he knew intimately and trusted completely. At the start, Jack was uncertain, knowing that charges of nepotism would be laid against him. "I don't know what's wrong with Jack," the Ambassador was quoted as saying. "He needs all the good men he can get around him down there. There's none better than Bobby." Then, when Jack finally embraced the idea, Bobby had to be convinced. Trying for a moment to escape his brother and confirm an independent identity, Bobby held out for days while his father kept insisting that his brother wanted and needed him. Bobby finally gave in.

And it was Joseph Kennedy, hurrying to finish up his work before the inauguration, who insisted that the family clear the way for Teddy to run for Jack's seat in the Senate. After coordinating the Western states for Jack during the 1960 campaign, Teddy had thought about making a career for himself in the Rocky Mountains. But this did not fit with the Ambassador's design. "Ted, you've got a base here [in Massachusetts]— family, friends. Why go off someplace and prove yourself for nothing?" Neither Jack nor Bobby wanted Teddy to run, but their father was adamant. "The person who was primarily interested in having him run was my father," Bobby said later, "just as I would never have been Attorney General if it hadn't been for him . . . He just felt that Teddy had worked all this time during the campaign and sacrificed himself for the older brother and we had our positions and so . . . he should have the right to run, that it was a mistake to run for any position lower than that."

There were many who would see in Joe Kennedy's design for his sons a monstrous arrogance, just as years before the press had criticized the Fitzgeralds for their "imperial dynasty." And arrogance it was. Built on a grand scale, with ambition, passion and will attaining in them a terrifying yet wondrous force, both the Fitzgeralds and the Kennedys seemed to live their lives with an uncommon intensity which drove them to seek out the heights of earthly greatness. Striking against the existing order of things in pursuance of their ambitions and their passions, they achieved more than they had ever dreamed, lending a magic to their family story that no tale of ordinary life could possibly rival. But the very nature of their search was for success of such towering proportions that, as history records, a terrible price was paid.

# CHAPTER 45
## A TIP
## OF THE
## HAT

F or more than one hundred years
a thick Catholic Bible with a
gold cross in the center of its
brown leather cover had accompanied the Fitzgerald family on their
varied journeys from the narrow streets and dark rooms of the North
End to the open fields of Concord; from the stately mansion on Welles
Avenue to the Bellevue Hotel. Then, with the death of Mayor Fitzgerald, the old Bible was brought to the dusty attic of the Dorchester home
of Thomas Fitzgerald, the mayor's youngest surviving son. There it

remained, its frayed pages standing witness to the lives of three generations, until the second week of January 1961, when John Fitzgerald
Kennedy dispatched two Secret Service agents to bring it from Boston
to Washington to be used in his swearing in as the thirty-fifth President
of the United States.

The Bible had originally belonged to Thomas Fitzgerald, the Irish
farmer with one cocked eye who heard the summons to America in the
late 1840s and sailed westward to a new life. Its front pages, used as a
family record, chronicle the births and deaths of the twelve Fitzgerald
children, beginning with the birth of Michael in 1858 and ending with
the death of two-day-old Mary Ellen in 1879. Along its lengthy scroll,
each generation makes room for the next. Recorded in a large, florid
hand, the twelve children of Tom Fitzgerald and Rosanna Cox are followed by the five children of John Fitzgerald and Josie Hannon, who
are followed in turn by the nine children of Rose Fitzgerald and Joseph
Kennedy.

Some of these children died before they had a chance to live, others
lived to see their dreams corrode, still others survived to bury their
young. But on the twentieth of January, 1961, they would share in a
collective moment of glory as the old Bible recording their names was
carefully placed on a large podium where it would play a central role in
the inauguration of the first Catholic President in the history of the
country.

During the years of the Kennedy family's rise in America, 35 million
immigrants had entered the United States, separating themselves forever from the old home, the whole circle of people and places, church
and kinfolk, from which they had derived their emotional security and
their personal identity. Westward from Ireland came 4.5 million people,
from Great Britain 4 million more. From the center of the Continent, from the lands that became the German Empire, came fully 6
million; from the north, 2 million Scandinavians; from the south, 5
million Italians; from the east, some 8 million Poles and Jews, Hungarians and Slovaks. And by the turn of the century perhaps 3 million more
were on their way from the Balkans and Asia Minor.

For these people and their children, Kennedy's dazzling rise to power
was a recognition that the great immigrant revolution was finally complete. In almost every field of endeavor, the new immigrants had already
broken through the barriers of fear and prejudice to reach the top of
their professions. Now the final barrier had been breached.

The Kennedy family tapped into this "Second American Revolution"
in just the right way. For more than a century, Americans had fashioned
an image of themselves as an invigorating new breed of men, risen out

of the blend of a half-dozen lesser breeds. "We are the heirs of all time," Melville had written at the start of the immigrant wave, "and with all nations we divide our inheritance. On this Western Hemisphere all tribes and peoples are forming into one federated whole; and there is a future which shall see the estranged children of Adam restored as the old hearthstone in [an American] Eden . . . The seed is sown, and the harvest must come."

Yet, as the nineteenth century gave way to the twentieth, there remained virulent strains of antipathy toward the immigrants, their institutions and their ideas; fear and hatred strong enough to obstruct the accession of an immigrant's child or a Catholic or a Jew to the presidency. With John Fitzgerald Kennedy's climb to power, the American people were being asked to make good on their age-old promise, the promise to turn "them" into "us."

But Kennedy was not simply a member of an excluded ethnic group whose time had come. As Garry Wills has observed, "It is the old story, for one of your own to get elected, he has to go out of his way to prove he is not just one of your own." John Kennedy had been inculcated from birth with the privileged sense that he could walk wherever he chose. His father had given him a prestigious secular education and had provided him with the opportunity to travel to dozens of countries around the world before he reached the age of thirty-five.

The Kennedy children had heard conflicting messages from their parents throughout their lives. From their father, whose internal battle for assimilation had never been resolved, they were taught to live beyond convention, to bow to no man and no institution, to act as if the land had always been theirs. From their mother they were told to remain true to the Catholic faith, to accept the limits and the pieties of the Church, to live by the rules. Detached in some measure from both of his parents, John Kennedy was able to draw strength from both traditions. Had he reached too fervently for the assimilation his father craved, he would have lost the richness of his Irish heritage and the pageantry of his Church. Yet had he remained too close to his mother's piety and the Catholic theology, he would have abandoned mainstream America and its assimilative myth. As it was, by shaping his own integration in his own way, he invented himself as "the first Irish Brahmin" and, in so doing, suggested a means of reinvention and identification for millions of others.

The close structure of the Kennedy family had a special appeal to the imagination of the American people. For every story that was written about Senator Kennedy in the 1950s, there were twice as many about the Kennedy family. For nearly a quarter of a century, ever since Joseph

Kennedy had become a source of public interest, reporters had invariably focused attention on the *esprit de corps* of the Kennedy family as a whole, projecting an affirmative image of kindred loyalties and commitment that seemed strangely and appealingly anachronistic in the modern world.

In a sense, the American people were right to be fascinated with the idea of the Kennedys. Whereas the typical American family was nuclear in structure, with each individual finding his own way of life, the Kennedys had done some basic thinking about themselves as a family, and that thinking had produced a series of rituals and mechanisms which kept them together. In the early days, these mechanisms had taken the form of religious celebrations, obligatory mealtimes, discussions and shared vacations. But with the emergence of John Kennedy as a public figure, the rituals of politics had replaced the rituals of the Church as the dominant means by which they strengthened their collective bonds. And now, after years of common effort, the family was about to witness the flourishing of the family tree.

The day before the inauguration, a raging snowstorm brought the capital to a standstill, leaving cars and taxis stranded on the streets, forcing thousands of visitors to trudge on foot to their hotels, their luggage in their hands. All night the snow had continued as three hundred workmen labored with plows to clear Pennsylvania Avenue for the inaugural parade. But then at dawn the snow began to stop and the sun, flooding down from a cloudless blue sky, lent radiance to the freshly scrubbed capital and to the colorful flags swirling in the wind.

Long before noon, the immense and varied crowd began to gather. There came the sons and daughters of John Fitzgerald's brothers, many of whom had never before been to Washington, and had come from Boston by car for the great event. There came the Duke and Duchess of Devonshire, the first members of British nobility to attend an American President's inauguration. There was Marion Davies, mistress of the late William Randolph Hearst. There were the crew members of Kennedy's *PT-109*, along with the commander of the Japanese destroyer that sank the boat. There also was Mary Moore, the widow of Eddie Moore, as well as two widows of former Presidents, Edith Galt Wilson and Eleanor Roosevelt.

At a few minutes before twelve, the crowd stirred as the Kennedy family and their special guests took their seats on the inaugural platform. At seventy-two, the ruddy-faced Joe Kennedy was still a vigorous man, handsomely dressed in a dark-blue topcoat with a blue-and-white dotted scarf at his neck. At his side, Rose Kennedy looked elegant in a white

mink hat and a ranch mink coat. Behind them followed the wives of the
highest notables, Jackie Kennedy, Mamie Eisenhower, Pat Nixon and
Lady Bird Johnson, flanked by all the sisters and brothers and sisters-in-
law and brothers-in-law of the President-elect.

At nine minutes past twelve, as President Eisenhower and Vice-President Nixon stepped onto the platform, the Marine Band struck up "Hail
to the Chief" in the General's honor for the last time. A few minutes
later, to the sounds of "Stars and Stripes Forever," John Kennedy
walked onto the Capitol steps wearing cutaway coat and silk top hat.
When General Eisenhower was inaugurated, he had elected to wear a
business suit and a black homburg, but Kennedy believed the occasion
called for something more elegant.

For Jack Kennedy, Lem Billings later observed, "romantic sentiment
mingled strangely with cool rationality." He understood the importance
of pageantry in tying the nation together. "He recognized," Billings said,
"that even as the people would reject a king, their hearts tugged for the
symbols of royalty. For that reason, he deliberately decided to invest his
inauguration with pomp and ceremony. He wanted to use the moment
to appeal to the imagination, to raise the ceremony to a heightened level
of feeling. Perhaps it was his Catholicism that created in him the appreciation for tradition and majesty, or perhaps it was just his instinctive
understanding of the American people, but whatever it was, it worked."

By reaching out to invest his inauguration with the trappings of mon-
archy, Jack Kennedy was reflecting a debate as old as the nation itself.
At the first inauguration, George Washington, ever mindful of the importance of setting a tone of dignity for the new nation, had originally
planned to wear a suit made of golden threads and to arrive in a golden
coach drawn by twelve white horses. But when his plans drew criticism
from Thomas Jefferson and other Republicans, he agreed to a compromise which saw him dressed in a brown suit with white silk stockings
and taken by a simple coach drawn by four brown horses. Even this was
too much for Jefferson, who disdained the slightest symbol of royalty,
preferring to walk to his own inauguration from his boardinghouse to
the Capitol for a simple ceremony. It remained for Andrew Jackson, the
first President elected by the people, to restore pageantry to the ceremony by inviting thousands of guests and arriving at the White House
on a white charger. But, in a sense, the issue was never settled, as each
President sought to interpret the ceremony in his own way.

To give the invocation Jack Kennedy had invited Richard Cardinal
Cushing, the Archbishop of Boston, to be followed by the recital of a
poem by the nation's unofficial poet laureate, Robert Frost. The idea of
inviting the poet had come from Jackie after she and Jack entertained

Frost in their Washington home. "If you can bear at your age the honor of being made President of the United States," the eighty-five-year-old poet replied, "I should be able at my age to bear the honor of taking part in your inauguration . . . It will please my family . . . if they were living, it would have pleased inordinately the kind of Grover Cleveland Democrats I had for parents."

Frost's recitation provided the most moving moment of the inauguration. As the old poet began reading the preface to his poem, the glare from the sun and the snow blinded him and he was unable to see the words on the page. After faltering for a minute, he gave up trying to read and proceeded from memory to recite his poem "The Gift Outright." When he finished, there was thunderous applause.

It was now nine minutes before one, time for the climax of the ceremony, the swearing in of the new President. Placing his left hand on the family Bible and raising his right hand, John Kennedy repeated the oath before Chief Justice Earl Warren. "I do solemnly swear," he said, in a loud, clear voice, "that I will faithfully execute the office of the President of the United States and will, to the best of my ability, preserve, protect and defend the Constitution of the United States. So help me God." There was no constitutional requirement that the oath be followed by the words "So help me God," but ever since George Washington had included them in his first inaugural all who entered the presidency had followed suit, calling upon God to witness and judge their faithful service to the people of their country.

During the swearing in, several people reported they saw tears glistening in Joe Kennedy's eyes. In so many ways, it was the father's triumph as well as the son's. He had not planned it this way, the second son having replaced the first, but it was surely an extraordinary end to a journey that had begun one hundred and eleven years before when his grandfather left the stone quay at New Ross, Ireland, to sail across the ocean. And now, even as Jack Kennedy was taking his oath, the entire town of New Ross was gathered at that same stone quay to celebrate the triumph of their native son.

The Irish ceremonies had begun earlier in the day as the harbormaster of New Ross raised the American flag and placed it beside the Irish flag. By midday, the *Irish Times* reported, "the town had experienced everything that was reminiscent of a major fair day or a Wexford team winning an all-Ireland final." There were dancing in the streets, fireworks and a gigantic bonfire of over a ton of old rubber tires. For this occasion Kennedy had sent a personal message, which was read to the cheering crowd. "Three generations have passed," Kennedy wrote, speaking of his great-grandfather's journey, "but across this long time I send all of you my very best wishes. New Ross and Washington, D.C., are tied together today."

If the imagination delights in remembering that more primitive time which had also become a permanent part of the Kennedys' heritage, there was a new balance in the making, a metaphor, perhaps, for the shifting balance of power between the United States and England, in the fact that the Duke and Duchess of Devonshire felt extremely honored by their attendance at the inauguration. "It will remain one of the greatest moments of our lives," the Duke stated in a letter to the Kennedys, "that we were privileged to hear the Presidential address and to be honored by sitting in the Presidential stand for the Parade to say nothing of a similar privilege at the Gala and the Inaugural Ball . . . I can only say thank you from the bottom of my heart."

As soon as the oath was completed, the President delivered his Inaugural Address, his Boston accent and his clipped voice now familiar to millions. "Let the word go forth," he said, "from this time and place, to friend and foe alike, that the torch has been passed to a new generation of Americans—born in this century, tempered by war, disciplined by a hard and bitter peace, proud of an ancient heritage. . . ."

In the famous peroration " . . . ask not what your country can do for you, but what you can do for your country," Kennedy evoked a theme of obligation that lay deep within the American tradition, the obligation to carry out God's will on earth. But even more impressive was the image of youth and vigor he conveyed to a world whose leaders seemed tired and old. At forty-three, Kennedy provided a sharp contrast to Konrad Adenauer, eighty-five, David Ben-Gurion, seventy-four, Jawaharlal Nehru, seventy-one, and Harold Macmillan and Nikita Khrushchev, both sixty-six.

After the speech, Jackie whispered to her husband, "Oh, Jack, what a day," and softly touched his face. The mood of celebration continued as the inaugural parade made its way down Pennsylvania Avenue toward the White House. In places, the crowds were eight and ten deep despite the freezing temperatures, and all along the route the people were friendly, good-humored and enthusiastic. Following tradition, the President and his wife rode at the front of the parade until they reached the White House, where they would go immediately to the special presidential stand to review the rest of the parade. Waiting in the front row at the reviewing stand were all the members of Kennedy's family.

As the President approached the stand, Eunice Shriver saw her father stand up and take off his hat in a gesture of deference to his son. "It was an extraordinary moment," Eunice said later. "Father had *never* stood up for any of us before. He was always proud of us, but he was always the authority we stood up for. Then, just as Jack passed by and saw Dad on his feet, Jack too stood up and tipped his hat to Dad, the only person he honored that day."

In the days before the inaugural it had been rumored that Joe Kennedy was looking for a house near Washington, but now the patriarch realized that nothing would ever be the same. "We're not going to live in Washington or anywhere near it," he told reporter Bob Considine. "If Jack ever feels he has anything to ask me—I've had lots of different experiences in life—he knows where he can find me and I'll tell him what I think.

"You probably know," he continued with a trace of sadness in his voice, "that we are a very close-knit family. But we've got to resign ourselves to the fact that he has much greater things to look out for now."

After the inaugural, the family Bible was returned to the Fitzgeralds in Boston, where it was largely forgotten until the opening of the John Fitzgerald Kennedy Library in Dorchester. There, resting in a plexiglass cradle, it remains today, its worn pages open to Ecclesiastes, one of Rose Kennedy's favorite books of the Old Testament:

> All things have their season, and in their times all things pass under heaven.
> A time to be born and a time to die; a time to plant, and a time to pluck up that which is planted.
> A time to kill, and a time to heal; a time to destroy, and a time to build.
> A time to weep, and a time to laugh; a time to mourn, and a time to dance . . .

In the family record at the front of the old Bible, the list of family deaths remains frozen where it was at the time of the inauguration.

On November 22, 1963, President John Fitzgerald Kennedy was assassinated in Dallas, Texas. He was forty-six. On June 6, 1968, Robert F. Kennedy, campaigning for the presidency, was assassinated in Los Angeles, California. He was forty-two. The following year, Joseph P. Kennedy died.

# NOTES

## ABBREVIATIONS

| | | | |
|---|---|---|---|
| AAB | Archives, Archdiocese of Boston. | HC | *Harvard Crimson.* |
| | | HU | Harvard University. |
| AF | Agnes Fitzgerald. | JFF | John Francis Fitzgerald and his Scrapbooks. |
| AKP | Arthur Krock Papers. | | |
| BA | *Boston American.* | JFK | John F. Kennedy Papers. |
| BCD | *Boston City Documents.* | JPK | Joseph P. Kennedy Papers. |
| BDA | *Boston Daily Advertiser.* | KK | Kathleen Kennedy. |
| BEA | *Boston Evening American.* | KKH | Kathleen Kennedy Hartington. |
| BER | *Boston Evening Record.* | RF | Rose Fitzgerald. |
| BET | *Boston Evening Transcript.* | RFK | Rose Fitzgerald Kennedy Papers. |
| BG | *Boston Globe.* | | |
| BH | *Boston Herald.* | LB | Lem Billings Papers. |
| BNB | *Boston News Bureau.* | LT | *London Times.* |
| BP | *Boston Post.* | MHS | Massachusetts Historical Society. |
| BRA | *Boston Record-American.* | | |
| BT | *Boston Traveler.* | NYT | *New York Times.* |
| CR | *Congressional Record.* | OH-JFKL | Kennedy Library Oral History Series. |
| DM | Diplomatic Memoirs of Joseph P. Kennedy. | | |
| | | PP | *Practical Politics.* |
| FRL | *Fore River Log.* | PRO | Public Records Office, London. |
| FRUS | *Foreign Relations of the United States.* | | |
| | | WSJ | *Wall Street Journal.* |
| FWP | Frank Waldron Papers. | | |

3 "below freezing" and "cloudy": *BET*, Feb. 12, 1863, p. 4.

3 three infants out of ten: *BCD*, 1863, No. 47, pp. 28–29.

3 visions of a little soul howling: Peter Gregg Slater, *Children in the New England Mind in Death and in Life* (1977), p. 30.

4 wooden tenement house on Ferry Street: Deed Book 890, p. 259, Oct. 28, 1869, Suffolk County Registry of Deeds. A drawing accompanying the deed indicated that 30 Ferry Street was one of six wooden row houses varying in size from 21 × 25 ft. to 25 × 25 ft.

4 through a maze: Various maps of the period are found in the rare-books room of the Boston Public Library, in particular C. Penney, *Atlas of the City of Boston* (1861).

4 turning north on Hanover: *Boston Almanac & Business Directory* (1863–64).

4 St. Stephen's Church: "St. Stephen's," pamphlet (1965); Harold Kirker, *Bulfinch's Boston* (1964), p. 74; Harold Kirker, *The Architecture of Charles Bulfinch* (1969), pp. 168–70; Peter Murray, *The Architecture of the Italian Renaissance* (1963), pp. 1–2.

4 the North End had become: Oscar Handlin, *Boston's Immigrants* (1975), pp. 63–64, 89–104; Robert Woods, *Americans in Process* (1903), p. 5.

4 baptismal ceremony: For descriptions of the ceremony see Rev. Challoner, *The Catholic Christian Instructed in the Sacraments, Sacrifices, Ceremonies, and Observances of the Catholic Church* (1908), pp. 23–24; Rev. John Sullivan, *The Externals of the Catholic Church* (1919), pp. 43–51; Rev. Philip Weller, *The Roman Ritual* (1950), Vol. 1, pp. 21–57.

5 the selection of a name: Interview, Prof. Thomas Wangler, Boston University.

5 "to procure and maintain . . .": Rev. Challoner, p. 30.

6 among the records: St. Stephen's Baptisms, AAB.

6 "space was the stuff . . .": Irving Howe, *World of Our Fathers* (1976), p. 171.

6 the Fitzgerald family shared: *8th Census of the U.S.* (1860), Boston, Ward 4, pp. 148–49.

7 "If there is any such thing . . .": James Parton, "Our Roman Catholic Brethren," *Atlantic Monthly*, Vol. XXI (1868), p. 565.

7 "You may be a poor man . . .": Interview, Prof. Thomas Wangler.

7 Acceptance of one's position: John Butler, *Rule of Life* (1807); Rt. Rev. Bishop, *Catholic Manual or Collection of Prayers, Anthems, Hymns, etc.* (1836).

7 "no slum was as fearful . . .": Cecil Woodham-Smith, *The Great Hunger: Ireland, 1815–1849* (1962), p. 248; see also Stephen Thernstrom, *The Other Bostonians* (1973), p. 132.

8 In the immigrant slums: Oscar Handlin, *Boston's Immigrants*, p. 87.

8 rooms no larger than closets: For descriptions of tenement furnishings see Henry Marcus Schreiber, "The Working People in the Middle of the 19th Century," Ph.D. dissertation, BU, 1950, pp. 52–54.

8 Behind a makeshift wall: *8th Census of the U.S.* (1860), pp. 148–49.

8 Of all the ills associated: BCD, 1870, No. 126, pp. 3–4; Massachusetts Senate Document 150 (1871), pp. 517–40.

8 "all the lower rooms . . .": Harold Estabrook, *Some Slums of Boston* (1898), pp. 16–17.

8 "sunlight comes right into . . .": Jacob Riis, *A Ten Years' War* (1900), p. 31.

9 Information about the events of the christening was passed from the Fitzgeralds to John F. Fitzgerald, who in turn spoke of it later to his friend Clem Norton: Interview, Clem Norton.

9 Information about Thomas' youngest brother, James: Interview, Julia Fitzgerald Hill.

10 when he listened to his father: Interview, Clem Norton.

10 It is now understood: Cecil Woodham-Smith, pp. 94–102.

11 Helpless before the fate: Ibid., p. 75.

11 Before the Great Famine: Ibid., pp. 206–7.

11 But now, terrified: For accounts of the famine and its effects see R. Dudley Edwards and T. Desmond Williams (eds.), *The Great Famine* (1957); Rev. T. O'Herlihy, *The Famine, 1845–1846* (1947).

11 The first major exodus: The numbers of alien passengers who arrived in the U.S. from Ireland are as follows: 1820–30: 57,278; 1831–40: 198,233; 1841–50: 733,434; 1851–60: 936,665; 1861–70: 774,883; *Statistical Abstract of the U.S.* (1879), p. 132. On immigration see Edith Abbott, *Historical Aspects of the Immigration Problem* (1969); William Forbes Adams, *Ireland and Irish Emigration to the New World from 1815 to the Famine* (1932).

11 "As I heard it told . . .": Interview, Mary Hannon Heffernan.

12 by 1857 he had moved back: Marriages, Vol. 110, p. 126, Mass. Vital Statistics.

13 Footnote: Jay Dolan, *The Yankee Peddlars of New England* (1964), pp. 225–27.

13 "backbreaking and soul destroying . . .": Irving Howe, p. 78.

13 On the fifteenth of November: Marriages at St. Stephen's, AAB.

14 "If we could sit . . .": *The Pilot*, Jan. 23, 1864, p. 4.

14 less than ten percent: Cecil Woodham-Smith, p. 267.

15 Possibly if when they first landed: John Maguire, *The Irish in America* (1969), p. 215.

15 remembered his father saying: Interview, Clem Norton.

15 The story that comes down: Interview, Julia Fitzgerald Hill.

16 Though the exact nature of the business: The schedule of property of Cornelius Doherty, after his death in 1862, indicated that he had loaned "J Fitz" $1,292.00 on Sept. 22, 1862. As of Dec. 1, 1862, "Jas. Fitz" had repaid $1.50. Suffolk County Probate Records, No. 44076.

16 James became "the grocer": *Boston City Directory*, 1861–1862.

16 the average salary of a clerk: Massachusetts Senate Document 150 (1871), p. 413; for salaries of the working class see NYT, Feb. 24, 1869, p. 2.

16 "Where they relied on the patronage . . .": Oscar Handlin, *Boston's Immigrants*, pp. 64–65.
17 All his life: Interview, Rose Kennedy.
17 For the typical immigrant family: Robert Woods, *The City Wilderness* (1898), p. 103.
17 In contrast to: For information on the food intake of the poor see George Derby, "The Food of the Poor of Massachusetts," 4th Annual Report of the State Board of Health (1873).
17 over 540 different establishments: *BCD*, 1863, No. 6, p. 30.
17 The typical "saloon": John Koren, *The Economic Aspects of the Liquor Problem* (1889), pp. 215, 225.
18 "Whenever anything bad . . .": Interview, Regis Fitzgerald Murphy.
18 The purchase of 435 Hanover Street: Book 880, p. 117, June 12, 1866, and Book 865, p. 64, March 27, 1865, Suffolk County Registry of Deeds, Boston.
19 "beyond his family . . .": Interview, Rose Kennedy.
19 "Only people who have . . .": Irving Howe, p. 154.
19 the Fitzgerald family boasted: Interview, Regis Fitzgerald Murphy.
19 there was a clear distinction: Interview, Clem Norton.
19 when he watched one of his: Ibid.
20 "the dingy tenement . . .": John Henry Cutler, *"Honey Fitz": Three Steps to the White House* (1962), p. 42.
20 at least twelve people: Boston Tax Assessors Records, 1868.
20 "like an apt pupil . . .": Jacob Riis, *How the Other Half Lives* (1970), p. 17.
20 And we do know: Book 1177, p. 313, July 16, 1870, Suffolk County Registry of Deeds.
21 Every night . . . all his brothers: Interview, Clem Norton.
22 he began winning some races: *BP*, Sun., Dec. 28, 1913, p. 29.
22 "We used to run . . .": Ibid.
23 "I attribute my good physical . . .": *BG*, Feb. 11, 1913, p. 10.
23 "a single blade of grass . . .": *BP*, Feb. 11, 1913, p. 11.
23 As long as there were streets: Joseph Sawyer, *The Last Leaf on the Tree: Reminiscences of Old North Church* (1930), p. 37, n. 2; in contrast to North End recreation see James D'Wolf Lovett, *Old Boston Boys and the Games They Played* (1906).
23 Johnny later remembered: Interview, Rose Kennedy.
24 "See that finger? . . .": *BP*, Feb. 11, 1913, p. 11; *BG*, Feb. 11, 1913, p. 12.
24 about the wide array of . . . festivals: Philip Aries, *Centuries of Childhood: A Social History of Family Life* (1962), pp. 72–73.
24 As the rhythmic world: Oscar Handlin, *The Uprooted* (1951), pp. 86–90.
24 the celebrations of the Catholic Church: Marguerite Ickis, *The Book of Religious Holidays and Celebrations* (1966), p. 35; see also Elfrieda Vipont, *Some Christian Festivals* (1963).
24 "times of waiting . . .": Maria Trapp, *Around the Year with the Trapp Family* (1955), p. 85.
25 the mystery and wonder of midnight Mass: Interview, Rose Kennedy.
26 All went well: Ibid.
26 help with the boys: Interviews, Regis Fitzgerald Murphy and Rose Kennedy; *BP*, Sun., Dec. 28, 1913, p. 29.
26 "the church stood desolate . . .": Interview, Rose Kennedy.
26 As Easter was preceded: Alan W. Watts, *Easter: Its Story and Meaning* (1950).
27 as children crowned: Robert A. Woods, *Americans* . . . , p. 250.
27 "Personally, I believe . . .": *Advance of Boston* (1913), p. 52.
27 "For some reason . . .": *BP*, Sun., Dec. 28, 1913, p. 29.
27 "the one who taught . . .": Interview, Thomas Fitzgerald.
27 "when was John Francis young?": Interview, Regis Fitzgerald Murphy; see also John Demos, *A Little Commonwealth: Family Life in Plymouth Colony* (1970), pp. 139–40.
28 One morning he decided: Interview, Rose Kennedy.
28 Classroom schedule described in *School Documents*, 1883, No. 11.
28 his body erect: J. M. Rice, "The Public Schools of Boston," *Forum*, February 1893, as cited in David B. Tyack, *Village School to Urban System* (1974), p. 53.

28 "There is no question . . .": *School Documents*, 1879, No. 2, p. 40.
29 "English grammar might be . . .": Ibid., 1880, No. 4, p. 47.
29 "History stands like a skeleton . . .": Ibid., 1878, No. 16, p. 15.
29 "That love of reading . . .": Ibid., 1879, No. 2, p. 13.
29 is clear from a sampling: Henry Adams, *The Education of Henry Adams: An Autobiography* (1961), p. 37; Henry Cabot Lodge, *Early Memories* (1975), pp. 20–21.
29 "We lived actually . . .": William O'Connell, *Recollections of Seventy Years* (1934), pp. 5–8.
30 For the story of Thomas Wall see James Cullen, *The Irish in Boston* (1889), pp. 137–38; Robert Lord, *The History of the Archdiocese of Boston* (1944), Vol. 2, pp. 587–97; Stanley Schultz, *The Culture Factory: Boston Public Schools, 1789–1860* (1973), pp. 307–8; *BDA*, March 18, 1859, p. 1.
31 Fitzgerald's memories of Ellen's birth and death: Interview, Rose Kennedy.
32 "The poor people . . .": Diary of Father Hilary Tucker, AAB.
32 "a dead child . . .": Peter Gregg Slater, p. 93.
32 that out of every one hundred children: *BCD*, 1871, No. 39, pp. 19–20.
32 shocking percentage of deaths: Charles Buckingham, *Sanitary Conditions of Boston* (1875), pp. 46, 51.
32 attributed Boston's high rate of death: Ibid., pp. 61–62.
32 of the total foreign-born: Charles Buckingham, p. 177.
32 "inborn predisposition . . .": Ibid., p. 78
33 "This whole district . . .": *BCD*, 1849, No. 66, p. 13.
33 "in the bloom of health . . .": Interview, Rose Kennedy.
33 "James Fitzgerald is making money . . .": Mass. Vol. 12, p. 82, R. G. Dun & Co. Collection, Harvard University Graduate School of Business Administration.
33 almost total absence of rain: *BCD*, 1871, No. 39, p. 13.
33 cholera came once again to the North End: Figures compiled from Death Records, Vol. 231 (1870), Mass. Vital Statistics.
33 "the most fatal disease . . .": Thomas Hawkes Tanner, *The Practice of Medicine* (1872), p. 667.
33 a group of physicians: *BCD*, 1870, No. 43, p. 3.
33 "open mouthed" cesspools: *BCD*, 1876, No. 3, pp. 8–11.
34 Fitzgerald's memories of Ellen's death: Interview, Rose Kennedy.
34 Yet, despite her precautions: Death Records, Vol. 231, p. 137, Mass. Vital Statistics.
34 "Indeed, it is folly to talk . . .": Thomas Hawkes Tanner, p. 675.
34 frequent doses of Dr. Strickland's: A. Strickland, *Cholera: Its Symptoms and Treatment* (1866), pp. 4, 22–25.
35 "The sickroom is to be emptied . . .": Thomas Hawkes Tanner, p. 678.
35 "In the epidemic among children . . .": Edward Everett Hale, *Workingmen's Homes and Other Stories* (1871), p. 177.
35 "I felt it was important . . .": Interview, Rose Kennedy.
35 For information on the Eliot Grammar School see *BH*, Sun., Feb. 16, 1913, p. 10; *BET*, Nov. 8, 1913, Sect. 3, p. 10; Historical Address by Harvey Shepard at the bicentennial celebration of the founding of the school, Dec. 12, 1913, files of the Boston School Department.
36 the aspiring teacher: Exam for Certificate of Teaching, in Examination Papers, 1886, files of the Boston School Department.
36 In contrast to the all-female: *School Documents*, 1878, No. 25, pp. 15–16.
36 A list of textbooks is provided in *BCD*, 1878, No. 111, pp. 320–21.
36 the thirty-five graduates: Ibid., p. 45.
36 And whatever his ranking: Grammar school exam for diploma, June 19, 1887, in the files of the Boston School Department.
37 "a needless indulgence . . .": *BCD*, loc. cit.
37 "A mother who had scrubbed . . .": Mary Antin, *The Promised Land* (1912), p. 276.
37 1,100 minors licensed as newsboys: In 1867 there were 500 newsboys; *BCD*, 1868, No. 83, p. 1. By 1900 there were 3,500; Everett W. Goodhue, "Boston Newsboys, How They Live and Work," *Charities*, June 1902, p. 529.
37 cleared an average of $2.50: *Charities*, loc. cit., p. 530.

37 fittingly described by one former hawker: Harry E. Burroughs, *Boys in Men's Shoes* (1944), p. 353.

38 "The unwritten story . . .": Frank Mott, *American Journalism* (1950), p. 314.

38 "the late hours . . .": *Charities*, June 1902, p. 530; *BCD*, 1868, No. 83, p. 5.

38 "brings them to school . . .": *Charities*, loc. cit., p. 528.

38 The account of Fitzgerald's days as a newsboy comes largely from an interview with Clem Norton.

38 For the location of newspaper offices see Louis B. Lyons, *Newspaper Story: One Hundred Years of the Boston Globe* (1971), p. 4.

39 permitting ten thousand copies: Ibid., p. 34. For descriptions of various components of newspaper production see *BH*, Feb. 9, 1878, pp. 1–3, 6.

39 the newcomers were obliged: Harry Burroughs, p. 2.

40 "the newspaper press . . .": Justin Winsor, *The Memorial History of Boston, 1630–1880* (1881), Vol. 3, p. 630. In the two decades following the Civil War the number of daily newspapers in the U.S. quadrupled from 381 to 1,147, and together they sold more than 4 million copies a day; Sidney Kobre, *Development of American Journalism* (1969), p. 350. See also S. W. D. North, *The Newspaper and Periodical Press* (1884), p. 74.

41 These years also witnessed: Sidney Kobre, pp. 349–63.

41 the war had whetted: Louis Lyons, p. 4; see also Alfred McLung Lee, *The Daily Newspaper in America* (1937), pp. 277–78.

41 he was fond of maintaining: Interview, Rose Kennedy.

41 The story of Johnny and Fred: Interview, Clem Norton.

42 once a boy had worked up a corner: Harry Burroughs, p. 2.

44 Fitzgerald saw "the other Boston": Interview, Rose Kennedy.

44 "the sunny street that holds . . .": Quoted in William S. Rossiter, *Days and Ways in Old Boston* (1915), pp. 35–36; see also Edward Stanhope, *Boston Illustrated* (1878), pp. 23, 25.

44 For the first time in his life: Interview, Rose Kennedy. For good descriptions of Boston social life in this era see Marjorie Drake Ross, *The Book of Boston: The Victorian Period, 1837–1901* (1964); Mark De Wolfe Howe, *Boston: The Place and the People* (1903); Samuel Eliot Morison, *One Boy's Boston* (1962); Rose Netzorg Kerr, *100 Years of Costumes in America, 1850–1950* (1951).

44 Restricted by their parents: Barbara Solomon, *Ancestors and Immigrants* (1972), p. 454.

44 "Homeric" and "savage": Henry Cabot Lodge, *Early Memories*, p. 19.

45 "It was no small deliverance . . .": Quoted in Henry James, *Charles W. Eliot* (1930), Vol. 1, p. 15.

45 the trading capital: For information on Boston shipping and trade see generally Samuel Eliot Morison, *Maritime History of Massachusetts* (1961); Ralph Paine, *The Ships and Sailors of Old Salem: The Record of a Brilliant Era of American Achievement* (1912); William Rossiter, pp. 1–20.

46 prosperity in manufacturing: See generally Daniel Boorstin, *The Americans: The National Experience* (1967).

46 a score of old Boston families: Arthur M. Johnson and Barry E. Supple, *Boston Capitalists and Western Railroads* (1967), pp. 15–17.

46 "when Boston was a great port . . .": "Boston," *Fortune*, Feb. 1933, p. 29.

46 "the hub of the Universe": As quoted in Van Wyck Brooks, *New England Indian Summer* (1950), p. 1.

46 New England . . . cultural renaissance: Perry Miller, *The Golden Age of American Literature* (1959), pp. 3–4; Vernon Parrington, *Main Currents in American Thought: The Romantic Revolution in America, 1800–1860* (1927), Vol. 3, pp. 271–472; Robert Ernest Spiller (ed.), *The Literary History of the United States* (1963), Vol. 1, pp. 232–34.

46 The wondrous parade began: Vernon Parrington, op. cit., pp. 435–37; Van Wyck Brooks, *The Flowering of New England* (1936), pp. 89–146, 323–42; E. Digby Baltzell, *Quaker Philadelphia and Puritan Boston* (1929), p. 54.

46 "still staggers our realization . . .": Perry Miller, p. 3.

47 the remarkable pattern: Martin Green, *The Problem of Boston: Some Readings in Cultural History* (1966), p. 22; Samuel Eliot Morison, *One Boy's Boston*, p. 68.

47 "there were so many of them . . .": Samuel Eliot Morison, *One Boy's Boston*, pp. 68–69.

48 "I must study politics and war . . .": Quoted in E. Digby Baltzell, p. 50.

48 "where the tone of society . . .": Charles Dickens, *American Notes* (1968), pp. 41, 43, 73; see also Van Wyck Brooks, *The Flowering . . .* , pp. 1–20.

49 Required to read Dickens': Interview, Rose Kennedy.

49 For the impact of the Civil War see Allan Nevins, *The Emergence of Modern America, 1865–1878* (1927), pp. 31–74; Brett Howard, *Boston: A Social History* (1976), pp. 243–44.

49 "The headlong growth . . .": John Higham, *Strangers in the Land: Patterns of American Nativism, 1860–1925* (1975), p. 16.

49 For an understanding of Boston's decline see Charles Francis Adams in Justin Winsor, Vol. 4, p. 111, and Hamilton Andrews Hill, ibid., pp. 229–30.

50 By 1880 Boston's export trade: *Professional and Industrial History of Suffolk County, Mass.* (1894), Vol. 2, p. 159.

50 By the mid-1880s: Elisha P. Douglass, *The Coming of Age of American Business* (1971), pp. 249, 404–5; 24th Annual Report of the Boston Board of Trade (1878), pp. 15–34.

50 it had increased its population: BCD, 1886, No. 104, pp. 4–5.

50 Before 1830: Oscar Handlin, *Boston's Immigrants*, pp. 51–52.

50 "Why, all these people . . .": Quoted in Van Wyck Brooks, *The Flowering . . .* , p. 6.

51 In the aftermath of the Civil War: Vernon Parrington, Vol. 3, pp. 7–17.

51 the Cunard Line: Lucius Beebe, *Boston and the Boston Legend* (1935), p. 245; Oscar Handlin, *Boston's Immigrants*, pp. 48–49.

51 In the nine years up to 1845: Cecil Woodham-Smith, pp. 246–47.

52 Irish newcomers had no choice: Walter Muir Whitehill, *Boston in the Age of JFK* (1966), p. 28.

52 Boston's population swelled: BCD, 1886, No. 104, pp. 4–5.

52 In contrast, New York: *New York City Guide* (1939), p. 3; Albert Langtry, *Metropolitan Boston: A Modern History* (1929), p. 25.

52 For even with the land: Walter Muir Whitehill, *Boston: A Topographical History* (1968), pp. 73–118.

52 The once fashionable North End: Ibid., pp. 141–73; William Dean Howells, *The Rise of Silas Lapham* (1951), pp. 21–22.

52 many of the Revolutionary landmarks: Rev. Edward Porter, *Rambles in Old Boston* (1887).

53 "power and arrogance . . .": John Higham, p. 37.

53 The recoil of fashionable Boston: Ibid., pp. 32–33; Cleveland Amory, *The Proper Bostonians* (1947), pp. 246–59.

53 "The more the center . . .": Van Wyck Brooks, *The Flowering . . .* , p. 91.

53 a substantial portion of Boston's elite: Samuel Bass Warner, *Streetcar Suburbs: The Process of Growth in Boston, 1870–1900* (1969), p. 13.

54 the shifting of their residential: Walter Muir Whitehill, *Boston: A Topographical . . .* , pp. 174–98; Oscar Handlin, *Boston's Immigrants*, pp. 207–29.

54 salt away their capital: *Fortune*, February 1933, pp. 35–36.

54 "The great family trusts . . .": Ibid., p. 106.

54 "I never invest . . .": Ibid., p. 36.

54 a genteel culture arrogant: Vernon Parrington, Vol. 3, pp. 55–60; Allan Nevins, *The Emergence . . .* , pp. 228–63.

55 The generation of Brahmins: Brett Howard, pp. 153–79; and generally Cleveland Amory, *The Proper Bostonians*; John P. Marquand, *The Late George Apley* (1940); Alexander W. Williams, *A Social History of Boston Clubs* (1970); Dixon Wecter, *The Saga of American Society: A Record of Social Aspirations, 1607–1937* (1970).

56 The visit to 31 Beacon Street: Interview, Rose Kennedy.

58 all the brothers continued to live: As indicated in the *Boston City Directories* Thomas

J. continued to live at 465 Hanover until his death in 1893; George F. until 1894; Joseph A. until 1899; and Edward, Michael and Henry S. until 1899, when they moved into the house John F. owned at 8 Unity St.

58 death certificate . . . "debility": Death Records, Vol. 231, p. 13, Mass. Vital Statistics.
59 after an early-March snowstorm: *BET*, March 11, 1879, p. 1.
59 Rosanna did not feel well: Interview, Regis Fitzgerald Murphy.
59 On her death certificate: Death Records, Vol. 231, p. 59, Mass. Vital Statistics.
59 The following day: *BH*, March 11, 1879, p. 4.
59 one of Fitzgerald's favorite memories: Interview, Rose Kennedy.
59 Hers is the familiar story: Carl Degler, *At Odds: Women and the Family in America from the Revolution to the Present* (1980), pp. 136–37.
60 "The only thing I remember . . .": Interview, Julia Fitzgerald Hill.
60 "bearing one baby after another . . .": Interview, Regis Fitzgerald Murphy.
61 There was never any question: Interview, Thomas Fitzgerald.
61 In an age when only 4 percent: *NYT Magazine*, Sun., April 28, 1935, p. 17.
61 "There are large numbers . . .": *School Documents*, 1878, No. 16, pp. 28–31.
61 "After Rosanna Fitzgerald's death . . .": Interview, Thomas Fitzgerald.
61 Latin School . . . founded: *School Documents*, 1929, No. 7, p. 13.
62 could read Virgil: *Catalogue of Boston Latin School*, 1883, Boston School Department.
62 the Brahmins were in full retreat: Barbara Solomon, p. 46.
62 Archbishop Williams announced: Ibid., p. 48.
62 the upper-class Yankees: Ibid., pp. 50–52.
62 Irish boys wishing: George Santayana, *Persons and Places* (1944), p. 179.
62 And in the process: Texts for Latin School in *Catalogue of Boston Latin School, 1635–1885*, pp. 77–80.
63 "It seemed a vast . . .": George Santayana, p. 153.
63 The Latin School on Warren Avenue was dedicated Feb. 22, 1881; see *BG*, Feb. 22, 1881, p. 4, and Feb. 23, p. 2.
63 For descriptions of sites on North End and Boston tours see Edward Stanhope; Moses King, *King's Handbook of Boston* (1878); *Illustrated Boston* (1889).
63 "these narrow old streets . . .": John Henry Cutler, p. 35.
63 Story of the tour taken with the British couple: Interview, Clem Norton.
64 Cavendish had arrived: *BG* Sun., May 7, 1882, p. 1.
65 "a brighter day had dawned . . .": *BG*, May 8, 1882, p. 1.
65 and there, at approximately: *NYT*, Sun., May 7, 1882, p. 1.
65 Footnote: Bernard Holland, *The Life of Spencer Compton, Eighth Duke of Devonshire* (1911), Vol. 1, p. 353.
66 In June 1884, along with thirty: *Catalogue of Graduates of the Public Latin School in Boston, 1816–1917* (1918), pp. 253–55.
66 admitted . . . to Harvard Medical School: Handwritten register of entering students, Countway Library, Harvard Medical School.
66 of the 102 students . . . : *102nd Annual Catalogue of the Medical School of Harvard University, 1884–1885* (1885), pp. 178–81.
66 young men with old Yankee: Ibid.
66 Harvard's experiment . . . one female: John Duffy, *The Healers: The Rise of the Medical Establishment* (1976), p. 273.
67 great improvement in the curriculum: John Duffy, pp. 260–62.
68 The last will: Suffolk County Probate Records, No. 73981.
68 "He was a plain . . .": *BP*, May 20, 1885, p. 4.
69 On Keany, see notes for page 94.
69 For descriptions of machine politics see James Bryce, *The American Commonwealth* (1895), Vol. 2, pp. 107–41.
70 Story of the meeting with Keany: Interview, Clem Norton.
72 "not the Politics of Aristotle . . .": Mosei Ostrogorski, *Organization and Party Politics* (1964), p. 367.
72 "Ye'd better get . . .": Joseph Dinneen, *Ward Eight* (1936), pp. 220–21.
72 the complexion of Ward Six: Robert Woods, *Americans . . .* , pp. 40–50.

73 Description of Fitzgerald's rise through the ranks and the checker story: Interview, Clem Norton.

75 Massachusetts had passed a law: Eldon Cobb Evans, *A History of the Australian Ballot System in the United States* (1917), p. 8.

76 position in the Customs House: In the lists of staff of the Customs House in the *City Directories* Fitzgerald is a clerk in the statistical department from 1888 to 1891. On the Customs House see *Bulletin of the Business Historical Society* (1934), pp. 42–43.

77 Story of the first meeting with Josie: Interview, Rose Kennedy.

77 "On both sides . . .": William F. Barnard, "A Day in Old Concord," *Marlboro Advertiser*, Aug. 27, 1884, 1880 Scrapbook, Concord Library.

78 the house . . . was rather small: Interview, Mary Heffernan.

78 "Irish families . . .": Joseph Dinneen, *Ward Eight*, pp. 81–82.

78 "The first time I saw . . .": John Henry Cutler, p. 43.

78 Josie's beauty: Rose Kennedy, *Times to Remember* (1975), p. 16.

78 "What I remember most . . .": Interview, Mary Jo Gargan Clasby.

79 he decided then and there: John Henry Cutler, p. 43.

79 "I can never imagine . . .": Interview, Geraldine Hannon.

79 "Father was an extrovert . . .": Rose Kennedy, p. 13.

79 "her shyness did not make . . .": Interview, Mary Jo Gargan Clasby.

80 "Politeness with proper . . .": *Donahoe's*, June 1885, p. 527.

80 the perfection of her mother's: Interview, Rose Kennedy.

80 "After Uncle Johnny's . . .": Interview, Geraldine Hannon.

80 "Butter was said . . .": G. Stanley Hall, "The Contents of Children's Minds on Entering School," *Pedagogical Seminary*, 1891, p. 155.

80 "Compared to Boston . . .": Interview, Geraldine Hannon.

81 "For medical expenses . . .": *Annual Report of the Selectmen of the Town of Acton, 1868–1869*, p. 6.

81 Boston totaled over $70,000: BCD, 1868, No. 57, pp. 1–7.

81 Josie . . . was born in Acton: *Annual Report of the Selectmen . . .*, 1865–1866, pp. 13–14.

81 die at the age of six: Ibid., 1861–1862, p. 36.

81 All births and deaths of the children are given in the Hannon family Bible now in the possession of the Kennedy Library.

82 The story of Lizzie's drowning: Interviews, Rose Kennedy and Mary Heffernan.

82 "When he was thirteen . . .": Interview, Geraldine Hannon.

83 Michael Hannon, Jr., died: *Annual Report of the Selectmen . . .*, 1881–1882, p. 15.

83 "It's the curse . . .": Interview, Mary Heffernan.

83 "James Hannon . . .": *Concord Enterprise*, April 26, 1889, p. 2.

83 "I married your mother . . .": Interview, Mary Heffernan.

83 "I can see how . . .": Interview, Geraldine Hannon.

84 "She could not help . . .": Interview, Rose Kennedy.

84 among the poorest residents: *Valuation List of Real and Personal Estate in the Town of Acton*, Sept. 1, 1872, pp. 1–46, and Sept. 1, 1889, pp. 1–63.

85 "There was always a great pride . . .": Interview, Geraldine Hannon.

85 "Even in her eighties . . .": Interview, Marion Fitzgerald Mullen.

85 "Whenever Josie . . .": Interview, Regis Fitzgerald Murphy.

85 "He was enchanted . . .": Interview, Rose Kennedy.

86 "Concord has a winsome . . .": *Concord Enterprise*, 1884, in 1880 Scrapbook, Concord Library.

86 Accounts of John and Josie's wanderings through Concord: Interview, Rose Kennedy.

87 "The girl who knows . . .": *Donahoe's*, October 1890, p. 358.

87 "That there has been . . .": *Annual Report of the School Committee of the Town of Acton*, 1869–1870, p. 5.

87 Ellen as "all rather sour": Interview, Mary Heffernan.

87 "This evil is becoming . . .": *Annual Report of the School Committee . . .*, loc. cit.

87 "When we lived in Concord . . .": Interview, Rose Kennedy.

88 "My mother loved riding . . .": Rose Kennedy, p. 16.
88 "not mere matters of form . . .": Lelia Bugg, *The Correct Thing for Catholics* (1891), p. 40.
88 "each week when John F. . . .": Interview, Mary Heffernan.
89 "Marriage impediment . . .": Dispensation Records: Consanguinity, 1889–1892, AAB.
89 "The marriage of Miss Mary . . .": *Concord Enterprise*, Sept. 27, 1889, p. 2.
90 "she always had her Johnny . . .": Interview, Rose Kennedy.
90 "John Fitzgerald always had . . .": Interview, Mary Jo Gargan Clasby.
90 "It was not easy . . .": Interview, Rose Keane Ellis.
90 July 22, 1890, dawned: Gail Cameron, *Rose* (1971), p. 23; *BP*, July 22, 1890, p. 1.
90 "All along John F. kept . . .": Interview, Geraldine Hannon.
91 his love for her: Interview, Clem Norton.
92 Fitzgerald's name appeared: *BP*, Dec. 16, 1981, pp. 1–2.
92 "The Council was the lowest . . .": Beatrice Webb, *American Diary, 1898* (1963), p. 83.
93 "The North End . . .": *Common Council Proceedings*, March 24, 1892, pp. 302–4, and May 19, 1892, pp. 509–15.
93 In 1893 property was acquired by the city for the park, which was completed for use during the summer of 1897: *BCD*, 1897, No. 65, pp. 1–3.
94 Account of Fitzgerald's reaction to Keany's death: Interview, Clem Norton.
94 "Never . . . such an imposing . . .": *The Republic*, March 5, 1892, p. 5; *BP*, Feb. 27, 1892, p. 1, and March 2, 1892, p. 4; *The Pilot*, March 5, 1892, p. 1
94 "Fitzgerald is as different . . .": *PP* Nov. 25, 1905, p. 89.
95 the Little Napoleon: Robert Woods, *Americans . . .* , pp. 181–82.
95 Later, Fitzgerald described: Interview, Clem Norton.
95 A thickset, well-muscled: Leslie Ainley, *Boston Mahatma* (1949), pp. 8–10; see also A. D. Van Nostrand, "The Lomasney Legend," *New England Quarterly*, Dec. 1948, pp. 435–58.
95 "the inquisitorial terrors . . .": Leslie Ainley, p. 12.
95 "more sleepless nights . . .": Thomas Carens, "Martin Lomasney: The Story of His Life," *BH*, Dec. 8, 1925, p. 15 (the series ran Dec. 2–27).
96 his character traits were not the issue: Leslie Ainley, p. 65.
96 "The United States in the eighties . . .": Arthur M. Schlesinger, *The Rise of the City, 1878–1898* (1933), p. xv.
96 During his years as a state senator: *Journal of the Senate*, 1893–1894.
96 "the most called for man . . .": *BDA*, June 11, 1894, p. 8.
97 O'Neil had served his district: Geoffrey Blodgett, *The Gentle Reformers: Massachusetts Democrats in the Cleveland Era* (1966), p. 145.
97 In the wake of the Wall Street panic: John T. Galvin, "Boston in the Panic of 1893," *BH*, Sept. 4, 1978, p. 31.
97 "what it had never gone through . . .": *BP*, Feb. 21, 1894, p. 1.
97 "allay the starvation": *BH*, Sept. 4, 1978, p. 31.
97 Mayor Matthews devoted: Ibid.
97 "the boy candidate": John Henry Cutler, p. 161.
97 "If noise, fireworks . . .": *BDA*, Sept. 21, 1894, p. 1.
98 The caucuses in September: Ibid.
98 The polls opened: *BDA*, Sept. 22, 1894, p. 1.
98 "Now that the fight . . .": *BRA*, Jan. 7, 1964, p. 23.
99 the formation of the . . . (APA): *BP*, Nov. 6, 1894, p. 6.
99 "a secret society . . .": *BG* (eve.), Nov. 5, 1894, p. 3.
99 "I cannot see . . .": Ibid.
99 "Fitzgerald will carry . . .": *BP*, Nov. 7, 1894, p. 4.
99 "Compared with New York . . .": As quoted in Constance M. Green, *Washington: Capital City, 1879–1950* (1963), p. 77; see also George Galloway, *History of the House of Representatives* (1962), p. 33; Neil MacNeil, *Forge of Democracy* (1963), pp. 5–16.
100 Fitzgerald found a room: *Washington, D.C., City Directory*, 1897.
100 requested a leave: *CR*, 54th Congress, 1st session, p. 26; *BET*, Dec. 3, 1895, p. 3.

100 During his prolonged stay: *BJ*, Dec. 25, 1895, p. 5, Feb. 27, 1896, p. 4, and April 10, 1896, p. 7.

100 Speech on the contract system: *CR*, 54th, 1st, June 6, 1896, p. 6229.

100 In the months that followed: *CR*, 54th, 2nd, "Boston Port," Feb. 23, 1897, p. 2152; "Constitution," Jan. 17, 1897, p. 798; "Immigration," Jan. 27, 1897, Appendix, p. 45. *CR*, 55th, 1st, "Tax," March 25, 1897, pp. 293–95. *CR*, 56th, 2nd, "Gypsy Moth," Jan. 30, 1901, pp. 1837–38.

100 Henry Cabot Lodge: See Alden Hatch, *The Lodges of Massachusetts* (1973).

101 "it involves, in a word . . .": Henry Cabot Lodge, *Speeches and Addresses, 1884–1909* (1909), pp. 245–46.

102 "the insidious arguments": Interview, Clem Norton.

102 "Mr. Speaker . . .": *CR*, 54th, 2nd, Jan. 27, 1897, Appendix, pp. 46–49.

102 when the vote was taken: Ibid., March 3, 1897, pp. 2946–47.

102 "You are an impudent . . .": John Henry Cutler, p. 64.

102 Fitzgerald later said: Ibid.

102 Cleveland veto: *CR*, 54th, 2nd, March 2, 1897, pp. 2667–68; see also Allan Nevins, *Grover Cleveland: A Study in Courage* (1932), pp. 725–26; *NYT*, March 3, 1897, p. 1.

103 "was to bring millions . . .": John Henry Cutler, p. 64.

103 "Once Mother got it . . .": Interview, Rose Kennedy.

103 Set back from the road: Rose Kennedy, p. 12; Gail Cameron, p. 34.

103 "These were wonderful . . .": Rose Kennedy, p. 12.

103 "she didn't have as much . . .": Rose Kennedy, "Notes for Times to Remember" (hereafter cited as "Notes for TTR"), RFK.

104 A deeply religious woman: Rose Kennedy, p. 15.

104 "This is the command . . .": *Donahoe's*, Nov. 1890, p. 346.

104 the public schools were training: Interview, Edward Fitzgerald.

104 "even if it were true . . .": *Donahoe's*, loc. cit., p. 347.

104 Josie would have much preferred: Interview, Rose Kennedy.

105 "Some children will study . . .": Rose Kennedy, "Notes for TTR," RFK.

105 "It is a price which members . . .": Ibid.

105 "the absolute thrill . . .": Interview, Rose Kennedy.

105 "Father knew that Lomasney . . .": Ibid.

106 *The Republic*: George Kibbe Turner, "The Mayor of Boston," *Collier's*, Nov. 16, 1907, p. 17.

106 "if he does have aspirations . . .": *PP*, Feb. 8, 1902, p. 144.

106 "I knew the success . . .": John Henry Cutler, p. 80.

106 "Sixty percent of the shoppers . . .": George K. Turner, loc. cit.

106 Fitzgerald's energetic promotion: Ibid.

106 "the entire demonstration . . .": *PP*, March 16, 1901, p. 229.

106 Patrick A. Collins . . . : *BH*, Dec. 14, 1925, p. 5.

107 death of Mayor Collins: *BH*, Sept. 15, 1905, p. 1.

107 "Fitzgerald did not have . . .": *BH*, Dec. 15, 1925, p. 11.

107 "Without Lomasney . . .": Ibid.

107 "I knew they were working . . .": Ibid. For biographical information on Donovan see *BP*, Oct. 22, 1905, p. 26.

107 "I am making my contest . . .": *BP*, Nov. 9, 1905, p. 9, and Nov. 13, 1905, p. 1.

108 "the gang in City Hall . . .": *PP*, Nov. 25, 1905, p. 830.

108 Donovan was not in the best of health: *BH*, Dec. 15, 1925, p. 11.

108 "no candidate has ever . . .": Ibid.

108 Boston "throbbed with excitement . . .": Ibid.

108 "surrounded by a procession . . .": *BG*, Nov. 16, 1905, p. 28.

108 Primary results: *BP*, Nov. 17, 1905, p. 1.

108 In the general election: George Nutter, "Political Boston, 1905–1933: A Cycle of Municipal History," read before the Mass. Historical Society, June 8, 1933, MHS.

109 "I am not going to support . . .": *BH*, Dec. 15, 1925, p. 11.

109 Election results: *BH*, Dec. 13, 1905, p. 1.

109 "Thank God for old Dewey": Interview, Clem Norton.

110 "the largest that has ever . . .": *BP*, Jan. 2, 1906, p. 5.

110 started with a midnight squall: *BER*, Jan. 1, 1906, p. 1.
111 City Hall, that "lunatic pile . . .": Edwin O'Connor, *The Last Hurrah* (1956), p. 40.
111 precedent was broken: *BET*, Jan. 1, 1906, p. 1.
111 the "monster automobile": Ibid.; see also *BP*, loc. cit.; *BH*, Jan. 2, 1906, p. 1.
111 "Never before . . .": *BET*, loc. cit.
111 "a continued ovation . . .": *BP*, loc. cit.
111 elegantly attired: Ibid., p. 5.
111 "What we need . . .": *BCD*, 1906, No. 1, pp. 3–4.
112 The applause at this point: *BG* (eve.), Jan. 1, 1906, p. 7; *BP*, loc. cit.
112 Yankees, reduced now to only 11 percent: Herbert M. Zolot, "Issues in Good Government: James Michael Curley and the Boston Scene 1897–1918," Ph.D. dissertation, State University at Stonybrook (1975), p. 37.
112 "go to school . . .": *BH*, Jan. 25, 1906, p. 5 (speech before the Young Men's Catholic Association of Boston College).
113 "the tendency of the American . . .": *BCD*, 1906, No. 1, p. 3.
113 it had been the custom: *BG* (eve.), Jan. 1, 1906, p. 7.
113 the pomp and revelry: Interview, Clem Norton.
114 "no more interesting . . .": *BG*, Jan. 2, 1906, p. 6.
114 "As Mayor . . . John Francis . . .": *PP*, Jan. 20, 1906, p. 46.
114 "a steady stream . . .": *BP*, Sun., April 29, 1906, p. 23.
115 "The doors opened . . .": Ibid.
115 "I had been in . . .": *BP*, June 30, 1906, p. 3.
115 the city had much more money: Herbert Zolot, p. 97; for city expenditures by department see *BCD*, 1906, No. 49, pp. vi–ix.
116 "familiarize himself . . .": John F. Fitzgerald, "The Duties of a Modern Mayor," *New England Magazine*, 1906, pp. 483–84.
116 One evening's "leisure": *Collier's*, Nov. 16, 1907, p. 18.
116 "The Mayor should go slow . . .": *PP*, Jan. 20, 1906, p. 46.
117 "the cohesive power . . .": As quoted in Herbert Zolot, p. 40.
117 "that no man . . .": Quoted from *The Republic* in *BP*, Jan. 13, 1906, p. 8.
117 "Fitzgerald would go . . .": *PP*, Nov. 25, 1905, p. 829.
118 he provided "provisional": *Collier's*, loc. cit; see also Francis Russell, *The Great Interlude* (1964), p. 76.
118 "a properly graded . . .": *BCD*, 1906, No. 1, p. 53.
119 "It is the most remarkable . . .": *BJ*, June 1, 1907, p. 12.
119 "Three men are still paid . . .": *BJ*, Jan. 3, 1907, p. 6.
119 "a record year . . .": *BJ*, June 5, 1907, p. 2.
119 "on a proper basis . . .": *The Republic*, Feb. 3, 1906, p. 11.
119 Because he had launched: *PP*, Dec. 1, 1906, p. 824, and March 16, 1907, p. 128.
120 "the huge leisure class . . .": Quoted in John Henry Cutler, p. 102.
120 Doyle's appointment: *BP*, Feb. 20, 1906, p. 4; *BH*, Feb, 20, 1906, pp. 1, 3.
120 "The Mayor's . . .": George Nutter Diary, MHS.
120 Fitzgerald's succeeding appointments: *BP*, April 24, 1906, p. 1.
120 "a steady deterioration . . .": Final Report, Boston Finance Commission, 1909, p. 11.
121 the conviction of the two Curleys: Herbert Zolot, pp. 171–83; Leonard White, *The Republican Era* (1958), pp. 278–302.
121 "to promote the welfare . . .": Quoted in Herbert Zolot, p. 62.
122 "His administration would likely . . .": Ibid., p. 24.
122 before the end of his first month . . . consumptives' hospital, *BP*, Jan. 30, 1906, p. 1; high school of commerce, *The Republic*, Feb. 10, 1906, p. 10. bill for taxing corporations, *BG*, Aug. 2, 1906, p. 9.
122 in the most routine tasks: Archbishop O'Connell, *BP*, April 19, 1906, p. 4. Deer Island, *BG*, May 24, 1906, p. 10. Dorchester High, *BP*, Sun., June 23, 1907, p. 11. Bryan, *BER*, Aug. 30, 1906, p. 4.
122 "He outdid himself . . .": *BER*, loc. cit.
123 "the city of the sea . . .": Samuel Adams Drake, *The Pine Tree Coast* (1891), pp. 114, 124–126.

124 "the most wonderful smile . . .": Interview, Rose Kennedy.
124 "I shall always . . .": Ibid.
124 "Mayor Fitzgerald shook . . .": BP, July 27, 1906, p. 6.
125 "displaced a hired pitcher . . .": Collier's, Nov. 16, 1907, p. 18.
125 "Hardly a day passed . . .": PP, Sept. 1, 1906, p. 566.
125 as "the royal family": Collier's, loc. cit.
125 "Henry S. and James T. . . .": PP, June 30, 1906, p. 410.
126 "an extremely wealthy man . . .": PP, July 14, 1906, p. 439.
126 It was said: Interviews, Mary Keane Campbell and Rose Keane Ellis.
126 his youngest brother, Henry: Interview, Edward Fitzgerald; obituary, BG, Feb. 23, 1955, p. 22.
127 "See Henry," was the Mayor's: Collier's, loc. cit.
127 Eddie was the most gregarious: Interviews, Thomas Fitzgerald and Regis Fitzgerald Murphy; obituary, The Pilot, March 9, 1940, p. 7.
127 "he had a good long run . . .": Interview, Thomas Fitzgerald.
127 Lizzy, "a dazzling beauty . . .": Interview, Margaret Curry.
127 Some of his relatives believe: Interview, Thomas Fitzgerald.
127 Michael, one year younger: Interviews, Thomas Fitzgerald and Regis Fitzgerald Murphy; obituary, BG (eve.), June 11, 1925, p. 8.
128 "a little dippy": Interview, Thomas Fitzgerald.
128 "the human postage stamp": PP, July 14, 1906, p. 439; obituary, The Republic, Oct. 23, 1920, p. 8.
128 "the Fitzgerald dynasty": PP, loc. cit.
128 "syndicated" the office: BP, Nov. 30, 1907, p. 2.
129 "no apology to make": BP, Dec. 2, 1907, p. 2.
129 "Two of the boys died . . .": BP, Sept. 15, 1909, p. 1.
129 "There was only one problem . . .": Interview, Rose Kennedy.
129 "Although it was late . . .": BER, Sept. 14, 1906, p. 4.
129 reporters found him: BP, Feb. 23, 1907, p. 1; The Republic, April 13, 1907, p. 10; BP, May 23, 1907, p.1, and June 19, 1907, p. 4.
131 "We all stood . . .": Interview, Margaret Curry.
131 "Brimming with animation . . .": Gail Cameron, p. 59.
132 "a golden afternoon": Interview, Rose Kennedy.
132 Background on Wellesley College: Florence Converse, The Story of Wellesley (1915).
132 Mary Calkins—had won: Wellesley College, 1875–1975: A Century of Women (1975), p. 208.
132 Wellesley faculty: Wellesley College Calendars, 1907–1911, Wellesley College Library. For information on Emily Balch see Mercedes Randall, Emily Greene Balch: Improper Bostonian (1964). On Vida Scudder and Ellen Hayes see Florence Converse, pp. 160–62; Mercedes Randall, pp. 105–6; Alice Payne Hachett, Wellesley: Part of the American Story (1949), pp. 184–90.
133 The various college groups are described in "Wellesley College Student Handbook" (1907); a list of guest speakers in 1907 appears in the "Annual Reports of the Presidents," Wellesley College Library.
133 At eleven o'clock Tuesday morning: Boston Finance Commission Report, 1907–1908, Vol. 1, p. 19; Sughrue obituary, BG, April 16, 1966, p. 1; an account of the first meeting, BP, Aug. 3, 1907, p. 4.
133 "the uneasy feeling . . .": George Nutter, "The Boston City Charter," National Municipal Review, 1913, p. 583; see also Elizabeth Herlihy (ed.), Fifty Years of Boston: A Memorial History (1932), pp. 99–102.
134 "the moral salvation . . .": John F. Moors, "Eighteen Months Work of the City," Survey, Oct. 2, 1909, p. 47.
134 In November 1906 the Boston Herald: Quoted in Herbert Zolot, p. 104.
134 "whitewashing committee": George Nutter, "Nathan Matthews," Harvard Graduates Magazine, March 1928, p. 9; see also Richard Abrams, Conservatism in a Progressive Era: Massachusetts Politics, 1910–1912 (1964), pp. 147–48; Herbert Zolot, p. 104.
135 "Usually when a committee . . .": Joseph Lee, "The Boston Finance Commission," Survey, Oct. 2, 1909, p. 12.

135 "As a matter of fact . . .": Ibid., p. 49.
135 "there was something . . .": Richard Hofstadter, *The Progressive Movement, 1900–1915* (1963), p. 1.
136 "made the work of the Commission . . .": Ibid., p. 50.
136 "so long as every line . . .": Ibid., p. 56.
136 "It was a report calculated . . .": Ibid., p. 12.
136 From the sands of Old Orchard: *BG*, Aug. 28, 1907, p. 1.
137 For information on Michael Mitchell see *PP*, April 28, 1907, p. 267; *BG*, Aug. 10, 1907, p. 1; *BER*, Aug. 10, 1907, p. 8.
137 "secure lower prices . . .": *BCD*, 1906, No. 1, p. 55; see also *The Republic*, Feb. 3, 1906, p. 10; *PP*, Jan. 13, 1906, p. 29; *BCD*, 1908, No. 45.
137 His preference, the *Boston*: *BER*, April 23, 1906, p. 4.
137 Mitchell's magnetic personality: *PP*, Feb. 3, 1906, p. 79, March 21, 1906, p. 194, and April 28, 1906, p. 267; *BP*, May 2, 1906, p. 11; *BER*, July 6, 1906, p. 4.
138 "We simply adored . . .": Interview, Rose Kennedy.
138 "He took the position . . .": *PP*, Sept. 14, 1907, p. 559.
138 When Fitzgerald received word: Interview, Edward Gallagher.
138 The first session: *BP*, Sept. 4, 1907, p. 1.
138 George P. Koch: *BG*, Sept. 4, 1907, p. 3; *BJ*, Sept. 4, 1907, p. 1.
138 During the intense questioning: *BER*, Sept. 4, 1907, p. 1.
139 He had not slept: Interview, Edward Gallagher.
139 he brought Mitchell to admit: *BER* and *BG*, loc. cit.
139 Sughrue produced two: *BER*, loc. cit.
140 "moistening his lips . . .": *BER*, Sept. 5, 1907, p. 3.
141 "Mitchell's loyalty . . .": Interview, Edward Gallagher.
141 "Hardly had the mayor . . .": *BJ*, Sept. 6, 1907, p. 1.
141 "lamentable picture of . . .": *BP*, Nov. 16, 1908, pp. 1 and 9.
141 On Mitchell's resignation see *PP*, Sept. 14, 1907, p. 559.
142 "There is absolutely . . .": *BP*, Sept. 7, 1907, p. 2.
142 Fitzgerald told a friend: Interview, Eddie Gallagher.
142 "right after the hearings . . .": Interview, Rose Kennedy.
143 "Your talk with me settled . . .": JFF to Cardinal O'Connell, Oct. 20, 1930, BAA.
143 On Cardinal O'Connell see Dorothy Wayman, *Cardinal O'Connell of Boston* (1955).
143 The disgraceful hearings: *PP*, Aug. 15, 1908, p. 450.
144 "My greatest regret . . .": Interview, Rose Kennedy.
145 For information on the Sacred Heart schools see Louise Callan, *The Society of the Sacred Heart in North America* (1937); Janet E. Stuart, *The Education of Catholic Girls* (1912).
145 the society had a definite plan: *Plan of Studies of the Boarding Schools of the Sacred Heart* (1931). The original plan was solidified in 1852, revised in 1927.
145 "the same blue and green . . .": Mary McCarthy, *Memories of a Catholic Girlhood*, p. 102.
146 "unusually concerned . . .": Rose Kennedy, p. 32.
146 "Linking the highest natural . . .": Janet Stuart, pp. 82–85.
146 "if fortune deals . . .": *Plan of Studies* . . .
146 "My studies did not dovetail . . .": Interview, Rose Kennedy.
146 "an anchorage in faith . . .": *Plan of Studies* . . .
147 "the world in which . . .": Interview, Rose Kennedy.
147 George Koch, the longtime clerk: *BJ*, Dec. 6, 1907, p. 6; *BER*, Dec. 5, 1907, p. 1.
147 his plan misfired: Unidentified clipping, Oct. 8, 1907, Herald Morgue Files, College of Communications, School of Journalism, Boston University.
147 "much worried over . . .": Ibid.
148 J. Wells Farley . . . to City Hospital: *BP*, Dec. 6, 1907, p. 11.
148 The story Koch told: *BJ*, Dec. 5, 1907, pp. 1–2; *BP*, Dec. 5, 1907, pp. 1, 11; *BER*, Dec. 5, 1907, p. 1.
148 "a perfected development . . .": Final Report, Boston Finance Commission, 1909, p. 34.
148 For Koch's "deathbed" testimony: *BJ*, Dec. 5, 1907, pp. 1–2, and Dec. 6, 1907, p. 6.

149 "In spite of the desperate . . .": As told to John B. Kennedy, labor representative of the commission, quoted in Fitzgerald campaign ad, Jan. 2, 1910, JFF.
149 "In view of the record of Mr. Koch . . .": BP, Dec. 6, 1907, p. 11.
150 "clean up the mess": John Henry Cutler, p. 118.
150 John A. Coulthurst: Ibid., pp. 117–19.
150 Election results: BH, Dec. 13, 1907, p. 1.
150 "We held a conference . . .": John Henry Cutler, p. 119.
151 to appear before a grand jury: BER, Dec. 23, 1907, pp. 1, 3.
151 "women, insane persons . . .": BP, July 18, 1909, p. 23.
151 "As nearly as can be learned . . .": BJ, Dec. 27, 1907, p. 1.
152 Fitzgerald was "smiling": Ibid.
152 "It was quite a new . . .": BH, Dec. 27, 1907, p. 12.
152 Fitzgerald also said: BER, June 29, 1909, p. 1.
153 "I say that as true . . .": BER, June 28, 1909, p. 1.
153 "Democratic politicians . . .": John Henry Cutler, p. 112.
153 "the biggest sensation . . .": BG (eve.), Jan. 6, 1908, p. 1.
153 "a grim face . . .": BP, Sun., Sept. 2, 1906, p. 26.
153 "most remarkable political . . .": Vera Goldwaite, "Our District Attorney," New England Magazine, July 1906, pp. 450–57.
154 "neither horse, dog . . .": BP, loc. cit.
154 "official freedom . . .": Vera Goldwaite, loc. cit., p. 450; see also "John B. Moran and Progressive Democracy in Massachusetts," Arena, Sept. 1906, pp. 300–302.
154 "So large a number . . .": BP, Jan. 7, 1908, p. 1.
154 As the indicted men: BH, Jan. 7, 1908, p. 4; BP, Jan. 7, 1908, p. 1.
154 his sister Catherine: PP, July 30, 1901, p. 1279.
155 Hibbard. . . . inaugural day: BP, loc. cit.; BJ, Jan. 6, 1908, p. 3.
155 in April he was forced: PP, April 11, 1908, p. 195.
155 "In those times . . .": Rose Kennedy, p. 31; see also BP, July 17, 1908, p. 2.
155 a trip to Europe: PP, July 11, 1908, p. 362.
156 a story leaked: PP, July 18, 1908, p. 374.
156 "investigation urged . . .": BP, July 17, 1908, p. 2.
156 Commissioner Sullivan: BP, July 18, 1908, p. 1.
156 As Fitzgerald explained it: BP, Sun., July 19, 1908, pp. 1–2.
156 government salaries: Common Council, Beatrice Webb, p. 83; Mass. Senate, Supplement of the Public Statutes of the Commonwealth of Mass., 1889–1895, p. 532; Congress, Constance Green, p. 17.
156 "glorious send-off party": PP, loc. cit.; BP, July 18, 1908, p. 1.
156 "trips to Europe . . .": Rose Kennedy, "Notes for TTR," RFK.
156 "smiling and defiant": BP, July 18, 1908, p. 1. See also BP, July 19, 1908, p. 2.; PP, July 25, 1908, p. 385.
158 When Fitzgerald first told Rose: Interview, Rose Kennedy.
158 "the fulfillment . . .": Rose Kennedy, p. 30.
158 "as comfortable and as nice . . .": Rose Fitzgerald to Thomas Fitzgerald, July 22, 1908, RFK.
158 "with as much affection . . .": BP, Sun., Aug. 30, 1908, p. 21.
158 Josie, for her part, enjoyed: RF to TF, July 22, 1908, RFK.
158 "the middle of the ocean . . .": Ibid.
158 Fitzgerald had originally: BP, loc. cit., p. 29.
158 From there they took the train: Rose Kennedy, "Notes for TTR," RFK.
159 "I hardly closed my eyes . . .": BP, Sun., Aug. 23, 1908, p. 21.
159 "indescribably lovely": Interview, Rose Kennedy.
159 her journal entry: Rose Kennedy "Notes for TTR," RFK.
159 "impressed with the neatness . . .": Rose Kennedy, p. 30.
159 the . . . district attorney died: BP, Sun., Feb. 7, 1909, p. 8.
160 there was already talk: Pelletier did win the election; see BP, Nov. 3, 1909, p. 1.
160 "one of the mildest . . .": Clement Pollock, "The Man Who Cleaned Up Boston," Harper's Weekly, Aug. 21, 1909, p. 11.
161 "the climax of excitement . . .": Ibid., p. 12.

161 The trial of Michael J. Mitchell: *BP*, June 22, 1909, p. 4.

161 "Gentlemen of the jury . . .": Ibid., p. 12.

161 "He seemed to take . . .": *BJ*, June 22, 1909, p. 12.

161 During an unusual career, Coakley: *BG*, Oct. 27, 1925, p. 32. Impeachment trial, *BG*, June 10, 1941, p. 1; obituary, *NYT*, Sept. 20, 1952, p. 15.

162 "a noticeable coolness . . .": *BJ*, loc. cit.

162 Coakley was planning to sue: *PP*, July 4, 1908, p. 353.

162 The second day of the trial: *BP*, June 23, 1909, p. 4.

162 Michael Cuddihy: *BH*, June 23, 1909, p. 3; *BJ*, June 24, 1909, p. 12.

162 Farley . . . on the stand: *BH*, June 26, 1909, p. 3.

163 "Mr. Farley, I don't know . . .": *BH*, June 29, 1909, p. 3.

163 Koch testified: *BJ*, June 29, 1909, p. 2.

163 Fitzgerald's testimony: *BER*, June 29, 1909, p. 3; *BP*, June 29, 1909, p. 1; *BH*, June 29, 1909, p. 3.

165 city papers were on the stands: *BH*, "Fitzgerald Fails to Remember in Flagstone Case"; *BJ*, "Fitzgerald's Memory Poor as to Deals."

165 "Necks were craned . . .": *BG*, June 30, 1909, p. 1.

165 "somewhat flushed": *BH*, June 30, 1909, p. 1.

166 "The fact remains . . .": *PP*, July 3, 1909, p. 1279.

166 "Hill: Have you thought . . .": *BG* and *BH*, loc. cit.; *BP*, June 30, 1909, p. 2; *BER*, June 29, 1909, p. 1.

166 "this unfortunate lapse . . .": *BP*, loc. cit.

166 "Hill: Did you realize . . .": *BER*, loc. cit.

167 it would seem that Coakley: Interview, Edward Gallagher.

167 "What was the custom . . .": *BH*, loc. cit., p. 9.

168 "Coakley: You are not . . .": Ibid.

168 In his closing statement: *BG*, July 1, 1909, p. 1; *BH*, July 1, 1909, p. 9; *BP*, June 30, 1909, p. 2.

169 the district attorney stood: *BG*, loc. cit.

170 The jury began: *BH*, loc. cit.

170 The fact that an agreement: *BP*, July 1, 1909, p. 1.

170 a tip was circulated: *PP*, July 3, 1909, p. 1279, and July 10, 1909, p. 1292.

171 Mr. Hill descended: *BP*, loc. cit.

171 All that night, Mitchell: Interview, Edward Gallagher.

171 The courtroom was packed: *BER*, July 1, 1909, p. 1.

171 "Mitchell was almost . . .": *BJ*, July 2, 1909, p. 12; *BH*, July 2, 1909, p. 14.

171 When the time for sentencing: *BG*, July 10, 1909, p. 1; *BG* (eve.), July 9, 1909, p. 1; *BH*, July 10, 1909, p. 1; *BP*, July 10, 1909, p. 1; *BJ*, July 10, 1909. p. 1.

172 "The fact that Mitchell . . .": *BH*, loc. cit, p. 2.

172 House of Correction: William Cole, "Boston's Penal Institutions," *New England Magazine*, Jan. 1898, pp. 613–29.

173 "John F. Fitzgerald is the . . .": *BG* and *BJ*, loc. cit.

173 Mitchell had fallen: *BDA*, July 10, 1909, p. 1; *BG*, July 11, 1909, p. 1; *BJ*, July 12, 1909, p. 4.

173 "a long nightmare . . .": Interview, Edward Gallagher.

174 Blumenthal was "an excellent . . .": RF to Mrs. JFF, April 21, 1909, RFK. The entire collection of Blumenthal letters is in Box 1 of a series of documents used in Mrs. Kennedy's memoirs, and portions are quoted in *Times to Remember*, pp. 32–38.

174 "we will be altogether . . .": AF to Mrs. JFF, Jan. 25, 1909. Agnes' letters to her parents were saved all these years in an attic and given to me by her daughter, Mary Jo Clasby.

174 "terribly disappointed": RF to Mrs. JFF, March 7, 1909, RFK.

175 "You can't imagine . . .": AF to Mrs. JFF, July 28, 1909.

175 "sudden feeling . . .": Interview, Rose Kennedy.

175 "I was the one . . .": Rose Kennedy, p. 31; see also Gail Cameron, p. 38.

176 For a description of Blumenthal at the time Rose was there see Mary Colum, *Life and the Dream* (1947), pp. 17–30.

176 For quarters: RF to Mrs. JFF, September 1908, RFK.

176 "so cold that they gave . . .": AF to Mrs. JFF, Nov. 8, 1908.
176 "a purplish bluish color": RF to Mrs. JFF, Jan. 29, 1909, RFK.
176 "nobody thought of complaining . . .": Mary Colum, p. 24.
176 "with penalties . . .": Ibid., p. 23.
176 "It is hard . . .": RF to Mrs. JFF, Oct. 1908, RFK.
176 "the same routine": RF to Mrs. JFF, Nov. 24, 1908, RFK.
177 "Not only the first . . .": Mary Colum, pp. 18–19.
177 The daily schedules and various rules are quoted from *Règlement des pensionnets et plan d'études* (1887).
177 "the loneliness of waking . . .": Interview, Rose Kennedy.
178 "The hardest thing . . .": Ibid.
178 "only here naturally . . .": RF to Mrs. JFF, Feb. 21, 1909, RFK.
178 "Even the time of private . . .": Mary Colum, p. 19.
178 "Without these moments . . .": Janet Stuart, p. 109.
179 "only one game . . .": AF to Mrs. JFF, Nov. 1908.
179 "Rose and I have been . . .": AF to Mrs. JFF, March 7, 1909.
179 "During these promenades . . .": RF to Mrs. JFF, June 21, 1909, RFK.
179 "particular friendships": Mary Colum, p. 21.
179 "throwing themselves . . .": *Règlement* . . .
179 "It gets a little mite . . .": RF to parents, April 21, 1909, RFK.
179 "I tell you frankly . . .": AF to Mrs. JFF, May 6, 1909.
179 For beneath the strict code: Janet Stuart, p. 213.
181 "Today . . . is the Feast . . .": AF to Mrs. JFF, Nov. 1, 1908.
181 "we wear our white . . .": RF to Mrs. JFF, Dec. 6, 1908, RFK.
181 On feast days: AF to Mrs. JFF, April 13, 1909.
181 "The Midnight Mass . . .": RF to Mrs. JFF, attached to Agnes' letter of Dec. 21, 1908.
181 "It was all so new . . .": AF to Mrs. JFF, April 13, 1909.
181 "We had the loveliest . . .": AF to Mrs. JFF, June 14, 1909, RFK.
182 "the gift of faith": Rose Kennedy, p. 482.
182 "While I had always . . .": Interview, Rose Kennedy.
182 "For me, faith . . .": Rose Kennedy, pp. 481–82.
182 "played the part . . .": Ibid., p. 33.
182 "So you see, my piety . . .": Ibid., p. 34.
183 "startled and amused . . .": Interview, Rose Kennedy.
183 Index of Forbidden Books: Redmond A. Burke, *What Is the Index?* (1952); see also Rev. Timothy Hurley, *A Commentary on the Present Index Legislation* (1908).
183 "When we were speaking . . .": RF to Mrs. JFF, Nov. 24, 1908, RFK.
184 We see her in mid-September: Rose Kennedy, p. 32.
184 she entreats them: Ibid., p. 34.
184 "Bryan has tried . . .": RF to Mrs. JFF, Nov. 15, 1908, RFK.
184 "perfectly glorious": RF to parents, Dec. 20, 1908, RFK.
184 "It was truly wonderful . . .": Rose Kennedy, p. 36.
185 ". . . Never mind, Fred": AF to Mrs. JFF, April 5, 1909.
185 "We sang the Dutch . . .": Rose Kennedy, p. 37.
185 "I realized when I came . . .": Interview, Rose Kennedy.
185 preparing for . . . retreat: For a description of the Sacred Heart retreat see Mary Colum, pp. 39–42. (The classic description is found in James Joyce, *A Portrait of the Artist as a Young Man* [1961], pp. 107–46.)
186 "You can imagine me . . .": AF to Mrs. JFF, Jan. 25, 1909.
186 "very beautiful . . .": AF to Mrs. JFF, Feb. 2, 1909.
186 "As I look back now . . .": Interview, Rose Kennedy.
186 "I used to be behind . . .": Gail Cameron, p. 58.
187 "Sometimes, it seemed . . .": Interview, Rose Kennedy.
187 "Rose was named . . .": AF to Mrs. JFF, May 23, 1909.
187 Among her pledges: Gail Cameron, pp. 58–59.
188 "If Papa runs . . .": RF to Mrs. JFF, May 23, 1909, RFK.
188 "I realize more . . .": RF to parents, May 23, 1909, RFK.

188 "You see, one year . . .": RF to parents, May 27, 1909, RFK.
188 she would never be: Interview, Rose Kennedy.
189 "We are certainly . . .": AF to Mrs. JFF, Aug. 5, 1909.
189 "Our mother greeted us . . .": Interview, Rose Kennedy.
191 "Plan Two": "Plan Two—A Hope," *City Affairs*, Oct. 1909, pp. 1–2.
191 "a group of schoolboys . . .": Justin Kaplan, *Lincoln Steffens: A Biography* (1974), p. 173.
191 On James Jackson Storrow see Henry Greenleaf Pearson, *Son of New England: James Jackson Storrow, 1864–1929* (1932).
192 "The growing cost . . .": JFF to Storrow, Nov. 24, 1909, unidentified clipping, JFF.
193 "an Irish boy . . .": Francis Russell, pp. 179–80.
193 "every father . . .": Fitzgerald campaign ad, Jan. 9, 1909, JFF.
193 "Of course . . . the sympathetic . . .": *PP*, Jan. 15, 1910, p. 1883.
193 under the common heading: *BG*, Jan 5, 1910, p. 6.
193 "I would awaken . . .": Interview, Rose Kennedy.
194 "an underground . . .": *BP*, Sun., Dec. 5, 1909, p. 2.
194 "blowing the bellows . . .": Unidentified clipping, Dec. 5, 1909, JFF.
194 "if he wants a certificate . . .": *BP*, Dec. 16, 1909, p. 4; *BG*, Dec. 6, 1909, p. 3.
195 "FITZGERALDISM IS CONSTRUCTIVE . . .": Fitzgerald campaign ad, Jan. 7, 1910, JFF.
195 "he was proud . . .": Unidentified clipping, Dec. 29, 1909, JFF.
195 "Can you conceive . . .": *BG*, Dec. 10, 1909, p. 6.
195 "The great issue . . .": Fitzgerald campaign ad, Jan. 6, 1909, JFF.
195 "as vociferous . . .": Unidentified clipping, Dec. 27, 1909, JFF.
196 "a simple unaffected . . .": *BG*, Jan. 2, 1909, JFF.
196 "It looks as if . . .": Lincoln Steffens, *The Letters of Lincoln Steffens* (1938), Vol. 1, p. 236.
196 "The whole town . . .": George Nutter Diaries, MHS.
196 official results: *BP*, Jan. 12, 1910, p. 1.
196 "It certainly is . . .": George Nutter Diaries, MHS.
196 "All my friends . . .": Justin Kaplan, p. 173.
196 "No man can ask . . .": John Henry Cutler, p. 142.
197 "He lived only a short . . .": Interview, Julia Fitzgerald Hill. Michael Mitchell died of heart failure Dec. 30, 1914: Death Records, Vol. 21, p. 707, Mass. Vital Statistics.
197 the new city charter: Clement Pollack, "The Reconstruction of Boston," *Harper's Weekly*, Dec. 25, 1909, p. 32.
197 Fitzgerald's accomplishments: discussed in *Advance of Boston* (1913), pp. 82–113.
197 "my father could relax . . .": Rose Kennedy, p. 48.
197 to "dedications . . .": Ibid., p. 56.
198 "He loved to travel . . .": Ibid.
198 "a time to laugh . . .": Ibid., p. 48.
198 "the inferior position . . .": *BP*, Aug. 17, 1911, p. 1.
198 "For reasons not only . . .": Rose Kennedy, p. 55.
199 It was, in Rose's words: Ibid., p. 56.
199 "I did not know . . .": *BP*, Sun., May 25, 1913, p. 32.
200 A lump rose in her throat: Interview, Rose Kennedy.
201 "Father says": Gail Cameron, p. 40.
201 "that control of her emotions . . .": Ibid., p. 61.
201 For a description of her spectacular debut and the preparations see *BP*, Jan. 2, 1911, pp. 1–2, and Jan. 3, 1911, p. 1; *BG*, Jan. 3, 1911, p. 1; see also Gail Cameron, p. 67.
202 "there were two societies . . .": Rose Kennedy, p. 50.
203 "As the leader . . .": Rose Kennedy, "Notes for TTR," RFK.
203 "The comment that I . . .": Ibid.
203 "one of those elementary . . .": Rose Kennedy, p. 53.
203 "it helped prevent . . .": Ibid., p. 54.
203 "On the one or two . . .": Rose Kennedy, "Notes for TTR," RFK.
203 "They had their Junior League . . .": Rose Kennedy, p. 53.
203 "*the* club for Catholic . . .": Interview, Debbie Green Muse.
204 "It was considered . . .": Rose Kennedy, "Notes for TTR," RFK.

204 "It has been my privilege . . .": *BG*, Sun., Sept. 24, 1911, p. 9.
205 Fitzgerald had warned: Interview, Rose Kennedy.
205 several prominent Irish: *BH*, Oct. 18, 1911, p. 2.
205 sending in his place: *BH*, Oct. 17, 1911, p. 12.
205 "I considered myself . . .": Interview, Rose Kennedy.
205 The details of Rose's reaction: Interview, Rose Kennedy.
206 "it had been just . . .": Rose Kennedy, "Notes for TTR," RFK.
206 Description of the audience reaction: *BP*, Dec. 17, 1911, pp. 1, 5, 7.
206 "If they start throwing . . .": Ibid., p. 5.
206 Rose confessed: Interview, Rose Kennedy.
208 Harvard College in the four years: Owen Johnson, "The Social Usurpation of Our Colleges," *Collier's*, May 15, 1912, p. 11.
209 more than 60 percent had graduated: Reports of the President and the Treasurer of Harvard College, 1907–1908, Appendix, pp. 329–44; see also Samuel Eliot Morison, *Three Centuries at Harvard, 1636–1936* (1936), p. 420; John Hays Gardiner, *Harvard* (1914), pp. 130–32.
209 the tone of college life: Charles Flandrau, *Harvard Episodes* (1897), p. 23.
209 "highly unattractive": Samuel Eliot Morison, loc. cit., p. 419.
209 The sons of the well-to-do: Walter Lippmann, "A Policy of Segregation," *Harvard Monthly*, 1916–17, pp. 153–54.
210 "At Dunster . . .": *Collier's*, May 15, 1912, p. 13.
210 Joe would long remember: Interview, Rose Kennedy.
210 the activities of the most prominent: *BA*, Sun., Oct. 15, 1911, p. 7E.
211 "I went up to Harvard . . .": John Reed, "Almost Thirty," *New Republic*, April 29, 1939, p. 332.
211 "Those who come to Harvard . . .": Owen Johnson, loc. cit., pp. 12, 14–15.
211 Tom Campbell: Edward M. Kennedy (ed.), *The Fruitful Bough: A Tribute to Joseph P. Kennedy* (1965), p. 18.
211 Bob Fisher: *Harvard Class of 1912: 6th Report* (1937), p. 237, HU Archives. See also *BG*, June 14, 1919, Herald Morgue Files; obituary, *BG*, July 7, 1942, p. 26.
211 start of triple friendship: Edward M. Kennedy (ed.), p. 18; Harvard University Directories, 1908–1912.
212 Robert Sturgis Potter: *Harvard Class of 1912: 6th Report* (1937), p. 600, HU Archives; obituary, *NYT*, April 13, 1947, p. 61.
212 "tremendous charm": quoted in Edward M. Kennedy (ed.), p. 18.
212 in a ritual excursion: Interview, Helen Barron.
212 Winthrop: William Clark, *History of Winthrop, 1630–1952* (1952), pp. 3, 181–86.
212 "the climax of the week": Margaret Burke in Edward M. Kennedy (ed.), p. 9.
213 whenever committees: *HC*, Feb. 20, 1909, p. 4; Harvard Class Album, 1912, pp. 101, 132. Campbell was class president 1910–11; Fisher was on the Student Council and class president 1909–10.
213 a badge of honor: Samuel Eliot Morison, loc. cit., p. 432.
213 Indeed, up until 1904: ibid., p. 277; Cleveland Amory, *The Proper Bostonians*, pp. 297–98.
213 The Institute conferred its membership: Samuel Eliot Morison, loc. cit., p. 423; see also "Constitution of the Hasty Pudding Club," Article VI, HU.
213 "It's a curious thing . . .": Interview, Rose Kennedy.
214 Those who made the Porcellian: Cleveland Amory, *The Proper Bostonians*, pp. 300–301; *Harvard University Handbook: An Official Guide* (1936), pp. 173–76.
214 On A. Lawrence Lowell's administration see Samuel Eliot Morison, loc. cit., pp. 439–81; inauguration, *BH*, Oct. 7, 1907, pp. 1, 2.
214 a progressive movement: "Report to the Board of Overseers for 1910–1911," General History File (1912), HU Archives.
215 Story of Joe's reaction: Interview, Rose Kennedy.
215 the Porcellian did not stand: *Harvard University Handbook* (1936), p. 175; Jack Frost, *Harvard and Cambridge: A Sketch Book* (1940), p. 35.
216 accepted less than 12 percent: *Harvard Class of 1912: 1st Report* (1913), HU Archives.
216 Lippmann was stunned: Ronald Steel, *Walter Lippmann and the American Century*

(1980), p. 14; see also Richard O'Connor, *Heywood Broun: A Biography* (1975), pp. 19–20.

217 "In college Albert . . .": Walter Lippmann, "Albert the Male," *New Republic*, July 22, 1916, p. 301.

217 "belated revenge": Ronald Steel, p. 30.

217 "the biggest disappointment": James M. Burns, *Roosevelt: The Lion and the Fox* (1956), p. 18.

218 "more and more in love" and description of courtship: Interview, Rose Kennedy.

218 For descriptions of Harvard Yard see Edwin M. Bacon, *Historic Pilgrimages in New England* (1898), p. 438; Rollo W. Brown, *Harvard Yard in the Golden Age* (1948), pp. 13–19.

218 "a worn and broken . . .": Edwin M. Bacon, p. 434.

219 Others have suggested: Rose Kennedy quotes Mary O'Connell in "Notes for TTR," RFK.

219 On Harry Nawn: "Harry Nawn," *New England Magazine*, Sept. 1910, p. 110.

219 Late at night, Fitzgerald: Interview, Rose Kennedy.

220 "There were no scenes . . .": Rose Kennedy, p. 64.

220 Rose would often agree: Gail Cameron, p. 68; Rose Kennedy, pp. 57, 66.

220 "I adored Joe": Rose Kennedy, p. 64.

221 she had romantic: Ibid., pp. 16–17.

221 "a bold and elegantly . . .": Ibid., p. 66.

221 he arranged for Rose: Interview, Rose Kennedy.

222 a classy white broadcloth: *BP*, Feb. 17, 1911, p. 16.

222 "a sinking feeling": Interview, Rose Kennedy.

222 As one of the fourteen: Harvard Class Album, 1912, p. 103.

222 "Oh, no, Daddy . . .": Interview, Rose Kennedy.

222 "Never dreaming of arguing . . .": Rose Kennedy, p. 61.

223 private meeting with President Taft: *BP*, loc. cit.

223 Description of typical day: *BP*, Feb. 23, 1911, p. 2.

224 Description of baseball game: Richard J. Whalen, *The Founding Father* (1964), p. 27; Bill Duncliffe, "Harvard 'Slights' Made Him Better," *BRA*, Jan. 10, 1964, p. 5.

224 only those players who played: John Gardiner, p. 136; *HC*, May 17, 1909, p. 5.

224 he was hurt once again: *HC*, Feb. 26, 1910, p. 6, March 16, 1910, p. 6, April 2, 1910, p. 1, and June 22, 1911, p. 8.

224 team captain was given: *HC*, Sept. 26, 1911, p. 1.

224 Yale tied the score: *BG*, June 24, 1911, p. 7.

225 throw to Kennedy at first: *BH*, June 24, 1911, p. 2; see also John A. Blanchard (ed.), *The Handbook of Harvard, 1851–1922* (1923), pp. 234, 236.

225 the game-winning ball: *BRA*, Jan. 10, 1964, p. 45; JPK awarded H, *HC*, Sept. 26, 1911, p. 9.

225 as a startling illustration: Richard J. Whalen, p. 27.

225 Others have suggested a more elaborate: David E. Koskoff, *Joseph P. Kennedy* (1974), p. 17.

226 for a description of P.J.'s temperament and for other background material on P.J. see Kathleen McCarthy, "The First Senator Kennedy," unpublished manuscript.

226 For a description of the Maverick House see Charles S. Damrell, *A Half Century of Boston's Buildings* (1895), p. 491.

227 "She was an amazingly . . .": Interview, Mary Lou McCarthy.

227 when his younger brother Francis: Death Records, Vol. 429, p. 227, Mass. Vital Statistics.

227 "The death of the baby . . .": Interview, Mary Lou McCarthy.

228 Constituting close to 40 percent: Herbert Zolot, p. 311.

228 "I never felt . . .": Interview, Clem Norton.

228 Every hour of every day: Interviews, Kerry and Mary Lou McCarthy; see also Bill Duncliffe, "Irish Surge as Pat Pulls Strings," *BRA*, Jan. 7, 1964, p. 5.

229 "everyone who ran for any political . . .": Interview, George Pumphret.

229 Years later, P.J.'s daughter: Interview, Mary Lou McCarthy.

229 "I remember looking into the eyes . . .": Interview, Edward Gallagher.

229 One day when the youngster: Fred Perkins and Anthony Merrill, "Family Ties Guide Kennedy Thought," *BEA* Dec. 17, 1937, p. 7.

230 "an open handed Santa Claus": Quoted in Bill Duncliffe, "Secret Charities Prove 'Hard Man' Soft Inside," *BRA*, Jan. 18, 1964, p. 25.

230 "Toward his close friends . . .": Interview, George Pumphret.

230 "It doesn't make . . .": *BA*, Sun., Jan. 25, 1914, RFK.

230 His decision to run: *PP*, Oct. 31, 1908, p. 752.

231 P.J.'s defeat: *BH*, Nov. 20, 1908, p. 3.

231 "There was no reason . . .": *PP*, Nov. 21, 1908, p. 798.

231 "The Democrats made the poorer . . .": *BET*, Nov. 20, 1908, p. 20.

231 Either Fitzgerald: *PP*, loc. cit; *BDA*, Nov. 19, 1908, p. 8; *BG*, Nov. 20, 1908, p. 1.

231 "No doubt you take it . . .": Sullivan letter in the possession of Mary Lou McCarthy.

231 thanked "most heartily": *BP*, Nov. 20, 1908, p. 6.

231 while his father succeeded: Interview, Edward Gallagher.

232 "After seeing the thanks . . .": Interview, George Pumphret.

232 "Joe Kennedy saw early . . .": Tom Corcoran as quoted in Richard J. Whalen, p. 34.

232 "with all the knowledge . . .": Theodore Dreiser, *The Financier* (1967), p. 11.

232 As a child Joe sold candies: Edward M. Kennedy (ed.), p. 16; Bill Duncliffe, "Joe Always 1st Around Corner," *BRA*, Jan. 8, 1964, p. 25.

232 operation of a sightseeing motorbus: Edward M. Kennedy (ed.), p. 16; *BRA*, loc. cit.

232 "let them have it": John B. Kennedy, "Joe Kennedy Never Liked Any Job He Tackled," *American Magazine*, May 1928, p. 146.

233 the South Station stand: Referred to later in Joe Donovan to JPK, Oct. 17, 1920, JPK.

233 profit of $10,000: Richard J. Whalen, p. 30.

234 troubles he had with an accounting course: Ibid.

235 "I saw, even in my limited . . .": John B. Kennedy, "Joe Kennedy . . . ," loc. cit., p. 146.

235 the age of the banker: Harold Faulkner, *American Economic History* (1960), p. 446; Arthur Link, *American Epoch* (1980), p. 47; Gabriel Kolko in Kurt H. Wolff and Barrington Moore, Jr., *The Critical Spirit: Essays in Honor of Herbert Marcuse* (1967), pp. 351–52.

235 "These bankers bestride as masters . . .": Louis D. Brandeis, *Other People's Money and How the Bankers Use It* (1914), p. 3.

235 John Pierpont Morgan: John Winkler, *Morgan the Magnificent* (1930), p. 7.

235 his summers . . . on the Hudson . . . : Cass Canfield, *The Incredible Pierpont Morgan* (1974), p. 101.

236 the Pujo Committee: Edwin Hoyt, *The House of Morgan* (1968), p. 313.

236 "tumbling cascade of facts . . .": John Winkler, p. 298.

236 clearly the most favored place: Oscar Handlin, *Boston's Immigrants*, p. 67.

236 a list of the directors: *Boston City Directory*, 1912, where directors are listed in ads for various banks; see also Isaac Marcosson, "The Millionaire Yield of Boston," *Munsey's Magazine*, Aug. 1912.

236 over 90 percent: Louis D. Brandeis, p. 26.

236 "ties of blood and sentiment . . .": Kolko essay in Kurt Wolff and Barrington Moore, Jr., p. 349.

237 "an occupation where . . .": Joe McCarthy, *The Remarkable Kennedys* (1960), p. 33.

237 Columbia Trust, which had opened: "Massachusetts Bank Commissioners Annual Report," *Mass. Public Documents*, 1895, No. 8, Part 2, p. xvi.

237 "Its birth was humble . . .": *East Boston Leader*, May 30, 1945, p. 4.

237 assets totaling nearly $700,000: *Mass. Public Documents*, 1912, No. 8, p. 417.

237 Wellington had started as a clerk: *East Boston Leader*, loc. cit.

238 years later he would still speak: Interview, Rose Kennedy.

238 a man like . . . Giannini: Marquis and Jesse James, *Biography of a Bank* (1954).

238 "first love": *East Boston Leader*, loc. cit.

238 Wellington to wait patiently: Wellington became president in 1929 following the death of P. J. Kennedy and retained the position until the bank was sold in 1945; obituaries, *East Boston Leader*, April 28, 1950, p. 5, and *BH*, April 22, 1950, p. 9.

238 "made their jobs routine . . .": *BEA*, Jan. 24, 1914, RFK.

239 Wellington suggested that Joe: Corrections by JPK of draft of 1937 *Fortune* article by a man named Looker (hereafter cited "Looker Draft"), JPK.

239 his name upon the official list: *List of Officials and Employees of the Commonwealth,* 1912–1913, p. 22.

239 "It was easy. I got him a job . . .": Interview, George Pumphret.

240 "John Fitzgerald may think . . .": "Looker Draft," JPK.

240 The bank commissioner's department: Report to the Governor of the Commonwealth, to Executive Council, and to Joint Committee of the Ways and Means of the General Court Concerning the Bank Commissioner's Department, Report No. 2, April 5, 1911, p. 1.

240 work load was staggering: *Mass. Public Documents,* 1912, No. 8, p. iii.

240 the public clamored noisily: Report to the Governor . . . , loc. cit.

240 "Inspection work took me . . .": *American Magazine,* May 1928, p. 146.

240 the most critical part of the examination: *An Outline of an Examination of a Bank* (1930), p. 1.

240 he knew the financial structure: Joseph F. Dinneen, *The Kennedy Family* (1959), p. 15.

240 "That bank examiner's job . . .": Quoted in Bill Duncliffe, "Headed Bank, Married Rose at 25," *BRA,* Jan. 11, 1964, p. 25.

241 "he learned far more . . .": Ibid.; see also Rose Kennedy, p. 67.

241 "There are no big shots": Morton Downey in Edward M. Kennedy (ed.), p. 34.

242 Fitzgerald appeared more popular: *BP,* Nov. 28, 1913, p. 11; *PP,* Dec. 20, 1913, p. 5959.

242 Much had been accomplished: *PP,* Jan. 24, 1914, p. 6034: *BH,* Nov. 29, 1914, p. 3; *BP,* Sun., Nov. 30, 1913, p. 10.

243 "And why should not the parks . . .": *Advance of Boston,* p. 33.

243 "Sometimes such things . . .": Ibid., p. 69.

243 Fitzgerald had been saying: Unidentified clipping, Nov. 10, 1913, JFF.

243 Curley began planning his own: James Michael Curley, *I'd Do It Again* (1957), pp. 110–11.

243 for taking the civil-service exam: Herbert Zolot, pp. 171–73.

244 he defiantly announced for mayor: Unidentified clipping, Nov. 10, 1913, JFF; *BH,* Nov. 10, 1913, p. 1, JFF.

244 much of the success of Fitzgerald's term: Herbert Zolot, pp. 315–16.

244 Curley's experience with the boss: James M. Curley, p. 113.

244 "I can't remember a time . . .": *Boston Advertiser,* Sun., Sept. 30, 1934, p. 1.

244 the frightened bosses put great: Unidentified clipping, Nov. 10, 1913, JFF; *BP,* Nov. 29, 1913, p. 14.

244 So the word spread: *BET,* Nov. 13, 1913, p. 2.

244 unanimous resolutions were adopted: *BH,* Nov. 27, 1913, p. 1.

245 colorful Fitzgerald badges: *BP,* Nov. 30, 1913, p. 10.

245 "a remarkable condition . . .": *BP,* Nov. 28, 1913, p. 11.

245 Curley was too much a realist: *BET,* Nov. 8, 1913, p. 2.

245 "Boston has done much . . .": *BP,* Sun., Nov. 30, 1913, p. 10.

245 Curley was more determined: *BP,* Nov. 29, 1913, p. 1.

245 "The stories that have come . . .": *BET,* Nov. 28, 1913, p. 16.

245 "For one hundred or more . . .": *BP,* Dec. 1, 1913, p. 1.

245 At this point, only death: *PP,* Nov. 15, 1913, p. 5884.

245 the most vicious: *BH,* Nov. 29, 1913, p. 1.

246 "had gnawed at Coakley": Interviews, Clem Norton and Tom Cabot.

246 she had come to ask Coakley: *BJ,* Jan. 4, 1915, p. 1.

246 According to her story: *BA,* Sun., Feb. 11, 1915, Sect. 2, p. 1.

247 "the event of her life": *BA,* Jan. 7, 1915, p. 1.

247 owner of a shellac business: *BA,* Jan. 20, 1915, p. 4.

247 all the witnesses agreed: *BA,* Feb. 8, 1915, p. 1.

247 whose job it was to lure: *BA,* Jan. 26, 1915, pp. 1, 4.

247 intensified for Coakley when Toodles listed: Interviews, Clem Norton and Tom Cabot.

247 All this would be made clear: *BG,* Sept. 30, 1921, p. 1; *BG* (eve.), July 3, 1922, p. 1.

248 there was no evidence . . . beyond his kisses: Mullen's report on JFF kissing Toodles, *BA*, Jan. 19, 1913, p. 1; deadlocked jury, *BA*, Feb. 19, 1915, p. 1.

248 Master of the unorthodox: *BA*, Nov. 13, 1913, p. 1.

248 Curley had a black-bordered letter: Interview, Clem Norton.

249 it was the worst moment: Ibid.

249 From the first, she had been strongly: Unidentified clippings, Nov. 8, 10 and 11, 1913, JFF.

249 walking in a nightmare: Eddie Moore as repeated to Edward Gallagher, Interview, Edward Gallagher.

249 devastating fire was raging: *BP*, Dec. 3, 1913, p. 1.

249 Fitzgerald was "visibly shocked": *BP*, Dec. 4, 1913, p. 1.

250 "scores of unfortunate men . . .": Ibid., p. 9.

250 By nightfall, reporters observed: *BP*, Dec. 5, 1913, pp. 1, 11.

250 "Mayor Fitzgerald collapsed . . .": *BH*, Dec. 5, 1913, p. 1.

250 "For several minutes . . .": *PP*, Dec. 6, 1913, p. 5937.

251 "on account of the Mayor's failing . . .": *BP*, Dec. 8, 1913, p. 1.

251 According to his own account: James M. Curley, pp. 114–15; Herbert Zolot, pp. 321–22.

251 Prepared with the help of: *BP*, Dec. 7, 1913, p. A.

251 on December 18, reluctantly: *BP*, Dec. 18, 1913, p. 1.

252 "as certain as anything . . .": Ibid., p. 11.

252 "Boston is deprived . . .": *BH*, Dec. 18, 1913, p. 5.

252 "petticoat element": *BA*, Dec. 18, 1913, p. 6.

252 launch his next campaign: Joe McCarthy, p. 40; see also *BH*, Nov. 8, 1916, p. 1.

253 Rose was profoundly disturbed: Interview, Mary Heffernan.

253 "Though she still did not conceive . . .": Ibid.

253 Under the caption "The Mayor's . . .": Unidentified clipping, Dec. 29, 1913, JFF.

253 "a start on his life work": *American Magazine*, May 1928, p. 146.

254 "a good price" and "most of them": Interview, Rose Kennedy.

254 turning first to his Hickey: Interviews, Kerry and Mary Lou McCarthy; see also *BRA*, Jan. 11, 1964, p. 25.

254 he did manage . . . to collect: "Looker Draft," JPK.

254 largest block of stock . . . Sullivan: The administrator's inventory of the estate of John Sullivan lists 308 shares of stock worth $30,800; Suffolk County Probate Records, No. 110997. On JPK's purchase of the stock see *BDA*, Jan. 22, 1914, p. 2. Price per share in *BNB*, Jan. 21, 1914, p. 5. As to the dispute between P.J. and the Sullivans, it is doubtful: Interviews, Kerry and Mary Lou McCarthy.

254 he turned to . . . Thayer: Richard J. Whalen, p. 38. JPK later mentions his thanks for help: JPK to E. Thayer, Feb. 4, 1921, JPK.

254 Biographical information on Thayer is in the files of the New England Merchants Bank.

254 On Merchants National Bank building: Edwin M. Bacon, *The Book of Boston* (1916), p. 217; interior details described in *Banker and Tradesman*, March 28, 1914, pp. 637–38, and *U.S. Investor*, March 28, 1914, p. 517, both from the files of the New England Merchants Bank.

255 Description of JPK meeting with Thayer: Interview, Rose Kennedy.

255 On Monday morning: Unidentified clipping, Jan. 24, 1914, RFK.

255 Kennedy was elected to the presidency: *BA*, Jan. 21, 1914, p. 2; *BDA*, Jan. 21, 1914, p. 2.; *BET*, Jan. 21, 1914, p. 19.

255 Wellington to the double role: *BH*, Jan. 21, 1914, p. 2.

255 "the youngest man to hold . . .": Unidentified clipping, Jan. 24, 1914, RFK.

256 "the story contained . . .": Tom Campbell in Edward M. Kennedy (ed.), p. 20.

257 There is not the slightest . . . evidence: Interview, Mary Lou McCarthy.

257 "the deep satisfaction": Interview, Rose Kennedy.

257 reputation as a people's bank: *East Boston Leader*, March 30, 1945, p. 4.

257 down-to-earth style: Unidentified clipping, Jan. 14, 1924, p. 14, and *BRA*, Jan. 11, 1914, p. 25, RFK.

258 "Some immediate steps . . .": JPK to Patrick J. Kennedy, Feb. 16, 1922, JPK.

258 deposits increased: Report of the Examining Commissioners on the Condition of Columbia Trust, Dec. 21, 1918, JPK.
258 "the Honorable John F. . . .": *BH*, Sun., June 21, 1914, RFK.
259 "I hope the next best man . . .": Eleanor King to RF, June 23, 1914, RFK.
259 "You are the first . . .": Cecile Murray to RF, undated, RFK.
259 "In those days . . .": Rose Kennedy, p. 68.
259 Catholic ceremony . . . Cardinal O'Connell: *BP*, Oct. 8, 1914, p. 11; *The Republic*, Oct. 10, 1914, p. 8. Chapel description, *BH*, Oct. 25, 1908, p. 5.
259 excited "much interest . . .": Unidentified clipping, undated, RFK.
259 "a public fiesta": Rose Kennedy, p. 71.
260 For a description of Greenbrier see William MacCorkle, *The White Sulphur Springs* (1916), pp. 346–53.
260 hardly an hour apart: Interview, Rose Kennedy.
260 a modest gray house: 83 Beals Street was designated a National Historic Site in May 1969, unidentified clipping in the files of the Brookline Public Library.
260 "From the very beginning . . .": Interview, Rose Kennedy.
261 Joe rented an airy gray house: Hank Searls, *The Lost Prince* (1969), p. 28.
261 For descriptions of Nantasket see William Bergen, *Old Nantasket* (1969).
261 "the fresh sheets, towels . . .": Rose Kennedy, p. 80.
261 "A boy," they said: *BP*, July 26, 1915, p. 12.
261 "It's Grandpa Now": Ibid.
262 "the best grandfather . . .": Interview, Mary Jo Gargan Clasby.
263 "the warmest and most . . .": Interview, Ann Gargan King.
263 "the best pal . . .": Interview, Mary Jo Gargan Clasby.
263 "greatest storyteller . . .": Edward Kennedy quoted in Rose Kennedy, p. 359.
263 "With Grandpa, everything . . .": Interview, Mary Jo Gargan Clasby.
263 leaving reporters to speculate: Unidentified clipping, undated, RFK.
267 When the first dispatches: Mark Sullivan, *Our Times: The United States, 1900–1925* (1932), Vol. 4, pp. 1–2.
267 "We assumed it would all . . .": Interview, Rose Kennedy.
268 "what Englishmen said . . .": D. F. Fleming, *The Origins and Legacies of World War I* (1968), p. 223.
268 "Through all the early years . . .": Interview, Rose Kennedy.
268 quite a few Irish Americans: Lawrence McCaffery, *The Irish Diaspora in America* (1976), p. 135.
269 Description of conversation between Joe and friends: Interview, Rose Kennedy.
269 Campbell had spent: *Harvard Class of 1912: 6th Report* (1937), p. 110, HU Archives.
269 Fisher too had received some: Ibid., p. 237.
269 Potter . . . stood the farthest: Ibid., p. 600.
270 the most extensive military: *BP*, July 3, 1917, p. 1.
270 glowing expectations: *BP*, June 29, 1916, p. 22.
270 "the last word in scientific warfare": *NYT*, June 30, 1916, p. 1.
270 immense and "sophisticated": *NYT*, July 2, 1916, pp. 1, 2.
270 "an extraordinary enthusiasm . . .": John Keegan, *The Face of Battle* (1976), p. 216.
270 "emptiness" and "silence": Reginald Pound, *The Lost Generation* (1963), p. 55.
270 "greatest of all adventures . . .": Robert Wohl, *The Generation of 1914* (1979), p. 92.
270 "It was a time of intense . . .": John Keegan, p. 217; see also John Buchan, *The Battle of the Somme* (1917), pp. 14–17, 24–26.
271 "the boys had a wonderful time . . .": Interview, Rose Kennedy.
271 announcing that at 7:30: *BG* (eve.), July 1, 1916, p. 1, "Allies Great Gain, Drove Germans Back 5–6 Miles."
271 "great waves of men": *NYT*, July 2, 1916, p. 1.
271 "cheering through the machine gun . . .": *NYT*, July 4, 1916, p. 1.
271 "with a spirit of self sacrifice . . .": *NYT*, July 7, 1916, pp. 1, 2.
271 "they went across toppingly": *NYT*, July 4, 1916, p. 6.
271 "with a whoop on their lips": *BP*, July 3, 1916, p. 4.
271 "There was a thrill . . .": *NYT*, July 3, 1916, pp. 1, 2.

272 "if they could achieve . . .": *BP*, July 2, 1916, p. 5.

272 "He merely shook his head . . .": Interview, Rose Kennedy.

272 "the single worst day . . .": James Stokesbury, *A Short History of World War I* (1981), p. 148; see also Martin Middlebrook, *The First Day of the Somme* (1972), p. 225.

272 "We can see now . . .": John Keegan, p. 236.

273 "practically annihilated . . .": Ibid., p. 244.

273 "volunteers who had willingly . . .": Martin Middlebrook, pp. 6–7.

273 Out of the 110,000 British: Paul Fussell, *The Great War and Modern Memory* (1975), p. 13.

273 total of 412,000: Charles Tansill, *America Goes to War* (1938), p. 587; see also Reginald Pound, p. 273, who puts the figure at less than 400,000.

273 more than two million men had already died: Reginald Pound, pp. 77–78; see also *Current History*, "The European War," April 1917–Sept. 1917, pp. 427–29.

274 "a vast transformation . . .": *Current History*, Oct. 1917–March 1918, pp. 9–13.

274 "only the draft system . . .": Florence Kelly, *What America Did* (1919), p. 3.

274 "It is needless to say . . .": *BP*, May 29, 1917, p. 6.

274 "certainly a bright one": Ibid.

274 Kennedy was "elected a trustee . . .": Unidentified clipping, May 30, 1917, Herald Morgue Files; *BP*, May 29, 1917, p. 1.

274 "The company's president admitted . . .": Joe McCarthy, p. 34.

275 sitting with him: Mass. General Electric, 17th Report (1916).

275 "wasted effort and wasted lives": Interview, Rose Kennedy.

275 "believed he was right . . .": Ibid.

275 For the activities of Harvard men in the war, see Frederick Mead (ed.), *Harvard Military Record in the World War* (1921).

276 "a sameness to his life . . .": Interview, Rose Kennedy.

276 from corset factories: Florence Kelly, pp. 34–36.

276 "a desire for action": Interview, Rose Kennedy.

276 "there was nothing . . .": Ibid.

276 "the itch to be in the great . . .": Randolph Bourne, *War and the Intellectuals: Essays, 1915–1919* (1964), p. 10.

276 "in the elemental blare of . . .": Ibid., p. 11.

277 The most direct reply: *FRL*, May 1918.

277 "We are in a crisis . . .": Mark Sullivan quoted, ibid.

277 Guy Currier . . . Young's Hotel: JPK to District Board 5, Feb. 18, 1918, JPK.

277 absolutely no knowledge . . .": Ibid.

277 "who combined the qualities . . .": J. Powell to District Board, Feb. 17, 1918, JPK.

278 "was doing something worthwhile . . .": JPK to District Board, Feb. 18, 1918, JPK.

278 "an investment instead of a waste": "Mobilizing the Shipyards," *The Nation*, April 12, 1917, p. 423.

278 Description and pictures of the main building and Fore River history: *FRL*, January 1919, p. 20.

278 Joe's duties were later outlined in a letter from John J. Ford to JPK, May 15, 1937, JPK.

279 Kennedy later acknowledged: Interview, Rose Kennedy.

279 construction of a second shipyard: *FRL*, January 1919, pp. 22–23.

279 construction of the restaurant: *FRL*, October 1918, p. 11, and January 1919, p. 38.

279 "was equivalent to building . . .": John J. Ford to JPK, loc. cit.

279 "The contractors began work . . .": *FRL*, January 1919, p. 38.

279 "It was substantial proof . . .": *FRL*, May 1918.

279 revising its draft regulations: 2nd Annual Report of the Provost Marshal to the Secretary of War (1921), p. 41.

280 required within seven days: *Brookline Townsman*, Nov. 19, 1917, p. 1; *Winthrop Sun*, Nov. 17, 1917, p. 1.

280 Breakdown of classes: *CR*, 65th, 2nd, June 25, 1918, pp. 8249–8350; *BET*, Jan. 3, 1918, p. 1.

280 "engaged in building . . .": 2nd Annual Report of the Provost Marshal . . . , p. 63.

280 he begged the district: JPK to District Board, Feb. 18, 1918, JPK.

281 "To draft him . . .": J. Powell to District Board, Feb. 17, 1918, JPK.
281 "There are not over six men . . .": Telegram, J. Powell to Meyer Bloomfield, Feb. 25, 1918, JPK. Meyer Bloomfield was head of the Industrial Service Department of the Emergency Fleet Corporation, NYT, March 15, 1938, p. 23.
281 disturbed by the growing: Interview, Rose Kennedy.
282 "I have been up to Devens . . .": JPK to J. Sheehan, April 9, 1918, JPK.
282 "I have written you two . . .": JPK to R. Potter, Jan. 9, 1918, JPK.
282 "Well, old top, I read . . .": C. Dunphy to JPK, undated, JPK.
283 "He always knew . . .": Interview, Rose Kennedy.
283 There were 371 Harvard men killed in the war, Frederick Mead, pp. 3–16.
283 Charles M. Schwab . . . : Samuel Moffett, "Captains of Industry," Cosmopolitan, July 1902, pp. 284–88; "The Great Steel Makers of Pittsburgh," The American Monthly Review of Reviews, April 1900, pp. 442–44.
284 Bethlehem's steel production soared: B. C. Forbes, "Gene Grace Whose Story Reads Like a Fairy Tale," American Magazine, July 1920, p. 16.
284 Encouraged by Wakeman: FRL, November 1917; Interview, Samuel Wakeman, Jr.
284 Kennedy led the insurance company: FRL, January 1919, p. 42.
285 "the medical catastrophe . . .": Richard Collier, The Plague of the Spanish Lady (1974), p. 310.
285 Boston was the first city . . . struck: Francis Russell, p. 29.
285 "After all, influenza, flu . . .": Alfred Crosby, Epidemic and Peace (1976), p. 5.
286 by the end of September 85,000: Ibid., p. 53.
286 Boston's mayor . . . had issued: BET, Sept. 27, 1918, p. 1.
286 "whole streets where every house . . .": Ibid., p. 12.
286 "I tell you . . .": Katherine Anne Porter, Pale Horse, Pale Rider (1939), pp. 232–33.
286 now with 26,000 men: John J. Ford to JPK, May 15, 1937, JPK.
286 "with the suddenness of a simoom": American Magazine, May 1928, p. 147.
286 the ones "who had been in the best . . .": Alfred Crosby, p. 26.
286 "They'd be sick one day . . .": Quoted ibid., p. 26.
286 an emergency task force: FRL, November 1918.
287 deaths in Quincy: BET, Sept. 25, 1918, p. 1.
287 "a drawn young man . . .": American Magazine, May 1928, p. 148.
287 Boston City Hospital . . . refuse admission: BET, Sept. 17, 1918, p. 1.
288 "a normal delivery . . . a beautiful . . .": Rose Kennedy, "Rose Kennedy: 'Rosemary Gave Us Strength,'" The Catholic Digest, March 1976, p. 36.
288 St. Aidan's Church: Rosemary was baptized Sept. 13, 1918, Baptismal Records, St. Aidan's Church.
289 Gazing one wintry evening: Interview, Rose Kennedy.
289 rotting at their wharves: Preston Slosson, The Great Crusade and After (1930), p. 75.
289 "As soon as the signal sounds . . .": FRL, August 1919.
290 "The key to Kennedy's . . . success . . .": J. J. Ford quote repeated by George Pumphret in an interview.
290 the highest standard of living: William E. Leuchtenburg, Perils of Prosperity, 1914–1932 (1958), p. 178; Arthur Link, American Epoch (1980), p. 249.
290 flourishing innovations . . . consumer products: Robert Sklar, The Plastic Age (1970), p. 98; Preston Slosson, pp. 163–64.
290 Never before in the financial history . . . : Albert Atwood, "The Great Bull Market," Saturday Evening Post, Jan. 12, 1929, pp. 6–7; Robert Sobel, Inside Wall Street (1977), p. 194.
291 Solidly established: NYT, Sun., Nov. 12, 1922, Sect. 2, p. 5.
291 "The peculiar genius that Hayden, Stone . . .": David Stone, "History of Hayden, Stone," unpublished manuscript, p. 1. The Stone estate was worth over $15 million at the time of Stone's death, NYT, Feb. 25, 1930, p. 28. Hayden's fortune was estimated at $60 million in 1924, Ferdinand Lundberg, America's 60 Families (1937), p. 26.
291 Kennedy . . . secured a seat next to Stone: "Mr. Kennedy, the Chairman," Fortune, Sept. 1937, p. 140. This statement was not refuted in JPK corrections of the Looker Draft.

292 Stone . . . produced in Kennedy: Richard J. Whalen, p. 53.

292 the plant was moving through: Arthur Pound and Samuel Moore, *They Told Barron: Conversations and Revelations of an American Pepys in Wall Street* (1930), p. 95.

292 warm letter of praise: Mentioned in JPK to J. Powell, June 30, 1919, JPK.

292 "for services rendered . . .": S. Wakeman to JPK, June 30, 1919, JPK.

292 trouble lay in a proposal: Terms of agreement spelled out in JPK to S. Wakeman, May 14, 1920; quoted to E. Grace in letter of Jan. 11, 1921, JPK.

292 Eugene R. Grace: *American Magazine*, July 1920, p. 16; Floyd Parsons, "Everybody's Business," *Saturday Evening Post*, Aug. 13, 1919, pp. 32, 34.

292 Thayer listened attentively: Interview, Rose Kennedy.

293 a generous settlement: E. Grace to JPK, Jan. 17, 1921; final letter with check enclosed, Feb. 2, 1921, JPK.

293 "I don't know when . . .": JPK to E. Thayer, Dec. 31,1920, JPK.

293 Thayer . . . nervous breakdown: NYT, Feb. 11, 1921, p. 6, and April 7, 1921, p. 28; WSJ, April 7, 1921, p. 6.

293 "I can't tell you . . .": JPK to E. Thayer, Feb. 14, 1921. This letter was followed by others suggesting various employment proposals.

293 the moment when his upward career: This point is clear from his obituaries, Jan. 2, 1937, NYT, p. 11, and BG, p. 13.

293 The offices of Hayden, Stone were housed in the New England Mutual Life Insurance Building. For photo and description see Moses King, *King's How to See Boston* (1895), p. 54.

294 "a total barometer": Bernard Baruch, *My Own Story* (1957), p. 84.

294 Hayden, Stone . . . occupied three floors: Interview, Edwin Hodder. The rooms are described from photographs in Mr. Hodder's office.

294 "It was a very elegant place . . .": Interview, Edwin Hodder.

294 only to put up 10 percent: Joseph P. Kennedy (as told to John B. Kennedy), "Shielding the Sheep," *Saturday Evening Post*, Jan. 18, 1936, p. 65.

295 Carbon steel netted him: Richardson & Hill to JPK, June 27, 1919, JPK; analysis in *Cumulative Digest of Corporate News*, 1st quarterly number, 1918, p. 45.

295 Waldorf Systems Syndicate: Richardson & Hill to JPK, May 27, 1919, JPK; analysis, *Poor's Manual*, 1925, Industrial Sect., p. 1108.

295 his losing investments: Stuart Mfg. Corp., *Moody's Analysis of Investments*, 1919, p. 1854; Utah Metal and Tunnel Co., *Poor's Manual*, loc. cit., p. 1157.

295 he was asked . . . to promptly send: Richardson & Hill to JPK, May 26, 1919, JPK.

295 "could help liking to work . . .": *American Magazine*, May 1928, p. 147.

296 not entitled to added income: Interview, Edwin Hodder.

296 For an understanding of the prerogatives of insidership and operations of the stock market before regulation by the SEC, the following were consulted: Frederick Lewis Allen, *Lords of Creation* (1966); *Hayden, Stone Weekly Market Letter*, January 1917– December 1918; S. S. Huebner, *The Stock Market* (1922); Sereno Pratt, *The Work of Wall Street* (1919); H. Parker Willis and J. I. Dogen, *Investment Banking* (1929).

296 one in which group of insiders: Robert Sobel, p. 194.

296 investment bankers . . . security issues: H. Parker Willis and J. I. Dogen, p. 31.

296 Galen Stone sat on the boards: BNB, Dec. 27, 1926, p. 1; see also *Who's Who in New England*, 1909–1910, p. 1029.

297 Eastern Steamship: *Poor's Manual*, 1925, p. 129.

297 he bought his first thousand shares: Course of stock activity traced through NYT and BNB; the price range of the stock in *Poor's Manual*, 1925, p. 130.

297 he was able to borrow: The three banks from which loans were secured were Brookline Trust, International Trust and Boston Trust. JPK to E. Turner, Aug. 16, 1921, JPK.

298 Kennedy decided to sell off: Ibid.

298 For a description of the recession see Peter Wyckoff, *Wall Street and the Stock Market* (1972), pp. 56-61.

298 "dark and dreary": JPK to C. Dunphy, Dec. 31, 1920, JPK.

298 at 160, only to watch it plunge: *Fortune*, Sept. 1937, p. 140; Bill Duncliffe, "And He Did Ultimately Stand By a Monarch," BRA, Jan. 14, 1964, p. 5.

298 Story of the meeting with Stone: Interview, Rose Kennedy.
299 his own losses: Richard J. Whalen, p. 53.
299 "When I see a danger signal . . .": Jesse Livermore, *How to Trade in Stocks* (1940), p. 25.
299 Aug. 26, 1921, the Dow Jones: Peter Wyckoff, p. 61.
299 "perfect Everest of prosperity": Frederick Lewis Allen, *Lords of Creation*, p. 391.
300 "Whatever money I have made . . . ": Quoted in Arthur Pound and Samuel Moore, p. 95.
300 "Eastern may look tough . . .": JPK to C. Dunphy, Aug. 12, 1920, JPK.
300 remarkable high of 127: *Poor's Manual*, 1925, p. 130.
301 Story of Rose's depression and flight to her family: Interview, Rose Kennedy.
301 a largely Protestant neighborhood: Of the sixteen churches in the town only three were Catholic, *Brookline Directory*, 1915.
302 social structure of suburban Brookline: Robert Boldston, *Suburbia: Civil Denial* (1970), p. 135; see also John Curtis, *History of the Town of Brookline* (1933), pp. 317–21.
302 the ideal "bedroom community": John Curtis, p. 316.
302 the child-rearing books stressed: L. Emmett Holt, *The Care and Feeding of Children* (1894), pp. 27–31.
303 "My husband changed jobs . . . ": Gail Cameron, p. 81.
304 "Dear Vera . . . ": JPK to V. Murray, Aug. 15, 1921, JPK.
304 "I hope you will have . . . ": JPK to A. Houghton, Sept. 19, 1921, JPK.
304 "the most beautiful . . . ": Interview, Rose Kennedy.
305 relatives recall it as a serious: Interview, Rose Keane Ellis.
305 November 1918 . . . Tague: *BET*, Oct. 2, 1919, p. 1, and Oct. 3, 1919, p. 5.
305 "would probably have been severely . . . ": *BP*, July 5, 1920, p. 6.
306 "the crowd cheered . . .": *BG*, July 5, 1920, p. 1.
306 "a beautiful young girl . . . ": Rose Kennedy, p. 99. For information on Eunice Fitzgerald's life see obituaries, *BP*, Sept. 26, 1923, p. 9; *BDA*, Sept. 25, pp. 1–2; *The Republic*, Sept. 29, p. 3.
307 attend a religious retreat: Rose Kennedy, *TTR* draft, RFK.
307 the participants would gather: Rose Kennedy, "Notes for TTR," RFK.
308 "a profession that was fully . . . ": Rose Kennedy, *TTR* draft, RFK.
309 "frantic terror": Interview, Rose Kennedy.
309 Brookline's hospital did not admit: "Report of the Board of Health," *215th Annual Report of the Town of Brookline* (1921), p. 249.
309 the South Department: John Byrne (ed.), *A History of the Boston City Hospital, 1905–1914* (1964), p. 337.
310 care of the great Dr. Edwin Place: Ibid., pp. 324–44.
310 he pressed his case: Interview, Rose Kennedy.
310 a "very, very sick . . . ": Rose Kennedy, p. 87.
310 Joe vividly recalled: Interview, Edward Gallagher.
310 "I had never experienced . . .": JPK to Dr. Place, July 2, 1920, JPK.
310 if Jack was spared: Rose Kennedy, p. 88.
311 "Jack has had to have . . . ": Sara Miller to JPK, undated (c. March 1, 1920), JPK.
311 On the Mansion House see *Poland Spring House* (1904, 1911).
311 "He is such a wonderful boy . . . ": Sara Miller to JPK, loc. cit.
311 "Jack is certainly . . . ": Anna Pope to JPK, May 14, 1920, JPK.
311 "there was an unusual spirit . . . ": John Byrne, p. 353.
311 "I enjoyed seeing *my Jack* . . . ": Sara Miller to L. Connelly, May 25, 1920, RFK.
311 "I am afraid I asked for too much . . . ": Anna Pope to JPK, loc. cit.
312 "My only hope . . . ": JPK to Dr. Place, loc. cit.
312 check to the Guild of St. Apollonia: Rose Kennedy, p. 87.
312 was able to purchase: *The Pilot*, Sept. 4, 1920, p. 1.
312 $3,750 . . . was exactly half: Rose Kennedy, p. 84.
312 the governesses were told: Alice Bastian in Edward M. Kennedy (ed.), p. 194.
312 "Joe was absolutely devoted . . . ": Rose Kennedy, p. 146.
313 "After Jack's illness . . . ": Interview, Rose Kennedy.

313 Rose was an excellent manager: Jerome Beatty, "The Nine Little Kennedys and How They Grew," *Woman's Day*, April 1939, p. 38.

313 in August 1920: A letter to the phone company dated Aug. 13, 1920, indicates the house had just been purchased and was to be occupied as of Oct. 1, JPK.

313 The new residence: Unidentified clipping, Nov. 12, 1964, Brookline Public Library.

314 this time Joe was intimately involved: JPK to Palais Rugs, July 26, 1920; JPK to Mr. Wheeler, Sept. 20, 1920, JPK.

314 "Kennedy could not get to New York . . . ": E. Turner to G. Currier, Jan. 5, 1921, JPK.

314 "Nothing I'd rather do . . . ": JPK to C. Dunphy, June 21, 1921, JPK.

314 Rose established certain times: Joseph Dinneen, *The Kennedy Family*, pp. 35–36.

314 shared religious exercises: Rev. Paul Furtey, *You and Your Children: A Book for Catholic Parents, Priests and Educators* (1929), pp. 1–5.

315 "to know and feel the past . . . ": Interview, Rose Kennedy.

315 feeling . . . out of joint with politics: Ibid.

315 "The great problems . . . ": George Jean Nathan as quoted in William Leuchtenburg, *Perils of Prosperity*, p. 150.

316 "We welcome you with open . . . ": J. Coolidge to JPK, Oct. 18, 1920, JPK.

316 Joe lent his name: *BET*, Sept. 22, 1919, p. 1.

316 "a first step toward . . . ": Francis Russell, p. 38.

316 police commissioner responded: *BG*, Sept. 9, 1919, p. 1.

316 Strike vote results: Ibid.; *BET*, Sept. 9, 1919, pp. 1, 5.

316 mobs took control: *BET*, Sept. 10, 1919, p. 1.

316 police commissioner issued: *BG*, Sept. 12, 1919, p. 1.

316 "You are levelheaded . . . ": *BG*, Sept. 10, 1919, p. 4.

316 He went out on strike: Interview, Mary Lou and Kerry McCarthy.

317 Wall Street bombing: John Brooks, *Once in Golconda* (1969), pp. 1–2.

317 "I felt a sudden shock . . . ": *BH*, Sept. 18, 1920, p. 4.

317 Breaking virtually every window: *BET*, Sept. 16, 1920, pp. 1, 5.

318 Rose recalled the argument: Interview, Rose Kennedy.

318 "I realize that you are anxious . . . ": JPK to L. Coolidge, Nov. 26, 1920, JPK.

318 Calling one day upon P.J.: Interview, Rose Kennedy.

318 The Church of the immigrants: William Halsey, *The Survival of American Innocence* (1980), pp. 10, 17–18, 40.

318 The Church of the twenties: Robert Leckie, *American and Catholic* (1970), pp. 285–86; Frances Lally, *The Catholic Church in a Changing America* (1962), p. 33.

319 Description of St. Aidan's: Brochure, June 1913, AAB.

319 "I wanted them to understand . . . ": Rose Kennedy, p. 85.

319 By establishing a fixed time: Ibid., pp. 108–09.

320 "I would have been bored . . . ": Ibid., p. 94.

320 epidemic of measles . . . Rose in California: Ibid., p. 98.

320 arrived home from a car accident: Ibid., pp. 81–82.

321 "Each time of life . . . ": Leo Tolstoy, *The Kreutzer Sonata and Other Tales* (1973), p. 104.

322 There is a picture: *BG*, June 22, 1922, p. 6.

322 The feature of the . . . afternoon: Ibid.; "Decennial at Harvard," circular from committee on program events, June 18, 1922, JPK.

323 "Joe loved fun . . . ": Quoted in Richard J. Whalen, p. 58.

323 Joe had pulled off a coup: Ibid.; see also *Harvard Class of 1912* (1923), p. xiii, HU Archives.

323 "the apparently unsuccessful . . .": *Harvard Class of 1912: 6th Report* (1937), p. 110, HU Archives.

323 Fisher had begun: Ibid., p. 237.

324 "no 1912 man sat in the wooden . . . ": Ibid., p. 110.

324 "There are certain persons . . . ": John P. Marquand, p. 68.

324 Living in a luxurious: *Boston City Directory*, 1923; *Harvard Class of 1912* (1927), p. 125.

324 the Somerset Club: Charles Bacon, pp. 372–73.

324 "It is all right to give . . .": JPK to A. Wellington, June 18, 1924, JPK.
325 From the porch . . . tricycles: Interview, Mrs. Samuel Wakeman, Jr.
325 "Mr. J. P. Kennedy's summer . . .": D. S. Dean to R. Fisher, May 7, 1922, JPK.
326 "I propose, Luce seconds . . .": D. S. Dean to H. Bancroft, June 8, 1922, JPK.
326 "You were going to let me know . . .": D. S. Dean to H. Bancroft, Aug. 14, 1922, JPK.
326 "Trying hard to get . . .": D. S. Dean to JPK, Aug. 18, 1922, JPK.
326 "It was petty . . .": Quoted in Richard J. Whalen, p. 59.
327 From 1922 to 1929: Harold Faulkner, *American* . . . , p. 93; Frederick Lewis Allen, *Lords of Creation*, p. 336.
327 the key industry: Harold Faulkner, loc. cit., pp. 99–100; Preston Slosson, p. 219; William Leuchtenburg, *Perils of Prosperity*, p. 185.
327 in 1916 . . . 4 million: *Historical Statistics of the United States: Colonial Times to 1957* (1960), p. 462.
327 By 1928 . . . over 24 million: Preston Slosson, p. 219.
327 Pond Creek Coal: *Hayden, Stone Weekly Market Letter*, March 22, 1918, p. 40; *Moody's Manual*, 1919, p. 1672.
328 the trading volume increased: NYT, Dec. 22, 1922, p. 22, and Dec. 23, 1922, p. 16.
328 Kennedy had borrowed to the limit: Richard J. Whalen, p. 54.
328 possibility of a merger: NYT, Dec. 23, 1922, p. 16, and Dec. 27, 1922, p. 22.
328 Ford and Stone reached: NYT, Dec. 29, 1922, p. 22.
328 Pond's stock jumped seven points: NYT, Dec. 22, 1922, p. 22.
328 sold his entire block: NYT, Dec. 29, 1922, p. 22.
329 Stone retired: NYT, Sun., Nov. 12, 1922, Sect. 2, p. 5.
329 After thirty years of unremitting: Arthur Pound and Samuel Taylor, p. 95.
329 Hayden, whose ancestry traced: NYT, Jan. 9, 1937, p. 19.
329 to head of the stock exchange department: Kennedy was made manager effective July 1, 1920, announcement to employees dated June 28, 1920, JPK.
329 "one of the noblest . . .": *American Magazine*, May 1928, p. 147.
329 loyalty to the firm: "Looker Draft," JPK.
330 Considered the greatest: J. P. McEvoy, "Here's Howey," *Cosmopolitan*, June 1948, p. 68; obituary, *Boston Daily Record*, March 22, 1954, p. 2.
330 model for Walter Burns: Paul H. Stevens, "Walter C. Howey," *The Palimpsest*, January–February 1975, pp. 25–31.
330 invested nearly all his life's savings: "Looker Draft," JPK; Richard J. Whalen, p. 67.
330 In January 1924 the stock: Stock quotes throughout this section are from WSJ unless otherwise indicated.
330 Yet the profits and earnings: WSJ, April, 10, 1924, p. 15.
330 Hertz was negotiating: NYT, Jan. 20, 1924, p. 2.
330 it was believed that the Checker Cab: Hertz obituary, NYT, Oct. 10, 1961, p. 43.
330 suffering from neuritis: Joe McCarthy, p. 47.
331 met two years earlier: *Fortune*, Sept. 1937, p. 140. The article appearing in the *American (Sunday Advertiser)* on p. 1 of Sect. 2 was the only piece of political news published that fall.
331 "I can never forget . . .": W. Howey to JPK, undated (c. 1937), JPK.
331 Details of his first day at the Waldorf as related to Rose that weekend in Providence: Interview, Rose Kennedy. The dinner at the Duck Inn, Rose Kennedy, "Notes for TRR," RFK.
331 Description of the Waldorf: Edward Hungerford, *The Story of the Waldorf-Astoria* (1925), pp. 207–23.
331 "the desire for the freedom . . .": Interview, Rose Kennedy.
332 "If ever I was scared . . .": *American Magazine*, May 1928, p. 148.
332 an additional three-point drop: WSJ, April 15, 1924, p. 16.
332 his plan for bolstering: "Looker Draft," JPK.
332 purchasing large blocks . . . with the intent: NYT, April 16, 1924, p. 1; WSJ, April 17, 1924, p. 4. When Hertz quit Yellow Cab he gave 7,000 shares of stock to about 60 employees "who threw in their lot with him 20 years ago . . .": NYT, Jan. 8, 1929, p. 3.

332  For information on John Hertz and Yellow Cab see Neil Clark, "John Hertz Supplies Taxicabs for Thirteen Hundred Cities," *American Magazine*, August 1925, pp. 54–56; Harry Shumway, *Famous Leaders of Business* (1936), pp. 190–96; obituary, *NYT*, Oct. 10, 1961, p. 43.
333  "It was ridiculously simple": John Hertz, "Why Our Business Has Grown to the Largest of Its Kind," *System: The Magazine of Business*, May 1923, p. 608.
333  to buy *and* sell: *Fortune*, Sept. 1937, p. 140; *American Magazine*, May 1928, p. 148.
334  "trusted implicitly . . .": Rose Kennedy, p. 91.
334  Biographical information on Moore from a one-page memo in the JPK papers and telephone conversation with Alice Lynch. See also *BG* (eve.), Dec. 14, 1937, p. 6.
335  shrouded his movements: *Fortune*, loc. cit.; *BRA*, Jan. 14, 1964, p. 25.
335  Never knowing what had hit them: *American Magazine*, loc. cit.
335  public-relations effort: *NYT*, April 21, 1924, p. 31, and April 25, 1924, p. 7; *WSJ*, April 10, 1924, p. 15, and April 28, 1924, p. 10.
335  the descent was halted: *Fortune*, loc. cit., p. 142.
336  Hertz's $5 million still intact: Ibid.
336  "I woke up one morning . . .": Joe McCarthy, p. 48.
336  "Daddy, Daddy! . . .": Rose Kennedy, p. 77.
336  the offer Hertz made in June 1924: JPK to J. Borden, June 19, 1924, JPK.
336  Hertz Rent-A-Car: *Moody's Industrial Manual*, 1983, Vol. 2, pp. 4251–52.
336  Omnibus Corporation: *NYT*, June 27, 1924, p. 21.
337  For information on Matthew Brush see Alfred Grunberg, "Top Notcher at 39," *American Magazine*, June 1917; obituary, *NYT*, Oct. 16, 1940, p. 23.
337  "the prince of speculators": Harold Faulkner, *From Versailles to the New Deal* (1950), p. 232.
337  "I bought some AGWI Common . . .": M. Brush to JPK, Sept. 21, 1925, JPK.
337  Kennedy's scribbled answer: JPK wrote "yes" next to the question.
337  he expected to see Stone: JPK to M. Brush, Oct. 1, 1925, JPK.
338  "before they pass a law . . .": Quoted in Richard J. Whalen, p. 66.
338  "the Wall Street racket . . .": Quoted in Harold Faulkner, *From Versailles . . .*, p. 232.
339  a special group of . . . immigrants: D. J. Wenden, *The Birth of the Movies* (1975), pp. 23–24.
340  investment of nearly $1.5 billion: Joseph P. Kennedy (ed), *The Story of Films* (1927), pp. 16, 27.
340  film industry was the sixth largest: *WSJ*, April 2, 1924, p. 2.
340  21,000 movie theaters: Joseph P. Kennedy (ed.), p. 27.
340  financing . . . on a personal basis: A. H. Giannini in ibid., pp. 80–81.
340  Samuel Goldwyn . . . had enough properties: *WSJ*, April 2, 1924, p. 5.
340  Only a half-dozen banks: Ibid.; see also Will Hays, *Memoirs* (1955), p. 465.
340  "This is . . . a gold mine. . . .": Joe Conway quoted in Edward M. Kennedy (ed.), p. 29.
340  The first operation: *Current Biography* (1940), p. 451.
341  The biggest test: Neville March Hunnings, *Film Censorship and the Law* (1967), p. 154.
341  "In New England . . .": JPK to W. Hays, Sept. 28, 1922, JPK.
341  Kennedy finally acquired: JPK to Ideal Amusement Co., Dec. 1, 1922, JPK.
341  "Kennedy learned [that] . . .": Richard J. Whalen, p. 71.
341  his widow was persuaded: *Motion Pictures Today*, Feb. 1926, JPK.
342  weekly payroll of nearly $60,000: *BP*, Feb. 8, 1926, p. 11.
342  given an exclusive option: E. Crum to JPK, June 17, 1921, JPK.
342  tried to interest . . . Hearst's: JPK to G. McFarland, June 18, 1921, JPK.
342  Traveling to Europe: *BH*, Aug. 17, 1925, p. 5.
342  the Grahams had sunk over $7 million: JPK to G. Currier, April 7, 1928, JPK.
342  the $1 million offer . . . small: *American Magazine*, May 1928, p. 148; *NYT*, Sun., June 3, 1928, Sect. 9, p. 10.
343  "Phone call for Mr. Kennedy . . .": Terry Ramsaye, "Intimate Visits to the Homes of Famous Film Magnates," *Photoplay*, Sept. 1927, p. 125.

343 Fitzgerald was convinced: Interview, Edward Gallagher.
343 with Guy Currier assuming: *Fortune*, Sept. 1937, p. 142.
343 "FITZGERALD A FILM MAGNATE": *BP*, Feb. 8, 1926, p. 1.
344 people would readily swap: Richard J. Whalen, p. 76.
344 to purchase a large block: Ibid.; for information on Prince see obituary, *NYT*, Feb. 3, 1953, p. 25.
344 "the greatest confidence . . .": JPK to J. Schnitzer, Feb. 11, 1926, JPK.
345 tight-lipped cronies: *Fortune*, loc. cit., p. 138.
345 "quite in a class by himself": *BP*, July 24, 1919, Herald Morgue Files.
345 "Little did we think . . .": E. E. Moore to JPK, Oct. 8, 1926, JPK.
346 The *Twentieth Century Ltd.*: John Marshall, *The Guinness Book of Rail Facts and Feats* (1975), pp. 178–80; Selwyn Kip Farrington, Jr., *Railroads of Today* (1949), pp. 21–35; Lucius Beebe, *High Iron: A Book of Trains* (1938), p. 190.
346 "Never before or since . . .": D. J. Wenden, p. 152.
346 Kennedy's offices . . . would later be seen: Interview, Marc Wanamaker.
346 HOLLYWOOD LAND sign: Bruce Torrence, *Hollywood: The First Hundred Years* (1982), p. 133.
347 entire Western village: Interview, Marc Wanamaker.
347 "It was more than . . .": *Photoplay*, Sept. 1927, p. 125.
347 "as an example of the sort . . .": Unidentified clipping, undated, RFK.
347 "We can't make pictures . . .": Final draft of unidentified speech, p. 16, JPK.
347 "It is out of the question . . .": *BG*, Aug. 4, 1926, RFK.
348 cost of an FBO film: JPK to G. Currier, April 7, 1928, JPK.
348 "Melodrama is our meat . . .": *Variety*, May 30, 1928, p. 22.
348 generating nearly $9 million: JPK to G. Currier, loc. cit.
349 "since it was Joe's duty . . .": Interview, Rose Kennedy.
350 "It was very exciting . . .": Quoted in Edward M. Kennedy (ed.), p. 15.
350 "Tickled to death . . .": JPK to JPK, Jr., July 1926, RFK.
351 "the look of wonder": Interview, Rose Kennedy.
351 Grandpa Fitzgerald stepped in: John Henry Cutler, pp. 243–44.
351 At the sheer sound of his voice: Interview, Rose Kennedy.
352 "If you bring up the eldest . . .": Ibid.
352 "I have always felt . . .": John F. Kennedy (ed.), *As We Remember Joe* (1945), p. 3.
352 Joe Junior's attitude: Lem Billings, "Notes," April 1, 1972, RFK.
352 "It wasn't the father . . .": Lem Billings quoted in Burton Hersh, *The Education of Edward Kennedy* (1972), p. 32.
352 a part of Joe's childhood was lost: For an analysis of the dilemma of the model child, see Alice Miller, *The Drama of the Gifted Child* (1981).
353 "I never heard him utter . . .": John F. Kennedy (ed.), p. 3.
353 "I suppose I knew Joe . . .": Ibid.
353 the "Pied Piper": Interview, Luella Hennessey Donovan.
353 Jack found it easy to pardon: L. Billings, "Notes," RFK.
353 "a tough, constant . . .": Ibid.
353 wish for a happy death: 1923 Diary, March 30, RFK.
353 "Gee, you're a great mother . . .": Ibid., April 3.
353 he used to cry: Interview, Lem Billings.
353 Rose would spend an hour: Herbert S. Parmet, *Jack: The Struggles of John F. Kennedy* (1980), p. 17.
354 Robert Kennedy remembered: Arthur M. Schlesinger, Jr., *Robert Kennedy and His Times* (1978), p. 13.
354 "would often find an excuse to slam . . .": Peter Collier and David Horowitz, *The Kennedys* (1984), p. 61.
354 "sarcastic and overbearing . . .": L. Billings, "Notes," RFK.
354 Joe suggested a bicycle race: James M. Burns, Notes, "Interview with Kennedy," March 22, 1959, JFK.
354 "frustrated and dominated": Interview, Lem Billings.
355 "invariably late . . .": Rose Kennedy, Transcript of CBS News Special, "JFK—The Childhood Years," Oct. 31, 1967, RFK.

355 "really very lonesome . . .": JPK to JFK, July 13, 1926, JPK.
355 he would "rather have spent . . .": John F. Kennedy (ed.), p. 3.
355 the Devotion School: Nina F. Little, *Some Old Brookline Houses* (1949), pp. 151–56.
355 Dexter provided: Dexter School for Boys, catalogues for 1931 and 1938.
356 "junior-grade Groton": James M. Burns, "Interview with Kennedy," loc. cit.
356 competing with Joe . . . greater athletic ability: Rose Kennedy in Bela Kornitzer, "My Son," *New York Herald Tribune*, Sept. 8, 1960, Magazine Sect., p. 11.
356 her teachers could not recommend her: Hank Searls, p. 37.
356 "She was a very pretty baby . . .": Rose Kennedy, pp. 160–61.
357 took delight in gazing: Interview, Rose Kennedy.
357 "My dear Rosemary . . .": E. E. Moore to Rosemary Kennedy, Easter 1921, JPK.
357 "Rosemary was constantly . . .": Interview, Rose Kennedy.
357 "I went to the head . . .": Ibid.
358 "We went from doctor . . .": *The Catholic Digest*, March 1976, p. 35.
358 "defective" children were divided: "Making Morons into Useful Citizens," *Literary Digest*, Jan. 29, 1927, pp. 19–20; see also Alfred F. Tredgold, *Mental Deficiency* (1929), pp. 65–72.
358 "They are born of . . .": Woods Hutchinson, "Children Who Never Grew Up," *Good Housekeeping*, April 1915, pp. 425–26.
359 Worse still . . . , the established wisdom: Alfred Tredgold, p. 422.
359 "What can they do in an institution . . .": Rose Kennedy, p. 162.
359 "Dear Santa Claus . . .": Rosemary letter, undated, RFK.
360 several problems in multiplication: Arithmetic papers, February 1927, RFK.
360 Eunice remembered watching: Eunice Kennedy Shriver, MS corrections for *TTR*, p. 16, RFK.
360 "She loved compliments. . . .": Interview, Eunice Kennedy Shriver.
360 "Even if I said to her . . .": *The Catholic Digest*, March 1976, p. 37.
360 "to do a work he cannot do . . .": Rose Kennedy, transcript of speech on mental retardation given in Chicago and Detroit, fall 1968, RFK.
361 In the middle of the night: Interview, Helen Barron.
361 Rosemary standing in the background: Rose Kennedy, p. 163.
361 "Then, one day we were all . . .": Interview, Marnie Devine.
362 the key to her children's compassion: *The Catholic Digest*, March 1976, p. 36.
362 "Never was there a girl . . .": Rose Kennedy, "Notes on the Children," RFK.
362 "the sunshine": Dinah Bridge, OH-JFKL and interview.
362 "Wherever she stood, there would be . . .": Interview, Dinah Bridge.
362 "All her life . . .": Interview, Lem Billings.
362 "They were the pick . . .": Quoted in Peter Collier and David Horowitz, p. 70.
363 "beyond all their advantages . . .": Interview, Rose Kennedy.
363 Eunice was aware: Rose Kennedy, "Notes on the Children," RFK.
363 "rather pale and of a nervous . . .": Ibid.
363 "If anyone in the family . . .": Interview, Luella Hennessey Donovan.
363 "Eunice . . . a sense of special . . .": Interview, Lem Billings.
363 "free from moral and physical . . .": Rose Kennedy, "Notes on the Children," RFK.
364 "particularly ambitious . . .": Ibid.
364 "Bobby had a lot going against . . .": L. Billings, "Notes," RFK.
364 "stuck by himself . . .": Rose Kennedy, p. 106.
364 "The gentlest and the shyest . . .": Arthur M. Schlesinger, Jr., *Robert Kennedy*, p. 22.
364 "on occasions impatient . . .": Ibid., p. 21.
364 "I was the seventh . . .": Ibid., p. 23.
364 Slow at swimming: Ibid., pp. 22–23.
364 "the least loved": L. Billings, "Notes," RFK.
365 Each afternoon when Jack returned: Interview, Lem Billings.
365 the Irish who went to Chicago: William Shannon, *The American Irish* (1966), p. 68.
366 Malcolm Cottage: The lease ran from June 1 to Oct. 1 at a cost of $3,500, JPK.
366 "coming in second . . .": Interview, Eunice Kennedy Shriver.
366 "No matter what anyone . . .": Leo Damore, *The Cape Cod Years of JFK* (1967), p. 24.

366 "Years ago we decided . . .": *Woman's Day*, April 1939, p. 16.
367 "I've seen you quoted . . .": Joe McCarthy, p. 42.
367 "Poor old Boston . . .": Elmer Davis, "Boston," *Harper's*, Jan. 1928, p. 152.
367 first city . . . to limit building heights: Elizabeth Herlihy (ed.), pp. 49–50.
367 "It was like a blow . . .": Interview, Rose Kennedy.
368 the death of his mother: *BET*, May 21, 1923, p. 7; *BG* (eve.), May 23, 1923, p. 12; *BP*, May 24, 1923, p. 3.
368 "many regrets . . .": JPK to J. Newbold, Treasurer, Sept. 22, 1927, JPK.
368 Moore produced a 13-room house: Rose Kennedy, p. 178; see also Lloyd Ultan, *The Beautiful Bronx, 1920–1950* (1979), pp. 15, 320.
368 Eunice . . . bad stomach: Health Index Cards, RFK.
369 December 1926 . . . Donham: JPK wired Will Hays, Jan. 13, 1927, that he had completed the negotiations, JPK.
369 Harvard could be the first: *BP* and *BH*, Jan. 24, 1927, RFK.
369 Five years earlier: Kenneth Anger, *Hollywood Babylon* (1975), pp. 27–60, 71–78; Kenneth MacGowen, *Behind the Screen: The History and Techniques of the Motion Picture* (1965), p. 352.
370 The appointment of . . . Hays: Hays accepted the appointment Jan. 14, 1922. See Neville M. Hunnings, p. 153; Henry F. Pringle, "Will Hays—Superior of Morals," *New Outlook*, April 11, 1928, pp. 576–78; Will Hays, "Motion Pictures and Their Censors," *Review of Reviews*, April 1927, pp. 393–98.
370 he offered . . . the full resources: Telegram, W. Hays to JPK, Jan. 14, 1927, JPK.
370 On Seabury see obituary, Nov. 9, 1949, p. 1.
370 "approximately four men . . .": W. M. Seabury to Dr. Lowell, Jan. 29, 1927, JPK.
371 $30,000 for . . . a film library: JPK to W. Donham, April 27, 1927, JPK: see also *HC*, March 16, 1927, p. 1.
371 "It's all right for you . . .": R. H. Cochrane to JPK, March 2, 1927, JPK.
371 "I told you at the station . . .": R. H. Cochrane to JPK, March 25, 1927, JPK.
372 "almost the entire inner cabinet . . .": Quoted in Joseph P. Kennedy (ed.), pp. ix–x.
372 For information on Adolph Zukor see Philip French, *The Movie Moguls* (1971), pp. 22–23; John B. Kennedy, "From a Penny Up," *Collier's*, June 2, 1928, pp. 18, 51–52; *New York Herald*, Sun., Sept. 18, 1921, p. 2, JPK.
372 Marcus Loew: Philip French, pp. 24–25.
372 "To a man like myself . . .": Joseph P. Kennedy (ed.), pp. 55–56.
373 For information on Marcus Loew see "Marcus Loew's Long Leap from Penny Arcades," *Literary Digest*, Sept. 24, 1927, pp. 39–40, 45; obituary, *NYT*, Sept. 6, 1927, pp. 1, 23.
373 "I cannot begin to tell . . .": Joseph P. Kennedy (ed.), pp. 285–86; see also *Christian Science Monitor*, March 31, 1927, RFK; *HC*, March 31, 1927, p. 1.
373 "Assembling all these men . . .": Richard J. Whalen, p. 82.
373 "We are beginning to . . .": Joseph P. Kennedy (ed.), pp. 175–76.
374 "the best day . . .": JPK to C. B. De Mille, March 18, 1927, JPK.
374 "very wonderful day . . .": Telegram, C. B. De Mille to JPK, April 28, 1927, JPK.
374 "It was not so long ago . . .": *Exhibitor's Daily Review*, April 29, 1927, p. 1, RFK.
374 "Kennedy should be tendered . . .": Quoted in ibid.
374 "White Hope" list: *New York Herald Tribune*, Dec. 18, 1927, JPK.
374 "The most ingenious maker . . .": *NYT*, Sun., Jan. 8, 1928, sect. 4, p. 18.
375 the Photophone . . . RCA: Eugene Lyons, *David Sarnoff* (1966), pp. 140–41.
375 Kennedy opened negotiations: *Boston Traveler*, Jan. 24, 1927, RFK.
375 the deal gave FBO the services: Unidentified clipping, Jan. 5, 1928, RFK.
375 Keith-Albee-Orpheum . . . KAO: *Variety*, Jan. 18, 1928, p. 25.
375 For information on Murdock see obituary, *NYT*, Dec. 9, 1948, p. 33.
375 Keith-Albee had merged: Charles Higham, *Cecil B. De Mille* (1973), p. 174.
375 Murdock recognized in Kennedy: *Variety*, Sept. 21, 1927, p. 5, Jan. 18, 1928, p. 5, and Feb. 15, 1928, p. 4.
375 For information on Albee see obituary, *NYT*, Nov. 12, 1930, p. 32.
375 offer to buy 200,000: JPK to E. Albee, May 10, 1928, JPK.
376 $21 a share: Douglas Gilbert, *American Vaudeville: Its Life and Times* (1940), p. 394.

376 Albee finally accepted: Agreement dated May 10, 1928, JPK.
376 "new blood and financial . . .": Press release from KAO, May 16, 1928, JPK; see also *NYT*, May 17, 1928, p. 23; *Variety*, May 23, 1928, p. 5.
376 to force Albee to resign: A letter from JPK to John Ford, July 2, 1928, indicates he had tried unsuccessfully to see Albee and asks Ford to find out how far they are obligated to pay Albee his salary, talk to Albee, explain conditions, and cut salary to $25,000, JPK.
376 "Didn't you know . . .": Douglas Gilbert, p. 394.
376 Pathé had enjoyed . . . monopoly: *BNB*, June 15, 1928, p. 73.
376 $70,000: *Variety*, June 13, 1928, p. 5.
376 "Employees [in motion picture . . .": *American Magazine*, May 1928, p. 148.
377 "When the banks came into . . .": Donald Hayne (ed.), *Autobiography of Cecil B. De Mille* (1959), pp. 288–89.
377 Kennedy would remember . . . De Mille: Interview, Rose Kennedy.
377 Built as a replica . . . Mount Vernon: Interview, Linda Hart; Charles Higham, *Cecil B. De Mille*, pp. 141–45.
378 Set alteration from *King of Kings* to the burning of Atlanta: see Charles Higham, *Cecil B. De Mille*, p. 166; Orville Goldner and George Turner, *The Making of King Kong* (1975), pp. 101, 103, 207; Rudy Behlmer (ed.), *Memo from David O. Selznick* (1972), p. 185.
378 urging him to attempt: Telegram, M. Flint to JPK, Jan. 12, 1927, JPK.
378 "Deeply appreciate your wire . . .": Telegram, JPK to M. Flint, Jan. 13, 1927, JPK.
379 Kennedy was asked: "Points for Consideration in Agreement with First National," Aug. 9, 1928, JPK: see also *Variety*, Aug. 15, 1928, p. 4.
379 "stirred an air . . .": Richard J. Whalen, p. 98.
379 refused to ratify: *BP*, Sun., Aug. 19, 1928, p. 3; *Variety*, Aug. 22, 1928, p. 9.
379 Kennedy went to dinner: Interview, Judge Charles Wyzansky.
379 moved out of Mount Vernon: Donald Hayne (ed.), p. 290; Charles Higham, *Cecil B. De Mille*, p. 190.
379 banner headline: *Variety*, Oct. 24, 1928, p. 5.
380 "The most intriguing . . .": Thomas Carens, "A New Mogul of the Movies," *New York Herald Tribune*, Sept. 16, 1928, pp. 8–9.
381 new Savoy Plaza: *NYT*, Nov. 28, 1925, p. 1, and Sept. 30, 1927, p. 5.
381 unseasonably warm . . . armistice: *NYT*, Nov. 11, 1927, p. 25.
382 "Gloria needs handling . . .": R. Kane to JPK, Nov. 7, 1927, JPK.
382 "Arriving New York . . .": Telegram, G. Swanson to JPK, Nov. 9, 1927, JPK.
382 "Will be very glad . . .": JPK to G. Swanson, Nov. 10, 1927, JPK.
382 Radiant with a passion: Hedda Hopper, *From Under My Hat* (1952), p. 164.
383 "every inch and every . . .": David Shipman, *The Great Movie Stars* (1979), p. 524.
383 alcoholic father . . . ambitious mother: Gloria Swanson, *Swanson on Swanson* (1980), pp. 13, 44, 48–51.
383 "There is no star . . .": Quoted in Charles Lockwood, *Dream Palaces* (1981), p. 127.
384 *Sadie Thompson*: *NYT*, Feb. 5, 1928, p. 6.
384 a concerted protest: Joe Kennedy was one of fifteen members of the Association who filed the "strongest protest" with Will Hays against the making of "Rain" or the story under any other name; producers to Will Hays, July 10, 1927, JPK.
384 "didn't resemble any banker . . .": Gloria Swanson, pp. 327–29.
385 "even dared to ask . . . his enthusiasm . . .": Ibid, p. 334.
385 "I would have been the second . . .": Ibid., p. 335.
385 "any possibility of doing business . . .": JPK to R. Kane, Nov. 15, 1927, JPK.
385 "the right business partner": Gloria Swanson, p. 340.
385 "she got herself . . .": JPK to R. Kane, loc. cit.
385 "more million dollar a year . . .": *Variety*, Jan. 23, 1929, p. 11.
386 a number of warrants: Among JPK's papers is correspondence between the IRS and Gloria's attorney from October 1926 through January 1928.
386 unpaid taxes: "Offer of Compromise Made on Client's Taxes Applicable Years 1921–1926 Inclusive," undated, JPK.
386 she had apparently deducted: T. Beener to T. Moore, Aug. 27, 1927, JPK.

386 "in attractive and fashionable . . .": Quoted from contract in IRS document dated Jan. 18, 1928, JPK.
386 average net income: *Statistical Abstract of the U.S.* (1930), p. 201.
387 Gloria Productions, Inc.: Incorporation certificate dated Jan. 24, 1928, JPK.
387 "My only job . . .": Gloria Swanson, p. 344.
387 For information on E. B. Derr see Florabel Muir, "Derr Starts Movie Career from Top," *Sunday News*, March 16, 1930, JPK.
387 loan of $20,000: Loan agreement dated January 1928, JPK.
387 Moore hold the check: E. B. Derr to E. E. Moore, Jan. 12, 1928, JPK.
388 "Ruthlessly speaking . . .": E. B. Derr to JPK, Jan. 25, 1928, JPK.
388 "I presume you know . . .": P. Bedard to G. Swanson, Feb. 28, 1928, JPK.
388 "A real friend . . .": Telegram, M. Cohen to G. Swanson, Jan. 24, 1928, JPK.
389 Rose safely ensconced: Rose Kennedy, p. 78.
389 "Besides, he always knew . . .": Interview, Rose Kennedy.
389 Gloria was still married: Hedda Hopper, p. 164; marriage, NYT, Jan. 29, 1925, p. 1.
389 "For the first time . . .": Gloria Swanson, p. 230.
389 marriage contract: Dated Jan. 27, 1925, it was registered in Paris on the 28th, JPK.
389 Gloria confessed . . . child: Gloria Swanson, p. 232.
390 "As soon as the holidays . . .": Ibid., pp. 348–49.
390 "the greatest aggregation . . .": Frank P. Stockbridge and John Perry, *Florida in the Making* (1926), p. 210; see also John Ney, *Palm Beach* (1966); Cleveland Amory, *The Last Resorts* (1948), pp. 329–404; E. W. Howe, "The Real Palm Beach," *Saturday Evening Post*, April 17, 1920, p. 42.
390 "the winter counterpart . . .": Federal Writers Project, *Florida* (1939), p. 228.
390 The meeting at the train and subsequent first encounter: Gloria Swanson, pp. 351–52, 356–57. Gloria and Henri arrived on the 29th; see *Variety*, Feb. 1, 1928, p. 11.
392 "Now, listen, Rosie . . .": Interview, Ann Gargan King.
392 According to the strictest: Richard Ginder, *Binding with Briars* (1975), pp. 87–95.
393 bill of Gloria's from Brentano's dated May 17, 1928, JPK.
393 "There is no question . . .": Interview, George Cukor.
393 "In those days . . .": Interview, Cy Howard.
394 El Mirasol: Cleveland Amory, *The Last Resorts*, pp. 379–81.
394 "There were great paintings . . .": Interview, Rose Kennedy; "Palm Beach notes," RFK.
394 "People will be arriving . . .": Gloria Swanson, pp. 353–54.
395 "manifested an endearing . . .": Ibid., p. 353.
395 "In an era of wonderful . . .": Interview, George Cukor.
395 "Everything all right . . .": Telegram, G. Swanson to JPK, Feb. 7, 1928, JPK.
395 "the financial morass" . . . : Interview, Rose Kennedy.
395 Fitzgerald had come: Interview, Ann Gargan King.
396 overhearing a loud argument: Interview, Geraldine Hannon.
396 "No matter what the mistress . . .": Interview, Cy Howard.
396 "My road to fame . . .": Telegram, F. Thompson to RFK, Feb. 22, 1928, RFK.
396 "Are you ready . . .": Telegram, W. Le Baron to RFK, Feb. 22, 1928, RFK.
396 "I have followed the growth . . .": Father Toohig to RFK, Feb. 27, 1928, RFK.
397 "Everything is going . . .": M. Moore to RFK, Feb. 24, 1928, RFK.
397 "How I envy you . . .": F. Thompson to RFK, March 5, 1928, RFK.
398 Santa Catalina Island: Federal Writers Project, *California* (1939), pp. 423–24; see also Josephine Hemphill, "Catalina, Isle of Magic and Beauty," *Sunset*, April 1928, p. 37.
398 The meeting with Stroheim: Thomas Quinn Curtis, *Von Stroheim* (1971), p. 244.
399 "That's precisely what all . . .": Gloria Swanson, p. 340.
399 "was the greatest director . . .": Quoted in Thomas Curtis, p. xvii. On Stroheim see also Charlotte Gobeil (ed.), *Hommage à Eric von Stroheim* (1966); Richard Koszarski, *The Man You Love to Hate* (1983).
399 critics remarked upon: Bob Thomas, *Thalberg* (1969), p. 73.
399 delayed shooting on *Foolish Wives*: Christopher Finch, *Gone Hollywood* (1957), p. 31.
399 believer in authenticity: Bosley Crowther, *The Great Films* (1967), p. 41.

399 regardless of the money: Eric von Stroheim, "The Seamy Side of Directing," in Richard Koszarski, *Hollywood Directory, 1914–1940* (1976), pp. 172–75; John Grierson, "Director of Directors," Appendix in Peter Noble, *Hollywood Scapegoat* (1972), pp. 202–3.

400 "an undisciplined spendthrift . . .": Gloria Swanson, p. 347.

400 melodramatic story: Original script in JPK.

400 Gloria was suddenly seized: Gloria Swanson, p. 347.

401 bringing out hidden depths: Bob Thomas, pp. 80–81.

401 reminded Gloria of a . . . puppy: Gloria Swanson, p. 346.

401 "Be sure your advance . . .": Telegram, E. B. Derr to C. Sullivan, May 4, 1928, JPK.

401 "putting a striped . . .": C. Sullivan to JPK, May 23, 1928, JPK.

401 contract signed May 9, 1928, JPK.

402 "the best film story ever written": Gloria Swanson, p. 358.

402 "we are having a final . . .": W. Le Baron to JPK, Sept. 25, 1928, JPK.

402 Kennedy sailed for Europe: *Variety*, Aug. 15, 1928, p. 32, and Aug. 22, 1928, p. 3.

402 "Don't see why I should pay . . .": Telegram, G. Swanson to JPK, Sept. 20, 1928, JPK.

402 on a silver platter: Thomas Curtis, p. 246.

402 "Oh, I tell you, Gloria . . .": Gloria Swanson, p. 359.

402 For descriptions of the sets see *Variety*, Oct. 24, 1928, p. 4; *Exhibitor's Herald World*, Jan. 12, 1929, p. 36.

403 "wouldn't have the right . . .": *Motion Picture Classic*, July 1929, p. 86.

403 "Never had he felt . . .": Gloria Swanson, p. 368.

403 "One naturally does as he . . .": *NYT*, Sun., Jan. 27, 1929, Sect. 9, p. 8.

403 "Every scene was alive . . .": Gloria Swanson, pp. 368–69.

404 "The experience of working . . .": Ibid., p. 369.

404 more arrestingly beautiful: E. B. Derr to JPK, Dec. 7, 1928, JPK.

404 14-hour days: *Variety*, Nov. 14, 1928, p. 4.

404 With Glazer's help: Telegram, E. B. Derr to JPK, Dec. 6, 1928; B. Glazer to Derr, Dec. 10, 1928, JPK.

405 "Had session last night . . .": Telegram, E. B. Derr to JPK, Dec. 7, 1928, JPK.

405 Gloria too began worrying: Gloria Swanson, p. 371.

405 Kennedy was making his own: *Variety*, Dec. 19, 1928, p. 5.

405 vocal lessons: C. Scollard to Mark Markoff, Jan. 8, 1929, JPK.

405 Irving Berlin to do the scoring: C. Scollard to E. B. Derr, Jan. 24, 1929, JPK.

405 "When Kennedy saw the first . . .": Peter Noble, p. 79.

406 romped away with the honors: *Motion Picture Classic*, July 1929, p. 6.

407 E. B. successful . . .": Telegram, G. Swanson to JPK, Jan. 21, 1929, JPK.

407 Walter report: E. Walter to JPK, Jan. 23, 1929, JPK.

407 Derr had become . . . concerned: *Variety*, Jan. 30, 1929, p. 4.

408 an ingenious plan: *Variety*, Feb. 6, 1929, p. 5, and March 6, 1929, p. 4.

408 her seamstress had come: Gloria Swanson, p. 370.

408 "Mr. von Stroheim began . . .": Ibid., p. 373.

409 "in very bad shape . . .": JPK to H. de la Falaise, March 13, 1929, JPK.

409 "would offend millions . . .": Rose Kennedy, "Notes for TTR," RFK, and *Fortune*, Sept. 1937, p. 142.

409 "We worked on this . . .": JPK to H. de la Falaise, loc. cit.

410 P.J. remained an exceptionally: Interview, Kerry and Mary Lou McCarthy.

410 "Go into my rolltop desk . . .": Interview, Mary Lou McCarthy.

411 *Variety* reported the death of his father May 21, 1929, p. 12.

411 "sea of despair": Interview, Rose Kennedy.

411 "You can't realize . . . shock . . .": JPK to A. H. Giannini, May 22, 1929, JPK.

411 "I had hoped to be able . . .": Telegram, JPK to R. Hunt, May 29, 1929, JPK.

411 "I know the great loss . . .": C. Dunphy to JPK, May 1929, JPK.

412 "meant in life . . .": BG, May 21, 1929, p. 16.

412 "With Mr. Kennedy . . .": BP, May 22, 1929, p. 6.

412 "Despite the rain . . .": BG, loc. cit.; *East Boston Argus Advocate*, May 25, 1929, p. 1.

412 behaved with incredible dignity: Interview, Rose Kennedy.
412 "I have heard such lovely . . .": JPK to JPK, Jr., June 3, 1929, JPK.
412 P.J. Kennedy left an estate: Suffolk County Probate Records, No. 235838.
413 "a beached whale": Gloria Swanson, p. 376.
413 The first correspondence between Boleslavsky and JPK is dated Dec. 3, 1929, JPK.
413 "all the accumulated excitement . . .": Gloria Swanson, p. 396.
413 "Kelly started and stopped . . .": Telegram, JPK to H. de la Falaise, Dec. 14, 1929, JPK.
413 "He was resigned. . . .": Gloria Swanson, p. 396.
413 Queen Kelly release: Thomas Quinn Curtis, p. 251.
413 "destined by fate . . .": Synopsis of story for Gloria Swanson, June 18, 1929, JPK.
414 "on a campaign . . .": Rose Kennedy, p. 199.
414 Gloria claims that she resisted: Gloria Swanson, p. 386.
414 "Virginia grasped . . .": Ibid.
414 "If she suspected me . . .": Ibid., p. 287.
414 Gloria and Virginia: Variety, Aug. 14, 1929, p. 3.
414 Joe and Rose were joined: NYT, Aug. 20, 1929, p. 16.
414 "Hope you had a fine trip": Telegram, JPK to G. Swanson. Aug. 16, 1929, JPK.
415 together in Paris: The story of their time in Paris is from Rose Kennedy, pp. 202–3; Gloria Swanson, pp. 386–90; interview, Rose Kennedy.
416 The London premiere: Variety, Sept. 11, 1929, p. 2; LT, Sept. 11, 1929, p. 10.
416 "The crowd gave . . .": New York Telegram, Sept. 11, 1929, JPK.
416 Joe reported that Gloria was not well: JPK to H. de la Falaise, Oct. 2, 1929, JPK.
416 "Gloria did a magnificent . . .": Interview, Rose Kennedy.
416 " Variety today carries . . .": JPK to H. de la Falaise, Oct. 2, 1929, JPK. Henri and Constance Bennett were married Nov. 22, 1931; see NYT, Nov. 23, 1931, p. 22.
417 "In fact she is in bed . . .": JPK to H. de la Falaise, Oct. 2, 1929, JPK.
417 the New York opening: Gloria Swanson, p. 391; see also NYT, Nov. 2, 1929, p. 4; Exhibitor's Herald World, Nov. 16, 1929, p. 68.
417 Gloria claims, she was summoned: Gloria Swanson, pp. 393–94. The archivist at AAB feels such a visit would definitely have been out of character; interview, James O'Toole.
417 What a Widow: Variety, Sept. 17, 1930, p. 21.
418 "It was as if two men . . .": Gloria Swanson, p. 404.
418 Sunset Boulevard: Variety, July 26, 1950, pp. 1, 119; Charles Lockwood, pp. 259–60.
418 "inside joke": Rose Kennedy, p. 205.
419 "Never before . . .": Saturday Evening Post, Jan. 12, 1929, p. 6; see also Literary Digest, Dec. 8, 1928, p. 8.
419 few voices . . . who warned: Alexander Dana Noyes, The Market Place (1939), pp. 322–24; John Kenneth Galbraith, The Great Crash (1972), p. 77.
420 "A few gloomy souls . . .": John Flynn, "Wall Street and the Depression," NEA Service, Oct. 15, 1934, p. 1.
420 visit to J. P. Morgan II: Gordon Thomas and Max Morgan-Witts, The Day the Bubble Burst (1980), pp. 59–60.
420 "It was a move he must . . .": John Brooks, p. 81.
420 "It looks to me . . .": G. Currier to L. Kirstein, April 1, 1929, Kirstein Papers.
420 Kennedy began to sell: G. Currier to JPK, May 6, 1929; JPK to G. Currier, May 7, 1929, JPK.
421 "When the time comes . . .": Joseph Dinneen, The Kennedy Family, p. 35.
421 "the fundamental business . . .": Quoted in Richard J. Whalen, p. 105.
421 sixteen million shares: Glen G. Munn, Meeting the Bear Market (1930), p. 41.
421 "to a levelling process . . .": John K. Galbraith, p. 118.
421 Bronxville estate . . . $250,000: NYT, June 6, 1929, p. 48.
422 For a comparison of Ben Smith and Joe Kennedy see John Brooks, pp. 122–23.
422 Despite glowing public relations: Variety, May 7, 1930, p. 3, and Dec. 17, 1930, p. 48.
422 the common stock ceased earning: John Flynn, "Other People's Money," The New Republic, July 18, 1934, p. 265.

422 "The Swanson pictures . . .": W. Brooks to H. Brown, Sept. 26, 1930, JPK.

422 negotiated . . . Hughes . . . Schenck against it: Unidentified person at *Variety* to JPK, Sept. 18, 1930, JPK.

422 worked out a deal: H. Brown to D. Sarnoff, Oct. 8, 1930, JPK; *Variety*, Oct. 15, 1930, p. 5.

422 less than $5 million: *Variety*, Nov. 12, 1930, p. 4.

422 "I can't tell you . . .": JPK to J. J. Murdock, Dec. 9, 1930, JPK.

423 a lawsuit was instituted: *Variety*, Dec. 24, 1930, p. 30.

423 "I purchased twenty shares . . .": A. Lawler to JPK, Dec. 30, 1930, JPK.

423 "We are going to put you . . .": Unsigned and undated to JPK, JPK.

424 four million . . . unemployed: Arthur M. Schlesinger, Jr., *The Crisis of the Old Order* (1957), p. 167; *Historical Statistics of the United States*, pp. 70, 73.

424 dismal era: Arthur M. Schlesinger, Jr., *The Crisis . . .* , p. 167. The NYT reported on Sept. 30, 1932, p. 14, "Starvation, illness, the moral evils of unemployment are eating away the very fibre of our national being."

424 "a golden interval": Rose Kennedy, p. 206.

424 "the same spacious rooms . . .": Interview, Rose Kennedy.

425 "But if he took out a good . . .": Interview, Cy Howard.

425 "I think that when Joe . . .": Interview, Edward Gallagher.

425 happiest of her married life: Interview, Rose Kennedy.

425 "Joe always had a sweet tooth . . .": Interview, Mary Lou McCarthy.

426 "Joe dear—I love you . . .": KK to JPK, Jan. 24, 1932, JPK.

426 being called George Washington: Interview, Lem Billings.

426 "the lines of friendship . . .": Arthur M. Schlesinger, Jr., *The Crisis . . .* , p. 168.

426 purchasing his third estate: John Ney, pp. 13–16.

426 "Joe didn't like traveling . . .": Interview, Rose Kennedy.

426 "Thank you. Twenty years . . .": Telegram, RFK to JPK, Oct. 6, 1934, JPK.

427 "Darling . . .": Telegram, JPK to RFK, Oct. 6, 1934, JPK.

427 "I had counted . . .": Telegram, RFK to JFK, Oct. 6, 1934, JPK.

427 "I am not ashamed . . .": Joseph P. Kennedy, *I'm for Roosevelt* (1936), p. 3.

427 "In the next generation . . .": Interview, Morton Downey.

428 first contact with Roosevelt: *New York Herald Tribune*, May 9, 1932, JPK; BG, Sun., Sept. 25, 1932, ed. sect., p. 3.

428 "I was really worried . . .": Joe McCarthy, p. 58.

428 journey to Warm Springs . . . AP first reported: NYT, May 9, 1932, p. 8.

428 correctly identified: BG, May 9, 1932, p. 13.

428 Democratic national convention: *NYT*, April 5, 1932, p. 1.

429 the delegates he controlled: W. A. Swanberg, *Citizen Hearst* (1961), p. 437.

429 Hearst . . . decided to hold out: Michael R. Beschloss, *Kennedy and Roosevelt* (1980), p. 71.

429 "Do you want that man Baker? . . .": Arthur Krock, Oral History, Columbia University.

429 Kennedy claimed full credit: Ralph Martin and Ed Plaut, *Front Runner, Dark Horse* (1960), p. 117.

429 raised over $150,000: *Fortune*, Sept. 1937, p. 57.

430 whistle-stop tour: NYT, Sept. 12, 1932, p. 2.

430 boarded the *Roosevelt Special*: NYT, Sept. 13, 1932, p. 4; BG (eve.), Sept. 13, 1932, p. 11.

430 he was to remember: JPK to Ernest K. Lindley, Dec. 9, 1960: "all I can say . . . may be there was a little more excitement in this campaign, but . . . it wasn't half as much fun as we witnessed in our cross-country runs in the '32 campaign," JPK.

430 The *Special* had nearly a dozen cars: NYT, loc. cit.

431 two cars for . . . permanent members: Raymond Moley, *After Seven Years* (1939), p. 53.

431 the intense pleasure Joe: Interview, Rose Kennedy.

431 Feeling at times: Raymond Moley, *After Seven Years*, pp. 54–55.

431 "a rather fabulous figure . . .": Quoted in Edward M. Kennedy (ed.), p. 68.

432 fleet of buses . . . Grand Canyon: NYT, Sept. 27, 1932, p. 1.

432 third day of the World Series: *NYT*, Oct. 1, 1932, p. 1; *Chicago Daily Tribune*, Oct. 1 and Oct. 2, 1932, both p. 1.
432 "a remarkably handsome . . .": Arthur Krock, OH-JFKL.
432 Paris, Illinois: *NYT*, Sept. 4, 1932, p. 5.
432 Mattoon: Ibid.
432 "For Roosevelt the faces . . .": Arthur M. Schlesinger, Jr., *The Crisis* . . . , pp. 429–30.
433 "an unadulterated joy": Raymond Moley, *After Seven Years*, p. 52.
433 members of the Laramie Post: *NYT*, Sept. 17, 1932, p. 1.
433 Denver: *NYT*, Sept. 16, 1932, p. 3; *Denver Post*, Sept. 16, 1932, p. 1.
433 Butte, Montana: *NYT*, Sept. 20, 1932, p. 1.
433 Seattle: *NYT*, Sept. 21, 1932, p. 1.
433 San Francisco: *San Francisco Examiner*, Sept. 14, 1932, p. 1.
433 "one of the greatest . . .": *NYT*, Oct. 1, 1932, p. 1.
433 Kennedy slipped away: *BG*, Sun., Sept. 25, 1932, ed. sect., p. 3.
433 delivered sixteen major speeches: Raymond Moley, *After Seven Years*, p. 52.
434 historic Hundred Days: Arthur M. Schlesinger, Jr., *The Coming of the New Deal* (1959), pp. 20–21; James M. Burns, *Roosevelt: The Lion* . . . , pp. 161–82.
434 Kennedy never hesitated to clash: *BG*, Sun., Sept. 29, 1932, ed. sect., p. 3.
434 "infinite capacity to make friends": Raymond Moley, *The First New Deal* (1966), p. 380.
434 "Capitalism is the wagon . . .": H. B. Swope to JPK, Sept. 9, 1932, JPK.
434 "We have no actual famine . . .": *NYT*, Sept. 24, 1932, p. 6.
435 "time never stopped": Arthur M. Schlesinger, Jr., *The Crisis* . . . , p. 429.
435 "I have had a lot of fun . . .": JPK to L. Ruppel, May 18, 1934, JPK.
435 victory over Hoover . . . lavish party: Richard J. Whalen, p. 128.
435 "Isn't it wonderful . . .": Ibid., p. 129.
436 considered filing a lawsuit: Ibid., p. 131.
436 "All night Joe kept trying . . .": Interview, Rose Kennedy.
437 Louis Howe . . . was unalterably: Richard J. Whalen, p. 121.
437 For information on Howe see Jerome Beatty, "Here's Howe," *American Magazine*, March 1933, p. 17; Arthur Smith, "Roosevelt's Pilots—Colonel House and Colonel Howe," *Scribner's Magazine*, Jan. 1933, p. 204; obituary, *Newsweek*, April 25, 1936, p. 30.
438 "Looking back now . . .": Interview, Rose Kennedy.
438 "I read and hear about you . . .": JPK to M. LeHand, Dec. 23, 1933, JPK.
438 "My interest in politics . . .": Telegram, JPK to W. R. Hearst, Dec. 23, 1933, JPK.
439 "By a strange coincidence . . .": JPK to L. Ruppel, May 18, 1934, JPK. Louis Ruppel was the managing editor of the *Chicago Times* from 1933 to 1938.
439 Financial statements in the JPK papers cover Halle & Steiglitz, 1931–33, and Redmond and Co., 1933–34. For Redmond, there are accounts in the name of E. E. Moore and Mrs. Rose Kennedy as well as numbered and lettered accounts.
440 Libby-Owens-Ford Glass: According to *Moody's*, 1932, p. 1495, the company was incorporated in 1916 to manufacture plate glass.
440 Mason Day came up with: "Stock Market Practices," Hearings Before Banking and Currency Committee of the Senate, 73rd Congress, 2nd Session, Vol. 441, Part 2, pp. 6218–43.
440 Elisha Walker: For information see obituary, *NYT*, Nov. 10, 1950, p. 27.
440 Owens-Illinois Glass: Company products included bottles, jars, vials and glass containers, *Moody's*, 1932, p. 2209; see also Hearings . . . , loc. cit., pp. 6242–43.
440 driving the price way up: Hearings . . . , loc. cit., pp. 6224–29.
440 Kennedy made a profit: Ibid., p. 6210. Kennedy's participation in the pool was brought out upon his appointment to the SEC; see *The New Republic*, July 11, 1934, p. 220; *NYT*, July 16, 1934, p. 2.
441 the liquor for his tenth reunion: JPK to M. Brush, June 26, 1922, JPK.
441 arranged to sell liquor at cost: JPK to R. Potter, Aug. 17, 1920, JPK.
441 "the hectic rush . . .": Interview, Helen Barron.
441 valued at thousands: JPK affidavit for Lloyds, undated, JPK.

441 "Before selling it to you . . .": JPK to M. Brush, loc. cit.
441 access to a large supply: J. T. Fitzgerald to JPK, July 27, 1933, JPK.
442 With $40,000 of his own money: Ibid.
442 major loophole in the Volstead Act: Thomas Coffey, *The Long Thirst* (1978), p. 31.
442 fourteen years of Prohibition: Andrew Sinclair, *Prohibition* (1962), p. 429.
442 "The drugstore and soda fountain . . .": Interview, Thomas Fitzgerald.
443 Frank Costello . . . claimed: *NYT*, July 27, 1973, p. 37.
443 "Talk about liquor, textile . . .": A. P. Giannini to JPK, Dec. 24, 1931, JPK.
443 Europe in September 1933: *NYT*, Sept. 21, 1933, p. 9; *BG* (eve.), Sept. 26, 1933, p. 1; Rose Kennedy, pp. 211–12.
443 Jimmy Roosevelt: Alva Johnson, "Jimmy's Got It," *Saturday Evening Post*, July 2, 1938, pp. 8–9.
443 "I can't tell you . . .": J. Roosevelt to JPK, May 19, 1933, JPK.
444 viewed as America's Prince of Wales: Alva Johnson article, loc. cit., p. 60.
444 closed "with the Englishmen . . .": JPK to JPK Jr., Dec. 4, 1933, JPK.
444 medicinal permits: Alva Johnson article, loc. cit.
444 "Cocktails will be a quarter . . .": *BET*, Dec. 4, 1933, p. 1.
444 Senate Banking and Currency Committee: Donald A. Ritchie, "The Pecora Wall Street Exposé, 1934," in Arthur M. Schlesinger, Jr., and Roger Bruns (eds.), *Congress Investigates: A Documented History, 1792–1974* (1975), pp. 2555–2578.
445 For information on Pecora see obituary, *NYT*, Dec. 8, 1971, p. 40; see also *Newsweek*, June 10, 1933, p. 16; *The Literary Digest*, Jan. 19, 1935, p. 7.
445 "I looked with astonishment . . .": John Flynn, "The Marines Land in Wall Street," *Harper's*, July 1934, p. 149.
446 drafted by a talented group: Ibid., pp. 150–51; *Newsweek*, July 13, 1935, pp. 24–25.
446 signing of the law: *NYT*, June 7, 1934, p. 7.
446 "Ferd, now that I have signed . . .": Donald Ritchie in Arthur M. Schlesinger, Jr., and Roger Bruns (eds.), pp. 2577–78.
446 makeup of the commission: Landis as possible chairman, *NYT*, May 27, 1934, p. 1; rumor of Pecora as chairman, *BG*, June 27, 1934, p. 14; first press on JPK as possible member, *New York Journal*, June 28, 1934, and *BP*, June 30, 1934, JPK.
447 "The best bet for Chairman . . .": Raymond Moley, *After Seven Years*, pp. 286–87.
447 like setting a cat: Michael Beschloss, p. 85.
447 Roy Howard visit: Raymond Moley, *After Seven Years*, pp. 287–90; Hugh Johnson of the *New York World Telegram* in a letter to JPK on June 26 states: "Howard told Swope to get the information to you . . . better not take the job . . . he would 'tear you to pieces' on your bull market record," JPK.
447 "The President cannot with impunity . . .": *Fortune*, Sept. 1937, p. 57.
447 start of a record heat wave: *Washington Post*, June 30, 1934, p. 1.
447 The account of the meeting: Raymond Moley, *After Seven Years*, pp. 288–89. Official announcement, *BG* (eve.), July 2, 1934, p. 1.
448 "Had FDR's dearest enemy . . .": John Flynn, "The World," *The New Republic*, July 11, 1934, p. 220.
449 wired the . . . subcommittee: *New York Journal*, June 28, 1934, JPK.
449 The swearing in: *Fortune*, Sept. 1937, p. 58. See also Federal Writers Project, *Washington: City and Capital* (1937), p. 980.
449 For information on the commissioners see Theodore Knappen, "The Rulers of the Stock Market," *Magazine of Wall Street*, July 21, 1934, pp. 329–31, 368.
449 were technically responsible for electing: *New York Journal*, loc. cit.; *NYT*, July 1, 1934, p. 1; *U.S. Statutes at Large, 1933–1934: Public Laws*, Vol. 48, Part 1, pp. 881–909.
449 scribbled note: Raymond Moley, *After Seven Years*, pp. 288–89.
449 "After that morning . . .": Donald L. Ritchie, *James Landis* (1980), p. 60.
450 "He looked very solemn . . .": *NYT*, July 3, 1934, p. 1.
450 "as chipper as two . . .": Ibid.
450 "I'm no sucker . . .": Michael Beschloss, p. 89.
450 "I believe that between now . . .": *New York Evening Journal*, July 2, 1934, JPK.
450 "Boys . . . I've got nine kids . . .": *Philadelphia Record*, Nov. 1934, JPK.

450 "I think Kennedy brings . . .": *BNB,* July 12, 1934, p. 1.
451 it made little sense to uproot: Rose Kennedy, pp. 214–15.
451 Marwood: *Newsweek,* Aug. 4, 1934, p. 28.
451 "Joe took good care of himself . . .": Quoted in Richard J. Whalen, p. 156.
451 "You dumb bastards . . .": Joe McCarthy, p. 66.
451 Account of Roosevelt's visit: Arthur Krock, *Memoirs: 60 Years on the Firing Line* (1968), pp. 169–70.
452 "an erstwhile alley gamin . . .": Ralph de Bedts, *The New Deal's SEC: The Formative Years* (1964), p. 108.
452 "We of the SEC . . .": Address, National Press Club, July 25, 1934, JPK; *NYT,* July 26, 1934, pp. 1, 3.
453 It was Kennedy's complex task: Ralph de Bedts, p. 76.
453 Kennedy outlined two goals: *Saturday Evening Post,* Jan. 18, 1934, p. 61.
453 "full and adequate disclosure . . .": Ibid.
454 "It was a real achievement . . .": *Kansas City Star,* Sept. 29, 1935, JPK.
454 "You are such a swell . . .": W. O. Douglas to JPK, Sept. 21, 1935, JPK.
454 "It was significant . . .": Ralph de Bedts, p. 106; on JPK's business background as an asset to the commission see Herring E. Pendleton, *Federal Commissioners* (1963), pp. 24–25.
454 Kennedy decided to resign: *NYT,* Sept. 21, 1935, p. 14; *Washington Post,* Sept. 21, 1935, pp. 1, 2.
454 "I'm proud of you . . .": C. Norton to JPK, Sept. 21, 1935, JPK.
455 "When Joseph Kennedy was named . . .": John Flynn, "Other People's Money," *The New Republic,* Oct. 9, 1935, p. 244.
457 "If Joe wouldn't accept . . .": Interview, Rose Kennedy.
457 "It was an astonishing . . .": Garry Wills, *The Kennedy Imprisonment* (1981), p. 67.
457 Jack confided . . . not even learned . . . slump: Jean Schoor, *Young Jack Kennedy* (1963), p. 37.
458 Joe Junior became a model student: L. Billings, "Notes," RFK.
458 Choate: *Choate Catalogue,* 1934–36.
458 "Is the boy in any part Hebraic?": Application form for admission to Choate, 1930–31, RFK.
458 George St. John's portrait appears in *The Brief,* the Choate yearbook, for 1933.
458 "efficient teaching, manly . . .": *Choate Catalogue,* p. 15.
458 school founded upon hierarchy: *The Choate Handbook,* 1931–32, pp. 13–14.
458 "He was roughhousing . . .": JFK to JPK, Dec. 9, year unknown, RFK.
459 "one of the most promising" . . . "watching . . .": Rowland C. Massie, Physical Director, June 1930, RFK.
459 his grades the first half: Hank Searls, p. 57.
459 "Mr. Hemenway says that . . .": JPK, Jr., to JPK, Feb. 5, 1933, RFK.
459 "It is rare . . .": Kenneth Miller, Report in French, June 1930, RFK.
459 "Joe's determination . . .": O. H. Morgan, Report in Latin, June 1930, RFK.
459 "Joe deserves a great deal . . .": Ray W. Tobey, Report in English, June 1930, RFK.
459 "one of the ablest . . .": F. W. Smith, Report in Algebra, June 1930, RFK.
459 "He has been one of the most . . .": Ben Davis, Housemaster, Report, June 1930, RFK.
459 "one of the most worthwhile . . .": G. St. John to JPK, Oct. 31, 1929, RFK.
460 "The minute we got . . .": Peter Collier and David Horowitz, p. 60.
460 "All day long . . .": L. Billings, "Notes," RFK.
460 Canterbury Prep . . . illness: Rose Kennedy, p. 187.
461 "He has a very attractive . . .": RFK to G. St. John, July 3, 1931, RFK.
461 Rose had a hard time: Interview, Lem Billings.
461 "had gained such an advantage . . .": Quoted in F. O. Matthiessen, *The James Family: A Group Biography* (1980), p. 74.
461 "one of the big boys . . .": Mrs. St. John to RFK, Oct. 7, 1931, RFK.
462 "a tower of strength": Earl G. Lernbach, Report, Oct. 1933, JPK.
462 "In looking over the monthly . . .": JPK to JFK, April 12, 1932, RFK.

462 "that it would be quite easy . . .": JPK to G. St. John, Nov. 21, 1933, JPK.

463 "Mr. Ayres told me . . .": JPK to JPK, Jr., Nov. 21, 1933, RFK.

463 "We have possibly contributed . . .": JPK to G. Steele, assistant headmaster, Jan. 5, 1935, RFK.

463 definitely decided to stop fooling: JFK to JPK, Dec. 4, 1934, RFK.

463 "In fact, I think the improvement . . .": JPK to JFK, Dec. 5, 1934, RFK.

464 large numbers of friendships: Herbert S. Parmet, p. 33; see also Joan and Clay Blair, Jr., *The Search for JFK* (1976), p. 37.

464 "When he flashed . . .": Quoted in Herbert S. Parmet, p. 33.

464 "it was the closest friendship . . .": Interview, Lem Billings.

464 Lem . . . was descended: Ibid.; see also David Michaelis, *The Best of Friends* (1983), p. 137.

464 "I was immediately . . .": Interview, Lem Billings.

465 rites of passage: Interview with Rip Horton in Joan and Clay Blair, Jr., p. 34.

465 Ralph Horton, or "Rip": Herbert S. Parmet, pp. 33–34; Joan and Clay Blair, Jr., p. 3.

465 "that Choate was *his*": Interview, Lem Billings.

465 Story of Prize Day: Ibid.

465 coveted prizes: listed in program for Prize Day, May 27, 1933, RFK.

465 Joe was awarded the Harvard Trophy: Hank Searls, pp. 60–61.

465 "very pleased for his brother . . .": Interview, Lem Billings.

465 three years before: *NYT*, Feb. 23, 1933, p. 15, and May 24, 1933, p. 9.

466 "This was the first time . . .": Interview, Lem Billings.

466 "Mother and I are very proud . . .": JPK to JPK, Jr., May 29, 1933, RFK.

467 Frankfurter had responded: F. Frankfurter, OH-JFKL.

467 "a little wild . . . beyond the pale": Interview, Rose Kennedy.

467 most articulate human being: Kingsley Martin, *Harold Laski* (1933), pp. x, 20–21.

467 crowds jostled: Ibid., p. 62.

468 "his eager zest for life . . .": Quoted in John F. Kennedy (ed.), p. 44.

468 "What he liked . . .": Ibid., p. 43.

468 "Joe would always come . . .": Quoted in Hank Searls, p. 68.

468 "students would sprawl . . .": Ibid.

468 "I am a socialist . . .": Ibid.

468 "He was with me during a year . . .": Quoted in John F. Kennedy (ed.), p. 44.

468 "I'm at Sir James Calder's . . .": JPK, Jr., to JPK, Dec. 10, 1933, RFK.

469 "My tastes seem to go for . . .": JPK, Jr., to RFK, March 9, 1934, RFK.

469 "solidarity, his real niceness . . .": F. Frankfurter to JPK, Oct. 24, 1933, JPK.

469 "Am getting along fine . . .": JPK, Jr., to JPK, Nov. 6, 1933, RFK.

470 "I can't tell you . . .": JPK to JPK, Jr., Nov. 21, 1933, RFK.

470 "Would like very much . . .": JPK to H. Greaves, Dec. 2, 1933, RFK.

470 "Hitler recognized this mood . . .": Alan Bullock, *Hitler—A Study in Tyranny* (1952), p. 278.

471 "One is struck . . .": JPK, Jr., to JPK, April 23, 1934, RFK.

471 "I had been to Laski's . . .": JPK, Jr., to JPK, Nov. 26, 1933, RFK.

471 "They had tried liberalism . . .": JPK, Jr., to JPK, April 23, 1934, RFK.

471 "They were at the heads . . .": Ibid.

472 Founded in orthodoxy . . . Jewish responsibility: "Causes of Anti-Semitism," Conference Bulletin, Archdiocese of New York, February 1937, JPK.

473 "couldn't compete with . . .": Interview, Clem Norton.

473 "a bunch of ignorant . . .": Ibid.

474 "We arrive tomorrow . . .": JPK, Jr., to RFK, June 1, 1967, RFK.

474 "If I were their age . . .": Rose Kennedy, p. 185.

475 a revolutionary "house": Benjamin Welles, "Harvard Has Class," *Town and Country*, Nov. 1939, p. 80; Helen Haring, "The Houses," *Harvard Alumni Bulletin*, May 7, 1939, pp. 880–83; Samuel Eliot Morison, *Three Centuries at Harvard*, p. 47.

476 "applications for entry . . .": Interview, John Kenneth Galbraith.

476 "Nowhere else in the world . . .": *Town and Country*, loc. cit., p. 78.

477 the Porcellian held sway: Ibid.; see also Robert E. Lane, "Analysis of the Harvard Community," undergraduate paper, HU Archives.
477 "Still, it was not easy . . .": Interview, John K. Galbraith. On Winthrop House see HC, March 23, 1937, p. 4.
477 Joe Junior "of Bronxville . . .": BH, Sept. 30, 1934, JPK.
477 "In those days . . . even though . . .": Interview, John K. Galbraith.
477 "he was so handsome . . .": Interview, Charles Burke.
477 freshman football: JPK wrote to JPK, Jr., Oct. 24, 1934: "Remember the first choice for freshman team does not . . . mean making . . . final team. . . . Remember, after you have done the best you can, nobody can do any more," JPK.
477 Hasty Pudding and the Spee: Hank Searls, p. 82.
477 close friendships: Ibid., pp. 73–74; see also on Reardon, Harvard Class of 1938 (1941); on Bilodeau, Harvard Class of 1937 (1940).
478 "For Joe . . . Harvard was simply . . .": Interview, Lem Billings.
478 "I have doubts about . . .": JPK to JPK, Jr., Oct. 2, 1934, RFK.
478 "The assistant graduate manager . . .": JPK to F. Frankfurter, Oct. 5, 1934, RFK.
478 "I stopped in and spent . . .": JPK to JPK, Jr., Dec. 7, 1934, RFK.
478 "The S.E.C. decision . . .": JPK, Jr., to JPK, April 11, 1936, RFK.
479 "Joe talked about his father . . .": Interview, John K. Galbraith.
479 "I congratulate you . . .": JPK to JPK, Jr., April 13, 1936, RFK.
479 "very good experience": JPK to JPK, Jr., Feb. 27, 1936, RFK.
479 "It really was tough luck . . .": JPK to JPK, Jr., Feb. 15, 1937, RFK.
479 "By the way, Barbara Cushing . . .": JPK, Jr., to JPK, February 1936, RFK.
480 "as 21 and 22 is still . . .": JPK to JPK, Jr., Feb. 27, 1936, RFK.
480 "certainly put an end . . .": JPK to J. Reilly, Oct. 7, 1936, JPK.
480 operation on Joe's knee: JPK to R. Bingham, Oct. 6, 1936, JPK.
480 "After all, he is only . . .": JPK to Dr. Jordan, Nov. 9, 1936, RFK.
480 "I am still a little concerned . . .": JPK to JPK, Jr., Feb. 15, 1937, RFK.
481 "When he came back to Choate . . .": Interview, Lem Billings.
481 "he had a very definite flair . . .": Harold Tinker as quoted by Ralph Horton, OH-JFKL.
481 But once again illness: G. St. John to RFK, Feb. 6, 1934, RFK.
481 home in March: JPK to Mrs. St. John, March 4, 1934, RFK.
481 prohibited from engaging in: JPK to G. St. John, Sept. 19, 1934, RFK.
481 "The girls really liked Jack . . .": Interview, Lem Billings.
482 "After parties, Kathleen liked . . .": Interview, John White.
482 "She was on the telephone . . .": Rose Kennedy, p. 179.
483 Noroton in 1933: Interviews, Sisters Alice and Gabriella Huson and Sister Jean Ford.
483 "In Kathleen's day . . .": Interview, Sister Gabriella Huson.
483 "The two of them were always . . .": Ibid.
484 "There were more boys who thought . . .": Interview, John White.
484 Lem's correspondence is now in the possession of Robert Kennedy, Jr.
484 "How about going up to Harvard . . .": LB to KK, October 1936, LB.
484 "Am afraid I couldn't work . . .": KK to LB, Oct. 10, 1936, LB.
484 "How is everything in Palm Beach? . . .": KK to RFK, Jan. 13, 1934, RFK.
485 "Kennedy's Palm Beach villa . . .": KK Scrapbook, RFK.
485 Kathleen's asthma: JPK to JFK, Oct. 10, 1934, RFK.
485 not at all sure Kathleen would . . . stick it out: Ibid.
485 "I am awfully sorry . . .": KK to JPK, Oct. 21, 1934, RFK.
485 "I was very proud of you . . .": JPK to KK, Dec. 8, 1934, RFK.
486 "I don't know when I have ever . . .": KK to JPK, Dec. 2, 1934, RFK.
486 "I didn't have any time . . .": KK to JPK, Dec. 1, 1936, RFK.
486 "We had lunch with Kathleen . . .": JPK to JFK, Feb. 6, 1935, RFK.
486 "put over festivities . . .": JFK Choate Scrapbook, JPK.
486 the Muckers Club: Herbert S. Parmet, pp. 34–35.
487 he called all the members: Lem Billings wrote for Mrs. Kennedy an explanation of the Muckers which is quoted in Rose Kennedy, pp. 194–95.
487 devoted an entire chapel: Rip Horton, OH-JFKL.

487 "They weren't wicked kids . . .": Quoted in Joan Meyers (ed.), *John F. Kennedy: As We Remember Him* (1965), p. 17.

487 Kathleen sent a funny telegram: Quoted in David Michaelis, p. 138. Kathleen, in a letter to Lem Feb. 27, 1935, apologized for the trouble caused by the telegram, LB.

487 "I was angry . . .": Quoted in Joan Meyers (ed.), p. 17.

487 "It was one thing to take on . . .": Interview, Lem Billings.

488 "In fact, he spoke . . .": Quoted in Joan Meyers (ed.), p. 17.

488 "I know you want to do all . . .": JPK to KK, Feb. 20, 1935, RFK.

488 "I went up to see Jack . . .": JPK to Dr. O'Leary, Feb. 18, 1935, RFK.

489 the donation was made two years earlier: G. St. John to JPK, March 11, 1932, and April 14, 1932, JPK.

489 "Something certainly soaked in . . .": Rose Kennedy, p. 196.

489 "Don't let me lose confidence . . .": JPK to JFK, April 29, 1934, RFK.

489 graduating in the middle of his class: Herbert S. Parmet, p. 32.

489 "most likely to succeed": Rip Horton, OH-JFKL.

489 Rose decided to send Kathleen: Rose Kennedy, "Notes for TTR," RFK.

489 wanted Kathleen to benefit: Rose Kennedy, pp. 215–16.

490 once again seriously ill: Ibid., p. 216.

490 "heartfelt appreciation . . .": JPK to R. Bingham, Oct. 21, 1935, Robert Bingham Papers, Library of Congress, Washington, D.C.

490 because his brother was *not* there: Joe in a letter to Jim Landis concerning Jack and law school states: "He thought he would go to Yale . . . because he felt it would be better not to be in direct competition with his brother," Landis Papers.

490 Joe would have preferred his going to Harvard: Interview, Rose Kennedy.

490 Swope, managed to get him admitted: David Koskoff, p. 402.

490 "I had a nice talk with Doctor Raycourt . . .": JPK to JFK, Nov. 11, 1935, RFK.

491 "Jack is far from being . . .": JPK to R. Bingham, Nov. 12, 1935, JPK.

491 "the most impressive thing . . .": KK to RFK, Nov. 4, 1935, RFK.

491 "Am rather sad at the prospect . . .": KK to LB, Nov. 24, 1935, LB.

491 her reading of *The Three Musketeers:* KK to parents, Feb. 17 and March 13, 1936, RFK.

491 "The best part of all . . .": KK to Bobby Kennedy, Jan. 23, 1936, RFK.

491 "Mother, please please come over . . .": KK to RFK, Jan. 24, 1936, RFK.

492 "Do you realize I haven't seen . . .": KK to Bobby Kennedy, April 26, 1936, RFK.

492 "She looked so pretty . . .": Interview, Rose Kennedy.

492 "the Soviet Union seemed as remote . . .": Rose Kennedy, pp. 221–22.

492 "When we first got back to Paris . . .": Interview, Rose Kennedy.

493 "Traveling with Kathleen was such a joy . . .": Ibid.

493 "Here I am . . .": RFK to KK, May 27, 1936, RFK.

494 Paramount Pictures hired him: *New York Evening Post*, May 2, 1936, JPK. On the report see *NYT*, July 3, 1936, p. 24, and July 17, 1936, p. 23.

494 "I am sure you will be interested . . .": A. Zukor to RFK, May 28, 1936, JPK.

494 fee of $150,000: *Fortune*, Sept. 1937, p. 144; Richard J. Whalen, pp. 179–80.

495 "I am asking a little group . . .": Telegram, J. Farley to JPK, June 11, 1936, JPK.

495 "I wonder if you could give me . . .": JPK to A. Krock, June 24, 1936, JPK.

495 Krock agreed: Typed response on Joe's letter, AKP.

495 "I haven't done much . . .": A. Krock to JPK, July 3, 1936, JPK.

495 "it ventured perilously . . .": Richard J. Whalen, p. 195.

495 "an organized functioning . . .": Joseph P. Kennedy, p. 14.

495 "Roosevelt must be gratified . . .": *Saturday Review of Literature*, Sept. 5, 1936, p. 11.

495 "As an American citizen . . .": Press release of speech at dinner of the Democratic Business Men's League, Oct. 24, 1936, JPK.

496 "Joseph Kennedy has grown": *Business Week*, Dec. 5, 1936, pp. 32–33.

496 sudden death of Agnes: BP, Sept. 17, 1936, p. 4; *NYT*, Sept. 19, 1936, p. 17.

496 Agnes had attracted many: Interview, Mary Jo Gargan Clasby.

496 met Joseph Gargan: Rose Kennedy, p. 114. Marriage, BP, Sun., April 28, 1936, p. 9.

496 "In those days the theory . . .": Interview, Joseph Gargan.

496 a "terrible blow": Interview, Rose Kennedy.
497 "As I told you last night . . .": JPK to M. LeHand, Dec. 29, 1936, JPK.
497 While the early reports: Reports from Devereux School, Berwyn, Pa., June 23, 1930. The 1936–37 course of study for Rosemary, who was being privately tutored, indicated that Grade 5 arithmetic was too difficult for her, JPK.
497 "I had a firm talk with Rosemary . . .": JPK to H. Newton, Oct. 15, 1934, JPK. JPK writes to Dr. Good asking about the possibility that glandular problems are contributing to Rosemary's backwardness: "We do not want to leave a stone unturned if there is anything possible to be done," Oct. 15, 1934, JPK.
497 "pray very hard that I will get . . .": Rosemary Kennedy to parents, June 2, 1934, JPK.
497 "I would do anything . . .": Rosemary Kennedy to JPK, Oct. 15, 1934, JPK.
497 "I have had from 15 to 20 years . . .": H. Newton to RFK, Aug. 17, 1936, JPK.
497 "Am wondering if Mrs. D. working her . . .": A. Rohde to RFK, Oct. 18, 1936, JPK.
498 "Rose will be in Boston . . .": JPK to JPK, Jr., April 11, 1938, RFK.
498 "Received your very nice letter . . .": JPK, Jr., to Rosemary Kennedy, Dec. 2, 1933, RFK.
498 "Rosemary had a marvelous time . . .": JPK to JFK, Feb. 15, 1937, RFK.
498 "We arrived in Washington . . .": Bobby Kennedy, "President Roosevelt's Second Inaugural," undated, RFK.
498 "I am very anxious to have . . .": FDR to JPK, Feb. 26, 1937, JPK.
499 "To be very honest with you . . .": JPK to J. Byrnes, March 15, 1937, JPK.
499 "he wanted nothing more . . .": Interview, Rose Kennedy.
499 "I am delighted that you are back . . .": H. Ickes to JPK, March 15, 1937, JPK.
499 "it would go down in the archives . . .": JPK to H. Ickes, April 3, 1937, JPK.
499 "I will not try your credulity . . .": Speech before Society of American Newspaper Editors, Washington, D.C., April 17, 1937, JPK.
500 "Just arrived home . . .": D. Pearson to JPK, Jan. 13, 1937, JPK.
500 Perhaps it was merely . . . convenience: Joan and Clay Blair, Jr., p. 17.
500 "I have just finished reading . . .": JPK to A. Krock, July 1, 1937, AKP.
500 "I may have lighted . . .": A. Krock to JPK, July 1, 1937, JPK.
501 "he was thrilled, for he knew . . .": Interview, Rose Kennedy.
501 the reporter assigned to the project: Eric Hodgins, managing editor, cabled JPK, March 30, 1937, that the article would be written by Fortune staff member Earle Looker. The letter of introduction for Looker indicated he was "an old hand in Washington and I am happily confident that you will find much of interest in common with him," JPK.
501 "Generally, my comment . . .": JPK to R. Davenport, May 17, 1937, JPK. JPK forwarded a 9-page review of the article with Looker's misstatements in one column and his observations in a second column (cited as "Looker Draft.")
501 "I have no trouble in trusting . . .": JPK to R. Davenport, May 25, 1937, JPK.
502 "I am convinced after talking with . . .": JPK to R. Davenport, May 28, 1937, JPK.
502 Fortune agreed to assign a new writer: R. Davenport to JPK, June 4, 1937, JPK.
502 consultant to the . . . Hearst organization: W. A. Swanberg, pp. 485–87.
502 Hearst was so burdened with debt: Arthur Poole prepared a statement entitled "Properties of W. R. Hearst: The Mistakes and Ineptitude of the Financial Management in Recent Years," and forwarded it to JPK June 23, 1937, JPK.
502 "forced to do a thousand things . . .": W. A. Swanberg, p. 488.
502 "We all realize this necessitates . . .": Telegram, JPK to W. R. Hearst, undated copy, JPK.
502 "While it will be all right . . .": A. Poole to JPK, May 5, 1937, JPK.
503 offered to purchase the two Boston papers: A. Poole to W. R. Hearst, June 23, 1937, JPK.
503 "should these properties come . . .": W. Howey to JPK, undated, JPK.
503 "I am receiving little information. . . .": Telegram, JPK to W. R. Hearst, Aug. 19, 1937, JPK.
503 debt totaled $126 million: W. A. Swanberg, p. 486; A. Poole to JPK, Oct. 12, 1937, JPK.
503 "Don't be surprised if Kennedy . . .": Newsweek, Aug. 28, 1937, p. 35. On Aug. 2,

JPK wrote to Walter Cummings, National Bank & Trust Co., Chicago: "I had a talk with Mr. Hearst and the men temporarily in charge of the management and tonight . . . meeting to see how they can arrange the legal situation to put me in control," JPK.

503 "not possessing family tradition . . .": *BP*, Sun., March 14, 1937, p. 4.

504 "It was with astonishment . . .": F. O'Hara to JPK, March 26, 1937, JPK.

504 Kennedy tried to assuage O'Hara: JPK to F. O'Hara, April 22, 1937, JPK.

504 Joe Junior was elected chairman: Noted in *HC*, March 4, 1937, p. 1.

504 student council: Election reported in *HC*, May 26, 1937, p. 1.

505 usher for Class Day: *HC*, May 21, 1937, p. 1.

505 business manager of the class album: *HC*, June 7, 1937, p. 1.

505 Jack failed to finish: *HC*, Feb. 24, 1937, p. 1.

505 "It was a matter of determination . . .": Quoted in John Henry Cutler, p. 292.

505 "Jack, if you want my opinion . . .": Quoted in *BG*, Nov. 19, 1964, HU Archives.

505 ruptured a spinal disc: Joe McCarthy, p. 75.

505 helped to lead his . . . freshman team: Activities File, Personal Papers, Box 2, JFK.

505 Torby Macdonald: Joan and Clay Blair, Jr., pp. 48–49; *Harvard Class of 1940* (1946), p. 237, HU Archives; obituary, *NYT*, May 22, 1976, p. 28.

506 annual freshman smoker: *HC*, April 1, 1937, p. 1.

506 managed to get Gertrude Niessen: *HC*, April 30, 1937, p. 1.

506 "I had no idea I was wishing . . .": JPK to J. Conway, May 3, 1937, JPK.

506 With Memorial Hall filled: *HC*, May 5, 1937, p. 1.

506 "one of the most popular . . .": on his application to Winthrop he wrote that his reason for choosing Winthrop was his brother, Personal Papers, Box 2, JFK.

506 Tutors recall: Ibid., Tutorial Reports.

506 Jack set off for Europe: *The New Yorker*, April 1, 1961, pp. 26–27; David Michaelis, pp. 153–59.

506 "the almost complete ignorance . . .": Quoted in James M. Burns, *John Kennedy: A Political Profile* (1963), pp. 32–33; Herbert S. Parmet, p. 53.

507 invited his father to be a guest speaker: Quoted in John F. Kennedy (ed.), p. 25.

507 "an absolutely wonderful talk . . .": Interview, John K. Galbraith.

507 at the Harvard–Yale game: Hank Searls, p. 91.

507 Tommy Campbell: *Harvard Class of 1912* (1937), p. 110, HU Archives.

507 The day of the big game: *HC*, Nov. 20, 1937, p. 1.; *BH*, Sun., Nov. 21, 1937, p. 36.

508 58,000 fans: *BG* (eve.), Nov. 20, 1937, p. 1.

508 "the hardest hitting . . .": *HC*, Nov. 22, 1937, p. 1.

508 score tied at 6–6 . . . last six minutes: *BG* (eve.), loc. cit., p. 4; Hank Searls, p. 92.

508 "Some seniors stayed . . .": Hank Searls, p. 92.

508 "like schoolboys . . .": *BH*, Sun., Nov. 21, 1937, pp. 1, 36.

508 fought his way through: Hank Searls, p. 93.

509 "Our first debt is to . . .": *HC*, Nov. 21, 1937, p. 3.

509 appointed ambassador: *NYT*, Dec. 9, 1937, p. 1.

509 Bingham . . . anxious to resign: Arthur Krock outlines the circumstances of the appointment in a "Private Memo," Dec. 23, 1937, AKP.

509 again hospitalized: *NYT*, Nov. 20, 1937, p. 6, and Nov. 26, 1937, p. 14. Ambassador Bingham died Dec. 18, 1937; see *NYT*, Dec. 19, 1937, pp. 1, 4.

509 "The moment the appointment . . .": Interview, Rose Kennedy.

509 The press reaction: "Capital Praises Kennedy Choice," *BG*, Dec. 10, 1937, p. 1; "London Opinion Laudatory," *NYT*, Dec. 18, 1937, p. 3.

509 "I am tickled to death . . .": L. Saltonstall to JPK, Dec. 10, 1937, JPK.

510 "I thank God I have lived . . .": "Mike" to JPK, Dec. 11, 1937, JPK.

510 "As in your case . . .": J. Tumulty to JPK, Dec. 11, 1937, JPK.

510 "I do not expect to get . . .": JPK to J. Tumulty, Dec. 21, 1937, JPK.

510 "You are a sincere man . . .": B. Carter to JPK, Dec. 28, 1937, JPK.

512 day was cool but sunny: *LT*, March 3, 1938, p. 16.

512 "soothing our sickness . . .": H. J. Massingham, *London Scene* (1933), p. 254.

512 Situated in . . . Grosvenor Square: John Winant, *A Letter from Grosvenor Square* (1947), p. 70; see also *Survey of London*, Vol. XL (1980), Part 2, pp. 112, 118, 167.

513 back to the late eighteenth century: "Embassy of the USA, London," undated pamphlet available at the United States Embassy in London.

513 "a mixture of amusement . . .": Herbert Ashley, "The Man Who Means Business," *Strand Magazine*, August 1938, p. 373, JPK.

513 "I have a beautiful blue . . .": JPK to J. Roosevelt, March 8, 1938, Hull Papers as cited in David Koskoff, p. 121.

514 "I am planning to take . . .": JPK to J. Breen, Dec. 31, 1937, JPK.

514 "You see, Herschel Johnson . . .": Interview, Page Huidekoper Wilson.

514 "There is little doubt . . .": Washington Chancery to American Department, Feb. 1938, Foreign Office F0371/21530/A1564/60/45, PRO.

514 formal accreditation: *LT*, March 9, 1938, p. 14. See also Christopher Hibbert, *The Court of St. James'* (1979), p. 3.

514 "It's a quarter past nine . . .": JPK to J. Byrnes, March 8, 1938, Byrnes Papers as cited in Michael Beschloss, p. 160.

514 three state carriages: *NYT*, March 9, 1938, p. 1.

515 "We were ushered into . . .": DM, Ch. 2, p. 7.

515 King George VI, who volunteered: Richard J. Whalen, p. 211.

515 "I have just been received . . .": JPK to A. Krock, March 8, 1938, AKP.

515 "You can't expect me to develop . . .": *Time*, March 14, 1938, p. 19.

516 "Dubious about hole in one": John Henry Cutler, p. 279.

516 "I am much happier . . .": Joe McCarthy, p. 5.

516 "When you feel that British . . .": DM, Ch. 1, p. 7; Elliott Roosevelt (ed.), *FDR: His Personal Letters, 1928–1945* (1950), Vol. 2, p. 769.

516 presenting American debutantes: DM, Ch. 1, pp. 7–8; *LT*, April 11, 1938, p. 12.

516 "The spectacle seemed to me: . . .": DM, Ch. 1, p. 8.

517 Seen in some quarters as the rebuke: Krock column, *NYT*, April 12, 1938, p. 22; John Corry, *Golden Clan: The Murrays, the McDonnells, and the Irish American Aristocracy* (1977), p. 74.

517 front-page coverage: *NYT*, April 10, 1938, p. 1.

517 "the curtain was rising . . .": Richard J. Whalen, p. 216.

518 Chamberlain convinced himself: Larry Fuchser, *Neville Chamberlain and Appeasement* (1982), p. 10; the Earl of Birkenhead, *Halifax: The Life of Lord Halifax* (1968), p. 363.

518 Chamberlain exerted: Ian Colvin, *The Chamberlain Cabinet* (1971), pp. 46–48.

518 Eden . . . had resigned: Winston Churchill, *The Gathering Storm* (1948), pp. 256–57.

518 "the dark waters . . .": Ibid., p. 257.

518 "During all the war soon to come . . .": Ibid.

518 "The more I talk with people . . .": JPK to A. Krock, March 21, 1938, JPK and AKP.

519 he could not see how "the Central . . .": Ibid.

519 He seemed at first to agree: DM, Ch. 2, pp. 8–9.

519 "with all due respect . . .": JPK to FDR, March 11, 1938, quoted in DM, Ch. 3, p. 6.

519 had announced a plebiscite: DM, Ch. 3, p. 1; William L. Shirer, *The Rise and Fall of the Third Reich* (1959), p. 334.

519 "I believe it was God's will . . .": Hitler quoted in William L. Shirer, loc. cit., p. 394.

520 "The hard fact is . . .": Quoted ibid., p. 353.

520 "Mussolini, I will never forget this . . .": DM, Ch. 3, p. 2.

520 "For the first few weeks . . .": William L. Shirer, loc. cit., p. 351.

520 Phone conversation with Cordell Hull: transcript in Hull Papers as cited in David Koskoff, p. 130.

520 "The Pilgrims' dinner . . .": Notes: "At Home Abroad," JPK.

520 submitted a draft: State Dept. MS 123, Kennedy, J.P./42, as cited in David Koskoff, p. 126; DM, Ch. 3, p. 8.

521 "We might, but then again . . .": DM, Ch. 3, p. 9.

521 "no plan to seek . . .": Ibid.

521 Hull wired Kennedy to delete: Ibid.; Hull to Kennedy, March 14, 1938, State Dept. MS 123, Kennedy, J.P./45, as cited in David Koskoff, p. 127.

521 "It must be realized . . .": DM, Ch. 3, p. 9.
521 one London paper: Ibid., p. 13; see also *LT*, March 19, 1938, p. 17.
522 "Hurry that boat up . . .": Telegram, JPK to RFK, March 12, 1938, JPK.
522 Eddie Moore sent him: E. E. Moore to JPK, March 16, April 6 and 19, 1938, JPK.
522 "Jack has had intestinal flue . . .": E. E. Moore to JPK, March 16, 1938, JPK.
522 "pictures of mother and dad . . .": JPK to L. Connelly, April 27, 1938, JPK.
523 When Rose finally arrived: RFK Diary, March 16, 1938, RFK; Richard J. Whalen, p. 211.
523 "as though they had become . . .": Lynne McTaggart, *Kathleen Kennedy: Her Life and Times* (1983), p. 25.
523 "His bouncing offspring . . .": "The Nine Kennedy Kids Delight Great Britain," *Life*, April 11, 1938, p. 17.
523 thirty-six-room embassy residence: Katy Carter, *London and the Famous* (1982), pp. 90–91; pictures of the facade and various rooms in *Vogue*, Aug. 3, 1938, pp. 41–42.
523 recalled the intense pleasure: Interview, Rose Kennedy.
523 blue plaque on the front door: Caroline Dakers, *The Blue Plaque Guide to London* (1981).
524 "Look at this, Rosie . . .": Interview, Rose Kennedy.
524 Never before, she confessed: Ibid.
524 "And Mrs. Kennedy . . .": Lesley Blanch, "Family Fugue: Theme and Variations on the Kennedys," *Vogue*, Aug. 3, 1938, p. 58.
525 steady round of parties: RFK Diary, June 1 and 14, 1938, RFK.
525 "It was a wonderful time . . .": Interview, Rose Kennedy.
525 April weekend . . . at Windsor: *LT*, April 11, 1938, p. 12; *Time*, April 18, 1938, p. 24; *BG*, April 9, 1938, p. 1.
525 "one of the most fabulous . . .": Interview, Rose Kennedy.
525 Joe and Rose motored down: Memo in RFK Diary, April 8, 1938, RFK; DM, Ch. 5, p. 6.
525 "Look, Joe. Let's write . . .": DM, Ch. 5, p. 6A.
526 "Rose, this is a helluva . . .": Rose Kennedy, p. 233.
526 At 8:20 P.M., the footmen: RFK Diary, April 9, 1938, RFK; repeated in Rose Kennedy, pp. 238–41.
526 "What the American people fear . . .": DM, Ch. 5, p. 6B.
526 "Fired by an idea . . .": Ibid., pp. 6B–6C.
527 "It was so incredibly beautiful . . .": Interview, Rose Kennedy.
527 "We all began laughing . . .": DM, Ch. 5, p. 6E.
528 "a scholar, a sportsman . . .": JPK to A. Krock, Mar. 21, 1938, AKP.
528 Having graduated from Eton and from Oxford: A. J. P. Taylor, *English History, 1914–1945* (1965), p. 129.
529 their long conversation: Taken from DM, Ch. 5, pp. 6E–6H.
529 "I'm just like that with . . .": *The Nation*, Dec. 14, 1940, pp. 593–94.
529 "if Chamberlain stays in power . . .": JPK to A. Krock, March 28, 1938, AKP.
529 Kennedy promised to help Halifax: DM, Ch. 6, pp. 4–6.
530 "Who would have thought . . .": John M. Blum, *From the Morgenthau Diaries* (1950), Vol. 1, p. 518.
530 showing "some of the same . . .": W. Lippmann to JPK, April 7, 1938, JPK.
531 Chairman of the Class Day committee: HC, March 17, 1938, p. 1.
532 "Plenty of excitement . . .": JFF to JPK, May 1938, JPK.
532 rumors centered upon two men: *BG* (eve.), June 9, 1938, pp. 1, 4. The rumor of JPK receiving an honorary degree was first reported in *BG*, May 17, 1938, p. 24.
532 "When Joe heard he was being . . .": Interview, Rose Kennedy.
532 both Kennedy and Disney: *BG* (eve.), June 9, 1938, p. 4.
532 "It was an honor he wanted . . .": Interview, Rose Kennedy.
532 the Archbishop . . . had waited in vain: Dorothy Wayman, p. 253.
532 "I'm just the same . . .": Quoted in Richard J. Whalen, p. 225.
532 Kennedy was met by: *NYT*, June 21, 1938, p. 6.
533 "a few connoisseurs of Presidential material . . .": Ernest K. Lindley, "Will Kennedy Run for President?" *Liberty*, May 21, 1938, p. 15.

533 the idea was picked up: *BP*, Sun., May 5, 1938, p. 6; *Washington Times-Herald*, June 12, 1938, JPK.

533 "the nearest to a Rooseveltian . . .": *Washington Post*, Sun., March 15, 1938, p. A; *Boston Traveler*, June 22, 1938, p. 21.

533 "I knew the time was not . . .": DM, Ch. 9, p. 1.

533 "I enlisted under President Roosevelt . . .": *BG* (eve.), June 20, 1938, p. 5; *NYT*, June 21, 1938, p. 6.

534 traveled to Hyde Park: *BG* (eve.), June 21, 1938, p. 19.

534 "It was on that train . . .": Interview, Rose Kennedy.

534 "There were some people . . .": Interview, Oscar Handlin.

534 the committee considered the award: Interview, Tom Cabot.

534 "It was a terrible blow . . .": Interview, Rose Kennedy.

535 "pretty good for one family . . ." *BG* (eve.), June 22, 1938, p. 1.

535 Class Day festivities: *BG*, June 23, 1938, pp. 1, 14.

535 would spend the day instead with . . . John: *Boston Traveler*, June 23, 1938, p. 13.

535 McMillan Cup races: *BG*, June 23, 1938, p. 14; *BP*, June 24, 1938, p. 7.

536 "heralded a beginning . . .": DM, Ch. 9, p. 6.

536 Stephen Early, gave out a story: Ibid., pp. 6–7. The article appeared in the *Chicago Tribune*, June 23, 1938, pp. 1, 8.

536 "It was a true Irish anger . . .": DM, Ch. 9, p. 8.

536 letters to the embassy: JFF wrote to E. E. Moore in May, "I wish you would see to it that anybody who comes to the Embassy with a card from me is properly taken care of," JPK.

537 he and Josie set sail for England: *BP*, June 15, 1939, p. 1.

537 a busy round of social: RFK Diary, June–July 1938, RFK; Rose Kennedy, p. 251.

537 "It was for Father . . .": Interview, Rose Kennedy.

537 helped himself to engraved . . . cards: Rose Kennedy, p. 252.

537 "John F. had a great time . . .": E. E. Moore to J. Sheehan, Sept. 14, 1938, JPK.

537 "an unparalleled . . .": F. Frankfurter to JPK, Jan. 8, 1938, JPK.

538 set off for Ireland: *The Irish Press*, July 6, 1938, JPK.

538 "came at just the right moment . . .": Interview, Rose Kennedy.

538 "It was about as rough . . .": E. E. Moore to J. J. Ford, July 20, 1938, JPK.

538 "in the best of spirits": *Dublin Evening Mail*, July 7, 1938, JPK.

538 "We welcome you . . .": *BP*, Sun., July 24, 1938, p. A1.

538 "Perchance my thrill . . .": Ibid.

539 "by far the happiest . . .": Interview, Rose Kennedy.

539 "wonderful years for all . . .": Interview, Luella Hennessey Donovan.

539 "as a psychologist . . .": Ibid.

540 "It was as if everything . . .": Interview, Rose Kennedy.

540 "so very few . . .": RFK Diary, Oct. 3, 1938, RFK.

540 ball given by Lady Baille . . . "Certainly everyone . . .": *LT*, May 24, 1938, p. 19; unidentified clipping, KK Scrapbook, RFK.

541 "When she came . . .": Dinah Bridge, OH-JFKL.

541 "Spent Easter weekend . . .": KK to LB, April 29, 1938, LB.

541 On Lady Astor see Maurice Collis, *Nancy Astor* (1960), pp. 12–22.

542 "Nancy Astor developed . . .": Interview, Rose Kennedy.

542 "Aunt Nancy really loved . . .": Interview, Dinah Bridge.

542 when Sissy's father was killed: Martin Page, "Hung on Lord Harlech," *Esquire*, Nov. 1968, pp. 106–7.

542 David Ormsby-Gore: Ibid.; Diane Lurie, "Lord Harlech's Family Talks About the Kennedys," *Ladies' Home Journal*, June 1968, p. 120.

542 David Rockefeller: *The New Yorker*, Nov. 16, 1940, p. 14.

542 William Douglas-Home: *The International Who's Who*, 1966, p. 1476.

542 Earl of Rosslyn: Ibid., p. 2650.

542 Kathleen's scrapbooks are included in RFK.

542 "Everyone is talking . . .": LB to KK, April 15, 1938, LB.

543 Henry Page: KK to LB, April 24, 1938, LB.

543 Byron . . . White: KK to LB, March 28, 1939, LB.

543 George and Lizzie: KK to LB, March 29, 1938, LB.
543 "I miss you an awful lot . . .": LB to KK, April 15, 1938, LB.
543 "Have to practice up . . .": KK to LB, April 29, 1938, LB.
543 Rose took her daughters to Paris: RFK Diary, April 19, 1938, RFK; Rose Kennedy, p. 244.
543 On the evening of the presentation: Interview, Rose Kennedy.
543 coming-out party: RFK Diary, June 2, 1938, RFK; Rose Kennedy, pp. 242–43.
544 "Our brawl . . . went off . . .": KK to LB, June 23, 1938, LB.
544 "This is where Kathleen . . .": Interview, Rose Kennedy.
544 William Cavendish: *Burke's Peerage* (1970), pp. 795–98.
545 garden party given by the King and Queen: *LT*, July 19, 1938, p. 19.
545 "The little Princesses . . .": E. E. Moore to the Fords, July 27, 1938, JPK.
545 Jack's outfit at the garden party: Memo to Mrs. Charlton, July 18, 1938, JPK.
545 Kathleen . . . looked especially beautiful: Interview, Rose Kennedy.
545 Only special guests: RFK Diary, July 18, 1938, RFK.
545 encountered Billy, David's best friend: *Esquire*, Nov. 1938, p. 180.
546 Billy invited Kathleen: Lynne McTaggart, p. 45.
546 on Chatsworth see the Duchess of Devonshire, *The House: Living at Chatsworth* (1982).
546 the ninth Duke, had died: *LT*, May 7, 1938, p. 17.
547 On Freemasonry see W. J. Whalen, *Handbook of Secret Organizations* (1966), pp. 45–65; J. Dewor, *The Unlocked Secret: Freemasonry Examined* (1966).
547 For the month of August: Rose left on July 27, Joe and Kick followed on Aug. 3, RFK Diary, RFK.
548 On Hitler and Czechoslovakia see William L. Shirer, *The Rise and Fall of the Third Reich*, pp. 358–66.
549 Churchill attacked Germany's mobilization: DM, Ch. 12, p. 15.
549 "the holidays were clearly over": Ibid., p. 16.
549 Kennedy met with Chamberlain: Ibid., Ch. 13, pp. 1–2.
549 "no state . . . certainly no democratic state . . .": Larry Fuchser, pp. 136–37.
549 "It is quite easy . . .": DM, Ch. 13, p. 1.
549 "Today Chamberlain is still . . .": JPK to Secretary of State, Aug. 30, 1938. *FRUS*, 1938, Vol. 1, p. 561; DM, Ch. 13, p. 2.
550 On August 31 . . . draft of the speech: DM, Ch. 13, p. 5; John Blum, Vol. 1, p. 518. On the speech see *NYT*, Sept. 3, 1938, p. 2.
550 "That young man needs . . .": John Blum, Vol. 1, p. 518.
550 wired a report that Halifax: JPK to Hull, Aug. 31, 1938, *FRUS*, 1938, Vol. 1, p. 565.
550 Hull wisely elected: Hull to JPK, Sept. 1, 1938, *FRUS*, loc. cit., pp. 568–69.
551 "I can't tell you how admirably . . .": S. Welles to JPK, Sept. 26, 1938, *FRUS*, loc. cit., pp. 660–61.
551 Ambassador Bullitt: *The Literary Digest*, Sept. 5, 1936, p. 10; *Saturday Evening Post*, March 11 and 18, 1939.
551 "terrifically expensive": RFK Diary, Sept. 6, 1938, RFK.
551 there was a solemn timbre: Interview, Rose Kennedy.
551 he admitted that a few years earlier: Henry L. Stimson Diaries, pp. 152–53.
552 "A petty segment of Europe . . .": William L. Shirer, *The Rise and Fall . . .*, p. 383.
552 "The shrill, almost whining . . .": DM, Ch. 14, p. 2.
552 "Since the days when we . . .": *NYT*, Sept. 13, 1938, p. 1.
552 it was "boastful, offensive . . .": DM, loc. cit.
553 "the Adolf" . . . never been "quite so full . . .": William L. Shirer, *Berlin Diary* (1941), p. 129.
553 "he would brook no interference . . .": DM, loc. cit.
553 "Hitler held out to the democracies . . .": Ibid., p. 3.
553 "They thought the speech . . .": Ibid., p. 4.
553 Without consulting . . . his Cabinet: Ibid., p. 7.
553 Hitler was "astounded . . .": William L. Shirer, *The Rise and Fall . . .*, p. 384.
553 one of "profound admiration . . .": DM, loc. cit., p. 10.

553 "everyone ready to weep for joy . . .": RFK Diary, Sept. 15, 1938, RFK.
553 But in Czechoslovakia: William L. Shirer, *Berlin Diary*, p. 131.
554 "we awaited anxiously . . .": DM, loc. cit., p. 12.
554 "sooner or later . . .": William L. Shirer, *The Rise and Fall . . .* , p. 389.
554 "had no other choice . . .": DM, loc. cit., p. 29.
554 reactions were mixed: Ibid., p. 23.
555 "there was little doubt . . .": Ibid.
555 "He is not the usual type . . .": Charles A. Lindbergh, *The Wartime Journals of Charles A. Lindbergh* (1970), p. 26.
555 enjoyed talking with Kennedy: Anne Morrow Lindbergh, *The Flower and the Nettle* (1976), p. 262.
555 "without doubt the German air fleet . . .": DM, Ch. 15, p. 3.
555 "Germany now has the means . . .": JPK to Secretary of State, Sept. 22, 1938, *FRUS*, 1938, Vol. 1, p. 73; DM, loc. cit., p. 41. For Lindbergh's version see *The Wartime Journals . . .* , pp. 72–73.
555 Lindbergh's evaluation was unrealistically bleak: Leonard Mosley, *Lindbergh* (1976), p. 230.
556 "It seems that Hitler has given Chamberlain . . .": William L. Shirer, *Berlin Diary*, p. 138.
556 "deprive us of every . . .": William L. Shirer, *The Rise and Fall . . .* , p. 396n.
556 "Finally cornered . . .": Ibid., p. 396.
556 "The Cabinet finally swung . . .": DM, Ch. 16, p. 3.
557 "All over London . . . fitted for . . .": Ibid., Ch. 15, p. 11.
557 "For a few days nobody knew . . .": E. E. Moore to H. Johnson, Oct. 4, 1938, JPK.
557 the worst state of excitement: William L. Shirer, *The Rise and Fall . . .* , p. 397.
557 "the most horrible . . .": Quoted in Larry Fuchser, p. 154.
557 "It seems to me that he left . . .": E. Walker to JPK, Sept. 27, 1938, JPK.
557 Welles called Kennedy: DM, Ch. 16, p. 5.
558 "starting to think about sending . . .": JPK to A. Krock, Sept. 26, 1938, JPK.
558 "How horrible, fantastic . . .": *LT*, Sept. 27, 1938, p. 1.
558 "his voice filled with sadness . . .": RFK Diary, Sept. 26, 1938, RFK.
558 "individual, brooding silence . . .": Ibid., Sept. 27, 1938.
558 "I shall not give up the hope . . .": *LT*, Sept. 27, 1938, p. 1; DM, Ch. 16, p. 11.
558 quickened its preparations for war: DM, loc. cit., p. 7.
559 "who wants to go to North America . . .": RFK Diary, Sept. 29, 1938, RFK.
559 the galleries had been filling up: *LT*, Sept. 29, 1938, p. 6; *Daily Express*, Sept. 29, 1938, p. 4; Sir Henry Channon, *Chips: The Diaries of Sir Henry Channon* (1967), p. 170.
559 "It was impossible . . .": John Wheeler-Bennett, *Munich* (1948), p. 168.
559 "I want you to know . . .": Hull to JPK, Sept. 27, 1938, State Dept. MS 123, Kennedy, J.P./120, as cited in David Koskoff, p. 154; DM, Ch. 16, p. 13.
559 "Narrow lanes for the . . . traffic . . .": DM, loc. cit., p. 14.
559 "Today we are faced . . .": *Parliamentary Debates*, 1937–1938, Vol. 339, p. 5; *LT*, Sept. 29, 1938, p. 6.
559 "As he passed from that part . . .": Larry Fuchser, p. 159.
560 "The House, poised so long . . .": *Daily Mail*, Sept. 29, 1938, p. 10, JPK.
560 "Sorry, excuse me . . .": Ibid.
560 "There is it": Ibid.
560 some believed they saw: Sir Henry Channon, p. 171.
560 "That is not all . . .": *Daily Mail*, loc. cit.
561 "like the biggest thunderstorm . . .": Ibid.
561 "Mr. Speaker. All of us are patriots . . .": Ibid.; *LT*, Sept. 29, 1938, p. 7.
561 "Was it possible that at this eleventh . . .": William L. Shirer, *The Rise and Fall . . .* , p. 411.
561 not to enter it again: Zbynek Zeman, *The Masaryks* (1976), p. 175; *LT*, March 11, 1948, p. 6.
561 "I hope this doesn't mean . . .": DM, Ch. 16, pp. 14–15.
561 "Well, boys . . .": Ibid., p. 16.

562 "If you have sacrificed my nation . . .": Quoted in William L. Shirer, *The Rise and Fall* . . . , p. 411.

562 "Munich itself was an anticlimax": DM, Ch. 17, p. 7.

562 "In the days of our sorrows . . .": Josef Hora as quoted in Telford Taylor, *Munich: The Price of Peace* (1979), p. 57.

562 Chamberlain was treated . . . as a conquering hero: *Evening News*, Sept. 30, 1938, pp. 1, 8, JPK; *LT*, Oct. 1, 1938, pp. 12, 14.

562 "I believe it is peace for . . .": *NYT*, Oct. 1, 1938, p. 4.

562 "he kissed me and twirled . . .": Interview, Rose Kennedy.

563 "I fully share your hope . . .": FDR to N. Chamberlain, Oct. 5, 1938, as quoted in William L. Langer and Everett S. Gleason, *The World Crisis and American Foreign Policy* (1952), Vol. 1, p. 35.

563 "the country had slept off . . .": John Wheeler-Bennett, p. 182.

563 "very deliverance from war . . .": Ibid.

563 "within a few days . . .": DM, Ch. 17, p. 3.

563 "The House was crowded . . .": Ibid., p. 2.

563 "in disregard of treaty obligations . . .": Ibid., p. 8; *Parliamentary Debates*, 1937–1938, Vol. 339, pp. 30–39.

564 "We are in the presence . . .": Winston Churchill, *The Gathering Storm*, pp. 327–28.

564 "the climax of the debate . . .": DM, loc. cit., p. 2.

564 "fascinating, delightful . . .": RFK Diary, Oct. 5, 1938, RFK.

564 "the pros and cons . . .": Ibid., Nov. 30, 1938.

565 "He was kind enough to add . . .": DM, loc. cit., pp. 2–3.

565 "Hi, there, Jan . . .": James Laver, *Between the Wars* (1961), p. 221.

565 he would end his life: *LT*, March 11, 1948, pp. 1, 6. There were rumors at the time that it was murder rather than suicide.

566 "It has long been a theory . . .": DM, Ch. 18, pp. 2–3; press release of speech, Oct. 19, 1938, JPK.

566 "For Mr. Kennedy . . . to propose . . .": Quoted in John Henry Cutler, p. 282.

566 Only after the speech . . . criticized: DM, loc. cit, pp. 4–5; *NYT*, Oct. 21, 1938, p. 8.

567 stab in the back: Richard J. Whalen, pp. 250–51.

567 "I wonder if Joe Kennedy understands . . .": F. Frankfurter to FDR, Oct. 27, 1938, in Max Freedman, *Roosevelt and Frankfurter* (1967), pp. 463–64.

567 "second Foreign Office": Claud Cockburn, "Britain's Cliveden Set," *Current History*, February 1938, p. 12.

567 Pearson . . . accused him: Michael Beschloss, p. 165.

567 "hardly prepared . . .": DM, loc. cit., p. 5.

567 "After all, the lives . . .": Ibid., p. 4.

568 "While it seemed to be unpopular . . .": Quoted in James M. Burns, *John Kennedy* . . . , p. 37.

568 "There are plenty of brickbats . . .": J. Boettiger to JPK, Oct. 28, 1938, as quoted in Michael Beschloss, p. 179.

568 terrible pogrom against the Jews: William L. Shirer, *The Rise and Fall* . . . , pp. 430–31; see also David S. Wyman, *Paper Walls: America and the Refugee Crisis, 1938–1945* (1968), pp. 71–72.

568 "the Third Reich . . .": William L. Shirer, *The Rise and Fall* . . . , p. 434.

568 "such things could occur . . .": *NYT*, Nov. 16, 1938, p. 1.

569 "it was not so much . . .": *Documents on German Foreign Policy*, Vol. 1, p. 715.

569 "This last drive on the Jews . . .": JPK to C. Lindbergh, quoted in DM, Ch. 20, p. 11.

569 "the Kennedy Plan": *Life*, Nov. 28, 1938, p. 24.

570 "If a reasonably good . . .": DM, Ch. 19, p. 5.

570 "What Mr. Kennedy has managed . . .": *NYT*, Sun., Nov. 11, 1938, Sect. 4, p. 3; see also *NYT*, Nov. 15, 1938, pp. 1, 5, and Nov. 16, 1938, pp. 1, 9.

570 "add new luster . . .": *Life*, loc. cit.

570 "It was plain . . . that most of them . . .": DM, Ch. 5, pp. 1–8.

571 "In spite of the complacency . . .": Ibid., Ch. 22, pp. 5–6.

571 "The destruction of Czechoslovakia . . .": John Wheeler-Bennett, p. 349.

571 "Chamberlain felt . . .": DM, Ch. 24, p. 2.
572 "His Majesty's Government . . .": Ibid., p. 15.
572 "That statement marked . . .": Ibid.
572 a host of powerful bankers: Charles Higham, *Trading with the Enemy* (1983), pp. 168–70.
573 seen his "friend Wohlthat . . .": JPK to M. Downey, Aug. 23, 1954, JPK.
574 "We hope to stay in England . . .": Quoted in Richard J. Whalen, p. 258.
574 "one of the loveliest . . .": RFK to FDR, Jan. 8, 1939, Roosevelt Papers.
575 "In fact . . . you cannot go . . .": RFK Diary, Nov. 4, 1938, RFK.
575 was terrifically upset: Ibid., July 20, 1938.
575 found it difficult to plan her clothes: Ibid., Nov. 21, 1938.
575 filling embassy bookcases: Ibid., Jan. 19–20, 27, 1939.
575 "from top to bottom": JPK, Jr., to JPK, Sept. 23, 1938, JPK.
575 to Rose he confided: Interview, Rose Kennedy.
575 "They have a small sled . . .": Quoted in Hank Searls, p. 111.
576 "He never complained . . .": Ibid., pp. 111–12.
576 "Everybody got pretty good . . .": JPK, Jr., to JPK, Jan. 25, 1939, JPK.
576 "a pretty good general idea . . .": Ibid.
576 On the Spanish Civil War see Hugh Thomas, *The Spanish War* (1961).
577 "It was just before Joe set off . . .": Interview, Rose Kennedy.
577 "Sorry I missed you . . .": *New York Herald Tribune*, Feb. 17, 1939, p. 1.
577 "And that is the reception . . .": Ibid.
577 "Crisis Hunter" . . . "Don José": Hank Searls, p. 116.
577 The tea with the Astors: Anne Morrow Lindbergh, p. 525.
578 "The theatres are packed . . .": JPK, Jr., to JPK, Feb. 19, 1939, JPK.
578 "very vivid and balanced . . .": Anne Morrow Lindbergh, p. 527.
579 looked "like a small boy . . .": Ibid., p. 529.
579 ended up quoting . . . at Chamberlain's urging: BG, April 20, 1939, p. 2.
580 chartered a whole *wagon-lit*: DM, Ch. 23, p. 1; *Daily Mail*, March 8, 1939, JPK.
580 disappointment at discovering: Interview, Rose Kennedy.
580 when she finally talked with Joe Junior: RFK Diary, April 7, 1939, RFK.
580 "Wire received. We are attending . . .": Telegram, JPK to JPK, Jr., March 9, 1939, JPK.
580 added specialness . . . Cardinal O'Connell: Rose Kennedy, p. 263; see also BH, March 13, 1939, pp. 1, 4; BP, March 11, 1939, pp. 1, 7.
580 For descriptions of the ceremony see NYT, March 12, 1939, pp. 1, 40; BG, March 13, 1939, pp. 1, 8, 9. Kathleen reported the event in *London Catholic Herald*, April 21, 1939, JPK.
580 "The great square in front . . .": DM, Ch. 23, pp. 4–6.
581 Teddy received his first communion: Ibid., p. 10; RFK Diary, March 16, 1939, RFK.
581 "It must have been a wonderful . . .": JPK, Jr., to JPK, March 15, 1939, JPK.
581 advised his son . . . to write a book: E. E. Moore to P. Murphy, July 28, 1939, JPK.
581 enlisted the skills of . . . Klemmer: Lynne McTaggart, p. 64.
581 Joe did publish a letter: *Atlantic Monthly*, Oct. 1939, JPK.
581 "a different Joe from the young man . . .": *Evening Chronicle*, April 21, 1939, JPK.
582 Dean's list: A. C. Hanford to JFK, March 17, 1939, Harvard Records, MS 65–185, JFK, as cited in Herbert S. Parmet, p. 61.
582 "Brother Jack is certainly doing well . . .": LB to KK, Oct. 1938, LB.
582 enthusiastic approval and support of his teachers: Payton Wild, OH-JFKL; Tutorial Records, Personal Papers, Box 2, JFK.
582 "Jack arrived looking . . .": KK to LB, March 25, 1938, LB.
583 "sitting in my office . . .": Orville Bullitt (ed.), *For the President, Personal and Secret: Correspondence Between Franklin D. Roosevelt and William C. Bullitt* (1972), p. 273.
583 "Probably the strongest impression . . .": Quoted in James M. Burns, *John Kennedy . . .*, p. 38.
583 "Yet in the midst of this confusion . . .": George F. Kennan, *Memoirs, 1925–1950* (1967), pp. 91–92.
584 "all you can hear or talk about . . .": KK to LB, Sept. 23, 1938, LB.

584 It was not British: Lynne McTaggart, p. 67.
584 "You'd be surprised to see . . .": LB to KK, April 12, 1939, LB.
584 "It really is amazing . . .": KK to LB, April 30, 1939, LB.
584 Billy Harrington . . . duty to fight: Lynne McTaggart, p. 67.
585 the British boys: RFK Diary, April 7, 1939, RFK.
585 Joe Kennedy was showing a film: Peter Collier and David Horowitz, p. 101.
585 "they are just getting back . . .": KK to LB, Aug. 2, 1939, LB.
586 "It was good to get away . . .": DM, Ch. 32, p. 1.
586 Hartington's coming-of-age party: LT, Aug. 15, 1939, p. 15; Derbyshire Times, Aug. 18, 1939, p. 1, JPK.
586 pleading with her: Interview, Rose Kennedy.
586 "Kennedy Girl May Wed Peer": BP, Aug. 15, 1939, pp. 1, 9.
586 Chamberlain "more depressed . . .": DM, Ch. 33, p. 2.
587 "The news . . . came with a rush . . .": Ibid., p. 16.
587 thousands of children: Daily Herald, Sept. 2, 1939, p. 6, JPK; PB, Sept. 5, 1939, p. 3.
587 "a day of ominous waiting . . .": DM, loc. cit., p. 18.
587 "There shall be no more . . .": Ibid.
587 "We were all terribly moved . . .": Ibid., Ch. 34, p. 1.
587 "We did the best we could . . .": Ibid.
587 for the House of Commons: RFK Diary, Sept. 3, 1939, RFK.
588 ". . . consequently, this county . . .": Parliamentary Debates, 1938–1939, Vol. 351, pp. 291–92.
588 "I trust I may live . . .": Ibid., p. 292.
588 "The Prime Minister . . ." and subsequent speeches: Ibid., pp. 295–300; see also Daily Herald, Sept. 4, 1939, p. 9, JPK.
590 "Rose, Kathleen . . .": JPK to A. Krock, Sept. 15, 1939, JPK.
591 "My feelings reminded me . . .": DM, Ch. 34, p. 9.
591 "was now committed": Ibid., Ch. 35, p. 11.
592 "a queer war": Janet Flanner, "Letter from Paris," New Yorker, Sept. 16, 1939, p. 30.
592 Were it not for the piles: Ibid.
592 "The only thing that does . . .": E. E. Moore to M. LeHand, Feb. 8, 1940, JPK.
592 "no one could have . . .": H. V. Morton, I Saw Two Englands (1933), p. 307.
592 "girding herself for war . . .": DM, Ch. 37, p. 6.
592 "In slightly over two months . . .": Ibid., p. 13.
592 For biographical information on Montagu Norman see Current Biography (1941), pp. 619–20; obituary, NYT, Sun., Feb. 5, 1950, p. 84.
592 opposed forcing her: Paul Einzig, "The Perennial Governor," Living Age, June 1941, pp. 345–50.
593 England was broke already: DM, Ch. 35, p. 14.
593 "If this struggle . . .": Ibid.
593 "to talk to any military . . .": Ibid., p. 19.
593 "place in the sun": Ibid., p. 20.
593 "It is now possible . . .": D. Gibbs to JPK, Jan. 10, 1940, JPK.
594 "she willingly puts herself . . .": D. Gibbs to E. E. Moore, Oct. 10, 1939, JPK.
594 "I see in the papper . . .": Rosemary Kennedy to E. E. Moore, Feb. 13, 1940, JPK.
594 responded with a long list: Mother Isabel to JPK, May 9, 1940, JPK.
594 two reporters . . . wrote her a letter: Mary and Harry Henry to Rosemary Kennedy, Nov. 5, 1939, JPK.
594 "When my mother and the rest . . .": E. E. Moore letter for Rosemary, undated, JPK.
595 "he couldn't stand it . . .": Interview, Rose Kennedy.
595 "Hopelessly impatient . . .": Telegram, JPK to RFK, Dec. 3, 1939, JPK.
595 "It was a treat . . .": DM, Ch. 35, p. 4.
595 "As you love America . . .": BP, Dec. 11, 1939, p. 1.
595 "a little difficult": DM, Ch. 40, pp. 6–7.
595 "One of the most important . . .": T. North Whitehead, "Concerning Mr. Kennedy," March 3, 1940, FO 371/24251/A1848/605/45, PRO.

596 "If you mean by isolation . . .": *NYT*, March 8, 1940, p. 8.
596 "With the greatest respect . . .": Beverly Baxter, "My Dear Ambassador—Why didn't you tell them?" *Sunday Graphic*, March 10, 1940, p. 15, JPK.
596 "lovely beyond even . . .": Clare Boothe Luce, *Europe in the Spring* (1940), p. 187.
597 "The news is stupefying . . .": William L. Shirer, *Berlin Diary*, p. 310.
597 "a revolution in British . . .": DM, Ch. 42, p. 13.
597 "because there is nothing . . .": *Parliamentary Debates*, 1939–1940, Vol. 340, p. 1283.
597 "my friends in the House . . .": Ibid., p. 1266.
597 "So difficult had been the upward . . .": Larry Fuchser, p. 189.
597 "he wanted to make Halifax . . .": DM, Ch. 50, p. 10.
597 "blood, toil, tears and sweat": *LT*, May 14, 1940, p. 3.
598 "All I can say . . .": JPK to D. Porter, May 6, 1940, JPK.
598 "He had a real zest . . .": Robert Rhodes James, *Churchill: A Study in Failure* (1970), pp. 65–66.
598 "I resented this . . .": DM, Ch. 36, pp. 4–5.
598 "the classic national . . .": Mollie Panter-Downes, *London War Notes* (1971), p. 66.
599 "both gaier and more . . .": Ibid., pp. 70–71.
599 "In fact betting on just . . .": DM, Ch. 39, p. 7.
599 "The finish may come . . .": JPK to JPK, Jr., June 6, 1940, RFK.
599 "Yet, to be fair . . .": Interview, John K. Galbraith.
600 "I realize it is an imposition . . .": JPK to B. Bracken, Aug. 8, 1940, JPK.
600 "Joe absolutely adored . . .": Interview, Rose Kennedy.
600 "Burke just phoned . . .": JPK, Jr., to JPK, Feb. 14, 1940, RFK.
601 "I've got to figure . . .": JPK, Jr., to JPK, April 5, 1940, RFK.
601 "thought he could arrange . . .": JPK, Jr., to E. E. Moore, April 13, 1940, JPK.
601 the Ambassador immediately wired: Interview, Rose Kennedy.
601 "I'm Joe Kennedy, Jr. . . .": Hank Searls, p. 140.
601 The day of the voting: BG, Sun., May 1, 1940, p. 4.
601 "Grandpa thought I did . . .": JPK, Jr., to JPK, May 4, 1940, JPK.
601 "if it were not for . . .": JFF to JPK, May 9, 1940, RFK.
602 Joe argued that America: BG, Jan. 6, 1941, p. 2; *NYT*, Jan. 7, 1941, p. 7; HC, Feb. 3, 1941, pp. 1, 3.
602 "Overnight the people have turned . . .": JPK, Jr., to JPK, May 18, 1941, RFK.
602 "I can't tell you . . .": JPK to JPK, Jr., June 6, 1941, RFK.
603 "an excellent grade . . .": J. Landis to JPK, July 17, 1940, Landis Papers.
603 the convention opened: *Chicago Tribune*, July 16, 1940, p. 1; BG, July 16, 1940, p. 1.
603 others, like William Burke: BG (eve.), July 17, 1940, p. 6.
603 Joe Kennedy, Jr., refused: BG, July 19, 1940, p. 3.
603 Clem Norton went up to Joe: Hank Searls, p. 146.
603 "No, I wouldn't think . . .": Bill Duncliffe, "Struggle with Europe's Madman 'Not Our War' ": BRA, Jan. 22, 1964, p. 27.
604 "I was pledged to Farley . . .": Quoted in J. Patterson to JPK, July 22, 1940, RFK.
604 first roll call: *Chicago Tribune*, July 18, 1940, p. 1; BG, July 18, 1940, p. 1.
604 "He seemed to gain . . .": J. Patterson to JPK, loc. cit.
604 "I will ever be grateful . . .": J. Farley to JPK, July 22, 1940, RFK.
604 "As you can imagine . . .": Quoted in Rose Kennedy, p. 288.
604 "Finished my thesis . . .": JFK to JPK, June 1940, Personal Papers, Box 2, JFK.
605 send it on to Arthur Krock: JPK to JFK, May 20, 1940, RFK; Arthur Krock, OH-JFKL.
605 had shown it to "various . . .": JPK to JFK, loc. cit.
605 "We should profit . . .": JFK thesis, Personal Papers, Box 2, JFK.
605 sold over forty thousand: James M. Burns, *John Kennedy . . .* , p. 44.
605 "So, whether you make a cent . . .": JPK to JFK, Aug. 2, 1940, RFK.
606 "young Jack was finding . . .": Herbert S. Parmet, p. 78.
606 "Jack was autographing . . .": Chuck Spalding, OH-JFKL.
606 "a person . . .": Interview, Lem Billings.
606 "It all seems like a . . .": KK to JPK, Sept. 18, 1939, RFK.

606 "a hell of a nice guy": LB to KK, undated, LB.
606 "Everyone likes him a great . . .": Eunice Kennedy to JPK, Aug. 6, 1940, RFK.
607 "insincerity": Lynne McTaggart, p. 71.
607 "and I wouldn't think . . .": JFK to JPK, spring 1940, Personal Papers, Box 2, JFK.
607 "I still keep telling everyone . . .": KK to JPK, May 21, 1940, RFK.
607 "I wish I could . . .": KK to JPK, Aug. 6, 1940, RFK.
607 "As to what is going . . .": JPK to RFK, Aug. 13, 1940, RFK.
608 "In spite of everything . . .": JPK to KK, Aug. 2, 1940, RFK.
608 "As far as I can see . . .": JPK to J. Landis, Aug. 6, 1940, Landis Papers.
608 early days of the Blitz: Ivan Maisky, *Memoirs of a Soviet Ambassador* (1967), pp. 112–13; Alexander McKee, *Strike from the Sky* (1960), p. 215; LT, Sept. 9, 1940, pp. 2, 4.
608 "I am sure, of course . . .": JPK to Edward Kennedy, Sept. 11, 1940, RFK.
609 "Last night they dropped . . .": JPK to Eunice Kennedy, Sept. 11, 1940, RFK.
609 "You get experienced . . .": as quoted in Angus Calder, *The People's War* (1971), p. 174.
609 "I did not know London . . .": *Time*, Nov. 4, 1940, p. 19.
610 On October 16 he sent a cablegram: Richard J. Whalen, p. 329; Arthur Krock, p. 335. JPK notes in his memoir that he wrote to Eddie Moore on Aug. 2, enclosing a diary account of his conversation with FDR; DM, Ch. 38, p. 2.
610 "one of the most misunderstood . . .": Ibid., Ch. 50, p. 9.
610 "I haven't had many successes . . .": Ibid., p. 11.
610 Kennedy arrived . . . "he looked for all . . .": *NYT*, Oct. 28, 1940, p. 1.
611 "The President sent you . . .": Arthur Krock, private memo, AKP.
611 "proving that Roosevelt . . .": James F. Byrnes, *All in One Life Time* (1958), p. 125; DM, Ch. 51, pp. 3–6.
611 "shaking a cocktail . . .": Quoted in Arthur M. Schlesinger, Jr., *Robert Kennedy . . .*, p. 35.
611 "acting as though . . .": DM, loc. cit., p. 3.
611 the President turned to Rose: Interview, Rose Kennedy.
612 "Since it doesn't seem possible . . .": Quoted in Michael Beschloss, p. 217.
612 "rather pale, rather ashen": Ibid.
612 "In the first place . . .": DM, Ch. 51, p. 4.
612 "many words not found . . .": James Byrnes, p. 126.
612 his wife tactfully: DM, loc. cit., p. 6.
612 "I stand in awe . . .": Interview, Rose Kennedy.
613 "All right, I will . . .": Arthur Krock, private memo, AKP.
613 paying for the special CBS hookup: *NYT*, Oct. 29, 1940, p. 19.
613 "renewed in my conviction . . .": *NYT*, Oct. 30, 1940, p. 8.
613 "As a vote getting . . .": *Life*, Jan. 27, 1941, p. 27.
614 Kennedy celebrated by tendering: DM, Ch. 52, p. 2.
614 "The Globe hopes . . .": L. Lyons to JPK, Nov. 7, 1940, JPK.
614 "It so happened . . .": J. Crider to A. Krock, Nov. 12, 1940, JPK; for Lyon's view see Louis Lyons, pp. 290–94.
614 "I'm willing to spend . . .": *BG*, Sun., Nov. 10, 1940, p. 1.
615 Coglan understood: R. Coglan to A. Krock, Nov. 12, 1940, AKP.
615 rushed for a cab: BG, loc. cit.
616 "Democracy is finished . . .": *St. Louis Post-Dispatch*, Sun., Nov. 10, 1940, p. 1.
616 "She bothered us more . . .": Quoted in Richard J. Whalen, p. 341.
616 "It is true Kennedy said . . .": R. Coglan to A. Krock, loc. cit.
616 Kennedy issued a statement: *Washington Post*, Nov. 12, 1940, p. 1.
616 "It is all to the good . . .": *News Chronicle*, Dec. 6, 1940, p. 4.
617 "Don't mind the attacks . . .": JPK to J. Seymour, Dec. 9, 1940, FO 371/24251/A1945/605/45, PRO.
617 "there was very strong . . .": FO 1941 File 391, PRO.
617 were it not for his family: Interview, Clem Norton.
617 "Having finished a rather busy . . .": JPK to A. C. Ralshesky, Feb. 10, 1941, JPK.
621 "There was something . . .": Interview, Rose Kennedy.

622 Mullins . . . long letter: B. Mullins to JPK, Sept. 3, 1941, JPK.
622 "I am more grateful . . .": JPK to B. Mullins, Sept. 5, 1941, JPK.
622 the "mess": Ibid. and JPK to J. Seymour, Nov. 18, 1941, JPK.
622 he signed up: Hank Searls, p. 156; noted in Boston papers Sun., July 13, 1941: BP, p. 14, and BH, p. 21.
622 "Wouldn't you know . . .": Hank Searls, p. 162.
622 Description of the ground school program: Ibid., p. 165.
622 top three in his class: Memo, G. R. Fairlamb to JPK, May 8, 1942, JPK.
623 "Student flies . . .": Hank Searls, p. 168.
623 "I saw young Joe . . .": JPK to T. McInerny, Jan. 26, 1942, JPK.
623 Maurice Sheehy: Hank Searls, p. 164.
623 the graduation exercises: BP, May 5, 1942, p. 1, and May 5, 1942, p. 5; BG, May 6, 1942, pp. 1, 16.
623 able to pin . . . wings: G. R. Fairlamb to JPK, loc. cit.
623 "The sight of those boys . . .": JPK to G. R. Fairlamb, May 12, 1942, JPK.
623 "We might just as well . . .": JPK, Jr., to JPK, June 11, 1942, RFK.
624 Joe wrote to his father . . . : JPK, Jr., to JPK, mid-June 1942, RFK.
624 decided the time had come: JPK to P. Murphy, June 29, 1942, RFK.
624 Paul Murphy drew up: P. Murphy to JPK, July 1, 1942, RFK.
624 "My own suggestion . . .": JPK to JPK, Jr., July 6, 1942, RFK.
624 "I was duty officer . . .": JPK, Jr., to parents, July 1942, RFK.
625 "Daddy's prerogative": Interview, John White.
625 rumors must have reached: RFK to JPK, Jr., July 23, 1942, RFK.
625 "regardless of reports . . .": JPK, Jr., to JPK, Oct. 1942, RFK.
625 Joe Casey: Clinton Courant, July 10, 1942, p. 7.
625 "You wouldn't think . . .": JPK to JPK, Jr., Aug. 7, 1942, RFK.
625 It is said that Joe Senior: Clinton Courant, Aug. 21, 1942, p. 1.
625 "Joe was anxious . . .": Interview, Rose Kennedy.
626 "We've had more fun . . .": JPK to F. Waldrop, Sept. 15, 1942, JPK.
626 "What a great old guy . . .": KK to LB, Aug. 6, 1942, LB.
626 "Look, I've got two boys . . .": Interview, Edward Hanify.
626 "Here is one of the things . . .": JPK to F. Waldrop, loc. cit.
626 "I think John F. will . . .": Ibid.
626 a very respectable showing: JPK to T. McInerny, Oct. 1, 1942, JPK.
626 "From John F.'s point . . .": Interview, Edward Hanify.
627 "I am awfully sorry . . .": JPK, Jr., to JPK, Oct. 1942, RFK.
627 "I am most deeply . . .": JPK to A. G. Kirk, Aug. 4, 1941, JPK.
627 reporter on the Times-Herald: Paul Healy, Cissy (1966), p. 349.
627 "Everything was done . . .": Interview, Page Huidekoper Wilson.
628 John White: Boston Monthly, Sept. 1979, p. 5.
628 "The only problem . . .": Interview, John White.
628 "Bickered with KK . . .": John White Diary (made available by White to the author).
629 "Took her to Haines . . .": Ibid.
629 "Another fight. . . .": Ibid.
630 Inga Arvad: Frank Waldrop, "Colson, Kennedy and the Nazi Spy," unpublished MS, p. 4, FWP (made available by Waldrop to the author).
630 "an insight into . . .": Ibid.
630 If Kathleen was the original: Lynne McTaggart, p. 95.
630 "he decided it was fine . . .": Interview, John White.
630 "Supper at Inga's . . .": John White Diary.
631 "How the hell . . .": Lynne McTaggart, pp. 100–101.
631 "lying in bed . . .": Ibid., p. 101.
631 "I enjoy your round robin . . .": JFK to RFK, Nov. 1941, RFK.
632 It was in this atmosphere: Frank Waldrop, "FDR & JFK & JEH & Inga: A Story of Love and War in Washington," unpublished MS, p. 5, FWP.
633 "One of ex-Ambassador Kennedy's . . .": Quoted in Lynne McTaggart, p. 108.
633 "All manner of to do . . .": John White Diary.
633 "Old Joe had learned . . .": Interview, Frank Waldrop.

633 At the Office of Naval Intelligence: Joan and Clay Blair, Jr., pp. 136–37.
633 Inga was very gloomy: John White Diary.
634 "like all kids . . .": JPK to A. Houghton, Dec. 29, 1941, JPK.
634 "He has become . . .": JPK to JPK, Jr., June 20, 1942, RFK.
634 Joe Kennedy stepped in: Lynne McTaggart, p. 111.
635 "parted forever . . .": John White Diary.
635 "She is going to marry . . .": KK to LB, Aug. 6, 1942, LB.
635 many phone calls: Interview, John White.
635 "Thank you for your latest . . .": JPK to RFK, spring 1942, RFK.
635 Kathleen had confided: John White Diary.
636 "In this great crisis . . .": Telegram, JPK to FDR, Dec. 7, 1941, RFK.
636 "I am afraid . . .": JPK to T. McInerny, Feb. 12, 1942, JPK.
636 Steve Early, had responded: JPK to B. Brickley, Dec. 18, 1941, JPK.
636 "I don't want to appear . . .": JPK to FDR, March 1942, Roosevelt Papers.
636 Kennedy believed the ice: JPK to J. McCormick, March 21, 1942, JPK.
636 "I am so damn . . .": JPK to F. Kent, March 2, 1942, JPK.
636 "which should turn out . . .": JPK to JFK, May 28, 1943, RFK.
636 "Mother insists that . . .": KK to LB, March 12, 1943, LB.
636 he agreed to meet . . . Howard Johnson: JPK to D. Gurnett, Oct. 18, 1943, JPK.
636 to sell the Bronxville estate: JPK to A. Houghton, Nov. 13, 1941, JPK.
637 "a loss of stability": Interview, Luella Hennessey Donovan.
637 "As a child, Bobby . . .": Interview, Lem Billings.
637 "While they all knew . . .": Interview, Rose Kennedy.
637 "little pet": RFK to Bobby Kennedy, Jan. 12, 1942, RFK.
637 "Unfortunately, none of us . . .": RFK to Mr. Brady, Nov. 4, 1940, RFK.
637 "I was so disappointed . . .": RFK to Bobby Kennedy, Jan. 12, 1942, RFK.
638 his letters reveal: JPK to Bobby Kennedy, Jan. 8, 1945, RFK.
638 "I wish Dad that you . . .": Bobby Kennedy to JPK, Jan. 1945, RFK.
638 When Kennedy responded: Cited in Arthur M. Schlesinger, Jr., *Robert Kennedy . . .* , p. 59.
638 "Thanks very much . . .": Bobby Kennedy to JPK, Feb. 1945, RFK.
638 he had attended ten different: Burton Hersh, p. 38.
638 it had been a serious mistake: Interview, Rose Kennedy.
639 Teddy was "a riot . . .": JPK to RFK, Nov. 23, 1942, RFK.
639 "Please do not mention . . .": RFK to Mother Patterson, Aug. 8, 1941, RFK.
639 "Don't go bothering your head . . .": JPK to RFK, loc. cit.
639 Joe took it upon himself: Interview, Rose Kennedy.
640 a marked deterioration: Rose Kennedy, p. 307.
640 "It had never been easy . . .": Interview, Lem Billings.
640 "I was always worried . . .": Rose Kennedy, "Notes on the Children," RFK.
640 "She was the most beautiful . . .": Interview, Ann Gargan King.
641 prefrontal lobotomy: Waldemar Kaempffert, "Turning the Mind Inside Out," *Saturday Evening Post*, May 24, 1941, p. 71.
641 In the early 1940s: Marguerite Clark, "Surgery in Mental Cases," *American Mercury*, March 1941, p. 293.
641 "Few surgical events . . .": Ibid., pp. 292, 295.
641 "The stark fears . . .": Ibid., p. 293.
642 Word . . . quickly spread: Richard Restak, "The Promise and Peril of Psychosurgery," *Saturday Review*, Sept. 25, 1973, pp. 55–56; Kurt Goldstein, "Prefrontal Lobotomy: Analysis and Warning," *Scientific American*, Feb. 1950, pp. 44–45.
642 "They knew right away . . .": Interview, Ann Gargan King.
642 Rose was simply told: Interview, Rose Kennedy.
643 "For Joe it was . . .": Interview, Ann Gargan King.
643 "Then she knew . . .": Ibid.
643 "Why didn't you advise me?": Interview, Luella Hennessey Donovan.
643 "He thought it would help . . .": Interview, Rose Kennedy.
643 "I am still very grateful . . .": JPK to Sister Anastasia, May 29, 1958, JPK.
645 John Harlee and John D. Bulkeley: John Harlee, OH-JFKL; Herbert S. Parmet, p. 96.

646 a "great enthusiasm": John Harlee, OH-JFKL.
646 "even when they are going . . .": Frank Henry, "Bucking Bronchos of the SEA," *Science Digest*, July 1944, p. 57.
646 "Jack came home . . .": JPK to JPK, Jr., Oct. 1, 1942, RFK.
646 Joe spoke with the doctors: JFK wrote to the chief, Bureau of Navigation, April 6, 1942, requesting inactive duty for six months for an operation and recuperation. He then spent time at the naval hospitals in South Carolina and Chelsea, Mass., but resumed regular duty June 24, 1942; Personal Papers, Box 11, JFK.
647 "You cannot believe . . .": RFK to JPK, Jr., Sept. 29, 1942, RFK.
647 "crazy about the school": KK to LB, Sept. 25, 1942, LB.
647 Jack performed excellently: James M. Burns, *John Kennedy* . . . , p. 48.
647 had to sleep with a piece of plywood: Joan and Clay Blair, Jr., pp. 161, 181.
647 Jack was sorely disappointed: John Harlee, OH-JFKL.
647 "causing his mother . . .": JPK to M. Sheehy, Oct. 28, 1942, JPK.
647 "the most powerful . . .": John Harlee, OH-JFKL.
648 "Frankly . . . I have not met . . .": D. I. Walsh to JFF, Dec. 21, 1942, Pre-Presidential Papers, Box 585, JFK.
648 "As to conditions . . .": JFK to parents, April 1943, RFK.
649 "what they say about Japs . . .": JFK to parents, May 10, 1943, RFK.
649 Lennie Thom . . . wrote: Joan and Clay Blair, Jr., p. 179; JFK to parents, April 1943, RFK.
649 "Jack was a big . . .": Joan and Clay Blair, Jr., p. 182.
649 "He was very brilliant . . .": Ibid., p. 183.
649 "He just seemed like . . .": Ibid.
649 "Going out every other . . .": JFK to parents, May 14, 1943, RFK.
650 "lying on a cool . . .": JFK to KK, June 3, 1943, RFK.
651 "to know that all nuns . . .": JFK to family, June 24, 1943, RFK.
651 assures his mother: JFK to parents, May 14, 1943, RFK.
651 "You will be pleased . . .": JFK to RFK, June 24, 1943, RFK.
651 "We were both Catholics . . .": quoted in Joan and Clay Blair, Jr., p. 182.
651 On the night of July 17–18: Ibid., pp. 201–5.
652 "We had a letter from Jack . . .": JPK to J. O'Leary, Aug. 16, 1943, JPK.
652 "He never really got over . . .": JFK to parents, Sept. 12, 1943, RFK.
652 On the *PT 109* incident see generally Robert J. Donovan, *PT 109* (1961); Richard Tregaskis, *John F. Kennedy and PT 109* (1962); John Hersey, "Survival," *New Yorker*, June 17, 1944, pp. 31–43.
653 "the most confused . . .": Robert Bulkeley, *At Close Quarters* (1962), p. 123.
653 It was now about 2:30: *New Yorker*, loc. cit., p. 31.
654 This is how it feels . . . : Ibid.
654 "Who's aboard?": Ibid.
655 "Mr. Kennedy! . . .": Ibid., p. 32.
656 He thought he had never known: Ibid., p. 34.
656 "Ross, you try it . . .": Ibid.
657 "I have a letter for you . . .": Ibid., p. 42.
657 "You've got to hand it . . .": Robert Donovan, p. 187.
657 Rose seems grateful: Rose Kennedy, p. 315.
658 "Kennedy's Son Is Hero . . .": NYT, Aug. 20, 1943, p. 1.
658 "blazing new saga . . .": *BH*, Aug. 20, 1943, p. 1.
658 "their least effective . . .": Bryan Cooper, *The Battle of the Torpedo Boats* (1970), p. 151.
658 "It was easy. They cut my PT boat . . .": Theodore C. Sorensen, *Kennedy* (1966), p. 18.
658 "What a splendid story . . .": M. Beaverbrook to JPK, Nov. 6, 1943, JPK.
659 "It certainly should occur . . .": JPK to Dr. Hall, Aug. 25, 1943, JPK.
659 "I imagine he's pretty well . . .": JPK to JPK, Jr., Aug. 31, 1943, RFK.
659 "I'm sure if he were John Doake's . . .": JPK to A. Houghton, Sept. 14, 1943, JPK.
659 "too young to be out . . .": JFK to JPK, Aug. 1943, RFK.
659 "It certainly brought home . . .": JFK to parents, Sept. 12, 1943, RFK.
659 he had finally learned: JPK to JFK, Oct. 30, 1943, RFK.

660 "It's a funny thing . . .": JFK to I. Arvad, Sept. 26, 1943, as quoted in Joan and Clay Blair, Jr., p. 386.
661 "fast and dangerous . . .": Hank Searls, p. 181.
662 "The most excited man . . .": Ibid.
662 "I read this about three hours . . .": JPK, Jr., to family, Aug. 29, 1943, RFK.
662 "considerably upset that during . . .": JPK to JPK, Jr., Aug. 31, 1943, RFK.
662 "With the great quantity . . .": JPK, Jr., to parents, Aug. 29, 1943, RFK.
663 At a festive dinner: Hank Searls, p. 183.
663 "Joe Darling . . .": RFK to JPK, Jr., Sept. 16, 1943, RFK.
663 "Feel all kinds of affection . . .": John White Diary.
663 "I love you . . .": Lynne McTaggart, p. 115.
663 "Here we are on the high seas . . .": LB to KK, July 1942, LB.
664 "He had been leaping . . .": LB to KK, Feb. 4, 1943, LB.
664 "He is the most amazing . . .": KK to LB, May 23, 1943, LB.
664 George Mead: Joan and Clay Blair, Jr., p. 89.
664 "He died trying to rescue . . .": KK to LB, Sept. 25, 1942, LB.
664 "Future days may bring . . .": Quoted in Lynne McTaggart, p. 120.
664 "He is buried near the beach . . .": JFK to parents, April 1943, RFK.
665 On the American Red Cross, see George Korson, At His Side (1945), pp. 258–66; Robert Bremmer et al., The History of the American Red Cross (1950), vol. 13, pp. 53–64.
665 Hans Crescent Club: KK to family, July 10, 1942, RFK.
665 "I consider ourselves most lucky . . .": T. McInerny to JPK, July 28, 1943, RFK.
665 "Don't get too upset . . .": JPK to KK, July 3, 1943, RFK.
666 "I'm not sure yet . . .": KK to F. Waldrop, July 20, 1943, FWP.
666 "The director . . . just had a little chat . . .": KK to family, Aug. 26, 1943, RFK.
666 "I don't know how much . . .": JFK to family, August 1943, RFK.
666 young woman was summarily dispatched: Lynne McTaggart, pp. 129–30.
666 "I judge . . . that you are not . . .": JPK to KK, Sept. 8, 1943, RFK.
667 she would much prefer: KK to family, Sept. 23, 1943, RFK.
667 "What a woman . . .": T. McInerny to JPK, Sept. 30, 1943, RFK.
667 "Aren't you longing . . .": KK to LB, March 25, 1943, LB.
667 "I am really so pleased . . .": KK to family, July 10, 1943, RFK.
667 "She has gone very far . . .": KK to family, July 20, 1943, RFK.
667 surrounded by her old friends: T. Rosslyn to JPK, July 1943, RFK.
667 "very good company": KK to JFK, July 29, 1943, RFK.
668 "It really is funny . . .": KK to family, July 14, 1943, RFK.
668 "For 24 hours I forgot . . .": KK to JFK, July 29, 1943, RFK.
668 "I wish his father . . .": KK to family, Aug. 10, 1943, RFK.
669 "She talks a lot about you . . .": Nancy Astor to RFK, Aug. 18, 1943, RFK.
669 "As far as I'm concerned . . .": JPK to KK, Sept. 8, 1943, RFK.
669 "absolutely thrilled . . .": KK to LB, Aug. 26, 1943, LB.
669 "Of course the news . . .": KK to family, Aug. 24, 1943, RFK.
669 "the biggest event of the week": KK to family, Sept. 29, 1943, RFK.
669 "They are so far ahead . . .": JPK, Jr., to parents, Sept. 30, 1943, RFK.
670 "easily the nicest girl . . .": JPK, Jr., to parents, Oct. 27, 1943, RFK.
670 Dining at the Savoy: Ibid.
670 Pat Wilson: Lynne McTaggart, pp. 144–45; marriage to the Earl of Jersey, NYT, Jan. 13, 1932, p. 27; marriage to Robin Wilson, NYT, Sun., Sept. 12, 1937, Sect. 6, p. 4.
670 reported to her father that Pat: KK to family, Nov. 11, 1943, RFK.
670 "living in a mud hole": JPK, Jr., to parents, Nov. 9, 1943, RFK.
670 "We hopped, skipped . . .": Quoted in Hank Searls, pp. 189–90.
671 "A small stove . . .": JPK, Jr., to parents, loc. cit., RFK.
671 "It was the first party . . .": KK to parents, Nov. 17, 1943, RFK.
671 Irving Berlin: Ibid.
671 "Kick handled herself . . .": JPK, Jr., to parents, Nov. 23, 1943, RFK.
671 Lists of guests attached to Kathleen's letter, Nov. 17, 1943, RFK.

671 Hartington, now stationed: Hank Searls, p. 260.
672 By 1943 many young married women: Lynne McTaggart, p. 146.
672 romance was "unknown . . .": JPK, Jr., to Pat Kennedy, Jan. 2, 1944, RFK.
672 "Next Saturday is Elizabeth Cavendish's . . .": KK to family, Jan. 2, 1944, RFK.
672 "Mother will long for them": KK to family, Jan. 6, 1944, RFK.
672 made her realize how much: KK to family, Jan. 12, 1944, RFK.
672 "I think it shows . . ." Ibid.
672 Billy had been granted leave: KK to family, Jan. 20, 1944, RFK.
673 His opponent was Charles White: R. W. P. Cockerton, recollection, unpublished; see also Angus Calder, pp. 637–40.
673 "Palace on the Peak": Lynne McTaggart, p. 149.
673 letter of support from Churchill: *Derbyshire Times*, Feb. 11, 1944, p. 1, RFK.
673 "I saw a by-election . . .": KK to LB, Feb. 23, 1944, LB.
673 Billy could not bring himself: KK to "Mother and Daddy only," week of Jan. 21, 1944, RFK.
674 "some stretch of the rules": Rose Kennedy, p. 319.
674 "He took the trouble . . .": KK to "Mother and Daddy only," loc. cit.
674 went to see Bishop Matthew: KK to family, Jan. 29, 1944, RFK.
674 "Please try and discover . . .": KK to JPK, Feb. 22, 1944, RFK.
674 he went to see Francis Spellman: Rose Kennedy, p. 319.
674 "As I've told you . . .": JPK to KK, Feb. 21, 1944, RFK.
675 "the benefit of your counsel . . .": JPK to JPK, Jr., Feb. 21, 1944, RFK.
675 "Daddy . . . feels terribly . . .": RFK to KK, Feb. 24, 1944, RFK.
675 "Dear Rose . . .": Marie Bruce to RFK, Jan. 23, 1944, RFK.
675 "Marie Bruce hasn't heard . . .": KK to parents, March 4, 1944, RFK.
675 "Billy also went . . .": KK to family, April 4, 1944, RFK.
676 "let all the rest of us . . .": JPK to KK, March 8, 1944, RFK.
676 Kathleen recalled the conversations: KK to LB, May 18, 1944, LB.
676 the Duke presented to her: KK to family, Feb. 22, 1944, RFK.
676 three days with Billy: KK to family, April 24, 1944, RFK.
676 "I have loved Kick . . .": B. Hartington to RFK, April 30, 1944, RFK.
677 "She said she would . . .": T. Rosslyn to JPK, May 6, 1944, RFK.
677 "heartbroken and horrified": Rose Kennedy, "Personal Reminiscences—Private," RFK.
677 "I thought it would . . .": Ibid.
677 "Heartbroken. Feel you have been . . .": Quoted in ibid.
677 "I can't help admiring Rose . . .": Interview, Dinah Bridge.
678 "Once she had definitely . . .": JPK, Jr., to parents, May 8, 1944, RFK.
678 with his potential Catholic constituency: KK to RFK, May 9, 1944, RFK.
678 "Billy is crazy about . . .": JPK, Jr., to parents, loc. cit.
678 "Never did anyone . . .": Quoted in John F. Kennedy (ed.), p. 54.
678 The wedding took place: *Derbyshire Times*, May 12, 1944, RFK; *LT*, May 7, 1944, p. 6; *BP*, May 6, 1944, pp. 1, 3; *Time*, May 13, 1944, p. 12.
679 "everything was wonderful": Telegram, JPK, Jr., to RFK, May 7, 1944, RFK.
679 "You would rejoice . . .": Telegram, Marie Bruce and Nancy Astor to RFK, May 7, 1944, RFK.
679 "The power of silence . . .": Telegram, JPK, Jr., to JPK, May 7, 1944, RFK.
679 the newspapers headlined the story: *Time*, loc. cit.
679 the press barraged: *Boston Traveler*, May 5, 1944, pp. 1, 12; JPK to JPK, Jr., May 24, 1944, RFK.
679 "May the Blessed Mother . . .": Rev. H. O'Donnell to RFK, May 1944, RFK.
679 she was praying: Grace C. Daumaine to RFK, May 24, 1944, RFK.
679 Rose was inconsolable: Interview, Rose Kennedy.
680 "With your faith . . .": Quoted in Lynne McTaggart, p. 160.
680 Rose to enter a hospital: *BG* (eve.), May 6, 1944, pp. 1–2.
680 "Your cable made my happiest . . .": Telegram, KK to JPK, May 8, 1944, RFK.
680 "I was very worried . . .": KK to RFK, May 9, 1944, RFK.
681 "She has done the best . . .": JPK to JPK, Jr., May 24, 1944, RFK.

681 "carried her over the tough time": Ibid.
681 to send a cable to Marie: KK to family, May 18, 1944, RFK.
681 "now I feel I can . . .": KK to RFK, May 8, 1944, RFK.
681 "It's very comfortable . . .": KK to family, loc. cit.
681 "Just lately she has . . .": Duke of Devonshire to JPK, Aug. 14, 1944, RFK.
681 "Billy and I talk . . .": Ibid.
682 "I'm delighted that you . . .": JPK to JPK, Jr., May 24, 1944, RFK.
682 "as Irish as . . .": KKH diary and scrapbook, May 17, 1944, RFK.
682 "Although I've been . . .": Ibid., June 13, 1944.
682 "Oh my darling . . .": B. Hartington to KKH, undated, ibid.
683 "I don't mind much . . .": JPK, Jr., to JPK, March 24, 1944, RFK.
683 "I sincerely hope . . .": JPK to JPK, Jr., April 7, 1944, RFK.
684 "I have finished . . .": JPK, Jr., to parents, May 8, 1944, RFK.
684 "In any case I am giving . . .": JPK, Jr., to parents, May 17, 1944, RFK.
684 Joe Junior took off from Dunkeswell: Hank Searls, pp. 210–11.
684 "I am delighted that I stayed . . .": JPK, Jr., to parents, June 12, 1944, RFK.
684 "I stayed with Pat Wilson . . .": JPK, Jr., to parents, June 23, 1944, RFK.
685 "Rumor hath it . . .": RFK to JPK, Jr., July 19, 1944, RFK.
685 "I had a wonderful birthday . . .": JPK, Jr., to parents, July 26, 1944, RFK.
685 For a thorough description of the mission see Hank Searls, pp. 223–56.
685 On the V-1 flying bombs see Peter G. Cooksley, *Flying Bomb* (1979), pp. 61–83.
685 "unmanned jet aircraft . . .": Hank Searls, p. 217.
685 "the doodlebugs": KKH diary and scrapbook, June 15 and July 3, 1944, RFK.
686 Civilian casualties: Peter G. Cooksley, p. 81.
686 begged Reedy to let him go: Hank Searls, p. 214.
686 "I am going to do . . .": JPK, Jr., to parents, July 26, 1944, RFK.
687 "I can quite understand . . .": JPK to JPK, Jr., Aug. 9, 1944, RFK.
687 "There was never an occasion . . .": L. Papas to JPK, Aug. 22, 1944, RFK.
688 "I'm about to go . . .": Hank Searls, p. 242.
688 "the biggest explosion I ever saw": Quoted ibid., p. 250.
688 It was early Sunday: Rose Kennedy, pp. 323–24.
689 "No. This cannot wait . . .": Interview, Rose Kennedy.
689 Rose ran upstairs: Rose Kennedy, p. 324.
689 "Children, your brother Joe . . .": Edward M. Kennedy (ed.), p. 207.
689 "loving him as much . . .": Pat Wilson to RFK, Aug. 14, 1944, RFK.
690 "I do not understand . . .": Pat Wilson to JFK, Sept. 8, 1944, RFK.
690 "Dear Kick has been . . .": Duke of Devonshire to JPK, Aug. 14, 1944, RFK.
690 "I'm so sorry I broke down . . .": Quoted in Hank Searls, p. 258.
690 Jack and Kathleen . . . church: Lynne McTaggart, p. 175.
691 "the blackest hours . . .": Interview, Rose Kennedy.
691 she confessed that because: Ibid.
691 "I have never known . . .": M. Soden to Mr. and Mrs. Kennedy, Aug. 18, 1944, RFK.
691 "Their words created . . .": JPK to Duke of Devonshire, Aug. 1944, RFK.
692 "There was something . . .": Interview, Rose Kennedy.
692 "Don't get worried . . .": JPK, Jr., to parents, Aug. 4, 1944, RFK.
692 "Joe threw the letter . . .": Interview, Rose Kennedy.
692 "As soon as I fully . . .": Ibid.
692 "I had been longing . . .": Mother Patterson to RFK, Aug. 27, 1944, RFK.
693 "When young Joe was killed . . .": JPK to W. Howey, March 4, 1954, JPK.
693 he could not regard: JPK to M. Sheehy, Jan. 6, 1945, RFK.
693 "It was one of the most . . .": Arthur Krock, OH-JFKL.
693 "I still can't read . . .": JPK to G. St. John, Dec. 7, 1944, JPK.
693 "I just can't get in the mood . . .": JPK to J. Calder, Sept. 26, 1944, JPK.
693 "because all my plans . . .": JPK to A. Houghton, Sept. 11, 1944, JPK.
693 "When the young bury . . .": JPK to B. Green, May 8, 1945, JPK.
694 "After almost nine years . . .": JPK to W. Howey, March 4, 1954, JPK.
694 Unable to relax with her mother: Lynne McTaggart, p. 177.

694 certain social niceties: Ibid., pp. 180–81.
694 brave and fearless . . .": J. Crowley to KKH, undated, RFK.
694 "The last six days . . .": B. Hartington to KKH, Sept. 4, 1944, RFK.
694 "They were deliriously happy . . .": Quoted in Michael Howard and John Sparrow, *The Coldstream Guards* (1951), p. 284.
695 "The reception we have had . . .": Billy Hartington to KKH, Sept. 4, 1944, RFK.
695 "That night a sharp dose . . .": Michael Howard and John Sparrow, p. 286.
695 On the morning of Sept. 8: Ibid., p. 289; Lynne McTaggart, pp. 182–83.
695 "Come on, you fellows . . .": *Derbyshire Times*, Sept. 22, 1944, RFK; *LT*, Sept. 20, 1944, p. 7.
696 news reached Kathleen: Lynne McTaggart, pp. 184–85.
696 she left for Quebec: Telegram, JPK to Duke of Devonshire, Sept. 19, 1944, JPK.
696 "So ends the story . . .": KKH diary and scrapbook, RFK.
696 "He loved his Derbyshire home . . .": *LT*, Sept. 20, 1944, p. 7.
697 "I guess God has taken . . .": Quoted in Richard J. Whalen, p. 375.
697 "This is a very hard . . .": KKH to LB, Nov. 29, 1944, LB.
697 "Please tell Kathleen . . .": Telegram, FDR to JPK, Sept. 1944, JPK.
697 "Repeated blows . . .": Telegram, JPK to Winston Churchill, Sept. 20, 1944, JPK.
697 "For a fellow who didn't . . .": JPK to M. Beaverbrook, Oct. 23, 1944, JPK.
698 "completely powerless . . .": Quoted in Lynne McTaggart, p. 176.
698 "his superiority sealed . . .": Interview, Lem Billings.
698 "terribly exposed . . .": Ibid.
699 "His worldly success . . .": John F. Kennedy (ed.), p. 5.
699 "could read only . . .": JPK to A. Krock, June 21, 1945, JPK.
699 "Joe used to talk about . . .": Francis Russell, *The President Makers* (1976), p. 361.
700 Kennedy had asked Kane: JPK to J. Kane, Feb. 8, 1944, JPK.
700 "There is something original . . .": J. Kane to JPK, Feb. 14, 1944, JPK.
700 "still his gay self . . .": JPK to R. Fay, March 26, 1945.
700 voiced the fear: JPK to Bobby Kennedy, March 19, 1945, RFK.
701 "You could set your clock . . .": Quoted in Joan and Clay Blair, Jr., p. 367.
701 "it was the one thing . . .": Interview, Rose Kennedy.
701 "his father had set up . . .": Joan and Clay Blair, Jr., p. 367.
701 "If I hadn't been warned . . .": Joseph P. Kennedy, "Notes on the 1944 Political Campaign," JPK.
702 "a huge and unprovable faith . . .": James M. Burns, *Roosevelt: The Soldier of Freedom* (1970), pp. 611–12.
702 Ruppel reached Jack: Telegram, L. Ruppel to P. O'Leary, April 23, 1945, Pre-Presidential Papers, Box 73, JFK.
702 "It would be very easy . . .": Arthur M. Schlesinger Jr., *A Thousand Days* (1965), p. 88.
703 "I think your column . . .": JPK to JFK, May 11, 1945, RFK.
703 his heart swelled: Interview, Rose Kennedy.
703 "offered him quite a responsible . . .": JPK to R. Wilson, June 21, 1945, JPK.
703 "Will see Eden . . .": JFK to JPK, May 28, 1945, RFK.
703 "was fighting a tide . . .": *New York Journal American*, June 24, 1945, JPK.
704 "this boy had the makings . . .": Arthur Krock, OH-JFKL.
704 "He's planning to go back . . .": JPK to L. Ruppel, Aug. 7, 1945, JPK.
704 Merchandise Mart: *NYT*, Sun., July 22, 1945, p. 32; *Time*, July 30, 1945, p. 84.
704 "Joe had a genius for seeing . . .": Interview, Rose Kennedy.
704 "At the time air-conditioning . . .": quoted in Edward M. Kennedy (ed.), p. 47.
705 "Harry Truman has taken . . .": JPK to J. Calder, Aug. 22, 1945, RFK.
705 Jack spent "hours on end": Interview, Rose Kennedy.
705 did not have "a temperament . . .": Ibid.
705 "It was like being drafted. . . .": Quoted in Joan and Clay Blair, Jr., p. 356.
705 "Jack arrived home . . .": JPK to J. Calder, loc. cit.
706 "a stranger in the city . . .": Richard J. Whalen, p. 393.
706 two-room suite at the Bellevue: "A Kennedy Runs for Congress," *Look*, June 11, 1946, p. 35.

706 public speaking did not come: James M. Burns, *John Kennedy* . . . , p. 65.
707 "It was a most interesting . . .": Mary R. Lincoln to JFK, Sept. 13, 1945, Pre-Presidential Papers, Box 11, JFK.
707 "Many a night when . . .": Interview, Eunice Kennedy Shriver.
707 "If I walked out on the stage . . .": Interview, Dave Powers.
708 "He never once said to anybody . . .": Kenneth O'Donnell and David F. Powers, *"Johnny, We Hardly Knew Ye"* (1970), p. 59.
708 "There was a basic dignity . . .": Interview, Dave Powers.
708 "in a state where money . . .": J. Kane to JPK, March 3, 1944, JPK.
708 "Your Jack is worth . . .": Ibid.
708 "Joe Kane had such . . .": Interview, Lem Billings.
708 "I thought Jack wouldn't last . . .": Interview, Dave Powers.
708 "It was a strange thing . . .": Ibid.
709 Curley ran a victorious campaign: *BP*, Nov. 7, 1945, pp. 1, 10, 14.
709 "Give the kid a break! . . .": J. Kane to JPK, March 7, 1946, RFK.
710 "Therefore, since he would have . . .": JPK to J. Kane, March 11, 1946, RFK.
710 "The temper of the times . . .": *BG*, April 23, 1946, p. 11.
710 On Mike Neville see *Cambridge Chronicle*, April 4, 1946, pp. 1, 10.
710 "The poor little rich . . .": James M. Burns, *John Kennedy* . . . , p. 65.
710 "During the bitter . . .": Cotter speech, undated, Pre-Presidential Papers, Box 73, JFK.
710 "People said he was simply . . .": Interview, Dave Powers.
711 "almost victory—politically speaking": J. Kane to JPK, Jan. 29, 1946, RFK.
711 "There was something about . . .": Interview, Dave Powers.
711 "There was only a twenty-watt . . .": Kenneth O'Donnell and David Powers, pp. 52–53; interview, Dave Powers.
712 recalled a similar: John Droney, OH-JFKL.
713 Powers recalled a similar: Interview, Dave Powers.
713 "It was the strangest . . .": Ibid.
713 "Joe Kennedy was the mastermind . . .": Joan and Clay Blair, Jr., p. 398.
713 "The Ambassador was the essential . . .": Mark Dalton, OH-JFKL.
713 "behind the scenes . . .": RFK to KKH, June 6, 1946, RFK.
714 working "like a beaver": JPK to J. Kane, Feb. 11, 1946, RFK.
714 Jack would be addressing: J. Kane to JPK, Feb. 25, 1946, RFK.
714 "Men who pushed back . . .": Pre-Presidential Papers, Box 11, JFK.
714 "My story about the collision . . .": Herbert S. Parmet, p. 111.
714 "After he'd been in a bar . . .": Interview, Dave Powers.
715 "I felt that his courage . . .": Kenneth O'Donnell and David Powers, pp. 66–67.
715 "I remember saying to the man . . .": Joe McCarthy, p. 20.
715 "Fitzgerald was a cheerleader . . .": Interview, Billy Sutton.
716 "All he had to do . . .": William De Marco, OH-JFKL.
716 "I seem to be the only . . .": Kenneth O'Donnell and David Powers, p. 59.
716 "Kennedy was at his best . . .": James M. Burns, *John Kennedy* . . . , p. 67.
717 "The older ladies seemed . . .": John Droney, OH-JFKL.
717 "Miss Kirby and Miss Norton . . .": May 21, 1946, Pre-Presidential Papers, Box 98, JFK.
717 "from Irish bartenders . . .": Bobby Kennedy to RFK, May 1946, RFK.
717 "hot weather campaigner": Billy Sutton, OH-JFKL.
718 The story is told: Interview, Dave Powers.
718 "everybody wanted . . .": Richard J. Whalen, p. 401.
718 "too effeminate": John Droney, OH-JFKL.
719 "It created a gigantic traffic . . .": Quoted in Joan and Clay Blair, Jr., p. 473.
719 "Every girl there . . .": Ibid.
719 "I have an obligation . . .": *Look*, June 11, 1946, p. 32.
719 "He has guts . . .": Ibid, pp. 34–36.
720 nearly $250,000: Ralph G. Martin and Ed Plaut, p. 133.
720 a contribution of $600,000: The newspaper reported the gift during the first weeks of August; see Pre-Presidential Papers, JFK.

720 "I'm not a politician . . .": Released June 17, 1946, Pre-Presidential Papers, Box 98, JFK.
720 votes were all counted: *BH*, June 19, 1946, pp. 1, 14.
720 It was a jubilant group: James M. Burns, *John Kennedy . . .*, p. 68; *BG* (eve.), June 19, 1946, p. 4; *BH*, June 19, 1946, p. 14.
720 "If Mr. Kennedy lives up to . . .": *BG*, July 9, 1946, Herald Morgue Files.
721 "I find myself with a new . . .": JPK to John Clark, Nov. 1, 1946, JPK.
721 "My crystal ball . . .": H. B. Swope to JFK, Nov. 6, 1946, Pre-Presidential Papers, Box 5, JFK.
722 Eunice . . . executive secretary: *NYT*, Jan. 17, 1947, p. 20; *Worcester Evening Gazette*, Jan. 20, 1947, JFK.
722 "substantial efforts . . .": *NYT*, loc. cit.
722 "Eunice was born . . .": Interview, Rose Kennedy.
723 "If that girl had been born . . .": Quoted in Peter Collier and David Horowitz, p. 159.
723 "Of all the kids . . .": Quoted in Joan and Clay Blair, Jr., p. 524.
723 The Georgetown house was a lively: Herbert S. Parmet, pp. 172–73; Joan and Clay Blair, Jr., pp. 518–26.
723 The women in Jack's life: Herbert S. Parmet, pp. 167–68; Joan and Clay Blair, Jr., pp. 499, 551–53.
723 "He was young, rich, handsome . . .": Quoted in Ralph G. Martin, *A Hero for Our Time* (1983), p. 54.
723 "I could walk with Jack . . .": Ibid., p. 53.
723 "I went to his house . . .": Quoted in Joan and Clay Blair, Jr., pp. 516–17.
724 "Jack liked girls . . .": Ibid., p. 526.
724 "I was at some posh restaurant . . .": Quoted in Ralph G. Martin, p. 54.
724 "his continual, almost heroic sexual . . .": Garry Wills, p. 33.
724 "He'd read everything . . .": Quoted in Peter Collier and David Horowitz, p. 175.
725 "The whole thing with him . . .": Ibid., p. 176.
725 "would strike down . . .": *Congressional Quarterly* fact sheet, week ending May 13, 1960, p. 846.
725 "While he loved the process . . .": Interview, Lem Billings.
726 "I don't think he really . . .": Quoted in Joan and Clay Blair, Jr., p. 512.
726 "I think time was heavy . . .": William O. Douglas, OH-JFKL.
726 Curley had been indicted: The trial began Nov. 19, 1945; see *BP*, Nov. 20, 1945, p. 1.
726 "most serious and precarious . . .": *BG*, June 24, 1947, p. 1.
726 there was a new numbness: *BG*, June 25, 1947, p. 6.
726 denied his plea: *BG*, June 26, 1947, pp. 1, 14.
727 Calling the sentence "cold": *BG*, June 27, 1947, p. 2; see also *CR*, 80th, 1st, June 26, 1947, pp. 7763–64.
727 "I don't know how many . . .": Mark Dalton, OH-JFKL.
727 he sided with Joe Kane: Charles Murphy, OH-JFKL.
727 implored Jack to find out: Ralph G. Martin and Ed Plaut, p. 153.
728 "I think they were so . . .": Garrett Byrne, OH-JFKL.
728 "If Jack signed . . .": Quoted in Joan and Clay Blair, Jr., p. 551.
728 "It was not easy . . .": Interview, Rose Kennedy.
728 singled him out in the press: *BG* (eve.), July 8, 1947, p. 1; unidentified clippings, July 8 and 9, 1947, Herald Morgue Files.
728 "Well I'm dead now, . . .": Ralph G. Martin and Ed Plaut, p. 153.
728 "I thought he made a . . .": Daniel O'Brien, OH-JFKL.
728 met by scores of jubilant: Unidentified clipping, Nov. 27, 1947, Herald Morgue Files.
728 "We do not begrudge . . .": Reprinted in unidentified clipping, Dec. 14, 1947, Herald Morgue Files.
729 "to study education . . .": *BG* (eve.), Sept. 10, 1947, JFK.
729 Leaving Boston on Sunday: *BH*, Sept. 1, 1947, p. 33.
729 "a picture book castle": Rose Kennedy, diary notes on Lismore Castle, RFK.
729 "the most perfect place": KKH to LB, Sept. 3, 1947, LB.

729 "Anthony Eden arrives . . .": Ibid.
729 "rather depressed": KKH to LB, April 1, 1945, LB.
729 "It nearly kills me . . .": KKH to parents, March 24, 1945, RFK.
730 "I try and do lots . . .": KKH to parents, April 25, 1945, RFK.
730 "Just got Daddy's letter . . .": KKH to parents, Feb. 27, 1945, RFK.
730 "Thinking of you . . .": Telegram, JPK to KKH, May 2, 1945, RFK.
730 "Why does that daughter . . .": Interview, Pamela Churchill Harriman.
730 "those attractive old . . .": RFK to JPK, Sept. 1947, RFK.
730 "I feel that I have . . .": KKH to LB, Sept. 20, 1945, LB.
730 found herself once more surrounded: Lynne McTaggart, pp. 205–6.
730 "I love your letters . . .": Anthony Eden to KKH, Jan. 10, 1948, RFK.
731 "We have a varied group . . .": KKH to JPK, Sept. 18, 1947, RFK.
731 "rather quietly, rather . . .": Quoted in Joan and Clay Blair, Jr., pp. 558–59. For description of Ireland trip, interview, Pamela Churchill Harriman.
732 It was during one of their long talks: Interview, Lem Billings.
732 On Peter Fitzwilliam see Lynne McTaggart, pp. 206–8, and his obituary, LT, May 15, 1948, p. 6.
733 all the tickets were sold: KKH to parents, June 16, 1946, RFK.
733 On the night of the ball: Lynne McTaggart, p. 209.
733 "Peter and Kathleen . . .": Quoted in Peter Collier and David Horowitz, p. 166.
733 "Peter had all the charm . . .": Ibid.
733 "like Joe Kennedy . . .": Ibid.
733 Kathleen told Jack: Interview, Lem Billings.
734 Kathleen shared with Jack: Ibid.
734 "she has all her friends . . .": RFK to JPK, Sept. 1947, RFK.
734 "got on terrifically well . . .": KKH to LB, Dec. 27, 1947, LB.
734 diagnosed a victim of Addison's: Joan and Clay Blair, Jr., p. 561.
734 "That young American . . .": Quoted ibid.
734 When the Boston papers: BH and BT, Oct. 6, 1947, and BP, Oct. 11, 1947, JFK.
735 "At least one half . . .": Robert Kennedy, "Tribute to JFK," Look, Feb. 25, 1964, p. 38.
735 "He went along . . .": Rose Kennedy, p. 217.
735 "Those who knew him . . .": Look, loc. cit., p. 38.
735 It was a bitter winter: BT, March 6, 1948, pp. 1, 2.
736 including Kathleen, who had arrived: KKH to LB, Feb. 21, 1948, LB; Lynne Mc-Taggart, p. 219.
736 before returning to England: KKH to LB, loc. cit.; Lynne McTaggart, p. 228.
736 Promising to be the social event: Life, May 10, 1948, p. 153; Time, April 26, 1948, p. 85.
736 "I don't know what to do . . .": Quoted in Lynne McTaggart, p. 228.
737 "She looked really alive . . .": Quoted in Peter Collier and David Horowitz, p. 169.
737 "I was going to take . . .": Marie Bruce to JPK, May 6, 1952, RFK.
737 absolutely "radiant": Lynne McTaggart, p. 129.
737 "If he objects . . .": Quoted ibid., p. 230.
738 Description of the airplane ride: Ibid., pp. 232–36.
739 "I'm not sure . . .": Ibid., pp. 236–37.
739 Jack was lying: Peter Collier and David Horowitz, p. 170.
739 had a sweet voice: Ibid.
739 Ambassador Kennedy heard the news: BH, May 14, 1948, p. 1.
739 Meanwhile, all the far-flung: BA, May 15, 1948, p. 8.
740 When Joe Kennedy called home: BH, loc. cit., pp. 1–2.
740 According to the New York Daily News: Lynne McTaggart, p. 243.
740 "only near him that she . . .": BP, May 14, 1948, pp. 1, 8.
740 Kathleen's burial: LT, May 21, 1948, p. 7.
740 "I can still see . . .": Quoted in Peter Collier and David Horowitz, p. 170.
742 "He was in terrible pain . . .": Interview, Lem Billings.
743 "The thing about Kathleen and Joe . . .": Quoted in James M. Burns, John Kennedy . . . , p. 54.

743 "a sort of slow-motion leukemia": Arthur M. Schlesinger, Jr., *A Thousand Days*, p. 96.
743 "runs through your mind . . .": Interview, Lem Billings.
743 "Tell me, Teddy boy . . .": Quoted in Peter Collier and David Horowitz, p. 171.
744 "After Kathleen's death . . .": Interview, Lem Billings.
744 "There was something . . .": Quoted in Peter Collier and David Horowitz, p. 172.
744 "Slowly he began to fight . . .": Interview, Lem Billings.
745 the Kennedys quickly stored away: Joan and Clay Blair, Jr., p. 567.
745 "a markedly increased sense . . .": Quoted ibid., pp. 567–68.
745 "When he was first told . . .": Interview, Lem Billings.
745 Mary Curley: *BG*, Feb. 11, 1950, pp. 1, 3; Interview, Francis Curley.
745 "Stunned by the news . . .": *BG*, Sun., Feb. 12, 1950, p. 34.
746 "an incredibly moving . . .": Interview, Dave Powers.
746 "The man must be made . . .": Ibid.
746 The visit to his grandfather: Interview, Lem Billings.
747 Eight months later: *BG*, Oct. 3, 1950, pp. 1, 15.
747 "one of Boston's most . . .": *BP*, Oct. 3, 1950, p. 1.
747 He had outlasted: Edward died March 3, 1940; James T., Jan. 22, 1950; Henry, Feb. 22, 1955.
747 "Grief-stricken" by the news: *BP*, Oct. 5, 1950, p. 1.
748 "In spite of his age . . .": Interview, Rose Kennedy.
748 "Bankers knelt side by side . . .": *BP*, Oct. 6, 1950, p. 19.
748 "All his life . . .": Interview, Clem Norton.
748 he decided to stick with politics: Interview, Lem Billings.
751 "the idea of the family . . .": Ibid.
751 "an inner eye": Ibid.
751 "In the process . . .": Interview, Rose Kennedy.
752 "He is such a wonderful . . .": Sara Miller to JPK, undated (c. March 1, 1920), JPK.
752 "Even in a crowded room . . .": Interview, Richard Goodwin.
752 "When we were reading . . .": Interview, Eunice Kennedy Shriver.
753 "Some people have their liberalism . . .": James M. Burns, *John Kennedy . . .*, p. 155.
754 "The world breaks . . .": Ernest Hemingway, *A Farewell to Arms*, p. 249.
754 "Whenever Mother traveled . . .": Interview, Lem Billings.
755 "Jack told me . . .": Kenneth O'Donnell and David Powers, p. 79. Joe Dinneen reported that by August 1952 Kennedy had spoken in 311 of the 351 cities in Massachusetts, *The Kennedy Family*, p. 143.
756 "sleeping in a crummy . . .": Kenneth O'Donnell and David Powers, p. 78.
756 Bickford . . . journeyed: L. Bickford to JPK, Sept. 1, 1951, JPK.
756 "As far as I'm concerned . . .": JPK to J. Calder, Nov. 24, 1951, RFK.
756 "When you've beaten Lodge . . .": *Time*, July 11, 1960, p. 19.
756 "You wonder why . . .": Richard J. Whalen, p. 417.
756 "He asked me what I thought . . .": William O. Douglas, OH-JFKL.
756 Paul Dever: Herbert S. Parmet, p. 232; see also *Current Biography* (1949), p. 148; *Chicago Tribune*, July 22, 1952, p. 6.
757 "It really was the Governor's . . .": Interview, Judge J. John Fox.
757 "We will all be anxiously . . .": L. Bickford to JPK, April 3, 1952, JPK.
757 "I've just talked to Dever . . .": Lawrence O'Brien, *No Final Victories* (1974), p. 26.
757 John Kennedy was known to only: Clifford Leach, "The Selling of the President," undergraduate thesis, HU, 1978.
757 On Lodge's background see William J. Miller, *Henry Cabot Lodge* (1967). See also obituaries, Feb. 28, 1985, *BG*, p. 1, and *BH*, pp. 1, 7.
757 "Rarely in American politics . . .": James M. Burns, *John Kennedy . . .*, p. 102.
757 "From the beginning . . .": Interview, Henry Cabot Lodge II.
758 "From the start . . .": Ibid.
758 "You must permit the use . . .": Dwight D. Eisenhower, *Mandate for Change* (1963), p. 18.
758 "It is a dangerous gamble . . .": *BP*, Sun., Nov. 18, 1951, p. 25.

759 "to be right in the swing . . .": Interview, Rose Kennedy.
759 "We had a beautiful brochure . . .": Interview, Dave Powers.
759 "This is one way to get . . .": J. Landis to JPK, May 13, 1952, JPK.
759 "because after all, they are . . .": JPK to B. Brickley, March 23, 1952, JPK.
759 "no limit on the number . . .": B. Brickley to JPK, June 12, 1952, JPK.
760 the father was the distinct: Ralph G. Martin and Ed Plaut, p. 161.
760 "I told Jack's father . . .": Ibid.
760 the callous treatment of Mark Dalton: Richard J. Whalen, p. 420.
760 "a grave disappointment": Mark Dalton, OH-JFKL.
760 "Dalton was at his desk . . .": Quoted in Richard J. Whalen, p. 420.
761 "The whole affair really hurt . . .": Interview, John Galvin.
761 "absolute disaster": Herbert S. Parmet, p. 238.
761 "Don't drag me into it.": Kenneth O'Donnell and David Powers, p. 83; Arthur M. Schlesinger, Jr., *Robert Kennedy* . . . , p. 59.
761 his academic record: Arthur M. Schlesinger, Jr., *Robert Kennedy* . . . , pp. 65–67.
761 he had "willed himself": Interview, Lem Billings.
761 "He is a remarkable boy. . . .": M. Beaverbrook to JPK, March 12, 1948, JPK.
761 "He is just starting off . . .": JPK to M. Beaverbrook, March 23, 1948, JPK.
761 "I am very grateful . . .": JPK to John Noonan, Jan. 20, 1949, JPK.
762 "Bobby could handle the father . . .": Kenneth O'Donnell, recorded interview, Oct. 8, 1968, Stein Papers (made available to the author by Jean Stein).
762 "prepared a magnificent . . .": Interview, Judge J. John Fox.
762 "Every afternoon Dever's people . . .": Interview, Phil Fine.
762 the Ambassador, argued that an open fight: Kenneth O'Donnell and David Powers, p. 88.
763 The more Kennedy's advisers studied Lodge: James M. Burns, *John Kennedy* . . . , pp. 104–5.
763 "We were in a real bind . . .": Interview, Phil Fine.
763 "What more do you want?": Quoted in Richard J. Whalen, p. 426.
763 "I can still remember . . .": Interview, Henry Cabot Lodge II.
764 "There was so little . . .": Ibid.
764 "a growing feeling . . .": Ibid.
765 the powerful paper printed: *BP*, Oct. 31, 1952, pp. 1, 20.
765 Fox admitted: Joe McCarthy, pp. 139–40.
765 "Oh yes, I've heard that story . . .": Interview, Henry Cabot Lodge II.
766 thirty-three teas: Interviews, Polly Fitzgerald and Helen Keyes.
766 "For approximately two hours . . .": Cabell Phillips, "Case History of a Senate Race," *NYT Magazine*, Sun., Oct. 26, 1952, p. 10.
766 "Mrs. Kennedy was a key . . .": Interview, Polly Fitzgerald.
766 "because she had always felt . . .": JPK to J. Calder, Dec. 31, 1952, JPK.
766 dramatic letter from Japan: Joseph Dinneen, *The Kennedy Family*, pp. 148–50.
767 "one of the very first . . .": *BG*, Nov. 4, 1952, p. 7.
767 election day, the early returns: *BP*, Nov. 5, 1952, pp. 1, 13.
767 "At five A.M. . . . we could feel . . .": Interview, Dave Powers.
767 "I extend my congratulations . . .": *BT*, Nov. 5, 1952, p. 20; *BG* (eve.), Nov. 5, 1952, p. 1.
767 "Until then I don't think Jack . . .": Interview, Lem Billings.
767 "This is probably one . . .": JPK to J. Calder, Dec. 31, 1952, JPK.
768 "I kept thinking . . .": Interview, Rose Kennedy.
769 On the night of January 20, 1953: *NYT*, Jan. 21, 1953, p. 1.
769 "From the beginning . . .": Interview, Lem Billings.
769 On Jackie see Gordon L. Hall and Ann Pinchot, *Jacqueline Kennedy* (1964); Kitty Kelley, *Jackie Oh!* (1978).
770 "I knew right away . . .": Interview, Lem Billings.
770 "the little boy, sick so much . . .": Theodore H. White, "For President Kennedy: Epilogue," *Life*, Dec. 6, 1963, p. 159.
770 "They were kindred . . .": Interview, Lem Billings.
771 "It was a very spasmodic . . .": James M. Burns, *John Kennedy* . . . , p. 127.

771 "his chariness of marriage . . .": Kitty Kelley, p. 30.
771 "For the Kennedy family . . .": Interview, Lem Billings.
771 "It was enough for me . . .": Conversation, Jacqueline Kennedy Onassis.
772 "I used to tell him . . .": Ibid.
772 "They are very nice . . .": JPK to B. Gimbel, July 13, 1953, JPK.
772 Rose let it be known: Gail Cameron, pp. 248–49.
772 For her part: Conversation, Jacqueline Kennedy Onassis.
772 "nearly crushing the bride": NYT, Sept. 13, 1953, p. 1.
772 "I was alone almost every weekend . . .": Kitty Kelley, p. 51.
773 his parents had experienced: Interview, Lem Billings.
773 "Jack kept assuring us . . .": Quoted in Peter Collier and David Horowitz, p. 197.
773 that a man is paying: Elinor Glyn, "Marriage," Good Housekeeping, September 1913, pp. 347–52.
773 "A woman cannot live . . .": The Pilot, March 9, 1907, p. 8.
773 "While on one level . . .": Interview, Lem Billings.
774 "This time the pain . . .": Ibid.
774 forced to use crutches: Evelyn Lincoln, My Twelve Years with John F. Kennedy (1965), pp. 53–54.
774 According to his doctors: Joe McCarthy, p. 150.
774 That same year: James A. Nicholas et al., "Management of Adrenocortical Insufficiency During Surgery," Archives of Surgery, November 1955, pp. 737–38.
774 "Jack was determined . . .": Interview, Rose Kennedy.
775 "to clear up a wartime injury": NYT, Oct. 11, 1943, p. 39.
775 the operation was postponed: NYT, Oct. 21, 1954, p. 17, James A. Nicholas et al., loc. cit., p. 739.
775 he was placed on the critical list: Evelyn Lincoln, p. 56.
775 Footnote: Interview, Lem Billings.
775 he dropped into a chair: Arthur Krock, OH-JFKL.
775 "it seemed inconceivable . . .": Interview, Rose Kennedy.
775 "The doctors don't understand . . .": Evelyn Lincoln, p. 56.
776 "It was a terrible time . . .": Interview, Lem Billings.
776 "By February, Joe came . . .": Interview, Rose Kennedy.
776 "The whole time I was there . . .": Interview, Lem Billings.
776 "Aside from experiencing . . .": BP, May 24, 1955, p. 6.
776 including a huge basket: BG (eve.), May 24, 1955, p. 11.
776 "there wasn't so much talk . . .": Interview, Lem Billings.
776 "a history . . .": BG, loc. cit.
777 "the sort to restore respect . . .": NYT Book Review, Jan. 1, 1956, p. 1.
777 the ancient ideal of individual: John W. Ward, Red, White and Blue: Men, Books and Ideas in American Culture (1969), p. 148.
777 Of all the virtues: Look, Feb. 25, 1964, p. 37.
777 "This kind of political production . . .": Garry Wills, p. 135.
777 In the first round of the selection: Ibid., pp. 136–37.
778 the prize was awarded: BG (eve.), May 6, 1957, p. 1.
778 "a distinguished American . . .": Herbert S. Parmet, p. 395.
778 "The gold ring . . .": Interview, Richard Goodwin.
779 Pointing out: James M. Burns, John Kennedy . . . , p. 125.
779 "a hopeless internecine . . .": Herbert S. Parmet, p. 285.
779 censure of McCarthy: David Crosby, God, Church, and Flag (1969), p. 21; Berkshire Eagle, Dec. 3, 1954, JFK.
780 "It was the goddamnedest thing . . .": Conversation, Lyndon B. Johnson.
780 "the most telegenic . . .": BG, July 22, 1956, JFK.
781 "He has youth . . .": BG, July 1956, JFK clipping in JFK scrapbook.
781 Joe Kennedy tried to hold: Joe McCarthy, p. 156.
781 "defeat would be a devastating blow . . .": JPK to JFK, May 23, 1956, JPK.
781 "although if it looks . . .": JFK to JPK, June 29, 1956, Sorensen Papers, Box 9, JFK.
781 "With Eisenhower running . . .": JPK to M. Downey, July 1956, JPK.
782 sentiment in Stevenson's headquarters: NYT, Aug. 16, 1956, p. 1.

782 "It was as if Jack's marriage . . .": Interview, Rose Kennedy.
782 "the personality of the Senator . . .": Quoted in Herbert S. Parmet, p. 367.
782 "Senator Kennedy came before . . .": Ibid., citing *NYT*, Aug. 14, 1956.
783 Eleanor Roosevelt refused: Eleanor Roosevelt, "Stevenson, Truman and Kennedy," *Saturday Evening Post*, March 8, 1958, pp. 32–33.
783 wanted Kennedy to deliver: Unidentified clipping, Aug. 17, 1956, Herald Morgue Files.
783 "the goddamned stupidest . . .": Conversation, Lyndon Johnson.
783 "tell him I'm going for it": Kenneth O'Donnell and David Powers, p. 122.
783 "a momentary paralysis": Interview, Lem Billings.
783 "The next twelve hours . . .": Evelyn Lincoln, p. 80.
783 "they kept Carmine de Sapio . . .": Joe McCarthy, p. 162.
783 Jack mistakenly approached Humphrey: Theodore C. Sorensen, pp. 99–100.
784 "Texas proudly casts its vote . . .": Joseph Dinneen, *The Kennedy Family*, p. 202.
784 "I've been thinking . . .": L. B. Johnson to JPK, Aug. 25, 1956, JPK.
784 "That's it, let's go": James M. Burns, *John Kennedy* . . . , p. 190.
784 "This was his great moment . . .": Ibid.
785 Jack flew: Unidentified clipping, Aug. 18, 1956, JFK.
785 "Jack arrived here . . .": JPK to M. Downey, Aug. 24, 1956, JPK.
785 Rushed to the hospital: James M. Burns, *John Kennedy* . . . , p. 164.
785 For three days, the Kennedy family: Kitty Kelley, p. 56; unidentified clipping, Aug. 28, 1956, JFK.
785 "Senator Kennedy . . .": Quoted in Kitty Kelley, p. 57.
785 For months, Jackie had been planning: Joseph Dinneen, *The Kennedy Family*, p. 207.
785 "Jackie losing the baby . . .": JPK to Michael Morrissey, Aug. 30, 1956, JPK.
786 "This was true for Bobby . . .": Interview, Lem Billings.
786 "People wrote of how . . .": Evelyn Lincoln, p. 87.
787 "After dinner . . . Jack . . .": Interview, Rose Kennedy.
789 "He brought the old ward boss . . .": Interview, Richard Goodwin.
790 "All of a sudden . . .": Conversation, Lyndon Johnson.
790 "one of the highest honors . . .": *NYT*, Jan. 9, 1956, p. 1.
790 "colonies are like fruit . . .": *NYT*, July 3, 1957, p. 1.
790 "perhaps the most . . .": Ibid.
790 "You don't know it . . .": James M. Burns, *John Kennedy* . . . , p. 196.
791 both Jack and his father were opposed: Arthur M. Schlesinger, Jr., *Robert Kennedy* . . . , p. 142; Ralph G. Martin and Ed Plaut, p. 202.
791 "a little more rumpled . . .": Harold Martin, "The Amazing Kennedys," *Saturday Evening Post*, Sept. 7, 1957, p. 49.
791 "This is the first time . . .": Aileen Marshall to Mr. and Mrs. Kennedy, July 31, 1957, RFK.
791 "I find Bobby a most . . .": M. Beaverbrook to JPK, Dec. 11, 1957, JPK.
791 "The Rise of the Brothers Kennedy," *Look*, Aug. 6, 1957, p. 18.
791 "the biggest and the best . . .": *Saturday Evening Post*, loc. cit., p. 44.
791 "Fervent admirers of the Kennedys . . .": Ibid., p. 49.
792 "You never really accept . . .": JPK to J. Knight, March 11, 1958, JPK.
792 "Jack is the greatest . . .": Ralph G. Martin and Ed Plaut, p. 461.
792 "Seldom in the annals . . .": *Time* (a Greenwich, Conn. paper), May 15, 1957, JFK.
792 Jackie gave birth: *BG* (eve.), Nov. 27, 1957, p. 1; *BG*, Nov. 28, 1957, pp. 1, 4.
792 "That child made all . . .": Kitty Kelley, p. 82.
793 "Jack was more emotional . . .": Interview, Lem Billings.
793 "Shall await the big . . .": RFK to children, Aug. 5, 1958, RFK.
793 a record turnout gave Kennedy: Kenneth O'Donnell and David Powers, p. 145.
793 "The vote was beyond our fondest . . .": JPK to Joe Conway, Nov. 18, 1958, RFK.
793 "How's Kennedy doing?" Joseph Dinneen, *The Kennedy Family*, p. 235.
794 "just another campaign": *BG*, Nov. 4, 1958, p. 1.
794 just sixteen days short: *BG*, Nov. 13, 1958, pp. 1, 3; *BH*, Sun., Nov. 16, 1958, pp. 1, 50.

794 "I am announcing today . . .": *NYT*, Jan. 3, 1960, p. 1.
795 "This is the most exclusive . . .": Quoted in Peter Collier and David Horowitz, p. 218.
795 "Jack knows the sorrow . . .": Miscellaneous Clippings, undated, RFK.
795 "Rose is sensational . . .": J. Fayne to JPK, Feb. 17, 1960, RFK.
796 "Whenever Uncle Joe would hear . . .": Interview, Ann Gargan King.
796 "What to do with books . . .": Father Cavanagh to RFK, March 23, 1959, RFK.
796 "I loved all the villages . . .": Interview, Rose Kennedy.
797 "The Wisconsin farmer . . .": Carroll Kilpatrick, OH-JFKL.
797 worked out an arrangement: Dave Powers, letter to the author, summer 1985.
797 the Sunday before the Tuesday election: Ira Kapenstein, OH-JFKL.
797 On primary night, his fears: Theodore H. White, *The Making of the President, 1960* (1967), p. 94.
797 "It means that we have to . . .": Ibid.; Kenneth O'Donnell and David Powers, p. 160.
797 "Here is where fate . . .": Pierre Salinger, *With Kennedy* (1966), p. 34.
797 "We have a few troubles . . .": JPK to M. Beaverbrook, April 20, 1960, RFK.
798 cartoon from a Baptist: *Western Voice*, Aug. 18, 1960, JPK.
798 "I am a Catholic . . .": Robert McDonough, OH-JFKL.
798 The reaction he got: Ibid.
798 first encounter with hunger: Theodore H. White, loc. cit., p. 106.
799 "There were more monuments . . .": Peter Lisagor, OH-JFKL.
799 "Any discussion of the war . . .": *NYT*, May 7, 1960, p. 11.
799 "The religious issue . . .": *BG* (eve.), May 11, 1960, p. 32.
799 "the unmistakable sound . . .": *NYT*, May 12, 1960, p. 1.
799 "Well the seven primaries . . .": JPK to M. Beaverbrook, May 27, 1960, RFK.
800 "I haven't had anything . . .": Stated before the West Virginia and Kentucky delegations, quoted in *New York Herald Tribune*, July 14, 1960, p. 12, JFK.
800 All spring long, the Ambassador: Eugene Kennedy, *Himself!* (1978), pp. 155–56.
800 Daley waited: Ibid., pp. 157–58; see also Len O' Connor, *Clout: Mayor Daley and His City* (1975), p. 153.
800 "With that the hope . . .": Theodore H. White, loc. cit., pp. 167–68.
800 Kennedy had successfully: Ibid., pp. 168–69.
800 Never leaving: Interview, Ann Gargan King.
801 "there was no question . . .": Ibid.
801 Rose later recalled trying: Interview, Rose Kennedy.
801 "Handsome as thoroughbreds . . .": *Time*, July 11, 1960, p. 19.
801 "It's just like the circus . . .": *BG*, July 14, 1960, p. 1.
801 The candidate himself was watching: Theodore H. White, loc. cit., pp. 169–70.
802 "They walked off into the corner . . .": Hugh Sidey, OH-JFKL.
802 the Ambassador had been arguing: Interview, Rose Kennedy.
802 "Lyndon Johnson and Joseph Kennedy . . .": Interview, Ann Gargan King.
802 Early Thursday morning, Kennedy telephoned: Thomas O'Neill, OH-JFKL.
802 "incredibly happy . . .": Interview, Lem Billings.
803 "We cannot turn our . . .": Lawrence Fuchs, *John F. Kennedy and American Catholicism* (1967), pp. 176–77.
803 "I believe in an America . . .": *Washington Post*, Sept. 13, 1960, p. A16.
803 "Neither man fell flat . . .": *BG*, Sept. 28, 1960, p. 19.
804 "maybe the audience . . .": Ibid.
804 "To be transferred from the Nixon . . .": Theodore H. White, loc. cit., p. 337.
804 The papers reported: *BG*, Nov. 9, 1960, p. 17.
804 "It was a festive meal. . . .": Interview, Ann Gargan King.
805 the key state was Illinois: Eugene Kennedy, pp. 179–87.
806 "I've brought a message . . .": Interview, Ann Gargan King.
806 his father was by his side: *BG*, Nov. 9, 1960, p. 31.
806 "I'm never there . . .": Kitty Kelley, p. 98.
807 "Jack doesn't belong . . .": Hugh Sidey, "Joe Kennedy's Feelings About His Son," *Life*, Dec. 19, 1960, p. 32.

807 "I don't know what's wrong . . .": Hugh Sidey in Lester Tanzer (ed.), *The Kennedy Circle* (1961), p. 186.

807 "Ted, you've got a base here . . .": Quoted in Peter Collier and David Horowitz, p. 285.

807 "The person who was primarily . . .": Arthur M. Schlesinger, Jr., *Robert Kennedy . . .* , p. 371.

810 35 million immigrants: Oscar Handlin, *The Uprooted*, p. 31.

811 "We are the heirs of all time . . .": Herman Melville, as quoted in John Higham, p. 21.

811 "It is the old story . . .": Garry Wills, p. 61.

812 a raging snowstorm: *BG*, Jan. 21, 1961, p. 1; *Washington Post*, Jan. 20, 1961, p. 1A.

812 There came the sons and daughters: Unidentified clipping, Jan. 18, 1961, Herald Morgue Files; *New York Herald Tribune*, Jan. 19, 1961, p. 3, and Jan. 20, p. 3.

812 At a few minutes before twelve: *Washington Post*, Jan. 21, 1961, p. 6A.

813 When General Eisenhower was inaugurated: *Washington Post*, Jan. 20, 1961, p. 1A.

813 "romantic sentiment mingled . . .": Interview, Lem Billings.

813 At the first inauguration: Joseph Nathan Kane, *Facts About the Presidents: A Compilation of Biographical and Historical Data* (1959), pp. 11–12, 30–31, 58–59.

813 The idea of inviting: *BG*, Sun., Jan. 22, 1961, p. 4A.

814 "If you can bear . . .": Ralph G. Martin, p. 6.

814 As the old poet began reading: *BG*, Jan. 21, 1961, p. 4; *Washington Post*, Jan. 21, 1961, p. 6A.

814 "the town had experienced . . .": *Irish Times*, Jan. 21, 1961, p. 9.

815 "It will remain one of the greatest . . .": Duke of Devonshire to JPK, Jan. 26, 1961, JPK.

815 "Oh, Jack, what a day": Arthur M. Schlesinger, Jr., *A Thousand Days*, p. 14.

815 "It was an extraordinary moment . . .": Interview, Eunice Kennedy Shriver.

816 "We're not going to live . . .": *New York Journal-American*, Jan. 8, 1961, p. 25.

# BIBLIOGRAPHY

MANUSCRIPTS AND PERSONAL PAPERS

Lem Billings Papers. Correspondence with Kathleen Kennedy. Now in the possession of
    Robert Kennedy, Jr.
Robert Bingham Papers. Library of Congress, Washington, D.C.
Boston Archdiocese Archives. Diaries of Father Hilary Tucker, 1862–67; St. Stephen's
    Baptisms, 1860–70; St. Stephen's Marriages, 1846–72; Dispensation Records.
R. W. P. Cockerton, "Recollections," unpublished.
R. G. Dunn and Company Collections. Baker Library, Harvard Graduate School of
    Business Administration, Cambridge, Mass.
John F. Fitzgerald Scrapbooks. College of the Holy Cross, Worcester, Mass.
John F. Kennedy Library, Boston, Mass.:
        John F. Kennedy Papers, Personal and Pre-Presidential.
        Joseph P. Kennedy Papers.
        Rose F. Kennedy Papers.
        Oral History Series.
        Theodore C. Sorensen Papers.
L. E. Kirstein Papers. Baker Library, Harvard Graduate School of Business Administra-
    tion, Cambridge, Mass.
Arthur Krock Papers. Princeton University, Princeton, N.J.
James Landis Papers. Library of Congress, Washington, D.C.
George Nutter Diaries. Massachusetts Historical Society, Boston, Mass.
Franklin D. Roosevelt Papers. Franklin D. Roosevelt Library, Hyde Park, N.Y.
Jean Stern Papers.
Henry L. Stimson Diaries. Yale University Library, New Haven, Conn.

GOVERNMENT DOCUMENTS (All found at the Boston Public Library unless otherwise
    noted.)

*Local*
Annual Reports of the Boston Board of Trade.
Annual Reports of the School Committee of the Town of Acton, Acton, Mass., Public
    Library.
Annual Reports of the Selectmen of the Town of Acton, Acton, Mass., Public Library.
Boston Almanac & Business Directories.
Boston City Documents.
Boston Finance Commission Reports.
Boston School Documents.
Boston Tax Assessors Records.
Common Council Proceedings.
Valuation Lists of Real and Personal Estates in the Town of Acton, Acton, Mass., Public
    Library.

*Commonwealth of Massachusetts*
Annual Reports of the State Board of Health.
Journal of the Senate.
Lists of Officials and Employees.
Massachusetts Public Documents.
Massachusetts Senate Documents.

Reports of the Chief of the Massachusetts District Police.
Suffolk County Probate Records and Registry of Deeds. Suffolk County Court House, Boston, Mass.
Vital Records and Statistics, Boston, Mass.

*Federal*
*Congressional Record.* Washington: U.S. Government Printing Office.
*Documents on German Foreign Policy, 1937–1945,* Series D. Washington: U.S. Government Printing Office.
*Foreign Relations of the United States.* Washington: U.S. Government Printing Office.
*Second Annual Report of the Provost Marshal to the Secretary of War, 1921.* Washington: U.S. Government Printing Office.
U.S. Bureau of the Census: *8th–12th Census of the United States, 1860–1900; Historical Statistics of the United States; Statistical Abstracts of the United States.*

*Other*
*Parliamentary Debates, 1937–40.* London: His Majesty's Printing Office.
*Foreign Office Paper.* London: Public Record Office.


BOOKS AND DISSERTATIONS


Abbott, Edith. *Historical Aspects of the Immigration Problem.* New York: Arno Press, 1969.
Abrams, Richard. *Conservatism in a Progressive Era: Massachusetts Politics, 1910–1912.* Cambridge, Mass.: Harvard University Press, 1964.
Adams, Henry. *The Education of Henry Adams: An Autobiography.* Boston: Houghton Mifflin, 1961.
Adams, William Forbes. *Ireland and Irish Emigration to the New World from 1815 to the Famine.* New York: Russell and Russell, 1932.
*Advance of Boston: A Pictorial Review of Municipal Progress by the City During Four Years, 1910–1913, John F. Fitzgerald, Mayor.* Boston: City of Boston Printing Office, 1913.
Ainley, Leslie. *Boston Mahatma: A Biography of Martin M. Lomasney.* New York: Bruce Humphries, 1949.
Allen, Frederick Lewis. *Lords of Creation.* Chicago: Quadrangle Books, 1966.
———. *Only Yesterday.* New York: Harper & Row, 1966.
Amory, Cleveland. *The Last Resorts.* New York: Harper & Row, 1948.
———. *The Proper Bostonians.* New York: E. P. Dutton, 1947.
Anger, Kenneth. *Hollywood Babylon.* New York: Simon and Schuster, 1975.
Antin, Mary. *The Promised Land.* Boston: Houghton Mifflin, 1912.
Appleton, William S. *Fathers and Daughters.* Garden City, N.Y.: Doubleday, 1981.
Arensberg, Conrad, and Solon Kimball. *Family and Community in Ireland.* Cambridge, Mass.: Harvard University Press, 1940.
Aries, Philip. *Centuries of Childhood: A Social History of Family Life,* translated by Robert Baldrick. New York: Alfred A. Knopf, 1962.
Astor, Sidney. *1939: The Making of the Second World War.* New York: Simon and Schuster, 1973.
Atwood, Albert W. *The Exchange and Speculation.* New York: Alexander Hamilton Institute, 1918–19.
Bacon, Charles. *Bacon's Dictionary of Boston.* Boston: Houghton Mifflin, 1886.
Bacon, Edwin M. *The Book of Boston.* Boston: Pilgrim Press, 1916.
———. *Historic Pilgrimages in New England.* New York: Silver, Burdett and Co., 1898.
Baldwin, Hanson. *World War I: Outline History.* New York: Harper & Row, 1962.
Baltzell, E. Digby. *Quaker Philadelphia and Puritan Boston.* New York: The Free Press, 1929.
Baruch, Bernard. *My Own Story.* New York: Henry Holt, 1957.

Beard, Charles A. *American Foreign Policy in the Making*. New Haven: Yale University Press, 1946.

Beebe, Lucius. *Boston and the Boston Legend*. New York: D. Appleton Century, 1935.

————. *High Iron: A Book of Trains*. New York: D. Appleton Century, 1938.

Behlmer, Rudy, ed. *Memo from David O. Selznick*. New York: Viking Press, 1972.

Bergen, William M. *Old Nantasket*. North Quincy, Mass.: Christopher Publishing House, 1969.

Beschloss, Michael R. *Kennedy and Roosevelt*. New York: W. W. Norton, 1980.

Birkenhead, Earl of. *Halifax: The Life of Lord Halifax*. Boston: Houghton Mifflin, 1968.

Bishop, Right Reverend. *Catholic Manual or Collection of Prayers, Anthems, Hymns, etc*. Boston: Devereux and Donahue, 1836.

Blair, Joan and Clay, Jr. *The Search for JFK*. New York: Berkley, 1976.

Blanchard, John A., ed. *The Handbook of Harvard, 1852–1922*. Cambridge, Mass.: Harvard Varsity Club, 1923.

Blodgett, Geoffrey. *The Gentle Reformers: Massachusetts Democrats in the Cleveland Era*. Cambridge, Mass.: Harvard University Press, 1966.

Blum, John Morton. *From the Morgenthau Diaries*, 3 vols. Boston: Houghton Mifflin, 1959–67.

Boldston, Robert. *Suburbia: Civil Denial*. New York: Macmillan, 1970.

Boorstin, Daniel. *The Americans: The National Experience*. New York: Vintage Books, 1967.

Bourne, Randolph Stillman. *War and the Intellectuals: Essays, 1915–1919*. New York: Harper & Row, 1964.

Brandeis, Louis D. *Other People's Money and How Bankers Use It*. New York: Frederick A. Stokes, 1914.

Bremmer, Robert, et al. *The History of the American National Red Cross*. Washington, D.C.: American National Red Cross, 1950.

Brooks, John. *Once in Golconda*. New York: Harper & Row, 1969.

Brooks, Van Wyck. *The Flowering of New England*. New York: E. P. Dutton, 1936.

————. *New England Indian Summer*. New York: E. P. Dutton, 1950.

Brown, Rollo W. *Harvard Yard in the Golden Age*. New York: Current Books, 1948.

Bryce, James. *The American Commonwealth*. New York: Macmillan, 1895.

Buchan, John. *The Battle of the Somme*. New York: G. H. Doran, 1917.

Buckingham, Charles E. *Sanitary Conditions of Boston*. Boston: Rockwell & Churchill, 1875.

Bugg, Lelia H. *The Correct Thing for Catholics*. New York: Benziger Brothers, 1891.

Bulkeley, Robert. *At Close Quarters*. Washington D.C.: U.S. Government Printing Office, 1962.

Bullitt, Orville H., ed. *For the President, Personal and Secret: Correspondence Between Franklin D. Roosevelt and William C. Bullitt*. Boston: Houghton Mifflin, 1972.

Bullock, Alan. *Hitler—A Study in Tyranny*. New York: Harper & Row, 1952.

Burke, Redmond A. *What Is the Index?* Milwaukee: Bruce Publishing Co., 1952.

*Burke's Peerage: Baronetage and Knightage*. London: Burke's Peerage, 1970.

Burns, James MacGregor. *John Kennedy: A Political Profile*. New York: Harcourt, Brace, 1960.

————. *Roosevelt: The Lion and the Fox*. New York: Harcourt, Brace, 1956.

————. *Roosevelt: The Soldier of Freedom*. New York: Harcourt Brace Jovanovich, 1970.

Burroughs, Harry E. *Boys in Men's Shoes*. New York: Macmillan, 1944.

Butler, John W. *Rule of Life*. Baltimore: Butler, 1807.

Byrne, John J., ed. *A History of the Boston City Hospital, 1905–1914*. Boston: Sheldon Press, 1964.

Byrnes, James F. *All in One Life Time*. New York: Harper and Brothers, 1958.

Calder, Angus. *The People's War: Britain, 1939–1945*. New York: Granada Publishing, 1971.

Calhoun, Arthur W. *A Social History of the American Family*. New York: Arno Press, 1919.

Callan, Louise. *The Society of the Sacred Heart in North America*. New York: Longmans, Green, 1937.

Camac, Charles B. *Classics of Medicine and Surgery*. New York: Dover Press, 1959.

Cameron, Gail. *Rose*. New York: G. P. Putnam's Sons, 1971.

Canfield, Cass. *The Incredible Pierpont Morgan*. New York: Harper & Row, 1974.

Cardozo, Arlene. *Women at Home*. Garden City, N.Y.: Doubleday, 1976.

Carter, Katy. *London and the Famous*. London: Fred Muller, 1982.

*Catalogue of Boston Latin School, 1635–1885*. Boston: Boston Latin School Association, 1886.

Challoner, Reverend Dr. *The Catholic Christian Instructed in the Sacraments, Sacrifices, Ceremonies, and Observances of the Church*. New York: Catholic Publication Society, 1809.

Chamberlain, Samuel. *Fair Harvard Photos*. New York: Hastings House, 1948.

Chandler, Alfred. *The Visible Hand*. Cambridge, Mass.: Belknap Press, 1977.

Channon, Sir Henry. *Chips: The Diaries of Sir Henry Channon*, edited by Robert Rhodes James. London: Weidenfeld & Nicolson, 1967.

Churchill, Winston S. *The Second World War*. Vol. I, *The Gathering Storm*; Vol. II, *The Finest Hour*. Boston: Houghton Mifflin, 1948, 1949.

Clark, William H. *History of Winthrop, 1630–1952*. Winthrop, Mass.: Winthrop Centennial Committee, 1952.

Clinch, Nancy Gager. *The Kennedy Neurosis*. New York: Grosset & Dunlap, 1973.

Coffey, Thomas. *The Long Thirst*. New York: W. W. Norton, 1978.

Coit, Margaret L. *Mr. Baruch*. Boston: Houghton Mifflin, 1957.

Collier, Peter, and David Horowitz. *The Kennedys*. New York: Summit Books, 1984.

Collier, Richard. *The Plague of the Spanish Lady: The Influenza Pandemic of 1918–1919*. New York: Atheneum, 1974.

Collis, Maurice. *Nancy Astor: An Informal Biography*. New York: E. P. Dutton, 1960.

Colum, Mary. *Life and the Dream*. Garden City N.Y.: Doubleday, 1947.

Colvin, Ian. *The Chamberlain Cabinet*. New York: Tuplinger Publishing, 1971.

Converse, Florence. *The Story of Wellesley*. Boston: Little, Brown, 1915.

Cooksley, Peter G. *Flying Bomb*. New York: Charles Scribner's Sons, 1979.

Cooper, Bryan. *The Battle of the Torpedo Boats*. New York: Stein and Day, 1970.

Corry, John. *Golden Clan: The Murrays, the McDonnells, and the Irish American Aristocracy*. Boston: Houghton Mifflin, 1977.

Cowles, Virginia. *Winston Churchill: The Era and the Man*. New York: Harper & Row, 1953.

Crosby, Alfred. *Epidemic and Peace*. Westport, Conn.: Greenwood Press, 1976.

Crosby, David. *God, Church, and Flag: Senator Joseph R. McCarthy and the Catholic Church, 1950–1957*. Chapel Hill: University of North Carolina Press, 1969.

Crowther, Bosley. *The Great Films*. New York: G. P. Putnam's Sons, 1967.

Cullen, James. *The Irish in Boston*. Boston: J. B. Cullen, 1889.

Culver, Davis M. "Tenement House Reform in Boston, 1846–1898." Ph.D. dissertation, Boston University, 1972.

*Cumulative Digest of Corporate News*. New York: Moody's Manufacturing Co., 1920–26.

Curley, James Michael. *I'd Do It Again*. Englewood Cliffs, N.J.: Prentice-Hall, 1957.

Curtis, John G. *History of the Town of Brookline*. Boston: Houghton Mifflin, 1933.

Curtis, Thomas Quinn. *Von Stroheim*. New York: Farrar, Straus & Giroux, 1971.

Cutler, John Henry. *"Honey Fitz": Three Steps to the White House*. Indianapolis: Bobbs-Merrill, 1962.

Dakers, Caroline. *The Blue Plaque Guide to London*. London: Mac Press, 1981.

Damore, Leo. *The Cape Cod Years of JFK*. Englewood Cliffs, N.J.: Prentice-Hall, 1967.

Damrell, Charles. *A Half Century of Boston's Building*. Boston: Louis P. Hagger, 1895.

Davis, John H. *The Kennedys: Dynasty and Disaster*. New York: McGraw-Hill, 1984.

de Bedts, Ralph. *The New Deal's SEC: The Formative Years*. New York: Columbia University Press, 1964.

Degler, Carl. *At Odds: Women and the Family in America from the Revolution to the Present*. New York: Oxford University Press, 1980.

Demos, John. *A Little Commonwealth: Family Life in Plymouth Colony*. New York: Oxford University Press, 1970.

Devonshire, Duchess of. *The House: Living at Chatsworth*. New York: Holt, Rinehart & Winston, 1982.

Dewor, J. *The Unlocked Secret: Freemasonry Examined*. London: William Kimber, 1966.

Dickens, Charles. *American Notes*. Gloucester, Mass.: Peter Smith, 1968.

Dinneen, Joseph F. *The Kennedy Family*. Boston: Little, Brown, 1959.

———. *Ward Eight*. New York: Harper & Row, 1936.

Dolan, Jay R. *The Yankee Peddlers of Early New England*. New York: Potter, 1964.

Donovan, Robert J. *PT 109: John F. Kennedy in World War II*. New York: McGraw-Hill, 1961.

Douglas, Elisha P. *The Coming of Age of American Business*. Chapel Hill: University of North Carolina Press, 1971.

Drake, Samuel Adams. *The Pine Tree Coast*. Boston: Estes & Lauriat, 1891.

Dreiser, Theodore. *The Financier*. New York: New American Library, 1967.

Drinkwater, Harry. *50 Years of Medical Progress, 1873–1922*. New York: Macmillan, 1924.

Duffy, John. *The Healers: The Rise of the Medical Establishment*. New York: McGraw-Hill, 1976.

Dupuy, Richard Ernest. *The Encyclopedia of Military History*. New York: Harper & Row, 1977.

Edwards, R. Dudley, and T. Desmond Williams, eds. *The Great Famine*. New York: New York University Press, 1957.

Eisenhower, Dwight D. *Mandate for Change*. Garden City, N.Y.: Doubleday, 1963.

*Encyclopedia of Practical Medicine*. Philadelphia: W. B. Sanders, 1902.

Estabrook, Harold. *Some Slums of Boston*. New York: 20th Century Club, 1898.

Evans, Eldon Cobb. *A History of the Australian Balloting System in the United States*. Chicago: University of Chicago Press, 1917.

Farrington, Selwyn Kip, Jr. *Railroads of Today*. New York: Coward-McCann, 1949.

Faulkner, Harold. *American Economic History*. New York: Harper & Row, 1960.

———. *From Versailles to the New Deal*. New York: United States Publishing Association, 1950.

Federal Writers Project. *California: A Guide to the Golden State*. New York: Hastings House, c. 1939.

———. *Florida*. New York: Oxford University Press, 1939.

———. *Maine*. Boston: Houghton Mifflin, 1937.

———. *Washington: City and Capital*. Washington, D.C.: U.S. Government Printing Office, 1937.

Feiling, Keith. *The Life of Neville Chamberlain*. London: Macmillan, 1970.

Fenner, Kay Toy. *American Catholic Etiquette*. Westminister, Md.: Newman Press, 1962.

Field, Carter. *Baruch: Park Bench Statesman*. New York: Whittlesey House, 1944.

Finch, Christopher. *Gone Hollywood*. Garden City. N.Y.: Doubleday, 1957.

Fitzgerald, F. Scott. *The Last Tycoon*. New York: Bantam Books, 1976.

Flandrau, Charles M. *Harvard Episodes*. Boston: Copeland & Day, 1897.

Fleming, D. F. *The Origins and Legacies of World War I*. Garden City, N.Y.: Doubleday, 1968.

Flynn, John T. *Security Speculation*. New York: Harcourt, Brace, 1934.

Freedman, Max. *Roosevelt and Frankfurter*. Boston: Little, Brown, 1967.

French, Philip. *The Movie Moguls*. Chicago: H. Regnery, 1971.

Frost, Jack. *Harvard and Cambridge: A Sketch Book*. New York: Coward-McCann, 1940.

Fuchs, Lawrence H. *John F. Kennedy and American Catholicism*. New York: Meredith Press, 1967.

Fuchser, Larry. *Neville Chamberlain and Appeasement*. New York: W. W. Norton, 1982.

Furtey, Reverend Paul. *You and Your Children: A Book for Catholic Parents, Priests and Educators*. New York: Benziger Brothers, 1929.

Fussell, Paul. *The Great War and Modern Memory*. New York: Oxford University Press, 1975.

Galbraith, John Kenneth. *The Great Crash*. Boston: Houghton Mifflin, 1972.

Galloway, George. *History of the House of Representatives*. New York: Crowell, 1962.

Gardiner, John Hays. *Harvard*. New York: Oxford University Press, 1914.

Gilbert, Douglas. *American Vaudeville: Its Life and Times.* New York: McGraw-Hill, 1940.

Ginder, Richard. *Binding with Briars.* Englewood Cliffs, N.J.: Prentice-Hall, 1975.

Gobeil, Charlotte, ed. *Hommage à Eric Von Stroheim.* Ottawa, Canada: Canadian Film Institute, 1966.

Goldner, Orville, and George Turner. *The Making of King Kong.* South Brunswick, N.J.: A. S. Barnes, 1975.

Green, Constance McLaughlin. *Washington: Capital City, 1879–1950.* Princeton, N.J.: Princeton University Press, 1963.

Green, Martin. *The Problem of Boston: Some Readings in Cultural History.* New York: W. W. Norton, 1966.

Habenstein, Robert, and William Lamers. *The History of American Funeral Directing.* Milwaukee: Bulfin Printers, 1962.

Hale, Edward Everett. *Workingmen's Homes and Other Stories.* Boston: James R. Osgood, 1871.

Hall, Gordon L., and Ann Pinchot. *Jacqueline Kennedy.* New York: Frederick Fell, 1964.

Halsey, William M. *The Survival of American Innocence.* Notre Dame, Ind.: University of Notre Dame Press, 1980.

Hampton, Benjamin B. *History of the American Film Industry.* New York: Dover Publications, 1970.

Handlin, Oscar. *Boston's Immigrants.* New York: Atheneum, 1975.

———. *The Uprooted.* Boston: Little, Brown, 1951.

Haskell, Molly. *From Reverence to Rape.* New York: Penguin Books, 1974.

Hatchett, Payne. *Wellesley: Part of the American Story.* New York: E. P. Dutton, 1949.

Hayne, Donald, ed. *Autobiography of Cecil B. De Mille.* Englewood Cliffs, N.J.: Prentice-Hall, 1959.

Hays, Will. *Memoirs.* Garden City, N.Y.: Doubleday, 1955.

Healy, Paul. *Cissy: The Biography of Eleanor M. Cissy Patterson.* Garden City, N.Y.: Doubleday, 1966.

Heilbrun, Carolyn. *Reinventing Womanhood.* New York: W. W. Norton, 1979.

Hemingway, Ernest. *A Farewell to Arms.* New York: Charles Scribner's Sons, 1929.

Herlihy, Elizabeth, ed. *Fifty Years of Boston: A Memorial History.* Boston: Subcommittee on Memorial History, 1932.

Hersh, Burton. *The Education of Edward Kennedy.* New York: William Morrow, 1972.

Hess, Stephen. *American Political Dynasties.* New York: Doubleday, 1966.

Hibbert, Christopher. *The Court of St. James'.* London: Weidenfeld & Nicolson, 1979.

Higham, Charles. *Cecil B. De Mille.* New York: Charles Scribner's Sons, 1973.

———. *Trading with the Enemy: An Exposé of the Nazi-American Money Plot, 1933–1948.* New York: Delacorte Press, 1983.

Higham, John. *Strangers in the Land: Patterns of American Nativism, 1860–1925.* New York: Atheneum, 1975.

Hofstadter, Richard. *The Progressive Movement, 1900–1915.* Englewood Cliffs, N.J.: Prentice-Hall, 1963.

Holland, Bernard. *The Life of Spencer Compton: Eighth Duke of Devonshire.* London: Longmans, Green & Co., 1911.

Holt, L. Emmett. *The Care and Feeding of Children.* New York: D. Appleton, 1894.

Homans, Abigail Adams. *Education by Uncles.* Boston: Houghton Mifflin, 1966.

Hopper, Hedda. *From Under My Hat.* Garden City, N.Y.: Doubleday, 1952.

Howard, Brett. *Boston: A Social History.* New York: Hawthorne Books, 1976.

Howard, Michael, and John Sparrow. *The Coldstream Guards.* London: Oxford University Press, 1951.

Howe, Irving. *World of Our Fathers.* New York: Harcourt Brace Jovanovich, 1976.

Howe, Mark De Wolfe. *Boston: The Place and the People.* New York: Macmillan, 1903.

Howells, William Dean. *The Rise of Silas Lapham.* New York: Modern Library, 1951.

Hoyt, Edwin. *The House of Morgan.* London: Frederick Muller, 1968.

Huddleston, Sisley. *Paris.* London: Methuen, 1928.

Huebner, S. S. *The Stock Market.* New York: D. Appleton, 1922.

Hull, Cordell. *The Memoirs of Cordell Hull,* 2 vols. New York: Macmillan, 1948.

Hulmes, Katherine. *The Nun's Story*. Boston: Little, Brown, 1956.

Hungerford, Edward. *The Story of the Waldorf-Astoria*. New York: G. P. Putnam's Sons, 1925.

Hunnings, Neville March. *Film Censorship and the Law*. London: George Allen & Unwin, 1967.

Hurley, Reverend Timothy. *A Commentary on the Present Index Legislation*. New York: Benziger Brothers, 1908.

Ickis, Marguerite. *The Book of Religious Holidays and Celebrations*. New York: Dodd, Mead, 1966.

*Illustrated Boston*. New York: American Publishing and Engraving Co., 1889.

*The International Who's Who*. London: Adam and Charles Black, 1966.

James, Henry. *Charles W. Eliot*. Boston: Houghton Mifflin, 1930.

James, Marquis and Jesse. *Biography of a Bank*. New York: Harper & Row, 1954.

James, Robert Rhodes. *Churchill: A Study in Failure*. Cleveland: World, 1970.

Johnson, Arthur M., and Barry E. Supple. *Boston Capitalists and Western Railroads*. Cambridge, Mass.: Harvard University Press, 1967.

Joyce, James. *A Portrait of the Artist as a Young Man*. New York: Viking Press, 1961.

Kaplan, Justin. *Lincoln Steffens: A Biography*. New York: Simon and Schuster, 1974.

Kazin, Alfred. *On Native Grounds*. New York: Harcourt, Brace, 1954.

Keegan, John. *The Face of Battle*. New York: Viking Press, 1976.

Kelley, Kitty. *Jackie Oh!* Secaucus, N.J.: Lyle Stuart, 1978.

Kelly, Florence. *What America Did*. New York: E. P. Dutton, 1919.

Keniston, Kenneth. *All Our Children*. New York: Harcourt Brace Jovanovich, 1977.

Kennan, George F. *Memoirs, 1925–1950*. Boston: Little, Brown, 1967.

Kennedy, Edward M., ed. *The Fruitful Bough: A Tribute to Joseph P. Kennedy*. Privately printed, 1965.

Kennedy, Eugene. *Himself! The Life and Times of Mayor Richard J. Daley*. New York: Viking Press, 1978.

Kennedy, John F., ed. *As We Remember Joe*. Privately printed, 1945.

Kennedy, Joseph P. *I'm for Roosevelt*. New York: Reynal and Hitchcock, 1936.

———, ed. *The Story of Films*, New York: A. W. Shaw, 1927.

Kennedy, Rose. *Times to Remember*. New York: Bantam Books, 1975.

Kerley, Charles. *Short Talks with Young Mothers*. New York: G. P. Putnam's Sons, 1901.

Kerr, Rose Netzorg. *100 Years of Costumes in America, 1850–1950*. Worcester, Mass.: Davis Press, 1951.

King, Moses. *King's Handbook of Boston*. Cambridge, Mass.: Moses King, 1878.

———. *King's How to See Boston*. Boston: Macullar, Parker, 1895.

Kirker, Harold. *The Architecture of Charles Bufinch*. Cambridge, Mass.: Harvard University Press, 1969.

———. *Bulfinch's Boston*. New York: Oxford University Press, 1964.

Kobre, Sidney. *Development of American Journalism*. Dubuque, Iowa: William C. Brown, 1963.

Koren, John. *The Economic Aspects of the Liquor Problem*. Boston: Houghton Mifflin, 1889.

Korson, George. *At His Side: The Story of the American Red Cross Overseas in World War II*. New York: Coward-McCann, 1945.

Koskoff, David E. *Joseph P. Kennedy*. Englewood Cliffs, N.J.: Prentice-Hall, 1974.

Koszarski, Richard. *Hollywood Directory, 1914–1940*. New York: Oxford University Press, 1976.

———. *The Man You Love to Hate*. New York: Oxford University Press, 1983.

Krock, Arthur. *Memoirs: 60 Years on the Firing Line*. New York: Funk & Wagnalls, 1968.

Lally, Francis. *The Catholic Church in a Changing America*. Boston: Little, Brown, 1962.

Langer, William L., and Everett S. Gleason. *The World Crisis and American Foreign Policy*, 2 vols. New York: Harper & Row, 1952–53.

Langtry, Albert P. *Metropolitan Boston: A Modern History*. New York: Lewis Historical Publishing Co., 1929.

Lasky, Jesse. *I Blow My Horn*. Garden City, N.Y.: Doubleday, 1957.

Lasky, Victor. *J.F.K.: The Man and the Myth*. New York: Macmillan, 1963.

Laver, James. *Between the Wars*. Boston: Houghton Mifflin, 1961.

Leach, Clifford, "The Selling of the President." PhD dissertation, Harvard University, 1978.

Leckie, Robert. *American and Catholic*. Garden City, N.Y.: Doubleday, 1970.

Lee, Alfred McLung. *The Daily Newspaper in America*. New York: Macmillan, 1937.

Leech, Margaret. *The Garfield Orbit*. New York: Harper & Row, 1978.

Leuchtenburg, William E. *Franklin D. Roosevelt and the New Deal, 1932–1940*. New York: Harper & Row, 1963.

———. *Perils of Prosperity, 1914–1932*. Chicago: University of Chicago Press, 1958.

Levy, Rosalie Marie. *Heavenly Friends*. Boston: St. Paul Editions, 1956.

Liddell Hart, B. H. *History of the Second World War*. London: Pan Books, 1970.

Lincoln, Evelyn. *My Twelve Years with John F. Kennedy*. New York: David McKay, 1965.

Lindbergh, Anne Morrow. *The Flower and the Nettle: Diaries and Letters of Anne Morrow Lindbergh, 1936–1956*. New York: Harcourt Brace Jovanovich, 1976.

Lindbergh, Charles A. *The Wartime Journals of Charles A. Lindbergh*. New York: Harcourt Brace Jovanovich, 1970.

Link, Arthur. *American Epoch*. New York: Alfred A. Knopf, 1980.

Little, Nina F. *Some Old Houses of Brookline*. Brookline, Mass.: Brookline Historical Society, 1949.

Livermore, Jesse. *How to Trade in Stocks*. New York: Duell, Sloan & Pearce, 1940.

Lockwood, Charles. *Dream Palaces*. New York: Viking Press, 1981.

Lodge, Henry Cabot. *Early Memories*. New York: Arno Press, 1975.

———. *Speeches and Addresses, 1884–1909*. Boston: Houghton Mifflin, 1909.

Lord, Robert. *History of the Archdiocese of Boston*, 3 vols. New York: Sheed Publishing Co., 1944.

Lovett, James D'Wolf. *Old Boston Boys and the Games They Played*. Boston: Riverdale Press, 1906.

Luce, Clare Boothe. *Europe in the Spring*. New York: Alfred A. Knopf, 1940.

Lundberg, Ferdinand. *America's 60 Families*. New York: Vanguard Press, 1937.

Lyons, Eugene. *David Sarnoff*. New York: Harper & Row, 1966.

———. *Herbert Hoover: A Biography*. Garden City, N.Y.: Doubleday, 1948.

Lyons, Louis B. *Newspaper Story: One Hundred Years of the Boston Globe*. Cambridge, Mass.: Belknap Press, 1971.

MacCorkle, William A. *The White Sulphur Springs*. New York: Neale Publishing Co., 1916.

MacGowen, Kenneth. *Behind the Screen: The History and Techniques of the Motion Picture*. New York: Delacorte Press, 1965.

MacLeod, Iain. *Neville Chamberlain*. London: Frederick Muller, 1961.

MacNeil, Neil. *Forge of Democracy*. New York: David McKay, 1963.

Maguire, John F. *The Irish in America*. New York: Arno Press, 1969.

Maisky, Ivan. *Memoirs of a Soviet Ambassador: The War, 1938–1943*, translated by Andrew Rothstein. London: Hutchinson, 1967.

Marquand, John P. *The Late George Apley*. New York: Modern Library, 1940.

Marshall, John. *The Guinness Book of Rail Facts and Feats*. Enfield, Conn.: Guinness Superlatives, 1975.

Martin, Kingsley. *Harold Laski*. New York: Viking Press, 1933.

Martin, Ralph G. *A Hero for Our Time*. New York: Macmillan, 1983.

———, and Ed Plaut. *Front Runner, Dark Horse*. Garden City, N.Y.: Doubleday, 1960.

Massingham, H. J. *London Scene*. London: Cobden-Sanderson, 1933.

Mast, Gerald. *A Short History of the Movies*. Indianapolis: Bobbs-Merrill, 1976.

Matthiessen, F. O. *The James Family: A Group Biography*. New York: Vintage Books, 1980.

McCaffery, Lawrence. *The Irish Diaspora in America*. Bloomington, Ind.: Indiana University Press, 1976.

McCarthy, Joe. *The Remarkable Kennedys*. New York: Dial Press, 1960.

McCarthy, Mary. *Memories of a Catholic Girlhood*. New York: Harcourt, Brace, 1957.

McKee, Alexander. *Strike from the Sky: The Story of the Battle of Britain*. Boston: Little, Brown, 1960.

McTaggart, Lynne. *Kathleen Kennedy: Her Life and Times*. New York: Dial Press, 1983.

Mead, Frederick S., ed. *Harvard's Military Record in the World War*. Boston: Harvard Alumni Association, 1921.

Meyers, Joan, ed. *John F. Kennedy: As We Remember Him*. New York: Atheneum, 1965.

Michaelis, David. *The Best of Friends*. New York: William Morrow, 1983.

Middlebrook, Martin. *The First Day of the Somme*. New York: W. W. Norton, 1972.

Miller, Alice. *The Drama of the Gifted Child*. New York: Basic Books, 1981.

Miller, Perry. *The Golden Age of American Literature*. New York: George Braziller, 1959.

Miller, William J. *Henry Cabot Lodge*. New York: Heinemann, 1967.

Moley, Raymond. *After Seven Years*. New York: Harper and Brothers, 1939.

———. *The First New Deal*. New York: Harcourt, Brace & World, 1966.

*Moody's Analysis of Investments*. New York: Moody's Manufacturing Co., 1920–26.

Morison, Samuel Eliot. *One Boy's Boston*. Boston: Houghton Mifflin, 1962.

———. *Maritime History of Massachusetts*. Boston: Houghton Mifflin, 1961.

———. *Three Centuries at Harvard, 1636–1936*. Cambridge, Mass.: Harvard University Press, 1936.

Morton, H. V. *I Saw Two Englands*. New York: Dodd, Mead, 1943.

Mosley, Leonard. *Lindbergh*. Garden City, N.Y.: Doubleday, 1976.

Mott, Frank. *American Journalism: A History of Newspapers in the United States Through 260 Years, 1690–1950*. New York: Macmillan, 1950.

Munn, Glenn G. *Meeting the Bear Market*. New York: Harper and Brothers, 1930.

Murray, Peter. *The Architecture of the Italian Renaissance*. New York: Schocken Books, 1963.

Nevins, Allan. *The Emergence of Modern America, 1865–1878*. New York: Macmillan, 1927.

———. *Grover Cleveland: A Study in Courage*. New York: Dodd, Mead, 1932.

*New York City Guide*. New York: Random House, 1939.

Ney, John. *Palm Beach*. Boston: Little, Brown, 1966.

Noble, Peter. *Hollywood Scapegoat*. New York: Arno Press, 1972.

North, S. W. D. *The Newspaper and Periodical Press*. Washington, D.C.: U.S. Government Printing Office, 1884.

Noyes, Alexander Dana. *The Market Place*. Boston: Little, Brown, 1939.

O'Brien, Lawrence. *No Final Victories*. Garden City, N.Y.: Doubleday, 1974.

O'Connell, William. *Recollections of Seventy Years*. Boston: Houghton Mifflin, 1934.

O'Connor, Edwin. *The Last Hurrah*. Boston: Little, Brown, 1956.

O'Connor, Len. *Clout: Mayor Daley and His City*. Chicago: Henry Regnery, 1975.

O'Connor, Richard. *Heywood Broun: A Biography*. New York: G. P. Putnam's Sons, 1975.

O'Donnell, Kenneth, and David F. Powers. *"Johnny, We Hardly Knew Ye."* Boston: Little, Brown, 1970.

*The Official Guide to Windsor Castle*. London: Orley & Son (Windsor), 1980.

O'Herlihy, Reverend T. *The Famine, 1845–1846*. Drogheda, Ireland: Drogheda Independent Co., 1947.

Ostrogorski, Mosei. *Organization and Party Politics*. Chicago: Quadrangle Books, 1964.

*Outline of an Examination of a Bank*. Boston: Commonwealth of Massachusetts Department of Banking and Insurance, 1930.

Paine, Ralph. *The Ships and Sailors of Old Salem: The Record of a Brilliant Era of American Achievement*. Chicago: A. C. McClung, 1912.

Panter-Downes, Mollie. *London War Notes*, edited by William Shawn. New York: Farrar, Straus & Giroux, 1971.

Parmet, Herbert S. *Jack: The Struggles of John F. Kennedy*. New York: Dial Press, 1980.

Parrington, Vernon. *Main Currents in American Thought: The Romantic Revolution in America, 1800–1860*, 3 vols. New York: Harcourt, Brace, 1927.

Patri, Angelo. *Child Training*. New York: D. Appleton, 1922.

Pendleton, Herring E. *Federal Commissioners*. Cambridge, Mass.: Harvard University Press, 1963.

Pearson, Henry Greenleaf. *Son of New England: James Jackson Storrow. 1846–1929*. Boston: Thomas Todd, 1932.

Penney, C. *Atlas of the City of Boston*. Boston: L. Prang, Lithographer, 1861.
*Plan of Studies of the Boarding Schools of the Sacred Heart*. Rome, Italy: Privately printed by the Society of the Sacred Heart, 1931.
*Poland Spring House*. South Portland, Me.: Hiram Ricker & Sons, 1904, 1911.
*Poor's Manual*. New York: Poor's Publishing Co., 1920–26.
Porter, Reverend Edward G. *Rambles in Old Boston*. Boston: Cupples & Hurd, 1887.
Porter, Katherine Anne. *Pale Horse, Pale Rider*. New York: Modern Library, 1939.
Pound, Arthur, and Samuel Taylor Moore, eds. *They Told Barron: Conversations and Revelations of an American Pepys in Wall Street*. New York: Harper & Row, 1930.
Pound, Reginald. *The Lost Generation*. New York: Coward-McCann, 1963.
Pratt, Sereno. *The Work of Wall Street*. New York: D. Appleton, 1919.
*Professional and Industrial History of Suffolk County, Mass.*, 4 vols. Boston: Boston History Co., 1894.
Randall, Mercedes. *Emily Green Balch: Improper Bostonian*. New York: Twayne Publishers, 1964.
*Règlement des pensionnets et plan d'études*. Rome, Italy: Privately printed by the Society of the Sacred Heart, 1887.
Richardson, Benjamin Ward. *The Field of Disease: A Book of Preventive Medicine*. Philadelphia: Henry C. Lea's Sons, 1884.
Riis, Jacob. *Children of the Poor*. New York: Johnson Reprint Co., 1970. (Originally published in 1872.)
———. *How the Other Half Lives*. Cambridge, Mass.: Belknap Press, 1970. (Originally published in 1890.)
———. *A Ten Years' War: An Account of the Battle with the Slums in New York*. Boston: Houghton Mifflin, 1900.
Ritchie, Donald L. *James Landis*. Cambridge, Mass.: Harvard University Press, 1980.
Robinson, David. *Hollywood in the 20's*. New York: A. S. Barnes, 1968.
Roosevelt, Elliott, ed. *FDR: His Personal Letters, 1928–1945*. New York: Duell, Sloan & Pearce, 1950.
Ross, Majorie Drake. *The Book of Boston: The Victorian Period, 1837–1901*. New York: Hastings House, 1964.
Rossiter, William S. *Days and Ways in Old Boston*. Boston: R. H. Stearns, 1915.
Rubin, Harry R. *Armistice, 1918*. New Haven: Yale University Press, 1944.
Russell, Francis. *The Great Interlude*. New York: McGraw-Hill, 1964.
———. *The President Makers*. Boston: Little, Brown, 1976.
Sage, Marchand. *Street Fighting at Wall and Broad*. New York: Macmillan, 1980.
Salinger, Pierre. *With Kennedy*. Garden City, N.Y.: Doubleday, 1966.
Santayana, George. *Persons and Places*. New York: Charles Scribner's Sons, 1944.
Sawyer, Joseph Dillaway. *The Last Leaf on the Tree: Reminiscences of Old North Church*. Boston, 1930.
Schlesinger, Arthur M. *The Rise of the City, 1878–1898*. New York: Macmillan, 1933.
Schlesinger, Arthur M., Jr. *The Age of Roosevelt*. Vol. I, *The Crisis of the Old Order*; Vol. II, *The Coming of the New Deal*. Boston: Houghton Mifflin 1957, 1959.
———. *Robert Kennedy and His Times*. Boston: Houghton Mifflin, 1978.
———. *A Thousand Days: John F. Kennedy in the White House*. Boston: Houghton Mifflin, 1965.
———, and Roger Bruns, eds. *Congress Investigates: A Documented History, 1792–1974*. New York: Chelsea House, 1975.
Schoor, Jean. *Young John Kennedy*. New York: Harcourt, Brace & World, 1963.
Schreiber, Henry Marcus. "The Working People in the Middle of the 19th Century." Ph.D. dissertation, Boston University, 1950.
Schultz, Stanley K. *The Culture Factory: Boston Public Schools, 1789–1860*. New York: Oxford University Press, 1973.
Searls, Hank. *The Lost Prince*. New York: Ballantine Books, 1969.
Shannon, William. *The American Irish*. New York: Macmillan, 1966.
Shipman, David. *The Great Movie Stars: The International Years*. New York: St. Martin's Press, 1973.
Shirer, William L. *Berlin Diary: The Journal of a Foreign Correspondent, 1939–1941*. New York: Alfred A. Knopf, 1941.

―――. *The Rise and Fall of the Third Reich.* New York: Simon and Schuster, 1959.

Shore, W. Teymouth. *Touring London.* London: B. T. Balsford, 1933.

Shumway, Harry I. *Famous Leaders of Industry.* Boston: L. C. Page, 1936.

Simpson, Lewis. *The Men of Letters in New England and the South.* Baton Rouge: Louisiana State University Press, 1973.

Sinclair, Andrew. *Prohibition.* Boston: Little, Brown, 1962.

Sklar, Robert. *The Plastic Age.* New York: George Braziller, 1970.

Slater, Peter Gregg. *Children in the New England Mind in Death and in Life.* New York: Archon Books, 1977.

Slosson, Preston. *The Great Crusade and After.* New York: Macmillan, 1930.

Sobel, Robert. *Inside Wall Street.* New York: W. W. Norton, 1977.

Solomon, Barbara. *Ancestors and Immigrants.* Chicago: University of Chicago Press, 1972.

Sorensen, Theodore C. *Kennedy.* New York: Harper & Row, 1965.

Sparling, Earl. *Mystery Men of Wall Street.* New York: Greenberg Publishers, 1930.

Spencer, Wilma B. *Palm Beach: A Century of Heritage.* Washington, D.C.: Mount Vernon Publishing Co., 1975.

Spiller, Robert Ernest, ed. *The Literary History of the United States.* New York: Macmillan, 1963.

Stanhope, Edward. *Boston Illustrated.* Boston: Houghton & Osgood, 1878.

Steel, Ronald. *Walter Lippmann and the American Century.* Boston: Little, Brown, 1980.

Steffens, Lincoln. *The Letters of Lincoln Steffens,* 2 vols. New York: Harcourt, Brace, 1938.

Stevens, Charles Wister. *Revelations of a Boston Physician.* Boston: A. Williams, 1881.

Stockbridge, Frank P., and John H. Perry. *Florida in the Making.* Kingsport, Tenn.: Kingsport Press, 1926.

Stokesbury, James. *A Short History of World War I.* New York: William Morrow, 1981.

Strickland, A. *Cholera: Its Symptoms and Treatment.* Cincinnati, 1866.

Stuart, Janet E. *The Education of Catholic Girls.* New York: Longmans, Green, 1912.

Sullivan, Reverend John F. *The Externals of the Catholic Church.* New York: P. J. Kenedy & Sons, 1919.

Sullivan, Mark. *Our Times,* Vol. 4, *The Twenties.* New York: Charles Scribner's Sons, 1932.

Swanberg, W. A. *Citizen Hearst.* New York: Charles Scribner's Sons, 1961.

Swanson, Gloria. *Swanson on Swanson.* New York: Random House, 1980.

Tanner, Thomas Hawkes. *The Practice of Medicine.* Philadelphia: Lindsay & Blakiston, 1872.

Tansill, Charles Callan. *America Goes to War.* Boston: Little, Brown, 1938.

Tanzer, Lester, ed. *The Kennedy Circle.* Washington, D.C.: Luce Publishing Co., 1961.

Taylor, A. J. P. *English History, 1914–1945.* New York: Oxford University Press, 1965.

―――, et al. *Churchill Revised: A Critical Assessment.* New York: Dial Press, 1969.

Taylor, Telford. *Munich: The Price of Peace.* Garden City, N.Y.: Doubleday, 1979.

Thernstrom, Stephen. *The Other Bostonians.* Cambridge, Mass.: Harvard University Press, 1973.

Thomas, Bob. *Thalberg.* Garden City, N.Y.: Doubleday, 1969.

Thomas, Gordon, and Max Morgan-Witts. *The Day the Bubble Burst.* New York: Penguin Books, 1980.

Thomas, Hugh. *The Spanish War.* New York: Harper and Brothers, 1961.

Thomson, William A. R. *Black's Medical Dictionary.* Totowa, N.J.: Barnes & Noble, 1984.

Tolstoy, Leo. *The Kreutzer Sonata and Other Tales.* London: Oxford University Press, 1973.

Torrence, Bruce T. *Hollywood: The First Hundred Years.* New York: Zoetrope, 1982.

Trapp, Maria Augusta. *Trapp: Around the Year with the Trapp Family.* New York: Pantheon, 1955.

Tredgold, Alfred F. *Mental Deficiency.* New York: W. Wood, 1929.

Tregaskis, Richard. *John F. Kennedy and PT 109.* New York: Random House, 1962.

Tyack, David B. *Village School to Urban System*. Cambridge, Mass.: Harvard University Press, 1974.

Ultan, Lloyd. *The Beautiful Bronx, 1920–1950*. New Rochelle, N.Y.: Arlington House, 1979.

Vipont, Elfride. *Some Christian Festivals*. London: M. Joseph, 1963.

Walker, Kenneth. *The Story of Medicine*. New York: Oxford University Press, 1955.

Ward, John William. *Red, White and Blue: Men, Books and Ideas in American Culture*. New York: Oxford University Press, 1969.

Warner, Samuel Bass. *Streetcar Suburbs: The Process of Growth in Boston, 1870–1900*. New York: Atheneum, 1969.

Watts, Allan W. *Easter: Its Story and Meaning*. New York: Henry Schuman, 1950.

Wayman, Dorothy. *Cardinal O'Connell of Boston*. New York: Farrar, Straus and Young, 1955.

Webb, Beatrice. *Beatrice Webb's American Diary, 1898*, edited by David A. Shannon. Madison: University of Wisconsin Press, 1963.

Wecter, Dixon. *The Saga of American Society: A Record of Social Aspirations, 1607–1937*. New York: Charles Scribner's Sons, 1970.

Weinberg, Herman G. *Stroheim: A Pictorial History of His Nine Films*. New York: Dover Publications, 1975.

Weller, Reverend Philip T. *The Roman Ritual*. New York: Bruce Publishing Co., 1950.

*Wellesley College, 1875–1975: A Century of Women*. Wellesley, Mass.: Wellesley College, 1975.

Wenden, D. J. *The Birth of the Movies*. London: MacDonald and James, 1975.

Whalen, Richard J. *The Founding Father*. New York: New American Library of World Literature, 1964.

Whalen, W. J. *Handbook of Secret Organizations*. Milwaukee: Bruce Publishing Co., 1966.

Wheeler-Bennett, John W. *Munich: Prologue to Tragedy*. London: Macmillan, 1948.

White, Leonard. *The Republican Era*. New York: Macmillan, 1958.

White, Theodore H. *The Making of the President, 1960*. New York: Atheneum, 1967.

Whitehill, Walter Muir. *Boston: A Topographical History*. Cambridge, Mass.: Belknap Press, 1968.

———. *Boston in the Age of JFK*. Norman: University of Oklahoma Press, 1966.

———. *Boston Public Library: A Centennial History*. Cambridge, Mass.: Harvard University Press, 1956.

Williams, Alexander W. *A Social History of Boston Clubs*. Barre, Mass.: Barre Publishing Co., 1970.

Willis, H. Parker, and J. I. Dogen. *Investment Banking*. New York: Harper & Row, 1929.

Wills, Garry. *The Kennedy Imprisonment: A Meditation on Power*. New York: Little, Brown, 1981.

Wilson, Delos. *Great Cities in America*. New York: Macmillan, 1910.

Winant, John. *A Letter from Grosvenor Square*. Boston: Houghton Mifflin, 1947.

*Windsor Castle*. London: Pitkin Pictorials, 1983.

Winkler, John. *Morgan the Magnificent*. New York: Vanguard Press, 1930.

Winsor, Justin. *The Memorial History of Boston, 1630–1880*, 5 vols. Boston: James R. Osgood, 1881.

Wohl, Robert. *The Generation of 1914*. Cambridge, Mass.: Harvard University Press, 1979.

Wolff, Kurt H., and Barrington Moore, Jr. *The Critical Spirit: Essays in Honor of Herbert Marcuse*. Boston: Beacon Press, 1967.

Woodham-Smith, Cecil. *The Great Hunger: Ireland, 1815–1849*. New York: Harper & Row, 1962.

Woods, Robert A. *Americans in Process*. Boston: Houghton Mifflin, 1903.

———. *The City Wilderness*. New York: Arno Press, 1898.

Wyckoff, Peter. *Wall Street and the Stock Market*. Philadelphia: Chilton Book Co., 1972.

Wyman, David S. *Paper Walls: America and the Refugee Crisis*. Boston: University of Massachusetts Press, 1968.

Zeman, Zbynek. *The Masaryks*. London: Weidenfeld & Nicolson, 1976.
Zolot, Herbert M. "Issues in Good Government: James Michael Curley and the Boston Scene from 1897–1918." Ph.D. dissertation, State University of New York at Stonybrook, 1975.

# INDEX

(Note: Subentries for persons are chronologically arranged. Abbreviations: FDR, Franklin Delano Roosevelt; JFF, John Francis Fitzgerald; JFK, John Fitzgerald Kennedy; JPK, Joseph Patrick Kennedy; P.J., Patrick Joseph Kennedy.)

Abbey Players, 204–7
Abbot, Gordon, 275
Abbott, Edith, 132
Abruzzi, Duke of the, 129
Ace of Clubs, 203–4, 261
Acorn, Thomas, 20
Acton, Mass., 12, 77–78, 80–81
Adams, Charles Francis (d. 1886), 537
Adams, Charles Francis (d. 1915), 50
Adams, Charles Francis (d. 1954), 275, 748
Adams, Henry, 29
Adams, John, 48, 513, 537
Adams, John Quincy, 275, 513, 777
Adams, Samuel, 52
Adams family, 47, 477
Addams, Jane, 132
Addison, Thomas, 734
Adenauer, Konrad, 815
*Affairs of Anatol, The* (film), 383
Ahmed Husain, Prince, 542
Airlie, Lady, 575
Aitken, Jane Kenyon-Slaney, 733, 737, 740
Aitken, Max, 737
Alba, Duke of, 672
Albee, Edward, 375–76
Albert, Raymond, 654
"Albert the Male" (Lippmann), 217
Alcott, Louisa May, 46, 87
Algerian war, 790
Allen, Frederick Lewis, 299, 323
Allen, Robert, 431, 567
Alsop, Joseph, 743, 803
*Amagiri* (Japanese destroyer), 653, 654, 658, 766–67, 812

Ambrose, Margaret, 722
American Association for the Study of the Feeble Minded, 358
American Federation of Labor, 316
*American Mercury, The*, 641
American Protective Association (APA), 99
American Red Cross, 664–65, 697
"America the Beautiful," 132
Amery, Leo, 557
Ames family, 236
Amory, Charles, 485
Amory family, 236
Anastasia, Sister, 643
Ancient Order of the Hibernians, 73
Anschluss, 519–20, 548
Antin, Mary, 37
"Appeasement at Munich" (Kennedy), 604–5
Appleton, Francis III, 356
*Arashi* (Japanese destroyer), 653
Arbuckle, Fatty, 370
Arcadia lodging-house fire, 249–51
Arvad, Inga, 630–35, 659, 734
Asquith, Margot, Lady, 564
Astaire, Adele and Fred, 546
Astor, John Jacob II, 134
Astor, John Jacob IV, 210
Astor, Nancy Langhorne, Lady Astor, 540, 555, 567, 577, 579, 597
  and Kathleen, 541–42, 584, 667, 668–69, 679, 740
Astor, Vincent, 210, 435
Astor, Waldorf, Lord Astor, 541, 555, 577, 584

*As We Remember Joe* (John F. Kennedy), 699
Atkins, Edward, 210
Atkinson, Joseph, 649
*Atlantic Monthly, The*, 6–7, 581
Atwood, Albert, 419
Auchincloss, Hugh, 770, 771, 772
Auchincloss, Janet Lee Bouvier, 769, 770, 772
Augusta Victoria, Kaiserin, 185
Austria, 268, 519–20, 548

Baillie, Lady, 540
Baillie, Pauline, 540
Baker, Newton D., 429
Balch, Emily Greene, 132
Baldwin, Stanley, Lord Baldwin, 559, 560, 604, 605
Bancroft, Edward Erastus, 66
Bancroft, George, 46
Bancroft, Hugh, 325
Bank for International Settlements, 572
Bank of America, 238, 340
Bank of England, 572, 592
Bank of Italy, 344
Barat, Sophie, 145
Barron, Helen, 361, 441
Bartlett, Charles, 769
Baruch, Bernard, 294, 296, 436, 447–48, 529
Bates, Katharine Lee, 132
Battis, George, 160
Baxter, Beverly, 596
Baxter, James Phinney III, 535
Beaverbrook, William Maxwell Aitken, Lord (Max), 598, 658, 697, 734, 737, 800
  lauds Robert Kennedy, 761, 791
  JPK's friendship with, 796
Bedard, Peter A., 388
Beery, Wallace, 383
Belgium, 268, 597–98
Bell, Alexander Graham, 278
Bemis, Samuel, 778
Benchley, Nathaniel, 504, 535
Benchley, Robert, 535
Beneš, Eduard, 557, 571
Ben-Gurion, David, 815
Bennett, Constance, 415–17
Benton, Thomas Hart, 777
Berchtesgaden Conference, 553, 556
Berkeley, Busby, 414
Berlin, Irving, 405
Berry, Seymour, 730, 740

Bethlehem Steel Corp., 277–81, 283–284, 286–87, 291–93
Bickford, Leland, 756, 758
Bigelow, Professor, 67
*Bigger than Barnum's* (film), 347
Bilainkin, George, 581
Billings, Josh, 465
Billings, Kirk Le Moyne (Lem), 460, 465–466, 485
  friendship with JFK, 353, 464–65, 486, 487, 490, 506, 717, 776, 802
  and Kathleen, 482, 484, 606, 742
  in North Africa, 663–64
Bilodeau, Thomas, 477
Bingham, Robert W., 490, 491, 509
*Birth of the Movies, The* (Wenden), 346
Black Tuesday, 421
Blitz, 608–9, 611
Bloomfield, Meyer, 281
Blumenthal, Holland, 155, 159, 174–89
Boettiger, John, 431, 568
Boleslavsky, Richard, 413
Bolton Abbey, 546
Boston
  Aldermen, Board of, 113, 121, 122, 243
  ascendancy and decline of, 45–55, 112
  Bath Department, 115
  Brahmin neighborhoods of, 44–45, 53, 55–57
  charter reform in, 191, 197
  "Coal Graft Hearings" in, 138–40, 147–48, 149
  "Codman Street land deal" case in, 154
  Collecting Department, 120
  Common Council (later, City Council), 70, 73–75, 92–93, 113, 122, 134, 157, 202, 243, 454
  Curley mayorship of, 252, 726–28
  education in, 28–31, 35–37, 55, 61–63, 66
  epidemics in 33–35, 285–88
  Finance Commission probe, 133–42, 147–50, 155–57, 191–95 *passim*, 251
  Fitzgerald mayorship of, 110–29, 133–153, 197–205, 242–46
  flagstone contract scandal in, 148–49, 151–54, 161–73
  Health, Board and Department of, 76, 115, 120
  Irish immigrants in, 3–35, 51–53, 80

Irish social set in, 202–4
Irish ward boss system in, 69–76, 92–99, 106–9, 117, 125, 228–30
Italians in, 94, 228
Jews in, 94, 99, 228
"July Fourth larceny" case in, 154, 160
Lamp Department, 115
Law Department, 141
Library Department, 115
newsboys in, 37–45
newspapers in, 38–41, 106
Parks Department, 115
police strike in, 316–17
population statistics, 32, 52, 112, 228
School Committee and Department, 37, 66, 122, 141, 192
Street Department, 120
Supply Department, 137–41, 147–49, 153, 161ff.
Water Department, 115
Weights and Measures, Department of, 118, 136
*Boston American*, 154, 173, 252, 502–3
Boston Braves, 270
Boston City Club, 192
Boston City Hospital, 287, 309–10
Boston College, 66
*Boston Daily Advertiser*, 38, 96, 98, 761–762
*Boston Daily Record*, 503
*Boston Evening Record*, 129, 137, 140
*Boston Evening Transcript*, 111, 231, 287
*Boston Globe*, 39, 56, 114, 271, 594, 614–617, 720
*Boston Herald*, 38, 122, 134, 252, 317
*Boston Journal*, 38, 119
Boston Latin School, 55, 61–63, 66, 81, 87, 124, 210, 214, 216, 228
*Boston Post*, 38, 114–15, 159, 261, 274, 747–48
  endorses JFK for Senate, 764–65
  and Fitzgeralds's home life, 199–201
Boston Red Sox, 227, 270
Boston Red Stockings, 128
*Boston's Immigrants* (Handlin), 8
Boston Stock Exchange, 293–94, 453
*Boston Transcript*, 39
*Boston Traveler*, 38
Bourne, Randolph, 276
Bouvier, Caroline Lee, 792
Bouvier, Jacqueline, *see* Kennedy, Jacqueline Bouvier

Bouvier, John III, 769, 770, 774
Bowen, Patrick, 148–49, 151, 157
Bradfield, Red, 687
Bradford, Robert, 758
Brain Trust, 431
Brand, Lord, 703
Brandeis, Louis D., 120, 235
Brant, Irving, 778
Breen, Joseph, 514
Brennan, John, 601
Brewer, Basil, 763, 764
Brickley, Bart, 759
Bridge, Dinah Brand, 362, 540, 542, 627, 677, 703
Britain
  and Austria, 519–20, 548
  and Czech crisis, 548ff.
  in First World War, 268, 270–73
  and German Jews, 568–69, 570–71
  Germany, ultimatum to, 587–88
  and Ireland, 10–11, 64–65, 268
  and Munich, 561–67, 571–72
  1945 election in, 703–4
  and Poland, 572, 587
  and Rhineland occupation, 517
  in Second World War, 588–600, 607–610, 694–95
Britain, Battle of, 607–8, 685
British Foreign Office, 595–96, 617
Broderick, Thomas, 711
Brook Farm, 48
Brookline, Mass., 301ff.
Brooks, John, 420
Brooks, Van Wyck, 53
Brooks, Walter, 422
Brown, Capability, 546
Brown, Hiram, 422
Bruce, Marie, 671, 675, 679, 681, 737
Bruff, Ireland, 9, 80, 159
Brush, Matthew, 337–38, 441
Bryan, William Jennings, 122, 184
Bryant, William Soher, 66
Buchan, John, 535
Buchanan, James, 513
Bulfinch, Charles, 4
Bulkeley, John D., 645, 646
Bulkeley, Robert, 653
Bullitt, William C., 492, 551, 583
Bullock, Alan, 470
Bundy, McGeorge, 356
Bundy, William, 356
Burke, Charles, 410, 477
Burke, Margaret Kennedy, 212–13, 228, 410, 412, 441, 643

Burke, Nancy, 662
Burke, Ned, 662
Burke, Thomas, 65fn.
Burke, William, 600, 603
Burns, James MacGregor, 702, 716, 753, 757, 778, 784–85
Burns, John J., 452, 454, 478, 522, 663
*Business Week*, 496
Butler, Alban, 5
Buttrick, Major, 86
Byrne, Garrett, 728
Byrne, John, 311
Byrnes, James F., 499, 514, 611, 612, 781
Byrnes, Mrs. James F., 611
Byron, George Gordon, Lord, 724
Byron, Walter, 402, 413

Cabot family, 46, 57, 191, 477
Cadogan, Sir Alexander, 553
Calder, Sir James, 468, 472, 540, 693, 705, 756, 766, 767
California Stock Exchange, 453
Calkins, Mary, 132
Cameron, Gail, 201
Campbell, Thomas, 211–16 *passim*, 256, 269–72, 275, 282, 323–24, 507, 508
Cannon, Frances Anne, 582, 650
Canterbury, Archbishop of, 575
Canterbury Preparatory School, 460
Carcano, Bebe and Chiquita, 670, 672
Carens, Thomas, 380
Carlyle, Thomas, 752, 753
Carnegie Steel Corp., 283
Carney, Francis, 164, 171–72
Carpentier, Georges, 323
Carr, Samuel, 135
Carroll, Charles, 92
Carter, Boake, 510–11
Casado, Sigismundo, 579, 581
Casey, Joseph, 625–27, 757, 799
Cass, Thomas, 16
*Catholic Digest, The*, 625
Catholicism
    Fitzgerald and, 24–27, 64, 88–89, 104, 142–43, 715
    Freemasons and, 547
    Harvard and, 216, 476
    Hitler and, 474
    and Irish immigrants, 3–7, 14, 24–27, 62
    JFK's unorthodoxy on, 353, 635, 651, 691, 716, 743, 753

JPK and, 310, 312, 580–81, 674, 676, 679–81, 693, 720
    and the Kathleen-Hartington marriage, 546–47, 673–81, 697
    loses ground in Boston, 318–19
    parochial-school system of, 30, 62, 104; *see also* Sacred Heart Convents
    as political issue for JFK, 781, 792, 795, 797–98, 799, 803
    prejudice against, 29–30, 99, 100
    Roosevelt and, 611
    Rose's commitment to, 185–89, 307–308, 677, 679, 690, 736, 773, 796
Catholic Literary Union, 114
Cavanagh, Father, 804
Cavendish, Adele Astaire, Lady Cavendish, 546
Cavendish, Lord Andrew, *see* Hartington, Andrew Cavendish, Marquess of
Cavendish, Anne, 679
Cavendish, Lord Charles, 546
Cavendish, Elizabeth, 672, 679, 696, 703, 736
Cavendish, Lord Frederick, 64–66, 544
Cavendish, William, *see* Hartington, William Cavendish (Billy), Marquess of
Cecil, Lord David, 672
Cecilian Club, 203
Celeste, Vincent, 793
Cermak, Anton, 433
Chamberlain, Joseph, 610
Chamberlain, Mrs. Neville, 526, 537
Chamberlain, Neville, 517–18, 605
    appeasement policy of, 518, 520, 529, 549–50, 552–65, 571–72, 604, 605
    JPK's first contacts with, 526, 528–30
    FDR and, 534, 557–58
    and German Jews, 568–71
    changes policy, 571–72
    and Franco, 579
    and invasion of Poland, 586–88
    declares war, 588
    as war leader, 590–91
    resigns, 597
    death of, 610, 611
Chamberlain, Norman, 528
Chambers, William, 778
Channing, William Ellery, 48
Chaplin, Charles, 385, 399
Charitable Irish Association, 73
Charles I, King, 527

Chase Manhattan Bank, 292–93
Chatsworth, 546, 586, 696, 740
Checker Cab Co., 330
Cherrill, Virginia, 669, 670
Chevalier, Maurice, 414
*Chicago Herald*, 502
*Chicago Herald-American*, 702, 704
Chichester, Earl of, 543
Children of Mary, 182–83, 185, 187
Childs, Marquis, 792
Choate family, 236
Choate School, 456–65, 477, 481, 486–
    489
Churchdale Hall, 546
Churchill, Pamela, 729, 730, 731–32, 734
Churchill, Randolph, 598, 740
Churchill, Winston, 530, 605, 610, 740
    and Eden's resignation, 518, 519
    and Czech crisis, 549, 555, 559
    attacks Munich policy, 564
    and declaration of war, 588
    and FDR, 550, 591
    leads Britain in war, 597–99
    and Hartington, 673, 697
    is turned out of office, 703–4
Cinema Credits Corp., 344
*Citizen Kane* (film), 402
Civil Rights Act (1957), 790
Civil War, 41, 45, 49, 51, 70
Clark, Marguerite, 641
Clasby, Mary Jo, 78, 79, 90
Cleveland, Grover, 102–3, 274
Cliveden, 537, 541, 567, 577–79, 584,
    667
Cliveden set, 567
*Clover Club*, 503
Coakley, Daniel, 153, 160, 161–62, 164,
    167–70, 172, 246–48, 601
Coakley, Timothy, 125
"Coal Graft Hearings," 138–40, 147,
    148, 149
Cochran, Thomas, 20
Cochrane, Robert, 371–72
Coglan, Ralph, 614–17, 758
Cogley, John, 803
Cohasset, Mass., 325–27
Cohen, Jack, 431
Cohen, Milton, 388
Colbert, James, 758
Coldstream Guards, 607, 668, 671, 695
Coleman, John (Zeke), 606
*Collier's Weekly*, 209–10
Collins, Patrick A., 106–7, 114, 128
Colum, Mary Magiore, 176–77, 178

Colum, Padraic, 176
Columbia Trust Co., 237–39, 253–58,
    387, 412, 442
Coman, Katharine, 132
Committee Against Military
    Intervention in Europe, 601
Committee of 50 (Boston, 1880s), 17
Commons, House of, 520, 559–61, 563–
    565, 572, 587–88, 597
*Commonweal*, 803
Compton Place, Eastbourne, 546, 680,
    696
Conant, James B., 532
Concord, Mass., 78, 86–87, 103–5
*Concord Enterprise*, 83, 89
Conlan, Michael, 20
Considine, Bob, 705, 816
*Constitution* (frigate), 100
Consumers League, 132
Conway, Joseph, 506, 793
Coolidge, Calvin, 316
Coolidge, Louis, 316
Coolidge family, 236
Cooper, Alfred Duff, 556, 563–64, 671
Cooper, Bryan, 658
Coral Sea, Battle of, 648
Corbett, Joseph, 98, 125, 150, 230
Corcoran, Thomas G., 452
Costello, Frank, 443
Cotter, John F., 710, 711
Coulthurst, John A., 150
Cox, Channing, 331
Cox, Mary, 13, 58
Cox, Philip, 13
Coxe, Betty, 627
Crider, John, 614
Crocker, George, 135
Crocker, G. Glover, 326
Crosby, Alfred, 285
Crowley, Timothy, 120
Crowther, Geoffrey, 703
Crum, Erskine, 342
Cuddihy, Michael, 162
Cuddihy Brothers, 148, 162
Cukor, George, 393, 395
Cummings, A. J., 616
Cunard, Samuel, 51
Cunard Line, 51
Curley, James Michael, 121, 334, 712
    elections of, 243–49, 251–52, 709
    imprisonment of, 726–28
    and family tragedies, 745–47
    defeated for Senate, 757
    death of, 793–94

Curley, Leo, 745
Curley, Mary, 726, 745
Curley, Thomas, 121
Currier, Guy, 277, 342, 344, 420
Curry, Margaret, 131
Cushing, Barbara, 479–80
Cushing, Harvey, 430
Cushing, Richard Cardinal, 230, 642, 720, 813
Customs House, Boston, 92
Cutler, John Henry, 106, 153
Cutler, Robert, 748
Cutten, Arthur, 296
*Cymric*, S.S., 156, 157–58, 189
Czechoslovakia, 548–65, 571, 573, 574, 583, 584

*Daily Mail*, London, 666
Daladier, Édouard, 560
Daley, Richard J., 755, 794, 800, 805–6
Dall, Anna Roosevelt, 430, 433
Dall, Curtis, 430
Dalton, Cornelius, 781
Dalton, Mark, 710, 713, 717, 727, 760–761
Daniels, Josephus, 279
Danzig, 583, 588
Davenport, Russell, 501–2
Davies, Marion, 393, 800–801, 812
Davis, Ben, 459
Davis, Sir Daniel, 734
Davis, Elmer, 367
Davis, Mary, 726
Dawson, Geoffrey, 577
Day, Henry Mason, 439, 440
D-Day, 684, 685
Dean, Dizzy, 506
Dean, Dudley, 325–26
de Bedts, Ralph, 454
Degnan, Ellen, 128
De Guglielmo, Lawrence, 719, 760
Dehan, Mr., 441
De Mille, Cecil B., 371, 374, 376–79, 383, 406–7
Democratic Business Men's League of Massachusetts, 495
Democratic national conventions
  1912: 198
  1932: 428–29
  1940: 600–604
  1956: 782–85, 786
  1960: 800–802
Dempsey, Jack, 323
Denison House, 132

Denmark, 596–97, 602, 605
Denver Stock Exchange, 453
Derby, Lord, 525
Derr, E. B., 345, 387, 388, 405, 406–7
de Valera, Eamon, 538
Dever, Paul, 756–57, 762–63
Devine, Marney, 361
Devonshire, Edward William Spencer Cavendish, 10th Duke of, 544, 546–547, 579, 586, 672, 675
  and son's wedding, 678–79
  and daughter-in-law Kathleen, 681, 690–91, 696, 729, 734, 740
  at JFK's inauguration, 812, 815
Devonshire, 8th Duke of, *see* Hartington, Spencer Compton Cavendish, Marquess of
Devonshire, 11th Duke of, *see* Hartington, Andrew Cavendish, Marquess of
Devonshire, Evelyn Fitzmaurice, Dowager Duchess of, 546
Devonshire, Mary Alice Gascoyne-Cecil, Duchess of, 546–47, 672, 690, 696, 703, 729, 734
  and son's marriage, 674, 678–79
  and Kathleen's burial, 740, 741
  at JFK's inauguration, 812, 815
Devonshire, Victor Cavendish, 9th Duke of, 546
Devotion, Edward, 355
Devotion School, 355, 356
Dewey, Henry, 108, 109
Dewey, Thomas E., 758
Dexter School, 355–56, 368
*Dial, The*, 48
Dickens, Charles, 48, 49
Dickerson, Nancy, 723
Dillingham, Charles, B., 303–4
Dineen, Joseph, 72, 78
Dirksen, Herbert von, 569
Disarmament Conference (Geneva), 470
Disney, Walt, 532, 535, 536
Dix, Dorothea, 48
Dodge, J. B., 414
Doherty, Cornelius, 16
Doherty, Neil, 92
*Donahoe's*, 80, 87, 104
Donham, Wallace, B., 369, 372
Donovan, James, 98, 107, 139, 150
Donovan, Joseph, 211, 216, 232–33, 275
Donovan, Ned, 96, 107–8
Douglas, William O., 454, 636, 726, 756

Douglas-Home, William, 542, 667, 740
Dowling, Eddie, 435
Downey, Morton, 427, 573, 781, 785
Doyle, James, 120, 125
Draper, Eben, 160
Draper family, 236
Drawdy, Leon, 652
Dreiser, Theodore, 232
Drew, Daniel, 13
Droney, John, 711, 712–13, 717, 718
Duncliffe, Bill, 241
Dunglass, Lord, 560
Dunkirk, 598, 599, 607
Dunn, Edward J., 764
Dunphy, Christopher, 282–83, 298, 300, 314, 411, 496
Du Pont Company, 572
Durant, William Crapo, 298
Dwan, Allan, 404
Dyer, Micah, 18

Early, Stephen, 536, 636
*East Boston Leader*, 237
Eastern Steamship Line, 296, 297–98, 300, 337, 420
Eden, Anthony, 518, 519, 528, 561, 597
    and the Kennedys, 703, 729–31, 740
Edmondson, Charles, 614
Eighteenth Amendment, 441
Eisenhower, Dwight D., 758, 763, 767, 769
    as President, 779, 780, 789, 795, 813
    runs for reelection, 781, 783
Eisenhower, Mamie, 813
El Alamein, Battle of, 663
Eleventh (earlier, Ninth) Congressional District, Mass., 97–99, 709, 710ff., 723, 725, 753
Eliot, Charles W., 45, 67
Eliot, Samuel, 28–29, 61
Eliot family, 47
Eliot Grammar School, 31, 35–37, 74
Elizabeth II, Queen (earlier, Princess Elizabeth), 527, 545, 558, 584, 733, 771
Elizabeth, Queen Consort (wife of George VI), 525–27, 543, 558, 584, 610, 615
Ellis, Rose, 90
Elphinstone, Lord and Lady, 526
Emergency Banking Act, 434
Emergency Fleet Corp., 279, 281
Emerson, Ralph Waldo, 46, 48, 86, 87
Entwhistle, Lillian, 346

Erie Canal, 50
Ernst, George, 135
Ethiopia, conquest of, 529
Eton College, 270, 458, 525, 528, 545
Evans, Ruth, 132

Fairbanks, Douglas, 372
Fairlamb, G. R., 623
Falaise de la Coudraye, Henri de la, 389–391, 393, 394–95, 408, 413, 415–18
Falvey, Catherine, 710
Famous Players Film Co., 372
Famous Players–Lasky, 382, 386
Farley, James A., 431, 495, 600, 601, 603–4
Farley, John Wells, 133, 148–49, 162–63
Farm Credit Act, 434
Fay, Paul "Red," 647, 700, 717
Fayne, Joseph, 795
FBO (Film Booking Offices), 341–48, 350, 375, 376, 379–80, 403, 422
Federal Bureau of Investigation (FBI), 632–33, 634
Federal Trade Commission, 446, 449
Fegan, Edward, 68
Ferguson Passage, 653, 655–56
Ferry, Dr., 507
Field, Henry, 628
Field, Marshall, 704
Field, Patsy White, 628, 736–37
Fifth Avenue Coach Co., 330, 335, 336
Finch College, 606
Fine, Philip, 762, 763
*Finian's Rainbow*, 739
Finnegan, Margaret, 186
Finnegan, Miriam, 221
First National Bank of Boston, 236, 293, 344, 443
First National Exhibitors' Circuit, 378–379, 381
First Ward National Bank, 253–55
First World War, *see* World War I
Fisher, Robert, 211–16 *passim*, 269–72, 275, 322–24, 325
Fisk, Jim, 13
Fitzgerald, Agnes, *see* Gargan, Agnes Fitzgerald
Fitzgerald, Bridget (JFF's aunt), 9
Fitzgerald, Edmond (JFF's great-uncle), 11, 88
Fitzgerald, Edward (JFF's brother), 18, 125, 126, 141, 157, 442, 747
Fitzgerald, Elizabeth Theresa Degnan, 128

Fitzgerald, Ellen (JFF's aunt), 9
Fitzgerald, Ellen Rosanna (JFF's sister), 31, 33–35, 288
Fitzgerald, Ellen Wilmouth (JFF's grandmother), 9, 11, 88
Fitzgerald, Eunice (JFF's daughter), 103, 111, 306–7, 314, 496
Fitzgerald, Fred, 103, 111, 185, 262, 496
Fitzgerald, F. Scott, 346
Fitzgerald, George, (JFF's brother), 21, 125, 126, 127, 157
Fitzgerald, Hannah (JFF's aunt), 9
Fitzgerald, Henry (JFF's brother), 21, 68, 92, 104, 125–27, 157, 747
Fitzgerald, James (JFF's great-grandfather), 88
Fitzgerald, James (JFF's uncle), 5, 9, 11–12, 14, 15–16, 33, 68
Fitzgerald, James T. (JFF's brother), 5, 18, 27, 28, 68, 69, 125–26
    and Mitchell case, 141, 153, 173
    investigation of, 251
    and Prohibition, 442
    death of, 747
Fitzgerald, John Francis (JFF), 3–6, 8–9, 14
    childhood of, 17, 18–37
    masters athletics, 21–24, 35
    early education of, 31, 35–37
    as newsboy, 37–45, 55–57, 768
    and friend Fred, 41–43, 76
    and the "other Boston," 44–45, 48–49, 55–57, 503
    and Lodge, 57, 102, 252, 768
    and his mother's death, 58–60
    at Boston Latin School, 61–62, 66, 81, 87
    conducts tours, 63–66
    Cavendish incident, 64–66
    at Harvard Medical School, 66–67, 69, 71
    and his father's death, 67–68
    learns ward politics, 69–76
    as customs clerk, 76, 85
    meets and courts Josie Hannon, 76–80, 83–89
    and consanguinity problem, 88–89, 361
    marriage of, 89–90
    and Rose's birth, 90–91
    in Council, 92–93
    and Keany's death, 93–94
    becomes ward boss, 94–95
    runs for state Senate, 95–96
    runs for Congress, 97–99

    as congressman, 99–100, 102–3
    residences of, 103, 105–6
    and his daughters' schooling, 104, 142–144, 155, 158, 159, 174, 189
    seeks and wins mayorship, 105–9, 162
    buys The Republic, 106
    first term as mayor, 110–29, 133–53
    and Finance Commission probe, 133–142, 148–50, 155–57
    defeated for reelection, 150
    and Mitchell/flagstone-contract case, 151–55, 161–75, 190
    European tours of, 155–56, 157–59, 189
    runs again for mayor, 190–96
    second term as mayor, 197–205, 242–246
    opposes Rose's romance, 217, 219–224, 233, 242, 253
    urges P.J. to seek office, 230–31
    claims to have helped JPK, 239–40
    runs for third term against Curley, 245–49
    and Toodles scandal, 247–49, 253
    collapses, withdraws from race, 249–252
    comeback attempts by, 252, 305, 331, 625–26, 746
    consents to Rose's marriage, 258
    as Grandpa Kennedy, 261–63, 274, 351, 465, 606
    and Rose's separation, 305–7
    is struck by truck, 305–6
    as "film magnate," 343–44
    and the JPK-Swanson affair, 395–96
    and FDR's election, 435
    and Jews, 473
    and JPK's honorary-degree chances, 532
    uses London embassy, 536–37
    and Joe Jr.'s political debut, 600, 601
    FDR anecdote about, 612
    and Jack's sea duty, 648
    and Curley's pardon petition, 728
    and Jack's career, 706, 715, 719, 720, 746–47, 753, 754
    death of, 747–48, 809
    and St. Lawrence Seaway, 779
Fitzgerald, John Francis, Jr., 103, 111
Fitzgerald, Joseph (JFF's brother), 21, 26, 125, 128
Fitzgerald, Josie, see Fitzgerald, Mary Josephine Hannon
Fitzgerald, Julia Adeline Brophy, 16
Fitzgerald, Lizzy, 127

Fitzgerald, Margaret Herlihy, 126
Fitzgerald, Mary (infant, d. 1879), 58
Fitzgerald, Mary Josephine Hannon
  (Josie)
  JFF's courtship of, 76, 77–89
  and consanguinity problem, 88–89,
    361
  at JFF's induction, 111
  as wife and mother, 89–91, 103–4,
    106, 111, 158–59, 189, 198–201,
    202, 220
  and Joe Kennedy, 220, 396, 435
  and the Toodles scandal, 248–49, 253
  and her grandchildren, 364, 465, 754
  visits Rose in London, 537
  in old age, 706, 747
Fitzgerald, Mary Linnehan, 88
Fitzgerald, Michael, (infant, d. 1860),
  5, 35
Fitzgerald, Michael (JFF's brother), 5,
  18, 60, 85, 125, 127–28
Fitzgerald, Michael (JFF's grandfather),
  5, 10, 11, 88
Fitzgerald, Mother, 485
Fitzgerald, Ned (JFF's nephew), 127
Fitzgerald, Polly, 766
Fitzgerald, Rosanna Cox, 5–6, 9, 13, 16–
  19, 26, 31, 32–34, 91
  death of, 58–61
Fitzgerald, Rose Elizabeth, see
  Kennedy, Rose Elizabeth
  Fitzgerald
Fitzgerald, Thomas (JFF's brother), 5,
  18, 27, 28, 69
Fitzgerald, Thomas, (JFF's father), 3–
  10, 12–20, 77, 80, 88, 159, 810
  and wife's death, 59, 60–61
  death and will of, 67–68, 71
Fitzgerald, Thomas (JFF's son), 103,
  111, 127, 158, 306, 442, 809
Fitzgerald, William (JFF's brother), 18
Fitzroy, Lady Mary Rose, 545, 547
Fitzwilliam, Olive Plunkett, Lady, 733
Fitzwilliam, Lord Peter, 732–34, 736–
  738, 740
Flagler, Henry M., 390
Flanagan, Daniel, 140
Flanner, Janet, 592
Fleeson, Doris, 804
Fleming, Donald, 268
Flint, Motley, 378
Flynn, John, 445, 448, 455
Fogg Museum, 371
Foley, Francis, 508
Foncannon, Eugene. 649

Foolish Wives (film), 399
Forbes, Alistair, 740
Ford, Henry, 14, 327–28
Ford, John (Henry Ford's grandfather),
  14
Ford, John J. (JPK's friend), 290, 345,
  758
Ford Motor Co., 572
Fore River Insurance Co., 284
Fore River shipyard, 277, 279, 284, 287–
  293, 334, 345, 387, 428
Forrestal, James V., 657, 703
Fortas, Abe, 454
Fortune magazine, 46, 54, 239–40, 501–
  502
Foss, Eugene, 239
Fox, J. John, 757, 762, 764–65
Fox, William, 371
France
  and Algeria, 790
  and Austria, 519, 548
  and Czech crisis, 549, 554, 556, 562
  fall of, 597, 598, 607
  First World War in, 270–73, 282–83
  and Jewish refugees, 570
  and Rhineland occupation, 517
  and Vietnam, 779
Franco, Francisco, 576, 578, 579, 585
Franconia, S.S., 198, 220
Frankfurter, Felix, 466–67, 468, 478,
  537, 567, 702
Fraser, Hugh, 585, 703, 729
Fred (newsboy), 41–43, 76
Frederick of Prussia, Prince, 543
Freeman, Walter, 642
Freemasons, 547
Frisch, Frankie, 506
Frohman, Charles, 268
Front Page, The (Hecht/MacArthur),
  330
Frost, Robert, 813–14
Frothingham, Louis, 108–9
Frothingham, Theodore, Jr., 215
Fruitful Bough, The, 212
Fuchser, Larry, 560
Fuller, Margaret, 48
Fussell, Paul, 273

Gable, Clark, 669
Gaddis, Hugh, 322
Galbraith, John Kenneth, 476, 477, 479,
  507, 599
Galeazzi, Enrico, 491
Gallagher, Eddie, 138, 157, 167, 173,
  229, 231, 426

Galluccio, Anthony, 711, 712
Galvin, John, 755–56, 760, 761
Gandhi, Mohandas, K., 541
Gardner, Isabella Stewart, 206
Gardner family, 236
Gargan, Agnes Fitzgerald, 103, 111, 158, 200, 305
    schooling of, 143, 155, 159, 174–89
    travels with Rose, 320, 353, 493
    death of, 496–97
Gargan, Ann, 496, 640, 643, 796, 801–6 passim
Gargan, Joseph, 496–97
Gargan, Mary Jo, 496, 497
Gaston family, 236
Gehrig, Lou, 432
General Motors Corp., 298, 572
George IV, King, 526
George VI, King, 562, 580
    the Kennedys and, 514–15, 525–27, 543, 610, 615
Germany
    Britain in WWII against, 588ff.
    in First World War, 268, 270–73, 277, 285, 288
    JFK in, 583
    Joe Jr. in, 470–72
    Rose Fitzgerald in, 184–85
    U.S. in WWII against, 632
    see also, Hitler, Adolf
Giannini, Amadeus Peter, 238, 340, 411, 443
Giannini, Attilio H., 411
Gibbs, Dorothy, 593–94
Gibson, Harvey, 665
Gibson, Mrs. Harvey, 666
"Gift Outright, The" (Frost), 814
Gillette, King, 383
Gimbel, Bernard, 772
Ginger (film), 452
Gladstone, William E. 65, 544
Glazer, Ben, 402, 404, 406, 408, 409
Gloria Productions, 387, 401
Glyn, Elinor, 773
Godesberg Conference, 556, 559, 562
Goering, Hermann, 552, 555, 572, 608, 632, 685
Goetz, Joseph A., 421
Goldwyn, Samuel, 340, 373
Gone with the Wind (film), 387
Good Government Association, 119
Good Housekeeping magazine, 358–59
Gore, Randolph, 99

Gorman, Peter, 543
Gould, Jack, 780
Goulding, Edmund, 407, 408, 409, 413
Grace, Eugene R., 292–93
Grace, Peter, 543, 606
Grace, W. R., 543
Granby, Charles Manners, Marquess of, 679
Grange, Red, 350
Gray, William, 340
Great Famine, 10–11, 51, 59
Great War, see World War I
Greaves, Harry, 470
Greed (film), 399, 408
Green, Buddy, 693
Greene, Marie, 350, 392
Greene, Vincent, 392
Greenwood, Arthur, 587
Gregory, Lady, 204
Grey, Charles Grey, Earl, 528
Griffith, D. W., 399
Groton preparatory school, 62, 209, 215, 476, 477
Guadalcanal, 648, 650, 664
Guadalcanal Diary (Tregaskis), 505
Guild of St. Apollonia, 312

Hagerty, James, 430
Hagikaze (Japanese destroyer), 653
Haig, Lady Irene, 545, 547
Hale, Edward Everett, 35
Halifax, Countess of, 526
Halifax, Edward Lindley Wood, Earl of, 515, 518, 526, 528–29, 605, 664
    and Czech crisis, 549, 550, 553, 556, 560
    and declaration of war, 591
    and Chamberlain's resignation, 597
Hall, C. Stanley, 80
Halle, Kay, 724
Halsey, William F., 651
Hanami, Kohei, 766–67, 812
Handlin, Oscar, 8, 16, 534
Hands Off Spain movement, 522, 576
Hanify, Edward, 625, 626
Hannon, Edmond, 81
Hannon, Elizabeth (Lizzie), 81–82, 91
Hannon, Emily, 81, 83, 253
Hannon, Geraldine, 79, 80, 82, 83, 85, 90, 396
Hannon, James (Jimmy), 79, 81, 82–83, 89
Hannon, John (d. 1854), 81
Hannon, John Edmond, 82, 103

Hannon, Josie, *see* Fitzgerald, Mary
Josephine Hannon
Hannon, Mary Ann Fitzgerald, 11, 12,
77–78, 80, 81, 84, 88–89
Hannon, Michael, 12, 77–78, 81, 82,
84, 88–89, 159
Hannon, Michael, Jr., 79, 81, 82–83
Hardwick Hall, 546
*Harlan Fiske Stone: Pillar of the Law*
(Mason), 778
Harlech, Lady, 740
Harlee, John, 645, 646, 647
Harlow, Dick, 508–9
*Harper's Weekly*, 161
Harriman, John, 758
Harriman, Pamela Churchill, *see*
Churchill, Pamela
Harris, Charles A., 655
Harrison, William, 444
Harte, Bret, 54
Hartington, Andrew Cavendish,
Marquess of, 547, 696, 729–30, 739
Hartington, Deborah Mitford
Cavendish, Marchioness of, 540,
547, 739
Hartington, Kathleen Kennedy
Cavendish ("Kick"), Marchioness
of, 65–66, 782
birth of, 309
as child, 361, 362–63, 397, 425
at school, 456, 482–86, 489–90, 491–
492
closeness to Jack, 362, 482, 486, 607,
627, 630–31, 729–34 *passim*
begins correspondence with Lem, 484
and Jack's school club, 487, 488
travels in Europe, 492–93, 506, 551,
585–86
as Ambassador's daughter, 514, 522,
523, 539–47, 582, 583–85, 587–88
falls in love with Hartington, 544–47,
586
returns to U.S., 606–7
in Washington, 627–31, 633, 635, 663
in wartime London, 663ff.
renews romance with Hartington, 668–
678
marriage to Hartington, 678–82, 717
and Pat Wilson, 684, 685
and V-1 bombs, 685
and Joe Jr.'s death, 690–92, 694
and Hartington's death, 696–97, 729–
730
at Lismore Castle, 729, 731–32

in love with Fitzwilliam, 732–34, 736–
738
death of, 738–41, 742–44
Hartington, Spencer Compton
Cavendish, Marquess of, 65, 544
Hartington, William Cavendish (Billy),
9th Marquess of, 66, 702, 729
romance of with Kathleen, 544–47,
586, 666, 668–78
and the coming war, 584–85
in France, 607, 692, 694–95
stands for Parliament, 672–73
marriage of, 678–82
death of, 695–97, 729–30
Harvard, John, 218
Harvard Business School, 369–74
Harvard College and University, 55
class reunions at, 322–24, 441, 535
football games vs. Yale, 507–9, 761
in Great War, 275–76, 283
honorary degrees from, 531–32, 534–
535
in JPK's day, 208–19, 224–25
in JPK Jr.'s day, 475–81, 504–9
*see also* Harvard Business School;
Harvard Medical School
Harvard *Crimson*, 504, 508
Harvard Medical School, 61, 66–67
Hasty Pudding Club, 213
Haussermann, Oscar, 322
Hawthorne, Nathaniel, 46, 48, 63, 86–
87
Hawthorne, Sophia Peabody, 86
Hayden, Charles, 291, 329
Hayden, Stone and Co., 275, 291–300,
323, 329, 337, 341–42, 443
Hayes, Ellen, 133
Hays, Will, 341, 370
Hays office, 370, 389–90, 407, 513
Healy, Robert, 446, 449
Hearst, Lorelle, 671, 688
Hearst, Randolph, 485
Hearst, William (Bill, son of W.R.),
670, 671
Hearst, William Randolph (W.R.) 150,
154, 342, 393, 428–29, 438, 502–3,
626
Hearst Company, 256, 502–3, 703
Heffernan, Ellen Hannon, 81, 82, 83,
87
Heffernan, Mary Hannon, 11, 82, 83,
88, 252–53
Heffernan, Maurice, 83
Heinze, Frederick A., 129

Hemingway, Ernest, 754
Henderson, Neville, 529
Hendricks Club, 95, 109
Heney, Francis, J., 196
Hennessey, Luella, 539, 576, 637
Henry VIII, King, 514
Hersey, John, 650, 658, 720
Hersh, Burton, 638
Hertz, John, 330–33, 335–36, 432, 435
Hibbard, George Albee, 149–50, 155
Hickey, Fred, 254
Hickey, James, 254, 316
Hickey, John, 254
Hickory Hill, 785
Higginson family, 46, 57, 191, 236
Higham, Charles, 572
Higham, John, 49
Hill, Arthur, 160–61, 163–68, 169–71
Hill, Julia Fitzgerald, 60, 197
Hinton, Harold, 514
Hiroshima, 705
Hitler, Adolf, 470–72, 474
  and Jews, 471–72, 519, 567–70
  moves into Rhineland, 517
  and Austria, 517, 519–20
  and Czechoslovakia, 548–65, 571
  and Poland, 572, 587
  requests gold loan, 572
  and British ultimatum, 587–88
  invades Scandinavia, 596–97, 602,
    605
  turns on Russia, 599
  launches Battle of Britain, 607
  Inga Arvad and, 632
Hoar, John, 222
Hoare, Sir Samuel, 553
Hodder, Edwin, 294
Hoffa, Jimmy, 791
Hofstadter, Richard, 135
Holker Hall, 546
Holland, occupation of, 597
Holmes, Burton, 158
Holmes, Oliver Wendell, 44, 46, 218
Holmes family, 47
Holt, L. Emmett, 302
Holy Cross College, 66
Home for Destitute Catholic Children,
  70
Hoover, Herbert, 419, 421, 427, 435,
  440
Hopkins, Harry, 603, 702
Hopper, Bruce, 582
Hora, Josef, 562
Horton, Ralph "Rip", 465, 484, 486, 723

Houghton, Arthur, 304, 514, 545, 580,
  634, 659, 693
House of Representatives, U.S.
  Education and Labor Committee,
    725
  Fitzgerald in, 99–100, 102–3
  JFK in, 722–29, 735, 753, 764
  Un-American Activities Committee,
    753
Howard, Cy, 393–94, 396, 425
Howard, Roy, 447
Howe, Irving, 6, 13
Howe, Louis, 437–39, 447, 448
Howe, Samuel Gridley, 48
Howey, Walter, 330–31, 503, 693–94
Hubert, René, 395
Hughes, Charles Evans, 270
Hughes, Howard, 422
Hugo, Victor, 796
Huidekoper, Page, 513–14, 627–28, 632
Hull, Cordell, 520, 521, 550–51, 556
Human Wreckage (film), 341
Humphrey, Hubert H., 782, 783, 797–
  799
Hundred Days, 434, 439
Hunloke, Anne, 696
Hunnewell, Arnold Welles, 215
Hunnewell, Thomas B., 356
Huntington, Collis P., 13
Husson, Sister Gabriella, 483
Hutchinson, Thomas, 90

Ickes, Harold L., 499
Île de France, S.S., 414, 489, 492
Iles, John, 649, 651
I'm for Roosevelt (JPK/Krock), 495
Ince, Ralph, 347
Ince, Thomas, 377
Independent League, 150
Index of Forbidden Books, 183, 796
Institute of 1770, 213, 214
Intergovernmental Committee on
  Refugees, 570
Into the Valley (Hersey), 650
Intolerance (film), 402
Ireland
  Britain and, 10–11, 64–65, 268
  Fitzgerald/Kennedy roots in, 9–11,
    159, 731, 814–15
  JPK honored in, 537–38
  potato famine in, 10–11, 51, 59
Irish Home Rule, 65, 114
Irish in the U.S.
  in Boston, see Boston

prejudice against, 29–30, 32–33, 216, 325–27, 477
*Irish Times*, 814
Isabel, Mother, 593, 594
Ivano, Paul, 402

Jackson, Andrew, 813
Jackson, Henry M., 723
Jackson family, 46, 191
Jacques, Jules, 315
James, Henry, 461
James, Robert Rhodes, 598
James, William, 461
*James Madison: The President* (Brant), 778
Japan, 623, 648–59 *passim*
*Jazz Singer, The* (film), 374
Jefferson, Thomas, 813
Jefferson Club, 95, 108
Jerome, William Travers, 107
Jersey, Earl of, 670
Jewett, Sophie, 132
Jews, 102
  in Boston, 94, 99, 228
  and Harvard, 216–17, 476, 477
  Hitler and, 471–72, 520, 567–70
  the Kennedys and, 471–74, 567–71
John XXIII, Pope, 798
*John Quincy Adams and the Union* (Bemis), 778
Johnson, Charles, 729
Johnson, Herschel, 514
Johnson, Howard, 636
Johnson, Lady Bird, 813
Johnson, Lyndon B., 735, 780, 783, 784, 790, 800, 802
Johnson, Owen, 209–10, 211
Johnson, Thomas "Golden Rule," 196
Johnston, Lynn, 758
Johnston, William, 720
Jones, J. Edward, 478
Jordan, Sara, 480
Juliana, Crown Princess of the Netherlands, 185

Kane, Joseph, 626, 699, 700, 708–11 *passim*, 714, 718, 727
Kane, Robert, 381–82, 384, 385
KAO, 422
*Kathleen ni Houlihan* (Yeats/Gregory), 204
Keany, Matthew, 68, 69–76, 92, 93–94, 142, 244
Keegan, John, 270, 272

Kefauver, Estes, 782, 783–84, 790
Keith-Albee-Orpheum circuit (KAO), 375–76, 379–80
Kelly, Arthur, 281
Kelly, William, 711
Kennan, George F., 583
Kennedy, Bridget, 226
Kennedy, Caroline Bouvier, 792–93
Kennedy, Edward Moore (Teddy), 363, 426, 460, 527, 608, 785
  in London, 522, 523, 539, 559
  and the Pope, 581
  at boarding schools, 638–39, 739
  marriage of, 771, 782
  and his children, 786
  in politics, 795, 804, 807
Kennedy, Ethel Skakel, 762, 772, 785, 804
Kennedy, Eunice, *see* Shriver, Eunice Kennedy
Kennedy, Francis (JPK's brother), 227
Kennedy, Jacqueline Bouvier, 769–74, 776, 801, 804, 813
  childbirths of, 782, 785–86, 792–93, 806
Kennedy, Jean, *see* Smith, Jean Kennedy
Kennedy, Joan Bennett, 771, 782, 804
Kennedy, John F., Commissioner, 135, 156, 157
Kennedy, John Fitzgerald (JFK, Jack), 430, 457, 474, 485, 498, 535
  birth of, 274, 275
  childhood of, 309–12, 314, 315, 350, 351, 353–56, 362–65, 397
  illnesses of, 309–12, 314, 353–54, 460, 481, 490–91; *see also reference to Addison's disease, below*
  religious unorthodoxy of, 353, 635, 651, 691, 743, 753
  rivalry with Joe Jr., 354–56, 458, 461, 465–66, 504–5, 698
  and Bobby, 354, 364–65
  closeness to Kathleen, 362, 482, 486, 607, 627, 630–31, 729–34 *passim*
  at Choate, 456–58, 460–65, 481, 486–489
  and women, 481–82, 607, 630–35, 723–725, 734, 773–74
  and Laski, 489–90
  at Princeton, 490–91
  at Harvard, 504–6, 516, 522, 568, 581–582

Kennedy, John Fitzgerald (JFK, Jack)
  *(cont.)*
  back problems of, 505, 646–67, 690,
    697, 700–701, 735, 774–76, 779
  on Spanish Civil War, 506
  in London, 524, 537, 538, 539, 545,
    577, 587–88
  praises JPK's coexistence speech, 568
  writes thesis on Britain, 582, 604–6
  tours eastern Europe, 583
  in Washington with Navy, 627, 630–
    633
  at midshipmen's school, 634, 635, 645–
    646
  at P-T boat school, 646–47
  in the Pacific, 648–60, 664
  commands *PT 109*, 649–58, 662, 669,
    714, 720
  and Joe Jr.'s death, 690–91, 698–99,
    743–44
  covers UN Conference, 702–3
  covers British election, 703–4
  enters politics, 705ff.
  seeks congressional nomination, 710–
    720
  wins seat, 721
  as congressman, 722–29, 735, 753,
    764
  and the Curley petition, 727–29
  visits Ireland, 729, 730–34
  afflicted with Addison's disease, 734–
    735, 743, 745, 749, 774, 788
  and Kathleen's death, 739, 742–44
  renews his commitment to politics,
    745, 748–49
  has last visit with JFF, 746–47, 749
  at JFF's funeral, 748
  character development of, 750–55
  pursues statewide constituency, 755–
    756
  runs against Lodge for Senate, 756–
    767, 771
  courts and marries Jacqueline
    Bouvier, 769–74
  and *Profiles in Courage*, 776–78
  in Senate, 753, 778–80, 789–92
  and vice-presidential nomination, 781–
    785
  and death of first baby, 785–86
  decides to run for President, 787ff.
  and Catholicism issue, 792, 795, 797–
    798, 799, 803
  and daughter's birth, 793
  reelected to Senate, 793

  seeks presidential nomination, 794–
    802
  debates with Nixon, 789–90, 803–4
  election of as President, 804–6
  as President-elect, 806–7
  inauguration of, 810–16
  assassination of, 817
Kennedy, John Fitzgerald, Jr., 806
Kennedy, Joseph Patrick (JPK)
  as a child, 98, 123, 227–28
  romance with Rose, 124, 158, 208,
    217–23, 225, 233, 242, 253
  at Boston Latin School, 124, 210,
    214, 216, 228
  at Harvard, 208–19, 224–26, 228, 230,
    234, 269
  social rejection of, 213–15, 269, 325–
    327, 365–67, 370, 535
  rejects politics as career, 228–32
  first business venture of, 232–33
  enters banking world, 234–41
  engagement and marriage of, 253,
    258–61
  prevents Columbia Trust takeover,
    253–54
  as "youngest bank president," 253–
    258, 276, 278
  and birth of Joe Jr., 261, 263
  is alienated by Great War, 268–72,
    275–76, 281–83, 323
  and birth of Jack, 274–75
  and the draft, 276, 280–81, 565, 799
  at Bethlehem shipyard, 277–81, 283–
    284, 286–87, 289–93
  becomes utility trustee, 274–75, 291–
    292
  in stock market, 290–91, 293–300,
    323, 327–38
  as "ladies' man," 303–4, 426, 724, 773;
    *see also* and Gloria Swanson, *below*
  and Rose's separation, 308, 313
  and Jack's near-death, 309–10
  flirts with Republican Party, 315–18
  and the police strike, 316–17
  becomes involved with his children,
    312–14, 320, 350–51, 539 and
    *passim*
  marital partnership of, 320–21, 391–
    392
  at tenth class reunion, 322–24, 441
  in movie industry, 339–48, 374–80,
    398–402, 404–13, 419, 422–24
  and Rosemary's retardation, 359, 360,
    497, 498, 593–95, 639–44, 652

moves family to New York, 367–68

arranges Harvard movie lectures, 369–374

and Gloria Swanson, 381–82, 384–97, 398–418 *passim*, 425–26

produces *Queen Kelly*, 398–402, 404–413

and father's illness and death, 409–412, 417

acquires Bronxville estate, 417, 421, 424

pulls out of stock market, 420–22

renews his commitment to marriage, 424–26

Palm Beach villa of, 426, 460, 473, 485

returns to politics, 427

supports FDR, 428–35

seeks post, 435–39, 635–36

returns to stock profiteering, 439–40

in liquor trade, 441–44

heads SEC, 447–55, 477, 485, 487, 507

plays host to FDR, 451

and his sons' schooling, 457, 461–70 *passim*, 477, 478, 487–89, 506, 507, 638

reputed anti-Semitism of, 473, 569, 763

and Kathleen's schooling, 485–86

as financial consultant to business, 494, 502–3

supports FDR in '36, 494–96

heads Maritime Commission, 498–499, 502, 507, 511

shapes his public image, 500–502

speaks on Irish and Puritans, 504

at '37 Harvard–Yale game, 507–9

as ambassador to Britain, 509–30, 534, 536–39, 549–68, 572–79, 583, 585–88, 590–600, 603, 605, 607–17

advocates isolationist/appeasement policies, 520–22, 529–30, 550, 564–568, 572–73, 585, 595, 596

at Windsor, 525–29

hopes for honorary degree, 531–32, 535–36

presidential boomlet for, 533–34, 536

honored in Ireland, 537–38

and German Jews, 567, 569–71

takes pride in Joe Jr.'s reports, 575, 577–79

at Pius XII's coronation, 580–81

helps Jack with tour, 583

antiwar outburst of, 585

and end of peace, 587, 588

defeatest attitude of, 590–93, 597–99, 607, 614–15

Foreign Office memos on, 595–96, 617

resented by British, 596, 598, 600, 616–617, 665–66

begins to live through his children, 600

and Joe Jr.'s entry into politics, 601, 603–4, 621–22

and family trust, 602, 624, 636

promotes Jack's book on England, 605

on the Blitz, 608–9

has last visit with Chamberlain, 610, 611

resignation of, 610–14, 617

makes radio speech for FDR, 613

controversial Lyons interview with, 614–17

at Joe Jr.'s naval-aviation graduation, 623

"spy" network of, 624–25

helps JFF against Casey, 625–27

and Jack's affair with Inga Arvad, 630–631, 633–35

sells Bronxville home, 636–37

and Jack's spinal problems, 646, 700–701, 704, 744–46

and Jack's *PT 109* exploit, 655, 657–659, 662

pulls strings for Kathleen, 665–67

backs Kathleen in her romance, 669, 672, 674, 676, 679–81

and Joe Jr.'s last mission, 687

and Joe Jr.'s death, 688–94, 697, 701, 792

and Hartington's death, 696, 697

focuses his hopes on Jack, 699–701, 705–7, 755

and FDR's death, 701–2, 704

buys Merchandise Mart, 704–5

runs Jack's congressional campaign, 713–21

and McCarthy, 723

and the Curley petition, 727–28

on Kathleen's decision to live in England, 730

and Kathleen's affair and death, 736, 737, 739–41

builds state organization for Jack, 756

runs Jack's Senate drives, 758–61, 763–767 *passim*, 793
and Jackie, 772
opposes Jack's vice-presidential bid, 781, 783, 785
and Jack's bid for the presidency, 787–788, 790, 792, 795–97, 799–801
and the election, 804–8
at JFK's inauguration, 812, 815–16
death of, 817
Kennedy, Joseph Patrick, Jr., 444, 485, 498, 506, 717
birth and infancy of, 261–63, 267, 272, 275
as favored child, 311, 315, 350–56, 362–63, 751
early schooling of, 355–56, 397
and Bobby, 364–65
at P.J.'s wake, 412
at Choate, 456–61, 465–66
studies with Laski, 467–69
visits Nazi Germany, 470–74
travels to Russia, 474, 492, 575, 606
at Harvard College, 475, 477–81, 504–505, 507–8, 516, 522, 531, 535–36, 576
"Hands Off Spain" thesis of, 522, 576
in Ireland and London as Ambassador's son, 537–40, 545, 587–588
at Paris embassy, 551, 575
traverses Continent, 575–76
sustains skiing accident, 576
in Spain, 576–79, 580–81, 585
at law school, 600, 602, 621, 622
enters politics, 600–604, 621–22
in naval-aviation training, 622–25, 627, 661–62
and Jack's *PT-109* exploit, 662–63
in England under RAF, 663, 669ff., 683–84, 686–88
and Pat Wilson, 670–72, 678, 684–685
and Kathleen's romance, 675, 678–679, 682
death of, 688–94, 698–99, 792
Kennedy, Katherine, 123, 254
Kennedy, Kathleen, *see* Hartington, Kathleen Kennedy Cavendish, Marchioness of
Kennedy, Loretta, 213, 228, 229, 311, 410, 412, 441, 522, 731
Kennedy, Margaret, *see* Burke, Margaret Kennedy

Kennedy, Mary Augusta Hickey (JPK's mother), 123, 212, 227, 229, 260, 308, 368, 410
Kennedy, Patricia, *see* Lawford, Patricia Kennedy
Kennedy, Patrick (JPK's grandfather), 263, 814
Kennedy, Patrick Joseph (P.J., father of JPK), 226–29, 260, 308, 318, 441, 754
as ward leader, 98, 100, 107, 125, 150, 157, 228–29, 338
defeated for public office, 230–32
and Columbia Trust, 237, 253–57, 278, 412
fatal illness and death, 409–12, 417
Kennedy, Robert Francis (Bobby), 492, 735, 739, 777, 785
birth of, 349
as child, 354, 363, 364–65, 397, 498
in London, 522, 523, 539
education of, 539, 637–38, 761
in wartime, 659, 700–701, 717
and father's womanizing, 724
in JFK's campaigns, 761–63, 767, 783, 795, 802, 804, 805
marriage of, 762
and his children, 786
and rackets hearings, 791
appointment of as attorney general, 807
assassination of, 817
Kennedy, Rose Elizabeth Fitzgerald
birth of, 90–91
childhood of, 103–5, 123
idolizes her father, 105, 200–201, 253
at father's induction as mayor, 111
high-school graduation of, 122
first meeting with JPK, 123
romance with JPK, 124, 158, 208, 217–223, 225, 233, 242, 253
as father's chosen companion, 125, 130–31, 197–201, 219, 221–22
girlhood radiance of, 130–31
sets her heart on Wellesley, 131–33, 142, 143, 144
is enrolled at Sacred Heart, 142–47
at convent school abroad, 155, 158, 159, 174–89, 217
travels with family, 157–59, 184–85, 189
religious commitment of, 185–89, 307–308, 319, 677, 679, 692, 736, 773, 796

reacts to attacks on father, 193
at Manhattanville, 197, 217, 259
debut of, 201–2
as leader of young Catholic set, 203–204, 302
shocked by Synge play, 204–7
disturbed by Toodles scandal, 249, 253
and father's collapse, 251
engagement of, 253, 258–59
marriage of, 259–61
pregnancies and childbirths of, 261, 274, 287–88, 301, 309, 314, 331, 336, 349, 389, 396–97, 426
and First World War, 267, 272, 287–288
and JPK's absences, 301, 346, 349–50, 389
feels isolated, 301–5
returns to parents' home, 305–7
goes on retreat, 307–8
builds close family structure, 313–15, 319–21, 366, 391–92, 396–97, 772
keeps her own space, 313–14, 786, 796
keeps JPK a Democrat, 317–18
and her children's early years, 351–362, 412, 637–38, 751
extramarital travels of, 353, 426–27, 492–93, 549, 551, 553, 577, 580, 639, 734, 747–48
on leaving Boston, 367–68
and the Swanson affair, 391–92, 395–397, 414–16, 425
has "golden interval" with JPK, 424–426
and JPK's SEC appointment, 450–451
and sons' schooling, 457, 460–61, 465, 467
chooses daughters' schooling, 457, 482–83, 489–90
and sister's death, 496–97
as Ambassador's wife, 522, 523–29, 536–39, 543–44, 558, 559, 563, 564, 574–75, 587
at Pope's coronation, 580–81
and JPK's resignation, 610–12
and sons' love affairs, 625, 630, 631, 685, 689–90
and Rosemary's lobotomy, 639–43 passim
learns that Jack is safe, 657–58
and Joe Jr.'s last visit, 663
and Kathleen's romance with Hartington, 669, 672, 674–81
and Joe Jr.'s death, 688–92
in Jack's campaigns, 717–19, 766, 768, 793, 795–96, 801, 804
and Kathleen's affair, 734, 736
and Kathleen's death, 739
and father's death, 747–48
and Jackie, 772, 801
at JFK's inauguration, 812
Kennedy, Rosemary, 607
as a child, 309, 356–63, 397
and her siblings, 360, 362, 363, 485, 498, 544, 772
is shielded by her family, 361, 544, 594–95, 735
at school, 497–98, 513, 522, 539, 593–595
debut of, 540
is presented at court, 543–44
lobotomy is performed on, 639–44, 652
Kennedy, Teddy, see Kennedy, Edward Moore
Kennedy Library, 816
Kent, George Edward, Duke of, 541, 545, 560
Kent, Marina, Duchess of, 541, 545
Kenyon-Slaney, Jane, 607, 733, 737, 740
Khrushchev, Nikita, 815
Kidder, Peabody and Co., 236, 293
King, Eleanor, 259
King Kong (film), 378
Kingman, Howard, 633
King of Kings, The (film), 377, 378
Kirk, Alan Goodrich, 627
Kirksey, Andrew, 652, 654
Kirstein, Louis, 342, 344, 420
Klemmer, Harvey, 513, 581
Klous, Maurice, 139–41, 148, 149
Knight, Jack, 792
Knights of Labor, 97
Koch, George P., 138–39, 147–49, 151, 163
Koch, Robert, 33
Koren, John, 17
Kowal, Maurice, 652
Kristallnacht, 568, 569, 571
Krock, Arthur, 615, 616, 693, 699, 775
friendship with JFK, 432, 500, 636
on JPK party for FDR, 451–52
helps with Kennedy books, 495, 605, 777
JPK letters to, 500, 515, 518, 558

and JPK's ambassadorship, 509, 514, 515
on JFK in politics, 704, 705
Kuhn, Leob and Co., 440
Kuroki, Tamemoto Tamesada, 129

Lambert, John, 533
Lamont, Thomas W., 421
Land, Emory, 532
Landis, James, M., 446, 449–50, 515fn., 608, 735, 758, 759
Landon, Alfred, 496
Lannan, Pat, 701
Laski, Harold, 467–68, 471, 474, 489, 490, 492, 605
Laski, Mrs., 468, 474
Lasky, Jesse, 371, 374, 384, 385, 409
Last Hurrah, The (O'Connor), 252, 728
Last Tycoon, The (Fitzgerald), 346
Late George Apley, The (Marquand), 55, 324, 504
Lawford, Christopher, 782
Lawford, Patricia Kennedy, 739, 748, 804
  birth of, 336
  as a child, 363–64, 397
  in London, 522, 523
  schooling of, 539, 637
  helps JFK's compaigns, 716, 795
  marriage of, 782, 795
Lawford, Peter, 782, 804
Lawler, Anne, 423
Lawrence, David L., 794–95
Lawrence, T. E., 541
Lawrence family, 236
League of Nations, 252, 429, 470, 529
Leahy, John, 120
Leahy, William, 205
Le Baron, William, 396, 402
Lee, Joseph, 136, 710
Lee family, 46, 191
Lee, Higginson and Co., 191, 236, 293
Legg, Vera, 132
LeHand, Missy, 431, 438, 452, 592, 613
Lehman brothers, 376
Lelong, Lucien, 416
Leslie, Sean, 729
Libby-Owens-Ford Glass Co., 440, 447
Liberal Party, Britain, 65, 544
Liberal Union Party, Britain, 65
Liberty magazine, 533
Life magazine, 523, 570, 613
Lincoln, Evelyn, 775, 783, 786
Lindbergh, Anne Morrow, 555, 577–79

Lindbergh, Charles A., 555, 569, 577, 615
Lindley, Ernest K., 431, 533
Lindsay, Peter, 737
Lippmann, Walter, 216–17, 530
Lisagor, Peter, 799
Lismore Castle, 65, 546, 729, 731–32, 734
Little American, The (film), 377
Livermore, Jesse, 296
Lives of the Saints (Butler), 5, 752
Lloyd, Harold, 377, 385
Lloyd George, David, 588, 597
Lodge, Henry Cabot I, 29, 100–102, 316
  JFF and, 57, 102, 109, 243, 252, 768
Lodge, Henry Cabot II, 626, 756–58, 763–65, 767
Lodge family, 47, 57, 708
Loew, Marcus, 372, 373
Login, Ella, 739
Lomasney, Joseph, 120
Lomasney, Martin, 95–96, 98, 105, 107–109, 150, 157, 244, 245, 804
London, University of, 489
London School of Economics, 490, 542
Lonely Crowd, The (Riesman), 777
Long, Breckinridge, 431
Long, Huey, 452
Longfellow, Henry Wadsworth, 46, 64, 218
Longworth, Nicholas, 114
Look, 719, 791
Looker, Earle, 501
Lords, House of, 597
Lothian, Lord, 577
Love of Sunya, The (film), 384, 387
Lowell, A. Lawrence, 214, 370
Lowell, James Russell, 62, 218
Lowell, Ralph, 222, 322, 326
Lowell family, 46, 47, 477
Lowrey, John, 653
Luce, Clare Boothe, 781
Luce, Matthew, 325–26
Lusitania, S.S., 268
Lyman family, 236
Lyons, Louis, 614–17

Macdonald, Torbert, 484, 505–6, 583, 606, 647, 717
Macmillan, Harold, 815
Madame Sans-Gêne (film), 389
Madrid, 576–79, 580, 581, 585
Maguire, John, 654

Maguire, P.J. "Pea Jacket," 97–98, 106, 214

Maguire, William, 318

Maher, Thomas F., 149, 152–54, 160, 161–73

Maher Brothers, 148–49, 152, 161–66 *passim*

Mahoney, Cornelius, 20

Maine–New Hampshire Theatres, 340–341, 343

*Male and Female* (film), 383

*Manchester Guardian*, 555

*Manhattan*,S.S., 537

Manhattanville College, 188, 189, 197, 217, 259, 782

Mann, Horace, 48

Mansfield, Henry, 246–48

Margaret Rose, Princess, 527, 545, 558, 584

Maritime Commission, 499, 502, 507, 511, 513, 532

Marlborough, Duke of, 540, 670

Marne, Battles of the, 282, 285

Marney, Harold, 654

Marquand, John P., 324

Marshall, George C., 729

Marshall, Tully, 402, 408, 413

Marshall Plan, 725, 729, 737

Martin, Harold, 791–92

Martin, Samuel Klump III, 451

Marwood, 451–52, 499

Marx, Robert, 431

Mary, Queen Mother, 526, 537, 559

Masaryk, Jan, 561–62, 565

Masaryk, Tomás, 561, 571

Mason, Alpheus T., 778

Massachusetts Civic League, 136

Massachusetts Electric Co., 274–75, 291–92

Massingham, H. J., 512

Mather, Cotton, 32

Mathew, Bishop, 674, 675, 680

Matthews, George, 446, 449–50

Matthews, Nathan, 97, 133, 135, 156

Maud, Queen, 575

Mauer, Edman, 654

Maugham, Somerset, 399

Mayer, Louis B., 373, 399

Mayflower bus enterprise, 232–33, 235

McCarthy, Eugene, 800

McCarthy, Joe (writer), 274

McCarthy, Joseph R., 723, 753, 779–80, 783

McCarthy, Mary, 145

McCarthy, Mary Lou, 227–28, 425

McClellan, James, 125

McClellan, John L., 791

McClellan, Joseph, 150

McCormack, John W., 727

McCormick, Cyrus H., 13

McCulloch, Charles, 332

McDonald, Charlotte, 483

McDonough, Robert, 798

McGahey, George, 95, 96

McGill, Ralph, 804

McGovern, John, 588

McInerny, Timothy, 623, 665, 666, 667, 669

McIntyre, Marvin, 449, 498

McKinley, William, 102

McLaughlin, Charles, 224–25

McLaughlin, Owen and Bridget, 8

McMahon, Patrick Henry "Pappy," 654–657, 715

McMillan Cup races, 535

*McTeague* (film), 399

Mead, George, 664

*Mein Kampf* (Hitler), 529

Melville, Herman, 811

*Memories of a Catholic Girlhood* (McCarthy), 145

Merchandise Mart, 704, 782

Merchants National Bank, 254–55

Merrill, Joseph, 211, 216, 275

*Merry Widow, The* (film), 399

Mestayer, Emily Stead, 414

Metro-Goldwyn-Mayer (MGM), 373, 379

Middlesex Club, 316, 318

Middlesex School, 62, 209, 476, 477

Midway, Battle of, 648

Milbank, Jeremiah, 376

Miller, Harlan, 533

Miller, Perry, 46

Miller, Sara, 311

*Milwaukee Journal*, 797

*Misérables, Les* (Hugo), 183, 796

Mitchell, Catherine, 154, 197

Mitchell, Charles E., 421

Mitchell, Michael, 137–42, 149, 151–155, 246, 248

  trial and conviction of, 161–73, 174–175, 190, 192

  release and death of, 196–97

Mitford, Deborah, 540, 547, 739

Mix, Tom, 350, 351, 385

Mizner, Harry, 426

Moley, Raymond, 431, 434, 436, 447–48

Monahan, Margaret Curry, 131
Moniz, Egas, 641
Monroe, James, 513
Montessori, Maria, 594
Mooney, James, 572–73
*Moon for the Misbegotten* (O'Neill), 411
Moore, Edward, 249, 250, 333–34, 345, 428, 580
  and JPK's children, 357, 397, 426, 513, 522, 576, 594, 607, 751
  finds home for JPK, 368
  and Swanson, 387, 390–91, 394
  rides the FDR train, 430, 431, 434
  fronts for JPK in stock deals, 439
  at Marwood with JPK, 450–51, 499
  and JPK's ambassadorship, 513, 537, 538, 545, 552, 557, 592, 610
  and JFK's campaigns, 713, 759
Moore, Mary, 397, 557, 580, 751, 872
Moors, John, 135
Moran, John B., 107, 149, 151–54, 159, 161, 164–65
Morey, Robert, 755
Morgan John Pierpont, 235–36, 317, 420, 523
Morgan, John Pierpont II, 445
Morgan, J. P., and Co., 317, 421, 445
Morgenthau, Henry, 530, 550
Morison, Samuel Eliot, 47, 209
Morrissey, Frank, 755
Mossarch, General, 585
*Mosses from an Old Manse* (Hawthorne), 86
Motion Picture Producers and Distributors of America, *see* Hays office
Motley, John, 46
Motor Torpedo Division, 647
Mott, Frank, 38
Mountbatten, Lady, 540
Muckers Club, 486–89
Mulkern, Patsy, 719
Mullen, Marian Fitzgerald, 85
Mullins, Bill, 622
Munich Conference and Agreement, 548, 560–65, 566–74, *passim*, 584
Municipal League, 119
Murdock, John J., 375, 376, 422
Murphy, Frank, 636
Murphy, Paul, 624
Murphy, Regis Fitzgerald, 27, 59, 60, 85
Murray, Cecile, 259
Murray, John Courtney, 803
Murray, Mae, 401

Murray, Vera, 303–4
Mussolini, Benito, 517, 518, 520, 560

Nasser, Gamal Abdel, 755
Nathan, George Jean, 315
*Nation, The*, 278
National Industrial Recovery Act, 434
National Labor Relations Act, 725
National Petroleum Council, 478
National Shawmut Bank, 236, 269, 324, 344, 443
National University, Dublin, 538
Navy League, British, 565
Nawn, Harry, 219
Nawn, Hugh, 219, 220
Nazi-Soviet Pact, 586
Negri, Pola, 372
Negrin, Juan, 579
Nehru, Jawaharlal, 815
Neptunes Associates, 71, 73
Neutrality Act, 577fn., 591
Neville, Michael, 710
*New Bedford Standard Times*, 763
New Deal (FDR Administration), 436–454 *passim*, 477, 478
*New England Magazine*, 115–16
New Hampshire primary (1960), 795–796, 799
Newport, Viscount, 543
New Ross, Ireland, 731–32, 814–15
*Newsweek*, 503
Newton, Rose, 497
*New York American*, 502
*New York Daily News*, 604, 740
*New Yorker, The*, 658
*New York Journal-American*, 703
*New York Mirror*, 633
*New York Post*, 566
New York Stock Exchange, 421, 445, 453
*New York Times, The*, 271, 274
*New York Times Book Review, The*, 777
*New York Times Magazine,The*, 766
Niessen, Gertrude, 506
Ninth Congressional District, Mass., *see* Eleventh Congressional District, Mass.
Niver Coal Co., 139–41, 148
Nixon, Pat, 813
Nixon, Richard M., 776, 790, 803–4, 805
Nobles and Greenough School, 355
Nolan, James, 120
Norfolk, Duke of, 580

Norman, Montagu, 592–93, 605
Normandie invasion, planned, 678, 682, 683–84
  see also, D-Day
Norris, Frank, 113, 399
Norton, Clem, 228, 249, 454, 473, 603, 748
Norton, Sally, 540
Norway, invasion of, 596–97, 602, 605
Noyes, Alexander, 419
Nuremberg rally (1938), 552–53
Nutter, George, 120, 134, 196

O'Brien, Daniel, 728
O'Brien, James, 68
O'Brien, Lawrence, 757
O'Callaghan, Marguerite, 132
O'Connell, William Cardinal, 29, 122, 259, 417, 580
  and Rose Fitzgerald's education, 143, 189
  gets honorary degree, 532
  on women and marriage, 773
O'Connor, Edwin, 111, 252
O'Donnell, Hugh, 679
O'Donnell, Kenneth, 761, 762
O'Farrell, Dennis J., 111
O'Farrell, Father, 157
Office of Naval Intelligence, 627, 632, 633
Offie, Carmel, 583
O'Hara, Francis, 504
Old Bullion Benton (Chambers), 778
Old Colony Trust Co., 275, 344
Old North Church, Boston, 64
Old Orchard Beach, 123–29 passim, 136, 138
O'Leary, Francis, 689
O'Leary, Jerry, 652
O'Leary, Paul, 488
O'Leary, Ted, 444
Ollman, Wally, 704
Olney, Richard, 274
Olympic, S.S., 414
Olympic Games, 632
Omnibus Corp., 336
O'Neil, Joseph, 97–98
O'Neill, Eugene, 411
Operation Cork, 684
Organization Man, The (Whyte), 777
Ormsby-Gore, David, 542, 545, 584–85, 607, 740
Ormsby-Gore, Sissy Thomas, 542, 545, 740

Ostrogorskii, M., 72
Owen, Seena, 402, 406, 413
Owens-Illinois Glass Co., 440

Page, Henry, 543
Page, Walter Hines, 530
Pale Horse, Pale Rider (Porter), 286
Palfrey, John, 46
Panama Canal, 198
Panter-Downes, Mollie, 598–99
Panic of 1893, 97
Papas, Louis, 687, 691
Paramount Pictures, 343, 372, 494
Paris Peace Conference (1919), 546
Parker, Francis Stanley, 356
Parkman, Francis, 46
Parliament, British, see Commons, House of
Parmet, Herbert S., 606
Parsons, Louella, 394
Pathé film company, 375, 376, 379–80, 393, 405, 409, 413, 422–24
Patterson, Eleanor M. (Cissy), 627, 633
Patterson, Joseph M., 604, 740
Patterson, Mother, 639
Peabody family, 47
Pearl Harbor attack, 623, 632, 636
Pearson, Drew, 500, 567
Pecora, Ferdinand, 445–50
Pelletier, Joseph, 247
Peters, Andrew, 286, 334
Pettijohn, Charles, 431
Phillips, Cabell, 766, 777
Phillips, David Graham, 113
Phillips family, 47
Pickford, Mary, 372, 385
Pilgrims Society, 520
Pilot, The, 14
Pittman, Key, 431
Pius XI, Pope, 491, 579
Pius XII (Eugenio Pacelli), Pope, 579–81
Place, Edwin, 310, 312
Plattsburgh, N.Y., training camp, 275, 281, 282
Playboy of the Western World (Synge), 204–7
Poland, 572, 583, 587
Pollock, Gordon, 402
Pond Creek Coal, 327–29
Poole, Arthur, 502
Poor's Manual, 295
Pope, Anna, 311
Porcellian Club, 214–17 passim, 269, 477, 535

Porter, Drew, 598
Porter, Katherine Anne, 286
Potter, Dorothy Tweedy, 324
Potter, Robert Sturgis, 212–16 *passim*,
  222, 224, 269–72, 275, 282, 323–25
Powell, Joseph, 277, 280–81, 292
Powers, David, 708, 710–13, 718, 746,
  755–56, 759, 783, 797
Powers, Patrick, 404
*Practical Politics*, 106, 114, 116, 125,
  138, 155, 166, 193, 231
Prescott, William, 46
Prince, Frederick, 344
Princeton University, 490–91
Pritchett, Florence, 723
Proctor, James, 726
*Profiles in Courage* (Kennedy), 777–78,
  779
Prohibition, 440–44, 534
*Promised Land, The* (Antin), 37
PT 59, 659
PT 109, 649, 651–55, 658, 659, 669, 720,
  766, 812
PT 157, 653
PT 159, 653
PT 162, 653
Puhl, Emil, 572
Pujo Committee, 236
Pulitzer Prize, 777–78, 780
Pumphret, George, 230, 232, 239

*Queen Elizabeth*, S.S., 558, 737
*Queen Kelly* (film), 398–418
*Queen Mary*, S.S., 493, 532, 582
Quincy, John, 52
Quincy, Josiah, 117, 121
Quincy family, 47

Radio Corporation of America (RCA),
  375, 379–80, 422, 494
Radio-Keith-Orpheum (RKO), 379–80,
  422
Rainoni, Charles, 4–6
Rambova, Natasha, 341
Ramsaye, Terry, 347
Raymond, George, 106
*Reader's Digest*, 658
Reardon, Ted, 477, 711, 723, 728, 739,
  743
Redesdale, Lady, 540
Reed, James, 773
Reed, John, 211
Reedy, James, 662, 663, 671, 686
Reichsbank, 572, 593

Reid, Charles, 171
Reid, Wallace, 341, 370
Reilly, James, 480
*Republic, The*, 41, 94, 106, 157
Revere, Paul, 63, 64
Richman, Harry, 543
Riesman, David, 777
Riis, Jacob, 8
Roach, Hal, 377
Robertson-Cole Co., 341
*Rochambeau*, U.S.S., 648
Roche, Jeffrey, 485
Rockefeller, David, 542
Rockefeller, Percy, 296
Roebuck, Alvah, 13fn.
Rogers, Will, 377
Rohde, Amanda, 497–98
Roman, Father, 157
Roosevelt, Alice, 114
Roosevelt, Betsy Cushing, 430, 443, 479
Roosevelt, Eleanor, 498, 534, 615, 616,
  783, 812
Roosevelt, Elliott, 688
Roosevelt, Franklin D., 217, 799
  JPK's first meetings with, 428
  nominated for President, 428–29
  campaign of, and JPK, 429–35
  physical handicap of, 432, 774
  JPK seeks appointment by, 436–39,
    635–36
  and Prohibition repeal, 441
  appoints JPK to head SEC, 446–50
  visits JPK, 451–52
  1936 campaign of, and JPK, 494–96
  second inaugural of, 498
  appoints JPK to head Maritime
    Commission, 498–99
  appoints JPK ambassador, 509
  gives "advice" to JPK, 516
  reacts to JPK's isolationist speeches,
    521, 550, 566–67
  on the JPK-Chamberlain intimacy,
    330
  and JPK's "boomlet," 533–34, 536
  and Chamberlain's policies, 534, 550,
    557, 559, 563
  leans toward Churchill, 550, 591
  and isolationists, 563, 566
  "quarantine" speech of, 566
  appalled at Nazi pogrom, 568
  predicts war over Poland, 572
  forbids JPK deal on German loan, 573
  sends JPK to Pope's coronation, 580
  bypasses JPK, 591

third-term nomination of, 603–4
and JPK's resignation, 610, 611–13
elected to third term, 613–14
JFK opposes supporter of, 625–27
fails to appoint JPK, 636
sends condolence to Kathleen, 697
death of, 701–2, 704
Roosevelt, Franklin D., Jr., 799
Roosevelt, James, 430, 431, 479, 480,
498, 584
friendship with JPK, 443–44, 513,
514, 532
Roosevelt, Kermit, 210, 215
Roosevelt, Theodore, 129, 193, 210
*Roosevelt: The Lion and the Fox*
(Burns), 778
Rosenblum, Carroll, 796, 804
Rosenman, Samuel I., 702
Ross, Edmund, 777
Ross, George "Barney," 653–57
Rosslyn, Anthony, Earl of, 542, 666,
667, 729, 740
Rotha, Paul, 609
Rothmere, Lord, 685
Rousseau, Jean-Jacques, 796
Royal Air Force (RAF), 607–8, 610,
662, 669, 690
Rublee, George, 570
Ruppel, Louis, 431, 435, 438–39, 702,
704
Russia, in First World War, 273
*see also* Soviet Union
Ruth, Babe, 350, 432
Rutland, Duke of, 679
Ryan, Elizabeth "Toodles," 246–48,
251, 252
*Rykov*, S.S., 474

Sacred Heart Convents, 142–47, 155,
174–89, 456, 482–86, 637
*see also* Manhattanville College
*Sadie Thompson* (film), 384, 387, 399
St. Albans School, 476, 477
St. Coletta's, 642–44
St. John, Adela Rogers, 384
St. John, George, 458, 459, 461, 462,
486–88, 693
St. John, Seymour, 464
St. Lawrence Seaway, 778–79
*St. Louis Post-Dispatch*, 614–17
St. Mark's School, 62, 209, 212
Saint-Moritz, 574, 575–76
St. Paul's School, 62, 209, 476, 477
St. Stephen's Catholic Lyceum, 129

St. Stephen's Church, Boston, 3–6, 13,
15, 73, 94, 111, 319
Salinger, Pierre, 797
Salisbury, Lady, 679
Saltonstall, Leverett, 510, 756
Saltonstall, Leverett, Jr., 356
Saltonstall, Philip, 275
Saltonstall family, 236, 708
Sanderson, George A., 163, 171–72
San Francisco Stock Exchange, 446
Santayana, George, 63
Santo Domingo, 570
Sarnoff, David, 375, 379
*Saturday Evening Post, The,* 791
*Saturday Review of Literature, The,* 495
Sawyer, Kate, 30
Schary, Dore, 782
Schenck, Joseph, 387, 422
Schlesinger, Arthur Meier, 96
Schlesinger, Arthur, M., Jr., 364, 426,
432, 530
Schnitzer, Joseph, 344
Schriber, Thomas, 575, 737
Schuschnigg, Kurt von, 519
Schwab, Charles M., 210, 283–84, 287,
345
Schwab, Herman Caspar, 210
Scollard, Patrick, 345
Scripps-Howard chain, 447
Scudder, Vida, 133
Seabury, Samuel, Bishop, 370, 550
Seabury, William Marston, 370–71
Sears, Henry Francis (Hank), 66, 468,
508
Sears, Richard W., 13fn.
Sears family, 236
Second World War, *see* World War II
Securities and Exchange Act, 445–46
453
Securities and Exchange Commission
(SEC), 334, 446–55, 478, 507
Selznick, David O., 378
Senate, U.S.
Banking and Currency Committee,
444–46, 447, 449
Foreign Relations Committee, 778,
779, 780
Government Operations Committee,
778
JFK in, 753, 778–80, 789–92
Labor and Public Welfare
Committee, 778, 790–91
Naval Committee, 647
Sennett, Mack, 383

Seymour, Charles, 535
Seymour, James, 513, 617
Seyss-Inquart, Artur von, 519
Shannon, William, 365
Shattuck family, 47
Shaughnessy, Frank, 446
Shaw, George Bernard, 541
Shaw family, 236
Sheehan, Joseph, 211, 216, 275, 281,
    537
Sheehy, Maurice, 623, 624, 625, 647,
    693
Sheen, Fulton J., 651, 736, 737
Sherwood, Robert E., 402
Shigure (Japanese destroyer), 653
Shirer, William L., 520, 553, 556, 557,
    568
Shriver, Eunice Kennedy, 397, 522,
    609, 639, 696, 707, 748
  birth of, 314
  ill health of, 363, 368
  and Rosemary, 363, 639, 644, 722
  schooling of, 513, 539, 637
  in London, 539, 584
  on Kathleen's beaux, 606
  helps JFK's campaigns, 716–18
  and juvenile delinquency, 722–23
  and Kathleen's affair, 736
  and Kathleen's death, 739
  marriage of, 782
  at JFK's inauguration, 815
Shriver, Maria, 782
Shriver, Robert Sargent, 723, 782, 804
Shriver, Robert (son), 782
Sidey, Hugh, 802, 807
Sills, Milton, 373
Simon, Sir John, 553, 560
Sinclair, Andrew, 442
Sinclair, Upton, 113
Slattery, Charles, 157
Smathers, George A., 723, 724, 781, 785
Smith, Ben, 422
Smith, Jean Kennedy, 363, 739, 748,
    804
  birth of, 396
  schooling of, 539, 637
  in London, 522, 523, 539
  marriage of, 782
  helps JFK's campaign, 795
Smith, Stephen, 782, 795, 804
Smith, William J., 141
Socialist Party, 133
Society of American Newspaper
    Editors, 499

Soden, Mark, 671, 690, 691
Solomon Islands, 648–60
Solynossy, Ilona, 741
Somborn, Herbert, 383, 388, 389
Somerset Club, 55, 214, 254, 324, 444
Somerset Company, 448, 468
Somme, Battles of the, 269–73, 282, 694
Soviet Union, 561, 562, 583, 599, 789
Spalding, Betty, 771
Spalding, Charles "Chuck," 606, 724,
    744
Spanish–American War, 128
Spanish Civil War, 506, 522, 576–79,
    585
Spellman, Francis Cardinal, 606, 674,
    677, 680–81
Sporberg, Henry, 733
Squantum shipyard, 279, 284
Squaw Man, The (film), 377
Stammers, Kay, 723
Standard Oil, 572
Stark, Harold R., 665
Steel, Ronald, 217
Steffens, Laura, 196
Steffens, Lincoln, 113, 191, 196
Stevenson, Adlai E., 767, 781–83, 784,
    794–95
Stimson, Henry L., 551
Stone, David, 291
Stone, Galen, 275, 291–92, 296–300,
    327–28, 329, 337
Storrow, James Jackson, 191–96
Storrow, James Jackson III, 356
Storrow family, 236
Story of the Films, The (published
    lectures), 374
Stotesbury, Mrs. E. T., 394–95
Stroheim, Erich von, 398–411, 413, 418
Stuart, Janet Erskine, 178
Sudetenland crisis, 548–65 passim
Sughrue, Michael, 133, 138–40, 147,
    156
Sukarno, 755
Sullivan, Charles, 345, 401
Sullivan, John, Commissioner, 135, 156
Sullivan, John H., 254
Sullivan, Mark, 277
Sullivan, Michael and Nancy, 8
Sullivan, Richard, 231
Sunday Graphic, 596
Sunset Boulevard (film), 418
Sutherland, Duke of, 575
Sutton, William, 708, 710, 715, 717,
    722, 739

Swanson, Gloria, 372, 381–418, 425–26, 724
Swope, Herbert Bayard, 434, 436, 490, 721
Sykes, Virginia Gilliat, Lady Sykes, 670, 689
Synge, John Millington, 204–7

Taft, Robert A. 758, 763, 764
Taft, William Howard, 122, 184, 223
Taft-Hartley bill, 725
Tague, Peter, 305
Talbot, Ted, 674
Tammany Club, Boston, 245
Tammany Hall, 134
Tanglewood Tales (Hawthorne), 63, 87
Tanner, Thomas Hawkes, 34
Taylor, William Desmond, 370
Teapot Dome, 439
Ten Commandments, The (film), 377
Tennessee Valley Authority, 438
Tenney, Nancy, 627
Thayer, Eugene, 254–55, 292–93
Thayer family, 236
They Were Expendable (White), 645, 650
Thom, Lennie, 649, 652–55
Thomas, Hugh, 542
Thompson, Frank, 723
Thomson, Frances, 397
Thomson, Fred, 396, 397
Thoreau, Henry David, 46, 86, 87
Thorndike, Augustus, 240
Ticknor, George, 46
Tierney, Gene, 723
Timilty, Joseph, 477, 663, 713
Tinker, Harold, 481
Tobin, Maurice, 706, 709, 748
Toland, Gregg, 402
Tolstoy, Leo, 321
Toohig, William, 396–97
Toscanini, Arturo, 479
Townshend, Peter, 738
Tracy, Spencer, 584
Tracy family, 46
Trading with the Enemy (Higham), 572
Trafalgar Day dinner (1938), 565–66, 567, 568
Tregaskis, Richard, 505
Trespasser, The (film), 413–18
Trilogy of Desire (Dreiser), 232
Trohan, Walter, 536
Truman, Harry, 705, 725, 727, 728, 729, 753, 779

Truth-in-Securities Act, 445
Tucker, Hilary, 32
Tulagi, 648, 650, 651
Tully, Grace, 452
Tumulty, Joseph, 510
Twain, Mark, 54
Tweed, William Marcy, 134
Twentieth Century Limited, 345–46
Twenty-first Amendment. 441, 444

U-boats (submarines), 268, 277, 279, 289, 662, 684
Underhill, Harriet, 374
Union Club, 214
United Artists, 382, 386, 387, 414, 422
United Nations Conference (1945), 702–703
United States Steel Corp., 284
Universal Pictures, 37
Unruh, Jesse, 794
Untermyer, Samuel, 236

Valentino, Rudolf, 341, 372
Van Buren, Martin, 513
Vanderbilt, Alfred Gwynne, 268
Variety, 385–86, 407–8, 414, 416, 422
Vernon, Bobby, 383
Versailles, Treaty of, 517, 548
Victoria, Queen, 545
Vietnam, 779
Vogue, 524
Volstead Act, 441–44
V-1 rocket bombs, 685–86
V-2 rocket bombs, 686

Wakeman, Sam, 280, 284, 292
Wakoff, I. R., 388
Waldorf-Astoria Hotel, 331–32, 435
Waldrop, Frank, 626, 628, 630, 632, 633, 666
Wales, Prince of (Edward VII), 542
Walker, Elisha, 376, 440, 557
Wall, Thomas, 30
Wall Street bombing (1920), 317
Walsh, David I., 647–48, 709, 757
Walsh, James, 251
Walsh, Raoul, 404
Walsh, Thomas J., 431
Walter, Eugene, 407
War and the Intellectuals (Bourne), 276
Warburg, Paul M., 419
Ward Eight (Dineen), 72
Warfield, Thomas E., 651, 652
Warner, Harry, 371

Warner Brothers, 374, 375
"War of the Worlds, The" (radio play), 582fn.
Warren, Earl, 814
Washington, George, 218, 813
*Washington*, S.S., 606
*Washington News*, 447
*Washington Times-Herald*, 502, 533, 627–33 *passim*, 663, 769
Waterhouse, Charles, 696
Watson, Thomas, 278
Watts, James, 642
Waugh, Evelyn, 672, 740
Weaver, John, 107
Webb, Beatrice, 92
Webster, Daniel, 101, 779
Weinberger, Caspar, 504
Welles, Benjamin, 476
Welles, Orson, 582fn.
Welles, Sumner, 551, 557, 610
Wellesley College, 131–33, 142, 143, 144, 188
Wellington, Alfred, 237–39, 240, 254, 255, 324
Wenden, D. J., 346
Wentworth Woodhouse, 732
West End Club, 192
West Virginia primary (1960), 797–99, 803
Whalen, Grover A., 483
Whalen, Richard, 225, 292, 379
*What a Widow* (film), 417
Wheeler-Bennett, John, 559, 563, 571
*When Love Grows Cold* (film), 341
*While England Slept* (Churchill), 605
White, Byron "Whizzer," 543
White, Charles, 673
White, John, 628–31, 633, 635, 663, 736
White, Theodore H., 800, 804
Whitelaw, Aubrey, 470
Whitney, Richard, 445
Whittier, John Greenleaf, 46
*Why Change Your Wife?* (film), 383
*Why England Slept* (John F. Kennedy), 605–6
Whyte, William, 777
Wiggin, Albert H., 293, 421

Wild, Payson, 582
Wilhelm II, Kaiser, 185
Wilhelm, Prince, 122
Wilhelmina, Queen of the Netherlands, 185
Wilkinson, Thomas, 444
Williams, John J., Archbishop, 62, 88
Williams, William Carlos, 286
Willkie, Wendell L., 611, 613
Wills, Garry 457, 724, 811
Willson, Russell, 703
Willy, Wilford, 687–88
Wilson, Edith Galt, 812
Wilson, Patricia, 670–72, 678, 684–85, 689–90, 740
Wilson, Robin, 670
Wilson, Woodrow, 198, 252, 270, 429, 431, 510
Winchell, Walter, 633
Windsor Castle, 525–29
Winsor, Justin, 40
Wisconsin primary (1960), 766–97, 799
Wohlthat, Helmuth, 572–73
*Wonder Book*, A (Hawthorne), 87
Wood, Frank, 254, 255
Wood, Sir Kingsley, 560
Wood, Peter, 529
Wood, Richard, 529, 664, 667, 730
*World of Our Fathers* (Howe), 6
World War I, 267–88, 274ff., 323, 387, 428, 574, 584–85, 586, 588
  Chamberlain and, 518, 528
  flu epidemic in, 285–88
World War II, 588–600, 602, 607–9, 622, 623, 632, 694–95
  in Pacific, 645–46, 648–60
Wrigley, William, 432
*Wuthering Heights* (film), 402, 584
Wyzansky, Charles, 379

Yeats, William Butler, 204
Yellow Cab Co., 330–36
Young Men's Catholic Association, 112, 129

Zola, Émile, 796
Zukor, Adolph, 372, 373, 494

# PHOTO CREDITS

## PHOTOS IN TEXT

*Page 3:* Boston Public Library
*Page 40:* Boston Public Library
*Page 110:* New York World
*Page 130:* Kennedy Family Collection
*Page 190:* Kennedy Family Collection
*Page 234:* Tupper, Boston
*Page 339:* Kennedy Family Collection
*Page 349:* Kennedy Family Collection
*Page 381:* United Artists
*Page 456:* Kennedy Family Collection
*Page 475:* Kennedy Family Collection
*Page 512:* unknown, photo in John F. Kennedy Library
*Page 531:* Kennedy Family Collection
*Page 621:* Frank Turgeon, Palm Beach
*Page 661:* Kennedy Family Collection
*Page 683:* George Woodruff
*Page 742:* Kennedy Family Collection
*Page 750:* John F. Kennedy Library
*Page 809:* Time/Life

## SECTION ONE

*Page One:* John F. Kennedy Library.
*Page Two:* Top, Bostonian Society; middle, Holy Cross College Archives, Worcester, MA; bottom, Kennedy Family Collection.
*Page Three:* Top, Kennedy Family Collection; bottom, John F. Kennedy Library.
*Pages Four and Five:* All photos, Kennedy Family Collection.
*Page Six:* Top, *Boston Globe*; bottom, Kennedy Family Collection.
*Page Seven:* "Norman," *Boston Post.*
*Page Eight:* Boston Globe.

## SECTION TWO

*Pages One, Two, Three, Four, Five and Six:* All photos, Kennedy Family Collection.
*Page Seven:* Top, Bachrach, Watertown, MA; bottom, Kennedy Family Collection.

*Page Eight:* Both photos, Kennedy Family Collection.

*Page Nine:* Top, Topical Press Agency, London; middle-right, Royal Atelier, New York; middle-left, Kennedy Family Collection; bottom, National Archives, Washington, DC.

*Pages Ten, Eleven and Twelve:* All photos, Kennedy Family Collection.

*Page Thirteen:* Top, Gordon Morris, New York; bottom, Kennedy Family Collection.

*Page Fourteen:* Top, Alfieri Picture Service, London; bottom-left, Kennedy Family Collection; bottom-right, Sport and General Press Agency, London.

*Page Fifteen:* Top, Planet News, London; bottom, G. Felici, Rome.

*Page Sixteen:* Kennedy Family Collection.


SECTION THREE:

*Page One:* Top and bottom, Kennedy Family Collection; middle, unknown.

*Page Two:* Top, Narvana Studio, London; middle, Kennedy Family Collection; bottom, Portman Press Bureau.

*Page Three:* Both photos, Kennedy Family Collection.

*Page Four:* Top and bottom, U.S. Navy photograph; middle, John F. Kennedy Library.

*Page Five:* Top and bottom-left, John F. Kennedy Library; bottom-right, Kennedy Family Collection.

*Page Six:* Top, Morgan Studio, Palm Beach; bottom, Kennedy Family Collection.

*Page Seven:* Both photos, Time-Life.

*Page Eight:* U.S. Army Signal Corps photograph.

# ABOUT THE AUTHOR

Doris Kearns Goodwin is the author of the brilliantly acclaimed *Lyndon Johnson and the American Dream*. She has been professor of Government at Harvard University. She lives in Concord, Massachusetts, with her husband, Richard Goodwin, and their three sons.